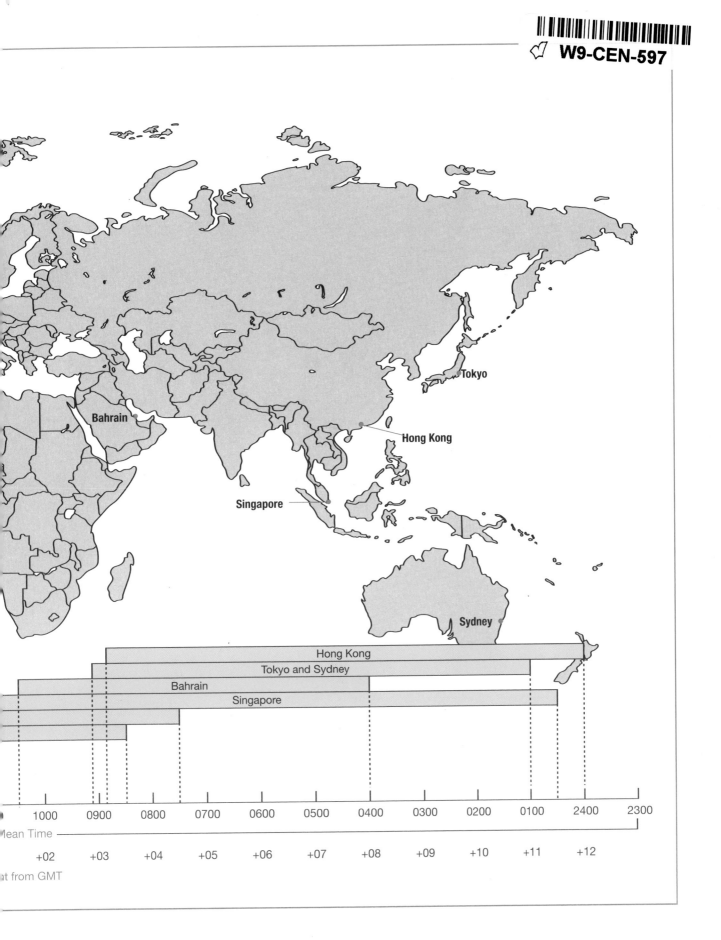

W9-CEN-597

MULTINATIONAL
BUSINESS FINANCE

12TH EDITION

The Prentice Hall Series in Finance

Alexander/Sharpe/Bailey
Fundamentals of Investments

Bear/Moldonado-Bear
Free Markets, Finance, Ethics, and Law

Berk/DeMarzo
Corporate Finance*

Berk/DeMarzo
Corporate Finance: The Core*

Berk/DeMarzo/Harford
Fundamentals of Corporate Finance*

Bierman/Smidt
The Capital Budgeting Decision:
Economic Analysis of Investment Projects

Bodie/Merton/Cleeton
Financial Economics

Brooks
Financial Management: Core Concepts*

Click/Coval
The Theory and Practice of International
Financial Management

Copeland/Weston/Shastri
Financial Theory and Corporate Policy

Cox/Rubinstein
Options Markets

Dietrich
Financial Services and Financial
Institutions: Value Creation in Theory
and Practice

Dorfman
Introduction to Risk Management
and Insurance

Dufey/Giddy
Cases in International Finance

Eakins
Finance in .learn

Eiteman/Stonehill/Moffett
Multinational Business Finance

Emery/Finnerty/Stowe
Corporate Financial Management

Fabozzi
Bond Markets: Analysis and Strategies

Fabozzi/Modigliani
Capital Markets: Institutions
and Instruments

Fabozzi/Modigliani/Jones/Ferri
Foundations of Financial Markets
and Institutions

Finkler
Financial Management for Public, Health,
and Not-for-Profit Organizations

Francis/Ibbotson
Investments: A Global Perspective

Fraser/Ormiston
Understanding Financial Statements

Geisst
Investment Banking in the Financial
System

Gitman
Principles of Managerial Finance*

Gitman
Principles of Managerial Finance—Brief
Edition*

Gitman/Joehnk
Fundamentals of Investing*

Gitman/Madura
Introduction to Finance

Guthrie/Lemon
Mathematics of Interest Rates
and Finance

Haugen
The Inefficient Stock Market: What Pays
Off and Why

Haugen
Modern Investment Theory

Haugen
The New Finance: Overreaction,
Complexity, and Uniqueness

Holden
Excel Modeling and Estimation in the
Fundamentals of Corporate Finance

Holden
Excel Modeling and Estimation in
the Fundamentals of Investments

Holden
Excel Modeling and Estimation
in Investments

Holden
Excel Modeling and Estimation
in Corporate Finance

Hughes/MacDonald
International Banking: Text and Cases

Hull
Fundamentals of Futures and Options
Markets

Hull
Options, Futures, and Other Derivatives

Hull
Risk Management and Financial
Institutions

Keown
Personal Finance: Turning Money
into Wealth

Keown/Martin/Petty/Scott
Financial Management: Principles
and Applications

Keown/Martin/Petty/Scott
Foundations of Finance: The Logic and
Practice of Financial Management

Kim/Nofsinger
Corporate Governance

Levy/Post
Investments

Madura
Personal Finance

May/May/Andrew
Effective Writing: A Handbook
for Finance People

Marthinsen
Risk Takers: Uses and Abuses
of Financial Derivatives

McDonald
Derivatives Markets

McDonald
Fundamentals of Derivatives Markets

Megginson
Corporate Finance Theory

Melvin
International Money and Finance

Mishkin/Eakins
Financial Markets and Institutions

Moffett
Cases in International Finance

Moffett/Stonehill/Eiteman
Fundamentals of Multinational Finance

Nofsinger
Psychology of Investing

Ogden/Jen/O'Connor
Advanced Corporate Finance

Pennacchi
Theory of Asset Pricing

Rejda
Principles of Risk Management
and Insurance

Schoenebeck
Interpreting and Analyzing Financial
Statements

Scott/Martin/Petty/Keown/Thatcher
Cases in Finance

Seiler
Performing Financial Studies:
A Methodological Cookbook

Shapiro
Capital Budgeting and Investment
Analysis

Sharpe/Alexander/Bailey
Investments

Solnik/McLeavey
Global Investments

Stretcher/Michael
Cases in Financial Management

Titman/Martin
Valuation: The Art and Science of
Corporate Investment Decisions

Trivoli
Personal Portfolio Management:
Fundamentals and Strategies

Van Horne
Financial Management and Policy

Van Horne
Financial Market Rates and Flows

Van Horne/Wachowicz
Fundamentals of Financial Management

Vaughn
Financial Planning for the Entrepreneur

Welch
Corporate Finance: An Introduction*

Weston/Mitchel/Mulherin
Takeovers, Restructuring, and Corporate
Governance

Winger/Frasca
Personal Finance

*denotes myfinancelab titles   Log onto www.myfinancelab.com to learn more

MULTINATIONAL BUSINESS FINANCE

12TH EDITION

David K.
EITEMAN

University of California,
Los Angeles

Arthur I.
STONEHILL

Oregon State University
and the University
of Hawaii at Manoa

Michael H.
MOFFETT

Thunderbird School
of Global Management

Prentice Hall

Boston San Francisco New York
London Toronto Sydney Tokyo Singapore Madrid
Mexico City Munich Paris Cape Town Hong Kong Montreal

Editor in Chief: Donna Battista
Project Manager: Kerri McQueen
Senior Marketing Manager: Elizabeth A. Averbeck
Marketing Assistant: Ian Gold
Managing Editor: Jeff Holcomb
Senior Production Supervisor: Meredith Gertz
Supplements Editor: Alison Eusden
Director of Media: Susan Schoenberg
Media Producer: Nicole Sackin
Senior Manufacturing Buyer: Carol Melville
Permissions Supervisor: Shannon Barbe
Permissions Coordinator: Warren Drabek
Project Coordination, Composition, Illustrations, Alterations, and Text Design:
    Gillian Hall, The Aardvark Group
Copy Editor: Kathleen Cantwell, C4 Technologies
Proofreader: Holly McLean-Aldis
Indexer: Jack Lewis
Design Manager: Linda Knowles
Cover Designer: Susan Paradise
Cover Image: © Dennis Degnan/Corbis

Credits and acknowledgments borrowed from other sources and reproduced, with permission, in this textbook appear on the appropriate page within the text or on the Credits pages.

Library of Congress Cataloging-in-Publication Data
Eiteman, David K.
  Multinational business finance / David K. Eiteman, Arthur I. Stonehill, Michael H. Moffett.
—12th ed.
    p. cm.
  Includes index.
  ISBN-13: 978-0-13-609668-9
  ISBN-10: 0-13-609668-9
  1. International business enterprises—Finance. I. Stonehill, Arthur I. II. Moffett, Michael
H. III. Title.
  HG4027.5.E36 2010
  658.15'99—dc22
2009024111

Prentice Hall
is an imprint of

www.pearsonhighered.com

ISBN-13: 978-0-13-609668-9
ISBN-10: 0-13-609668-9
2 3 4 5 6 7 8 9 10–EB–13 12 11 10

Preface

As the field of international finance has evolved, so has the content of *Multinational Business Finance*. As in previous editions, we perceive the multinational enterprise (MNE) to be a unique institution that acts as a catalyst and facilitator of international trade and as an important producer and distributor in host countries where its subsidiaries are located. The success of a multinational enterprise continues to depend on its ability to recognize and benefit from imperfections in national markets for products, factors of production, and financial assets.

Also carried over from earlier editions is the theme that volatile exchange rates may not only increase risk, but also they may create opportunities for both investors and firms to profit, given a proper understanding of exchange risk management.

The 12th edition continues to recognize the increasing importance of global integration of money and capital markets, a trend that is creating expanded opportunities for both investors and organizations that must raise capital. Although global integration of financial markets removes some market imperfections that impede the flow of capital internationally, excellent opportunities continue to exist for investors to increase their returns while lowering their risk through international portfolio diversification and for firms to lower their cost of capital by sourcing it internationally.

The 12th edition views the MNE as an organization that poses unique demands on the business leaders of tomorrow. Those leaders—possibly some of the readers of this text—will be confronted with a multitude of challenges that will test not only their ability to *comprehend* global markets, but also, more importantly, to *lead* their organizations through the constantly shifting currents and tides of global change. Competent leadership may indeed be the scarcest global commodity.

This book is about multinational management, and more specifically, the financial management dimensions of leading a multinational enterprise. The MNE's potential success, however, rests in the hands of the truly competent global leader. The success of any MNE depends on its leadership's ability to guide and manage the global organization.

Our vision for this book is to aid in the development of tomorrow's MNE leaders. Their ability to recognize and benefit from business opportunities such as imperfections in national markets, unequal costs and efficiencies of the factors of production, wellsprings of intellectual property, and sources of global funding to facilitate growth adds value.

The financial managers of MNEs face numerous foreign exchange and political risks. These risks can be daunting, but if properly understood they present opportunities for creating value. These risks and opportunities are most effectively understood in the context of the global business itself, and the ability of management to integrate the strategic and financial challenges that business faces.

Audience

Multinational Business Finance, 12th edition, is appropriate for university-level courses in international financial management, international business finance, international finance, and similar titles. It can be used at the undergraduate and graduate level as well as in executive education courses.

A prerequisite course or experience in corporate finance or financial management would be ideal. However, we review the basic finance concepts before we extend them to the multinational case. We also review the basic concepts of international economics and international business.

We recognize that many of our potential adopters live outside of the United States and Canada. Therefore, we use a significant number of non-U.S. examples, mini-cases, and *Global Finance in Practice* boxes, as seen in the business and news press (anecdotes and illustrations).

Organization

Multinational Business Finance, 12th edition, is organized into six parts, unified by the common thread of the globalization process by which a firm moves from a domestic to a multinational business orientation.

- Part 1 introduces the global financial environment.
- Part 2 explains foreign exchange theory and markets.
- Part 3 analyzes foreign exchange exposure.
- Part 4 analyzes financing the global firm.
- Part 5 analyzes international investment decisions.
- Part 6 examines managing multinational operations.

New in the 12th Edition

- Chapter 1, *Globalization and the Multinational Enterprise*, traces the logical development of globalization forces, comparative advantage, foreign direct investment by multinational enterprises, and financial globalization principles of multinational financial management.
- Chapter 2, *Financial Goals and Corporate Governance*, expands on the discussion of corporate governance, and now includes private ownership of business—the still dominant form of ownership globally—and differing perspectives on the value of good global governance.
- Chapter 5, *Current Multinational Financial Challenges: The Credit Crisis of 2007–2009*, is completely new. It details the origins and dissemination of the securities and derivatives and market developments behind the current global financial crisis and proposed solutions.
- Chapter 18, *Foreign Direct Investment Theory and Political Risk*, includes a new section on emerging market MNEs.
- There are 22 Mini-Cases. Four are new and 18 are retained in response to reader feedback.
- There are additional *Global Finance in Practice* boxes throughout the text, highlighting current events as tied to the chapter material.
- Complete answers to starred (*) end-of-chapter Problems are provided at the rear of the book in a section called *Answers to Selected Problems*.

In this book, we use foreign exchange quotations that sometimes may differ from the latest computer code quotation symbols (three-digit symbols). This results from the constant change in the marketplace and because sometimes we prefer to use traditional symbols—$, ¥, £—rather than three-digit codes, which we consider to be more sterile. We acknowledge that this decision may make the material seem out of date. But then again, this book is somewhat about the difficulties and challenges of managing businesses in a rapidly changing financial environment. We also understand that many professors have prepared additional teaching materials based on our existing foreign exchange quotations. Therefore, we continue to use a mix of selected existing quotations (from previous editions) and the latest rates and movements in the marketplace. In any case, the quotations are meant to illustrate a particular problem, not to support up-to-the-minute solutions.

A Rich Array of Support Materials

A robust package of materials for the instructor and student accompanies the text to facilitate learning and to support teaching and testing. All instructor resources are available for download from the online catalog page for this book (www.pearsonhighered.com/irc).

- **Instructor's Manual.** The Online Instructor's Manual, prepared by the authors, contains answers to end-of-chapter questions and mini-cases. Excel® solutions for all end-of-chapter problems are available as well as PowerPoint teaching solutions for all mini-cases. The Instructor's Manual is available for download as Microsoft® Word files or as Adobe® PDF files and the solutions to the problems are available for download as Microsoft Excel® files from the Instructor Resource Center or from your local sales representative.

- **Test Bank.** The Test Bank, prepared by Curtis J. Bacon of Southern Oregon University, contains more than 700 multiple choice and true/false questions. The multiple choice questions are labeled by topic and category—recognition, conceptual, and analytical. The test bank is available for download from the Instructor's Resource Center.

- **Computerized Test Bank.** The Test Bank is also available in Pearson Education's TestGen software for Windows® and Macintosh®. TestGen's graphical interface enables the instructor to view, edit, and add questions; transfer questions to tests; and print different forms of tests. Search-and-sort features enable the instructor to locate questions quickly and arrange them as preferred. The Quizmaster application allows the instructor to administer TestGen tests over the school's computer network. More information on TestGen software is available at www.pearsoned.com/testgen.

- **PowerPoint Presentation.** The PowerPoint presentation slides, prepared by Mark. J. Bradt, provide lecture outlines and selected graphics from the text for each chapter. The PowerPoint presentation is also available for download from the Instructor's Resource Center.

- **Companion Web Site.** A dedicated Web site (www.pearsonhighered.com/eiteman) contains access to chapter exhibits, Excel solutions for select end-of chapter problems (denoted with an asterisk), Internet exercises, and glossary flashcards. Instructors have access to spreadsheet solutions for all problems from the Instructor Resource Center.

International Editions

Multinational Business Finance has been used throughout the world to teach students of international finance. It is published in a number of languages, including Chinese, French, Spanish, Indonesian, Portuguese, and Ukrainian.

Acknowledgments

The authors are very thankful for the many detailed reviews and suggestions from numerous colleagues. These reviews, by more than 100 adopters and non-adopters, include detailed chapter-by-chapter reviews and answers to a comprehensive questionnaire. The current edition of Multinational Business Finance reflects most of the suggestions provided by these reviewers. The survey participants are anonymous. The detailed reviewers are as follows:

Gordon M. Bodnar, *John Hopkins University*
Imad A. Elhah, *University of Louisville*
Larry Fauver, *University of Tennessee*
John P. Lajaunie, *Nicholls State University*

Sheryl Winston Smith, *University of Minnesota*
Masahiro Watanabe, *Rice University*
Gwinyai Utete, *Auburn University*

Special thanks are extended to the reviewers and survey participants of the previous editions:

Otto Adleberger
Essen University, Germany
Alan Alford
Northeastern University
Stephen Archer
Williamette University
Bala Arshanapalli
Indiana University Northwest
Hossein G. Askari
George Washington University
Robert T. Aubey
University of Wisconsin at Madison
David Babbel
University of Pennsylvania
James Baker
Kent State University
Morten Balling
Arhus School of Business, Denmark
Arindam Bandopadhyaya
University of Massachusetts at Boston
Ari Beenhakker
University of South Florida
Carl Beidleman
Lehigh University
Robert Boatler
Texas Christian University
Nancy Bord
University of Hartford
Finbarr Bradley
University of Dublin, Ireland
Tom Brewer
Georgetown University

Michael Brooke
University of Manchester, England
Robert Carlson
Assumption University, Thailand
Kam C. Chan
University of Dayton
Chun Chang
University of Minnesota
Sam Chee
Boston University Metropolitan College
Kevin Cheng
New York University
It-Keong Chew
University of Kentucky
Frederick D. S. Choi
New York University
Jay Choi
Temple University
Nikolai Chuvakhin
Pepperdine University
Mark Ciechon
University of California, Los Angeles
J. Markham Collins
University of Tulsa
Alan N. Cook
Baylor University
Kerry Cooper
Texas A&M University
Robert Cornu
Cranfield School of Management, U.K.
Roy Crum
University of Florida

Steven Dawson
University of Hawaii at Manoa
David Distad
University of California, Berkeley
Gunter Dufey
University of Michigan, Ann Arbor
Mark Eaker
Duke University
Rodney Eldridge
George Washington University
Vihang Errunza
McGill University
Cheol S. Eun
Georgia Tech University
Mara Faccio
University of Notre Dame
Joseph Finnerty
University of Illinois at Urbana-Champaign
William R. Folks, Jr.
University of South Carolina
Lewis Freitas
University of Hawaii at Manoa
Anne Fremault
Boston University
Fariborg Ghadar
George Washington University
Ian Giddy
New York University
Martin Glaum
Justus-Lievig-Universitat Giessen, Germany
Manolete Gonzales
Oregon State University

Deborah Gregory
University of Georgia

Robert Grosse
Thunderbird

Christine Hekman
Georgia Tech University

Steven Heston
University of Maryland

James Hodder
University of Wisconsin, Madison

Alfred Hofflander
University of California, Los Angeles

Janice Jadlow
Oklahoma State University

Veikko Jaaskelainen
Helsinki School of Economics and Business Administration

Benjamas Jirasakuldech
University of the Pacific

Ronald A. Johnson
Northeastern University

John Kallianiotis
University of Scranton

Charles Kane
Boston College

Fred Kaen
University of New Hampshire

Robert Kemp
University of Virginia

W. Carl Kester
Harvard Business School

Seung Kim
St. Louis University

Yong Kim
University of Cincinnati

Gordon Klein
University of California, Los Angeles

Steven Kobrin
University of Pennsylvania

Paul Korsvold
Norwegian School of Management

Chris Korth
University of South Carolina

Chuck C. Y. Kwok
University of South Carolina

Sarah Lane
Boston University

Martin Laurence
William Patterson College

Eric Y. Lee
Fairleigh Dickinson University

Donald Lessard
Massachusetts Institute of Technology

Arvind Mahajan
Texas A&M University

Rita Maldonado-Baer
New York University

Anthony Matias
Palm Beach Atlantic College

Charles Maxwell
Murray State University

Sam McCord
Auburn University

Jeanette Medewitz
University of Nebraska at Omaha

Robert Mefford
University of San Francisco

Paritash Mehta
Temple University

Antonio Mello
University of Wisconsin at Madison

Eloy Mestre
American University

Kenneth Moon
Suffolk University

Gregory Noronha
Arizona State University

Edmund Outslay
Michigan State University

Lars Oxelheim
Lund University, Sweden

Jacob Park
Green Mountain College

Yoon Shik Park
George Washington University

Harvey Poniachek
New York University

Yash Puri
University of Massachusetts at Lowell

R. Ravichandrarn
University of Colorado at Boulder

Scheherazade Rehman
George Washington University

Jeff Rosenlog
Emory University

David Rubinstein
University of Houston

Alan Rugman
Oxford University, U.K.

R. J. Rummel
University of Hawaii at Manoa

Mehdi Salehizadeh
San Diego State University

Michael Salt
San Jose State University

Roland Schmidt
Erasmus University, the Netherlands

Lemma Senbet
University of Maryland

Alan Shapiro
University of Southern California

Hany Shawky
State University of New York, Albany

Hamid Shomali
Golden Gate University

Vijay Singal
Virginia Tech University

Luc Soenen
California Polytechnic State University

Marjorie Stanley
Texas Christian University

Joseph Stokes
University of Massachusetts-Amherst

Jahangir Sultan
Bentley College

Lawrence Tai
Loyola Marymount University

Kishore Tandon
CUNY—Bernard Baruch College

Russell Taussig
University of Hawaii at Manoa

Lee Tavis
University of Notre Dame

Sean Toohey
University of Western Sydney, Australia

Norman Toy
Columbia University

Joseph Ueng
University of St. Thomas

Harald Vestergaard
Copenhagen Business School

K. G. Viswanathan
Hofstra University

Joseph D. Vu
University of Illinois, Chicago

Mahmoud Wahab
University of Hartford

Michael Williams
University of Texas at Austin

Brent Wilson
Brigham Young University

Bob Wood
Tennessee Technological University

Alexander Zamperion
Bentley College

Emilio Zarruk
Florida Atlantic University

Tom Zwirlein
University of Colorado, Colorado Springs

Industry (present or former affiliation)

Paul Adaire
Philadelphia Stock Exchange

Barbara Block
Tektronix, Inc.

Holly Bowman
Bankers Trust

Payson Cha
HKR International, Hong Kong

John A. Deuchler
Private Export Funding Corporation

Kåre Dullum
Gudme Raaschou Investment Bank, Denmark

Steven Ford
Hewlett Packard

David Heenan
Campbell Estate, Hawaii

Sharyn H. Hess
Foreign Credit Insurance Association

Aage Jacobsen
Gudme Raaschou Investment Bank, Denmark

Ira G. Kawaller
Chicago Mercantile Exchange

Kenneth Knox
Tektronix, Inc.

Arthur J. Obesler
Eximbank

I. Barry Thompson
Continental Bank

Gerald T. West
Overseas Private Investment Corporation

Willem Winter
First Interstate Bank of Oregon

Inevitably woven into the fabric of this book are ideas received from faculty and students from institutions where we have taught from all over the world. They include our home universities of University of California, Los Angeles; Oregon State University; University of Hawaii; and Thunderbird. Our visiting stints have been at the Hong Kong University of Science and Technology; University of California, Berkeley; University of Michigan, Ann Arbor; Cranfield School of Management, United Kingdom; University of Hawaii at Manoa; Northern European Management Institute, Norway; Copenhagen Business School, Denmark; Aarhus School of Business, Denmark; Helsinki School of Economics and Business Administration, Finland; Indian School of Business, Hyderabad; Institute for the Development of Executives, Argentina; National University of Singapore; International Centre for Public Enterprises, Yugoslavia; Beijing Institute of Chemical Engineering and Management; and Dalian University of Science & Technology, China. Further ideas came from consulting assignments in Argentina, Belgium, Canada, Denmark, Finland, Guatemala, Hong Kong, Indonesia, Japan, Malaysia, Mexico, the Netherlands, Norway, People's Republic of China, Peru, Sweden, Taiwan, the United Kingdom, and Venezuela.

We would also like to thank two key individuals at Pearson who worked diligently on this 12th edition: Donna Battista and Kerri McQueen.

Finally, we would like to rededicate this book to our parents, the late Wilford and Sylvia Eiteman, the late Harold and Norma Stonehill, and Bennie Ruth and the late Hoy Moffett, who motivated us to become academicians and authors. We thank our wives, Keng-Fong, Kari, and Megan for their patience throughout the years spent preparing this edition.

Pacific Palisades, California   D.K.E.
Honolulu, Hawaii   A.I.S.
Glendale, Arizona   M.H.M.

About the Authors

Arthur I. Stonehill is a Professor of Finance and International Business, Emeritus, at Oregon State University, where he taught for 24 years (1966–1990). During 1991–1997 he held a split appointment at the University of Hawaii at Manoa and Copenhagen Business School. From 1997 to 2001 he continued as a Visiting Professor at the University of Hawaii at Manoa. He has also held teaching or research appointments at University of California, Berkeley; Cranfield School of Management (U.K.); and the North European Management Institute (Norway). He was a former president of the Academy of International Business and a western director of the Financial Management Association.

Professor Stonehill received a B.A. (History) from Yale University (1953), an M.B.A. from Harvard Business School (1957), and a Ph.D. in Business Administration from University of California, Berkeley (1965). He was awarded honorary doctorates from the Aarhus School of Business (Denmark, 1989), the Copenhagen Business School (Denmark, 1992), and Lund University (Sweden, 1998).

He has authored or coauthored nine books and twenty-five other publications. His articles have appeared in *Financial Management*, *Journal of International Business Studies*, *California Management Review*, *Journal of Financial and Quantitative Analysis*, *Journal of International Financial Management and Accounting*, *International Business Review*, *European Management Journal*, *The Investment Analyst* (U.K.), *Nationaløkonomisk Tidskrift* (Denmark), *Sosialøkonomen* (Norway), *Journal of Financial Education*, and others.

David K. Eiteman is Professor Emeritus of Finance at the John E. Anderson Graduate School of Management at UCLA. He has also held teaching or research appointments at the Hong Kong University of Science & Technology, Showa Academy of Music (Japan), the National University of Singapore, Dalian University (China), the Helsinki School of Economics and Business Administration (Finland), University of Hawaii at Manoa, University of Bradford (U.K.), Cranfield School of Management (U.K.), and IDEA (Argentina). He is a former president of the International Trade and Finance Association, Society for Economics and Management in China, and Western Finance Association.

Professor Eiteman received a B.B.A. (Business Administration) from the University of Michigan, Ann Arbor (1952); M.A. (Economics) from University of California, Berkeley (1956); and a Ph.D. (Finance) from Northwestern University (1959).

He has authored or coauthored four books and twenty-nine other publications. His articles have appeared in *The Journal of Finance*, *The International Trade Journal*, *Financial Analysts Journal*, *Journal of World Business*, *Management International*, *Business Horizons*, *MSU Business Topics*, *Public Utilities Fortnightly*, and others.

Michael H. Moffett is Continental Grain Professor of Finance at Thunderbird School of Global Management. He was formerly Associate Professor of Finance at Oregon State University (1985–1993). He has also held teaching or research appointments at the University of Michigan, Ann Arbor (1991–1993); the Brookings Institution, Washington, D.C., the University of Hawaii at Manoa; the Aarhus School of Business (Denmark); the Helsinki School of Economics and Business Administration (Finland); the International Centre for Public Enterprises (Yugoslavia); and the University of Colorado, Boulder.

Professor Moffett received a B.A. (Economics) from the University of Texas at Austin (1977), an M.S. (Resource Economics) from Colorado State University (1979), an M.A. (Economics) from the University of Colorado, Boulder (1983), and a Ph.D. (Economics) from the University of Colorado, Boulder (1985).

He has authored, coauthored, or contributed to six books and 15 other publications. His articles have appeared in the *Journal of Financial and Quantitative Analysis*, *Journal of Applied Corporate Finance*, *Journal of International Money and Finance*, *Journal of International Financial Management and Accounting*, *Contemporary Policy Issues*, *Brookings Discussion Papers in International Economics*, and others. He has contributed to a number of collected works including the *Handbook of Modern Finance*, the *International Accounting and Finance Handbook*, and the *Encyclopedia of International Business*. He is also coauthor of two books on multinational business with Michael Czinkota and Ilkka Ronkainen, *International Business* (7th edition) and *Global Business*.

Brief Contents

Contents

Global Financial Environment

CHAPTER 1

Globalization and the Multinational Enterprise

I define globalization as producing where it is most cost-effective, selling where it is most profitable, and sourcing capital where it is cheapest, without worrying about national boundaries.

—Narayana Murthy, President and CEO, Infosys.

This book is about international financial management with special emphasis on the *multinational enterprise*. The multinational enterprise (MNE) is defined as one that has operating subsidiaries, branches, or affiliates located in foreign countries. It also includes firms in service activities such as consulting, accounting, construction, legal, advertising, entertainment, banking, telecommunications, and lodging.

MNEs are globally headquartered. Many of them are owned by a mixture of domestic and foreign shareholders. The ownership of some firms is so dispersed internationally that they are known as transnational corporations. The transnationals are usually managed from a global perspective rather than from the perspective of any single country.

Although *Multinational Business Finance* emphasizes MNEs, purely domestic firms also often have significant international activities. These include the import and export of products, components, and services. Domestic firms can also license foreign firms to conduct their foreign business. They have exposure to foreign competition in their domestic market. They also have indirect exposure to international risks through their relationships with customers and suppliers. Therefore, domestic firm managers need to understand international financial risk, especially those related to foreign exchange rates and the credit risks related to trade payments.

Multinational Business Finance is written in English and usually uses the U.S. dollar in its exposition. However, we have tried to make it relevant for all multinational enterprises by using numerous non–U.S.-based MNEs. We will use the term *multinational enterprise* (MNE) throughout this text for two very important reasons. First, the term *multinational* is used rather than *international* because we will focus on the third phase of the globalization process in which firms operate businesses in many different countries. Second, the term *enterprise* is used instead of *corporation* because as businesses move into many emerging markets, they will enter into joint ventures, strategic alliances, or simply operating agreements with enterprises that may not be publicly traded or even privately owned (and therefore not corporations), but actually extensions of government.

Globalization and Creating Value in the Multinational Enterprise

Global business, like any business, is the social science of managing people to organize, maintain, and grow the collective productivity toward accomplishing productive goals, typically to generate profit and value for its owners and stakeholders. Reaching that goal—building firm value—requires combining three critical elements: 1) an *open marketplace*; 2) high quality *strategic management*; and 3) *access to capital*. As shown in Exhibit 1.1, any MNE attempting to create value would need to combine these three critical elements composing the sides of the firm value pyramid.

An Open Marketplace

Market economics is the fundamental condition for value creation. The MNE has little opportunity to thrive and grow if it is not operating within a marketplace that allows free movement and competition of labor, capital, technology, and the spirits of innovation and entrepreneurship. The rapid economic development of China, and the many businesses arising within China today, are ready examples of the power of the increasingly open marketplace. There are, however, many complexities to fostering healthy market economics in any country, and many countries have yet to find the magical mix.

Strategic Management

Although the ability to compete in a marketplace is a requirement, the ability to see business opportunities, and then to design, develop, and execute a corporate strategy through all levels of leadership and management is needed to create value. Although the basic elements of innovation and entrepreneurship are probably embedded in the human DNA, good strategy and management are not. Yet insightful strategy and adept leadership is critical to creating value. It is not something that has yet been quantified or captured; as any business student

EXHIBIT 1.1   Creating Firm Value in Global Markets

The challenge to building firm value—value for all stakeholders including stockholders, corporate stakeholders, and social community—is in the expansion and development of all three sides of the global pyramid: an *open marketplace*; *access to affordable capital*; and *high-quality strategic management*.

knows, if computers could strategize and manage, companies wouldn't hire people (or students).

Access to Capital

Open markets and insightful leadership is all for nought, however, if the MNE cannot gain ready access to affordable capital. It is the capital that allows the investment needed to obtain the technology, execute the strategy, and expand across global markets. It is the "capital" in *capitalism*; it is the ability of the enterprise to reach out and obtain resources from outside of the firm to pursue the firm's vision and create the value for all of the key stakeholders in the enterprise itself, and subsequently for the community and society of which it is an integral element.

The level of development of these three combined elements, Levels I–III shown in Exhibit 1.1, is representative of the degrees of depth, breadth, and sophistication accessible by the MNE. For example:

- General Electric (USA) may be considered a resident of Level III. It is a global MNE with widely recognized strategic leadership and management quality, ready access to cheap and plentiful capital, and a key competitor in the most competitive and open marketplaces in the world.

- Cemex (Mexico) may be an example of a resident of Level II. A rapidly growing competitor in its global industry, it is based in Mexico, which is rapidly emerging as a market economy of nearly limitless potential. Yet Cemex is still sometimes hampered in its access to ready and affordable capital to support its business goals.

- The Haier Group (China) may be representative of an MNE resident in Level I of the value pyramid. Although highly successful and an MNE to be reckoned with in a growing number of marketplaces, Haier is still struggling to overcome barriers and limitations of all three critical elements from its Chinese base.

As described in *Global Finance in Practice 1.1*, the evolution of the domestic company to multinational and "a-national" is generating significant benefits for all stakeholders.

These three firms are residents of the pyramid. Their positions in the pyramid are the result of the complex interaction of the three key elements—the three sides of the pyramid—with the level of economic development and openness of the countries of their business activities. The mini-case on Porsche at the end of the chapter will challenge the reader to determine where it might fall within the architecture of the value pyramid.

As we shall see throughout this book, the global economy is seeing an unprecedented growth in the resident MNEs in the value pyramid, and the size and shape of the pyramid tomorrow is probably limitless. We now move to the underlying principle driving the growth of the global business—*comparative advantage*.

The Theory of Comparative Advantage

The *theory of comparative advantage* provides a basis for explaining and justifying international trade in a model world assumed to enjoy free trade, perfect competition, no uncertainty, costless information, and no government interference. The theory's origins lie in the work of Adam Smith, and particularly with his seminal book *The Wealth of Nations* published in 1776. Smith sought to explain why the division of labor in productive activities, and subsequently international trade of those goods, increased the quality of life for all citizens. Smith based his work on the concept of *absolute advantage*, where every country should specialize in the production of that good it was uniquely suited for. More would be

GLOBAL FINANCE IN PRACTICE 1.1

National Multinational or 'A-National'?

When Isaac Merritt Singer set up a branch of his sewing machine maker in Paris in 1855, he probably did not think he was blazing a trail US companies would still be following more than 150 years later. Singer's expansion in France turned the New York-based company into the first US multinational, pioneering a business model that would be adopted by other icons of American capitalism, from Ford to Standard Oil to General Electric. But perhaps the most important legacy of Singer's daring move was that it worked: within six years of the French opening, foreign sales had exceeded US revenues. It is a lesson not lost on today's corporate leaders.

Over the past three months, blue-chips such as General Electric, the conglomerate, IBM, the technology giant, and UPS, the logistics group, have hitched a ride on a global economy growing faster than the US. By contrast, companies that depend on domestic consumers such as Wal-Mart, the retail bell-wether, and Home Depot, the do-it-yourself chain, have released disappointing results and gloomy predictions.

But if foreign earnings have helped US multinationals stave off a fall in profitability, the question is whether the current reliance on the rest of the world is just a cyclical phase or the harbinger of a transformation in corporate America. Could the importance of overseas markets destroy—as Sam Palmisano, IBM's chief executive, has argued—the old multinational model whereby companies decentralised manufacturing and sales operations but kept key functions such as the executive office, research and product design in the "home country"? And if so, are some US companies ready to become truly "transnational" by scattering their top executives around the world?

At first sight, there are significant cyclical forces behind the recent rise of US multinationals—forces, in other words, that could change in the near future. First, the dollar has lost nearly a third of its value against America's largest trading partners over the past seven years, making it easier for US exporters to sell to the world and boosting the dollar value of overseas earnings. Second, US multinationals have been boosted by global economic growth, which has largely been driven by emerging markets hungry for infrastructure and consumer goods—two of America Inc's strongest suits.

But even if economic changes and internal revolutions at companies mean, in the words of Steve Mills, head of IBM's global software business, that "things cannot go back to the way they were", will more companies abandon national allegiance and become truly "a-national"? "Big Blue"—as IBM is known—claims to be just that, with operations in more than 150 countries and key functions spread around the world. Its head of procurement, for example, is based in Shenzhen, China, half a world away from Mr Palmisano's headquarters in Armonk, New York. "Ours is a boundary-less way of thinking," says Mr Mills.

However, many US chief executives regard such moves as impractical, if not outright dangerous. They argue that being rooted in the US is not only an insurance policy in case the globalisation tide turns, but also a way of maintaining order and focus in increasingly complex and dispersed enterprises—of letting everybody know where the buck stops and who is in charge. Jeffrey Immelt, who heads GE, one of the most "global" companies in the US, recently distilled this view: "We're an American company but in order to be successful we've got to win in every corner of the world." In other words, global aspirations tinged with national pride—which Singer would have understood—is just as recognisable today among US business leaders.

Source: Excerpted from "US Companies Choose: National Multinational or 'A-National'?," Francesco Guerrera, *Financial Times*, August 16, 2007, p. 7.

produced for less. Thus, by each country specializing in products for which it possessed absolute advantage, countries could produce more in total and exchange products—trade—for goods that were cheaper in price than those produced at home.

David Ricardo, in his work *On the Principles of Political Economy and Taxation* published in 1817, sought to take the basic ideas set down by Adam Smith a few logical steps further. Ricardo noted that even if a country possessed absolute advantage in the production of two products, it might still be relatively more efficient than the other country in one good's product than the other. Ricardo termed this *comparative advantage*. Each country would then possess comparative advantage in the production of one of the two products, and both countries would then benefit by specializing completely in one product and trading for the other.

Although international trade might have approached the comparative advantage model during the nineteenth century, it certainly does not today, for a variety of reasons. Countries do not appear to specialize only in those products that could be most efficiently produced by that country's particular factors of production. Instead, governments interfere with comparative advantage for a variety of economic and political reasons, such as to achieve full employment, economic development, national self-sufficiency in defense-related industries, and protection of an agricultural sector's way of life. Government interference takes the form of tariffs, quotas, and other non-tariff restrictions.

At least two of the factors of production, capital and technology, now flow directly and easily between countries, rather than only indirectly through traded goods and services. This direct flow occurs between related subsidiaries and affiliates of multinational firms, as well as between unrelated firms via loans, and license and management contracts. Even labor flows between countries such as immigrants into the United States (legal and illegal), immigrants within the European Union, and other unions.

Modern factors of production are more numerous than in this simple model. Factors considered in the location of production facilities worldwide include local and managerial skills, a dependable legal structure for settling contract disputes, research and development competence, educational levels of available workers, energy resources, consumer demand for brand name goods, mineral and raw material availability, access to capital, tax differentials, supporting infrastructure (roads, ports, and communication facilities), and possibly others.

Although the terms of trade are ultimately determined by supply and demand, the process by which the terms are set is different from that visualized in traditional trade theory. They are determined partly by administered pricing in oligopolistic markets.

Comparative advantage shifts over time as less developed countries become more developed and realize their latent opportunities. For example, over the past 150 years comparative advantage in producing cotton textiles has shifted from the United Kingdom to the United States, to Japan, to Hong Kong, to Taiwan, and to China. The classical model of comparative advantage also did not really address certain other issues such as the effect of uncertainty and information costs, the role of differentiated products in imperfectly competitive markets, and economies of scale.

Nevertheless, although the world is a long way from the classical trade model, the general principle of comparative advantage is still valid. The closer the world gets to true international specialization, the more world production and consumption can be increased, provided the problem of equitable distribution of the benefits can be solved to the satisfaction of consumers, producers, and political leaders. Complete specialization, however, remains an unrealistic limiting case, just as perfect competition is a limiting case in microeconomic theory.

Supply Chain Outsourcing: Comparative Advantage Today

Comparative advantage is still a relevant theory to explain why particular countries are most suitable for exports of goods and services that support the global supply chain of both MNEs and domestic firms. The comparative advantage of the twenty-first century, however, is one that is based more on services, and their cross border facilitation by telecommunications and the Internet. The source of a nation's comparative advantage, however, still is created from the mixture of its own labor skills, access to capital, and technology.

Many locations for supply chain outsourcing exist today. Exhibit 1.2 presents a geographical overview of this modern reincarnation of trade-based comparative advantage. To prove that these countries should specialize in the activities shown you would need to know how costly the same activities would be in the countries that are importing these

EXHIBIT 1.2   Global Outsourcing of Comparative Advantage

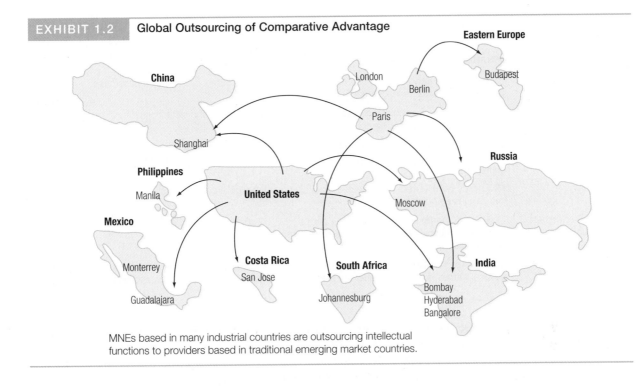

MNEs based in many industrial countries are outsourcing intellectual functions to providers based in traditional emerging market countries.

services compared to their own other industries. Remember that it takes a *relative advantage* in costs, not just an *absolute advantage*, to create *comparative advantage*.

For example, India has developed a highly efficient and low-cost software industry. This industry supplies not only the creation of custom software, but also call centers for customer support, and other information technology services. The Indian software industry is composed of subsidiaries of MNEs and independent companies. If you own a Hewlett-Packard computer and call the customer support center number for help, you are likely to reach a call center in India. Answering your call will be a knowledgeable Indian software engineer or programmer who will "walk" you through your problem. India has a large number of well-educated, English-speaking technical experts who are paid only a fraction of the salary and overhead earned by their U.S. counterparts. The overcapacity and low cost of international telecommunication networks today further enhances the comparative advantage of an Indian location.

The extent of global outsourcing is already reaching out to every corner of the globe. From financial back-offices in Manila, to information technology engineers in Hungary, modern telecommunications now take business activities to labor rather than moving labor to the places of business.

What Is Different about Global Financial Management?

Exhibit 1.3 details some of the main differences between international and domestic financial management. These component differences include institutions, foreign exchange and political risks, and the modifications required of financial theory and financial instruments.

International financial management requires an understanding of cultural, historical, and institutional differences such as those affecting corporate governance. Although both

EXHIBIT 1.3	What Is Different about International Financial Management?	
Concept	**International**	**Domestic**
Culture, history, and institutions	Each foreign country is unique and not always understood by MNE management	Each country has a known base case
Corporate governance	Foreign countries' regulations and institutional practices are all uniquely different	Regulations and institutions are well known
Foreign exchange risk	MNEs face foreign exchange risks due to their subsidiaries, as well as import/export and foreign competitors	Foreign exchange risks from import/export and foreign competition (no subsidiaries)
Political risk	MNEs face political risks because of their foreign subsidiaries and high profile	Negligible political risks
Modification of domestic finance theories	MNEs must modify finance theories like capital budgeting and cost of capital because of foreign complexities	Traditional financial theory applies
Modification of domestic financial instruments	MNEs utilize modified financial instruments such as options, futures, swaps, and letters of credit	Limited use of financial instruments and derivatives because of fewer foreign exchange and political risks

domestic firms and MNEs are exposed to foreign exchange risks, MNEs alone face certain unique risks, such as political risks, that are not normally a threat to domestic operations.

MNEs also face other risks that can be classified as extensions of domestic finance theory. For example, the normal domestic approach to the cost of capital, sourcing debt and equity, capital budgeting, working capital management, taxation, and credit analysis needs to be modified to accommodate foreign complexities. Moreover, a number of financial instruments that are used in domestic financial management have been modified for use in international financial management. Examples are foreign currency options and futures, interest rate and currency swaps, and letters of credit.

The main theme of this book is to analyze how a multinational enterprise's financial management evolves as it pursues global strategic opportunities and new constraints emerge. In this opening chapter, we will take a brief look at the challenges and risks associated with Trident Corporation (Trident), a company evolving from domestic in scope to being truly multinational. The discussion will include the constraints that a company will face in terms of managerial goals and governance as it becomes increasingly involved in multinational operations. But first we need to clarify the unique value proposition and advantages which the MNE was created to exploit.

Market Imperfections: A Rationale for the Existence of the Multinational Firm

MNEs strive to take advantage of imperfections in national markets for products, factors of production, and financial assets. Imperfections in the market for products translate into market opportunities for MNEs. Large international firms are better able to exploit such competitive factors as economies of scale, managerial and technological expertise, product differentiation, and financial strength than are their local competitors. In fact, MNEs thrive best in markets characterized by international oligopolistic competition, where these factors are particularly critical. In addition, once MNEs have established a physical presence abroad, they are in a better position than purely domestic firms to identify and implement market opportunities through their own internal information network.

Why Do Firms become Multinational?

Strategic motives drive the decision to invest abroad and become an MNE. These motives can be summarized under the following five categories:

1. **Market seekers** produce in foreign markets either to satisfy local demand or to export to markets other than their home market. U.S. automobile firms manufacturing in Europe for local consumption are an example of market-seeking motivation. Porsche, a European automaker discussed in this chapter's mini-case, has chosen *not* to follow this path.

2. **Raw material seekers** extract raw materials wherever they can be found, either for export or for further processing and sale in the country in which they are found— the host country. Firms in the oil, mining, plantation, and forest industries fall into this category.

3. **Production efficiency seekers** produce in countries where one or more of the factors of production are underpriced relative to their productivity. Labor-intensive production of electronic components in Taiwan, Malaysia, and Mexico is an example of this motivation.

4. **Knowledge seekers** operate in foreign countries to gain access to technology or managerial expertise. For example, German, Dutch, and Japanese firms have purchased U.S.-located electronics firms for their technology.

5. **Political safety seekers** acquire or establish new operations in countries that are considered unlikely to expropriate or interfere with private enterprise. For example, Hong Kong firms invested heavily in the United States, United Kingdom, Canada, and Australia in anticipation of the consequences of China's 1997 takeover of the British colony.

These five types of strategic considerations are not mutually exclusive. Forest products firms seeking wood fiber in Brazil, for example, may also find a large Brazilian market for a portion of their output.

In industries characterized by worldwide oligopolistic competition, each of the above strategic motives should be subdivided into *proactive* and *defensive* investments. Proactive investments are designed to enhance the growth and profitability of the firm itself. Defensive investments are designed to deny growth and profitability to the firm's competitors. Examples of the latter are investments that try to preempt a market before competitors can get established in it, or capture raw material sources and deny them to competitors.

The Globalization Process

Trident is a hypothetical U.S.-based firm that will be used as an illustrative example throughout the book to demonstrate the *globalization process*—the structural and managerial changes and challenges experienced by a firm as it moves its operations from domestic to global.

Global Transition I: Trident Moves from the Domestic Phase to the International Trade Phase

Trident is a young firm that manufactures and distributes an array of telecommunication devices. Its initial strategy is to develop a sustainable competitive advantage in the U.S. market. Like many other young firms it is constrained by its small size, competitors, and lack of access to cheap and plentiful sources of capital. The top half of Exhibit 1.4 shows Trident

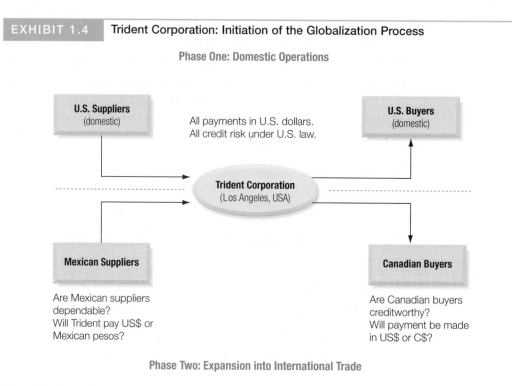

EXHIBIT 1.4 Trident Corporation: Initiation of the Globalization Process

Phase One: Domestic Operations

Phase Two: Expansion into International Trade

in its early *domestic phase*. Trident sells its products in U.S. dollars to U.S. customers and buys its manufacturing and service inputs from U.S. suppliers, paying U.S. dollars. The creditworth of all suppliers and buyers is established under domestic U.S. practices and procedures. A potential issue for Trident at this time is that although Trident is not international or global in its operations, some of its competitors, suppliers, or buyers may be. This is often the impetus to push a firm like Trident into the first transition of the globalization process, into international trade.

Trident was founded by James and Edgar Winston in Los Angeles in 1948 to make telecommunications equipment. The family-owned business expanded slowly but steadily over the following 40 years. The demands of continual technological investment in the 1980s, however, required that the firm raise additional equity capital in order to compete. This need led to its initial public offering (IPO) in 1988. As a U.S.-based publicly traded company on NASDAQ, Trident's management sought to *create value for its shareholders*.

As Trident became a visible and viable competitor in the U.S. market, strategic opportunities arose to expand the firm's market reach by exporting product and services to one or more foreign markets. The North American Free Trade Area (NAFTA) made trade with Mexico and Canada attractive. This second phase of the globalization process is shown in the lower-half of Exhibit 1.4. Trident responded to these globalization forces by importing inputs from Mexican suppliers and making export sales to Canadian buyers. We define this stage of the globalization process as the *International Trade Phase*.

Exporting and importing products and services increases the demands of financial management over and above the traditional requirements of the domestic-only business. First, direct *foreign exchange risks* are now borne by the firm. Trident may now need to quote prices in foreign currencies, accept payment in foreign currencies, or pay suppliers in foreign currencies. As the value of currencies change from minute to minute in the global marketplace, Trident will now experience significant risks from the changing values associated with these foreign currency payments and receipts. As discussed in this chapter's mini-case on Porsche, foreign exchange risks may result in gains as well as losses!

Second, the evaluation of the credit quality of foreign buyers and sellers is now more important than ever. Reducing the possibility of non-payment for exports and non-delivery of imports becomes one of two main financial management tasks during the international trade phase. This *credit risk management* task is much more difficult in international business, as buyers and suppliers are new, subject to differing business practices and legal systems, and generally more challenging to assess.

Global Transition II: The International Trade Phase to the Multinational Phase

If Trident is successful in its international trade activities, the time will come when the globalization process will progress to the next phase. Trident will soon need to establish foreign sales and service affiliates. This step is often followed by establishing manufacturing operations abroad or by licensing foreign firms to produce and service Trident's products. The multitude of issues and activities associated with this second larger global transition is the true purpose of this book.

Trident's continued globalization will require it to identify the sources of its competitive advantage, and with that knowledge, expand its intellectual capital and physical presence globally. A variety of strategic alternatives are available to Trident—the *foreign direct investment sequence*—as shown in Exhibit 1.5. These alternatives include the creation of foreign sales offices, the licensing of the company name and everything associated with it, and

EXHIBIT 1.5	Trident's Foreign Direct Investment Sequence

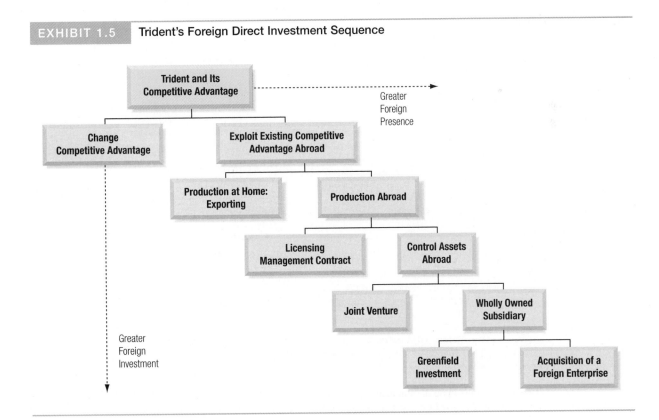

the manufacturing and distribution of its products to other firms in foreign markets. As Trident moves farther down and to the right in Exhibit 1.9, the degree of its physical presence in foreign markets increases. It may now own its own distribution and production facilities, and ultimately, may want to acquire other companies. Once Trident owns assets and enterprises in foreign countries it has entered the *multinational phase* of its globalization.

The Limits to Financial Globalization

The theories of international business and international finance introduced in this chapter have long argued that with an increasingly open and transparent global marketplace in which capital may flow freely, capital will increasingly flow and support countries and companies based on the *theory of comparative advantage*. Since the mid-twentieth century this has indeed been the case as more and more countries have pursued more open and competitive markets. But the past decade has seen the growth of a new kind of limit or impediment to *financial globalization*: the growth in the influence and self-enrichment of organizational insiders.[1]

One possible representation of this process can be seen in Exhibit 1.6. If influential insiders in corporations and sovereign states continue to pursue the increase in firm value, there will be a definite and continuing growth in financial globalization. But, if these same influential insiders pursue their own personal agendas, which may increase their personal power and influence or personal wealth, or both, then capital will not flow into these sovereign states and corporations. The result is the growth of financial inefficiency and the segmentation of globalization outcomes—creating winners and losers. As we will see

---

EXHIBIT 1.6   **The Potential Limits of Financial Globalization**

There is a growing debate over whether many of the insiders and rulers of organizations with enterprises globally are taking actions consistent with creating firm value or consistent with increasing their own personal stakes and power.

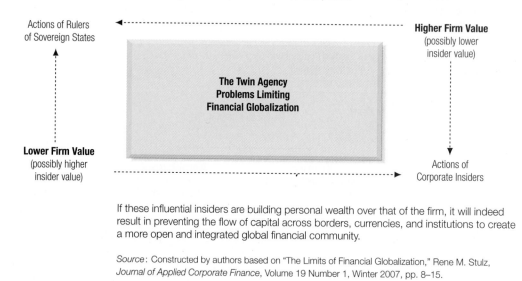

If these influential insiders are building personal wealth over that of the firm, it will indeed result in preventing the flow of capital across borders, currencies, and institutions to create a more open and integrated global financial community.

Source: Constructed by authors based on "The Limits of Financial Globalization," Rene M. Stulz, *Journal of Applied Corporate Finance*, Volume 19 Number 1, Winter 2007, pp. 8–15.

---

[1]This section draws upon the stimulating thoughts presented in "The Limits of Financial Globalization," Rene M. Stulz, *Journal of Applied Corporate Finance*, Volume 19, Number 1, Winter 2007, pp. 8–15.

throughout this book, this barrier to international finance may indeed be increasingly troublesome.

This growing dilemma is also something of a composite of what this book is about. The three fundamental elements—*financial theory*, *global business*, and *management beliefs and actions*—combine to present either the problem or the solution to the growing debate over the benefits of globalization to countries and cultures worldwide. The mini-case on Porsche sets the stage for our debate and discussion. Are the controlling family members of this company creating value for themselves or their shareholders?

SUMMARY POINTS

- The creation of value requires combining three critical elements: 1) an open marketplace; 2) high quality strategic management; and 3) access to capital.

- The basic theory, comparative advantage, and its requirements should be considered for the explanation and justification for international trade and commerce.

- The theory of comparative advantage provides a basis for explaining and justifying international trade in a model world assumed to enjoy free trade, perfect competition, no uncertainty, costless information, and no government interference.

- International financial management requires an understanding of cultural, historical, and institutional differences such as those affecting corporate governance.

- Although both domestic firms and MNEs are exposed to foreign exchange risks, MNEs alone face certain unique risks, such as political risks, that are not normally a threat to domestic operations.

- MNEs strive to take advantage of imperfections in national markets for products, factors of production, and financial assets.

- Large international firms are better able to exploit such competitive factors as economies of scale, managerial and technological expertise, product differentiation, and financial strength than are their local competitors.

- A firm may first enter into international trade transactions, then international contractual arrangements such as sales offices and franchising, and ultimately the acquisition of foreign subsidiaries. It is at this final stage that it truly becomes a multinational enterprise (MNE).

- The decision whether or not to invest abroad is driven by strategic motives, and may require the MNE to enter into global licensing agreements, joint ventures, cross-border acquisitions, or Greenfield Investments.

- If influential insiders in corporations and sovereign states pursue their own personal agendas which may increase their personal power, influence, or wealth, then capital will not flow into these sovereign states and corporations. In turn, this will create limitations to globalization in finance.

MINI-CASE   **Porsche Changes Tack[1]**

"Yes, of course we have heard of shareholder value. But that does not change the fact that we put customers first, then workers, then business partners, suppliers, and dealers, and then shareholders."

—*Dr. Wendelin Wiedeking, CEO, Porsche, Die Zeit,* April 17, 2005.

Porsche had always been different. Statements by Porsche leadership, like the one shown here, always made Veselina (Vesi) Dinova nervous about the company's attitude about creating shareholder value. The company was a paradox. Porsche's attitudes and activities were like that of a family-owned firm, but it had succeeded in creating substantial shareholder value for more than a decade.

Porsche's CEO, Dr. Wendelin Wiedeking, had been credited with clarity of purpose and sureness of execution. As one colleague described him: "He grew up PSD: poor, smart, and driven."

Porsche's management had created confusion in the marketplace as to which value proposition Porsche presented. Was Porsche continuing to develop an organizational focus on *shareholder value*, or was it returning to its more traditional German roots of *German cronyism*? Simply put, was Porsche's leadership pursuing family objectives at the expense of its shareholders?

Porsche AG

Porsche AG was a publicly traded, closely held German-based auto manufacturer. Porsche's President and Chief Executive Officer, Dr. Wendelin Wiedeking, had returned the company to both status and profitability since taking over the company in 1993. Immediately after taking over, he had killed the 928 and 968 model platforms to reduce complexity and cost, although at the time this left the company with only one platform, the 911. Wiedeking had then brought in a group of Japanese manufacturing consultants, in the Toyota tradition, who led the complete overhaul of the company's manufacturing processes.

Although Porsche was traded on the Frankfurt Stock Exchange (and associated German exchanges), control of the company remained firmly in the hands of the founding families, the Porsche and Piëch families. Porsche had two classes of shares, *ordinary* and *preference*. The two families held all 8.75 million *ordinary shares*—the shares which held all voting rights. The second class of share, *preference shares*, participated only in profits. All 8.75 million preference shares were publicly traded. Approximately 50% of all preference shares were held by large institutional investors in the United States, Germany, and the United Kingdom, 14% were held by the Porsche and Piëch families, and 36% were held by small private investors. As noted by the Chief Financial Officer, Holger Härter, "As long as the two families hold on to their stock portfolios, there won't be any external influence on company-related decisions. I have no doubt that the families will hang on to their shares."

Porsche was somewhat infamous for its independent thinking and occasional stubbornness when it came to disclosure and compliance with reporting requirements—the prerequisites of being publicly traded. In 2002 the company had chosen not to list on the New York Stock Exchange after the passage of the Sarbanes-Oxley Act. The company pointed to the specific requirement of Sarbanes-Oxley that senior management sign off on the financial results of the company personally as being inconsistent with German law (which it largely was) and illogical for management to accept. Management had also long been critical of the practice of quarterly reporting, and had in fact been removed from the Frankfurt Exchange's stock index in September 2002 because of its refusal to report quarterly financial results.

But, after all was said and done, the company had just reported record profits for the 10th consecutive year (see Exhibit 1). Returns were so good and had grown so steadily that the company had paid out a special dividend of €14 per share in 2002, in addition to increasing the size of the regular dividend. There was a continuing concern that management came first. In the words of one analyst "... we think there is the potential risk that management may not rate shareholders' interests very highly." The compensation packages of Porsche's senior management team were nearly exclusively focused on current year profitability (83% of executive board compensation was performance-related pay), with no management incentives or stock option awards related to the company's share price.

Porsche's Growing Portfolio

Porsche had three major vehicle platforms: the premier luxury sports car, the *911*; the competitively priced *Boxster* roadster; and the recently introduced off-road sport utility vehicle, the *Cayenne*. Porsche had also recently announced that it would be adding a fourth platform, the *Panamera*, which would be a high-end sedan to compete with Jaguar, Mercedes, and Bentley.

911. The 911 series was still the focal point of the Porsche brand, but many believed that it was growing old and due for replacement. Sales had seemingly peaked in 2001/02, and fallen back more than 15% in 2002/03. The 911 had always enjoyed nearly exclusive ownership of its market segment. Prices continued to be high, and margins were some of the very highest in the global auto industry for production models. The 911 was the only Porsche model that was manufactured and assembled in-house.

Boxster. The Boxster roadster had been introduced in 1996 as Porsche's entry into the lower price end of the sports car market. The Boxster was also considered an anticyclical move because the traditional 911 was so high-priced. The Boxster's lower price made it affordable and less sensitive to the business cycle. It did, however, compete in an increasingly competitive market segment. Boxster sales volumes had peaked in 2000/01.

Cayenne. The third major platform innovation was Porsche's entry into the sports utility vehicle (SUV)

EXHIBIT 1   **Porsche's Growth in Sales, Income, and Margin**

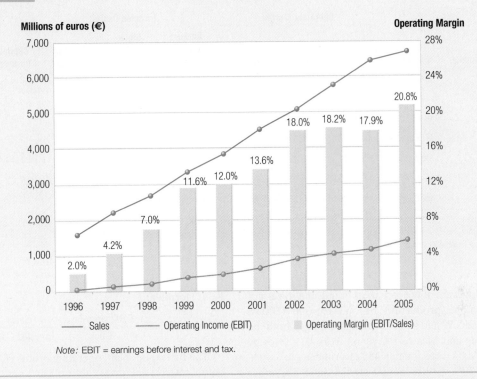

Note: EBIT = earnings before interest and tax.

segment, the Cayenne. Clearly at the top end of the market (2002/03 Cayenne sales averaged more than $70,000 each), the Cayenne had been a very quick success, especially in the SUV-crazed American market. It was considered the most successful new product launch in auto history. The Cayenne's success had been even more dramatic given much pre-launch criticism that the market would not support such a high-priced SUV, particularly one that shared a strong bloodline with the Volkswagen (VW) Touareg. The Porsche Cayenne and VW Touareg shared a common chassis, and in fact were both manufactured at the same factory in Bratislava, Slovakia. Porsche shipped the Cayenne chassis to its facility in Leipzig where the engine, drive train, and interior were combined in final assembly.

Panamera. On July 27, 2005, Porsche announced that it would proceed with the development and production of a fourth major model—the *Panamera*. The name was derived from the legendary *Carrera Panamericana* long-distance road race held for many years in Mexico. The Panamera would be a premium class four-door four-seat sports coupe, and would compete with the premium sedan models. Pricing was expected to begin at $125,000, rising to $175,000. Production was scheduled to begin in 2009 at a scale of 20,000 units per year.

The Most Profitable Automobile Company in the World

Porsche's financial performance and health, by auto manufacturer standards, European or elsewhere, was excellent. It was clearly the smallest of the major European-based manufacturers with total sales of €6.4 billion in 2004. But, as shown in Exhibit 2, Porsche was outstanding by all metrics of profitability and return on invested capital. Porsche's EBITDA, EBIT, and net income margins were the highest among all European automakers in 2004.

Foreign Exchange. Porsche's financial results, however, had been the subject of substantial debate in recent years as upwards of 40% of operating earnings were thought to be derived from currency hedging. Porsche's cost-base was purely European euro; it produced in only two countries, Germany and Finland, and both were euro area members. Porsche believed that the quality of its engineering and

| EXHIBIT 2 | Return on Invested Capital (ROIC) for European Automakers, 2004 |

European Automaker	Sales (millions)	Operating Margin			Invested Capital			Capital Turnover	ROIC
		EBIT	Taxes	EBIT After-tax	Interest-Bearing Debt	Stock-holders' Equity	Invested Capital		
BMW	€44,335	€3,745	€1,332	€2,413	€1,555	€17,517	€19,072	2.32	12.65%
DaimlerChrysler	€142,059	€4,612	€1,177	€3,435	€9,455	€33,541	€42,996	3.30	7.99%
Fiat	€46,703	€22	−€29	€51	€24,813	€5,946	€30,759	1.52	0.17%
Peugeot	€56,797	€1,916	€676	€1,240	€6,445	€13,356	€19,801	2.87	6.26%
Porsche	€6,359	€1,141	€470	€671	€2,105	€2,323	€4,428	1.44	15.15%
Renault	€40,715	€2,148	€634	€1,514	€7,220	€16,444	€23,664	1.72	6.40%
Volkswagen	€88,963	€1,620	€383	€1,237	€14,971	€23,957	€38,928	2.29	3.18%

Source: "European Autos," Deutsche Bank, July 20, 2005; "Porsche," Deutsche Bank, September 26, 2005; Thomson Analytics; author estimates. "Invested Capital" = total stockholders' equity + gross interest-bearing debt. Capital turnover = sales / Invested capital. ROIC (return on invested capital) = EBIT – taxes / Invested capital.

manufacturing were at the core of its brand, and it was not willing to move production beyond Europe (BMW, Mercedes, and VW had all been manufacturing in both the United States and Mexico for years). Porsche's sales by currency in 2004 were roughly 45% European euro, 40% U.S. dollar, 10% British pound sterling, and 5% other (primarily the Japanese yen and Swiss franc).

Porsche's leadership had undertaken a very aggressive currency hedging strategy beginning in 2001 when the euro was at a record low against the U.S. dollar. In the following years these financial hedges (currency derivatives) proved extremely profitable. For example, nearly 43% of operating earnings in 2003 were thought to have been derived from hedging activities. Although profitable, many analysts argued the company was increasingly an investment banking firm rather than an automaker, and was heavily exposed to the unpredictable fluctuations between the world's two most powerful currencies, the dollar and the euro.

ROIC. It was Porsche's return on invested capital (ROIC), however, which had been truly exceptional over time. The company's ROIC in 2004—following Deutsche Bank's analysis presented in Exhibit 2, was 15.15%. This was clearly superior to all other European automakers.

This ROIC reflected Porsche's two-pronged financial strategy: 1) superior margins on the narrow but selective product portfolio and 2) leveraging the capital and capabilities of manufacturing partners in the development and production of two of its three products. The company had successfully exploited the two primary drivers of the

ROIC formula:

$$\text{ROIC} = \frac{\text{EBIT after-tax}}{\text{Sales}} \times \frac{\text{Sales}}{\text{Invested Capital}}$$

The first component, operating profits (EBIT, earnings before interest and taxes) after-tax as a percent of sales—*operating margin*—was exceptional at Porsche due to the premium value pricing derived from its global brand of quality and excellence. This allowed Porsche to charge premium prices and achieve some of the largest margins in the auto industry. As shown in Exhibit 2, Porsche's operating profits after-tax of €671 million produced an operating margin after tax of 10.55% (€671 divided by €6,359 in sales), the highest in the industry in 2004.

The second component of ROIC, the *capital turnover ratio* (sales divided by invested capital)—*velocity*—although quite high compared to other automakers in the past, was one of the lowest in 2004 as seen in Exhibit 2. In recent years, however, *invested capital* had risen faster than sales. But Porsche was not adding fixed assets to its invested capital basis, but cash. The rising cash balances were the result of retained profits (undistributed to shareholders) and new debt issuances (raising more than €600 million in 2004 alone). As a result, fiscal 2003/04 had proven to be one of Porsche's poorest years in ROIC. Porsche's minimal levels of invested capital resulted from some rather unique characteristics.

Invested capital is defined a number of ways, but Vesi used her employer's standardized definition of cash plus net working capital plus net fixed assets. Porsche's invested capital was growing primarily because of its

EXHIBIT 3   Porsche's Velocity, Margin, and ROIC

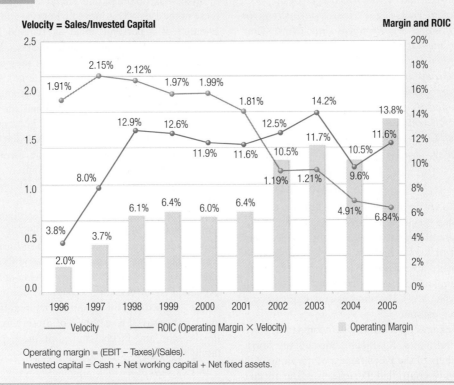

Operating margin = (EBIT − Taxes)/(Sales).
Invested capital = Cash + Net working capital + Net fixed assets.

accumulation of cash. Vesi was concerned that using this measure of "invested capital" led to a distorted view of the company's actual performance. Porsche's minimal fixed asset capital base resulted from the explicit strategy of the company as executed over the past decade.

Porsche Changes Tack

The summer and fall of 2005 saw a series of surprising moves by Porsche. First, Porsche announced that the €1 billion investment to design and manufacture the new Panamera would be largely funded by the company itself. Although the introduction of the Panamera had been anticipated for quite some time, the market was surprised that Porsche intended to design and build the car—and its manufacturing facility—nearly totally in-house. As opposed to the previous new product introductions, the Boxster and the Cayenne, there would be no major production partner involved. Porsche CEO Wendelin Wiedeking specifically noted this in his press release: "There are no plans for a joint venture with another car maker. But to ensure the profitability of this new model series we will cooperate more closely than so far with

selected system suppliers." The *German share* of the value of the Panamera would be roughly 70%. Like the 911, Boxster, and Cayenne, the Panamera would bear the *Made in Germany* stamp. The second surprise occurred on September 25, 2005, with the announcement to invest €3 billion in VW.

Porsche AG, Stuttgart, seeks to acquire a share of approximately 20 per cent in the stock capital of Volkswagen AG, Wolfsburg, entitled to vote. Porsche is taking this decision because Volkswagen is now not only an important development partner for Porsche, but also a significant supplier of approximately 30 per cent of Porsche's sales volume. In the words of Porsche's President and CEO: "Making this investment, we seek to secure our business relations with Volkswagen and make a significant contribution to our own future plans on a lasting, long-term basis." Porsche is in a position to finance the acquisition of the planned share in Volkswagen through its own, existing liquidity. After careful examination of this business case, Porsche is confident that the investment will prove profitable for both parties.

... The planned acquisition is to ensure that ... there will not be a hostile takeover of Volkswagen by investors not committed to Volkswagen's long-term interests. In the words of Porsche's President and CEO: "Our planned investment is the strategic answer to this risk. We wish in this way to ensure the independence of the Volkswagen Group in our own interest. This 'German solution' we are seeking is an essential prerequisite for stable development of the Volkswagen Group and, accordingly, for continuing our cooperation in the interest of both Companies."

> —"Acquisition of Stock to Secure Porsche's Business," Porsche AG (press release), September 25, 2005.

Porsche would spend approximately €3 billion to take a 20% ownership position in VW. This would make Porsche VW's single largest investor, slightly larger than the government of Lower Saxony.[2] It clearly eliminated any possible hostile acquisitions that may have been on the horizon (DaimlerChrysler was rumored to have been interested in raiding VW). The announcement was met by near universal opposition.

The family linkages between the two companies were well known. Ferdinand K. Piëch, one of the most prominent members of the Piëch family, which along with the Porsche family controlled Porsche, was the former CEO (he retired in 2002) and still Chairman of Volkswagen. He was the grandson of Ferdinand Porsche, the founder of Porsche. Accusations of conflict of interest were immediate, as were calls for his resignation, and the denial of Porsche's request for a seat on VW's board. Although VW officially welcomed the investment by Porsche, Christian Wulff, VW's board member representing the state of Lower Saxony where VW was headquartered, publicly opposed the investment by Porsche. In the eyes of many, the move by Porsche was a return to German corporate cronyism.

For years, "Deutschland AG" was emblematic of the cosy network of cross-shareholdings and shared non-executive directorships that insulated Germany from international capitalism. Wendelin Wiedeking, Porsche's chief executive, himself invoked the national angle, saying this "German solution" was essential to secure VW, Europe's largest carmaker, against a possible hostile takeover by short-term investors.

> —"Shield for corporate Germany or a family affair? VW and Porsche close ranks,"*Financial Times*, Tuesday, September 27, 2005, p. 17.

Germany, although long known for complex networks of cross-shareholdings, had effectively unwound most of these in the 1990s. This move by Porsche and VW was seen as more of a personal issue—Ferdinand Piëch—rather than a national issue of German alliances. Many Porsche investors had agreed, arguing that if they had wanted to invest in VW they would have done it themselves. Although the arguments for solidifying and securing the Porsche/VW partnership were rational, the cost was not. At €3 billion, this was an enormous investment in a non-performing asset. Analysts concluded that the potential returns to shareholders, even in the form of a special dividend, were now postponed indefinitely.

The announcement of Porsche's intention to take a 20% equity interest in VW was greeted with outright opposition on the part of many shareholders in both VW and Porsche. Major investment banks immediately downgraded Porsche from a *buy* to a *sell*, arguing that the returns on the massive investment, some €3 billion, would likely never accrue to shareholders. Although Porsche had explained its investment decision to be one that would assure the stability of its future cooperation with VW, many critics saw it as a choice of preserving the stakes of the Porsche and Piëch families at the expense of non-family shareholders.

"Why should a small and highly-profitable maker of sports cars suddenly hitch its fortunes to a lumbering and struggling mass-producer? That was the question that some alarmed shareholders asked this week when Porsche, the world's most profitable carmaker, announced plans to buy 20% stake in Volkswagen (VW), Europe's biggest carmaker. To some critics of the deal, Porsche's move looked like a return to cosy, German corporatism at its worst. Since January 2002, when a change in the law encouraged German companies to sell their cross-shareholdings in each other, free of capital gains tax, new foreign shareholders have often shaken up fossilized German management. A deal with friendly compatriots from Porsche might rescue VW from this distasteful fate, particularly since foreign hedge funds and corporate raiders have been rumored to be circling VW."

> —"Business: Keeping It in the Family," *The Economist*, October 1, 2005.

Case Questions

1. What strategic decisions made by Porsche over recent years had given rise to its extremely high return on invested capital?

---

[2] The resulting ownership structure of Volkswagen in October 2005 was: 18.53% Porsche; 18.2% State of Lower Saxony; 13.0% Volkswagen; 8.58% Brandes Investment Partners; 3.5% Capital Group; and 38.19% widely distributed.

2. Vesi wondered if her position on Porsche might have to distinguish between the company's *ability* to generate results for stockholders versus its *willingness* to do so. What do you think?

3. Is pursuing the interests of Porsche's controlling families different from maximizing the returns to its public share owners?

QUESTIONS

1. Globalization and the MNE. The term *globalization* has become very widely used in recent years. How would you define it?

2. Globalization and Value Creation. What does an MNE need in order for it to create value through the globalization process?

3. Value Creation and the Concept of Capitalism. How does the concept of *capitalism* actually apply to the globalization process of a business, as it moves from elemental to multinational stages of development?

4. Theory of Comparative Advantage. Define and explain the theory of comparative advantage.

5. Limitations of Comparative Advantage. Key to understanding most theories is what they say and what they don't. What are four or five key limitations to the theory of comparative advantage?

6. Trident's Globalization. After reading this chapter's description of Trident's globalization process, how would you explain the distinctions between *international*, *multinational*, and *global* companies?

7. Trident, the MNE. At what point in the globalization process did Trident become a multinational enterprise (MNE)?

8. Trident's Advantages. What are the main advantages that Trident gains by developing a multinational presence?

9. Trident's Phases. What are the main phases that Trident passed through as it evolved into a truly global firm? What are the advantages and disadvantages of each?

10. Financial Globalization. How do the motivations of individuals, both inside and outside the organization or business, define the limits of financial globalization?

PROBLEMS

Comparative Advantage

Problems 1–5 illustrate an example of trade induced by comparative advantage. They assume that China and France each have 1,000 production units. With one unit of production (a mix of land, labor, capital, and technology), China can produce either ten containers of toys or seven cases of wine. France can produce either two containers of toys or seven cases of wine. Thus, a production unit in China is five times as efficient compared to France when producing toys, but equally efficient when producing wine. Assume at first that no trade takes place. China allocates 800 production units to building toys and 200 production units to producing wine. France allocates 200 production units to building toys and 800 production units to producing wine.

1. Production and Consumption. What is the production and consumption of China and France without trade?

2. Specialization. Assume complete specialization, where China produces only toys and France produces only wine. What would be the effect on total production?

3. Trade at China's Domestic Price. China's domestic price is ten containers of toys equals seven cases of wine. Assume China produces 10,000 containers of toys and exports 2,000 containers to France. Assume France produces 7,000 cases of wine and exports 1,400 cases to China. What happens to total production and consumption?

4. Trade at France's Domestic Price. France's domestic price is two containers of toys equals seven cases of wine. Assume China produces 10,000 containers of toys and exports 400 containers to France. Assume France in turn produces 7,000 cases of wine and exports 1,400 cases to China. What happens to total production and consumption?

5. Trade at Negotiated Mid-price. The mid-price for exchange between France and China can be calculated as follows:

	Toys		Wine
China's domestic price	10	to	7
France's domestic price	2	to	7
Negotiated mid-price	6	to	7

What happens to total production and consumption?

Luzon Industries—2007

Problems 6 through 10 are based on Luzon Industries. Luzon is a U.S.-based multinational manufacturing firm, with wholly owned subsidiaries in Brazil, Germany, and China, in addition to domestic operations in the United States. Luzon is traded on the NASDAQ. Luzon currently has 650,000 shares outstanding. The basic operating characteristics of the various business units are as follows:

(000s, local currency)	USA (dollars, $)	Brazil (reais, R$)	Germany (euros, €)	China (yuan, Y)
Earnings before tax (EBT)	$4,500	R$6,250	€4,500	Y2,500
Corporate income tax rate	35%	25%	40%	30%
Average exchange rate for period	—	R$1.80/$	€0.7018/$	Y7.750/$

*6. **Luzon Corporation's Consolidated Earnings.** Luzon must pay corporate income tax in each country in which it currently has operations.
   a. After deducting taxes in each country, what are Luzon's consolidated earnings and consolidated earnings per share in U.S. dollars?
   b. What proportion of Luzon's consolidated earnings arise from each individual country?
   c. What proportion of Luzon's consolidated earnings arise from outside the United States?

7. **Luzon's EPS Sensitivity to Exchange Rates (A).** Assume a major political crisis wracks Brazil, first affecting the value of the Brazilian reais and, subsequently, inducing an economic recession within the country. What would be the impact on Luzon's consolidated EPS if the Brazilian reais were to fall to R$3.00/$, with all other earnings and exchange rates remaining the same?

8. **Luzon's EPS Sensitivity to Exchange Rates (B).** Assume a major political crisis wracks Brazil, first affecting the value of the Brazilian reais and, subsequently, inducing an economic recession within the country. What would be the impact on Luzon's consolidated EPS if, in addition to the fall in the value of the reais to R$3.00/$, earnings before taxes in Brazil fell as a result of the recession to R$5,800,000?

*9. **Luzon's Earnings and the Fall of the Dollar.** The U.S. dollar has experienced significant swings in value against most of the world's currencies in recent years.

   a. What would be the impact on Luzon's consolidated EPS if all foreign currencies were to appreciate 20% against the U.S. dollar?
   b. What would be the impact on Luzon's consolidated EPS if all foreign currencies were to depreciate 20% against the U.S. dollar?

   Note: Calculate the percentage changes by dividing the initial currency value by (1 + the percentage change) to calculate the new currency value.

10. **Luzon's Earnings and Global Taxation.** All MNEs attempt to minimize their global tax liabilities. Return to the original set of baseline assumptions and answer the following questions regarding Luzon's global tax liabilities.
   a. What is the total amount—in U.S. dollars—which Luzon is paying across its global business in corporate income taxes?
   b. What is Luzon's effective tax rate on a global basis (total taxes paid as a percentage of pre-tax profits)?
   c. What would be the impact on Luzon's EPS and global effective tax rate if Germany instituted a corporate tax reduction to 28%, and Luzon's earnings before tax in Germany rose to €5,000,000?

INTERNET EXERCISES

1. **International Capital Flows: Public and Private.** Major multinational organizations (some of which follow) attempt to track the relative movements and magnitudes of global capital investment. Using the following Web pages and others, prepare a two-page executive briefing on the question of whether capital generated in the industrialized countries is finding its way to the less developed and emerging markets. Is there some critical distinction between "less developed" and "emerging"?

The World Bank	www.worldbank.org/
OECD	www.oecd.org/
European Bank for Reconstruction	www.ebrd.org/

2. **International Management and Strategy Consultancies.** The management consulting industry has been one of the primary resources utilized by MNEs throughout the world in the 1990s to design and develop their corporate strategies. The following Web pages provide some insight into the industry, the job opportunities available for professionals in

consulting, as well as some interesting features such as the Boston Consulting Group's online interactive case study:

A.T. Kearney	www.atkearney.com/
Bain and Company	www.rec.bain.com/
Booze, Allen & Hamilton	www.bah.com/
Boston Consulting Group	www.bcg.com/
McKinsey & Company	www.mckinsey.com/

3. **External Debt.** The World Bank regularly compiles and analyzes the external debt of all countries globally. As part of their annual publication on World Development Indicators (WDI), they provide summaries of the long-term and short-term external debt obligations of selected countries online like that of Poland shown here. Go to the following Web site

and find the decomposition of external debt for Brazil, Mexico, and the Russian Federation:

The World Bank   www.worldbank.org/data

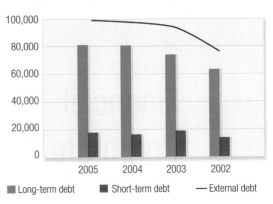

Country: Poland; Data are in millions

CHAPTER 2

Financial Goals and Corporate Governance

Gerald L. Storch, CEO of Toys 'R' Us, says all CEOs share the same fundamental goals: enhance the value for the customer, maximize return to the shareholders, and develop a sustainable competitive advantage. "Largely, I believe that the differences are more subtle than what I've read in many articles. On a day-to-day basis, I do the same thing. I get to work every morning. I try to make the company better."

—"Public Vs. Private," *Forbes*, September 1, 2006.

This chapter examines how cultural, legal, political, and institutional differences affect a firm's choice of financial goals and corporate governance.

Who Owns the Business?

We begin our discussion of financial goals by asking a sequence of two basic questions: 1) who owns the business? and 2) do the owners of the business manage the business themselves? Most companies are created by entrepreneurs who are either individuals or a small set of partners. In either case they may be the members of a family. (Do not forget that even Microsoft started its existence as the brain-child of two partners, Bill Gates and Paul Allen.) As shown in Exhibit 2.1, companies begin on the left-hand side as ownership version A, a 100% privately held business.

Over time, however, some firms may choose to go public via an initial public offering, or IPO. Typically, only a relatively small percentage of the company is initially sold to the public, resulting in a company that may still be controlled by a small number of private investors, but who also have public shares outstanding, which are generating a market-based share price on a daily basis. This is ownership version B, as shown in Exhibit 2.1.

Whether the ownership structure ever actually moves from version B to C or D is very case specific. Some companies may sell more and more of their equity interests into the public marketplace, possibly eventually becoming totally publicly traded. Or the private owner or family may choose to retain a major share but does not have explicit control. Possibly, as has been the case in recent years, a firm that has reached ownership versions C

EXHIBIT 2.1   Who Owns the Business?

Who owns the business—whether it's privately held or publicly traded—has a significant impact on the relationship between ownership and operational ownership.

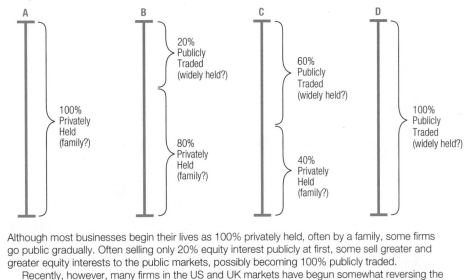

Although most businesses begin their lives as 100% privately held, often by a family, some firms go public gradually. Often selling only 20% equity interest publicly at first, some sell greater and greater equity interests to the public markets, possibly becoming 100% publicly traded.

Recently, however, many firms in the US and UK markets have begun somewhat reversing the process, with private equity funds buying all outstanding shares, taking the firm private once more.

or D may move back toward B or even A as the company becomes owned outright by a private owner. For example, in late 2005 a very large private firm, Koch Industries (U.S.), purchased all outstanding shares of Georgia-Pacific (U.S.), a very large publicly traded forest products company. Koch took Georgia-Pacific private.

An added consideration is that even when the firm's ownership is publicly traded, it may still be controlled by a single investor or a small group of investors, including major institutional investors. This means that the control of the company is much like the privately held company, and therefore reflects the interests and goals of the individual investor. And as shown in *Global Finance in Practice 2.1*, family controlled firms all over the world, including France, may outperform publicly traded firms.

As discussed in the "Corporate Governance" section later in this chapter, something else of significance results from the initial sale of shares to the public: the firm becomes subject to many of the increased legal, regulatory, and reporting requirements in most countries surrounding the sale and trading of securities. In the United States, for example, going public means the firm will now have to disclose a sizable degree of financial and operational detail, publish this information at least quarterly, comply with Securities and Exchange Commission (SEC) rules and regulations, and comply with all the specific operating and reporting requirements of the specific exchange on which it is traded. Obviously, the move to public trading of shares comes with a lot of luggage!

Separation of Ownership from Management

The change in ownership from version A to B or C or D in Exhibit 2.1 carries with it another major change—the possibility that the firm is managed by hired professionals, not owners. This raises the possibility that ownership and management may not be perfectly aligned in their business and financial objectives, the so-called *agency problem*.

GLOBAL FINANCE IN PRACTICE 2.1

Family Controlled Firms in France Outperform the Public Sector

Translation: "Why do family firms outperform the CAC 40 index?"

Among the major industrial countries, France has the highest number of family businesses (about 65% of the CAC 40 firms are family owned versus only about 24% in the UK). This includes Bouygues, Dassault, Michelin and Peugeot. Over the 1990–2006 period, French family firms generated a 639% return to their owners, whereas the major French index, the CAC 40, returned only 292%. This family owned firm dominance is attributed to three factors: 1) they focus on the long-term; 2) they stick to their core business; and 3) because the owners are closer to management, fewer conflicts arise between management and ownership (fewer agency problems in the terminology of Finance).

Source: Le Figaro, June 2007.

The U.S. and U.K. stock markets have been characterized by widespread ownership of shares. Management owns only a small proportion of stock in their firms. In contrast, in the rest of the world ownership is usually characterized by controlling shareholders. Typical controlling shareholders are as follows:

- Government (for example privatized utilities)
- Institutions (such as banks in Germany)
- Family (such as in France and Asia)
- Consortiums (such as *keiretsus* in Japan and *chaebols* in South Korea)

Control is enhanced by ownership of shares with dual voting rights, interlocking directorates, staggered election of the board of directors, takeover safeguards, and other techniques not used in the Anglo-American markets. However, the recent emergence of huge equity funds and hedge funds in the United States and the United Kingdom has led to the privatization of some very prominent publicly traded firms.

What Is the Goal of Management?

As Trident becomes more deeply committed to multinational operations, a new constraint develops—one that springs from divergent worldwide opinions and practices as to just what the firms' overall goal should be from the perspective of top management, as well as the role of corporate governance.

What do investors want? First, of course, investors want performance: strong predictable earnings and sustainable growth. Second, they want transparency, accountability, open communications and effective corporate governance. Companies that fail to move toward international standards in each of these areas will fail to attract and retain international capital.

—"The Brave New World of Corporate Governance," *LatinFinance*, May 2001.

An introductory course in finance is usually taught within the framework of maximizing shareholders' wealth as *the goal of management*. In fact, every business student memorizes the concept of *maximizing shareholder value* sometime during his or her college education. This rather rote memorization, however, has at least two major challenges: 1) it is not necessarily the accepted goal of management across countries to maximize the wealth of shareholders—other stakeholders may carry substantial weight and 2) it is extremely difficult to carry out. *Creating value* is—like so many lofty goals—much easier said than done.

Although the idea of maximizing shareholder wealth is probably realistic both in theory and in practice in the Anglo-American markets, it is not always exclusive elsewhere. Some basic differences in corporate and investor philosophies exist between the Anglo-American markets and those in the rest of the world. Therefore, one must realize that the so-called *universal truths* taught in basic finance courses are actually *culturally determined norms*.

Shareholder Wealth Maximization Model

The Anglo-American markets have a philosophy that a firm's objective should follow the *shareholder wealth maximization (SWM)* model. More specifically, the firm should strive to maximize the return to shareholders, as measured by the sum of capital gains and dividends, for a given level of risk. Alternatively, the firm should minimize the risk to shareholders for a given rate of return.

The SWM model assumes as a universal truth that the stock market is *efficient*. This means that the share price is always correct because it captures all the expectations of return and risk as perceived by investors. It quickly incorporates new information into the share price. Share prices, in turn, are deemed the best allocators of capital in the macro economy.

The SWM model also treats its definition of risk as a universal truth. Risk is defined as the added risk that the firm's shares bring to a diversified portfolio. The total operational risk of the firm can be eliminated through portfolio diversification by the investors. Therefore, this *unsystematic risk*, the risk of the individual security, should not be a prime concern for management unless it increases the prospect of bankruptcy. *Systematic risk*, the risk of the market in general, cannot be eliminated. This reflects risk that the share price will be a function of the stock market.

Agency Theory. The field of *agency theory* is the study of how shareholders can motivate management to accept the prescriptions of the SWM model.[1] For example, liberal use of stock options should encourage management to think like shareholders. Whether these inducements succeed is open to debate. However, if management deviates too much from SWM objectives of working to maximize the returns to the shareholders—the board of directors should replace them. In cases where the board is too weak or ingrown to take this action, the discipline of the equity markets could do it through a takeover. This discipline is made possible by the one-share-one-vote rule that exists in most Anglo-American markets.

---

[1] Michael Jensen and W. Meckling, "Theory of the Firm: Managerial Behavior, Agency Costs, and Ownership Structure," *Journal of Financial Economics*, No. 3, 1976, and Michael C. Jensen, "Agency Cost of Free Cash Flow, Corporate Finance and Takeovers," *American Economic Review*, 76, 1986, pp. 323–329.

Long-Term versus Short-Term Value Maximization. During the 1990s the economic boom and rising stock prices in the United States and abroad exposed a flaw in the SWM model, especially in the United States. Instead of seeking long-term value maximization, several large U.S. corporations sought short-term value maximization (e.g., the continuing debate about meeting the market's expected quarterly earnings). This strategy was partly motivated by the overly generous use of stock options to motivate top management. In order to maximize growth in short-term earnings and to meet inflated expectations by investors, firms such as Enron, Global Crossing, Health South, Adelphia, Tyco, Parmalat, and WorldCom undertook risky, deceptive, and sometimes dishonest practices for the recording of earnings and/or obfuscation of liabilities, which ultimately led to their demise. It also led to highly visible prosecutions of their CEOs, CFOs, accounting firms, legal advisers, and other related parties. This destructive short-term focus by both management and investors has been correctly labeled *impatient capitalism*. This point of debate is also sometimes referred to as the firm's *investment horizon* in reference to how long it takes the firm's actions, its investments and operations, to result in earnings.

In contrast to impatient capitalism is *patient capitalism*, which focuses on long-term shareholder wealth maximization. Legendary investor Warren Buffett, through his investment vehicle Berkshire Hathaway, represents one of the best of the patient capitalists. Buffett has become a multibillionaire by focusing his portfolio on mainstream firms that grow slowly but steadily with the economy such as Coca Cola. He was not lured into investing in the high growth but risky dot.coms of 2000 or the "high tech" sector that eventually imploded in 2001.

Stakeholder Capitalism Model

In the non–Anglo-American markets, controlling shareholders also strive to maximize long-term returns to equity. However, they are more constrained by powerful other stakeholders. In particular, labor unions are more powerful than in the Anglo-American markets. Governments interfere more in the marketplace to protect important stakeholder groups, such as local communities, the environment, and employment. Banks and other financial institutions are more important creditors than securities markets. This model has been labeled the stakeholder capitalism model (SCM).

Market Efficiency. The SCM model does not assume that equity markets are either efficient or inefficient. It does not really matter because the firm's financial goals are not exclusively shareholder-oriented since they are constrained by the other stakeholders. In any case, the SCM model assumes that long-term "loyal" shareholders, typically controlling shareholders, should influence corporate strategy rather than the transient portfolio investor.

Risk. The SCM model assumes that *total risk,* that is, operating and financial risk, does count. It is a specific-corporate objective to generate growing earnings and dividends over the long run with as much certainty as possible, given the firm's mission statement and goals. Risk is measured more by product market variability than by short-term variation in earnings and share price.

Single versus Multiple Goals. Although the SCM model typically avoids a flaw of the SWM model, namely impatient capital that is short-run oriented, it has its own flaw. Trying to meet the desires of multiple stakeholders leaves management without a clear signal about the trade-offs. Instead, management tries to influence the trade-offs through written and oral disclosures and complex compensation systems.

The Score Card. In contrast to the SCM model, the SWM model requires a single goal of value maximization with a well-defined score card. In the words of Michael Jensen:

Maximizing the total market value of the firm—that is, the sum of the market values of the equity, debt and any other contingent claims outstanding on the firm—is the objective function that will guide managers in making the optimal tradeoffs among multiple constituencies (or stakeholders). It tells the firm to spend an additional dollar of resources to satisfy the desires of each constituency as long as that constituency values the result at more than a dollar. In this case, the payoff to the firm from the investment of resources is at least a dollar (in terms of market value).[2]

Although both models have their strengths and weaknesses, in recent years two trends have led to an increasing focus on the shareholder wealth form. First, as more of the non–Anglo-American markets have increasingly privatized their industries, the shareholder wealth focus is seemingly needed to attract international capital from outside investors, many of whom are from other countries. Second, and still quite controversial, many analysts believe that shareholder-based MNEs are increasingly dominating their global industry segments. Nothing attracts followers like success.

Operational Goals

It is one thing to say *maximize value*, but it is another to actually do it. The management objective of maximizing profit is not as simple as it sounds, because the measure of profit used by ownership/management differs between the privately held firm and the publicly traded firm. In other words, is management attempting to maximize current income, capital appreciation, or both?

The return to a shareholder in a publicly traded firm combines current income in the form of dividends and capital gains from the appreciation of share price:

$$\text{Shareholder return} = \frac{\text{Dividend}}{\text{Price}_1} + \frac{\text{Price}_2 - \text{Price}_1}{\text{Price}_1}$$

where the initial price, P_1, is equivalent to the initial investment by the shareholder, and P_2 is the price of the share at the end of period. The shareholder theoretically receives income from both components. For example, over the past 50 or 60 years in the U.S. marketplace, a diversified investor may have received a total average annual return of 14%, split roughly between dividends, 2%, and capital gains, 12%.

Management generally believes it has the most direct influence over the first component—the *dividend yield*. Management makes strategic and operational decisions that grow sales and generate profits. Then it distributes those profits to ownership in the form of dividends. *Capital gains*—the change in the share price as traded in the equity markets—is much more complex, and reflects many forces that are not in the direct control of management. Despite growing market share, profits, or any other traditional measure of business success, the market may not reward these actions directly with share price appreciation. Many top executives believe that stock markets move in mysterious ways and are not always consistent in their valuations.

A privately held firm has a much simpler shareholder return objective function: maximize current and sustainable income. The privately held firm does not have a share price (it does have a value, but this is not a definitive market-determined value in the way in which we believe markets work). It therefore simply focuses on generating current income, dividend income, to generate the returns to its ownership. If the privately held ownership is a

[2]Michael C. Jensen, "Value Maximization, Stakeholder Theory, and the Corporate Objective Function," *Journal of Applied Corporate Finance*, Fall 2001, Volume 14, No. 3, pp. 8–21, p. 12.

family, the family may also place a great emphasis on the ability to sustain those earnings over time while maintaining a slower rate of growth, which can be managed by the family itself. It is therefore critical that ownership and ownership's specific financial interests be understood from the very start if we are to understand the strategic and financial goals and objectives of management.

Operational Goals for MNEs. The MNE must be guided by operational goals suitable for various levels of the firm. Even if the firm's goal is to maximize shareholder value, the manner in which investors value the firm is not always obvious to the firm's top management. Therefore, most firms hope to receive a favorable investor response to the achievement of operational goals that can be controlled by the way in which the firm performs, and then hope—if we can use that term—that the market will reward their results.

The MNE must determine the proper balance between three common operational financial objectives:

1. Maximization of consolidated after-tax income
2. Minimization of the firm's effective global tax burden
3. Correct positioning of the firm's income, cash flows, and available funds as to country and currency

These goals are frequently incompatible, in that the pursuit of one may result in a less desirable outcome in regard to another. Management must make decisions about the proper trade-offs between goals (which is why people rather than computers are employed as managers).

Consolidated Profits. The primary operational goal of the MNE is to *maximize consolidated profits, after-tax. Consolidated profits* are the profits of all the individual units of the firm originating in many different currencies expressed in the currency of the parent company. This is not to say that management is not striving to maximize the present value of all future cash flows. It is simply the case that most of the day-to-day decision making in global management is about current earnings. The leaders of the MNE, the management team who are developing and implementing the firm's strategy, must think far beyond current earnings.

For example, foreign subsidiaries have their own set of traditional financial statements: 1) a statement of income, summarizing the revenues and expenses experienced by the firm over the year; 2) a balance sheet, summarizing the assets employed in generating the unit's revenues, and the financing of those assets; and 3) a statement of cash flows, summarizing those activities of the firm that generate and then use cash flows over the year. These financial statements are expressed initially in the local currency of the unit for tax and reporting purposes to the local government, but they must be consolidated with the parent company's financial statements for reporting to shareholders.

Corporate Governance

Although the governance structure of any company, domestic, international, or multinational, is fundamental to its very existence, this very subject has become the lightning rod of political and business debate in the past few years as failures in governance in a variety of forms has led to corporate fraud and failure. Abuses and failures in corporate governance have dominated global business news in recent years. Beginning with the accounting fraud and questionable ethics of business conduct at Enron culminating in its bankruptcy in the fall of 2001, failures in corporate governance have raised issues about the very ethics and culture of the conduct of business.

The Goal of Corporate Governance

The single overriding objective of corporate governance in the Anglo-American markets is the optimization over time of the returns to shareholders. In order to achieve this, good governance practices should focus the attention of the board of directors of the corporation on this objective by developing and implementing a strategy for the corporation, which ensures corporate growth and improvement in the value of the corporation's equity. At the same time, it should assure an effective relationship with stakeholders.[3] One of the most widely accepted statements of good corporate governance practices are those established by the Organization for Economic Cooperation and Development (OECD):[4]

- **The rights of shareholders:** The corporate governance framework should protect shareholders' rights.

- **The equitable treatment of shareholders:** The corporate governance framework should ensure the equitable treatment of all shareholders, including minority and foreign shareholders. All shareholders should have the opportunity to obtain effective redress for violation of their rights.

- **The role of stakeholders in corporate governance:** The corporate governance framework should recognize the rights of stakeholders as established by law and encourage active cooperation between corporations and stakeholders in creating wealth, jobs, and the sustainability of financially sound enterprises.

- **Disclosure and transparency:** The corporate governance framework should ensure that timely and accurate disclosure is made on all material matters regarding the corporation, including the financial situation, performance, ownership, and governance of the company.

- **The responsibilities of the board:** The corporate governance framework should ensure the strategic guidance of the company, the effective monitoring of management by the board, and the board's accountability to the company and the shareholders.

These principles obviously focus on several key areas—shareholder rights and roles, disclosure and transparency, and the responsibilities of boards—which we will discuss in more detail.

The Structure of Corporate Governance

Our first challenge is to try to capture what people mean when they use the expression "corporate governance." Exhibit 2.2 provides an overview of the various parties and their responsibilities associated with the governance of the modern corporation. The modern corporation's actions and behaviors are directed and controlled by both *internal forces* and *external forces*.

The *internal forces*, the officers of the corporation (such as the chief executive officer or CEO) and the board of directors of the corporation (including the chairman of the board), are those directly responsible for determining both the strategic direction and the execution of the

---

[3]This definition of the corporate objective is based on that supported by the International Corporate Governance Network (ICGN), a nonprofit organization committed to improving corporate governance practices globally.

[4]"OECD Principles of Corporate Governance," The Organization for Economic Cooperation and Development, 1999, revised 2004.

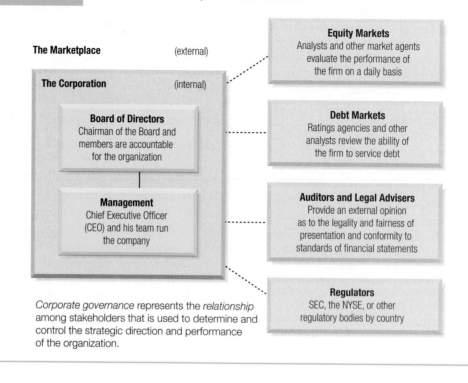

EXHIBIT 2.2   The Structure of Corporate Governance

The Marketplace   (external)

The Corporation   (internal)

Board of Directors
Chairman of the Board and members are accountable for the organization

Management
Chief Executive Officer (CEO) and his team run the company

Equity Markets
Analysts and other market agents evaluate the performance of the firm on a daily basis

Debt Markets
Ratings agencies and other analysts review the ability of the firm to service debt

Auditors and Legal Advisers
Provide an external opinion as to the legality and fairness of presentation and conformity to standards of financial statements

Regulators
SEC, the NYSE, or other regulatory bodies by country

Corporate governance represents the *relationship* among stakeholders that is used to determine and control the strategic direction and performance of the organization.

company's future. But they are not acting within a vacuum; they are subject to the constant prying eyes of the *external forces* in the marketplace who question the validity and soundness of their decisions and performance. These include the equity markets in which the shares are traded, the analysts who critique their investment prospects, the creditors and credit agencies who lend them money, the auditors and legal advisers who testify to the fairness and legality of their reporting, and the multitude of regulators who oversee their actions in order to protect the investment public.

The Board of Directors. The legal body that is accountable for the governance of the corporation is its board of directors. The board is composed of both employees of the organization (inside members) and senior and influential nonemployees (outside members). Areas of debate surrounding boards include the following: 1) the proper balance between inside and outside members; 2) the means by which board members are compensated for their service; and 3) the actual ability of a board to adequately monitor and manage a corporation when board members are spending sometimes less than five days a year in board activities. Outside members, often the current or retired chief executives of other major companies, may bring with them a healthy sense of distance and impartiality, which although refreshing, may also result in limited understanding of the true issues and events within the company.

Officers and Management. The senior officers of the corporation, the chief executive officer (CEO), the chief financial officer (CFO), and the chief operating officer (COO), are not only the most knowledgeable of the business, but the creators and directors of its strategic and operational direction. The management of the firm is, according to theory, acting as a contractor—as an *agent*—of shareholders to pursue value creation. They are motivated by salary, bonuses, and stock options (positively) or the risk of losing their jobs (negatively). They may, however, have biases of self-enrichment or personal agendas, which the board and other corporate stakeholders are responsible for overseeing and policing. Interestingly enough, in more than 80% of the companies in the Fortune 500, the CEO is also the chairman of the board. This is, in the opinion of many, a conflict of interest and not in the best interests of the company and its shareholders.

Equity Markets. The publicly traded company, regardless of country of residence, is highly susceptible to the changing opinion of the marketplace. The equity markets themselves, whether they are the New York Stock Exchange, London Stock Exchange, or Mexico City Bolsa, should reflect the market's constant evaluation of the promise and performance of the individual company. The analysts are those self-described experts employed by the many investment banking firms who also trade in the client company shares. They are expected (sometimes naïvely) to evaluate the strategies, plans for execution of the strategies, and financial performance of the firms on a real-time basis. Analysts depend on the financial statements and other public disclosures of the firm for their information.

Debt Markets. Although the debt markets (banks and other financial institutions providing loans and various forms of securitized debt like corporate bonds), are not specifically interested in building shareholder value, they are indeed interested in the financial health of the company. Their interest, specifically, is in the company's ability to repay its debt in a timely and efficient manner. These markets, like the equity markets, must rely on the financial statements and other disclosures (public and private in this case) of the companies with which they work.

Auditors and Legal Advisers. Auditors and legal advisers are responsible for providing an external professional opinion as to the fairness, legality, and accuracy of corporate financial statements. In this process, they attempt to determine whether the firm's financial records and practices follow what in the United States is termed *generally accepted accounting principles* (GAAP) in regard to accounting procedures. But auditors and legal advisers are hired by the firms they are auditing, leading to a rather unique practice of policing their employers. The additional difficulty that has arisen in recent years is that the major accounting firms pursued the development of large consulting practices, often leading to a conflict of interest. An auditor not giving a clean bill of health to a client could not expect to gain many lucrative consulting contracts from that same firm in the near future.

Regulators. Publicly traded firms in the United States and elsewhere are subject to the regulatory oversight of both governmental organizations and non-governmental organizations. In the United States, the Securities and Exchange Commission (SEC) is a careful watchdog of the publicly traded equity markets, both in the behavior of the companies themselves in those markets and of the various investors participating in those markets. The SEC and other authorities like it outside of the United States require a regular and orderly disclosure process of corporate performance in order that all investors may evaluate the company's investment value with adequate, accurate, and fairly distributed information. This regulatory oversight is often focused on when and what information is released by the company, and to whom.

A publicly traded firm in the United States is also subject to the rules and regulations of the exchange upon which they are traded (New York Stock Exchange, American Stock Exchange, and NASDAQ are the largest). These organizations, typically categorized as self-regulatory in nature, construct and enforce standards of conduct for both their member companies and themselves in the conduct of share trading.

Comparative Corporate Governance[5]

The origins of the need for a corporate governance process arise from the separation of ownership from management, and from the varying views by culture of who the stakeholders are and of what significance. This assures that corporate governance practices will differ across countries, economies, and cultures. As described in Exhibit 2.3, though, the various corporate governance regimes may be classified by regime. The regimes in turn reflect the evolution of business ownership and direction within the countries over time.

Market-based regimes, like that of the United States, Canada, and the United Kingdom, are characterized by relatively efficient capital markets in which the ownership of publicly traded companies is widely dispersed. *Family-based systems*, like those characterized in many of the emerging markets, Asian markets, and Latin American markets, not only started with strong concentrations of family ownership (as opposed to partnerships or small investment groups which are not family-based), but have continued to be largely controlled by families even after going public. *Bank-based* and *government-based* regimes are those reflecting markets in which government ownership of property and industry has been the constant force over time, resulting in only marginal "public ownership" of enterprise, and even then, subject to significant restrictions on business practices.

These regimes are therefore a function of at least four major factors in the evolution of corporate governance principles and practices globally: 1) the financial market development; 2) the degree of separation between management and ownership; 3) the concept of disclosure and transparency; and 4) the historical development of the legal system.

Financial Market Development. The depth and breadth of capital markets is critical to the evolution of corporate governance practices. Country markets that have had relatively slow growth, as in the emerging markets, or have industrialized rapidly utilizing neighboring capital markets (as is the case of Western Europe), may not form large public equity market systems. Without significant public trading of ownership shares, high concentrations of ownership are preserved and few disciplined processes of governance developed.

Separation of Management and Ownership. In countries and cultures in which the ownership of the firm has continued to be an integral part of management, agency issues and fail-

EXHIBIT 2.3	Comparative Corporate Governance Regimes	
Regime Basis	**Characteristics**	**Examples**
Market-based	Efficient equity markets; Dispersed ownership	United States, United Kingdom, Canada, Australia
Family-based	Management and ownership is combined; Family/majority and minority shareholders	Hong Kong, Indonesia, Malaysia, Singapore, Taiwan, France
Bank-based	Government influence in bank lending; Lack of transparency; Family control	Korea, Germany
Government affiliated	State ownership of enterprise; Lack of transparency; No minority influence	China, Russia

Source: Based on "Corporate Governance in Emerging Markets: An Asian Perspective," by J. Tsui and T. Shieh, in *International Finance and Accounting Handbook*, Third Edition, Frederick D.S. Choi, editor, Wiley, 2004, pp. 24.4–24.6.

[5]For a summary of comparative corporate governance see R. La Porta, F. Lopez-de-Silanes, and A. Schleifer, "Corporate Ownership Around the World," *Journal of Finance*, 54, 1999, pp. 471–517. See also A. Schleifer and R. Vishny, "A Survey of Corporate Governance," *Journal of Finance*, 52, 1997, pp. 737–783, and the Winter 2007 issue, Volume 19 Number 1, of the *Journal of Applied Corporate Finance*.

ures have been less problematic. In countries like the United States, in which ownership has become largely separated from management (and widely dispersed), aligning the goals of management and ownership is much more difficult.

Disclosure and Transparency. The extent of disclosure regarding the operations and financial results of a company vary dramatically across countries. Disclosure practices reflect a wide range of cultural and social forces, including the degree of ownership which is public, the degree to which government feels the need to protect investor's rights versus ownership rights, and the extent to which family-based and government-based business remains central to the culture. Transparency, a parallel concept to disclosure, reflects the visibility of decision making processes within the business organization.

Historical Development of the Legal System. Investor protection is typically better in countries in which *English common law* is the basis of the legal system, compared to the *codified civil law* that is typical in France and Germany (the so-called *Code Napoleon*). English common law is typically the basis of the legal systems in the United Kingdom and former colonies of the United Kingdom, including the United States and Canada. The Code Napoleon is typically the basis of the legal systems in former French colonies and the European countries that Napoleon once ruled, such as Belgium, Spain, and Italy. In countries with weak investor protection, controlling shareholder ownership is often a substitute for a lack of legal protection.

Note that the word *ethics* has not been used. All of the principles and practices described so far have assumed that the individuals in roles of responsibility and leadership pursue them truly and fairly. That, however, has not always been the case.

Family Ownership and Corporate Governance

Although much of the discussion about corporate governance concentrates on the market-based regimes (see Exhibit 2.3), family-based regimes are arguably more common and more important worldwide, including the United States and Western Europe. For example, in a study of 5,232 corporations in 13 Western European countries, family-controlled firms represented 44% of the sample compared to 37% that were widely held.[6]

Recent research indicates that, as opposed to popular belief, family-owned firms in some highly developed economies typically outperform publicly owned firms. This is true not only in Western Europe but also in the United States. A recent study of firms included in the S&P500 found that families are present in fully one-third of the S&P500 and account for 18% of their outstanding equity. And, as opposed to popular opinion, family firms outperform nonfamily firms. (An added insight is that firms possessing a CEO from the family also perform better than those with outside-CEOs.) Interestingly, it seems that minority shareholders are actually better off according to this study when part of a family-influenced firm.[7]

Another study based on 120 Norwegian, founding-family controlled and nonfounding family-controlled firms, concluded that founding family control was associated with higher firm value. Furthermore, the impact of founding family directors on firm value is not affected by corporate governance conditions such as firm age, board independence, and number of share classes. The authors also found that the positive relation between founding family ownership and firm value is greater among older firms, firms with larger boards, and particularly

[6]Mara Faccio and Larry H.P. Lang, "The Ultimate Ownership of Western European Corporations," *Journal of Financial Economics*, 65 (2002), p. 365. See also: Torben Pedersen and Steen Thomsen, "European Patterns of Corporate Ownership," *Journal of International Business Studies*, Vol. 28, No. 4, Fourth Quarter, 1997, pp. 759–778.

[7]Ronald C. Anderson and David M. Reeb, "Founding Family Ownership and Firm Performance from the S&P500," *The Journal of Finance*, June 2003, p. 1301.

when these firms have multiple classes of stock.[8] It is common for Norwegian firms and firms based in several other European countries to have dual classes of stock with differential voting rights.

Failures in Corporate Governance

Failures in corporate governance have become increasingly visible in recent years. The Enron scandal in the United States is described in the mini-case at the end of this chapter. In addition to Enron, other firms that have revealed major accounting and disclosure failures, as well as executives looting the firm, are WorldCom, Parmalat, Global Crossing, Tyco, Adelphia, and HealthSouth.

In each case, prestigious auditing firms, such as Arthur Andersen, missed the violations or minimized them possibly because of lucrative consulting relationships or other conflicts of interest. Moreover, security analysts and banks urged investors to buy the shares and debt issues of these and other firms that they knew to be highly risky or even close to bankruptcy. Even more egregious, most of the top executives who were responsible for the mismanagement that destroyed their firms, walked away (initially) with huge gains on shares sold before the downfall, and even overly generous severance payments.

It appears that the day of reckoning has come. The first to fall (due to its involvement with Enron) was Arthur Andersen, one of the former "Big Five" U.S. accounting firms. However, many more legal actions against former executives are underway. Although the corruption scandals were first revealed in the United States, they have spread to Canada and the European Union countries.

Good Governance and Corporate Reputation

Does good corporate governance matter? This is actually a difficult question, and the realistic answer has been largely dependent on outcomes historically. For example, as long as Enron's share price continued to rise dramatically throughout the 1990s, questions over transparency, accounting propriety, and even financial facts were largely overlooked by all of the stakeholders of the corporation. Yet, eventually, the fraud, deceit, and failure of the multitude of corporate governance practices resulted in the bankruptcy of the firm. It not only destroyed the wealth of investors, but the careers, incomes, and savings of so many of its basic stakeholders—its own employees. Ultimately, *yes*, good governance does matter. A lot.

Good corporate governance is dependent on a variety of factors, one of which is the general governance reputation of the country of incorporation and registration. Exhibit 2.4 presents selected recent country rankings compiled by Governance Metrics International (GMI) as of September 23, 2008. Studies by many different organizations and academics, including GMI, have continued to show a number of important linkages between good governance (at both the country and corporate levels) and the cost of capital (lower), returns to shareholders (higher), and corporate profitability (higher). An added dimension of interest is the role of country governance as it may influence the country in which international investors may choose to invest. Early studies indicate that good governance does indeed attract international investor interest.

Exhibits 2.5 and 2.6 present the results of another recent international corporate governance study, which compared the premiums that shareholders in selected markets were willing to pay for what was perceived as good governance. Exhibit 2.5 measures good governance

---

[8]Chandra S. Mishra, Trond Randøy, and Jan Inge Jenssen, "The Effect of Founding Family Influence on Firm Value and Corporate Governance," *Journal of International Financial Management and Accounting*, Volume 12, Number 3, Autumn 2001, pp. 235–259.

EXHIBIT 2.4	Country Governance Rankings 2008

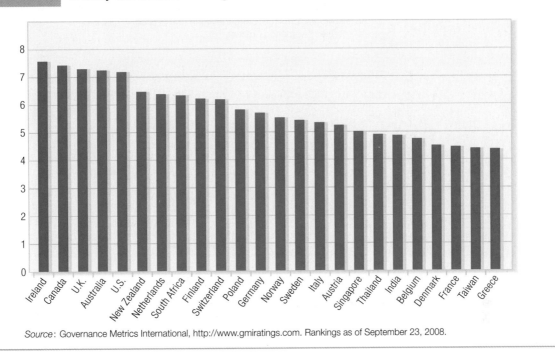

Source: Governance Metrics International, http://www.gmiratings.com. Rankings as of September 23, 2008.

EXHIBIT 2.5	The Premium Paid for Voting Shares: Accounting Standards

The lower the premium paid, the higher the perceived quality of corporate governance present.

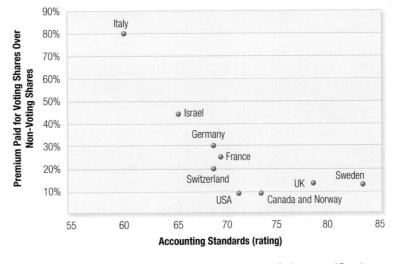

Source: The Owner ship Structure, Governance, and Performance of French Companies," Peter Harbula, *Journal of Applied Corporate Finance*, Volume 19 Number 1, Winter 2007, pp. 88–99.

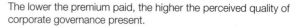

EXHIBIT 2.6   The Premium Paid for Voting Shares: Law Enforcement

The lower the premium paid, the higher the perceived quality of corporate governance present.

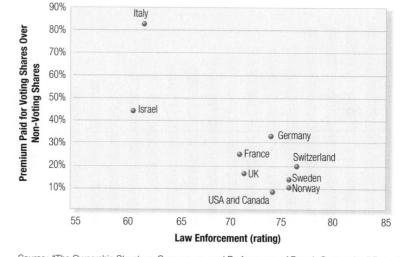

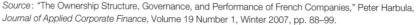

Source: "The Ownership Structure, Governance, and Performance of French Companies," Peter Harbula, *Journal of Applied Corporate Finance*, Volume 19 Number 1, Winter 2007, pp. 88–99.

on the basis of accounting standards, while Exhibit 2.6 uses a measure of perceived legal standards in the country of incorporation. In both cases, the value measure used is what premium, if any, investors appear willing to pay for voting shares over non-voting shares. The idea is that if the country is perceived to have relatively good corporate governance, the investor would not need to obtain voting rights to try to protect his or her investment.

A third way to signal good corporate governance in non–Anglo-American firms is to elect one or more Anglo-American board members. This was shown to be true for a select group of Scandinavian firms. A study by Oxelheim and Randøy of a database of Norwegian and Swedish firms concluded the following:[9]

This study examines the influence of foreign (Anglo-American) board membership on corporate performance measured in terms of valuation (Tobin's Q). Based on firms headquartered in Norway and Sweden this study indicates a significantly higher value for firms having outsider Anglo-American board member(s) after controlling for a variety of firm-specific and corporate governance related factors. We argue that the superior performance reflects that these companies have successfully broken away from a partly segmented domestic capital market by "importing," through their outsider Anglo-American board member(s), an Anglo-American corporate governance system offering improved monitoring opportunities and enhanced investor recognition.

A follow-up study of the same firms found that CEO pay increased because of the perceived reduction in tolerance for bad performance and increased monitoring required.[10]

[9]Lars Oxelheim and Trond Randøy, "The Impact of Foreign Board Membership on Firm Value," *Journal of Banking and Finance*, Volume 27, Number 12, 2003, pp. 2369–2392.

[10]Lars Oxelheim and Trond Randøy, "The Anglo-American Financial Influence on CEO Compensation in Non–Anglo-American Firms," *Journal of International Business Studies*, Volume 36, Number 4, July 2005, pp. 470–483.

Corporate Governance Reform

Within the United States and the United Kingdom, the main corporate governance problem is the one treated by agency theory: with widespread share ownership, how can a firm align management's interest with that of the shareholders? Since individual shareholders do not have the resources or the power to monitor management, the U.S. and U.K. markets rely on regulators to assist in the agency theory monitoring task. Outside the United States and the United Kingdom, large controlling shareholders (including Canada) are in the majority. They are able to monitor management in some ways better than regulators. However, controlling shareholders pose a different agency problem. How can minority shareholders be protected against the controlling shareholders?

In recent years, reform in the United States and Canada has been largely regulatory. Reform elsewhere has been largely adoption of principles rather than stricter legal regulations. The principles approach is softer, less costly, and less likely to conflict with other existing regulations.

Sarbanes-Oxley Act. The U.S. Congress passed the Sarbanes-Oxley Act (SOX) in July 2002. Named after its two primary congressional sponsors, SOX had four major requirements: 1) CEOs and CFOs of publicly traded firms must vouch for the veracity of the firm's published financial statements; 2) corporate boards must have audit and compensation committees drawn from independent (outside) directors; and 3) companies are prohibited from making loans to corporate officers and directors; and 4) companies must test their internal financial controls against fraud.

The first provision—the so-called *signature clause*, has already had significant impacts on the way in which companies prepare their financial statements. The provision was intended to instill a sense of responsibility and accountability in senior management (and therefore fewer explanations of "the auditors signed off on it"). The companies themselves have pushed the same procedure downward in their organizations, often requiring business unit managers and directors at lower levels to sign their financial statements. Severe penalties were enacted in case of non-compliance.

SOX has been much more expensive to implement than was originally expected during the debate in the U.S. Congress. Apart from the obvious costs of filling out more forms, many critics argue that too much time is consumed in meeting the new regulations, modifying internal controls to combat fraud, and restating past earnings, rather than running the operations of the firms. This cost may be disproportionately high for small firms that must meet the same regulatory requirements as large firms. In particular, auditing and legal fees have skyrocketed.

Everyone is afraid of following in the footsteps of Arthur Andersen that collapsed as a result of the Enron scandal. (The "Big Five" accounting firms became the "Big Four" overnight!) The net result may lead to more small but growing firms choosing to sell out to larger firms instead of going the initial public offering (IPO) route. Other firms may simply choose to stay private, feeling that the costs of public offerings outweigh the benefits. Moreover, many firms may become more risk averse. Lower level employees might pass all risky decisions up the line to a more central risk assessment level. Such an action would slow down decision making, and potentially, growth.

SOX has been quite controversial internationally. Its "one size fits all" style conflicts with a number of the corporate governance practices already in place in markets that view themselves as having better governance records than the United States. A foreign firm wishing to list or continue listing their shares on a U.S. exchange must comply with the law. Some companies, such as Porsche, withdrew plans for a U.S. listing specifically in opposition to SOX. Other companies, however, including many of the largest foreign companies traded on U.S. exchanges such as Unilever, Siemens, and ST Microelectronics, have stated their willingness to comply—if they can find acceptable compromises between U.S. law and the governance requirements and principles in their own countries. One example is Germany, where supervisory board audit committees must include employee representatives. But according to U.S. law, employees are not independent. Many of these listed firms have concluded they need access to the U.S. capital market and therefore must comply.

Board Structure and Compensation. Many critics have argued for the United States to move more toward structural reforms more consistent with European standards (e.g., prohibiting CEOs from also being chairmen). Although this is increasingly common, there is no regulatory or other legal requirement to force the issue. Secondly, and more radically, would be to move toward the two-tiered structure of countries like Germany, in which there is a supervisory board (largely outsiders, and typically large—Siemens has 18 members) and a management board (predominantly insiders, and small—Siemens has eight members). As shown in Exhibit 2.7, it is not clear that the director composition of boards is truly the problem.

Although SOX addresses the agency theory problem of transparency, it does not address the agency theory problem of aligning the goals of boards and managers with the interests of shareholders. In the past, the United States was characterized by compensation schemes to reward directors and management with a combination of an annual stipend or salary with significant stock options. However, when stock options go *underwater* (become essentially value-less because they are so far out-of-the-money), it does not cost the recipient any direct cost, only the loss of a potential future benefit. Indeed, some firms simply rewrite the options so that they have higher values immediately. It now appears that many firms are changing their compensation schemes to replace options with *restricted stock*. Restricted stock cannot be sold publicly for some specified period of time. If the price of the firm's shares falls, the recipient has actually lost money and is normally not recompensated by receiving more restricted shares.

Transparency, Accounting, and Auditing. The concept of *transparency* is also one which has been raised in a variety of different markets and contexts. Transparency is a rather common term used to describe the degree to which an investor—either existing or potential—can discern the true activities and value drivers of a company from the disclosures and financial results reported. For example, Enron was often considered a "black box" when it came to what the actual operational and financial results and risks were for its multitude of business lines. The consensus of corporate governance experts is that all firms, globally, should work toward increasing the transparency of the firm's risk-return profile.

EXHIBIT 2.7	U.S. Director Independence 2008

Shearman and Sterling LLP conduct an annual survey of selected corporate governance practices of the Top 100 Companies. Here are selected notes and highlights from their 2008 survey.

- Both the NYSE and NASDAQ listing standards require that a majority of a listed company's directors be independent.

- Of the Top 100 Companies, 52 in 2008 have adopted and disclosed stricter standards regarding the minimum number of independent directors than required by the relevant listing standards.

- Most of the Top 100 Companies do not explicitly require that 75% or more of their directors be independent. In practice, however, the Top 100 Companies continue to exceed their own requirements.

- Independent directors constitute 75% or more of the boards of 89 of the Top 100 Companies surveyed this year. The CEO is the only non-independent director at 44 of the Top 100 Companies. CFOs and COOs were members of the board at seven and nine of the Top 100 Companies, respectively.

Source: "2008 Trends in Corporate Governance of the Large US Public Companies," Shearman & Sterling LLP, pp. 14–15. The Top 100 Companies consist of the 100 largest U.S. public companies as ranked in *Fortune* magazine's *Fortune 500* list by revenue for the most recently ended fiscal year that have equity securities listed on the NYSE or NASDAQ.

The accounting process itself has now come under debate. The U.S. system is characterized as strictly rule based, rather than conceptually based, as is common in Western Europe. Many critics of U.S. corporate governance practices point to this as a fundamental flaw, in which constantly more clever accountants find ways to follow the rules, yet not meet the underlying purpose for which the rules were intended. An extension of the accounting process debate is that of the role and remuneration associated with auditing. This is the process of using third parties, paid by the firm, to vet their reporting practices as being consistent with generally accepted accounting principles. As the collapse of Arthur Andersen following the Enron debacle illustrated, serious questions remain as to the validity of this current practice.

Minority Shareholder Rights. Finally, the issue of minority shareholder rights continues to rage in many of the world's largest markets. Many of the emerging markets are still characterized by the family-based corporate governance regime, where the family remains in control even after the firm has gone public. But what of the interests and voices of the other shareholders? How are their interests preserved in organizations where families or controlling investors make all true decisions, including the boards? As *Global Finance in Practice 2.2* points out, minority shareholder rights is an issue in all markets today, including China.

GLOBAL FINANCE IN PRACTICE 2.2

Corporate Governance Reform in China

China has made many positive improvements to its corporate governance structure in recent times by revising its securities and company laws. Notable changes include greater financial disclosure requirements, improved protection of minority shareholders' rights, and clearer guidelines on the role of supervising boards.

Significant progress has also been made in improving corporate governance in both the banking and equity markets. Foreign banks are now allowed to invest in PRC banks and to bring with them their corporate governance concepts. The government has also introduced a share reform program, making it mandatory for nontradable shares in state-owned enterprises (SOEs) to be converted into tradable shares. Efforts have also been made to decrease financial risk in China's banking system by reducing the large number of nonperforming loans held by local banks.

While there have been significant improvements in the corporate governance structure in China, it still lags behind that of many developed countries. What are the shortcomings in China's corporate governance system? China has a two-tier board governance structure for companies, which is very similar to the German system, with a board of directors and a supervisory board. Unfortunately, in reality, supervisory boards in China usually just rubber-stamp decisions taken by the board of directors. This duplication in the system does not do any good except to create redundancy and increase administrative costs for companies. Also, although Chinese companies are required to have at least a third of their boards constitute

independent directors, in practice, these directors have very limited ability to influence how their companies are run.

Moreover, the financial disclosure requirements of Chinese listed companies are still weak compared to those of many developed jurisdictions. The continued uncertain reform of SOEs' share structures and the lack of good financial information make it extremely difficult for China's equity markets to grow and function properly.

The PRC government has been encouraging companies to improve their awareness of good corporate governance. One method adopted by the government has been to actively encourage local companies to list on the Hong Kong stock exchange, which has a more internationally-accepted corporate governance system for listed companies. However, this plan could backfire and hinder the development of China's equity markets, as it creates the perception that the local stock exchanges in Shanghai and Shenzhen—and the companies listed on them—are weaker and less professionally managed.

Another corporate governance problem for big PRC companies (most of which are majority government-owned) is of the government trying to exert a strong management influence on them. Many of the senior management of these majority state-owned companies see their role as that of keeping the government happy at all costs. Clearly, there is plenty of room to improve China's corporate governance system.

Source: "Shortcomings in China's Corporate Governance Regime," Johnny KW Cheung, *China Law & Practice*, February 2007, p. 1.

Poor performance of management usually requires changes to management, ownership, or both. Exhibit 2.8 illustrates some of the alternative paths available to shareholders when dissatisfied with firm performance. Depending on the culture and accepted practices, it is not unusual for many investors to—at least for an extended time—remain quietly disgruntled regarding share price performance. If more active in response, they may sell their shares. It is the third and fourth responses, shareholder activist responses, in which management hears a much louder voice of the dissatisfied shareholder.

EXHIBIT 2.8   Potential Responses to Shareholder Dissatisfaction

What counts is that the management of a publicly quoted company, and its board of directors, know that the company can become the subject of a hostile takeover bid if they fail to perform. The growth of equity and hedge funds in the United States and elsewhere in recent years has strengthened this threat as leveraged buyouts are once again common.

SUMMARY POINTS

- Most companies are created by entrepreneurs who are either individuals or a small set of partners or members of a family.

- Over time, some firms may choose to go public via an initial public offering, or IPO.

- The U.S. and U.K. stock markets are characterized by widespread ownership of shares. In the rest of the world, ownership is usually characterized by controlling shareholders. Typical controlling shareholders are government, institutions, family, and consortiums.

- When a firm becomes widely owned it is typically managed by hired professionals. Professional managers' interests may not be perfectly aligned with the interests of owners thus creating an *agency problem*.

- The Anglo-American markets have a philosophy that a firm's objective should follow the *shareholder wealth maximization (SWM)* model. More specifically, the firm should strive to maximize the return to shareholders, as measured by the sum of capital gains and dividends, for a given level of risk.

- In the non–Anglo-American markets, controlling shareholders also strive to maximize long term returns to equity. However, they are more constrained by powerful other stakeholders. In particular, labor unions are more powerful than in the Anglo-American markets. Governments interfere more in the marketplace to protect important stakeholder groups, such as local communities, the environment, and employment. Banks and other financial institutions are more important creditors than securities markets. This model has been labeled the stakeholder capitalism model (SCM).

- The return to a shareholder in a publicly traded firm combines current income in the form of dividends and capital gains from the appreciation of share price.

- A privately held firm tries to maximize current and sustainable income; since it has no share price, it does not use time or resources in attempting to influence the market's opinion of its business.

- The MNE must determine for itself the proper balance between three common operational objectives: maximization of consolidated after tax income; minimization of the firm's effective global tax burden; and correct positioning of the firm's income, cash flows, and available funds as to country and currency.

- The relationship among stakeholders used to determine and control the strategic direction and performance of an organization is termed corporate governance.

- Dimensions of corporate governance include agency theory; composition and control of boards of directors; and cultural, historical and institutional variables.

- As MNEs become more dependent on global capital markets for financing they may need to modify their policies of corporate governance.

- A trend exists for firms resident in non–Anglo-American markets to move toward being more "shareholder friendly." Simultaneously, firms from the Anglo-American markets may be moving toward being more "stakeholder friendly."

- Failures in corporate governance, especially in the United States, have recently been in the spotlight and have been given partial blame for the decline in value of the U.S. stock markets.

- Shareholders who are dissatisfied with their firm's performance have four typical choices: remain quietly disgruntled; sell their shares; change management; or initiate a takeover.

- The recent failures in corporate governance in the United States have spawned a flurry of government and private initiatives to prevent the same kind of future failures.

- The United States has reacted to the failures in corporate governance by passing the Sarbanes-Oxley Act of 2002.

- Sarbanes-Oxley Act (SOX) has four major requirements: 1) CEOs and CFOs of publicly traded firms must vouch for the veracity of the firm's published financial statements; 2) corporate boards must have audit and compensation committees drawn from independent (outside) directors; 3) companies are prohibited from making loans to corporate officers and directors; and 4) companies must test their internal financial controls against fraud.

- According to the OECD, good corporate governance practices would include clear and detailed definition of shareholder rights and roles, disclosure and transparency, and the responsibilities of boards.

MINI-CASE   Governance Failure at Enron

"The tragic consequences of the related-party transactions and accounting errors were the result of failures at many levels and by many people: a flawed idea, self-enrichment by employees, inadequately-designed controls, poor implementation, inattentive oversight, simple (and not so simple) accounting mistakes, and overreaching in a culture that appears to have encouraged pushing the limits. Our review indicates that many of these consequences could and should have been avoided."

— "Report of Investigation: Special Investigative Committee of the Board of Directors of Enron Corporation," Board of Directors, Enron, February 1, 2002, pp. 27–28.

On December 2, 2001, Enron Corporation filed for bankruptcy protection under Chapter 11. Enron failed as a result of a complex combination of business and governance failures. As noted in the quotation from the report reprinted here, the failures involved organizations and individuals both inside and outside of Enron. But outside of the courts and sensational press, the question remains as to how the system allowed it to happen. Why did the many structures and safeguards within the U.S. corporate governance system not catch, stop, or prevent the failure of Enron?

Enron's Collapse

According to former Enron CEO Jeffrey Skilling, Enron failed because of a "run on the bank." This in fact, is probably technically correct. When Enron's credit rating was downgraded to below investment grade in November 2001 by the credit rating agencies, its business was effectively stopped. This was because as a trading company it needed to maintain an investment grade rating in order for other companies to trade with it. No grade, no trade.

But that answer largely begs the question of *why* the company was downgraded? Because Enron's total indebtedness was now determined to be $38 billion, not $13 billion. Why was the debt now, suddenly, so high? Because much of the debt which had been classified as *off-balance sheet* was now reclassified to *on-balance sheet*. Why the reclassification? Because many of the *special purpose entities* (SPEs) and off-balance sheet partnerships carrying this debt were now either found to have been misclassified to begin with or were reconsolidated with the company as a result of their equity falling in value (Enron shares). Which leads us back to the beginning—why did Enron's share price tumble in 2001? Was it simply a natural result of a failing business, or had Enron's reported and prospective earnings, in combination with its general financial health, not been honestly reported and evaluated?

Failure of Corporate Governance at Enron

Enron's senior management team, primarily CEO Kenneth Lay and COO Jeffrey Skilling (later CEO) were responsible for the formulation and implementation of the company's strategy, including its operating and financial results. Like most companies of its size, it had literally hundreds of accountants and lawyers on its permanent staff. It was the concerns of one accountant, Sherron Watkins, which became particularly public in August and September 2001 and contributed to the rapidly escalating examination of Enron and its operations in the fall of 2001.

In the case of Enron, the external corporate governance bodies have been the focus of much criticism.

- **Auditor.** Arthur Andersen (one of the so-called *Big Five*) was Enron's auditor. Andersen's job was to determine and testify annually as to whether Enron had followed generally accepted accounting practices in the statements of its financial results. Andersen, like all auditors, was hired and paid by Enron itself. Andersen also provided a large variety of consulting activities for Enron, the sum of which was a much larger line of business than the basic audit practice itself.

- **Legal Counsel.** Enron's legal counsel, primarily the firm of Vinson & Elkins of Houston, also hired by the firm, was responsible for providing legal opinions on the many strategies, structures, and general legality of much of what Enron did. As was also the case with Arthur Andersen, when questioned later as to why it did not oppose certain ideas or practices, the company explained that it had not been fully informed of all of the details and complexities of the management and ownership of the SPEs.

- **Regulators.** Enron actually fell between the cracks of most U.S. regulatory bodies by industry. As a trader in the energy markets, the Federal Energy Regulatory Commission (FERC) had some distant oversight responsibilities in regard to some of the markets and trading which the company participated in, but these were largely separate issues from Enron's overall activities.

- **Equity Markets.** As a publicly traded company, Enron was subject to the rules and regulations of the Securities and Exchange Commission (SEC). The SEC, however, does little first-hand investigation or confirmation of reporting diligence itself, relying instead on the testimonials of other bodies like the company's auditor.

  As a share traded on the New York Stock Exchange (NYSE), Enron was governed by the rules and regulations of that exchange. At this time, however, the reporting requirements of the NYSE differed little if any from those of the SEC. The NYSE did no independent first-hand verification of compliance.

  As a share followed by a multitude of investment banking firms, analysts for these firms were responsible for following, analyzing, and evaluating Enron's results constantly. Enron's relationships with its investment bankers involved a frequent 'tit-for-tat' behavior, in which those firms which cooperated with Enron and supported its performance stories were rewarded with new business and new mandates for other investment banking activities that were profitable to the firms.

- **Debt Markets.** Enron, like all companies who desired and needed a credit rating, paid companies like Standard & Poor's and Moody's to provide it with a credit rating. These ratings are needed for the company's debt securities to be issued and traded in the marketplace. Again, one of the problems that the credit ratings agencies had with Enron was that they could only provide analysis on what was known to them of Enron's operational and financial activities and results. And, in the case of debt knowingly held by off-balance sheet special purposes entities, there is considerable debate continuing as to whether the credit rating agencies had full detail and knowingly chose to overlook them in the company's total indebtedness or not.

And finally, let's not forget the banks and bankers themselves, who provided the access to the debt capital. Most of these banks made millions and millions of dollars on interest and fee income as a result of leading and managing debt issuances for Enron.

Feeding the Beast

A particularly troublesome feature of Enron's emerging business model in the late 1990s was that revenues grew much faster than earnings. The cost of undertaking large international power projects (such as in India), electrical power trading, and even new trading ventures such as the trading in water rights and Broadband, were, in the words of one former executive, *hideous*. The salaries, bonuses, startup costs, and general lack of control over all operating costs drown whatever profits arose from the new ventures. Even the more successful trading lines, including electricity, did not generate the margins the marketplace had come to expect from Enron and its older portfolio of businesses (primarily natural gas trading). As shown in Exhibit 1, the actual operating income (IBIT, income before interest and taxes) by business line was not growing in line with revenues.

The growing deficit in corporate cash flows also led to a more fundamental financial management problem for Enron, the growing need for external capital, or as it was described in-house, "feeding the beast." Rapidly escalat-

ing investments in new businesses, whether they were the Portland General Electric (PGE) acquisition of 1997 or the power projects pursued by Rebecca Mark (the Director of Enron's international development group) globally, were absorbing more capital than the current business could self finance. Enron's cash flows fell increasingly behind its investments and sales.

Enron needed additional external capital—new debt and new equity. Ken Lay and Jeff Skilling, however, were both reluctant to issue large amounts of new equity because it would dilute earnings and the holdings of existing shareholders. The debt option was also limited, given the already high debt levels Enron was carrying (and which it had carried since its inception) which left it in the continuously precarious position of being rated BBB, just barely *investment grade* by credit agency standards.

Although Jeff Skilling had first employed the concept of a fund of capital to be created to support business development within Enron with the creation of the *Cactus Fund* in 1991, Andrew Fastow took the concept to a new level. Fastow's experience in banking, specifically in the use of *special purpose entities* (SPEs), a common tool in financial services, was his ticket up the corporate ladder at Enron. He eventually rose to the Chief Financial Officer position.

Many of the transactions involve an accounting structure known as a "special purpose entity" or "special purpose vehicle" (referred to as an "SPE" in this Summary

---

EXHIBIT 1	Enron's Actual Operating Income

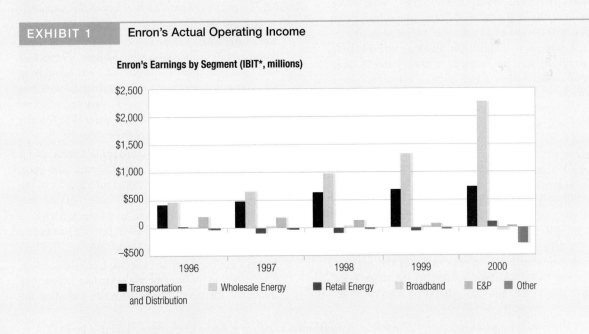

Enron's Earnings by Segment (IBIT*, millions)

Legend: ■ Transportation and Distribution   Wholesale Energy   ■ Retail Energy   Broadband   E&P   ■ Other

* IBIT is income before interest and taxes

and in the Report). A company that does business with an SPE may treat that SPE as if it were an independent, outside entity for accounting purposes if two conditions are met: (1) an owner independent of the company must make a substantive equity investment of at least 3% of the SPE's assets, and that 3% must remain at risk throughout the transaction; and (2) the independent owner must exercise control of the SPE. In those circumstances, the company may record gains and losses on transactions with the SPE, and the assets and liabilities of the SPE are not included in the company's balance sheet, even though the company and the SPE are closely related. It was the technical failure of some of the structures with which Enron did business to satisfy these requirements that led to Enron's restatement.[1]

The SPEs created by Andy Fastow and his assistant Michael Kopper served two very important purposes. First, by selling troubled assets to the partnerships, Enron removed them from its balance sheet, taking pressure off the firm's total indebtedness and simultaneously hiding underperforming investments. This also freed up additional room on the balance sheet to fund new investment opportunities. Second, the sale of the troubled investments to the partnerships generated income which Enron could then use to make its quarterly earnings commitments to Wall Street.

The problem with this solution was that it was only temporary. The SPEs were largely funded from three sources: 1) equity in the form of Enron shares by Enron; 2) equity in the form of a minimum 3% of assets by an unrelated third-party (in principle, although this was later found to not be true in a number of cases); and 3) large quantities of debt from major banks. This capital base made up the right-hand side of the SPE's balance sheet. On the left-hand side, the capital was used to purchase a variety of assets from Enron. Fastow sold these partnership deals to the banks on the premise that because he was uniquely positioned as both the CFO of Enron and the Managing Partner in the SPE, he could essentially cherry-pick the assets to be purchased by the SPE. Fastow did indeed *cherry-pick*, but they were the rotten cherries. Most of the assets purchased by the SPEs were troubled or underperforming.

A final detail of the SPEs proved in the end devastating to the financial future of Enron. Since the primary equity in the SPEs was Enron stock, as the share price rose throughout 1999 and 2000, the SPEs could periodi-

cally be marked-to-market, resulting in an appreciation in the value of the SPE and contributing significant earnings to Enron. These same shares, once their price began sliding in 2001, resulted in partnerships which should have been marked-to-market for substantial losses, but were not. As Enron's share price plummeted in the early fall of 2001, the equity in the SPEs would no longer meet accounting guidelines for remaining off balance sheet. The SPEs were becoming something of a synthetic business for Enron.

"The trouble was, the Raptors, like the rest of LJM2, had become something of a dumping ground for bad properties. In an effort to make quarterly earnings (and, of course, annual bonuses), Enron originators were hooked on making deals with Fastow instead of outside third parties—who would have asked a lot of questions, slowed down the process, and, in many cases, killed deals. Again, none of this mattered to most people at Enron, as long as the stock kept rising."[2]

The Failure of People

As it turns out, much of what Enron reported as *earnings* were not. Much of the debt raised by the company via the partnerships which was not disclosed in corporate financial statements, should have been. Simultaneously to the over reporting of profits and the under reporting of debt, was the massive compensation packages and bonuses earned by corporate officers. So how could this happen?

- It appears that the executive officers of the firm were successful in managing the Board of Directors toward their own goals. Management had moved the company into a number of new markets in which the firm suffered substantial losses, resulting in redoubled attempts on their part to somehow generate the earnings needed to meet Wall Street's unquenchable thirst for profitable growth.

- The Board failed in its duties to protect shareholder interests due to lack of due diligence and most likely a faith in the competence and integrity of the company's senior officers. It is also notable that Enron's legal advisers, some of whom reported to the Board directly, also failed to provide leadership on a number of instances of malfeasance.

- Enron's auditors, Arthur Andersen, committed serious errors in its judgments regarding accounting treatment for many Enron activities including the

[1]"Report of Investigation: Special Investigative Committee of the Board of Directors of Enron Corporation," Board of Directors, Enron, February 1, 2002 (often called *The Powers Report*), p. 5.

[2]*Power Failure*, by Sherron Watkins, p. 232. The *Raptors* and *LJM2* refer to special-purpose entities.

partnerships discussed here. Andersen was reported to have had serious conflicts of interest, earning $5 million in auditing fees from Enron in 2001, but more than $50 million in consulting fees in the same year.

■ Enron's analysts were, in a few cases, blinded by the sheer euphoria over Enron's successes in the mid to late 1990s, or working within investment banks which were earning substantial investment banking fees related to the complex partnerships. Although a few analysts continued to note that the company's earnings seemed strangely large relative to the falling cash flows reported, Enron's management was generally successful in arguing their point.

The rise and fall of Enron is a story which is far from complete. It may be in the end, however, that the true moral of the story is not in the failure of any specific process in place within the American system of corporate governance, nor in the mistaken focus on fair value accounting, nor in the lack of diligence of the Board's own audit committee, but simply the failure of people in a wide variety of positions in a great many different organizations to act reputably and responsibly.

Case Questions

1. Which parts of the corporate governance system, *internal* and *external*, do you believe failed Enron the most?

2. How do you think each of the individual stakeholders and components of the corporate governance system should have either prevented the problems at Enron or acted to resolve the problems before they reached crisis proportions?

3. If all publicly traded firms in the United States are operating within the same basic corporate governance system as Enron, why would some people believe this was an isolated incident, and not an example of many failures to come?

QUESTIONS

1. **Ownership of the Business.** How does ownership alter the goals and governance of a business?

2. **Separation of Ownership and Management.** Why is this separation so critical to the understanding of how businesses are structured and led?

3. **Corporate Goals: Shareholder Wealth Maximization.** Explain the assumptions and objectives of the shareholder wealth maximization model.

4. **Corporate Goals: Stakeholder Wealth Maximization.** Explain the assumptions and objectives of the stakeholder wealth maximization model.

5. **Corporate Governance.** Define the following terms:
   a. Corporate governance
   b. The market for corporate control
   c. Agency theory
   d. Cronyism
   e. Stakeholder capitalism

6. **Operational Goals.** What should be the primary operational goal of an MNE?

7. **Knowledge Assets.** "Knowledge assets" are a firm's intangible assets, the sources and uses of its intellectual talent—its competitive advantage. What are some of the most important "knowledge assets" that create shareholder value?

8. **Labor Unions.** In Germany and Scandinavia, among others, labor unions have representation on boards of directors or supervisory boards. How might such union representation be viewed under the shareholder wealth maximization model compared to the corporate wealth maximization model?

9. **Interlocking Directorates.** In an interlocking directorate members of the board of directors of one firm also sit on the board of directors of other firms. How would interlocking directorates be viewed by the shareholder wealth maximization model compared to the stakeholder wealth maximization model?

10. **Leveraged Buyouts.** A leveraged buyout is a financial strategy in which a group of investors gain voting control of a firm and then liquidate its assets in order to repay the loans used to purchase the firm's shares. How would leveraged buyouts be viewed by the shareholder wealth maximization model compared to the stakeholder wealth maximization model?

11. **High Leverage.** How would a high degree of leverage (debt/assets) be viewed by the shareholder wealth maximization model compared to the stakeholder wealth maximization model?

12. **Conglomerates.** Conglomerates are firms that have diversified into unrelated fields. How would a policy of conglomeration be viewed by the shareholder wealth maximization model compared to the stakeholder wealth maximization model?

13. Risk. How is risk defined in the shareholder wealth maximization model compared to the stakeholder wealth maximization model?

14. Stock Options. How would stock options granted to a firm's management and employees be viewed by the shareholder wealth maximization model compared to the stakeholder wealth maximization model?

15. Shareholder Dissatisfaction. If shareholders are dissatisfied with their company what alternative actions can they take?

16. Dual Classes of Common Stock. In many countries it is common for a firm to have two or more classes of common stock with differential voting rights. In the United States the norm is for a firm to have one class of common stock with one-share-one-vote. What are the advantages and disadvantages of each system?

17. Emerging Markets Corporate Governance Failures. It has been claimed that failures in corporate governance have hampered the growth and profitability of some prominent firms located in emerging markets. What are some typical causes of these failures in corporate governance?

18. Emerging Markets Corporate Governance Improvements. In recent years emerging market MNEs have improved their corporate governance policies and become more shareholder friendly. What do you think is driving this phenomenon?

19. Developed Markets Corporate Governance Failures. What have been the main causes of recent corporate governance failures in the United States and Europe?

20. Family Ownership. What are the key differences in the goals and motivations of family ownership of a business as opposed to a widely held publicly traded business?

21. Value of Good Governance. Do markets appear to be willing to pay for good governance?

22. Corporate Governance Reform. What are the primary principles behind corporate governance reform today? Are these culturally specific in your opinion?

PROBLEMS

Use the following formula for shareholder returns to answer questions 1 through 3, where P_t is the share price at time t, and D_t is the dividend paid at time t.

$$\text{Shareholder return} = \frac{P_2 - P_1 + D_2}{P_1} = \frac{P_2 - P_1}{P_1} + \frac{D_2}{P_1}$$

*1. Suvari Returns. If the share price of Suvari, a Florida-based shipping company, rises from $16 to $18 over a one-year period, what was the rate of return to the shareholder if:
a. The company paid no dividends
b. The company paid a dividend of $1 per share
c. Assuming the company paid the dividend, separate the total return to the shareholder into the dividend yield and the capital gain

2. Fong's Choices. Alexander Fong, a prominent investor, is evaluating investment alternatives. If he believes an individual equity will rise in price from $62 to $74 in the coming one year period, and the share is expected to pay a dividend of $2.25 per share, and he expects at least a 12% rate of return on an investment of this type, should he invest in this particular equity?

*3. Legrand Returns (A). Tony Varga is a New York-based investor. He has been following his investment in 100 shares of Legrand, a French firm that went public in March 2005 very closely. When he purchased his 100 shares, at a price of €19.75 per share, the euro was trading at $1.2250/€. Currently the share is trading at €25.28 per share, and the dollar has fallen to $1.4280/€.
a. If Tony sold his shares today, what is the percentage change in the share price he would receive?
b. What has been the percentage change in the value of the euro versus the dollar over the same period?
c. What would be the total return Tony would earn on his shares if he sold them at these rates?

4. Legrand Returns (B). Tony Varga chose not to sell his shares at the time described in the previous problem. He waited, expecting the share price to rise further after the announcement of quarterly earnings. His expectations proved correct, the share price rose to €29.46 per share after the announcement. He now wishes to recalculate his returns at this time. The current spot exchange rate is $1.1840/€.
a. If Tony sold his shares today, what is the percentage change in the share price he would receive?
b. What has been the percentage change in the value of the euro versus the dollar over the same period?
c. What would be the total return Tony would earn on his shares if he sold them at these rates?

5. Legrand Returns (C). Using the same prices and exchange rates as in the previous problem, Legrand (B), what would be the total return on the Legrand shares by Raid Gaule, a Paris-based investor?

6. **Microsoft's Dividend.** In January 2003 Microsoft announced that it would begin paying a dividend of $0.16 per share. Given the following share prices for Microsoft stock in the recent past, how would a constant dividend of $0.16 per share per year have changed the company's return to its shareholders over this period?

First Trading Day	Closing Share Price	First Trading Day	Closing Share Price
1998 (Jan 2)	$131.13	2001 (Jan 2)	$43.38
1999 (Jan 4)	$141.00	2002 (Jan 2)	$67.04
2000 (Jan 3)	$116.56	2003 (Jan 2)	$53.72

7. **Powlitz Manufacturing (A).** Dual classes of common stock are common in a number of countries. Assume that Powlitz Manufacturing has the following capital structure at book value:

Powlitz Manufacturing	Local Currency (millions)
Long-term debt	200
Retained earnings	300
Paid-in common stock: 1 million A-shares	100
Paid-in common stock: 4 million B-shares	400
Total long-term capital	1,000

The A-shares each have ten votes, the B-shares each have one vote per share.
   a. What proportion of the total long-term capital has been raised by A-shares?
   b. What proportion of voting rights is represented by A-shares?
   c. What proportion of the dividends should the A-shares receive?

8. **Powlitz Manufacturing (B).** Assuming all of the same debt and equity values for Powlitz Manufacturing in problem 7, with the sole exception that both A-shares and B-shares have the same voting rights, one vote per share:
   a. What proportion of the total long-term capital has been raised by A-shares?
   b. What proportion of voting rights is represented by A-shares?

   c. What proportion of the dividends should the A-shares receive?

9. **Pharmaceutical Acquisitions.** During the 1960s, many conglomerates were created by a firm enjoying a high price/earnings ratio (P/E). They then used their highly valued stock to acquire other firms that had lower P/E ratios, usually in unrelated domestic industries. These conglomerates went out of fashion during the 1980s when they lost their high P/E ratios, thus making it more difficult to find other firms with lower P/E ratios to acquire.

   During the 1990s, the same acquisition strategy was possible for firms located in countries where high P/E ratios were common compared to firms in other countries where low P/E ratios were common. Consider the hypothetical firms in the pharmaceutical industry shown in table at the bottom of this page.

   Pharm-USA wants to acquire Pharm-Italy. It offers 5,500,000 shares of Pharm-USA, with a current market value of $220,000,000 and a 10% premium on Pharm-Italy's shares, for all of Pharm-Italy's shares.
   a. How many shares would Pharm-USA have outstanding after the acquisition of Pharm-Italy?
   b. What would be the consolidated earnings of the combined Pharm-USA and Pharm-Italy?
   c. Assuming the market continues to capitalize Pharm-USA's earnings at a P/E ratio of 40, what would be the new market value for Pharm-USA?
   d. What is the new earnings per share of Pharm-USA?
   e. What is the new market value of a share of Pharm-USA?
   f. How much did Pharm-USA's stock price increase?
   g. Assume that the market takes a negative view of the merger and lowers Pharm-USA's P/E ratio to 30. What would be the new market price per share of stock? What would be its percentage loss?

10. **Corporate Governance: Overstating Earnings.** A number of firms, especially in the United States, have had to lower their previously reported earnings due to accounting errors or fraud. Assume that Pharm-USA had to lower their earnings to $5,000,000 from the previously reported $10,000,000. What might be its new market value prior to the acquisition? Could it still do the acquisition?

	P/E ratio	Number of shares	Market value per share	Earnings	EPS	Total market value
Pharm-Italy	20	10,000,000	$20	$10,000,000	$1.00	$200,000,000
Pharm-USA	40	10,000,000	$40	10,000,000	$1.00	$400,000,000

11. Pacific Precision (A): European Sales. Pacific Precision is a Hong Kong-based exporter of machine tools, and files all of its financial statements in Hong Kong dollars (HK$). The company's European sales director, Jacque Mayal, has been criticized of late for his performance. He disagrees, arguing that sales in Europe have grown steadily in recent years. Who is correct?

	2002	2003	2004
Total net sales, HK$	171,275	187,500	244,900
Percent of total sales from Europe	48%	44%	39%
Total European sales, HK$	_____	_____	_____
Average exchange rate, HK$/€	7.4	8.5	9.4
Total European sales, €	_____	_____	_____
Growth rate of European sales	_____	_____	_____

12. Pacific Precision (B): Japanese Yen Debt. Pacific Precision of Hong Kong borrowed Japanese yen under a long-term loan agreement several years ago. The company's new CFO believes, however, that what was originally thought to have been relatively "cheap debt" is no longer true. What do you think?

	2002	2003	2004
Annual yen payments on debt agreement (¥)	12,000,000	12,000,000	12,000,000
Average exchange rate, ¥/HK$	15.9	14.7	13.7
Annual yen debt service, HK$	_____	_____	_____

13. Chinese Sourcing and the Yuan. Harrison Equipment of Denver, Colorado, purchases all of its hydraulic tubing from manufacturers in mainland China. In June 2005 the company completed a corporate-wide initiative in six sigma/lean manufacturing. Completed oil field hydraulic system costs were reduced 4% over a one year period, from $880,000 to $844,800. The company is now worried that all of the hydraulic tubing that goes into these systems (making up 20% of their total costs) will be hit by the potential revaluation of the Chinese

yuan—if some in Washington get their way. How would a 12% revaluation of the yuan against the dollar impact total system costs? A 12% revaluation of the yuan would be calculated as follows:

$$\frac{\text{Yuan } 8.28/\$}{1+\% \text{ change}} = \frac{\text{Yuan } 8.28/\$}{1.012} = \text{Yuan } 7.39/\$.$$

14. Mattel's Global Performance. As illustrated in the table opposite, Mattel (U.S.) achieved significant sales growth in its major international regions between 2001 and 2004. In its filings with the United States Security and Exchange Commission (SEC), it reported both the amount of regional sales and what percentage change in regional sales occurred as a result of exchange rate changes.
a. What was the percentage change in sales, in U.S. dollars, by region?
b. What was the percentage change in sales by region net of currency change impacts?
c. What relative impact did currency changes have on the level and growth of Mattel's consolidated sales for the 2001 to 2004 period?

INTERNET EXERCISES

1. Multinational Firms and Global Assets/Income. The differences across MNEs are striking. Using a sample of firms such as those listed here, pull from their individual Web pages the proportions of their incomes which are earned outside their country of incorporation.
a. Walt Disney — disney.go.com/
b. Nestlé S.A. — www.nestle.com/
c. Intel — www.intel.com/
d. Daimler-Benz — www.daimlerchrysler.de
e. Mitsubishi Motors — www.mitsubishi.com/
f. Nokia — www.nokia.com/
g. Royal Dutch/Shell — www.shell.com/

(Note how Nestlé calls itself a "transnational company.")

Also note the way in which international business is now conducted via the Internet. Several of the above home pages allow the user to choose the language of the presentation viewed.

2. Corporate Governance. There is no hotter topic in business today than corporate governance. Use the following sites to view recent research, current events and news items, and other information related to the relationships between a business and its stakeholders.

Corporate Governance Net   www.corpgov.net/

Mattel's Global Sales

(thousands of US$)	2001 Sales ($)	2002 Sales ($)	2003 Sales ($)	2004 Sales ($)
Europe	$ 933,450	$ 1,126,177	$ 1,356,131	$ 1,410,525
Latin America	471,301	466,349	462,167	524,481
Canada	155,791	161,469	185,831	197,655
Asia Pacific	119,749	136,944	171,580	203,575
Total International	$ 1,680,291	$ 1,890,939	$ 2,175,709	$ 2,336,236
United States	3,392,284	3,422,405	3,203,814	3,209,862
Sales Adjustments	(384,651)	(428,004)	(419,423)	(443,312)
Total Net Sales	$ 4,687,924	$ 4,885,340	$ 4,960,100	$ 5,102,786

Impact of Change in Currency Rates

Region	2001–2002	2002–2003	2003–2004
Europe	7.0%	15.0%	8.0%
Latin America	–9.0%	–6.0%	–2.0%
Canada	0.0%	11.0%	5.0%
Asia Pacific	3.0%	13.0%	6.0%

Source: Mattel, Annual Report, 2002, 2003, 2004.

3. **Fortune Global 500.** *Fortune* magazine is relatively famous for its listing of the Fortune 500 firms are in the global marketplace. Use *Fortune's* Web site to find the most recent listing of which firms from which countries are in this distinguished club.

Fortune   www.fortune.com/fortune/

4. **Financial Times.** The *Financial Times*, based in London—the global center of international finance, has a Web site that possesses a wealth of information. After going to the home page, go to the Markets Data & Tools page, and examine the recent stock market activity around the globe. Note the similarity in movement on a daily basis among the world's major equity markets.

Financial Times   www.ft.com/

CHAPTER 3

The International Monetary System

The price of every thing rises and falls from time to time and place to place; and with every such change the purchasing power of money changes so far as that thing goes.

—Alfred Marshall

This chapter begins with a brief history of the international monetary system from the days of the classical gold standard to the present time. The history includes the development of the Eurocurrency market and its reference rate of interest known as the London Interbank Offered Rate (LIBOR). The next section describes contemporary currency regimes, fixed versus flexible exchange rates, and the attributes of the ideal currency. The next section analyzes emerging markets and regime choices, including currency boards and dollarization. The following section describes the birth of the euro and the path toward monetary unification, including the expansion of the European Union on May 1, 2004. The final section analyzes the trade-offs between exchange rate regimes based on rules, discretion, cooperation, and independence.

History of the International Monetary System

Over the ages currencies have been defined in terms of gold and other items of value, and the international monetary system has been subject to a variety of international agreements. A review of these systems provides a useful perspective against which to understand today's system and to evaluate weaknesses and proposed changes in the present system.

The Gold Standard, 1876–1913

Since the days of the pharaohs (about 3000 B.C.), gold has served as a medium of exchange and a store of value. The Greeks and Romans used gold coins and passed on this tradition through the mercantile era to the nineteenth century. The great increase in trade during the free-trade period of the late nineteenth century led to a need for a more formalized system for settling international trade balances. One country after another set a par value for its currency in terms of gold and then tried to adhere to the so-called rules of the game. This later came to be known as the classical gold standard. The gold standard as an international monetary system gained acceptance in Western Europe in the 1870s. The United States was something of a latecomer to the system, not officially adopting the standard until 1879.

Under the gold standard, the "rules of the game" were clear and simple. Each country set the rate at which its currency unit (paper or coin) could be converted to a weight of gold.

The United States, for example, declared the dollar to be convertible to gold at a rate of $20.67 per ounce (a rate in effect until the beginning of World War I). The British pound was pegged at £4.2474 per ounce of gold. As long as both currencies were freely convertible into gold, the dollar/pound exchange rate was:

$$\frac{\$20.67/\text{ounce of gold}}{£4.2474/\text{ounce of gold}} = \$4.8665/£$$

Because the government of each country on the gold standard agreed to buy or sell gold on demand with anyone at its own fixed parity rate, the value of each individual currency in terms of gold, and therefore exchange rates between currencies, was fixed. Maintaining adequate reserves of gold to back its currency's value was very important for a country under this system. The system also had the effect of implicitly limiting the rate at which any individual country could expand its money supply. Any growth in the amount of money was limited to the rate at which official authorities could acquire additional gold.

The gold standard worked adequately until the outbreak of World War I interrupted trade flows and the free movement of gold. This event caused the main trading nations to suspend operation of the gold standard.

The Interwar Years and World War II, 1914–1944

During World War I and the early 1920s, currencies were allowed to fluctuate over fairly wide ranges in terms of gold and in relation to each other. Theoretically, supply and demand for a country's exports and imports caused moderate changes in an exchange rate about a central equilibrium value. This was the same function that gold had performed under the previous gold standard. Unfortunately, such flexible exchange rates did not work in an equilibrating manner. On the contrary: international speculators sold the weak currencies short, causing them to fall further in value than warranted by real economic factors. *Selling short* is a speculation technique in which an individual speculator sells an asset such as a currency to another party for delivery at a future date. The speculator, however, does not yet own the asset, and expects the price of the asset to fall by the date when the asset must be purchased in the open market by the speculator for delivery.

The reverse happened with strong currencies. Fluctuations in currency values could not be offset by the relatively illiquid forward exchange market except at exorbitant cost. The net result was that the volume of world trade did not grow in the 1920s in proportion to world gross domestic product but instead declined to a very low level with the advent of the Great Depression in the 1930s.

The United States adopted a modified gold standard in 1934 when the U.S. dollar was devalued to $35 per ounce of gold from the $20.67 per ounce price in effect prior to World War I. Contrary to previous practice, the U.S. Treasury traded gold only with foreign central banks, not private citizens. From 1934 to the end of World War II, exchange rates were theoretically determined by each currency's value in terms of gold. During World War II and its chaotic aftermath, however, many of the main trading currencies lost their convertibility into other currencies. The dollar was the only major trading currency that continued to be convertible.

Bretton Woods and the International Monetary Fund, 1944

As World War II drew to a close in 1944, the Allied Powers met at Bretton Woods, New Hampshire, in order to create a new postwar international monetary system. The Bretton Woods Agreement established a U.S. dollar-based international monetary system and provided for two new institutions: the International Monetary Fund and the World Bank. The

International Monetary Fund (IMF) aids countries with balance of payments and exchange rate problems. The International Bank for Reconstruction and Development (World Bank) helped fund postwar reconstruction and since then has supported general economic development. *Global Finance in Practice 3.1* provides some insight into the debates at Bretton Woods.

The IMF was the key institution in the new international monetary system, and it has remained so to the present. The IMF was established to render temporary assistance to member countries trying to defend their currencies against cyclical, seasonal, or random occurrences. It also assists countries having structural trade problems if they promise to take

GLOBAL FINANCE IN PRACTICE 3.1

Hammering Out an Agreement at Bretton Woods

The governments of the Allied powers knew that the devastating impacts of World War II would require swift and decisive policies. Therefore, a full year before the end of the war, representatives of all 45 allied nations met in the summer of 1944 (July 1–22) at Bretton Woods, New Hampshire, for the United Nations Monetary and Financial Conference. Their purpose was to plan the postwar international monetary system. It was a difficult process, and the final synthesis of viewpoints was shaded by pragmatism and significant doubt.

Although the conference was attended by 45 nations, the leading policy makers at Bretton Woods were the British and the Americans. The British delegation was led by Lord John Maynard Keynes, termed "Britain's economic heavyweight." The British argued for a postwar system that would be decidedly more flexible than the various gold standards used before the war. Keynes argued, as he had after World War I, that attempts to tie currency values to gold would create pressures for deflation (a general fall in the level of prices in a country) in many of the war-ravaged economies. And these economies were faced with enormous re-industrialization needs that would likely cause inflation, not deflation.

The American delegation was led by the director of the U.S. Treasury's monetary research department, Harry D. White, and the U.S. Secretary of the Treasury, Henry Morgenthau, Jr. The Americans argued for stability (fixed exchange rates) but not a return to the gold standard itself. In fact, although the United States at that time held most of the gold of the Allied powers, the U.S. delegates argued that currencies should be fixed in parities, but redemption of the gold should occur only between official authorities (central banks of governments).

On the more pragmatic side, all parties agreed that a postwar system would be stable and sustainable only if there was sufficient credit available for countries to defend their currencies in the event of payment imbalances, which they knew to be inevitable in a reconstructing world order.

Mount Washington Hotel, Bretton Woods, New Hampshire

The conference divided up into three commissions for weeks of negotiation. One commission, led by U.S. Treasury Secretary Morgenthau, was charged with the organization of a fund of capital to be used for exchange rate stabilization. A second commission, chaired by Lord Keynes, was charged with the organization of a second "bank" whose purpose would be for long-term reconstruction and development. A third commission was to hammer out details such as what role silver would have in any new system.

After weeks of meetings the participants came to a three-part agreement—the *Bretton Woods Agreement*. The plan called for: 1) fixed exchange rates, termed an "adjustable peg" among members; 2) a fund of gold and constituent currencies available to members for stabilization of their respective currencies, called the *International Monetary Fund* (IMF); and 3) a bank for financing long-term development projects (eventually known as the *World Bank*). One proposal resulting from the meetings, which was not ratified by the United States, was the establishment of an international trade organization to promote free trade. That would take many years and conferences to come.

adequate steps to correct their problems. If persistent deficits occur, however, the IMF cannot save a country from eventual devaluation. In recent years, it has attempted to help countries facing financial crises. It has provided massive loans as well as advice to Russia and other former Russian republics, Brazil, Indonesia, and South Korea, to name but a few.

Under the original provisions of the Bretton Woods Agreement, all countries fixed the value of their currencies in terms of gold but were not required to exchange their currencies for gold. Only the dollar remained convertible into gold (at $35 per ounce). Therefore, each country established its exchange rate vis-à-vis the dollar, and then calculated the gold par value of its currency to create the desired dollar exchange rate. Participating countries agreed to try to maintain the value of their currencies within 1% (later expanded to 2.25%) of par by buying or selling foreign exchange or gold as needed. Devaluation was not to be used as a competitive trade policy, but if a currency became too weak to defend, a devaluation of up to 10% was allowed without formal approval by the IMF. Larger devaluations required IMF approval. This became known as the *gold-exchange standard.*

The *Special Drawing Right* (SDR) is an international reserve asset created by the IMF to supplement existing foreign exchange reserves. It serves as a unit of account for the IMF and other international and regional organizations, and is also the base against which some countries peg the exchange rate for their currencies.

Defined initially in terms of a fixed quantity of gold, the SDR has been redefined several times. It is currently the weighted average of four major currencies: the U.S. dollar, the euro, the Japanese yen, and the British pound. The weights are updated every five years by the IMF. Individual countries hold SDRs in the form of deposits in the IMF. These holdings are part of each country's international monetary reserves, along with official holdings of gold, foreign exchange, and its reserve position at the IMF. Members may settle transactions among themselves by transferring SDRs.

Eurocurrencies

Eurocurrencies are domestic currencies of one country on deposit in a second country. Eurodollar time deposit maturities range from call money and overnight funds to longer periods. Certificates of deposit are usually for three months or more and in million-dollar increments. A Eurodollar deposit is not a demand deposit; it is not created on the bank's books by writing loans against required fractional reserves, and it cannot be transferred by a check drawn on the bank having the deposit. Eurodollar deposits are transferred by wire or cable transfer of an underlying balance held in a correspondent bank located within the United States. A domestic analogy in most countries would be the transfer of deposits held in nonbank savings associations. These are transferred by having the association write its own check on a commercial bank.

Any convertible currency can exist in "Euro-" form. (Note that this use of the expression "Euro-" should not be confused with the new common European currency called the *euro.*) The Eurocurrency market includes Eurosterling (British pounds deposited outside the United Kingdom), Euroeuros (euros on deposit outside the euro zone), and Euroyen (Japanese yen deposited outside Japan), as well as Eurodollars. The exact size of the Eurocurrency market is difficult to measure because it varies with daily decisions by depositors on where to hold readily transferable liquid funds, and particularly on whether to deposit dollars within or outside the United States.

Eurocurrency markets serve two valuable purposes: 1) Eurocurrency deposits are an efficient and convenient money market device for holding excess corporate liquidity; and 2) the Eurocurrency market is a major source of short-term bank loans to finance corporate working capital needs, including the financing of imports and exports.

Banks in which Eurocurrencies are deposited are called *Eurobanks.* A Eurobank is a financial intermediary that simultaneously bids for time deposits and makes loans in a currency other than that of the country in which it is located. Eurobanks are major world banks that conduct a Eurocurrency business in addition to all other banking functions. Thus, the Eurocurrency operation that qualifies a bank for the name "Eurobank" is in fact a department of a large commercial bank, and the name springs from the performance of this function.

The modern Eurocurrency market was born shortly after World War II. Eastern European holders of dollars, including the various state trading banks of the Soviet Union, were afraid to deposit their dollar holdings in the United States because these deposits might be attached by U.S. residents with claims against communist governments. Therefore, Eastern European holders deposited their dollars in Western Europe, particularly with two Soviet banks: the Moscow Narodny Bank in London, and the Banque Commerciale pour l'Europe du Nord in Paris. These banks redeposited the funds in other Western banks, especially in London. Additional dollar deposits were received from various central banks in Western Europe, which elected to hold part of their dollar reserves in this form to obtain a higher yield. Commercial banks also placed their dollar balances in the market for the same reason, as well as because specific maturities could be negotiated in the Eurodollar market. Additional dollars came to the market from European insurance companies with a large volume of U.S. business. Such companies found it financially advantageous to keep their dollar reserves in the higher-yielding Eurodollar market. Various holders of international refugee funds also supplied funds.

Although the basic causes of the growth of the Eurocurrency market are economic efficiencies, the following unique institutional events during the 1950s and 1960s helped its growth:

- In 1957, British monetary authorities responded to a weakening of the pound by imposing tight controls on U.K. bank lending in sterling to nonresidents of the United Kingdom. Encouraged by the Bank of England, U.K. banks turned to dollar lending as the only alternative that would allow them to maintain their leading position in world finance. For this they needed dollar deposits.

- Although New York was home base for the dollar and had a large domestic money and capital market, London became the center for international trading in the dollar because of that city's expertise in international monetary matters and its proximity in time and distance to major customers.

- Additional support for a European-based dollar market came from the balance of payments difficulties that the United States experienced during the 1960s, which temporarily separated the U.S. domestic capital market from that of the rest of the world.

Ultimately, however, the Eurocurrency market continues to thrive because it is a large international money market relatively free from governmental regulation and interference.

Eurocurrency Interest Rates: LIBOR

In the Eurocurrency market, the reference rate of interest is the *London Interbank Offered Rate* (LIBOR). LIBOR is now the most widely accepted rate of interest used in standardized quotations, loan agreements, and financial derivatives valuations. LIBOR is officially defined by the *British Bankers Association* (BBA). For example, U.S. dollar LIBOR is the mean of 16 multinational banks' interbank offered rates as sampled by the BAA at 11 A.M. London time.

Similarly, the BBA calculates the Japanese yen LIBOR, euro LIBOR, and other currency LIBOR rates at the same time in London from sample groups of banks.

The interbank interest rate is not, however, confined to London. Most major domestic financial centers construct their own interbank offered rates for local loan agreements. These rates include PIBOR (Paris Interbank Offered Rate), MIBOR (Madrid Interbank Offered Rate), SIBOR (Singapore Interbank Offered Rate), and FIBOR (Frankfurt Interbank Offered Rate), to name but a few.

The key factor attracting both depositors and borrowers to the Eurocurrency loan market is the narrow interest rate spread within that market. The difference between deposit and loan rates is often less than 1%. Interest spreads in the Eurocurrency market are small for a number of reasons. Low lending rates exist because the Eurocurrency market is a *wholesale market,* where deposits and loans are made in amounts of $500,000 or more on an unsecured basis. Borrowers are usually large corporations or government entities that qualify for low rates because of their credit standing and because the transaction size is large. In addition, overhead assigned to the Eurocurrency operation by participating banks is small.

Deposit rates are higher in the Eurocurrency markets than in most domestic currency markets because the financial institutions offering Eurocurrency activities are not subject to many of the regulations and reserve requirements imposed on traditional domestic banks and banking activities. With these costs removed, rates are subject to more competitive pressures, deposit rates are higher, and loan rates are lower. A second major area of cost avoided in the Eurocurrency markets is the payment of deposit insurance fees (such as the Federal Deposit Insurance Corporation (FDIC) assessments paid on deposits in the United States). Exhibit 3.1 illustrates how Eurodollar deposit and loan rates, including dollar LIBOR rates, compare with traditional domestic interest rates.

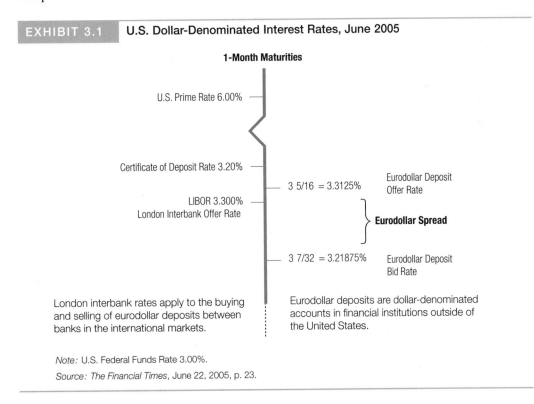

EXHIBIT 3.1   U.S. Dollar-Denominated Interest Rates, June 2005

1-Month Maturities

U.S. Prime Rate 6.00%

Certificate of Deposit Rate 3.20%

3 5/16 = 3.3125%   Eurodollar Deposit Offer Rate

LIBOR 3.300%
London Interbank Offer Rate

Eurodollar Spread

3 7/32 = 3.21875%   Eurodollar Deposit Bid Rate

London interbank rates apply to the buying and selling of eurodollar deposits between banks in the international markets.

Eurodollar deposits are dollar-denominated accounts in financial institutions outside of the United States.

Note: U.S. Federal Funds Rate 3.00%.

Source: The Financial Times, June 22, 2005, p. 23.

Fixed Exchange Rates, 1945–1973

The currency arrangement negotiated at Bretton Woods and monitored by the IMF worked fairly well during the post-World War II period of reconstruction and rapid growth in world trade. However, widely diverging national monetary and fiscal policies, differential rates of inflation, and various unexpected external shocks eventually resulted in the system's demise. The U.S. dollar was the main reserve currency held by central banks and was the key to the web of exchange rate values. Unfortunately, the United States ran persistent and growing deficits in its balance of payments. A heavy capital outflow of dollars was required to finance these deficits and to meet the growing demand for dollars from investors and businesses. Eventually, the heavy overhang of dollars held by foreigners resulted in a lack of confidence in the ability of the United States to meet its commitment to convert dollars to gold.

This lack of confidence forced President Richard Nixon to suspend official purchases or sales of gold by the U.S. Treasury on August 15, 1971, after the United States suffered outflows of roughly one-third of its official gold reserves in the first seven months of the year. Exchange rates of most of the leading trading countries were allowed to float in relation to the dollar and thus indirectly in relation to gold. By the end of 1971, most of the major trading currencies had appreciated vis-à-vis the dollar. This change was—in effect—a devaluation of the dollar.

A year and a half later, the U.S. dollar once again came under attack, thereby forcing a second devaluation on February 12, 1973; this time by 10% to $42.22 per ounce of gold. By late February 1973, a fixed-rate system no longer appeared feasible given the speculative flows of currencies. The major foreign exchange markets were actually closed for several weeks in March 1973. When they reopened, most currencies were allowed to float to levels determined by market forces. Par values were left unchanged. The dollar floated downward an average of another 10% by June 1973.

An Eclectic Currency Arrangement, 1973–Present

Since March 1973, exchange rates have become much more volatile and less predictable than they were during the "fixed" exchange rate period, when changes occurred infrequently. Exhibit 3.2 illustrates the wide swings exhibited by the IMF's nominal exchange rate index of the U.S. dollar since 1957. Clearly, volatility has increased for this currency measure since 1973.

Exhibit 3.3 summarizes the key events and external shocks that have affected currency values since March 1973. The most important shocks in recent years have been the European Monetary System (EMS) restructuring in 1992 and 1993; the emerging market currency crises, including that of Mexico in 1994, Thailand (and a number of other Asian currencies) in 1997, Russia in 1998, and Brazil in 1999; the introduction of the euro in 1999; the economic crisis in Turkey in 2001; and the currency crises and changes in Argentina and Venezuela in 2002.

Contemporary Currency Regimes

Today, the international monetary system is composed of national currencies, artificial currencies (such as the SDR), and one entirely new currency (euro) that replaced the 11 national European Union currencies on January 1, 1999. All of these currencies are linked to one another via a "smorgasbord" of currency regimes.

IMF's Exchange Rate Regime Classifications

The IMF classifies all exchange rate regimes into eight specific categories. The eight categories span the spectrum of exchange rate regimes from rigidly fixed to independently floating.

1. **Exchange arrangements with no separate legal tender.** The currency of another country circulates as the sole legal tender or the member belongs to a monetary or

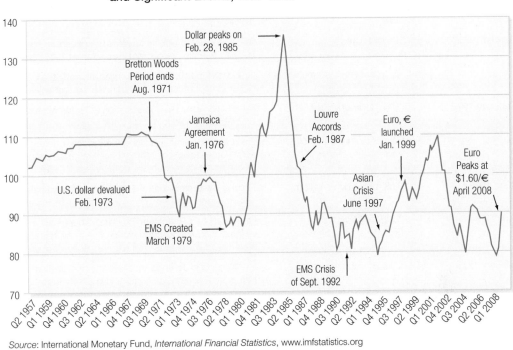

EXHIBIT 3.2   **The IMF's Nominal Exchange Rate Index of the U.S. Dollar and Significant Events, 1957–2008**

Source: International Monetary Fund, *International Financial Statistics*, www.imfstatistics.org

currency union in which the same legal tender is shared by the members of the union.

2. **Currency board arrangements.** A monetary regime based on an implicit legislative commitment to exchange domestic currency for a specified foreign currency at a fixed exchange rate, combined with restrictions on the issuing authority to ensure the fulfillment of its legal obligation.

3. **Other conventional fixed peg arrangements.** The country pegs its currency (formally or *de facto*) at a fixed rate to a major currency or a basket of currencies (a *composite*), where the exchange rate fluctuates within a narrow margin or at most ±1% around a central rate.

4. **Pegged exchange rates within horizontal bands.** The value of the currency is maintained within margins of fluctuation around a formal or *de facto* fixed peg that are wider than ±1% around a central rate.

5. **Crawling pegs.** The currency is adjusted periodically in small amounts at a fixed, preannounced rate or in response to changes in selective quantitative indicators.

6. **Exchange rates within crawling pegs.** The currency is maintained within certain fluctuation margins around a central rate that is adjusted periodically at a fixed preannounced rate or in response to changes in selective quantitative indicators.

7. **Managed floating with no preannounced path for the exchange rate.** The monetary authority influences the movements of the exchange rate through active intervention in the foreign exchange market without specifying, or precommitting to, a preannounced path for the exchange rate.

EXHIBIT 3.3	World Currency Events, 1971–2008

Date	Event	Impact
August 1971	Dollar floated	Nixon closes the U.S. gold window, suspending purchases or sales of gold by U.S. Treasury; temporary imposition of 10% import surcharge
December 1971	Smithsonian Agreement	Group of Ten reaches compromise whereby the US$ is devalued to $38/oz. of gold; most other major currencies are appreciated versus US$
February 1973	U.S. dollar devalued	Devaluation pressure increases on US$, forcing further devaluation to $42.22/oz. of gold
February–March 1973	Currency markets in crisis	Fixed exchange rates no longer considered defensible; speculative pressures force closure of international foreign exchange markets for nearly two weeks; markets reopen on floating rates for major industrial currencies
June 1973	U.S. dollar depreciation	Floating rates continue to drive the now freely floating US$ down by about 10% by June
Fall 1973–1974	OPEC oil embargo	Organization of Petroleum Exporting Countries (OPEC) impose oil embargo, eventually quadrupling the world price of oil; because world oil prices are stated in US$, value of US$ recovers some former strength
January 1976	Jamaica Agreement	IMF meeting in Jamaica results in the "legalization" of the floating exchange rate system already in effect; gold is demonetized as a reserve asset
1977–1978	U.S. inflation rate rises	Carter administration reduces unemployment at the expense of inflation increases; rising U.S. inflation causes continued depreciation of the US$
March 1979	EMS created	The European Monetary System (EMS) is created, establishing a cooperative exchange rate system for participating members of the European Economic Community (EEC)
Summer 1979	OPEC raises prices	OPEC nations raise price of oil again
Spring 1980	U.S. dollar begins rise	Worldwide inflation and early signs of recession coupled with real interest differential advantages for dollar-denominated assets contribute to increased demand for dollars
August 1982	Latin American debt crisis	Mexico informs U.S. Treasury on Friday 13, 1982, that it will be unable to make debt service payments; Brazil and Argentina follow within months
February 1985	U.S. dollar peaks	The U.S. dollar peaks against most major industrial currencies, hitting record highs against the deutsche mark and other European currencies
September 1985	Plaza Agreement	Group of Ten members meet at the Plaza Hotel in New York City to sign an international cooperative agreement to control the volatility of world currency markets and to establish target zones
February 1987	Louvre Accords	Group of Six members state they will "intensify" economic policy coordination to promote growth and reduce external imbalances
December 1991	Maastricht Treaty	European Union concludes a treaty to replace all individual currencies with a single currency—the euro
September 1992	EMS crisis	High German interest rates induce massive capital flows into deutsche mark-denominated assets, causing the withdrawal of the Italian lira and British pound from the EMS's common float
July 31, 1993	EMS realignment	EMS adjusts allowable deviation band to ±15% for all member countries (except the Dutch guilder); U.S. dollar continues to weaken; Japanese yen reaches ¥100.25/$
1994	EMI founded	European Monetary Institute (EMI), the predecessor to the European Central Bank, is founded in Frankfurt, Germany

EXHIBIT 3.3   World Currency Events, 1971–2008 (continued)

Date	Event	Impact
December 1994	Peso collapse	Mexican peso suffers major devaluation as a result of increasing pressure on the managed devaluation policy; peso falls from Ps3.46/$ to Ps5.50/$ within days; the peso's collapse results in a fall in most major Latin American exchanges in a contagion process—the "tequila effect"
August 1995	Yen peaks	Japanese yen reaches an all-time high versus the U.S. dollar of ¥79/$; yen slowly depreciates over the following two-year period, rising to over ¥130/$
June 1997	Asian crisis	The Thai baht is devalued in July, followed soon after by the Indonesian rupiah, Korean won, Malaysian ringgit, and Philippine peso; following the initial exchange rate devaluations, the Asian economy plummets into recession
August 1998	Russian crisis	On Monday, August 17, the Russian Central Bank devalues the ruble by 34%; the ruble continues to deteriorate in the following days, sending the already weak Russian economy into recession
January 1, 1999	Euro launched	Official launch date for the euro, the single European currency; 11 European Union member states elect to participate in the system, which irrevocably locks their individual currencies rates among them
January 1999	Brazilian reais crisis	The reais, initially devalued 8.3% by the Brazilian government on January 12, is allowed to float against the world's currencies
January 1, 2002	Euro coinage	Euro coins and notes are introduced in parallel with home currencies; national currencies are phased out during the six-month period beginning January 1
January 8, 2002	Argentine peso crisis	The Argentine peso, its value fixed to the U.S. dollar at 1:1 since 1991 through a currency board, is devalued to Ps1.4/$, then floated
February 13, 2002	Venezuelan bolivar floated	The Venezuelan bolivar, fixed to the dollar since 1996, is floated as a result of increasing economic crisis
February 14, 2004	Venezuelan bolivar devalued	Venezuela devalues the bolivar by 17% versus the U.S. dollar, in an attempt to deal with its growing fiscal deficit
May 1, 2004	EU enlargement	Ten more countries join the European Union, thereby enlarging it to 25 members; in the future, when they qualify, most of these countries are expected to adopt the euro
July 21, 2005	Yuan reform	The Chinese government and the People's Bank of China abandon the peg of the Chinese yuan (renminbi) to the U.S. dollar, announcing that it will be instantly revalued from Yuan8.28/$ to Yuan8.11/$, and reform the exchange rate regime to a managed float in the future; Malaysia announces a similar change to its exchange rate regime
April 2008	Euro peaks	The euro peaks in strength against the U.S. dollar at $1.60/€. In the following months the euro falls substantially, hitting $1.25/€ by late October 2008.

8. **Independent floating.** The exchange rate is market-determined, with any foreign exchange intervention aimed at moderating the rate of change and preventing undue fluctuations in the exchange rate, rather than establishing a level for it.

The most prominent example of a rigidly fixed system is the euro area, in which the euro is the single currency for its member countries. However, the euro itself is an independently floating currency against all other currencies. Other examples of rigidly fixed exchange regimes include Ecuador and Panama, which use the U.S. dollar as their official currency; the Central African Franc (CFA) zone, in which countries such as Mali, Niger, Senegal, Cameroon, and Chad among others use a single common currency (the franc, tied to the euro) and the Eastern Caribbean Currency Union (ECCU), whose members use a single common currency (the Eastern Caribbean dollar).

At the other extreme are countries with independently floating currencies. These include many of the most developed countries, such as Japan, the United States, the United Kingdom, Canada, Australia, New Zealand, Sweden, and Switzerland. However, this category also includes a number of unwilling participants—emerging market countries that tried to maintain fixed rates but were forced by the marketplace to let them float. Among these are Korea, the Philippines, Brazil, Indonesia, Mexico, and Thailand.

It is important to note that only the last two categories, including 80 of the 186 countries covered, are actually "floating" to any real degree. Although the contemporary international monetary system is typically referred to as a "floating regime," it is clearly not the case for the majority of the world's nations.

Fixed versus Flexible Exchange Rates

A nation's choice as to which currency regime to follow reflects national priorities about all facets of the economy, including inflation, unemployment, interest rate levels, trade balances, and economic growth. The choice between fixed and flexible rates may change over time as priorities change.

At the risk of over generalizing, the following points partly explain why countries pursue certain exchange rate regimes. They are based on the premise that, other things being equal, countries would prefer fixed exchange rates.

- Fixed rates provide stability in international prices for the conduct of trade. Stable prices aid in the growth of international trade and lessen risks for all businesses.
- Fixed exchange rates are inherently anti-inflationary, requiring the country to follow restrictive monetary and fiscal policies. This restrictiveness, however, can often be a burden to a country wishing to pursue policies that alleviate continuing internal economic problems, such as high unemployment or slow economic growth.

Fixed exchange rate regimes necessitate that central banks maintain large quantities of international reserves (hard currencies and gold) for use in the occasional defense of the fixed rate. As international currency markets have grown rapidly in size and volume, increasing reserve holdings has become a significant burden to many nations.

Fixed rates, once in place, may be maintained at levels that are inconsistent with economic fundamentals. As the structure of a nation's economy changes, and as its trade relationships and balances evolve, the exchange rate itself should change. Flexible exchange rates allow this to happen gradually and efficiently, but fixed rates must be changed administratively—usually too late, too highly publicized, and at too large a onetime cost to the nation's economic health.

Attributes of the "Ideal" Currency

If the ideal currency existed in today's world, it would possess three attributes (illustrated in Exhibit 3.4), often referred to as the "impossible trinity":

1. **Exchange rate stability.** The value of the currency would be fixed in relationship to other major currencies, so traders and investors could be relatively certain of the foreign exchange value of each currency in the present and into the near future.

2. **Full financial integration.** Complete freedom of monetary flows would be allowed, so traders and investors could willingly and easily move funds from one country and currency to another in response to perceived economic opportunities or risks.

3. **Monetary independence.** Domestic monetary and interest rate policies would be set by each individual country to pursue desired national economic policies, especially as they might relate to limiting inflation, combating recessions, and fostering prosperity and full employment.

These qualities are termed "the impossible trinity" because a country must give up one of the three goals described by the sides of the triangle: monetary independence, exchange rate stability, or full financial integration. The forces of economics do not allow the simultaneous achievement of all three. For example, a country with a pure float exchange rate regime can have monetary independence and a high degree of financial integration with the outside capital markets, but the result must be a loss of exchange rate stability (the case of the United States). Similarly, a country that maintains very tight controls over the inflow and outflow of capital will retain its monetary independence and a stable exchange rate, but at the loss of being integrated with global financial and capital markets (the case of Malaysia in the 1998–2002 period).

As shown in Exhibit 3.4, the consensus of many experts is that the force of increased capital mobility has been pushing more and more countries toward full financial integration in an attempt to stimulate their domestic economies and feed the capital appetites of their own MNEs. As a result, their currency regimes are being "cornered" into being either purely floating (like the United States) or integrated with other countries in monetary unions (like the European Union).

EXHIBIT 3.4   The Impossible Trinity

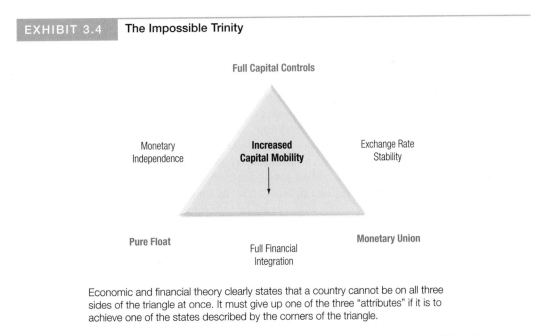

Economic and financial theory clearly states that a country cannot be on all three sides of the triangle at once. It must give up one of the three "attributes" if it is to achieve one of the states described by the corners of the triangle.

Source: Adapted from Lars Oxelheim, *International Financial Integration*, Springer-Verlag, 1990, p. 10.

Emerging Markets and Regime Choices

The 1997–2005 period saw increasing pressures on emerging market countries to choose among more extreme types of exchange rate regimes. The increased capital mobility pressures noted in the previous section have driven a number of countries to choose between either a free-floating exchange rate (as in Turkey in 2002) or the opposite extreme, a fixed-rate regime—such as a *currency board* (as in Argentina throughout the 1990s and detailed in the following section) or even *dollarization* (as in Ecuador in 2000).

Currency Boards

A *currency board* exists when a country's central bank commits to back its monetary base—its money supply—entirely with foreign reserves at all times. This commitment means that a unit of domestic currency cannot be introduced into the economy without an additional unit of foreign exchange reserves being obtained first. Eight countries, including the Hong Kong territory, utilize currency boards as a means of fixing their exchange rates.

Argentina. In 1991, Argentina moved from its previous managed exchange rate of the Argentine peso to a currency board structure. The currency board structure fixed the Argentine peso's value to the U.S. dollar on a one-to-one basis. The Argentine government preserved the fixed rate of exchange by requiring that every peso issued through the Argentine banking system be backed by either gold or U.S. dollars held on account in banks in Argentina. This 100% reserve system made the monetary policy of Argentina dependent on the country's ability to obtain U.S. dollars through trade or investment. Only after Argentina had earned these dollars through trade could its money supply be expanded. This requirement eliminated the possibility of the nation's money supply growing too rapidly and causing inflation.

An additional feature of the Argentine currency board system was the ability of all Argentines or foreigners to hold dollar-denominated accounts in Argentine banks. These accounts were in actuality *Eurodollar accounts*—dollar-denominated deposits in non-U.S. banks. These accounts provided savers and investors with the ability to choose whether or not to hold pesos.

From the very beginning, however, there was substantial doubt in the market that the Argentine government could maintain the fixed exchange rate. Argentine banks regularly paid slightly higher interest rates on peso-denominated accounts than on dollar-denominated accounts. This interest differential represented the market's assessment of the risk inherent in the Argentine financial system. Depositors were rewarded for accepting risk—for keeping their money in peso-denominated accounts. This was an explicit signal by the marketplace that there was a perceived possibility that what was then "fixed" would not always be so.

The market proved to be correct. In January 2002, after months of economic and political turmoil and nearly three years of economic recession, the Argentine currency board was ended. The peso was first devalued from Peso1.00/$ to Peso1.40/$, then floated completely. It fell in value dramatically within days. The Argentine decade-long experiment with a rigidly fixed exchange rate was over. The devaluation followed months of turmoil, including continuing bank holidays and riots in the streets of Buenos Aires. The Argentina crisis is presented in detail in Chapter 7.

Dollarization

Several countries have suffered currency devaluation for many years, primarily as a result of inflation, and have taken steps toward dollarization. Dollarization is the use of the U.S. dollar as the official currency of the country. Panama has used the dollar as its official currency since 1907. Ecuador, after suffering a severe banking and inflationary crisis in 1998 and 1999, adopted the U.S. dollar as its official currency in January 2000. One of the primary attributes of dollarization was summarized well by *BusinessWeek* in a December 11, 2000, article entitled "The Dollar Club":

> *One attraction of dollarization is that sound monetary and exchange-rate policies no longer depend on the intelligence and discipline of domestic policymakers. Their monetary policy becomes essentially the one followed by the U.S., and the exchange rate is fixed forever.*

The arguments for dollarization follow logically from the previous discussion of the impossible trinity. A country that dollarizes removes any currency volatility (against the dollar) and would theoretically eliminate the possibility of future currency crises. Additional benefits are expectations of greater economic integration with the United States and other dollar-based markets, both product and financial. This last point has led many to argue in favor of regional dollarization, in which several countries that are highly economically integrated may benefit significantly from dollarizing together.

Three major arguments exist against dollarization. The first is the loss of sovereignty over monetary policy. This is, however, the point of dollarization. Second, the country loses the power of *seignorage,* the ability to profit from its ability to print its own money. Third, the central bank of the country, because it no longer has the ability to create money within its economic and financial system, can no longer serve the role of lender of last resort. This role carries with it the ability to provide liquidity to save financial institutions that may be on the brink of failure during times of financial crisis.

Ecuador. Ecuador officially completed the replacement of the Ecuadorian sucre with the U.S. dollar as legal tender on September 9, 2000. This step made Ecuador the largest national adopter of the U.S. dollar, and in many ways set it up as a test case of dollarization for other emerging market countries to watch closely. As shown in Exhibit 3.5, this was the last stage of a massive depreciation of the sucre in a brief two-year period.

EXHIBIT 3.5	The Ecuadorian Sucre Exchange Rate, November 1998–March 2000

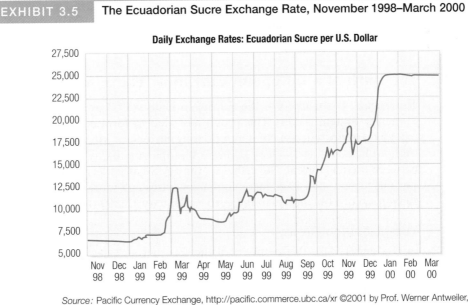

Daily Exchange Rates: Ecuadorian Sucre per U.S. Dollar

Source: Pacific Currency Exchange, http://pacific.commerce.ubc.ca/xr ©2001 by Prof. Werner Antweiler, University of British Columbia, Vancouver, BC, Canada.

During 1999, Ecuador suffered a rising rate of inflation and a falling level of economic output. In March 1999, the Ecuadorian banking sector was hit with a series of devastating "bank runs," financial panics in which all depositors attempted to withdraw all of their funds simultaneously. Although there were severe problems in the Ecuadorian banking system, the truth was that even the healthiest financial institution would fail under the strain of this financial drain. Ecuador's president at that time, Jamil Mahuad, immediately froze all deposits (what was termed a bank holiday in the United States in the 1930s, in which banks closed their doors). The Ecuadorian sucre, which in January 1999 was trading at roughly Sucre7,400/$, plummeted in early March to Sucre12,500/$. Ecuador defaulted on more than $13.6 billion in foreign debt in 1999 alone. President Mahuad moved quickly to propose dollarization to save the failing Ecuadorian economy.

By January 2000, when the next president took office (after a rather complicated military coup and subsequent withdrawal), the sucre had fallen in value to Sucre25,000/$. The new president, Gustavo Naboa, continued the dollarization initiative. Although unsupported by the U.S. government and the IMF, Ecuador completed its replacement of its own currency with the dollar over the next nine months.

The results of dollarization in Ecuador are still unknown. Ecuadorian residents immediately returned over $600 million into the banking system, money that they had withheld from the banks in fear of bank failure. This added capital infusion, along with new IMF loans and economic restructurings, allowed the country to actually close 2000 with a small economic gain of 1%. Inflation, however, remained high, closing the year at over 91% (up from 66% in 1999). Clearly, dollarization alone did not eliminate inflationary forces. Ecuador continues to struggle to find both economic and political balance with its new currency regime.

There is no doubt that for many emerging markets, a currency board, dollarization, and free-floating exchange rate regimes are all extremes. In fact, many experts feel that the global financial marketplace will drive more and more emerging market nations toward one of these extremes. As shown in Exhibit 3.6, there is a distinct lack of middle ground between rigidly fixed and free-floating extremes. In anecdotal support of this argument, a poll of the general population in Mexico in 1999 indicated that 9 out of 10 people would prefer dollarization over a floating-rate peso. Clearly, there are many in the emerging markets of the world who have little faith in their leadership and institutions to implement an effective exchange rate policy.

The Birth of a European Currency: The Euro

The original 15 members of the European Union (EU) are also members of the European Monetary System (EMS). This group has tried to form an island of fixed exchange rates among themselves in a sea of major floating currencies. Members of the EMS rely heavily on trade with each other, so they perceive that the day-to-day benefits of fixed exchange rates between them are great. Nevertheless, the EMS has undergone a number of major changes since its inception in 1979, including major crises and reorganizations in 1992 and 1993, and conversion of 11 members to the euro on January 1, 1999 (Greece joined in 2001).

The Maastricht Treaty

In December 1991, the members of the EU met at Maastricht, the Netherlands, and concluded a treaty that changed Europe's currency future.

Timetable. The Maastricht Treaty specified a timetable and a plan to replace all individual ECU currencies with a single currency called the euro. Other steps were adopted that would lead to a full European Economic and Monetary Union (EMU).

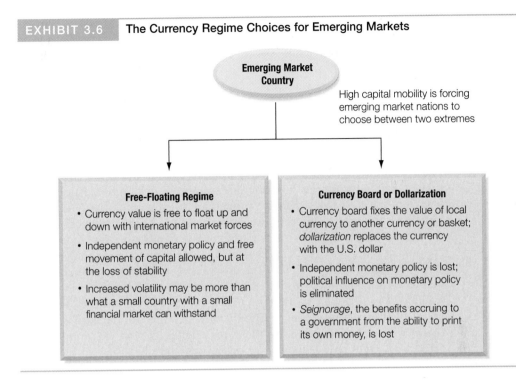

EXHIBIT 3.6   The Currency Regime Choices for Emerging Markets

Emerging Market Country

High capital mobility is forcing emerging market nations to choose between two extremes

Free-Floating Regime

- Currency value is free to float up and down with international market forces
- Independent monetary policy and free movement of capital allowed, but at the loss of stability
- Increased volatility may be more than what a small country with a small financial market can withstand

Currency Board or Dollarization

- Currency board fixes the value of local currency to another currency or basket; *dollarization* replaces the currency with the U.S. dollar
- Independent monetary policy is lost; political influence on monetary policy is eliminated
- *Seignorage*, the benefits accruing to a government from the ability to print its own money, is lost

Convergence Criteria. To prepare for the EMU, the Maastricht Treaty called for the integration and coordination of the member countries' monetary and fiscal policies. The EMU would be implemented by a process called convergence. Before becoming a full member of the EMU, each member country was originally expected to meet the following convergence criteria:

- Nominal inflation should be no more than 1.5% above the average for the three members of the EU with the lowest inflation rates during the previous year.
- Long-term interest rates should be no more than 2% above the average for the three members with the lowest interest rates.
- The fiscal deficit should be no more than 3% of gross domestic product.
- Government debt should be no more than 60% of gross domestic product.

The convergence criteria were so tough that few, if any, of the members could satisfy them at that time, but 11 countries managed to do so just prior to 1999. Greece adopted the euro on January 1, 2001.

Strong Central Bank. A strong central bank, called the European Central Bank (ECB), has been established in Frankfurt, Germany, in accordance with the Treaty. The bank is modeled after the U.S. Federal Reserve System. This independent central bank dominates the countries' central banks, which continue to regulate banks resident within their borders; all financial market intervention and the issuance of euros remain the sole responsibility of the ECB. The single most important mandate of the ECB is to promote price stability within the European Union.

As part of its development of cross-border monetary policy, the ECB has formed the Transeuropean Automated Real-time Gross settlement Express Transfer system (TARGET).

TARGET is the mechanism by which the ECB will settle all cross-border payments in the conduct of EU banking business and regulation. It will allow the ECB to conduct monetary policy and other intrabanking system capital movements quickly and without cost.

Why Monetary Unification?

According to the EU, EMU is a single-currency area within the EU single market, now known informally as the *euro zone,* in which people, goods, services, and capital are supposed to move without restrictions. Beginning with the Treaty of Rome in 1957 and continuing with the Single European Act of 1987, the Maastricht Treaty of 1991–1992, and the Treaty of Amsterdam of 1997, a core set of European countries worked steadily toward integrating their individual countries into one larger, more efficient, domestic market. Even after the launch of the 1992 Single Europe program, however, a number of barriers to true openness remained. The use of different currencies required both consumers and companies to treat the individual markets separately. Currency risk of cross-border commerce still persisted. The creation of a single currency is designed to move beyond these vestiges of separated markets.

The official abbreviation of the euro, EUR, has been registered with the International Standards Organization (letter abbreviations are needed for computer-based worldwide trading). This is similar to the three-letter computer symbols used for the U.S. dollar, USD, and the British pound sterling, GBP. The official symbol of the euro is €. According to the EU, the € symbol was inspired by the Greek letter *epsilon* (ε), simultaneously referring to Greece's ancient role as the source of European civilization and recalling the first letter of the word *Europe.*

The Launch of the Euro

On January 4, 1999, 11 member states of the EU initiated the EMU. They established a single currency, the euro, which replaced the individual currencies of the participating member states. The 11 countries were Austria, Belgium, Finland, France, Germany, Ireland, Italy, Luxembourg, the Netherlands, Portugal, and Spain. The United Kingdom, Sweden, and Denmark chose to maintain their individual currencies. Greece did not qualify for EMU but joined the Euro group in 2001. On December 31, 1998, the final fixed rates between the 11 participating currencies and the euro were put into place. On January 4, 1999, the euro was officially launched. Although it was the result of a long-term and methodical program for the alignment of all political and economic forces in the EU, the launch of the euro was only the first of many steps to come. The impacts of the euro on the economic environment and on society in general within the participating countries have been and will continue to be dramatic. It is only now becoming apparent what some of the impacts might be.

The euro affects markets in three ways: 1) countries within the euro zone enjoy cheaper transaction costs; 2) currency risks and costs related to exchange rate uncertainty are reduced; and 3) all consumers and businesses both inside and outside the euro zone enjoy price transparency and increased price-based competition.

Achieving Monetary Unification

If the euro is to be a successful replacement for the currencies of the participating EU states, it must have a solid economic foundation. The primary driver of a currency's value is its ability to maintain its purchasing power (money is worth what money can buy). The single largest threat to maintaining purchasing power is inflation. So, job one for the EU since the beginning has been to construct an economic system that would work to prevent inflationary forces from undermining the euro.

Fiscal Policy and Monetary Policy. Monetary policy for the EMU is conducted by the ECB, which has one responsibility: to safeguard the stability of the euro. Following the basic structures that were used in the establishment of the Federal Reserve System in the United States and the Bundesbank in Germany, the ECB is free of political pressures that have historically caused monetary authorities to yield to employment pressures by inflating economies. The ECB's independence allows it to focus simply on the stability of the currency without falling victim to this historical trap.

Fixing the Value of the Euro. The December 31, 1998, fixing of the rates of exchange between national currencies and the euro were permanent fixes for these currencies. The United Kingdom has been skeptical of increasing EU infringement on its sovereignty, and has opted not to participate. Sweden, which has failed to see significant benefits from EU membership (although it is one of the newest members), has also been skeptical of EMU participation. Denmark, like the United Kingdom and Sweden, has a strong political element that is highly nationalistic, and so far has opted not to participate. Norway has twice voted down membership in the EU and thus does not participate in the euro system.

On January 4, 1999, the euro began trading on world currency markets. Its introduction was a smooth one. The euro's value slid steadily following its introduction, however, primarily as a result of the robustness of the U.S. economy and U.S. dollar, and continuing sluggish economic sectors in the EMU countries. Exhibit 3.7 illustrates the euro's value since its introduction in January 1999. After declining in value against the U.S. dollar over 1999 and 2000, the euro

EXHIBIT 3.7	The U.S. Dollar/Euro Spot Exchange Rate, 1999–2008 (Monthly Average)

Source: ©2009 by Prof. Werner Antweiler, University of British Columbia, Vancouver BC, Canada. Permission is granted to reproduce the above image provided that the source and copyright are acknowledged.

Time period shown in diagram: 1 January 1999–2 March 2009

traded in a relatively narrow band throughout 2001. Beginning in early 2002, however, the euro started a strong and steady rise in value versus the dollar, peaking at $1.50/€ in late 2007.

Causes of the Dollar Decline. Since the introduction of the euro, the United States has experienced severe balance of payments deficits on the current account (explained in Chapter 4). The biggest bilateral deficits were with China and Japan. However, in order to protect their export competitiveness, both China and Japan followed macroeconomic policies that would maintain relatively fixed rates of exchange between their currencies and the U.S. dollar. In order to accomplish this result, both China and Japan had to intervene in the foreign exchange market by buying massive amounts of U.S. dollars while selling corresponding amounts of their own currencies, the Chinese yuan, and the Japanese yen. These purchases showed up as capital inflows into the United States. However, as the United States has continued to maintain historically low interest rates—both to stimulate the domestic economy and to promote liquidity in the financial system following the subprime mortgage failures in 2007—some critics wonder whether China and Japan will continue to hold such large quantities of U.S. dollars.

Furthermore, several Asian and Middle Eastern governments are beginning to create so-called sovereign wealth funds to use their accumulating U.S. dollar balances. Sovereign wealth funds are government owned and funded investment funds that are either acquiring or taking a significant interest in private companies and major foreign banks in the United States and other Western countries. They are the subject of growing concern as foreign nations invest within other countries.

Expansion of the European Union and the Euro. In January 2007, two more countries were added to the EU's growing membership—Bulgaria and Romania. Their entry was little more than two years after the EU had added 10 more countries to its ranks. As shown in *Global Finance in Practice 3.2*, to date, only one of these 12 new members has actually adopted the

GLOBAL FINANCE IN PRACTICE 3.2

New EU Members and Adoption of the Euro

These new members will not automatically adopt the euro as their currency. They will be allowed to adopt the euro only after they have met the criteria all euro members have had to meet from the very beginning: a high degree of price stability, sustainable government finances, a stable exchange rate, and convergence in long-term interest rates.

The following eight countries are currently slated to join the euro zone:

Country	Currency	Current Exchange Rate Regime	Expected Euro Adoption
Bulgaria	lev	Pegged to the euro	2010, though possibly as late as 2015
Czech Republic	koruna	Free-floating; managed against the euro	2012
Estonia	kroon	Pegged to the euro	2011
Hungary	forint	Free-floating, but references the euro	2010–2012 (under debate)
Latvia	lat	Pegged to the euro	2012 (earliest)
Lithuania	litas	Pegged to the euro	2010
Poland	zloty	Free-floating, but references the euro	2012 (tentative)
Romania	leu	Free-floating	2014

euro. Although all members are expected eventually to replace their currencies with the euro, recent years have seen growing debates and continual postponements by the new members in moving toward full euro adoption.

The Euro and Growth. Prior to the introduction of the euro, opponents thought political and economic conditions were unfavorable for a common currency. Most of the countries that eventually adopted the euro, such as Germany, France, and Italy, lacked the flexible labor markets they would need to compensate for losing individual (country-level) control over monetary policy as a tool to promote growth. Since the individual members of the EU cannot devalue their currencies, they would need to rely mainly on coordinated fiscal policies to stimulate growth. It is probably impossible to conduct a centralized monetary policy that fits all member countries, as illustrated by the impossible trinity discussed earlier. Some members are growing and some are not. Unemployment has been fairly high in some members but lower in others.

Exchange Rate Regimes: What Lies Ahead?

All exchange rate regimes must deal with the trade-off between *rules* and *discretion,* as well as between *cooperation* and *independence.* Exhibit 3.8 illustrates the trade-offs between exchange rate regimes based on rules, discretion, cooperation, and independence.

- Vertically, different exchange rate arrangements may dictate whether the country's government has strict intervention requirements—*rules*—or whether it may choose whether, when, and to what degree to intervene in the foreign exchange markets—*discretion.*

- Horizontally, the trade-off for countries participating in a specific system is between consulting and acting in unison with other countries—*cooperation*—or operating as a member of the system, but acting on their own—*independence.*

EXHIBIT 3.8   The Trade-offs between Exchange Rate Regimes

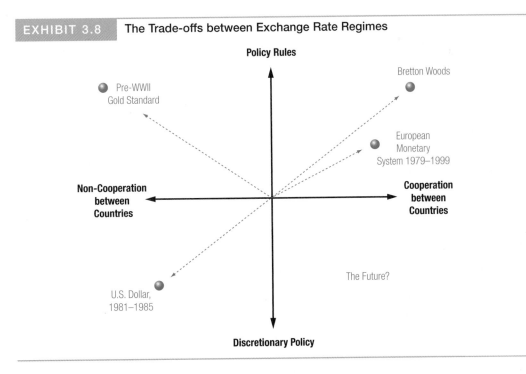

Regime structures like the gold standard required no cooperative policies among countries, only the assurance that all would abide by the "rules of the game." Under the gold standard in effect prior to World War II, this assurance translated into the willingness of governments to buy or sell gold at parity rates on demand. The Bretton Woods Agreement, the system in place between 1944 and 1973, required more in the way of cooperation, in that gold was no longer the "rule," and countries were required to cooperate to a higher degree to maintain the dollar-based system. Exchange rate systems, like the European Monetary System's fixed exchange rate band system used from 1979 to 1999, were hybrids of these cooperative and rule regimes.

The present international monetary system is characterized by no rules, with varying degrees of cooperation. Although there is no present solution to the continuing debate over what form a new international monetary system should take, many believe that it could succeed only if it combined cooperation among nations with individual discretion to pursue domestic social, economic, and financial goals.

SUMMARY POINTS

- Under the gold standard (1876–1913), the "rules of the game" were that each country set the rate at which its currency unit could be converted to a weight of gold.

- During the inter-war years (1914–1944), currencies were allowed to fluctuate over fairly wide ranges in terms of gold and each other. Supply and demand forces determined exchange rate values.

- The Bretton Woods Agreement (1944) established a U.S. dollar-based international monetary system. Under the original provisions of the Bretton Woods Agreement, all countries fixed the value of their currencies in terms of gold but were not required to exchange their currencies for gold. Only the dollar remained convertible into gold ($35 per ounce).

- A variety of economic forces led to the suspension of the convertibility of the dollar into gold in August 1971. Exchange rates of most of the leading trading countries were then allowed to float in relation to the dollar and thus indirectly in relation to gold. After a series of continuing crises in 1972 and 1973, the U.S. dollar and the other leading currencies of the world have floated in value since that time.

- Eurocurrencies are domestic currencies of one country on deposit in a second country.

- Although the basic causes of the growth of the Eurocurrency market are economic efficiencies, a number of unique institutional events during the 1950s and 1960s helped its growth. In 1957, British monetary authorities responded to a weakening of the pound by imposing tight controls on U.K. bank lending in sterling to nonresidents of the United Kingdom. Encouraged by the Bank of England, U.K. banks

turned to dollar lending as the only alternative that would allow them to maintain their leading position in world finance. For this they needed dollar deposits. Although New York was "home base" for the dollar and had a large domestic money and capital market, international trading in the dollar centered in London because of that city's expertise in international monetary matters and its proximity in time and distance to major customers.

- Additional support for a European-based dollar market came from the balance of payments difficulties of the United States during the 1960s, which temporarily segmented the U.S. domestic capital market from that of the rest of the world.

- If the ideal currency existed in today's world, it would possess three attributes: a fixed value, convertibility, and independent monetary policy.

- Emerging market countries must often choose between two extreme exchange rate regimes, either a free-floating regime or an extremely fixed regime such as a *currency board* or *dollarization*.

- The 15 members of the European Union are also members of the European Monetary System (EMS). This group has tried to form an island of fixed exchange rates among themselves in a sea of major floating currencies. Members of the EMS rely heavily on trade with each other, so the day-to-day benefits of fixed exchange rates between them are perceived to be great.

- On May 1, 2004, the European Union admitted an additional 10 countries, reaching a total of 25 countries as members. The 10 new members are expected to work toward adoption of the euro gradually over the next six to seven years.

- The euro affects markets in three ways: 1) countries within the euro zone enjoy cheaper transaction costs; 2) currency risks and costs related to exchange rate uncertainty are reduced; and 3) all consumers and businesses both inside and outside the euro zone enjoy price transparency and increased price-based competition.

MINI-CASE   The Revaluation of the Chinese Yuan[1]

"They started talking about something that wasn't very useful, then started to collect mobile phones and BlackBerrys," said a banker who was briefed later. The Chinese then distributed a four-point statement: Beijing was unlinking the yuan from the U.S. dollar effective immediately."

— "Behind Yuan Move, Open Debate and Closed Doors," *The Wall Street Journal*, July 25, 2005, p. A1.

"This a cautious move," said Zhong Wei, a finance expert at Beijing Normal University. "This is more like a political stance than real currency reform."

— "China Ends Fixed-Rate Currency," Peter S. Goodman, *The Washington Post*, July 22, 2005, p. A01.

On July 21, 2005, the Chinese government and the People's Bank of China officially changed the value of the Chinese yuan (or renminbi, RMB). On the morning of July 21, a number of key foreign banks in Beijing were asked to send representatives to the People's Bank of China for a meeting with an unannounced agenda. The People's Bank announced to the assembled banking group that it would abandon the peg of the yuan to the dollar, allow the value of the yuan to rise to Yuan8.11/$ immediately, and allow the value of the yuan to fluctuate 0.3% per day over the previous day's closing price going forward (see the Mini-Case Appendix for the complete text of the announcement). The change in value and regime—a revaluation against the U.S. dollar and a movement to an unknown basket of currencies peg—was both expected and a surprise.

The Revaluation Debate

Throughout 2004 and 2005, the U.S. government had continued to urge China to revalue the yuan from its decade-long peg to the U.S. dollar of Yuan8.28/$. The U.S. argued that the growing Chinese trade surplus with the U.S. indicated that the yuan was significantly undervalued. The political sparring had reached levels of veiled threats, as members of the U.S. Treasury had warned Chinese officials that a revaluation of at least 10% would be needed to prevent protectionist legislation in Congress. Even many within China acknowledged that maintaining the pegged rate was costly, as China's central bank continued to buy up the U.S. dollars that continued to pour in from trade and investment. By early 2005, China's foreign exchange reserves had swelled to more than $700 billion, including $190 billion in U.S. government bonds.

The Chinese government and many international trade experts, however, did not agree that the yuan was undervalued, arguing that the bilateral trade surplus with the United States was a result of competitiveness, cost of production, and changing global industry structures. Regardless, the move to revalue the yuan was seen as a political move to reduce pressures growing between governments, while simultaneously starting the process of moving the Chinese economy into a prominent role in the global economy.

In May 2004, the Chinese government had convened a panel of academic experts in Dalian to debate the future of the Chinese yuan. The debate boiled down to a "stay the course" philosophy advocated by Ronald McKinnon of Stanford University and Robert Mundell of Columbia University, as opposed to the "pro-revaluation" position of Jeffrey Frankel of Harvard University and Morris Goldstein of the Institute for International Economics. Interestingly, the risk that both camps agreed upon was that if the revaluation was too small, the currency markets—specifically, speculators—would demand more, leading to additional instability. That risk was now a clear possibility.

Pressure had continued to mount and rumors circulated. As recently as July 15, the headlines of the *Financial Times* had proclaimed "U.S. Expects Chinese Currency Revaluation," speculating that it would occur sometime in August. China moved even faster. Late on Wednesday, July 20, 2005, the U.S. Treasury and Hong Kong banking authorities were both informed, just hours before the rest of the world, that China was on the brink of altering its exchange regime from a dollar-peg to a managed float.

New Currency Regime

The Chinese yuan had been pegged to the U.S. dollar at Yuan8.28/$ since early 1997. This peg had been sustained through the Asian Financial Crisis of 1997/1998, and had provided a fixed and stable currency base for the rapid development and growth of the Chinese economy into the new millennium. The Chinese economy continued to grow extremely rapidly—more than 10% in real GDP terms—and the growth rate was expected to continue at this rate for at least a decade to come. Clearly, the economy was increasingly too large to remain a second-rate exchange rate country. More and more voices from outside China called for the Chinese yuan to be transitioned to a floating exchange rate and join the U.S. dollar, the euro, and the Japanese yen in the forefront of the global financial system.

The new currency regime announced by the People's Bank of China would change how the currency's value was managed. Although not saying exactly how the value would be determined, it was clear that the Chinese policy makers would consider the values of other major currencies such as the euro and the yen in addition to the dollar in moving to a *managed float*. Without knowing the contents of this *conceptual basket,* however, outsiders would be unable to predict specific policy maker movements on the currency's value.

The immediate change, however, was a revaluation of approximately 2.1%, a much smaller change than the 10% to 20% suggested by Chinese critics like the United States government:

$$\frac{\text{Yuan8.28/\$} - \text{Yuan8.11/\$}}{\text{Yuan8.11/\$}} \times 100 = 2096\% \approx 21\%$$

The implication of the 0.3% accepted deviation was potentially more significant. Although this deviation would limit the day-to-day movement of the yuan's value (in many ways protecting investors and companies alike against large sudden changes), it would permit the yuan to begin a minimal float. And it would not prevent the yuan from slowly and gradually *appreciating* against other currencies like the dollar over time. A number of currency experts were quick to point out that the previous yuan regime also officially allowed gradual rate adjustment,

and that the yuan had actually been revalued from Yuan8.70/$ to Yuan8.28/$ between 1994 and 1997.

Regional Impacts

The Chinese economy has become increasingly integral to the economies of Asia; specifically, to the economies of Thailand, Malaysia, Korea, and Taiwan. In recent years, a number of major industries have migrated from other Southeast Asian countries to China, so the revaluation of the yuan alters the competitive dynamics in the region. Several countries immediately reacted to the revaluation by announcing exchange rate changes of their own. Hong Kong, however, maintained its peg to the dollar.

The Malaysian government, within hours, announced the introduction of a similar managed-float exchange rate regime like that of China. Malaysia had maintained a fixed exchange rate since the onslaught of the Asian financial crisis in 1997. The new regimes in China and Malaysia were both remarkably similar to Singapore's regime, the so-called "basket, band, and crawl" or BBC, which that country had used successfully since the 1980s.

Competitive Implications

One well-known U.S. company with a big exposure to China is Mattel Inc., the world's largest toy manufacturer, which gets about 70% of its Barbie Dolls, Hot Wheels cars, and other toys from China, including from factories it owns there. A Mattel spokeswoman said the stronger yuan could mean higher materials costs next year when it renegotiates contracts with factories that it doesn't own. At its own plants, the impact "is mostly labor-related, rather than raw-material related, and is not sizeable," she added.

—"Companies See Little Impact from Costlier Yuan—For Now," *The Wall Street Journal*, July 22, 2005, p. B1.

The revaluation of the Chinese yuan had not been something most multinational companies had sought. Most multinational companies operating in China had invested for the purpose of using China as a manufacturing base for global sourcing. As such, they wished the currency to remain both stable and relatively "cheap." A foreign multinational company like Mattel, one of the world's foremost toy manufacturers, sourced more than 70% of its toys from within China. Any revaluation of the yuan would mean that in dollar or euro terms, the cost of goods sold would rise and the resulting margins and profitability reduced when those same products were sold in euro or dollar markets.

For some companies, like Boeing, revaluation would have a marginally positive impact, if any. Boeing did little sourcing in China, but had been making larger and larger sales to China. The revaluation of the yuan would slightly increase the purchasing power of Boeing's Chinese customers, as it used U.S. dollar-based pricing for its export sales, including those to China. Other companies anticipated more complex competitive impacts. For example, General Motors actually welcomed the revaluation. Although GM did increasingly source parts and sub-assemblies from China, the 2.1% revaluation was thought to be a small cost increase. Simultaneously, the revaluation of the yuan was expected to give the Japanese yen a substantial boost in the international financial markets, driving the value of the yen up against the dollar and the euro. From GM's perspective, any increase in the value of the yen would benefit it by hurting arch-competitor Toyota, with much of its global manufacturing still in Japan.

The competitive impacts on Chinese companies—specifically, Chinese multinationals like the Haier Group (manufacturer of small appliances like the mini-refrigerators in many college dorm rooms around the globe)—were potentially major over the long term. Although they would suffer only a 2% increase in cost versus foreign market pricing immediately, the yuan's new freedom to float incrementally over time presented them with a new and

growing operational risk from exchange rates over time.

Clearly, for all companies moving rapidly into China for either access to manufacturing or markets, only time would tell whether the yuan's newfound freedom would represent an opportunity or a threat.

Case Questions

1. Many Chinese critics had urged China to revalue the yuan by 20% or more. What would the Chinese yuan's value be in U.S. dollars if it had indeed been devalued by 20%?

2. Do you believe that the revaluation of the Chinese yuan was politically or economically motivated?

3. If the Chinese yuan were to change by the maximum allowed per day, 0.3% against the U.S. dollar, consistently over a 30- or 60-day period, what extreme values might it reach?

4. Chinese multinationals would now be facing the same exchange-rate related risks borne by U.S., Japanese, and European multinationals. What impact do you believe this rising risk will have on the strategy and operations of Chinese companies in the near future?

MINI-CASE APPENDIX   Public Announcement of the People's Bank of China on Reforming the RMB Exchange Rate Regime

July 21, 2005—With a view to establish and improve the socialist market economic system in China, enable the market to fully play its role in resource allocation as well as to put in place and further strengthen the managed floating exchange rate regime based on market supply and demand, the People's Bank of China, with authorization of the State Council, is hereby making the following announcements regarding reforming the RMB exchange rate regime:

1. Starting from July 21, 2005, China will reform the exchange rate regime by moving into a managed floating exchange rate regime based on market supply and demand with reference to a basket of currencies. RMB will no longer be pegged to the U.S. dollar and the RMB exchange rate regime will be improved with greater flexibility.

2. The People's Bank of China will announce the closing price of a foreign currency such as the U.S. dollar traded against the RMB in the interbank foreign exchange market after the closing of the market on each working day, and will make it the central par-

ity for the trading against the RMB on the following working day.

3. The exchange rate of the U.S. dollar against the yuan will be adjusted to 8.11 yuan per U.S. dollar at the time of 19:00 hours of July 21, 2005. The foreign exchange designated banks may since adjust quotations of foreign currencies to their customers.

4. The daily trading price of the U.S. dollar against the RMB in the interbank foreign exchange market will continue to be allowed to float within a band of ±0.3 percent around the central parity published by the People's Bank of China, while the trading prices of the non-U.S. dollar currencies against the RMB will be allowed to move within a certain band announced by the People's Bank of China.

The People's Bank of China will make adjustment of the RMB exchange rate band when necessary according to market development as well as the economic and financial situation. The RMB exchange rate will be more flexible based on market condition with reference to a basket of currencies. The People's Bank of China is responsible for maintaining the RMB exchange rate basically stable at an adaptive and equilibrium level, so as to promote the basic equilibrium of the balance of payments

and safeguard macroeconomic and financial stability (see Exhibit 1 on the following page).

Source: http://www.pbc.gov.cn/english/xinwen/.

EXHIBIT 1   **Monthly Average Exchange Rates: Chinese Renminbi per U.S. Dollar**

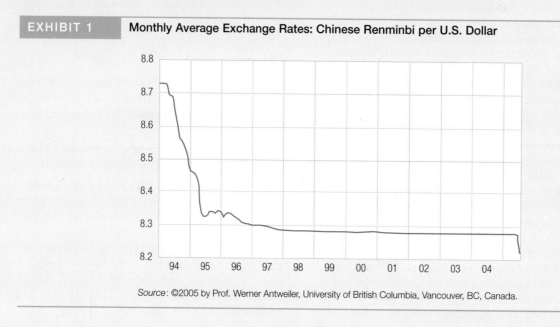

Source: ©2005 by Prof. Werner Antweiler, University of British Columbia, Vancouver, BC, Canada.

QUESTIONS

1. The Gold Standard and the Money Supply. Under the gold standard all national governments promised to follow the "rules of the game." This meant defending a fixed exchange rate. What did this promise imply about a country's money supply?

2. Causes of Devaluation. If a country follows a fixed exchange rate regime, what macroeconomic variables could cause the fixed exchange rate to be devalued?

3. Fixed versus Flexible Exchange Rates. What are the advantages and disadvantages of fixed exchange rates?

4. The Impossible Trinity. Explain what is meant by the term *impossible trinity* and why it is true.

5. Currency Board or Dollarization. Fixed exchange rate regimes are sometimes implemented through a *currency board* (Hong Kong) or *dollarization* (Ecuador). What is the difference between the two approaches?

6. Emerging Market Exchange Rate Regimes. High capital mobility is forcing emerging market nations to choose between free-floating regimes and currency

board or dollarization regimes. What are the main outcomes of each of these regimes from the perspective of emerging market nations?

7. Argentine Currency Board. How did the Argentine currency board function from 1991 to January 2002 and why did it collapse?

8. The Euro. On January 4, 1999, 11 member states of the European Union initiated the European Monetary Union (EMU) and established a single currency, the *euro,* which replaced the individual currencies of participating member states. Describe three of the main ways that the euro affects the members of the EMU.

9. Mavericks. The United Kingdom, Denmark, and Sweden have chosen not to adopt the *euro* but rather maintain their individual currencies. What are the motivations of each of these three countries that are also members of the European Union?

10. International Monetary Fund (IMF). The IMF was established by the Bretton Woods Agreement (1944). What were its original objectives?

11. Special Drawing Rights. What are *Special Drawing Rights?*

12. **Exchange Rate Regime Classifications.** The IMF classifies all exchange rate regimes into eight specific categories that are summarized in this chapter. Under which exchange rate regime would you classify the following countries?
    a. France
    b. The United States
    c. Japan
    d. Thailand

13. **The Ideal Currency.** What are the attributes of the ideal currency?

14. **Bretton Woods Failure.** Why did the fixed exchange rate regime of 1945–1973 eventually fail?

15. **EU and Euro Expansion.** With so many new countries joining the European Union in 2004, when will they officially move to the euro—if ever?

PROBLEMS

1. **Brussels and New York.** If in Brussels, one can buy a U.S. dollar for €0.8200. In New York, one can buy a euro for $1.22. What is the foreign exchange rate between the dollar and the euro?

*2. **Mexican Peso Changes.** In December 1994, the government of Mexico officially changed the value of the Mexican peso from 3.2 pesos per dollar to 5.5 pesos per dollar. What was the percentage change in the value of the peso? Was this a *devaluation, revaluation, depreciation,* or *appreciation?* Explain.

3. **Gold Standard.** Before World War I, $20.67 was needed to buy one ounce of gold. If, at the same time one ounce of gold could be purchased in France for FF310.00, what was the exchange rate between French francs and U.S. dollars?

4. **Good as Gold.** Under the gold standard, the price of an ounce of gold in U.S. dollars was $20.67, while the price of that same ounce of gold in British pounds was £4.2474. What would the exchange rate between the dollar and the pound be if the U.S. dollar price had been $38 per ounce?

5. **Mexican Peso Spot Rate.** The spot rate for Mexican pesos is Ps10.74/$. If your company buys Ps350,000 spot from your bank on Monday, how much must your company pay and on what date?

6. **Hong Kong Dollar and the Chinese Yuan.** The Hong Kong dollar has long been pegged to the U.S. dollar at HK$7.80/$. When the Chinese yuan was revalued in July 2005 against the U.S. dollar from Yuan8.28/$ to Yuan8.11/$, how did the value of the Hong Kong dollar change against the yuan?

*7. **Loonie Parity.** If the price of former Chairman of the U.S. Federal Reserve Alan Greenspan's memoir, *The Age of Turbulence* is listed on the dust jacket as C$26.45, but costs just US$20.99, what exchange rate does that imply between the two currencies?

8. **Porsche Pricing (A).** Porsche plans on introducing a new four-door luxury automobile in 2009 called the Panamera. Although pricing is not yet set, some automotive analysts believe the basic production model will be sold in Europe at a price of €120,000. At this price they believed the company stood to earn a 20% margin on each car.
    a. If the spot rate in 2009 was $1.4400/€, what would be its projected price in the United States?
    b. If the price in the U.S. market was set at $158,000, and the spot exchange rate averaged $1.4240/€, what would be the margin on the Panamera?

9. **Porsche Pricing (B).** Using the same basic data as in the previous problem, consider the following. If the dollar continues to fall throughout the year, and the spot rate in 2009 averages $1.6250/€, but the U.S. dollar price is held constant since its introduction in January 2009 at $158,000, what would be the profit margin on each car sold in the United States?

10. **Toyota Exports to the United Kingdom.** Toyota manufactures most of the vehicles it sells in the United Kingdom in Japan. The base platform for the Toyota Tundra truck line is ¥1,650,000. The spot rate of the Japanese yen against the British pound has recently moved from ¥197/£ to ¥190/£. How does this change the price of the Tundra to Toyota's British subsidiary in British pounds?

11. **Ranbaxy (India) in Brazil.** Ranbaxy, an India-based pharmaceutical firm, has continuing problems with its cholesterol reduction product's price in Brazil, one of its rapidly growing markets. All product is produced in India, with costs and pricing initially stated in Indian rupees (Rps), but converted to Brazilian reais (R$) for distribution and sale in Brazil. In 2004, the unit volume was priced at Rps12,500, with a Brazilian reais price set at R$825. But in 2005 the reais appreciated in value versus the rupee, averaging Rps17.5/R$. In order to preserve the reais price and product profit margin in rupees, what should the new rupee price be set at?

12. **Chunnel Choices.** The Channel Tunnel or Chunnel passes underneath the English Channel between

Great Britain and France, a land link between the Continent and the British Isles. Therefore, one side is an economy of British pounds, the other euros. If you were to check the Chunnel's rail ticket Internet rates you would find that they would be denominated in U.S. dollars. For example, a first class round trip fare for a single adult from London to Paris via the Chunnel through RailEurope may cost $170. This currency neutrality, however, means that customers on both ends of the Chunnel pay differing rates in their home currencies from day to day. What is the British pound and euro denominated prices for the $170 round trip fare in local currency if purchased on the following dates at the accompanying spot rates drawn from the *Financial Times?*

Date	Pound Spot Rate	Euro Spot Rate
July 17, 2005	£0.5702/$	€0.8304/$
July 18, 2005	£0.5712/$	€0.8293/$
July 19, 2005	£0.5756/$	€0.8340/$

*13. **Middle East Exports.** A European-based manufacturer ships a machine tool to a buyer in Jordan. The purchase price is €375,000. Jordan imposes a 12% import duty on all products purchased from the European Union. The Jordanian importer then re-exports the product to a Saudi Arabian importer, but only after imposing its own resale fee of 22%. Given the following spot exchange rates on May 25, 2004, what is the total cost to the Saudi Arabian importer in Saudi Arabian riyal, and what is the U.S. dollar equivalent of that price?

Spot rate, Jordanian dinar (JD) per euro (€)	JD 0.8700/€
Spot rate, Jordanian dinar (JD) per U.S. dollar ($)	JD 0.7080/$
Spot rate, Saudi Arabian riyal (SRI) per U.S. dollar	SRI 3.750/$

14. **Chinese Yuan Revaluation.** Many experts believe that the Chinese currency should not only be revalued against the U.S. dollar as it was in July 2005, but also be revalued by 20% or 30%. What would be the new exchange rate value be if the yuan was revalued an additional 20% or 30% from its initial post-revaluation rate of Yuan8.11/$?

15. **Vietnamese Coffee Coyote.** Many people were surprised when Vietnam became the second largest coffee producing country in the world in recent years,

second only to Brazil. The Vietnamese dong, VND or d, is managed against the U.S. dollar but is not widely traded. If you were a traveling coffee buyer for the wholesale market (a *coyote* by industry terminology), which of the following currency rates and exchange commission fees would be in your best interest if traveling to Vietnam on a buying trip?

Currency Exchange	Rate	Commission
Vietnamese bank rate	d14,000	1.50%
Saigon Airport exchange bureau rate	d13,800	2.00%
Hotel exchange bureau rate	d13,750	1.50%

INTERNET EXERCISES

1. **Personal Transfers.** As anyone who has traveled internationally learns, the exchange rates available to private retail customers are not always as attractive as those accessed by companies. The OzForex Web site has a section on "customer rates" which illustrates the difference. Use the site to calculate the percentage difference between Australian dollar/U.S. dollar spot exchange rates for retail customers versus interbank rates.

   OzForex   www.ozforex.com

2. **International Monetary Fund's Special Drawing Rights.** The Special Drawing Right (SDR) is a composite index of six key participant currencies. Use the IMF's Web site to find the current weights and valuation of the SDR.

   International Monetary Fund   www.imf.org/external/np/
                                 tre/sdr/basket.htm

3. **Recent Exchange Rate History.** Use the Pacific Exchange Rate database and plot capability to track the U.S. dollar's value—it's down—against the following major global currencies over the past decade: the euro, the Japanese yen, the British pound, the Swiss franc, and the Chinese yuan.

   Pacific Exchange Rate Service   fx.sauder.ubc.ca

4. **Capital Controls.** One of the key "sides" of the impossibility trinity discussed in this chapter is the degree of capital mobility into and out of a country. Use the International Finance subsection of Yahoo! to determine the current state of capital movement freedom for the following countries: Chile, China, Malaysia, Taiwan, and Russia.

   Yahoo!   biz.yahoo.com/intl.html

5. **Currency Boards.** Use the following Web sites, and any others, to track the ongoing debate of the relative success of dollarization and currency boards.

International Monetary Fund	www.imf.org/external/pubs
National Bureau of Economic Research	papers.nber.org/papers
Cato Institute	www.cato.org/pubs/pubs.html

6. **Malaysian Currency Controls.** The institution of currency controls by the Malaysian government in the aftermath of the Asian currency crisis is a classic response by government to unstable currency conditions. Use the following Web site to increase your knowledge of how currency controls work.

EconEdLink	www.econedlink.org/lessons/index.cfm?lesson=EM25

CHAPTER 4

The Balance of Payments

The sort of dependence that results from exchange, i.e., from commercial transactions, is a reciprocal dependence. We cannot be dependent upon a foreigner without his being dependent on us. Now, this is what constitutes the very essence of society. To sever natural interrelations is not to make oneself independent, but to isolate oneself completely.

—Frederic Bastiat.

International business transactions occur in many different forms over the course of a year. The measurement of all international economic transactions between the residents of a country and foreign residents is called the *balance of payments* (BOP). The official terminology used throughout this chapter is that of the IMF. Because the IMF is the primary source of similar statistics for balance of payments and economic performance by nations worldwide, its language is more general than other terminology such as that employed by the U.S. Department of Commerce. Government policy makers need such measures of economic activity in order to evaluate the general competitiveness of domestic industry, to set exchange rate or interest rate policies or goals, and for many other purposes. MNEs use various BOP measures to gauge the growth and health of specific types of trade or financial transactions by country and regions of the world against the home country.

Home-country and host-country BOP data are important to business managers, investors, consumers, and government officials, because the data influences and is influenced by other key macroeconomic variables such as gross domestic product, employment levels, price levels, exchange rates, and interest rates. Monetary and fiscal policy must take the BOP into account at the national level. Business managers and investors need BOP data to anticipate changes in host-country economic policies that might be driven by BOP events. BOP data is also important for the following reasons:

- The BOP is an important indicator of pressure on a country's foreign exchange rate, and thus of the potential for a firm trading with or investing in that country to experience foreign exchange gains or losses. Changes in the BOP may predict the imposition or removal of foreign exchange controls.

- Changes in a country's BOP may signal the imposition or removal of controls over payment of dividends and interest, license fees, royalty fees, or other cash disbursements to foreign firms or investors.

- The BOP helps to forecast a country's market potential, especially in the short run. A country experiencing a serious trade deficit is not as likely to expand imports as it would be if running a surplus. It may, however, welcome investments that increase its exports.

Typical Balance of Payments Transactions

International transactions take many forms. Each of the following examples is an international economic transaction that is counted and captured in the U.S. balance of payments:

- Honda U.S. is the U.S. distributor of automobiles manufactured in Japan by its parent company, Honda of Japan.
- A U.S.-based firm, Fluor Corporation, manages the construction of a major water treatment facility in Bangkok, Thailand.
- The U.S. subsidiary of a French firm, Saint Gobain, pays profits (dividends) back to its parent firm in Paris.
- An American tourist purchases a small Lapponia necklace in Finland.
- The U.S. government finances the purchase of military equipment for its NATO (North Atlantic Treaty Organization) military ally, Norway.
- A Mexican lawyer purchases a U.S. corporate bond through an investment broker in Cleveland.

This is a small sample of the hundreds of thousands of international transactions that occur each year. The balance of payments provides a systematic method for classifying these transactions. One rule of thumb always aids the understanding of BOP accounting: "Follow the cash flow."

The BOP is composed of a number of subaccounts that are watched quite closely by groups as diverse as investment bankers, farmers, politicians, and corporate executives. These groups track and analyze the major subaccounts, the *current account*, the *capital account*, and the *financial account*, on a continuing basis. Exhibit 4.1 provides an overview of these major subaccounts of the BOP.

EXHIBIT 4.1   **Generic Balance of Payments**

A. Current Account

1. Net exports/imports of goods (balance of trade)
2. Net exports/imports of services
3. Net income (investment income from direct and portfolio investment plus employee compensation)
4. Net transfers (sums sent home by migrants and permanent workers abroad, gifts, grants, and pensions)

   A (1-4) = Current Account Balance

B. Capital Account

Capital transfers related to the purchase and sale of fixed assets such as real estate

C. Financial Account

1. Net foreign direct investment
2. Net portfolio investment
3. Other financial items

   A + B + C = Basic Balance

D. Net Errors and Omissions

Missing data such as illegal transfers

   A + B + C + D = Overall Balance

E. Reserves and Related Items

Changes in official monetary reserves including gold, foreign exchange, and IMF position

---

Fundamentals of Balance of Payments Accounting

The BOP must balance. If it does not, something has not been counted or has been counted improperly. Therefore, it is incorrect to state that the BOP is in disequilibrium. It cannot be. The supply and demand for a country's currency may be imbalanced, but supply and demand are not the same thing as the BOP. A subaccount of the BOP, such as the merchandise trade balance, may be imbalanced, but the entire BOP of a single country is always balanced.

There are three main elements of the actual process of measuring international economic activity: 1) identifying what is and is not an international economic transaction; 2) understanding how the flow of goods, services, assets, and money create debits and credits to the overall BOP; and 3) understanding the bookkeeping procedures for BOP accounting.

Defining International Economic Transactions

Identifying international transactions is ordinarily not difficult. The export of merchandise—goods such as trucks, machinery, computers, telecommunications equipment and so forth—is obviously an international transaction. Imports such as French wine, Japanese cameras, and German automobiles are also clearly international transactions. But this merchandise trade is only a portion of the thousands of different international transactions that occur in the United States or any other country each year.

Many other international transactions are not so obvious. The purchase of a glass figure in Venice, Italy, by a U.S. tourist is classified as a U.S. merchandise import. In fact, all expenditures made by U.S. tourists around the globe for services (e.g., restaurants and hotels), but not for goods, are recorded in the U.S. balance of payments as imports of travel services in the current account. The purchase of a U.S. Treasury bill by a foreign resident is an international financial transaction and is duly recorded in the financial account of the U.S. balance of payments.

The BOP as a Flow Statement

The BOP is often misunderstood because many people infer from its name that it is a balance sheet, whereas in fact it is a *cash flow statement*. By recording all international transactions over a period of time such as a year, the BOP tracks the continuing flows of purchases and payments between a country and all other countries. It does not add up the value of all assets and liabilities of a country on a specific date like a balance sheet does for an individual firm.

Two types of business transactions dominate the balance of payments:

1. **Exchange of Real Assets.** The exchange of goods (e.g., automobiles, computers, watches, and textiles) and services (e.g., banking, consulting, and travel services) for other goods and services (barter) or for money.

2. **Exchange of Financial Assets.** The exchange of financial claims (e.g., stocks, bonds, loans, and purchases or sales of companies) for other financial claims or money.

Although assets can be identified as real or financial, it is often easier simply to think of all assets as goods that can be bought and sold. The purchase of a hand-woven area rug in a shop in Bangkok by a U.S. tourist is not all that different from a Wall Street banker buying a British government bond for investment purposes.

BOP Accounting

The measurement of all international transactions in and out of a country over a year is a daunting task. Mistakes, errors, and statistical discrepancies will occur. The primary problem is that double-entry bookkeeping is employed in theory, but not in practice. Individual purchase and sale transactions should—in theory—result in financing entries in the balance of payments that match. In reality, the entries are recorded independently. Current, financial, and capital account entries are recorded independently of one another, not together as double-entry bookkeeping would prescribe. Thus, there will be serious discrepancies (to use a nice term for it) between debits and credits.

The Accounts of the Balance of Payments

The balance of payments is composed of three primary subaccounts: the current account, the financial account, and the capital account. In addition, the *official reserves account* tracks government currency transactions, and a fifth statistical subaccount, the *net errors and omissions account*, is produced to preserve the balance in the BOP. The international economic relationships between countries, however, continue to evolve, as the recent revision of the major accounts within the BOP discussed in the following sections indicates.

The Current Account

The *current account* includes all international economic transactions with income or payment flows occurring within the year, the *current* period. The current account consists of four subcategories:

1. **Goods Trade.** The export and import of goods. Merchandise trade is the oldest and most traditional form of international economic activity. Although many countries depend on imports of goods (as they should, according to the theory of comparative advantage), they also normally work to preserve either a balance of goods trade or even a surplus.

2. **Services Trade.** The export and import of services. Common international services are financial services provided by banks to foreign importers and exporters, travel services of airlines, and construction services of domestic firms in other countries. For the major industrial countries, this subaccount has shown the fastest growth in the past decade.

3. **Income.** Predominantly *current income* associated with investments that were made in previous periods. If a U.S. firm created a subsidiary in South Korea to produce metal parts in a previous year, the proportion of net income that is paid back to the parent company in the current year (the dividend) constitutes current investment income. Additionally, wages and salaries paid to nonresident workers are also included in this category.

4. **Current Transfers.** The financial settlements associated with the change in ownership of real resources or financial items. Any transfer between countries that is one-way—a gift or grant—is termed a *current transfer*. For example, funds provided by the U.S. government to aid in the development of a less-developed nation would be a current transfer. Transfers associated with the transfer of fixed assets are included in a separate account, the *capital account*.

All countries possess some amount of trade, most of which is merchandise. Many smaller and less-developed countries have little in the way of service trade, or items that fall under the income or transfers subaccounts.

The *current account* is typically dominated by the first component described, the export and import of merchandise. For this reason, the *balance of trade* (BOT) which is so widely quoted in the business press in most countries refers to the balance of exports and imports of goods trade only. If the country is a larger industrialized country, however, the BOT is somewhat misleading, in that service trade is not included.

Exhibit 4.2 summarizes the current account and its components for the United States for the 1998–2005 period. As illustrated, the U.S. goods trade balance has been consistently negative, but has been partially offset by the continuing surplus in services trade balance.

Goods Trade

Exhibit 4.3 places the current account values of Exhibit 4.2 in perspective over time by dividing the current account into its two major components: 1) *goods trade* and 2) *services trade and investment income*. The first and most striking message is the magnitude of the goods trade deficit in the period shown (a continuation of a position created in the early 1980s). The balance on services and income, although not large in comparison to net goods trade, has with few exceptions run a surplus over the past two decades.

The deficits in the BOT of the past decade have been an area of considerable concern for the United States, in both the public and private sectors. Merchandise trade is the original core of international trade. The manufacturing of goods was the basis of the industrial revolution and the focus of the theory of comparative advantage in international trade. Manufacturing is traditionally the sector of the economy that employs most of a country's workers. The goods trade deficit of the 1980s saw the decline of traditional heavy industries in the United States, industries that through history employed many U.S. workers. Declines in the BOT in areas such as steel, automobiles, automotive parts, textiles, and shoe manufacturing caused massive economic and social disruption.

Understanding merchandise import and export performance is much like understanding the market for any single product. The demand factors that drive both are income, the economic growth rate of the buyer, and price of the product in the eyes of the consumer after passing through an exchange rate. For example, U.S. merchandise imports reflect the income level of U.S. consumers and growth of industry. As income rises, so does the demand for imports.

| **EXHIBIT 4.2** | The United States Current Account, 1998–2007 (billions of U.S. dollars) |

	1998	1999	2000	2001	2002	2003	2004	2005	2006	2007
Goods exports	672	686	775	722	686	717	811	898	1027	1153
Goods imports	−917	−1030	−1227	−1148	−1167	−1264	−1477	−1682	−1861	−1968
Goods trade balance (BOT)	−245	−344	−452	−426	−481	−548	−666	−783	−835	−815
Services trade credits	261	280	296	283	289	301	350	385	430	493
Services trade debits	−181	−199	−224	−222	−231	−250	−291	−314	−349	−378
Services trade balance	80	80	72	61	58	51	58	72	81	115
Income receipts	262	294	351	291	281	320	414	535	685	818
Income payments	−258	−280	−330	−259	−254	−275	−347	−463	−628	−736
Income balance	4	14	21	32	27	45	67	72	57	82
Current transfers, credits	10	9	11	9	12	15	20	19	25	22
Current transfers, debits	−63	−59	−69	−60	−77	−87	−105	−109	−117	−135
Net transfers	−53	−50	−59	−51	−65	−72	−84	−90	−92	−113
Current Account Balance	**−213**	**−300**	**−417**	**−385**	**−461**	**−523**	**−625**	**−729**	**−788**	**−731**

Totals may not add due to rounding.

Source : Derived from International Monetary Fund, *Balance of Payments Statistics Yearbook 2008*, p. 1054.

EXHIBIT 4.3   U.S. Trade Balances on Goods & Services, 1985–2007
(billions of U.S. dollars)

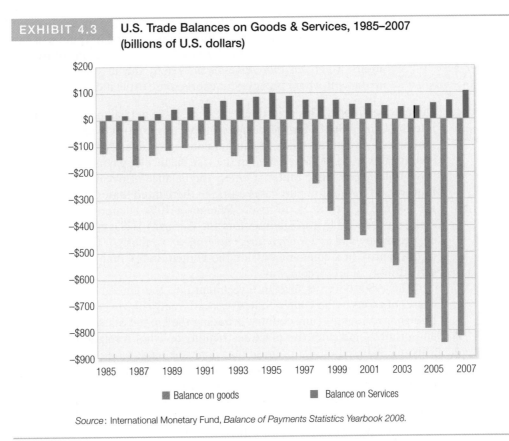

Source: International Monetary Fund, Balance of Payments Statistics Yearbook 2008.

Exports follow the same principles, but in the reversed position. U.S. manufacturing exports depend not on the incomes of U.S. residents, but on the incomes of buyers of U.S. products in all other countries around the world. When these economies are growing, the demand for U.S. products will also rise.

The service component of the U.S. current account is a mystery to many. As illustrated in Exhibit 4.2 and Exhibit 4.3, the United States has consistently achieved a surplus in services trade income. The major categories of services include travel and passenger fares; transportation services; expenditures by U.S. students abroad and foreign students pursuing studies in the United States; telecommunications services; and financial services.

The Capital and Financial Accounts

The capital and financial accounts of the balance of payments measure all international economic transactions of financial assets.

- **The Capital Account.** The capital account is made up of transfers of financial assets and the acquisition and disposal of nonproduced/nonfinancial assets. This account has been introduced as a separate component in the IMF's balance of payments only recently. The magnitude of capital transactions covered is relatively minor, and we will include it in principle in all of the following discussion of the financial account.

- **The Financial Account.** The financial account consists of three components: *direct investment*, *portfolio investment*, and *other asset investment*. Financial assets can be classified in a number of different ways, including by the length of the life of the asset (its maturity) and the nature of the ownership (public or private). The financial account, however, uses a third method, the degree of control over assets or operations, as in *portfolio investment*, where the investor has no control, or *direct investment*, where the investor exerts some explicit degree of control over the assets.

Direct Investment. This investment measure is the net balance of capital dispersed from and into the United States for the purpose of exerting control over assets. If a U.S. firm builds a new automotive parts facility in another country or actually purchases a company in another country, this is a *direct investment* in the U.S. balance of payments accounts. When the capital flows out of the United States, it enters the balance of payments as a negative cash flow. If, however, a foreign firm purchases a firm in the United States, it is a capital inflow and enters the balance of payments positively. Whenever 10% or more of the voting shares in a U.S. company are held by foreign investors, the company is classified as the U.S. affiliate of a foreign company, and as a *foreign direct investment*. Similarly, if U.S. investors hold 10% or more of the control in a company outside the United States, that company is considered the foreign affiliate of a U.S. company.

The 1980s boom in foreign investment into the United States, or foreign resident purchases of assets in the United States, was extremely controversial. The source of concern over foreign investment in any country, including the United States, focuses on two topics: control and profit. Some countries place restrictions on what foreigners may own in their country. This rule is based on the premise that domestic land, assets, and industry in general should be owned by residents of the country. On the other hand, the United States has traditionally had few restrictions on what foreign residents or firms can own or control; most restrictions remaining today relate to national security concerns. Unlike the case in the traditional debates over whether international trade should be free, there is no consensus that international investment should necessarily be free. This question is still very much a domestic political concern first, and an international economic issue second.

The second major source of concern over foreign direct investment is who receives the profits from the enterprise. Foreign companies owning firms in the United States will ultimately profit from the activities of the firms, or put another way, from the efforts of U.S. workers. In spite of evidence that indicates foreign firms in the United States reinvest most of their profits in their U.S. businesses (in fact, at a higher rate than domestic firms), the debate on possible profit drains has continued. Regardless of the actual choices made, workers of any nation feel that the profits of their work should remain in their own hands. Once again, this is in many ways a political and emotional concern more than an economic one.

The choice of words used to describe foreign investment can also influence public opinion. If these massive capital inflows are described as "capital investments from all over the world showing their faith in the future of U.S. industry," the net capital surplus is represented as decidedly positive. If, however, the net capital surplus is described as resulting in "the United States being the world's largest debtor nation," the negative connotation is obvious. Both are essentially spins on the economic principles at work.

Capital, whether short-term or long-term, flows to where the investor believes it can earn the greatest return for the level of risk. And although in an accounting sense this is "international debt," when the majority of the capital inflow is in the form of direct investment, a long-term commitment to jobs, production, services, technological, and other competitive investments, the impact on the competitiveness of industry located within the United States is increased. When the "net debtor" label is applied to equity investment, it is misleading, in that it invites comparison with large debt crisis conditions suffered by many countries in the past.

Portfolio Investment. This is net balance of capital that flows in and out of the United States but does not reach the 10% ownership threshold of direct investment. If a U.S. resident purchases shares in a Japanese firm but does not attain the 10% threshold, we define the purchase as a *portfolio investment* (and in this case an outflow of capital). The purchase or sale of debt securities (like U.S. Treasury bills) across borders is also classified as portfolio investment, because debt securities by definition do not provide the buyer with ownership or control.

Portfolio investment is capital invested in activities that are purely profit-motivated (return), rather than ones made to control or manage the investment. Purchases of debt securities, bonds, interest-bearing bank accounts, and the like are intended only to earn a return. They provide no vote or control over the party issuing the debt. Purchases of debt issued by the U.S. government (U.S. Treasury bills, notes, and bonds) by foreign investors constitutes *net portfolio investment* in the United States. It is worth noting that most U.S. debt purchased by foreigners is U.S. dollar-denominated—denominated in the currency of the issuing country. Most foreign debt issued by countries such as Russia, Mexico, Brazil, and Southeast Asian countries is also U.S. dollar-denominated—in this case, the currency of a foreign country. The foreign country must earn dollars to repay its foreign-held debt. The United States need not earn any foreign currency to repay its foreign debt.

As illustrated in Exhibit 4.4, portfolio investment has shown much more volatile behavior than net foreign direct investment has over the past decade. Many U.S. debt securities

EXHIBIT 4.4	The United States Financial Account and Components, 1998-2007 (billions of U.S. dollars)									
	1998	**1999**	**2000**	**2001**	**2002**	**2003**	**2004**	**2005**	**2006**	**2007**
Direct Investment										
Direct investment abroad	−143	−225	−159	−142	−154	−150	−316	−36	−241	−333
Direct investment in the U.S.	179	289	321	167	84	64	146	113	242	238
Net direct investment	36	65	162	25	−70	−86	−170	76	1	−96
Portfolio Investment										
Assets, net	−130	−122	−128	−91	−49	−123	−177	−258	−499	−295
Liabilities, net	188	286	437	428	428	550	867	832	1127	1145
Net portfolio investment	57	163	309	338	379	427	690	575	628	851
Financial Derivatives										
Derivatives assets									0	0
Derivatives liabilities									30	7
									30	7
Other Investment										
Other investment assets	−74	−166	−273	−145	−88	−54	−510	−267	−514	−662
Other investment liabilities	57	165	280	187	283	244	520	303	692	675
Net other investment	−17	0	7	43	195	190	10	36	178	13
Net Financial Account Balance	**77**	**227**	**478**	**405**	**504**	**532**	**530**	**687**	**837**	**774**

Totals may not add due to rounding.

Source: Derived from International Monetary Fund, *Balance of Payments Statistics Yearbook 2008*, p. 1054. Note that "Financial Derivatives" were added in 2006.

such as U.S. Treasury securities and corporate bonds were in high demand in the late 1980s, while surging emerging markets in both debt and equities caused a reversal in direction in the 1990s. The motivating forces for portfolio investment flows are always the same—return and risk. This fact, however, does not make the flows any more predictable.

Other Investment Assets/Liabilities. This final category consists of various short-term and long-term trade credits, cross-border loans from all types of financial institutions, currency deposits and bank deposits, and other accounts receivable and payable related to cross-border trade.

Exhibit 4.5 shows the major subcategories of the U.S. financial account balance from 1985 to 2007: direct investment, portfolio investment, and other long-term and short-term capital investment.

Current and Financial Account Balance Relationships

Exhibit 4.6 illustrates the current and financial account balances for the United States over recent years. What the exhibit shows is one of the basic economic and accounting relationships of the balance of payments: *the inverse relation between the current and financial accounts*. This inverse relationship is not accidental. The methodology of the balance of payments, double-entry bookkeeping in theory, requires that the current and financial accounts be offsetting, unless the country's exchange rate is being highly manipulated or controlled by governmental authorities. Countries experiencing large current account deficits "finance" these purchases through equally large surpluses in the financial account, and vice versa.

Net Errors and Omissions. As previously noted, because current and financial account entries are collected and recorded separately, errors or statistical discrepancies will occur. The *net errors and omissions account* ensures that the BOP actually balances.

| EXHIBIT 4.5 | The United States Financial Account, 1985–2007 (billions of U.S. dollars) |

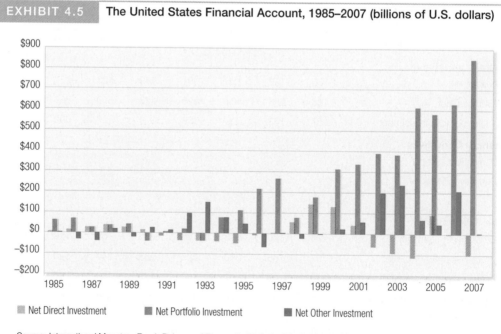

Source: International Monetary Fund, *Balance of Payments Statistics Yearbook, 2008.*

EXHIBIT 4.6	Current and Combined Financial/Capital Account Balances for the United States, 1992–2007 (billions of U.S. dollars)

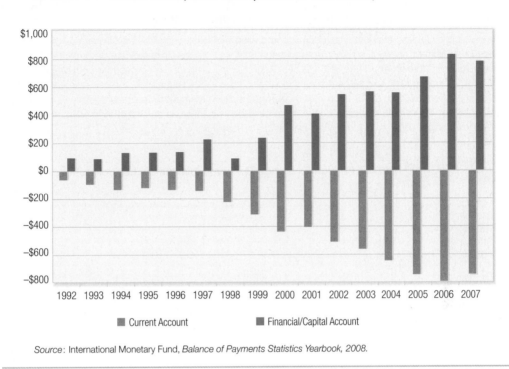

Source: International Monetary Fund, *Balance of Payments Statistics Yearbook, 2008.*

Official Reserves Account. The Official Reserves Account is the total reserves held by official monetary authorities within the country. These reserves are normally composed of the major currencies used in international trade and financial transactions (so-called "hard currencies" like the U.S. dollar, European euro, and the Japanese yen; gold; and special drawing rights, SDRs).

The significance of official reserves depends generally on whether the country is operating under a *fixed exchange rate* regime or a *floating exchange rate* system. If a country's currency is fixed, the government of the country officially declares that the currency is convertible into a fixed amount of some other currency. For example, the Chinese yuan was fixed to the U.S. dollar for many years. It was the Chinese government's responsibility to maintain this fixed rate, also called *parity rate*. If for some reason there was an excess supply of Chinese yuan on the currency market, to prevent the value of the yuan from falling, the Chinese government would have to support the yuan's value by purchasing yuan on the open market (by spending its hard currency reserves, its official reserves) until the excess supply was eliminated. Under a floating rate system, the Chinese government possesses no such responsibility and the role of official reserves is diminished. But as discussed in *Global Finance in Practice 4.1*, the Chinese government's foreign exchange reserves are now the largest in the world, and if need be, it probably possesses sufficient reserves to manage the yuan's value for years to come.

GLOBAL FINANCE IN PRACTICE 4.1

Official Foreign Exchange Reserves: The Rise of China

The rise of the Chinese economy has been accompanied by a rise in its current account surplus, and subsequently, its accumulation of foreign exchange reserves. As illustrated in Exhibit A, China's foreign exchange reserves increased by a factor of 10 from 2001 to 2008—from $200 billion to nearly $2,000 billion. There is no real precedent for this build-up in foreign exchange reserves in global financial history. These reserves allow the Chinese government to manage the value of the Chinese *yuan* (also referred to as the *renminbi*) and its impact on Chinese competitiveness in the world economy. The magnitude of these reserves will allow the Chinese government to maintain a relatively stable managed fixed rate of the yuan against other major currencies like the U.S. dollar as long as it chooses.

EXHIBIT A	China's Foreign Exchange Reserves (billions of U.S. dollars)

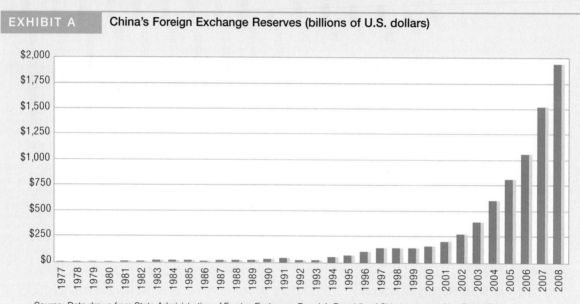

Source: Data drawn from State Administration of Foreign Exchange, People's Republic of China, as quoted by Chinability, www.chinability.com/Reserve.htm.

The Balance of Payments in Total

Exhibit 4.7 provides the official balance of payments for the United States as presented by the IMF, which collects these statistics for over 160 different countries around the globe. Now that the individual accounts and the relationships among the accounts have been discussed, Exhibit 4.7 allows us a comprehensive overview of how the individual accounts are combined to create some of the most useful summary measures for multinational business managers.

The current account (line A in Exhibit 4.7), the capital account (line B), and the financial account (line C) combine to form the *basic balance* (*Total, Groups A through C*). This balance is one of the most frequently used summary measures of the BOP. It describes the international economic activity of the nation, which is determined by market forces, not by government decisions (such as currency market intervention). The U.S. *basic balance* totaled a surplus of $41 billion in 2007. A second frequently used measure, the *overall balance*, also called the *official settlements balance* (*Total, Groups A through D* in Exhibit 4.7), was at a small surplus of $0.13 billion in 2007.

The sheer size and magnitude of China's official reserves (excluding gold) is illustrated by Exhibit B, which shows the 20 largest countries in terms of their reserve holdings in 2008. China's reserves are more than double those of the second largest country reserves, those of Japan. Note that only five countries even have reserves that exceed $200 billion. The United States, with roughly $65 billion in reserves, pales in comparison to the growing caches of the booming Asian economies.

There have been a variety of suggestions made as to what China could do with its growing reserves. Most of the proposals—stockpiling oil or other commodities for example— would only result in pushing up the price of these other critical global commodities, while not really stopping the accumulation of official reserves. The only real solution to this "problem," if it is a problem, is to reduce the Chinese current account surplus or allow the yuan to float to a stronger value. Both solutions, however, are not in-line with China's current political plan.

EXHIBIT B   **Rising Reserves in Asia (billions of U.S. dollars)**

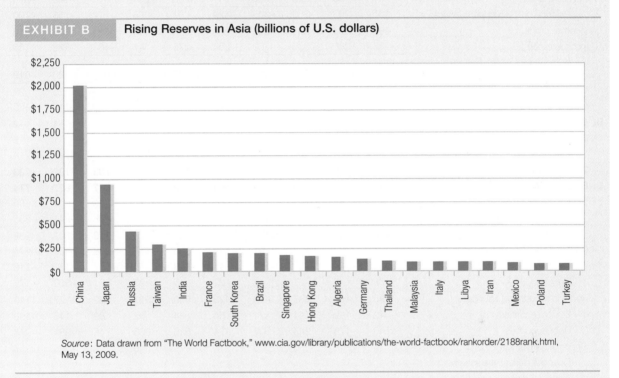

Source: Data drawn from "The World Factbook," www.cia.gov/library/publications/the-world-factbook/rankorder/2188rank.html, May 13, 2009.

The meaning of the BOP has changed over the past 30 years. As long as most of the major industrial countries were still operating under fixed exchange rates, the interpretation of the BOP was relatively straightforward:

- A surplus in the BOP implied that the demand for the country's currency exceeded the supply and that the government should allow the currency value to increase— in value—or intervene and accumulate additional foreign currency reserves in the official reserves account. This intervention would occur as the government sold its own currency in exchange for other currencies, thus building up its stores of hard currencies.

- A deficit in the BOP implied an excess supply of the country's currency on world markets, and the government would then either *devalue* the currency or expend its official reserves to support its value.

The transition to floating exchange rate regimes in the 1970s (described in Chapter 3) changed the focus from the total BOP to its various subaccounts like the current and financial

EXHIBIT 4.7   The United States Balance of Payments, Analytic Presentation, 1998–2007 (billions of U.S. dollars)

	1998	1999	2000	2001	2002	2003	2004	2005	2006	2007
A. Current Account	−213	−300	−417	−385	−461	−523	−625	−729	−788	−731
Goods: exports fob	672	686	775	722	686	717	811	898	1027	1153
Goods: imports fob	−917	−1030	−1227	−1148	−1167	−1264	−1477	−1682	−1861	−1968
Balance on Goods	−245	−344	−452	−426	−481	−548	−666	−783	−835	−815
Services: credit	261	280	296	283	289	301	350	385	430	493
Services: debit	−181	−199	−224	−222	−231	−250	−291	−314	−349	−378
Balance on Goods and Services	−165	−263	−380	−365	−424	−497	−608	−712	−753	−700
Income: credit	262	294	351	291	281	320	414	535	685	818
Income: debit	−258	−280	−330	−259	−254	−275	−347	−463	−628	−736
Balance on Goods, Services, and Income	−160	−249	−359	−333	−396	−452	−541	−639	−696	−619
Current transfers: credit	10	9	11	9	12	15	20	19	25	22
Current transfers: debit	−63	−59	−69	−60	−77	−87	−105	−109	−117	−135
B. Capital Account	−1	−5	−1	−1	−1	−3	−2	−4	−4	−2
Capital account: credit	1	1	1	1	1	1	1	1	1	2
Capital account: debit	−2	−6	−2	−2	−2	−4	−3	−5	−5	−4
Total, Groups A Plus B	−214	−305	−418	−386	−463	−527	−627	−733	−792	−733
C. Financial Account	77	227	478	405	504	532	530	687	837	774
Direct investment	36	65	162	25	−70	−86	−170	76	1	−96
Direct investment abroad	−143	−225	−159	−142	−154	−150	−316	−36	−241	−333
Direct investment in United States	179	289	321	167	84	64	146	113	242	238
Portfolio investment assets	−130	−122	−128	−91	−49	−123	−177	−258	−499	−295
Equity securities	−101	−114	−107	−109	−17	−118	−85	−187	−137	−118
Debt securities	−29	−8	−21	18	−32	−5	−93	−71	−362	−177
Portfolio investment liabilities	188	286	437	428	428	550	867	832	1127	1145
Equity securities	42	112	194	121	54	34	62	89	146	198
Debt securities	146	173	243	307	374	516	806	743	981	948
Financial derivatives	0	0	0	0	0	0	0	0	30	7
Financial derivatives assets										
Financial derivatives liabilities										30	7
Other investment assets	−74	−166	−273	−145	−88	−54	−510	−267	−514	−662
Monetary authorities	0	0	0	0	0	0	0	0	0	0
General government	0	3	−1	0	0	1	2	6	5	−22
Banks	−36	−71	−133	−136	−38	−26	−359	−151	−329	−516
Other sectors	−38	−98	−139	−9	−50	−29	−153	−121	−190	−124
Other investment liabilities	57	165	280	187	283	244	520	303	692	675
Monetary authorities	7	25	−11	35	70	11	13	8	2	−11
General government	−3	−1	−2	−2	0	−1	0	0	3	5
Banks	30	67	123	88	118	136	347	232	343	477
Other sectors	23	74	171	66	96	98	160	62	344	204
Total, Groups A Through C	−138	−77	60	19	41	5	-98	-46	45	41
D. Net Errors and Omissions	144	69	−59	−14	−38	−6	95	32	−47	−41
Total, Groups A Through D	7	−9	0.31	4.88	3.71	−1.33	−2.80	−14.10	−2.40	0.13
E. Reserves and Related Items	−7	9	0	−5	−4	2	3	14	2	0

Source: International Monetary Fund, *Balance of Payments Statistics Yearbook 2008*, p.1054.
Note: Totals may not match original source due to rounding.

account balances. These subaccounts are the indicators of economic activities and currency repercussions to come.

The Balance of Payments Interaction with Key Macroeconomic Variables

A nation's balance of payments interacts with nearly all of its key macroeconomic variables. *Interacts* means that the balance of payments affects and is affected by such key macroeconomic factors as the following:

- Gross domestic product (GDP)
- Exchange rate
- Interest rates
- Inflation rates

The BOP and GDP

In a static (accounting) sense, a nation's GDP can be represented by the following equation:

$$GDP = C + I + G + X - M$$

C = consumption spending
I = capital investment spending
G = government spending
X = exports of goods and services
M = imports of goods and services
$X - M$ = the balance on current account (when including current income and transfers)

Thus, a positive current account balance (surplus) contributes directly to increasing the measure of GDP, but a negative current account balance (deficit) decreases GDP.

In a dynamic (cash flow) sense, an increase or decrease in GDP contributes to the current account deficit or surplus. As GDP grows, so does disposable income and capital investment. Increased disposable income leads to more consumption, a portion of which is supplied by more imports. Increased consumption eventually leads to more capital investment.

Growth in GDP also should eventually lead to higher rates of employment. However, some of that theoretical increase in employment may be blunted by foreign sourcing (that is, the purchase of goods and services from other enterprises located in other countries).

Supply chain management has increasingly focused on cost reduction through imports from less costly (lower wages) foreign locations. These imports can be from foreign-owned firms or from foreign subsidiaries of the parent firm. In the latter case, foreign subsidiaries tend to buy components and intellectual property from their parent firms, thus increasing exports. Although outsourcing has always been a factor in determining where to locate or procure manufactured goods and commodities, as mentioned in Chapter 1, during the past decade, an increasing amount of high-tech goods and services have been sourced from abroad. Foreign sourcing from the United States and Western Europe has been to countries such as India (software and call centers), China, Eastern Europe, Mexico, and the Philippines. This pattern has caused a loss of some white collar jobs in the United States and Western Europe and a corresponding increase elsewhere.

The BOP and Exchange Rates

A country's BOP can have a significant impact on the level of its exchange rate and vice versa, depending on that country's exchange rate regime. The relationship between the BOP and exchange rates can be illustrated by use of a simplified equation that summarizes BOP data:

Current account balance		Capital account balance		Financial account balance		Reserve balance		Balance of payments
$(X - M)$	+	$(CI - CO)$	+	$(FI - FO)$	+	FXB	=	BOP

$$
\begin{aligned}
X &= \text{exports of goods and services} \\
M &= \text{imports of goods and services} \\
CI &= \text{capital inflows} \\
CO &= \text{capital outflows} \\
FI &= \text{financial inflows} \\
FO &= \text{financial outflows} \\
FXB &= \text{official monetary reserves such as foreign exchange and gold}
\end{aligned}
$$

The effect of an imbalance in the BOP of a country works somewhat differently depending on whether that country has fixed exchange rates, floating exchange rates, or a managed exchange rate system.

Fixed Exchange Rate Countries. Under a fixed exchange rate system, the government bears the responsibility to ensure that the BOP is near zero. If the sum of the current and capital accounts do not approximate zero, the government is expected to intervene in the foreign exchange market by buying or selling official foreign exchange reserves. If the sum of the first two accounts is greater than zero, a surplus demand for the domestic currency exists in the world. To preserve the fixed exchange rate, the government must then intervene in the foreign exchange market and sell domestic currency for foreign currencies or gold so as to bring the BOP back near zero.

If the sum of the current and capital accounts is negative, an excess supply of the domestic currency exists in world markets. Then the government must intervene by buying the domestic currency with its reserves of foreign currencies and gold. It is obviously important for a government to maintain significant foreign exchange reserve balances, sufficient to allow it to intervene effectively. If the country runs out of foreign exchange reserves, it will be unable to buy back its domestic currency and will be forced to devalue.

Floating Exchange Rate Countries. Under a floating exchange rate system, the government of a country has no responsibility to peg its foreign exchange rate. The fact that the current and capital account balances do not sum to zero will automatically (in theory) alter the exchange rate in the direction necessary to obtain a BOP near zero. For example, a country running a sizable current account deficit, with a capital and financial accounts balance of zero will have a net BOP deficit. An excess supply of the domestic currency will appear on world markets. Like all goods in excess supply, the market will rid itself of the imbalance by lowering the price. Thus, the domestic currency will fall in value, and the BOP will move back toward zero. Exchange rate markets do not always follow this theory, particularly in the short to intermediate term. This delay is known as the *J-curve effect* (see also the later section "Trade Balances and Exchange Rates"). The deficit gets worse in the short run, but moves back toward equilibrium in the long term.

Managed Floats. Although still relying on market conditions for day-to-day exchange rate determination, countries operating with managed floats often find it necessary to take action to maintain their desired exchange rate values. Therefore, they seek to alter the market's valuation of a specific exchange rate by influencing the motivations of market activity, rather than through direct intervention in the foreign exchange markets.

The primary action taken by such governments is to change relative interest rates, thus influencing the economic fundamentals of exchange rate determination. In the context of the equation discussed, a change in domestic interest rates is an attempt to alter the term ($CI - CO$), especially the short-term portfolio component of these capital flows, in order to restore an imbalance caused by the deficit in the current account. The power of interest rate changes on international capital and exchange rate movements can be substantial. A country with a managed float that wishes to defend its currency may choose to raise domestic interest rates to attract additional capital from abroad. This step will alter market forces and create additional market demand for the domestic currency. In this process, the government signals to exchange market participants that it intends to take measures to preserve the currency's value within certain ranges. The process also raises the cost of local borrowing for businesses, however, so the policy is seldom without domestic critics.

The BOP and Interest Rates

Apart from the use of interest rates to intervene in the foreign exchange market, the overall level of a country's interest rates compared to other countries does have an impact on the financial account of the balance of payments. Relatively low real interest rates should normally stimulate an outflow of capital seeking higher interest rates in other country currencies. However, in the case of the United States, the opposite effect has occurred. Despite relatively low real interest rates and large BOP deficits on current account, the U.S. BOP financial account has experienced offsetting financial inflows due to relatively attractive U.S. growth rate prospects, high levels of productive innovation, and perceived political safety. Thus, the financial account inflows have helped the United States to maintain its lower interest rates and to finance its exceptionally large fiscal deficit.

However, it is beginning to appear that the favorable inflow on the financial account is diminishing while the U.S. balance on current account is worsening. *Global Finance in Practice 4.2* shows that the United States is becoming a bigger debtor nation vis-à-vis the rest of the world.

The BOP and Inflation Rates

Imports have the potential to lower a country's inflation rate. In particular, imports of lower-priced goods and services places a limit on what domestic competitors charge for comparable goods and services. Thus, foreign competition substitutes for domestic competition to maintain a lower rate of inflation than might have been the case without imports.

On the other hand, to the extent that lower-priced imports substitute for domestic production and employment, gross domestic product will be lower and the balance on current account will be more negative.

Trade Balances and Exchange Rates

A country's import and export of goods and services is affected by changes in exchange rates. The transmission mechanism is in principle quite simple: changes in exchange rates change relative prices of imports and exports, and changing prices in turn result in changes in quantities demanded through the price elasticity of demand. Although the theoretical economics appear straightforward, the reality of global business is a bit more complex.

The United States as the World's Largest Debtor Nation

The United States has become the world's largest debtor nation, rather than the world's largest creditor, the position it held in earlier years. Net foreign purchases of U.S. securities have retreated from their peak in 2001, while the U.S. balance on current accounts has worsened, as shown in the chart on the left. The chart on the right shows that the U.S.

net international investment position at market value, as a percentage of GDP is also sinking—to a negative 25%.

Losing Their Lustre

$bn

Net Foreign Purchases of U.S. Securities*

U.S. Current account balance*

91 92 93 94 95 96 97 98 99 00 01 02 03

*12-Month Moving Total

Source: Deutsche Bank; U.S. Bureau of Economic Analysis

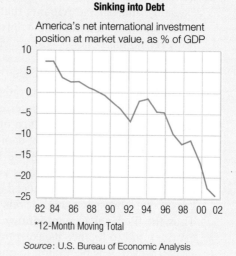

Sinking into Debt

America's net international investment position at market value, as % of GDP

82 84 86 88 90 92 94 96 98 00 02

*12-Month Moving Total

Source: U.S. Bureau of Economic Analysis

Trade and Devaluation

Countries occasionally devalue their own currencies as a result of persistent and sizable trade deficits. Many countries in the not-too-distant past have intentionally devalued their currencies in an effort to make their exports more price-competitive on world markets. The devaluation of the New Taiwan dollar in 1997 during the Asian financial crisis is believed by many to have been one such competitive devaluation. These competitive devaluations are often considered self-destructive, however, as they also make imports relatively more expensive. So what is the logic and likely results of intentionally devaluing the domestic currency to improve the trade balance?

The J-Curve Adjustment Path

International economic analysis characterizes the trade balance adjustment process as occurring in three stages: 1) the *currency contract period*; 2) the *pass-through period*; and 3) the *quantity adjustment period*. These three stages, and the resulting time-adjustment path of the trade balance in whole, is illustrated in Exhibit 4.8. Assuming that the trade balance is already in deficit prior to the devaluation, a devaluation at time t_1 results initially in a further deterioration in the trade balance before an eventual improvement—the path of adjustment taking on the shape of a flattened "j".

In the first period, the *currency contract period*, a sudden unexpected devaluation of the domestic currency has a somewhat uncertain impact, simply because all of the contracts for

EXHIBIT 4.8   Trade Balance Adjustment to Exchange Rate Changes: The J-Curve

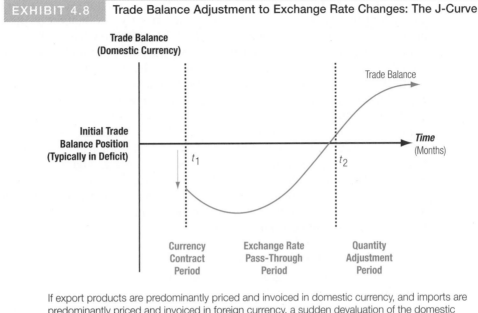

If export products are predominantly priced and invoiced in domestic currency, and imports are predominantly priced and invoiced in foreign currency, a sudden devaluation of the domestic currency can possibly result—initially—in a deterioration of the balance on trade. After exchange rate changes are passed-through to product prices, and markets have time to respond to price changes by altering market demands, the trade balance will improve. The currency contract period may last from three to six months, with pass-through and quality adjustment following for an additional three to six months.

exports and imports are already in effect. Firms operating under these agreements are required to fulfill their obligations, regardless of whether they profit or suffer losses. Assume that the United States experienced a sudden fall in the value of the U.S. dollar. Most exports were priced in U.S. dollars but most imports were contracts denominated in foreign currency. The result of a sudden depreciation would be an increase in the size of the trade deficit at time t_1, because the cost to U.S. importers of paying their import bills would rise as they spent more and more dollars to buy the foreign currency they needed, while the revenues earned by U.S. exporters would remain unchanged. Although this is the commonly cited scenario regarding trade balance adjustment, there is little reason to believe that most U.S. imports are denominated in foreign currency and most exports in U.S. dollars.

The second period of the trade balance adjustment process is termed the *pass-through period*. As exchange rates change, importers and exporters eventually must pass these exchange rate changes through to their own product prices. For example, a foreign producer selling to the U.S. market after a major fall in the value of the U.S. dollar will have to cover its own domestic costs of production. This need will require that the firm charge higher dollar prices in order to earn its own local currency in large enough quantities. The firm must raise its prices in the U.S. market. U.S. import prices rise substantially, eventually passing through the full exchange rate changes into prices. American consumers see higher import-product prices on the shelf. Similarly, the U.S. export prices are now cheaper compared to foreign competitors' because the dollar is cheaper. Unfortunately for U.S. exporters, many of the inputs for their final products may actually be imported, causing them also to suffer from rising prices after the fall of the dollar.

The third and final period, the *quantity adjustment period*, achieves the balance of trade adjustment that is expected from a domestic currency devaluation or depreciation. As the import and export prices change as a result of the pass-through period, consumers both in the United States and in the U.S. export markets adjust their demands to the new prices. Imports are relatively more expensive; therefore the quantity demanded decreases. Exports are relatively cheaper; and therefore the quantity demanded increases. The balance of trade—the expenditures on exports less the expenditures on imports—improves.

Unfortunately, these three adjustment periods do not occur overnight. Countries, like the United States, that have experienced major exchange rate changes also have seen this adjustment take place over a prolonged period. Empirical studies have concluded that for industrial countries, the total time elapsing between time t_1 and t_2 can vary from 3 to 12 months—sometimes longer. To complicate the process, new exchange rate changes often occur before the adjustment is completed. Trade adjustment to exchange rate changes does not occur in a sterile laboratory environment, but in the messy and complex world of international business and economic events.

Trade Balance Adjustment Path: The Equations

A country's trade balance is essentially the net of import and export revenues, where each is a multiple of prices ($P_X^\$$ and P_M^{fc})—the prices of exports and imports, respectively. Export prices are assumed to be denominated in U.S. dollars, and import prices are denominated in foreign currency. The quantity of exports and the quantity of imports are denoted as Q_x and Q_M respectively. Import expenditures are then expressed in U.S. dollars by multiplying the foreign currency denominated expenditures by the spot exchange rate, $S^{\$/fc}$. The U.S. trade balance, expressed in U.S. dollars, is then expressed as follows:

$$\text{U.S. trade balance} = (P_X^\$ Q_x) - (S^{\$/fc}\, P_M^{fc}\, Q_M)$$

The immediate impact of a devaluation of the domestic currency is to increase the value of the spot exchange rate S, resulting in an immediate deterioration in the trade balance (currency contract period). Only after a period in which the current contracts have matured, and new prices reflecting partial to full pass-through have been instituted, would improvement in the trade balance been evident (pass-through period). In the final stage, in which the price elasticity of demand has time to take effect (quantity adjustment period), is the actual trade balance—in theory—which is expected to rise above where it started in Exhibit 4.8.

Capital Mobility

The degree to which capital moves freely across borders is critically important to a country's balance of payments. We have already seen how the United States, while experiencing a deficit in its current account balance over the past 20 years, has simultaneously enjoyed a financial account surplus. This financial account surplus has probably been one of the major reasons that the U.S. dollar has been able to maintain its value until recently. Other countries, however—for example, Brazil in 1998–1999 and Argentina in 2001–2002—have experienced massive financial account outflows, which were major components of their economic and financial crises.

Historical Patterns of Capital Mobility

Before finishing our discussion of the balance of payments, we need to gain additional insights into the history of capital mobility and the contribution of capital outflows—*capital flight*—to balance of payments crises. Has capital always been free to move in and out of a country? Definitely not. The ability of foreign investors to own property, buy businesses, or purchase stocks and bonds in other countries has been controversial. Obstfeld and Taylor (2001) studied the globalization of capital markets and concluded that the pattern illustrated in Exhibit 4.9 is a fair representation of the conventional wisdom on the openness of global capital markets in recent history. Since 1860 the gold standard in use prior to the World War I and the post-1971 period of floating exchange rates has seen the greatest ability of capital to flow cross-border. Note that Obstfeld and Taylor use no specific quantitative measure of mobility. The diagram uses only a stylized distinction between "low" and "high," combining two primary factors: the exchange rate regimes and the state of international political and economic relations.

The authors argue that the post-1860 era can be subdivided into four distinct periods:

1. The first, 1860–1914, was a period characterized by continuously increasing capital openness, as more and more countries adopted the gold standard and expanded international trade relations.

2. The second, 1914–1945, was a period of global economic destruction. The combined destructive forces of two world wars and a worldwide depression led most nations to move toward highly nationalistic and isolationist political and economic policies, effectively eliminating any significant movement of capital between countries.

3. The third, 1945–1971, the Bretton Woods era, saw a great expansion of international trade in goods and services. This time also saw the slow but steady recovery of cap-

---

EXHIBIT 4.9   A Stylized View of Capital Mobility in Modern History

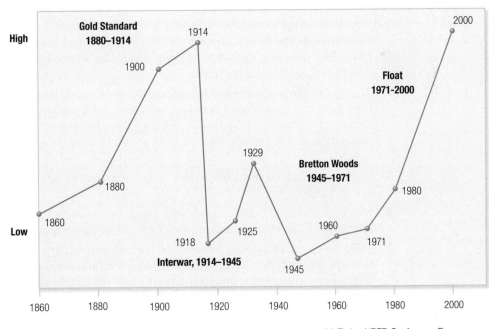

Source: "Globalization and Capital Markets," Maurice Obstfeld and Alan M. Taylor, NBER Conference Paper, May 4-5, 2001, p. 6.

ital markets. The fixed exchange rate regime of Bretton Woods may have failed because the sheer forces of global capital could no longer be held in check.

4. The fourth, 1971–2000 [2007], was a period characterized by floating exchange rates and economic volatility, but rapidly expanding cross-border capital flows. The major industrial countries either no longer tried to, needed to, or could control the movement of capital. Because currency markets are free to reflect underlying economic fundamentals and investor sentiments about the future, capital movements increased in response to this openness.

The currency crises of the latter half of the 1990s and the early twenty-first century may result in the reversal of this freedom of cross-border capital movement; it is still too early to tell. It is clear, however, that the ability of capital to move instantaneously and massively across borders has been one of the major factors in the severity of recent currency crises.

Capital Flight

A final issue is *capital flight*. Although no single accepted definition of capital flight exists, Ingo Walter's discussion has been one of the more useful:

> *International flows of direct and portfolio investments under ordinary circumstances are rarely associated with the capital flight phenomenon. Rather, it is when capital transfers by residents conflict with political objectives that the term "flight" comes into general usage.*[1]

Although it is not limited to heavily indebted countries, the rapid and sometimes illegal transfer of convertible currencies out of a country poses significant economic and political problems. Many heavily indebted countries have suffered significant capital flight, which has compounded their problems of debt service.

Five primary mechanisms exist by which capital may be moved from one country to another:

1. Transfers via the usual international payments mechanisms (regular bank transfers) are obviously the easiest and lowest cost, and are legal. Most economically healthy countries allow free exchange of their currencies, but of course for such countries "capital flight" is not a problem.

2. Transfer of physical currency by bearer (the proverbial smuggling out of cash in the false bottom of a suitcase) is more costly and, for transfers out of many countries, illegal. Such transfers may be deemed illegal for balance of payments reasons or to make difficult the movement of money from the drug trade or other illegal activities.

3. Cash is transferred into collectibles or precious metals, which are then transferred across borders.

4. Money laundering is the cross-border purchase of assets that are then managed in a way that hides the movement of money and its ownership.

5. False invoicing of international trade transactions occurs when capital is moved through the underinvoicing of exports or the overinvoicing of imports, where the difference between the invoiced amount and the actual agreed upon payment is deposited in banking institutions in a country of choice.

---

[1]Ingo Walter, "The Mechanisms of Capital Flight," in *Capital Flight and Third World Debt*, edited by Donald R. Lessard and John Williamson, Institute for International Economics, Washington, D.C., 1987, p. 104.

SUMMARY POINTS

- The balance of payments is the summary statement of all international transactions between one country and all other countries.

- The balance of payments is a flow statement, summarizing all the international transactions that occur across the geographic boundaries of the nation over a period of time, typically a year.

- Although the BOP must always balance in theory, in practice there are substantial imbalances as a result of statistical errors and misreporting of current account and financial/capital account flows.

- The two major sub-accounts of the balance of payments, the current account and the financial/capital account, summarize the current trade and international capital flows of the country respectively.

- The current account and financial/capital account are typically inverse on balance, one in surplus while the other experiences deficit.

- Although most nations strive for current account surpluses, it is not clear that a balance on current or capital account, or a surplus on current account, is either sustainable or desirable.

- Although merchandise trade is more easily observed (for example, goods flowing through ports of entry), the growth of services trade is more significant to the balance of payments for many of the world's largest industrialized countries today.

- Monitoring of the various sub-accounts of a country's balance of payment activity is helpful to decision makers and policy makers on all levels of government and industry in detecting the underlying trends and movements of fundamental economic forces driving a country's international economic activity.

- Changes in exchange rates change relative prices of imports and exports, and changing prices in turn result in changes in quantities demanded through the price elasticity of demand.

- A devaluation results initially in a further deterioration in the trade balance before an eventual improvement—the path of adjustment taking on the shape of a flattened "j".

- The ability of capital to move instantaneously and massively cross-border has been one of the major factors in the severity of recent currency crises. In a number of cases, such as Malaysia in 1997 and Argentina in 2001, the national governments concluded that they had no choice but to impose drastic restrictions on the ability of capital to flow.

- Although not limited to heavily indebted countries, the rapid and sometimes illegal transfer of convertible currencies out of a country poses significant economic and political problems. Many heavily indebted countries have suffered significant capital flight, which has compounded their problems of debt service.

 **MINI-CASE**

Turkey's Kriz (A): Deteriorating Balance of Payments

It was only when optimistic Turks started snapping up imports that investors began to doubt that foreign capital inflows would be sufficient to fund both spendthrift consumers and the perennially penurious government.

—"On the Brink Again," *The Economist*, February 24, 2001.

In February 2001 Turkey's rapidly escalating economic *kriz*, or crisis, forced the devaluation of the Turkish lira. The Turkish government had successfully waged war on the inflationary forces embedded in the country's economy in 1999 and early 2000. But just as the economy began to boom in the second half of 2000, pressures on the country's balance of payments and currency rose. The

question asked by many analysts in the months following the crisis was whether the crisis had been predictable, and what early signs of deterioration should have been noted by the outside world.

The Accounts

Exhibit 1 presents the Turkish balance on current account and financial account between 1993 and 2000 (ending less than two months prior to the devaluation). Several issues are immediately evident:

- First, Turkey seemingly suffered significant volatility in the balances on key international accounts. The financial account swung between surplus

Turkey's Balance of Payments, 1993–2000

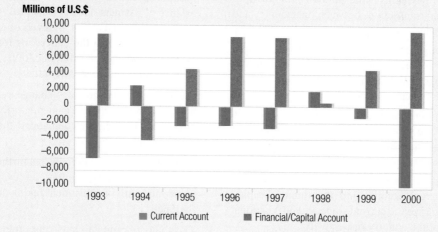

- Current Account   - Financial/Capital Account

(1993) and deficit (1994), and back to surplus again (1995–1997). After plummeting in 1998, the financial surplus returned in 1999 and 2000.

- Second, as is typically the case, the current account behaved in a relatively inverse manner to the financial account, running deficits in most of the years shown. But significantly, the deficit on current account grew dramatically in 2000, to over $9.8 billion, from a deficit in 1999 of only $1.4 billion.

Many analysts are quick to point out that the sizable increase in the current account deficit should have been

seen as a danger signal of imminent collapse. Others, however, point out quite correctly that most national economies experience rapid increases in trade and current account deficits during rapid periods of economic growth. And to add weight to the argument, the net surplus on the financial account seemed to indicate a growing confidence in the Turkish economy's outlook by foreign investors.

An examination of the subcomponents of these major account balances is helpful. As illustrated in Exhibit 2, the rapid deterioration of the current account in 2000 was largely the result of a rapid jump in imported goods and merchandise. The goods import bill rose from $39.8 billion

Subaccounts of the Turkish Current Account, 1998–2000 (millions of U.S. dollars)

	1998	1999	2000
Goods: exports	31,220	29,325	31,664
Goods: imports	−45,440	−39,768	−54,041
Balance on goods	−14,220	−10,443	−22,377
Services: credit	23,321	16,398	19,484
Services: debit	−9,859	−8,953	−8,149
Balance on services	13,462	7,445	11,335
Income: credit	2,481	2,350	2,836
Income: debit	−5,466	−5,887	−6,838
Balance on income	−2,985	−3,537	−4,002
Current transfers: credit	5,860	5,294	5,317
Current transfers: debit	−133	−119	−92
Balance on transfers	5,727	5,175	5,225
Balance on current account	1,984	−1,360	−9,819

Source: International Monetary Fund, *Balance of Payments Statistics Yearbook 2001*, p. 913.

in 1999 to over $54.0 billion in 2000, an increase of 36% in one year. At the same time, services trade and current income accounts, both credits and debits subcomponents, showed little change. Unfortunately, the statistics reported to the IMF provide little in additional detail as to the composition of these rapid imports, their industry or nature, and their financing.

A similar decomposition of the surplus on the financial account also allows us to identify where in the various inflows and outflows of capital in Turkey there was a significant change. Exhibit 3 provides this financial account decomposition. According to Exhibit 3, the doubling of the Turkish financial account surplus in 2000 was largely the result of a massive increase—over $7 billion—in "net other investment."

One very important determinant of these account balances was the telecommunications sector. Throughout 2000, TelSim, the national telecommunications provider in Turkey, imported billions of dollars worth of equipment from Nokia (Finland) and Motorola (United States). The equipment was purchased on trade credit, meaning that TelSim would repay Nokia and Motorola at a future date for the equipment, primarily from the proceeds of activating the equipment for telecommunications services. TelSim, however, defaulted on its payments, and Nokia and Motorola were left with billions of dollars in losses.

Case Questions

1. Where in the current account would the imported telecommunications equipment be listed? Would this location correspond to the increase in magnitude and timing of the financial account?

2. Why do you think that net direct investment declined from $573 million in 1998 to $112 million in 2000?

3. Why do you think that TelSim defaulted on its payments for equipment imports from Nokia and Motorola?

EXHIBIT 3	Subaccounts of the Turkish Financial Account, 1998–2000 (millions of U.S. dollars)		
	1998	1999	2000
Net direct investment	573	138	112
Net portfolio investment	−6,711	3,429	1,022
Net other investment	6,586	1,103	8,311
Balance of financial account	448	4,670	9,445

Source: International Monetary Fund, Balance of Payments Statistics Yearbook 2001, p. 915.

QUESTIONS

1. **Balance of Payments Defined.** The measurement of all international economic transactions between the residents of a country and foreign residents is called the balance of payments (BOP). What institution provides the primary source of similar statistics for balance of payments and economic performance worldwide?

2. **Importance of BOP.** Business managers and investors need BOP data to anticipate changes in host country economic policies that might be driven by BOP events. From the perspective of business managers and investors list three specific signals that a country's BOP data can provide.

3. **Economic Activity.** What are the two main types of economic activity measured by a country's BOP?

4. **Balance.** Why does the BOP always "balance"?

5. **BOP Accounting.** If the BOP were viewed as an accounting statement, would it be a balance sheet of the country's wealth, an income statement of the country's earnings, or a funds flow statement of money into and out of the country?

6. **Current Account.** What are the main component accounts of the current account? Give one debit and one credit example for each component account for the United States.

7. **Real versus Financial Assets.** What is the difference between a "real" asset and a "financial" asset?

8. **Direct versus Portfolio Investments.** What is the difference between a direct foreign investment and a portfolio foreign investment? Give an example of each. Which type of investment is a multinational industrial company more likely to make?

9. **Capital and Financial Accounts.** What are the main components of the financial accounts? Give one debit and one credit example for each component account for the United States.

10. **Classifying Transactions.** Classify the following as a transaction reported in a sub-component of the current account or the capital and financial accounts of the two countries involved:
    a. A U.S. food chain imports wine from Chile.
    b. A U.S. resident purchases a euro-denominated bond from a German company.
    c. Singaporean parents pay for their daughter to study at a U.S. university.
    d. A U.S. university gives a tuition grant to a foreign student from Singapore.
    e. A British company imports Spanish oranges, paying with Eurodollars on deposit in London.
    f. A Spanish orchard deposits half the proceeds of its sale in a New York bank.
    g. A Spanish orchard deposits half the proceeds in a Eurodollar account in London.
    h. A London-based insurance company buys U.S. corporate bonds for its investment portfolio.
    i. An American multinational enterprise buys insurance from a London insurance broker.
    j. A London insurance firm pays for losses incurred in the United States because of an international terrorist attack.
    k. Cathay Pacific Airlines buys jet fuel at Los Angeles International Airport so it can fly the return segment of a flight back to Hong Kong.
    l. A California-based mutual fund buys shares of stock on the Tokyo and London stock exchanges.
    m. The U.S. army buys food for its troops in South Asia from vendors in Thailand.
    n. A Yale graduate gets a job with the International Committee of the Red Cross in Bosnia and is paid in Swiss francs.
    o. The Russian government hires a Dutch salvage firm to raise a sunken submarine.
    p. A Colombian drug cartel smuggles cocaine into the United States, receives a suitcase of cash, and flies back to Colombia with that cash.
    q. The U.S. government pays the salary of a Foreign Service Officer working in the U.S. embassy in Beirut.
    r. A Norwegian shipping firm pays U.S. dollars to the Egyptian government for passage of a ship through the Suez Canal.
    s. A German automobile firm pays the salary of its executive working for a subsidiary in Detroit.
    t. An American tourist pays for a hotel in Paris with his American Express card.
    u. A French tourist from the provinces pays for a hotel in Paris with his American Express card.
    v. A U.S. professor goes abroad for a year on a Fulbright grant.

11. **The Balance.** What are the main summary statements of the balance of payments accounts and what do they measure?

12. **Drugs and Terrorists.** Where in the balance of payments accounts do the flows of "laundered" money by drug dealers and international terrorist organizations flow?

13. **Capital Mobility—United States.** The U.S. dollar has maintained or increased its value over the past 20 years despite running a gradually increasing current account deficit. Why has this phenomenon occurred?

14. **Capital Mobility—Brazil.** Brazil has experienced periodic depreciation of its currency over the past 20 years despite occasionally running a current account surplus. Why has this phenomenon occurred?

15. **BOP Transactions.** Identify the correct BOP account for each of the following transactions:
    a. A German-based pension fund buys U.S. government 30-year bonds for its investment portfolio.
    b. Scandinavian Airlines System (SAS) buys jet fuel at Newark Airport for its flight to Copenhagen.
    c. Some Hong Kong students pay tuition to the University of California, Berkeley.
    d. A Japanese auto company pays the salaries of its executives working for its U.S. subsidiaries.
    e. A U.S. tourist pays for a restaurant meal in Bangkok.
    f. A U.K. corporation purchases a euro-denominated bond from an Italian MNE.

PROBLEMS

Australia's Current Account

Use the following data from the International Monetary Fund (all items are for the current account) to answer questions 1 through 4.

*1. What is Australia's balance on goods trade?

*2. What is Australia's balance on services?

*3. What is Australia's balance on goods and services?

*4. What is Australia's current account balance?

Australia's Current Account

Assumptions (million US$)	1998	1999	2000	2001	2002	2003	2004	2005	2006
Goods: exports	55,884	56,096	64,052	63,676	65,099	70,577	87,207	106,969	124,913
Goods: imports	−61,215	−65,857	−68,865	−61,890	−70,530	−85,946	−105,238	−120,372	−134,509
Services: credit	16,181	17,399	18,677	16,689	17,906	21,205	26,362	28,442	33,088
Services: debit	−17,272	−18,330	−18,388	−16,948	−18,107	−21,638	−27,040	−29,360	−32,219
Income: credit	6,532	7,394	8,984	8,063	8,194	9,457	13,969	16,969	21,748
Income: debit	−17,842	−18,968	−19,516	−18,332	−19,884	−24,245	−35,057	−43,746	−54,131
Current transfers: credit	2,651	3,003	2,622	2,242	2,310	2,767	3,145	3,262	3,698
Current transfers: debit	−2,933	−3,032	−2,669	−2,221	−2,373	−2,851	−3,414	−3,625	−4,092

China's (Mainland) Balance of Payments

Use the following Chinese balance of payments data from the IMF to answer questions 5 through 8.

5. Is China experiencing a net capital inflow or outflow?

6. What is China's total for Groups A and B?

7. What is China's total for Groups A through C?

8. What is China's total for Groups A through D?

People's Republic of China (Mainland) Balance of Payments

Assumptions (million US$)	1998	1999	2000	2001	2002	2003	2004	2005	2006
A. Current account balance	31,472	21,115	20,518	17,401	35,422	45,875	68,659	160,818	253,268
B. Capital account balance	−47	−26	−35	−54	−50	−48	−69	4,102	4,020
C. Financial account balance	−6,275	5,204	1,958	34,832	32,341	52,774	110,729	58,862	2,642
D. Net errors and omissions	−18,902	−17,641	−11,748	−4,732	7,504	17,985	26,834	−16,441	−13,075
E. Reserves and related items	−6,248	−8,652	−10,693	−47,447	−75,217	−116,586	−206,153	−207,342	−246,855

India's Current Account

Use the following India balance of payments data from the IMF (all items are for the current account) to answer questions 9 through 13.

9. What is India's balance on goods?

10. What is India's balance on services?

11. What is India's balance on goods and services?

12. What is India's balance on goods, services, and income?

13. What is India's current account balance?

India's Current Account

Assumptions (millions of US$)	1998	1999	2000	2001	2002	2003	2004	2005	2006
Goods: exports	34,076	36,877	43,247	44,793	51,141	60,893	77,939	102,176	123,617
Goods: imports	−44,828	−45,556	−53,887	−51,212	−54,702	−68,081	−95,539	−134,702	−166,695
Services: credit	11,691	14,509	16,684	17,337	19,478	23,902	38,281	55,831	75,354
Services: debit	−14,540	−17,271	−19,187	−20,099	−21,039	−24,878	−35,641	−47,989	−63,537
Income: credit	1,806	1,919	2,521	3,524	3,188	3,491	4,690	5,082	7,795
Income: debit	−5,443	−5,629	−7,414	−7,666	−7,097	−8,386	−8,742	−11,475	−12,059
Current transfers: credit	10,402	11,958	13,548	15,140	16,789	22,401	20,615	24,120	27,449
Current transfers: debit	−67	−35	−114	−407	-698	−570	−822	−877	−1,340

Euro Area Balance of Payments

Use the following Euro Area balance of payments data from the IMF to answer questions 14 through 17.

14. Is the Euro Area experiencing a net capital inflow?

15. What is the Euro Area's total for Groups A and B?

16. What is the Euro Area's total for Groups A through C?

17. What is the Euro Area's total for Groups A through D?

Euro Area Balance of Payments

Assumptions (billion US$)	1998	1999	2000	2001	2002	2003	2004	2005	2006
A. Current account balance	31.3	−25.5	−81.8	−19.7	54.8	38.8	79.8	22.5	1.5
B. Capital account balance	13.9	13.5	8.4	5.6	9.7	14.3	20.6	13.9	11.7
C. Financial account balance	−86.1	2.6	50.9	−41.2	−16.9	−49.0	−39.0	−14.4	129.9
D. Net errors and omissions	31.2	−2.2	6.4	38.8	−44.6	−36.9	−76.9	−44.9	−140.6
E. Reserves and related items	9.6	11.6	16.2	16.4	−3.0	32.8	15.6	22.9	−2.6

Argentina's Balance of Payments

Argentina used a currency board to maintain its peso on a par with the U.S. dollar. However, in January 2002 the peso collapsed. Argentina's BOP could have signaled this event. Listed below is Argentina's BOP for the period 1998–2006. Use this data to answer questions 18 through 24.

18. What is Argentina's balance on services?

19. What is Argentina's current account balance?

20. What seems to have been the primary driver of Argentina's current account between 1998 and 2000?

21. What is Argentina's financial account balance?

22. What is Argentina's total for Groups A through C?

23. What is Argentina's total for Groups A through D?

24. What indications of impending crisis do you observe in the years leading up to the 2002 collapse of the peso?

Argentina's Balance of Payments

Assumptions (million US$)	1998	1999	2000	2001	2002	2003	2004	2005	2006
A. Current Account									
Goods: exports	26,434	23,309	26,341	26,543	25,651	29,939	34,576	40,387	46,546
Goods: imports	−29,531	−24,103	−23,889	−19,158	−8,473	−13,134	−21,311	−27,300	−32,588
Services: credit	4,854	4,719	4,936	4,627	3,495	4,500	5,288	6,635	7,987
Services: debit	−9,298	−8,830	−9,219	−8,490	−4,956	−5,693	−6,619	−7,620	−8,529
Income: credit	6,134	6,075	7,420	5,358	3,039	3,104	3,721	4,313	5,674
Income: debit	−13,538	−13,566	−14,968	−13,085	−10,530	−11,080	−13,004	−11,617	−11,834
Current transfers: credit	802	790	792	856	818	942	1,110	1,226	1,412
Current transfers: debit	−338	−337	-393	−431	−278	−438	-549	−742	−962
B. Capital Account (Group B)	73	149	106	157	406	70	196	89	97
C. Financial Account									
Direct investment abroad	−2,325	−1,730	-901	−161	627	-774	-676	−1,311	−2,438
Direct investment in Argentina	7,291	23,988	10,418	2,166	2,149	1,652	4,125	5,265	5,537
Portfolio investment assets, net	−1,906	−2,005	−1,252	212	477	-95	-77	1,368	−1
Portfolio investment liabilities, net	10,693	−4,780	−1,331	−9,715	−5,117	−7,663	−9,339	−1,731	7,921
Balance on other assets & liabilities, net	5,183	−1,024	919	−7,473	−18,821	−8,980	−4,982	−1,693	−6,132
D. Net Errors and Omissions	−437	−642	−154	−2,810	−1,890	−1,428	548	377	1,556
E. Reserves and Related Items	−4,090	−2,013	1,176	21,405	13,402	9,077	6,993	−7,644	−14,247

25. Trade deficits and J-curve adjustment paths. Assume the United States has the following import/export volumes and prices. It undertakes a major "devaluation" of the dollar, say 18% on average against all major trading partner currencies. What is the pre-devaluation and post-devaluation trade balance?

Initial (pre-devaluation) spot rate ($/foreign currency)	2.00	
Price of exports ($)	20.00	
Price of imports (foreign currency, fc)	12.00	
Quantity of exports, units		100.00
Quantity of imports, units		120.00
Price elasticity of demand, imports		−0.90

INTERNET EXERCISES

1. World Organizations and the Economic Outlook. The IMF, World Bank, and United Nations are only a few of the major world organizations that track, report, and aid international economic and financial development. Using these Web sites and others that may be linked, briefly summarize the economic outlook for the developed and emerging nations of the world. For example, the full text of Chapter 1 of the *World Economic Outlook* published annually by the World Bank is available through the IMF's Web page.

International Monetary Fund	www.imf.org/external/index.htm
United Nations	www.un.org/databases/index.html
The World Bank Group	www.worldbank.org

Europa (EU) Homepage	europa.eu/
Bank for International Settlements	www.bis.org/index.htm

2. St. Louis Federal Reserve. The Federal Reserve Bank of St. Louis provides a large amount of recent open-economy macroeconomic data online. Use the following addresses to track down recent BOP and GDP data for the major industrial countries:

Recent international economic data	research.stlouisfed.org/publications/iet/
Balance of payments statistics	research.stlouisfed.org/fred2/categories/125

3. U.S. Bureau of Economic Analysis. Use the following Bureau of Economic Analysis (U.S. government) and the Ministry of Finance (Japanese government) Web sites to find the most recent balance of payments statistics for both countries:

Bureau of Economic Analysis	www.bea.gov/International/Index.htm
Ministry of Finance	www.mof.go.jp/english/index.htm

4. World Trade Organization and Intellectual Property. The World Trade Organization (WTO) is currently in a multiple-year round of negotiations on international trade. The current round is taking place in Doha, Qatar. Visit the WTO's Web site, including some online video segments, and find the most recent evidence presented by the WTO on the progress of talks on issues including international trade in services and international recognition of intellectual property.

World Trade Organization	www.wto.org/

CHAPTER 5

Current Multinational Financial Challenges: The Credit Crisis of 2007–2009

Confidence in markets and institutions, it's a lot like oxygen. When you have it, you don't even think about it. Indispensable. You can go years without thinking about it. When it's gone for five minutes, it's the only thing you think about. The confidence has been sucked out of the credit markets and institutions.

—Warren Buffett, October 1, 2008.

Beginning in the summer of 2007, first the United States, followed by the European and Asian financial markets, incurred financial crises. This chapter will provide an overview of the origins, dissemination, and repercussions of these credit crises on the conduct of global business. The impacts on the multinational enterprise have been significant and lasting. This chapter is a new addition to this text—representing, in our eyes, the significance of the subject. No student of multinational business should be without a clear understanding of the causes and consequences of this breakdown in global financial markets.

The Seeds of Crisis: Subprime Debt

The origins of the current crisis lie within the ashes of the equity bubble and subsequent collapse of the equity markets at the end of the 1990s. As the so-called *dot.com bubble* collapsed in 2000 and 2001, capital flowed increasingly toward the real estate sectors in the United States. Some economists have argued that much of the wealth accumulated from the equity markets during that period was now used to push housing prices and general real estate demands upwards. Although corporate lending was still relatively slow, the U.S. banking sector found mortgage lending a highly profitable and rapidly expanding market. The following years saw investment and speculation in the real estate sector increase rapidly. This included both residential housing and commercial real estate. As prices rose and speculation increased, a growing number of the borrowers were of lower and lower credit quality. These borrowers and their associated mortgage agreements, the *subprime debt* which has been so widely discussed, now carried higher debt service obligations with lower and lower income and cash flow capabilities. In traditional financial management terms, *debt-service coverage* was increasingly inadequate.

Repeal of Glass-Steagall

The market was also more competitive than ever, as a number of deregulation efforts in the United States in 1999 and 2000 now opened these markets up to more and more financial organizations and institutions than ever before. One of the major openings was the U.S. Congress' passage of the Gramm-Leach-Bliley Financial Services Modernization Act of 1999, which repealed the last vestiges of the Glass-Steagall Act of 1933, eliminating the last barriers between commercial and investment banks. The Act now allowed commercial banks to enter into more areas of risk, including underwriting and proprietary dealing.[1] One key result was that the banks now competed aggressively for the loan business of customers of all kinds, offering borrowers more and more creative mortgage forms at lower and lower interest rates—at least initial interest rates.

Another negative result of banking deregulation was that extra pressure was placed on the existing regulators. The Federal Deposit Insurance Corporation (FDIC) was established to insure the deposits of customers in commercial banks. The FDIC's main tools were to require an adequate capital base for each bank and periodic inspections to assure the credit quality of the banks' loans. This worked very well for the period 1933–1999. There were very few bank failures and almost no major failure.

Investment banks and stock brokerage firms were regulated by the Securities and Exchange Commission (SEC). These banks and brokerage firms dealt in much riskier activities than the commercial banks. These activities included stock and bond underwriting, active participation in derivatives and insurance markets and investments in subprime debt and other mortgages, using their own equity and debt capital—not the deposits of consumers.

The Housing Sector and Mortgage Lending

One of the key outcomes of this new market openness and competitiveness was that many borrowers who in previous times could not have qualified for mortgages now could. Many of these loans were quite transparent in terms of both risks and returns. Borrowers often borrowed at floating rates, often priced at LIBOR, plus a small interest rate spread. The loans would then reset at much higher fixed rates within two to five years. Other forms included loan agreements that were interest only in the early years, requiring a subsequent step up in payments with principal reduction or complete refinancing at later dates. In some cases, the interest-only loan payment structures were at initial interest rates that were far below market rates.

Credit Quality. Mortgage loans in the U.S. marketplace are normally categorized as *prime* (or A-paper), *Alt-A* (Alternative-A paper), and *subprime*, in increasing order of riskiness.[2] A prime mortgage would be categorized as *conforming* (also referred to as *conventional loans),* meaning it would meet the guarantee requirements and resale to Government-Sponsored

---

[1] The Act now allowed corporate combinations like that between Citibank, a commercial bank, and the Travelers Group, an insurance company. The combined entity could now provide banking, insurance, and underwriting services under a variety of different brands. This combination would have been strictly forbidden under the Glass-Steagall and Bank Holding Company Acts.

[2] *Prime* is the 30-year fixed interest rate reported by the Freddie Mac Primary Mortgage Market Survey. *Subprime* is the average 30-year fixed interest rate at origination as calculated by the LoanPerformance data set. *Subprime premium* is the difference between the prime and subprime rates.

Enterprises (GSEs) Fannie Mae and Freddie Mac. Alt-A mortgages, however, would still be considered a relatively low risk loan and the borrower creditworthy, but for some reason were not initially conforming. (They could, however, still be sold to GSEs if certain minimums like 20% down payments were included.) As the housing and real estate markets boomed in 2003 and 2004, more and more mortgages were originated by lenders which were in the Alt-A category, as it was the preferred loan for many non–owner-occupied properties. Investors wishing to buy homes for resale purposes, *flipping*, would typically qualify for an Alt-A mortgage, but not a prime. By the end of 2008 there was more than $1.3 trillion in Alt-A debt outstanding.

The third category of mortgage loans, *subprime*, is difficult to define. In principle, it reflects borrowers who do not meet underwriting criteria. Subprime borrowers have a higher perceived risk of default, normally as a result of some credit history elements which may include bankruptcy, loan delinquency, default, or simply limited experience or history of debt. They are nearly exclusively floating-rate structures, and carry significantly higher interest rate spreads over the floating bases like LIBOR.

Subprime borrowers typically pay a 2% premium over prime—the *subprime differential*. From a traditional lender's perspective, the key metric for any loan is the *termination profile*, the likelihood that the borrower will either prepay or default on the loan. Historically, the actual interest rate any specific borrower would pay is determined by a host of factors including the borrower's credit score, the specific mortgage loan-to-value (LTV) ratio, and the size of the down payment. Interestingly, the interest rate charged does not change significantly until the down payment drops below 10%.

Subprime lending was itself the result of deregulation. Until 1980, most states in the United States had stringent interest rate caps on lenders/borrowers. Even if a lender was willing to extend a mortgage to a subprime borrower—at a higher interest rate, and the borrower was willing to pay the higher rate, state law prohibited it. With the passage of the 1980 Depository Institutions Deregulation and Monetary Control Act (DIDMCA) federal law superceded state law. But it wasn't until the passage of the Tax Reform Act of 1986 that subprime debt became a viable market. The TRA of 1986 eliminated tax deductibility of consumer loans, but allowed tax deductibility on interest charges associated with both a primary residence and a second mortgage loan. The subprime loan was born.

The growing demand for loans or mortgages by these borrowers led more and more originators to provide the loans at above market rates beginning in the late 1990s. By the 2003–2005 period, these subprime loans were a growing segment of the market.[3] As illustrated in Exhibit 5.1, the growth in financial assets of all kinds (measured here as a percentage of gross domestic product, GDP) more than doubled between the late 1980s and 2008, in a little less than 20 years.

Asset Values. One of the key financial elements of this growing debt was the value of the assets collateralizing the mortgages—the houses and real estate itself. As the market demands pushed up prices, housing assets rose in market value. The increased values were then used as collateral in refinancing, and in some cases, additional debt in the form of second mortgages based on the rising equity value of the home.

Unfortunately, one particularly complex component of this process was that as existing homes rose in value, many homeowners were now enticed and motivated to refinance existing mortgages. As a result, many mortgage holders who were previously stable became more

---

[3]Subprime mortgages may have never exceeded 7% to 8% of all outstanding mortgage obligations by 2007, but by the end of 2008, they were the source of more than 65% of bankruptcy filings by homeowners in the United States.

EXHIBIT 5.1	U.S. Financial Assets as a Percent of GDP

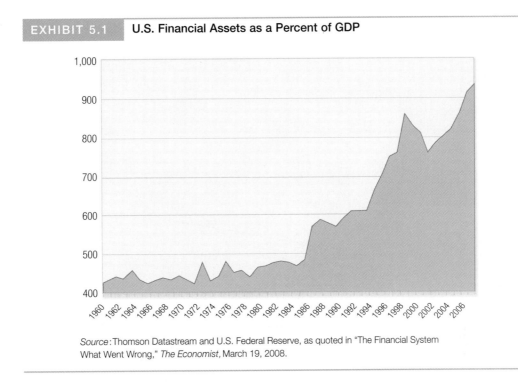

Source: Thomson Datastream and U.S. Federal Reserve, as quoted in "The Financial System What Went Wrong," *The Economist,* March 19, 2008.

indebted and were participants in more aggressively constructed loan agreements. The mortgage brokers and loan originators themselves also provided fuel to the fire, as the continuing prospects for refinancing generated additional fee income, a staple of the industry's returns. The industry was itself providing the feedstock for its own growth. Students of financial history will recognize this as a common story behind some of the most famous financial bubbles in history.

Mortgage debt as a percentage of household disposable income continued to climb in the United States rapidly in the post-2000 business environment. But it was not a uniquely American issue, as debt obligations were rising in a variety of countries including Great Britain, France, Germany, and Australia. Exhibit 5.2 illustrates the rising household debt levels for three selected countries through mid-2008. In the end, Great Britain was significantly more indebted in mortgage debt than even the United States.

The U.S. Federal Reserve, at the same time, intentionally aided the debt growth mechanism by continuing to lower interest rates. The Fed's monetary policy actions were predictably to lower interest rates to aid the U.S. economy in its recovery from the 2000–2001 recession. These lower rates provided additional incentive and aid for borrowers of all kinds to raise new and ever cheaper debt.

The Transmission Mechanism: Securitization and Derivatives of Securitized Debt

If subprime debt was the malaria, then securitization was the mosquito carrier, the airborne transmission mechanism of the protozoan parasite. The transport vehicle for the growing lower quality debt was a combination of securitization and repackaging provided by a series of new financial derivatives.

| EXHIBIT 5.2 | Household Debt as a Percentage of Disposable Income, 1990–2008 |

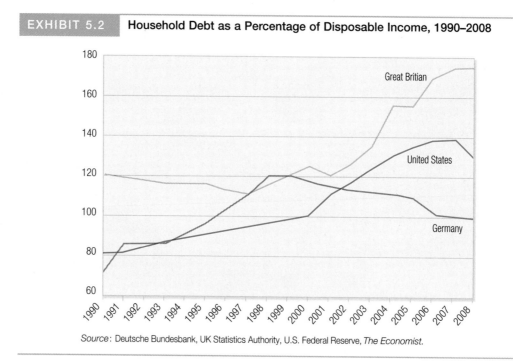

Source: Deutsche Bundesbank, UK Statistics Authority, U.S. Federal Reserve, *The Economist*.

Securitization

Securitization has long been a force of change in global financial markets. *Securitization* is the process of turning an illiquid asset into a liquid salable asset. The key element is in the interpretation of the word *liquid*. *Liquid*, in the field of finance, is the ability to exchange an asset for cash, instantly, at fair market value.[4] Although a multitude of countries had used securitization as a method of creating liquid markets for debt and equity funding since World War II, the United States had been one of the last major industrial countries to use securitization in its savings and loan and commercial banking systems. The 1980s, however, saw the introduction of securitization in U.S. debt markets, and its growth had been unchecked since. In its purest form, securitization essentially bypasses the traditional financial intermediaries, typically banks, to go directly to investors in the marketplace in order to raise funds. As a result, it may often reduce the costs of lending and borrowing, while possibly raising the returns to investors, as the financial middleman is eliminated.

The growth in subprime lending and Alt-A lending in the post-2000 U.S. debt markets depended upon this same securitization force. Financial institutions extended more and more loans of all kinds, mortgage, corporate, industrial, and asset-backed, and then moved these loan and bond agreements off their balance sheets to special purpose vehicles and ultimately into the ever-growing liquid markets using securitization. The securitized assets took two major forms, *mortgage-backed securities* (MBSs) and *asset-backed securities* (ABSs). ABSs included second mortgages and home-equity loans based on mortgages, in addition to credit card receivables, auto loans, and a variety of others.

---

[4]Liquidity is not widely understood. A relevant example would be the ability of a homeowner to sell their home for cash today. Although they could do it, they would most likely receive a cash payment which is far below the asset's true value —the fair market value.

Growth was rapid, as illustrated in Exhibit 5.3, *mortgage-backed securities* (MBS) totaled more than $27 trillion by the end of 2007, five times that of 1990, and representing 39% of all loans outstanding in the U.S. marketplace. Of the $1.3 trillion in Alt-A debt outstanding at the end of 2008, more than $600 billion of it had been securitized, roughly the same as the outstanding subprime securities outstanding.

The credit crisis of 2007–2008 renewed much of the debate over the use of securitization. Historically, securitization has been viewed as a successful device for creating liquid markets for many loan and other debt instruments which were not tradable, and therefore could not be moved off the balance sheets of banks and other financial organizations which are originating the debt. By securitizing the debt, portfolios of loans and other debt instruments could be packaged and resold into a more liquid market, freeing up the originating institutions to make more loans and increase access to debt financing for more mortgage seekers or commercial loan borrowers.

The problem, however, is that securitization may degrade credit quality. As long as the lender, the originator, was 'stuck' with the loan, the lender was keen to assure the quality of the loan and the capability of the borrower to repay in a timely manner. The lender had a vested interest in continuing to monitor borrower behavior over the life of the debt.

Securitization, however, severed that link. Now the originator could originate and sell, not being held accountable for the ultimate capability of the borrower to fulfill the loan obligation. Critics argue that securitization provides incentives for rapid and possibly sloppy credit quality assessment. Originators could now focus on generating more and more fees through more loans, origination, while not being concerned over the actual loan performance over time. The originate-to-distribute (OTD) model was now fragmenting traditional banking risks and returns. Under the OTD framework, once the loan was made and resold, the ability for any institution trading the portfolio of loans to track and monitor borrower behavior was negligible.

EXHIBIT 5.3	Securitized Loans Outstanding (trillions of U.S. dollars)

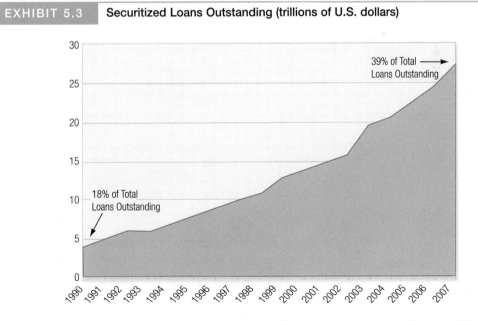

Source: U.S. Federal Reserve, NERA Economic Consulting as quoted in "Securitisation: Fear and Loathing and A Hint of Hope," *The Economist*, February14, 2008.

Proponents of securitization acknowledge that it did allow more subprime mortgages and loans to be written. But those same credits allowed more and more home buyers and commercial operators lower-cost financing, making home ownership and small business activities more affordable and more accessible. Moreover, although there was clearly abuse in the origination of subprime mortgages, many believe that the U.S. system was particularly vulnerable, not having sufficient requirements or principles in place over key credit quality criteria like credit histories. Proponents of securitization argue that if these errors are corrected, securitization would have the ability to truly reach its objectives of creating more liquid and efficient markets without degrading the quality of the instruments and obligations.

Of course securitization alone did not assure a market for the obligations. Securitization simply changed their form, but there was still the need for a market for the nonconforming obligations.

Structured Investment Vehicles

The organization that filled that market niche, the buyer of much of the securitized nonconforming debt, was the structured investment vehicle. The *structured investment vehicle* (SIV) was the ultimate financial intermediation device: it borrowed short and invested long. The SIV was an off-balance sheet entity first created by Citigroup in 1988. It was designed to allow a bank to create an investment entity that would invest in long-term and higher yielding assets such as speculative grade bonds, mortgage-backed securities (MBSs), and collateralized debt obligations (CDOs), while funding itself through commercial paper (CP) issuances. CP has long been one of the lowest-cost funding sources for any business. The problem, of course, is that the buyers of CP issuances must have full faith in the credit quality of the business unit. And that, in the end, was the demise of the SIV.

Exhibit 5.4 provides a brief overview of the SIV's basic structure. The funding of the typical SIV was fairly simple: using minimal equity, the SIV borrowed very short—commercial paper, interbank, or medium-term-notes. Sponsoring banks provided backup lines of credit

EXHIBIT 5.4   Structured Investment Vehicles (SIVs)

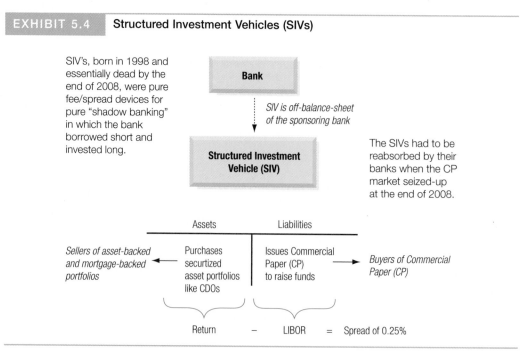

SIV's, born in 1998 and essentially dead by the end of 2008, were pure fee/spread devices for pure "shadow banking" in which the bank borrowed short and invested long.

Bank

SIV is off-balance-sheet of the sponsoring bank

Structured Investment Vehicle (SIV)

The SIVs had to be reabsorbed by their banks when the CP market seized-up at the end of 2008.

	Assets	Liabilities	
Sellers of asset-backed and mortgage-backed portfolios	Purchases securitized asset portfolios like CDOs	Issues Commercial Paper (CP) to raise funds	*Buyers of Commercial Paper (CP)*

Return − LIBOR = Spread of 0.25%

to assure the highest credit ratings for CP issuances. The SIV then used the proceeds to purchase portfolios of higher yielding securities that held investment grade credit ratings. The SIV then generated an interest margin, roughly 0.25% on average, acting as a middleman in the shadow banking process.

It is the credit quality of many of the purchased assets—for example, collateralized debt obligations (CDOs), as described in the following section, which has been the subject of much *ex post* debate. A portfolio of subprime mortgages, which by definition are not of investment grade credit quality, was often awarded investment grade quality because of the belief in portfolio theory. The theory held that whereas a single large subprime borrower constituted significant risk, a portfolio of subprime borrowers which was securitized (chopped up pieces in a sense), represented significantly less risk of credit default and could therefore be awarded investment grade status.

The theory proved false, however. As the housing boom collapsed in 2007, the subprime mortgages underlying these CDOs failed, causing the value of the SIV's asset portfolios to be instantly written down in value (mark-to-market accounting required real-time revaluation of the assets). As the asset values fell, buyers of SIV-based CP disappeared. Because the sponsoring banks of many SIVs had to provide backup lines of credit for their SIVs to obtain A1/P1 credit quality to begin with, the banks were forced to step back in and fund their own SIVs. In the second half of 2007 and the first half of 2008, most SIVs were either closed down or re-consolidated with their sponsoring banks. By October 2008, SIVs were a thing of the past.

In the end, both the birth and death of the SIV were somewhat symbolic of the three major forces many believe were behind the credit crisis of 2007 and 2008: complex financial instruments, off-balance sheet accounting entities, and increased use of leverage.

> *"SIVs are only one part of the story of credit problems in 2007 and 2008, but they are instructive because they include three features that contributed disturbance elsewhere. First, they involved the use of innovative securities, which were hard to value in the best of circumstances and which had little history to indicate how they might behave in a severe market downturn. Second, risks were underestimated: the SIVs were a form of highly leveraged speculation, which was dependent on the assumption that the markets would always supply liquidity. Finally, they were off balance sheet entities: few in the markets (or perhaps in the regulatory agencies) had an accurate idea of the scope or nature of their activities until the trouble came. The result of the interaction of these factors with a sharp housing market downturn is the most sustained period of instability in U.S. financial markets since the Great Depression."*
>
> —"Averting Financial Crisis," CRS Report for Congress, by Mark Jickling, Congressional Research Service, October 8, 2008, p. CRS-5.

As the credit crisis of 2008 deepened into the recession of 2009, many lawmakers and regulators in a variety of countries and continents debated the possible regulation of financial derivatives that may have contributed to the crisis. Both the European Union and the United States governments looked hard and close at two specific derivatives—*collateralized debt obligations* (CDOs) and *credit default swaps* (CDSs)—to determine what role they played in the crisis, and if and how they might be brought under greater control.

Collateralized Debt Obligations (CDOs)

One of the key instruments in this new growing securitization was the *collateralized debt obligation*, or CDO, pictured in Exhibit 5.5. Banks originating mortgage loans, and corporate loans and bonds, could now create a portfolio of these debt instruments and package them as

---

EXHIBIT 5.5   The Collateralized Debt Obligation

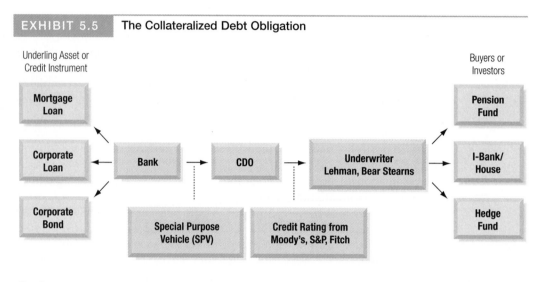

The Collateralized Debt Obligation, CDO, is a derivative instrument created from bank-originated mortgages and loans, combined with similar debt obligations into a portfolio, and then re-sold through investment banking underwriters to a variety of investors. The credit rating of the CDO, based on its constituent components, is critical to the salability to investors.

---

an asset-backed security. Once packaged, the bank passed the security to a *special purpose vehicle* (SPV), often located in an offshore financial center like the Cayman Islands for legal and tax advantages.[5] SPVs offered a number of distinct advantages, such as the ability to remain off-balance sheet if financed and operated properly. From there the CDO was sold into a growing market through underwriters. This freed up the bank's financial resources to originate more and more loans, earning a variety of fees. A typical fee was 1.1% up-front to the CDO underwriter. The collateral in the CDO was the real estate or aircraft or heavy equipment or other property the loan was used to purchase.

These CDOs were sold to the market in categories representing the credit quality of the borrowers in the mortgages—*senior tranches* (rated AAA), *mezzanine* or *middle tranches* (AA down to BB), and *equity tranches* (below BB, junk bond status, many of which were unrated). The actual marketing and sales of the CDOs was done by the major investment banking houses which now found the fee income easy and profitable. These houses, Lehman Brothers, Bear Stearns, AIG, and others, would later rue the day they committed their future to their new addiction to CDOs. Exhibit 5.5 traces this flow of CDOs to buyer.

Although at first glance this appeared relatively straightforward, it turned out in practice to be quite messy. A collection of corporate bonds or subprime mortgages would be combined into a portfolio—the CDO. The CDO would then be passed to a ratings firm, firms such as Moody's, S&P, and Fitch, for a rating for the security. The rating firms were paid for their rating, and were often under severe pressure to complete their analysis and rating of the CDO quickly. As a result, it was common practice to use the ratings information provided by the underwriter, rather than doing ground-up credit analysis on their own. A second, and somewhat confounding issue, was that it was also possible for a collection of bonds, say BB bonds, to be rated above BB when combined into a CDO. In the end, the ratings provided by

---

[5]Some readers may remember the ignominious past of the SPV from its widespread use by Enron in acquiring more and more debt—off-balance sheet—to feed its continuously failing business model in the late 1990s.

the ratings firms were critical for the underwriter to be able to market the CDOs quickly and at a favorable price. Many investing institutions had strict investment policy statements in place which required investment grade status (BBB and above) for purchase.

The CDO now became the preferred asset *du jour*, as financial institutions of all kinds, from pension funds to hedge funds, purchased the assets and earned the relatively high rates of interest and returns as the economy, real estate, and mortgage lending markets boomed from 2001 to 2007. These markets, aided substantially by slowly performing equity markets and relatively low interest rates, benefited from investors moving rapidly toward real estate investment and speculation. By 2007, the CDO market had reached a record level of more than $600 billion.

Of course, the actual value of the CDO was no better or worse than its two primary value drivers. The first was the performance of the debt collateral it held, the ongoing payments being made by the original borrowers on their individual mortgages. If for any reason those borrowers were unable to make timely debt service payments, from changing interest rates or income levels, CDO values would fall. The second driver, the one to go unnoticed until crisis occurred, was the willingness of the many institutions and traders of CDOs to continue to make a market in the derivative. This liquidity component would later prove to be disastrous.

Ownership. One of the concerns about CDOs from the very beginning, voiced by a number of people including Warren Buffett, the famous American investor, was that the CDO originator had no continuing link or responsibility to the mortgage. Once the mortgage loan was made and the CDO structured and sold, the mortgage lender had no further responsibility toward the performance of the loan. This was commonly seen as a fatal flaw. It provided a significant incentive for mortgage originators to make more and more loans of questionable credit quality, earning their fees while passing the securities along to the marketplace. Of course, the buyers in the market were also responsible for their due diligence on the quality of the assets they were buying. They too found it somewhat easy to pass the CDOs along to more and more market participants, whether they are institutions like Freddie Mac in the United States, or commercial or investment banking organizations in London, Paris, Hong Kong, or Tokyo.

Mind the Gap. A second feature of potential failure was how the CDOs fit within the organizational structures of the financial institutions themselves. The original mortgage loans were a highly illiquid asset, and were typically carried on what might be called the "loan book" of a financial institution. Once the mortgages were combined into a securitized portfolio, the CDO, they were now traded in a market that was relatively invisible, with no real regulation or reporting of market activity. The CDOs were carried on the "market book" of the financial institutions. In a number of organizations, these different books meant different departments, people, and monitoring activities. Accountability often failed.

The CDO market reached what some investment bankers characterized as a "feeding frenzy" in the fall of 2006, as the appetite for new issues seemed insatiable. *Synthetic CDOs* were born. These were structures in which the CDO itself did not actually hold debt, but were constructed purely of derivative contracts combined to "mimic" the cash flows of many other CDOs. One issue, the *Mantoloking CDO* offered by Merrill Lynch in October 2006, was representative of another new extreme. *Mantoloking* was a "CDO-squared," a CDO that held other CDOs. As more and more CDOs were created, all of the subprime components that were not wanted or acceptable to potential investors were grouped; Mantoloking was effectively a dumping ground.[6] The CDO-squared instruments not only held lower and lower

---

[6]"Frenzy," Jill Drew, *The Washington Post*, Tuesday, December 16, 2008, p. A1.

quality loans and bonds, but also they were typically highly subordinated CDOs to the original instruments that they supported.

Regardless of the CDO's weaknesses, it became a mainstay of investment banking activity globally by 2007. By the time the first real cracks in the market appeared in 2007, the CDO had spread far and wide within the global financial marketplace. Many would later argue that it would act as a cancer to the future of the system's health. The beginning of the end was the collapse of two Bear Stearns' hedge funds in July 2007. Both funds were made up nearly entirely of CDOs. Within a month the market for CDOs was completely illiquid. Anyone trying to liquidate a CDO was met with bids approaching $0.08 on the dollar. The market effectively collapsed, as illustrated in Exhibit 5.6.

Credit Default Swaps (CDSs)

"Despite its forbidding name, the CDS is a simple idea: it allows an investor to buy insurance against a company defaulting on its debt payments. When it was invented, the CDS was a useful concept because more people felt comfortable owning corporate debt if they could eliminate the risk of the issuer failing. The extra appetite for debt helped lower the cost of capital."

—"Derivatives: Giving Credit Where It Is Due," *The Economist*, November 6, 2008.

The second derivative of increasing note—or concern—was the *credit default swap* (CDS). The credit default swap was a contract, a derivative, which derived its value from the credit quality and performance of any specified asset. The CDS was new, invented by a team at JPMorgan in 1997, and designed to shift the risk of default to a third party. In short, it was a way to bet whether a specific mortgage or security would either fail to pay on time or fail to pay at all. In some cases, for hedging, it provided insurance against the possibility that a borrower might not pay. In other instances, it was a way in which a speculator could bet against

---

EXHIBIT 5.6   Global CDO Issuance, 2004–2008 (billions of U.S. dollars)

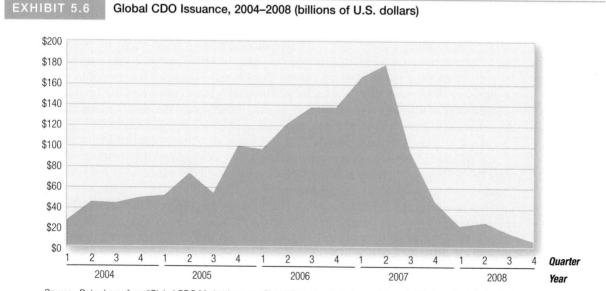

Source: Data drawn from "Global CDO Market Issuance Data," Securities Industry and Financial Markets Association (SIFMA), sigma.org.

the increasingly risky securities (like the CDO), to hold their value. And uniquely, you could make the bet without ever holding or being directly exposed to the credit instrument itself.

The CDS was completely outside the regulatory boundaries, having obtained unique protection as a result of the Commodity Futures Modernization Act of 2000. The CDS was in fact a position or play which had been outlawed for more than a century—that is until major financial market deregulatory steps were taken in 1999 and 2000. A *bucket shop* was a type of gambling house in which one could speculate on whether stocks were going to rise or fall in price without owning the stock. Note that this is not the same as a *short position*. A *short position* is when a speculator bets on a security to fall in price, and agrees to sell an actual share to a second party at a future date at a specified price. The speculator is hoping that the share price does fall, so that it can be purchased on the open market at a lower price. It could then use that share to fulfill the resale obligation. In order to write or sell the positions one needed only to find a counterparty willing to take the opposite position (as opposed to actually owning the shares). As a result, the CDS market, estimated at $62 trillion at its peak, grew to a size many times the size of the underlying credit instruments it was created to protect.

The cash flows and positions of CDSs are illustrated in Exhibit 5.7. The organization that wishes to acquire insurance against a potential credit quality fall (a hedger), or any organization possessing a view that a specific negative credit event will occur in the near-term (a speculator), is the *protection buyer*. The *protection seller* is any organization wishing to take the opposite side of the transaction, regardless of whether the institution has any specific holdings or interests in the asset or credit instrument in question. It is this dimension of CDSs

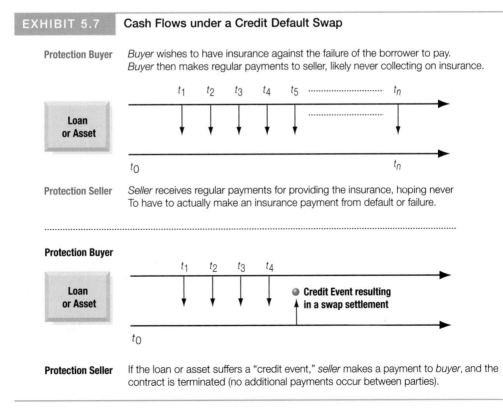

EXHIBIT 5.7   **Cash Flows under a Credit Default Swap**

Protection Buyer   *Buyer* wishes to have insurance against the failure of the borrower to pay. *Buyer* then makes regular payments to seller, likely never collecting on insurance.

Loan or Asset

t_1 t_2 t_3 t_4 t_5 .... t_n

t_0 t_n

Protection Seller   *Seller* receives regular payments for providing the insurance, hoping never To have to actually make an insurance payment from default or failure.

Protection Buyer

Loan or Asset

t_1 t_2 t_3 t_4

● **Credit Event resulting in a swap settlement**

t_0

Protection Seller   If the loan or asset suffers a "credit event," *seller* makes a payment to *buyer*, and the contract is terminated (no additional payments occur between parties).

that has been the subject of concern; that the participants in the market do not have to have any actual holdings or interests in the credit instruments at the center of the protection. They simply have to have a viewpoint. It turns out that they also needed to have more money than they had to fulfill their promise of protection. Another growing concern is that CDSs actually allow banks to sever their links to their borrowers, thereby reducing incentives to screen and monitor the ability of borrowers to repay.

The top of Exhibit 5.7 illustrates what is generally expected to happen over time to the positions and obligations of the protection buyer and seller. The buyer makes regular nominal premium payments to the seller for the length of the contract. There is no significant negative credit event during the term of the contract, and the protection seller earns its premiums over time, never having to payoff a significant claim. In essence, it's simple insurance.

The bottom half of Exhibit 5.7, however, tells a very different story. This is the case in which, say in Period 4 of the swap agreement, the credit instrument at the core of the contract suffers a credit event (e.g., bankruptcy). Then the protection seller has to fulfill its obligation to make a settlement payment to the protection buyer. All that is needed for a successful contract completion is for the protection seller to actually have sufficient capital or insurance of its own to cover its obligations. But to quote Shakespeare, "ay, that's the rub."[7] Questions continue over the adequacy of capital. According to *The Economist*, the sellers of CDSs in 2007 were widespread across a variety of financial institutions. Everyone then piled into the market: 44% banks, 32% hedge funds, 17% insurance companies, 4% pension funds, and 3% other.[8]

As a result of the CDS market growth in a completely deregulated segment, there was no real record or registry of issuances, no requirements on writers and sellers that they had adequate capital to assure contractual fulfilment, and no real market for assuring liquidity — depending on one-to-one counterparty settlement. As seen in Exhibit 5.8, the market boomed. New proposals for regulation of the market have centered on first requiring participants to have an actual exposure to a credit instrument or obligation. This eliminated the outside speculators simply wishing to take a position in the market. Also needed was the formation of some type of clearinghouse to provide systematic trading and valuation of all CDS positions at all times.

Critics of regulation argue that the market has weathered many challenges, such as the failures of Bear Stearns and Lehman Brothers (at one time estimated to have been a seller of 10% of global CDS obligations), the near failure of AIG, and the defaults of Freddie Mac and Fannie Mae. Despite these challenges, the CDS market continues to function and may have learned its lessons. Proponents argue that increased transparency of activity alone might provide sufficient information for growing market resiliency and liquidity.

> *"All of which leaves a $55 trillion question. If companies fail en masse, what will happen to the derivatives that insure against default, known as credit default swaps (CDS)? The collapse of Lehman Brothers, an investment bank, and other financial disasters, raise fears that the sellers of these products, namely banks and insurance firms, will not honour their commitments. A cascade of defaults could be multiplied many times through derivatives, blowing yet another hole in the financial system. Once considered a marvelous tool of risk management, CDSs now look as though they will magnify, not mitigate, risk."*
>
> — "Dirty Words: Derivatives, Defaults, Disaster …,"
> by Henry Tricks, *The World*, November 19, 2008.

---

[7]From Hamlet's famous "to be or not to be" speech by William Shakespeare, 1603.

[8]"Credit Derivatives: The Great Untangling," *The Economist*, November 6, 2008.

EXHIBIT 5.8   Credit Default Swap Market Growth

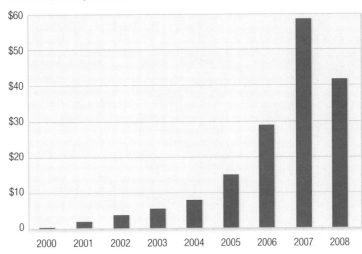

Amount outstanding in trillions of U.S. dollars

Source: Data drawn from Table 19: Amounts Outstanding of Over-the-Counter-Derivatives, by Risk Category and Instrument, *BIS Quarterly Review*, June 2009, bis.org.

Credit Enhancement

A final element quietly at work in credit markets beginning in the late 1990s was the process of *credit enhancement. Credit enhancement* is the method of making investments more attractive to prospective buyers by reducing their perceived risk. In the mid-1990s underwriters of a variety of asset-backed securities (ABSs) often used bond insurance agencies to make their products 'safer' for both them and the prospective buyers. These bond insurance agencies were third parties, not a direct part of the underwriting and sale, but a guarantor in the case of default. The practice was widely used specifically in the underwriting of home equity loan ABSs.

Beginning in 1998, however, a more innovative approach to credit enhancement was introduced in the form of *subordination*. The process of *subordination*, illustrated in Exhibit 5.9, combined different asset pools (corporate bonds, MBSs, ABSs, etc.) of differing credit quality into different tranches by credit quality. Senior tranches contained high quality loans, with mezzanine and junior tranches made up of relatively lower quality loans such as Alt-A and jumbo loans. These were loans that were in many ways nonconforming—technically, but were still considered of relatively high quality and believed to be of low risk to the investor. The final tranches, the subordinated tranches, were composed of subprime loans which were clearly considered higher risk, and as a result were paying higher interest. It was the higher interest of the subprime components that made the entire combined package higher yield, possessing a higher weighted average interest return. These subordinated structures were particularly attractive to the senior tranche holders as they earned a higher return as a result of the junior and mezzanine components, but held first-call rights on being repaid in the event of default.

EXHIBIT 5.9   CDO Construction and Credit Enhancement

CDOs were constructed as portfolios of securitized instruments which mixed assets of differing risk in order to provide greater returns to investors. A typical CDO would combine tranches based on both debt rating (AAA, A, etc.) and equity.

By including lower credit quality tranche components, it was hoped that the overall return on the CDO would be enhanced while overall risk—as a result of the portfolio—was acceptable.

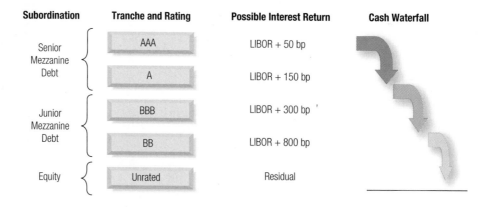

Subordination	Tranche and Rating	Possible Interest Return	Cash Waterfall
Senior Mezzanine Debt	AAA	LIBOR + 50 bp	
	A	LIBOR + 150 bp	
Junior Mezzanine Debt	BBB	LIBOR + 300 bp	
	BB	LIBOR + 800 bp	
Equity	Unrated	Residual	

In the event of portfolio asset default and failure, the *cash waterfall* would fill from the top-down, with lower mezzanine and equity/residual positions likely receiving little of cash flow on redemption.

A third method of credit enhancement in the post high-tech bubble era (post 2000) was the use of the credit default swaps (CDSs) described in the previous section. A credit default swap could be used by the buyer of a CDO holding a variety of asset-backed or mortgage-backed securities to gain additional protection against the default of the CDOs at what proved to be relatively cheap rates.

The Fallout: The Crisis of 2007 and 2008

The housing market began to falter in late 2005, with increasing signs of collapse throughout 2006. The bubble finally burst in the spring of 2007. The United States was not alone, as housing markets in the United Kingdom and Australia followed similar paths. What followed was a literal domino effect of collapsing loans and securities, followed by the funds and institutions that were their holders. In July 2007 two hedge funds at Bear Stearns holding a variety of CDOs and other mortgage-based assets failed. Soon thereafter, Northern Rock, a major British banking organization, was rescued from the brink of collapse by the Bank of England. In early September 2007, global financial markets turned to near panic, as a multitude of financial institutions on several continents suffered bank runs. Interest rates rose, equity markets fell, and the first stages of crisis rolled through the global economy.

2008 proved even more volatile than 2007. Crude oil prices—as well as nearly every other commodity price—rose at astronomical rates in the first half of the year. The massive growth in the Chinese and Indian economies, and in fact in many emerging markets globally, continued unabated. And just as suddenly, it stopped. Crude oil peaked at $147/barrel in July, and then plummeted, as did nearly every other commodity price including copper, nickel, timber, concrete, and steel.

As mortgage markets faltered, the U.S. Federal Reserve stepped in. On August 10, 2008, the Fed purchased a record $38 billion in mortgage-backed securities in an attempt to inject liquidity into the credit markets. On September 7, 2008, the U.S. government announced that it was placing Fannie Mae (the Federal National Mortgage Association) and Freddie Mac (the Federal Home Loan Mortgage Corporation) into conservatorship. In essence, the government was taking over the institutions as result of their near insolvency. Over the following week, Lehman Brothers, one of the oldest investment banks on Wall Street, struggled to survive. Finally on September 14, Lehman filed for bankruptcy. As described in the mini-case at the end of this chapter, this was by the far the largest single bankruptcy in American history.

On Monday September 15 the markets reacted. Equity markets plunged. In many ways much more important for the financial security of multinational enterprises, U.S. dollar LIBOR rates shot skywards, as illustrated in Exhibit 5.10, as a result of the growing international perception of financial collapse by U.S. banking institutions. The following day, American International Group (AIG), the U.S. insurance conglomerate, received an $85 billion injection from the U.S. Federal Reserve in exchange for an 80% equity interest. AIG had extensive credit default swap exposure. Although dollar markets seemingly calmed, the following weeks saw renewed periods of collapse and calm as more and more financial institutions failed, merged, or were bailed out by a bewildering array of bailout packages and capital injections.

The credit crisis now began in full force. Beginning in September 2008 and extending into the spring of 2009, the world's credit markets—lending of all kinds—nearly stopped. The corporate lending markets now demonstrated the following complex combination of crisis conditions:

■ In the end, the risky investment banking activities undertaken post-deregulation, especially in the mortgage market, overwhelmed the banks' commercial banking

EXHIBIT 5.10   USD & JPY LIBOR Rates (September—October 2008)

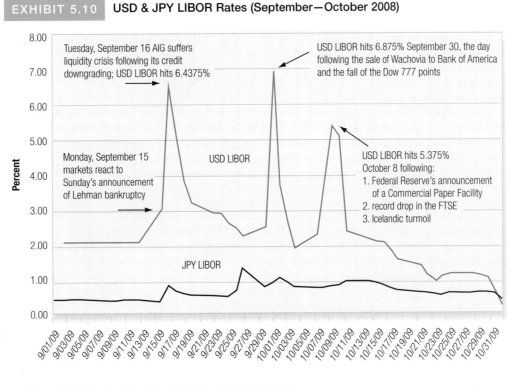

Source: British Bankers Association (BBA). Overnight lending rates.

activities. Traditional commercial bank lending for working capital financing, automobile loans, student loans, and credit card debt were squeezed out by the huge losses from the investment banking activities. Thus began the credit squeeze worldwide, a decline of asset prices, increased unemployment, burgeoning real estate foreclosures, and a general global economic malaise.

- The indebtedness of the corporate sector was tiered, with the biggest firms actually being extremely well positioned to withstand the crisis. The middle and lower tier companies by size, however, were heavily dependent on debt, particularly short-term debt for working capital financing. Many were now having trouble in both servicing existing debt and gaining access to new debt to stave off declining business conditions.

- The Fortune 500 companies had two balance sheet characteristics that seemed to have predicted the crisis. First, the right-hand side of their balance sheets was extremely clean. They held record-low levels of debt, having reduced borrowing and paying down debt over the previous five-year period. Second, they were holding record-high levels of cash and marketable securities on the left-hand side of the balance sheet. This gave them ready cash even if their bank lines did dry up.

- Even within the top tier, the lowest indebted firms, the repercussions continued. Many corporate treasurers in the Fortune 500 now discovered that much of their marketable security portfolio, invested so safely and carefully with high quality mutual funds and banks, had actually been invested in a variety of securities, derivatives, and funds that were now failing, despite all policy statements in place and supposedly adhered to.

- All corporate borrowers were suddenly confronted by banks reducing their access to credit. Companies that did not have preexisting lines of credit could not gain access to funds at any price. Companies with preexisting lines of credit were now receiving notification that their lines were being reduced. (This was particularly heavy in London, but also seen in New York.) As a result, many companies, although not needing the funds, chose to draw down their existing lines of credit before they could be reduced. This was clearly a panic response, and in fact worked to reduce credit availability for all.

- The commercial paper market nearly ceased to operate in September and October. Although the CP market had always been a short-term money market, more than 90% of all issuances in September 2008 were overnight. The markets no longer trusted the credit quality of any counterparty—whether they be hedge funds, money market funds, mutual funds, investment banks, commercial banks, or corporations. The U.S. Federal Reserve stepped in quickly, announcing that it would now buy billions in CP issuances in order to add liquidity into the system.

Global Contagion

Although it is difficult to ascribe causality, the rapid collapse of the mortgage-backed securities markets in the United States definitely spread to the global marketplace. Capital invested in equity and debt instruments in all major financial markets fled not only for cash, but for cash in traditional safe-haven countries and markets. Equity markets fell worldwide, while capital fled many of the world's most promising emerging markets. Exhibit 5.11 illustrates clearly how markets fell in September and October 2008, and how they remained volatile ("jittery" in the Street's lexicon) in the months that followed.

EXHIBIT 5.11	Selected Stock Markets during the Crisis

Stock Market Indices (1 October 2007 = 100)

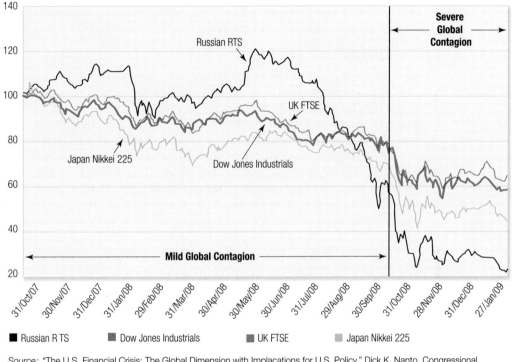

Source: "The U.S. Financial Crisis: The Global Dimension with Implacations for U.S. Policy," Dick K. Nanto, Congressional Research Service, Wahington D.C., January 29, 2009, p.11.

The impact was felt immediately in the currencies of a multitude of the more financially open emerging markets. Many currencies now fell against the traditional three safe-haven currencies, the dollar, the euro, and the yen: the Icelandic krona, Hungarian forint, Pakistani rupee, Indian rupee, South Korean won, Mexican peso, Brazilian real, to name a few.

The spring of 2009 saw a mortgage marketplace that continued to deteriorate. Alt-A mortgages were now reaching record delinquency levels, higher than even subprime mortgages. It was now apparent that many of the mortgages that were pumped into the system near the end of the housing boom as Alt-A or "near-prime" mortgages were in fact subprime. Although possessing an historical average delinquency rate of less than 1%, the Alt-A mortgage debt originated in 2006 was now above 11%. Credit ratings of outstanding securities were at horrendous levels. Moody's, for example, downgraded more than $59 billion in Alt-A securities in a three-day period alone in January 2009, most of which fell instantly to speculative grade. Eventually it was expected that 25% of all Alt-A mortgage security debt would fail.

By January 2009 the credit crisis was having additionally complex impacts on global markets—and global firms. As financial institutions and markets faltered in many industrial countries, pressure of all kinds, business, market, and political, increased to focus on the needs of "their own." A new form of antiglobalization force arose, the differentiation of the domestic from the multinational. This new form of *financial mercantilism* focused on supporting the home-country financial and nonfinancial firms first, all others second.

Multinational companies, even in emerging markets, now saw increasing indicators that they were being assessed higher credit risks and lower credit qualities, even though they theoretically had greater business diversity and the wherewithal to withstand the onslaught. The financial press categorized the credit dynamics as *homeward flow*. Credit conditions and a variety of new government bailout plans were underway in Australia, Belgium, Canada, France, Germany, Iceland, Ireland, Italy, Luxembourg, Spain, Sweden, the United Kingdom, and the United States.

The credit crisis, which had first started in the summer of 2007, now moved to a third stage. The first stage had been the failure of specific mortgage-backed securities. These had caused the fall of specific funds and instruments. The second stage had seen the crisis spread to the very foundations of the organizations at the core of the global financial system, the commercial and investment banks on all continents. This third new stage had been feared from the beginning—a credit-induced global recession of potential depression-like depths. Not only had lending stopped, but also in many cases, borrowing and investing had ceased. Although interest rates in U.S. dollar markets hovered little above zero, the price was not the issue. The prospects for investment returns of all types were now dim. The corporate sector did not see economic opportunities and returns to new investment. Budgets were slashed, layoffs continued, and the economies of the industrial world retrenched.

Was Mark-to-Market Accounting a Contributor to the Crisis?

One of the continuing debates about the global credit crisis is whether the use of *mark-to-market* (MTM) accounting contributed significantly to the failure of financial institutions. MTM accounting is the methodology of revaluing financial instruments and derivatives to their market values on a daily basis. It is based on the basic financial principle that market values, not historical book values, should be used in the recorded value of financial assets.

A long-term practice of the futures markets, the method requires that a financial institution revalue all financial assets and derivatives daily, even though there is no intention to liquidate the asset at that time. Financial Accounting Standard No. 157, "Fair Value Measurements," effective beginning November 15, 2007, expanded the adoption of MTM by U.S. companies, financial and nonfinancial alike. Although the last in a series of new financial standards over the valuation of financial instruments and assets, FAS 157 did emphasize that the fair value of the assets should be based on an *exit price*—the sale value of the asset, not the purchase price—and that the valuation should be market-based.

The problem, of course, is that many instruments either do not trade in markets, or trade only in very thin markets. If revaluing an asset or highly complex derivative that does not trade, so that there is not really a market value, the revaluation must follow a theoretical process of simulating value called *mark-to-model*. During a financial crisis such as occurred in September 2008, an additional problem arises. What was the previous day a liquid market may suddenly become illiquid; there are in effect no buyers willing to pay anything close to what is considered by some a fair market value.[9] As a result, if a financial institution must revalue all of its securities, derivatives, and assets in markets that are essentially in panic-induced free fall, the asset values are extremely low, and may result in significant destruction of the organization's equity; insolvency results. This is despite the fact that the organization had no intention of liquidating the asset at that time.

---

[9]This is a highly contentious point among industry analysts, regulators, and investors. Many, for example Warren Buffett, argue that regardless of what someone else considers 'illiquid,' if the market says the price is x, then the price is x. Anything else he considers pure conjecture, and opening a virtual Pandora's Box of market valuation abuses.

What's Wrong with LIBOR?

> *"Today's failure of confidence is based on three related issues: the solvency of banks, their ability to fund themselves in illiquid markets and the health of the real economy."*
>
> —"The Credit Crunch: Saving the System," *The Economist*, October 9, 2008.

The global financial markets have always depended upon commercial banks for their core business activity. The banks in turn, have always depended on the interbank market for the liquid linkage to all of their non-bank activity, their loans and financing of multinational business. But throughout 2008 and early 2009, the interbank market was, in one analyst's words, "behaving badly." LIBOR was clearly the culprit.

The interbank market has historically operated, on its highest levels, as a "no-name" market. This meant that for the banks at the highest level of international credit quality, interbank transactions could be conducted without discriminating by name. They therefore traded among themselves at no differential credit risk premiums. A major money center bank trading on such a level was said to be *trading on the run*. Banks that were considered to be of slightly less credit quality, sometimes reflecting more country risk than credit risk, paid slightly higher to borrow in the interbank market. The market itself still preferred not to price on an individual basis, often categorizing many banks by tier.

But much of this changed in the summer of 2007 as many subprime mortgages began to fail. As they fell, the derivatives that had fed on those mortgages fell, the Credit Default Obligations (CDOs), and with them a number of hedge funds. As individual financial institutions, commercial and investment banks alike, started suffering more and more losses related to bad loans and credits, the banks themselves became the object of much debate.

LIBOR's Role

The British Bankers Association (BBA), the organization charged with the daily tabulation and publication of LIBOR Rates, became worried in the spring of 2008 about the validity of its own published rate. The growing stress in the financial markets had actually created incentives for banks surveyed for LIBOR calculation to report lower rates than they were actually paying. A bank that had historically been considered to be *on the run*, but now suddenly reported having to pay higher rates in the interbank market, would be raising concerns that it no longer was of the same steadfast credit quality. The BBA collects quotes from 16 banks of seven different countries daily, including the United States, Switzerland, and Germany. Rate quotes are collected for 15 different maturities, ranging from one day to one year across 10 different currencies.[10] But the BBA has become concerned that even its survey wording— "at what rate could the bank borrow a reasonable amount?"—was leading to some reporting irregularities. There were increasing differences in the interpretation of "reasonable."

As the crisis deepened in September and October 2008, many corporate borrowers began to argue publicly that LIBOR rates published were in fact understating their problems. Many loan agreements with banks have *market disruption* clauses that allow banks to actually charge corporate borrowers their "real cost of funds," not just the published LIBOR. When markets are under stress and banks have to pay more and more to fund themselves, they need to pass the higher costs on to their corporate clients. Of course, this is only for corporate borrowers with preexisting loan agreements with the banks. Corporate borrowers attempting to arrange new loan agreements were being quoted ever-higher prices at considerable spreads over LIBOR.

---

[10]After collecting the 16 quotes by maturity and currency, the BBA eliminates the four highest and four lowest rates reported, and averages the remaining ones to determine various published LIBOR rates.

LIBOR, although only one of several key interest rates in the global marketplace, has been the focus of much attention and anxiety of late. In addition to its critical role in the interbank market, it has become widely used as the basis for all floating rate debt instruments of all kinds. This includes mortgages, corporate loans, industrial development loans, and the multitudes of financial derivatives sold throughout the global marketplace. The BBA recently estimated that LIBOR was used in the pricing of more than $360 trillion in assets globally. LIBOR's central role in the markets is illustrated in Exhibit 5.12. It was therefore a source of much concern when LIBOR rates literally skyrocketed in September 2008.

In principle, central banks around the world set the level of interest rates in their currencies and economies. But these rates are for lending between the central bank and the banks of the banking system. The result is that although the central bank sets the rate it lends at, it does not dictate the rate at which banks lend either between themselves or to non-bank borrowers. As illustrated in Exhibit 5.13, in July and August prior to the September crises, three-month LIBOR was averaging just under 80 basis points higher than the three-month interest rate swap index—the difference being termed the *TED Spread*. In September and October 2008, however, the spread rose to more than 350 basis points, 3.5%, as the crisis caused many banks to question the credit quality of other banks. Even this spread proved misleading. The fact was that many banks were completely "locked-out" of the interbank market. Regardless of what they may or may not have been willing to pay for funds, they could not get them.

What is also apparent from Exhibit 5.13 is the impact of the various U.S. Treasury and Federal Reserve actions to "re-float" the market. As banks stopped lending in mid- to late-September, and many interbank markets became illiquid, the U.S. financial authorities worked feverishly to inject funds into the marketplace. The result was the rapid reduction in the three-month Interest Rate Swap Index. The TED Spread remained relatively wide only

EXHIBIT 5.12   LIBOR and the Crisis in Lending

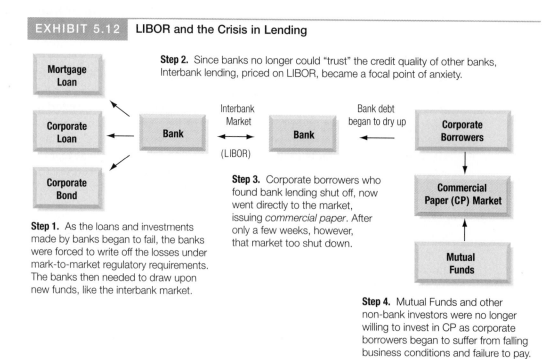

Step 2. Since banks no longer could "trust" the credit quality of other banks, Interbank lending, priced on LIBOR, became a focal point of anxiety.

Step 1. As the loans and investments made by banks began to fail, the banks were forced to write off the losses under mark-to-market regulatory requirements. The banks then needed to draw upon new funds, like the interbank market.

Step 3. Corporate borrowers who found bank lending shut off, now went directly to the market, issuing *commercial paper*. After only a few weeks, however, that market too shut down.

Step 4. Mutual Funds and other non-bank investors were no longer willing to invest in CP as corporate borrowers began to suffer from falling business conditions and failure to pay.

EXHIBIT 5.13   **The U.S. Dollar TED Spread (July 2008–January 2009)**

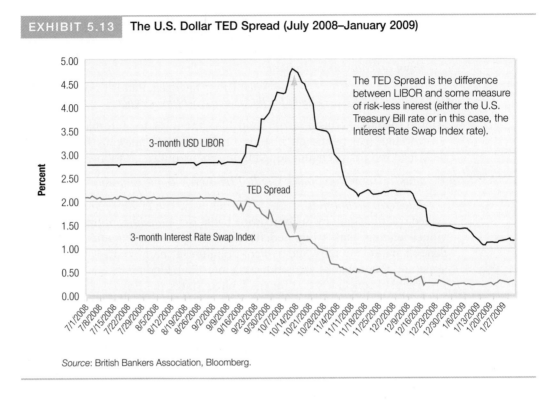

Source: British Bankers Association, Bloomberg.

a short period of time, with LIBOR actually falling to under 1.5% by the end of 2008. In January 2009 the TED Spread returned to a more common spread of under 80 basis points.[11]

Of course, the larger, more creditworthy companies do not have to borrow exclusively from banks, but may issue debt directly to the market in the form of *commercial paper*. In September 2008, when many commercial banks were no longer answering the phone, many corporate borrowers did just that. The Commercial Paper market, however, also quickly fell as many of the market's traditional buyers of commercial paper—other commercial banks, hedge funds, private equity funds, and even the SIVs discussed earlier—all now shied away from buying the paper. By mid-October the commercial paper market saw issuances fall from an already low $1.75 billion weekly to just above $1.4 billion. Even CP sold by the traditionally secure General Electric jumped up 40 basis points. Many of the buyers of CP now worried that the declining economy would result in an increasing default rate by CP issuers. As the CP market locked-up, the corporate sector saw another door to capital close.

LIBOR's Elements

"The risk premiua contained in the interest rates on three-month interbank deposits at large, internationally active banks increased sharply in August 2007 and risk premia have remained at an elevated level since. While there is evidence of a role played by credit risk,

---

[11]The TED Spread is often calculated using the maturity equivalent to LIBOR in U.S. Treasuries, in this case, the three-month U.S. Treasury Bill yield. In fact, in late 2008 the U.S. three-month Treasury Bill yield hovered around zero.

at least at lower frequencies, the absence of a close relationship between the risk of default and risk premia in the money market, as well as the reaction of the interbank markets to central bank liquidity provisions, point to the importance of liquidity factors for banks' day-to-day quoting behavior."

—"What Drives Interbank Rates? Evidence from the LIBOR Panel,"
Bank for International Settlements Quarterly Review, March 2008, pp. 47–58.

Amidst the credit crunch of 2007 and 2008, the Bank for International Settlements in Basel, Switzerland, had published a study of the LIBOR market's behavior of late. The study described the risk premium added to interbank quotes as follows:

Risk Premium = Term Premium + Credit Premium + Bank Liquidity + Market Liquidity + Micro

The *term premium* is a charge for maturity. The *credit premium* is a charge for the perceived risk of default by the borrowing bank. *Bank liquidity* premium is the access of the individual lending bank to immediate funds. The *market liquidity* premium is a measure of general market liquidity, and a *micro* premium, a charge representative of the market microstructure of how banks are conducting interbank lending.[12]

The BIS concluded that for the United States, the Euro Area, and the United Kingdom, although there seemed to be some evidence of a small credit premium charge, most of the total risk premium was explained by bank and market liquidity. The study was careful to note that its evidence was somewhat complex and sometimes inconsistent. The results, however, would seem to argue that much of what ails the LIBOR market is more a result of the multitude of instruments and markets sporadically trading (reduced liquidity) than banks discriminating amongst themselves over differing perceptions of credit quality. Exhibit 5.14 illustrates the study's results for the January 2007 to January 2008 period.

One additional finding of interest made by the BIS study was that "in several currencies the gap between the rates quoted by international banks and domestic money market rates widened noticeably," as compared to gaps between rates quoted between domestic banks.[13] This seemed to indicate that the cross border activities by the larger international banks were resulting in increased perceptions of exposure and risk.

The results of the BIS study also support the relatively more successful credit crisis bailout programs associated with market liquidity. In the case of the U.S. government, the bail-out programs focusing on injecting equity into selected banks had been largely unsuccessful. This finding is complicated by the government's inconsistency, first 'saving' Bear Stearns, then allowing Lehman to fail. The U.S. government's willingness to allow Lehman to fail is seen by many as one of the true mistakes made during the credit crisis. Programs of injecting liquidity into the financial markets, particularly the willingness of the U.S. Federal Reserve to buy commercial paper directly, have resulted in increased market liquidity. This is seen in the recovery of the LIBOR system. It is clear, however, that regardless of either government or market solutions, a healthy and stable LIBOR is a cornerstone for the health of the international interbank marketplace.

---

[12]The BIS study used an index of *overnight interest rate swaps* (OISs) rather than Treasury rates to calculate the spread, in this case, LIBOR-OIS. OISs are interest rate swaps in which the floating leg is linked to a published index of overnight rates. The two parties agree to exchange at maturity, on an agreed notional amount, the difference between interest accrued at the agreed fixed rate and interest accrued through the geometric average of the floating index rate.

[13]*BIS Quarterly Review*, March 2008, p. 48.

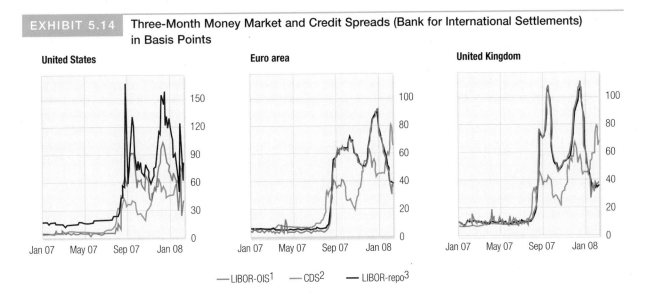

EXHIBIT 5.14 **Three-Month Money Market and Credit Spreads (Bank for International Settlements) in Basis Points**

[1]Three-month LIBOR rates minus corresponding OIS rates (for the euro area, EONIA swap; for the United Kingdom, SONIA swap).

[2]Average of the five-year on-the-run CDS spreads for the panel banks reporting LIBOR quotes in the domestic currency's panel.

[3]Three-month LIBOR rates minus general collateral repo rates (for the United States, ICAP government general collateral repo; for the euro area, EBF eurepo; for the United Kingdom, BBA repo) in the same currency and maturity.

Sources: Bloomberg; BIS calculations.

The Remedy: Prescriptions for an Infected Global Financial Organism

> *Put crudely, the bright new finance is the highly leveraged, lightly regulated, market-based system of allocating capital dominated by Wall Street. It is the spivvy successor to "traditional banking", in which regulated commercial banks lent money to trusted clients and held the debt on their books. The new system evolved over the past three decades and saw explosive growth in the past few years thanks to three simultaneous but distinct developments: deregulation, technological innovation and the growing international mobility of capital.*
>
> —"The World Economy: Taming the Beast," *The Economist*, October 8, 2008.

So where now for the global financial markets? Dismissing the absolute extremes, on one end that capitalism has failed, and on the other end that extreme regulation is the only solution, what practical solutions fall in between? What if we return to the sequence of events which has led to the most recent global credit crisis?

Debt. Was the mortgage boom itself the problem? The market largely boomed as a result of the combination of few competing investments (equity markets had fallen) with the low cost and great availability of capital. Of greater concern was the originate-to-distribute behavior combined with questionable credit assessments and classifications. New guidelines for credit quality and access to mortgages are already underway.

As illustrated by *Global Finance in Practice 5.1*, there were a number of additional surprises—unintended consequences—from the financial bailout.

GLOBAL FINANCE IN PRACTICE 5.1

Refinancing Opportunities and the Credit Crisis

One of the more unusual outcomes of the credit crisis in fall of 2008 was the opportunity for many companies to buy back their own debt at fractions of face value. The crisis had driven secondary market prices of debt, particularly speculative grade debt, extremely low. In some cases, outstanding debt was trading at 30% of face value. Now, if the issuing company had available cash, or access to new lower cost sources of debt, it could repurchase its outstanding debt at fire-sale prices. The actual repurchase could be from the public market, or via a debt tender, where an offer would be extended directly to all current debt holders.

A multitude of companies including FreeScale, First Data, GenTek, and Weyerhauser have taken advantage of the opportunity to retire more costly debt at discount prices. Many companies currently held by private equity investors, who have access to additional financial resources, have moved aggressively to repurchase. Firms have focused particularly on debt issuances which are coming due in the short-term, particularly if they feared difficulty in refinancing.

There have been a number of unintended consequences, however. A number of the distressed financial institutions have used some of the government funds provided under bailout lending to repurchase their own debt. Morgan Stanley reported earnings of more than $2.1 billion in the fourth quarter of 2008 from just buying back $12 billion of its own debt. Although this does indeed shore up the balance sheets, the primary intent of the government-backed capital had been to renew lending and financing by the banks to the non-bank financial sector—commercial businesses—in hopes of restarting general business activity, not to generate bank profits from the refinancing of its own portfolio.

Securitization. Was the financial technique of combining assets into packaged portfolios for trading the problem, or the lack of transparency and accountability for the individual elements within the portfolio? Although portfolio theory itself has been used for risk reduction since the 1960s, it was always used in the construction of assets with uncorrelated movements. In the case of mortgage-backed securities, however, the portfolio components were so similar that the only benefit was that the holder "hoped" that all the same securities would not fall into delinquency simultaneously. This was not the premise of portfolio theory.

Derivatives. This is not the first time that derivatives have been the source of substantial market failures, and it will most likely not be the last. They are the core of financial technological innovation. But derivatives are only devices and tools, and they are not better or worse than those using them. The creation of complex mortgage-backed assets and derivative structures which ultimately made the securities nearly impossible to value, particularly in thin markets, was in hindsight a very poor choice. Renewed regulatory requirements, increasing reporting, and greater degrees of transparency in pricing and valuation will aid in pulling derivatives back from the brink.

Deregulation. Regulation itself is complex enough in today's rapidly changing financial marketplace, and deregulation has the tendency to put very dangerous tools and toys in the hands of the uninitiated. Certain corrections have clearly been needed from the beginning. For example, the lack of regulatory oversight and exchange trading of credit default swaps is already in the works. There are many today who argue that financial markets do indeed need to be regulated, but of course the degree and type is unclear. This will be a growing arena of debate in the coming years.

Capital Mobility. Capital is more mobile today than ever before. This increased capital mobility, when combined with the growth in capital markets in general and the new openness in many economies in particular, will likely produce more and more cases of financial-induced crisis. The dilemmas of Iceland and New Zealand in recent years are only the beginning of this phenomenon.

Illiquid Markets. This finally, will be the most troublesome. Most of the mathematics and rational behavior behind the design of today's sophisticated financial products, derivatives, and investment vehicles are based on principles of orderly and liquid markets. When the trading of highly commoditized securities or positions as clean as overnight bank loans between banks becomes the core source of instability in the system then all traditional knowledge and assumptions of finance have indeed gone out the window. *Global Finance in Practice 5.2* explains why history-based models can lead to flawed conclusions—at least in the eyes of one rather famous investor.

GLOBAL FINANCE IN PRACTICE 5.2

Warren Buffett on the Credit Crisis

The type of fallacy involved in projecting loss experience from a universe of noninsured bonds onto a deceptively similar universe in which many bonds are insured pops up in other areas of finance. "Back-tested" models of many kinds are susceptible to this sort of error. Nevertheless, they are frequently touted in financial markets as guides to future action. (If merely looking up past financial data would tell you what the future holds, the Forbes 400 would consist of librarians.)

Indeed, the stupefying losses in mortgage-related securities came in large part because of flawed, history-based models used by salesmen, rating agencies, and investors. These parties looked at loss experience over periods when home prices rose only moderately and speculation in houses was negligible. They then made this experience a yardstick for evaluating future losses. They blissfully ignored the fact

that house prices had recently skyrocketed, loan practices had deteriorated and many buyers had opted for houses they couldn't afford. In short, universe "past" and universe "current" had very different characteristics. But lenders, government and media largely failed to recognize this all-important fact.

Investors should be skeptical of history-based models. Constructed by a nerdy sounding priesthood using esoteric terms such as beta, gamma, sigma, and the like, these models tend to look impressive. Too often, though, investors forget to examine the assumptions behind the symbols. Our advice: Beware of geeks bearing formulas.

Source: Bershire Hathaway Annual Report, 2008, Letter to Shareholders, pp. 14–15.

SUMMARY POINTS

- The origins of the current crisis lie within the ashes of the equity bubble and subsequent collapse of the equity markets at the end of the 1990s.

- A large part of the current global financial crisis resulted from the rapid expansion of mortgage-based lending on all credit levels—prime, Alt-A, and subprime—in the years following the 2000–2001 economic downturn.

- Mortgage debt as a percentage of household disposable income reached historical highs never seen before in the United States in the post-2000 business environment.

- If subprime debt was the malaria, then securitization was the mosquito carrier, the airborne transmission mechanism of the protozoan parasite. The transport

vehicle for the growing lower quality debt was a combination of securitization and repackaging via mortgage-backed securities (MBSs) provided by a series of new financial derivatives.

- The growth in subprime lending and Alt-A lending in the post-2000 U.S. debt markets depended upon the use of securitization. Financial institutions extended more and more loans of all kinds, mortgage, corporate, industrial, and asset-backed, and then moved these loan and bond agreements off their balance sheets into the ever-growing liquid markets using securitization.

- By securitizing debt, portfolios of loans and other debt instruments could be packaged and resold into a more liquid market, freeing up the originating institutions to make more loans and increase access to debt financing for more mortgage seekers or commercial loan borrowers. Securitization, however, may degrade credit quality.

▪ The Structured Investment Vehicle (SIV) was designed to allow a bank to create an investment entity which would invest in long-term and higher yielding assets such as speculative grade bonds and collateralized debt obligations (CDOs), while funding itself through commercial paper (CP) issuances.

▪ One of the key instruments used in the securitization of mortgage-backed securities was the *collateralized debt obligation*, or CDO. Banks originating mortgage loans, and corporate loans and bonds, could now create a portfolio of these debt instruments and package them as an asset-backed security.

▪ The second derivative of increasing concern was the *credit default swap* (CDS). The credit default swap is a derivative which derives its value from the credit quality and performance of any specified asset. In some cases, it provided insurance against the possibility that a borrower might not pay. In other instances, it was a way in which to speculate against increasingly risky securities (like the CDO) to hold their value.

▪ On September 7, 2008, the U.S. government announced that it was placing Fannie Mae (the Federal National Mortgage Association) and Freddie Mac (the Federal Home Loan Mortgage Corporation) into conservatorship. On September 14, Lehman Brothers, one of the oldest investment banks on Wall Street, filed for bankruptcy. Two days later the Federal Reserve provided an $85 billion injection into AIG.

▪ LIBOR is used in the pricing of more than $360 trillion in assets globally. It was therefore a source of much concern when LIBOR rates literally skyrocketed in September 2008. As questions regarding the credit quality of many international banks rose, the interbank market—via LIBOR—literally locked up.

▪ Market liquidity will be one of the lasting questions about the global financial crisis. Most of the mathematics and rational behavior behind the design of today's sophisticated financial products, derivatives, and investment vehicles are based on principles of orderly and liquid markets. When the trading of highly commoditized securities or positions as clean as overnight bank loans between banks becomes the core source of instability in the system, then many basic assumptions of finance are called into question.

MINI-CASE   Letting Go of Lehman Brothers[1]

There are other things the Treasury might do when a major financial firm assumed to be "too big to fail" comes knocking, asking for free money. Here's one: Let it fail.

Not as chaotically as Lehman Brothers was allowed to fail. If a failing firm is deemed "too big" for that honor, then it should be explicitly nationalized, both to limit its effect on other firms and to protect the guts of the system. Its shareholders should be wiped out, and its management replaced. Its valuable parts should be sold off as functioning businesses to the highest bidders— perhaps to some bank that was not swept up in the credit bubble. The rest should be liquidated, in calm markets. Do this and, for everyone except the firms that invented the mess, the pain will likely subside.

— "How to Repair a Broken Financial World," by Michael Lewis and David Einhorn, *The New York Times*, January 4, 2009.

Should Lehman Brothers have been allowed to fail? This is one of the lasting debates over the U.S. government's actions, or in this case inaction, in its attempts to fix the failing U.S. financial system in late 2008. Allowing Lehman to fail—it filed for bankruptcy on September 15, 2008— was in the eyes of many in the global financial markets the individual event which caused the global credit crisis which followed.

Lehman Brothers was founded in 1850 in Alabama by a pair of enterprising brothers. After moving the firm to New York following the American Civil War, the firm had long been considered one of the highest return, highest risk small investment banking firms on Wall Street. Although it had lived and nearly died by the sword many times over the years, by 2008 the firm was holding an enormous portfolio of failing mortgage-backed securities and the future was not bright.

Lehman's demise was not a shock, but a slow and painful downward spiral. After two major Bear Stearn's hedge funds collapsed in July 2007, Lehman was the constant focus of much speculation over its holdings of many of the distressed securities behind the credit crisis—the collateralized debt obligations and credit default swaps that had flooded the market as a result of the real estate and mortgage lending boom of the 2000 to 2007 period.

Too Big to Fail

The "too big to fail" doctrine has long been a mainstay of the U.S. financial system. The U.S. Federal Reserve has long held the responsibility as the *lender of last resort*, the institution that is charged with assuring the financial stability and viability of the U.S. financial system. Although it has exercised its powers only rarely in history, the Fed, in conjunction with the Comptroller of the Currency and the Federal Deposit Insurance Corporation (FDIC), has on a few occasions determined that an individual large bank's failure would threaten the health and functioning of the financial system. In those cases, for example Continental Illinois of Chicago in 1984, the three organizations had stepped in to effectively nationalize the institution and arrange for its continued operation to prevent what were believed to be disastrous results.

The doctrine, however, had largely been confined to commercial banks, not investment banks who made their money by intentionally taking on riskier classes of securities and positions on behalf of their investors—who expected greater returns. Lehman was clearly a risk taker. But the distinction between commercial and investment banking was largely gone, as more and more deregulation efforts had successfully reduced the barriers between taking deposits and making consumer and commercial loans, with traditional investment banking activities of underwriting riskier debt and equity issuances with a lessened fiduciary responsibility.

Many critics have argued that for some reason Lehman was singled out for failure. One week prior to Lehman's bankruptcy the Federal Reserve and U.S. Treasury under Secretary of the Treasury Hank Paulson, Jr., had bailed out both Fannie Mae and Freddie Mac, putting them into U.S. government receivership. Two days following Lehman's bankruptcy filings the Federal Reserve had extended AIG, an insurance conglomerate, an $85 billion loan package to prevent its failure. So why not Lehman?

Why Not Lehman?

Lehman had already survived one near miss. When Bear Stearns had failed in March 2008 and its sale arranged by the U.S. government, Lehman had been clearly in the cross-hairs of the financial speculators, particularly the short sellers. Its longtime CEO, Richard Fuld Jr., had been a vocal critic of the short sellers who continued to pound Lehman in the summer of 2008. But CEO Fuld had been encouraged by investors, regulators, and critics to find a way out of its mess following the close call in March. Secretary Paulson had gone on record following Lehman's June earnings reports (which showed massive losses) that if Lehman had not arranged a sale by the end of the third quarter there would likely be a crisis.

But repeated efforts by Fuld at finding buyers for different parts of the company failed, from Wall Street to the Middle East to Asia. Fuld has since argued that one of the reasons he wasn't able to arrange a sale was the U.S. government was not offering the same attractive guarantees it had put forward when arranging the sale of Bear Stearns.[2] The Fed has successfully arranged the sale of Bear Stearns to JPMorgan Chase only after the Fed agreed to cover $29 billion in losses. In fact, in August 2008, just weeks prior to its failure, Lehman believed it had found two suitors, Bank of America and Barclays, that would quickly step up if the Federal Reserve would guarantee $65 billion in potential bad loans on Lehman's books. The Fed declined.

Another proposal that had shown promise had been a self-insurance approach by Wall Street. Lehman would be split into a "good bank" and a "bad bank." The good bank would be composed of the higher quality assets and securities, and would be purchased by either Bank of America or Barclays. The bad bank would be a dumping ground of failing mortgage-backed securities which would be purchased by a consortium of 12 to 15 Wall Street financial institutions, not requiring any government funding or taxpayer dollars. The plan ultimately failed when the potential bad bank borrowers could not face their own losses and acquire Lehman's losses, while either Bank of America or Barclays walked away with high quality assets at the price of a song. In the end, only one day after Lehman's collapse, Barclays announced that it would buy Lehman's United States capital markets division for $1.75 billion, a "steal" according to one analyst.

Secretary Paulson has argued that in fact his hands were tied. The Federal Reserve is required by law only to lend to, and is limited by, the amount of asset collateral

---

[2]Fuld's own wealth and compensation had been the subject of much criticism. It has been estimated that Fuld's total compensation by Lehman over the previous five years had totaled more than $500 million, and that his personal wealth had been more than $1 billion early in 2008 (prior to the fall in Lehman's share price).

any specific institution has to offer against rescue loans. (This is in fact the defining principle behind the Fed's discount window operations.) But many critics have argued that it was not possible to determine the collateral value of the securities held by Lehman or AIG or Fannie Mae and Freddie Mac accurately at this time because of the credit crisis and the illiquidity of markets. Secretary Paulson had never been heard to make the argument before the time of the bankruptcy.

It also became readily apparent that following the AIG rescue the U.S. authorities moved quickly to try to create a systemic solution, rather than continuing to be bounced from one individual institutional crisis to another. Secretary Paulson has noted that it was increasingly clear that a larger solution was required, and that saving Lehman would not have stopped the larger crisis. Others have noted, however, that Lehman was one of the largest commercial paper issuers in the world. In the days following Lehman's collapse, the commercial paper market literally locked up. The seizing of the commercial paper market in turn eliminated the primary source of liquid funds between mutual banks, hedge funds, and banks of all kinds. The crisis was now in full bloom.

Executives on Wall Street and officials in European financial capitals have criticized Mr. Paulson and Mr. Bernanke for allowing Lehman to fail, an event that sent shock waves through the banking system, turning a financial tremor into a tsunami.

"For the equilibrium of the world financial system, this was a genuine error," Christine Lagarde, France's finance minister, said recently. Frederic Oudea, chief executive of Société Générale, one of France's biggest banks, called the failure of Lehman "a trigger" for events leading to the global crash. Willem Sels, a credit strategist with Dresdner Kleinwort, said that "it is clear that when Lehman defaulted, that is the date your money markets freaked out. It is difficult to not find a causal relationship."

—"The Reckoning: Struggling to Keep Up as the Crisis Raced On," by Joe Nocera and Edmund L. Andrews, *The New York Times*, October 22, 2008.

Case Questions

1. Do you believe that the U.S. government treated some financial institutions differently during the crisis? Was that appropriate?

2. Many experts argue that when the government bails out a private financial institution it creates a problem called "moral hazard," meaning that if the institution knows it will be saved, it actually has an incentive to take on more risk, not less. What do you think?

3. Do you think that the U.S. government should have allowed Lehman Brothers to fail?

QUESTIONS

1. **Three Forces.** What were the three major forces behind the credit crisis of 2007 and 2008?

2. **MBS.** What is a mortgage-backed security (MBS)?

3. **SIV.** What is a structured investment vehicle (SIV)?

4. **CDO.** What is a collateralized debt obligation (CDO)?

5. **CDS.** What is a credit default swap (CDS)?

6. **LIBOR's Role.** Why does LIBOR receive so much attention in the global financial markets?

7. **Interbank Market.** Why do you believe it is important for many of the world's largest commercial and investment banks to be considered on-the-run in the interbank market?

8. **LIBOR Treasury Spread.** Why were LIBOR rates so much higher than Treasury yields in 2007 and 2008? What is needed to return LIBOR rates to the lower, more stable levels of the past?

PROBLEMS

*1. **U.S. Treasury Bill Auction Rates—March 2009.** The interest yields on U.S. Treasury securities in early 2009 fell to very low levels as a result of the combined events surrounding the global financial crisis. Calculate the simple and annualized yields for the 3-month and 6-month Treasury bills auctioned on March 9, 2009, listed here.

	3-Month T-Bill	6-Month T-Bill
Treasury bill, face value	$10,000.00	$10,000.00
Price at sale	$9,993.93	$9,976.74
Discount	$6.07	$23.26

2. **The Living Yield Curve.** *SmartMoney* magazine has what they term a *Living Yield Curve* graphic on their Internet page. This yield curve graphic simulates the U.S. dollar Treasury yield curve from 1977 through the

current day. Using this graphic at www .smartmoney.com (then go to investing/bonds/living-yield-curve), answer the following questions.

a. After checking the box which says "Average," what is the average 90-day Treasury bill rate for the 1977 to current day time interval?

b. In what year does the U.S. Treasury yield curve appear to have reached its highest levels for the 1977 to 2009 or 2010 period?

c. In what year does the U.S. Treasury yield curve appear to have reached its lowest levels for the 1977 to 2009 or 2010 period?

3. **Credit Crisis, 2008.** The global credit crisis became globally visible in September 2007. Interest rates, particularly extremely short-term interest rates, will often change quickly (typically up) as indications that markets are under severe stress. The interest rates shown in the table below are for selected dates in September and October 2008. Different publications define the *TED Spread* different ways, but one measure is the differential between the overnight LIBOR interest rate and the 3-month U.S. Treasury bill rate.

a. Calculate the spread between the two market rates shown here in September and October 2008.

b. On what date is the spread the narrowest? The widest?

c. When the spread widens dramatically, presumably demonstrating some form of financial anxiety or crisis, which of the rates moves the most and why?

4. **U.S. Treasury Bill Auction Rates – May 2009.** The interest yields on U.S. Treasury securities continued to fall in the spring of 2009. Calculate the discount, and then the simple and annualized yields for the 3-month and 6-month Treasury bills auctioned on May 4, 2009, listed here.

	3-Month T-Bill	6-Month T-Bill
Treasury bill, face value	$10,000.00	$10,000.00
Price at sale	$9,995.07	$9,983.32

5. **Underwater Mortgages.** Bernie Madeoff pays $240,000 for a new four-bedroom 2400-square-foot home outside of Tonopah, Nevada. He plans to make a 20% down payment, but is having trouble deciding whether he wants a 15-year fixed rate mortgage (6.400%) or a 30-year fixed rate (6.875%).

a. What is the monthly payment for both the 15- and 30-year mortgages, assuming a fully amortizing loan of equal payments for the life of the mortgage? Use a spreadsheet calculator for the payments.

b. Assume that instead of making a 20% down payment, he makes a 10% down payment, and finances the remainder at 7.125% fixed interest for 15 years. What is his monthly payment?

c. Assume that the home's total value falls by 25%. If the homeowner is able to now sell the house, but at the new home value, what would be his gain or

Date	Overnight USD LIBOR	3-Month U.S. Treasury	TED Spread	Date	Overnight USD LIBOR	3-Month U.S. Treasury	TED Spread
9/8/2008	2.15%	1.70%	_____	9/29/2008	2.57%	0.41%	_____
9/9/2008	2.14%	1.65%	_____	9/30/2008	6.88%	0.89%	_____
9/10/2008	2.13%	1.65%	_____	10/1/2008	3.79%	0.81%	_____
9/11/2008	2.14%	1.60%	_____	10/2/2008	2.68%	0.60%	_____
9/12/2008	2.15%	1.49%	_____	10/3/2008	2.00%	0.48%	_____
9/15/2008	3.11%	0.83%	_____	10/6/2008	2.37%	0.48%	_____
9/16/2008	6.44%	0.79%	_____	10/7/2008	3.94%	0.79%	_____
9/17/2008	5.03%	0.04%	_____	10/8/2008	5.38%	0.65%	_____
9/18/2008	3.84%	0.07%	_____	10/9/2008	5.09%	0.55%	_____
9/19/2008	3.25%	0.97%	_____	10/10/2008	2.47%	0.18%	_____
9/22/2008	2.97%	0.85%	_____	10/13/2008	2.47%	0.18%	_____
9/23/2008	2.95%	0.81%	_____	10/14/2008	2.18%	0.27%	_____
9/24/2008	2.69%	0.45%	_____	10/15/2008	2.14%	0.20%	_____
9/25/2008	2.56%	0.72%	_____	10/16/2008	1.94%	0.44%	_____
9/26/2008	2.31%	0.85%	_____	10/17/2008	1.67%	0.79%	_____

loss on the home and mortgage assuming all of the mortgage principal remains? Use the same assumptions as in part a.

6. **Ted Spread, 2009.** If we use the same definition of the TED Spread noted in problem 3, the differential between the overnight LIBOR rate and the 3-month U.S. Treasury bill rate, we can see how the market may have calmed by the spring of 2009. Use the following data to answer the questions below.

a. Calculate the TED Spread for the dates shown.
b. On which dates is the spread the narrowest and the widest?
c. Looking at both the spread and the underlying data series, how would you compare these values with the rates and spreads in problem 3?

Date	Overnight USD LIBOR	3-Month U.S. Treasury	TED Spread	Date	Overnight USD LIBOR	3-Month U.S. Treasury	TED Spread
3/12/2009	0.33%	0.19%	_____	3/27/2009	0.28%	0.13%	_____
3/13/2009	0.33%	0.18%	_____	3/30/2009	0.29%	0.12%	_____
3/16/2009	0.33%	0.22%	_____	3/31/2009	0.51%	0.20%	_____
3/17/2009	0.31%	0.23%	_____	4/1/2009	0.30%	0.21%	_____
3/18/2009	0.31%	0.21%	_____	4/2/2009	0.29%	0.20%	_____
3/19/2009	0.30%	0.19%	_____	4/3/2009	0.27%	0.20%	_____
3/20/2009	0.28%	0.20%	_____	4/6/2009	0.28%	0.19%	_____
3/23/2009	0.29%	0.19%	_____	4/7/2009	0.28%	0.19%	_____
3/24/2009	0.29%	0.21%	_____	4/8/2009	0.26%	0.18%	_____
3/25/2009	0.29%	0.18%	_____	4/9/2009	0.26%	0.18%	_____
3/26/2009	0.29%	0.14%	_____	4/14/2009	0.27%	0.17%	_____

INTERNET ACTIVITIES

1. *The New York Times* **& Times Topics.** The online version of the *The New York Times* has a special section entitled "Times Topics"—issues of continuing interest and coverage by the publication. The current financial crisis is covered and updated regularly here.

   The New York Times & Times Topics   topics.nytimes.com/topics/reference/timestopics/subjects/c/credit_crisis/

2. **British Bankers Association and LIBOR.** The British Bankers Association (BBA), the author of LIBOR, provides both current data for LIBOR of varying maturities as well as timely studies of interbank market behavior and practices.

   British Bankers Association and LIBOR   www.bbalibor.com

3. **Bank for International Settlements.** The Bank for International Settlements (BIS) publishes regular assessments of international banking activity. Use the BIS Web site to find up-to-date analysis of the ongoing credit crisis.

   Bank for International Settlements   www.bis.org/

4. **Federal Reserve Bank of New York.** The New York Fed maintains an interactive map of mortgage and credit card delinquencies for the United States. Use the following Web site to view the latest in default rates according to the Fed.

   Federal Reserve Bank of New York   data.newyorkfed.org/creditconditionsmap/

Foreign Exchange Theory and Markets

CHAPTER 6

The Foreign Exchange Market

The best way to destroy the capitalist system is to debauch the currency. By a continuing process of inflation, governments can confiscate, secretly and unobserved, an important part of the wealth of their citizens.

—John Maynard Keynes.

The foreign exchange market provides the physical and institutional structure through which the money of one country is exchanged for that of another country, the rate of exchange between currencies is determined, and foreign exchange transactions are physically completed. *Foreign exchange* means the money of a foreign country; that is, foreign currency bank balances, banknotes, checks, and drafts. A *foreign exchange transaction* is an agreement between a buyer and seller that a fixed amount of one currency will be delivered for some other currency at a specified rate.

This chapter describes the following features of the foreign exchange market:

- Its geographical extent
- Its three main functions
- Its participants
- Its immense daily transaction volume
- Types of transactions, including spot, forward, and swap transactions
- Methods of stating exchange rates, quotations, and changes in exchange rates

Geographical Extent of the Foreign Exchange Market

The foreign exchange market spans the globe, with prices moving and currencies trading somewhere every hour of every business day. Major world trading starts each morning in Sydney and Tokyo, moves west to Hong Kong and Singapore, passes on to Bahrain, shifts to the main European markets of Frankfurt, Zurich, and London, jumps the Atlantic to New York, goes west to Chicago, and ends in San Francisco and Los Angeles. Many large international banks operate foreign exchange trading rooms in each major geographic trading center in order to serve important commercial accounts on a 24-hour-a-day basis. Global currency trading is indeed a 24-hour-a-day process. As shown in Exhibit 6.1, the volume of currency transactions ebbs and flows across the globe as the major currency trading centers of London, New York, and Tokyo open and close throughout the day.

In some countries, a portion of foreign exchange trading is conducted on an official trading floor by open bidding. Closing prices are published as the official price, or "fixing," for the day and certain commercial and investment transactions are based on this official price. Business firms in countries with exchange controls often must surrender foreign exchange earned from exports to the central bank at the daily fixing price.

Banks engaged in foreign exchange trading are connected by highly sophisticated telecommunications networks. Professional dealers and brokers obtain exchange rate quotes on desktop computer screens and communicate with each other by telephone, computer, fax, and telex. The foreign exchange departments of many nonbank business firms also use computer networks to keep in touch with the market and to seek out the best quotations. Reuters, Telerate, and Bloomberg are the leading suppliers of foreign exchange rate information and trading systems. A recent development has been the introduction of automated "matching" systems into computerized quotation systems. Many dealers think computer-executed transactions will replace other, more conventional trading systems in the near future.

Functions of the Foreign Exchange Market

The foreign exchange market is the mechanism by which participants transfer purchasing power between countries, obtain or provide credit for international trade transactions, and minimize exposure to the risks of exchange rate changes.

■ Transfer of purchasing power is necessary because international trade and capital transactions normally involve parties living in countries with different national currencies. Each party usually wants to deal in its own currency, but the trade or

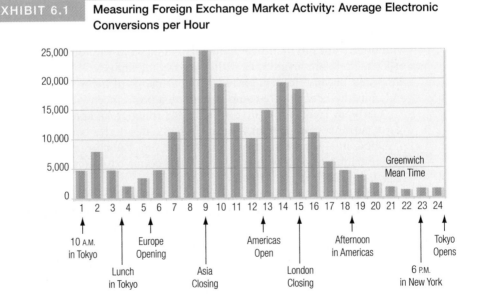

EXHIBIT 6.1   Measuring Foreign Exchange Market Activity: Average Electronic Conversions per Hour

Source: Federal Reserve Bank of New York, "The Foreign Exchange Market in the United States," 2001, http://www.ny.frb.org.

capital transaction can be invoiced in only one currency. Hence, one party must deal in a foreign currency.

- Because the movement of goods between countries takes time, inventory in transit must be financed. The foreign exchange market provides a source of credit. Specialized instruments, such as bankers' acceptances and letters of credit, are available to finance international trade. These documents will be explained in Chapter 20.

- The foreign exchange market provides "hedging" facilities for transferring foreign exchange risk to someone else more willing to carry risk. These facilities are explained in Chapter 9.

Market Participants

The foreign exchange market consists of two tiers: the interbank or wholesale market, and the client or retail market. Individual transactions in the interbank market are usually for large sums that are multiples of a million U.S. dollars or the equivalent value in other currencies. By contrast, contracts between a bank and its clients are usually for specific amounts.

Four broad categories of participants operate within these two tiers: bank and nonbank foreign exchange dealers, individuals and firms conducting commercial or investment transactions, speculators and arbitragers, and central banks and treasuries.

Bank and Nonbank Foreign Exchange Dealers

Banks, and a few nonbank foreign exchange dealers, operate in both the interbank and client markets. They profit from buying foreign exchange at a *bid* price and reselling it at a slightly higher *ask* (also called *offer*) price. Competition among dealers worldwide narrows the spread between bid and ask and so contributes to making the foreign exchange market efficient in the same sense as in securities markets.

Dealers in the foreign exchange departments of large international banks often function as *market makers*. Such dealers stand willing at all times to buy and sell those currencies in which they specialize and thus maintain an inventory position in those currencies. They trade with other banks in their own monetary centers and with other centers around the world in order to maintain inventories within the trading limits set by bank policy. Trading limits are important because foreign exchange departments of many banks operate as profit centers, and individual dealers are compensated on a profit incentive basis.

Currency trading is quite profitable for commercial and investment banks. Many of the major currency-trading banks in the United States derive between 10% and 20% on average of their annual net income from currency trading. But currency trading is also very profitable for the bank's traders, who typically earn a bonus based on the profitability to the bank of their individual trading activities.

Small- to medium-size banks are likely to participate but not be market makers in the interbank market. Instead of maintaining significant inventory positions, they buy from and sell to larger banks to offset retail transactions with their own customers. Of course, even market-making banks do not make markets in every currency. They trade for their own account in those currencies of most interest to their customers and become participants when filling customer needs in less important currencies. *Global Finance in Practice 6.1* describes a typical foreign exchange dealer's day.

Individuals and Firms Conducting Commercial and Investment Transactions

Importers and exporters, international portfolio investors, MNEs, tourists, and others use the foreign exchange market to facilitate execution of commercial or investment transactions.

GLOBAL FINANCE IN PRACTICE 6.1

The Foreign Exchange Dealer's Day

How do foreign exchange dealers prepare for their working day? Foreign exchange dealing in Europe is officially opened at 8 A.M., but the dealer's work starts at least one hour earlier. Every morning, the chief dealers give their staff guidelines for their dealing activities. They will reassess their strategy on the basis of their estimation of the market over the next few months. They will also decide their tactics for the day, based on the following factors:

- **Trading activities in the past few hours in New York and the Far East.** Because of the time difference, banks in New York will have continued trading for several hours longer than the banks in Europe, while in the Far East the working day is already closing when the European day begins.

- **New economic and political developments.** Following the theoretical forces that determine exchange rates, changes in interest rates, economic indicators, and monetary aggregates are the fundamental factors influencing exchange rates. Political events such as military conflicts, social unrest, the fall of a government, and so on, can also influence, and sometimes even dominate, the market scene.

- **The bank's own foreign exchange position.**

Early in the morning, market makers use electronic information systems to catch up on any events of the past night that might impact exchange rates. Charts, graphic presentations of market movements, and screen-based rate boards allow dealers to study the latest developments in exchange rates in New York and the Far East. As soon as this preparatory work is completed, the dealers will be ready for international trades (between 8 A.M. and 5 P.M.).

The day starts with a series of telephone calls between the key market players; the aim being to sound out what intentions are. Until recently, brokers also acted as intermediaries in foreign exchange and money market operations. Nowadays, however, the Electronic Broking System (EBS) has largely replaced the activities of the brokers themselves. The original brokers used to work with minimum amounts, such as US$5 million, whereas the EBS allows flexible trading from US$1 to $999 million. EBS does not only deal in U.S. dollars, however. Currencies such as EUR/CHF, EUR/JPY, and EUR/GBP are also traded. This means that the continuity of rate determination is substantially higher, as a larger number of smaller amounts, previously negotiated privately between banks, now play a role in setting rates. Another advantage of this system is that the rates are always available onscreen.

Source: Foreign Exchange and Money Market Transactions, UBS Investment Bank, Spring 2004.

Their use of the foreign exchange market is necessary but nevertheless incidental to their underlying commercial or investment purpose. Some of these participants use the market to "hedge" foreign exchange risk.

Speculators and Arbitragers

Speculators and arbitragers seek to profit from trading in the market itself. They operate in their own interest, without a need or obligation to serve clients or to ensure a continuous market. Where dealers seek profit from the spread between bid and offer in addition to what they might gain from changes in exchange rates, speculators seek all of their profit from exchange rate changes. Arbitragers try to profit from simultaneous exchange rate differences in different markets.

A large proportion of speculation and arbitrage is conducted on behalf of major banks by traders employed by those banks. Thus, banks act both as exchange dealers and as speculators and arbitragers. (However, banks seldom admit to speculating; they characterize themselves as "taking an aggressive position"!)

Central Banks and Treasuries

Central banks and treasuries use the market to acquire or spend their country's foreign exchange reserves as well as to influence the price at which their own currency is traded. They may act to support the value of their own currency because of policies adopted at the national level or because of commitments entered into through membership in joint float agreements, such as the European Monetary System (EMS) central bank's agreements that preceded introduction of the euro. Consequently, the motive is not to earn a profit as such, but rather to influence the foreign exchange value of their currency in a manner that will benefit the interests of their citizens. In many instances they do their job best when they willingly take a loss on their foreign exchange transactions. As willing loss takers, central banks and treasuries differ in motive and behavior from all other market participants.

Communications in the Interbank Market

Rapidly evolving technology in telecommunications is quickly changing the communications of the interbank market. There is little face-to-face trading (except in those few countries still using trading floors). Currently, most foreign exchange transactions are still executed by phone. However, electronic trading will probably soon replace the phone.

Continuous Linked Settlement and Fraud

In September 2002, the Continuous Linked Settlement (CLS) system was introduced. CLS eliminates losses if either party of a foreign exchange transaction is unable to settle with the other party. CLS system links the Real-Time Gross Settlement (RTGS) systems in seven major currencies. It is expected to eventually result in same-day settlement rather than needing the current two days.

The CLS system should help counteract fraud in the foreign exchange markets. In the United States, the Commodity Futures Modernization Act of 2000 gives the responsibility for regulating foreign exchange trading fraud to the U.S. Commodity Futures Trading Commission (CFTC).

Transactions in the Interbank Market

Transactions in the foreign exchange market can be executed on a *spot*, *forward*, or *swap* basis. A broader definition of the foreign exchange market includes foreign currency options and futures (covered in Chapter 8). A *spot* transaction requires almost immediate delivery of foreign exchange. A *forward* transaction requires delivery of foreign exchange at some future date, either on an "outright" basis or through a "futures" contract. A *swap* transaction is the simultaneous exchange of one foreign currency for another.

Spot Transactions

A spot transaction in the interbank market is the purchase of foreign exchange, with delivery and payment between banks to take place, normally, on the second following business day. The Canadian dollar settles with the U.S. dollar on the first following business day.

The date of settlement is referred to as the *value date*. On the value date, most dollar transactions in the world are settled through the computerized Clearing House Interbank Payments System (CHIPS) in New York, which provides for calculation of net balances owed by any one bank to another and for payment by 6 P.M. that same day in Federal Reserve Bank of New York funds.

A typical spot transaction in the interbank market might involve a U.S. bank contracting on a Monday for the transfer of £10,000,000 to the account of a London bank. If the spot exchange rate were $1.8420/£, the U.S. bank would transfer £10,000,000 to the London bank on Wednesday, and the London bank would transfer $18,420,000 to the U.S. bank at the same time. A spot transaction between a bank and its commercial customer would not necessarily involve a wait of two days for settlement.

Outright Forward Transactions

An *outright forward transaction* (usually called just a *forward*) requires delivery at a future value date of a specified amount of one currency for a specified amount of another currency. The exchange rate is established at the time of the agreement, but payment and delivery are not required until maturity. Forward exchange rates are normally quoted for value dates of one, two, three, six, and twelve months. Actual contracts can be arranged for other numbers of months or, on occasion, for periods of more than one year. Payment is on the second business day after the even-month anniversary of the trade. Thus, a two-month forward transaction entered into on March 18 will be for a value date of May 20, or the next business day if May 20 falls on a weekend or holiday.

Note that as a matter of terminology we can speak of "buying forward" or "selling forward" to describe the same transaction. A contract to deliver dollars for euros in six months is buying euros forward for dollars and selling dollars forward for euros.

Swap Transactions

A swap transaction in the interbank market is the simultaneous purchase and sale of a given amount of foreign exchange for two different value dates. Both purchase and sale are conducted with the same counterparty. A common type of swap is a *spot against forward*. The dealer buys a currency in the spot market and simultaneously sells the same amount back to the same bank in the forward market. Because this is executed as a single transaction with one counterparty, the dealer incurs no unexpected foreign exchange risk. Swap transactions and outright forwards combined made up 57% of all foreign exchange market activity in April 2004.

Forward-Forward Swaps. A more sophisticated swap transaction is called a *forward-forward swap*. A dealer sells £20,000,000 forward for dollars for delivery in, say, two months at $1.8420/£ and simultaneously buys £20,000,000 forward for delivery in three months at $1.8400/£. The difference between the buying price and the selling price is equivalent to the interest rate differential—that is, interest rate parity; between the two currencies. Thus, a swap can be viewed as a technique for borrowing another currency on a fully collateralized basis.

Nondeliverable Forwards (NDFs). Created in the early 1990s, the *nondeliverable forward*, or NDF, is now a relatively common derivative offered by the largest providers of foreign exchange derivatives. NDFs possess the same characteristics and documentation requirements as traditional forward contracts, except that they are settled only in U.S. dollars and the foreign currency being sold forward or bought forward is not delivered. The dollar-settlement feature reflects the fact that NDFs are contracted offshore—for example, in New York for a Mexican investor—and so are beyond the reach and regulatory frameworks of the home country governments (Mexico in this case). NDFs are traded internationally using standards set by the International Swaps and Derivatives Association (ISDA). Although originally envisioned to be a method of currency hedging, it is now estimated that more than 70% of all NDF trading is for speculation purposes.

NDFs are used primarily for emerging market currencies, currencies that typically do not have open spot market currency trading, liquid money markets, or quoted Eurocurrency interest rates. Although most NDF trading focused on Latin American currencies in the 1990s, many Asian currencies have been very widely traded in the post-1997 Asian crisis era. In general, NDF markets normally develop for country currencies having large cross-border capital movements, but still subject to convertibility restrictions. Trading in recent years has been dominated by the Korean won, Chilean peso, Taiwanese dollar, Brazilian reais, and Chinese renminbi.

Pricing of NDFs reflects basic interest differentials, as with regular forward contracts, plus some additional premium charged by the bank for dollar settlement. If, however, there is no accessible or developed money market for interest rate setting, the pricing of the NDF takes on a much more speculative element. Without true interest rates, traders often price on the basis of what they believe spot rates may be at the time of settlement. For example, in the fall of 2003, NDFs on the Chinese renminbi fell to record lows (meaning a very strong renminbi against the dollar) because most currency traders and analysts were expecting the Chinese government to revalue the renminbi very soon.[1]

NDFs are traded and settled outside the country of the subject currency, and therefore are beyond the control of the country's government. In the past this has created a difficult situation, in which the NDF market then serves as something of a gray market in the trading of that currency. For example, in late 2001 Argentina was under increasing pressure to abandon its fixed exchange rate regime of one peso equaling one U.S. dollar. The NDF market began quoting rates of Ps1.05/$ and Ps1.10/$, in effect a devalued peso, for NDFs settling within the next year. This led to increasing speculative pressure against the peso, and the ire of the Argentine government.

NDFs, however, have proven to be something of an imperfect replacement for traditional forward contracts. The problems with NDFs typically involve its "fixing of spot rate on the fixing date." This the spot rate at the end of the contract used to calculate the settlement. In times of financial crisis, for example the Venezuelan bolivar in 2003, the government of the subject currency may suspend foreign exchange trading in the spot market for an extended period of time. Without an official fixing rate, the NDF cannot be settled. In the case of Venezuela, the problem was compounded when a new official "devalued bolivar" was announced, but still not traded. As described in *Global Finance in Practice 6.2*, NDFs are particularly active in the Chinese renminbi.

GLOBAL FINANCE IN PRACTICE 6.2

A Hedge Against Foreign Exchange Exposure?

When Beijing announced the 2.1 per cent revaluation of the renminbi late on July 21, traders at Deutsche Bank in Singapore had to rejig their plans for the evening. "It was chaotic because everyone had already left the office," says Mirza Baig, currency strategist at Deutsche. "Traders had to rush back to their desks to look at their exposure, particularly in terms of short positions." Currency traders were focusing on the market for renminbi non-deliverable forwards; offshore derivatives that are mainly traded by big international banks in Singapore.

NDFs are widely used by hedge funds betting on the value of currencies that are not fully convertible. However, Beijing policymakers have not publicly expressed any interest in the informational value of the market, despite the paucity of other credible indicators for the Chinese currency. Nor does the NDF market receive much attention in the Chinese press, which focuses on trading in the central

bank-dominated domestic foreign exchange market. Forwards are over-the-counter agreements in which assets are traded at current prices for delivery after a specified period, normally ranging from one month to one year. Renminbi forwards are "non-deliverable," because they are settled in US dollars.

One official at the People's Bank of China, the country's central bank, dismisses suggestions that NDF prices might play a role in the renminbi's new rate-setting regime, which is formally known as a managed float based on "market supply and demand with reference to a basket of currencies." "NDFs are not a currency; they are just a kind of contract, so they are not in our basket," the official says. "It's not in this basket, so it will certainly not be considered [in setting the exchange rate]."

Still, with an average daily trading volume of about US$500m, the renminbi NDF market is more than just a playground for a few trigger-happy hedge funds. For example, big

---

[1]For an excellent in-depth analysis of the NDF market see "An Overview of Non-Deliverable Foreign Forward Exchange Markets," by Laura Lipscomb, Federal Reserve Bank of New York, May 2005.

international companies with operations in mainland China tend to use NDFs to hedge their foreign currency exposure. One Hong Kong-based treasurer at a big international group says US companies are particularly keen to avoid currency translation effects on their balance sheets. "They tend to have very conservative internal accounting policies," he adds. "They are saying: 'we understand that the renminbi is a one-way bet at the moment, but we don't care.'"

International companies might also want to use NDF contracts because they are sourcing from Chinese suppliers and because some of their costs are denominated in renminbi. Mr Baig at Deutsche believes some companies will be

keen to "lock in" bullish market expectations. One-year NDF contracts suggest the renminbi will rise by about 5 per cent from its revalued level. "Hedging gives them certainty for their profit forecasts for the next 12 months," he adds.

Others, however, remain skeptical. "Often, the expectations in the NDF market are quite exaggerated, compared with what companies [on the ground] think," says Stephen Green, senior economist at Standard Chartered Bank. "There is no point in using this market for hedging if you think it is out of line."

Source: "A Hedge Against Forex Exposure," *Financial Times*, August 2, 2005.

Size of the Market

The Bank for International Settlements (BIS), in conjunction with central banks around the world, conducts a survey of currency trading activity every three years. The most recent survey, conducted in April 2007, estimated *daily* global net turnover in foreign exchange market activity to be $3.2 trillion. This was a massive increase of nearly 70% over the 2004 survey's estimate of $1.9 trillion. The BIS data for surveys between 1989 and 2007 is shown in Exhibit 6.2.

Global foreign exchange turnover in Exhibit 6.2 is divided into three categories of currency instruments: spot transactions, forward transactions, and swap transactions. All three

EXHIBIT 6.2   Global Foreign Exchange Market Turnover, 1989–2007 (daily averages in April, billions of U.S. dollars)

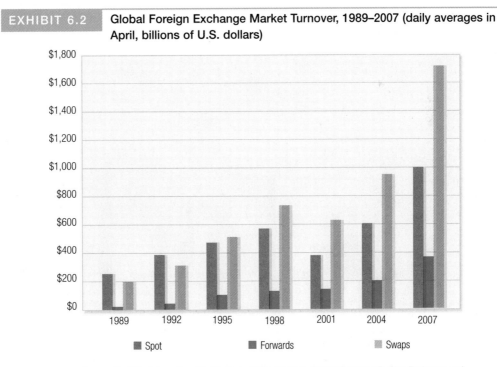

Source: Bank for International Settlements, "Triennial Central Bank Survey of Foreign Exchange and Derivatives Market Activity in April 2007: Preliminary Global Results," October 2007, www.bis.org.

categories of currency transactions rose significantly between 2004 and 2007, a distinct change relative to what had been seen in the 2001 and 2004 surveys.

- Spot transactions grew from $621 billion per day in 2004 to $1,005 billion in 2007, an increase of 62%.

- Outright forward transactions grew from $208 billion per day in 2004 to $363 billion in 2007, an increase of 74%.

- Swap transactions, showing the greatest growth, grew from $944 billion per day in 2004 to more than $1,714 billion in 2007, an increase of 82%.

Why the enormous increase? The BIS believes a combination of three main forces drove the growth. First, a significant expansion in the activity of a variety of specialized investment groups including hedge funds. Second, a trend for institutional investors with a longer term investment horizon toward holding more internationally diversified portfolios—which in turn requires the exchange of currencies. And third, a marked increase in the levels of technical computer-based trading—most notably algorithmic trading.

Exhibit 6.3 shows the proportionate share of foreign exchange trading for the most important national markets in the world in 2007. Note that although the data is collected and reported on a national basis, designations like "the United States" should largely be interpreted as "New York," due to the fact that the great majority of foreign exchange trading takes place in the major city of each country. This is most true for "the United Kingdom" and "London."

EXHIBIT 6.3 Top 10 Geographic Trading Centers in the Foreign Exchange Market, 1992–2007 (daily averages in April, billions of U.S. dollars)

Source: Bank for International Settlements, Triennial Central Bank Survey of Foreign Exchange and Derivatives Market Activity in April 2007: Preliminary Global Results," September 2007, www.bis.org.

Clearly, the United Kingdom (London) continues to be the center of world foreign exchange activity, with $1,359 billion in daily foreign exchange turnover, a dominant 34.1% of daily world exchange. The United States (New York) remains second largest at $664 billion in daily activity, making up 16.6% of global trading. London and New York alone now make up 50% of all foreign exchange market activity, a concentration not seen since the BIS has been surveying the markets.

There has been also significant change in the activity levels of other major foreign exchange trading nations. Switzerland has moved up markedly in recent years, now being the third largest trading center with 6.1% of world trading, followed by Japan (6%), Singapore (5.8%), Hong Kong (4.4%), Australia (4.2%), France (3%), Germany (2.5%), and at tenth—Denmark (2.2%). Hong Kong is another center of trading activity that has grown markedly in recent years, primarily as in its role as a key economic and financial linkage to the rapidly rising Chinese economy. Interestingly, Australia has grown considerably in recent years reflecting the demand for currency trading related to what is termed the *carry trade*, in which capital flows into the country in pursuit of high interest rate returns. This topic is covered in detail in Chapter 7.

The currency composition of turnover, shown in Exhibit 6.4, also has demonstrated change in recent years. Because all currencies are traded against some other currency, all percentages shown in Exhibit 6.4 are for that currency versus another currency; in this case, the U.S. dollar. The trends are relatively clear: the U.S. dollar/euro cross-rate and the Japanese yen/U.S. dollar cross-rate have been slowly trending downward, although quite slowly. What is clear, however, is that a number of other currencies such as the Australian dollar, have increased in their volume activity. The rising share of the Hong Kong dollar was also notable, probably reflecting Hong Kong's economic and financial linkages to China's economic growth. An added note, which is not reflected in Exhibit 6.4 itself, is the growth in emerging market currencies. For the first time the share of emerging market currencies increased, constituting more than 20% of all transactions in April 2007.

EXHIBIT 6.4   Foreign Exchange Market Turnover by Currency Pair (Daily averages in April)

Note: All currencies are versus the U.S. dollar.
Source: Bank for International Settlements, "Triennial Central Bank Survey for Foreign Exchange and Derivatives Market Activity in April 2007: Preliminary Global Results," September 2007. www.bis.org.

Foreign Exchange Rates and Quotations

A foreign exchange *rate* is the price of one currency expressed in terms of another currency. A foreign exchange *quotation* (or *quote*) is a statement of willingness to buy or sell at an announced rate.

In the retail market (including newspapers and foreign exchange booths at airports), quotes are most often given as the home currency price of the foreign currency and are also given for many currency pairs. However, this practice is not uniform worldwide. As described in the next section, the professional interbank market has standardized its quotation system.

Interbank Quotations

Recall from Exhibit 6.4 that most foreign exchange transactions are through the U.S. dollar. Professional dealers and brokers may state foreign exchange quotations in one of two ways: the foreign currency price of one dollar or the dollar price of one unit of foreign currency. Most foreign currencies in the world are stated in terms of the number of units of foreign currency needed to buy one dollar. For example, the exchange rate between U.S. dollars and Swiss francs is normally stated as follows:

SF1.6000/$, read as "1.6000 Swiss francs per dollar"

This method, called *European terms*, expresses the rate as the foreign currency price of one U.S. dollar. An alternative method is called *American terms*. The same exchange rate expressed in American terms is as follows:

$0.6250/SF, read as "0.6250 dollars per Swiss franc"

Under American terms, foreign exchange rates are stated as the U.S. dollar price of one unit of foreign currency. Note that European terms and American terms are reciprocals:

$$\frac{1}{\text{SF1.6000/\$}} = \$0.6250/\text{SF}$$

With several exceptions, including two important ones, most interbank quotations around the world are stated in European terms. Thus, throughout the world, the normal way of quoting the relationship between the Swiss franc and U.S. dollar is SF1.6000/$; this method may also be called "Swiss terms." A Japanese yen quote of ¥118.32/$ is called "Japanese terms," although the expression "European terms" is often used as the generic name for Asian as well as European currency prices of the dollar. European terms were adopted as the universal way of expressing foreign exchange rates for most (but not all) currencies in 1978 to facilitate worldwide trading through telecommunications.

As mentioned, several exceptions exist to the use of European terms quotes. The two most important are quotes for the euro and for the U.K. pound sterling. The euro, first traded in January 1999, and the U.K. pound sterling are both normally quoted in American terms; that is, the U.S. dollar price of a euro or a pound sterling. Additionally, Australian dollars and New Zealand dollars are normally quoted on American terms. Sterling is quoted as the foreign currency price of one pound for historical reasons. For centuries, the British pound sterling consisted of 20 shillings, each of which had 12 pence. Multiplication and division with the nondecimal currency were difficult. The custom evolved for foreign exchange prices in London, then the undisputed financial capital of the world, to be stated in foreign currency units per pound. This practice remained even after sterling changed to decimals in 1971.

American terms are used in quoting rates for most foreign currency options and futures, as well as in retail markets that deal with tourists and personal remittances. Foreign exchange traders use nicknames for major currencies. *Cable* means the exchange rate between U.S.

dollars and U.K. pound sterling, the name dating from the time when transactions in dollars and pounds were carried out over the transatlantic telegraph cable. A Canadian dollar is a *loonie*, named after the waterfowl on Canada's one-dollar coin. *Paris* means the French franc, *kiwi* stands for the New Zealand dollar, *Aussie* for the Australian dollar, *Swissie* for Swiss francs, and *Sing dollar* for the Singapore dollar.

Currency amounts must be precise in foreign exchange conversations to avoid major blunders. Unfortunately, British and U.S. English meaning differs for the word "billion." For the British, "one billion" is 1 followed by 12 zeros: 1,000,000,000,000 or a million million. In the United States and France, where the system of numeration is based on groups of threes rather than fours, "one billion" is a thousand million, or 1,000,000,000. For the British, a "trillion" is a million billions, while in U.S. and French usage a "trillion" is a thousand billions, the same as one British billion.[2] To avoid confusion, foreign exchange traders use the word *yard* to describe a U.S. billion.

Direct and Indirect Quotes

Foreign exchange quotes are at times described as either *direct or indirect*. In this pair of definitions, the home or base country of the currencies being discussed is critical.

A *direct quote* is a home currency price of a unit of foreign currency, and an *indirect quote* is a foreign currency price of a unit of home currency. The form of the quote depends on what the speaker regards as home.

The foreign exchange quote SF1.6000/$ is a direct quote in Switzerland—it is the Swiss home currency (Swiss franc) price of a foreign currency (U.S. dollar). Exactly the same quotation, SF1.6000/$, is an indirect quotation when used in the United States—it is now the foreign currency (Swiss franc) price of the home currency (U.S. dollar). The reciprocal of this quote, $0.6250/SF, is a direct quote in the United States and an indirect quote in Switzerland.

The direct dollar quote against the Swiss franc, $0.6250/SF in the previous example, may also be referred to as the "external value of the Swiss franc"—that is, the value of one Swiss franc outside of Switzerland. The internal value of the Swiss franc is SF1.6000/$—the number of Swiss francs that can be purchased for one dollar.

Bid and Ask Quotations

Interbank quotations are given as a *bid* and *ask* (also referred to as *offer*). A bid is the price (that is, exchange rate) in one currency at which a dealer will buy another currency. An ask is the price (that is, exchange rate) at which a dealer will sell the other currency. Dealers bid (buy) at one price and ask (sell) at a slightly higher price, making their profit from the spread between the buying and selling prices.

Bid and ask quotations in the foreign exchange markets are superficially complicated by the fact that the bid for one currency is also the offer for the opposite currency. A trader seeking to buy dollars with Swiss francs is simultaneously offering to sell Swiss francs for dollars. Assume a bank makes the quotations shown in the top half of Exhibit 6.5 for the Japanese yen. The spot quotations on the first line indicate that the bank's foreign exchange trader will buy dollars (that is, sell Japanese yen) at the bid price of ¥118.27 per dollar. The trader will sell dollars (that is, buy Japanese yen) at the ask price of ¥118.37 per dollar.

As illustrated in Exhibit 6.5, however, the full *outright quotation* (the full price to all of its decimal points) is typically shown only for the current spot rate. Traders, however, tend to abbreviate when talking on the phone or putting quotations on a video screen. The first term,

---

[2]*The Shorter Oxford English Dictionary on Historical Principles*, third edition, Volumes I and II, Oxford: Clarendon Press, 1973.

EXHIBIT 6.5	Spot and Forward Quotations for the Euro and Japanese Yen

	Term	Euro: Spot and Forward ($/€)			Yen: Spot and Forward (¥/$)		
		Mid Rates	Bid	Ask	Mid Rates	Bid	Ask
	Spot	1.0899	1.0897	1.0901	118.32	118.27	118.37
Cash rates	1 week	1.0903	3	4	118.23	−10	−9
	1 mo	1.0917	17	19	117.82	−51	−50
	2 mo	1.0934	35	36	117.38	−95	−93
	3 mo	1.0953	53	54	116.91	−143	−140
	4 mo	1.0973	72	76	116.40	−195	−190
	5 mo	1.0992	90	95	115.94	−240	−237
	6 mo	1.1012	112	113	115.45	−288	−287
	9 mo	1.1075	175	177	114.00	−435	−429
	1 yr	1.1143	242	245	112.50	−584	−581
Swap rates	2 yr	1.1401	481	522	106.93	−1150	−1129
	3 yr	1.1679	750	810	101.09	−1748	−1698
	4 yr	1.1899	960	1039	96.82	−2185	−2115
	5 yr	1.2102	1129	1276	92.91	−2592	−2490

Note: *mo* is month, *yr* is year. Mid rates are the numerical averages of bid and ask.

the bid, of a spot quotation may be given in full: that is, "118.27." However, the second term, the ask, will probably be expressed only as the digits that differ from the bid. Hence, on a video screen the bid and ask for spot yen would probably be shown as "118.27–37."

Expressing Forward Quotations on a Points Basis

The spot quotations given in the top line for each currency in Exhibit 6.5 are *outright*: ¥118.27/$ for the spot bid and ¥118.37/$ for the spot ask. The forward rates are, however, typically quoted in terms of *points*, also referred to as *cash rates* and *swap rates*, depending on maturity. A point is the last digit of a quotation, with convention dictating the number of digits to the right of the decimal point. Currency prices for the U.S. dollar are usually expressed to four decimal points. Hence, a point is equal to 0.0001 of most currencies. Some currencies, such as the Japanese yen shown in Exhibit 6.5, are quoted only to two decimal points. A forward quotation expressed in points is not a foreign exchange rate as such. Rather, it is the difference between the forward rate and the spot rate. Consequently the spot rate itself can never be given on a points basis.

The three-month points quotations for the Japanese yen in Exhibit 6.5 are −143 bid and −140 ask. The first number (−143) refers to points away from the spot bid, and the second number (−140) to points away from the spot ask. Given the outright quotes of 118.27 bid and 118.37 ask, the outright three-month forward rates are calculated as follows:

	Bid	Ask
Outright spot:	¥118.27	¥118.37
plus points (three months)	−1.43	−1.40
Outright forward:	¥116.84	¥116.97

The forward bid and ask quotations in Exhibit 6.5 for two years or longer are called *swap rates*. As mentioned earlier, many forward exchange transactions in the interbank market involve a simultaneous purchase for one date and sale (reversing the transaction) for another date. This "swap" is a way to borrow one currency for a limited time while giving up the use of another currency for the same time. In other words, it is a short-term borrowing of one currency combined with a short-term loan of an equivalent amount of another currency. The two parties could, if they wanted, charge each other interest at the going rate for each of the currencies. However, it is easier for the party with the higher-interest currency to simply pay the net interest differential to the other. The swap rate expresses this *net* interest differential on a points basis rather than as an interest rate.

Forward Quotations in Percentage Terms

Forward quotations may also be expressed as the percent-per-annum deviation from the spot rate. This method of quotation facilitates comparing premiums or discounts in the forward market with interest rate differentials. However, the percent premium or discount depends on which currency is the home, or base, currency. Assume the following quotations, where the dollar is the home currency:

	Foreign currency/home currency	Home currency/foreign currency
Spot rate	¥105.65/$	$0.009465215/¥
Three-month forward	¥105.04/$	$0.009520183/¥

Quotations Expressed in Foreign Currency Terms (Indirect Quotations). When the foreign currency price of the home currency is used, the formula for the percent-per-annum premium or discount becomes

$$f^{\yen} = \frac{\text{Spot} - \text{Forward}}{\text{Forward}} \times \frac{360}{n} \times 100$$

Substituting ¥/$ spot and forward rates, as well as the number of days forward (90), we have

$$f^{\yen} = \frac{105.65 - 105.04}{105.04} \times \frac{360}{90} \times 100 = +2.32\% \text{ per annum}$$

The sign is positive, indicating that the forward yen is selling at a 2.32% per annum premium over the dollar.

Quotations Expressed in Home Currency Terms (Direct Quotations). When the home currency price for a foreign currency is used, the formula for the percent premium or discount ($f^{\yen}$) is

$$f^{\yen} = \frac{\text{Forward} - \text{Spot}}{\text{Spot}} \times \frac{360}{n} \times 100$$

where n is the number of days in the contract. (n may also be the number of months, in which case the numerator is 12.) Substituting the $/¥ spot and forward rates, as well as the number of days forward (90), we have

$$f^{\yen} = \frac{0.009520183 - 0.009465215}{0.009465215} \times \frac{360}{90} \times 100 = +2.32\% \text{ per annum}$$

The sign is positive, indicating that the forward yen is selling at a 2.32% per annum premium over the dollar.

Foreign Exchange Market Information

It is very important for all market participants to access "real-time" prices and news events. The main commercial information providers are Moneyline Telerate, Reuters, and Bloomberg. These commercial services offer computer-based service screens in all their customers' offices.

Foreign exchange rates are quoted in all major world newspapers. The manner of quotation in *The Wall Street Journal* and the *Financial Times*, the world's two major English-language business newspapers, is shown in Exhibit 6.6. Although these quotes for the pound are for the same day, they are not identical because of time zone differences and the banks surveyed for the quotes.

The Wall Street Journal gives American terms quotes under the heading "US$ equivalent" and European terms quotes under the heading "Currency per US$." Quotes are for the last two trading days and are given on an outright basis for spot, one-, three-, and six-month forwards. The exchange rates quoted are mid rates, the average of the bid-ask. Quotes are for trading among banks in amounts of $1 million or more, as quoted at 4 P.M. U.S. Eastern Standard Time by Reuters and other sources. The *Journal* states that retail transactions provide fewer units of foreign currency per dollar.

The *Financial Times* presents the latest day's closing mid rates as well, plus the absolute change in the rate from the previous trading day's close. One-month, three-month, and one-year forward rates are quoted in direct terms, U.S. dollars per pound. The rate in parentheses next to "U.K." is the current spot rate in British pounds per U.S. dollar.

Cross Rates

Many currency pairs are only inactively traded, so their exchange rate is determined through their relationship to a widely traded third currency. For example, a Mexican importer needs Japanese yen to pay for purchases in Tokyo. Both the Mexican peso (Ps) and the Japanese

---

EXHIBIT 6.6   Foreign Exchange Rate Quotations on the U.S. Dollar/British Pound in the Financial Press

The Wall Street Journal

	US$ Equivalent		Currency per US$	
	Thu	**Wed**	**Thu**	**Wed**
U.K. (pound)	1.8410	1.8343	.5432	.5452
one-month forward	1.8360	1.8289	.5447	.5468
three-months forward	1.8259	1.8187	.5477	.5498
six-months forward	1.8120	1.8048	.5519	.5541

Source: "Exchange Rates," *The Wall Street Journal*, Friday, June 4, 2004 (quotes for Thursday, June 3, 2004), p. B5.

Financial Times

	Closing Mid	**Day's Change**
U.K. (0.5429) (£)	1.8418	−0.0015
one month	1.8368	−0.0011
three month	1.8268	−0.0008
one year	1.7885	−0.0007

Source: "Currencies, Bonds & Interest Rates," *Financial Times*, June 4, 2004 (quotes are for June 3, 2004), p. 25.

yen (¥) are commonly quoted against the U.S. dollar. Assume the following quotes:

Japanese yen	¥110.73/$
Mexican peso	Ps11.4456/$

The Mexican importer can buy one U.S. dollar for 11.4456 Mexican pesos, and with that dollar buy 110.73 Japanese yen. The cross-rate calculation would be as follows:

$$\frac{\text{Japanese yen/U.S. dollar}}{\text{Mexican pesos/U.S. dollar}} = \frac{¥110.73/\$}{Ps\,11.4456/\$} = ¥\,9.6745/Ps$$

The cross rate could also be calculated as the reciprocal:

$$\frac{\text{Mexican peso/U.S. dollar}}{\text{Japanese yen/U.S. dollar}} = \frac{Ps\,11.4456/\$}{¥110.73/\$} = Ps\,0.1034/¥$$

In financial publications, cross rates often appear in the form of a matrix, as shown in Exhibit 6.7. This matrix shows the amount of each currency (columns) needed to buy a unit of the currency of the country on the line (row), as quoted by *The Wall Street Journal*.

Intermarket Arbitrage

Cross rates can be used to check on opportunities for intermarket arbitrage. Suppose that the following exchange rates are quoted:

Citibank quotes U.S. dollars per euro:	$1.2223/€
Barclays Bank quotes U.S. dollars per pound sterling:	$1.8410/£
Dresdner Bank quotes euros per pound sterling:	€1.5100/£

The cross rate between Citibank and Barclays is

$$\frac{\$1.8410/£}{\$1.2223/€} = €1.5062/£$$

This cross rate is not the same as Dresdner's quotation of €1.5100/£, so an opportunity exists to profit from arbitrage between the three markets. Exhibit 6.8A shows the steps in what is called *triangular arbitrage*.

EXHIBIT 6.7   Key Currency Cross Rates

	Dollar	Euro	Pound	Sfranc	Peso	Yen	CdnDir
Canada	1.3618	1.6646	2.5071	1.0889	.11898	.01230	—
Japan	110.73	135.34	203.85	88.539	9.674	—	81.309
Mexico	11.4456	13.9899	21.071	9.1519	—	.10336	8.4045
Switzerland	1.2506	1.5286	2.3024	—	.10927	.01129	.9183
U.K.	.54320	.6639	—	.4343	.04746	.00491	.39886
Euro	.81810	—	1.5062	.65418	.07148	.00739	.60075
U.S.	—	1.2223	1.8410	.79960	.08737	.00903	.73430

Source: Reuters, as quoted in "Key Currency Cross Rates," *The Wall Street Journal*, Friday, June 4, 2004. Quotes are for late New York trading, Thursday, June 3, 2004.

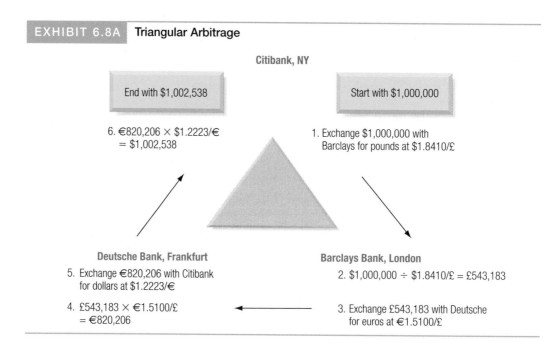

EXHIBIT 6.8A   Triangular Arbitrage

Citibank, NY

End with $1,002,538

Start with $1,000,000

6. €820,206 × $1.2223/€
   = $1,002,538

1. Exchange $1,000,000 with
   Barclays for pounds at $1.8410/£

Deutsche Bank, Frankfurt

5. Exchange €820,206 with Citibank
   for dollars at $1.2223/€

4. £543,183 × €1.5100/£
   = €820,206

Barclays Bank, London

2. $1,000,000 ÷ $1.8410/£ = £543,183

3. Exchange £543,183 with Deutsche
   for euros at €1.5100/£

A market trader with $1,000,000 can sell that sum spot to Barclays Bank for $1,000,000 ÷ $1.8410/£ = £543,183. Simultaneously, these pounds can be sold to Dresdner Bank for £543,183 × €1.5100/£ = €820,206, and the trader can then immediately sell these euro to Citibank for dollars: €820,206 × $1.2223/€ = $1,002,538. The profit on one such turn is a risk-free $2,538. Such triangular arbitrage can continue until exchange rate equilibrium is reestablished; that is, until the calculated cross rate equals the actual quotation, less any tiny margin for transaction costs.

Exhibit 6.8B shows a sensitivity analysis and the equilibrium exchange rate (no gain or loss) for the triangular arbitrage shown in Exhibit 6.8A. Note that when the Dresdner quote is less than the Barclays/Citibank, cross-rate, the loss can be reversed by moving money counter-clockwise to the triangular flow shown in Exhibit 6.8A. Therefore, it is always possible to profit when the intermediate quote and cross rate are different.

Exhibit 6.8B is the first time we use a spreadsheet construction of an exhibit. Spreadsheets have become a very common tool in all functional areas of business management in addition to their traditional uses in finance and accounting. Some exhibits in this book will use a spreadsheet form. The purpose is both to present important content and to give you some insight into how the content was constructed or calculated. We assume that you are already familiar with basic spreadsheet operations (calculation components are secondary to the purpose of the exhibit).

Two aspects should be noted: 1) Such arbitrage is practical only if the participants have instant access to quotes and executions. Hence, except in rare instances, such arbitrage is conducted only by foreign exchange traders. Public participation is most difficult. 2) Bank traders can conduct such arbitrage without an initial sum of money, other than their bank's credit standing, because the trades are entered into and subsequently "washed" (that is, offset) by electronic means before the normal settlement two days later.

EXHIBIT 6.8B Triangular Arbitrage

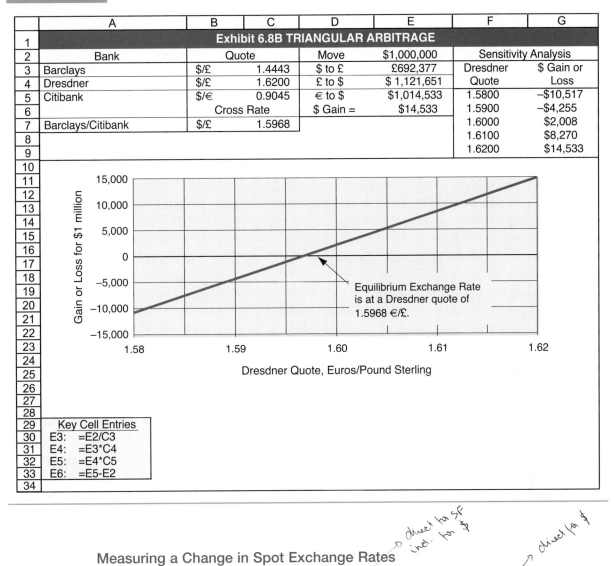

	A	B	C	D	E	F	G
1			Exhibit 6.8B TRIANGULAR ARBITRAGE				
2	Bank	Quote		Move	$1,000,000	Sensitivity Analysis	
3	Barclays	$/£	1.4443	$ to £	£692,377	Dresdner	$ Gain or
4	Dresdner	$/£	1.6200	£ to $	$ 1,121,651	Quote	Loss
5	Citibank	$/€	0.9045	€ to $	$1,014,533	1.5800	–$10,517
6		Cross Rate		$ Gain =	$14,533	1.5900	–$4,255
7	Barclays/Citibank	$/£	1.5968			1.6000	$2,008
8						1.6100	$8,270
9						1.6200	$14,533

Equilibrium Exchange Rate is at a Dresdner quote of 1.5968 €/£.

Dresdner Quote, Euros/Pound Sterling

	Key Cell Entries
E3:	=E2/C3
E4:	=E3*C4
E5:	=E4*C5
E6:	=E5-E2

Measuring a Change in Spot Exchange Rates

Assume that the Swiss franc, quoted at SF1.6351/$ (which is the same as $0.61158/SF), suddenly strengthens to SF1.5000/$ (which is the same as $0.66667/SF). What is the percent increase in the dollar value of the franc, and thus in the value of Swiss franc-denominated accounts receivable or payable held by Americans? As with forward quotations in percentage form, the home currency is critical.

Quotations Expressed in Home Currency Terms (Direct Quotations). When the home currency price for a foreign currency is used, the formula for the percent change in the foreign currency is as follows:

$$\%\Delta = \frac{\text{Ending rate} - \text{Beginning rate}}{\text{Beginning rate}} \times 100 = \frac{\$0.66667/\text{SF} - \$0.61158/\text{SF}}{\$0.61158/\text{SF}} \times 100 = +9.008\%$$

In this instance, the Swiss franc is 9.008% stronger at the ending rate. Holders of Swiss francs receivables will receive 9.008% more dollars, but those who owe Swiss francs will have to pay 9.008% more to buy them.

Quotations Expressed in Foreign Currency Terms (Indirect Quotations). When the foreign currency price of the home currency is used, the formula for the percent change in the foreign currency becomes

$$\%\Delta = \frac{\text{Beginning rate} - \text{Ending rate}}{\text{Ending rate}} \times 100 = \frac{\text{SF1.6351/\$} - \text{SF1.5000/\$}}{\text{SF1.5000/\$}} \times 100 = +9.008\%$$

By both methods of calculation, the Swiss franc increased 9.008% in value relative to the dollar.

A final note of clarity on this calculation. Many students perform these two calculations and find the two very close, but still differing values. If the second calculation (or vice versa) is calculated as follows, using the precise inverse quotes, the resulting percentage change will be precisely the same, + 9.008%.

$$\%\Delta = \frac{\text{Beginning rate} - \text{Ending rate}}{\text{Ending rate}} \times 100 = \frac{\dfrac{1}{\$0.61158/\text{SF}} - \dfrac{1}{\$0.66667/\text{SF}}}{\dfrac{1}{\$0.66667/\text{SF}}} \times 100 = +9.008\%$$

SUMMARY POINTS

- The three functions of the foreign exchange market are to transfer purchasing power, provide credit, and minimize foreign exchange risk.

- The foreign exchange market is composed of two tiers: the interbank market and the client market. Participants within these tiers include bank and non-bank foreign exchange dealers, individuals and firms conducting commercial and investment transactions, speculators and arbitragers, central banks and treasuries, and foreign exchange brokers.

- Geographically, the foreign exchange market spans the globe, with prices moving and currencies traded somewhere every hour of every business day.

- A foreign exchange *rate* is the price of one currency expressed in terms of another currency. A foreign exchange *quotation* is a statement of willingness to buy or sell currency at an announced price.

- Transactions within the foreign exchange market are executed either on a spot basis, requiring settlement two days after the transaction, or on a forward or swap basis, which requires settlement at some designated future date.

- *European terms* quotations are the foreign currency price of a U.S. dollar. *American terms* quotations are the dollar price of a foreign currency.

- Quotations can also be *direct* or *indirect*. A direct quote is the home currency price of a unit of foreign currency, while an indirect quote is the foreign currency price of a unit of home currency.

- Direct and indirect are *not* synonyms for American and European terms, because the home currency will change depending on who is doing the calculation, while European terms are always the foreign currency price of a dollar.

- A cross rate is an exchange rate between two currencies, calculated from their common relationships with a third currency. When cross rates differ from the direct rates between two currencies, intermarket arbitrage is possible.

MINI-CASE

The Venezuelan Bolivar Black Market[1]

Rumor has it that during the year and a half that Venezuelan President Hugo Chávez spent in jail for his role in a 1992 coup attempt against the government, he was a voracious reader. Too bad his prison syllabus seems to have been so skimpy on economics and so heavy on Machiavelli.

— *"Money Fun in the Venezuela of Hugo Chávez," The Economist, February 13, 2004.*

One late afternoon on March 10, 2004, Santiago opened the window of his office in Caracas, Venezuela. Immediately he was hit with the sounds rising from the plaza—cars honking, protesters banging their pots and pans, street vendors hawking their goods. Since the imposition of a new set of economic policies by President Hugo Chávez in 2002, such sights and sounds had become a fixture of city life in Caracas. Santiago sighed as he wished for the simplicity of life in the old Caracas.

Santiago's once-thriving pharmaceutical distribution business had hit hard times. Since capital controls were implemented in February 2003, dollars had been hard to come by. He had been forced to pursue various methods—methods that were more expensive and not always legal—to obtain dollars, causing his margins to decrease by 50%. To add to the strain the Venezuelan currency, the bolivar (Bs), had been recently devalued (repeatedly). This had instantly squeezed his margins as his costs had risen directly with the exchange rate. He could not find anyone to sell him dollars. His customers needed supplies and they needed them quickly, but how was he going to come up with the $30,000—the hard currency—to pay for his most recent order?

Political Chaos

Hugo Chávez's tenure as president of Venezuela had been tumultuous at best since his election in 1998. After repeated recalls, resignations, coups, and reappointments, the political turmoil had taken its toll on the Venezuelan economy as a whole, and on its currency in particular. The short-lived success of the anti-Chávez coup in 2001, and his nearly immediate return to office, had set the stage for a retrenchment of his isolationist economic and financial policies.

On January 21, 2003, the bolivar closed at a record low—Bs1891.50/$. The next day, President Chávez suspended the sale of dollars for two weeks. Nearly instantaneously, an unofficial or black market for the exchange of Venezuelan bolivars for foreign currencies (primarily U.S. dollars) sprouted. As investors of all kinds sought ways to exit the Venezuelan market, or simply to obtain the hard currency needed to continue to conduct their businesses (as was the case for Santiago), the escalating capital flight caused the black market value of the bolivar to plummet to Bs2500/$ in weeks. As markets collapsed and exchange values fell, the Venezuelan inflation rate soared to more than 30% per annum.

Capital Controls and CADIVI

To combat the downward pressures on the bolivar, on February 5, 2003, the Venezuelan government announced the passage of the *2003 Exchange Regulations Decree*.

The decree took the following actions:

1. Set the official exchange rate at Bs1596/$ for purchase (*bid*) and Bs1600/$ for sale (*offer*).

2. Established the Comisión de Administración de Divisas (CADIVI) to control the distribution of foreign exchange.

3. Implemented strict price controls to stem inflation triggered by the weaker bolivar and the exchange control-induced contraction of imports.

CADIVI was both the official means and the cheapest means by which Venezuelan citizens could obtain foreign currency. In order to receive an authorization from CADIVI to obtain dollars, an applicant was required to complete a series of forms. The applicant was then required to prove that they had paid taxes the previous three years, provide proof of business and asset ownership and lease agreements for company property, and document current Social Security payments.

Unofficially, however, there was an additional unstated requirement for permission to obtain foreign currency: that authorizations by CADIVI would be reserved for Chávez supporters. In August 2003, an anti-Chávez petition had gained widespread circulation. One million signatures had been collected. Although the government ruled that the petition was invalid, it had used the list of signatures to create a database of names and Social Security numbers that CADIVI utilized to cross-check identities when deciding who would receive hard currency. President Chávez was quoted as saying, "Not one more dollar for the *putschits* ("radicals" or coup-backers"); the bolivars belong to the people."[2]

Santiago's Alternatives

Santiago had little luck obtaining dollars via CADIVI to pay for his imports. Because he had signed the petition calling for President Chávez's removal, he had been listed in the CADIVI database as anti-Chávez, and now could not obtain permission to exchange bolivars for dollars.

The transaction in question was an invoice for $30,000 in pharmaceutical products from his U.S.-based supplier. Santiago would in turn sell to a large Venezuelan customer who would distribute the products. This transaction, however, was not the first time that Santiago had had to search out alternative sources for meeting his U.S. dollar obligations. Since the imposition of capital controls, the search for dollars had become a weekly activity for Santiago. In addition to the official process, through CADIVI, he could also obtain dollars through the *gray market*, or the *black market*.

The Gray Market: CANTV Shares

In May 2003, three months following the implementation of the exchange controls, a window of opportunity had opened up for Venezuelans—an opportunity that allowed investors in the Caracas stock exchange to avoid the tight foreign exchange curbs. This loophole circumvented the government-imposed restrictions by allowing investors to purchase local shares of the leading telecommunications company CANTV on the Caracas bourse, and to then convert them into dollar-denominated American Depositary Receipts (ADRs) traded on the NYSE.

The sponsor for CANTV ADRs on the NYSE was the Bank of New York, the leader in ADR sponsorship and management in the United States. The Bank of New York had suspended trading in CANTV ADRs in February after the passage of the exchange regulations decree, wishing to determine the legality of trading under the new Venezuelan currency controls. On May 26, after concluding that trading was indeed legal under the decree, the bank resumed trading in CANTV shares. CANTV's share price and trading volume soared in the following week.[3]

The share price of CANTV quickly became the primary method of calculating the implicit gray market exchange rate. For example, CANTV shares closed at Bs7945/share on the Caracas bourse on February 6, 2004. That same day, CANTV ADRs closed in New York at $18.84/ADR. Each New York ADR was equal to seven shares of CANTV in Caracas. The implied gray market exchange rate was then calculated as follows:

$$\text{Implicit gray market rate} = \frac{7 \times \text{Bs7945/Share}}{\$18.84/\text{ADR}}$$

$$= \text{Bs2952/\$}$$

The official exchange rate on that same day was Bs1598/$. This meant that the gray market rate was quoting the bolivar approximately 46% weaker against the dollar than what the Venezuelan government officially declared its currency to be worth.

Exhibit 1 illustrates both the official exchange rate and the gray market rate (calculated using CANTV shares) for the January 2002–March 2004 period. The divergence between the official and gray market rates beginning in February 2003 coincided with the imposition of capital controls.[4]

The Black Market

A third method of obtaining hard currency by Venezuelans was through the rapidly expanding black market. The black market was, as is the case with black markets all over the world, essentially unseen and illegal. It was, however, quite sophisticated, using the services of a stockbroker or

[2]"Venezuela Girds for Exchange Controls," *The Wall Street Journal* (Eastern edition), February 5, 2003, p. A14.

[3]In fact, CANTV's share price continued to rise over the 2002–2004 period as a result of its use as an exchange rate mechanism. The use of CANTV ADRs as a method of obtaining dollars by Venezuelan individuals and organizations was typically described as "not illegal."

[4]On November 26, 2003, Morgan Stanley Capital International (MSCI) announced that it would change its standard spot rate for the Venezuelan bolivar to the notional rate based on the relationship between the price of its CANTV Telefonos de Venezuela D in the local market in bolivars and the price of its ADR in U.S. dollars.

EXHIBIT 1	Venezuelan Official and Gray Market Exchange Rates, Venezuelan Bolivar/U.S. Dollar (January 2002–March 2004)

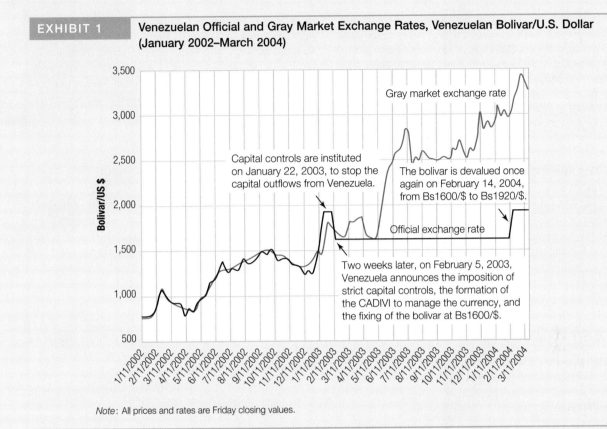

Note: All prices and rates are Friday closing values.

banker in Venezuela who simultaneously held U.S. dollar accounts offshore. The choice of a black market broker was a critical one; in the event of a failure to complete the transaction properly, there was no legal recourse.

If Santiago wished to purchase dollars on the black market, he would deposit bolivars in his broker's account in Venezuela. The agreed upon black market exchange rate was determined on the day of the deposit, and usually was within a 20% band of the gray market rate derived from the CANTV share price. Santiago would then be given access to a dollar-denominated bank account outside of Venezuela in the agreed amount. The transaction took, on average, two business days to settle. The unofficial black market rate was Bs3300/$.

Spring 2004

In early 2004, President Chávez had asked Venezuela's Central Bank to give him "a little billion"—*millardito*—of its $21 billion in foreign exchange reserves. Chávez argued that the money actually belonged to the people, and he wished to invest some of it in the agricultural sector. The Central Bank refused. Not to be thwarted in its search for

funds, the Chávez government announced another devaluation on February 9, 2004. The bolivar was devalued 17%, falling in official value from Bs1600/$ to Bs1920/$ (see Exhibit 1). With all Venezuelan exports of oil being purchased in U.S. dollars, the devaluation of the bolivar meant that the country's proceeds from oil exports grew by the same 17% as the devaluation itself.

The Chávez government argued that the devaluation was necessary because the bolivar was "a variable that cannot be kept frozen, because it prejudices exports and pressures the balance of payments," according to Finance Minister Tobias Nobriega. Analysts, however, pointed out that Venezuelan government actually had significant control over its balance of payments: oil was the primary export, the government maintained control over the official access to hard currency necessary for imports, and the Central Bank's foreign exchange reserves were now over $21 billion.

It's not clear whether Mr. Chávez understands what a massive hit Venezuelans take when savings and earnings in dollar terms are cut in half in just three years. Perhaps the political-science student believes that more devalued bolivars makes everyone richer. But one unavoidable conclusion is that he recognized the devaluation as a way to pay for his Bolivarian "missions," government projects that might restore his popularity long enough to allow him to survive the recall, or survive an audacious decision to squelch it.

— "Money Fun in the Venezuela of Hugo Chávez," *The Wall Street Journal* (Eastern edition), February 13, 2004, p. A13.

Time Was Running Out

Santiago received confirmation from CADIVI on the afternoon of March 10 that his latest application for dollars was approved and that he would receive $10,000 at the official exchange rate of Bs1920/$. Santiago attributed his good fortune to the fact that he paid a CADIVI insider an extra 500 bolivars per dollar to expedite his request. Santiago noted with a smile that "the Chavistas need to make money too." The noise from the street seemed to be dying with the sun. It was time for Santiago to make some decisions. None of the alternatives were *bonita*, but if he was to preserve his business, dollars—at some price—had to be obtained.

Case Questions

1. Why does a country like Venezuela impose capital controls?

2. In the case of Venezuela, what is the difference between the gray market and the black market?

3. Create a financial analysis of Santiago's choices and use it to recommend a solution to his problem.

QUESTIONS

1. **Definitions.** Define the following terms:
   a. Foreign exchange market
   b. Foreign exchange transaction
   c. Foreign exchange

2. **Functions of the Foreign Exchange Market.** What are the three major functions of the foreign exchange market?

3. **Market Participants.** For each of the foreign exchange market participants, identify their motive for buying or selling foreign exchange.

4. **Transaction.** Define each of the following types of foreign exchange transactions:
   a. Spot
   b. Outright forward
   c. Forward-forward swaps

5. **Foreign Exchange Market Characteristics.** With reference to foreign exchange turnover in 2007:
   a. Rank the relative size of spot, forwards, and swaps as of 2007.
   b. Rank the five most important geographic locations for foreign exchange turnover.
   c. Rank the three most important currencies of denomination.

6. **Foreign Exchange Rate Quotations.** Define and give an example of each of the following quotes:
   a. Bid quote
   b. Ask quote

7. **Reciprocals.** Convert the following indirect quotes to direct quotes and direct quotes to indirect quotes:
   a. Euro: €1.22/$ (indirect quote)
   b. Russia: Rub 30/$ (indirect quote)
   c. Canada: $0.72/C$ (direct quote)
   d. Denmark: $0.1644/DKr (direct quote)

8. **Geographical Extent of the Foreign Exchange Market.** With reference to the foreign exchange market:
   a. What is the geographical location?
   b. What are the two main types of trading systems?
   c. How are foreign exchange markets connected for trading activities?

9. **American and European Terms.** With reference to interbank quotations, what is the difference between American terms and European terms?

10. **Direct and Indirect Quotes.** Define and give an example of the following:
    a. A direct quote between the U.S. dollar and the Mexican peso, where the United States is designated as the home country
    b. An example of an indirect quote between the Japanese yen and the Chinese renminbi (yuan), where China is designated as the home country

PROBLEMS

*1. **Paris to St. Petersburg.** On your post-graduation celebratory trip you are leaving Paris for St. Petersburg, Russia. You leave Paris with 10,000 euros in your money pouch. Wanting to exchange all of these for

Russian rubles, you obtain the following quotes:

Spot rate on the dollar/euro cross rate	$1.4260/€
Spot rate on the ruble/dollar cross rate	Rbl 24.75/$

a. What is the Russian ruble/euro cross rate?
b. How many rubles will you obtain for your euros?

*2. **Basel Trading.** You receive the following quotes for Swiss francs against the dollar for spot, one-month forward, three-months forward, and six-months forward.

1.2575 to 1.2585, 10 to 15, 14 to 22, 20 to 30.

a. Calculate the outright quotes for bid and ask, and the number of points spread between each.
b. What do you notice about the spread as quotes evolve from spot toward six months?

3. **Asian Financial Crisis.** The Asian financial crisis which began in July 1997 wreaked havoc throughout the currency markets of East Asia. Which of the following currencies had the largest depreciations or devaluations during the July to November period? Which seemingly survived the first five months of the crisis with the least impact on their currencies?

Country	Currency	July 1997 (per US$)	November 1997 (per US$)
China	yuan	8.4	8.4
Hong Kong	dollar	7.75	7.73
Indonesia	rupiah	2400	3600
Korea	won	900	1100
Malaysia	ringgit	2.5	3.5
Philippines	peso	27	34
Singapore	dollar	1.43	1.60
Taiwan	dollar	27.8	32.7
Thailand	baht	25	40

4. **Forward premiums on the Japanese yen.** Use the following spot and forward bid-ask rates for the yen/dollar (¥/$) exchange rate to answer the following questions:
a. What is the mid-rate for each maturity?
b. What is the annual forward premium for all maturities?
c. Which maturities have the smallest and largest forward premiums?

Period	¥/$ Bid Rate	¥/$ Ask Rate
spot	114.23	114.27
1 month	113.82	113.87
2 months	113.49	113.52
3 months	113.05	113.11
6 months	112.05	112.11
12 months	110.20	110.27
24 months	106.83	106.98

5. **Bloomberg Cross Rates.** Use the cross-rate table from Bloomberg shown at the bottom of this page to determine the following rates. If you are not familiar with all of the three-letter currency codes, refer to the table inside the back cover of this text.
a. Japanese yen/U.S. dollar
b. U.S. dollars per Japanese yen
c. U.S. dollars per euro
d. Euros per U.S. dollar
e. Japanese yen per euro
f. Euros per Japanese yen
g. Canadian dollars per U.S. dollar
h. U.S. dollars per Canadian dollar
i. Australian dollars per U.S. dollar
j. U.S. dollars per Australian dollar
k. British pounds per U.S. dollar
l. U.S. dollars per British pound
m. U.S. dollars per Swiss franc
n. Swiss francs per U.S. dollar

Currency	USD	EUR	JPY	GBP	CHF	CAD	AUD	HKD
HKD	7.7508	11.1496	0.0679	15.9061	6.6564	8.052	7.1088	
AUD	1.0903	1.5684	0.0096	2.2375	0.9364	1.1327		0.1407
CAD	0.9626	1.3847	0.0084	1.9754	0.8267		0.8829	0.1242
CHF	1.1644	1.675	0.102	2.3896		1.2097	1.068	0.1502
GBP	0.4873	0.701	0.0043		0.4185	0.5062	0.4469	0.0629
JPY	114.156	164.2134		234.2687	98.0368	118.5913	104.7005	14.7282
EUR	0.6952		0.0061	1.4266	0.597	0.7222	0.6376	0.0897
USD		1.4385	0.0088	2.0522	0.8588	1.0389	0.9172	0.129

6. **Forward Premiums on the Dollar/Euro.** Use the following spot and forward bid-ask rates for the U.S. dollar/euro (US$/€) exchange rate to answer the following questions:

Period	$/€ Bid Rate	$/€ Ask Rate
spot	1.4389	1.4403
1 month	1.4440	1.4410
2 months	1.4400	1.4415
3 months	1.4403	1.4418
6 months	1.4407	1.4422
12 months	1.4408	1.4424
24 months	1.4417	1.4436

a. What is mid-rate for each maturity?
b. What is the annual forward premium for each maturity?
c. Which maturities have the smallest and largest forward premiums?

7. **Riskless Profit on the Swiss Franc.** The following exchange rates are available to you. (You can buy or sell at the stated rates.)

Mt. Fuji Bank	¥120.00/$
Mt. Rushmore Bank	SF1.6000/$
Mt. Blanc Bank	¥80.00/SF

Assume you have an initial SF10,000,000. Can you make a profit via triangular arbitrage? If so, show steps and calculate the amount of profit in Swiss francs.

8. **Forward Premiums on the Australian Dollar.** Use the following spot and forward quotations on the U.S. dollar/Australian dollar (US$/A$) from October 26, 2007, to answer the questions that follow.

Period	US$/A$ Bid Rate	US$/A$ Ask Rate
Spot	0.91630	0.91700
1 month	0.91477	0.91551
2 months	0.91313	0.91388
3 months	0.91156	0.91233
6 months	0.90542	0.90621
12 months	0.89155	0.89242
24 months	0.86488	0.86602

a. What are the mid-rates (average) from the bid-ask quotations?
b. What is the forward premium for each maturity using the mid-rates calculated in part (a)?
c. Which maturities have the smallest and largest forward premiums?

9. **Transatlantic Arbitrage.** A corporate treasury with operations in New York simultaneously calls Citibank in New York City and Barclays in London, where it receives the following quotes at the same time:

Citibank NYC	Barclays London
$0.9650–70/€	$0.9640–60/€

Using $1 million or its euro equivalent, show how the corporate treasury could make geographic arbitrage profit with the two different exchange rate quotes.

10. **Victoria Exports.** A Canadian exporter, Victoria Exports, will be receiving six payments of €10,000, ranging from now to 12 months in the future. Since the company keeps cash balances in both Canadian dollars and U.S. dollars, it can choose which currency to change the euros to at the end of the various periods. Which currency appears to offer the better rates in the forward market?

Period	Days Forward	US$/euro Bid Rate	US$/euro Ask Rate
spot		1.38390	1.1914
1 month	30	1.38439	1.1926
2 months	60	1.38444	1.1941
3 months	90	1.38590	1.1956
6 months	180	1.38750	1.2013
12 months	360	1.39189	1.2130

11. **Venezuelan Bolivar (A).** The Venezuelan government officially floated the Venezuelan bolivar (Bs) in February 2002. Within weeks, its value had moved from the pre-float fix of Bs778/$ to Bs1025/$.
a. Is this a devaluation or a depreciation?
b. By what percentage did its value change?

12. **Venezuelan Bolivar (B).** The Venezuelan political and economic crisis deepened in late 2002 and early 2003. On January 1, 2003, the bolivar was trading at Bs1400/$. By February 1, its value had fallen to

Bs1950/$. Many currency analysts and forecasters predicted that the bolivar would fall an additional 40% from its February 1 value by early summer 2003.
   a. By what percentage did the bolivar change in value in January 2003?
   b. If the currency forecasters are correct, what would the bolivar's value be against the dollar in June 2003?

13. **Indirect Quotation on the Dollar.** Calculate the forward premium on the dollar (the dollar is the home currency) if the spot rate is €1.0200/$ and the three-month forward rate is €1.0300/$.

14. **Direct Quotation on the Dollar.** Calculate the forward discount on the dollar (the dollar is the home currency) if the spot rate is $1.5500/£ and the six-month forward rate is $1.5600/£.

15. **Mexican Peso-European Euro Cross Rates.** Calculate the cross rate between the Mexican peso (Ps) and the euro (€) from the following two spot rates: Ps11.43/$; €0.6944/$.

16. **Around the Horn.** Assuming the following quotes, calculate how a market trader at Citibank with $1,000,000 can make an intermarket arbitrage profit:

Citibank quotes U.S. dollars per pound:	$1.5400/£
National Westminster quotes euro per pound:	€1.6000/£
Deutsche Bank quotes dollars per euro:	$0.9700/€

INTERNET EXERCISES

1. **Bank for International Settlements.** The Bank for International Settlements (BIS) publishes a wealth of effective exchange rate indices. Use its database and analyses to determine the degree to which the dollar, the euro, and the yen (the "big three currencies") are currently overvalued or undervalued.

Bank for International Settlements   bis.org/statistics/eer/index.htm

2. **Bank of Canada Exchange Rate Index (CERI).** The Bank of Canada regularly publishes the CERI, an index of the Canadian dollar's value. The CERI is a multilateral trade-weighted index of the Canadian dollar's value against other major global currencies relevant to the Canadian economy and business landscape. Use the CERI from the Bank of Canada's Web site to evaluate the relative strength of the *loonie* in recent years.

Bank of Canada exchange rates   www.bankofcanada.ca/en/rates/ceri.html

3. **Forward Quotes.** OzForex Foreign Exchange Services provides representative forward rates on a multitude of currencies online. Use the following Web site to search out forward exchange rate quotations on a variety of currencies. (Note the London, New York, and Sydney times listed on the quotation screen.)

OzForex   www.ozforex.com.au

4. **Federal Reserve Statistical Release.** The United States Federal Reserve provides daily updates of the value of the major currencies traded against the U.S. dollar on its Web site. Use the Fed's Web site to determine the relative weights used by the Fed to determine the index of the dollar's value.

Federal Reserve   www.federalreserve.gov/releases/h10/update/

5. **Exotic Currencies.** Although major currencies like the U.S. dollar and the Japanese yen dominate the headlines, there are nearly as many currencies as there are countries in the world. Many of these currencies are traded in extremely thin and highly regulated markets, making their convertibility suspect. Finding quotations for these currencies is sometimes very difficult. Using the following Web pages, see how many African currency quotes you can find:

Forex-Markets.com   www.forex-markets.com/quotes_exotic.htm

Oanda.com   oanda.com

6. **Daily Market Commentary.** Many different online currency trading and consulting services provide daily assessments of global currency market activity. Use the GCI Web site to find the market's current assessment of how the euro is trading against both the U.S. dollar and the Canadian dollar.

GCI Financial Ltd   www.gcitrading.com/fxnews/

7. **Pacific Exchange Rate Service.** The Pacific Exchange Rate Service Web site, headed up by Professor Werner Antweiler of the University of British Columbia, possesses a wealth of current information on currency exchange rates and related statistics. Use the service to plot the recent performance of currencies which have recently suffered significant devaluations or depreciations, such as the Argentine peso, the Venezuelan bolivar, the Turkish lira, and the Egyptian pound.

Pacific Exchange Rate Service   fx.sauder.ubc.ca/plot.html

International Parity Conditions

... if capital freely flowed towards those countries where it could be most profitably employed, there could be no difference in the rate of profit, and no other difference in the real or labour price of commodities, than the additional quantity of labour required to convey them to the various markets where they were to be sold.

—David Ricardo, *On the Principles of Political Economy and Taxation*, 1817, Chapter 7.

What are the determinants of exchange rates? Are changes in exchange rates predictable? These are fundamental questions that managers of MNEs, international portfolio investors, importers and exporters, and government officials must deal with every day. This chapter describes the core financial theories surrounding the determination of exchange rates. Chapter 10 will introduce two other major theoretical schools of thought regarding currency valuation, and combine the three different theories in a variety of real-world applications.

The economic theories that link exchange rates, price levels, and interest rates are called *international parity conditions*. In the eyes of many, these international parity conditions form the core of the financial theory that is considered unique to the field of international finance. These theories do not always work out to be "true" when compared to what students and practitioners observe in the real world, but they are central to any understanding of how multinational business is conducted and funded in the world today. And, as is often the case, the mistake is not always in the theory itself, but in the way it is interpreted or applied in practice.

Prices and Exchange Rates

If identical products or services can be sold in two different markets, and no restrictions exist on the sale or transportation costs of moving the product between markets, the product's price should be the same in both markets. This is called the *law of one price*.

A primary principle of competitive markets is that prices will equalize across markets if frictions or costs of moving the products or services between markets do not exist. If the two markets are in two different countries, the product's price may be stated in different currency terms, but the price of the product should still be the same. Comparing prices would require only a conversion from one currency to the other. For example,

$$P^\$ \times S = P^\yen$$

where the price of the product in U.S. dollars ($P^\$$), multiplied by the spot exchange rate (S, yen per U.S. dollar), equals the price of the product in Japanese yen ($P^¥$). Conversely, if the prices of the two products were stated in local currencies, and markets were efficient at competing away a higher price in one market relative to the other, the exchange rate could be deduced from the relative local product prices:

$$S = \frac{P^¥}{P^\$}$$

Purchasing Power Parity and the Law of One Price

If the law of one price were true for all goods and services, the *purchasing power parity* (PPP) exchange rate could be found from any individual set of prices. By comparing the prices of identical products denominated in different currencies, one could determine the "real" or PPP exchange rate that should exist if markets were efficient. This is the absolute version of the theory of purchasing power parity. Absolute PPP states that the spot exchange rate is determined by the relative prices of similar baskets of goods.

The "Big Mac Index," as it has been christened by *The Economist* (see Exhibit 7.1) and calculated regularly since 1986, is a prime example of this law of one price. Assuming that the Big Mac is indeed identical in all countries listed, it serves as one form of comparison of whether currencies are currently trading at market rates which are close to the exchange rate implied by Big Macs in local currencies.

For example, using Exhibit 7.1, a Big Mac in China cost Yuan 12.5 (local currency), while the same Big Mac in the United States cost $3.57. The actual spot exchange rate was Yuan 6.83/$ at this time. The price of a Big Mac in China in U.S. dollar terms was therefore

$$\frac{\text{Price of Big Mac in China in Yuan}}{\text{Yuan/\$ spot rate}} = \frac{\text{Yuan } 12.5}{\text{Yuan } 6.83/\$} = \$1.83$$

This is the value in the second column of Exhibit 7.1 for China. *The Economist* then calculates the *implied purchasing power parity rate of exchange* using the actual price of the Big Mac in China (Yuan 12.5) over the price of the Big Mac in the United States in U.S. dollars ($3.57):

$$\frac{\text{Price of Big Mac in China in Yuan}}{\text{Price of Big Mac in the U.S. in \$}} = \frac{\text{Yuan } 12.5}{\$3.57} \approx \text{Yuan } 3.50/\$$$

This is the value in the third column in Exhibit 7.1 for China. In principle, this is what the Big Mac Index is saying the exchange rate between the yuan and the dollar should be according to the theory.

Now comparing this implied PPP rate of exchange, Yuan 3.50/$, with the actual market rate of exchange at that time, Yuan 6.83/$, the degree to which the yuan is either *undervalued* (−%) or *overvalued* (+%) versus the U.S. dollar is calculated as follows:

$$\frac{\text{Implied Rate} - \text{Actual Rate}}{\text{Actual Rate}} = \frac{\text{Yuan } 3.50/\$ - \text{Yuan } 6.83/\$}{\text{Yuan } 6.83/\$} = -.4876 \approx -49\%$$

In this case, the Big Mac Index indicates that the Chinese yuan is undervalued by 49% versus the U.S. dollar as indicated in the far right-hand column for China in Exhibit 7.1. *The Economist* is also quick to note that although this indicates a sizable undervaluation of the managed value of the Chinese yuan versus the dollar, the theory of purchasing power parity

| EXHIBIT 7.1 | The McCurrency Menu—the Hamburger Standard |

	Big Mac Prices		Implied PPP[†] of the Dollar	Actual Exchange Rate	Under (−)/Over (+) Valuation against Dollar
	In Local Currency	In Dollars*			
United States[‡]	$3.57	3.57	–	–	
Argentina	Peso 11.0	3.64	3.08	3.02	+2
Australia	A$3.45	3.36	0.97	1.03	−6
Brazil	Real 7.50	4.73	2.10	1.58	+33
Britain	£ 2.29	4.57	1.56§	2.00	+28
Canada	C$4.09	4.08	1.15	1.00	+14
Chile	Peso 1,550	3.13	434	494	−12
China	Yuan 12.5	1.83	3.50	6.83	−49
Czech Republic	Koruna 66.1	4.56	18.5	14.5	+28
Denmark	DK28.0	5.95	7.84	4.70	+67
Egypt	Pound 13.0	2.45	3.64	5.31	−31
Euro Area**	€ 3.37	5.34	1.06[††]	1.59	+50
Hong Kong	HK$13.3	1.71	3.73	7.80	−52
Hungary	Forint 670	4.64	187.7	144.3	+30
Indonesia	Rupiah 18,700	2.04	5,238	9,152	−43
Japan	Yen 280	2.62	78.4	106.8	−27
Malaysia	Ringgit 5.50	1.70	1.54	3.2	−52
Mexico	Peso 32.0	3.15	8.96	10.2	−12
New Zealand	NZ$4.90	3.72	1.37	1.32	+4
Norway	Kroner 40.0	7.88	11.2	5.08	+121
Poland	Zloty 7.00	3.45	1.96	2.03	−3
Russia	Ruble 59.0	2.54	16.5	23.2	−29
Saudi Arabia	Riyal 10.0	2.67	2.80	3.75	−25
Singapore	S$3.95	2.92	1.11	1.35	−18
South Africa	Rand 16.9	2.24	4.75	7.56	−37
South Korea	Won 3,200	3.14	896	1,018	−12
Sweden	SKr38.0	6.37	10.6	5.96	+79
Switzerland	SFr6.50	6.36	1.82	1.02	+78
Taiwan	NT$75.0	2.47	21.0	30.4	−31
Thailand	Baht 62.0	1.86	17.4	33.4	−48
Turkey	Lire 5.15	4.32	1.44	1.19	+21
UAE	Dirhams 10.00	2.72	2.80	3.67	−24
Colombia	Peso 7000.00	3.89	1960.78	1798.65	9
Costa Rica	Colones 1800.00	3.27	504.20	551.02	−8
Estonia	Kroon 32.00	3.24	8.96	9.87	−9
Iceland	Kronur 469.00	5.97	131.37	78.57	67
Latvia	Lats 1.55	3.50	0.43	0.44	−2
Lithuania	Litas 6.90	3.17	1.93	2.18	−11
Pakistan	Rupee 140.00	1.97	39.22	70.90	−45
Peru	New Sol 9.50	3.35	2.66	2.84	−6
Philippines	Peso 87.00	1.96	24.37	44.49	−45
Slovakia	Koruna 77.00	4.03	21.57	19.13	13
Sri Lanka	Rupee 210.00	1.95	58.82	107.55	−45
Ukraine	Hryvnia 11.00	2.39	3.08	4.60	−33
Uruguay	Peso 61.00	3.19	17.09	19.15	−11

*At current exchange rates; [†]Purchasing-power parity; local price divided by price in the United States; [‡]Average of New York, Chicago, Atlanta, and San Francisco; §Dollars per pound; **Weighted average of prices in euro area; [††]Dollars per euro

Source: "The Big Mac Index: Sandwiched," The Economist, July 24, 2008.

is supposed to give an indication of where the value of currencies are supposed to go over the long-term, and not necessarily what its value is today.

It is important to understand why the Big Mac may be a good candidate for the application of the law of one price and measurement of under or overvaluation. First, the product itself is nearly identical in each and every market. This is the result of product consistency, process excellence, and brand image and pride by McDonald's. Second, and just as important, is that the product is a result of predominantly local materials and input costs. This means that its price in each country is representative of domestic costs and prices and not imported ones—which would be influenced by exchange rates themselves. But as *The Economist* points out, the Big Mac Index is not perfect.

> *The index was never intended to be a precise predictor of currency movements, simply a take-away guide to whether currencies are at their "Acorrect" long-run level. Curiously, however, burgernomics has an impressive record in predicting exchange rates: currencies that show up as overvalued often tend to weaken in later years. But you must always remember the Big Mac's limitations. Burgers cannot sensibly be traded across borders and prices are distorted by differences in taxes and the cost of non-tradable inputs, such as rents.*

> —"Happy 20th Anniversary," *The Economist*, May 25, 2006.

A less extreme form of this principle would be that in relatively efficient markets the price of a basket of goods would be the same in each market. Replacing the price of a single product with a price index allows the PPP exchange rate between two countries to be stated as

$$S = \frac{PI^{¥}}{PI^{\$}}$$

where $PI^{¥}$ and $PI^{\$}$ are price indices expressed in local currency for Japan and the United States, respectively. For example, if the identical basket of goods cost ¥1,000 in Japan and $10 in the United States, the PPP exchange rate would be

$$\frac{¥1000}{\$10} = ¥100/\$.$$

Relative Purchasing Power Parity

If the assumptions of the absolute version of PPP theory are relaxed a bit more, we observe what is termed *relative purchasing power parity*. Relative PPP holds that PPP is not particularly helpful in determining what the spot rate is today, but that the relative change in prices between two countries over a period of time determines the change in the exchange rate over that period. More specifically, *if the spot exchange rate between two countries starts in equilibrium, any change in the differential rate of inflation between them tends to be offset over the long run by an equal but opposite change in the spot exchange rate.*

Exhibit 7.2 shows a general case of relative PPP. The vertical axis shows the percentage change in the spot exchange rate for foreign currency, and the horizontal axis shows the percentage difference in expected rates of inflation (foreign relative to home country). The diagonal parity line shows the equilibrium position between a change in the exchange rate and relative inflation rates. For instance, point P represents an equilibrium point where inflation in the foreign country, Japan, is 4% lower than in the home country, the United States. Therefore, relative PPP would predict that the yen would appreciate by 4% per annum with respect to the U.S. dollar.

EXHIBIT 7.2	Relative Purchasing Power Parity (PPP)

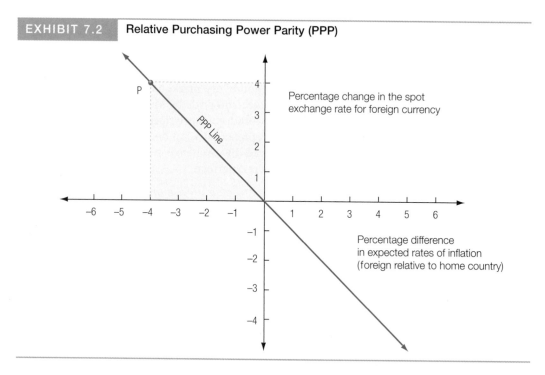

The main justification for purchasing power parity is that if a country experiences inflation rates higher than those of its main trading partners, and its exchange rate does not change, its exports of goods and services become less competitive with comparable products produced elsewhere. Imports from abroad become more price-competitive with higher-priced domestic products. These price changes lead to a deficit on current account in the balance of payments unless offset by capital and financial flows.

Empirical Tests of Purchasing Power Parity

Extensive testing of both the absolute and relative versions of purchasing power parity and the law of one price has been done.[1] These tests have, for the most part, not proved PPP to be accurate in predicting future exchange rates. Goods and services do not in reality move at zero cost between countries, and in fact many services are not "tradable"—for example, haircuts. Many goods and services are not of the same quality across countries, reflecting differences in the tastes and resources of the countries of their manufacture and consumption.

Two general conclusions can be made from these tests: 1) PPP holds up well over the very long run but poorly for shorter time periods and 2) the theory holds better for countries with relatively high rates of inflation and underdeveloped capital markets.

Exchange Rate Indices: Real and Nominal

Because any single country trades with numerous partners, we need to track and evaluate its individual currency value against all other currency values in order to determine relative purchasing power. The objective is to discover whether its exchange rate is "overvalued" or

[1]See, for example, Kenneth Rogoff, "The Purchasing Power Parity Puzzle," *Journal of Economic Literature*, Volume 34, Number 2, June 1996, pp. 647–668; and Barry K. Goodwin, Thomas Greenes, and Michael K. Wohlgenant, "Testing the Law of One Price When Trade Takes Time," *Journal of International Money and Finance*, March 1990, pp. 21–40.

"undervalued" in terms of PPP. One of the primary methods of dealing with this problem is the calculation of *exchange rate indices*. These indices are formed by trade-weighting the bilateral exchange rates between the home country and its trading partners.

The *nominal effective exchange rate index* uses actual exchange rates to create an index, on a weighted average basis, of the value of the subject currency over time. It does not really indicate anything about the "true value" of the currency, or anything related to PPP. The nominal index simply calculates how the currency value relates to some arbitrarily chosen base period, but it is used in the formation of the real effective exchange rate index. The *real effective exchange rate index* indicates how the weighted average purchasing power of the currency has changed relative to some arbitrarily selected base period. Exhibit 7.3 plots the real effective exchange rate indexes for the United States and Japan over the past 22 years.

The real effective exchange rate index for the U.S. dollar, $E_R^\$$, is found by multiplying the nominal effective exchange rate index, $E_N^\$$ by the ratio of U.S. dollar costs, $C^\$$, over foreign currency costs, C^{FC}, both in index form:

$$E_R^\$ = E_N^\$ \times \frac{C^\$}{C^{FC}}$$

If changes in exchange rates just offset differential inflation rates—if purchasing power parity holds—all the real effective exchange rate indices would stay at 100. If an exchange rate strengthened more than was justified by differential inflation, its index would rise above 100. If the real effective exchange rate index is above 100, the currency would be considered "overvalued" from a competitive perspective. An index value below 100 would suggest an "undervalued" currency.

Exhibit 7.3 shows that the real effective exchange rate of the dollar, yen, and euro have changed over the past three decades. The dollar's index value was substantially above 100 in

EXHIBIT 7.3   **IMF's Real Effective Exchange Rate Indexes for the United States, Japan, and the Euro Area (2000 = 100)**

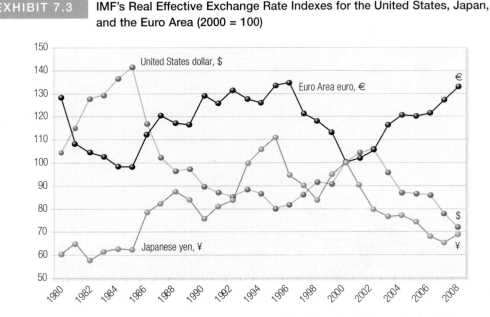

Source: *International Financial Statistics*, International Monetary Fund, December 2008, annual, series REU. 2008 values are for the January–September period.

the 1980s (overvalued), but has remained below 100 (undervalued) since the late 1980s (it did rise slightly above 100 briefly in 1995–1996 and again in 2001–2002). The Japanese yen's real effective rate has remained above 100 for nearly the entire 1980 to 2006 period (overvalued). The euro, whose value has been back-calculated for the years prior to its introduction in 1999, has been largely below 100 and undervalued in its real lifetime.

Apart from measuring deviations from PPP, a country's real effective exchange rate is an important tool for management when predicting upward or downward pressure on a country's balance of payments and exchange rate, as well as being an indicator of the desirability to produce for export from that country. *Global Finance in Practice 7.1* shows deviations from PPP in the twentieth century.

GLOBAL FINANCE IN PRACTICE 7.1

Deviations from Purchasing Power Parity in the Twentieth Century

The recent seminal work by Dimson, Marsh, and Staunton (2002) found that for the 1900–2000 period, relative purchasing power parity generally held. They noted also, however, that significant short-run deviations from PPP did occur. "When deviations from PPP appear to be present, it is likely that exchange rates are responding not only to relative inflation but also to other economic and political factors. Changes in productivity differentials, such as Japan's post-war productivity growth in the traded-goods sector, can bring similar wealth effects, with domestic inflation that does not endanger the country's exchange rate."

"While real exchange rates do not appear to exhibit a long-term upward or downward trend, they are clearly volatile, and on year-to-year basis, PPP explains little of the fluctuations in foreign exchange rates. Some of the extreme changes [in the table] reflect exchange rates or inflation indexes that are not representative, typically (as in Germany) because of wartime controls, and this may amplify the volatility of real exchange rate changes. Given the potential measurement error in inflation indexes, and the fact that real exchange rates involve a ratio of two different price index series, it is all the more striking that, with the exception of South Africa, all real exchange rates appreciate or depreciate annually by no more than a fraction of one percentage point."

Source: Elroy Dimson, Paul Marsh, and Mike Staunton, *Triumph of the Optimists: 101 Years of Global Investment Returns*, Princeton University Press, 2002, pp. 97–98.

Real Exchange Rate Changes Against the U.S. Dollar, Annually 1900–2000

Country	Geometric Mean (%)	Arithmetic Mean (%)	Standard Deviation (%)	Minimum Change (Year, %)	Maximum Change (Year, %)
Australia	−0.6	−0.1	10.7	1931: −39.0	1933: 54.2
Belgium	0.2	1.0	13.3	1919: −32.1	1933: 54.2
Canada	−0.5	−0.4	4.6	1931: −18.1	1933: 12.9
Denmark	0.1	1.0	12.7	1946: −50.3	1933: 37.2
France	−0.4	2.5	24.0	1946: −78.3	1943: 141.5
Germany	−0.1	15.1	134.8	1945: −75.0	1948: 1302.0
Ireland	−0.1	0.5	11.2	1946: −37.0	1933: 56.6
Italy	−0.2	4.0	39.5	1946: −64.9	1944: 335.2
Japan	0.2	3.2	29.5	1945: −78.3	1946: 253.0
The Netherlands	−0.1	0.8	12.6	1946: −61.6	1933: 55.7
South Africa	−1.3	−0.7	10.5	1946: −35.3	1986: 37.3
Spain	−0.4	1.1	18.8	1946: −56.4	1939: 128.7
Sweden	−0.4	0.2	10.7	1919: −38.0	1933: 43.5
Switzerland	0.2	0.8	11.2	1936: −29.0	1933: 53.3
United Kingdom	−0.3	0.3	11.7	1946: −36.7	1933: 55.2

Exchange Rate Pass-Through

Incomplete *exchange rate pass-through* is one reason that a country's real effective exchange rate index can deviate for lengthy periods from its PPP-equilibrium level of 100. The degree to which the prices of imported and exported goods change as a result of exchange rate changes is termed *pass-through*. Although PPP implies that all exchange rate changes are passed through by equivalent changes in prices to trading partners, empirical research in the 1980s questioned this long-held assumption. For example, sizable current account deficits of the United States in the 1980s and 1990s did not respond to changes in the value of the dollar.

To illustrate exchange rate pass-through, assume that BMW produces an automobile in Germany and pays all production expenses in euros. When the firm exports the auto to the United States, the price of the BMW in the U.S. market should simply be the euro value converted to dollars at the spot exchange rate

$$P^{\$}_{BMW} = P^{\euro}_{BMW} \times S$$

where $P^{\$}_{BMW}$ is the BMW price in dollars, $P^{\euro}_{BMW}$ is the BMW price in euros, and S is the number of dollars per euro. If the euro appreciated 10% versus the U.S. dollar, the new spot exchange rate should result in the price of the BMW in the United States rising a proportional 10%. If the price in dollars increases by the same percentage change as the exchange rate, the pass-through of exchange rate changes is complete (or 100%).

However, if the price in dollars rises by less than the percentage change in exchange rates (as is often the case in international trade), the pass-through is *partial*, as illustrated in Exhibit 7.4. The 71% pass-through (U.S. dollar prices rose only 14.29% when the euro appreciated 20%) implies that BMW is absorbing a portion of the adverse exchange rate change. This absorption could result from smaller profit margins, cost reductions, or both. For example, components and raw materials imported to Germany cost less in euros when the euro appreciates. It is also likely that some time may pass before all exchange rate changes are finally reflected in the prices of traded goods, including the period over which previously

---

EXHIBIT 7.4   **Exchange Rate Pass-Through**

Pass-through is the measure of response of imported and exported product prices to exchange rate changes. Assume that the price in dollars and euros of a BMW automobile produced in Germany and sold in the United States at the spot exchange rate is

$$P^{\$}_{BMW} = P^{\euro}_{BMW} \times (\$ / \euro) = \euro 35,000 \times \$1,000 / \euro = \$35,000$$

If the euro were to appreciate 20% versus the U.S. dollar, from \$1.0000/€ to \$1.2000/€, the price of the BMW in the U.S. market should theoretically be \$42,000. But if the price of the BMW in the U.S. does not rise by 20%—for example, it rises only to \$40,000—then the degree of pass-through is partial:

$$\frac{P^{\$}_{BMW,2}}{P^{\$}_{BMW,1}} - \frac{\$40,000}{\$35,000} = 1.1429, \text{ or a } 14.29\% \text{ increase.}$$

The degree of pass-through is measured by the proportion of the exchange rate change reflected in dollar prices. In this example, the dollar price of the BMW rose only 14.29%, while the euro appreciated 20% against the U.S. dollar. The degree of pass-through is partial: 14.29% ÷ 20.00%, or approximately 0.71. Only 71% of the exchange rate change was passed through to the U.S. dollar price. The remaining 29% of the exchange rate change has been absorbed by BMW.

signed contracts are delivered upon. It is obviously in the interest of BMW to keep the appreciation of the euro from raising the price of its automobiles in major export markets.

The concept of *price elasticity of demand* is useful when determining the desired level of pass-through. Recall that the own-price elasticity of demand for any good is the percentage change in quantity of the good demanded as a result of the percentage change in the good's own price:

$$\text{Price elasticity of demand} = e_p = \frac{\%\Delta Q_d}{\%\Delta P}$$

where Q_d is quantity demanded and P is product price. If the absolute value of e_p is less than 1.0, the good is relatively "inelastic," and greater than 1.0 indicates a relatively "elastic" good.

A German product that is relatively price-inelastic, meaning that the quantity demanded is relatively unresponsive to price changes, may often demonstrate a high degree of pass-through. This is so because a higher dollar price in the United States market would have little noticeable effect on the quantity of the product demanded by consumers. Dollar revenue would increase, but euro revenue would remain the same. However, products that are relatively price-elastic would respond in the opposite direction. If the 20% euro appreciation resulted in 20% higher dollar prices, U.S. consumers would decrease the number of BMWs purchased. If the price elasticity of demand for BMWs in the United States were greater than one, total dollar sales revenue of BMWs would decline.

Interest Rates and Exchange Rates

We have already seen how prices of goods in different countries should be related through exchange rates. We now consider how interest rates are linked to exchange rates.

The Fisher Effect

The Fisher effect, named after economist Irving Fisher, states that nominal interest rates in each country are equal to the required real rate of return plus compensation for expected inflation. More formally, this is derived from $(1 + r)(1 + \pi) - 1$:

$$i = r + \pi + r\pi$$

where i is the nominal rate of interest, r is the real rate of interest, and π is the expected rate of inflation over the period of time for which funds are to be lent. The final compound term, $r\pi$, is frequently dropped from consideration due to its relatively minor value. The Fisher effect then reduces to (approximate form):

$$i = r + \pi$$

The Fisher effect applied to the United States and Japan would be as follows:

$$i^\$ = r^\$ + \pi^\$; \, i^\yen = r^\yen + \pi^\yen$$

where the superscripts $\$$ and $\yen$ pertain to the respective nominal (i), real r, and expected inflation (π) components of financial instruments denominated in dollars and yen, respectively. We need to forecast the future rate of inflation, not what inflation has been. Predicting the future can be difficult.

Empirical tests using *ex-post* national inflation rates have shown that the Fisher effect usually exists for short-maturity government securities such as treasury bills and notes. Comparisons based on longer maturities suffer from the increased financial risk inherent in fluctuations of the market value of the bonds prior to maturity. Comparisons of private sector securities are influenced by unequal creditworthiness of the issuers. All the tests are inconclusive to the extent that recent past rates of inflation are not a correct measure of future expected inflation.

The International Fisher Effect

The relationship between the percentage change in the spot exchange rate over time and the differential between comparable interest rates in different national capital markets is known as the *international Fisher effect*. "Fisher-open," as it is often termed, states that the spot exchange rate should change in an equal amount but in the opposite direction to the difference in interest rates between two countries. More formally,

$$\frac{S_1 - S_2}{S_2} = i^{\$} - i^{¥}$$

where $i^{\$}$ and $i^{¥}$ are the respective national interest rates, and S is the spot exchange rate using indirect quotes (an indirect quote on the dollar is, for example, ¥/$) at the beginning of the period (S_1) and the end of the period (S_2). This is the approximation form commonly used in industry. The precise formulation is as follows:

$$\frac{S_1 - S_2}{S_2} = \frac{i^{\$} - i^{¥}}{1 + i^{¥}}$$

Justification for the international Fisher effect is that investors must be rewarded or penalized to offset the expected change in exchange rates. For example, if a dollar-based investor buys a 10-year yen bond earning 4% interest, instead of a 10-year dollar bond earning 6% interest, the investor must be expecting the yen to appreciate vis- à-vis the dollar by at least 2% per year during the 10 years. If not, the dollar-based investor would be better off remaining in dollars. If the yen appreciates 3% during the 10-year period, the dollar-based investor would earn a bonus of 1% higher return. However, the international Fisher effect predicts that with unrestricted capital flows, an investor should be indifferent to whether his bond is in dollars or yen, because investors worldwide would see the same opportunity and compete it away.

Empirical tests lend some support to the relationship postulated by the international Fisher effect, although considerable short-run deviations occur. A more serious criticism has been posed, however, by recent studies that suggest the existence of a foreign exchange risk premium for most major currencies. Also, speculation in uncovered interest arbitrage (described shortly) creates distortions in currency markets. Thus, the expected change in exchange rates might consistently be more than the difference in interest rates.

The Forward Rate

A *forward rate* is an exchange rate quoted today for settlement at some future date. A forward exchange agreement between currencies states the rate of exchange at which a foreign currency will be *bought forward* or *sold forward* at a specific date in the future (typically after 30, 60, 90, 180, 270, or 360 days).

The forward rate is calculated for any specific maturity by adjusting the current spot exchange rate by the ratio of euro currency interest rates of the same maturity for the two subject currencies. For example, the 90-day forward rate for the Swiss franc/U.S. dollar exchange rate ($F_{90}^{SF/\$}$) is found by multiplying the current spot rate ($S^{SF/\$}$) by the ratio of the 90-day euro-Swiss franc deposit rate (i^{SF}) over the 90-day Eurodollar deposit rate ($i^\$$):

$$F_{90}^{SF/\$} = S^{SF/\$} \times \frac{\left[1 + \left(i^{SF} \times \frac{90}{360}\right)\right]}{\left[1 + \left(i^\$ \times \frac{90}{360}\right)\right]}$$

Assuming a spot rate of SF1.4800/$, a 90-day euro Swiss franc deposit rate of 4.00% per annum, and a 90-day Eurodollar deposit rate of 8.00% per annum, the 90-day forward rate is SF1.4655/$:

$$F_{90}^{SF/\$} = SF1.4800/\$ \times \frac{\left[1 + \left(0.0400 \times \frac{90}{360}\right)\right]}{\left[1 + \left(0.0800 \times \frac{90}{360}\right)\right]} = SF1.4800/\$ \times \frac{1.01}{1.02} = SF1.4655/\$$$

The *forward premium* or *discount* is the percentage difference between the spot and forward exchange rate, stated in annual percentage terms. When the foreign currency price of the home currency is used, as in this case of SF/$, the formula for the percent-per-annum premium or discount becomes

$$f^{SF} = \frac{Spot - Forward}{Forward} \times \frac{360}{days} \times 100$$

Substituting the SF/$ spot and forward rates, as well as the number of days forward (90),

$$f^{SF} = \frac{SF1.4800/\$ - SF1.4655/\$}{SF1.4655/\$} \times \frac{360}{90} \times 100 = +3.96\% \text{ per annum}$$

The sign is positive, indicating that the Swiss franc is *selling forward at a 3.96% per annum premium* over the dollar (it takes 3.96% more dollars to get a franc at the 90-day forward rate).

As illustrated in Exhibit 7.5, the forward premium on the Eurodollar forward exchange rate series arises from the differential between Eurodollar interest rates and Swiss franc interest rates. Because the forward rate for any particular maturity utilizes the specific interest rates for that term, the forward premium or discount on a currency is visually obvious—the currency with the higher interest rate (in this case the U.S. dollar) will sell forward at a discount, and the currency with the lower interest rate (in this case the Swiss franc) will sell forward at a premium.

The forward rate is calculated from three observable data items—the spot rate, the foreign currency deposit rate, and the home currency deposit rate—and is not a forecast of the future spot exchange. It is, however, frequently used by managers within MNEs as a forecast, with mixed results, as the following section describes.

Interest Rate Parity (IRP)

The theory of *interest rate parity* (IRP) provides the link between the foreign exchange markets and the international money markets. The theory states: *The difference in the national*

EXHIBIT 7.5	Currency Yield Curves and the Forward Premium

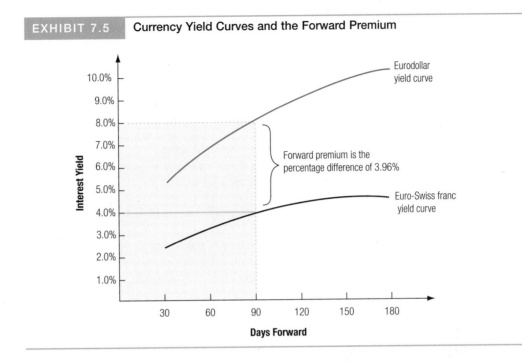

interest rates for securities of similar risk and maturity should be equal to, but opposite in sign to, the forward rate discount or premium for the foreign currency, except for transaction costs.

Exhibit 7.6 shows how the theory of interest rate parity works. Assume that an investor has $1,000,000 and several alternative but comparable Swiss franc (SF) monetary investments. If the investor chooses to invest in a dollar money market instrument, the investor

EXHIBIT 7.6	Interest Rate Parity (IRP)

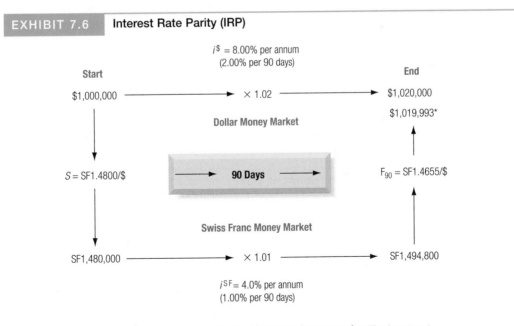

*Note that the Swiss franc investment yields $1,019,993, $7 less on a $1 million investment.

would earn the dollar rate of interest. This results in $(1 + i^\$)$ at the end of the period, where $i^\$$ is the dollar rate of interest in decimal form. The investor may, however, choose to invest in a Swiss franc money market instrument of identical risk and maturity for the same period. This action would require that the investor exchange the dollars for francs at the spot rate of exchange, invest the francs in a money market instrument, sell the francs forward (in order to avoid any risk that the exchange rate would change), and at the end of the period convert the resulting proceeds back to dollars.

A dollar-based investor would evaluate the relative returns of starting in the top-left corner and investing in the dollar market (straight across the top of the box) compared to investing in the Swiss franc market (going down and then around the box to the top-right corner). The comparison of returns would be as follows:

$$\left(1+i^\$\right)= S^{SF/\$} \times \left(1+i^{SF}\right)\times \frac{1}{F^{SF/\$}}$$

where S = the spot rate of exchange and F = the forward rate of exchange. Substituting in the spot rate (SF1.4800/\$) and forward rate (SF1.4655/\$) and respective interest rates ($i^\$$ = 0.02, i^{SF} = 0.01) from Exhibit 7.6, the interest rate parity condition is as follows:

$$(1+0.02) = 1.4800 \times (1+0.01) \times \frac{1}{1.4655}$$

The left-hand side of the equation is the gross return the investor would earn by investing in dollars. The right-hand side is the gross return the investor would earn by exchanging dollars for Swiss francs at the spot rate, investing the franc proceeds in the Swiss franc money market, and simultaneously selling the principal plus interest in Swiss francs forward for dollars at the current 90-day forward rate.

Ignoring transaction costs, if the returns in dollars are equal between the two alternative money market investments, the spot and forward rates are considered to be at IRP. The transaction is "covered," because the exchange rate back to dollars is guaranteed at the end of the 90-day period. Therefore, as in Exhibit 7.6, in order for the two alternatives to be equal, any differences in interest rates must be offset by the difference between the spot and forward exchange rates (in approximate form):

$$\frac{F}{S} = \frac{\left(1+i^{SF}\right)}{\left(1+i^\$\right)} \quad \text{or} \quad \frac{SF1.4655/\$}{SF1.4800/\$} = \frac{1.01}{1.02} = 0.9902 \approx 1\%$$

Covered Interest Arbitrage (CIA)

The spot and forward exchange markets are not constantly in the state of equilibrium described by interest rate parity. When the market is not in equilibrium, the potential for "riskless" or arbitrage profit exists. The arbitrager who recognizes such an imbalance will move to take advantage of the disequilibrium by investing in whichever currency offers the higher return on a covered basis. This is called *covered interest arbitrage* (CIA).

Exhibit 7.7 describes the steps that a currency trader, most likely working in the arbitrage division of a large international bank, would implement to perform a CIA transaction. The currency trader, Fye Hong, may utilize any of a number of major eurocurrencies that his bank holds to conduct arbitrage investments. The morning conditions indicate to Fye Hong that a CIA transaction that exchanges 1 million U.S. dollars for Japanese yen, invested in a six-month euroyen account and sold forward back to dollars, will yield a profit of \$4,638 (\$1,044,638 − \$1,040,000) over and above that available from a eurodollar investment. Conditions in the exchange markets and euromarkets change rapidly however, so if Fye

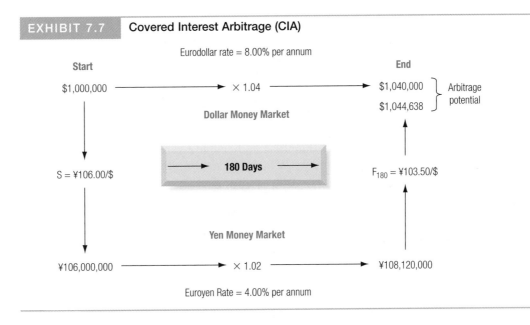

EXHIBIT 7.7   Covered Interest Arbitrage (CIA)

Hong waits even a few minutes, the profit opportunity may disappear. Fye Hong executes the following transaction:

Step 1: Convert $1,000,000 at the spot rate of ¥106.00/$ to ¥106,000,000 (see "Start" in Exhibit 7.7).

Step 2: Invest the proceeds, ¥106,000,000, in a euroyen account for six months, earning 4.00% per annum, or 2% for 180 days.

Step 3: Simultaneously sell the future yen proceeds (¥108,120,000) forward for dollars at the 180-day forward rate of ¥103.50/$. This action "locks in" gross dollar revenues of $1,044,638 (see "End" in Exhibit 7.7).

Step 4: Calculate the cost (opportunity cost) of funds used at the eurodollar rate of 8.00% per annum, or 4% for 180 days, with principal and interest then totaling $1,040,000. Profit on CIA ("End") is $4,638 ($1,044,638 − $1,040,000).

Note that all profits are stated in terms of the currency in which the transaction was initialized, but that a trader may conduct investments denominated in U.S. dollars, Japanese yen, or any other major currency.

Rule of Thumb. All that is required to make a covered interest arbitrage profit is for interest rate parity not to hold. Depending on the relative interest rates and forward premium, Fye Hong would have started in Japanese yen, invested in U.S. dollars, and sold the dollars forward for yen. The profit would then end up denominated in yen. But how would Fye Hong decide in which direction to go around the box in Exhibit 7.7?

The key to determining whether to start in dollars or yen is to compare the differences in interest rates to the forward premium on the yen (the *cost of cover*). For example, in Exhibit 7.7, the difference in 180-day interest rates is 2.00% (dollar interest rates are higher by 2.00%). The premium on the yen for 180 days forward is as follows:

$$f^{\ast} = \frac{\text{Spot} - \text{Forward}}{\text{Forward}} \times \frac{360}{180} \times 100 = \frac{¥106.00/\$ - ¥103.50/\$}{¥103.50/\$} \times 200 = 4.8309\%$$

In other words, by investing in yen and selling the yen proceeds forward at the forward rate, Fye Hong earns 4.83% per annum, whereas he would earn only 4% per annum if he continues to invest in dollars.

> **Arbitrage rule of thumb:** If the difference in interest rates is greater than the forward premium (or expected change in the spot rate), invest in the higher interest yielding currency. If the difference in interest rates is less than the forward premium (or expected change in the spot rate), invest in the lower yielding currency.

Using this rule of thumb should enable Fye Hong to choose in which direction to go around the box in Exhibit 7.7. It also guarantees that he will always make a profit if he goes in the right direction. This rule assumes that the profit is greater than any transaction costs incurred.

This process of CIA drives the international currency and money markets toward the equilibrium described by interest rate parity. Slight deviations from equilibrium provide opportunities for arbitragers to make small riskless profits. Such deviations provide the supply and demand forces that will move the market back toward parity (equilibrium).

Covered interest arbitrage opportunities continue until interest rate parity is reestablished, because the arbitragers are able to earn risk-free profits by repeating the cycle as often as possible. Their actions, however, nudge the foreign exchange and money markets back toward equilibrium for the following reasons:

1. Purchase of yen in the spot market and sale of yen in the forward market narrows the premium on the forward yen. This is so because the spot yen strengthens from the extra demand and the forward yen weakens because of the extra sales. A narrower premium on the forward yen reduces the foreign exchange gain previously captured by investing in yen.

2. The demand for yen-denominated securities causes yen interest rates to fall, and the higher level of borrowing in the United States causes dollar interest rates to rise. The net result is a wider interest differential in favor of investing in the dollar.

Uncovered Interest Arbitrage (UIA)

A deviation from covered interest arbitrage is *uncovered interest arbitrage* (UIA), wherein investors borrow in countries and currencies exhibiting relatively low interest rates and convert the proceeds into currencies that offer much higher interest rates. The transaction is "uncovered," because the investor does not sell the higher yielding currency proceeds forward, choosing to remain uncovered and accept the currency risk of exchanging the higher yield currency into the lower yielding currency at the end of the period. Exhibit 7.8 demonstrates the steps an uncovered interest arbitrager takes when undertaking what is termed the "yen carry-trade."

The "yen carry-trade" is an age-old application of UIA. Investors, from both inside and outside Japan, take advantage of extremely low interest rates in Japanese yen (0.40% per annum) to raise capital. Investors exchange the capital they raise for other currencies like U.S. dollars or euros. Then they reinvest these dollar or euro proceeds in dollar or euro money markets where the funds earn substantially higher rates of return (5.00% per annum in Exhibit 7.8). At the end of the period—a year, in this case—they convert the dollar proceeds back into Japanese yen in the spot market. The result is a tidy profit over what it costs to repay the initial loan.

The trick, however, is that the spot exchange rate at the end of the year must not change significantly from what it was at the beginning of the year. If the yen were to appreciate significantly against the dollar, as it did in late 1999, moving from ¥120/$ to ¥105/$, these "uncov-

EXHIBIT 7.8 Uncovered Interest Arbitrage (UIA): The Yen Carry-Trade

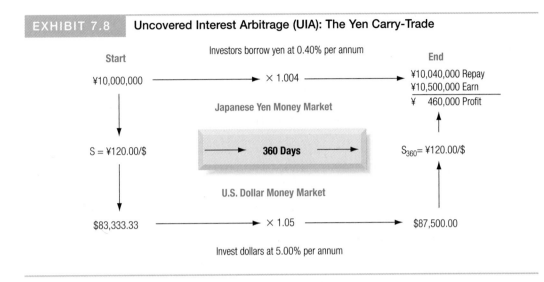

Investors borrow yen at 0.40% per annum

Start   **End**

¥10,000,000 ──────► × 1.004 ──────► ¥10,040,000 Repay
                                                    ¥10,500,000 Earn
                                                    ─────────────
                                                    ¥   460,000 Profit

Japanese Yen Money Market

S = ¥120.00/$ **360 Days** S_{360} = ¥120.00/$

U.S. Dollar Money Market

$83,333.33 ──────► × 1.05 ──────► $87,500.00

Invest dollars at 5.00% per annum

ered" investors would suffer sizable losses when they convert their dollars into yen to repay the yen they borrowed. The higher return does indeed come at higher risk! *Global Finance in Practice 7.2* highlights the multitude of impacts the carry-trade may have.

GLOBAL FINANCE IN PRACTICE 7.2

Shopping, Cooking, Cleaning... Playing The Yen Carry Trade

Nakako Ishiyama sits quietly in the living room of her apartment in the old Nihonbashi quarter of Tokyo, not far from its famous stone bridge—the point from which, in Edo times, all distances in Japan were measured. She has been telling me about her investment history since around 2000—the time, not coincidentally, when the Bank of Japan first pushed interest rates down to within a hair's breadth of zero. Largely without the knowledge of her husband, Ishiyama began investing the couple's money, mainly in lots of around $50,000. And didn't stop. Each fund in which she entrusted their retirement nest egg—or toranoko, "tiger's cub," in Japanese—has a more elaborate name than the last. As she lists each one she invariably adds as a suffix the words nantoka nantoka— "something or other" or "thingamajig." It is not altogether reassuring.

"Now let's see, there was the Global Infrastructure Thingamajig Fund," she says. "And the Emerging Currency Something or Other Fund. And the Australian Fixed Term Whatever-You-Call-It Fund." Shy and anxious (she refused to be photographed), 66-year-old Ishiyama does not look like someone who has played a role—however modest—in the drama that has engulfed the global financial system. Yet she and many of her peers have done exactly that. Japan's housewives have acted as the guardians of the country's vast household savings built up since its rise to prosperity after the

devastation of war. At more than ¥1,500,000bn (some $16,800bn), these savings are considered the world's biggest pool of investable wealth. Most of it is stashed in ordinary Japanese bank accounts; a surprisingly large amount is kept at home in cash, in tansu savings, named for the traditional wooden cupboards in which people store their possessions. But from the early 2000s, the housewives—often referred to collectively as "Mrs. Watanabe," a common Japanese surname—began to hunt for higher returns.

Many were dissatisfied with the paltry interest rates banks were offering. The 0.02 percent return on a typical fixed-term deposit was so derisory that the annual payment on even substantial lifetime savings might come to a mere few hundred yen. "If you got a puncture on the way to the bank, you'd be out of pocket," scoffs Ishiyama. She, like hundreds of thousands of others, found more appealing returns in foreign bonds and other overseas investments. "I was walking in the street and I saw a poster advertising a 5 percent interest rate. I got quite giddy with the idea," she says. "I saw TV advertisements with everyone grinning and I thought: 'I suppose it should be OK.'"

It wasn't long before the markets began to notice something was stirring. In the first half of 2003, individual Japanese investors bought ¥2,700bn of foreign bonds, easily a record.

Brokers were delighted, partly because they made a killing on fees. But there was nervous chatter, too: if Japanese housewives opened the floodgates and sluiced money abroad, there could be a collapse in Japan's enormous government bond market. Hitherto, the large sums of money trapped inside the country in savings had allowed the government to negotiate remarkably low rates of interest on the country's massive foreign debt.

Professional traders began to study Mrs. Watanabe's every move. She impressed them by holding her nerve whenever the yen temporarily strengthened, using each occasion as an opportunity to buy more foreign assets at knockdown prices. The lines of Mrs. Watanabes outside banks and brokerages became a barometer of what might happen to the yen. While highly-paid foreign-exchange traders dithered, Mrs. Watanabe cashed in and began to acquire the reputation of an investing genius. Some professionals quietly began to do whatever Mrs. Watanabe was doing.

Those who did made money hand over fist. Even in 2006, by which time the Bank of Japan had inched overnight rates up to 0.25 percent, Australian rates were a full six percentage points higher. Many Japanese holiday in Australia and quite a few were comfortable parking a portion of their savings in Australian banks. Others opted for South African rand, where the interest-rate differential in 2006 was 8.25 percent, or even Turkish lira, offering a miraculous 17.25 percent. Others still went for foreign-currency-denominated bonds (uridashis) or foreign-invested mutual funds yielding an annual dividend of 6 per cent or more.

Nakako Ishiyama was one of those seduced. Before she realised it, many of her investments had been savaged by the sudden collapse of equity prices and the switchback of the yen. Ishiyama blames no one but herself. "It's all my own fault. I take responsibility. My grandmother always told me not to poke my nose into things I didn't understand," she says, quoting a slightly dubious old saying about a woman and a crowing cockerel. She says she read about subprime loans and wobbling American banks but couldn't imagine that such far-off happenings had anything to do with her or that she had anything to do with them. Reaching for another of her grandmother's expressions, she sums up her investment experience: "Like a blind person with no fear of snakes, I have acted like a fool."

Source: Abstracted from "Shopping, Cooking, Cleaning... Playing The Yen Carry Trade; Stories—Inquiry; Why Japanese housewives added international finance to their list of daily chores," David Pilling. *Financial Times*. London (UK): February 21, 2009, p. 30.

Equilibrium between Interest Rates and Exchange Rates

Exhibit 7.9 illustrates the conditions necessary for equilibrium between interest rates and exchange rates. The vertical axis shows the difference in interest rates in favor of the foreign currency, and the horizontal axis shows the forward premium or discount on that currency. The interest rate parity line shows the equilibrium state, but transaction costs cause the line to be a band rather than a thin line. Transaction costs arise from foreign exchange and investment brokerage costs on buying and selling securities. Typical transaction costs in recent years have been in the range of 0.18% to 0.25% on an annual basis. For individual transactions like Fye Hong's arbitrage activity in the previous example, there is no explicit transaction cost per trade; rather, the costs of the bank in supporting Fye Hong's activities are the transaction costs. Point X shows one possible equilibrium position, where a 4% lower rate of interest on yen securities would be offset by a 4% premium on the forward yen.

The disequilibrium situation, which encouraged the interest rate arbitrage in the previous CIA example, is illustrated by point U. It is located off the interest rate parity line because the lower interest on the yen is –4% (annual basis), whereas the premium on the forward yen is slightly over 4.8% (annual basis). Using the formula for forward premium presented earlier, we find the premium on the yen thus:

$$\frac{¥106.00/\$ - 103.50/\$}{¥103.50/\$} \times \frac{360 \text{ days}}{180 \text{ days}} \times 100 = 4.83\%$$

The situation depicted by point U is unstable, because all investors have an incentive to execute the same covered interest arbitrage. Except for a bank failure, the arbitrage gain is virtually risk-free.

EXHIBIT 7.9   Interest Rate Parity (IRP) and Equilibrium

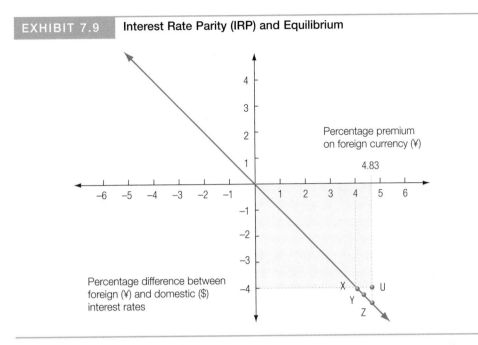

Some observers have suggested that political risk does exist, because one of the governments might apply capital controls that would prevent execution of the forward contract. This risk is fairly remote for covered interest arbitrage between major financial centers of the world, especially because a large portion of funds used for covered interest arbitrage is in Eurodollars. The concern may be valid for pairings with countries not noted for political and fiscal stability.

The net result of the disequilibrium is that fund flows will narrow the gap in interest rates and/or decrease the premium on the forward yen. In other words, market pressures will cause point U in Exhibit 7.9 to move toward the interest rate parity band. Equilibrium might be reached at point Y, or at any other locus between X and Z, depending on whether forward market premiums are more or less easily shifted than interest rate differentials.

Forward Rate as an Unbiased Predictor of the Future Spot Rate

Some forecasters believe that foreign exchange markets for the major floating currencies are "efficient" and forward exchange rates are *unbiased predictors* of future spot exchange rates.

Exhibit 7.10 demonstrates the meaning of "unbiased prediction" in terms of how the forward rate performs in estimating future spot exchange rates. If the forward rate is an unbiased predictor of the future spot rate, the expected value of the future spot rate at time 2 equals the present forward rate for time 2 delivery, available now, $E_1(S_2) = F_{1,2}$.

Intuitively, this means that the distribution of possible actual spot rates in the future is centered on the forward rate. The fact that it is an unbiased predictor, however, does not mean that the future spot rate will actually be equal to what the forward rate predicts. Unbiased prediction simply means that the forward rate will, on average, overestimate and underestimate the actual future spot rate in equal frequency and degree. The forward rate may, in fact, never actually equal the future spot rate.

EXHIBIT 7.10 Forward Rate as Unbiased Predictor for Future Spot Rate

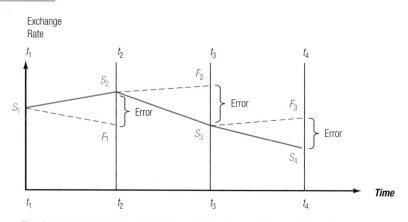

The forward rate available today (F_t, $t + 1$), time t, for delivery at future time $t + 1$, is used as a "predictor" of the spot rate that will exist at that day in the future. Therefore, the forecast spot rate for time S_{t2} is F_1; the actual spot rate turns out to be S_2. The vertical distance between the prediction and the actual spot rate is the forecast error.

  When the forward rate is termed an "unbiased predictor of the future spot rate," it means that the forward rate over- or underestimates the future spot rate with relatively equal frequency and amount. It therefore "misses the mark" in a regular and orderly manner. The sum of the errors equals zero.

The rationale for this relationship is based on the hypothesis that the foreign exchange market is reasonably efficient. Market efficiency assumes that 1) all relevant information is quickly reflected in both the spot and forward exchange markets; 2) transaction costs are low; and 3) instruments denominated in different currencies are perfect substitutes for one another.

Empirical studies of the efficient foreign exchange market hypothesis have yielded conflicting results. Nevertheless, a consensus is developing that rejects the efficient market hypothesis. It appears that the forward rate is not an unbiased predictor of the future spot rate and that it does pay to use resources to attempt to forecast exchange rates.

If the efficient market hypothesis is correct, a financial executive cannot expect to profit in any consistent manner from forecasting future exchange rates, because current quotations in the forward market reflect all that is presently known about likely future rates. Although future exchange rates may well differ from the expectation implicit in the present forward market quotation, we cannot know today which way actual future quotations will differ from today's forward rate. The expected mean value of deviations is zero. The forward rate is therefore an "unbiased" estimator of the future spot rate.

Tests of foreign exchange market efficiency, using longer time periods of analysis, conclude that either exchange market efficiency is untestable or, if it is testable, that the market is not efficient. Furthermore, the existence and success of foreign exchange forecasting services suggest that managers are willing to pay a price for forecast information even though they can use the forward rate as a forecast at no cost. The "cost" of buying this information is, in many circumstances, an "insurance premium" for financial managers who might get fired for using their own forecast, including forward rates, when that forecast proves incorrect. If they "bought" professional advice that turned out wrong, the fault was not in their forecast!

If the exchange market is not efficient, it would be sensible for a firm to spend resources on forecasting exchange rates. This is the opposite conclusion to the one in which exchange markets are deemed efficient.

Prices, Interest Rates, and Exchange Rates in Equilibrium

Exhibit 7.11 illustrates all of the fundamental parity relations simultaneously, in equilibrium, using the U.S. dollar and the Japanese yen. The forecasted inflation rates for Japan and the United States are 1% and 5%, respectively; a 4% differential. The nominal interest rate in the U.S. dollar market (one-year government security) is 8%, a differential of 4% over the Japanese nominal interest rate of 4%. The spot rate, S_1, is ¥104/$, and the one-year forward rate is ¥100/$.

- **Relation A: Purchasing Power Parity (PPP).** According to the relative version of purchasing power parity, the spot exchange rate one year from now, S_2, is expected to be ¥100/$:

$$S_2 = S_1 \times \frac{1 + \pi^{¥}}{1 + \pi^{\$}} = ¥104/\$ \times \frac{1.01}{1.05} = ¥100/\$$$

  This is a 4% change and equal, but opposite in sign, to the difference in expected rates of inflation (1% − 5% or 4%).

- **Relation B: The Fisher Effect.** The real rate of return is the nominal rate of interest less the expected rate of inflation. Assuming efficient and open markets, the real rates of return should be equal across currencies. Here, the real rate is 3% in U.S. dollar markets ($r = i - \pi = 8\% - 5\%$), and in Japanese yen markets (4% − 1%). Note

EXHIBIT 7.11   International Parity Conditions in Equilibrium (Approximate Form)

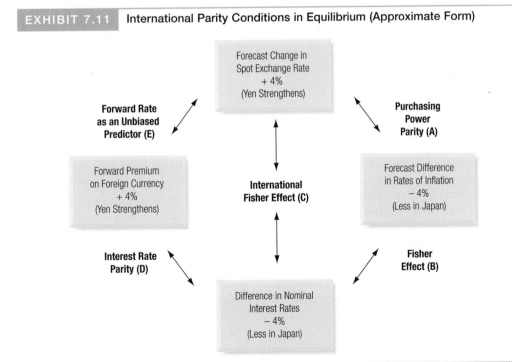

that the 3% real rate of return is not in Exhibit 7.11, but rather the Fisher effect's relationship—that nominal interest rate differentials equal the difference in expected rates of inflation, –4%.

■ **Relation C: International Fisher Effect.** The forecast change in the spot exchange rate, in this case 4%, is equal to, but opposite in sign to, the differential between nominal interest rates:

$$\frac{S_1 - S_2}{S_2} \times 100 = i^{¥} - i^{\$} = 4\% - 8\% = -4\%$$

■ **Relation D: Interest Rate Parity (IRP).** According to the theory of interest rate parity, the difference in nominal interest rates is equal to, but opposite in sign to, the forward premium. For this numerical example, the nominal yen interest rate (4%) is 4% less than the nominal dollar interest rate (8%):

$$i^{¥} - i^{\$} = 4\% - 8\% = -4\%$$

and the forward premium is a positive 4%:

$$f^{¥} = \frac{S_1 - F}{F} \times 100 = \frac{¥104/\$ - ¥100/\$}{¥100/\$} \times 100 = 4\%$$

■ **Relation E: Forward Rate as an Unbiased Predictor.** Finally, the one-year forward rate on the Japanese yen, ¥100/$, if assumed to be an unbiased predictor of the future spot rate, also forecasts ¥100/$.

SUMMARY POINTS

■ Parity conditions have traditionally been used by economists to help explain the long run trend in an exchange rate.

■ Under conditions of freely floating rates the expected rate of change in the spot exchange rate, differential rates of national inflation and interest, and the forward discount or premium are all directly proportional to each other and mutually determined. A change in one of these variables has a tendency to change all of them with a feedback on the variable that changes first.

■ If the identical product or service can be sold in two different markets, and there are no restrictions on its sale or transportation costs of moving the product between markets, the product's price should be the same in both markets. This is called the law of one price.

■ The absolute version of the theory of purchasing power parity states that the spot exchange rate is determined by the relative prices of similar baskets of goods.

■ The relative version of the theory of purchasing power parity states that if the spot exchange rate between two countries starts in equilibrium, any change in the differential rate of inflation between them tends to be offset over the long run by an equal but opposite change in the spot exchange rate.

■ The Fisher effect, named after economist Irving Fisher, states that nominal interest rates in each country are equal to the required real rate of return plus compensation for expected inflation.

■ The international Fisher effect, "Fisher-open" as it is often termed, states that the spot exchange rate should change in an equal amount but in the opposite direction to the difference in interest rates between two countries.

■ Some forecasters believe that for the major floating currencies, foreign exchange markets are "efficient" and forward exchange rates are unbiased predictors of future spot exchange rates.

■ The theory of interest rate parity (IRP) states that the difference in the national interest rates for securities of similar risk and maturity should be equal to, but opposite in sign to, the forward rate discount or premium for the foreign currency, except for transaction costs.

■ When the spot and forward exchange markets are not in equilibrium as described by interest rate parity, the potential for "riskless" or arbitrage profit exists. This is called covered interest arbitrage (CIA).

MINI-CASE

Currency Pass-Through at Porsche

Based in Germany, and with manufacturing and assembly exclusively located in Germany, Slovakia, and Finland, Porsche's entire cost base is the euro or Slovakian koruna (which is managed by the Slovakian government to maintain stability against the euro). This means that all of the direct costs in its automobile manufacturing are incurred (for practical purposes) in euro-denominated operations (cost, markup, and basic pricing). Porsche's products are then exported to its major markets around the world, including the United States, the United Kingdom, China, and Japan.

Exhibit 1 illustrates a possible scenario of the European cost and market pricing for the North American launch of the Porsche 911 4S Cabriolet in 2003 (a 3.6-liter six cylinder engine with a top track speed of 174 mph; 0 to 62 mph in 5.3 seconds). Assuming that Porsche first established the price of the car in euros, and then—in April 2003—set the U.S. dollar price at the then current exchange rate of $1.0862/€, approximately $93,200.

As illustrated in the exhibit, in the months following the price-setting, the company's margin would have been largely eliminated as a result of the continued appreciation of the euro versus the dollar. The analysis highlights the squeeze suffered by a European producer exporting to the US dollar markets. Independent of what method, degree, or effectiveness of hedging was undertaken by Porsche, the company is faced with a continuing pricing dilemma for all of its North American sales.

Case Questions

1. Which do you believe is most important for sustaining the sale of the new Carrera model, maintaining a profit margin or maintaining the U.S. dollar price?

2. Given the change in exchange rates and the strategy employed by Porsche, would you say that the purchasing power of the U.S. dollar customer has grown stronger or weaker?

3. In the long run, what do most automobile manufacturers do to avoid these large exchange rate squeezes?

EXHIBIT 1   Pass-Through Analysis for the 911 Carrera 4S Cabriolet, 2003

Assume that Porsche established what it considered the target price in April 2003, when the exchange rate was $1.0862/€. This allowed Porsche to price in a margin of approximately 15% on a full-cost basis, with a European price of €85,900 and a target North American price of $93,200, which preserved the 15% margin.

Actual North American launch of the 4S Cabriolet did not occur until July. By then, the spot exchange rate had effectively reduced the margin earned by Porsche on the new model. As 2003 continued, the margin continued to erode.

Price Component	Pricing Apr	May	Jun	NA Launch Jul	Aug	Sep	Oct	Nov	Dec
Full cost	€74,696	€74,696	€74,696	€74,696	€74,696	€74,696	€74,696	€74,696	€74,696
Margin (@ 15%)	€11,204	€11,204	€11,204	€11,204	€11,204	€11,204	€11,204	€11,204	€11,204
European price	€85,900	€85,900	€85,900	€85,900	€85,900	€85,900	€85,900	€85,900	€85,900
Spot rate ($/€)	1.0862	1.1565	1.1676	1.1362	1.1286	1.1267	1.1714	1.1710	1.2298
Base price in US$ if 100% pass-through	$93,305	$99,343	$100,297	$97,600	$96,947	$96,784	$100,623	$100,589	$105,640

Effective Margin on 4S Cabriolet with Capped US$ Price

Price Component	Apr	May	Jun	Jul	Aug	Sep	Oct	Nov	Dec
Target price in US$	$93,200	$93,200	$93,200	$93,200	$93,200	$93,200	$93,200	$93,200	$93,200
Spot rate ($/€)	1.0862	1.1565	1.1676	1.1362	1.1286	1.1267	1.1714	1.1710	1.2298
Price received in euros	€85,804	€80,588	€79,822	€82,028	€82,580	€82,719	€79,563	€79,590	€75,785
Less full cost	(€74,696)	(€74,696)	(€74,696)	(€74,696)	(€74,696)	(€74,696)	(€74,696)	(€74,696)	(€74,696)
Residual margin	€11,108	€5,892	€5,126	€7,332	€7,885	€8,024	€4,867	€4,894	€1,089
Margin (%)	14.9%	7.9%	6.9%	9.8%	10.6%	10.7%	6.5%	6.6%	1.5%

QUESTIONS

1. **Purchasing Power Parity.** Define the following terms:
   a. The law of one price
   b. Absolute purchasing power parity
   c. Relative purchasing power parity

2. **Nominal Effective Exchange Rate Index.** Explain how a nominal effective exchange rate index is constructed.

3. **Real Effective Exchange Rate Index.** What formula is used to convert a nominal effective exchange rate index into a real effective exchange rate index?

4. **Real Effective Exchange Rates: Japan and the United States.** Exhibit 7.3 compares the real effective exchange rates for Japan and the United States. If the comparative real effective exchange rate was the main determinant, does Japan or the United States have a competitive advantage in exporting? Which of the two has an advantage in importing? Explain why.

5. **Exchange Rate Pass-Through.** Incomplete *exchange rate pass-through* is one reason that a country's real effective exchange rate can deviate for lengthy periods from its purchasing power equilibrium level of

100. What is meant by the term *exchange rate pass-through*?

6. **The Fisher Effect.** Define the *Fisher effect*. To what extent do empirical tests confirm that the *Fisher effect* exists in practice?

7. **The International Fisher Effect.** Define the *international Fisher effect*. To what extent do empirical tests confirm that the *international Fisher effect* exists in practice?

8. **Interest Rate Parity.** Define *interest rate parity*. What is the relationship between *interest rate parity* and forward rates?

9. **Covered Interest Arbitrage.** Define the terms *covered interest arbitrage* and *uncovered interest arbitrage*. What is the difference between these two transactions?

10. **Forward Rate as an Unbiased Predictor of the Future Spot Rate.** Some forecasters believe that foreign exchange markets for the major floating currencies are "efficient" and forward exchange rates are *unbiased predictors* of future spot exchange rates. What is meant by "unbiased predictor" in terms of how the forward rate performs in estimating future spot exchange rates?

PROBLEMS

1–5. The Latin American Big Mac Index: Historical Comparison. This textbook has used *The Economist* magazine's Big Mac Index for many years. Below are the Big Mac prices and actual exchange rates for select Latin American countries as printed in previous editions. Use the data in the table to complete the calculation of the implied PPP value of the currency versus the U.S. dollar and the calculation as to whether that currency is undervalued or overvalued versus the U.S. dollar.

Big Mac Index: April 1997 Country	(1) Big Mac Prices in Local Currency	(2) Actual Exchange Rate (April 7,1997)	(3) Big Mac Prices Prices in Dollars	(4) Implied PPP of the Dollar	(5) Local Currency Under (–) / Over (+) Valuation
United States (dollar)	2.42	—	2.42	1.00	
Argentina (peso)	2.50	1.00	_____	_____	_____
Brazil (reais)	2.97	1.06	_____	_____	_____
Chile (peso)	1,200.00	417.00	_____	_____	_____
Mexico (peso)	14.90	7.90	_____	_____	_____

Big Mac Index: March 1999 Country	(1) Big Mac Prices in Local Currency	(2) Actual Exchange Rate (March 30, 1999)	(3) Big Mac Prices Prices in Dollars	(4) Implied PPP of the Dollar	(5) Local Currency Under (–) / Over (+) Valuation
United States (dollar)	2.43	—	2.43	1.00	
Argentina (peso)	2.50	1.00	_____	_____	_____
Brazil (reais)	2.95	1.73	_____	_____	_____
Chile (peso)	1,250.00	484.00	_____	_____	_____
Mexico (peso)	19.90	9.54	_____	_____	_____

Big Mac Index: April 2002	(1) Big Mac Prices in Local Currency	(2) Actual Exchange Rate (April 23, 2002)	(3) Big Mac Prices Prices in Dollars	(4) Implied PPP of the Dollar	(5) Local Currency Under (–) / Over (+) Valuation
Country					
United States (dollar)	2.49	—	2.49	1.00	
Argentina (peso)	2.50	3.13	_____	_____	_____
Brazil (reais)	3.60	2.34	_____	_____	_____
Chile (peso)	1,400.00	655.00	_____	_____	_____
Mexico (peso)	21.90	9.28	_____	_____	_____

Big Mac Index: April 2005	(1) Big Mac Prices in Local Currency	(2) Actual Exchange Rate (April 2005)	(3) Big Mac Prices Prices in Dollars	(4) Implied PPP of the Dollar	(5) Local Currency Under (–) / Over (+) Valuation
Country					
United States (dollar)	3.06	—	3.06	1.00	
Argentina (peso)	4.75	2.90	_____	_____	_____
Brazil (reais)	5.90	2.47	_____	_____	_____
Chile (peso)	1,500	594.00	_____	_____	_____
Mexico (peso)	28.00	10.84	_____	_____	_____

Notes: Column 3 = Column 1 / Column 2; Column 4 = Column 1 / Big Mac US$ Price; Column 5 = Column 4/Column 2.

*6. **Argentine Peso and PPP.** The Argentine peso was fixed through a currency board at Ps1.00/$ throughout the 1990s. In January 2002 the Argentine peso was floated. On January 29, 2003, it was trading at Ps3.20/$. During that one year period Argentina's inflation rate was 20% on an annualized basis. Inflation in the United States during that same period was 2.2% annualized.

a. What should have been the exchange rate in January 2003 if purchasing power parity held?

b. By what percentage was the Argentine peso undervalued on an annualized basis?

c. What were the probable causes of undervaluation?

7. **Akira Numata—CIA Japan.** Akira Numata, a foreign exchange trader at Credit Suisse (Tokyo), is exploring covered interest arbitrage possibilities. He wants to invest $5,000,000 or its yen equivalent, in a covered interest arbitrage between U.S. dollars and Japanese yen. He faced the following exchange rate and interest rate quotes:

Spot exchange rate:	¥118.60/$	180-day forward exchange rate:	¥117.80/$
180-day dollar interest rate:	4.800% per year		
180-day yen interest rate:	3.400% per year		

The bank does not calculate transaction costs on any individual transaction because these costs are part of the overall operating budget of the arbitrage depart-ment. Explain and diagram the specific steps Akira must take to make a covered interest arbitrage profit.

8. **Akira Numata—UIA Japan.** Akira Numata, Credit Suisse (Tokyo), observes that the ¥/$ spot rate has been holding steady, and both dollar and yen interest rates have remained relatively fixed over the past week. Akira wonders if he should try an uncovered interest arbitrage (UIA) transaction and thereby save the cost of forward cover. Many of Akira's research associates—and their computer models—are predicting the spot rate to remain close to ¥118.00/$ for the coming 180 days. Using the same data as in the previous problem, analyze the UIA potential.

a. Calculate how much profit Akira could make if his expectations prove correct.

b. What is the risk he is taking? What if the spot rate in 180 days is ¥106.00/$?

9. **Joseph Yazzie and Japanese/United States Parity Conditions.** Joseph Yazzie is attempting to determine whether U.S./Japanese financial conditions are at parity. The current spot rate is a flat ¥120.00/$, while the 360-day forward rate is ¥115.40/$. Forecast inflation is 1.00% for Japan, 5.00% for the United States. The 360-day euro-yen deposit rate is 4.000%, and the 360-day euro-dollar deposit rate is 8.000%. Using this data, diagram and calculate whether international parity conditions hold between Japan and the United States. What is the forecasted change in the Japanese yen/U.S. dollar (¥/$) exchange rate one year hence?

*10. XTerra Exports and Pass-Through. Assume that the export price of a Nissan XTerra from Osaka, Japan, is ¥3,250,000. The exchange rate is ¥115.20/$. The forecast rate of inflation in the United States is 2.2% per year and is 0.0% per year in Japan.

a. What is the export price of the XTerra at the beginning of the year expressed in U.S. dollars?

b. Assuming purchasing power parity holds, what should the exchange rate be at the end of the year?

c. Assuming 100% pass-through of exchange rate changes, what should be the dollar price of an XTerra at the end of the year?

d. Assuming 75% pass-through, what should be the price of an XTerra at the end of the year?

11. Copenhagen CIA (A). John Duell, a foreign exchange trader at JPMorgan Chase can invest $5 million or the foreign currency equivalent of the bank's short-term funds in a covered interest arbitrage with Denmark. Using the following quotes, can John Duell make a covered interest arbitrage (CIA) profit?

Spot exchange rate:	kr 6.1720/$
Three-month forward rate:	kr 6.1980/$
Three-month dollar interest:	3.0% per year (0.75% for 90 days)
Three-month krone interest:	5.0% per year (1.25% for 90 days)

12. Copenhagen CIA (B). John Duell is now evaluating the arbitrage profit potential in the same market after interest rates change.

a. Assume that interest rates in the United States increase to 4% per year (1% for 90 days) but all other rates remain the same. Can John make a 90-day covered interest arbitrage profit?

b. Assume that Danish kroner interest rates increase to 6% per year (1.5% for 90 days) but all other rates remain the same, including the original U.S. interest rate of 3% per year. Calculate if John could make a 90-day covered interest arbitrage profit.

13. Luis Pinzon—CIA New York. Luis Pinzon is a foreign exchange dealer for a bank in New York. He has $1,000,000 (or its Swiss franc equivalent) for a short-term money market investment and wonders if he should invest in U.S. dollars for three months or make a covered interest arbitrage investment in the Swiss franc. He faces the rates shown in the table:

a. Where do you recommend Luis invest, and why?

b. What is Luis's rate of return, on an annual basis, on this investment?

Spot exchange rate:	SFr.1.2810/$
Three-month forward rate:	SFr.1.2740/$
Three-month U.S. interest rate:	4.800% p.a. (1.200% per quarter)
Three-month Swiss interest rate:	3.200% p.a. (0.800% per quarter)

14. Luis Pinzon—UIA. Luis Pinzon, using the same values and assumptions as in the previous question, now decides to seek the full 4.800% return available in U.S. dollars by not covering his forward dollar receipts—an uncovered interest arbitrage (UIA) transaction. Assess this decision.

*15. Luis Pinzon—30 Days Later. One month after the events described in the previous questions, Luis Pinzon again has $1,000,000 (or its Swiss franc equivalent) to invest for three months. He now faces the following rates. Should he again enter into a covered interest arbitrage (CIA) investment?

Spot exchange rate:	SF1.3392/$
Three-month forward rate:	SF1.3286/$
Three-month U.S. interest rate:	4.750% per annum
Three-month Swiss rate:	3.625% per annum

16. Langkawi Island Resort. You are planning a 30-day vacation on Langkawi Island, Malaysia, one year from now. The present charge for a luxury suite plus meals in Malaysian ringgit (RM) is RM1,050/day. The Malaysian ringgit presently trades at RM3.75/$. Hence, the dollar cost today for a 30-day stay would be $8,400. The hotel has informed you that any increase in its room charges will be limited to any increase in the Malaysian cost of living. Malaysian inflation is expected to be 4% per annum, while U.S. inflation is expected to be only 1%.

a. How many dollars might you expect to need one year hence to pay for your 30-day vacation?

b. By what percent has the dollar cost gone up? Why?

17. Statoil of Norway's Arbitrage. Statoil, the national oil company of Norway, is a large, sophisticated, and active participant in both the currency and petrochemical markets. Although it is a Norwegian company, because it operates within the global oil market it considers the U.S. dollar as its functional currency, not the Norwegian krone. Ari Karlsen is a currency trader for Statoil, and has immediate use of either $4 million or the Norwegian krone equivalent. Faced with the following market rates, he wonders whether he can make some arbitrage profits in the coming 90 days.

Spot rate, Norwegian krone (kr) per dollar:	kr 6.5520/
Three-month forward rate:	kr 6.5264/
U.S. three-month treasury bill rate:	5.625% per annum
Norwegian three-month treasury bill rate:	4.250% per annum

18. **London and New York.** Money and foreign exchange markets in London and New York are very efficient. The following information is available:

	London	New York
Spot exchange rate	$1.3860/€	$1.3860/€
One-year treasury bill rate	3.800%	4.20%
Expected inflation rate	unknown	2.00%

  a. What do the financial markets suggest for inflation in Europe next year?
  b. Estimate today's one-year forward exchange rate between the dollar and the euro.

19. **Chamonix Chateau Rentals.** You are planning a ski vacation to Mt. Blanc in Chamonix, France, one year from now. You are negotiating the rental of a chateau. The chateau's owner wishes to preserve his real income against both inflation and exchange rate changes, and so the present weekly rent of €9,800 (Christmas season) will be adjusted upward or downward for any change in the French cost of living between now and then. You are basing your budgeting on purchasing power parity (PPP). French inflation is expected to average 3.5% for the coming year, while U.S. dollar inflation is expected to be 2.5%. The current spot rate is $1.3620/€. What should you budget as the U.S. dollar cost of the one week rental?

20. **East Asiatic Company—Thailand.** The East Asiatic Company (EAC), a Danish company with subsidiaries all over Asia, has been funding its Bangkok subsidiary primarily with U.S. dollar debt because of the cost and availability of dollar capital as opposed to Thai baht (B) funds. The treasurer of EAC-Thailand is considering a one-year bank loan for $350,000. The current spot exchange rate is B42.84/$, and the dollar-based interest is 8.885% for the one year period. The current spot exchange rate is B42.84/$. One year loans are 14% in baht but only 8.885% in dollars.
  a. Assuming expected inflation rates of 4.50% and 2.20% in Thailand and the United States, respec-

tively, for the coming year, according to purchasing power parity, what would the effective cost of funds be in Thai baht terms?
  b. If EAC's foreign exchange advisers believe strongly that the Thai government wishes to push the value of the baht down against the dollar by 5% over the coming year (to promote its export competitiveness in dollar markets), what might the effective cost of funds end up being in baht terms?
  c. If EAC could borrow Thai baht at 14% per annum, would this be cheaper than either part (a) or part (b) above?

21. **Maltese Falcon: March 2003–2004.** The infamous solid gold falcon, initially intended as a tribute to the King of Spain by the Knights of Malta in appreciation for his gift of the island of Malta to the order in 1530, has recently been recovered. The falcon is 14 inches high, solid gold, and weighs approximately 48 pounds. Gold prices in late 2002 and early 2003, primarily as a result of increasing international political tensions, have risen to $440/ounce.

The falcon is currently held by a private investor in Istanbul, who is actively negotiating with the Maltese government for its purchase and prospective return to its island home. The sale and payment are to take place in March 2004, and the parties are negotiating over the price and currency of payment. The investor has decided, in a show of goodwill, to base the sales price only on the falcon's *specie value*—its gold value.

The current spot exchange rate is 0.39 Maltese lira (ML) per U.S. dollar. Maltese inflation is expected to be about 8.5% for the coming year, while U.S. inflation, on the heels of a double-dip recession, is expected to come in at only 1.5%. If the investor bases value in the U.S. dollar, would he be better off receiving Maltese lira in one year—assuming purchasing power parity, or receiving a guaranteed dollar payment assuming a gold price of $420 per ounce?

22. **London Money Fund.** Tim Hogan is the manager of an international money market fund managed out of London. Unlike many money funds that guarantee their investors a near-risk-free investment with variable interest earnings, Tim Hogan's fund is a very aggressive fund, which searches out relatively high interest earnings around the globe, but at some risk. The fund is pound-denominated.

Tim is currently evaluating a rather interesting opportunity in Malaysia. The Malaysian government has been periodically enforcing substantive currency

CHAPTER 7 International Parity Conditions

and capital restrictions since the Asian Crisis of 1997 to protect and preserve the value of the Malaysian ringgit (RM). The current spot exchange rate of RM3.750/$ has been maintained with little deviation since late 1997. Local currency (Malaysian ringgit) time deposits of 180-day maturities are hovering at about 9.600% per annum ($500,000 minimum deposit). The London eurocurrency market, for pounds, is offering only about 4.200% per annum for the same 180-day maturities. The current spot rate on the British pound is $1.7640/£, and the 180-day forward rate is $1.7420/£. What do you recommend Tim Hogan do about the Malaysian money market opportunity assuming he is investing £1 million?

23. **The Beer Standard.** In 1999 *The Economist* magazine reported the creation of an index or standard for the evaluation of currency values in Africa. Beer was chosen as the product for comparison because McDonald's had not penetrated the African continent beyond South Africa, and Beer met most of the same product and market characteristics required for the construction of a proper currency index.

Investec, a South African investment banking firm, has replicated the process of creating a measure of purchasing power parity like that of the Big Mac Index of The Economist, *for Africa. The index compares the cost of a 375 milliliter bottle of clear lager beer across sub-Sahara Africa. As a measure of purchasing power parity, the beer needs to be relatively homogeneous in qualities across countries, and needs to possess sub-*

stantial elements of local manufacturing, distribution, and service, in order to actually provide a measure of relative purchasing power.

The beers are first priced in local currency (purchased in the taverns of the local man, and not in the high-priced tourist centers and servers), then converted to South African rand. The prices of the beers in rand are then compared to form one measure of whether the local currencies are either undervalued (−%) or overvalued (+%) versus the South African rand.

Use the data in the table at the bottom of this page and complete the calculation of whether the individual African currencies listed are overvalued or undervalued.

24. **Brynja Johannsdottir and the Icelandic Carry-Trade.** Brynja Johannsdottir is Icelandic by birth, but is working for Magma Capital, a currency hedge fund run out of New York. The high money market rates offered in Iceland have been supporting the carry-trade, as investors borrow in cheaper currencies (nearly any currency at this point) and invest for the short term in Icelandic krona. But they do so on an uncovered basis. Brynja believes that—at least for the coming three- to six-month period—the krona will continue to stay strong, sticking at kr.70/$. Her bank requires that any position she takes yields at least 4.0% for the period in question (16% annually). Using the assumptions in the preceding table, she wishes to evaluate the uncovered interest arbitrage (UIA) potential.

The Beer Standard

Country	Beer	Beer Prices In Local Currency	In Rand	Implied PPP Rate	Spot Rate 3/15/99	Under or Overvalued to Rand %
South Africa	Castle	Rand 2.30	2.30	—	—	—
Botswana	Castle	Pula 2.20	2.94	0.96	0.75	_____
Ghana	Star	Cedi 1,200	3.17	521.74	379.10	_____
Kenya	Tusker	Shilling 41.25	4.02	17.93	10.27	_____
Malawi	Carlsberg	Kwacha 18.50	2.66	8.04	6.96	_____
Mauritius	Phoenix	Rupee 15.00	3.72	6.52	4.03	_____
Namibia	Windhoek	N$ 2.50	2.50	1.09	1.00	_____
Zambia	Castle	Kwacha 1,200	3.52	521.74	340.68	_____
Zimbabwe	Castle	Z$ 9.00	1.46	3.91	6.15	_____

Beer price in rand = Price in local currency/spot rate.
Implied PPP rate = Price in rand/2.30.
Under/Overvalued to rand = Implied PPP rate/spot rate.

Source: The Economist, May 8, 1999, p. 78.

Arbitrage funds available ($)	$2,000,000
Spot exchange rate (kr./$)	71.6350
Three-month forward rate (kr./$)	72.9127
Expected spot rate in 90 days (kr.$)	70.0000
U.S. dollar three-month interest rate	4.800%
Icelandic krona three-month interest rate	12.020%

Arbitrage funds available ($)	$1,000,000
Spot exchange rate (¥/$)	118.00
Three-month forward rate (¥/$)	117.33
Expected spot rate in 90 days (¥/$)	118.00
U.S. dollar three-month interest rate	4.800%
New U.S. dollar three-month interest rate (August 15)	4.400%
Japanese yen three-month interest rate	2.500%

25. **Plummeting Yen Carry-Trade.** The Japanese yen, long the home of the global carry-trade as the lowest interest cost source of funds of any major industrial market, began strengthening in August 2007. The yen had remained relatively quiet and above ¥118/$ for several months. Most analysts and arbitragers believed it would stay at 118, maybe falling to 120. As the U.S. subprime mortgage crisis hit in August 2007, U.S. dollar interest rates starting rising, initially adding some momentum to the carry-trade.

But then on August 14, the rising concerns over the financial health of the U.S. economy caused a fall in the dollar, and the yen starting appreciating significantly against the dollar (rising quickly to ¥114/$). This was devastating for the carry-trade, as a rising yen undermined the uncovered interest arbitrage benefits. Within days, things worsened. In an effort to increase the liquidity of the U.S. financial sector fearing rising mortgage-backed securities defaults, the U.S. Federal Reserve lowered the discount rate, which caused a fall in short-term interest rates.

Daily Exchange Rates: Japanese Yen per U.S. Dollar

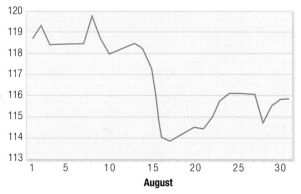

Source: Pacific Exchange Rate Service

Using the following inputs and the exchange rate graphic above, using a $1,000,000 notional principal (or Japanese yen equivalent), show how the Japanese yen carry-trade results in a negative investment return after the rise of the yen and the fall of U.S. dollar interest rates:

INTERNET EXERCISES

1. **Big Mac Index Updated.** Use *The Economist's* Web site to find the latest edition of the Big Mac Index of currency overvaluation and undervaluation. (You will need to do a search for "Big Mac Currencies.") Create a worksheet to compare how the British pound, the euro, the Swiss franc, and the Canadian dollar have changed from the version presented in this chapter.

   The Economist   www.economist.com/markets/ Bigmac/Index.cfm

2. **Purchasing Power Parity Statistics.** The Organization for Economic Cooperation and Development (OECD) publishes detailed measures of prices and purchasing power for its member countries. Go to the OECD's Web site and download the spreadsheet file with the historical data for purchasing power for the member countries.

   OECD Purchasing Power   www.oecd.org/department/ 0,3355,en_2649_34357_1_1_1_ 1_1,00.html

3. **International Interest Rates.** A number of Web sites publish current interest rates by currency and maturity. Use the *Financial Times* Web site to isolate the interest rate differentials between the U.S. dollar, the British pound, and the euro for all maturities up to and including one year.

   Financial Times
   Market Data   www.ft.com/markets

   Data Listed by the *Financial Times*:
   - International money rates (bank call rates for major currency deposits)
   - Money rates (LIBOR, CD rates, etc.)
   - 10-year spreads (individual country spreads versus the euro and U.S. 10-year treasuries) Note: Which

countries actually have lower 10-year government bond rates than the United States and the euro? Probably Switzerland and Japan. Check.

- Benchmark government bonds (sampling of representative government issuances by major countries and recent price movements) Note which countries are showing longer maturity benchmark rates.
- Emerging market bonds (government issuances, Brady bonds, etc.)
- Eurozone rates (miscellaneous bond rates for assorted European-based companies; includes debt ratings by Moodys and S&P)

4. **World Bank's International Comparison Program.** The World Bank has an ongoing research program that focuses on the relative purchasing power of 107 different economies globally, specifically in terms of household consumption. Download the latest data tables and highlight which economies seem to be showing the greatest growth in recent years in relative purchasing power.

World Bank International   go.worldbank.org/
Comparison Program   7UQYBDJZAO

An Algebraic Primer to International Parity Conditions

The following is a purely algebraic presentation of the parity conditions explained in this chapter. It is offered to provide those who wish additional theoretical detail and definition ready access to the step-by-step derivation of the various conditions.

The Law of One Price

The *law of one price* refers to the state in which, in the presence of free trade, perfect substitutability of goods, and costless transactions, the equilibrium exchange rate between two currencies is determined by the ratio of the price of any commodity i denominated in two different currencies. For example,

$$S_t = \frac{P_{i,t}^{\$}}{P_{i,t}^{\mathrm{SF}}}$$

where $P_i^{\$}$ and P_i^{SF} refer to the prices of the same commodity i, at time t, denominated in U.S. dollars and Swiss francs, respectively. The spot exchange rate, S_t, is simply the ratio of the two currency prices.

Purchasing Power Parity

The more general form in which the exchange rate is determined by the ratio of two price indexes is termed the absolute version of purchasing power parity (PPP). Each price index reflects the currency cost of the identical "basket" of goods across countries. The exchange rate that equates purchasing power for the identical collection of goods is then stated:

$$S_t = \frac{P_t^{\$}}{P_t^{\mathrm{SF}}}$$

where $P_t^{\$}$ and P_t^{SF} are the price index values in U.S. dollars and Swiss francs at time t, respectively. If π represents the rate of inflation in each country, the spot exchange rate at time $t + 1$ would be

$$S_{t+1} = \frac{P_t^{\$}\left(1+\pi^{\$}\right)}{P_t^{\mathrm{SF}}\left(1+\pi^{\mathrm{SF}}\right)} = S_t \left[\frac{\left(1+\pi^{\$}\right)}{\left(1+\pi^{\mathrm{SF}}\right)} \right]$$

The change from period t to $t + 1$ is then

$$\frac{S_{t+1}}{S_t} = \frac{\dfrac{P_t^\$\left(1+\pi^\$\right)}{P_t^{SF}\left(1+\pi^{SF}\right)}}{\dfrac{P_t^\$}{P_t^{SF}}} = \frac{S_t\left[\dfrac{\left(1+\pi^\$\right)}{\left(1+\pi^{SF}\right)}\right]}{S_t} = \frac{\left(1+\pi^\$\right)}{\left(1+\pi^{SF}\right)}$$

Isolating the percentage change in the spot exchange rate between periods t and $t + 1$ is then

$$\frac{S_{t+1} - S_t}{S_t} = \frac{S_t\left[\dfrac{\left(1+\pi^\$\right)}{\left(1+\pi^{SF}\right)}\right] - S_t}{S_t} = \frac{\left(1+\pi^\$\right) - \left(1+\pi^{SF}\right)}{\left(1+\pi^{SF}\right)}$$

This equation is often approximated by dropping the denominator of the right-hand side if it is considered to be relatively small. It is then stated as

$$\frac{S_{t+1} - S_t}{S_t} = \left(1+\pi^\$\right) - \left(1+\pi^{SF}\right) = \pi^\$ - \pi^{SF}$$

Forward Rates

The forward exchange rate is that contractual rate which is available to private agents through banking institutions and other financial intermediaries who deal in foreign currencies and debt instruments. The annualized percentage difference between the forward rate and the spot rate is termed the forward premium:

$$f^{SF} = \left[\frac{F_{t,t+1} - S_t}{S_t}\right] \times \left[\frac{360}{n_{t,t+1}}\right]$$

where f^{SF} is the forward premium on the Swiss franc, $F_{t,t+1}$ is the forward rate contracted at time t for delivery at time $t + 1$, S_t is the current spot rate, and $n_{t,t+1}$ is the number of days between the contract date (t) and the delivery date ($t + 1$).

Covered Interest Arbitrage (CIA) and Interest Rate Parity (IRP)

The process of covered interest arbitrage is when an investor exchanges domestic currency for foreign currency in the spot market, invests that currency in an interest-bearing instrument, and signs a forward contract to "lock in" a future exchange rate at which to convert the foreign currency proceeds (gross) back to domestic currency. The net return on CIA is

$$\text{Net return} = \left[\frac{\left(1+i^{SF}\right)F_{t,t+1}}{S_t}\right] - \left(1+i^\$\right)$$

where S_t and $F_{t,t+1}$ are the spot and forward rates (\$/SF), i^{SF} is the nominal interest rate (or yield) on a Swiss franc-denominated monetary instrument, and $i^\$$ is the nominal return on a similar dollar-denominated instrument.

If they possess exactly equal rates of return—that is, if CIA results in zero riskless profit—interest rate parity (IRP) holds, and appears as

$$\left(1+i^{\$}\right) = \left[\frac{\left(1+i^{SF}\right)F_{t,t+1}}{S_t}\right]$$

or alternatively as

$$\frac{\left(1+i^{\$}\right)}{\left(1+i^{SF}\right)} = \frac{F_{t,t+1}}{S_t}$$

If the percent difference of both sides of this equation is found (the percentage difference between the spot and forward rate is the forward premium), then the relationship between the forward premium and relative interest rate differentials is

$$\frac{F_{t,t+1} - S_t}{S_t} = f^{SF} = \frac{i^{\$} - i^{SF}}{i^{\$} + i^{SF}}$$

If these values are not equal (thus the markets are not in equilibrium), there exists a potential for riskless profit. The market will then be driven back to equilibrium through CIA by agents attempting to exploit such arbitrage potential, until CIA yields no positive return.

Fisher Effect

The Fisher effect states that all nominal interest rates can be decomposed into an implied real rate of interest (return) and an expected rate of inflation:

$$i^{\$} = \left[\left(1+r^{\$}\right)\left(1+\pi^{\$}\right)\right] - 1$$

where $r^{\$}$ is the real rate of return, and $\pi^{\$}$ is the expected rate of inflation, for dollar-denominated assets. The sub-components are then identifiable:

$$i^{\$} = r^{\$} + \pi^{\$} + r^{\$}\,\pi^{\$}$$

As with PPP, there is an approximation of this function that has gained wide acceptance. The cross-product term of $r^{\$}\,\pi^{\$}$ is often very small and therefore dropped altogether:

$$i^{\$} = r^{\$} + \pi^{\$}$$

International Fisher Effect

The international Fisher effect is the extension of this domestic interest rate relationship to the international currency markets. If capital, by way of covered interest arbitrage (CIA), attempts to find higher rates of return internationally resulting from current interest rate differentials, the real rates of return between currencies are equalized (e.g., $r^{\$} = r^{SF}$):

$$\frac{S_{t+1} - S_t}{S_t} = \frac{\left(1+i^{\$}\right) - \left(1+i^{SF}\right)}{\left(1+i^{SF}\right)} = \frac{i^{\$} - i^{SF}}{\left(1+i^{SF}\right)}$$

If the nominal interest rates are then decomposed into their respective real and expected inflation components, the percentage change in the spot exchange rate is

$$\frac{S_{t+1}-S_t}{S_t} = \frac{\left(r^\$ + \pi^\$ + r^\$\pi^\$\right) - \left(r^{SF} + \pi^{SF} + r^{SF}\pi^{SF}\right)}{1 + r^{SF} + \pi^{SF} + r^{SF}\pi^{SF}}$$

The international Fisher effect has a number of additional implications, if the following requirements are met: (1) capital markets can be freely entered and exited; (2) capital markets possess investment opportunities that are acceptable substitutes; and (3) market agents have complete and equal information regarding these possibilities.

Given these conditions, international arbitragers are capable of exploiting all potential riskless profit opportunities, until real rates of return between markets are equalized ($r^\$ = r^{SF}$). Thus, the expected rate of change in the spot exchange rate reduces to the differential in the expected rates of inflation:

$$\frac{S_{t+1}-S_t}{S_t} = \frac{\pi^\$ + r^\$\pi^\$ - \pi^{SF} - r^{SF}\pi^{SF}}{1 + r^{SF} + \pi^{SF} + r^{SF}\pi^{SF}}$$

If the approximation forms are combined (through the elimination of the denominator and the elimination of the interactive terms of r and π), the change in the spot rate is simply

$$\frac{S_{t+1}-S_t}{S_t} = \pi^\$ - \pi^{SF}$$

Note the similarity (identical in equation form) of the approximate form of the international Fisher effect to purchasing power parity, discussed previously (the only potential difference is that between *ex post* and *ex ante*, or expected, inflation).

CHAPTER 8

Foreign Currency Derivatives

Unless derivatives contracts are collateralized or guaranteed, their ultimate value also depends on the creditworthiness of the counterparties to them. In the meantime, though, before a contract is settled, the counterparties record profits and losses—often huge in amount—in their current earnings statements without so much as a penny changing hands. The range of derivatives contracts is limited only by the imagination of man (or sometimes, so it seems, madmen).

—Warren Buffett, *Berkshire Hathaway Annual Report, 2002.*

Financial management of the multinational enterprise in the twenty-first century will need to consider the use of *financial derivatives*. These derivatives, so named because their values are derived from an underlying asset like a stock or a currency, are a powerful tool used in business today for two very distinct management objectives, speculation and hedging. The financial manager of an MNE may purchase these financial derivatives in order to take positions in the expectation of profit, *speculation*, or may use these instruments to reduce the risks associated with the everyday management of corporate cash flow, *hedging*. Before these financial instruments can be used effectively, however, the financial manager must understand certain basics about their structure and pricing. We will cover two common foreign currency financial derivatives in this chapter, foreign currency futures and foreign currency options. We focus here on the fundamentals of their valuation and their use for speculative purposes. Chapter 9 will describe the valuation and use of interest rate swaps, the financial derivative most widely used by firms today. Chapter 11 will describe how these foreign currency derivatives can be used to hedge commercial transactions.

A word of caution—of reservation—before we proceed. Financial derivatives are a powerful tool in the hands of careful and competent financial managers. They can also be very destructive devices when used recklessly. The 1990s were littered with cases in which financial managers lost control of their derivatives, resulting in significant losses for their companies and occasionally outright collapse. In the right hands and with proper controls, however, financial derivatives may provide management with opportunities to enhance and protect their corporate financial performance. On the other hand, the mini-case at the end of this chapter describes how one rogue trader, Nicholas Leeson, brought down Baring Brothers & Co. through uncontrolled speculation. We begin with the relatively easier foreign currency derivative, the foreign currency future.

Foreign Currency Futures

A *foreign currency futures contract* is an alternative to a forward contract that calls for future delivery of a standard amount of foreign exchange at a fixed time, place, and price. It is similar to futures contracts that exist for commodities (hogs, cattle, lumber, and so on), interest-bearing deposits, and gold.

Most world money centers have established foreign currency futures markets. In the United States the most important market for foreign currency futures is the International Monetary Market (IMM) of Chicago, a division of the Chicago Mercantile Exchange.

Contract Specifications

Contract specifications are established by the exchange on which futures are traded. For example, in the Chicago IMM, the major features that must be standardized are the following:

- **Size of the Contract.** Called the *notional principal*; trading in each currency must be done in an even multiple of currency units.

- **Method of Stating Exchange Rates.** "American terms" are used; that is, quotations are the U.S. dollar cost of foreign currency units, also known as direct quotes.

- **Maturity Date.** Contracts mature on the third Wednesday of January, March, April, June, July, September, October, or December.

- **Last Trading Day.** Contracts may be traded through the second business day prior to the Wednesday on which they mature. Therefore, unless holidays interfere, the last trading day is the Monday preceding the maturity date.

- **Collateral and Maintenance Margins.** The purchaser must deposit a sum as an initial margin or collateral. This requirement is similar to requiring a performance bond, and it can be met by a letter of credit from a bank, Treasury bills, or cash. In addition, a maintenance margin is required. The value of the contract is marked to market daily, and all changes in value are paid in cash daily. *Marked to market* means that the value of the contract is revalued using the closing price for the day. The amount to be paid is called the *variation margin*.

- **Settlement.** Only about 5% of all futures contracts are settled by the physical delivery of foreign exchange between buyer and seller. Most often, buyers and sellers offset their original position prior to delivery date by taking an opposite position. That is, if one party buys a futures contract, that party will normally close out its position by selling a futures contract for the same delivery date. The complete buy/sell or sell/buy is called a "round turn."

- **Commissions.** Customers pay a commission to their broker to execute a round turn and a single price is quoted. This practice differs from that of the interbank market, where dealers quote a bid and an offer and do not charge a commission.

- **Use of a Clearing House as a Counterparty.** All contracts are agreements between the client and the exchange clearing house, rather than between the two clients involved. Consequently clients need not worry that a specific counterparty in the market will fail to honor an agreement. The clearing house is owned and guaranteed by all members of the exchange.

Using Foreign Currency Futures

To illustrate the use of currency futures for speculating on currency movements, we will focus on the Mexican peso futures traded on the Chicago Mercantile Exchange (CME). Exhibit 8.1

presents typical Mexican peso (Ps) futures quotations from *The Wall Street Journal*. Each contract is for 500,000 "new Mexican pesos," and is quoted in U.S. dollars per Mexican peso.

Any investor wishing to speculate on the movement of the Mexican peso versus the U.S. dollar could pursue one of the following strategies. Keep in mind that the principle of a futures contract is that if a speculator buys a futures contract, they are locking in the price at which they must buy that currency on the specified future date, and if they sell a futures contract, they are locking in the price at which they must sell that currency on that future date.

Short Positions. If Amber McClain, a speculator working for International Currency Traders, believes the Mexican peso will fall in value versus the U.S. dollar by March, she could sell a March futures contract, taking a *short position*. By selling a March contract, Amber locks in the right to sell 500,000 Mexican pesos at a set price. If the price of the peso does fall by the maturity date as she expects, Amber has a contract to sell pesos at a price above their current price on the spot market. Hence, she makes a profit.

Using the quotes on Mexican peso futures in Exhibit 8.1, Amber sells one March futures contract for 500,000 pesos at the closing price, termed *settle price*, of $.10958/Ps. The value of her position at maturity—at the expiration of the futures contract in March—is then

$$\text{Value at maturity (Short position)} = -\text{Notional principal} \times (\text{Spot} - \text{Futures})$$

Note that the short position is entered into the valuation as a negative notional principal. If the spot exchange rate at maturity is $.09500/Ps, the value of her position on settlement is

$$\text{Value} = -\text{Ps}500{,}000 \times (\$.09500/\text{Ps} - \$.10958/\text{Ps}) = \$7{,}290$$

Amber's expectation proved correct: the Mexican peso fell in value versus the U.S. dollar. We could say that "Amber ends up buying at $.09500 and sells at $.10958 per peso."

All that was really required of Amber to speculate on the Mexican peso's value was that she formed an opinion on the Mexican peso's future exchange value versus the U.S. dollar. In this case, she opined that it would fall in value by the March maturity date of the futures contract.

Long Positions. If Amber McClain expected the peso to rise in value versus the dollar in the near term, she could take a *long position*, by buying a March future on the Mexican peso. Buying a March future means that Amber is locking in the price at which she must buy Mexican pesos at the future's maturity date. Amber's futures contract at maturity would have the following value:

$$\text{Value at maturity (Long position)} = \text{Notional principal} \times (\text{Spot} - \text{Futures})$$

| EXHIBIT 8.1 | Mexican Peso Futures, US$/Peso (CME) |

Maturity	Open	High	Low	Settle	Change	High	Low	Open Interest
Mar	.10953	.10988	.10930	.10958	...	.11000	.09770	34,481
June	.10790	.10795	.10778	.10773	...	.10800	.09730	3,405
Sept	.10615	.10615	.10610	.10573	...	.10615	.09930	1,481

All contracts are for 500,000 new Mexican pesos. "Open" means the opening price on the day. "High" means the high price on the day. "Low" indicates the lowest price on the day. "Settle" is the closing price on the day. "Change" indicates the change in the settle price from the previous day's close. "High" and "Low" to the right of Change indicate the highest and lowest prices this specific contract (as defined by its maturity) has experienced over its trading history. "Open Interest" indicates the number of contracts outstanding.

Again using the March settle price on Mexican peso futures in Exhibit 8.1, $.10958/Ps, if the spot exchange rate at maturity is $.1100/Ps, Amber has indeed guessed right. The value of her position on settlement is then

$$\text{Value} = \text{Ps500,000} \times (\$.11000/\text{Ps} - \$.10958/\text{Ps}) = \$210$$

In this case, Amber makes a profit in a matter of months of $210 on the single futures contract. We could say that "Amber buys at $.10958 and sells at $.11000 per peso."

But what happens if Amber's expectation about the future value of the Mexican peso proves wrong? For example, if the Mexican government announces that the rate of inflation in Mexico has suddenly risen dramatically, and the peso falls to $.08000/Ps by the March maturity date, the value of Amber's futures contract on settlement is

$$\text{Value} = \text{Ps500.000} \times (\$.08000/\text{Ps} - \$.10958/\text{Ps}) = (\$14,790)$$

In this case, Amber McClain suffers a major speculative loss. Such is the life of the currency speculator!

Futures contracts could obviously be used in combinations to form a variety of more complex positions. When we are combining contracts, however, valuation is fairly straightforward and additive in character.

Foreign Currency Futures versus Forward Contracts

Foreign currency futures contracts differ from forward contracts in a number of important ways, as shown in Exhibit 8.2. Individuals find futures contracts useful for speculation because they usually do not have access to forward contracts. For businesses, futures contracts are often considered inefficient and burdensome because the futures position is marked to market on a daily basis over the life of the contract. Although this does not require the business to pay or receive cash on a daily basis, it does result in more frequent margin calls from its financial service providers than the business typically wants.

EXHIBIT 8.2   Currency Futures and Forwards Compared

Characteristic	Foreign Currency Futures	Forward Contracts
Size of contract	Standardized contracts per currency	Any size desired
Maturity	Fixed maturities, longest typically being one year	Any maturity up to one year, sometimes longer
Location	Trading occurs on an organized exchange	Trading occurs between individuals and banks with other banks by telecom linkages
Pricing	Open outcry process on the exchange floor	Prices are determined by bid and ask quotes
Margin/Collateral	Initial margin that is marked to market on a daily basis	No explicit collateral, but standard bank relationship necessary
Settlement	Rarely delivered upon; settlement normally takes place through purchase of offsetting position	Contract is normally delivered upon, although the taking of offsetting positions is possible
Commissions	Single commission covers both purchase and sale (roundtrip)	No explicit commission; banks earn effective commissions through the bid-ask spreads
Trading hours	Traditionally traded during exchange hours; some exchanges have moved to 24 hours	Negotiated by phone or Internet, 24 hours a day, through bank global networks
Counterparties	Unknown to each other due to the auction market structure	Parties are in direct contact in settling forward specifications
Liquidity	Liquid but relatively small in total sales volume and value	Liquid and relatively large in sales volume compared to futures contracts

Currency Options

A *foreign currency option* is a contract giving the option purchaser (the buyer) the right, but not the obligation, to buy or sell a given amount of foreign exchange at a fixed price per unit for a specified time period (until the maturity date). The most important phrase in this definition is "but not the obligation"; this means that the owner of an option possesses a valuable choice.

In many ways buying an option is like buying a ticket to a benefit concert. The buyer has the right to attend the concert, but does not have to do so. The buyer of the concert ticket risks nothing more than what she paid for the ticket. Similarly, the buyer of an option cannot lose anything more than what she paid for the option. If the buyer of the ticket decides later not to attend the concert—prior to the day of the concert, the ticket can be sold to someone else who does wish to go.

- There are two basic types of options, *calls* and *puts*. A call is an option to buy foreign currency, and a put is an option to sell foreign currency.

- The buyer of an option is termed the *holder*, while the seller of an option is referred to as the *writer* or *grantor*.

Every option has three different price elements: 1) the *exercise* or *strike price,* the exchange rate at which the foreign currency can be purchased (call) or sold (put); 2) the *premium*, which is the cost, price, or value of the option itself; and 3) the underlying or actual spot exchange rate in the market.

- An *American option* gives the buyer the right to exercise the option at any time between the date of writing and the expiration or maturity date. A *European option* can be exercised only on its expiration date, not before. Nevertheless, American and European options are priced almost the same because the option holder would normally sell the option itself before maturity. The option would then still have some "time value" above its "intrinsic value" if exercised (explained later in this chapter).

- The *premium* or option price is the cost of the option, usually paid in advance by the buyer to the seller. In the over-the-counter market (options offered by banks), premiums are quoted as a percentage of the transaction amount. Premiums on exchange-traded options are quoted as a domestic currency amount per unit of foreign currency.

- An option whose exercise price is the same as the spot price of the underlying currency is said to be *at-the-money* (ATM). An option that would be profitable, excluding the cost of the premium, if exercised immediately is said to be *in-the-money* (ITM). An option that would not be profitable, again excluding the cost of the premium, if exercised immediately is referred to as *out-of-the-money* (OTM).

Foreign Currency Options Markets

In the past three decades the use of foreign currency options as a hedging tool and for speculative purposes has blossomed into a major foreign exchange activity. A number of banks in the United States and other capital markets offer flexible foreign currency options on transactions of $1 million or more. The bank market, or *over-the-counter market* as it is called, offers custom-tailored options on all major trading currencies for any time period up to one year, and in some cases, two to three years.

In 1982 the Philadelphia Stock Exchange introduced trading in standardized foreign currency option contracts in the United States. The Chicago Mercantile Exchange and other exchanges in the United States and abroad have followed suit. Exchange-traded contracts are particularly appealing to speculators and individuals who do not normally have access to the over-the-counter market. Banks also trade on the exchanges because it is one of several ways they can offset the risk of options they have transacted with clients or other banks.

Increased use of foreign currency options is a reflection of the explosive growth in the use of other kinds of options and the resultant improvements in option pricing models. The original option pricing model developed by Black and Scholes in 1973 has been commercialized since then by numerous firms offering software programs and even built-in routines for handheld calculators. Several commercial programs are available for option writers and traders to utilize.

Options on the Over-the-Counter Market

Over-the-counter (OTC) options are most frequently written by banks for U.S. dollars against British pounds sterling, Swiss francs, Japanese yen, Canadian dollars, and the euro.

The main advantage of over-the-counter options is that they are tailored to the specific needs of the firm. Financial institutions are willing to write or buy options that vary by amount (notional principal), strike price, and maturity. Although the over-the-counter markets were relatively illiquid in the early years, the market has grown to such proportions that liquidity is now quite good. On the other hand, the buyer must assess the writing bank's ability to fulfill the option contract. Termed *counterparty risk*, the financial risk associated with the counterparty is an increasing issue in international markets as a result of the increasing use of financial contracts like options and swaps by MNE management. Exchange-traded options are more the territory of individuals and financial institutions themselves than of business firms.

If Maria Gonzalez, the Chief Financial Officer of Trident, wishes to purchase an option in the over-the-counter market, she will normally place a call to the currency option desk of a major money center bank, specify the currencies, maturity, strike rate(s), and ask for an *indication*—a bid-ask quote. The bank will normally take a few minutes to a few hours to price the option and return the call.

Options on Organized Exchanges

Options on the physical (underlying) currency are traded on a number of organized exchanges worldwide, including the Philadelphia Stock Exchange (PHLX) and the Chicago Mercantile Exchange.

Exchange-traded options are settled through a clearing house, so that buyers do not deal directly with sellers. The clearing house is the counterparty to every option contract and it guarantees fulfillment. Clearing-house obligations are in turn the obligation of all members of the exchange, including a large number of banks. In the case of the Philadelphia Stock Exchange, clearing-house services are provided by the Options Clearing Corporation (OCC).

Currency Option Quotations and Prices

Typical quotes in *The Wall Street Journal* for options on Swiss francs are shown in Exhibit 8.3. The *Journal*'s quotes refer to transactions completed on the Philadelphia Stock Exchange on the previous day. Quotations usually are available for more combinations of strike prices and expiration dates than were actually traded and thus reported in the newspaper. Currency option strike prices and premiums on the U.S. dollar are typically quoted as direct quotations on the U.S. dollar and indirect quotations on the foreign currency ($/SF, $/¥, and so on).

Exhibit 8.3 illustrates the three different prices that characterize any foreign currency option. The three prices that characterize an "August 58.5 call option" (highlighted in Exhibit 8.3) are the following:

EXHIBIT 8.3	Swiss Franc Option Quotations (U.S. cents/SF)						
		Calls—Last			Puts—Last		
Option and Underlying	Strike Price	Aug	Sep	Dec	Aug	Sept	Dec
58.51	56	–	–	2.76	0.04	0.22	1.16
58.51	56.5	–	–	–	0.06	0.30	–
58.51	57	1.13	–	1.74	0.10	0.38	1.27
58.51	57.5	0.75	–	–	0.17	0.55	–
58.51	58	0.71	1.05	1.28	0.27	0.89	1.81
58.51	58.5	0.50	–	–	0.50	0.99	–
58.51	59	0.30	0.66	1.21	0.90	1.36	–
58.51	59.5	0.15	0.40	–	2.32	–	–
58.51	60	–	0.31	–	2.32	2.62	3.30

Each option = 62,500 Swiss francs. The August, September, and December listings are the option maturities or expiration dates.

1. **Spot Rate.** In Exhibit 8.3, "Option & Underlying" means that 58.51 cents, or $0.5851, was the spot dollar price of one Swiss franc at the close of trading on the preceding day.

2. **Exercise Price.** The exercise price, or "Strike Price" listed in Exhibit 8.3, means the price per franc that must be paid if the option is exercised. The August call option on francs of 58.5 means $0.5850/SF. Exhibit 8.3 lists nine different strike prices, ranging from $0.5600/SF to $0.6000/SF, although more were available on that date than are listed here.

3. **Premium.** The premium is the cost or price of the option. The price of the August 58.5 call option on Swiss francs was 0.50 U.S. cents per franc, or $0.0050/SF. There was no trading of the September and December 58.5 call on that day. The premium is the market value of the option, and therefore the terms premium, cost, price, and value are all interchangeable when referring to an option.

The August 58.5 call option premium is 0.50 cents per franc, and in this case, the August 58.5 put's premium is also 0.50 cents per franc. Since one option contract on the Philadelphia Stock Exchange consists of 62,500 francs, the total cost of one option contract for the call (or put in this case) is SF62,500 × $0.0050/SF = $312.50.

Foreign Currency Speculation

Speculation is an attempt to profit by trading on expectations about prices in the future. In the foreign exchange markets, speculators take an open (unhedged) position in a foreign currency and then close that position after the exchange rate has moved in—they hope—the expected direction. In the following section we analyze the manner in which speculation is undertaken in spot, forward, and options markets. It is important to understand this phenomenon because it has a major impact on our inability to accurately forecast future exchange rates.

Speculating in the Spot Market

Hans Schmidt is a currency speculator in Zurich, Switzerland. He is willing to risk money on his own opinion about future currency prices. Hans may speculate in the spot, forward, or options markets. To illustrate, assume the Swiss franc is currently quoted as follows:

Spot rate:	$0.5851/SF
Six-month forward rate:	$0.5760/SF

Hans has $100,000 with which to speculate, and he believes that in six months the spot rate for the franc will be $0.6000/SF. Speculation in the spot market requires only that the speculator believe the foreign currency will appreciate in value. Hans should take the following steps:

1. Use the $100,000 today to buy SF170,910.96 spot at $0.5851/SF.

2. Hold the SF170,910.96 indefinitely. Although the franc is expected to rise to the target value in six months, Hans is not committed to that time horizon.

3. When the target exchange rate has been reached, sell SF170,910.96 at the new spot rate of $0.6000/SF, receiving SF170,910.96 × $0.6000/SF = $102,546.57.

This results in a profit of $2,546.57, or 2.5% on the $100,000 committed for six months (5.0% per annum). This ignores for the moment interest income on the Swiss francs and opportunity cost on the dollars.

The potential maximum gain is unlimited, while the maximum loss will be $100,000 if the francs purchased in step 1 drop in value to zero. Having initially undertaken a spot market speculation for six months, Hans is nevertheless not bound by that target date. He may sell the francs earlier or later if he wishes.

Speculating in the Forward Market

Forward market speculation occurs when the speculator believes that the spot price at some future date will differ from today's forward price for that same date. Success does not depend on the direction of movement of the spot rate, but on the relative position of the future spot rate and the current forward rate. Given the above data and expectations, Hans Schmidt should take the following steps:

1. Today buy SF173,611.11 forward six months at the forward quote of $0.5760/SF. Note that this step requires no outlay of cash.

2. In six months fulfill the forward contract, receiving SF173,611.11 at $0.5760/SF for a cost of $100,000.

3. Simultaneously sell the SF173,611.11 in the spot market, at Hans' expected future spot rate of $0.6000/SF, receiving SF173,611.11 × $0.6000/SF = $104,166.67.

This is a profit of $4,166.67 ($104,166.67 – $100,000.00).

The profit of $4,166.67 cannot be related to an investment base to calculate a return on investment because the dollar funds were never needed. On the six-month anniversary, Hans simply crosses the payment obligation of $100,000 with receipts of $104,166.67, and accepts a net $4,166.67. Nevertheless, some financial institutions might require him to deposit collateral as margin to ensure his ability to complete the trade.

In this particular forward speculation, the maximum loss is $100,000, the amount needed to buy francs via the forward contract. This loss would be incurred only if the value of the spot franc in six months were zero. The maximum gain is unlimited, since francs acquired in the forward market can in theory rise to an infinite dollar value.

Forward market speculation cannot be extended beyond the maturity date of the forward contract. However, if Hans wants to close out his operation before maturity, he may buy an offsetting contract. In the above example, after, say, four months Hans could sell SF173,611.11 forward two months at whatever forward price then existed. Two months after that he would close the matured six-month contract to purchase francs against the matured two-month contract to sell francs, pocketing any profit or paying up any loss. The amount of profit or loss would be fixed by the price at which Hans sold forward two months.

This example is only one of several possible types of forward speculations and ignores any interest earned. In a spot speculation, the speculator can invest the principal amount in the foreign money market to earn interest. In the various forward speculations, a speculator who is holding cash against the risk of loss can invest those funds in the home money market. Thus, relative profitability will be influenced by interest differentials.

Speculating in Option Markets

Options differ from all other types of financial instruments in the patterns of risk they produce. The option owner has the choice of exercising the option or allowing it to expire unused. The owner will exercise it only when exercising is profitable, which means only when the option is in the money. In the case of a call option, as the spot price of the underlying currency moves up, the holder has the possibility of unlimited profit. On the down side, however, the holder can abandon the option and walk away with a loss never greater than the premium paid. As described in *Global Finance in Practice 8.1*, some have made large profits in option speculation in the past.

GLOBAL FINANCE IN PRACTICE 8.1

The New Zealand Kiwi, Key, and Krieger

What has long been considered one of the most dramatic currency plays in history has moved back into the limelight. New Zealand elected Mr. John Key as its new prime minister in November 2008. Key's career has been a long and storied one, a large part of it involving speculation on foreign currencies. Strangely enough, Key had at one time worked with another currency speculator, Andrew Krieger, who is believed to have single-handedly caused the fall of the New Zealand dollar, the kiwi, way back in 1987.

In 1987 Andrew Krieger was a 31-year-old currency trader for Bankers Trust of New York (BT). Following the U.S. stock market crash in October 1987, the world's currency markets moved rapidly to exit the dollar. Many of the world's other currencies—including small ones which were in stable, open, industrialized markets like that of New Zealand—became the subject of interest. As the world's currency traders dumped dollars and bought kiwis, the value of the kiwi rose rapidly.

Krieger believed that the markets were overreacting, and would overvalue the kiwi. So he took a short position on the kiwi, betting on its eventual fall. And he did so in a big way, not limiting his positions to simple spot or forward market positions, but through currency options as well. (Krieger supposedly had approval for positions rising to nearly $700 million in size, when all other BT traders were restricted to $50 million.) Krieger, on behalf of Bankers Trust, is purported to have shorted 200 million kiwi—more than the entire New Zealand money supply at the time. His view proved correct. The kiwi fell, and Krieger was able to earn millions in currency gains for BT. Ironically, only months later, Krieger resigned from BT when annual bonuses were announced and he reportedly earned only $3 million on the more than $300 million he had made for the bank.

Eventually the New Zealand central bank lodged complaints with Bankers Trust, in which the CEO of BT at the time Charles S. Sanford Jr., who seemingly added insult to injury when he is reported to have remarked "We didn't take too big a position for Bankers Trust," he grumbled, "but we may have taken too big a position for that market."

Buyer of a Call

The position of Hans as a buyer of a call is illustrated in Exhibit 8.4. Assume he purchases the August call option on Swiss francs described previously, the one with a strike price of 58.5 ($0.5850/SF), and a premium of $0.005/SF. The vertical axis measures profit or loss for the option buyer at each of several different spot prices for the franc up to the time of maturity.

At all spot rates below the strike price of 58.5, Hans would choose not to exercise his option. This is obvious because at a spot rate of 58.0 for example, he would prefer to buy a Swiss franc for $.580 on the spot market rather than exercising his option to buy a franc at $0.585. If the spot rate remains below 58.0 until August when the option expired, Hans would not exercise the option. His total loss would be limited to only what he paid for the option, the $0.005/SF purchase price. At any lower price for the franc, his loss would similarly be limited to the original $0.005/SF cost.

Alternatively, at all spot rates above the strike price of 58.5, Hans would exercise the option, paying only the strike price for each Swiss franc. For example, if the spot rate were 59.5 cents per franc at maturity, he would exercise his call option, buying Swiss francs for $0.585 each instead of purchasing them on the spot market at $0.595 each. He could sell the Swiss francs immediately in the spot market for $0.595 each, pocketing a gross profit of $0.010/SF, or a net profit of $0.005/SF after deducting the original cost of the option of

EXHIBIT 8.4   Buying a Call Option on Swiss Francs

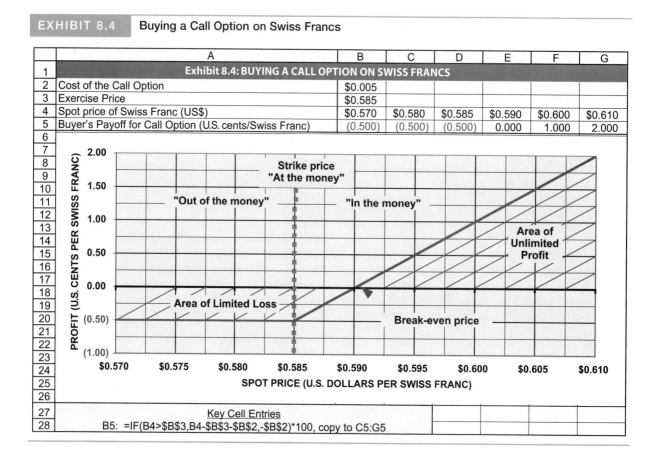

	A	B	C	D	E	F	G
1	Exhibit 8.4: BUYING A CALL OPTION ON SWISS FRANCS						
2	Cost of the Call Option	$0.005					
3	Exercise Price	$0.585					
4	Spot price of Swiss Franc (US$)	$0.570	$0.580	$0.585	$0.590	$0.600	$0.610
5	Buyer's Payoff for Call Option (U.S. cents/Swiss Franc)	(0.500)	(0.500)	(0.500)	0.000	1.000	2.000

Key Cell Entries
B5: =IF(B4>$B$3,B4-$B$3-$B$2,-$B$2)*100, copy to C5:G5

$0.005/SF. Hans' profit, if the spot rate is greater than the strike price, with strike price $0.585, a premium of $0.005, and a spot rate of $0.595, is

$$\text{Profit} = \text{Spot Rate} - (\text{Strike Price} + \text{Premium})$$
$$= \$0.595/SF - (\$0.585/SF + \$0.005/SF)$$
$$= \$0.005/SF$$

More likely, Hans would realize the profit through executing an offsetting contract on the options exchange rather than taking delivery of the currency. Because the dollar price of a franc could rise to an infinite level (off the upper right-hand side of the page in Exhibit 8.4), maximum profit is unlimited. The buyer of a call option thus possesses an attractive combination of outcomes: limited loss and unlimited profit potential.

Note that the *break-even price* of $0.590/SF is the price at which Hans neither gains nor loses on exercise of the option. The premium cost of $0.005, combined with the cost of exercising the option of $0.585, is exactly equal to the proceeds from selling the francs in the spot market at $0.590. Note that he will still exercise the call option at the break-even price. This is so because by exercising it he at least recoups the premium paid for the option. At any spot price above the exercise price but below the break-even price, the gross profit earned on exercising the option and selling the underlying currency covers part (but not all) of the premium cost.

Writer of a Call

The position of the writer (seller) of the same call option is illustrated in Exhibit 8.5. If the option expires when the spot price of the underlying currency is below the exercise price of 58.5, the option holder does not exercise. What the holder loses, the writer gains. The writer keeps as profit the entire premium paid of $0.005/SF. Above the exercise price of 58.5, the writer of the call must deliver the underlying currency for $0.585/SF at a time when the value of the franc is above $0.585. If the writer wrote the option "naked," that is, without owning the currency, that writer will now have to buy the currency at spot and take the loss. The amount of such a loss is unlimited and increases as the price of the underlying currency rises. Once again, what the holder gains, the writer loses, and vice versa. Even if the writer already owns the currency, the writer will experience an opportunity loss, surrendering against the option the same currency that could have been sold for more in the open market.

For example, the profit to the writer of a call option of strike price $0.585, premium $0.005, a spot rate of $0.595/SF is

$$\text{Profit} = \text{Premium} - (\text{Spot Rate} - \text{Strike Price})$$
$$= \$0.005/SF - (\$0.595/SF - \$0.585/SF)$$
$$= -\$0.005/SF$$

but only if the spot rate is greater than or equal to the strike rate. At spot rates less than the strike price, the option will expire worthless and the writer of the call option will keep the premium earned. The maximum profit that the writer of the call option can make is limited to the premium. The writer of a call option would have a rather unattractive combination of potential outcomes—limited profit potential and unlimited loss potential—but there are ways to limit such losses through other offsetting techniques.

Buyer of a Put

Hans' position as buyer of a put is illustrated in Exhibit 8.6. The basic terms of this put are similar to those we just used to illustrate a call. The buyer of a put option, however, wants to

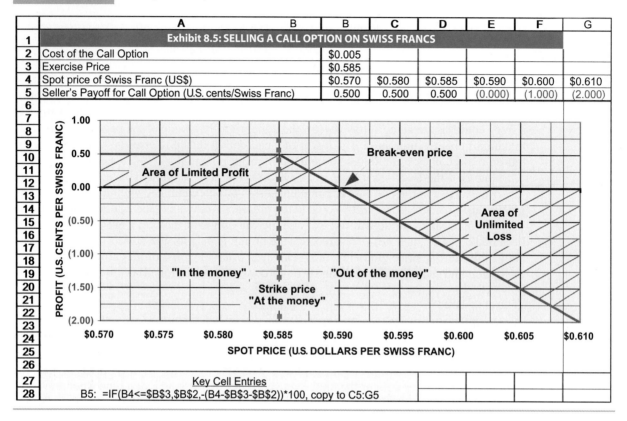

EXHIBIT 8.5 Selling a Call Option on Swiss Francs

	A	B	B	C	D	E	F	G
1	Exhibit 8.5: SELLING A CALL OPTION ON SWISS FRANCS							
2	Cost of the Call Option		$0.005					
3	Exercise Price		$0.585					
4	Spot price of Swiss Franc (US$)		$0.570	$0.580	$0.585	$0.590	$0.600	$0.610
5	Seller's Payoff for Call Option (U.S. cents/Swiss Franc)		0.500	0.500	0.500	(0.000)	(1.000)	(2.000)
27	Key Cell Entries							
28	B5: =IF(B4<=$B$3,$B$2,-(B4-$B$3-$B$2))*100, copy to C5:G5							

be able to sell the underlying currency at the exercise price when the market price of that currency drops (not rises as in the case of a call option). If the spot price of a franc drops to, say, $0.575/SF, Hans will deliver francs to the writer and receive $0.585/SF. The francs can now be purchased on the spot market for $0.575 each and the cost of the option was $0.005/SF, so he will have a net gain of $0.005/SF.

Explicitly, the profit to the holder of a put option if the spot rate is less than the strike price, with a strike price $0.585/SF, premium of $0.005/SF, and a spot rate of $0.575/SF, is

$$Profit = Strike\ Price - (Spot\ Rate + Premium)$$
$$= \$0.585/SF - (\$0.575/SF + \$0.005/SF)$$
$$= \$0.005/SF$$

The break-even price for the put option is the strike price less the premium, or $0.580/SF in this case. As the spot rate falls further and further below the strike price, the profit potential would continually increase, and Hans' profit could be unlimited (up to a maximum of $0.580/SF, when the price of a franc would be zero). At any exchange rate above the strike price of 58.5, Hans would not exercise the option and so would lose only the $0.005/SF premium paid for the put option. The buyer of a put option has an almost unlimited profit potential with a limited loss potential. Like the buyer of a call, the buyer of a put can never lose more than the premium paid up front.

EXHIBIT 8.6   Buying a Put Option on Swiss Francs

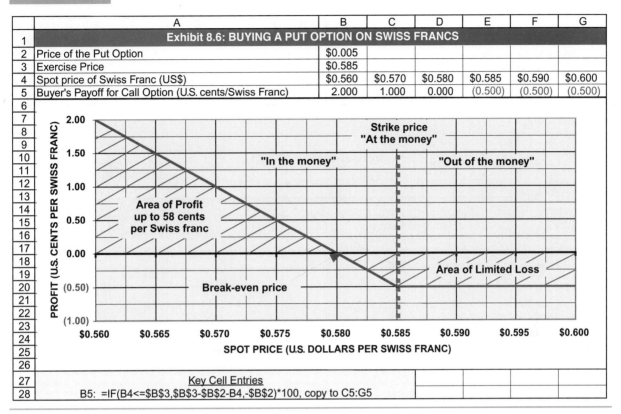

	A	B	C	D	E	F	G
1	Exhibit 8.6: BUYING A PUT OPTION ON SWISS FRANCS						
2	Price of the Put Option	$0.005					
3	Exercise Price	$0.585					
4	Spot price of Swiss Franc (US$)	$0.560	$0.570	$0.580	$0.585	$0.590	$0.600
5	Buyer's Payoff for Call Option (U.S. cents/Swiss Franc)	2.000	1.000	0.000	(0.500)	(0.500)	(0.500)

Key Cell Entries

B5: =IF(B4<=$B$3,$B$3-$B$2-B4,-$B$2)*100, copy to C5:G5

Writer of a Put

The position of the writer who sold the put to Hans is shown in Exhibit 8.7. Note the symmetry of profit/loss, strike price, and break-even prices between the buyer and the writer of the put. If the spot price of francs drops below 58.5 cents per franc, Hans will exercise the option. Below a price of 58.5 cents per franc, the writer will lose more than the premium received from writing the option ($0.005/SF), falling below break-even. Between $0.580/SF and $0.585/SF the writer will lose part, but not all, of the premium received. If the spot price is above $0.585/SF, Hans will not exercise the option, and the option writer will pocket the entire premium of $0.005/SF.

The profit (loss) earned by the writer of a $0.585 strike price put, premium $0.005, at a spot rate of $0.575, is

$$\text{Profit (loss)} = \text{Premium} - (\text{Strike Price} - \text{Spot Rate})$$
$$= \$0.005/\text{SF} - (\$0.585/\text{SF} - \$0.575/\text{SF})$$
$$= -\$0.005/\text{SF}$$

but only for spot rates that are less than or equal to the strike price. At spot rates greater than the strike price, the option expires out-of-the-money and the writer keeps the premium. The writer of the put option has the same basic combination of outcomes available to the writer of a call: limited profit potential and unlimited loss potential.

EXHIBIT 8.7   Selling a Put Option on Swiss Francs

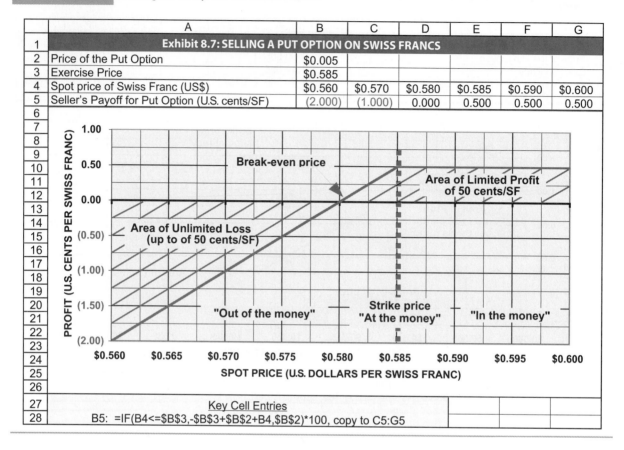

	A	B	C	D	E	F	G
1	Exhibit 8.7: SELLING A PUT OPTION ON SWISS FRANCS						
2	Price of the Put Option	$0.005					
3	Exercise Price	$0.585					
4	Spot price of Swiss Franc (US$)	$0.560	$0.570	$0.580	$0.585	$0.590	$0.600
5	Seller's Payoff for Put Option (U.S. cents/SF)	(2.000)	(1.000)	0.000	0.500	0.500	0.500

Break-even price

Area of Limited Profit of 50 cents/SF

Area of Unlimited Loss (up to of 50 cents/SF)

"Out of the money"   Strike price "At the money"   "In the money"

SPOT PRICE (U.S. DOLLARS PER SWISS FRANC)

PROFIT (U.S. CENTS PER SWISS FRANC)

Key Cell Entries			
B5: =IF(B4<=$B$3,-$B$3+$B$2+B4,$B$2)*100, copy to C5:G5			

Option Pricing and Valuation

Exhibit 8.8 illustrates the profit/loss profile of a European-style call option on British pounds. The call option allows the holder to buy British pounds at a strike price of $1.70/£. It has a 90-day maturity. The value of this call option is actually the sum of two components:

Total value (Premium) = Intrinsic value + Time value

The pricing of any currency option combines six elements. For example, this European-style call option on British pounds has a premium of $0.033/£ (3.3 cents per pound) at a spot rate of $1.70/£. This premium is calculated using the following assumptions:

1. Present spot rate: $1.70/£

2. Time to maturity: 90 days

3. Forward rate for matching maturity (90 days): $1.70/£

4. U.S. dollar interest rate: 8.00% per annum

5. British pound sterling interest rate: 8.00% per annum

6. Volatility, the standard deviation of daily spot price movement: 10.00% per annum

EXHIBIT 8.8	Analysis of Call Option on British Pounds with a Strike Price = $1.70/£	

	A	B	C	D
1	**Exhibit 8.8: ANALYSIS OF CALL OPTION ON BRITISH POUNDS**			
2	**Input Data**			
3	Present spot rate, $/£			$1.70
4	Strike price, $/£			$1.70
5	Time to maturity, days			90
6	Forward rate for matching maturity (90 days), $/£			$1.70
7	U.S. dollar interest rate, percent/year			8.0%
8	British pound sterling interest rate, percent/year			8.0%
9	Standard deviation of daily spot price movement, percent/year			10.0%
10	**Effect of Spot Rate on Intrinsic, Time, and Total Value**			
11		Intrinsic value,	Time value,	Total value,
12	Spot rate, $/£	U.S. cents/£	U.S. cents/£	U.S. cents/£
13	1.65	0.00	1.37	1.37
14	1.66	0.00	1.67	1.67
15	1.67	0.00	2.01	2.01
16	1.68	0.00	2.39	2.39
17	1.69	0.00	2.82	2.82
18	1.70	0.00	3.30	3.30
19	1.71	1.00	2.82	3.82
20	1.72	2.00	2.39	4.39
21	1.73	3.00	2.01	5.01
22	1.74	4.00	1.67	5.67

42	Key Cell Entries
43	B12: =IF(A12<$D$3,0,A12-$D$3)*100, copy to B13:B21
44	C12: Calculated with option-pricing software.
45	D12: =B12+C12, copy to D13:D21

Intrinsic value is the financial gain if the option is exercised immediately. It is shown by the shaded line in Exhibit 8.8, which is zero until it reaches the strike price, then rises linearly (one cent for each one-cent increase in the spot rate). Intrinsic value will be zero when the option is out-of-the-money—that is, when the strike price is above the market price—as no gain can be derived from exercising the option. When the spot rate rises above the strike price, the intrinsic value becomes positive, because the option is always worth at least this value if exercised. On the date of maturity, an option will have a value equal to its intrinsic value (zero time remaining means zero time value).

- When the spot rate is $1.74/£, the option is in-the-money and has an intrinsic value of $1.74 − $1.70/£, or 4 cents per pound.

- When the spot rate is $1.70/£, the option is at-the-money and has an intrinsic value of $1.70 − $1.70/£, or 0 cents per pound.

- When the spot rate is $1.66/£, the option is out-of-the-money and has no intrinsic value. This is shown by the shaded line for intrinsic value lying on the horizontal axis. Only a fool would exercise this call option at this spot rate instead of buying pounds more cheaply on the spot market.

The *time value* of an option exists because the price of the underlying currency, the spot rate, can potentially move further and further into the money between the present time and the option's expiration date. Time value is shown in Exhibit 8.8 as the area between the *total value* of the option and its intrinsic value.

Exhibit 8.9 separates the total value into intrinsic and time values for the call option depicted in Exhibit 8.8. For example, at a spot rate of $1.72/£, the option's total value is made up of 2 cents per pound intrinsic value and 2.39 cents per pound in time value, for a total value of 4.39 cents per pound.

Note that the time value component is the same in value—symmetric—as you move in either direction away from the strike price of $1.70/£. For example, the time value is 2.39 cents at spot rates of 1.68 (2 cents below strike) and 1.72 (2 cents above strike). This result demonstrates the underlying principle that option pricing is based on an expected distribution of possible outcomes around the forward rate, which in this case is the same as the strike price, $1.70.

An investor will pay something today for an out-of-the-money option (i.e., zero intrinsic value) on the chance that the spot rate will move far enough before maturity to move the option in-the-money. Consequently, the price of an option is always somewhat greater than its intrinsic value, because there is always some chance that the intrinsic value will rise between the present and the expiration date.

EXHIBIT 8.9   The Intrinsic, Time, and Total Value Components of the 90-Day Call Option on British Pounds at Varying Spot Exchange Rates

Strike Price: $1.70/£								
Spot ($/£)	1.66	1.67	1.68	1.69	1.70	1.71	1.72	1.73	1.74
Intrinsic	0.00	0.00	0.00	0.00	0.00	1.00	2.00	3.00	4.00
Time	1.67	2.01	2.39	2.82	3.30	2.82	2.39	2.01	1.67
Total value	1.67	2.01	2.39	2.82	3.30	3.82	4.39	5.01	5.67

Currency Option Pricing Sensitivity

If currency options are to be used effectively, either for the purposes of speculation or risk management (covered in the coming chapters), the individual trader needs to know how option values—*premiums*—react to their various components. The following section will analyze these six basic sensitivities:

1. The impact of changing forward rates
2. The impact of changing spot rates
3. The impact of time to maturity
4. The impact of changing volatility
5. The impact of changing interest differentials
6. The impact of alternative option strike prices

Forward Rate Sensitivity

Although rarely noted, standard foreign currency options are priced around the forward rate, because the current spot rate and both the domestic and foreign interest rates (home currency and foreign currency rates) are included in the option premium calculation.[1] Regardless of the specific strike rate chosen and priced, the forward rate is central to valuation. The option-pricing formula calculates a subjective probability distribution centered on the forward rate. This approach does not mean that the market expects the forward rate to be equal to the future spot rate. It is simply a result of the arbitrage-pricing structure of options.

The forward rate focus also provides helpful information for the trader managing a position. When the market prices a foreign currency option, it does so without any bullish or bearish sentiment on the direction of the foreign currency's value relative to the domestic currency. If the trader has specific expectations about the future spot rate's direction, those expectations can be put to work. A trader will not be inherently betting against the market. In a following section, we will also describe how a change in the interest differential between currencies, the theoretical foundation of forward rates, also alters the value of the option.

Spot Rate Sensitivity (delta)

The call option on British pounds depicted in Exhibit 8.8 possesses a premium that exceeds the intrinsic value of the option over the entire range of spot rates surrounding the strike rate. As long as the option has time remaining before expiration, the option will possess this time value element. This characteristic is one of the primary reasons why an American-style option, which can be exercised on any day up to and including the expiration date, is seldom actually exercised prior to expiration. If the option holder wishes to liquidate it for its value, it would normally be sold, not exercised, so any remaining time value can also be captured by the holder. If the current spot rate falls on the side of the option's strike price, which would induce the option holder to exercise the option upon expiration, the option also has an intrinsic value. The call option illustrated in Exhibit 8.8 is in-the-money at spot rates to the right of the strike rate of $1.70/£, at-the-money at $1.70/£, and out-of-the-money at spot rates less than $1.70/£.

---

[1] Recall that the forward rate is calculated from the current spot rate and the two subject currency interest rates for the desired maturity. For example, the 90-day forward rate for the call option on British pounds described earlier is calculated as follows:

$$F_{90} = \$1.70/£ \times \left[\frac{1 + 0.08\left(\dfrac{90}{360}\right)}{1 + 0.08\left(\dfrac{90}{360}\right)} \right] = \$1.70/£$$

The vertical distance between the market value and the intrinsic value of a call option on pounds is greatest at a spot rate of $1.70/£. At $1.70/£, the spot rate equals the strike price (at-the-money). This premium of 3.30 cents per pound consists entirely of time value. In fact, the value of any option that is currently out-of-the-money is made up entirely of time value. The further the option's strike price is out-of-the-money, the lower the value or premium of the option. This is true because the market believes the probability of this option actually moving into the exercise range prior to expiration is significantly less than one that is already at-the-money. If the spot rate were to fall to $1.68/£, the option premium falls to 2.39 cents/£—again, entirely time value. If the spot rate were to rise above the strike rate to $1.72/£, the premium rises to 4.39 cents/£. In this case, the premium represents an intrinsic value of 2.00 cents ($1.72/£ – $1.70/£) plus a time value element of 2.39 cents. Note the symmetry of time value premiums (2.39 cents) to the left and to the right of the strike rate.

The symmetry of option valuation about the strike rate is seen by decomposing the option premiums into their respective intrinsic and time values. Exhibit 8.10 illustrates how varying the current spot rate by ±$0.05 about the strike rate of $1.70/£ alters each option's intrinsic and time values.

The sensitivity of the option premium to a small change in the spot exchange rate is called the *delta*. For example, the delta of the $1.70/£ call option, when the spot rate changes from $1.70/£ to $1.71/£, is simply the change in the premium divided by the change in the spot rate:

$$delta = \frac{\Delta \text{ Premium}}{\Delta \text{ Spot rate}} = \frac{\$0.038/£ - \$0.033/£}{\$1.71/£ - \$1.70/£} = 0.5$$

If the delta of the specific option is known, it is easy to determine how the option's value will change as the spot rate changes. If the spot rate changes by 1 cent ($0.01/£), given a delta of 0.5, the option premium would change by 0.5 × $0.01, or $0.005. If the initial premium were $0.033/£, and the spot rate increased by 1 cent (from $1.70/£ to $1.71/£), the new option premium would be $0.033 + $0.005 = $0.038/£. Delta varies between +1 and 0 for a call option, and −1 and 0 for a put option.

Traders in options categorize individual options by their delta rather than in-the-money, at-the-money, or out-of-the-money. As an option moves further in-the-money, like the in-the-money option in Exhibit 8.10, delta rises toward 1.0 (in this case to 0.71). As an option moves further out-of-the-money, delta falls toward zero. Note that the out-of-the-money option in Exhibit 8.10 has a delta of only 0.28.[2]

Rule of thumb: The higher the delta (deltas of 0.7 or 0.8 and more are considered high), the greater the probability of the option expiring in-the-money.

EXHIBIT 8.10   Decomposing Call Option Premiums: Intrinsic Value and Time Value

Strike Rate ($/£)	Spot Rate ($/£)	Money	Call Premium (cents/£)	=	Intrinsic Value (cents/£)	+	Time Value (cents/£)	Delta (0 to 1)
1.70	1.75	ITM	6.37		5.00		1.37	0.71
1.70	1.70	ATM	3.30		0.00		3.30	0.50
1.70	1.65	OTM	1.37		0.00		1.37	0.28

[2]The expected change in the option's delta resulting from a small change in the spot rate is termed *gamma*. It is often used as a measure of the stability of a specific option's delta. Gamma is utilized in the construction of more sophisticated hedging strategies that focus on deltas (delta-neutral strategies).

Time to Maturity: Value and Deterioration (theta)

Option values increase with the length of time to maturity. The expected change in the option premium from a small change in the time to expiration is termed *theta*. Theta is calculated as the change in the option premium over the change in time. If the $1.70/£ call option were to age one day from its initial 90-day maturity, the theta of the call option would be the difference in the two premiums, 3.30 cents/£ and 3.28 cents/£ (assuming a spot rate of $1.70/£):

$$theta = \frac{\Delta \text{ Premium}}{\Delta \text{ Time}} = \frac{\text{cents } 3.30/£ - \text{cents } 3.28/£}{90 - 89} = 0.02$$

Theta is based not on a linear relationship with time, but rather the square root of time. Exhibit 8.11 illustrates the time value deterioration for our same $1.70/£ call option on pounds. The at-the-money strike rate is $1.70/£, and the out-of-the-money and in-the-money spot rates are $1.75/£ and $1.65/£, respectively. Option premiums deteriorate at an increasing rate as they approach expiration. In fact, the majority of the option premium—depending on the individual option—is lost in the final 30 days prior to expiration.

This exponential relationship between option premium and time is seen in the ratio of option values between the three-month and the one-month at-the-money maturities. The ratio for the at-the-money call option is not 3 to 1 (holding all other components constant), but rather

$$\frac{\text{premium of three-month}}{\text{premium of one-month}} = \frac{\sqrt{3}}{\sqrt{1}} = \frac{1.73}{1.00} = 1.73$$

The three-month option's price is only 1.73 times that of the one-month, not 3 times the price.

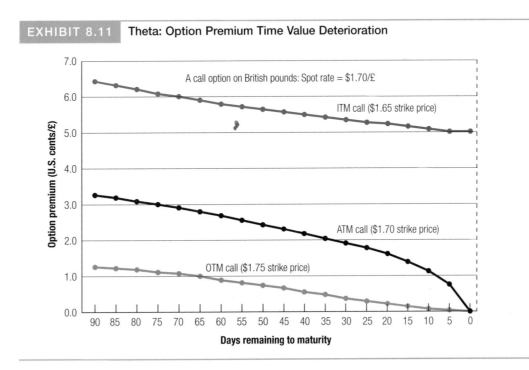

EXHIBIT 8.11   **Theta: Option Premium Time Value Deterioration**

A call option on British pounds: Spot rate = $1.70/£

ITM call ($1.65 strike price)

ATM call ($1.70 strike price)

OTM call ($1.75 strike price)

Option premium (U.S. cents/£)

Days remaining to maturity

The rapid deterioration of option values in the last days prior to expiration is seen by once again calculating the theta of the $1.70/£ call option, but now as its remaining maturity moves from 15 days to 14 days:

$$theta = \frac{\Delta \text{ Premium}}{\Delta \text{ Time}} = \frac{\text{cents } 1.37/£ - \text{cents } 1.32/£}{15 - 14} = 0.05$$

A decrease of one day in the time to maturity now reduces the option premium by 0.05 cents/£, rather than only 0.02 cents/£ as it did when the maturity was 90 days.

Exhibit 8.11 also illustrates the basic spot rate–option premium relations noted previously. The out-of-the-money call option's premium is logically smaller than the at-the-money option throughout its life, but deteriorates at a slower rate due to an initially smaller level to fall from. The in-the-money option is of greater value throughout its life relative to the at-the-money, falling toward its intrinsic value (5 cents/£) at expiration. The at-the-money option, however, falls particularly quickly in the final periods prior to expiration. As any specific option ages, moving continually toward expiration, the time value will constantly decrease (assuming that nothing else has changed). This situation would be illustrated by the total value line of the call option initially shown in Exhibit 8.8 collapsing inward toward the strike price of $1.70.

The implications of time value deterioration for traders are quite significant. A trader purchasing an option with only one or two months until expiration will see the option's value deteriorate rapidly. If the trader were then to sell the option, it would have a significantly smaller market value in the periods immediately following its purchase.

At the same time, however, a trader who is buying options of longer maturities will pay more, but not proportionately more, for the longer maturity option. A six-month option's premium is approximately 2.45 times more expensive than the one-month, yet the twelve-month option would be only 3.46 times more expensive than the one-month. This information implies that two three-month options do not equal one six-month option.

> *Rule of thumb:* A trader will normally find longer-maturity options better values, giving the trader the ability to alter an option position without suffering significant time value deterioration.

Sensitivity to Volatility (lambda)

There are few words in the financial field more used and abused than *volatility.* Option volatility is defined as the standard deviation of daily percentage changes in the underlying exchange rate. Volatility is important to option value because of an exchange rate's perceived likelihood to move either into or out of the range in which the option would be exercised. If the exchange rate's volatility is rising, and therefore the risk of the option being exercised is increasing, the option premium would be increasing.

Volatility is stated in percent per annum. For example, an option may be described as having a 12.6% annual volatility. The percentage change for a single day can be found as follows:

$$\frac{12.6\%}{\sqrt{365}} = \frac{12.6\%}{19.105} = 0.66\% \quad \text{Daily volatility}$$

For our $1.70/£ call option, an increase in annual volatility of one percentage point—for example, from 10.0% to 11.0%—will increase the option premium from $0.033/£ to $0.036/£.

The marginal change in the option premium is equal to the change in the option premium itself divided by the change in volatility, called *lambda*:

$$lambda = \frac{\Delta \text{ Premium}}{\Delta \text{ Volatility}} = \frac{\$0.036/£ - \$0.033/£}{0.11 - 0.10} = 0.30$$

The primary problem with volatility is that it is unobservable; it is the only input into the option pricing formula that is determined subjectively by the trader pricing the option. No single correct method for its calculation exists. The problem is one of forecasting; historical volatility is not necessarily an accurate predictor of the future volatility of the exchange rate's movement, yet there is little to go on except history.

Volatility is viewed three ways: *historic,* where the volatility is drawn from a recent period of time; *forward-looking,* where the historic volatility is altered to reflect expectations about the future period over which the option will exist; and *implied,* where the volatility is backed out of the market price of the option.

- **Historic volatility.** Historic volatility is normally measured as the percentage movement in the spot rate on a daily, 6-, or 12-hour basis over the previous 10, 30, or 90 days.

- **Forward-looking volatility.** Alternatively, an option trader may adjust recent historic volatilities for expected market swings or events, either upward or downward.

- **Implied volatility.** Implied volatility is equivalent to having the answers to the test; implied volatilities are calculated by being backed out of the market option premium values traded. Because volatility is the only unobservable element of the option premium price, after all other components are accounted for, the residual value of volatility implied by the price is used.

If option traders believe that the immediate future will be the same as the recent past, the historic volatility will equal the forward-looking volatility. If, however, the future period is expected to experience greater or lesser volatility, the historic measure must be altered for option pricing.

Selected implied volatilities for a number of currency pairs on January 30, 2008, are listed in Exhibit 8.12. These volatilities are *mid rates,* the average of the bid and ask rates quoted for option contracts. Exhibit 8.12 clearly illustrates that option volatilities vary considerably across currencies, and that the relationship between volatility and maturity (time to expiration) does not move in just one direction. For example, the first exchange rate quoted, the US$/euro cross rate, falls from a 9.3% volatility at one week to 8.7% for the three-year maturity before rising again to 9.3% at three years. The US$/Canadian dollar cross rate, however, moves in one direction; from 8.9% for one week to 7.9% for the three-year maturity.

Because volatilities are the only judgmental component that the option writer contributes, they play a critical role in the pricing of options. All currency pairs have historical series that contribute to the formation of the expectations of option writers. But in the end, the truly talented option writers are those with the intuition and insight to price the future effectively.

Like all futures markets, option volatilities react instantaneously and negatively to unsettling economic and political events (or rumor). A doubling of volatility for an at-the-money option will result in an equivalent doubling of the option's price. Most currency option traders focus their activities on predicting movements of currency volatility in the short run,

| EXHIBIT 8.12 | Foreign Exchange Implied Volatility for Foreign Currency Options, January 30, 2008 |

Implied Volatility Rates

The implied volatility rates are averages of mid-level rates for bid and ask "at-money-quotations" on selected currencies at 11:00 A.M. on the last business day of the month.

Implied Volatility Rates for Foreign Currency Options*

March 31, 2009

	1WK	1MO	2MO	3MO	6MO	1YR	2YR	3YR
EUR	20.2	18.2	18.1	17.9	17.7	17.5	16.5	15.1
JPY	20.4	18.4	17.3	16.5	15.4	14.2	12.3	11.6
CHF	17.5	16.0	15.9	15.7	15.6	15.2	14.2	12.9
GBP	19.8	18.2	18.0	17.8	17.7	17.5	17.1	17.0
CAD	16.7	16.6	16.5	16.5	16.5	16.5	16.5	16.4
AUD	23.8	22.3	21.8	21.3	20.5	19.7	18.4	17.5
GBPEUR	16.3	15.8	15.8	15.7	15.7	15.6	14.9	14.4
EURJPY	24.4	22.5	22.0	21.5	21.0	20.6	20.4	20.3

This release provides survey ranges of implied volatility mid rates for the money options as of 11:00 A.M. The quotes are for contracts of at least $10 million with a prime counterparty.

This information is based on data collected by the Federal Reserve Bank of New York from a sample of market participants and is intended only for informational purposes.

The data were obtained from sources believed to be reliable but this bank does not guarantee their accuracy, completeness, or correctness.

because short-run movements move price the most. For example, option volatilities rose significantly in the months preceding the Persian Gulf War, in September 1992 when the European Monetary System was in crisis, in 1997 after the onset of the Asian financial crisis, and in the days following the terrorist attacks on the United States in September 2001. In all instances, option volatilities for major cross-currency combinations such as the SF/$ rose to nearly 20% for extended periods. As a result, premium costs rose by corresponding amounts.

> *Rule of thumb*: Traders who believe that volatilities will fall significantly in the near term will sell (write) options now, hoping to buy them back for a profit immediately after volatilities fall, causing option premiums to fall.

Sensitivity to Changing Interest Rate Differentials (rho and phi)

At the start of this section, we pointed out that currency option prices and values are focused on the forward rate. The forward rate is in turn based on the theory of Interest Rate Parity, as discussed in Chapter 7. Interest rate changes in either currency will alter the forward rate, which in turn will alter the option's premium or value. The expected change in the option premium from a small change in the domestic interest rate (home currency) is termed *rho*. The expected change in the option premium from a small change in the foreign interest rate (foreign currency) is termed *phi*.

Continuing with our numerical example, an increase in the U.S. dollar interest rate from 8.0% to 9.0% *increases* the at-the-money call option premium on British pounds from $0.033/£ to $0.035/£. This is a *rho* value of positive 0.2:

$$rho = \frac{\Delta \text{ Premium}}{\Delta \text{ U.S. dollar interest rate}} = \frac{\$0.035/£ - \$0.033/£}{9.0\% - 8.0\%} = 0.2$$

A similar 1% increase in the foreign interest rate—the pound sterling rate, in this case—*reduces* the option value (premium) from $0.033/£ to $0.031/£. The *phi* for this call option premium is therefore –0.2:

$$phi = \frac{\Delta \text{ Premium}}{\Delta \text{ Foreign interest rate}} = \frac{\$0.031/£ - \$0.033/£}{9.0\% - 8.0\%} = -0.2$$

For example, throughout the 1990s, U.S. dollar (domestic currency) interest rates were substantially lower than pound sterling (foreign currency) interest rates. This meant that the pound consistently sold forward at a discount versus the U.S. dollar. If this interest differential were to widen (either from U.S. interest rates falling or foreign currency interest rates rising, or some combination of both), the pound would sell forward at a larger discount. An increase in the forward discount is the same as a decrease in the forward rate (in U.S. dollars per unit of foreign currency). The option premium condition states that the premium must increase as interest rate differentials increase (assuming that spot rates remain unchanged).

Exhibit 8.13 demonstrates how European call option premiums on the British pound change with interest differentials. If we use the same call option value assumptions as before, an increase in pound sterling interest rates relative to U.S. dollar interest rates, $i_{US\$} - i_{£}$ a movement from left to right results in a decline in call option premiums.

For the option trader, an expectation of the differential between interest rates can obviously help in the evaluation of where the option value is headed. For example, when foreign interest rates are higher than domestic interest rates, the foreign currency sells forward at a discount. This results in relatively lower call option premiums (and higher put option premiums).

Rule of thumb: A trader who is purchasing a call option on foreign currency should do so before the domestic interest rate rises. This timing will allow the trader to purchase the option before its price increases.

EXHIBIT 8.13 Interest Differentials and Call Option Premiums

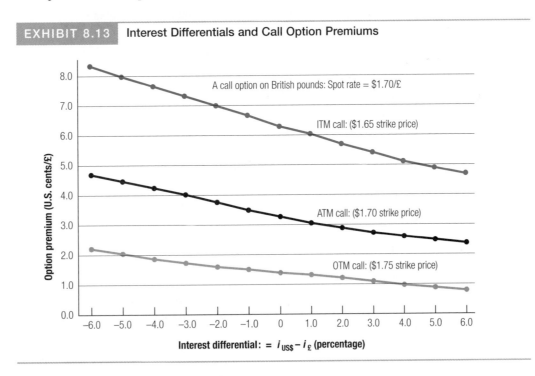

Alternative Strike Prices and Option Premiums

The sixth and final element that is important in option valuation (but, thankfully, has no Greek alias) is the selection of the actual strike price. Although we have conducted all of our sensitivity analysis using the strike price of $1.70/£ (a forward at-the-money strike rate), a firm purchasing an option in the over-the-counter market may choose its own strike rate. The question is how to choose.

Exhibit 8.14 illustrates call option premiums required for a series of alternative strike rates above and below the forward at-the-money strike rate of $1.70/£ using our benchmark example. The option premium for the call option used throughout, $1.70/£, is 3.3 cents/£. Call options written with strike prices less than $1.70/£, when the present spot rate is $1.70/£, are already profitable or in-the-money. For example, a call option with a strike rate of $1.65/£ would have an intrinsic value of $0.05/£ ($1.70/£ – $1.65/£), which the option premium must cover. The call option premium for the $1.65/£ strike rate is 6.3 cents/£, which is higher than the benchmark.

Similarly, call options on pounds at strike rates above $1.70/£ become increasingly cheap at the underlying spot rate of $1.70/£. At present they have no intrinsic value. For example, a call option on pounds with a strike rate of $1.75/£ possesses a premium of only 1.5 cents/£, because the option is at present very much out-of-the-money. The option has no intrinsic value but time value only; intrinsic value is zero.

Exhibit 8.15 briefly summarizes the various "Greek" elements and impacts discussed in the previous sections. The option premium is one of the most complex concepts in financial theory, and the application of option pricing to exchange rates does not make it any simpler. Only with a considerable amount of time and effort can the individual be expected to attain a "second sense" in the management of currency option positions.

EXHIBIT 8.14   **Option Premiums for Alternative Strike Rates**

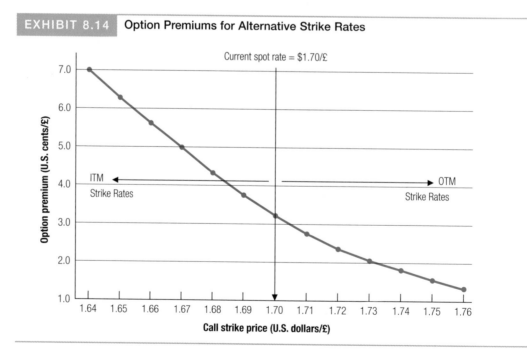

EXHIBIT 8.15	Summary of Option Premium Components	

Greek	Definition	Interpretation
Delta Δ	Expected change in the option premium for a small change in the **spot rate**	The higher the delta, the more likely the option will move in-the-money.
Theta θ	Expected change in the option premium for a small change in **time to expiration**	Premiums are relatively insensitive until the final 30 or so days.
Lambda λ	Expected change in the option premium for a small change in **volatility**	Premiums rise with increases in volatility.
Rho ρ	Expected change in the option premium for a small change in the **domestic interest rate**	Increases in domestic interest rates cause increasing call option premiums.
Phi φ	Expected change in the option premium for a small change in the **foreign interest rate**	Increases in foreign interest rates cause decreasing call option premiums.

Prudence in Practice

As illustrated in *Global Finance in Practice 8.2*, major corporate financial disasters related to financial derivatives continue to be a problem in global business. As is the case with so many issues in modern society, technology is not at fault, rather human error in its use. We conclude our discussion of financial derivatives with a note of caution and humility from an essay by Peter Bernstein published in the *Harvard Business Review*:

> *More than any other development, the quantification of risk defines the boundary between modern times and the rest of history. The speed, power, movement, and instant communication that characterize our age would have been inconceivable before science replaced superstition as a bulwark against risks of all kinds.*
>
> *It is hubris that we believe that we can put reliable and stable numbers on the impact of a politician's power, on the probability of a takeover boom like the one that occurred in the 1980s, on the return on the stock market over the next 2, 20, or 50 years, or on subjective factors like utility and risk aversion. It is equally silly to limit our deliberations only to those variables that do lend themselves to quantification, excluding all serious consideration of the unquantifiable. It is irrational to confuse probability with timing and to assume that an event with low probability is therefore not imminent. Such confusion, however, is by no means unusual. And it surely is naive to define discontinuity as anomaly instead of as normality; only the shape and the timing of the disturbances are hidden from us, not their inevitability.*
>
> *Finally, the science of risk management is capable of creating new risks even as it brings old risk under control. Our faith in risk management encourages us to take risk we otherwise would not take. On most counts, that is beneficial. But we should be wary of increasing the total amount of risk in the system. Research shows that the security of seat belts encourages drivers to behave more aggressively, with the result that the number of accidents rises even as the seriousness of injury in any one accident may diminish.*
>
> —Reprinted by permission of *Harvard Business Review*. Excerpt from "The New Religion of Risk Management" by Peter L. Bernstein, March–April 1996. Copyright 1996 by the Harvard Business School Publishing Corporation; all rights reserved.

GLOBAL FINANCE IN PRACTICE 8.2

A Select List of Derivative and Managerial Disasters

Date	Company	Description
1991	Allied-Lyons (U.K.)	Losses of £165 million related to speculation on currency options.
1993	Shell Showa Sekiyu (Japan)	Over ¥1.5 billion in losses arising from recognition of cumulative losses on forward contracts continually rolled over between 1989 and 1993.
1993	Metallgesellschaft (Germany)	A flawed petroleum futures hedging strategy essentially caused the collapse of the organization.
1994	Codelco (Chile)	A copper futures trader for the national copper company of Chile, Codelco loses approximately 0.5% of Chile's gross domestic product for 1994 through speculative futures trading.
1994	Kashima Oil (Japan)	Hundreds of millions of yen are lost on a failed forward speculation on the Japanese yen.
1994	Procter & Gamble (U.S.), Gibson Greeting Cards (U.S.), Air Products (U.S.), Dharmala (Indonesia)	All suffer material losses in the millions of dollars on leveraged swap agreements with Bankers Trust of the United States.
1995	Barings Brothers (U.K.)	The oldest investment bank in London fails as a result of the losses on futures trading suffered by one trader in its Singapore office, a Mr. Nicholas Leeson. (See the following mini-case.)
2002	Allied Irish Bank (U.S./U.K.)	A rogue currency trader in the Baltimore offices of Allied Irish Bank is credited with losing more than $691 million.

SUMMARY POINTS

- A foreign currency futures contract is an exchange-traded agreement calling for future delivery of a standard amount of foreign exchange at a fixed time, place, and price.

- Foreign currency futures contracts are in reality standardized forward contracts. Unlike forward contracts, however, trading occurs on the floor of an organized exchange rather than between banks and customers. Futures also require collateral and are normally settled through the purchase of an offsetting position.

- As summarized in Exhibit 8.2, futures differ from forward contracts by size of contract, maturity, location of trading, pricing, collateral/margin requirements, method of settlement, commissions, trading hours, counterparties, and liquidity.

- Financial managers typically prefer foreign currency forwards over futures because of forwards' simplicity of use and position maintenance. Financial speculators typically prefer foreign currency futures over forwards because of the liquidity of the futures markets.

- Foreign currency options are financial contracts that give the holder the right, but not the obligation, to buy (in the case of calls) or sell (in the case of puts) a specified amount of foreign exchange at a predetermined price on or before a specified maturity date.

- The use of a currency option as a speculative device for the buyer of an option arises from the fact that an option gains in value as the underlying currency rises (for calls) or falls (for puts). The amount of loss when the underlying currency moves opposite to the desired direction is limited to the premium of the option.

- The use of a currency option as a speculative device for the writer (seller) of an option arises from the option premium. If the option—either a put or call—expires out-of-the-money (valueless), the writer of the option has earned, and retains, the entire premium.

- Speculation is an attempt to profit by trading on expectations about prices in the future. In the foreign exchange market, one speculates by taking a position in a foreign currency and then closing that position after the exchange rate has moved; a profit results only if the rate moves in the direction that the speculator expected.

- The buyer of a call or put option has a limited loss potential and an unlimited profit potential; the buyer of a call or put cannot lose more than the option premium initially paid.

- The writer (seller) of a call or put option has a limited profit potential (the option premium earned is the limit to profit), with an unlimited loss potential of covering the option sold.

- Currency option valuation, the determination of the option's premium, is a complex combination of the current spot rate, the specific strike rate, the forward rate (which itself is dependent on the current spot rate and interest differentials), currency volatility, and time to maturity.

- The total value of an option is the sum of its intrinsic value and time value. Intrinsic value depends on the relationship between the option's strike price and the current spot rate at any single point in time, whereas time value estimates how this current intrinsic value may change—for the better—prior to the option's maturity or expiration.

MINI-CASE

Warren Buffett's Love-Hate Relationship with Derivatives

Warren Buffett has long been considered one of the true voices of reason in the vast wasteland of bad business decisions. As Chairman of the Board of Berkshire Hathaway, along with his friend and colleague, Vice Chairman Charlie Munger, he has one of the finest reputations in investing. He is also renowned for his outspoken nature, tough talk, and in some cases, downright bluntness. One of the targets of his relentless criticism has been *the derivative*. In the following excerpt from one of his famous letters to shareholders, he holds nothing back in vilifying what he sees as a definitive threat to the future of both the financial system and business in general.

But one added note before proceeding. In his 2007 letter to shareholders (published in March 2008), this same Warren Buffett described in detail how the company had 94 derivative contracts of two types, credit default swaps and put options on stock indices. Buffett noted that "...in all cases we hold the money, which means that we have no counterparty risk." He also gave a very interesting explanation of how mark-to-market accounting of the derivatives held by the firm would be viewed:

"Changes in the value of a derivative contract, however, must be applied each quarter to earnings. Thus, our derivatives positions will sometimes cause large swings in reported earnings, even though Charlie and I might believe the intrinsic value of these positions has changed little. He and I will not be bothered by these swings—even though they could easily amount to $1 billion or more in a quarter—and we hope you won't be either. You will recall that in our catastrophe insurance

business, we are always ready to trade increased volatility in reported earnings in the short run for greater gains in net worth in the long run. This is our philosophy in derivatives as well."

—Letter to Shareholders, Berkshire Hathaway, Annual Report, 2007, p. 16.

With those comforting thoughts, the following describes Mr. Buffett's thoughts on derivatives five years previous.

Berkshire Hathaway *Annual Report, 2002*: Excerpt on Derivatives

Charlie and I are of one mind in how we feel about derivatives and the trading activities that go with them: We view them as time bombs, both for the parties that deal in them and the economic system.

Having delivered that thought, which I'll get back to, let me retreat to explaining derivatives, though the explanation must be general because the word covers an extraordinarily wide range of financial contracts. Essentially, these instruments call for money to change hands at some future date, with the amount to be determined by one or more reference items, such as interest rates, stock prices or currency values. If, for example, you are either long or short an S&P 500 futures contract, you are a party to a very simple derivatives transaction—with your gain or loss derived from movements in the index. Derivatives contracts are of varying duration (running sometimes to 20 or more years) and their value is often tied to several variables.

Unless derivatives contracts are collateralized or guaranteed, their ultimate value also depends on the creditworthiness of the counterparties to them. In the meantime, though, before a contract is settled, the counterparties record profits and losses—often huge in amount—in their current earnings statements without so much as a penny changing hands.

The range of derivatives contracts is limited only by the imagination of man (or sometimes, so it seems, madmen). At Enron, for example, newsprint and broadband derivatives, due to be settled many years in the future, were put on the books. Or say you want to write a contract speculating on the number of twins to be born in Nebraska in 2020. No problem—at a price, you will easily find an obliging counterparty.

When we purchased Gen Re, it came with General Re Securities, a derivatives dealer that Charlie and I didn't want, judging it to be dangerous. We failed in our attempts to sell the operation, however, and are now terminating it. But closing down a derivatives business is easier said than done. It will be a great many years before we are totally out of this operation (though we reduce our exposure daily). In fact, the reinsurance and derivatives businesses are similar: Like Hell, both are easy to enter and almost impossible to exit. In either industry, once you write a contract—which may require a large payment decades later—you are usually stuck with it. True, there are methods by which the risk can be laid off with others. But most strategies of that kind leave you with residual liability.

Another commonality of reinsurance and derivatives is that both generate reported earnings that are often wildly overstated. That's true because today's earnings are in a significant way based on estimates whose inaccuracy may not be exposed for many years.

Errors will usually be honest, reflecting only the human tendency to take an optimistic view of one's commitments. But the parties to derivatives also have enormous incentives to cheat in accounting for them. Those who trade derivatives are usually paid (in whole or part) on "earnings" calculated by mark-to-market accounting. But often there is no real market (think about our contract involving twins) and "mark-to-model" is utilized. This substitution can bring on large-scale mischief. As a general rule, contracts involving multiple reference items and distant settlement dates increase the opportunities for counterparties to use fanciful assumptions. In the twins scenario, for example, the two parties to the contract might well use differing models allowing both to show substantial profits for many years. In extreme cases, mark-to-model degenerates into what I would call mark-to-myth.

Of course, both internal and outside auditors review the numbers, but that's no easy job. For example, General Re Securities at year end (after ten months of winding down its operation) had 14,384 contracts outstanding, involving 672 counterparties around the world. Each contract had a plus or minus value derived from one or more reference items, including some of mind-boggling complexity. Valuing a portfolio like that, expert auditors could easily and honestly have widely varying opinions.

The valuation problem is far from academic: In recent years, some huge-scale frauds and near-frauds have been facilitated by derivatives trades. In the energy and electric utility sectors, for example, companies used derivatives and trading activities to report great "earnings"—until the roof fell in when they actually tried to convert the derivatives-related receivables on their balance sheets into cash. "Mark-to-market" then turned out to be truly "mark-to-myth."

I can assure you that the marking errors in the derivatives business have not been symmetrical. Almost invariably, they have favored either the trader who was eyeing a multi-million dollar bonus or the CEO who wanted to report impressive "earnings" (or both). The bonuses were paid, and the CEO profited from his options. Only much later did shareholders learn that the reported earnings were a sham.

Another problem about derivatives is that they can exacerbate trouble that a corporation has run into for completely unrelated reasons. This pile-on effect occurs because many derivatives contracts require that a company suffering a credit downgrade immediately supply collateral to counterparties. Imagine, then, that a company is downgraded because of general adversity and that its derivatives instantly kick in with their requirement, imposing an unexpected and enormous demand for cash collateral on the company. The need to meet this demand can then throw the company into a liquidity crisis that may, in some cases, trigger still more downgrades. It all becomes a spiral that can lead to a corporate meltdown.

Derivatives also create a daisy-chain risk that is akin to the risk run by insurers or reinsurers that lay off much of their business with others. In both cases, huge receivables from many counterparties tend to build up over time. (At Gen Re Securities, we still have $6.5 billion of receivables, though we've been in a liquidation mode for nearly a year.) A participant may see himself as prudent, believing his large credit exposures to be diversified and therefore not dangerous. Under certain circumstances, though, an exogenous event that causes the receivable from Company A to go bad will also affect those from Companies B through Z. History teaches us that a crisis often causes problems to correlate in a manner undreamed of in more tranquil times.

In banking, the recognition of a "linkage" problem was one of the reasons for the formation of the Federal Reserve System. Before the Fed was established, the failure of weak banks would sometimes put sudden and unanticipated liquidity demands on previously-strong banks, causing them to fail in turn. The Fed now insulates the strong from the troubles of the weak. But there is no central bank assigned to the job of preventing the dominoes toppling in insurance or derivatives. In these industries, firms that are fundamentally solid can become troubled simply because of the travails of other firms further down the chain. When a "chain reaction" threat exists within an industry, it pays to minimize links of any kind. That's how we conduct our reinsurance business, and it's one reason we are exiting derivatives.

Many people argue that derivatives reduce systemic problems, in that participants who can't bear certain risks are able to transfer them to stronger hands. These people believe that derivatives act to stabilize the economy, facilitate trade, and eliminate bumps for individual participants. And, on a micro level, what they say is often true. Indeed, at Berkshire, I sometimes engage in large-scale derivatives transactions in order to facilitate certain investment strategies.

Charlie and I believe, however, that the macro picture is dangerous and getting more so. Large amounts of risk, particularly credit risk, have become concentrated in the hands of relatively few derivatives dealers, who in addition trade extensively with one other. The troubles of one could quickly infect the others. On top of that, these dealers are owed huge amounts by non-dealer counterparties. Some of these counterparties, as I've mentioned, are linked in ways that could cause them to contemporaneously run into a problem because of a single event (such as the implosion of the telecom industry or the precipitous decline in the value of merchant power projects). Linkage, when it suddenly surfaces, can trigger serious systemic problems.

Indeed, in 1998, the leveraged and derivatives-heavy activities of a single hedge fund, Long-Term Capital Management, caused the Federal Reserve anxieties so severe that it hastily orchestrated a rescue effort. In later Congressional testimony, Fed officials acknowledged that, had they not intervened, the outstanding trades of LTCM—a firm unknown to the general public and employing only a few hundred people—could well have posed a serious threat to the stability of American markets. In other words, the Fed acted because its leaders were fearful of what might have happened to other financial institutions had the LTCM domino toppled. And this

affair, though it paralyzed many parts of the fixed-income market for weeks, was far from a worst-case scenario.

One of the derivatives instruments that LTCM used was total-return swaps, contracts that facilitate 100% leverage in various markets, including stocks. For example, Party A to a contract, usually a bank, puts up all of the money for the purchase of a stock while Party B, without putting up any capital, agrees that at a future date it will receive any gain or pay any loss that the bank realizes.

Total-return swaps of this type make a joke of margin requirements. Beyond that, other types of derivatives severely curtail the ability of regulators to curb leverage and generally get their arms around the risk profiles of banks, insurers and other financial institutions. Similarly, even experienced investors and analysts encounter major problems in analyzing the financial condition of firms that are heavily involved with derivatives contracts. When Charlie and I finish reading the long footnotes detailing the derivatives activities of major banks, the only thing we understand is that we don't understand how much risk the institution is running.

The derivatives genie is now well out of the bottle, and these instruments will almost certainly multiply in variety and number until some event makes their toxicity clear. Knowledge of how dangerous they are has already permeated the electricity and gas businesses, in which the eruption of major troubles caused the use of derivatives to diminish dramatically. Elsewhere, however, the derivatives business continues to expand unchecked. Central banks and governments have so far found no effective way to control, or even monitor, the risks posed by these contracts.

Charlie and I believe Berkshire should be a fortress of financial strength—for the sake of our owners, creditors, policyholders and employees. We try to be alert to any sort of megacatastrophe risk, and that posture may make us unduly apprehensive about the burgeoning quantities of long-term derivatives contracts and the massive amount of uncollateralized receivables that are growing alongside. In our view, however, derivatives are financial weapons of mass destruction, carrying dangers that, while now latent, are potentially lethal.

Case Questions

1. In his 2002 letter to shareholders, what does Warren Buffett seem to fear most about financial derivatives?
2. In his 2007 letter to shareholders, what does Warren Buffett admit that he and Charlie had done?
3. Do you think there is an underlying consistency in his viewpoint on the proper use of derivatives?

QUESTIONS

1. **Options versus Futures.** Explain the difference between foreign currency *options* and *futures* and when either might be used most appropriately.

2. **Trading Location for Futures.** Check *The Wall Street Journal* to find where in the United States foreign exchange future contracts are traded.

3. **Futures Terminology.** Explain the meaning and probable significance for international business of the following contract specifications:
   a. Specific-sized contract
   b. Standard method of stating exchange rates
   c. Standard maturity date
   d. Collateral and maintenance margins
   e. Counterparty

4. **A Futures Trade.** A newspaper shows the following prices for the previous day's trading in U.S. dollar-euro currency futures:

Month:	December
Open:	0.9124
Settlement:	0.9136
Change:	+0.0027
High:	0.9147
Low:	0.9098
Estimated volume:	29,763
Open interest:	111,360
Contract size:	€125,000

   What do the above terms indicate?

5. **Puts and Calls.** What is the basic difference between a *put* on British pounds sterling and a *call* on sterling?

6. **Call Contract Elements.** You read that exchange-traded American call options on pounds sterling having a strike price of 1.460 and a maturity of next March are now quoted at 3.67. What does this mean if you are a potential buyer?

7. **The Option Cost.** What happens to the premium you paid for the option in question 6 in the event you decide to let the option expire unexercised? What happens to this amount in the event you decide to exercise the option?

8. **Buying a European Option.** You have the same information as in question 6, except that the pricing is for a European option. What is different?

9. **Writing Options.** Why would anyone write an option, knowing that the gain from receiving the option premium is fixed but the loss if the underlying price goes in the wrong direction can be extremely large?

10. **Option Valuation.** The value of an option is stated to be the sum of its *intrinsic value* and its *time value*. Explain what is meant by these terms.

PROBLEMS

*1. **Peregrine Funds—Jakarta.** Samuel Samosir trades currencies for Peregrine Funds in Jakarta, Indonesia. He focuses nearly all of his time and attention on the U.S. dollar/Singapore dollar ($/S$) cross-rate. The current spot rate is $0.6000/S$. After considerable study this week, he has concluded that the Singapore dollar will appreciate versus the U.S. dollar in the coming 90 days, probably to about $0.7000/S$. He has the following options on the Singapore dollar to choose from:

Option	Strike Price	Premium
Put on Sing $	$0.6500/S$	$0.00003/S$
Call on Sing $	$0.6500/S$	$0.00046/S$

   a. Should Samuel buy a put on Singapore dollars or a call on Singapore dollars?
   b. Using your answer to part (a), what is Samuel's break-even price?
   c. Using your answer to part (a), what is Samuel's gross profit and net profit (including the premium) if the spot rate at the end of the 90 days is indeed $0.7000/S$?
   d. Using your answer to part (a), what is Samuel's gross profit and net profit (including the premium) if the spot rate at the end of the 90 days is indeed $0.8000/S$?

2. **Paulo's Puts.** Paulo writes a put option on Japanese yen with a strike price of $0.008000/¥ (¥125.00/$) at a premium of 0.0080 cents per yen and with an expiration date six months from now. The option is for ¥12,500,000. What is Paulo's profit or loss at maturity if the ending spot rates are ¥110/$, ¥115/$, ¥120/$, ¥125/$, ¥130/$, ¥135/$, and ¥140/$.

3. **Amber McClain.** Amber McClain, the currency speculator we met earlier in the chapter, now sells eight June futures contracts for 500,000 pesos at the closing price quoted in Exhibit 8.1.

a. What is the value of her position at maturity if the ending spot rate is $.12000/Ps?

b. What is the value of her position at maturity if the ending spot rate is $.09800/Ps?

c. What is the value of her position at maturity if the ending spot rate is $.11000/Ps?

4. **Black River Investments.** Jennifer Magnussen, a currency trader for Chicago-based Black River Investments, uses the futures quotes (shown at the bottom of this page) on the British pound to speculate on its value:

a. If Jennifer buys 5 June pound futures, and the spot rate at maturity is $1.3980/pound, what is the value of her position?

b. If Jennifer sells 12 March pound futures, and the spot rate at maturity is $1.4560/pound, what is the value of her position?

c. If Jennifer buys 3 March pound futures, and the spot rate at maturity is $1.4560/pound, what is the value of her position?

d. If Jennifer sells 12 June pound futures, and the spot rate at maturity is $1.3980/pound, what is the value of her position?

5. **Madera Capital.** Katya Berezovsky is a currency speculator for Madera Capital of Los Angeles. Her latest speculative position is to profit from her expectation that the U.S. dollar will rise significantly against the Japanese yen. The current spot rate is ¥120.00/$. She must choose between the following 90-day options on the Japanese yen:

Option	Strike Price	Premium
Put on yen	¥125/$	$0.00003/¥
Call on yen	¥125/$	$0.00046/¥

a. Should Katya buy a put on yen or a call on yen?

b. Using your answer to part (a), what is Katya's break-even price?

c. Using your answer to part (a), what is Katya's gross profit and net profit (including the premium) if the spot rate at the end of the 90 days is ¥140/$?

6. **Gnome Capital (A).** Stefan Weir trades currency for Gnome Capital of Geneva. Stefan has $10 million to begin with, and he must state all profits at the end of any speculation in U.S. dollars. The spot rate on the euro is $1.3558/€, while the 30-day forward rate is $1.3550/€.

a. If Stefan believes the euro will continue to rise in value against the U.S. dollar, so that he expects the spot rate to be $1.3600/€ at the end of 30 days, what should he do?

b. If Stefan believes the euro will depreciate in value against the U.S. dollar, so that he expects the spot rate to be $1.2800/€ at the end of 30 days, what should he do?

7. **Gnome Capital (B).** Stefan Weir believes the Swiss franc will appreciate versus the U.S. dollar in the coming three-month period. He has $100,000 to invest. The current spot rate is $0.5820/SF, the three-month forward rate is $0.5640/SF, and he expects the spot rates to reach $0.6250/SF in six months.

a. Calculate Stefan's expected profit assuming a pure spot market speculation strategy.

b. Calculate Stefan's expected profit assuming he buys or sells SF three months forward.

8. **Call Profits.** Assume that a call option on euros is written with a strike price of $1.25/€ at a premium of 3.80 cents per euro ($0.0380/€) and with an expiration date three months from now. The option is for €100,000. Calculate your profit or loss should you exercise before maturity at a time when the euro is traded spot at

a. $1.10/€
b. $1.15/€
c. $1.20/€
d. $1.25/€
e. $1.30/€
f. $1.35/€
g. $1.40/€

British Pound Futures, US$/pound (CME)

Contract = 62,500 pounds

Maturity	Open	High	Low	Settle	Change	High	Low	Open Interest
March	1.4246	1.4268	1.4214	1.4228	.0032	1.4700	1.3810	25,605
June	1.4164	1.4188	1.4146	1.4162	.0030	1.4550	1.3910	809

9. **Giri the Contrarian.** Giri Patel works for CIBC Currency Funds in Toronto. Giri is something of a *contrarian*—as opposed to most of the forecasts, he believes the Canadian dollar (C$) will appreciate versus the U.S. dollar over the coming 90 days. The current spot rate is $0.6750/C$. Giri may choose between the following options on the Canadian dollar:

Option	Strike Price	Premium
Put on C$	$0.7000	$0.0003/C$
Call on C$	$0.7000	$0.0249/C$

a. Should Giri buy a put on Canadian dollars or a call on Canadian dollars?
b. Using your answer to part (a), what is Giri's break-even price?
c. Using your answer to part (a), what is Giri's gross profit and net profit (including the premium) if the spot rate at the end of the 90 days is indeed $0.7600/C$?
d. Using your answer to part (a), what is Giri's gross profit and net profit (including the premium) if the spot rate at the end of the 90 days is indeed $0.8250/C$?

10. **Downing Street.** Sydney Reeks is a currency trader for Downing Street, a private investment house in London. Downing Street's clients are a collection of wealthy private investors who, with a minimum stake of £250,000 each, wish to speculate on the movement of currencies. The investors expect annual returns in excess of 25%. Although located in London, all accounts and expectations are based in U.S. dollars.

Sydney is convinced that the British pound will slide significantly—possibly to $1.3200/£—in the coming 30 to 60 days. The current spot rate is $1.4260/£. Andy wishes to buy a put on pounds which will yield the 25% return expected by his investors. Which of the put options shown below would you recommend he purchase? Prove your choice is the preferable combination of strike price, maturity, and up-front premium expense.

Strike Price	Maturity	Premium
$1.36/£	30 days	$0.00081/£
$1.34/£	30 days	$0.00021/£
$1.32/£	30 days	$0.00004/£
$1.36/£	60 days	$0.00333/£
$1.34/£	60 days	$0.00150/£
$1.32/£	60 days	$0.00060/£

Pricing Your Own Options

An Excel workbook entitled FX Option Pricing *is downloadable from the book's Web site. The workbook has four spreadsheets constructed for pricing currency options for the following five currency pairs (shown top of next page): U.S. dollar/euro, U.S. dollar/Japanese yen, euro/Japanese yen, U.S. dollar/British pound, and euro/British pound. Use the appropriate spreadsheet from the workbook to answer the following questions.*

11. **U.S. Dollar/Euro.** The exhibit at the top of the following page indicates that a one-year call option on euros at a strike rate of $1.25/€ will cost the buyer $0.0366/€, or 4.56%. But that assumed a volatility of 10.5% when the spot rate was $1.2674/€. What would that same call option cost if the volatility was 12% and the spot rate $1.2480/€?

12. **U.S. Dollar/Japanese Yen.** What would be the premium expense, in home-currency, for Nakagama of Japan's purchase of an option to sell 750,000 U.S. dollars, assuming the initial values listed in the *FX Option Pricing* workbook?

13. **Euro/Japanese Yen.** Legrand (France) is expecting to receive ¥10.4 million in 90 days as a result of an export sale to a Japanese semiconductor firm. What will it cost, in total, to purchase an option to sell the yen at €0.0072/¥?

14. **U.S. Dollar/British Pound.** Assuming the same initial values for the dollar/pound cross rate in the *FX Option Pricing* workbook, how much more would a call option on pounds be if the maturity was doubled from 90 to 180 days? What percentage increase is this for twice the length of maturity?

15. **Euro/British Pound.** How would the call option premium change on the right to buy pounds with euros if the euro interest rate changed to 4.000% from the initial values listed in the *FX Option Pricing* workbook?

Pricing Currency Options on the Euro	A U.S.-based firm wishing to buy or sell euros (the foreign currency)		A European firm wishing to buy or sell dollars (the foreign currency)	
	Variable	Value	Variable	Value
Spot rate (domestic/foreign)	S_0	$1.248	S_0	€ 0.8013
Strike rate (domestic/foreign)	X	$1.2500	X	€ 0.8000
Domestic interest rate (% p.a.)	r_d	1.453%	r_d	2.187%
Foreign interest rate (% p.a.)	r_f	2.187%	r_f	1.453%
Time (years, 365 days)	T	1.000	T	1.000
Days equivalent		365.00		365.00
Volatility (% p.a.)	s	10.500%	s	10.500%
Call option premium (per unit fc)	c	$0.0461	c	€ 0.0366
Put option premium (per unit fc)	p	$0.0570	p	€ 0.0295
(European pricing)				
Call option premium (%)	c	3.69%	c	4.56%
Put option premium (%)	p	4.57%	p	3.68%

INTERNET EXERCISES

1. **Financial Derivatives and the ISDA.** The ISDA, the International Swaps and Derivatives Association, publishes a wealth of information about financial derivatives, their valuation, and their use, in addition to providing master documents for their contractual use between parties. Use the following ISDA Web site to find the definitions to 31 basic financial derivative questions and terms.

   ISDA   www.isda.org/educat/faqs.html

2. **Risk Management of Financial Derivatives.** If you think this book is long, take a look at the freely downloadable U.S. Comptroller of the Currency's handbook on risk management related to the care and use of financial derivatives!

   Comptroller of
   the Currency   www.occ.treas.gov/handbook/deriv.pdf

3. **Option Pricing.** OzForex Foreign Exchange Services is a private firm with an enormously powerful foreign currency derivative-enabled Web site. Use the following Web site to evaluate the various "Greeks" related to currency option pricing.

   OzForex   www.ozforex.com.au/reference/fxoptions/

4. **Garman-Kohlhagen Option Formulation.** For the brave of heart and quantitatively adept, check out the following Internet site's detailed presentation of the Garman-Kohlhagen option formulation used in business and finance so widely today.

   Riskglossary.com   www.riskglossary.com/link/garman_kohlhagen_1983.htm

5. **Chicago Mercantile Exchange.** The Chicago Mercantile Exchange trades futures and options on a variety of currencies, including the Brazilian reais. Use the following Web site to evaluate the uses of these currency derivatives.

   Chicago Mercantile   www.cme.com/trading/dta/del/
   Exchange   product_list.html?ProductType=cur

6. **Implied Currency Volatilities.** The single unobservable variable in currency option pricing is the volatility, since volatility inputs are the expected standard deviation of the daily spot rate for the coming period of the option's maturity. Use the New York Federal Reserve's Web site to obtain current implied currency volatilities for major trading cross-rate pairs.

   Federal Reserve   www.ny.frb.org/markets/
   Bank of New York   impliedvolatility.html

7. **Montreal Exchange.** The Montreal Exchange is a Canadian exchange devoted to the support of financial derivatives in Canada. Use its Web site to view the latest on MV volatility—the volatility of the Montreal Exchange Index itself—in recent trading hours and days.

   Montreal Exchange   www.m-x.ca/marc_options_en.php

Currency Option Pricing Theory

The foreign currency option model presented here, the European-style option, is the result of the work of Black and Scholes (1972); Cox and Ross (1976); Cox, Ross, and Rubinstein (1979); Garman and Kohlhagen (1983); and Bodurtha and Courtadon (1987). Although we do not explain the theoretical derivation of the following option-pricing model, the original model derived by Black and Scholes is based on the formation of a riskless hedged portfolio composed of a long position in the security, asset, or currency, and a European call option. The solution to this model's expected return yields the option *premium*.

The basic theoretical model for the pricing of a European call option is:

$$C = e^{-r_f T}\, SN(d_1) - E_e^{-r_d T}\, N(d_2)$$

where

  C = premium on a European call
  e = continuous time discounting
  S = spot exchange rate ($/foreign currency)
  E = exercise or strike rate
  T = time to expiration
  N = cumulative normal distribution function
  r_f = foreign interest rate
  r_d = domestic interest rate
  σ = standard deviation of asset price (volatility)
  ln = natural logarithm

The two density functions, d_1 and d_2, are defined as

$$d_1 = \frac{\ln\left(\dfrac{S}{E}\right) + \left(r_d - r_f + \dfrac{\sigma^2}{2}\right)T}{\sigma\sqrt{T}}$$

and

$$d_2 = d_1 - \sigma\sqrt{T}$$

This expression can be rearranged so the premium on a European call option is written in terms of the forward rate

$$C = e^{-r_f T}\, FN(d_1) - e^{-r_d T}\, EN(d_2)$$

where the spot rate and foreign interest rate have been replaced with the forward rate, F, and both the first and second terms are discounted over continuous time, e. If we now slightly simplify, we find that the option premium is the present value of the difference between two cumulative normal density functions:

$$C = \left[FN(d_1) - EN(d_2) \right] e^{-r_d T}$$

The two density functions are now defined as

$$d_1 = \frac{\ln\left(\dfrac{F}{E}\right) + \left(\dfrac{\sigma^2}{2}\right) T}{\sigma\sqrt{T}}$$

and

$$d_2 = d_1 - \sigma\sqrt{T}$$

Solving each of these equations for d_1 and d_2 allows the determination of the European call option premium. The premium for a European put option, P, is similarly derived as

$$P = \left[F\left(N(d_1) - 1\right) - E\left(N(d_2) - 1\right) \right] e^{-r_d T}$$

The European Call Option: Numerical Example

The actual calculation of the option premium is not as complex as it appears from the preceding set of equations. Assuming the following basic exchange rate and interest rate values, computation of the option premium is relatively straightforward.

Spot rate	= \$1.7000/£
90-day forward	= \$1.7000/£
Strike rate	= \$1.7000/£
U.S. dollar interest rate	= 8.00% (per annum)
Pound sterling interest rate	= 8.00% (per annum)
Time (days)	= 90
Std. dev. (volatility)	= 10.00%
e (infinite discounting)	= 2.71828

The value of the two density functions are first derived as

$$d_1 = \frac{\ln\left(\dfrac{F}{E}\right) + \left(\dfrac{\sigma^2}{2}\right) T}{\sigma\sqrt{T}} = \frac{\ln\left(\dfrac{1.7000}{1.7000}\right) + \left(\dfrac{0.1000^2}{2}\right)\dfrac{90}{365}}{0.1000\sqrt{\dfrac{90}{365}}} = 0.025$$

and

$$d_2 = 0.025 - 0.1000\sqrt{\dfrac{90}{365}} = -0.025$$

The values of d_1 and d_2 are then found in the cumulative normal probability table:

$$N(d_1) = N(0.025) = 0.51; \qquad N(d_2) = N(-0.025) = 0.49$$

The premium of the European call with a "forward-at-the-money" strike rate is

$$C = [(1.7000)(0.51)] - (1.7000)(0.49)]2.71828^{-0.08(90/365)} = \$0.033/£$$

This is the call option premium, price, value, or cost.

Cumulative Normal Probability Table

The probability that a drawing from a unit normal distribution will produce a value less than the constant d is

$$\text{Prob}(z < d) = \int_{-\infty}^{d} \frac{1}{\sqrt{2\pi}} e^{-z^2/2} dz = N(d)$$

EXHIBIT 8A.1

Range of d: −2.49 ≤ d ≤ 0.00

D	−0.00	−0.01	−0.02	−0.03	−0.04	−0.05	−0.06	−0.07	−0.08	−0.09
−2.40	0.00820	0.00798	0.00776	0.00755	0.00734	0.00714	0.00695	0.00676	0.00657	0.00639
−2.30	0.01072	0.01044	0.01017	0.00990	0.00964	0.00939	0.00914	0.00889	0.00866	0.00842
−2.20	0.01390	0.01355	0.01321	0.01287	0.01255	0.01222	0.01191	0.01160	0.01130	0.01101
−2.10	0.01786	0.01743	0.01700	0.01659	0.01618	0.01578	0.01539	0.01500	0.01463	0.01426
−2.00	0.02275	0.02222	0.02169	0.02118	0.02068	0.02018	0.01970	0.01923	0.01876	0.01831
−1.90	0.02872	0.02807	0.02743	0.02680	0.02619	0.02559	0.02500	0.02442	0.02385	0.02330
−1.80	0.03593	0.03515	0.03438	0.03362	0.03288	0.03216	0.03144	0.03074	0.03005	0.02938
−1.70	0.04457	0.04363	0.04272	0.04182	0.04093	0.04006	0.03920	0.03836	0.03754	0.03673
−1.60	0.05480	0.05370	0.05262	0.05155	0.05050	0.04947	0.04846	0.04746	0.04648	0.04551
−1.50	0.06681	0.06552	0.06426	0.06301	0.06178	0.06057	0.05938	0.05821	0.05705	0.05592
−1.40	0.08076	0.07927	0.07780	0.07636	0.07493	0.07353	0.07215	0.07078	0.06944	0.06811
−1.30	0.09680	0.09510	0.09342	0.09176	0.09012	0.08851	0.08691	0.08534	0.08379	0.08226
−1.20	0.11507	0.11314	0.11123	0.10935	0.10749	0.10565	0.10383	0.10204	0.10027	0.09853
−1.10	0.13567	0.13350	0.13136	0.12924	0.12714	0.12507	0.12302	0.12100	0.11900	0.11702
−1.00	0.15866	0.15625	0.15386	0.15150	0.14917	0.14686	0.14457	0.14231	0.14007	0.13786
−0.90	0.18406	0.18141	0.17879	0.17619	0.17361	0.17106	0.16853	0.16602	0.16354	0.16109
−0.80	0.21186	0.20897	0.20611	0.20327	0.20045	0.19766	0.19489	0.19215	0.18943	0.18673
−0.70	0.24196	0.23885	0.23576	0.23270	0.22965	0.22663	0.22363	0.22065	0.21770	0.21476
−0.60	0.27425	0.27093	0.26763	0.26435	0.26109	0.25785	0.25463	0.25143	0.24825	0.24510
−0.50	0.30854	0.30503	0.30153	0.29806	0.29460	0.29116	0.28774	0.28434	0.28096	0.27760
−0.40	0.34458	0.34090	0.33724	0.33360	0.32997	0.32636	0.32276	0.31918	0.31561	0.31207
−0.30	0.38209	0.37828	0.37448	0.37070	0.36693	0.36317	0.35942	0.35569	0.35197	0.34827
−0.20	0.42074	0.41683	0.41294	0.40905	0.40517	0.40129	0.39743	0.39358	0.38974	0.38591
−0.10	0.46017	0.45620	0.45224	0.44828	0.44433	0.44038	0.43644	0.43251	0.42858	0.42465

(continues)

Range of d: $-2.49 \leq d \leq 0.00$

D	−0.00	−0.01	−0.02	−0.03	−0.04	−0.05	−0.06	−0.07	−0.08	−0.09
0.00	0.50000	0.49601	0.49202	0.48803	0.48405	0.48006	0.47608	0.47210	0.46812	0.46414
0.00	0.50000	0.50399	0.50798	0.51197	0.51595	0.51994	0.52392	0.52790	0.53188	0.53586
0.01	0.53983	0.54380	0.54776	0.55172	0.55567	0.55962	0.56356	0.56749	0.57142	0.57535
0.20	0.57926	0.58317	0.58706	0.59095	0.59483	0.59871	0.60257	0.60642	0.61026	0.61409
0.30	0.61791	0.62172	0.62552	0.62930	0.63307	0.63683	0.64058	0.64431	0.64803	0.65173
0.40	0.65542	0.65910	0.66276	0.66640	0.67003	0.67364	0.67724	0.68082	0.68439	0.68793
0.50	0.69146	0.69497	0.69847	0.70194	0.70540	0.70884	0.71226	0.71566	0.71904	0.72240
0.60	0.72575	0.72907	0.73237	0.73565	0.73891	0.74215	0.74537	0.74857	0.75175	0.75490
0.70	0.75804	0.76115	0.76424	0.76730	0.77035	0.77337	0.77637	0.77935	0.78230	0.78524
0.80	0.78814	0.79103	0.79389	0.79673	0.79955	0.80234	0.80511	0.80785	0.81057	0.81327
0.90	0.81594	0.81859	0.82121	0.82381	0.82639	0.82894	0.83147	0.83398	0.83646	0.83891
1.00	0.84134	0.84375	0.84614	0.84850	0.85083	0.85314	0.85543	0.85769	0.85993	0.86214
1.10	0.86433	0.86650	0.86864	0.87076	0.87286	0.87493	0.87698	0.87900	0.88100	0.88298
1.20	0.88493	0.88686	0.88877	0.89065	0.89251	0.89435	0.89617	0.89796	0.89973	0.90147
1.30	0.90320	0.90490	0.90658	0.90824	0.90988	0.91149	0.91309	0.91466	0.91621	0.91774
1.40	0.91924	0.92073	0.92220	0.92364	0.92507	0.92647	0.92785	0.92922	0.93056	0.93189
1.50	0.93319	0.93448	0.93574	0.93699	0.93822	0.93943	0.94062	0.94179	0.94295	0.94408
1.60	0.94520	0.94630	0.94738	0.94845	0.94950	0.95053	0.95154	0.95254	0.95352	0.95449
1.70	0.95543	0.95637	0.95728	0.95818	0.95907	0.95994	0.96080	0.96164	0.96246	0.96327
1.80	0.96407	0.96485	0.96562	0.96637	0.96712	0.96784	0.96856	0.96926	0.96995	0.97062
1.90	0.97128	0.97193	0.97257	0.97320	0.97381	0.97441	0.97500	0.97558	0.97615	0.97670
2.00	0.97725	0.97778	0.97831	0.97882	0.97932	0.97982	0.98030	0.98077	0.98124	0.98169
2.10	0.98214	0.98257	0.98300	0.98341	0.98382	0.98422	0.98461	0.98500	0.98537	0.98574
2.20	0.98610	0.98645	0.98679	0.98713	0.98745	0.98778	0.98809	0.98840	0.98870	0.98899
2.30	0.98928	0.98956	0.98983	0.99010	0.99036	0.99061	0.99086	0.99111	0.99134	0.99158
2.40	0.99180	0.99202	0.99224	0.99245	0.99266	0.99286	0.99305	0.99324	0.99343	0.99361

Source: Hans R. Stoll and Robert E. Whaley, *Futures and Options,* Southwestern Publishing, 1993, pp. 242–243. Reprinted with permission.

CHAPTER 9

Interest Rate and Currency Swaps

The objects of a financier are, then, to secure an ample revenue; to impose it with judgment and equality; to employ it economically; and, when necessity obliges him to make use of credit, to secure its foundations in that instance, and forever, by the clearness and candor of his proceedings, the exactness of his calculations, and the solidity of his funds.

—Edmund Burke (1729–1797).

This chapter discusses the variety of strategies for managing interest rate and currency risks associated with an MNE's capital structure. Our main tools are interest rate and currency swaps. Moreover, many of the same tools we observed earlier in foreign exchange risk management have parallels in interest rate and currency risk management.

The management of financial risks—exchange rates, interest rates, and commodity prices—is a rapidly expanding area of multinational financial management. All of these financial prices introduce risk into the cash flows of the firm. The identification, measurement, and management of interest rate risk now receive roughly the same level of attention and effort as foreign exchange risk did just a few years ago.

Defining Interest Rate Risk

All firms—domestic or multinational, small or large, leveraged or unleveraged—are sensitive to interest rate movements in one way or another. Although a variety of interest rate risks exist in theory and industry, this book focuses on the financial management of the nonfinancial firm. Hence, our discussion is limited to the interest rate risks associated with the multinational firm. The interest rate risks of financial firms, such as banks, are not covered here.

The single largest interest rate risk of the nonfinancial firm is debt service. The debt structure of the MNE will possess differing maturities of debt, different interest rate structures (such as fixed versus floating rate), and different currencies of denomination. Interest rates are currency-specific. Each currency has its own interest rate yield curve and credit spreads for borrowers. Therefore, the multicurrency dimension of interest rate risk for the MNE is a serious concern. As illustrated in Exhibit 9.1, even the interest rate calculations vary on occasion across currencies and countries.

The second most prevalent source of interest rate risk for the MNE lies in its holdings of interest-sensitive securities. Unlike debt, which is recorded on the right-hand side of the

EXHIBIT 9.1	International Interest Rate Calculations

International interest rate calculations differ by the number of days used in the period's calculation and the definition of how many days there are in a year (for financial purposes). The following example highlights how the different methods result in different one-month payments of interest on a $10 million loan, 5.500% per annum interest, for an exact period of 28 days.

Practice	Day Count in Period	Days/Year	Days Used	$10 million @ 5.500% per annum Interest Payment
International	Exact number of days	360	28	$42,777.78
British	Exact number of days	365	28	$42,191.78
Swiss (Eurobond)	Assumed 30 days/month	360	30	$45,833.33

Source: Adapted from "Hedging Instruments for Foreign Exchange, Monday Market, and Precious Metals," Union Bank of Switzerland, pp. 41–42.

firm's balance sheet, the marketable securities portfolio of the firm appears on the left-hand side. Marketable securities represent potential earnings or interest inflows to the firm. Ever-increasing competitive pressures have pushed financial managers to tighten their management of both the left and right sides of the firm's balance sheet.

Whether it is on the left or right side, the *reference rate* of interest calculation merits special attention. A *reference rate*—for example, U.S. dollar LIBOR—is the rate of interest used in a standardized quotation, loan agreement, or financial derivative valuation. LIBOR, the London Interbank Offered Rate, is by far the most widely used and quoted, as described in Chapter 3. It is officially defined by the British Bankers Association (BBA). U.S. dollar LIBOR is the mean of 16 multinational banks' interbank offered rates as sampled by the BBA at approximately 11 A.M. London time in London. Similarly, the BBA calculates the Japanese yen LIBOR, euro LIBOR, and other currency LIBOR rates at the same time in London from samples of banks.

The interbank interest rate market is not, however, confined to London. Most major domestic financial centers construct their own interbank offered rates for local loan agreement purposes. These rates include PIBOR (Paris Interbank Offered Rate), MIBOR (Madrid Interbank Offered Rate), SIBOR (Singapore Interbank Offered Rate), and FIBOR (Frankfurt Interbank Offered Rate), to name but a few. Exhibit 9.2 illustrates the close relationship between LIBOR and other short-term interest rates and deposit rates.

Credit Risk and Repricing Risk

Prior to describing the management of the most common interest rate pricing risks, it is important to distinguish between credit risk and repricing risk. *Credit risk*, sometimes termed *roll-over risk*, is the possibility that a borrower's creditworth, at the time of renewing a credit, is reclassified by the lender. This can result in changing fees, changing interest rates, altered credit line commitments, or even denial. *Repricing risk* is the risk of changes in interest rates charged (earned) at the time a financial contract's rate is reset.

Consider the following three different debt strategies being considered by a corporate borrower. Each is intended to provide $1 million in financing for a three-year period:

■ *Strategy 1*: Borrow $1 million for three years at a fixed rate of interest

■ *Strategy 2*: Borrow $1 million for three years at a floating rate, LIBOR + 2%, to be reset annually

■ *Strategy 3*: Borrow $1 million for one year at a fixed rate, then renew the credit annually

EXHIBIT 9.2   U.S. Dollar-Denominated Interest Rates (February 2004)

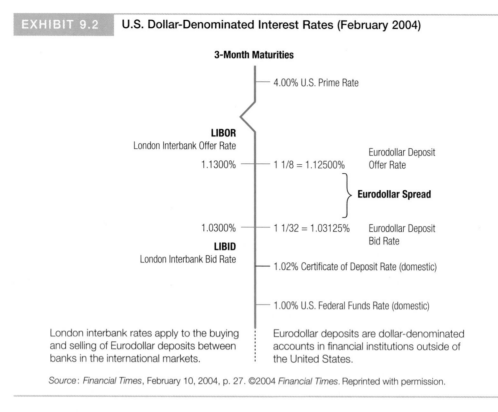

3-Month Maturities

— 4.00% U.S. Prime Rate

LIBOR
London Interbank Offer Rate

1.1300% —— 1 1/8 = 1.12500%   Eurodollar Deposit Offer Rate

} **Eurodollar Spread**

1.0300% —— 1 1/32 = 1.03125%   Eurodollar Deposit Bid Rate

LIBID
London Interbank Bid Rate

— 1.02% Certificate of Deposit Rate (domestic)

— 1.00% U.S. Federal Funds Rate (domestic)

London interbank rates apply to the buying and selling of Eurodollar deposits between banks in the international markets.

Eurodollar deposits are dollar-denominated accounts in financial institutions outside of the United States.

Source: *Financial Times*, February 10, 2004, p. 27. ©2004 *Financial Times*. Reprinted with permission.

Although the lowest cost of funds is always a major selection criterion, it is not the only one. If the firm chooses strategy 1, it assures itself of the funding for the full three years at a known interest rate. It has maximized the predictability of cash flows for the debt obligation. What it has sacrificed, to some degree, is the ability to enjoy a lower interest rate in the event that interest rates fall over the period. Of course, it has also eliminated the risk that interest rates could rise over the period, increasing debt servicing costs.

Strategy 2 offers what strategy 1 did not—flexibility (repricing risk). It too assures the firm of full funding for the three-year period. This eliminates credit risk. Repricing risk is, however, alive and well in strategy 2. If LIBOR changes dramatically by the second or third year, the LIBOR rate change is passed through fully to the borrower. The spread, however, remains fixed (reflecting the credit standing that has been locked in for the full three years). Flexibility comes at a cost in this case, the risk that interest rates could go up as well as down.

Strategy 3 offers more flexibility and more risk. First, the firm is borrowing at the shorter end of the yield curve. If the yield curve is positively sloped, as is commonly the case in major industrial markets, the base interest rate should be lower. But the short end of the yield curve is also the more volatile. It responds to short-term events in a much more pronounced fashion than longer-term rates. The strategy also exposes the firm to the possibility that its credit rating may change dramatically by the time for credit renewal, for better or worse. Noting that credit ratings in general are established on the premise that a firm can meet its debt-service obligations under worsening economic conditions, firms that are highly creditworthy (investment rated grades) may view strategy 3 as a more relevant alternative than do firms of lower quality (speculative grades). This is not a strategy for firms that are financially weak.

Although the previous example gives only a partial picture of the complexity of funding decisions within the firm, it demonstrates the many ways credit risks and repricing risks are inextricably intertwined. The expression *interest rate exposure* is a complex concept, and the proper measurement of the exposure prior to its management is critical. We now proceed to describe the interest rate risk of the most common form of corporate debt, floating rate loans.

Management of Interest Rate Risk

The Management Dilemma

Before they can manage interest rate risk, treasurers and financial managers of all types must resolve a basic management dilemma: the balance between risk and return. Treasury has traditionally been considered a service center (cost center) and is therefore not expected to take positions that incur risk in the expectation of profit. Treasury activities are rarely managed or evaluated as profit centers. Treasury management practices are therefore predominantly conservative, but opportunities to reduce costs or actually earn profits are not to be ignored. History, however, is littered with examples in which financial managers have strayed from their fiduciary responsibilities in the expectation of profit. Unfortunately, much of the time they have realized only loss. Losses on derivatives by specific companies have already been chronicled in Chapter 8. The many derivative disasters, combined with the wider use of financial derivatives, has helped more and more firms realize the value of well-constructed policy statements such as those listed in Exhibit 9.3.

Both foreign exchange and interest rate risk management must focus on managing existing or anticipated cash flow exposures of the firm. As in foreign exchange exposure management, the firm cannot undertake informed management or hedging strategies without forming expectations—a *directional* and/or *volatility view*—of interest rate movements. Fortunately, interest rate movements have historically shown more stability and less volatility than exchange rates. Financial management has frequently found it valuable to err on the conservative side, adding to the predictability of commitments and cash flows. This conservatism in turn improves the strategic decision-making capability of the firm. Finally, similar to exchange rate risks, the question still exists as to whether stockholders want management to hedge interest rate risk or prefer to diversify the risk away through their ownership of other securities.

Once management has formed expectations about future interest rate levels and movements, it must choose the appropriate implementation, a path which includes the selective

---

EXHIBIT 9.3	Treasury Policy Statements

The major derivative disasters of the 1990s highlighted the need for the proper construction and implementation of corporate financial management policy statements. Policy statements are, however, frequently misunderstood by those writing and enforcing them. A few helpful fundamentals may be in order.

- **A policy is a rule, not a goal.** A policy is intended to limit or restrict management actions, not set priorities or goals. For example, "Thou shalt not write uncovered options" is a policy. "Management will pursue the lowest cost of capital at all times" is a goal.

- **A policy is intended to restrict some subjective decision making.** Although at first glance this aspect seems to indicate that management is not to be trusted, it is actually intended to make management's decision-making easier in potentially harmful situations.

- **A policy is intended to establish operating guidelines independently of staff.** Although many policies may appear overly restrictive given the specific talents of financial staff, the fiduciary responsibility of the firm needs to be maintained independently of the specific personnel onboard. Changes in personnel frequently place new managers in uncomfortable and unfamiliar surroundings. Errors in judgment may result. Proper policy construction provides a constructive and protective base for management's learning curve.

use of various techniques and instruments. Fortunately, management of interest rate risk is helped by the availability of several interest rate derivative instruments, such as forward rate agreements, swaps, and options. Their use is illustrated by Trident's floating rate loan as an example. The growth in use of these instruments in general is presented in *Global Finance in Practice 9.1*.

Trident's Floating Rate Loans

Floating rate loans are a widely used source of debt for firms worldwide as illustrated by *Global Finance in Practice 9.2*. They are also the source of the single largest and most frequently observed corporate interest rate exposure.

Exhibit 9.4 shows the costs and cash flows for a three-year floating rate loan taken out by Trident Corporation. The loan of US$10 million will be serviced with annual interest payments and total principal repayment at the end of the three-year period.

- ■ The loan is *priced* at U.S. dollar LIBOR + 1.500% (note that the cost of money, interest, is often referred to as *price*). The LIBOR base will be reset each year on an agreed-upon date (say two days prior to payment). Whereas the LIBOR component is truly floating, the spread of 1.500% is actually a fixed component of the interest payment, which is known with certainty for the life of the loan.

- ■ When the loan is drawn down initially, at year zero, an up-front fee of 1.500% is charged by the lender. This fee results in a reduction in the net proceeds of the loan by US$150,000. Although the loan agreement states the amount as $10,000,000 and Trident is required to repay it in full, the actual net proceeds to the firm are only $9,850,000.

GLOBAL FINANCE IN PRACTICE 9.1

Interest Rate Derivatives—Booming in 2007

As part of the Bank for International Settlement's survey of foreign exchange turnover every three years (the Triennial Survey), the bank also collects data on the use of interest rate derivatives.

As illustrated by the graphic, it is clear that interest rate derivatives—forward rate agreements (FRAs), interest rate options, and interest rate swaps—are showing substantial growth in recent years. The April 2007 survey indicates that more than $1.6 trillion in daily trading occurred in the over-the-counter (OTC) market. The majority of this was in interest rate swaps, $1.2 trillion, which are demonstrating much greater growth than options.

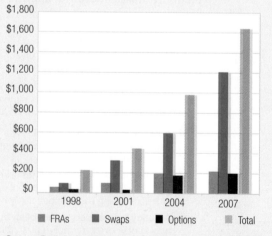

Over-the-Counter (OTC) Interest Rate Derivatives Turnover, 1998–2007 (daily averages in April, billions of U.S. dollars)

Source: Bank for International Settlements, Triennial Central Bank Survey of Foreign Exchange and Derivatives Market Activity in April, 2007: Preliminary Global Results," October 2007, p. 13, www.bis.org.

GLOBAL FINANCE IN PRACTICE 9.2

A Fixed-Rate or Floating-Rate World?

The *BIS Quarterly Review* of March 2009 provides a detailed statistical breakdown of the types of international notes and bonds newly issued and outstanding, by issuer, by type of instrument, and by currency of denomination. The data provides some interesting insights into the international securities market.

■ At of end of year 2008 there were $22.7 trillion outstanding in international notes and bonds issued by all types of institutions.

■ The market continues to be dominated by issuances of financial institutions. The issuers by dollar value were: financial institutions, $17.9 trillion or 79%; governments, $1.8 trillion or 8%; international organizations, $0.6 trillion or 3%; and corporate issuers, $2.4 trillion or 10% of the total outstanding.

■ The instruments are still largely fixed-rate issuances, with 64% of all outstanding issuances being fixed-rate, 34% floating-rate, and roughly 2% equity-related.

■ The euro continues to dominate international note and bond issuances, making up more than 48% of the total. The euro is followed by the dollar, 36%; the pound sterling, 8%; the Japanese yen, 3%; and the Swiss franc, just under 2%.

The data continues to support two long-standing fundamental properties of the international debt markets. First, that the euro's domination reflects the long-term use of the international security markets by the institutions in the countries constituting the euro—Western Europe. Second, that fixed-rate issuances are still the foundation of the market. Although floating-rate issuances did rise marginally in the 2003–2006 period, the international credit crisis of 2007–2008 and the response by central banks to push interest rates downwards created new opportunities for the issuance of longer-term fixed-rate issuances by issuers of all kinds.

Source: Data drawn from Table 13B, *BIS Quarterly Review*, March 2009, p. 91, www.bis.org/statistics/secstats.htm

---

EXHIBIT 9.4   Trident Corporation's Costs and Cash Flows in Servicing a Floating Rate Loan

The expected interest rates and cash flows associated with a three-year $10,000,000 floating rate loan. Trident pays an initiation fee of 1.500% of principal up front (which reduces proceeds).

Loan Interest Rates	Year 0	Year 1	Year 2	Year 3
LIBOR (floating)	5.000%	5.000%	5.000%	5.000%
Spread (fixed)		1.500%	1.500%	1.500%
Total interest payable		6.500%	6.500%	6.500%
Interest cash flows on loan				
LIBOR (floating)		($500,000)	($500,000)	($500,000)
Spread (fixed)		(150,000)	(150,000)	(150,000)
Total interest		($650,000)	($650,000)	($650,000)
Loan proceeds (repayment)	$9,850,000			($10,000,000)
Total loan cash flows	$9,850,000	($650,000)	($650,000)	($10,650,000)
IRR of total cash flows	7.072%		All-in-cost (AIC)	

Sensitivities to LIBOR	LIBOR (yr 0)	LIBOR (yr 1)	LIBOR (yr 2)	LIBOR (yr 3)	AIC
Baseline case above	5.000%	5.000%	5.000%	5.000%	7.072%
LIBOR rises 25 basis points/yr		5.250%	5.500%	5.750%	7.565%
LIBOR falls 25 basis points/yr		4.750%	4.500%	4.250%	6.578%

Note: The effective cost of funds (before-tax) for Trident, all-in-cost (AIC), is found by determining the internal rate of return (IRR) of the total cash flows associated with the loan. The AIC of the original loan agreement, without fees, is 6.500%.

■ Trident will not know the actual interest cost of the loan until the loan has been completely repaid. Maria Gonzalez, the CFO of Trident, may forecast what LIBOR will be for the life of the loan, but she will not know with certainty until all payments have been completed. This uncertainty is not only an interest rate risk, but it is also an actual cash flow risk associated with the interest payment. (A fixed interest rate loan has *interest rate risk*, in this case opportunity cost, which does not put actual cash flows at risk.)

Exhibit 9.4 illustrates the *all-in-costs* (AIC) of the loan under a number of different sensitivities. The AIC is found by calculating the internal rate of return (IRR) of the total cash flows for repayment. The baseline analysis assumes that LIBOR remains at 5.000% for the life of the loan. Including the up-front fees, the AIC to Trident is 7.072% (or 6.500% flat without fees). If, however, LIBOR were to rise steadily over the three-year period by 25 basis points (0.25%) per year, the AIC of the loan would rise to 7.565%. If LIBOR were to fall by the same 25 basis points per year, the AIC would fall to 6.578%. We must remember, however, that only the LIBOR component of the loan price creates cash flow risk.

If Trident Corporation decided, after it had taken out the loan, that it wished to manage the interest rate risk associated with the loan agreement, it would have a number of management alternatives:

■ **Refinancing.** Trident could go back to its lender and restructure and refinance the entire agreement. This is not always possible and it is often expensive.

■ **Forward Rate Agreements (Fras).** Trident could lock in the future interest rate payments with FRAs, much the same way that exchange rates are locked in with forward contracts.

■ **Interest Rate Futures.** Although companies rarely use foreign currency futures for foreign exchange risk management, interest rate futures have gained substantially more acceptance. Trident could lock in the future interest rate payments by taking an interest rate futures position.

■ **Interest Rate Swaps.** Trident could enter into an additional agreement with a bank or swap dealer in which it exchanged cash flows in such a way that the interest rate payments on the floating rate loan would become fixed.

Forward Rate Agreements

A *forward rate agreement* (FRA) is an interbank-traded contract to buy or sell interest rate payments on a notional principal. These contracts are settled in cash. The buyer of an FRA obtains the right to lock in an interest rate for a desired term that begins at a future date. The contract specifies that the seller of the FRA will pay the buyer the increased interest expense on a nominal sum (the notional principal) of money if interest rates rise above the agreed rate, but the buyer will pay the seller the differential interest expense if interest rates fall below the agreed rate. Maturities available are typically 1, 3, 6, 9, and 12 months, much like traditional forward contracts for currencies.

For example, Trident may decide that it wishes to lock in the first interest payment (due at the end of year 1), so it buys an FRA that locks in a total interest payment of 6.500%. If LIBOR rises above 5.000% by the end of year 1, Trident would receive a cash payment from the FRA seller that would reduce the interest rate to 5.000%. Similarly, if LIBOR were to fall during year 1 to below 5.000% (not what Maria Gonzalez expects to happen), Trident would make a cash payment to the seller of the FRA, effectively raising its LIBOR payment to 5.000% and the total loan interest to 6.500%.

Like foreign currency forward contracts, FRAs are useful on individual exposures. They are contractual commitments of the firm that allow little flexibility to enjoy favorable movements, such as when LIBOR is falling as was just described. Firms also use FRAs if they plan to invest in securities at future dates but fear that interest rates might fall prior to the investment date. Because of the limited maturities and currencies available, however, FRAs are not widely used outside the largest industrial economies and currencies.

Interest Rate Futures

Unlike foreign currency futures, *interest rate futures* are relatively widely used by financial managers and treasurers of nonfinancial companies. Their popularity stems from the relatively high liquidity of the interest rate futures markets, their simplicity of use, and the rather standardized interest rate exposures most firms possess. The two most widely used futures contracts are the Eurodollar futures traded on the Chicago Mercantile Exchange (CME) and the U.S. Treasury Bond Futures of the Chicago Board of Trade (CBOT). Interestingly, the third-largest volume of a traded futures contract in the latter 1990s was the U.S. dollar/Brazilian reais currency futures contract traded on the Bolsa de Mercadorias y Futuros in Brazil.

To illustrate the use of futures for managing interest rate risks we will focus on the three-month Eurodollar futures contracts. Exhibit 9.5 presents Eurodollar futures for two years (they actually trade 10 years into the future).

The yield of a futures contract is calculated from the *settlement price*, which is the closing price for that trading day. For example, a financial manager examining the Eurodollar quotes in Exhibit 9.5 for a March 2003 contract would see that the *settlement price* on the previous day was 94.76, an annual yield of 5.24%:

$$Yield = (100.00 - 94.76) = 5.24\%$$

Since each contract is for a three-month period (quarter) and a notional principal of $1 million, each basis point is actually worth $2,500 (.01 × $1,000,000 × 90/360).

If Maria Gonzalez were interested in hedging a floating rate interest payment due in March 2003, she would need to *sell a future,* to take a *short position.* This strategy is referred to as a short position because Maria is selling something she does not own (as in shorting common stock). If interest rates rise by March—as Maria fears—the futures price will fall and she will be able to close the position at a profit. This profit will roughly offset the losses associated with rising interest payments on her debt. If she is wrong, however, and interest

EXHIBIT 9.5	Eurodollar Futures Prices					
Maturity	**Open**	**High**	**Low**	**Settle**	**Yield**	**Open Interest**
June 02	94.99	95.01	94.98	95.01	4.99	455,763
Sept	94.87	94.97	94.87	94.96	5.04	535,932
Dec	94.60	94.70	94.60	94.68	5.32	367,036
Mar 03	94.67	94.77	94.66	94.76	5.24	299,993
June	94.55	94.68	94.54	94.63	5.37	208,949
Sept	94.43	94.54	94.43	94.53	5.47	168,961
Dec	94.27	94.38	94.27	94.36	5.64	130,824

Note: Typical presentation by *The Wall Street Journal*. Only regular quarterly maturities shown. All contracts are for $1 million; points of 100%. Open interest is number of contracts outstanding.

rates actually fall by the maturity date, causing the futures price to rise, Maria will suffer a loss that will wipe out the "savings" derived by making a lower floating rate interest payment than she expected. So by selling the March 2003 futures contract, she will be locking in an interest rate of 5.24%.

Obviously, interest rate futures positions could be—and are regularly—purchased purely for speculative purposes. Although that is not the focus of the managerial context here, the example shows how any speculator with a directional view on interest rates could take positions in expectations of profit.

As mentioned previously, the most common interest rate exposure of the nonfinancial firm is interest payable on debt. Such exposure is not, however, the only interest rate risk. As more and more firms aggressively manage their entire balance sheet, the interest earnings from the left-hand side are under increasing scrutiny. If financial managers are expected to earn higher interest on interest-bearing securities, they may well find a second use of the interest rate futures market: to lock in future interest earnings. Exhibit 9.6 provides an overview of these two basic interest rate exposures and the strategies needed to manage interest rate futures.

Interest Rate Swaps

Swaps are contractual agreements to exchange or *swap* a series of cash flows. These cash flows are most commonly the interest payments associated with debt service, such as the floating rate loan previously described.

- If the agreement is for one party to swap its fixed interest rate payment for the floating interest rate payments of another, it is termed an *interest rate swap*.

- If the agreement is to swap currencies of debt service obligation—for example, Swiss franc interest payments in exchange for U.S. dollar interest payments—it is termed a *currency swap*.

- A single swap may combine elements of both interest rate and currency swaps.

In any case, however, the swap serves to alter the firm's cash flow obligations, as in changing floating rate payments into fixed rate payments associated with an existing debt obligation. The swap itself is not a source of capital, but rather an alteration of the cash flows associated with payment. What is often termed the *plain vanilla swap* is an agreement between two parties to exchange fixed rate for floating rate financial obligations. This type of swap forms the largest single financial derivative market in the world.

EXHIBIT 9.6	Interest Rate Futures Strategies for Common Exposures		
Exposure	**Futures Action**	**Interest Rates**	**Position Outcome**
Paying interest on future date	Sell a future (short position)	If rates go up	Futures price falls; short earns a profit
		If rates go down	Futures price rises; short earns a loss
Earning interest on future date	Buy a future (long position)	If rates go up	Futures price falls; long earns a loss
		If rates go down	Futures price rises; long earns a profit

The two parties may have various motivations for entering into the agreement. For example, a very common position is as follows. A corporate borrower of good credit standing has existing floating rate debt service payments. The borrower, after reviewing current market conditions and forming expectations about the future, may conclude that interest rates are about to rise. In order to protect the firm against rising debt-service payments, the company's treasury may enter into a swap agreement to *pay fixed/receive floating*. This means the firm will now make fixed rate interest payments and receive from the swap counterparty floating rate interest payments. The floating rate payments that the firm receives are used to service the debt obligation of the firm, so the firm, on a net basis, is now making fixed rate interest payments. Using derivatives it has synthetically changed floating rate debt into fixed rate debt. It has done so without going through the costs and intricacies of refinancing existing debt obligations.

Similarly, a firm with fixed rate debt that expects interest rates to fall can change fixed rate debt to floating rate debt. In this case, the firm would enter into a *pay floating/receive fixed* interest rate swap. Exhibit 9.7 presents a summary table of the recommended interest rate swap strategies for firms holding either fixed rate debt or floating rate debt.

The cash flows of an interest rate swap are interest rates applied to a set amount of capital (*notional principal*). For this reason they are also referred to as *coupon swaps*. Firms entering into interest rate swaps set the notional principal so that the cash flows resulting from the interest rate swap cover their interest rate management needs.

Interest rate swaps are contractual commitments between a firm and a swap dealer and are completely independent of the interest rate exposure of the firm. That is, the firm may enter into a swap for any reason it sees fit and then swap a notional principal that is less than, equal to, or even greater than the total position being managed. For example, a firm with a variety of floating rate loans on its books may enter into interest rate swaps for only 70% of the existing principal, if it wishes.

The reason for entering into a swap, and the swap position the firm enters into, is purely at management's discretion. It should also be noted that the interest rate swap market is filling a gap in market efficiency. If all firms had free and equal access to capital markets, regardless of interest rate structure or currency of denomination, the swap market would most likely not exist. The fact that the swap market not only exists but also flourishes and provides benefits to all parties is in some ways the proverbial "free lunch," due to comparative advantage.

Comparative Advantage

Companies of different credit quality are treated differently by the capital markets. For example, Unilever (U.K.) and Xerox (U.S.) are both in the market for $30 million of debt for a five-year period. Unilever has an AAA credit rating (the highest) and therefore has access to both fixed and floating rate interest debt at attractive rates. Unilever would prefer to borrow at floating rates, since it already has fixed rate funds and wishes to increase the

EXHIBIT 9.7	Interest Rate Swap Strategies	
Position	**Expectation**	**Interest Rate Swap Strategy**
Fixed rate debt	Rates to go up	Do nothing
	Rates to go down	Pay floating/Receive fixed
Floating rate debt	Rates to go up	Pay fixed/Receive floating
	Rates to go down	Do nothing

proportion of its debt portfolio which is floating. Xerox has a BBB credit rating (the lowest major category of investment-grade debt ratings) and would prefer to raise the debt at fixed rates of interest. Although Xerox has access to both fixed rate and floating rate funds, the fixed rate debt is considered expensive. The firms, through Citibank, could actually borrow in their relatively advantaged markets and then swap their debt service payments. This is illustrated in Exhibit 9.8.

Implementation of the Interest Rate Swap

Each company first borrows in the market in which it has relative comparative advantage. As illustrated in Exhibit 9.8, Unilever can borrow fixed rate funds 1.000% cheaper than Xerox (7.000% as opposed to 8.000%), and can borrow floating rate funds 0.5% cheaper (0.25% relative to Xerox's 0.75%). This means that Unilever's *relative comparative advantage* is to borrow fixed rate funds, and therefore Xerox should borrow floating rate funds.

1. Unilever borrows at the fixed rate of 7.000% per annum, and then enters into a *receive fixed pay floating* interest rate swap with Citibank. The bank then agrees to make the debt service payments of 7.000% on behalf of Unilever for the life of the swap agreement (five years).

2. Unilever agrees in turn to pay Citibank a floating rate of interest, one-year LIBOR, enabling it to make debt service payments on a floating rate basis, which it prefers. The interest rate it negotiates with Citibank is lower than the rate it could have acquired on its own.

3. Xerox borrows at the floating rate of LIBOR + 0.75%, and then swaps the payments with Citibank. Citibank agrees to service the floating rate debt payments on behalf of Xerox.

4. Xerox agrees in turn to pay Citibank a fixed rate of interest, 7.875%, enabling Xerox to make fixed rate debt service payments—which it prefers—but at a lower cost of funds than it could have acquired on its own.

EXHIBIT 9.8   Comparative Advantage and Structuring a Swap Agreement

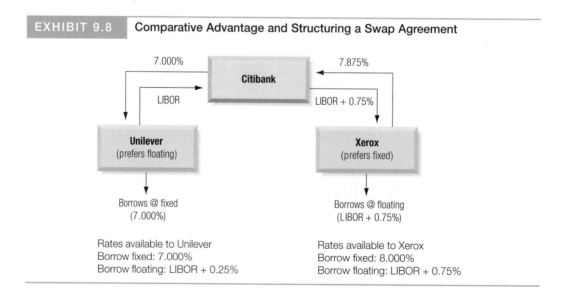

Benefits of the Interest Rate Swap

Unilever borrowed funds at 7.000% fixed rate. It has now entered into a swap agreement in which it will pay floating, LIBOR + 0%, in return for Citibank making its 7.000% interest payments on its debt. Unilever then has the following combined interest payments:

Unilever borrows at fixed rates:	(7.000%)
Swaps *fixed for floating* rates:	+ 7.000% Receives fixed
	(LIBOR) Pays floating
Net interest (debt + swap)	(LIBOR)

Xerox borrowed funds at LIBOR + 0.75%, a floating rate of interest. It has now entered into a swap agreement to swap *floating for fixed*, meaning that it will receive a floating rate of LIBOR + 0.25% and pay a fixed rate of interest, 7.875%.

Xerox borrows at floating rates:	(LIBOR + 0.75%)	
Swaps *floating for fixed* rates:	+ LIBOR + 0.75%	Receives floating
	(7.875%)	Pays fixed
Net interest (debt + swap)	(7.875%)	

Each of the borrowers benefits from the interest rate swap by being able to borrow capital in the preferred interest rate structure and at a lower rate than obtainable on their own.

	Unilever (U.K.)	Xerox (U.S.)
If borrowing directly	LIBOR + 0.25%	8.000%
If borrowing through swap	LIBOR + 0%	7.875%
Savings	+ 0.25%	+ 0.125%

How is this possible? Each benefits as a result of the specialization of each borrower acquiring funds in their market of preferred access, and then exchanging interest payment streams, redistributing the benefits of specialization.

Trident Corporation: Swapping to Fixed Rates

Trident Corporation's existing floating rate loan is now the source of some concern to Maria Gonzalez. Recent events have led her to believe that interest rates, specifically LIBOR, may be rising in the three years ahead. Because the loan agreement is relatively new (Trident is still in the first year of the loan and has yet to make an interest payment), refinancing is considered too expensive at this point. Maria believes that a *pay fixed/receive floating* interest rate swap may be the better alternative for fixing future interest rates now. Upon contacting several of its primary banks, Trident is quoted a fixed rate of 5.750% against LIBOR. If Trident enters into the swap agreement, for the next three years it will receive LIBOR and pay out 5.750% on a notional principal of $10 million. A quick analysis of the combined existing loan and pay fixed/receive floating swap undertaken by Trident's treasury group is presented in Exhibit 9.9.

The swap agreement does not replace the existing loan agreement; it supplements it. Trident is still responsible for making all payments on the floating rate loan. Note that the swap agreement applies only to the interest payments on the loan and does not include the

EXHIBIT 9.9	Trident Corporation's Interest Rate Swap to Pay Fixed/Receive Floating				
Loan Interest Rates	**Variability**		**Year 1**	**Year 2**	**Year 3**
LIBOR (floating)	Could go up or down		− 5.000%	− 5.000%	− 5.000%
Spread (fixed)	Fixed		− 1.500%	− 1.500%	− 1.500%
Total interest payable			− 6.500%	− 6.500%	− 6.500%
Swap Interest Rates					
Pay fixed	Fixed		− 5.750%	− 5.750%	− 5.750%
Receive floating LIBOR	Could go up or down		+ 5.000%	+ 5.000%	+ 5.000%
Combined Loan and Swap Position					
LIBOR on loan	Paying		− 5.000%	− 5.000%	− 5.000%
Spread (fixed)	Paying		− 1.500%	− 1.500%	− 1.500%
Pay fixed on swap	Paying		− 5.750%	− 5.750%	− 5.750%
Receive floating LIBOR on swap	Receiving		+ 5.000%	+ 5.000%	+ 5.000%
Net interest due after swap	Net payment		− 7.250%	− 7.250%	− 7.250%

Note: On the date the interest rate swap agreement is made, the actual LIBOR rates for all years (1, 2, and 3) are unknown. However, on the basis of the expectations of swap traders, the present value of the floating rate cash flow streams and fixed rate cash flow streams are equal on the agreement date.

principal repayment. The portion of the debt service payment that Trident is concerned about—the LIBOR base rate—now would be offset by the receipt of a cash flow of LIBOR from the swap bank. This arrangement leaves Trident responsible for payment of the 1.500% fixed spread on the loan plus the fixed payment to the swap bank of 5.750%. These payments combine to create a total fixed interest rate payment of 7.250% on the $10 million debt, as illustrated in Exhibit 9.9.

The question that remains for Maria Gonzalez is whether this is a good deal. Trident now has a fixed rate debt of $10 million for three years. If current market rates quoted to Trident by its lenders are at fixed rates above 7.250%, the answer is *yes*. Trident would be well advised to secure the swap agreement now, assuming its goal is to lock in fixed rates of interest for the coming three years.

Currency Swaps

Since all swap rates are derived from the yield curve in each major currency, the fixed to floating rate interest rate swap existing in each currency allows firms to swap across currencies. Exhibit 9.10 lists typical swap rates for the euro, the U.S. dollar, the Japanese yen, and the Swiss franc. These swap rates are based on the government security yields in each of the individual currency markets, plus a credit spread applicable to investment grade borrowers in the respective markets.

Note that the swap rates in Exhibit 9.10 are not rated or categorized by credit ratings. This is because the swap market itself does not carry the credit risk associated with individual borrowers. We saw that in the previous interest rate swap example when Trident, which borrowed on its own at LIBOR plus a spread of 1.500% (the spread representing the credit spread specific to the borrower), swapped out of the LIBOR component only. The fixed spread, a credit risk premium, was still borne by the firm itself. For example, lower-rated firms

EXHIBIT 9.10 Interest Rate and Currency Swap Quotes

Years	Euro-€ Bid	Ask	Swiss franc Bid	Ask	U.S. dollar Bid	Ask	Japanese yen Bid	Ask
1	2.99	3.02	1.43	1.47	5.24	5.26	0.23	0.26
2	3.08	3.12	1.68	1.76	5.43	5.46	0.36	0.39
3	3.24	3.28	1.93	2.01	5.56	5.59	0.56	0.59
4	3.44	3.48	2.15	2.23	5.65	5.68	0.82	0.85
5	3.63	3.67	2.35	2.43	5.73	5.76	1.09	1.12
6	3.83	3.87	2.54	2.62	5.80	5.83	1.33	1.36
7	4.01	4.05	2.73	2.81	5.86	5.89	1.55	1.58
8	4.18	4.22	2.91	2.99	5.92	5.95	1.75	1.78
9	4.32	4.36	3.08	3.16	5.96	5.99	1.90	1.93
10	**4.42**	**4.46**	**3.22**	**3.30**	**6.01**	**6.04**	**2.04**	**2.07**
12	4.58	4.62	3.45	3.55	6.10	6.13	2.28	2.32
15	4.78	4.82	3.71	3.81	6.20	6.23	2.51	2.56
20	5.00	5.04	3.96	4.06	6.29	6.32	2.71	2.76
25	5.13	5.17	4.07	4.17	6.29	6.32	2.77	2.82
30	5.19	5.23	4.16	4.26	6.28	6.31	2.82	2.88
LIBOR	3.0313	3.0938	1.3125	1.4375	4.9375	5.0625	0.1250	0.2188

Note: Typical presentation by the *Financial Times*. Bid and ask spreads as of close of London business. US$ is quoted against three-month LIBOR; Japanese yen against six-month LIBOR; euro and Swiss franc against six-month LIBOR.

may pay spreads of 3% or 4% over LIBOR, while some of the world's largest and most financially sound MNEs may actually raise capital at rates of LIBOR−0.40%. The swap market does not differentiate the rate by the participant; all swap at fixed rates versus LIBOR in the respective currency.

The usual motivation for a currency swap is to replace cash flows scheduled in an undesired currency with flows in a desired currency. The desired currency is probably the currency in which the firm's future operating revenues (inflows) will be generated. Firms often raise capital in currencies in which they do not possess significant revenues or other natural cash flows. The reason they do so is cost; specific firms may find capital costs in specific currencies attractively priced to them under special conditions. Having raised the capital, however, the firm may wish to swap its repayment into a currency in which it has future operating revenues.

The utility of the currency swap market to an MNE and government institutions is significant. An MNE wishing to swap a 10-year fixed 6.04% U.S. dollar cash flow stream could swap to 4.46% fixed in euros, 3.30% fixed in Swiss francs, or 2.07% fixed in Japanese yen. It could swap from fixed dollars not only to fixed rates, but also to floating LIBOR rates in the various currencies as well. All are possible at the rates quoted in Exhibit 9.10.

Trident Corporation: Swapping Floating Dollars into Fixed Rate Swiss Francs

We return to Trident Corporation to demonstrate how to use a currency swap. After raising $10 million in floating rate financing, and subsequently swapping into fixed rate payments,

Trident decides that it would prefer to make its debt service payments in Swiss francs. Trident had recently signed a sales contract with a Swiss buyer that will be paying francs to Trident over the next three-year period. This would be a natural inflow of Swiss francs for the coming three years, and Trident may decide it wishes to match the currency of denomination of the cash flows through a currency swap.

Trident Corporation now enters into a three-year *pay Swiss francs and receive U.S. dollars* currency swap. Both interest rates are fixed. Trident will pay 2.01% (ask rate) fixed Swiss franc interest, and receive 5.56% (bid rate) fixed U.S. dollars.

As illustrated in Exhibit 9.11, the three-year currency swap entered into by Trident is different from the plain vanilla interest rate swap described above in two important ways:

1. The spot exchange rate in effect on the date of the agreement establishes what the notional principal is in the target currency. The target currency is the currency Trident is swapping into, in this case the Swiss franc. The $10,000,000 notional principal converts to a Sfr15,000,000 notional principal. This is the principal used to establish the actual cash flows Trident is committing to making (2.01% × Sfr15,000,000 = Sfr301,500).

2. The notional principal itself is part of the swap agreement. In the interest rate swaps described previously, both interest payment cash flows were based on the same U.S. dollar notional principal. Hence, there was no need to include the principal in the agreement. In a currency swap, however, because the notional principals are denominated in two different currencies, and the exchange rate between those two currencies may change over the life of the swap, the notional principals are actually part of the swap agreement.

At the time of the swap's inception, both positions have the same net present value. Trident's swap commits it to three future cash payments in Swiss francs. In turn, it will receive three payments in U.S. dollars. The payments are set. Financial accounting practices will require Trident to track and value its position regularly, *mark-to-market* the swap, on the basis of current exchange rates and interest rates. If after the swap is initiated the Swiss franc appreciates versus the dollar, and Trident is paying francs, Trident will record a loss on the swap for accounting purposes. (Similarly, the swap dealer's side of the transaction will record a gain.) At the same time, if interest rates in Swiss franc markets rise, and Trident's swap

---

EXHIBIT 9.11   Trident Corporation's Currency Swap: Pay Swiss Francs and Receive U.S. Dollars

Swap Component	Year 0	Year 1	Year 2	Year 3
Trident will receive fixed US$ at this rate		5.56%	5.56%	5.56%
On a notional principal of	$10,000,000			
Cash flows Trident will receive		$556,000	$556,000	$10,556,000
Exchange rate	Sfr.1.5000/$			
Trident will pay fixed Sfr at rate		2.01%	2.01%	2.01%
On a notional principal of	Sfr15,000,000			
Cash flows Trident will pay		Sfr301,500	Sfr301,500	Sfr15,301,500

The pay fixed US$ rate of 5.56% is the three-year bid rate in Exhibit 9.10. The receive fixed Swiss franc rate of 2.01% is the three-year ask rate from Exhibit 9.10. Once Trident Corporation determines the notional principal of $10,000,000, the current spot rate is used to determine the notional principal for the Swiss franc side of the swap (or vice versa depending on Trident's goals). The present value of each side of the swap at inception is $10,000,000 (Sfr15,000,000).

commits it to a fixed rate of 2.01%, then a gain will result from the interest component of the swap's value. In short, gains and losses on the swap, at least for accounting purposes, will persist throughout the swap's life.

The currency swaps described here are nonamortizing swaps. A *nonamortizing swap* repays the entire principal at maturity, rather than over the life of the swap agreement. Swap dealers will of course be more than happy to provide the firm with the form of its choice. We use nonamortizing swap examples throughout this chapter for simplicity of presentation.

Trident Corporation: Unwinding Swaps

As with all original loan agreements, it may happen that at some future date the partners to a swap may wish to terminate the agreement before it matures. If, for example, after one year Trident Corporation's Swiss sales contract is terminated, Trident will no longer need the swap as part of its hedging program. Trident could terminate or *unwind* the swap with the swap dealer.

Unwinding a currency swap requires the discounting of the remaining cash flows under the swap agreement at current interest rates, then converting the target currency (Swiss francs here) back to the home currency of the firm (U.S. dollars for Trident). If Trident has two payments remaining on the swap agreement of Sfr301,500 and Sfr15,301,500 (an interest-only payment, and a principal and interest payment), and the two-year fixed rate of interest for francs is now 2.000%, the present value of Trident's commitment in Swiss francs is as follows:

$$PV(Sfr) = \frac{Sfr301,500}{(1.020)^1} + \frac{Sfr15,301,500}{(1.020)^2} = Sfr15,002,912$$

At the same time, the present value of the remaining cash flows on the dollar side of the swap is determined using the current two-year fixed dollar interest rate, which is now 5.500%:

$$PV(\$) = \frac{\$556,000}{(1.055)^1} + \frac{\$10,556,000}{(1.055)^2} = \$10,011,078$$

Trident's currency swap, if unwound at this time, would yield a present value of net inflows (what it receives under the swap) of $10,011,078 and a present value of outflows (what it pays under the swap) of Sfr15,002,912. If the spot exchange rate is now Sfr1.4650/$, the net settlement of this currency swap will be as follows:

$$\text{Settlement} = \$10,011,078 - \frac{Sfr15,002,912}{Sfr1.4650/\$} = (\$229,818)$$

Trident makes a cash payment to the swap dealer of $229,818 to terminate the swap. Trident lost on the swap, largely as a result of the appreciation of the Swiss franc (the interest rates barely changed). Since Trident had promised to pay in the currency which is now stronger in value—the franc—unwinding the swap is costly. The swap, however, was entered into as a hedge rather than as a financial investment.

Counterparty Risk

Counterparty risk is the potential exposure any individual firm bears that the second party to any financial contract will be unable to fulfill its obligations under the contract's specifications. Concern over counterparty risk has risen in the interest rate and currency swap markets as a result of a few large and well publicized swap defaults. The rapid growth in the currency and interest rate financial derivatives markets has actually been accompanied by a surprisingly low default rate to date, particularly in a global market that is, in principle, unregulated.

Counterparty risk has long been one of the major factors that favor the use of exchange-traded derivatives rather than over-the-counter derivatives. Most exchanges, like the Philadelphia Stock Exchange for currency options or the Chicago Mercantile Exchange for Eurodollar futures, are themselves the counterparty to all transactions. This allows all firms a high degree of confidence that they can buy or sell exchange-traded products quickly and with little concern over the credit quality of the exchange itself. Financial exchanges typically require a small fee of all traders on the exchanges, to fund insurance funds created expressly for the purpose of protecting all parties. Over-the-counter products, however, are direct credit exposures to the firm because the contract is generally between the buying firm and the selling financial institution. Most financial derivatives in today's world financial centers are sold or brokered only by the largest and soundest financial institutions. This structure does not mean, however, that firms can enter continuing agreements with these institutions without some degree of real financial risk and concern.

A firm entering into a currency or interest rate swap agreement retains ultimate responsibility for the timely servicing of its own debt obligations. Although a swap agreement may constitute a contract to exchange U.S. dollar payments for euro payments, the firm that actually holds the dollar debt is still legally responsible for payment. The original debt remains on the borrower's books. In the event a swap counterparty does not make the payment as agreed, the firm legally holding the debt is still responsible for debt service. In the event of such a failure, the euro payments would be stopped, by the right of *offset*, and the losses associated with the failed swap would be mitigated.

The real exposure of an interest or currency swap is not the total notional principal, but the mark-to-market values of differentials in interest or currency interest payments (replacement cost) since the inception of the swap agreement. This differential is similar to the change in swap value discovered by unwinding a swap. This amount is typically only 2% to 3% of the notional principal.

SUMMARY POINTS

- The single largest interest rate risk of the nonfinancial firm is debt service. The debt structure of the MNE will possess different maturities of debt, different interest rate structures (such as fixed versus floating rate), and different currencies of denomination.

- The increasing volatility of world interest rates, combined with the increasing use of short-term and variable-rate debt by firms worldwide, has led many firms to actively manage their *interest rate risks*.

- The primary sources of interest rate risk to a multinational nonfinancial firm are short-term borrowing and investing, as well as long-term sources of debt.

- The techniques and instruments used in interest rate risk management in many ways resemble those used in currency risk management: the tried and true methods of lending and borrowing.

- The primary instruments and techniques used for interest rate risk management include forward rate agreements (FRAs), interest rate futures, and interest rate swaps.

- The interest rate and currency swap markets allow firms that have limited access to specific currencies and interest rate structures to gain access at relatively low costs. This in turn allows these firms to manage their currency and interest rate risks more effectively.

- A cross-currency interest rate swap allows a firm to alter both the currency of denomination of cash flows in debt service and the fixed-to-floating or floating-to-fixed interest rate structure.

MINI-CASE   McDonald's Corporation's British Pound Exposure

McDonald's Corporation has investments in over 100 countries. It considers its equity investment in foreign subsidiaries to be at risk, subject to hedging depending on the individual country, currency, and market.

British Subsidiary as an Exposure

McDonald's parent company has three different pound-denominated exposures arising from ownership and operation of its British subsidiary.

- First, the British subsidiary has equity capital, which is a pound-denominated asset of the parent company.

- Second, in addition to the equity capital invested in the British subsidiary, the parent company provides intra-company debt in the form of a four-year £125 million loan. The loan is denominated in British pounds and carries a fixed 5.30% per annum interest payment.

- Third, the British subsidiary pays a fixed percentage of gross sales in royalties to the parent company. This too is pound-denominated. The three different exposures sum to a significant exposure problem for McDonald's.

- An additional technical detail further complicates the situation. When the parent company makes an intracompany loan to the British subsidiary, it must designate—according to U.S. accounting and tax law practices—whether the loan is considered to be *permanently invested* in that country. (Although on the surface it seems illogical to consider four years "permanent," the parent company could continually roll the loan over and never actually repay it.) If it is not considered permanent, the foreign exchange gains and losses related to the loan flow directly to the parent company's profit and loss statement, according to FAS#52.[1] If, however, the loan is designated as permanent, the foreign exchange gains and losses related to the intracompany loan flow only to the cumulative translation adjustment (CTA) on the consolidated balance sheet. To date, McDonald's has chosen to designate the loan as *permanent*. The functional currency of the British

subsidiary for consolidation purposes is the local currency, the British pound.

Anka Gopi is Manager for Financial Markets/Treasury and a McDonald's shareholder. She is currently reviewing the existing hedging strategy employed by McDonald's against the pound exposure. The company has been hedging the pound exposure by entering into a cross-currency U.S. dollar/British pound sterling swap. The current swap is a seven-year swap to receive dollars and pay pounds. Like all cross-currency swaps, the agreement requires McDonald's-U.S. to make regular pound-denominated interest payments and a bullet principal repayment (notional principal) at the end of the swap agreement. McDonald's considers the large notional principal payment a hedge against the equity investment in its British subsidiary.

According to FAS#52, a company may elect to take the interest associated with a foreign currency denominated loan and carry that directly to the parent company's P&L. This has been done in the past, and McDonald's has benefited from the inclusion of this interest payment.

FAS#133, *Accounting for Derivative Instruments and Hedging Activities*, issued in June 1998, was originally intended to be effective for all fiscal quarters within fiscal years beginning after June 15, 1999 (for most firms this meant January 1, 2000). The new standard, however, was so complex and potentially of such material influence to U.S.-based MNEs that the Financial Accounting Standards Board has been approached by dozens of major firms and asked to postpone mandatory implementation. The standard's complexity, combined with the workloads associated with Y2K (year 2000) risk controls, persuaded the Financial Accounting Standards Board to delay FAS#133's mandatory implementation date indefinitely.

Anka Gopi wishes to consider the potential impact of FAS#133 on the hedging strategy currently employed. Under FAS#133, the firm will have to mark-to-market the entire cross-currency swap position, including principal, and carry this to *other comprehensive income* (OCI). OCI, however, is actually a form of income required under U.S. GAAP and reported in the footnotes to the financial statements, but not the income measure used in reported

---

[1]FAS#52 is the accounting standard that sets most of the financial reporting practices by firms related to foreign exchange rates and exchange rate changes.

earnings per share. Although McDonald's has been carrying the interest payments on the swap to income, it has not previously had to carry the present value of the swap principal to OCI. In Anka's eyes, this poses a substantial material risk to OCI.

Anka Gopi also wishes to reconsider the current strategy. She begins by listing the pros and cons of the current strategy, comparing these to alternative strategies, and then deciding what if anything should be done about it at this time.

Case Questions

1. How does the cross-currency swap effectively hedge the three primary exposures McDonald's has relative to its British subsidiary?

2. How does the cross-currency swap hedge the long-term equity exposure in the foreign subsidiary?

3. Should Anka—and McDonald's—worry about OCI?

QUESTIONS

1. **Triumvirate of Risks.** Define and explain the three main financial risks facing a multinational enterprise.

2. **Reference Rates.** What is an interest "reference rate" and how is it used to set rates for individual borrowers?

3. **Risk and Return.** Some corporate treasury departments are organized as service centers (cost centers), while others are set up as profit centers. What is the difference and what are the implications for the firm?

4. **Forecast Types.** What is the difference between a specific forecast and a directional forecast?

5. **Policy Statements.** Explain the difference between a goal statement and a policy statement.

6. **Credit and Repricing Risk.** From the point of view of a borrowing corporation, what are credit and repricing risks? Explain steps a company might take to minimize both.

7. **Forward Rate Agreement.** How can a business firm that has borrowed on a floating-rate basis use a forward rate agreement to reduce interest rate risk?

8. **Eurodollar Futures.** The newspaper reports that a given June Eurodollar future settled at 93.55. What was the annual yield?

9. **Defaulting on an Interest Rate Swap.** Smith Company and Jones Company enter into an interest rate swap, with Smith paying fixed interest to Jones, and Jones paying floating interest to Smith. Smith now goes bankrupt and so defaults on its remaining interest payments. What is the financial damage to Jones Company?

10. **Currency Swaps.** Why would one company with interest payments due in pounds sterling want to swap those payments for interest payments due in U.S. dollars?

11. **Counterparty Risk.** How does organized exchange trading in swaps remove any risk that the counterparty in a swap agreement will not complete the agreement?

PROBLEMS

*1. **Chavez S.A.** Chavez S.A., a Venezuelan company, wishes to borrow $8,000,000 for eight weeks. A rate of 6.250% per annum is quoted by potential lenders in New York, Great Britain, and Switzerland using, respectively, international, British, and the Swiss-Eurobond definitions of interest (day count conventions). From which source should Chavez borrow?

2. **Botany Bay Corporation.** Botany Bay Corporation of Australia seeks to borrow US$14,000,000 in the Eurodollar market. Funding is needed for two years. Investigation leads to three possibilities:
   Option 1: Borrow the US$14,000,000 for two years at a fixed 5.375% rate of interest
   Option 2: Borrow the US$14,000,000 at LIBOR + 1.5%. LIBOR is currently 3.885%, and the rate would be reset every six months
   Option 3: Borrow the US$14,000,000 for one year only at 4.625%; at the end of the first year the company would have to negotiate for a new one-year loan

   Compare the alternatives and make a recommendation.

3. **Raid Gauloises.** Raid Gauloises is a rapidly growing French sporting goods and adventure racing outfitter. The company has decided to borrow €20,000,000 via a euro-euro floating rate loan for four years. Raid must decide between two competing loan offerings from two of its banks.

   Banque de Paris has offered the four-year debt at euro-LIBOR + 2.00% with an up-front initiation fee of 1.8%. Banque de Sorbonne, however, has offered euro-LIBOR + 2.5%, a higher spread, but with no loan initiation fees up front, for the same term and principal. Both banks reset the interest rate at the end of each year.

Euro-LIBOR is currently 4.00%. Raid's economist forecasts that LIBOR will rise by 0.5 percentage points each year. Banque de Sorbonne, however, officially forecasts euro-LIBOR to begin trending upward at the rate of 0.25 percentage points per year. Raid Gauloises's cost of capital is 11%. Which loan proposal do you recommend for Raid Gauloises?

*4. **Agnelli Motors.** Agnelli Motors of Italy recently took out a four-year €5 million loan on a floating rate basis. It is now worried, however, about rising interest costs. Although it had initially believed interest rates in the Eurozone would be trending downward when taking out the loan, recent economic indicators show growing inflationary pressures. Analysts are predicting that the European Central Bank will slow monetary growth driving interest rates up.

Agnelli is now considering whether to seek some protection against a rise in euro-LIBOR, and is considering a Forward Rate Agreement (FRA) with an insurance company. According to the agreement, Agnelli would pay to the insurance company at the end of each year the difference between its initial interest cost at LIBOR + 2.50% (6.50%) and any fall in interest cost due to a fall in LIBOR. Conversely, the insurance company would pay to Agnelli 70% of the difference between Agnelli's initial interest cost and any increase in interest costs caused by a rise in LIBOR.

Purchase of the floating Rate Agreement will cost €100,000, paid at the time of the initial loan. What are Agnelli's annual financing costs now if LIBOR rises and if LIBOR falls? Agnelli uses 12% as its weighted average cost of capital. Do you recommend that Agnelli purchase the FRA?

5. **Chrysler LLC.** Chrysler LLC, the now privately held company sold off by DaimlerChrysler, must pay floating rate interest three months from now. It wants to lock in these interest payments by buying an interest rate futures contract. Interest rate futures for three months from now settled at 93.07, for a yield of 6.93% per annum.

a. If the floating interest rate three months from now is 6.00%, what did Chrysler gain or lose?

b. If the floating interest rate is 8.00% three months from now, what did Chrysler gain or lose?

6. **Cañon Chemicals.** Amanda Suvari, the treasurer of Cañon Chemical Company believes interest rates are going to rise, so she wants to swap her future floating rate interest payments for fixed rates. At present she is paying LIBOR + 2% per annum on $5,000,000 of debt for the next two years, with payments due semiannually. LIBOR is currently 4.00% per annum. Ms. Suvari has just made an interest payment today, so the next payment is due six months from today.

Ms. Suvari finds that she can swap her current floating rate payments for fixed payments of 7.00% per annum. (Cañon Chemical's weighted average cost of capital is 12%, which Ms. Suvari calculates to be 6% per six month period, compounded semiannually.)

a. If LIBOR rises at the rate of 50 basis points per six-month period, starting tomorrow, how much does Ms. Suvari save or cost her company by making this swap?

b. If LIBOR falls at the rate of 25 basis points per six-month period, starting tomorrow, how much does Ms. Suvari save or cost her company by making this swap?

7. **Xavier and Zulu.** Xavier Manufacturing and Zulu Products both seek funding at the lowest possible cost. Xavier would prefer the flexibility of floating rate borrowing, while Zulu wants the security of fixed rate borrowing. Xavier is the more creditworthy company. They face the following rate structure. Xavier, with the better credit rating, has lower borrowing costs in both types of borrowing:

	Xavier	Zulu
Credit rating	AAA	BBB
Fixed rate cost of borrowing	8%	12%
Floating rate cost of borrowing	LIBOR + 1%	LIBOR + 2%

Xavier wants floating rate debt, so it could borrow at LIBOR + 1%. However it could borrow fixed at 8% and swap for floating rate debt. Zulu wants fixed rate, so it could borrow fixed at 12%. However, it could borrow floating at LIBOR + 2% and swap for fixed rate debt. What should they do?

8. **Trident's Cross-Currency Swap: Sfr for US$.** Trident entered into a three-year cross currency interest rate swap in the chapter to receive U.S. dollars and pay Swiss francs. Trident, however, decided to unwind the swap after one year—thereby having two years left on the settlement costs of unwinding the swap after one year. Repeat the calculations for unwinding, but assume that the following rates now apply:

Two-year Swiss franc interest rate	5.20% per annum
Two-year U.S. dollar interest rate	2.20% per annum
Spot exchange rate	SF1.5560/$

9. **Trident's Cross-Currency Swap: Yen for Euros.** Using the same table of swap rates (Exhibit 9.8), assume Trident enters into a swap agreement to *receive euros and pay Japanese yen*, on a notional principal of €5,000,000. The spot exchange rate at the time of the swap is ¥104/€.
   a. Calculate all principal and interest payments, in both euros and Swiss francs, for the life of the swap agreement. (Use Exhibit 9.9 as a guide.)
   b. Assume that one year into the swap agreement Trident decides it wishes to unwind the swap agreement and settle it in euros. Assuming that a two-year fixed rate of interest on the Japanese yen is now 0.80%, and a two-year fixed rate of interest on the euro is now 3.60%, and the spot rate of exchange is now ¥114/€, what is the net present value of the swap agreement? Who pays whom what?

10. **Delphi.** Delphi is the U.S.-based automotive parts supplier which was spun off from General Motors in 2000. With annual sales of over $26 billion, the company has expanded its markets far beyond the traditional automobile manufacturers in the pursuit of a more diversified sales base. As part of the general diversification effort, the company wishes to diversify the currency of denomination of its debt portfolio as well. Assume Delphi enters into a $50 million seven-year cross currency interest rate swap to do just that—pay euros and receive dollars. Using the data in Exhibit 9.10,
   a. Calculate all principal and interest payments in both currencies for the life of the swap.
   b. Assume that three years later Delphi decides to unwind the swap agreement. If four-year fixed rates of interest in euros have now risen to 5.35%, four-year fixed rate dollars have fallen to 4.40%, and the current spot exchange rate of $1.02/€, what is the net present value of the swap agreement? Who pays who what?

INTERNET EXERCISES

1. **Living Yield Curve.** SmartMoney's Web site allows the user to see a detailed graphic exposition of the U.S. Treasury yield curve in motion from 1977 to the present. Use the graphic to see how interest rates in general in the United States have fallen over time, and how the current yield curve is positioned relative to what it was over the historical time period.

| SmartMoney | www.smartmoney.com/investing/bonds/the-living-yield-curve-7923/ |

2. **International Interest Rates.** A number of Web sites publish current interest rates by currency and maturity. Use the following *Financial Times* Web site to isolate the interest rate differentials between the U.S. dollar, the British pound, and the euro for all maturities up to and including one year.

| *Financial Times* Market Data | www.ft.com/markets |

Data Listed by the *Financial Times*:

- *International money rates (bank call rates for major currency deposits)*
- *Money rates (LIBOR, CD rates, etc.)*
- *Ten-year spreads (individual country spreads versus the euro and U.S. 10-year treasuries). Which countries actually have lower 10-year government bond rates than the United States and the euro? Probably Switzerland and Japan. Check.*
- *Benchmark government bonds (sampling of representative government issuances by major countries and recent price movements). Which countries are showing longer maturity benchmark rates?*
- *Emerging market bonds (government issuances, Brady bonds, etc.)*
- *Eurozone rates (miscellaneous bond rates for assorted European-based companies; includes debt ratings by Moodys and S&P)*

3. **Euro Yield Curve.** Eurstat, the statistics unit of the European Union (EU), posts an up-to-date graphic of the yield curve for euro-denominated European Central Bank debt outstanding. Use the site to take a detailed look at the following: a) yields, b) volatility, and c) historical yield curve structures.

| Eurostat europar | www.ecb.int/stats/acc/html/index.en.html |

4. **Current Interest Rates and Yield Curves.** Use the New York Federal Reserve Bank's Web page for recent interest rates on all maturities of U.S. dollar-denominated debt issues. Historical data is also available so that it is relatively easy to plot how the Treasury's Constant Maturity yields have changed from week to week and month to month for maturities varying between 3 months and 10 years.

| Federal Reserve Bank of New York | www.ny.frb.org/ |

5. **The International Swaps and Derivatives Association (ISDA).** The ISDA is the primary global organization that attempts to both standardize the use of interest rates and cross-currency swaps and track the market's size. Use ISDA's Web site to determine which type of interest rate derivative is growing the fastest.

| International Swaps & Derivatives Association | www.isda.org |

6. **Pounds and Dollar Interest Rates.** The Web site yieldcurve.com provides real-time quotes on major maturities of both U.S. dollar-denominated fixed income securities and British pound-denominated bonds (bunds). Use the site's information to compare the difference in interest rate structures at the present time.

| Yieldcurve.com | www.yieldcurve.com/marketyieldcurve.asp |

CHAPTER 10

Foreign Exchange Rate Determination and Forecasting

He who lives by the crystal ball soon learns to eat ground glass. The herd instinct among forecasters makes sheep look like independent thinkers.

—Edgar R. Fiedler.

Exchange rate determination is complex. Chapter 4 explained how a country's balance of payments can have a significant impact on the level of its exchange rate and vice versa, depending on that country's exchange rate regime. Chapter 7 analyzed the international parity conditions that integrate exchange rates with inflation and interest rates, and provided a theoretical framework for the global financial markets and the management of international financial activities. This chapter extends the discussion of exchange rate determination to another major school of thought on the determination of exchange rates: the *asset market approach.*

Exhibit 10.1 provides an overview of the many determinants of exchange rates. This road map is first organized by the three major schools of thought (parity conditions, balance of payments approach, and asset market approach), and second by the individual drivers within those approaches. At first glance, the idea that there are three sets of theories may appear daunting, but it is important to remember that these are not *competing theories,* but rather *complementary theories.* Without the depth and breadth of the various approaches combined, our ability to capture the complexity of the global market for currencies is lost.

In addition to gaining an understanding of the basic theories, it is equally important to gain a working knowledge of how the complexities of international political economy; societal and economic infrastructures; and random political, economic, or social events affect the exchange rate markets. Here are a few examples:

- *Infrastructure weaknesses* were among the major causes of the exchange rate collapses in emerging markets in the late 1990s. On the other hand, infrastructure strengths help explain why the U.S. dollar continued to be strong, at least until the September 11, 2001, terrorist attack on the United States, despite record balance of payments deficits on current account.

- *Speculation* contributed greatly to the emerging market crises that are described later in this chapter. Some characteristics of speculation are hot money flowing

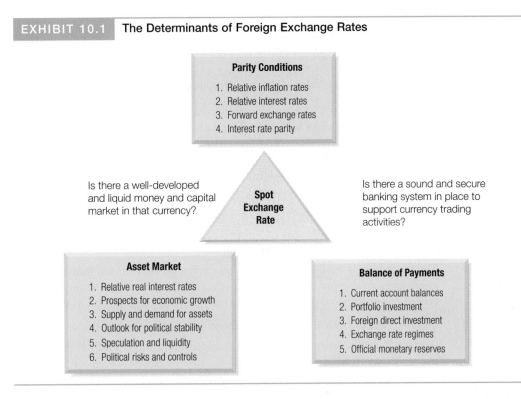

EXHIBIT 10.1 The Determinants of Foreign Exchange Rates

Parity Conditions
1. Relative inflation rates
2. Relative interest rates
3. Forward exchange rates
4. Interest rate parity

Is there a well-developed and liquid money and capital market in that currency?

Spot Exchange Rate

Is there a sound and secure banking system in place to support currency trading activities?

Asset Market
1. Relative real interest rates
2. Prospects for economic growth
3. Supply and demand for assets
4. Outlook for political stability
5. Speculation and liquidity
6. Political risks and controls

Balance of Payments
1. Current account balances
2. Portfolio investment
3. Foreign direct investment
4. Exchange rate regimes
5. Official monetary reserves

into and out of currencies, securities, real estate, and commodities. Uncovered interest arbitrage caused by exceptionally low borrowing interest rates in Japan coupled with high real interest rates in the United States was a problem for much of the 1990s. Borrowing yen to invest in safe U.S. government securities, hoping that the exchange rate did not change, was popular.

■ *Cross-border foreign direct investment and international portfolio investment* into the emerging markets dried up during their crises.

■ *Foreign political risks* have been much reduced in recent years as capital markets became less segmented from each other and more liquid. More countries adopted democratic forms of government. However, recent occurrences of terrorism may be changing perceptions of political risk.

Finally, note that most determinants of the spot exchange rate are also in turn affected by changes in the spot rate. In other words, they are not only linked but also mutually determined.

Exchange Rate Determination: The Theoretical Thread[1]

Under the skin of an international economist lies a deep-seated belief in some variant of the PPP theory of the exchange rate.

—Paul Krugman, 1976.

[1]This section draws upon a variety of sources, including *Currency Forecasting: A Guide to Fundamental and Technical Models of Exchange Rate Determination,* Michael R. Rosenberg, Chicago: Irwin Professional Publishing, 1996.

There are basically three views of the exchange rate. The first takes the exchange rate as the relative price of monies (the monetary approach); the second, as the relative price of goods (the purchasing-power-parity approach); and the third, the relative price of bonds.

—Rudiger Dornbusch, "Exchange Rate Economics: Where Do We Stand?"
Brookings Papers on Economic Activity 1, 1980, pp. 143–194.

Professor Dornbusch's tripartite categorization of exchange rate theory is a good starting point, but in some ways not robust enough—in our humble opinion—to capture the multitude of theories and approaches. So, in the spirit of both tradition and completeness, we have amended Dornbusch's three categories with several additional streams of thought in the following discussion. The next section will provide a brief overview of the many different but related theories of exchange rate determination, and their relative usefulness in forecasting for business purposes.

Purchasing Power Parity Approaches

The most widely accepted theory of all exchange rate determination theories, the theory of *purchasing power parity* (PPP), states that the long-run equilibrium exchange rate is determined by the ratio of domestic prices relative to foreign prices, as explained in Chapter 6.

- PPP is both the oldest and most widely followed of the exchange rate theories.
- Most theories of exchange rate determination have PPP elements embedded within their frameworks.
- PPP calculations and forecasts, however, may be plagued with structural differences across countries and significant data challenges in estimation.

Balance of Payments (Flows) Approaches

After purchasing power parity, the most frequently used theoretical approach to exchange rate determination is probably the *balance of payments approach*, involving the supply and demand for currencies in the foreign exchange market. These exchange rate *flows* reflect current account and financial account transactions recorded in a nation's balance of payments, as described in Chapter 4.

- The basic *balance of payments approach* argues that the equilibrium exchange rate is found when the net inflow (outflow) of foreign exchange arising from current account activities matches the net outflow (inflow) of foreign exchange arising from financial account activities.
- The balance of payments approach continues to enjoy a wide degree of appeal as balance of payments transactions are one of the most frequently captured and reported of international economic activity.
- Criticisms of the balance of payments approach arise from the theory's emphasis on flows of currency and capital rather than stocks of money or financial assets.
- Relative stocks of money or financial assets play no role in exchange rate determination in this theory, a weakness explored in the following monetary and asset market approaches.
- Curiously, the balance of payments approach is largely dismissed by the academic community today, while the practitioner public—market participants, including currency traders themselves—still rely on different variations of the theory for their decision making.

Monetary Approaches

The *monetary approach* in its simplest form states that the exchange rate is determined by the supply and demand for national monetary stocks, as well as the expected future levels and rates of growth of monetary stocks. Other financial assets, such as bonds (covered later), are not considered relevant for exchange rate determination, as both domestic and foreign bonds are viewed as perfect substitutes. It is all about money stocks.

- Changes in the supply and demand for money are the primary determinants of inflation. Changes in relative inflation rates in turn alter exchange rates through an assumed purchasing power parity affect.

- The monetary approach also assumes that prices are flexible in the short run as well as the long run, so that the transmission mechanism is immediate in impact.

- In monetary models of exchange rate determination, real economic activity is relegated to a role in which it influences only exchange rates through any alterations to the demand for money.

- The monetary approach omits a number of factors, which are generally agreed by subject area experts as important to exchange rate determination, including 1) the failure of PPP to hold in the short to medium term; 2) money demand appearing to be relatively unstable over time; and 3) the level of economic activity and the money supply appearing to be interdependent, not independent. As a result, we will not pursue the monetary approach further.

Asset Market Approach (Relative Price of Bonds)

The *asset market approach,* sometimes called the *relative price of bonds* or *portfolio balance approach*, argues that exchange rates are determined by the supply and demand for a wide variety of financial assets.

- Shifts in the supply and demand for financial assets alter exchange rates.

- Changes in monetary and fiscal policy alter expected returns and perceived relative risks of financial assets, which in turn alter exchange rates.

- Many of the macroeconomic theoretical developments in the 1980s focused on how monetary and fiscal policy changes altered the relative perceptions of return and risk to the stocks of financial assets driving exchange rate changes. The frequently cited works of Mundell-Fleming are in this genre.

- Theories of *currency substitution*, the ability of individual and commercial investors to alter the composition of their monetary holdings in their portfolios, follow the same basic premises of the portfolio balance and rebalance framework.

Unfortunately, for all of the good work and research over the past 50 years, the ability to forecast exchange rate values in the short-term to long-term is—in the word of the following quotation—*sorry*. Although academics and practitioners alike agree that in the long run, fundamental principles such as purchasing power and external balances drive currency values, none of the fundamental theories have proven that useful in the short to medium term.

> *... [T]he case for macroeconomic determinants of exchange rates is in a sorry state.... [The] results indicate that no model based on such standard fundamentals like money supplies, real income, interest rates, inflation rates and current account balances will ever succeed in explaining or predicting a high percentage of the variation in the exchange rate, at least at short- or medium-term frequencies.*

> —Jeffrey A. Frankel and Andrew K. Rose, "A Survey of Empirical Research on Nominal Exchange Rates," *NBER Working Paper* no. 4865, 1994.

Technical Analysis

The forecasting inadequacies of fundamental theories has led to the growth and popularity of *technical analysis*, the belief that the study of past price behavior provides insights into future price movements.

- The primary feature of technical analysis is the assumption that exchange rates, or for that matter any market-driven price, follows trends. And those trends may be analyzed and projected to provide insights into short-term and medium-term price movements in the future.

- Most theories of technical analysis differentiate fair value from market value. Fair value is the true long-term value that the price will eventually reattain. The market value is subject to a multitude of changes and behaviors arising from widespread market participant perceptions and beliefs.

The Asset Market Approach to Forecasting

The *asset market approach* assumes that whether foreigners are willing to hold claims in monetary form depends on an extensive set of investment considerations or drivers. These drivers, as shown in Exhibit 10.1, include the following:

- Relative real interest rates are a major consideration for investors in foreign bonds and short-term money market instruments.

- Prospects for economic growth and profitability are an important determinant of cross-border equity investment in both securities and foreign direct investment.

- Capital market liquidity is particularly important to foreign institutional investors. Cross-border investors are not only interested in the ease of buying assets, but also in being able to sell those assets quickly for fair market value.

- A country's economic and social infrastructure is an important indicator of that country's ability to survive unexpected external shocks and to prosper in a rapidly changing world economic environment.

- Political safety is exceptionally important to both foreign portfolio and direct investors. The outlook for political safety is usually reflected in political risk premiums for a country's securities and for purposes of evaluating foreign direct investment in that country.

- The credibility of corporate governance practices is important to cross-border portfolio investors. A firm's poor corporate governance practices can reduce foreign investors' influence and cause subsequent loss of the firm's focus on shareholder wealth objectives.

- *Contagion* is defined as the spread of a crisis in one country to its neighboring countries and other countries that have similar characteristics, at least in the eyes of cross-border investors. Contagion can cause an "innocent" country to experience capital flight and a resulting depreciation of its currency.

- Speculation can cause a foreign exchange crisis or make an existing crisis worse. We will observe this effect through the two illustrative cases that follow later in this chapter.

The Asset Market Approach in Highly Developed Countries

Foreign investors are willing to hold securities and undertake foreign direct investment in highly developed countries based primarily on relative real interest rates and the outlook for economic growth and profitability. All the other drivers described in Exhibit 10.1 and detailed previously are assumed to be satisfied.

For example, during 1981–1985, the U.S. dollar strengthened despite growing current account deficits. This strength was due partly to relatively high real interest rates in the United States. Another factor, however, was the heavy inflow of foreign capital into the U.S. stock market and real estate, motivated by good long-run prospects for growth and profitability in the United States.

The same cycle was repeated in the United States between 1990 and 2000. Despite continued worsening balances on current account, the U.S. dollar strengthened in both nominal and real terms due to foreign capital inflow motivated by rising stock and real estate prices, a low rate of inflation, high real interest returns, and a seemingly endless "irrational exuberance" about future economic prospects.

This time the bubble burst following the September 11, 2001, terrorist attack on the United States. The attack and its aftermath caused a negative reassessment of long-term growth and profitability prospects in the United States as well as a newly formed level of political risk for the United States itself. This negative outlook was reinforced by a very sharp drop in the U.S. stock markets based on lower expected earnings. Further damage to the economy was caused by a series of revelations about failures in corporate governance of several large corporations. These failures included accounting overstatement of earnings, insider trading, and self-serving loans by firms to their own executives, as described in Chapter 2.

Loss of confidence in the U.S. economy led to a large withdrawal of foreign capital from U.S. security markets. As would be predicted by both the balance of payments and asset market approaches, the U.S. dollar depreciated. Indeed, its nominal rate depreciated by 18% between mid-January and mid-July 2002 relative to the euro alone. Further depreciation occurred due to the war in Iraq and the terrorism and instability that followed.

The experience of the United States, as well as other highly developed countries, illustrates why some forecasters believe that exchange rates are more heavily influenced by economic prospects than by the current account. One scholar summarizes this belief using an interesting anecdote:

Many economists reject the view that the short-term behavior of exchange rates is determined in flow markets. Exchange rates are asset prices traded in an efficient financial market. Indeed, an exchange rate is the relative price of two currencies and therefore is determined by the willingness to hold each currency. Like other asset prices, the exchange rate is determined by expectations about the future, not current trade flows.

A parallel with other asset prices may illustrate the approach. Let's consider the stock price of a winery traded on the Bordeaux stock exchange. A frost in late spring results in a poor harvest, in terms of both quantity and quality. After the harvest the wine is finally sold, and the income is much less than the previous year. On the day of the final sale there is no reason for the stock price to be influenced by this flow. First, the poor income has already been discounted for several months in the winery stock price. Second, the stock price is affected by future, in addition to current, prospects. The stock price is based on expectations of future earnings, and the major cause for a change in stock price is a revision of these expectations.

A similar reasoning applies to exchange rates: Contemporaneous international flows should have little effect on exchange rates to the extent they have already been expected. Only news about future economic prospects will affect exchange rates. Since economic expectations are potentially volatile and influenced by many variables, especially variables of a political nature, the short-run behavior of exchange rates is volatile.[2]

[2]Bruno H. Solnik, *International Investments*, 3rd Edition, Reading, MA: Addison Wesley 1996, p. 58. Reprinted with permission of Pearson Education, Inc.

The asset market approach to forecasting is also applicable to emerging markets. In this case, however, a number of additional variables contribute to exchange rate determination. These variables, as described previously, are illiquid capital markets, weak economic and social infrastructure, political instability, corporate governance, contagion effects, and speculation. These variables will be illustrated in the sections on crises that follow.

Disequilibrium: Exchange Rates in Emerging Markets

Although the three schools of thought on exchange rate determination (parity conditions, balance of payments approach, and asset approach) make understanding exchange rates appear to be straightforward, that is rarely the case. The large and liquid capital and currency markets follow many of the principles outlined so far relatively well in the medium to long term. The smaller and less liquid markets, however, frequently demonstrate behaviors that seemingly contradict theory. The problem lies not in the theory, but in the relevance of the assumptions underlying the theory. An analysis of the emerging market crises illustrates a number of these seeming contradictions.

After a number of years of relative global economic tranquility, the second half of the 1990s was racked by a series of currency crises that shook all emerging markets. The devaluation of the Mexican peso in December 1994 was a harbinger. The Asian crisis of July 1997 and the fall of the Argentine peso in 2002 provide a spectrum of emerging market economic failures, each with its own complex causes and unknown outlooks. These crises also illustrated the growing problem of capital flight and short-run international speculation in currency and securities markets. We will use each of the individual crises to focus on a specific dimension of the causes and consequences:

1. **The Asian Crisis.** Although this was not the collapse of any one currency, economy, or system, the complex structures combining government, society, and business throughout the Far East provide a backdrop for understanding the tenuous link between business, government, and society.

2. **The Argentine Crisis.** In 1991, Argentina adopted a currency board structure. The Argentine peso was tied to the U.S. dollar on a one-to-one basis. The resulting austerity program caused by the need to defend its fixed exchange rate caused Argentina to plunge into recession. Starting in 1998 and continuing for the next four years, the austerity program and recession caused increasing political turmoil, capital flight, and eventually the demise of the currency board itself.

Illustrative Case: The Asian Crisis

The roots of the Asian currency crisis extended from a fundamental change in the economics of the region: the transition of many Asian nations from being net exporters to net importers. Starting as early as 1990 in Thailand, the rapidly expanding economies of the Far East began importing more than they exported, requiring major net capital inflows to support their currencies. As long as the capital continued to flow in—capital for manufacturing plants, dam projects, infrastructure development, and even real estate speculation—the pegged exchange rates of the region could be maintained. When the investment capital inflows stopped, however, crisis was inevitable.

The most visible roots of the crisis were in the excesses of capital inflows into Thailand in 1996 and early 1997. With rapid economic growth and rising profits forming the backdrop, Thai firms, banks, and finance companies had ready access to capital on the international markets, finding U.S. dollar debt cheap offshore. Thai banks continued to raise capital internationally, extending credit to a variety of domestic investments and enterprises beyond what the Thai economy could support. As capital flows into the Thai market hit record rates, financial flows poured into investments of all kinds, including manufacturing, real estate, and even equity market margin-lending. As the investment bubble expanded, some participants raised questions about the economy's ability to repay the rising debt. The Thai baht came under attack.

Currency Collapse

The Thai government and central bank intervened in the foreign exchange markets directly (using up precious hard currency reserves) and indirectly (by raising interest rates to attempt to stop the continual outflow). The Thai investment markets ground to a halt, which caused massive currency losses and bank failures. On July 2, 1997, the Thai central bank finally allowed the baht to float (or sink in this case). The baht fell 17% against the U.S. dollar and more than 12% against the Japanese yen in a matter of hours. By November, the baht had fallen from Baht25/$ to Baht40/$, a fall of about 38%. In the aftermath, the international speculator and philanthropist George Soros was the object of much criticism, primarily by the Prime Minister of Malaysia, Dr. Mahathir Mohamad, for being the cause of the crisis because of massive speculation by his and other hedge funds. Soros, however, was likely only the messenger.

Within days, in Asia's own version of what is called the *tequila effect*, a number of neighboring Asian nations, some with and some without characteristics similar to Thailand's, came under speculative attack by currency traders and capital markets. ("Tequila effect" is the term used to describe how the Mexican peso crisis of December 1994 quickly spread to other Latin American currency and equity markets, a form of financial panic termed *contagion*.) The Philippine peso, the Malaysian ringgit, and the Indonesian rupiah all fell in the months following the July baht devaluation (see Exhibit 10.2 and Exhibit 10.3).

In late October 1997, Taiwan caught the markets off balance with a surprise competitive devaluation of 15%. The Taiwanese devaluation seemed only to renew the momentum of the

EXHIBIT 10.2	The Economies and Currencies of Asia, July–November 1997				
				Exchange Rate	
	1996 Current Acct (billions of U.S. dollars)	Liabilities to Foreign Banks (billions of U.S. dollars)	July (per U.S. dollars)	November (per U.S. dollars)	% Change
Weaker Economies					
Indonesia (rupiah)	−9.0	29.7	2,400	3,600	−33.3%
Korea (won)	−23.1	36.5	900	1,100	−18.2%
Malaysia (ringgit)	−8.0	27.0	2.5	3.5	−28.6%
Philippines (peso)	−3.0	2.8	27	34	−20.6%
Thailand (baht)	−14.7	48.0	25	40	−37.5%
Stronger Economies					
China (yuan)	47.2	56.0	8.4	8.4	+0.0%
Hong Kong (dollar)	0.0	28.8	7.75	7.73	+0.0%
Singapore (dollar)	14.3	55.3	1.43	1.60	−10.6%
Taiwan (dollar)	11.0	17.6	27.8	32.7	−15.0%

Source: International Monetary Fund, *International Financial Statistics*, October–November 1997.

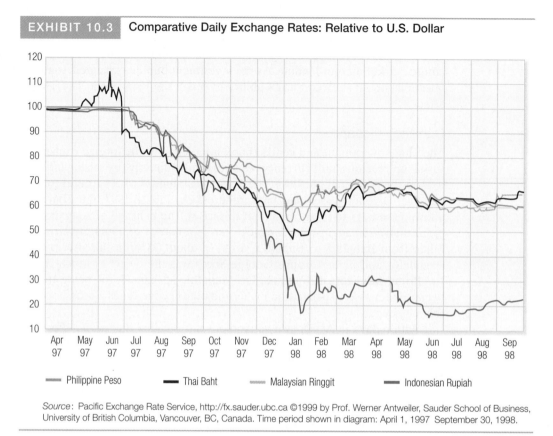

EXHIBIT 10.3   Comparative Daily Exchange Rates: Relative to U.S. Dollar

— Philippine Peso   — Thai Baht   — Malaysian Ringgit   — Indonesian Rupiah

Source: Pacific Exchange Rate Service, http://fx.sauder.ubc.ca ©1999 by Prof. Werner Antweiler, Sauder School of Business, University of British Columbia, Vancouver, BC, Canada. Time period shown in diagram: April 1, 1997 September 30, 1998.

crisis. Although the Hong Kong dollar survived (at great expense to the central bank's foreign exchange reserves), the Korean won was not so lucky. In November 1997, the historically stable Korean won fell from Won900/$ to more than Won1100/$. The only currency that had not fallen besides the Hong Kong dollar was the Chinese yuan, which was not freely convertible. Although the yuan was not devalued, there was rising speculation that the Chinese government would devalue it soon for competitive reasons (it did not).

Causal Complexities

The Asian economic crisis—for it was more than just a currency collapse—had many roots besides traditional balance of payments difficulties. The causes were different in each country, yet there are specific underlying similarities that allow comparison: corporate socialism, corporate governance, and banking stability and management.

Corporate Socialism. Although Western markets have long known the volatility of the free market, the countries of post-World War II Asia have largely known only stability. Because of the influence of government and politics in the business arena, even in the event of failure, it was believed that government would not allow firms to fail, workers to lose their jobs, or banks to close. That was true until the problems reached the size seen in 1997 and business liabilities exceeded the capacities of governments to bail businesses out. Practices that had persisted for decades without challenge, such as lifetime employment, were no longer sustainable. The result was a painful lesson in the harshness of the marketplace.

Corporate Governance. Little doubt exists that many local firms operating within the Far Eastern business environments were controlled either by families or by groups related to the governing party or body of the country. This tendency has been labeled *cronyism*. Cronyism means that the interests of minority stockholders and creditors are often secondary, at best, to the primary motivations of corporate management. When management did not focus on "the bottom line," the bottom line deteriorated.

Banking Liquidity and Management. The banking sector has fallen out of favor in the past two decades. Bank regulatory structures and markets have been deregulated nearly without exception across the globe. The central role played by banks in the conduct of business, however, has largely been ignored and underestimated. As firms across Asia collapsed, government coffers were emptied and speculative investments made by the banks themselves failed. Without banks, the "plumbing" of business conduct was shut down. Firms could not obtain the necessary working capital financing to manufacture and sell their products or provide their services. This pivotal role of banking liquidity was the focus of the IMF's bailout efforts.

The Asian economic crisis had global impacts. What started as a currency crisis quickly became a region-wide recession. The magnitude of economic devastation in Asia is still largely unappreciated by Westerners. At a 1998 conference sponsored by the Milken Institute, a speaker noted that the world's preoccupation with the economic problems of Indonesia was incomprehensible because "the total gross domestic product of Indonesia is roughly the size of North Carolina." The following speaker observed, however, that the last time he had checked, "North Carolina did not have a population of 220 million people." The slowed economies of the region quickly caused major reductions in world demands for many products, especially commodities. World oil, metal, and agricultural products markets all saw severe price falls as demand fell. These price drops were immediately noticeable in declining earnings and growth prospects for other emerging economies.

Illustrative Case: The Argentine Crisis of 2002

Now, most Argentines are blaming corrupt politicians and foreign devils for their ills. But few are looking inward, at mainstream societal concepts such as viveza criolla, an Argentine cultural quirk that applauds anyone sly enough to get away with a fast one. It is one reason behind massive tax evasion here: One of every three Argentines does so—and many like to brag about it.

—Anthony Faiola, "Once-Haughty Nation's Swagger Loses Its Currency,"
The Washington Post, March 13, 2002.

Argentina's economic ups and downs have historically been tied to the health of the Argentine peso. South America's southernmost country—which oftentimes considered itself more European than Latin American—had been wracked by hyperinflation, international indebtedness, and economic collapse in the 1980s. By early 1991, the people of Argentina had had enough. Economic reform in the early 1990s was a common goal of the Argentine people. They were not interested in quick fixes, but in lasting change and a stable future. They nearly got it.

The Currency Board

In 1991, the Argentine peso had been fixed to the U.S. dollar at a one-to-one rate of exchange. The policy was a radical departure from traditional methods of fixing the rate of a currency's value. Argentina adopted a *currency board*, a structure for—rather than merely a commitment to—limiting the growth of money in the economy. Under a currency board, the central bank of a country may increase the money supply in the banking system only with increases in its holdings of hard currency reserves. The reserves in this case were U.S. dollars. By removing the ability of government to expand the rate of growth of the money supply, Argentina believed it was eliminating the source of inflation that had devastated its standard of living.

The idea was elegantly simple and in many ways simplistic: limit the rate of growth in the country's money supply to the rate at which the country receives net inflows of U.S. dollars as a result of trade growth and general surplus. It was both a recipe for conservative and prudent financial management, and a decision to eliminate the power of politicians, elected and unelected, to exercise judgment both good and bad. It was an automatic and unbendable rule. And from the beginning, it had shown the costs and benefits of its rigor.

Exhibit 10.4 illustrates the three traditional measures of a country's macroeconomic performance: real growth in gross domestic product (GDP), inflation, and unemployment. But Exhibit 10.4 also illustrates the austerity dimension to the currency board structure. Although hyperinflation had indeed been the problem, the cure was a restrictive monetary policy, which slowed economic growth in the coming years. The first and foremost cost of the slower economic growth had been in unemployment. Beginning with a decade low unemployment rate of 6.3% in 1991, unemployment rose to double-digit levels in 1994 and stayed there. The real GDP growth rate, which opened the decade with booming levels over 10%, settled into recession in late 1998. GDP growth shrank in 1999 (–3.5%) and 2000 (–0.4%). Preliminary estimates for 2001 indicated a further deterioration in GDP: –3% for the year.

As part of the continuing governmental commitment to the currency board's fixed exchange rate for the peso, Argentine banks allowed depositors to hold their money in either form—pesos or dollars. This approach was intended to provide a market-based discipline to the banking and political systems, and to demonstrate the government's unwavering commitment to maintaining the peso's value parity with the dollar. Although considered by many an excellent policy to build confidence, in the end it proved disastrous to the Argentine banking system.

Economic Crisis, 2001

The 1998 recession proved to be unending. Three and a half years later, Argentina was still in recession. By 2001, crisis conditions had revealed three very important underlying problems with Argentina's economy: 1) the Argentine peso was overvalued; 2) the currency board regime had eliminated monetary policy alternatives for macroeconomic policy; and 3) the Argentine government budget deficit—and deficit spending—was out of control.

The Argentine Peso. The peso had indeed been stabilized, but inflation had not been eliminated, and the other factors that are important in the global market's evaluation of a currency's value—economic growth, corporate profitability, and so on—had not necessarily always been positive. The inability of the peso's value to change with market forces led many

EXHIBIT 10.4	Argentina's Economic Performance, 1991–2000									
	1991	1992	1993	1994	1995	1996	1997	1998	1999	2000
Real GDP growth rate (%)	10.5	9.6	5.8	5.8	–2.8	5.5	8.2	3.9	–3.5	–0.4
Unemployment rate (%)	6.3	7.2	9.1	11.7	15.9	16.3	14.2	14.1	15.5	15.0
Inflation rate (%)	172.0	24.6	10.6	4.3	3.3	0.2	0.5	0.9	–1.2	–0.9

Source: International Monetary Fund, Political Risk Services, Argentina Economic Development Agency.

to believe increasingly that it was overvalued, and that the overvaluation gap was rising as time passed.

Argentina's large neighbor to the north, Brazil, had also suffered many of the economic ills of hyperinflation and international indebtedness in the 1980s and early 1990s. Brazil's response, the *Real Plan*, was introduced in July 1994.[3] The Real Plan worked for a while, but eventually collapsed in January 1999 as a result of the rising gap between the reais's official value and the market's assessment of its true value.

Brazil was by far Argentina's largest trading partner. With the fall of the Brazilian reais, however, Brazilian consumers could no longer afford Argentine exports. It simply took too many reais to purchase a peso. In fact, Argentine exports became some of the most expensive in all of South America, as other countries saw their currencies slide marginally against the dollar over the decade. But not the Argentine peso.

The Currency Board and Monetary Policy. The increasingly sluggish economic growth in Argentina warranted expansionary economic policies, argued many policy makers in and out of the country. But the currency board's basic premise was that the money supply to the financial system could not be expanded any further or faster than the ability of the economy to capture dollar reserves. This rule eliminated monetary policy as an avenue for macroeconomic policy formulation, leaving only fiscal policy for economic stimulation.

Government Budget Deficits. Government spending was not slowing, however. As the unemployment rate grew higher, as poverty and social unrest grew, government in the civil center of Argentina, Buenos Aires and in the outer provinces was faced with growing expansionary spending, needed to close the economic and social gaps. Government spending continued to increase, but tax receipts did not. Lower income led to lower taxes on income.

Argentina then turned to the international markets to aid in the financing of its government's deficit spending. As illustrated in Exhibit 10.5, the total foreign debt of the country began rising dramatically in 1997 and 1998. Only a number of IMF capital injections in 2000 and 2001 prevented the total foreign debt of the country from skyrocketing. When the decade was over, however, total foreign debt had effectively doubled and the economy's earning power had not.

Also seen in Exhibit 10.5 is Argentina's failure to turn the current account toward surplus. Although this failure is not surprising, given the overvalued currency relative to its major South American neighbors, it was only through running a trade surplus that Argentina could earn additional dollar reserves and allow a loosening of monetary policy constraints.

EXHIBIT 10.5	Argentina's Debt and Key Balances, 1991–2000									
	1991	**1992**	**1993**	**1994**	**1995**	**1996**	**1997**	**1998**	**1999**	**2000**
Foreign debt (billion $)	65.4	71.9	60.3	69.6	68.2	105.2	123.2	139.0	149.0	123.7
Current account (billion $)	−0.65	−5.49	−8.03	−11.22	−5.30	−6.94	−12.43	−14.55	−11.95	−8.90
Budget balance (billion $)	−1.01	−0.07	−1.58	−1.88	−1.42	−5.24	−4.35	−4.15	−8.13	−6.86

Source: International Monetary Fund, Political Risk Services, Argentina Economic Development Agency.

[3]Brazil introduced a new currency at that time, the *reais*. The reais's value was not, however, fixed to the U.S. dollar but pegged to the dollar with a predictable and promised rate of daily devaluation. This allowed the reais to weaken commensurate with Brazil's still higher rate of inflation and lower rate of growth, but control its value change over time.

In the end, the government budget deficit continued to grow. Continuing recession required large fiscal expenditures by federal and local governments. Government spending was increasingly financed by international capital. International investors were beginning to doubt Argentina's ability to repay them.

Social Repercussions

As economic conditions continued to deteriorate, banks suffered increasing runs. Depositors, fearing that the peso would be devalued, lined up to withdraw their money, both Argentine peso cash balances and U.S. dollar cash balances. Pesos were converted to dollars, once again adding fuel to the growing fire of currency collapse. The government, fearing that the increasing financial drain on banks would cause their collapse, closed the banks on December 1, 2001, in an effort to stop the flight of cash and capital out of Argentina. Consumers, unable to withdraw more than $250 per week, were instructed to use debit cards and credit cards to make purchases and conduct everyday transactions.

In December 2001, riots in the streets of Buenos Aires intensified the need for rapid change. As the new year of 2002 arrived, the second president in two weeks, Fernando de la Rua, was driven from office. He was succeeded by a Peronist, President Adolfo Rodriguez Saa, who lasted all of one week as president before he too was driven from office. President Saa did, however, leave his legacy. In his one week as president of Argentina, Saa declared the largest sovereign debt default in history. Argentina announced it would not be able to make interest payments due on $155 billion in sovereign (government) debt.

Saa was succeeded by Eduardo Duhalde, Argentina's fifth president in a little more than two weeks. A presidential candidate in 1999 and a senator for Buenos Aires province, Duhalde faced a massive task. He was immediately granted emergency powers to try to save what was left of the Argentine economic system.

Devaluation

On Sunday, January 6, 2002, in the first act of his presidency, Duhalde devalued the peso from Ps1.00/$ to Ps1.40/$. It was hoped that once the peso was devalued, the country could calm the nerves of its people.

But the economic pain continued. Two weeks after the devaluation, the banks were still closed. Most of the state governments outside of Buenos Aires, basically broke and without access to financing resources, began printing their own money—*script*—promissory notes of the provincial governments. The provincial governments were left with little choice—the economy of Argentina was nearing complete collapse as people and businesses could not obtain money to conduct the day-to-day commercial transactions of life.

But the notes were only a partial answer. Because the notes were promissory notes of the provincial governments, not the federal government, people and businesses would not accept notes from other provinces. Store shelves stood empty, because although consumers could buy what was already in the store, the store could not make acceptable payment to regional, national, or international suppliers. The population became trapped within its own province, because their money was not accepted in the outside world in exchange for goods, services, travel, or anything else.

On February 3, 2002, the Argentine government announced that the peso would be floated. The government would no longer attempt to fix or manage its value to any specific level, allowing the market to find or set the exchange rate. The value of the peso now began a gradual depreciation.[4]

---

[4]When a currency that is under a fixed exchange rate regime is officially reduced in value against some other benchmark currency, it is termed a *devaluation*. When a currency that is freely floated on exchange markets moves downward in value, it is termed *depreciation*.

As the year wore on, the country was confronted with issue after issue of social, political, and economic collapse. The banks and bankers were increasingly the target of the ire of the population. As banks collapsed, business fell with them. In February and March, a growing series of investigations into illegal trading and financial fraud covered the Buenos Aires headlines. In February and March 2002, continued negotiations between the IMF and Argentina went in fits and starts as the IMF demanded increasing fiscal reform over the growing government budget deficits and bank mismanagement. The IMF itself became an increasing target of the Argentine population's discontent.

On March 24 and 25, the peso was once again hit by massive sell-offs. In a country long considered the wealthiest and most sophisticated in all of South America, the people were increasingly opposed to all politicians, all banks and financial service providers, and in many cases each other. The path of the peso's collapse is presented in Exhibit 10.6. In the spring of 2002, Argentina was a country in considerable trouble.

Harvard professor and member of the U.S. President's Council of Economic Advisors Martin Feldstein summed up the hard lessons of the Argentine story.

> *In reality, the Argentines understood the risk that they were taking at least as well as the IMF staff did. Theirs was a calculated risk that might have produced good results. It is true, however, that the IMF staff did encourage Argentina to continue with the fixed exchange rate and currency board. Although the IMF and virtually all outside economists believe that a floating exchange rate is preferable to a "fixed but adjustable" system, in which the government recognizes that it will have to devalue occasionally, the IMF (as well as some outside economists) came to believe that the currency board system of a firmly fixed exchange rate (a "hard peg" in the jargon of international finance) is a viable long-term policy for an economy. Argentina's experience has proved that wrong.[5]*

EXHIBIT 10.6   Daily Exchange Rates: Argentine Pesos per U.S. Dollar

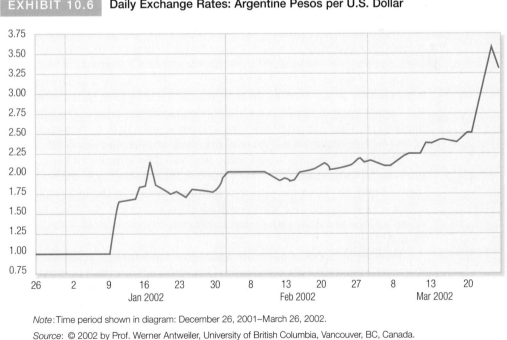

Note: Time period shown in diagram: December 26, 2001–March 26, 2002.

Source: © 2002 by Prof. Werner Antweiler, University of British Columbia, Vancouver, BC, Canada.

[5]Martin Feldstein, "Argentina's Fall," *Foreign Affairs* (March/April 2002), Volume 81, Issue 2, pp. 8–14.

Forecasting in Practice

In addition to the three approaches to forecasting depicted in Exhibit 10.1, forecasting practitioners use *technical analysis*.

Technical Analysis

Technical analysts, traditionally referred to as *chartists*, focus on price and volume data to determine past trends that are expected to continue into the future. The single most important element of technical analysis is that future exchange rates are based on the current exchange rate. Exchange rate movements, similar to equity price movements, can be divided into three periods: 1) day-to-day movement, which is seemingly random; 2) short-term movements extending from several days to several months; and 3) long-term movements, characterized by up-and-down long-term trends. Long-term technical analysis has gained popularity as a result of recent research into the possibility that long-term "waves" in currency movements exist under floating exchange rates.

The longer the time horizon of the forecast, the more inaccurate the forecast is likely to be. Whereas forecasting for the long run must depend on economic fundamentals of exchange rate determination, many of the forecast needs of the firm are short- to medium-term in their time horizon and can be addressed with less theoretical approaches. Time series techniques infer no theory or causality but simply predict future values from the recent past. Forecasters freely mix fundamental and technical analysis, presumably because forecasting is like horseshoes: getting close counts!

Forecasting Services

Numerous foreign exchange forecasting services exist, many of which are provided by banks and independent consultants. In addition, some multinational firms have their own in-house forecasting capabilities. Predictions can be based on elaborate econometric models, technical analysis of charts and trends, intuition, and a certain measure of gall.

Whether any of the forecasting services are worth their cost depends partly on the motive for forecasting as well as the required accuracy of the forecast. For example, long-run forecasts may be motivated by a multinational firm's desire to initiate a foreign investment in Japan, or perhaps to raise long-term funds denominated in Japanese yen. Or a portfolio manager may be considering diversifying for the long term in Japanese securities. The longer the time horizon of the forecast, the more inaccurate but also the less critical the forecast is likely to be. The forecaster will typically use annual data to display long-run trends in such economic fundamentals as Japanese inflation, growth, and the BOP.

Short-term forecasts are typically motivated by a desire to hedge a receivable, payable, or dividend for perhaps a period of three months. In this case, the long-run economic fundamentals may not be as important as technical factors in the marketplace, government intervention, news, and passing whims of traders and investors. Accuracy of the forecast is critical, as most of the exchange rate changes are relatively small, even though the day-to-day volatility may be high.

Forecasting services normally undertake fundamental economic analysis for long-term forecasts, and some base their short-term forecasts on the same basic model. Others base their short-term forecasts on technical analysis similar to that conducted in security analysis. They attempt to correlate exchange rate changes with various other variables, regardless of whether there is any economic rationale for the correlation. The chance of these forecasts being consistently useful or profitable depends on whether one believes the foreign exchange market is efficient. The more efficient the market is, the more likely it is that exchange rates are "random walks," with past price behavior providing no clues to the future. The less efficient the foreign exchange market is, the better the chance that forecasters may get lucky and find a key relationship that holds, at least for the short run. If the relationship is really consistent, however, others will soon discover it and the market will become efficient again with respect to that piece of information.

Exhibit 10.7 summarizes the various forecasting periods, regimes, and the authors' opinions on the preferred methodologies. Opinions, however, are subject to change without notice! (And remember, if the authors could predict the movement of exchange rates with regularity, we surely wouldn't write books.)

Cross-Rate Consistency in Forecasting

International financial managers must often forecast their home currency exchange rates for the set of countries in which the firm operates, not only to decide whether to hedge or to make an investment, but also as an integral part of preparing multicountry operating budgets in the home country's currency. These are the operating budgets against which the performance of foreign subsidiary managers will be judged. Checking the reasonableness of the cross rates implicit in individual forecasts acts as a reality check to the original forecasts.

To illustrate, assume that the U.S. parent home office forecasts the yen-to-dollar exchange rate a year hence to be ¥105/$ and the U.K. pound sterling rate to be $1.85/£. This creates an implied spot rate one year hence of ¥194.25/£. However, both the Japanese and the British financial managers, with good reason, have forecast a spot rate one year hence of ¥190.00/£.

EXHIBIT 10.7   Exchange Rate Forecasting in Practice

Forecast Period	Regime	Recommended Forecast Methods
Short run	Fixed rate	1. Assume the fixed rate is maintained 2. Indications of stress on fixed rate 3. Capital controls; black market rates 4. Indicators of government's 5. Changes in official foreign currency reserves

	Floating rate	1. Technical methods that capture trend
		2. Forward rates as forecasts
		  a. <30 days; assume a random walk
		  b. 30–90 days; forward rates
		3. 90–360 days; combine trend with fundamental analysis
		4. Fundamental analysis of inflationary concerns
		5. Government declarations and agreements regarding exchange rate goals
		6. Cooperative agreements with other countries

Long run	Fixed rate	1. Fundamental analysis 2. BOP management 3. Ability to control domestic inflation 4. Ability to generate hard currency reserves to use for intervention 5. Ability to run trade surpluses
	Floating rate	1. Focus on inflationary fundamentals and PPP 2. Indicators of general economic health, such as economic growth and stability 3. Technical analysis of long-term trends; new research indicates possibility of long-term technical "waves"

Obviously, the two foreign subsidiary managers (forecasting ¥190.00/£) and the home office (with an implicit forecast of ¥194.25/£) cannot both be correct. The time to reconcile these conflicting forecasts is the present, not one year hence when managers in Japan or the United Kingdom claim that their performance against budget is better than measured by the U.S. parent. Additionally, checking the reasonableness of implied cross rates is an exercise in improving the accuracy of the forecasting process.

Forecasting: What to Think?

Obviously, with the variety of theories and practices, forecasting exchange rates into the future is a daunting task. Here is a synthesis of our thoughts and experience:

- It appears, from decades of theoretical and empirical studies, that exchange rates do adhere to the fundamental principles and theories outlined in the previous sections. Fundamentals do apply in the long term. There is, therefore, something of a *fundamental equilibrium path* for a currency's value.

- It also seems that in the short term, a variety of random events, institutional frictions, and technical factors may cause currency values to deviate significantly from their long-term fundamental path. This behavior is sometimes referred to as *noise*. Clearly, therefore, we might expect deviations from the long-term path not only to occur, but to occur with some regularity and relative longevity.

Exhibit 10.8 illustrates this synthesis of forecasting thought. The long-term equilibrium path of the currency—although relatively well defined in retrospect—is not always apparent in the short term. The exchange rate itself may deviate in something of a cycle or wave about the long-term path.

If market participants agree on the general long-term path and possess *stabilizing expectations*, the currency's value will periodically return to the long-term path. It is critical, however, that when the currency's value rises above the long-term path, most market participants

EXHIBIT 10.8   Differentiating Short-Term Noise from Long-Term Trends

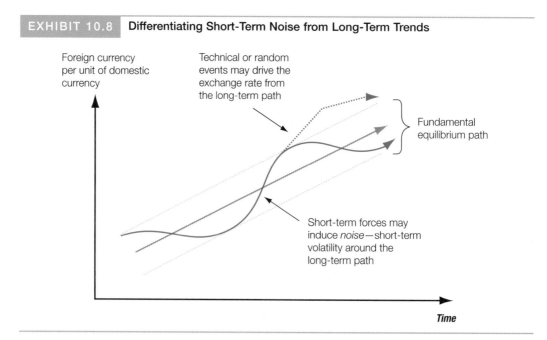

see it as being overvalued and respond by selling the currency, causing its price to fall. Similarly, when the currency's value falls below the long-term path, market participants respond by buying the currency driving its value up. This is what is meant by *stabilizing expectations*: market participants must continually respond to deviations from the long-term path by buying or selling to drive the currency back to the long-term path.

If, for some reason, the market becomes unstable, as illustrated by the dotted deviation path in Exhibit 10.8, the exchange rate may move significantly away from the long-term path for longer periods of time. Causes of these destabilizing movements, such as weak infrastructure (for example, the banking system), and political or social events that dictate economic behaviors, are often the result of actions of speculators and inefficient markets.

Exchange Rate Dynamics: Making Sense of Market Movements

Although the various theories surrounding exchange rate determination are clear and sound, it may appear on a day-to-day basis that the currency markets do not pay much attention to the theories—they don't read the books! The difficulty is understanding which fundamentals are driving markets at which points in time.

One example of this relative confusion over exchange rate dynamics is the phenomenon known as *overshooting*. Assume that the current spot rate between the dollar and the euro, as illustrated in Exhibit 10.9, is S_0. The U.S. Federal Reserve announces an expansionary monetary policy that cuts U.S. dollar interest rates. If euro-denominated interest rates remain unchanged, the new spot rate expected by the exchange markets on the basis of interest differentials is S_1. This immediate change in the exchange rate is typical of how the markets react to *news*, distinct economic and political events that are observable. The immediate change in the value of the dollar/euro is therefore based on interest differentials.

EXHIBIT 10.9   **Exchange Rate Dynamics: Overshooting**

If the U.S. Federal Reserve were to announce a change in monetary policy, an expansion in money supply growth, it could potentially result in an overshooting " exchange rate change.

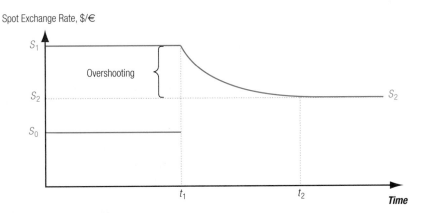

The Fed announces a monetary expansion at a time t_1. This announcement results immediately in lower dollar interest rates. The foreign exchange markets immediately respond to the lower dollar interest rates by driving the value of the dollar down from S_0 to S_1. this new rate is based on *interest differentials*. However, in the coming days and weeks, as the fundamental price effects of the monetary policy actions work their way through the economy, *purchasing power parity* takes hold and the market moves toward a longer-term valuation of the dollar—by time—t_2—of S_2, a weaker dollar than S_0, but not as weak as initially set at S_1.

As time passes, however, the price impacts of the monetary policy change start working their way through the economy. As price changes occur over the medium to long term, purchasing power parity forces drive the market dynamics, and the spot rate moves from S_1 toward S_2. Although both S_1 and S_2 were rates determined by the market, they reflected the dominance of different theoretical principles. As a result, the initial lower value of the dollar of S_1 is often explained as an *overshooting* of the longer-term equilibrium value of S_2.

This is of course only one possible series of events and market reactions. Currency markets are subject to *new* news every hour of every day, making it very difficult to forecast exchange rate movements in short periods of time. In the longer term, as shown here, the markets do customarily return to fundamentals of exchange rate determination.

SUMMARY POINTS

- The asset approach to forecasting suggests that whether foreigners are willing to hold claims in monetary form depends partly on relative real interest rates and partly on a country's outlook for economic growth and profitability.

- Longer-term forecasting, over one year, requires a return to the basic analysis of exchange rate fundamentals such as BOP, relative inflation rates, relative interest rates, and the long-run properties of purchasing power parity.

- Technical analysts (chartists) focus on price and volume data to determine past trends that are expected to continue into the future.

- Exchange rate forecasting in practice is a mix of both fundamental and technical forms of exchange rate analysis.

- The Asian currency crisis was primarily a balance of payments crisis in its origins and impacts on exchange rate determination. A weak economic and financial infrastructure, corporate governance problems and speculation were also contributing factors.

- The Argentine crisis of 2002 was probably a combination of a disequilibrium in international parity conditions (differential rates of inflation) and balance of payments disequilibrium (current account deficits combined with financial account outflows).

MINI-CASE   JPMorgan Chase's Forecasting Accuracy [1]

Veselina (Vesi) Dinova was asked by her director at Teknekron (U.S.) to review the exchange rate forecasting accuracy of her company's primary financial services provider, JPMorgan Chase (JPMC). Vesi focused on the three primary currencies the company's operations revolved around: the dollar, the euro, and the yen. Teknekron had relied upon JPMC for most of its currency advisory services for years, and the forecasts provided by JPMC were regularly used in sales and sourcing decisions—including pricing. The rise of the euro against the dollar in recent years had, however, raised the interest in the accuracy of these forecasts. Assessing that accuracy was now Vesi's task.

Focusing first on the U.S. dollar/euro spot exchange rate, Vesi plotted the forecasts provided by JPMC and the actual spot exchange rate for the 2002–2005 period, in 90-day increments. As illustrated by Exhibit 1, the results were not encouraging. Although JPMC had hit the actual spot rate dead-on in both May and November 2002, the size of the forecasting errors and direction of movement seemed to increase over time.

What was most worrisome to Vesi was that in a good part of 2004, JPMC was getting the direction wrong. In February 2004, they had forecast the spot rate to move from the current rate of \$1.27/€ to \$1.32/€, but in fact the dollar had appreciated dramatically in the following three-month period to close at \$1.19/€. This was in fact a massive difference. Although Teknekron used a weighted moving average of the actual spot and forecasted rate in its foreign currency pricing (in this case, in euros), the directional error had caused the firm to average in a much weaker dollar than what had happened. The buyer had been irritated.

[1]This case study uses exchange rate data, both actual and forecast, as published in the print edition of *The Economist,* appearing quarterly. The source of the exchange rate forecasts, as noted in *The Economist,* is JPMorgan Chase.

EXHIBIT 1   Monthly Average Exchange Rates: US$/€

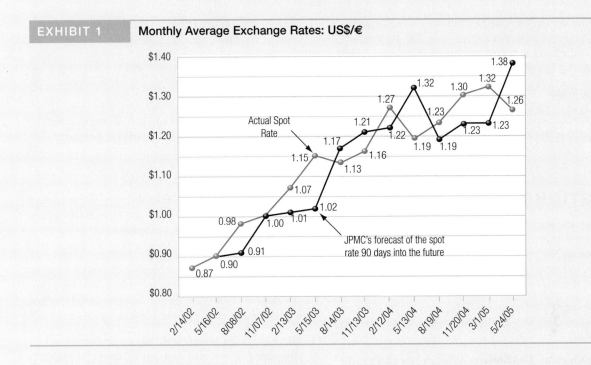

Whereas Teknekron did most of its sales in North America and Europe (hence the euro-based pricing), its sourcing was confined to the United States and Japan. Teknekron's Japanese suppliers provided 3% discounts for Japanese yen-denominated invoicing, which Teknekron had traditionally been happy to take (the discount) and provide (yen payments). But this approach required Vesi's company to manage and control its cost of goods sold—including the yen-denominated costs.

Vesi now turned to the predicted accuracy of JPMC on the yen. Exhibit 2 provides an overview of that analysis. Once again, although the dollar was consistently falling

EXHIBIT 2   Monthly Average Exchange Rates: Japanese Yen per U.S. Dollar

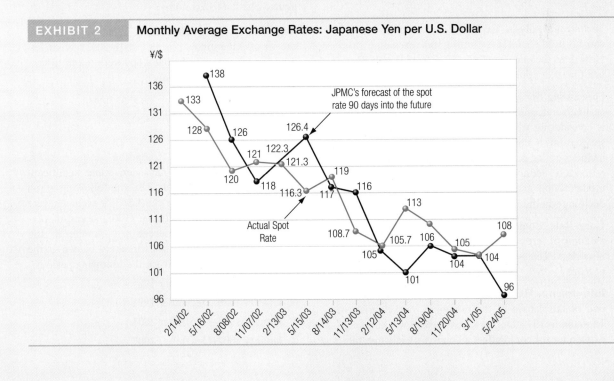

against the yen, the forecasting accuracy—at least by eye-balling the graphic, was not encouraging. The most recent quarter had closed at ¥108/$, although the forecast had been to follow trend to ¥96/$.

Case Questions

1. How would you actually go about calculating the statistical accuracy of these forecasts? Would Vesi have been better off using the current spot rate as the forecast of the future spot rate, 90 days out?

2. Forecasting the future is obviously a daunting challenge. All things considered, how well do you think JPMC is doing?

3. If you were Vesi, what would you conclude about the relative accuracy of JPMC's spot rate forecasts?

QUESTIONS

1. **Term Forecasting.** What are the major differences between short-term and long-term forecasts for the following?
   a. A fixed exchange rate
   b. A floating exchange rate

2. **Exchange Rate Dynamics.** What is meant by the term "overshooting"? What causes it and how is it corrected?

3. **Fundamental Equilibrium.** What is meant by the term "fundamental equilibrium path" for a currency value? What is "noise"?

4. **Asset Market Approach to Forecasting.** Explain how the asset market approach can be used to forecast future spot exchange rates. How does the asset market approach differ from the BOP approach to forecasting?

5. **Technical Analysis.** Explain how technical analysis can be used to forecast future spot exchange rates. How does technical analysis differ from the BOP and asset market approaches to forecasting?

6. **Forecasting Services.** Numerous exchange rate forecasting services exist. Trident's CFO Maria Gonzalez is considering whether to subscribe to one of these services at a cost of $20,000 per year. The price includes online access to the forecasting services' computerized econometric exchange rate prediction model. What factors should Maria consider when deciding whether or not to subscribe?

7. **Cross-Rate Consistency in Forecasting.** Explain the meaning of "cross-rate consistency" as used by MNEs. How do MNEs use a check of cross-rate consistency in practice?

8. **Infrastructure Weakness.** *Infrastructure weakness* was one of the causes of the emerging market crisis in Thailand in 1997. Define infrastructure weakness and explain how it could affect a country's exchange rate.

9. **Infrastructure Strength.** Explain why infrastructure strengths have helped to offset the large BOP deficits on current account in the United States.

10. **Speculation.** The emerging market crises of 1997–2002 were worsened because of rampant speculation. Do speculators cause such crisis or do they simply respond to market signals of weakness? How can a government manage foreign exchange speculation?

11. **Foreign Direct Investment.** Swings in foreign direct investment flows into and out of emerging markets contribute to exchange rate volatility. Describe one concrete historical example of this phenomenon during the last 10 years.

12. **Thailand's Crisis of 1997.** What were the main causes of Thailand's crisis of 1997? What lessons were learned and what steps were eventually taken to normalize Thailand's economy?

13. **Argentina's Crisis of 2001–2002.** What were the main causes of Argentina's crisis of 2001–2002? What lessons were learned and what steps were taken to normalize Argentina's economy?

PROBLEMS

1. **Canadian Loonie.** The Canadian dollar's value against the U.S. dollar has seen some significant changes over recent history. Use the following graph (top left on next page) of the C$/US$ exchange rate for the 27-year period between 1980 and end-of-year 2007 to estimate the percentage change in the Canadian dollar's value (affectionately known as the "loonie") versus the dollar for the following periods:
   a. January 1980–December 1985
   b. January 1986–December 1991
   c. January 1992–December 2001
   d. January 2002–December 2007

Monthly Average Exchange Rates:
Canadian Dollars per U.S. Dollar

Source: Pacific Exchange Rate Service ©2007 by Prof. Werner Antweiler, University of British Columbia, Vancouver, BC, Canada.

Monthly Average Exchange Rates:
Japanese Yen per European Euro

Source: Pacific Exchange Rate Service ©2007 by Prof. Werner Antweiler, University of British Columbia, Vancouver, BC, Canada.

*2. **Brazilian Reais.** The Brazilian reais's (R$) value was R$1.21/$ on Monday January 11, 1999. Its value fell to R$1.43/$ on Friday January 15, 1999. What was the percentage change in its value?

3. **Turkish Lira.** The Turkish lira (TL) was officially devalued by the Turkish government in February 2001 during a severe political and economic crisis. The Turkish government announced on February 21 that the lira would be devalued by 20%. The spot exchange rate on February 20 was TL68,000/$.

   a. What was the exchange rate after a 20% devaluation?

   b. Within three days the lira had plummeted to more than TL100,000/$. What percentage change was this from the pre-devaluation rate?

4. **Euros and Yen.** The Japanese yen-euro cross-rate is one of the more significant currency values for global trade and commerce. The following graph (top of next column) shows this cross-rate back-calculated from early 1994 through the end-of-year 2007. (Remember the euro was not launched until January 1999, but its value can be back-calculated from its component currencies.) Estimate the change in the value of the yen over the following three periods of change:

   a. January 1994–August 1998

   b. September 1998–October 2000

   c. November 2000–December 2007

*5. **Seis Anos.** Mexico was famous—or infamous—for many years in having two things every six years (*seis anos* in Spanish): a presidential election and a currency devaluation. This was the case in 1976, 1982, 1988, and 1994. In its last devaluation on December 20, 1994, the value of the Mexican peso (Ps) was officially changed from Ps3.30/$ to Ps5.50/$. What was the percentage devaluation?

6. **Russian Ruble.** The Russian ruble (R) traded at R6.25/$ on August 7, 1998. By September 10, 1998, its value had fallen to R20.00/$. What was the percentage change in its value?

7. **Thai Baht.** The Thai baht (Bt) was devalued by the Thai government from Bt25/$ to Bt29/$ on July 2, 1997. What was the percentage devaluation of the baht?

8. **Ecuadorian Sucre.** The Ecuadorian sucre (S) suffered from hyper-inflationary forces throughout 1999. Its value moved from S5,000/$ to S25,000/$. What was the percentage change in its value?

9. **Forecasting the Argentine Peso.** As illustrated in the graph on the next page, the Argentine peso moved from its fixed exchange rate of Ps1.00/$ to over Ps2.00/$ in a matter of days in early January 2002. After a brief period of high volatility, the peso's value appeared to settle down into a range varying between 2.0 and 2.5 pesos per dollar.

If you were forecasting the Argentine peso further into the future, how would you use the information in the graphic—the value of the peso freely floating in the weeks following devaluation—to forecast its future value?

Daily Exchange Rates: Argentine Pesos per U.S. Dollar

Source: ©2007 by Prof. Werner Antweiler, University of British Columbia, Vancouver, BC, Canada.

Forecasting the Pan-Pacific Pyramid

Use the table at the top of the next page containing economic, financial, and business indicators from the October 20, 2007, issue of The Economist *(print edition) to answer problems 10 through 15.*

10. **Current Spot Rates.** What are the current spot exchange rates for the following cross-rates?
    a. Japanese yen/U.S. dollar
    b. Japanese yen/Australian dollar
    c. Australian dollar/U.S. dollar

11. **Purchasing Power Parity Forecasts.** Using the theory of purchasing power parity, and assuming that forecasted changes in consumer prices are the best measures of expected inflation, forecast the following spot exchanges for one year into the future:
    a. Japanese yen/U.S. dollar
    b. Japanese yen/Australian dollar
    c. Australian dollar/U.S. dollar

12. **International Fisher Forecasts.** Using International Fisher, and that the latest government bond rates are the most appropriate interest rates for applying International Fisher, forecast the following spot exchanges for one year into the future:
    a. Japanese yen/U.S. dollar
    b. Japanese yen/Australian dollar
    c. Australian dollar/U.S. dollar

13. **Implied Real interest Rates.** Use the latest government bond rates and the forecast changes in consumer prices to forecast the real interest rates for the following:
    a. Australian dollar
    b. Japanese yen
    c. United States dollar

14. **Forward Rates.** Using the spot rates and 90-day market interest rates listed, calculate the 90-day forward rates for the following exchange rates:
    a. Japanese yen/U.S. dollar
    b. Japanese yen/Australian dollar
    c. Australian dollar/U.S. dollar

15. **Real Economic Activity and Misery.** One of the common general measures of national economic health is sometimes referred to as the "misery index," the sum of the country's inflation rate and unemployment rate. Using the previously calculated forward rates (problem 14), calculate the country's misery index and use it as a relative measure for forecasting (in the same way as inflation differentials or interest differentials are used to forecast) one year into the future.
    a. Japanese yen/U.S. dollar
    b. Japanese yen/Australian dollar
    c. Australian dollar/U.S. dollar

INTERNET EXERCISES

1. **Exchange Rate and Interest Rate Six Month Forecasts.** Use the following independent source of forecasts for all key international data to view the outlook for the US$/€, ¥/$, and $/£ exchange rates.

   | Financial Forecast Center | www.forecasts.org/exchange-rate/index.htm |

2. **Bank of Canada Exchange Rate Statistics.** One of the most comprehensive and freely available Internet sites for exchange rate statistics and analysis is that maintained by the Bank of Canada. Use the Bank's Web site to view the latest indicators of how relative interest rate changes will affect the all-important exchange rate of the Canadian dollars with both the U.S. dollar and the euro.

   | Bank of Canada Exchange Rates | www.bankofcanada.ca/en/rates/exchange.html |

3. **Mellon FX Forecast Update.** One of the more interesting and complete economic and exchange rate forecasting newsletters is the Mellon Financial. Use Mellon's Web site to download the latest version of their foreign exchange forecast. It often includes significant analysis of prospective real rates of return in

Forecasting the Pan-Pacific Pyramid

Australia, Japan, and the United States

Country	Gross Domestic Product				Industrial Production	Unemployment Rate
	Latest Qtr	Qtr*	Forecast 2007e	Forecast 2008e	Recent Qtr	Latest
Australia	4.3%	3.8%	4.1%	3.5%	4.6%	4.2%
Japan	1.6%	−1.2%	2.0%	1.9%	4.3%	3.8%
United States	1.9%	3.8%	2.0%	2.2%	1.9%	4.7%

Country	Consumer Prices			Interest Rates	
					1-yr Govt Bond
	Year Ago	Latest	Forecast 2007e	3-month Latest	Latest
Australia	4.0%	2.1%	2.4%	6.90%	6.23%
Japan	0.9%	−0.2%	0.0%	0.73%	1.65%
United States	2.1%	2.8%	2.8%	4.72%	4.54%

Country	Trade Balance	Current Account		Current Units (per US$)	
	Last 12 months (billion $)	Last 12 months (billion $)	Forecast 07 (% of GDP)	October 17th	Year Ago
Australia	−13.0	−$47.0	−5.7%	1.12	1.33
Japan	98.1	$197.5	4.6%	117	119
United States	−810.7	−$793.2	−5.6%	1.00	1.00

Source: Data abstracted from *The Economist*, October 20, 2007, print edition.

Note: Unless otherwise noted, percentages are percentage changes over one-year. Rec Qtr = recent quarter.

Values for 2007e are estimates or forecasts.

the United States, Europe, Japan, Canada, the United Kingdom, Australia, and New Zealand.

Mellon Foreign Exchange	www.mellon.com/assetservicing/ productservices/foreignexchange.html

4. **Recent Economic and Financial Data.** Use the following Web sites to obtain recent economic and financial data used for all approaches to forecasting presented in this chapter.

Economist.com	www.economist.com
FT.com	www.ft.com
EconEdLink	www.econedlink.org/datalinks/ index.cfm

5. **OzForex Weekly Comment.** The OzForex Foreign Exchange Services Web site provides a weekly commentary on major political and economic factors and events that move current markets. Using their Web site, see what they expect to happen in the coming week on the three major global currencies—the dollar, yen, and euro.

OzForex	www.ozforex.com.au/marketwatch.htm

6. **Bloomberg Exchange Rates, Interest Rates, and Global Markets.** The magnitude of market data can seem overwhelming on occasion. Use the following Bloomberg markets page to organize your mind and your global data.

Bloomberg Financial News	www.bloomberg.com/markets

Foreign Exchange Exposure

CHAPTER 11

Transaction Exposure

There are two times in a man's life when he should not speculate: when he can't afford it and when he can.

— "Following the Equator," *Pudd'nhead Wilson's New Calendar*, Mark Twain.

Foreign exchange exposure is a measure of the potential for a firm's *profitability, net cash flow,* and *market value* to change because of a change in exchange rates. An important task of the financial manager is to measure foreign exchange exposure and to manage it so as to maximize the profitability, net cash flow, and market value of the firm. These three components—profits, cash flows, and market value—are the key financial elements of how we view the relative success or failure of a firm. The first two—profits and cash flows—largely give rise to the third, market value. And, although the theory of finance teaches us that cash flows matter and accounting does not, any true businessperson knows that currency-related gains and losses can have destructive impacts on reported earnings. The reported earnings of any publicly traded company are fundamental to the market's opinion of that company.

Types of Foreign Exchange Exposure

What happens to a firm when foreign exchange rates change? The effect can be measured in several ways. Exhibit 11.1 reviews the three main types of foreign exchange exposure—*transaction*, *operating*, and *translation*.

Transaction Exposure

Transaction exposure measures changes in the value of outstanding financial obligations incurred prior to a change in exchange rates but not due to be settled until after the exchange rates change. Thus, it deals with changes in cash flows that result from existing contractual obligations. The purpose of this chapter is to analyze how transaction exposure is measured and managed.

Operating Exposure

Operating exposure, also called *economic exposure*, *competitive exposure*, or *strategic exposure*, measures the change in the present value of the firm resulting from any change in expected future operating cash flows of the firm caused by an *unexpected* change in exchange rates. The change in value depends on the effect of the exchange rate change on future sales volume, prices, and costs. Chapter 12 analyzes operating exposure.

| EXHIBIT 11.1 | Conceptual Comparison of Transaction, Operating, and Translation Foreign Exchange Exposure |

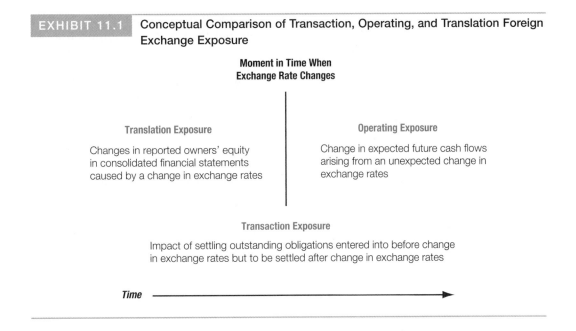

Transaction exposure and operating exposure exist because of unexpected changes in future cash flows. The difference between the two is that transaction exposure is concerned with future cash flows already contracted for, while operating exposure focuses on expected (not yet contracted for) future cash flows that might change because a change in exchange rates has altered international competitiveness.

Translation Exposure

Translation exposure, also called *accounting exposure,* is the potential for accounting-derived changes in owner's equity to occur because of the need to "translate" foreign currency financial statements of foreign subsidiaries into a single reporting currency to prepare worldwide consolidated financial statements. Chapter 13 analyzes translation exposure.

Tax Exposure

The tax consequence of foreign exchange exposure varies by country. As a general rule, however, only *realized* foreign exchange losses are deductible for purposes of calculating income taxes. Similarly, only *realized* gains create taxable income. *Realized* means that the loss or gain involves cash flows.

Losses from transaction exposure usually reduce taxable income in the year in which they are realized. Losses from operating exposure reduce taxable income over a series of future years. As Chapter 13 will show, losses from translation exposure are not cash losses and so are not deductible. Some steps taken to minimize one or another of the types of exposure, such as entering into a forward exchange contract, create taxable income or loss. Other steps taken to obtain the same protection have no income tax implications. Because tax exposure is determined by the country of domicile of each subsidiary, an MNE needs to plan its foreign exchange management policies to minimize the worldwide after-tax consequences of foreign exchange losses and to maximize after-tax gains. However, since many MNEs manage foreign exchange exposures centrally, gains or losses are often not matched with the country of origin.

Currency exposures do not always result in losses to the firm. They may, in fact, occasionally result in gains—gains that are not the result of the firm's true operations or core competence—but from the luck and timing associated with exchange rate changes and currency movements. As illustrated in *Global Finance in Practice 11.1*, there are many continuing debates over the management of foreign exchange exposure.

Why Hedge?

MNEs possess a multitude of cash flows that are sensitive to changes in exchange rates, interest rates, and commodity prices. These three financial price risks are the subject of the growing field of *financial risk management*. In this chapter, we will focus on the sensitivity of the individual firm's future cash flows to exchange rates alone.

Definition of Hedging

Many firms attempt to manage their currency exposures through hedging. *Hedging* is the taking of a position—either acquiring a cash flow, an asset, or a contract (including a forward contract)—that will rise (or fall) in value and offset a fall (or rise) in the value of an existing position. Therefore, hedging protects the owner of the existing asset from loss. However, it also eliminates any gain from an increase in the value of the asset hedged against. The question remains: What is to be gained by the firm from hedging?

The value of a firm according to financial theory is the net present value of all expected future cash flows. The fact that these cash flows are *expected* emphasizes that nothing about

---

GLOBAL FINANCE IN PRACTICE 11.1

FX Risk Management—A Rose by Any Other Name

There are many different opinions in both industry and academia today as to the focus, the objectives, and even the categorization of foreign exchange risk management.

Focus of Foreign Exchange Risk Management

The choices for focus are typically summarized as either *cash flow* or *earnings*. Academia often stresses the pure financial theoretical objective of focusing on cash flow-based events, and not spending "real money" managing accounting results. Many in industry, however, believe that if the markets, particularly the public equity markets, make many value judgments on reported earnings, then it is the firm's management responsibility to protect reported earnings from foreign exchange risk.

Objective of Foreign Exchange Risk Management

The objective of FX risk management may be even more contentious. Although most firms will quickly acknowledge that eliminating foreign exchange risk is nearly impossible, particularly in time horizons beyond the immediate short-run (say 90 days), there are obviously differences in opinion. Many

firms will specifically note that their objective is to *maximize the home currency value of all exposures*, but *minimizing realized home currency value deviation to budget* is often frequently noted, as is *minimizing the cost of hedging*.

Categorization of Foreign Exchange Exposure

This book uses a traditional method of exposure categorization, separating FX exposure into three categories: *operating exposure, transaction exposure*, and *translation exposure*. But this is far from standardized, and many companies internally use very different classification and management systems. One common methodology is to classify exposures on the basis of *accounting* (balance sheet, earnings translation, etc.) and *non-accounting* (anticipated transactions and contingent exposures). Even when using this simple distinction, many exposures that are not on the balance sheet, like *anticipated exposures* on intrafirm purchases, will soon be. Some exposures, like the investment a parent company has in a foreign subsidiary, is particularly complex depending on intracompany dividend policy and the functional currency of the foreign subsidiary.

the future is certain. If the reported currency value of many of these cash flows is altered by exchange rate changes, a firm that hedges its currency exposures reduces some of the variance in the value of its future expected cash flows. Therefore, *currency risk* can be defined roughly as the variance in expected cash flows arising from unexpected exchange rate changes.

Exhibit 11.2 illustrates the distribution of expected net cash flows of the individual firm. Hedging these cash flows narrows the distribution of the cash flows about the mean of the distribution. Currency hedging reduces risk. Reduction of risk is not, however, the same as adding value or return. The value of the firm presented in Exhibit 11.2 would be increased only if hedging actually shifted the mean of the distribution to the right. In fact, if hedging is not "free," meaning that the firm must expend resources to undertake hedging activity, then hedging will add value only if the rightward shift is sufficiently large to compensate for the cost of hedging.

Reasons Not to Hedge

Hence the key question: Is a reduction in the variability of cash flows sufficient reason for currency risk management? This question is actually a continuing debate in multinational financial management. Opponents of currency hedging commonly make the following arguments:

1. Shareholders are much more capable of diversifying currency risk than the management of the firm. If shareholders do not wish to accept the currency risk of any specific firm, they can diversify their portfolios to manage the currency risk in a way that satisfies their individual preferences and risk tolerance.

2. As previously noted, currency risk management does not increase the expected cash flows of the firm. Currency risk management normally consumes some of a firm's

---

EXHIBIT 11.2 Impact of Hedging on the Expected Cash Flows of the Firm

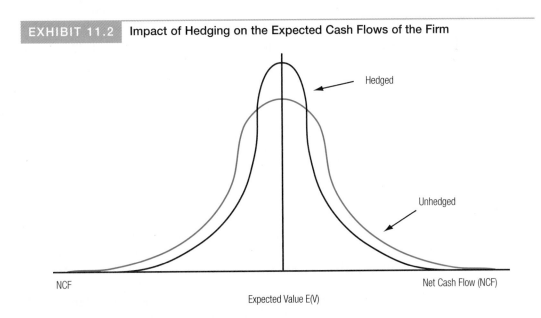

Hedging reduces the variability of expected cash flows about the mean of the distribution.
This reduction of distribution variance is a reduction of risk.

resources and so reduces cash flow. The impact on value is a combination of the reduction of cash flow (which by itself lowers value) and the reduction in variance (which by itself increases value).

3. Management often conducts hedging activities that benefit management at the expense of the shareholders. The field of finance called *agency theory* frequently argues that management is generally more risk-averse than shareholders. If the firm's goal is to maximize shareholder wealth, hedging is probably not in the best interest of the shareholders.

4. Managers cannot outguess the market. If and when markets are in equilibrium with respect to parity conditions, the expected net present value of the hedging is zero.

5. Management's motivation to reduce variability is sometimes driven by accounting reasons. Management may believe that it will be criticized more severely for incurring foreign exchange losses in its financial statements than for incurring similar or even higher cash costs in avoiding the foreign exchange loss. Foreign exchange losses appear in the income statement as a highly visible separate line item or as a footnote, but the higher costs of protection are buried in operating or interest expenses.

6. Efficient-market theorists believe that investors can see through the "accounting veil" and therefore have already factored the foreign exchange effect into a firm's market valuation.

Reasons to Hedge

Proponents of hedging cite the following reasons for supporting it:

- Reduction in risk in future cash flows improves the planning capability of the firm. If the firm can predict future cash flows more accurately, it may be able to undertake specific investments or activities that it might otherwise not consider.

- Reduction of risk in future cash flows reduces the likelihood that the firm's cash flows will fall below a necessary minimum. A firm must generate sufficient cash flows to make debt-service payments in order for it to continue to operate. This minimum cash flow point, often referred to as the point of *financial distress,* lies left of the center of the distribution of expected cash flows. Hedging reduces the likelihood of the firm's cash flows falling to this level.

- Management has a comparative advantage over the individual shareholder in knowing the actual currency risk of the firm. Regardless of the level of disclosure provided by the firm to the public, management always possesses an advantage in the depth and breadth of knowledge concerning the real risks and returns inherent in any firm's business.

- Markets are usually in disequilibrium because of structural and institutional imperfections, as well as unexpected external shocks (such as an oil crisis or terrorist attack). Management is in a better position than shareholders to recognize disequilibrium conditions and to take advantage of one-time opportunities to enhance firm value through *selective hedging.* "Selective hedging" refers to the hedging of large, singular, exceptional exposures or the occasional use of hedging when management has a definite expectation of the direction of exchange rates.

Measurement of Transaction Exposure

Transaction exposure measures gains or losses that arise from the settlement of existing financial obligations whose terms are stated in a foreign currency. Transaction exposure arises from the following:

- Purchasing or selling on credit goods or services when prices are stated in foreign currencies
- Borrowing or lending funds when repayment is to be made in a foreign currency
- Being a party to an unperformed foreign exchange forward contract
- Otherwise acquiring assets or incurring liabilities denominated in foreign currencies

The most common example of transaction exposure arises when a firm has a receivable or payable denominated in a foreign currency. As illustrated in Exhibit 11.3, the total transaction exposure consists of *quotation, backlog,* and *billing exposures.* A transaction exposure is actually created at the first moment the seller quotes a price in foreign currency terms to a potential buyer (t_1). The quote can be verbal, as in a telephone quote, or written, as in a bid or a printed price list. The placing of an order (t_2) converts the potential exposure created at the time of the quotation (t_1) into actual exposure, called backlog exposure because the product has not yet been shipped or billed. Backlog exposure lasts until the goods are shipped and billed (t_3), at which time it becomes billing exposure. Billing exposure remains until the seller receives payment (t_4).

Purchasing or Selling on Open Account

Suppose that Trident Corporation sells merchandise on open account to a Belgian buyer for €1,800,000, payment to be made in 60 days. The current exchange rate is $1.2000/€, and Trident expects to exchange the euros received for €1,800,000 × $1.2000/€ = $2,160,000 when payment is received.

EXHIBIT 11.3   The Life Span of a Transaction Exposure

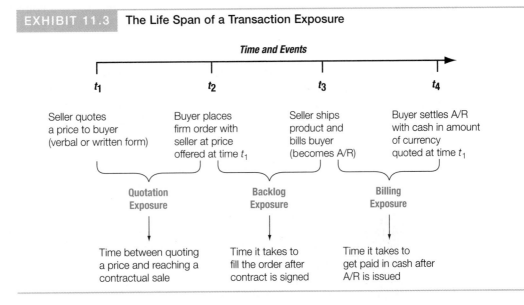

Transaction exposure arises because of the risk that Trident will receive something other than the $2,160,000 expected. For example, if the euro weakens to $1.1000/€ when payment is received, Trident will receive only €1,800,000 × $1.1000/€ = $1,980,000, or some $180,000 less than expected. If the euro should strengthen to $1.3000/€, however, Trident receives €1,800,000 × $1.3000/€ = $2,340,000, an increase of $180,000 over the amount expected. Thus, exposure is the chance of either a loss or a gain.

Trident might have avoided transaction exposure by invoicing the Belgian buyer in dollars. Of course, if Trident attempted to sell only in dollars it might not have obtained the sale in the first place. Avoiding transaction exposure by not having a sale is counterproductive to the well-being of the firm! Even if the Belgian buyer agrees to pay in dollars, transaction exposure is not eliminated. Instead, it is transferred to the Belgian buyer, whose dollar account payable has an unknown cost in euros 60 days hence.

Borrowing and Lending

A second example of transaction exposure arises when funds are borrowed or loaned, and the amount involved is denominated in a foreign currency. For example, PepsiCo's largest bottler outside of the United States in 1994 was Grupo Embotellador de Mexico (Gemex). In mid-December 1994, Gemex had U.S. dollar debt of $264 million. At that time, Mexico's new peso (Ps) was traded at Ps3.45/US$, a pegged rate that had been maintained with minor variations since January 1, 1993, when the new currency unit was created. On December 22, 1994, the new peso was allowed to float because of economic and political events within Mexico, and in one day it sank to Ps4.65/US$. For most of the following January it traded in a range near Ps5.50/US$.

For Gemex, the increase in the peso amount of its dollar debt was as follows:

Dollar debt in mid-December 1994: US$264,000,000 × Ps3.45/US$ =	Ps910,800,000
Dollar debt in mid-January 1995: US$264,000,000 × Ps5.50/US$ =	Ps1,452,000,000
Dollar debt increase measured in new Mexican pesos	Ps541,200,000

The number of pesos needed to repay the dollar debt increased by 59%! In U.S. dollar terms, the drop in the value of the pesos caused Gemex to need the peso-equivalent of an additional US$98,400,000 to repay. This increase in debt was the result of transaction exposure.

Other Causes of Transaction Exposure

When a firm buys a forward exchange contract, it deliberately creates a transaction exposure. This risk is usually incurred to hedge an existing transaction exposure. For example, a U.S. firm might want to offset an existing obligation to purchase ¥100 million to pay for an import from Japan in 90 days. One way to offset this payment is to purchase ¥100 million in the forward market today for delivery in 90 days. In this manner the firm neutralizes any change in value of the Japanese yen relative to the dollar. If the yen increases in value, an unhedged account payable would cost more dollars, a transaction loss. The forward contract, however, has already fixed the amount of dollars needed to buy the ¥100 million. Thus, the potential transaction loss (or gain) on the account payable has been offset by the transaction gain (or loss) on the forward contract.

Note that foreign currency cash balances do not create transaction exposure, even though their home-currency value changes immediately with a change in exchange rates. No legal obligation exists to move the cash from one country and currency to another. If such an obligation did exist, it would show on the books as a payable (for example, dividends declared and payable) or receivable and then be counted as part of transaction exposure. Nevertheless, the foreign exchange value of cash balances does change when exchange rates change. Such a change is reflected in the consolidated statement of cash flows and the consolidated balance sheet, as we will discuss in Chapter 12.

Contractual Hedges

Foreign exchange transaction exposure can be managed by *contractual, operating,* and *financial hedges.* The main contractual hedges employ the forward, money, futures, and options markets. Operating and financial hedges use risk-sharing agreements, leads and lags in payment terms, swaps, and other strategies to be discussed in later chapters.

The term *natural hedge* refers to an offsetting operating cash flow, a payable arising from the conduct of business. A *financial hedge* refers to either an offsetting debt obligation (such as a loan) or some type of financial derivative such as an interest rate swap. It is important to distinguish hedges in the same way finance distinguishes cash flows—*operating* from *financing.*

The following case illustrates how contractual hedging techniques may protect against transaction exposure.

Trident's Transaction Exposure

Maria Gonzalez is the chief financial officer of Trident. She has just concluded negotiations for the sale of telecommunications equipment to Regency, a British firm, for £1,000,000. This single sale is quite large in relation to Trident's present business. The sale is made in March with payment due three months later in June. Maria has collected the following financial and market information for the analysis of her currency exposure problem:

- Spot exchange rate: $1.7640/£
- Three-month forward rate: $1.7540/£ (a 2.2676% per annum discount on the pound)
- Trident's cost of capital: 12.0%
- U.K. three-month borrowing interest rate: 10.0% (or 2.5%/quarter)
- U.K. three-month investment interest rate: 8.0% (or 2.0%/quarter)
- U.S. three-month borrowing interest rate: 8.0% (or 2.0%/quarter)
- U.S. three-month investment interest rate: 6.0% (or 1.5%/quarter)
- June put option in the over-the-counter (bank) market for £1,000,000; strike price $1.75 (nearly at-the-money); 1.5% premium
- Trident's foreign exchange advisory service forecasts that the spot rate in three months will be $1.76/£.

Like many manufacturing firms, Trident operates on relatively narrow margins. Although Maria and Trident would be very happy if the pound appreciated versus the dollar, concerns center on the possibility that the pound will fall. When Maria budgeted this specific contract, she determined that its minimum acceptable margin was at a sales price of $1,700,000. The *budget rate,* the lowest acceptable dollar per pound exchange rate, was therefore established at $1.70/£. Any exchange rate below this budget rate would result in Trident actually losing money on the transaction.

The following four options are available to Trident to manage the exposure:

1. Remain unhedged
2. Hedge in the forward market
3. Hedge in the money market
4. Hedge in the options market

Unhedged Position

Maria may decide to accept the transaction risk. If she believes the foreign exchange adviser, she expects to receive £1,000,000 × $1.76 = $1,760,000 in three months. However, that amount is at risk. If the pound should fall to, say, $1.65/£, she will receive only $1,650,000. Exchange risk is not one-sided, however; if the transaction is left uncovered and the pound strengthened even more than forecast by the adviser, Trident will receive considerably more than $1,760,000.

The essence of an unhedged approach is as follows:

(Today)   (Three months hence)

Do nothing.   Receive £1,000,000.
                                                 Sell £1,000,000 spot and receive
                                                 dollars at that day's spot rate.

Forward Market Hedge

A "forward hedge" involves a forward (or futures) contract and a source of funds to fulfill that contract. The forward contract is entered into at the time the transaction exposure is created. In Trident's case, that would be in March, when the sale to Regency was booked as an account receivable.

When a foreign currency-denominated sale such as this is made, it is booked at the spot rate of exchange existing on the booking date. In the case of Trident, the spot rate on the day it is booked as an account receivable is $1.7640/£, so the sale is recorded on Trident's books as a sale of $1,764,000. Funds to fulfill the contract will be available in June, when Regency pays £1,000,000 to Trident. If funds to fulfill the forward contract are on hand or are due because of a business operation, the hedge is considered *covered*, *perfect*, or *square* because no residual foreign exchange risk exists. Funds on hand or to be received are matched by funds to be paid.

In some situations, funds to fulfill the forward exchange contract are not already available or due to be received later, but must be purchased in the spot market at some future date. Such a hedge is *open* or *uncovered*. It involves considerable risk because the hedger must take a chance on purchasing foreign exchange at an uncertain future spot rate in order to fulfill the forward contract. Purchase of such funds at a later date is referred to as "covering."

Should Trident wish to hedge its transaction exposure in the forward market, it will sell £1,000,000 forward today at the three-month forward quotation of $1.7540 per pound. This is a covered transaction in which the firm no longer has any foreign exchange risk. In three months the firm will receive £1,000,000 from the British buyer, deliver that sum to the bank against its forward sale, and receive $1,754,000. This certain sum is $6,000 less than the uncertain $1,760,000 expected from the unhedged position because the forward market quotation differs from the firm's three-month forecast. This would then be recorded on Trident's books as a foreign exchange loss of $10,000 ($1,764,000 as booked, $1,754,000 as settled).

The essence of a forward hedge is as follows:

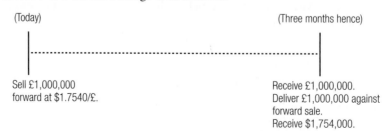

(Today)   (Three months hence)

Sell £1,000,000   Receive £1,000,000.
forward at $1.7540/£.   Deliver £1,000,000 against
                                                 forward sale.
                                                 Receive $1,754,000.

If Maria's forecast of future rates were identical to that implicit in the forward quotation, that is, $1.7540, expected receipts would be the same whether or not the firm hedges. However, realized receipts under the unhedged alternative could vary considerably from the certain receipts when the transaction is hedged. Believing that the forward rate is an unbiased estimate of the future spot rate does not prevent us from using the forward hedge to eliminate the risk of an unexpected change in the future spot rate.

Money Market Hedge

Like a forward market hedge, a money market hedge also includes a contract and a source of funds to fulfill that contract. In this instance the contract is a loan agreement. The firm seeking the money market hedge borrows in one currency and exchanges the proceeds for another currency. Funds to fulfill the contract—that is, to repay the loan—may be generated from business operations, in which case the money market hedge is covered. Alternatively, funds to repay the loan may be purchased in the foreign exchange spot market when the loan matures. In this instance, the money market hedge is uncovered or open.

A money market hedge can cover a single transaction, such as Trident's £1,000,000 receivable, or repeated transactions. Hedging repeated transactions is called *matching*. It requires the firm to match the expected foreign currency cash inflows and outflows by currency and maturity. For example, if Trident had numerous sales denominated in pounds to British customers over a long period of time, it would have somewhat predictable U.K. pound cash inflows. The appropriate money market hedge technique would be to borrow U.K. pounds in an amount matching the typical size and maturity of expected pound inflows. Then, if the pound depreciated or appreciated, the foreign exchange effect on cash inflows in pounds would be approximately offset by the effect on cash outflows in pounds from repaying the pound loan plus interest.

The structure of a money market hedge resembles that of a forward hedge. The difference is that the cost of the money market hedge is determined by differential interest rates, while the cost of the forward hedge is a function of the forward rate quotation. In efficient markets, interest rate parity should ensure that these costs are nearly the same, but not all markets are efficient at all times. Furthermore, the difference in interest rates facing a private firm borrowing in two separate national markets may not be the same as the difference in risk-free government bill rates or Eurocurrency interest rates in these same markets. It is the latter differential that is relevant for interest rate parity.

To hedge in the money market, Maria will borrow pounds in London at once, immediately convert the borrowed pounds into dollars, and repay the pound loan in three months with the proceeds from the sale. How much should she borrow? She will need to borrow just enough to repay both the principal and interest with the sale proceeds. The borrowing interest rate will be 10% per annum, or 2.5% for three months. Therefore, the amount to borrow now for repayment in three months is

$$\frac{£1,000,000}{1+.025} = £975,610$$

Maria should borrow £975,610 now and in three months repay that amount plus £24,390 of interest from the sale proceeds of the account receivable. Trident would exchange the £975,610 loan proceeds for dollars at the current spot exchange rate of $1.7640/£, receiving $1,720,976 at once.

The money market hedge, if selected by Trident, actually creates a pound-denominated liability, that is, a pound bank loan, to offset the pound-denominated asset, the account receivable. The money market hedge works as a hedge by matching assets and liabilities according to their currency of denomination. Using a simple T-account to illustrate Trident's balance sheet, we see that the loan (principal and interest payable) in British pounds offsets the pound-denominated account receivable:

Assets		Liabilities and Net Worth	
Account receivable	£1,000,000	Bank loan (principal)	£975,610
		Interest payable	24,390
	£1,000,000		£1,000,000

The loan acts as a *balance sheet hedge*—a money market hedge in this case—against the pound-denominated account receivable.

To compare the forward hedge with the money market hedge we must analyze how Trident's loan proceeds will be utilized for the next three months. Remember that the loan proceeds are received today but the forward contract proceeds are received in three months. For comparison purposes, we must calculate either the future value in three months of the loan proceeds or the present value of the forward contract proceeds. (We will use future value for pedagogical reasons, but the correct use of present value would give the same comparative results.)

Because both the forward contract proceeds and the loan proceeds are relatively certain, it is possible to choose from the two alternatives the one that yields the higher dollar receipts. This result, in turn, depends on the assumed rate of investment of the loan proceeds.

At least three logical choices exist for an assumed investment rate for the loan proceeds for the next three months. First, if Trident is cash rich, the loan proceeds might be invested in U.S. dollar money market instruments that have been assumed to yield 6% per annum. Second, Maria might simply use the pound loan proceeds to substitute for an equal dollar loan that Trident would otherwise have undertaken at an assumed rate of 8% per annum. Third, Maria might invest the loan proceeds in the general operations of the firm, in which case the cost of capital of 12% per annum would be the appropriate rate. The future value of the loan proceeds at the end of three months under each of these three investment assumptions would be as follows:

Received Today	Invested In	Rate	Future Value in Three Months
$1,720,976	Treasury bill	6%/yr or 1.5%/quarter	$1,746,791
$1,720,976	Debt cost	8%/yr or 2.0%/quarter	$1,755,396
$1,720,976	Cost of capital	12%/yr or 3.0%/quarter	$1,772,605

Because the proceeds in three months from the forward hedge would be $1,754,000, the money market hedge is superior to the forward hedge if Maria used the loan proceeds to replace a dollar loan (8%) or to conduct general business operations (12%). The forward hedge would be preferable if Trident merely invested the pound loan proceeds in dollar-denominated money market instruments at 6% annual interest.

A break-even investment rate can be calculated that would make Trident indifferent between the forward hedge and the money market hedge. Assume that r is the unknown three-month investment rate—expressed as a decimal—that would equalize the proceeds from the forward and money market hedges. We have

$$(\text{Loan proceeds})\,(1 + \text{rate}) = (\text{forward proceeds})$$
$$\$1{,}720{,}976(1 + r) = \$1{,}754{,}000$$
$$r = 0.0192$$

We can convert this three-month (90-day) investment rate to an annual whole percentage equivalent, assuming a 360-day financial year, as follows:

$$0.0192 \times \frac{360}{90} \times 100 = 7.68\%$$

In other words, if Maria can invest the loan proceeds at a rate higher than 7.68% per annum, she would prefer the money market hedge. If she can only invest at a rate lower than 7.68%, she would prefer the forward hedge.

The essence of the money market hedge is as follows:

(Today)   (Three months hence)

Borrow £975,610.   Receive £1,000,000.
Exchange £975,610 for   Repay £975,610 loan plus £24,390
dollars at $1.7640/£.   interest, for a total of £1,000,000.
Receive $1,720,976 cash.

The money market hedge results in cash received up front (at the start of the period), which can then be carried forward in time for comparison with the other hedging alternatives.

Exhibit 11.4 shows the value of Trident's £1,000,000 account receivable over a range of possible ending spot exchange rates. The value of the receivable is shown uncovered, covered with a forward contract hedge, and covered with a money market hedge. Exhibit 11.4 makes it clear that the firm's view of likely exchange rate changes aids in the hedging choice. If the firm expects the exchange rate to move against Trident—to the left of $1.76/£—the money market hedge is the clearly preferred alternative. At a guaranteed value of $1,772,605, the money market hedge is by far the most profitable choice. If Trident expects the exchange rate

EXHIBIT 11.4   Valuation of Cash Flows by Hedging Alternative for Trident

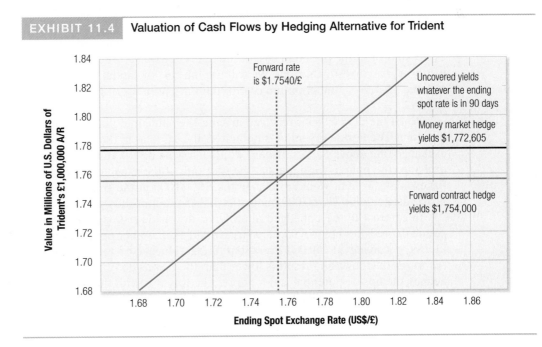

to move in Trident's favor, to the right of $1.76/£, the choice of the hedge is more complex. Consider the following points:

- If the spot rate is expected to move to the right of $1.77/£, the unhedged alternative always provides the highest U.S. dollar value for the receivable.

- If Maria is worried that her expectations may prove incorrect, the decision to remain unhedged does not assure Trident of meeting its budgeted exchange rate of $1.70/£. This is an outcome the firm cannot afford. The possibility always exists of a major political or economic event disrupting international currency markets unexpectedly.

- If the spot rate is expected to move to the right of $1.77/£, but not far to the right, for example to $1.78/£, the expected benefits of remaining unhedged are probably outweighed by the risks of remaining unhedged. The money market hedge is still the preferred choice.

Exhibit 11.4 also helps Maria focus on exactly what she wishes she could achieve: a position that provides her protection on the downside (to the left of $1.76/£), but still allows her to benefit on the upside (to the right of $1.76/£). This is the basic advantage of an option hedge.

Options Market Hedge

Maria could also cover her £1,000,000 exposure by purchasing a put option. This technique allows her to speculate on the upside potential for appreciation of the pound while limiting downside risk to a known amount.

Given the earlier quote, Maria could purchase from her bank a three-month put option on £1,000,000 at an at-the-money (ATM) strike price of $1.75/£ and a premium cost of 1.50%. The cost of this option with a strike price of $1.75, a strike price that would be considered close to forward-at-the-money, is

$$\text{(Size of option)} \times \text{(premium)} \times \text{(spot rate)} = \text{cost of option}$$
$$£1,000,000 \times 0.015 \times \$1,7640 = \$26,460$$

Because we are using future value to compare the various hedging alternatives, it is necessary to project the premium cost of the option forward three months. Once again we could justify several investment rates. We will use the cost of capital of 12% per annum or 3% per quarter. Therefore, the premium cost of the put option as of June would be $26,460(1.03) = $27,254.

When the £1,000,000 is received in June, the value in dollars depends on the spot rate at that time. The upside potential is unlimited, the same as in the unhedged alternative. At any exchange rate above $1.75/£ Trident would allow its option to expire unexercised and would exchange the pounds for dollars at the spot rate. If the expected rate of $1.76/£ materializes, for example, Trident would exchange the £1,000,000 in the spot market for $1,760,000. Net proceeds would be $1,760,000 minus the $27,254 cost of the option, or $1,732,746.

In contrast to the unhedged alternative, downside risk is limited with an option. If the pound depreciates below $1.75/£, Maria would exercise her option to sell (put) £1,000,000 at $1.75/£, receiving $1,750,000 gross, but $1,722,746 net of the $27,254 cost of the option. Although this downside result is lower than the downside of the forward or money market hedges, the upside potential is not limited the way it is with those hedges. Thus, whether the option strategy is superior to a forward or money market hedge depends on the degree to which management is risk averse.

The essence of the at-the-money (ATM) option market hedge is as follows:

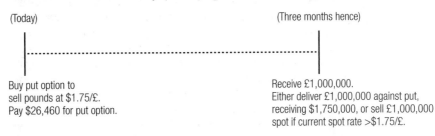

(Today)   (Three months hence)

Buy put option to
sell pounds at $1.75/£.
Pay $26,460 for put option.

Receive £1,000,000.
Either deliver £1,000,000 against put,
receiving $1,750,000, or sell £1,000,000
spot if current spot rate >$1.75/£.

We can calculate a trading range for the pound that defines the break-even points for the option compared with the other strategies. The upper bound of the range is determined by comparison with the forward rate. The pound must appreciate enough above the $1.7540/£ forward rate to cover the $0.0273/£ cost of the option. Therefore, the break-even upside spot price of the pound must be $1.7540 + $0.0273 = $1.7813. If the spot pound appreciates above $1.7813/£, proceeds under the option strategy will be greater than under the forward hedge. If the spot pound ends up below $1.7813/£, the forward hedge would be superior in retrospect.

The lower bound of the range is determined by a comparison with the unhedged strategy. If the spot price falls below $1.75/£, Maria will exercise her put option and sell the proceeds at $1.75/£. The net proceeds per pound will be $1.75/£ less the $0.0273 cost of the option, or $1.7221/£. If the spot rate falls below $1.7221/£, the net proceeds from exercising the option will be greater than the net proceeds from selling the unhedged pounds in the spot market. At any spot rate above $1.7221/£, the spot proceeds from the unhedged alternative will be greater. These rates and values are summarized as follows:

Put Option Strike Price	ATM Option $1.75/£
Option cost (future value)	$27,254
Proceeds if exercised	$1,750,000
Minimum net proceeds	$1,722,746
Maximum net proceeds	Unlimited
Break-even spot rate (upside)	$1.7813/£
Break-even spot rate (downside)	$1.7221/£

Comparison of Alternatives

The four alternatives available to Maria Gonzalez and Trident are shown in Exhibit 11.5. The forward hedge yields a certain $1,754,000 in three months. The money market hedge, if the loan proceeds are invested at the 12% cost of capital, yields $1,772,605, preferable to the forward market hedge.

If Maria does not hedge, she can expect $1,760,000 in three months (calculated at the expected spot rate of $1.76/£). However, this sum is at risk and might be greater or smaller. Under conditions when the forward rate is accepted as the most likely future spot rate, the expected results from an unhedged position are identical to the certain results from the forward hedge. Under such circumstances the advantage of hedging over remaining unhedged is the reduction of uncertainty.

The put option offers a unique alternative. If the exchange rate moves in Trident's favor, the option offers nearly the same upside potential as the unhedged alternative except for the upfront costs. If, however, the exchange rate moves against Trident, the put option limits the downside risk to net receipts of $1,722,746.

EXHIBIT 11.5   Trident's Hedging Alternatives, Including an ATM Put Option

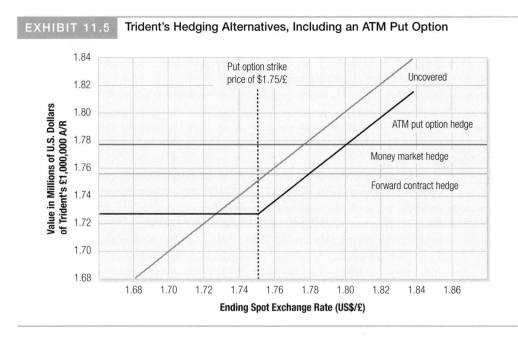

Foreign currency options have a variety of hedging uses beyond the one illustrated here. A put option is useful to construction firms or other exporters when they must submit a fixed-price bid in a foreign currency without knowing until some later date whether their bid is successful. A put option can be used to hedge the foreign exchange risk either for the bidding period alone or for the entire period of potential exposure if the bid is won. If the bid is rejected, the loss is limited to the cost of the option. In contrast, if the risk is hedged by a forward contract and the bid is rejected, the forward contract must be reversed or eventually fulfilled at an unknown potential loss or gain. The bidder has been holding what turned out to be an uncovered forward contract.

Strategy Choice and Outcome

The preceding section compared hedging alternatives available to Trident. Trident, like all firms attempting to hedge transaction exposure, must decide on a strategy before the exchange rate changes occur. How will Maria Gonzalez of Trident choose among the alternative hedging strategies? She must select on the basis of two decision criteria: 1) the *risk tolerance* of Trident, as expressed in its stated policies and 2) her own *view* or expectation of the direction (and distance) the exchange rate will move over the coming 90-day period.

Trident's risk tolerance is a combination of management's philosophy toward transaction exposure and the specific goals of treasury activities. Many firms believe that currency risk is simply a part of doing business internationally, and therefore start their analysis from an unhedged baseline. Other firms, however, view currency risk as unacceptable. They either start their analysis from a full forward contract cover baseline or simply mandate that all transaction exposures be fully covered by forward contracts regardless of the value of other hedging alternatives. The treasury in such firms operates as a cost or service center for the firm. On the other hand, if the treasury in a firm operates as a profit center, it might tolerate more risk.

The final choice among hedges—if Maria Gonzalez does expect the pound to appreciate—combines the firm's risk tolerance, Maria's view, and Maria's confidence in her view. Transaction exposure management with contractual hedges requires managerial judgment.

Management of an Account Payable

The Trident case as we've discussed it so far assumes a foreign currency-denominated receivable. The management of an account payable, where the firm is required to make a foreign currency payment at a future date, is similar but not identical in form.

If Trident had a £1,000,000 account payable in 90 days, the hedging choices would appear as follows:

1. **Remain Unhedged.** Trident could wait 90 days, exchange dollars for pounds at that time, and make its payment. If Trident expects the spot rate in 90 days to be $1.76/£, the payment would be expected to cost $1,760,000. This amount is, however, uncertain; the spot exchange rate in 90 days could be very different from that expected.

2. **Use Forward Market Hedge.** Trident could buy £1,000,000 forward, locking in a rate of $1.7540/£ and a total dollar cost of $1,754,000. This is $6,000 less than the expected cost of remaining unhedged, and it is less risky. Therefore, it might be deemed preferable.

3. **Use Money Market Hedge.** The money market hedge is distinctly different for a payable as opposed to a receivable. To implement a money market hedge in this case, Trident would exchange U.S. dollars spot and invest them for 90 days in a pound-denominated interest-bearing account. It would then use the principal and interest in British pounds at the end of the 90-day period to pay the £1,000,000 account payable.

   In order to ensure that the principal and interest exactly equal the £1,000,000 due in 90 days, Trident would discount the £1,000,000 by the pound investment interest rate of 8% per annum for 90 days (2%) in order to determine the pounds needed today:

$$\frac{£1,000,000}{\left[1+\left(.08 \times \frac{90}{360}\right)\right]} = £980,392.16$$

   This £980,392.16 needed today would require $1,729,411.77 at the current spot rate of $1.7640/£:

$$£980,392.16 \times \$1,7640/£ = \$1,729,411.77$$

   Finally, in order to compare the money market hedge outcome with the other hedging alternatives, the $1,729,411.77 cost today must be carried forward 90 days to the same future date as the other hedge choices. If the current dollar cost is carried forward at Trident's weighted average cost of capital (WACC) of 12%, the total future value cost of the money market hedge is

$$\$1,792,411.77 \times \left[1+\left(.12 \times \frac{90}{360}\right)\right] = \$1,781,294.12$$

   This is higher than the forward hedge and therefore unattractive.

4. **Use Option Hedge.** Trident could cover its £1,000,000 account payable by purchasing a call option on £1,000,000. A June call option on British pounds with a near at-the-money strike price of $1.75/£ would cost 1.5% (premium) or

$$£1,000,000 \times 0.015 \times \$1,7640/£ = £26,460$$

This premium, regardless of whether the call option is exercised or not, will be paid up front. Its value carried forward 90 days at the WACC of 12%, as it was in the receivable example, would raise its end-of-period cost to $27,254.

If the spot rate in 90 days is less than $1.75/£, the option would be allowed to expire and the £1,000,000 for the payable would be purchased on the spot market. The total cost of the call option hedge if the option is not exercised is theoretically smaller than any other alternative (with the exception of remaining unhedged), because the option premium is still paid and lost.

If the spot rate in 90 days exceeds $1.75/£, the call option would be exercised. The total cost of the call option hedge if exercised is as follows:

Exercise call option (£1,000,000 × $1.75/£)	$1,750,000
Call option premium (carried forward 90 days)	27,254
Total maximum expense of call option hedge	$1,777,254

The four hedging methods of managing a £1,000,000 account payable for Trident are summarized in Exhibit 11.6. The costs of the forward hedge and money market hedge are certain. The cost of using the call option hedge is calculated as a maximum, and the cost of remaining unhedged is highly uncertain.

As with Trident's account receivable, the final hedging choice depends on the confidence of Maria's exchange rate expectations and her willingness to bear risk. The forward hedge provides the lowest cost of making the account payable payment that is certain. If the dollar strengthens against the pound, ending up at a spot rate less than $1.75/£, the call option could potentially be the lowest cost hedge. Given an expected spot rate of $1.76/£, however, the forward hedge appears to be the preferred alternative.

EXHIBIT 11.6   Valuation of Hedging Alternatives for an Account Payable

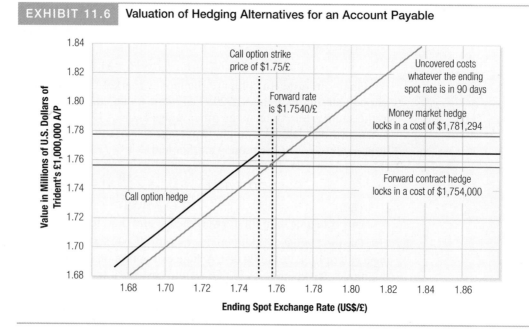

Risk Management in Practice

As many different approaches to exposure management exist as there are firms. A variety of surveys of corporate risk management practices in recent years in the United States, the United Kingdom, Finland, Australia, and Germany indicate no real consensus exists regarding the best approach. The following is our attempt to assimilate the basic results of these surveys and combine them with our personal experiences in industry.

Which Goals?

The treasury function of most firms, the functional group typically responsible for transaction exposure management, is usually considered a cost center. It is not expected to add profit to the firm's bottom line (which is not the same thing as saying it is not expected to add value to the firm). Currency risk managers are expected to err on the conservative side when managing the firm's money.

Which Exposures?

Transaction exposures exist before they are actually booked as foreign currency-denominated receivables and payables. However, many firms do not allow the hedging of quotation exposure or backlog exposure as a matter of policy. The reasoning is straightforward: Until the transaction exists on the accounting books of the firm, the probability of the exposure actually occurring is considered to be less than 100%. Conservative hedging policies dictate that contractual hedges be placed only on existing exposures.

An increasing number of firms, however, are not only actively hedging backlog exposures but also selectively hedging both quotation and anticipated exposures. Anticipated exposures are transactions for which there are—at present—no contracts or agreements between parties, but such contracts are anticipated on the basis of historical trends and continuing business relationships. Although on the surface hedging anticipated exposures would appear to be overly speculative behavior on the part of these firms, it may be that hedging expected foreign-currency payables and receivables for future periods is the most conservative approach to protect the firm's future operating revenues against unexpected exchange rate changes.

Which Contractual Hedges?

As might be expected, transaction exposure management programs are generally divided along an option line: those that use options and those that do not. Firms that do not use currency options rely almost exclusively on forward contracts and money market hedges. A few firms with appreciable quantities of transaction exposure actually do no hedging at all. And as described in *Global Finance in Practice 11.2*, options can be expensive.

Proportional Hedges. Many MNEs have established rather rigid transaction exposure risk management policies that mandate proportional hedging. These policies generally require the use of forward contract hedges on a percentage (for instance, 50%, 60%, or 70%) of existing transaction exposures. As the maturity of the exposures lengthens, the percentage of forward cover required decreases. The remaining portion of the exposure is then selectively hedged on the basis of the firm's risk tolerance, view of exchange rate movements, and confidence level.

Although rarely acknowledged by the firms themselves, the continual use of selective hedging programs is essentially speculation against the currency markets. Significant theoretical questions remain as to whether a firm or a financial manager can consistently predict

The Credit Crisis and Option Volatilities in 2009

The global credit crisis had a number of lasting impacts on corporate foreign exchange hedging practices in late 2008 and early 2009. Currency volatilities rose to some of the highest levels seen in years, and stayed there. This caused option premiums to rise so dramatically that many companies were much more selective in their use of currency options in their risk management programs.

The dollar-euro volatility was a prime example. As recently as July 2007, the implied volatility for the most widely traded currency cross was below 7% for maturities from one week to three years. By October 31, 2008, the one-month

implied volatility had reached 29%. Although this was seemingly the peak, one month implied volatilities were still over 20% on January 30, 2009.

This makes options very expensive. For example, the premium on a one month call option on the euro with a strike rate forward-at-the-money at the end of January 2009 rose from $0.0096/€ to $0.0286/€ when volatility is 20%, not 7%. For a notional principal of €1 million, that is an increase in price from $9,580 to $28,640. That will put a hole in any treasury department's budget.

the future direction of exchange rate movements. Gunter Dufey (the University of Michigan) once noted, "it may occasionally be possible to find money lying in the street, but I would not expect to make a living at it."

SUMMARY POINTS

- MNEs encounter three types of currency exposure: 1) transaction exposure, 2) operating exposure, and 3) translation exposure.

- *Transaction exposure* measures gains or losses that arise from the settlement of financial obligations whose terms are stated in a foreign currency.

- *Operating exposure*, also called *economic exposure*, measures the change in the present value of the firm resulting from any change in future operating cash flows of the firm caused by an unexpected change in exchange rates.

- *Translation exposure* is the possibility that accounting-derived changes in owner's equity will occur because of the need to "translate" foreign currency financial statements of foreign subsidiaries into a single reporting currency to prepare worldwide consolidated financial statements.

- Transaction exposure arises from 1) purchasing or selling on credit goods or services whose prices are stated in foreign currencies; 2) borrowing or lending funds when repayment is to be made in a foreign currency; 3) being a party to an unperformed forward foreign exchange contract; and 4) otherwise acquiring assets or liabilities denominated in foreign currencies.

- Considerable theoretical debate exists as to whether firms should hedge currency risk. Theoretically, hedging reduces the variability of the cash flows to the firm.

- It does not increase the cash flows to the firm. In fact, the costs of hedging may potentially lower cash flows.

- Transaction exposure can be managed by contractual techniques that include forward, futures, money market, and option hedges.

- The choice of which contractual hedge to use depends on the individual firm's currency risk tolerance and its expectation of the probable movement of exchange rates over the transaction exposure period.

- In general, if an exchange rate is expected to move in a firm's favor, the preferred contractual hedges are probably those that allow it to participate in some upside potential (remaining unhedged or using a currency option), but protect it against significant adverse exchange rate movements.

- In general, if the exchange rate is expected to move against the firm, the preferred contractual hedge is one that locks in an exchange rate, such as the forward contract hedge or money market hedge.

- Risk management in practice requires a firm's treasury department to identify its goals. Is treasury a cost center or profit center?

- Treasury must also choose which contractual hedges to use and what proportion of the currency risk should be hedged. Additionally, treasury must determine whether the firm should buy and/or sell currency options, a historically risky strategy for some firms and banks.

MINI-CASE   Xian-Janssen Pharmaceutical (China) and the Euro

It was December 2003, and Paul Young, the financial controller of Xian-Janssen Pharmaceutical Ltd (XJP), was preparing for a meeting with the CEO of the company, Christian Velmer, to discuss the 2004 business plan. XJP was Johnson & Johnson's (J&J) joint venture entry into the Chinese market. XJP was one of J&J's largest single operating companies, and was now expected to close 2003 with Rmb 1.006 billion in earnings ($121.6 million). The CEO of XJP had already passed on corporate's earnings objectives for 2004: Rmb 1.205 billion, just under a 20% increase. Although XJP had performed well in recent years, averaging 20% annual earnings growth despite many challenges including the SARS epidemic in 2003, meeting corporate's objectives this time would be difficult. Many of XJP's direct and indirect expenses had been rising, including foreign exchange losses.

Christian Velmer had been CEO of XJP only six months, and Paul Young knew that Velmer would likely accept the corporate directive on earnings. He had little choice. XJP's earnings were core to J&J, and with a number of its traditional markets slowing, the need for growth would be increasingly borne by units like XJP. The management team also knew that if the unit failed to meet its earnings objectives, in addition to management performance reviews and job security, the unit's new product development position could be threatened. Without new products, XJP could lose its number one position in the Chinese market.

XJP of China

XJP produced and marketed prescription and over-the-counter (OTC) medications. The company was the number one foreign pharmaceutical company operating in China, and had been there since 1985. The company's operations were roughly equally divided between Ethical and OTC businesses. 2003 had proven to be a very busy year, with the company successfully weathering two different price cuts, three new Ethical product introductions, not to mention closing the year with a 98% success rate on over 1,200 tender sales.[1]

The drug market in China was largely hospital-based, with over 80% of all drug sales reaching consumers

through government-run hospitals. The 20% balance of the market was then split between drugstores, small collective or work-unit clinics, and a few but growing private hospitals. The Chinese pharmaceutical market had averaged 12.5% annual growth for the past decade, and was expected to continue at close to that growth rate in the near future. Increases in income and purchasing power by large segments of the urban population, combined with a multitude of medical insurance and health care reforms, had opened the door for many Chinese to Western drugs. The problem was that these same reforms were now channeling insurance reimbursements toward generic drugs, putting more and more pressure on prices. The hospitals themselves were now regularly purchasing through the tender market, in which XJP often found itself making smaller and smaller margins.

Cost and Currency Pressures

XJP's product line covered a wide range of pharmaceutical products, most of which had been either discovered or developed by its parent company. In recent years the company had also licensed a number of third-party drugs through J&J Europe. Historically, 100% of XJP's raw material and finished product was imported from J&J Europe. In 2003, the company had initiated some local sourcing in China, but this still did not constitute more than 5% of purchased inventory. Both pricing and invoicing of XJP's core business still originated in Europe, which meant pricing and invoicing in euros. Paul had also determined in recent months that the transfer prices imposed upon XJP were relatively high compared to other intrafirm purchasers globally.

XJP purchased its materials and products from J&J Europe's Belgian treasury center. All payments would be in euros, with XJP incurring the currency risks and expenses internally. Corporate policy required that XJP hedge a minimum of 80% of its anticipated currency exposures, with hedges not to exceed 100%. Currency hedging alternatives were few. After netting whatever payments it could by law per quarter, XJP then purchased forward contracts (buy euro, sell Rmb) from its foreign currency bank in Shanghai. Chinese law restricted the pur-

---

[1] *Tender sales* were periodic auction purchases by many Chinese hospitals of generic product lines. The sales were conducted like Dutch auctions, in which the buyer rank-ordered bids by lowest price first, accumulating volume until reaching the purchase need. The price of the last incremental offer set the price for that entire auction.

EXHIBIT 1   Chinese Renminbi/Euro Spot Exchange Rate (monthly average, 1999–2003)

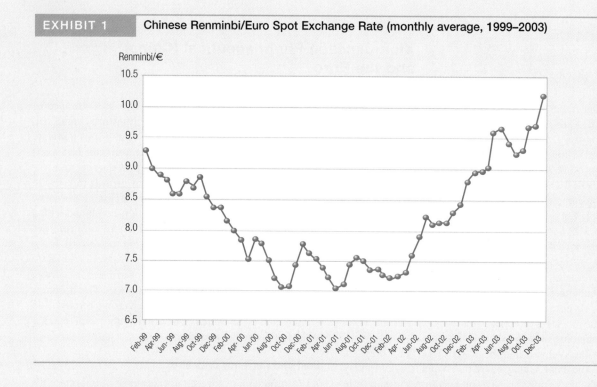

chase of forward contracts to commercial transactions only (forwards could not be purchased for investment purposes).

The Chinese renminbi (Rmb) was fixed to the U.S. dollar at Rmb8.27/$. The dramatic rise of the euro against the dollar throughout 2003 had therefore translated directly into an equally weak Rmb against the euro. Paul Young's bank advisers had recently forecast the euro to remain strong, if not gaining further strength, in 2004. The consensus forecast for the first half of 2004 was $1.30/€, or a cross rate of Rmb10.75/€, what Paul Young considered "off the chart" when he looked at Exhibit 1.

XJP's financial results for 2003 had been greatly affected by the cost of hedging. XJP had budgeted for 2003 (in December 2002) at an average expected spot exchange rate of Rmb8.60/€. But the run-up in the euro had resulted in an average 90-day forward rate for all of 2003 of Rmb9.22/€, culminating in total foreign exchange losses (differences between budgeted spot and forward rate) of Rmb75 million (see Exhibit 2). Of the total Rmb75 million, Rmb60 million would be charged against XJP's 2003 results, and Rmb 15 million would be absorbed in inventory that would be pushed into 2004. Fortunately, as illustrated in Paul Young's financial worksheets in Exhibit 2, the Chinese unit had earned Rmb70 million in one-time (extraordinary) gains on a housing fund adjustment and an inventory valuation reversal. These gains had

obviously mitigated the negative impact of the currency losses, but 2004 would most likely not be such a lucky year.

With the dollar closing on $1.30/€ in December (Rmb10.75/€), the 90-day forward rate was also moving up. Paul Young knew that he would have to use a budget rate for 2004 (forecast for the average spot exchange rate for the year) of somewhere between Rmb9.8/€ and Rmb10.0/€. But given the rough forward premium he had been forced to pay in 2003, his after-hedging effective rate could rise to Rmb10.50/€ in 2004. Paul stared at the numbers—specifically his estimate of earnings for 2004—and wondered how in the world he was going to reach corporate's earnings objectives of Rmb 1.205 billion.

Case Questions

1. How significant an impact do foreign exchange gains and losses have on corporate performance at XJP? What is your opinion of how they structure and manage their currency exposures?

2. Johnson & Johnson has roughly 200 foreign subsidiaries worldwide. It has always pursued a highly decentralized organizational structure, in which the individual units are responsible for much of their own performance from the top to the bottom line of the income statement. How is this reflected in the situation XJP finds itself?

EXHIBIT 2	Xian-Janssen Pharmaceutical (China)

Assumed growth in sales and costs: 20%

Chinese renminbi (Rmb)	2003 Actual	2004 Budget
Total sales	3,353,600,000	4,024,320,000
Gross cost of products sold	(1,040,600,000)	(1,422,960,000)
Gross margin	2,313,000,000	2,601,360,000
Selling, marketing & admin expenses	(1,263,000,000)	(1,515,600,000)
Net operating earnings	1,050,000,000	1,085,760,000
Extraordinary gains (losses)	70,000,000	—
Foreign currency gains (losses)	(60,000,000)	(75,020,000)
Net earnings	1,060,000,000	1,010,740,000
Import purchases worksheet:		
Expected import purchases (euros)	€121,000,000	€145,200,000
Budget spot exchange rate (euro/Rmb)	8.60	9.80
Expected import purchases (Rmb)	1,040,600,000	1,422,960,000
Actual average forward rate (euro/Rmb)	9.22	10.50
Actual cost of imports hedged (Rmb)	1,115,620,000	1,524,600,000
Cost of hedging (Rmb)	(75,020,000)	(101,640,000)
Cost of hedging, to current year (Rmb)	(60,000,000)	(80,000,000)
Cost of hedging, inventory (Rmb)	(15,020,000)	(21,640,000)

Note: Financial values have been fictionalized to preserve confidentiality. 2004 Budget assumes same growth rate in revenues and sales. 2004 foreign currency gains (losses) assume 80% of current year gains (losses) incurred in addition to the inventory costs from the previous year.

3. What is the relationship between actual spot exchange rate, the budgeted spot exchange rate, the forward rate, and the expectations for the Chinese subsidiary's financial results by the U.S. parent company?

4. If you were Paul Young, what would you do?

QUESTIONS

1. **Foreign Exchange Exposure.** Give a general definition of "foreign exchange exposure" as it relates to the operations of a multinational enterprise.

2. **Exposure Types.** Explain the differences among transaction, operating, and translation exposure.

3. **Translation versus Transaction Exposure.** How do translation exposures and transaction exposures alter corporate cash flow?

4. **Tax Exposure.** What is tax exposure and how does it relate to the triumvirate of transaction, operating, and translation exposure?

5. **Hedging.** What is a hedge?

6. **Cash Flow Variability.** Exhibit 11.2 shows two normal distributions about a mean called expected value.
   a. What is the implication of the areas toward the center of the distributions where the hedged line is higher than the unhedged line?
   b. What is the implication of the areas toward the outlying edges of the distributions where the unhedged line is higher than the hedged line?
   c. Can an argument be made that the mean of the hedged distribution should be to the left or right of, but not the same as, the mean of the unhedged distribution? Discuss.

7. **Investor Expectations.** Proponents of the efficient market hypothesis argue that an MNE should not hedge because investors can hedge themselves if they

do not like the foreign exchange risks carried by the firm. Assess this argument.

8. **Creating Transaction Exposure.** Identify and create a hypothetical example for each of the four causes of transaction exposure.

9. **Cash Balances.** Why does the holding of foreign currency cash balances not lead to transaction exposure?

10. **Natural versus Contractual Hedges.** Explain the difference between a natural hedge and a contractual hedge. Give a hypothetical example of each.

11. **Risk Tolerance.** What is risk tolerance? Can it be measured?

PROBLEMS

1. **Siam Cement.** Siam Cement, the Bangkok-based cement manufacturer, suffered enormous losses with the coming of the Asian crisis in 1997. The company had been pursuing a very aggressive growth strategy in the mid-1990s, taking on massive quantities of foreign currency denominated debt (primarily U.S. dollars). When the Thai baht (B) was devalued from its pegged rate of B25.0/$ in July 1997, Siam's interest payments alone were over $900 million on its outstanding dollar debt (with an average interest rate of 8.40% on its U.S. dollar debt at that time). Assuming Siam Cement took out $50 million in debt in June 1997 at 8.40% interest, and had to repay it in one year when the spot exchange rate had stabilized at B42.0/$, what was the foreign exchange loss incurred on the transaction?

2. **Hindustan Lever.** Unilever's affiliate in India, Hindustan Lever, procures much of its toiletries product line from a Japanese company. Because of the shortage of working capital in India, payment terms by Indian importers are typically 180 days or longer. Hindustan Lever wishes to hedge an 8.5 million Japanese yen payable. Although options are not available on the Indian rupee (Rs), forward rates are available against the yen. Additionally, a common practice in India is for companies like Hindustan Lever to work with a currency agent who will, in this case, lock in the current spot exchange rate in exchange for a 4.85% fee. Using the following exchange rate and interest rate data, recommend a hedging strategy.

Spot rate, yen/dollar:	¥120.60/$	180-day rupee investment rate:	8.000%
Spot rate, rupees/dollar:	Rs47.75/$	180-day yen investment rate:	1.500%
180-day forward rate, yen/rupee:	¥2.4000/Rs	Hindustan cost of capital:	12.00%
Expected spot rate in 180 days:	¥2.6000/Rs		

*3. **Seattle Scientific, Inc.** Josh Miller is chief financial officer of a medium-sized Seattle-based medical device manufacturer. The company's annual sales of $40 million have been growing rapidly, and working capital financing is a common source of concern. He has recently been approached by one of his major Japanese customers, Yokasa, with a new payment proposal. Yokasa typically orders ¥12,500,000 in product every other month and pays in Japanese yen. The current payment terms extended by Seattle are 30 days, with no discounts given for early or cash payment. Yokasa has suggested that it would be willing to pay in cash—in Japanese yen—if it were given a 4.5% discount on the purchase price. Josh Miller gathered the following quotes from his bank on current spot and forward exchange rates, and estimated Yokasa's cost of capital.

Spot rate:	¥111.40/$	Yokasa's WACC:	8.850%
30-day forward rate:	¥111.00/$	Seattle Scientific's WACC:	9.200%
90-day forward rate:	¥110.40/$		
180-day forward rate:	¥109.20/$		

How much in U.S. dollars will Seattle Scientific receive 1) with the discount and 2) with no discount but fully covered with a forward contract?

4. **Warner Indonesia.** Warner, the U.S.-based multinational pharmaceutical company, is evaluating an export sale of its cholesterol reduction drug with a prospective Indonesian distributor. The purchase would be for 1,650 million Indonesian rupiah (Rp), which at the current spot exchange rate of Rp9,450/$, translates into nearly $175,000. Although not a big sale by company standards, company policy dictates that sales must be settled for at least a minimum gross margin, in this case, a cash settlement of $168,000 on the sale. The current 90-day forward rate is

Rp9,950/$. Although this rate appeared unattractive, Warner had to contact several major banks before even finding a forward quote on the rupiah. The consensus of currency forecasters at the moment, however, is that the rupiah will hold relatively steady, possibly falling to Rp9,400 over the coming 90 to 120 days. Analyze the prospective sale and make a hedging recommendation.

5. **Embraer of Brazil.** Embraer of Brazil is one of the two leading global manufacturers of regional jets (Bombardier of Canada is the other). Regional jets are smaller than the traditional civilian airliners produced by Airbus and Boeing, seating between 50 and 100 people on average.

Embraer has concluded an agreement with a regional U.S. airline to produce and deliver four aircraft one year from now for $80 million. Although Embraer will be paid in U.S. dollars, it also possesses a currency exposure of inputs—it must pay foreign suppliers $20 million for inputs one year from now (but they will be delivering the sub-components throughout the year). The current spot rate on the Brazilian reais (R$) is R$1.8240/$, but it has been steadily appreciating against the U.S. dollar over the past three years. Forward contracts are difficult to acquire and considered expensive. Citibank Brasil has not explicitly provided Embraer a forward rate quote, but has stated that it will probably be pricing a forward off the current 4.00% U.S. dollar Eurocurrency rate and the 10.50% Brazilian government bond rate. Advise Embraer on its currency exposure.

6. **Caterpillar.** Caterpillar (U.S.) just purchased a Korean company that produces plastic nuts and bolts for heavy equipment. The purchase price was Won7,030 million. Won1,000 million has already been paid, and the remaining Won6,030 million is due in six months. The current spot rate is Won1,200/$, and the six-month forward rate is Won1,260/$. Additional data:

Six-month Korean interest rate:	16.00% p.a.
Six-month U.S. interest rate:	4.00% p.a.
Six-month call option on Korean won atW1200/$:	3.0% premium
Six-month put option on Korean won atW1200/$:	2.4% premium

Caterpillar can invest at the rates given in the preceding table, or borrow at 2% per annum above those rates. Cat's weighted average cost of capital is 10%. Compare alternate ways that Caterpillar might deal with its foreign exchange exposure. What do you recommend and why?

7. **Mattel Toys.** Mattel is a U.S.-based company whose sales are roughly two-thirds in dollars (Asia and the Americas) and one-third in euros (Europe). In September, Mattel delivers a large shipment of toys (primarily Barbies and Hot Wheels) to a major distributor in Antwerp. The receivable, €30 million, is due in 90 days, standard terms for the European toy industry. Mattel's treasury team has collected the following currency and market quotes. The company's foreign exchange advisers believe the euro will be at about $1.4200/€ in 90 days. Mattel's management does not use currency options in currency risk management activities. Advise Mattel on which hedging alternative is probably preferable.

Spot rate:	$1.4158/€	90-day eurodollar interest rate	4.000%
Credit Suisse 90-day forward quote:	$1.4172/€	90-day euro interest rate	3.885%
Barclays 90-day forward quote:	$1.4195/€	90-day dollar borrowing rate	5.000%
Mattel's capital:	9.600%	90-day euro borrowing rate	5.000%

8. **South Face.** South Face, Ltd., a Canadian manufacturer of raincoats, does not selectively hedge its transaction exposure. Instead, if the date of the transaction is known with certainty, all foreign currency-denominated cash flows must utilize the following mandatory forward contract cover formula:

	Exposure coverage required according to maturity		
If South Face Is:	**0–90 days**	**91–180 days**	**>180 days**
"paying the points forward"	75%	60%	50%
"receiving the points forward"	100%	90%	50%

South Face expects to receive multiple payments in Danish kroner over the next year. DKr 3,000,000 is due in 90 days; DKr 2,000,000 is due in 180 days; and DKr 1,000,000 is due in one year. Using the following spot and forward exchange rates, what would be the amount of forward cover required by company policy by period?

Spot rate:	DKr 4.70/C$
Three-month forward rate:	DKr 4.71/C$
Six-month forward rate:	DKr 4.72/C$
One-year forward rate:	DKr 4.74/C$

9. Translucent/H20. Translucent/H2O is a U.S.-based company that manufactures, sells, and installs water purification equipment. On April 20, the company sold a system to the City of Nagasaki, Japan, for installation in Nagasaki's famous Glover Gardens (where Puccini's Madame Butterfly waited for the return of Lt. Pinkerton). The sale was priced in yen at ¥20,000,000, with payment due in three months. On the day of the sale the *Financial Times* published the following mid-rates for the yen:

Spot exchange rate:	¥118.255/$ (closing mid-rate)
One-month forward rate:	¥117.760/$, a 5.04% p.a. premium
Three-month forward:	¥116.830/$, a 4.88% p.a. premium
One-year forward:	¥112.450/$, a 5.16% p.a. premium

Money rates (% p.a.)	United States	Japan	Differential
One month	4.8750%	0.09375%	4.78125%
Three months	4.9375 %	0.09375%	4.84375%
Twelve months	5.1875%	0.31250%	4.87500%

Note: The interest rate differentials vary slightly from the forward discounts on the yen because of time differences for the quotes. The spot ¥118.255/$, for example, is a mid-point range. On April 20, the spot yen traded in London from ¥118.30/$ to ¥117.550/$.

Additional information: Translucent/H2O's Japanese competitors are currently borrowing yen from Japanese banks at a spread of two percentage points above the Japanese money rate. Translucent/H2O's weighted average cost of capital is 16%, and the company wishes to protect the dollar value of this receivable.

Three-month options from Kyushu Bank:

- Call option on ¥20,000,000 at exercise price of ¥118.00/$: a 1% premium.
- Put option on ¥20,000,000 at exercise price of ¥118.00/$: a 3% premium.

a. What are the costs and benefits of alternative hedges? Which would you recommend, and why?

b. What is the break-even reinvestment rate when comparing forward and money market alternatives?

10. Farah Jeans. Farah Jeans of San Antonio, Texas, is completing a new assembly plant near Guatemala City. A final construction payment of Q8,400,000 is due in six months. ("Q" is the symbol for Guatemalan *quetzals*.) Farah uses 20% per annum as its weighted average cost of capital. Today's foreign exchange and interest rate quotations are as follows:

Present spot rate:	Q7.0000/$
Six-month forward rate:	Q7.1000/$
Guatemalan six-month interest rate:	14.00% per annum
U.S. dollar six-month interest rate:	6.00% per annum

Farah's treasury manager, concerned about the Guatemalan economy, wonders if Farah should be hedging its foreign exchange risk. The manager's own forecast is as follows:

Highest expected rate:	Q8.0000/$, reflecting a significant devaluation
Expected rate:	Q7.3000/$
Lowest expected rate:	Q6.4000/$, reflecting a strengthening of the quetzal

What realistic alternatives are available to Farah for making payment? Which method would you select, and why?

*11. PanAmerican Travel. PanAmerican Travel, a Honolulu, Hawaii-based 100% privately owned travel company has signed an agreement to acquire a 50% ownership share of Taipei Travel, a Taiwan-based privately owned travel agency specializing in servicing inbound customers from the United States and Canada. The acquisition price is 7 million Taiwan dollars (T$ 7,000,000) payable in cash in three months.

Susan Takaga, PanAmerican's owner, believes the Taiwan dollar will either remain stable or decline a little over the next three months. At the present spot rate of T$35/$, the amount of cash required is only $200,000 but even this relatively modest amount will need to be borrowed personally by Susan Takaga. Taiwanese interest-bearing deposits by nonresidents are regulated by the government, and are currently set at 1.5% per year. She has a credit line with Bank of Hawaii for $200,000 with a current borrowing interest rate of 8%

per year. She does not believe that she can calculate a credible weighted average cost of capital since she has no stock outstanding and her competitors are all also privately owned without disclosure of their financial results. Since the acquisition would use up all her available credit, she wonders if she should hedge this transaction exposure. She has the quotes from Bank of Hawaii shown in the table below.

Spot rate:	T$33.40/$
Three-month forward rate:	T$32.40/$
Three-month dollar borrowing rate:	6.50% per year
Three-month T$ deposit rate:	1.50% per year
Three-month call options:	not available

Analyze the costs and risks of each alternative, and then make a recommendation as to which alternative Susan Takaga should choose.

12. **Chronos Time Pieces.** Chronos Time Pieces of Boston exports watches to many countries, selling in local currencies to stores and distributors. Chronos prides itself on being financially conservative. At least 70% of each individual transaction exposure is hedged, mostly in the forward market, but occasionally with options. Chronos's foreign exchange policy is such that the 70% hedge may be increased up to a 120% hedge if devaluation or depreciation appears imminent.

Chronos has just shipped to its major North American distributor. It has issued a 90-day invoice to its buyer for €1,560,000. The current spot rate is $1.2224/€, the 90-day forward rate is $1.2270/€. Chronos's treasurer, Manny Hernandez, has a very good track record in predicting exchange rate movements. Currently he believes the euro will weaken against the dollar in the coming 90 to 120 days, possibly to around $1.16/€.

a. Evaluate the hedging alternatives for Chronos if Manny is right (Case #1: $1.16/€) and if Manny is wrong (Case #2: $1.26/€). What do you recommend?

b. What does it mean to hedge 120% of a transaction exposure?

c. What would be considered the most conservative transaction exposure management policy by a firm? How does Chronos compare?

13. **Micca Metals, Inc.** Micca Metals, Inc. is a specialty materials and metals company located in Detroit, Michigan. The company specializes in specific precious metals and materials that are used in a variety

of pigment applications in many other industries including cosmetics, appliances, and a variety of high tinsel metal fabricating equipment. Micca just purchased a shipment of phosphates from Morocco for 6,000,000 dirhams, payable in six months. Micca's cost of capital is 8.600%. The following quotes are available in the market.

	United States	Morocco
Six-month interest rate for borrowing:	6.00% p.a.	8.00% p.a.
Six-month interest rate for investing:	5.00% p.a.	7.00% p.a.
Spot exchange rate:	$1.00 = 10.00 dirhams	
Six-month forward rate:	$1.00 = 10.40 dirhams	

Six-month call options on 6,000,000 dirhams at an exercise price of 10.00 dirhams per dollar are available from Bank Al-Maghrub at a premium of 2%. Six-month put options on 6,000,000 dirhams at an exercise price of 10.00 dirhams per dollar are available at a premium of 3%. Compare and contrast alternative ways that Micca might hedge its foreign exchange transaction exposure. What is your recommendation?

14. **Pixel's Financial Metrics.** Leo Srivastava is the director of finance for Pixel Manufacturing, a U.S.-based manufacturer of hand-held computer systems for inventory management. Pixel's system combines a low-cost active bar code used on inventory (the bar code tags emit an extremely low-grade radio frequency) with custom-designed hardware and software that tracks the low-grade emissions for inventory control. Pixel has completed the sale of a bar-code system to a British firm, Grand Metropolitan (U.K.), for a total payment of £1,000,000. The following exchange rates were available to Pixel on the dates corresponding to the events of this specific export sale. Assume that each month is 30 days.

Date	Spot Rate ($/£)	Forward Rate ($/£)	Description
Feb 1	1.7850	$F_{210} = 1.7771$	Price quotation by Pixel (U.S.) to Grand Met (U.K.)
Mar 1	1.7465	$F_{180} = 1.7381$	Contract signed for the sale totaling £1,000,000
Jun 1	1.7689	$F_{90} = 1.7602$	Product shipped to Grand Met
Aug 1	1.7840	$F_{30} = 1.7811$	Product received by Grand Met
Sept 1	1.7290	_____	Grand Met makes payment of £1,000,000

a. Pixel's income statement will reflect the sale both as booked sales and as a potential foreign exchange gain (loss). Assume Leo decides not to hedge this transaction exposure. What is the value of the sale as booked? What is the foreign exchange gain (loss) on the sale?

b. Now assume Leo decides that he should hedge the exposure with a forward contract. The financial statements will reflect a different set of values when hedged. What is the value of the sale as booked? What is the foreign exchange gain (loss) on the sale if hedged with a forward contract?

15. **Maria Gonzalez and Trident (A).** Trident—the same U.S.-based company as discussed throughout this chapter, has concluded a second larger sale of telecommunications equipment to Regency (U.K.). Total payment of £3,000,000 is due in 90 days. Maria Gonzalez has also learned that Trident will only be able to borrow in the United Kingdom at 14% per annum (due to credit concerns of the British banks). Given the following exchange rates and interest rates, what transaction exposure hedge is now in Trident's best interest?

Spot rate:	$1.7620/£
Expected spot rate in 90 days:	$1.7850/£
90-day forward rate:	$1.7550/£
90-day dollar deposit rate:	6.0% per annum
90-day dollar borrowing rate:	8.0% per annum
90-day pound deposit rate:	8.0% per annum
90-day pound borrowing rate:	14.0% per annum
Trident's12.0% per annum	

Maria has collected data on two specific options as well:

	Strike Rate	Premium
90-day put option on £	$1.75/£	1.5%
90-day put option on £	$1.71/£	1.0%

16. **Maria Gonzalez and Trident (B).** One year later Maria Gonzalez is still on the job at Trident. Trident's business is booming, and sales have now expanded to include exports to Germany and Japan, besides continuing sales to the United Kingdom. All export sales are invoiced in the local currency of the buyer. Maria Gonzalez will book the following sales this period:

Domestic sales	$7,300,000 (45-day credit terms)
Export sales	€2,340,000; £1,780,000; ¥125,000,000 (all export terms are 90 days)

Other income statement items are as follows:

Cost of goods sold	65% of sales
G&A expenses	9% of sales
Depreciation	$248,750 per period
U.S. corporate tax	40% of earnings before tax
Shares outstanding	1,000,000

Maria Gonzalez has collected the following spot rates (sales will be booked at these rates), 90-day forward rates, and 90-day forecasts by Trident's foreign exchange adviser for the three currencies:

Spot	90-day Forward	FX Adviser Forecast
$1.5900/£	$1.5875/£	$1.5600/£
$1.0560/€	$1.0250/€	$1.0660/€
¥122.43/$	¥120.85/$	¥126.00/$

Creating a *pro forma* income statement for Trident, answer the following questions:

a. If Maria Gonzalez leaves all positions uncovered, and the final spot rates at settlement are exactly what the FX adviser had forecast, what are the foreign exchange gains (losses) for the period, and what is the final net income and earnings per share (EPS) figures?

b. If Maria Gonzalez covers all positions with full forward cover, and the final spot rates at settlement are exactly what the FX adviser forecast, what are the foreign exchange gains (losses) for the period, and the final net income and earnings per share (EPS) figures?

c. If Maria Gonzalez uses a common industry practice of covering all positions 100% with forward cover if the forward rate earns her the points, while only covering half the positions in which she is paying the forward points, what are the foreign exchange gains (losses) for the period and the final net income and earnings per share (EPS) figures, assuming the following final settlement spot rates: $1.0480/€, $1.6000/£, ¥122.50/$?

17. **Solar Turbines.** On March 1, Solar Turbines, a wholly owned subsidiary of Caterpillar (U.S.), sold a 12 megawatt compression turbine to Vollendam Dike Company of the Netherlands for €4,000,000, payable €2,000,000 on June 1 and €2,000,000 on September 1st. Solar derived its price quote of €4,000,000 on February 1 by dividing its normal U.S. dollar sales price of $4,320,000 by the then current spot rate of $1.0800/€.

By the time the order was received and booked on March 1, the euro had strengthened to $1.1000/€, so the sale was in fact worth €4,000,000 × $1.1000/€ = $4,400,000. Solar had already gained an extra $80,000 from favorable exchange rate movements! Nevertheless, Solar's director of finance now wondered if the firm should hedge against a reversal of the recent trend of the euro. Four approaches were possible:

1. Hedge in the forward market. The three-month forward exchange quote was $1.1060/€ and the six-month forward quote was $1.1130/€.
2. Hedge in the money market. Solar could borrow euros from the Frankfurt branch of its U.S. bank at 8.00% per annum.
3. Hedge with foreign currency options. June put options were available at strike price of $1.1000/€ for a premium of 2.0% per contract, and September put options were available at $1.1000/€ for a premium of 1.2%. June call options at $1.1000/€ could be purchased for a premium of 3.0%, and September call options at $1.1000/€ were available at a 2.6% premium.
4. Do nothing. Solar could wait until the sales proceeds were received in June and September, hope the recent strengthening of the euro would continue, and sell the euros received for dollars in the spot market.

Solar estimates its cost of equity capital to be 12% per annum. As a small firm, Solar Turbines is unable to raise funds with long-term debt. U.S. T-bills yielded 3.6% per annum. What should Solar do?

Tektronix

The following five problems are based on the hypothetical but typical foreign exchange transaction exposures that might be faced by Tektronix, Inc. (TEK), an actual MNE based in Beaverton, Oregon. TEK's sales in the fiscal year ending May 31, 2004, were about $1 billion. Its main products are scientific measuring instruments such as protocol analyses and simulators, network monitoring systems, transmission and cable test products, and a broad range of oscilloscopes. Part of the foreign sales were direct exports from TEK's Beaverton manufacturing and research facility. A second part of sales were passed through TEK's own foreign sales and assembly subsidiaries. A third part of sales were through joint ventures such as in Japan (Sony) and China. TEK also imported components and other materials that were used in the manufacturing operations in Beaverton. TEK's main competitors are Agilent (formerly Hewlett Packard's measuring instruments business) and Siemens (a very large German conglomerate).

18. **TEK—Italian Account Receivable (Spreadsheet on Web Site)** TEK wishes to hedge a €4,000,000 account receivable arising from a sale to Olivetti (Italy). Payment is due in three months. TEK's Italian unit does not have ready access to local currency borrowing, eliminating the money market hedge alternative. Citibank has offered TEK the following quotes:

Spot rate:	$1.2000/€
Three-month forward rate:	$1.2180/€
Three-month euro interest rate:	4.200% per year
Three-month put option on euros at strike price of $1.0800/€:	3.40%
TEK's weighted average cost of capital:	9.80%

a. What are the costs of each alternative?
b. What are the risks of each alternative?
c. Which alternative should TEK choose if it prefers to "play it safe"?
d. Which alternative should TEK choose if it is willing to take a reasonable risk and has a directional view that the euro may be appreciating versus the dollar during the next three months?

19. **TEK—Japanese Account Payable.** TEK has imported components from its joint venture in Japan, Sony–TEK, with payment of ¥8,000,000 due in six months. Citibank has offered TEK the following quotes:

Spot rate:	¥108.20/$
Six-month forward rate:	¥106.20/$
Six-month yen deposit rate:	1.250% per year
Six-month dollar interest rate:	4.000% per year
Six-month call option on yen at a strike price of ¥108/$:	2.5%
TEK's weighted average cost of capital:	9.80%

a. What are the costs of each alternative?
b. What are the risks of each alternative?
c. Which alternative should TEK choose if it is willing to take a reasonable risk and has a directional view that the yen may be depreciating versus the dollar during the next six months?

20. **TEK—British Telecom Bidding.** TEK has made a £1,500,000 bid to supply and install a network monitoring system for British Telecom in Manchester, U.K. The bid is good for 30 days at which time the winner of the bidding process will be announced. Other bidders are expected to be Agilent, Siemens, and at least two British firms. If TEK wins the bid it

will have 60 days to build and install the system. During this 90-day period the £1,500,000 will be accounted for as backlog. Upon delivery and testing of the system British Telecom will make full payment 30 days later. During this month TEK will account for the £1,500,000 as an account receivable. Barclay's Bank (U.K.) has offered TEK the following quotes:

Spot rate:	$1.8418/£
One-month forward rate:	1.8368/£
Four-month forward rate:	1.8268/£
One-month £ investment rate:	4.000% per year
One-month £ borrowing rate:	6.500% per year
Four-month £ investment rate:	4.125% per year
Four-month £ borrowing rate:	6.500% per year
One-month put option on pound ($1.85/£ strike) $0.006/£ premium	
Four-month put option on pound ($1.85/£ strike) $0.012/£ premium	
TEK's weighted average cost of capital:	9.80%

What should TEK do to hedge this bid?

21. **TEK—Swedish Price List.** TEK offers oscilloscopes and other off-the-shelf products through foreign-currency-denominated price lists. The prices are valid for three months only. One example is a Swedish price list expressed in Swedish kronor. In effect, customers are given a cost-free call option on products with a fixed dollar/krona exchange rate. During a typical three-month period, TEK could expect to sell SKr 5,000,000–SKr 10,000,000 worth of products based on the price list. Since the SKr/$ exchange rate is likely to change during any three-month period, TEK would like to hedge this transaction exposure (TEK's Swedish business unit does believe the krona will be strengthening versus the dollar in the coming months.) Nordea Bank (Sweden) has offered TEK the following quotes:

Spot rate:	SKr 7.4793/$
Three-month forward rate:	SKr 7.4937/$
Three-month krona interest rate:	4.780% per year
Three-month krona borrowing rate:	6.50% per year
Three-month dollar interest rate:	4.00% per year
Three-month put option on krona @ strike price of SKr 7.50/$:	2.5%
TEK's weighted average cost of capital:	9.80%

a. What are the costs of each alternative for hedging SKr 5,000,000?
b. What are the risks of each alternative? How much kronor should TEK hedge if it wants to "play it safe"?
c. Which alternative should TEK choose if it is willing to take a reasonable risk and has a directional view that the Swedish krona will appreciate versus the U.S. dollar during the next three months?

22. **TEK—Swiss Dividend Payable.** TEK's European subsidiaries are formally owned by a holding company, TEK-Switzerland. Thus, the subsidiaries pay dividends to the Swiss holding company, which in turn pays dividends to TEK-Beaverton. TEK has declared a dividend of 5 million Swiss francs payable in three months from Switzerland to TEK-Beaverton. If TEK-Beaverton wishes to hedge this transaction exposure it could utilize the following quotes from Swiss Bank Corporation:

Spot rate:	SFr1.2462/$
Expected spot rate in three months:	SFr1.2200/$
Three-month forward rate:	SFr1.2429/$
Three-month Swiss franc interest rate:	3.75% per year
Three-month dollar interest rate:	4.00% per year
Three-month put option on SF @ strike price of SFr1.25/$:	$0.0150/SFr premium
TEK's weighted average cost of capital:	9.80%

What are the costs of each alternative for hedging the dividend payable? What are the risks of each alternative? Which alternative should TEK choose? Explain your assumption about TEK's motivation in choosing your suggested alternative.

INTERNET EXERCISES

1. **Foreign Currency Volatilities.** You wish to price your own options, but you need current volatilities on the euro, British pound, and Japanese yen. Using the following Web sites, collect spot rates and volatilities in order to price forward at-the-money put options for your option pricing analysis:

Rates FX   www.ratesfx.com/summaries/volatility.html

2. **Hedging Objectives.** All multinational companies will state the goals and objectives of their currency risk management activities in their annual reports.

Beginning with the following firms, collect samples of corporate "why hedge?" discussions for a contrast and comparison discussion:

Nestlé   www.nestle.com

Disney   www.disney.com

Nokia   www.nokia.com

BP   www.bp.com

3. **New Zealand Government Policy.** The New Zealand government has specific policies and guidelines for the management of transaction exposure. Visit the following Web site to follow the detailed analysis of their recommendations:

New Zealand Treasury   www.treasury.govt.nz/
                          publicsector/fxexposure/5.asp

Complex Options

Dayton Manufacturing, a U.S.-based firm, possesses a long £1,000,000 exposure—an account receivable—to be settled in 90 days. Exhibit 11A.1 summarizes the assumptions, exposure, and traditional option alternatives to be used throughout this appendix. The firm believes that the exchange rate will move in its favor over the 90-day period (the British pound will appreciate versus the U.S. dollar). Despite having this *directional view* or *currency expectation,* the firm wishes downside protection in the event the pound were to depreciate instead.

The exposure management zones that are of most interest to the firm are the two opposing *triangles* formed by the uncovered and forward rate profiles. The firm would like to retain all potential area in the upper-right triangle, but minimize its own potential exposure to the bottom-left triangle. The put option's "kinked-profile" is consistent with what the firm wishes if it believes the pound will appreciate.

EXHIBIT 11A.1   Dayton Manufacturing's Problem and Put Option Hedges

Spot rate	$1.4790/£			
90-day forward rate	$1.4700/£	Put Option	Strike Rates	Premium
90-day euro-$ interest rate	3.250%	Forward ATM put	$1.4700/£	$0.0318/£
90-day euro-£ interest rate	5.720%	OTM put	$1.4400/£	$0.0188/£
90-day $/£ volatility	11.000%			

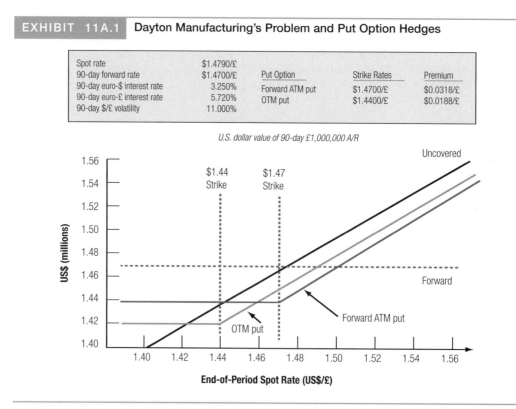

U.S. dollar value of 90-day £1,000,000 A/R

End-of-Period Spot Rate (US$/£)

The firm could consider any number of different put option strike prices, depending on what minimum assured value—degree of self-insurance—the firm is willing to accept. Exhibit 11A.1 illustrates two different put option alternatives: a forward-ATM put of strike price $1.4700/£, and a forward-OTM put with strike price $1.4400/£. Because foreign currency options are actually priced about the forward rate (see Chapter 8), not the spot rate, the correct specification of whether an option, put or call, is ITM, ATM, or OTM is in reference to the same maturity forward rate. The forward-OTM put provides protection at lower cost, but also at a lower level of protection.

The Synthetic Forward

At a forward rate of $1.4700/£, the proceeds of the forward contract in 90 days will yield $1,470,000. A second alternative for the firm would be to construct a *synthetic forward* using options. The synthetic forward requires the firm to combine three different elements:

1. Long position in £ (A/R of £1,000,000)

2. Buy a put option on £ bought at a strike price of $1.4700/£, paying a premium of $0.0318/£

3. Sell a call option on £ at a strike price of $1.4700/£, earning a premium of $0.0318/£

The purchase of the put option requires a premium payment, and the sale of the call option earns the firm the premium payment. If both options are struck at the forward rate (forward-ATM), the premiums should be identical and the net premium payment have a value of zero.

Exhibit 11A.2 illustrates the uncovered position, the basic forward rate hedge, and the individual profiles of the put and call options for the possible construction of a synthetic for-

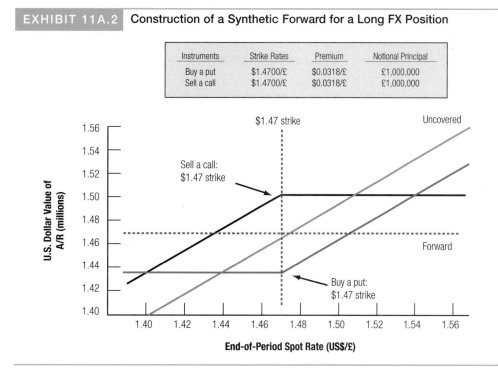

EXHIBIT 11A.2   **Construction of a Synthetic Forward for a Long FX Position**

Instruments	Strike Rates	Premium	Notional Principal
Buy a put	$1.4700/£	$0.0318/£	£1,000,000
Sell a call	$1.4700/£	$0.0318/£	£1,000,000

ward. The outcome of the combined position is easily confirmed by simply tracing what would happen at all exchange rates to the left of $1.4700/£, and what would happen to the right of $1.4700/£.

At all exchange rates to the left of $1.4700/£:

1. The firm would receive £1,000,000 in 90 days.
2. The call option on pounds sold by the firm would expire out-of-the-money.
3. The firm would exercise the put option on pounds to sell the pounds received at $1.4700/£.

At all exchange rates below $1.4700/£, the U.S.-based firm would earn $1,470,000 from the receivable. At all exchange rates to the right of $1.4700/£:

1. The firm would receive £1,000,000 in 90 days.
2. The put option on pounds purchased by the firm would expire out-of-the-money.
3. The firm would turnover the £1,000,000 received to the buyer of the call, who now exercises the call option against the firm. The firm receives $1.4700/£ from the call option buyer.

Thus, at all exchange rates above or below $1.4700/£, the U.S.-based firm nets $1,470,000 in domestic currency. The combined spot-option position has behaved identically to that of a forward contract. A firm with the exact opposite position, a £1,000,00 payable 90 days in the future, could similarly construct a synthetic forward using options.[1]

But why would a firm undertake this relatively complex position in order to simply create a forward contract? The answer is found by looking at the option premiums earned and paid. We have assumed that the option strike prices used were precisely forward-ATM rates, and the resulting option premiums paid and earned were exactly equal. But this need not be the case. If the option strike prices (remember that they must be identical for both options, bought and sold) are not precisely on the forward-ATM, the two premiums may differ by a slight amount. The net premium position may then end up as a net premium earning or a net premium payment. If positive, this amount would be added to the proceeds from the receivable to result in a higher total dollar value received.[2]

Second-Generation Currency Risk Management Products

Second-generation risk management products are constructed from the two basic derivatives used throughout this book: the forward and the option. We will subdivide them into two groups: (1) the *zero-premium option products*, which focus on pricing in and around the forward rate and (2) the *exotic option products* (for want of a better name), which focus on alternative pricing targets. Although all of the following derivatives are sold as financial products by risk management firms, we will present each as the construction of the position from

[1] A U.S.-resident firm possessing a future foreign currency–denominated payment of £1,000,000 could construct a synthetic forward in the following way: (1) the firm would pay £1,000,000 in 90 days; (2) buy a call option on pounds at a strike price of $1.4700/£; and (3) sell a put option on pounds at a strike price of $1.4700/£.

[2] An additional possibility is that the firm finds, for the moment at which the position is taken, that the call option premium earned may actually slightly exceed the put option premium paid. This result means that the options market is temporarily out of equilibrium (parity). This situation is quite possible, given the judgment required in the pricing of options (different banks' pricing options do not necessarily use the identical volatilities at all times) and the inherent decentralized structure of the currency and currency option markets.

common building blocks, or LEGO^R_S, as they have been termed, used in traditional currency risk management, forwards and options. As a group, they are collectively referred to as *complex options.*

Zero-Premium Option Products

The primary "problem" with the use of options for risk management in the eyes of the firms is the up-front premium payment. Although the premium payment is only a portion of the total payoff profile of the hedge, many firms view the expenditure of substantial funds for the *purchase* of a financial derivative as prohibitively expensive. In comparison, the forward contract that eliminates currency risk requires no out-of-pocket expenditure by the firm (and requires no real specification of expectations regarding exchange rate movements).

Zero-premium option products (or financially engineered derivative combinations) are designed to require no out-of-pocket premium payment at the initiation of the hedge. This set of products includes what are most frequently labeled the *range forward* and the *participating forward.* Both of these products are (1) priced on the basis of the forward rate; (2) constructed to provide a zero-premium payment up-front; and (3) allow the hedger to take advantage of expectations of the direction of exchange rate movements. For the case problem at hand, this means that all of the following products are applicable to an expectation that the U.S. dollar will depreciate versus the pound. If the hedger has no such *view,* they should turn back now (and buy a forward, or nothing at all)!

Ratio Spreads

Before describing the most widely accepted second-generation option products, it is helpful to demonstrate one of the older methods of obtaining a zero-premium option combination: an alternative that leaves the hedger with a large uncovered exposure.

The U.S.-based firm in our chapter problem decides that it wishes to establish a floor level of protection by purchasing a $1.4700/£ put option (forward-ATM) at a cost of $0.0318/£ (total cost of $31,800). This is a substantial outlay of up-front capital for the option premium, and the firm's risk management division has no budget funding for this magnitude of expenditures. The firm, feeling strongly that the dollar will depreciate against the pound, decides to "finance" the purchase of the put with the sale of an OTM call option. The firm reviews market conditions and considers a number of call option strike prices that are significantly OTM, strike prices of $1.5200/£, $1.5400/£, or further out.

It is decided that the $1.5400/£ call option, with a premium of $0.0089/£, is to be written and sold to earn the premium and finance the put purchase. However, because the premium on the OTM call is so much smaller than the forward-ATM put premium, the size of the call option written must be larger. The firm determines the amount of the call by solving the simple problem of premium equivalency as follows:

$$\text{Cost of put premium} = \text{Earnings call premium}$$

Substituting in the put and call option premiums yields

$$\$0.0318/£ \times £1,000,000 = \$0.0089/£ \times £ \text{ call}$$

Solving for the size of the call option to be written as follows:

$$\frac{\$31,800}{\$0.0089/£} = £3,573,034$$

The reason that this strategy is called a *ratio spread* is that the final position, call option size to put option size, is a ratio greater than 1 (£3,573,034 ÷ £1,000,000, or a ratio of about 3.57).

An alternative form of the ratio spread is the *calendar spread*. The calendar spread would combine the 90-day put option with the sale of an OTM call option with a maturity that is longer; for example, 120 or 180 days. The longer maturity of the call option written earns the firm larger premium earnings requiring a smaller "ratio." As a number of firms using this strategy have learned the hard way, however, if the expectations of the hedger prove incorrect, and the spot rate moves past the strike price of the call option written, the firm is faced with delivering a foreign currency that it does not have. In this example, if the spot rate moved above $1.5400/£, the firm would have to cover a position of £2,573,034.

The Range Forward

The basic *range forward* has been marketed under a variety of other names, including the *collar*, *flexible forward*, *cylinder option*, *option fence* or simply *fence*, *mini-max*, or *zero-cost tunnel*. The range forward is constructed via two steps:

1. Buying a put option with a strike rate *below* the forward rate, for the full amount of the long currency exposure (100% coverage)
2. Selling a call option with a strike rate *above* the forward rate, for the full amount of the long currency exposure (100% coverage)

The hedger chooses one side of the "range" or spread, normally the downside (put strike rate), which then dictates the strike rate at which the call option will be sold. The call option must be chosen at an equal distance from the forward rate as the put option strike price from the forward rate. If the hedger believes there is a significant possibility that the currency will move in the firm's favor, and by a sizable degree, the put-floor rate may be set relatively low in order for the ceiling to be higher or further out from the forward rate and still enjoy a zero net premium. How far down the downside protection is set is a difficult issue for the firm to determine. Often the firm's treasurer will determine at what bottom exchange rate the firm would be able to recover the minimum necessary margin on the business underlying the cash flow exposure, sometimes called the *budget rate*.

Exhibit 11A.3 illustrates the final outcome of a range forward constructed by buying a put with strike price $1.4500/£, paying a premium of $0.0226/£, with selling a call option with strike price $1.4900/£, earning a premium of $0.0231/£. The hedger has bounded the range over which the firm's A/R value moves as an uncovered position, with a put option floor and a sold call option ceiling.

A number of variations on the basic range forward exist. If both strike prices are the same, it is a *synthetic forward*. If both strike prices chosen are equal to the actual forward rate, the synthetic equals the actual forward contract. This synthetic forward will have a near-zero net premium. Although the put and call option premiums are in this case not identical, they are close enough to result in a near-zero net premium:

$$\text{Net premium} = (\$0.0226/£ - \$0.0231/£) \times £1,000,000 = -\$500$$

The benefits of the combined position are readily observable, given that the put option premium alone amounts to $22,600. If the strike rates of the options are selected independently of the desire for an exact zero-net premium up-front (still bracketing the forward rate), it is termed an *option collar* or *cylinder option*.

The Participating Forward

The *participating forward*, also called a *zero-cost ratio option* and *forward participation agreement*, is an option combination that allows the hedger to share in potential upside move-

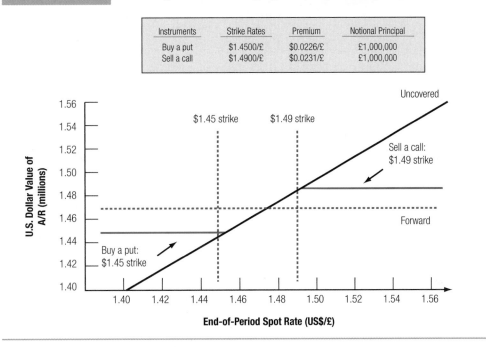

EXHIBIT 11A.3 The Range Forward: Hedging a £1,000,000 Long Position

Instruments	Strike Rates	Premium	Notional Principal
Buy a put	$1.4500/£	$0.0226/£	£1,000,000
Sell a call	$1.4900/£	$0.0231/£	£1,000,000

ments while providing option-based downside protection, all at a zero net premium. The participating forward is constructed via two steps:

1. Buying a put option with a strike price *below* the forward rate, for the full amount of the long currency exposure (100% coverage)

2. Selling a call option with a strike price *that is the same as the put option*, for a *portion* of the total currency exposure (less than 100% coverage)

Similar to the range forward, the buyer of a participating forward will choose the put option strike rate first. Because the call option strike rate is the same as the put, all that remains is to determine the *participation rate,* the proportion of the exposure sold as a call option.

Exhibit 11A.4 illustrates the construction of a participating forward for the chapter problem. The firm first chooses the put option protection level, in this case $1.4500/£, with a premium of $0.0226/£. A call option sold with the same strike rate of $1.4500/£ would earn the firm $0.0425/£. The call premium is substantially higher than the put premium because the call option is already in-the-money (ITM). The firm's objective is to sell a call option only on the number of pounds needed to fund the purchase of the put option. The total put option premium is

$$\text{Total put premium} = \$0.0226/£ \times £1,000,000 = \$22,600$$

which is then used to determine the size of the call option that is needed to exactly offset the purchase of the put:

$$\$22,600 = \$0.0425/£ \times \text{call principal}$$

EXHIBIT 11A.4 The Participating Forward: Hedging a £1,000,000 Long Position

Instruments	Strike Rates	Premium	Notional Principal
Buy a put	$1.4500/£	$0.0226/£	£1,000,000
Sell a call	$1.4500/£	$0.0425/£	£531,765

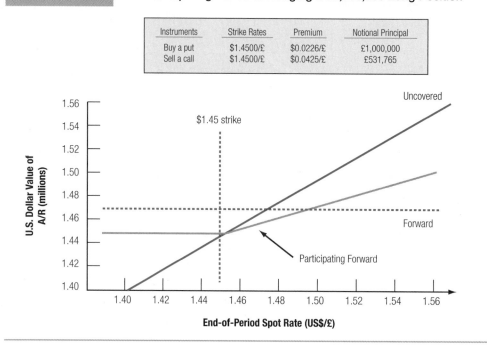

Solving for the call principal:

$$\text{Call principal} = \frac{\$22,600}{\$0.0425/£} = £531,765$$

The firm must therefore sell a call option on £531,765 with a strike rate of $1.4500/£ to cover the purchase of the put option. This mismatch in option principals is what gives the participating forward its unique shape.[3] The ratio of option premiums, as well as the ratio of option principals, is termed the *percent cover*:

$$\text{Percent cover} = \frac{\$0.026/£}{\$0.0425/£} = \frac{£531,765}{£1,000,000} = 0.5318 \approx 53.18\%$$

The *participation rate* is the residual percentage of the exposure that is not covered by the sale of the call option. For example, if the percent cover is 53.18%, the participation rate would be 1—the percent cover, or 46.82%. This means that for all favorable exchange rate movements (those above $1.4500/£), the hedger would "participate" or enjoy 46.8% of the differential. However, like all option-based hedges, downside exposure is bounded by the put option strike rate.

The expectations of the buyer are similar to the range forward; only the degree of foreign currency bullishness is greater. For the participating forward to be superior in outcome

---

[3]Note that if both options had the same strike rate and the same principal, the result would be a positive premium synthetic forward. The positive premium would result from the strike rate that places the call option in-the-money and the put option out-of-the-money. A true net-zero synthetic forward would use a strike rate that was the same as the forward rate.

to the range forward, it is necessary for the exchange rate to move further in the favorable direction than the range forward.

The Average Rate Option

These options are normally classified as "path-dependent" currency options because their values depend on averages of spot rates over some pre-specified period of time. Here we describe two examples of path-dependent options, the *average rate option* and the *average strike option*:

1. *Average rate option (ARO)*, also known as an *Asian Option*, sets the option strike rate upfront, and is exercised at maturity if the average spot rate over the period (as observed by scheduled sampling) is less than the preset option strike rate.

2. *Average strike option (ASO)* establishes the option strike rate as the average of the spot rate experienced over the option's life, and is exercised if the strike rate is greater than the end of period spot rate.

Like the knock-out option, the average rate option is difficult to depict because its value depends not on the ending spot rate, but rather the path the spot rate takes over its specified life span. For example, an average rate option with strike price $1.4700/£ would have a premium of only $0.0186/£. The average rate would be calculated by weekly observations (12 full weeks, the first observation occurring 13 days from purchase) of the spot rate. Numerous different averages or paths of spot rate movement obviously exist. A few different scenarios aid in understanding how the ARO differs in valuation.

1. The spot rate moves very little over the first 70 to 80 days of the period, with a sudden movement in the spot rate below $1.4700/£ in the days prior to expiration. Although the final spot rate is below $1.4700/£, the average for the period is above $1.4700, so the option cannot be exercised. The receivable is exchanged at the spot rate (below $1.4700/£) and the cost of the option premium is still incurred.

2. The dollar slowly and steadily depreciates versus the pound, the rate rising from $1.4790/£ to $1.48, $1.49, and on up. At the end of the 90 days the option expires out of the money, the receivable is exchanged at the favorable spot rate, and the firm has enjoyed average rate option protection at substantially lower premium expense.

A variation on the average rate is the *lookback option, with strike* and *without strike*. A *lookback option with strike* is a European-style option with a preset strike rate that on maturity is valued versus the highest or lowest spot rate reached over the option life. A *lookback option without strike* is typically a European-style option that sets the strike rate at maturity as the lowest exchange rate achieved over the period for a call option, or the highest exchange rate experienced over the period for a put option, and is exercised on the basis of this strike rate versus the ending spot rate.

A variety of different types of average rate currency option products are sold by financial institutions, each having a distinct pay-off structure. Because of the intricacy of the path-dependent option's value, care must be taken in the use of these instruments. As in all markets, let the buyer beware.

CHAPTER 12

Operating Exposure

The essence of risk management lies in maximizing the areas where we have some control over the outcome while minimizing the areas where we have absolutely no control over the outcome and the linkage between effect and cause is hidden from us.

—Peter Bernstein, *Against the Gods*, 1996.

This chapter extends the concept of *transaction exposure*, described in Chapter 11, further into time and across the multitudes of future cash flows that create the value of any multinational firm. *Operating exposure*, also called *economic exposure*, *competitive exposure*, and even *strategic exposure* on occasion, measures any change in the present value of a firm resulting from changes in future operating cash flows caused by any unexpected change in exchange rates. *Operating exposure analysis* assesses the impact of changing exchange rates on a firm's own operations over coming months and years and on its competitive position vis-à-vis other firms. The goal is to identify strategic moves or operating techniques the firm might wish to adopt to enhance its value in the face of unexpected exchange rate changes.

Operating exposure and transaction exposure are related in that they both deal with future cash flows. They differ in terms of which cash flows management considers and why those cash flows change when exchange rates change.

Attributes of Operating Exposure

Measuring the operating exposure of a firm requires forecasting and analyzing all the firm's future individual transaction exposures together with the future exposures of all the firm's competitors and potential competitors worldwide. A simple example will clarify the point.

An MNE like Eastman Kodak (U.S.) has a number of transaction exposures at any time. Kodak has sales in the United States, Japan, and Europe and therefore posts a continuing series of foreign currency receivables (and payables). Sales and expenses that are already contracted for are traditional *transaction exposures*. Sales that are highly probable based on Kodak's historical business line and market share but have no legal basis yet are *anticipated transaction exposures*. (This term is used quite specifically in accounting for foreign exchange rate gains and losses.)

What if the analysis of the firm's exposure to exchange rate changes is extended even further into the future? What are the longer-term exposures of Kodak to exchange rate changes? Future exchange rate changes will not only alter the domestic currency value (U.S. dollars in this case) of the firm's foreign currency cash flows, but also it will change the quantity of foreign currency cash flows generated. Any change in Kodak's cash flows in the future depends on how competitive it is in various markets. Kodak's international competitiveness will in turn be affected by the operating exposures of its major competitors like Fuji (Japan) and Agfa (Germany). The analysis of this longer term—where exchange rate changes are unpredictable and therefore unexpected—is the goal of operating exposure analysis.

Operating and Financing Cash Flows

The cash flows of the MNE can be divided into *operating cash flows* and *financing cash flows*. Operating cash flows arise from intercompany (between unrelated companies) and intracompany (between units of the same company) receivables and payables, rent and lease payments for the use of facilities and equipment, royalty and license fees for the use of technology and intellectual property, and assorted management fees for services provided.

Financing cash flows are payments for the use of intercompany and intracompany loans (principal and interest) and stockholder equity (new equity investments and dividends). Each of these cash flows can occur at different time intervals, in different amounts, and in different currencies of denomination, and each has a different predictability of occurrence. We summarize cash flow possibilities in Exhibit 12.1 for an MNE which supports its foreign subsidiary.

Expected versus Unexpected Changes in Cash Flow

Operating exposure is far more important for the long-run health of a business than changes caused by transaction or translation exposure. However, operating exposure is inevitably subjective because it depends on estimates of future cash flow changes over an arbitrary time horizon. Thus, it does not spring from the accounting process but rather from operating

EXHIBIT 12.1   **Financial and Operating Cash Flows between Parent and Subsidiary**

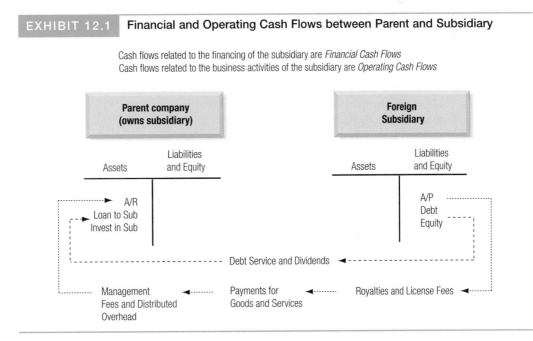

Cash flows related to the financing of the subsidiary are *Financial Cash Flows*
Cash flows related to the business activities of the subsidiary are *Operating Cash Flows*

analysis. Planning for operating exposure is a total management responsibility because it depends on the interaction of strategies in finance, marketing, purchasing, and production.

An expected change in foreign exchange rates is not included in the definition of operating exposure, because both management and investors should have factored this information into their evaluation of anticipated operating results and market value. From a management perspective, budgeted financial statements already reflect information about the effect of an expected change in exchange rates. For example, under equilibrium conditions the forward rate might be used as an unbiased predictor of the future spot rate. In such a case, management would use the forward rate when preparing the operating budgets, rather than assume the spot rate would remain unchanged.

Another example is that expected cash flow to amortize debt should already reflect the international Fisher effect. The level of expected interest and principal repayment should be a function of expected exchange rates rather than existing spot rates.

From an investor's perspective, if the foreign exchange market is efficient, information about expected changes in exchange rates should be widely known and thus reflected in a firm's market value. Only unexpected changes in exchange rates, or an inefficient foreign exchange market, should cause market value to change.

From a broader perspective, operating exposure is not only the sensitivity of a firm's future cash flows to unexpected changes in foreign exchange rates, but also its sensitivity to other key macroeconomic variables. This factor has been labeled as *macroeconomic uncertainty*. Chapter 7 described the parity relationships among exchange rates, interest rates, and inflation rates. However, these variables are often in disequilibrium with one another. Therefore, unexpected changes in interest rates and inflation rates could also have a simultaneous but differential impact on future cash flows.

Illustrating Operating Exposure: Trident

To illustrate the consequences of operating exposure we use Trident's European subsidiary, Trident Europe. Exhibit 12.2 presents the dilemma facing Trident Corporation as a result of an unexpected change in the value of the euro, the currency of economic consequence for the German subsidiary. Trident Corporation (U.S.) derives much of its reported profits (earnings and earnings per share—EPS—as reported to Wall Street) from its European subsidiary. If the euro unexpectedly falls in value, how will Trident Europe's revenues change (prices, in euro terms, and volumes)? How will its costs change (primarily input costs, in euro terms)? How will competitors respond? We explain the sequence of likely events over the short and medium run in the following section.

Base Case

Trident Europe manufactures in Germany from European material and labor. Half of production is sold within Europe for euros and half is exported to non-European countries. All sales are invoiced in euros, and accounts receivable are equal to one-fourth of annual sales. In other words, the average collection period is 90 days. Inventory is equal to 25% of annual direct costs. Trident Europe can expand or contract production volume without any significant change in per-unit direct costs or in overall general and administrative expenses. Depreciation on plant and equipment is €600,000 per year, and the corporate income tax in Germany is 34%.

The December 31, 2010, balance sheet and alternative scenarios are shown in Exhibit 12.3. We assume that on January 1, 2011, before any commercial activity begins, the euro unexpectedly drops 16.67% in value, from $1.2000/€ to $1.0000/€. If no devaluation had occurred, Trident Europe was expected to perform in 2011 as shown in the base case of

EXHIBIT 12.2 Trident Corporation and Its European Subsidiary: Operating Exposure of the Parent and Its Subsidiary

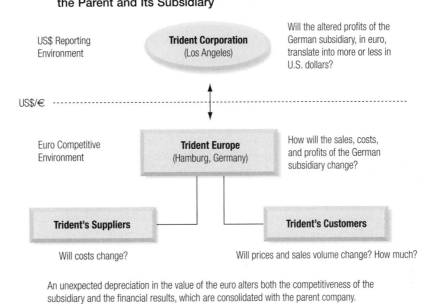

US$ Reporting Environment

Trident Corporation (Los Angeles)

Will the altered profits of the German subsidiary, in euro, translate into more or less in U.S. dollars?

US$/€

Euro Competitive Environment

Trident Europe (Hamburg, Germany)

How will the sales, costs, and profits of the German subsidiary change?

Trident's Suppliers

Will costs change?

Trident's Customers

Will prices and sales volume change? How much?

An unexpected depreciation in the value of the euro alters both the competitiveness of the subsidiary and the financial results, which are consolidated with the parent company.

Exhibit 12.3, generating a dollar cash flow from operations for Trident Corporation of $2,074,320.

Operating exposure depends on whether an unexpected change in exchange rates causes unanticipated changes in sales volume, sales prices, or operating costs. Following a euro devaluation, Trident Europe might choose to maintain its domestic sales prices constant in euro terms, or it might try to raise domestic prices because competing imports are now priced higher in Europe. The firm might choose to keep export prices constant in terms of foreign currencies, in terms of euros, or somewhere in between (partial pass-through). The strategy undertaken depends to a large measure on management's opinion about the price elasticity of demand. On the cost side, Trident Europe might raise prices because of more expensive imported raw material or components, or perhaps because all domestic prices in Germany have risen and labor is now demanding higher wages to compensate for domestic inflation.

Trident Europe's domestic sales and costs might also be partly determined by the effect of the euro devaluation on demand. To the extent that the devaluation, by making prices of German goods initially more competitive, stimulates purchases of European goods in import competing sectors of the economy as well as exports of German goods, German national income should increase. This assumes that the favorable effect of a euro devaluation on comparative prices is not immediately offset by higher domestic inflation. Thus, Trident Europe might be able to sell more goods domestically because of price and income effects and internationally because of price effects.

To illustrate the effect of various postdevaluation scenarios on Trident Europe's operating exposure, consider three simple cases:

Case 1: Devaluation; no change in any variable

Case 2: Increase in sales volume, other variables remain constant

Case 3: Increase in sales price, other variables remain constant

To calculate the net change in present value under each of the scenarios, we will use a five-year horizon for any change in cash flow induced by the change in the dollar/euro exchange rate.

Case 1: Devaluation; No Change in Any Variable

Assume that in the five years ahead no changes occur in sales volume, sales price, or operating costs. Profits for the coming year in euros will be as expected, and cash flow from operations will be €1,728,600, as shown in Exhibit 12.3. With a new exchange rate of $1.0000/€, this cash flow measured in dollars during 2011 will be €1,728,600 × $1.0000/€ = $1,728,600. Exhibit 12.3 shows that the change in year-end cash flows from the base case is $345,720 for each of the next five years (2011–2015).

Exhibit 12.3 shows that the discounted present value of this series of diminished dollar value cash flows is $1,033,914.

Case 2: Volume Increases; Other Variables Remain Constant

Assume that sales within Europe double following the devaluation because German-made telecom components are now more competitive with imports. Additionally, export volume doubles because German-made components are now cheaper in countries whose currencies have not weakened. The sales price is kept constant in euro terms because management of Trident Europe has not observed any change in local German operating costs and because it sees an opportunity to increase market share.

Exhibit 12.3 shows expected cash flow for the first year (2011) would be $3,840,600. This amount, however, is not available because a doubling of sales volume will require additional investment in accounts receivable and in inventory. Although a portion of this additional investment might be financed by increasing accounts payable, we assume additional working capital is financed by cash flow from operations.

At the end of 2011, accounts receivable will be equal to one-fourth of annual sales, or €6,400,000. This amount is twice receivables of €3,200,000 at the end of 2010, and the incremental increase of €3,200,000 must be financed from available cash. Year-end inventory would be equal to one-fourth of annual direct costs, or €4,800,000, an increase of €2,400,000 over the year-beginning level. Receivables and inventory together increase by €5,600,000. At the end of five years (2015), these incremental cash outflows will be recaptured because any investment in current assets eventually rolls back into cash.

Assuming no further change in volume, price, or costs, cash inflows for the five years would be as described in Exhibit 12.3. In this instance, the devaluation causes a major drop in first-year cash flow from the $2,074,320 anticipated in 2011 without devaluation to a negative cash flow of $1,759,400. However, the remaining four years' cash flow is substantially enhanced by the operating effects of the devaluation. Over time, Trident Europe generates significantly more cash for its owners. The devaluation produces an operating *gain* over time, rather than an operating *loss*.

The reason that Trident Corporation is better off in Case 2 following the devaluation is that sales volume doubled while the per-unit dollar-equivalent sales price fell only 16.67%—the percent amount of the devaluation. In other words, the product faced a price elasticity of demand greater than one.

Case 3: Sales Price Increases; Other Variables Remain Constant

Assume the euro sales price is raised from €12.80 to €15.36 per unit to maintain the same U.S. dollar-equivalent price (the change offsets the depreciation of the euro). Assume further that volume remains constant in spite of this price increase; that is, customers expect to pay the same dollar-equivalent price, and local costs do not change.

EXHIBIT 12.3   Trident Europe

	A	B	C	D	E	F
1				Exhibit 12.3: TRIDENT EUROPE		
2			Balance Sheet Information, End of Fiscal 2010			
3	Assets		Liabilities and Net Worth			
4	Cash	€ 1,600,000	Accounts payable		€ 800,000	
5	Accounts receivable	3,200,000	Short-term bank loan		1,600,000	
6	Inventory	2,400,000	Long-term debt		1,600,000	
7	Net plant and equipment	4,800,000	Common stock		1,800,000	
8			Retained earnings		6,200,000	
9	Sum	€ 12,000,000	Sum		€ 12,000,000	
10			Important Ratios to be Maintained and Other Data			
11			Accounts receivable, as percent of sales		25.00%	
12			Inventory, as percent of annual direct costs		25.00%	
13			Cost of capital (annual discount rate)		20.00%	
14			Income tax rate		34.00%	
15			Base Case	Case 1	Case 2	Case 3
16			Assumptions			
17	Exchange rate, $/€		1.2000	1.0000	1.0000	1.0000
18	Sales volume (units)		1,000,000	1,000,000	2,000,000	1,000,000
19	Sales price per unit		€12.80	€12.80	€12.80	€15.36
20	Direct cost per unit		€9.60	€9.60	€9.60	€9.60
21			Annual Cash Flows before Adjustments			
22	Sales revenue		€ 12,800,000	€ 12,800,000	€ 25,600,000	€ 15,360,000
23	Direct cost of goods sold		9,600,000	9,600,000	19,200,000	9,600,000
24	Cash operating expenses (fixed)		890,000	890,000	890,000	890,000
25	Depreciation		600,000	600,000	600,000	600,000
26	Pretax profit		€ 1,710,000	€ 1,710,000	€ 4,910,000	€ 4,270,000
27	Income tax expense		581,400	581,400	1,669,400	1,451,800
28	Profit after tax		€ 1,128,600	€ 1,128,600	€ 3,240,600	€ 2,818,200
29	Add back depreciation		600,000	600,000	600,000	600,000
30	Cash flow from operations, in euros		€ 1,728,600	€ 1,728,600	€ 3,840,600	€ 3,418,200
31	Cash flow from operations, in dollars		$ 2,074,320	$ 1,728,600	$ 3,840,600	$ 3,418,200
32			Adjustments to Working Capital for 2011 and 2015 Caused by Changes in Conditions			
33	Accounts receivable		€ 3,200,000	€ 3,200,000	€ 6,400,000	€ 3,840,000
34	Inventory		2,400,000	2,400,000	4,800,000	2,400,000
35	Sum		€ 5,600,000	€ 5,600,000	€ 11,200,000	€ 6,240,000
36	Change from base conditions in 2011		€ -	€ -	€ 5,600,000	€ 640,000
37		Year	Year-End Cash Flows			
38		1 (2011)	$ 2,074,320	$ 1,728,600	$ (1,759,400)	$ 2,778,200
39		2 (2012)	$ 2,074,320	$ 1,728,600	$ 3,840,600	$ 3,418,200
40		3 (2013)	$ 2,074,320	$ 1,728,600	$ 3,840,600	$ 3,418,200
41		4 (2014)	$ 2,074,320	$ 1,728,600	$ 3,840,600	$ 3,418,200
42		5 (2015)	$ 2,074,320	$ 1,728,600	$ 9,440,600	$ 4,058,200
43		Year	Change in Year-End Cash Flows from Base Conditions			
44		1 (2011)	na	$ (345,720)	$ (3,833,720)	$ 703,880
45		2 (2012)	na	$ (345,720)	$ 1,766,280	$ 1,343,880
46		3 (2013)	na	$ (345,720)	$ 1,766,280	$ 1,343,880
47		4 (2014)	na	$ (345,720)	$ 1,766,280	$ 1,343,880
48		5 (2015)	na	$ (345,720)	$ 7,366,280	$ 1,983,880
49			Present Value of Incremental Year-End Cash Flows			
50			na	$ (1,033,914)	$ 2,866,106	$ 3,742,892
51			Base Case	Case 1	Case 2	Case 3

52	Key Cell Entries
53	C22: =C$18*C19, copy to D22:F23 C33: =$E11*C22, copy to D33:F34
54	C24: Enter as data value, copy to D24:F24 C35: =SUM(C33:C34), copy to D35:F35
55	C25: Enter as data value, copy to D25:F25 C36: =C35-$C$35, copy to D36:F36
56	C26: =C22-SUM(C23:C25), copy to D26:F26 C38: =C31-C36, copy to D38:F38
57	C27: =$E$14*C26, copy to D27:F27 C39: =C$31, copy to C38:F41
58	C28: =C26-C27, copy to D28:F28 C42: =C31+C36, copy to D42:F42
59	C29: =C25, copy to D29:F29 D44: =D38-$C38, copy to D44:F48
60	C30: =C28+C29, copy to D30:F30 D50: =NPV($E$13,D44:D48), copy to E44:F48
61	C31: =C30*C17, copy to D31:F31

Trident Europe is now better off following the devaluation than it was before because the sales price, which is pegged to the international price level, increased. However, volume did not drop. The new level of accounts receivable would be one-fourth of the new sales level of €15,360,000, or €3,840,000, an increase of €640,000 over the base case. The investment in inventory is $2,400,000, which is the same as the base case because annual direct costs did not change.

Expected dollar cash flow in every year exceeds the cash flow of $2,074,320 that had been anticipated with no devaluation. The increase in working capital causes net cash flow to be only $2,778,200 in 2011, but thereafter the cash flow is $3,418,200 per year, with an additional $640,000 working capital recovered in the fifth year.

The key to this improvement is operating leverage. If costs are incurred in euros and do not increase after a devaluation, an increase in the sales price by the amount of devaluation will lead to sharply higher profits.

Other Possibilities

If any portion of sales revenues were incurred in other currencies, the situation would be different. Trident Europe might leave the foreign sales price unchanged, in effect raising the euro-equivalent price. Alternatively it might leave the euro-equivalent price unchanged, thus lowering the foreign sales price in an attempt to gain volume. Of course, it could also position itself between these two extremes. Depending on elasticities and the proportion of foreign to domestic sales, total sales revenue might rise or fall.

If some or all raw material or components were imported and paid for in hard currencies, euro operating costs would increase after the devaluation of the euro. Another possibility is that local (not imported) euro costs would rise after a devaluation.

Measurement of Loss

Exhibit 12.3 summarizes the change in expected year-end cash flows for the three cases and compares them with the cash flow expected should no devaluation occur (Base Case). These changes are then discounted by Trident Corporation's assumed weighted average cost of capital of 20% to obtain the present value of the gain (loss) on operating exposure.

In Case 1, in which nothing changes after the euro is devalued, Trident Corporation incurs an operating loss with a present value of $1,033,914. In Case 2, in which volume doubled with no price change after devaluation, Trident Corporation experienced an operating gain with a present value of $2,866,106. In Case 3, in which the euro sales price was increased and volume did not change, the present value of the operating gain from devaluation was $3,742,892. An almost infinite number of combinations of volume, price, and cost could follow any devaluation, and any or all of them might take effect immediately after a devaluation or only after the passage of time.

Strategic Management of Operating Exposure

The objective of both operating and transaction exposure management is to anticipate and influence the effect of unexpected changes in exchange rates on a firm's future cash flows, rather than merely hoping for the best. To meet this objective, management can *diversify the firm's operating and financing base*. Management can also *change the firm's operating and financing policies*.

The key to managing operating exposure at the strategic level is for management to recognize a disequilibrium in parity conditions when it occurs and to be prepositioned to react most appropriately. This task can best be accomplished if a firm *diversifies* internationally both its operating and its financing bases. Diversifying operations means diversifying sales, location of production facilities, and raw material sources. Diversifying the financing base means raising funds in more than one capital market and in more than one currency.

A diversification strategy permits the firm to react either actively or passively, depending on management's risk preference, to opportunities presented by disequilibrium conditions in the foreign exchange, capital, and product markets. Such a strategy does not require management to predict disequilibrium but only to *recognize* it when it occurs. It does require management to consider how competitors are prepositioned with respect to their own operating exposures. This knowledge should reveal which firms would be helped or hurt competitively by alternative disequilibrium scenarios.

Diversifying Operations

If a firm's operations are diversified internationally, management is prepositioned both to recognize disequilibrium when it occurs and to react competitively. Consider the case where purchasing power parity is temporarily in disequilibrium. Although the disequilibrium may have been unpredictable, management can often recognize its symptoms as soon as they occur. For example, management might notice a change in comparative costs in the firm's own plants located in different countries. It might also observe changed profit margins or sales volume in one area compared to another, depending on price and income elasticities of demand and competitors' reactions.

Recognizing a temporary change in worldwide competitive conditions permits management to make changes in operating strategies. Management might make marginal shifts in sourcing raw materials, components, or finished products. If spare capacity exists, production runs can be lengthened in one country and reduced in another. The marketing effort can be strengthened in export markets where the firm's products have become more price competitive because of the disequilibrium condition.

Even if management does not actively distort normal operations when exchange rates change, the firm should experience some beneficial portfolio effects. The variability of its cash flows is probably reduced by international diversification of its production, sourcing, and sales because exchange rate changes under disequilibrium conditions are likely to increase the firm's competitiveness in some markets while reducing it in others. In that case, operating exposure would be neutralized. *Global Finance in Practice 12.1* shows Goodyear's response to the Mexican peso devaluation through a timely shift in operating strategy.

In contrast to the internationally diversified MNE, a purely domestic firm might be subject to the full impact of foreign exchange operating exposure even though it does not have

GLOBAL FINANCE IN PRACTICE 12.1

Goodyear's Response to the Mexican Peso's Devaluation

On December 20, 1994, when Goodyear's manager in Mexico heard on his car radio that the peso had crashed, he met with his managers immediately to assess the damage. Within days, he figured that domestic demand for Goodyear tires would plunge more than 20%, or 3,000 a day. His choices: lay off workers or find new export markets—right away, before his warehouse overflowed.

His team members, aided by the Goodyear Tire and Rubber company headquarters in Akron, Ohio, not only found enough export buyers to make up for what turned out to be a 3,500 tire drop in domestic sales, but also they found spots to sell 1,600 more, setting an output record at the plant some 15 miles north of Mexico City. A factory that had imported supplies but exported not a single tire in 1992 now shipped half its production, mostly to the United States but also to South America and Europe. The company quickly moved from being a net importer to being a net exporter.

foreign currency cash flows. For example, it could experience intense import competition in its domestic market from competing firms producing in countries with undervalued currencies. *Global Finance in Practice 12.2* provides one example of such competition.

A purely domestic firm does not have the option to react to an international disequilibrium condition in the same manner as an MNE. In fact, a purely domestic firm will not be positioned to recognize that a disequilibrium exists because it lacks comparative data from its

GLOBAL FINANCE IN PRACTICE 12.2

Detroit Dreams of a Rising Yen in the Fall of 2007

The financial gods work in mysterious ways. While many unfortunates are being punished by the subprime maelstrom, the US auto industry could receive a much needed boost if the yen continues to rise. On top of its myriad home-grown failings, Detroit has suffered from Japanese companies' success at winning market share. While factors such as build quality and a fashion for smaller cars have played a part, there is no doubt that the likes of Toyota and Honda have priced aggressively. True, the Japanese are more efficient producers, but a weak yen over the past few years has helped their cause.

Historically, there is a strong correlation between the volume of automobile exports from Japan to the US and the yen/dollar exchange rate. Over the past 15 years there have been two periods of prolonged yen strength versus the dollar. The most marked was the two years before 1995, when the dollar fell to ¥80. Over that time the number of cars offloaded at US ports almost halved to about 80,000 vehicles a month. Imports from Japan also flagged between 2002 and 2004, the previous period of yen strength.

Of course, the US market has moved on since the 1990s. Companies like Toyota now have a considerable manufacturing presence on US soil. They also have a far bigger market share to protect and Detroit is arguably in even worse shape. But Japanese auto companies remain very sensitive to the dollar: Honda's earnings per share, for example, would fall by about a third should the dollar fall from ¥120 to ¥100. And with a global reach, they can quickly change their emphasis from the US to, say, Europe.

The "Big Three" US carmakers would have to lift their game to capitalise on any exchange rate move. With luck Chrysler, in new hands, will also shake up Ford and General Motors. But Detroit will have to be quick, for there is likely to be an economic hit from the subprime crisis, too. Still, if US manufacturers can grab back some market share regardless of a downturn, they may well, in relative terms, emerge stronger.

Source: "Detroit Winners," *Financial Times*, Wednesday September 5, 2007, p.12.

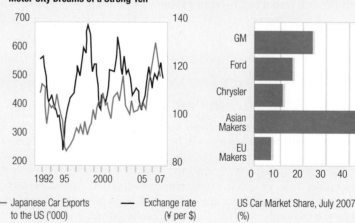

Motor City Dreams of a Strong Yen

— Japanese Car Exports to the US ('000)   — Exchange rate (¥ per $)

US Car Market Share, July 2007 (%)

Source: Datastream; Ward's AutoInfoBank: Citigroup

own internal sources. By the time external data are available from published sources, it is often too late to react. Even if a domestic firm recognizes the disequilibrium, it cannot quickly shift production and sales into foreign markets in which it has had no previous presence.

Diversifying Financing

If a firm diversifies its financing sources, it will be prepositioned to take advantage of temporary deviations from the international Fisher effect. If interest rate differentials do not equal expected changes in exchange rates, opportunities to lower a firm's cost of capital will exist. However, to be able to switch financing sources, a firm must already be well known in the international investment community, with banking contacts firmly established. Once again, this is not an option for a domestic firm that has limited its financing to one capital market.

Although we recommend diversification as a strategy for foreign exchange risk management, such a strategy has a potentially favorable impact on other risks as well. In particular, it could reduce the variability of future cash flows due to domestic business cycles, provided these are not perfectly correlated with international cycles. It could increase the availability of capital, and reduce its cost, by diversifying such risks as restrictive capital market policies or government borrowing competition in the capital market. It could mitigate political risks such as expropriation, war, blocked funds, or unfavorable changes in laws that reduce or eliminate profitability. The list of advantages from international diversification can even be extended to such areas as spreading the risk of technological obsolescence and reducing portfolio risk in the context of the capital asset pricing model. Now we are verging on the diversification strategy theme that appears throughout the rest of this book.

Constraints exist that may limit the feasibility of a diversification strategy for foreign exchange risk management or one of the other risks just mentioned. For example, the technology of a particular industry may require such large economies of scale that it is not economically feasible to diversify production locations. Firms in this industry could still diversify sales and financing sources, however. On the other hand, a firm may be too small or too unknown to attract international equity investors or lenders. Yet it could at least diversify its sales internationally. Thus, a diversification strategy can be implemented only as far as is feasible.

Proactive Management of Operating Exposure

Operating and transaction exposures can be *partially managed* by adopting operating or financing policies that offset anticipated foreign exchange exposures. Six of the most commonly employed proactive policies are as follows:

1. Matching currency cash flows
2. Risk-sharing agreements
3. Back-to-back or parallel loans
4. Currency swaps
5. Leads and lags
6. Reinvoicing centers

Matching Currency Cash Flows

One way to offset an anticipated continuous long exposure to a particular currency is to acquire debt denominated in that currency. Exhibit 12.4 demonstrates the exposure of a U.S. firm with continuing export sales to Canada. In order to compete effectively in Canadian

EXHIBIT 12.4   Matching: Debt Financing as a Financial Hedge

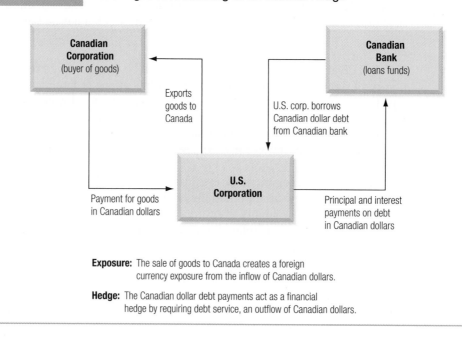

Exposure: The sale of goods to Canada creates a foreign
currency exposure from the inflow of Canadian dollars.

Hedge: The Canadian dollar debt payments act as a financial
hedge by requiring debt service, an outflow of Canadian dollars.

markets, the firm invoices all export sales in Canadian dollars. This policy results in a continuing receipt of Canadian dollars month after month. If the export sales are part of a continuing supplier relationship, the long Canadian dollar position is relatively predictable and constant. This endless series of transaction exposures could of course be continually hedged with forward contracts or other contractual hedges, as discussed in Chapter 11.

But what if the firm sought out a continual use, an outflow, for its continual inflow of Canadian dollars? If the U.S. firm were to acquire part of its debt-capital in the Canadian dollar markets, it could use the relatively predictable Canadian dollar cash inflows from export sales to service the principal and interest payments on Canadian dollar debt and be *cash flow matched*. The U.S.-based firm has hedged an operational cash inflow by creating a financial cash outflow, and so it does not have to actively manage the exposure with contractual financial instruments such as forward contracts. This form of hedging, sometimes referred to as *matching*, is effective in eliminating currency exposure when the exposure cash flow is relatively constant and predictable over time.

The list of potential matching strategies is nearly endless. A second alternative would be for the U.S. firm to seek potential suppliers of raw materials or components in Canada as a substitute for U.S. or other foreign firms. The firm would then possess not only an operational Canadian dollar cash inflow, the receivable, but also a Canadian dollar operational cash outflow, a payable. If the cash flows were roughly the same in magnitude and timing, the strategy would be a *natural hedge*. The term *natural* refers to operating-based activities of the firm.

A third alternative, often referred to as *currency switching*, would be to pay foreign suppliers with Canadian dollars. For example, if the U.S. firm imported components from Mexico, the Mexican firms themselves might welcome payment in Canadian dollars because they are short Canadian dollars in their multinational cash flow network.

Currency Clauses: Risk-Sharing

An alternative arrangement for managing a long-term cash flow exposure between firms with a continuing buyer-supplier relationship is *risk-sharing*. Risk-sharing is a contractual arrangement in which the buyer and seller agree to "share" or split currency movement impacts on payments between them. If the two firms are interested in a long-term relationship based on product quality and supplier reliability and not on the whims of the currency markets, a cooperative agreement to share the burden of currency risk management may be in order.

If Ford's North American operations import automotive parts from Mazda (Japan) every month, year after year, major swings in exchange rates can benefit one party at the expense of the other. Ford is a major stockholder of Mazda, but it does not exert control over its operations. Therefore, the risk-sharing agreement is particularly appropriate; transactions between the two are both intercompany and intracompany. A risk-sharing agreement solidifies the partnership. One potential solution would be for Ford and Mazda to agree that all purchases by Ford will be made in Japanese yen at the current exchange rate, as long as the spot rate on the date of invoice is between, say, ¥115/$ and ¥125/$. If the exchange rate is between these values on the payment dates, Ford agrees to accept whatever transaction exposure exists (because it is paying in a foreign currency). If, however, the exchange rate falls outside this range on the payment date, Ford and Mazda will *share* the difference equally.

For example, Ford has an account payable of ¥25,000,000 for the month of March. If the spot rate on the date of invoice is ¥110/$, the Japanese yen would have appreciated versus the dollar, causing Ford's costs of purchasing automotive parts to rise. Since this rate falls outside the contractual range, Mazda would agree to accept a total payment in Japanese yen which would result from a difference of ¥5/$ (¥115 − ¥110). Ford's payment would be as follows:

$$\left[\frac{¥25,000,000}{¥115.00/\$ - \dfrac{¥5.00/\$}{2}} \right] = \frac{¥25,000,000}{¥112.50/\$} = \$222,222.22$$

Ford's total payment in Japanese yen would be calculated using an exchange rate of ¥112.50/$, and saves Ford $5,050.51. At a spot rate of ¥110/$, Ford's costs for March would be $227,272.73. The risk-sharing agreement between Ford and Mazda allows Ford to pay $222,222.22, a savings of $5,050.51 over the cost without risk-sharing (this "savings" is a reduction in an increased cost, not a true cost reduction). Both parties therefore incur costs and benefits from exchange rate movements outside the specified band. Note that the movement could just as easily have been in Mazda's favor if the spot rate had moved to ¥130/$.

The risk-sharing arrangement is intended to smooth the impact on both parties of volatile and unpredictable exchange rate movements. Of course, a sustained appreciation of one currency versus the other would require the negotiation of a new sharing agreement, but the ultimate goal of the agreement is to alleviate currency pressures on the continuing business relationship. Risk-sharing agreements like these have been in use for nearly 50 years on world markets. They became something of a rarity during the 1960s when exchange rates were relatively stable under the Bretton Woods Agreement. But with the return to floating exchange rates in the 1970s, firms with long-term customer-supplier relationships across borders have returned to some old ways of maintaining mutually beneficial long-term trade.

Back-to-Back Loans

A *back-to-back loan*, also referred to as a *parallel loan* or *credit swap*, occurs when two business firms in separate countries arrange to borrow each other's currency for a specific period of time. They return the borrowed currencies at an agreed terminal date. The operation is conducted outside the foreign exchange markets, although spot quotations may be used as the reference point for determining the amount of funds to be swapped. Such a swap creates a covered hedge against exchange loss, since each company, on its own books, borrows the same currency it repays. Back-to-back loans are also used at a time of actual or anticipated legal limitations on the transfer of investment funds to or from either country.

The structure of a typical back-to-back loan is illustrated in Exhibit 12.5. A British parent firm wanting to invest funds in its Dutch subsidiary locates a Dutch parent firm that wants to invest funds in the United Kingdom. Avoiding the exchange markets entirely, the British parent lends pounds to the Dutch subsidiary in the United Kingdom, while the Dutch parent lends euros to the British subsidiary in the Netherlands. The two loans would be for equal values at the current spot rate and for a specified maturity. At maturity the two separate loans would each be repaid to the original lender, again without any need to use the foreign exchange markets. Neither loan carries any foreign exchange risk, and neither loan normally needs the approval of any governmental body regulating the availability of foreign exchange for investment purposes.

Parent company guarantees are not needed on the back-to-back loans because each loan carries the right of offset in the event of default of the other loan. A further agreement can provide for maintenance of principal parity in case of changes in the spot rate between the two countries. For example, if the pound dropped by more than, say, 6% for as long as 30 days, the British parent might have to advance additional pounds to the Dutch subsidiary to bring the principal value of the two loans back to parity. A similar provision would protect the British if the euro should weaken. Although this parity provision might lead to changes in the amount of home currency each party must lend during the period of the agreement, it does not increase foreign exchange risk, because at maturity all loans are repaid in the same currency loaned.

EXHIBIT 12.5   Using a Back-to-Back Loan for Currency Hedging

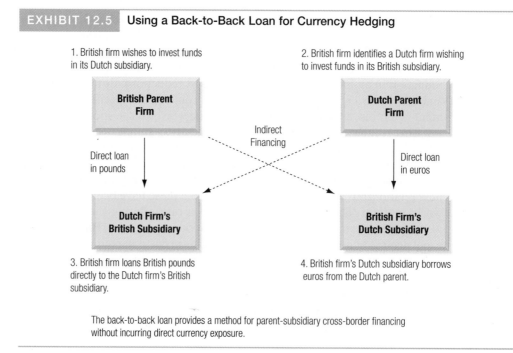

1. British firm wishes to invest funds in its Dutch subsidiary.

2. British firm identifies a Dutch firm wishing to invest funds in its British subsidiary.

British Parent Firm

Dutch Parent Firm

Indirect Financing

Direct loan in pounds

Direct loan in euros

Dutch Firm's British Subsidiary

British Firm's Dutch Subsidiary

3. British firm loans British pounds directly to the Dutch firm's British subsidiary.

4. British firm's Dutch subsidiary borrows euros from the Dutch parent.

The back-to-back loan provides a method for parent-subsidiary cross-border financing without incurring direct currency exposure.

There are two fundamental impediments to widespread use of the back-to-back loan. First, it is difficult for a firm to find a partner, termed a *counterparty*, for the currency, amount, and timing desired. Second, a risk exists that one of the parties will fail to return the borrowed funds at the designated maturity—although this risk is minimized because each party to the loan has, in effect, 100% collateral, albeit in a different currency. These disadvantages have led to the rapid development and wide use of the currency swap.

Currency Swaps

A *currency swap* resembles a back-to-back loan except that it does not appear on a firm's balance sheet. As we noted briefly in Chapter 6, the term *swap* is widely used to describe a foreign exchange agreement between two parties to exchange a given amount of one currency for another and, after a period of time, to give back the original amounts swapped. Care should be taken to clarify which of the many different swaps is being referred to in a specific case.

In a currency swap, a firm and a swap dealer or swap bank agree to exchange an equivalent amount of two different currencies for a specified period of time. Currency swaps can be negotiated for a wide range of maturities up to at least 10 years. If funds are more expensive in one country than another, a fee may be required to compensate for the interest differential. The swap dealer or swap bank acts as a middleman in setting up the swap agreement.

A typical currency swap first requires two firms to borrow funds in the markets and currencies in which they are best known. For example, a Japanese firm would typically borrow yen on a regular basis in its home market. If, however, the Japanese firm were exporting to the United States and earning U.S. dollars, it might wish to construct a *matching cash flow hedge*, which would allow it to use the U.S. dollars earned to make regular debt service payments on U.S. dollar debt. If, however, the Japanese firm is not well known in the U.S. financial markets, it may have no ready access to U.S. dollar debt.

One way in which it could, in effect, borrow dollars, is to participate in a *cross-currency swap* (see Exhibit 12.6). The Japanese firm could swap its yen-denominated debt service payments with another firm that has U.S. dollar-debt service payments. This swap would have the Japanese firm "paying dollars" and "receiving yen." The Japanese firm would then have dollar debt service without actually borrowing U.S. dollars. Simultaneously, a U.S. corporation could actually be entering into a cross-currency swap in the opposite direction—"paying yen" and "receiving dollars." The swap dealer is a middleman.

Swap dealers arrange most swaps on a blind basis, meaning that the initiating firm does not know who is on the other side of the swap arrangement—the counterparty. The firm views the dealer or bank as its counterparty. Because the swap markets are dominated by the major money center banks worldwide, the counterparty risk is acceptable. Because the swap dealer's business is arranging swaps, the dealer can generally arrange for the currency, amount, and timing of the desired swap.

Accountants in the United States treat the currency swap as a foreign exchange transaction rather than as debt and treat the obligation to reverse the swap at some later date as a forward exchange contract. Forward exchange contracts can be matched against assets, but they are entered in a firm's footnotes rather than as balance sheet items. The result is that both translation and operating exposures are avoided, and neither a long-term receivable nor a long-term debt is created on the balance sheet. The risk of changes in currency rates to the implied collateral in a long-term currency swap can be treated with a clause similar to the maintenance-of-principal clause in a back-to-back loan. If exchange rates change by more than some specified amount, say 10%, an additional amount of the weaker currency might have to be advanced.

EXHIBIT 12.6   Using a Cross-Currency Swap to Hedge Currency Exposure

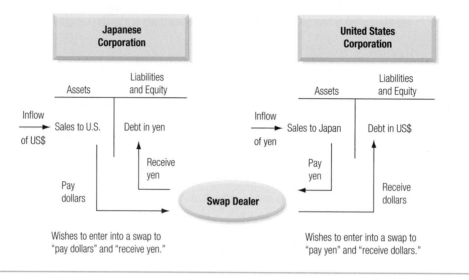

Both the Japanese corporation and the U.S. corporation would like to enter into a cross-currency swap that would allow them to use foreign currency cash inflows to service debt.

After being introduced on a global scale in the early 1980s, currency swaps have grown to be one of the largest financial derivative markets in the world. Chapter 9 provides a detailed explanation of the theory and application of currency swaps in the context of interest rate risk management.

Leads and Lags: Retiming the Transfer of Funds

Firms can reduce both operating and transaction exposure by accelerating or decelerating the timing of payments that must be made or received in foreign currencies. *To lead* is to pay early. A firm holding a soft currency or that has debts denominated in a hard currency will lead by using the soft currency to pay the hard currency debts as soon as possible. The object is to pay the currency debts before the soft currency drops in value. *To lag* is to pay late. A firm holding a hard currency and having debts denominated in a soft currency will lag by paying those debts late, hoping that less of the hard currency will be needed. If possible, firms will also lead and lag their collection of receivables, collecting soft foreign currency receivables early and collecting hard foreign currency receivables later.

Leading and lagging can be done between related firms (intracompany) or with independent firms (intercompany). Assuming that payments will be made eventually, leading or lagging always results in changing the cash and payables position of one firm, with the reverse effect on the other firm.

Intracompany Leads and Lags. Leading and lagging between related firms is more feasible because they presumably embrace a common set of goals for the consolidated group. Furthermore, the many periodic payments between units of an MNE provide opportunities for many types of leads or lags. Because opportunities for leading or lagging payments depend on the requirement for payments of this nature, the device is more readily adaptable to a company that operates on an integrated worldwide basis. If each unit functions as a separate and self sufficient entity, the motivation for leading or lagging diminishes. In the case of financing cash flows with foreign subsidiaries, there is an additional motivation for early or late payments to position funds for liquidity reasons. For example, a subsidiary that is allowed to lag payments to the parent company is in reality borrowing from the parent.

Because the use of leads and lags is an obvious technique for minimizing foreign exchange exposure and for shifting the burden of financing, many governments impose limits on the allowed range. Terms allowed by governments are often subject to negotiation when a good argument can be presented. Thus, some limits are subject to exceptions. For example, in the past, Italy has placed no limit on export and import lags on trade payments with other OECD countries. However, a 180-day limit on export lags and a five-year limit on import lags was applied to trade with non-OECD countries.

Intercompany Leads and Lags. Leading or lagging between independent firms requires the time preference of one firm to be imposed to the detriment of the other firm. For example, Trident Europe may wish to lead in collecting its Brazilian accounts receivable that are denominated in reais because it expects the reais to drop in value compared with the euro. But why should the Brazilian customers prepay their accounts payable? Credit in reais was part of the inducement for them to purchase from Trident Europe to begin with. The only way the Brazilians would be willing to pay their accounts payable early would be for the German creditor to offer a discount about equal to the forward discount on the reais or, in equilibrium, the difference between Brazilian and German interest rates for the period of prepayment. In equilibrium this "discount" would eliminate the benefit to Trident Europe of collecting the "soft" currency earlier.

Reinvoicing Centers

A *reinvoicing center* is a separate corporate subsidiary that serves as a type of middleman between the parent or related unit in one location and all foreign subsidiaries in a geographic region. Manufacturing subsidiaries sell goods to distribution subsidiaries of the same firm only by selling to a reinvoicing center, which in turn resells to the distribution subsidiary. Title passes to the reinvoicing center, but the physical movement of goods is direct from the manufacturing plant, in this case Trident USA, to the foreign subsidiary, Trident Brazil. Thus, the reinvoicing center handles paperwork but has no inventory.

As shown in Exhibit 12.7, the U.S. manufacturing unit of Trident Corporation invoices the firm's reinvoicing center—located within the corporate headquarters facilities in Los Angeles—in U.S. dollars. However, the actual goods are shipped directly to Trident Brazil. The reinvoicing center in turn resells to Trident Brazil in Brazilian reais. Consequentially, all operating units deal only in their own currency, and all transaction exposure lies with the reinvoicing center.

To avoid accusations of profit-shifting through transfer pricing, most reinvoicing centers resell at cost plus a small commission for their services. The resale price is frequently the manufacturer's price times the forward exchange rate for the date on which payment from the buyer is expected, although other combinations are possible. The commission covers the cost of the reinvoicing center, but does not shift profits away from operating subsidiaries.

There are three basic benefits that arise from the creation of a reinvoicing center:

1. **Managing Foreign Exchange Exposure.** The formation of the center allows the management of all foreign exchange transaction exposure for intracompany sales to be located in one place. Reinvoicing center personnel can develop a specialized expertise in choosing which hedging technique is best at any moment, and they are likely to obtain more competitive foreign exchange quotations from banks because they are dealing in larger transactions.

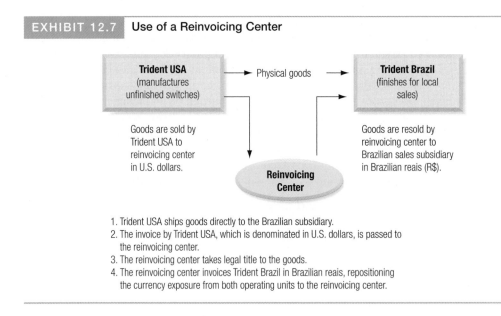

EXHIBIT 12.7   Use of a Reinvoicing Center

1. Trident USA ships goods directly to the Brazilian subsidiary.
2. The invoice by Trident USA, which is denominated in U.S. dollars, is passed to the reinvoicing center.
3. The reinvoicing center takes legal title to the goods.
4. The reinvoicing center invoices Trident Brazil in Brazilian reais, repositioning the currency exposure from both operating units to the reinvoicing center.

2. **Guaranteeing the Exchange Rate for Future Orders.** By guaranteeing the exchange rate for future orders, the reinvoicing center can set firm local currency costs in advance. This enables distribution subsidiaries to make firm bids to unrelated final customers, and to protect against the exposure created by a backlog of unfilled orders. Backlog exposure does not appear on the corporate books because the sales are not yet recorded. Sales subsidiaries can focus on their marketing activities and their performance can be judged without distortion because of exchange rate changes.

3. **Managing Intra-Subsidiary Cash Flows.** The center can manage intra-subsidiary cash flows, including leads and lags of payments. With a reinvoicing center all subsidiaries settle intracompany accounts in their local currencies. The reinvoicing center need only hedge residual foreign exchange exposure.

The main disadvantage is one of cost relative to benefits received. One additional corporate unit must be created, and a separate set of books must be kept. The initial setup cost can be high because existing order-processing procedures must be reprogrammed. The center will have an impact on the tax status and customs duties of all subsidiaries, as well as on the amount of foreign exchange business directed to local banks in each country. Establishment of a reinvoicing center is likely to bring increased scrutiny by tax authorities to be sure that it is not functioning as a tax haven. Consequently, a variety of professional costs will be incurred for tax and legal advice, in addition to the costs of personnel operating the center.

Contractual Approaches: Hedging the Unhedgeable

Some MNEs now attempt to hedge their operating exposure with contractual strategies. Firms like Eastman Kodak (U.S.) and Merck (U.S.) have undertaken long-term currency option positions hedges designed to offset lost earnings from adverse exchange rate changes. This hedging of what many of these firms refer to as *strategic exposure* or *competitive exposure* seems to fly in the face of traditional theory.

The ability of firms to hedge the "unhedgeable" is dependent upon *predictability*: 1) the predictability of the firm's future cash flows and 2) the predictability of the firm's competitor's responses to exchange rate changes. Although the management of many firms may believe they are capable of predicting their own cash flows, few in practice feel capable of accurately predicting competitor response.

Merck is an example of a firm whose management feels capable of both. The company possesses relatively predictable long-run revenue streams due to the niche-product nature of the pharmaceuticals industry. As a U.S.-based exporter to foreign markets, markets in which sales levels by product are relatively predictable and prices are often regulated by government, Merck can accurately predict net long-term cash flows in foreign currencies five and ten years into the future. Merck has a relatively undiversified operating structure. It is highly centralized in terms of where research, development, and production costs are located. Merck's managers feel Merck has no real alternatives but contractual hedging if it is to weather long-term unexpected exchange rate changes. Merck has purchased over-the-counter (OTC) long-term put options on foreign currencies versus the U.S. dollar as insurance against potential lost earnings from exchange rate changes. In Merck's case, the predictability of competitor response to exchange rate changes is less pertinent given the niche-market nature of pharmaceutical products.

Eastman Kodak is another MNE that has in the past undertaken contractual hedging of its operating exposure. Kodak management believes its markets are largely price driven and is aware that its major competitor, Fuji, has a Japanese cost base. If the U.S. dollar were to strengthen in the medium to long term, Kodak's market share in the United States and in foreign markets would decline. Kodak leadership also believes that whatever sales Kodak loses, its competitors will gain. Kodak has therefore also purchased long-term put options on foreign currencies, which would replace long-term earnings if the value of the U.S. dollar rose unexpectedly.

The magnitude of the option position depends on the nature of desired replacement. For example, if Kodak wished to insure only the lost net earnings from exchange rate induced losses, the option position would be considerably smaller than a position attempting to replace gross sales revenues. Given the premium expenses associated with long-term put option positions of this type, replacing earnings is preferred to replacing sales.

A significant question remains as to the true effectiveness of hedging operating exposure with contractual hedges. The fact remains that even after feared exchange rate movements and put option position payoffs have occurred, the firm is competitively disadvantaged. The capital outlay required for the purchase of such sizable put option positions is capital not used for the potential diversification of operations, which in the long run might have more effectively maintained the firm's global market share and international competitiveness.

SUMMARY POINTS

- *Foreign exchange exposure* is a measure of the potential for a firm's profitability, net cash flow, and market value to change because of a change in exchange rates. The three main types of foreign exchange risk are *operating*, *transaction*, and *translation exposures*.

- *Operating exposure* measures the change in value of the firm that results from changes in future operating cash flows caused by an unexpected change in exchange rates.

- Strategies for the management of operating exposure emphasize the structuring of firm operations in order to create matching streams of cash flows by currency. This is termed *natural hedging*.

- The objective of operating exposure management is to anticipate and influence the effect of unexpected changes in exchange rates on a firm's future cash flow, rather than being forced into passive reaction to such changes. This task can best be accomplished if a firm diversifies internationally both its operations and its financing base.

■ Proactive policies include matching currency of cash flow, currency risk-sharing clauses, back-to-back loan structures, and cross-currency swap agreements.

■ Contractual approaches (that is, options and forwards) have occasionally been used to hedge operating exposure but are costly and possibly ineffective.

MINI-CASE   Toyota's European Operating Exposure

It was January 2002, and Toyota Motor Europe Manufacturing (TMEM) had a problem. More specifically, Mr. Toyoda Shuhei, the new President of TMEM, had a problem. He was on his way to Toyota Motor Company's (Japan) corporate offices outside Tokyo to explain the continuing losses of European manufacturing and sales operations. The CEO of Toyota Motor Company, Mr. Hiroshi Okuda, was expecting a proposal from Mr. Shuhei to reduce and eventually eliminate these losses. The situation was intense given that TMEM was the only major Toyota subsidiary losing money.

Toyota and Auto Manufacturing

Toyota Motor Company was the number one automobile manufacturer in Japan, the third largest manufacturer in the world by unit sales (5.5 million units or one auto every six seconds), but number eight in sales in continental

Europe. The global automobile manufacturing industry, like many industries, had been experiencing continued consolidation in recent years as margins were squeezed, economies of scale and scope pursued, and global sales slowed.

Toyota was no different. It had continued to rationalize its manufacturing along regional lines and to increase the amount of local manufacturing in North America. In 2001, over 60% of Toyota's North American sales were locally manufactured. But Toyota's European sales were nowhere close to this yet. Most of Toyota's automobile and truck manufacturing for Europe was still done in Japan. In 2001, only 26% of the autos sold in Europe were manufactured in Europe (including the U.K.), the remainder being imported from Japan (see Exhibit 1).

Toyota Motor Europe sold 634,000 automobiles in 2000. Europe was the second largest foreign market for Toyota, second only to North America. TMEM expected

EXHIBIT 1   Toyota Motor's European Currency Operating Structure

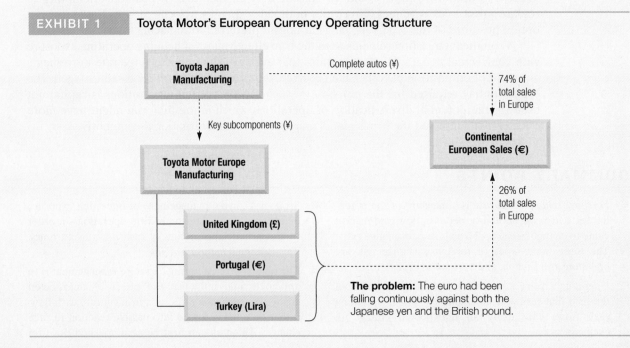

significant growth in European sales and was planning to expand European manufacturing and sales to 800,000 units by 2005. But for fiscal 2001 the unit reported operating losses of ¥9.897 billion ($82.5 million at ¥120/$). TMEM had three assembly plants in the United Kingdom, one plant in Turkey, and one in Portugal. In November 2000, Toyota Motor Europe announced publicly that it would not generate profits for the next two years due to the weakness of the euro.

Toyota had recently introduced a new model to the European market, the Yaris, which was proving very successful. The Yaris, a super-small vehicle with a 1,000cc engine, had sold more than 180,000 units in 2000. Although the Yaris had been specifically designed for the European market, the decision had been made early on to manufacture it in Japan.

Currency Exposure

One source of the continuing operating losses suffered by TMEM was the falling value of the euro. Throughout 1999 and the first half of 2000 the yen strengthened against the euro (see Exhibit 2). Although the euro regained some ground in late 2000, it remained relatively weak.

As demonstrated in Exhibit 1, the cost base for most of the autos sold within the Continental European market was the Japanese yen. As the yen rose against the euro, costs increased significantly when measured in euro terms. If Toyota wished to preserve its price competitiveness in the European market, it had to absorb most of the exchange rate changes, suffering reduced or negative margins on both completed cars and key subcomponents shipped to its European manufacturing centers. Deciding to manufacture the Yaris in Japan had only exacerbated the problem.

Management Response

Toyota management was not passively sitting by. In 2001, they had started up some assembly operations in Valenciennes, France. Although Valenciennes still constituted a relatively small percentage of total European sales as of January 2002, Toyota planned to continue to expand its capacity and capabilities to source about 25% of European sales by 2004. Assembly of the Yaris was scheduled to be moved to Valenciennes in 2002. The continuing problem, however, was that it was an assembly facility, which meant that much of the expensive value-added content of the cars being assembled was still based in either Japan or the United Kingdom.

Mr. Shuhei, with the approval of Mr. Okuda, had also initiated a local sourcing and procurement program for the United Kingdom manufacturing operations. TMEM wished to decrease the number of key components imported from Toyota Japan to reduce the currency exposure of the U.K. unit. But again, the continuing problem of the euro's weakness against the British pound, as shown in Exhibit 3, reduced the effectiveness of even this solution.

| EXHIBIT 2 | Daily Exchange Rates: Japanese Yen per Euro |

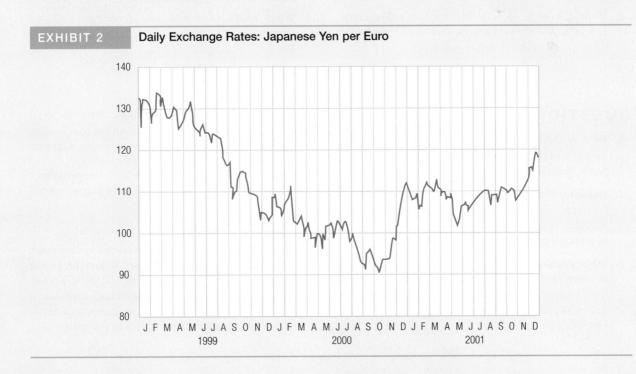

EXHIBIT 3	Daily Exchange Rates: British Pounds per Euro

Case Questions

1. Why do you think Toyota waited so long to move much of its manufacturing for European sales to Europe?

2. If Britain were to join the European Monetary Union, would the problem be resolved? How likely do you think it is that Britain will join?

3. If you were Mr. Shuhei, how would you categorize your problems and solutions? What was a short-term and what was a long-term problem?

4. What measures would you recommend Toyota Europe take to resolve the continuing operating losses?

QUESTIONS

1. **By Any Other Name.** Operating exposure has other names. What are they, and what do the words in these names suggest about the nature of operating exposure?

2. **Exposure Type Comparison.** From a cash flow measurement perspective, what is the major difference between losses from transaction exposure and from operating exposure?

3. **Intracompany Cash Flows.** What are the differences between operating cash flows and financial cash flows from parent to subsidiary or vice versa? List several cash flows in both categories and indicate why that flow takes place.

4. **Expected Exchange Rate Changes.** Why do unexpected exchange rate changes contribute to operating exposure, but expected exchange rate changes do not?

5. **Macroeconomic Uncertainty.** What is *macroeconomic uncertainty* and how does it relate to measuring operating exposure?

6. **Who Owns Whom?** *The Economist* (December 1–7, 2001, p. 4 of "Survey" insert) reported on a French company that had a subsidiary in India. The Indian subsidiary in turn had its own subsidiary in France. How would you conjecture the operating exposure to the international French firm of an unexpected devaluation of the Indian rupee relative to the euro?

7. **Strategic Responses.** What strategic responses can a multinational firm make to avoid loss from its operating exposure?

8. **Proactive Policies to Offset Foreign Exchange Exposure.** A fine line exists between fully anticipated exchange rate changes and possible-but-not-assured exchange rate changes. If management believes an exchange rate change might take place but cannot estimate the timing or amount of such change, what might management do to alleviate the possible consequences of such an uncertain devaluation?

9. **Paradox?** The possibility of a gain or loss on operating exposure offset by an opposite loss or gain on transaction exposure may appear contradictory. Explain why, when the currency in which a foreign subsidiary operates falls in value, the parent firm may experience both an operating gain and a transaction loss.

10. **Subsidiary Borrowing from Parent.** Newly established foreign subsidiaries are often financed with debt supplied by the parent, perhaps because a new subsidiary has no financial credit record or worthiness of its own, or maybe because the parent firm can acquire capital more cheaply. As soon as the subsidiary is operational, however, parent firms usually encourage or require their subsidiaries to arrange their own local debt financing. How would this approach serve as a natural hedge for most subsidiaries?

PROBLEMS

1. **Kona Macadamia Nuts.** Kona Macadamia Nuts, based in Hilo, Hawaii, exports Macadamia nuts worldwide. The Japanese market is its biggest export market, with average annual sales invoiced in yen to Japanese customers of ¥1,200,000,000. At the present exchange rate of ¥125/$ this is equivalent to $9,600,000. Sales are relatively equally distributed during the year. They show up as a ¥250,000,000 account receivable on Kona Macadamia Nuts' balance sheet. Credit terms to each customer allow for 60 days before payment is due. Monthly cash collections are typically ¥100,000,000.

Kona would like to hedge its yen receipts, but it has too many customers and transactions to make it practical to sell each receivable forward. It does not want to use options because they are considered to be too expensive for this particular purpose. Therefore, they have decided to use a "matching" hedge by borrowing yen.

a. How much should Kona borrow in yen?
b. What should be the terms of payment on the yen loan?

*2. **Newport Lifts (A).** Newport Lifts (U.S.) exports heavy crane equipment to several Chinese dock facilities. Sales are currently 10,000 units per year at the yuan equivalent of $24,000 each. The Chinese yuan (renminbi) has been trading at Yuan8.20/$, but a Hong Kong advisory service predicts the renminbi will drop in value next week to Yuan9.20/$, after which it will remain unchanged for at least a decade. Accepting this forecast as given, Newport Lifts faces a pricing decision in the face of the impending devaluation. It may 1) maintain the same yuan price and in effect sell for fewer dollars, in which case Chinese volume will not change or 2) maintain the same dollar price, raise the yuan price in China to offset the devaluation, and experience a 10% drop in unit volume. Direct costs are 75% of the U.S. sales price.

a. What would be the short-run (one year) impact of each pricing strategy?
b. Which do you recommend?

3. **Newport Lifts (B).** Assume the same facts as in problem 2. Additionally, financial management believes that if it maintains the same yuan sales price, volume will increase at 12% per annum for eight years. Dollar costs will not change. At the end of ten years, Newport Lift's patent expires and it will no longer export to China. After the yuan is devalued to Yuan9.20/$, no further devaluations are expected. If Newport Lifts raises the yuan price so as to maintain its dollar price, volume will increase at only 1% per annum for eight years, starting from the lower initial base of 9,000 units. Again dollar costs will not change and at the end of eight years, Newport will stop exporting to China. Newport's weighted average cost of capital is 10%. Given these considerations, what should be Newport's pricing policy?

4. **Pucini's Risk-Sharing.** Pucini Fashionwear, based in New York City, imports leather coats from Boselli Leather Goods, a reliable and longtime supplier, based in Buenos Aires. Payment is in Argentine pesos. When the peso lost its parity with the U.S. dollar in January 2002, it collapsed in value to Ps 4.0/$ by October 2002. The outlook was for a further decline

in the peso's value. Since both Pucini Fashionwear and Boselli Leather Goods wanted to continue their longtime relationship, they agreed on a risk-sharing arrangement. As long as the spot rate on the date of an invoice is between Ps3.5/$ and Ps4.5/$ Pucini Fashionwear will pay based on the spot rate. If the exchange rate falls outside this range they will share the difference equally with Boselli Leather Goods. The risk-sharing agreement will last for six months, at which time the exchange rate limits will be reevaluated. Pucini Fashionwear contracts to import leather coats from Boselli Leather Goods for Ps8,000,000 or $2,000,000 at the current spot rate of Ps4.0/$ during the next six months.

a. If the exchange rate changes immediately to Ps6.00/$ what will be the dollar cost of six months of imports to Pucini Fashionwear?

b. At Ps6.0/$ what will be the peso export sales of Boselli Leather Goods to Pucini Fashionwear?

5. **Morris Garage, Ltd.** Morris Garage, Ltd., of Coventry, England, manufactures British style sports cars, a number of which are exported to New Zealand for payment in pounds sterling. The distributor sells the sports cars in New Zealand for New Zealand dollars. The New Zealand distributor is unable to carry all of the foreign exchange risk, and would not sell Morris models unless Morris could share some of the foreign exchange risk. Morris Garage has agreed that sales for a given model year will initially be priced at a "base" spot rate between the New Zealand dollar and pound sterling set to be the spot mid-rate at the beginning of that model year. As long as the actual exchange rate is within ±5% of that base rate, payment will be made in pounds sterling. That is, the New Zealand distributor assumes all foreign exchange risk. However if the spot rate at time of shipment falls outside of this ±5% range, Morris Garage will share equally (that is, 50/50) the difference between the actual spot rate and the base rate. For the current model year the base rate is NZ$1.6400/£.

a. What are the outside ranges within which the New Zealand importer must pay at the then current spot rate?

b. If Morris ships 10 sports cars to the New Zealand distributor at a time when the spot exchange rate is NZ$1.7000/£, and each car has an invoice cost of £12,000, what will be the cost to the distributor in New Zealand dollars? How many pounds will Morris receive, and how does this compare with Morris's expected sales receipts of £12,000 per car?

c. If Morris Garage ships the same 10 sports cars to New Zealand at a time when the spot exchange rate is NZ$1.6500/£, how many New Zealand dollars will the distributor pay. How many pounds will Morris Garage receive?

d. Does a risk-sharing agreement such as this one shift the currency exposure from one party of the transaction to the other?

e. Why is such a risk-sharing agreement of benefit to Morris? To the New Zealand distributor?

6. **Trident Europe: Case 4.** Trident Europe (see Exhibit 12.3) decides not to change its domestic price of €12.80 per unit within Europe, but to raise its export price (in euros) from €12.80 per unit to €15.36 per unit, thus preserving its original dollar equivalent price of $15.36 per unit. Volume in both markets remains the same because no buyer perceives that the price has changed.

a. What is the impact on cash flow?

b. What is the impact on working capital needed?

c. What is the impact on the present value approach to measuring operating exposure?

7. **Trident Europe: Case 5.** Trident Europe (see Exhibit 12.3) finds that domestic costs increase in proportion to the drop in value of the euro because of local inflation and a rise in the cost of imported raw materials and components. This rise in costs (+20%) applies to all cash costs, including direct costs and fixed cash operating costs. However, it does not apply to depreciation. Because of the increase in its costs Trident Europe increases its sales price in euros from €12.80 per unit to €15.36 per unit.

a. What is the impact on cash flow?

b. What is the impact on working capital needed?

c. What is the impact on the present value approach to measuring operating exposure?

8. **Dzell Printers, Inc. (A).** Dzell Printers, Inc. (DP) of the United States exports computer printers to Brazil, whose currency, the reais (symbol R$) has been trading at R$3.40/US$. Exports to Brazil are currently 50,000 printers per year at the reais equivalent of $200 each. A strong rumor exists that the reais will be devalued to R$4.00/$ within two weeks by the Brazilian government. Should the devaluation take place, the reais is expected to remain unchanged for another decade.

Accepting this forecast as given, DP faces a pricing decision which must be made before any actual devaluation: DP may either 1) maintain the same reais price and in effect sell for fewer dollars, in which case Brazilian volume will not change or 2) maintain the same dollar price, raise the reais price in Brazil to compensate for the devaluation, and experience a 20% drop in volume. Direct costs in the U.S. are 60% of the U.S. sales price.

What would be the short-run (one-year) implication of each pricing strategy? Which do you recommend?

9. **Dzell Printers, Inc. (B).** Assume the same facts as in problem 8. DP also believes that if it maintains the same price in Brazilian reais as a permanent policy, volume will increase at 10% per annum for six years. Dollar costs will not change. At the end of six years DP's patent expires and it will no longer export to Brazil. After the reais is devalued to R$4.00/US$ no further devaluation is expected.

If DP raises the price in reais so as to maintain its dollar price, volume will increase at only 4% per annum for six years, starting from the lower initial base of 40,000 units. Again, dollar costs will not change, and at the end of six years DP will stop exporting to Brazil. DP's weighted average cost of capital is 12%. Given these considerations, what do you recommend for DP's pricing policy? Justify your recommendation.

10. **Risk-Sharing at Harley Davidson.** Harley-Davidson (U.S.) reportedly uses risk-sharing agreements with its own foreign subsidiaries and with independent foreign distributors. Because these foreign units typically sell to their local markets and earn local currency, Harley would like to ease their individual currency exposure problems by allowing them to pay for merchandise from Harley (U.S.) in their local functional currency.

The spot rate between the U.S. dollar and the Australian dollar on January 1 is A$1.2823/US$. Assume that Harley uses this rate as the basis for setting its *central rate* or base exchange rate for the year at A$1.2800/US$. Harley agrees to price all contracts to Australian distributors at this exact exchange rate

as long as the current spot rate on the order date is within ±2.5% of this rate. If the spot rate falls outside of this range, but is still within ±5% of the central rate, Harley will "share" equally (that is, 50/50) the difference between the new spot rate and the neutral boundary with the distributor.

a. What are the specific exchange rates at the boundaries of the neutral and risk-sharing zones?
b. If Harley (U.S.) ships a motorcycle, a "hog," with an invoice of $8,500 to Australia, and the exchange rate on the order date is A$1.3442/US$, what is the price in Australian dollars?
c. If Harley (U.S.) ships the same hog to Australia, and the exchange rate on the order date is A$1.2442/US$, what is the price in Australian dollars to the foreign distributor?

INTERNET EXERCISES

1. **Operating Exposure: Recent Examples.** Using the following major periodicals as starting points, find a current example of a firm with a substantial operating exposure problem. To aid in your search, you might focus on businesses having major operations in countries with recent currency crises, either through depreciation or major home currency appreciation.

Financial Times	www.ft.com/
The Economist	www.economist.com/
The Wall Street Journal	www.wsj.com/

2. **SEC Edgar Files.** In order to analyze an individual firm's operating exposure more carefully, it is necessary to have more detailed information available than in the normal annual report. Choose a specific firm with substantial international operations, for example Coca-Cola or PepsiCo, and search the Security and Exchange Commission's Edgar Files for more detailed financial reports of their international operations.

Search SEC EDGAR Archives	www.sec.gov/cgi-bin/srch-edgar

CHAPTER 13

Translation Exposure

The pen is mightier than the sword, but no match for the accountant.

—Jonathan Glancey.

Translation exposure, also called *accounting exposure*, arises because financial statements of foreign subsidiaries—which are stated in foreign currency—must be restated in the parent's reporting currency for the firm to prepare consolidated financial statements. Foreign subsidiaries of U.S. companies, for example, must restate local euro, pound, yen, and so on statements into U.S. dollars so the foreign values can be added to the parent's U.S. dollar-denominated balance sheet and income statement. This accounting process is called "translation." Translation exposure is the potential for an increase or decrease in the parent's net worth and reported net income caused by a change in exchange rates since the last translation.

Although the main purpose of translation is to prepare consolidated statements, translated statements are also used by management to assess the performance of foreign subsidiaries. Although such assessment might be performed from the local currency statements, restatement of all subsidiary statements into the single "common denominator" of one currency facilitates management comparison.

Overview of Translation

Translation in principle is quite simple. Foreign currency financial statements must be restated in the parent company's reporting currency for consolidation purposes. If the same exchange rate were used to remeasure each and every line item on the individual statement (income statement and balance sheet), there would be no imbalances resulting from the remeasurement. But if a different exchange rate were used for different line items on an individual statement, an imbalance would result.

Why would we use a different exchange rate in remeasuring different line items? It is because translation principles in many countries are often a complex compromise between historical and current market valuation. Historical exchange rates may be used for certain equity accounts, fixed assets, and inventory items, while current exchange rates may be used for current assets, current liabilities, income, and expense items. The question, then, is what—if anything—is to be done with the imbalance? It is taken to either current income or equity reserves.

344

Translation methods differ by country along two overall dimensions, as well as by individual account. One dimension is a difference in the way a foreign subsidiary is characterized based on its degree of independence of the parent firm. The second dimension is the definition of which currency is most important for the foreign subsidiary's operations.

Subsidiary Characterization

Today, most countries specify the translation method used by a foreign subsidiary based on the subsidiary's business operations. For example, a foreign subsidiary's business can be categorized as either an *integrated foreign entity* or a *self-sustaining foreign entity*. An integrated foreign entity is one that operates as an extension of the parent company, with cash flows and general business lines that are highly interrelated with those of the parent. A self-sustaining foreign entity is one that operates in the local economic environment independent of the parent company. The differentiation is important to the logic of translation. A foreign subsidiary should be valued principally in terms of the currency that is the basis of its economic viability.

It is not unusual to find two different foreign subsidiaries of a single company that have different characters. For example, a U.S.-based manufacturer that produces subassemblies in the United States that are then shipped to a Spanish subsidiary for finishing, assembly, and resale in the European Union would likely characterize the Spanish subsidiary as an *integrated foreign entity*. The dominant currency of economic operation is likely the U.S. dollar. That same U.S. parent may, however, also own an agricultural marketing business in Venezuela, which has few cash flows or operations related to the U.S. parent company (or U.S. dollar). The Venezuelan subsidiary may purchase almost all materials and expend all costs of operations in Venezuelan bolivar, while selling exclusively in Venezuela. Because the Venezuelan subsidiary's operations are independent of its parent, and its functional currency is the Venezuelan bolivar, it would be classified as a *self-sustaining foreign entity*.

Functional Currency

A foreign subsidiary's *functional currency* is the currency of the primary economic environment in which the subsidiary operates and in which it generates cash flows. In other words, it is the dominant currency used by that foreign subsidiary in its day-to-day operations. It is important to note that the geographic location of a foreign subsidiary and its functional currency may be different. The Singapore subsidiary of a U.S. firm may find that its functional currency is the U.S. dollar (integrated subsidiary), the Singapore dollar (self-sustaining subsidiary), or a third currency such as the British pound (also a self-sustaining subsidiary).

The United States, rather than distinguishing a foreign subsidiary as either integrated or self-sustaining, follows a parallel approach that requires that the functional currency of the subsidiary be determined. Current U.S. translation practices are delineated in *Statement of Financial Accounting Standards Number 52*, usually referred to as FAS#52. It was issued by the Financial Accounting Standards Board (FASB) in December 1981, superseding FAS#8, which had been in effect since 1975. The FASB defines approved accounting practices for U.S. firms.

Management must evaluate the nature and purpose of each of its individual foreign subsidiaries to determine the appropriate functional currency for each. Exhibit 13.1 lists the indicators the FASB uses in determining the functional currency of a foreign subsidiary. If a foreign subsidiary of a U.S.-based company is determined to have the U.S. dollar as its functional currency, it is essentially an extension of the parent company (equivalent to the integrated foreign entity designation used by most countries). If, however, the functional

---

EXHIBIT 13.1   Economic Indicators for Determining the Functional Currency

According to the Financial Accounting Standards Board (FASB), the following economic indicators should be used to determine the functional currency of any foreign subsidiary:

A. Cash Flow Indicators

1. Foreign Currency—Cash flows related to the foreign entity's individual assets and liabilities are primarily in the foreign currency and do not impact the parent company's cash flows.

2. Parent's Currency—Cash flows related to the foreign entity's individual assets and liabilities directly impact the parent's cash flows on a current basis and are readily available for remittance to the parent company.

B. Sales Price Indicators

1. Foreign Currency—Sales prices for the foreign entity's products are not primarily responsive on a short-term basis to changes in exchange rates but are determined more by local competition or by local government regulation.

2. Parent's Currency—Sales prices for the foreign entity's products are primarily responsive on a short-term basis to changes in exchange rates; for example, sales prices are determined more by worldwide competition or by international prices.

C. Sales Market Indicators

1. Foreign Currency—There is an active local sales market for the foreign entity's products, although there might also be significant amounts of exports.

2. Parent's Currency—The sales market is mostly in the parent's country or sales contracts are denominated in the parent's currency.

D. Expense Indicators

1. Foreign Currency—Labor, materials, and other costs for the foreign entity's products or services are primarily local costs, even though there might also be imports from other countries.

2. Parent's Currency—Labor, materials, and other costs for the foreign entity's products or services, on a continuing basis, are primarily costs for components obtained from the country in which the parent company is located.

E. Financing Indicators

1. Foreign Currency—Financing is primarily denominated in foreign currency, and funds generated by the foreign entity's operations are sufficient to service existing and normally expected debt obligations.

2. Parent's Currency—Financing is primarily from the parent or other dollar-denominated obligations, or funds generated by the foreign entity's operations are not sufficient to service existing and normally expected debt obligations without the infusion of additional funds from the parent. Infusion of additional funds from the parent for expansion is not a factor, provided funds generated by the foreign entity's expanded operations are expected to service that additional financing.

F. Intercompany Transactions and Arrangements Indicators

1. Foreign Currency—There is a low volume of intercompany transactions and there is not an extensive interrelationship between the operations of the foreign entity and the parent company. However, the foreign entity's operations may rely on the parent's subsidiaries' competitive advantages, such as patents and trademarks.

2. Parent's Currency—There is a high volume of intercompany transactions and there is an extensive interrelationship between the foreign entity and the parent company. Additionally, the parent's currency generally would be the functional currency if the foreign entity is a device or shell corporation for holding investments, obligations, intangible assets, and so on, that could readily be carried on the parent's or an affiliate's books.

Reprinted with permission of the FASB.

---

currency of the foreign subsidiary is determined to be different from the U.S. dollar, the subsidiary is considered a separate entity from the parent (equivalent to the self-sustaining entity designation).

Translation Methods

Two basic methods for the translation of foreign subsidiary financial statements are employed worldwide, the *current rate method* and the *temporal method*. Regardless of which method is employed, a translation method must not only designate at what exchange rate individual balance sheet and income statement items are remeasured, but also designate where any imbalance is to be recorded (typically either in current income or in an equity reserve account in the balance sheet). The significance of this decision is that imbalances passed through the income statement affect the firm's current reported income, while imbalances transferred directly to the balance sheet do not.

Current Rate Method

The current rate method is the most prevalent in the world today. Under this method, all financial statement line items are translated at the "current" exchange rate with few exceptions. Line items include the following:

- **Assets and Liabilities.** All assets and liabilities are translated at the current rate of exchange; that is, at the rate of exchange in effect on the balance sheet date.

- **Income Statement Items.** All items, including depreciation and cost of goods sold, are translated at either the actual exchange rate on the dates the various revenues, expenses, gains, and losses were incurred or at an appropriately weighted average exchange rate for the period.

- **Distributions.** Dividends paid are translated at the exchange rate in effect on the date of payment.

- **Equity Items.** Common stock and paid-in capital accounts are translated at historical rates. Year-end retained earnings consist of the original year-beginning retained earnings plus or minus any income or loss for the year.

Gains or losses caused by translation adjustments are *not* included in the calculation of consolidated net income. Rather, translation gains or losses are reported separately and accumulated in a separate equity reserve account (on the consolidated balance sheet) with a title such as *cumulative translation adjustment* (CTA). A multitude of different names are used for this reserve account adjustment. In Spain, for example, the CTA is termed the *diferencias de conversión*. If a foreign subsidiary is later sold or liquidated, translation gains or losses of past years accumulated in the CTA account are reported as one component of the total gain or loss on sale or liquidation. The total gain or loss is reported as part of the net income or loss for the time period in which the sale or liquidation occurs. This is the subject of this chapter's Mini-Case.

The biggest advantage of the current rate method is that the gain or loss on translation does not pass through the income statement but goes directly to a reserve account. This eliminates the variability of reported earnings due to foreign exchange translation gains or losses. A second advantage of the current rate method is that the relative proportions of individual balance sheet accounts remain the same. Hence, the process of translation does not distort such balance sheet ratios as the current ratio or the debt-to-equity ratio. The main disadvantage of the current rate method is that it violates the accounting principle of carrying balance sheet accounts at historical cost. For example, foreign assets purchased with dollars and then recorded on a subsidiary's statements at their foreign currency historical cost are translated into dollars at a different rate. Thus, they are reported in the consolidated statement in dollars at something other than their historical dollar cost.

Temporal Method

Under the temporal method, specific assets and liabilities are translated at exchange rates consistent with the timing of the item's creation. The *temporal method* assumes that a number of individual line item assets such as inventory and net plant and equipment are restated regularly to reflect market value. If these items were not restated but were instead carried at historical cost, the temporal method becomes the *monetary/nonmonetary method* of translation, a form of translation that is still used by a number of countries today. Line items include the following:

- **Monetary assets (primarily cash, marketable securities, accounts receivable, and long-term receivables).** Are translated at current exchange rates.

- **Monetary liabilities (primarily current liabilities and long-term debt).** Are translated at current exchange rates.

- **Nonmonetary assets and liabilities (primarily inventory and fixed assets).** Are translated at historical rates.

- **Income statement items.** Are translated at the average exchange rate for the period, except for items such as depreciation and cost of goods sold that are directly associated with nonmonetary assets or liabilities. These accounts are translated at their historical rate.

- **Distributions.** Dividends paid are translated at the exchange rate in effect on the date of payment.

- **Equity items.** Common stock and paid-in capital accounts are translated at historical rates. Year-end retained earnings consist of the original year-beginning retained earnings plus or minus any income or loss for the year, plus or minus any imbalance from translation, as explained next.

Under the temporal method, gains or losses resulting from remeasurement are carried directly to current consolidated income and not to equity reserves. Hence, foreign exchange gains and losses arising from the translation process do introduce volatility to consolidated earnings.

The basic advantage of the temporal method is that foreign nonmonetary assets are carried at their original cost in the parent's consolidated statement. In most countries, this approach is consistent with the original cost treatment of domestic assets of the parent firm. In practice, however, if some foreign accounts are translated at one exchange rate while others are translated at different rates, the resulting translated balance sheet will not balance. Hence, there is a need for a "plug" to remove what has been called the "dangling debit or credit." The true nature of the gain or loss created by use of such a plug is open to question. Unrealized foreign exchange gains or losses are included in quarterly primary *earnings per share* (EPS), thus increasing variability of reported earnings.

U.S. Translation Procedures

As mentioned previously, the United States differentiates foreign subsidiaries on the basis of functional currency, not subsidiary characterization. The result, however, is equivalent. Exhibit 13.2 illustrates the translation procedures used by U.S.-based companies under current U.S. generally accepted accounting principles (GAAP). As shown in Exhibit 13.2:

- If the financial statements of the foreign subsidiary of a U.S. company are maintained in U.S. dollars, translation is not required.

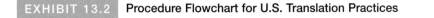

| EXHIBIT 13.2 | Procedure Flowchart for U.S. Translation Practices |

Purpose: Foreign currency financial statements must be translated into U.S. dollars

If the financial statements of the foreign subsidiary are expressed in a foreign currency, the following determinations need to be made.

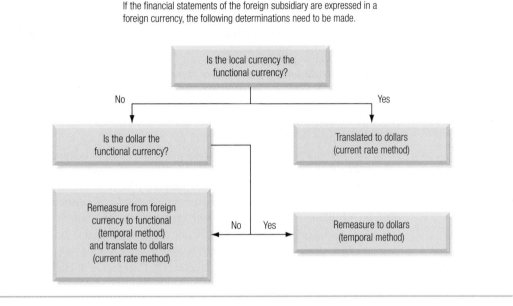

- If the financial statements of the foreign subsidiary are maintained in the local currency and the local currency is the functional currency, they are translated by the *current rate method*.

- If the financial statements of the foreign subsidiary are maintained in the local currency and the U.S. dollar is the functional currency, they are remeasured by the *temporal method*. (Terminology can be tricky; under U.S. accounting and translation practices, use of the current rate method is termed *translation* while use of the temporal method is termed *remeasurement*.)

- If the financial statements of foreign subsidiaries of U.S. companies are maintained in the local currency and neither the local currency nor the dollar is the functional currency, then the statements must first be remeasured into the functional currency by the temporal method, and then translated into dollars by the current rate method.

Hyperinflation Countries

FAS#52 has a special provision for translating statements of foreign subsidiaries of U.S. companies operating in countries where cumulative inflation has been approximately 100% or more over a three-year period. Financial statements of these subsidiaries must be translated into the reporting currency using the temporal method.

The rationale is to correct the problem of the "disappearing asset." If the current rate were used, depreciation would be understated relative to replacement costs, profits would be overstated in real terms, and the book value of plant and equipment would eventually nearly disappear from the balance sheet as its value diminished in reporting currency terms. Translating plant, equipment, and depreciation expenses at the historical exchange rate yields a higher asset value in the reporting currency than would use of the current (depreciated) exchange rate. This leads to a less distorted income statement and balance sheet. In effect, FAS#52 declares the functional currency of subsidiaries in hyperinflation countries to be the reporting currency (U.S. dollars for U.S. firms).

The hyperinflation standard has precedence in business practice.

> *When a country is plagued with hyperinflation, it often uses the U.S. dollar or other hard currency as its de facto functional currency for actual transactions regardless of accounting standards. For example, most Israeli retailers in 1982 priced their merchandise in U.S. dollars, not shekels. In the face of triple-digit inflation, they cannot change their prices every other day. The U.S. dollar becomes the unit of account. Also, when an Israeli holds U.S. dollars and the shekel is devalued, his holding in dollars remains the same, whereas if he holds currency in shekels and the shekel is devalued, his holding declines in purchasing power. The U.S. dollar becomes the storehouse of value. Consistent with the mercantile practice of businessmen in highly inflationary economies, the FASB promulgates the accounting standard that the home currency becomes the functional currency when inflation is rampant; otherwise the local currency is the functional currency. Accounting standards-setting simply is patterned after accepted business practice.*
>
> —Russell A. Taussig, "Impact of SFAS 52 on the Translation of Foreign Financial Statements of Companies in Highly-Inflationary Economies," *Journal of Accounting, Auditing, and Finance*, Winter 1983, pp. 145–176.

In summary, U.S. translation practices require the parent company to first determine the functional currency of the foreign subsidiary, which then dictates whether the subsidiary's financial statements will be translated by the current rate method or remeasured by the temporal method. A final point of emphasis: The selection of the functional currency is determined by the economic realities of the subsidiary's operations and is not a discretionary management decision on preferred procedures or elective outcomes. Since many U.S.-based multinationals have numerous foreign subsidiaries, some U.S. dollar-functional and some foreign currency-functional, foreign currency gains and losses may be both passing through current consolidated income and/or accruing in equity reserves.

International Translation Practices

As illustrated in Exhibit 13.3, many of the world's largest industrial countries—as well as the relatively newly formed International Accounting Standards Committee (IASC)—follow the same basic translation procedure:

- A foreign subsidiary is an *integrated foreign entity* or a *self-sustaining foreign entity*.
- Integrated foreign entities are typically remeasured using the *temporal method* (or some slight variation thereof).
- Self-sustaining foreign entities are translated at the *current rate method*, also termed the *closing-rate method*.

Translation Example: Trident Europe

Let us continue the example of Trident from Chapter 12, focusing here on its European subsidiary. We will also illustrate translation by the temporal method in order to show the very arbitrary nature of a translation gain or loss. Selection of the accounting method is the major factor in determining the magnitude of gain or loss. The example that follows deals with

EXHIBIT 13.3   Comparison of Translation Methods Employed in Selected Countries

Country	Integrated Foreign Entity	Self-Sustaining Foreign Entity
United States	Financial statements are remeasured using the temporal method with adjustments included in current net income.	Current rate method. Translation adjustments are reported as a separate component of shareholders' equity.
International	Temporal method. Translation adjustments are included in net income currently, except that translation adjustments on long-term monetary items may be deferred and amortized over the life of the item.	Current rate method. Translation adjustments are reported as a separate component of shareholders' equity.
Australia	Temporal method. Translation adjustments are included in current net income.	Current rate method. Translation adjustments are reported as a separate component of shareholders' equity.
Canada	Temporal method. Translation adjustments are included in current net income.	Current rate method. Translation adjustments are reported as a separate component of shareholders' equity.
France	Temporal method. Translation adjustments are included in current net income.	Current rate method. Translation adjustments are reported as a separate component of shareholders' equity.
Germany	Temporal method or current rate method is acceptable. Translation adjustments are included in net income currently if the temporal method is used and as a separate component if the current rate method is used.	Same as for integrated foreign entity.
Japan	Temporal method. Adjustments related to foreign subsidiaries are reported separately as an asset or a liability; adjustments related to divisions or branches are included in current net income.	Same as for integrated foreign entity.
Netherlands	Temporal method. Translation adjustments are included in current net income. The current rate method is used if the entity utilizes current value accounting.	Current rate method. Translation adjustments are reported as a separate component of shareholders' equity.
United Kingdom	Temporal method. Translation adjustments are included in current net income.	Current rate method. Translation adjustments are reported as a separate component of shareholders' equity.

Source: *Survey of International Accounting Practices*, Arthur Andersen & Co., Coopers & Lybrand, Deloitte & Touche, Ernst & Young, KPMG Peat Marwick, and Price Waterhouse, 1991.

balance sheet translation only. The somewhat more complex procedures for translating income statements are described in international accounting texts.

The functional currency of Trident Europe is the euro, and the reporting currency of its parent, Trident Corporation, is the U.S. dollar. Assume the following:

- Plant and equipment and long-term debt were acquired and common stock issued by Trident Europe sometime in the past when the exchange rate was $1.2760/€. Although the euro never traded at this rate against the dollar, the historic deutschemark rate in use at the time the initial investment was made must be converted to a "historic euro rate" which, in effect, backdates euro rates against the deutschemark.

- Inventory currently on hand was purchased or manufactured during the immediately prior quarter when the average exchange rate was $1.2180/€. At the close of business on Monday, December 31, 2010, the current spot exchange rate was $1.2000/€.

■ When business reopened on January 2, 2011, after the New Year holiday, the euro had dropped 16.67% in value versus the dollar to $1.0000/€.

The example will also look at the consequences had the euro strengthened by 10% overnight to $1.3200/€.

Current Rate Method

The top half of Exhibit 13.4 illustrates translation loss using the current rate method. Assets and liabilities on the predepreciation balance sheet are translated at the current exchange

EXHIBIT 13.4	Trident Europe: Translation Loss Just after Depreciation of the Euro				
		December 31, 2010		January 2, 2011	
	In Euros		Just before Depreciation		Just after Depreciation
Current Rate Method					
Cash	€1,600,000	1.2000	$1,920,000	1.0000	$1,600,000
Accounts receivable	3,200,000	1.2000	3,840,000	1.0000	3,200,000
Inventory	2,400,000	1.2000	2,880,000	1.0000	2,400,000
Net plant and equipment	4,800,000	1.2000	5,760,000	1.0000	4,800,000
	€12,000,000		$14,400,000		$12,000,000
Accounts payable	€800,000	1.2000	$960,000	1.0000	$800,000
Short-term bank loan	1,600,000	1.2000	1,920,000	1.0000	1,600,000
Long-term debt	1,600,000	1.2000	1,920,000	1.0000	1,600,000
Common stock	1,800,000	1.2760	2,296,800	1.2000	2,296,800
Retained earnings	6,200,000	(a)	7,440,000	1.2000(b)	7,440,000
Translation adjustment (CTA)	—	—	(136,800)	—	(1,736,800)
	€12,000,000		$14,400,000		$12,000,000
Temporal Method					
Cash	€1,600,000	1.2000	$1,920,000	1.0000	$1,600,000
Accounts receivable	3,200,000	1.2000	3,840,000	1.0000	3,200,000
Inventory	2,400,000	1.2180	2,923,200	1.2180	2,923,200
Net plant and equipment	4,800,000	1.2760	6,124,800	1.2760	6,124,800
	€12,000,000		$14,808,000		$13,848,000
Accounts payable	€800,000	1.2000	$960,000	1.0000	$800,000
Short-term bank loan	1,600,000	1.2000	1,920,000	1.0000	1,600,000
Long-term debt	1,600,000	1.2000	1,920,000	1.0000	1,600,000
Common stock	1,800,000	1.2760	2,296,800	1.2760	2,296,800
Retained earnings	6,200,000	(a)	7,711,200	(b)	7,711,200
Translation gain (loss)	—	—	—	(c)	(160,000)
	€12,000,000		$14,808,000		$13,848,000

(a) Dollar retained earnings before depreciation are the cumulative sum of additions to retained earnings of all prior years, translated at exchange rates in each year. See text for assumptions used in this example.

(b) Translated into dollars at the same rate as before depreciation of the euro.

(c) Under the temporal method, the translation loss of $160,000 would be closed into retained earnings via the income statement rather than left as a separate line item shown here. Hence, under the temporal method, ending retained earnings would actually be $7,711,200–$160,000 = $7,551,200.

rate of $1.1600/€. Capital stock is translated at the historical rate of $1.2760/€, and retained earnings are translated at a composite rate that is equivalent to having each past year's addition to retained earnings translated at the exchange rate in effect in that year.

The sum of retained earnings and the cumulative translation adjustment (CTA) account must "balance" the liabilities and net worth section of the balance sheet with the asset side. For this hypothetical text example, we have assumed the two amounts used for the December 31, 2010, balance sheet. The assumption does not affect the final measure of the increase in the CTA account because the retained earnings account is carried over at whatever arbitrary amount is assigned for this example.

As shown in the top half of Exhibit 13.4, the "just before depreciation" dollar translation reports an accumulated translation loss from prior periods of $136,800. This balance is the cumulative gain or loss from translating euro statements into dollars in prior years, and it had been carried separately in the CTA account. Statements from 1998 and earlier would have originally been deutschemark statements, translated into euros after January 1, 1999, when the euro was introduced.

After the 16.67% depreciation, Trident Corporation translates assets and liabilities at the new exchange rate of $1.0000/€. Equity accounts, including retained earnings, are translated just as they were before depreciation, and as a result the cumulative translation loss increases to $1,736,800. The increase of $1,600,000 in this account (from a cumulative loss of $136,800 to a new cumulative loss of $1,736,800) is the translation loss measured by the current rate method.

This translation loss is a decrease in equity, measured in the parent's reporting currency, of net exposed assets. An *exposed asset* is an asset whose value drops with the depreciation of the functional currency and rises with an appreciation of that currency. *Net* exposed assets in this context means exposed assets minus exposed liabilities. Net exposed assets are positive ("long") if exposed assets exceed exposed liabilities. They are negative ("short") if exposed assets are smaller than exposed liabilities.

Exposure can be measured by creating a before-and-after translated balance sheet, as shown in Exhibit 13.4. A simpler method is to multiply net exposed assets by the percentage amount of depreciation. We did this calculation for the current rate method in the left column of Exhibit 13.5, which illustrates that a 16.67% depreciation of the euro means that net exposed assets of $9,600,000 lose 16.67% of their value, a translation loss of $1,600,000.

Suppose instead that the euro had appreciated. If, by the end of the year, the euro had appreciated from $1.2000/€ to $1.3200/€, the appreciation would be 10%. The effect of this appears in Panel B of Exhibit 13.5, which starts with the same net exposed assets calculated in Panel A. Under the current rate method, the U.S. parent would have a translation gain of $960,000.

Temporal Method

Translation of the same accounts under the temporal method shows the arbitrary nature of any gain or loss from translation. This is illustrated in the bottom half of Exhibit 13.4. Monetary assets and monetary liabilities in the predepreciation euro balance sheet are translated at the current rate of exchange, but other assets and the equity accounts are translated at their historic rates. For Trident Europe, the historical rate for inventory differs from that for net plant and equipment because inventory was acquired more recently.

Under the temporal method, translation losses are not accumulated in a separate equity account but passed directly through each quarter's income statement. Thus, in the dollar balance sheet translated before depreciation, retained earnings were the cumulative result of earnings from all prior years translated at historical rates in effect each year, plus translation

EXHIBIT 13.5   Trident Europe: Translation Loss or Gain: Comparison of Current Rate and Temporal Methods

Panel A: Depreciation of the Euro, from $1.2000/€ to $1.0000/€ (−16.67%)

	Current Rate Method	Temporal Method
Exposed Assets		
Cash	$1,920,000	$1,920,000
Accounts receivable	3,840,000	3,840,000
Inventory	2,880,000	not exposed
Net plant and equipment	5,760,000	not exposed
Total exposed assets ("A")	$14,400,000	$5,760,000
Exposed Liabilities		
Accounts payable	$960,000	$960,000
Short-term bank loan	1,920,000	1,920,000
Long-term debt	1,920,000	1,920,000
Total exposed liabilities ("L")	$4,800,000	$4,800,000
Gain (loss) if euro depreciates		
Net exposed assets ("A" − "L")	$9,600,000	$960,000
Times amount of depreciation	× (0.1667)	× (0.1667)
Translation gain (loss)	($1,600,000)	($160,000)

Panel B: Appreciation of the Euro, from $1.2000/€ to $1.3200/€ (+10.00%)

	Current Rate Method	Temporal Method
Gain (loss) if euro appreciates		
Net exposed assets ("A" − "L")	$9,600,000	$960,000
Times amount of appreciation	× 0.1000	× 0.1000
Translation gain (loss)	$960,000	$96,000

gains or losses from all prior years. In Exhibit 13.4, no translation loss appears in the predepreciation dollar balance sheet because any losses would have been closed to retained earnings.

The effect of the 16.67% depreciation is to create an immediate translation loss of $160,000. This amount is shown as a separate line item in Exhibit 13.4 in order to focus attention on it for this textbook example. Under the temporal method, this translation loss of $160,000 would pass through the income statement, reducing reported net income and reducing retained earnings. Ending retained earnings would in fact be $7,711,200 minus $160,000, or $7,551,200. Other countries using the temporal method do not necessarily require gains and losses to pass through the income statement.

When translation loss is viewed in terms of changes in the value of exposed accounts, as shown in the right column of Exhibit 13.5, the loss under the temporal method is 16.67% of net exposed assets of $960,000, or $160,000. If the euro should appreciate 10%, the translation gain to the U.S. parent would be $96,000, as shown at the bottom of the right column in Exhibit 13.5.

Managerial Implications

In Exhibit 13.4 and Exhibit 13.5, translation loss or gain is larger under the current rate method because inventory and net plant and equipment, as well as all monetary assets, are deemed exposed. When net exposed assets are larger, gains or losses from translation are also larger.

The managerial implications of this fact are very important. If management expects a foreign currency to depreciate, it could minimize translation exposure by reducing net exposed assets. If management anticipates an appreciation of the foreign currency, it should increase net exposed assets to benefit from a gain.

Depending on the accounting method of the moment, management might select different assets and liabilities for reduction or increase. Thus, "real" decisions about investing and financing might be dictated by which accounting technique is required, when in fact the method of reporting should be neutral in its influence on operating and financing decisions.

Comparing Translation Exposure with Operating Exposure

In Exhibit 13.6 translation gains or losses in the event of a currency depreciation are compared with the operating gains or losses from Chapter 12, Exhibit 12.3. Obviously, translation gains or losses can be quite different from operating gains or losses, not only in magnitude but also in sign (a gain or loss). A manager focusing only on translation losses, in a situation such as Trident Europe, might avoid doing business in Germany because of the likelihood of such a loss. The manager might fear losing a bonus tied to reported profits, or possibly losing a job if the investment in Germany were made and the income statement reported severe translation losses back to the home office.

Operating exposure presents an entirely different view of the same situation. As summarized in Exhibit 13.6, Germany and Europe became more (not less) desirable locations for investment because of the *operating* consequences that followed depreciation in two of the three cases shown here. This illustrates the importance of focusing decisions primarily on the operating consequences of changes in exchange rates and only secondarily on the accounting-based measurements of performance.

Managing Translation Exposure

The main technique to minimize translation exposure is called a *balance sheet hedge*. Some firms have attempted to hedge translation exposure in the forward market. Such action amounts to speculating in the forward market in the hope that a cash profit will be realized to offset the noncash loss from translation. Success depends on a precise prediction of future exchange rates, for such a hedge will not work over a range of possible future spot rates. In

EXHIBIT 13.6 Comparison of Translation Exposure with Operating Exposure, Depreciation of Euro from $1.200/€ to $1.0000/€ for Trident Europe

Exposure	Amount	Gain or Loss
Translation Exposure (Exhibits 13.4 and 13.5)		
Current rate method	($1,600,000)	**Loss** on translation
Temporal method	($160,000)	**Loss** on translation
Operating Exposure (in present value terms; Exhibit 12.3)		
Case 1: Depreciation of euro	($1,033,914)	**Loss** on operations
Case 2: Volume doubles	$2,866,106	**Gain** on operations
Case 3: Sales price increases	$3,742,892	**Gain** on operations

addition, such a hedge will increase the tax burden, since the profit from the forward hedge (speculation) is taxable, but the translation loss does not reduce taxable income. As illustrated by *Global Finance in Practice 13.1*, hedging translation is in general, still quite controversial.

Balance Sheet Hedge Defined

A balance sheet hedge requires an equal amount of *exposed* foreign currency assets and liabilities on a firm's consolidated balance sheet. If this can be achieved for each foreign currency, net translation exposure will be zero. A change in exchange rates will change the value of exposed liabilities in an equal amount but in a direction opposite to the change in value of exposed assets. If a firm translates by the temporal method, a zero net exposed position is called *monetary balance*. Complete monetary balance cannot be achieved under the current rate method because total assets would have to be matched by an equal amount of debt, but the equity section of the balance sheet must still be translated at historic exchange rates.

The cost of a balance sheet hedge depends on relative borrowing costs. If foreign currency borrowing costs, after adjusting for foreign exchange risk, are higher than parent currency borrowing costs, the balance sheet hedge is costly, and vice versa. Normal operations, however, already require decisions about the magnitude and currency denomination of specific balance sheet accounts. Thus, balance sheet hedges are a compromise in which the denomination of balance sheet accounts is altered, perhaps at a cost in terms of interest expense or operating efficiency, to achieve some degree of foreign exchange protection.

Balance Sheet Hedge Illustrated

To illustrate a balance sheet hedge, let us return to the translation exposure previously identified for Trident Europe and its parent, Trident Corporation. Earlier data from Exhibit 13.4 is restated in a different format in Exhibit 13.7.

GLOBAL FINANCE IN PRACTICE 13.1

Gyrus (UK): Translation Exposure or Transaction Exposure?

Shares in Gyrus dropped after the surgical equipment maker said that it remained exposed to the weak US dollar after unveiling first-half profits in line with expectations. Gyrus, which has 80 per cent of revenue denominated in dollars, said sales for the six months to June 30 rose 2 per cent to £109m (£107m) compared with an 11 per cent rise on a constant currency basis.

"We look to the second half and beyond with confidence … but somewhat temper our enthusiasm as a result of the continued weakness of the dollar," Gyrus said. The company reported strong growth from its urological/gynaecological and surgical divisions in the US where revenues increased 22 per cent and 11 per cent, respectively. The general surgery division saw sales jump 136 per cent to $6.6m (£3.3m).

Simon Shaw, chief financial officer, said the currency impact was translational and not transactional. "Translation is not economically viable to hedge, it's terribly expensive."

Andy Smith, investment manager at the International Biotechnology Trust, which holds about 3 per cent of its portfolio in Gyrus, said: "This is the second year in a row that this has hit their share price. They do hedge a certain proportion but obviously it needs to be more. "There are several ways to get out of this—hedge the dollar exposure more, re-list on Nasdaq or be acquired by a US company. Gyrus is a great company and should address these issues."

Mr Shaw said the option to re-list on Nasdaq had been discussed, but the "risks that come with Sarbanes Oxley and the cost of compliance outweigh the potential valuation uplift", he added. Mr Smith said Gyrus was a prime acquisition target. Interested parties could include rivals Smith & Nephew, Johnson & Johnson and Tyco. Pre-tax profits, before restructuring costs, rose to £10.3m (£5.5m). Earnings per share were 3.5p (2.5p). Shares in Gyrus fell 35p to close at 398p.

Source: "Gyrus Hurt by Dollar Weakness," *Financial Times*, September 18, 2007.

EXHIBIT 13.7	Trident Europe, Balance Sheet Exposure		
	Balance Sheet Accounts	**Current Rate Exposure**	**Temporal Exposure**
Assets			
Cash	€1,600,000	€1,600,000	€1,600,000
Accounts receivable	3,200,000	3,200,000	3,200,000
Inventory	2,400,000	2,400,000	
Net plant and equipment	4,800,000	4,800,000	
Total assets	€12,000,000		
Exposed assets		€12,000,000	€4,800,000
Liabilities and Capital			
Accounts payable	€800,000	€800,000	€800,000
Short-term bank debt	1,600,000	1,600,000	1,600,000
Long-term debt	1,600,000	1,600,000	1,600,000
Capital stock	1,800,000		
Retained earnings	6,200,000		
Total liabilities and net worth	€12,000,000		
Exposed liabilities		€4,000,000	€4,000,000
Net exposed assets in euros		€8,000,000	€800,000
Times exchange rate ($/€)		× 1.2000	× 1.2000
Net exposed assets in dollars		$9,600,000	$960,000
Times amount of devaluation		× 0.1667	× 0.1667
Expected translation gain (loss)		$(1,600,000)	$(160,000)

Trident Europe expects the euro to drop 16.67% in value from its year-beginning value to a new exchange rate of $1.0000/€. Under the current rate method, the expected loss is 16.67% of the exposure of $9,600,000, or $1,600,000. Under the temporal method, the expected loss is 16.67% of the exposure of $960,000, or $160,000.

To achieve a balance sheet hedge, Trident Corporation must either 1) reduce exposed euro assets without simultaneously reducing euro liabilities or 2) increase euro liabilities without simultaneously increasing euro assets. One way to do this is to exchange existing euro cash for dollars. If Trident Europe does not have large euro cash balances, it can borrow euros and exchange the borrowed euros for dollars. Another subsidiary could borrow euros and exchange them for dollars. That is, the essence of the hedge is for the parent or any of its subsidiaries to create euro debt and exchange the proceeds for dollars.

Current Rate Method. Under the current rate method, Trident Europe should borrow as much as €8,000,000. The initial effect of this first step is to increase both an exposed asset (cash) and an exposed liability (notes payable) on the balance sheet of Trident Europe, with no immediate effect on net exposed assets. The required follow-up step can take two forms: 1) Trident Europe can exchange the acquired euros for U.S. dollars and hold those dollars itself or 2) it can transfer the borrowed euros to Trident Corporation, perhaps as a euro dividend or as repayment of intracompany debt. Trident Corporation could then exchange the euros for dollars. In some countries, of course, local monetary authorities will not allow their currency to be so freely exchanged.

Another possibility would be for Trident Corporation or a sister subsidiary to borrow the euros, thus keeping the euro debt entirely off Trident Europe's books. However, the second step is still essential to eliminate euro exposure; the borrowing entity must exchange the euros for dollars or other unexposed assets. Any such borrowing should be coordinated with all other euro borrowings to avoid the possibility that one subsidiary is borrowing euros to reduce translation exposure at the same time as another subsidiary is repaying euro debt. (Note that euros can be "borrowed," by simply delaying repayment of existing euro debt; the goal is to increase euro debt, not borrow in a literal sense.)

Temporal Method. If translation is by the temporal method, only the much smaller amount of €800,000 need be borrowed. As before, Trident Europe could use the proceeds of the loan to acquire U.S. dollars. However, Trident Europe could also use the proceeds to acquire inventory or fixed assets in Europe. Under the temporal method these assets are not regarded as exposed and do not drop in dollar value when the euro depreciates.

When Is a Balance Sheet Hedge Justified?

If a firm's subsidiary is using the local currency as the functional currency, the following circumstances could justify when to use a balance sheet hedge:

- The foreign subsidiary is about to be liquidated, so that the value of its CTA would be realized.
- The firm has debt covenants or bank agreements that state the firm's debt/equity ratios will be maintained within specific limits.
- Management is evaluated on the basis of certain income statement and balance sheet measures that are affected by translation losses or gains.
- The foreign subsidiary is operating in a hyperinflationary environment.

If a firm is using the parent's home currency as the functional currency of the foreign subsidiary, all transaction gains/losses are passed through to the income statement. Hedging this consolidated income to reduce its variability may be important to investors and bond rating agencies. *Global Finance in Practice 13.2* describes an alternative hedging of accounting results, foreign currency-denominated income.

Choice between Minimizing Transaction or Translation Exposure

Management will find it almost impossible to offset both translation and transaction exposure at the same time. Reduction of one exposure usually changes the amount of the other exposure. For example, the easiest way to offset translation exposure is to require the parent and all subsidiaries to denominate all exposed assets and liabilities in the parent's reporting currency. For U.S. firms and their subsidiaries, all assets and liabilities would be held in dollars. Such firms would have no translation exposure, but each subsidiary would have its own transaction exposure.

To illustrate, assume that a U.S. parent company instructs its Japanese subsidiary to bill an export to the parent in dollars. The account receivable on the Japanese subsidiary's books is shown as the yen equivalent of the dollar amount, and yen profit is recorded at the time of sale. If, before the parent pays dollars to the Japanese subsidiary, the yen appreciates 5%, the parent still pays only the contracted dollar amount. The Japanese subsidiary receives 5% fewer yen than were expected and booked as profit. Hence, the Japanese subsidiary will experience a 5% foreign exchange loss on its dollar-denominated accounts receivable. Lower yen profit will eventually be translated into lower dollar profit when the subsidiary's income statement is consolidated with that of the parent. Eventually the consolidated U.S.-based MNE will show a foreign exchange loss—in dollars!

GLOBAL FINANCE IN PRACTICE 13.2

Hedging the Euro Away

In 2000, a number of major U.S. multinationals grew increasingly concerned over the sliding value of the euro. Given the significant contribution of continental profits earned in euros, the declining value of the euro versus the dollar represented a continuing degradation of potential reported profits. Some, like Coca-Cola, hedged the dollar value of their projected euro earnings. The hedges protected the dollar value of their euro earnings, and as a result, the companies suffered no material declines in consolidated earnings. Others, however,

like Goodyear and Caterpillar, suffered double-digit percentage reductions in consolidated earnings as a result of the unhedged euro decline.

Although a number of companies have admittedly been able to prevent their consolidated earnings from being hurt by falling foreign currencies—for a quarter or a series of quarters, at least—it is still highly controversial for a firm to expend resources and acquire hedging positions with forwards and swaps to hedge accounting results.

The Impact of the Falling Value of the Euro on Selected U.S.-Based Multinationals

Company	Operating Income Third Quarter 2000 (millions)	Reduction because of Euro (percent)
Goodyear	$68	30%
Caterpillar	$294	12%
McDonald's	$910	5%
Kimberly-Clark	$667	2.5%

Source: "Business Won't Hedge the Euro Away," *Business Week*, December 4, 2000.

Similar reasoning will show that if a firm chooses to eliminate transaction exposure, translation exposure might even be increased. The easiest way to be rid of transaction exposure is to require the parent and all subsidiaries to denominate all accounts subject to transaction exposure in its local currency. Thus, every subsidiary would avoid transaction gains or losses. However, each subsidiary would be creating net translation exposure by being either long or short in terms of local currency—exposed assets or liabilities. The consolidated financial statement of the parent firm would show translation exposure in each local currency.

As a general matter, firms seeking to reduce both types of exposure usually reduce transaction exposure first. They then recalculate translation exposure (which may have changed), and decide if any residual translation exposure can be reduced without creating more transaction exposure. Taxes complicate the decision to seek protection against transaction or translation exposure. Transaction losses are normally considered "realized" losses and are therefore deductible from pretax income. However, translation losses are only "paper" losses, involving no cash flows, and are not deductible from pretax income. It is highly debatable whether protective techniques that necessitate cash payments, and so reduce net cash flow, should be incurred to avoid noncash losses.

SUMMARY POINTS

- Translation exposure results from translating foreign currency denominated statements of foreign subsidiaries into the parent's reporting currency so the parent can prepare consolidated financial statements. Translation exposure is the potential for loss or gain from this translation process.

- A foreign subsidiary's functional currency is the currency of the primary economic environment in which the subsidiary operates and in which it generates cash flows. In other words, it is the dominant currency used by that foreign subsidiary in its day-to-day operations.

- The two basic procedures for translation used in most countries today are the current rate method and the temporal method.

- Technical aspects of translation include questions about when to recognize gains or losses in the income statement, the distinction between functional and reporting currency, and the treatment of subsidiaries in hyperinflation countries.

- Translation gains and losses can be quite different from operating gains and losses, not only in magnitude but in sign. Management may need to determine which is of greater significance prior to deciding which exposure is to be managed first.

- The main technique for managing translation exposure is a balance sheet hedge. This calls for having an equal amount of exposed foreign currency assets and liabilities.

- Even if management chooses to follow an active policy of hedging translation exposure, it is nearly impossible to offset both transaction and translation exposure simultaneously. If forced to choose, most managers will protect against transaction losses because these are realized cash losses, rather than protect against translation losses.

MINI-CASE   LaJolla Engineering Services

Meaghan O'Connor had inherited a larger set of problems in the Engineering Equipment Division than she had ever expected.[1] After taking over as the CFO of the division in March 2004, Meaghan had discovered that LaJolla's Engineering Equipment Division's Latin American subsidiaries were the source of recent losses and growing income threats. The rather unusual part of the growing problem was that both the losses and the threats were arising from currency translation.

Latin American Subsidiaries

LaJolla was a multinational engineering services company with an established reputation in electrical power system design and construction. Although most of LaJolla's business was usually described as "services," and therefore using or owning few real assets, that was not the case with the Engineering Equipment Division. This specific business unit was charged with owning and operating the very high-cost and specialized heavy equipment involved in certain electrical power transmission and distribution system construction. In Meaghan's terminology, she was in charge of the "Big Iron" in a company of consultants.

LaJolla's recent activity had been focused in four countries—Argentina, Jamaica, Venezuela, and Mexico. Unfortunately, the last few years had not been kind to the value of these currencies—particularly against the U.S. dollar. Each of LaJolla's subsidiaries in these countries was local currency functional. Each subsidiary generated the majority of its revenues from local service contracts, and many of the operating expenses were also local. But

each of the units had invested in some of the specialized equipment—the so-called Big Iron—which had led to *net exposed assets* when LaJolla had completed its consolidation of foreign activities each year for financial reporting purposes. The translation gains and losses (mostly losses in recent years as the Argentine peso, Jamaican dollar, Venezuelan bolivar, and Mexican peso had weakened against the U.S. dollar), had accumulated in the cumulative translation adjustment line item on the company's consolidated books. But the problem had become more real of late.

Ordinarily, these translation losses would not have been a large managerial issue for LaJolla and Meaghan, except for a minor document filing error in Argentina in the fall of 2003. LaJolla, like many multinational companies operating in Argentina in recent years, had simply given up on conducting any real business of promise in the severely depressed post-crisis Argentina. It had essentially closed up shop there in the summer of 2003. But its legal counsel in Buenos Aires had made a mistake. Instead of ceasing current operations and mothballing the existing assets of LaJolla Engineering Argentina, the local counsel had filed papers stating that LaJolla was liquidating the business. Although it seemed a minor distinction, according to U.S. GAAP and FAS52, LaJolla would now have to realize in current earnings the cumulative translation losses that had grown over the years from the Argentine business. And these were substantial: $7 million in losses in the fourth quarter of 2003. LaJolla's management had not been happy.

[1]This case concerns a real company. The names and countries have been changed to preserve confidentiality.

LaJolla 2004

As a result of this recent experience, LaJolla was taking a close look at all of the translation gains and losses of its various business units worldwide. Once again, the company's Latin American operations were the focal point, as collectively many of the Latin currencies had weakened recently against the dollar, although the dollar itself was quite weak against the euro. Jamaica, Venezuela, and Mexico each posed their individual problems and challenges, but all posed translation adjustment threats to LaJolla.

Jamaica. The company had been fairly concerned about the Jamaican business and its contracts from the very beginning.[2] The company had initially agreed to take all revenues in Jamaican dollars (sealing the local currency functional currency designation), but after the fall of the Jamaican dollar in early 2003 (see Exhibit 1), the company had renegotiated a risk-sharing agreement. The agreement restructured the relationship to one where, although LaJolla would continue to be paid in local currency, the two companies would share any changes in the exchange rate beginning in the fourth quarter of 2003 when establishing the charges as invoiced. Regardless, the continuing decline of the Jamaican dollar had created substantial translation losses for LaJolla in Jamaica.

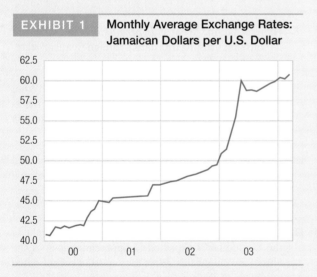

EXHIBIT 1 Monthly Average Exchange Rates: Jamaican Dollars per U.S. Dollar

Mexico. Although the Mexican peso had been quite stable for a number of years, it clearly had started to slide against the dollar in 2002 and 2003 (see Exhibit 2).

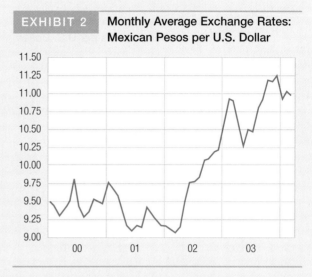

EXHIBIT 2 Monthly Average Exchange Rates: Mexican Pesos per U.S. Dollar

Meaghan had become particularly frustrated with the Mexican situation the deeper she looked into it. LaJolla had only initiated the subsidiary's operations in Mexico in early 2000, yet the reported translation losses from Mexico had grown much more rapidly than what she would have expected. She had also become quite agitated when she realized that the financial reports coming from her Mexican offices were seemingly "writing-up" the translation losses every quarter. When she had asked questions, first by phone and then later in person, her local financial controller simply stopped talking (she was working through an interpreter), claiming they simply did not understand her questions. Meaghan was no beginner in international finance, and she knew that Mexican financial statements did regularly index foreign currency denominated accounts in line with government published indexes of asset values related to currencies. She wondered if the indexing could be at the source of the rapid growth in translation losses.

Venezuela. The continuing political crisis in Venezuela surrounding the presidency of Hugo Chavez had taken its toll on the Venezuelan bolivar (see Exhibit 3). Not only was LaJolla suffering declining U.S. dollar proceeds from its Venezuelan operations, but also it had continued to suffer severe late payments from the various government agencies to which the company was exclusively providing services. The average invoice was now taking more than

[2]All exchange rate diagrams courtesy of the Pacific Exchange Rate Service (http://fx.sauder.ubc.ca), a service for academic research and teaching; ©2004 by Prof. Werner Antweiler, University of British Columbia, Vancouver, BC, Canada. Time period shown in each diagram is 1/Jan/2000–9/Mar/2004.

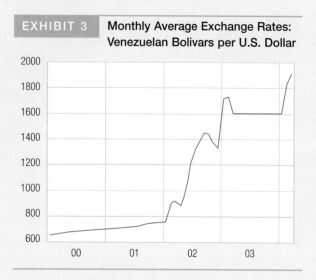

EXHIBIT 3   Monthly Average Exchange Rates: Venezuelan Bolivars per U.S. Dollar

180 days to be settled, and the bolivar's decline had added to the losses. Translation losses were accumulating here, again from a subsidiary whose functional currency was the local currency. The LaJolla controller in Venezuela had

faxed a proposal that would involve changing the currency used for the books in Venezuela to U.S. dollars, as well as a suggestion that they consider moving the subsidiary offshore (out of Venezuela) for accounting and consolidation purposes. He had suggested either the Cayman Islands or the Netherlands Antilles just off the coast.

All in all, Meaghan was beginning to think she made a big mistake when she had accepted the promotion to CFO of this division. She turned her eyes once more to look out over the Pacific and ponder what alternatives she might have to manage these exposures, and what—if anything— she should do immediately.

Case Questions

1. Do you believe Meaghan should spend time and resources attempting to manage translation losses, what many consider purely an accounting phenomenon?

2. How would you characterize or structure your analysis of each of the individual country threats to LaJolla? What specific features of their individual problems seem to be intertwined with currency issues?

3. What would you recommend that Meaghan do?

QUESTIONS

1. **By Any Other Name.** What does the word *translation* mean? Why is translation exposure sometimes called *accounting exposure*?

2. **Converting Financial Assets.** In the context of preparing consolidated financial statements, are the words *translate* and *convert* synonyms?

3. **The Central Problem.** What is the central problem in consolidating the financial statements of a foreign subsidiary?

4. **Self-Sustaining Subsidiaries.** What is the difference between a *self-sustaining foreign subsidiary* and an *integrated foreign subsidiary*?

5. **Functional Currency.** What is a *functional currency*? What is a *nonfunctional currency*?

6. **Translating Assets.** What are the major differences in translating assets between the current rate method and the temporal method?

7. **Translating Liabilities.** What are the major differences in translating liabilities between the current rate method and the temporal method?

8. **Hyperinflation.** What is *hyperinflation* and what are its consequences for translating foreign financial statements?

9. **Foreign Exchange Losses by Any Other Name.** What are the primary differences among losses from transaction exposure, operating exposure, and translation exposure?

10. **Reacting to Potential Losses.** How should financial managers react to any differences between potential losses from operating exposure and translation exposure?

11. **Trident and a Strong Dollar.** During the year ahead the U.S. dollar is expected to appreciate vis-à-vis the euro. How might this affect the reported consolidated earnings of Trident and its operating subsidiary in Germany?

12. **Trident and a Weak Dollar.** During the year ahead the U.S. dollar is expected to weaken vis-à-vis the euro. How might this affect the reported consolidated earnings of Trident and its operating subsidiary in Germany?

PROBLEMS

1. **Trident Europe (A).** Using facts in the chapter for Trident Europe, assume that the exchange rate on January 2, 2011, in Exhibit 13.4 *dropped in value* from $1.2000/€ to $0.9000/€ rather than to $1.0000/€. Recalculate Trident Europe's translated balance sheet for January 2, 2011, with the new exchange rate using the *current rate method*.
   a. What is the amount of translation gain or loss?
   b. Where should it appear in the financial statements?

2. **Trident Europe (B).** Using facts in the chapter for Trident Europe, assume as in question 1 that the exchange rate on January 2, 2011, in Exhibit 13.4 dropped in value from $1.2000/€ to $0.9000/€ rather than to $1.0000/€. Recalculate Trident Europe's translated balance sheet for January 2, 2011, with the new exchange rate using the *temporal method*.
   a. What is the amount of translation gain or loss?
   b. Where should it appear in the financial statements?
   c. Why does the translation loss or gain under the temporal method differ from the loss or gain under the current rate method?

3. **Trident Europe (C).** Using facts in the chapter for Trident Europe, assume that the exchange rate on January 2, 2011, in Exhibit 13.4 *appreciated* from $1.2000/€ to $1.500/€. Calculate Trident Europe's translated balance sheet for January 2, 2011, with the new exchange rate using the *current rate method*.
   a. What is the amount of translation gain or loss?
   b. Where should it appear in the financial statements?

4. **Trident Europe (D).** Using facts in the chapter for Trident Europe, assume as in question 3 that the exchange rate on January 2, 2011 in Exhibit 13.4 *appreciated* from $1.2000/€ to $1.5000/€. Calculate Trident Europe's translated balance sheet for January 2, 2011, with the new exchange rate using the *temporal method*.
   a. What is the amount of translation gain or loss?
   b. Where should it appear in the financial statements?

*5. **Productos Montevideo, S.A. (A).** Montevideo Products, S.A., is the Uruguayan subsidiary of a U.S. manufacturing company. Its balance sheet for January 1 follows. The January 1 exchange rate between the U.S. dollar and the *peso Uruguayo* ($U) is $U20/US$.

Montevideo Products, S.A.

Balance Sheet, January 1, thousands of *pesos Uruguayo*

Assets		Liabilities and Net Worth	
Cash	$U 60,000	Current liabilities	$U30,000
Accounts receivable	120,000	Long-term debt	90,000
Inventory	120,000	Capital stock	300,000
Net plant and equipment	240,000	Retained earnings	120,000
	$U540,000		$U540,000

   a. Determine Montevideo's contribution to the translation exposure of its parent on January 1, using the current rate method.
   b. Calculate Montevideo's contribution to its parent's translation loss if the exchange rate on December 31 is $U20/US$. Assume all peso Uruguayo accounts remain as they were at the beginning of the year.

6. **Productos Montevideo, S.A. (B).** Calculate Montevideo's contribution to its parent's translation loss if the exchange rate on December 31 is $U22/$. Assume all peso accounts remain as they were at the beginning of the year.

7. **Productos Montevideo, S.A. (C).** Calculate Montevideo's contribution to its parent's translation gain or loss using the current rate method if the exchange rate on December 31 is $U12/$. Assume all peso accounts remain as they were at the beginning of the year.

8. **Bangkok Instruments, Ltd. (A).** Bangkok Instruments, Ltd., the Thai subsidiary of a U.S. corporation, is a seismic instrument manufacturer. Bangkok Instruments manufactures the instruments primarily for the oil and gas industry globally, though with recent commodity price increases of all kinds—including copper—its business has begun to grow rapidly. Sales are primarily to multinational companies based in the United States and Europe. Bangkok Instruments' balance sheet in thousands of Thai bahts (B) as of March 31 is shown in the table on the following page.

Bangkok Instruments, Ltd.
Balance Sheet, March 1, thousands of Thai bahts

Assets		Liabilities and Net Worth	
Cash	B 24,000	Accounts payable	B 18,000
Accounts receivable	36,000	Bank loans	60,000
Inventory	48,000	Common stock	18,000
Net plant and equipment	60,000	Retained earnings	72,000
	B168,000		B168,000

Exchange rates for translating Bangkok's balance sheet into U.S. dollars are as follows:

B40.00/$	April 1 exchange rate after 25% devaluation.
B30.00/$	March 31 exchange rate, before 25% devaluation. All inventory was acquired at this rate.
B20.00/$	Historic exchange rate at which plant and equipment were acquired.

The Thai baht dropped in value from B30/$ to B40/$ between March 31 and April 1. Assuming no change in balance sheet accounts between these two days, calculate the gain or loss from translation by both the current rate method and the temporal method. Explain the translation gain or loss in terms of changes in the value of exposed accounts.

9. **Bangkok Instruments, Ltd. (B).** Using the original data provided for Bangkok Instruments, assume that the Thai baht *appreciated* in value from B30/$ to B25/$ between March 31 and April 1. Assuming no change in balance sheet accounts between those two days, calculate the gain or loss from translation by both the current rate method and the temporal method. Explain the translation gain or loss in terms of changes in the value of exposed accounts.

10. **Cairo Ingot, Ltd.** Cairo Ingot, Ltd. is the Egyptian subsidiary of Trans-Mediterranean Aluminum, a British multinational that fashions automobile engine blocks from aluminum. Trans-Mediterranean's home reporting currency is the British pound. Cairo Ingot's December 31 balance sheet follows. At the date of this balance sheet the exchange rate between Egyptian pounds (£E) and British pounds (UK£) was £E5.50/UK£.

Assets		Liabilities and Net Worth	
Cash	£E 16,500,000	Accounts payable	£E 24,750,000
Accounts receivable	33,000,000	Long-term debt	49,500,000
Inventory	49,500,000	Invested capital	90,750,000
Net plant and equipment	66,000,000		
	£E165,000,000		£E165,000,000

What is Cairo Ingot's contribution to the translation exposure of Trans-Mediterranean on December 31, using the current rate method? Calculate the translation exposure loss to Trans-Mediterranean if the exchange rate at the end of the following quarter is £E6.00/UK£. Assume all balance sheet items remain unchanged.

INTERNET EXERCISES

1. **Translation Practices: FASB.** The Financial Accounting Standards Board promulgates standard practices for the reporting of financial results by companies in the United States. However, it also often leads the way in the development of new practices and emerging issues around the world. Use the FASB's home page to track current proposed accounting standards and the current state of reaction to the proposed standards.

FASB home page   www.fasb.org/

2. **Professional Treasury Associations.** Corporate treasury, the unit within the typical MNE that manages cash balances and foreign exchange positions, is an area of specialized services. There are a number of major organizations—two are listed here—that provide continuing education and updates on regulatory, technological, and topical advancement.

Association for Financial Professionals	www.afponline.org/
Treasury and Risk	www.treasuryandrisk.com/

3. **Nestlé's Financial Statements and Exchange Rates.** Using Nestlé's Web page, check Current Press Releases for more recent financial results, including what the company reports as the primary currencies and average exchange rates used for translation during the most recent period.

Nestlé: The World Food Company	www.nestle.com/MediaCenter/ PressReleases/PressReleases.htm

PART IV

Financing the Global Firm

CHAPTER 14

The Global Cost and Availability of Capital

Ideas and leadership, however, are not enough. They need to be nurtured with money. Companies that cannot depend on steady access to the capital markets will not prosper. ... What do investors want? First, of course, investors want performance: strong predictable earnings and sustainable growth. Second, they want transparency, accountability, open communications and effective corporate governance. Companies that fail to move toward international standards in each of these areas will fail to attract and retain international capital.

—"The Brave New World of Corporate Governance," LatinFinance, May 2001.

How can firms tap global capital markets for the purpose of minimizing their cost of capital and maximizing capital's availability? Why should they do so?

Global integration of capital markets has given many firms access to new and cheaper sources of funds beyond those available in their home markets. These firms can then accept more long-term projects and invest more in capital improvements and expansion. If a firm is located in a country with illiquid and/or segmented capital markets, it can achieve this lower global cost and greater availability of capital by a properly designed and implemented strategy. The dimensions of the cost and availability of capital are presented in Exhibit 14.1. The impact of firm-specific characteristics, market liquidity for the firm's securities, and the definition and effect of market segmentation on the prices of a firm's capital are the focus of most of this chapter.

A firm that must source its long-term debt and equity in a *highly illiquid domestic securities market* will probably have a relatively high cost of capital and will face limited availability of such capital, which in turn will lower its competitiveness both internationally and vis-à-vis foreign firms entering its home market. This category of firms includes both firms resident in emerging countries, where the capital market remains undeveloped, and firms too small to gain access to their own national securities markets. Many family-owned firms find themselves in this category because they choose not to utilize securities markets to source their long-term capital needs.

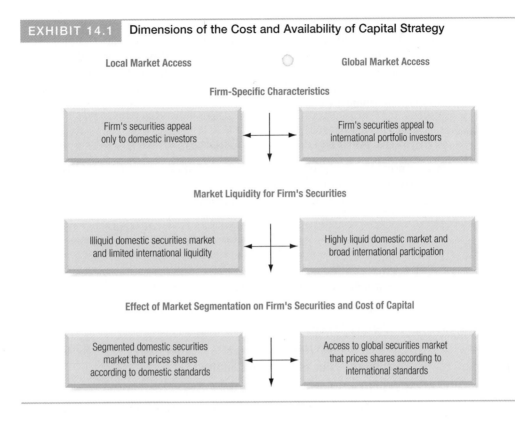

EXHIBIT 14.1   Dimensions of the Cost and Availability of Capital Strategy

Firms resident in industrial countries with *small capital markets* often source their long-term debt and equity at home in these partially liquid domestic securities markets. The firms' cost and availability of capital is better than that of firms in countries with illiquid capital markets. However, if these firms can tap the highly liquid global markets, they can also strengthen their competitive advantage in sourcing capital.

Firms resident in countries with *segmented capital markets* must devise a strategy to escape dependence on that market for their long-term debt and equity needs. A national capital market is segmented if the required rate of return on securities in that market differs from the required rate of return on securities of comparable expected return and risk traded on other securities markets. Capital markets become segmented because of such factors as excessive regulatory control, perceived political risk, anticipated foreign exchange risk, lack of transparency, asymmetric availability of information, cronyism, insider trading, and many other market imperfections.

Firms constrained by any of these conditions must develop a strategy to escape their own limited capital markets and source some of their long-term capital abroad. First, this chapter will review how a firm calculates its weighted average cost of capital when international portfolio investors are able to invest in its equity and debt securities. Trident will be our example.

Then, the chapter analyzes how a firm can attract international portfolio investors to its securities. This ability depends on firm-specific characteristics, a regulatory environment that permits unrestricted cross-border investment flows, and a financial strategy that creates market liquidity and global pricing for the firm's securities, whether or not its domestic market is segmented from other capital markets.

Next, the focus is on the link between the cost and availability of capital. Achieving this link requires improving market liquidity for the firm's securities and escaping from a segmented domestic market. If the firm is successful in implementing these strategies, it will reduce its weighted average cost of capital and increase its availability.

Finally, we analyze whether MNEs have reduced their cost of capital below that of their comparable domestic competitors.

Weighted Average Cost of Capital

A firm normally finds its *weighted average cost of capital* (WACC) by combining the cost of equity with the cost of debt in proportion to the relative weight of each in the firm's optimal long-term financial structure. More specifically:

$$k_{WACC} = k_e \frac{E}{V} + k_d (1-t) \frac{D}{V}$$

where

k_{WACC} = weighted average after-tax cost of capital

k_e = risk-adjusted cost of equity

k_d = before-tax cost of debt

t   = marginal tax rate

E   = market value of the firm's equity

D   = market value of the firm's debt

V   = total market value of the firm's securities (D + E)

Cost of Equity

The *capital asset pricing model* (CAPM) approach is to define the cost of equity for a firm by the following formula:

$$k_e = k_{rf} + \beta_j (k_m - k_{rf})$$

where

k_e = expected (required) rate of return on equity

k_{rf} = rate of interest on risk-free bonds (Treasury bonds, for example)

β_j = coefficient of *systematic risk* for the firm

k_m = expected (required) rate of return on the market portfolio of stocks

Systematic risk is a function of the total variability of expected returns of the firm's stock relative to the market index (k_m) and the degree to which the variability of expected returns of the firm is correlated to the expected returns on the market index. More formally:

$$\beta_j = \frac{\rho_{jm} \sigma_j}{\sigma_m}$$

where

β_j (beta)   = measure of systematic risk for security j

ρ (rho)   = correlation between security j and the market

σ_j (sigma) = standard deviation of the return on firm j

σ_m (sigma) = standard deviation of the market return

Beta will have a value of less than 1.0 if the firm's returns are less volatile than the market, 1.0 if the same as the market, or greater than 1.0 if more volatile—or risky—than the market. CAPM analysis assumes that the required return estimated is an indication of what more is necessary to keep an investor's capital invested in the equity considered. If the equity's return does not reach the expected return, CAPM assumes that individual investors will liquidate their holdings.

Cost of Debt

The normal procedure for measuring the cost of debt requires a forecast of interest rates for the next few years, the proportions of various classes of debt the firm expects to use, and the corporate income tax rate. The interest costs of the different debt components are then averaged according to their proportion in the debt structure. This before-tax average, k_d, is then adjusted for corporate income taxes by multiplying it by the expression (1 – tax rate), to obtain $k_d (1 - t)$, the weighted average after-tax cost of debt.

The weighted average cost of capital is normally used as the risk-adjusted discount rate whenever a firm's new projects are in the same general risk class as its existing projects. On the other hand, a project-specific required rate of return should be used as the discount rate if a new project differs from existing projects in business or financial risk.

Trident's Weighted Average Cost of Capital

Maria Gonzalez, Trident's chief financial officer, calculates the weighted average cost of capital to be 12.28%, as shown in Exhibit 14.2.

EXHIBIT 14.2   Calculation of Trident's Weighted Average Cost of Capital

Cost of Equity (k_e) Inputs

$k_{rf} = 5.000\%$ — k_{rf} is the risk-free rate of interest estimated by using the U.S. government Treasury bond rate.

$k_m = 15.000\%$ — k_m is the expected rate of return on the market portfolio held by a well-diversified global investor. Over 40% of Trident's stock is held by foreign portfolio investors, as part of their globally diversified portfolios. Trident's U.S. investors also typically hold globally diversified portfolios.

$\beta = 1.2$ — β is Trident's estimate of its own systematic risk using the correlation of Trident's returns with those of the market (ρ), Trident's standard deviation (σ_c), and the market's standard deviation (σ_m).

The cost of equity is then — $k_e = k_{rf} + \beta (k_m - k_{rf}) = 5.000\% + 1.2 (15.000\% - 5.000\%) = 17.000\%$

Cost of Debt (k_d) Inputs

$k_d = 8.000\%$ — k_d is the before tax cost of debt estimated by observing the current yield on Trident's outstanding bonds combined with bank debt.

$t = 35\%$ — t is the U.S. corporate income tax rate.

The after-tax cost of debt is then — $k_d (1 - t) = 8.000 (1 - 0.35) = 8.000 (0.65) = 5.200\%$

Financial Structure

$E/V = 60\%$ — E/V is the equity ratio; the percentage of Trident's securities (E + D) that is equity.

$D/V = 40\%$ — D/V is the debt ratio; the percentage of Trident's securities (E + D) that is debt (bonds and bank loans).

$V = 100\%$ — V is the market value of Trident's securities (E + D).

The weighted average cost of capital (k_{WACC}) is then

$$k_{WACC} = k_e \frac{E}{V} + k_d (1-t)\frac{D}{V} = 17.00\%(0.60) + 5.20\%(0.40) = 12.28\%$$

She believes that Trident's cost of capital is already at a global level. It is fully competitive with Trident's main rivals in the telecommunications hardware industry segment worldwide, which are mainly headquartered in the United States, the United Kingdom, Canada, Finland, Sweden, Germany, Japan, and the Netherlands. Their shares are listed on prominent stock exchanges and international portfolio investors can freely trade in their shares. Trident itself is listed on the very liquid NASDAQ. The key to Trident's favorable global cost and availability of capital is its ability to attract and hold the international portfolio investors that own its stock.

Nestlé: An Application of the International CAPM

In theory, the primary distinction in the estimation of the cost of equity for an individual firm using an internationalized version of the CAPM is the definition of the market and a recalculation of the firm's beta for that market. The case of Nestlé (Switzerland) provides an illustration of the possible impact of this globalization of portfolios.

Nestlé, the Swiss-based multinational firm that produces and distributes a variety of confectionery products, serves as an excellent example of how the international investor may view the global cost of capital differently from a domestic investor.[1]

Estimating the required return on Nestlé, a prospective Swiss investor might assume a risk-free return of 3.3% (index of Swiss government bond issues, in Swiss francs), an average return on a portfolio of Swiss equities of 10.2% (*Financial Times Swiss Index*, in Swiss francs), and a $\beta_{Nestlé}$ of 0.885. An investor would then expect Nestlé to yield 9.4065% for the coming year:

$$k_e^{Nestlé} = k_{rf} + \left(k_m - k_{rf}\right)\beta_{Nestlé} = 3.3 + \left(10.2 - 3.3\right)0.885 = 9.4065\%$$

One problem with this traditional domestic CAPM approach is that it assumes that investors in the Swiss market, and potentially in Nestlé, hold portfolios limited to stocks available in the Swiss market alone—a purely domestic portfolio. If Swiss investors held internationally diversified portfolios instead, both the expected market return (k_m) and the beta estimate for Nestlé ($\beta_{Nestlé}$) would be defined and determined differently.

A Swiss investor may hold a global portfolio, rather than a domestic portfolio. Given the trends toward deregulation and integration of international capital markets, the Swiss investor's portfolio expectations would be more accurately represented by a global portfolio index rather than by a purely domestic index.

We follow Stulz's (1995) preference here for describing the internationally diversified portfolio as the global portfolio rather than the world portfolio. The distinction is important. The world portfolio is an index of all securities in the world. However, even with the increasing trend of deregulation and financial integration, a number of securities markets still remain segmented or restricted in their access. Those securities actually available to an investor are the *global portfolio*.

In the case of Nestlé, for the same time period as before, a global portfolio index such as the *Financial Times* index in Swiss francs (FTA-Swiss) would show a market return of 13.7% (as opposed to the domestic Swiss index return of 10.2%). In addition, a beta for Nestlé estimated on Nestlé's returns versus the global portfolio index would be much smaller: 0.585 (as opposed to the 0.885 found previously). An internationally diversified Swiss investor would expect a return on Nestlé of

$$k_e^{Nestlé} = k_{rf} + \left(k_m - k_{rf}\right)\beta_{Nestlé} = 3.3 + \left(13.7 - 3.3\right)0.585 = 9.384\%$$

[1]René Stulz, "The Cost of Capital in Internationally Integrated Markets: The Case of Nestlé," *European Financial Management,* Volume 1, Number 1, March 1995, pp. 11–22.

Admittedly, there is not a lot of difference in the end. Exhibit 14.3 summarizes the values and results of the comparison. However, given the magnitude of change in both the values of the market return average and the beta for the firm, it is obvious that the final result could easily have varied by several hundred basis points. The proper construction of the investor's portfolio and the proper portrayal of the investor's perceptions of risk and opportunity cost are clearly important to identifying the global cost of a company's equity capital.

Calculating Equity Risk Premiums in Practice

In practice, calculating a firm's equity risk premium is more controversial. Although the capital asset pricing model (CAPM) has now become very widely accepted in global business as the preferred method of calculating the cost of equity for a firm, there is rising debate over what numerical values should be used in its application, especially for the equity risk premium. The *equity risk premium* is the average annual return of the market expected by investors over and above riskless debt, the term $(k_m - k_{rf})$.

Equity Risk Premium History. The field of finance does agree that a cost of equity calculation should be forward-looking, meaning that the inputs to the equation should represent what is expected to happen over the relevant future time horizon. As is typically the case, however, practitioners use historical evidence as the basis for their forward-looking projections. The current debate begins with a debate over what has happened in the past.

Exhibit 14.4 presents the results of a large study originally completed in 2001 and updated in 2003. The study calculates the equity risk premium in 16 different developed countries for 1900 through 2002. There are clearly significant differences in equity returns over time by country. Comparing arithmetic returns, Italy was the highest (10.3%) with Germany (9.4%) and Japan (9.3%) following. Denmark, with an average arithmetic return of only 3.8%, had the lowest premium. The United States had an average arithmetic return of 7.2%, while the United Kingdom had 5.9%. The average return for the 16 listed countries was 6.9%. The world, as defined by the authors of the study, had an arithmetic return of 5.7%.

There is less debate regarding the use of arithmetic returns over geometric returns. The mean arithmetic return is simply the average of the annual percentage changes in capital appreciation plus dividend distributions. This is a rate of return calculation with which every business student is familiar. The mean geometric return, however, is a more specialized calculation that takes into account only the beginning and ending values over an extended period of history. Then it calculates the annual average rate of compounded growth from the

EXHIBIT 14.3   Estimating the Global Cost of Equity for Nestlé (Switzerland)

Domestic Portfolio for Swiss Investor

k_{rf} = 3.3% (Swiss bond index yield)

k_m = 10.2% (Swiss market portfolio in SF)

$\beta_{Nestlé}$ = 0.885 (Nestlé versus Swiss market portfolio)

Global Portfolio for Swiss Investor

k_{rf} = 3.3% (Swiss bond index yield)

k_m = 13.7% (*Financial Times* Global index in SF)

$\beta_{Nestlé}$ = 0.585 (Nestlé versus FTA-Swiss index)

$$k_{Nestlé} = k_{rf} + (k_m - k_{rf})\, \beta_{Nestlé}$$

Required return on Nestlé:

$k_e^{Nestl} = 9.4065\%$

Required return on Nestlé:

$k_e^{Nestlé} = 9.3840\%$

Source: All values are taken from René Stulz, "The Cost of Capital in Internationally Integrated Markets: The Case of Nestlé," *European Financial Management*, March 1995, Volume 1, Number 1, pp. 11–22.

| EXHIBIT 14.4 | Equity Risk Premiums around the World, 1900–2002 | | | | | |
</br>

	Relative to Bills			Relative to Bonds		
	Geometric Mean	Arithmetic Mean	SD	Geometric Mean	Arithmetic Mean	SD
Australia	6.8	8.3	17.2	6.0	7.6	19.0
Belgium	2.2	4.4	23.1	2.1	3.9	20.2
Canada	4.2	5.5	16.8	4.0	5.5	18.2
Denmark	2.2	3.8	19.6	1.5	2.7	16.0
France	6.4	8.9	24.0	3.6	5.8	22.1
Germany	3.9	9.4	35.5	5.7	9.0	28.8
Ireland	3.6	5.5	20.4	3.2	4.8	18.5
Italy	6.3	10.3	32.5	4.1	7.6	30.2
Japan	6.1	9.3	28.0	5.4	9.5	33.3
The Netherlands	4.3	6.4	22.6	3.8	5.9	21.9
South Africa	5.9	7.9	22.2	5.2	6.8	19.4
Spain	2.8	4.9	21.5	1.9	3.8	20.3
Sweden	5.2	7.5	22.2	4.8	7.2	2.5
Switzerland	3.2	4.8	18.8	1.4	2.9	17.5
United Kingdom	4.2	5.9	20.1	3.8	5.1	17.0
United States	5.3	7.2	19.8	4.4	6.4	20.3
Average	4.5	6.9	22.8	3.8	5.9	21.6
World	4.4	5.7	16.5	3.8	4.9	15.0

Source: Elroy Dimson, Paul Marsh, and Mike Staunton, "Global Evidence on the Equity Risk Premium," *Journal of Applied Corporate Finance,* 2003, Volume 15, Number 4, p. 31. The equity risk premium is measured as 1 + equity rate of return divided by 1 + risk-free return, minus 1. The statistics reported in this table are based on 103 annual observations for each country, except Germany, which excludes 1922–1923, when bill and bondholders experienced returns of –100% due to hyperinflation. The row labeled "Average" is a simple, unweighted average of the statistics for the 16 individual countries. The row marked "World" is for the world index. SD is standard deviation.

beginning to the end, without paying attention to the specific path taken in between. Exhibit 14.5 provides a simple example of how the two methods would differ for a very short historical series of stock prices.

Arithmetic returns capture the year-to-year volatility in markets; geometric returns do not. For this reason, most practitioners prefer the arithmetic measurement, as it embodies

EXHIBIT 14.5	Arithmetic versus Geometric Returns: A Sample Calculation					
Year	**1**	**2**	**3**	**4**	**5**	**Mean**
Share price	10	12	10	12	14	
Arithmetic change		+20.00%	−16.67%	+20.00%	+16.67%	+10.00%
Geometric change		+8.78%	+8.78%	+8.78%	+8.78%	+ 8.78%

Arithmetic change is calculated year-by-year as $[P_2/P_1 − 1]$. The simple average of the series is the mean. The geometric change is calculated using only the beginning and ending values, 10 and 14, and the geometric root of $[(14/10)^{1/4} − 1]$ is found (four periods of change). The geometric change assumes reinvested compounding, whereas the arithmetic mean only assumes point-to-point investment.

more of the volatility so often characteristic of equity markets globally. Note that the geometric change will in all but a few extreme circumstances yield a smaller mean return.

The United States Looking Forward. The debate over which equity risk premium to use in practice was highlighted in this same study by looking at what equity risk premiums are being recommended for the United States by a variety of sources. As illustrated in Exhibit 14.6, a hypothetical firm with a beta of 1.0 (estimated market risk equal to that of the market) might have a cost of equity as low as 9.000% and as high as 12.800% using this set of alternative values. Note that here the authors used geometric returns, not arithmetic returns.

How important is it for a company to predict its cost of equity accurately? The corporation must annually determine which potential investments it will accept and reject due to its limited capital resources. If the company is not accurately estimating its cost of equity—and therefore its general cost of capital—it will not be accurately estimating the net present value of potential investments if it uses its own cost of capital as the basis for discounting expected cash flows.

The Demand for Foreign Securities: The Role of International Portfolio Investors

Gradual deregulation of equity markets during the past three decades not only elicited increased competition from domestic players but also opened up markets to foreign competitors. International portfolio investment and cross-listing of equity shares on foreign markets have become commonplace.

What motivates portfolio investors to purchase and hold foreign securities in their portfolio? The answer lies in an understanding of "domestic" portfolio theory and how it has been extended to handle the possibility of global portfolios. More specifically, it requires an understanding of the principles of portfolio risk reduction, portfolio rate of return, and foreign currency risk. These principles are explained in detail in Chapter 17.

Both domestic and international portfolio managers are asset allocators. Their objective is to maximize a portfolio's rate of return for a given level of risk, or to minimize risk for a given rate of return. International portfolio managers can choose from a larger bundle of assets than portfolio managers limited to domestic-only asset allocations. As a result, internationally diversified portfolios often have higher expected rates of return, and they nearly always have lower levels of portfolio risk, because national securities markets are imperfectly correlated with one another.

Portfolio asset allocation can be accomplished along many dimensions, depending on the investment objective of the portfolio manager. For example, portfolios can be diversified according to the type of securities. They can be composed of stocks only or bonds only or a

EXHIBIT 14.6   Alternative Estimates of Cost of Equity for a Hypothetical U.S. Firm Assuming $\beta = 1$ and $k_{rf} = 4\%$

Source	Equity Risk Premium	Cost of Equity	Differential
Ibbotson	8.800%	12.800%	3.800%
Finance textbooks	8.500%	12.500%	3.500%
Investor surveys	7.100%	11.100%	2.100%
Dimson, et al.	5.000%	9.000%	Baseline

Source: Equity risk premium quotes from "Stockmarket Valuations: Great Expectations," *The Economist*, January 31, 2002.

combination of both. They also can be diversified by industry or by size of capitalization (small-cap, mid-cap, and large-cap stock portfolios).

For our purposes, the most relevant dimensions are diversification by country, geographic region, stage of development, or a combination of these (global). An example of diversification by country is the Korea Fund. At one time it was the only vehicle for foreign investors to hold South Korean securities, but foreign ownership restrictions have more recently been liberalized. A typical regional diversification would be one of the many Asian funds. These performed exceptionally well until the "bubble" burst in Japan and Southeast Asia during the second half of the 1990s. Portfolios composed of emerging market securities are examples of diversification by stage of development. They comprise securities from different countries, geographic regions, and stage of development.

The Link between Cost and Availability of Capital

Trident's weighted average cost of capital was calculated assuming that equity and debt capital would always be available at the same required rate of return even if Trident's capital budget were to expand. This is a reasonable assumption, considering Trident's excellent access through the NASDAQ to international portfolio investors in global capital markets. It is a bad assumption, however, for firms resident in illiquid or segmented capital markets, small domestic firms, and family-owned firms resident in any capital market. We will now examine how market liquidity and market segmentation can affect a firm's cost of capital. This is followed by an illustrative case showing how NOVO Industri A/S, a Danish firm, was able to overcome the disadvantages of being resident in an illiquid and segmented market.

Improving Market Liquidity

Although no consensus exists about the definition of *market liquidity,* we can observe market liquidity by noting the degree to which a firm can issue a new security without depressing the existing market price, as well as the degree to which a change in price of its securities elicits a substantial order flow.

In the domestic case, an underlying assumption is that total availability of capital to a firm at any time is determined by supply and demand in the domestic capital markets. A firm should always expand its capital budget by raising funds in the same proportion as its optimal financial structure. As its budget expands in absolute terms, however, its marginal cost of capital will eventually increase. In other words, a firm can tap the capital market only for some limited amount in the short run before suppliers of capital balk at providing further funds, even if the same optimal financial structure is preserved. In the long run, this setup may not be a limitation, depending on market liquidity.

In the multinational case, a firm is able to improve market liquidity by raising funds in the Euromarkets (money, bond, and equity), by selling security issues abroad, and by tapping local capital markets through foreign subsidiaries. Such activity should logically expand the capacity of an MNE to raise funds in the short run over what might have been raised if the firm were limited to its home capital market. This situation assumes that the firm preserves its optimal financial structure.

Market Segmentation

If all capital markets are fully integrated, securities of comparable expected return and risk should have the same required rate of return in each national market after adjusting for foreign exchange risk and political risk. This definition applies to both equity and debt, although it often happens that one or the other may be more integrated than its counterpart.

As introduced earlier, capital market segmentation is a financial market imperfection caused mainly by government constraints, institutional practices, and investor perceptions. The following are the most important imperfections:

- Asymmetric information between domestic and foreign-based investors
- Lack of transparency
- High securities transaction costs
- Foreign exchange risks
- Political risks
- Corporate governance differences
- Regulatory barriers

Market imperfections do not necessarily imply that national securities markets are inefficient. A national securities market can be efficient in a domestic context, yet segmented in an international context. According to finance theory, a market is *efficient* if security prices in that market reflect all available relevant information and adjust quickly to any new relevant information. Therefore, the price of an individual security reflects its "intrinsic value" and any price fluctuations will be "random walks" around this value. Market efficiency assumes that transaction costs are low, that many participants are in the market, and that these participants have sufficient financial strength to move security prices. Empirical tests of market efficiency show that most major national markets are reasonably efficient.

An efficient national securities market might very well correctly price all securities traded in that market on the basis of information available to the investors who participate in that market. However, if that market were segmented, foreign investors would not be participants. Thus, securities in the segmented market would be priced on the basis of domestic rather than international standards.

In the rest of this chapter, and in the next chapter, we will use the term MNE to describe all firms that have access to a global cost and availability of capital. This includes qualifying MNEs, whether they are located in highly developed or emerging markets. It also includes large firms that are not multinational but have access to global capital markets. They too could be located in highly developed or emerging capital markets. We will use the term *domestic firm* (DF) for all firms that do not have access to a global cost and availability of capital, no matter where they are located.

Availability of capital depends on whether a firm can gain liquidity for its debt and equity securities and a price for those securities based on international rather than national standards. In practice, this means that the firm must define a strategy to attract international portfolio investors and thereby escape the constraints of its own illiquid or segmented national market.

The Effect of Market Liquidity and Segmentation

The degree to which capital markets are illiquid or segmented has an important influence on a firm's marginal cost of capital and thus on its weighted average cost of capital. The marginal cost of capital is the weighted average cost of the next currency unit raised. This is illustrated in Exhibit 14.7, which shows the transition from a domestic to a global marginal cost of capital.

Exhibit 14.7 shows that the MNE has a given marginal return on capital at different budget levels, represented in the line MRR. This demand is determined by ranking potential projects according to net present value or internal rate of return. Percentage rate of return to both users and suppliers of capital is shown on the vertical scale. If the firm is limited to

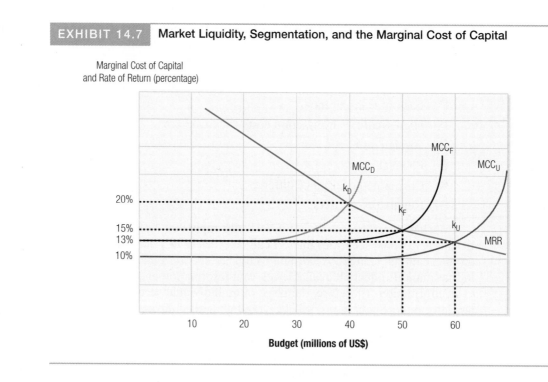

raising funds in its domestic market, the line MCC_D shows the marginal domestic cost of capital (vertical axis) at various budget levels (horizontal axis). Remember that the firm continues to maintain the same debt ratio as it expands its budget, so that financial risk does not change. The optimal budget in the domestic case is $40 million, where the marginal return on capital (MRR) just equals the marginal cost of capital (MCC_D). At this budget, the marginal domestic cost of capital, k_D would be equal to 20%.

If the MNE has access to additional sources of capital outside an illiquid domestic capital market, the marginal cost of capital should shift to the right (the line MCC_F). In other words, foreign markets can be tapped for long-term funds at times when the domestic market is saturated because of heavy use by other borrowers or equity issuers, or when it is unable to absorb another issue of the MNE in the short run. Exhibit 14.7 shows that by a tap of foreign capital markets, the firm has reduced its marginal international cost of capital, k_F, to 15%, even while it raises an additional $10 million. This statement assumes that about $20 million is raised abroad, as only about $30 million could be raised domestically at a 15% marginal cost of capital.

If the MNE is located in a capital market that is both illiquid and segmented, the line MCC_U represents the decreased marginal cost of capital if it gains access to other equity markets. As a result of the combined effects of greater availability of capital and international pricing of the firm's securities, the marginal cost of capital, k_U, declines to 13% and the optimal capital budget climbs to $60 million.

Most of the tests of market segmentation suffer from the usual problem for models—namely, the need to abstract from reality in order to have a testable model. In our opinion, a realistic test would be to observe what happens to a single security's price when it has been traded in only a domestic market, is "discovered" by foreign investors, and then is traded in a foreign market. Arbitrage should keep the market price equal in both markets. However, if during the transition we observe a significant change in the security's price uncorrelated with price movements in either of the underlying securities markets, we can infer that the domestic market was segmented.

In academic circles, tests based on case studies are often considered to be "casual empiricism," because no theory or model exists to explain what is being observed. Nevertheless, something may be learned from such cases, just as scientists learn from observing nature in an uncontrolled environment. Furthermore, case studies that preserve real-world complications may illustrate specific kinds of barriers to market integration and ways in which they might be overcome.

Unfortunately, few case studies have been documented in which a firm has "escaped" from a segmented capital market. In practice, escape usually means being listed on a foreign stock market such as New York or London, and/or selling securities in foreign capital markets. We will illustrate something more specific by using the example of Novo Industri A/S, a Danish firm.[2]

Globalization of Securities Markets

During the 1980s, numerous other Nordic and other European firms followed Novo's example. They cross-listed on major foreign exchanges such as London and New York. They placed equity and debt issues in major securities markets. In most cases, they were successful in lowering their WACC and increasing its availability.

During the 1980s and 1990s, national restrictions on cross-border portfolio investment were gradually eased under pressure from the Organization for Economic Cooperation and Development (OECD), a consortium of most of the world's most industrialized countries. Liberalization of European securities markets was accelerated, because of the European Union's efforts to develop a single European market without barriers. Emerging nation markets followed suit, as did the former East bloc countries after the breakup of the Soviet Union. Emerging national markets have often been motivated by the need to source foreign capital to finance large-scale privatization.

Presently, market segmentation has been significantly reduced, although the liquidity of individual national markets remains limited. Most observers believe that for better or for worse, we have achieved a global market for securities. The good news is that many firms have been assisted to become MNEs because they now have access to a global cost and availability of capital. The bad news is that the correlation among securities markets has increased, thereby reducing but not eliminating the benefits of international portfolio diversification. Globalization of securities markets has also led to more volatility and speculative behavior, as shown by the emerging market crises of the 1995–2001 period, and the 2008 global credit crisis.

Corporate Governance and the Cost of Capital. Would global investors be willing to pay a premium for a share in a good corporate governance company? A recent study of Norwegian and Swedish firms measured the impact of foreign board membership (Anglo-American) on firm value. They summarized their findings as follows:

> *Using a sample of firms with headquarters in Norway or Sweden, the study indicates a significantly higher value for firms that have outsider Anglo-American board member(s), after a variety of firm-specific and corporate governance related factors have been controlled for. We argue that this superior performance reflects the fact that these companies*

[2]The Novo case material, presented at the end of this chapter, is a condensed version of Arthur Stonehill and Kåre B. Dullum, *Internationalizing the Cost of Capital in Theory and Practice: The Novo Experience and National Policy Implications* (Copenhagen: Nyt Nordisk Forlag Arnold Busck, 1982; and New York: Wiley, 1982). Reprinted with permission.

have successfully broken away from a partly segmented domestic capital market by "importing" an Anglo-American corporate governance system. Such an "import" signals a willingness on the part of the firm to expose itself to improved corporate governance and enhances its reputation in the financial market.[3]

Strategic Alliances

Strategic alliances are normally formed by firms that expect to gain synergies from one or more of the following joint efforts. They might share the cost of developing technology, or pursue complementary marketing activities. They might gain economies of scale or scope or a variety of other commercial advantages. However, one synergy that may sometimes be overlooked is the possibility for a financially strong firm to help a financially weak firm to lower its cost of capital by providing attractively priced equity or debt financing. This is illustrated in the *Global Finance in Practice 14.1* on the strategic alliance between Bang & Olufsen and Philips N.V.

GLOBAL FINANCE IN PRACTICE 14.1

Bang & Olufsen and Philips N.V.

One excellent example of financial synergy that lowered a firm's cost of capital was provided by the cross-border strategic alliance of Philips N.V. of the Netherlands and Bang & Olufsen (B&O) of Denmark in 1990. Philips N.V. is one of the largest multinational firms in the world and the leading consumer electronics firm in Europe. B&O is a small European competitor but with a nice niche at the high end of the audio-visual market.

Philips was a major supplier of components to B&O, a situation it wished to continue. It also wished to join forces with B&O in the upscale consumer electronics market, where Philips did not have the quality image enjoyed by B&O. Philips was concerned that financial pressure might force B&O to choose a Japanese competitor for a partner. That would be very unfortunate. B&O had always supported Philips' political efforts to gain EU support to make the few remaining European-owned consumer electronics firms more competitive than their strong Japanese competitors.

B&O's Motivation

B&O was interested in an alliance with Philips to gain more rapid access to its new technology and assistance in converting that technology into B&O product applications. B&O wanted assurance of timely delivery of components at volume discounts from Philips itself, as well as access to Philip's large network of suppliers under terms enjoyed by Philips. Equally important, B&O wanted to get an equity infusion from Philips to strengthen its own shaky financial position. Despite its commercial artistry, in recent years B&O had been only

marginally profitable, and its publicly traded shares were considered too risky to justify a new public equity issue either in Denmark or abroad. It had no excess borrowing capacity.

The Strategic Alliance

A strategic alliance was agreed upon that would give each partner what it desired commercially. Philips agreed to invest DkK342 million (about $50 million) to increase the equity of B&O's main operating subsidiary. In return, it received a 25% ownership of the expanded subsidiary.

When B&O's strategic alliance was announced to the public on May 3, 1990, the share price of B&O Holding, the listed company on the Copenhagen Stock Exchange, jumped by 35% in two days. It remained at that level until the Gulf War crisis temporarily depressed B&O's share price. The share price has since recovered and the expected synergies eventually materialized. B&O eventually bought back its shares from Philips at a price that had been predetermined at the start.

In evaluating what happened, we recognize that an industrial purchaser might be willing to pay a higher price for a firm that will provide it some synergies than would a portfolio investor who does not receive these synergies. Portfolio investors are only pricing firms' shares based on the normal risk versus return trade-off. They cannot normally anticipate the value of synergies that might accrue to the firm from an unexpected strategic alliance partner. The same conclusion should hold for a purely domestic strategic alliance, but this example happens to be a cross-border alliance.

---

[3]Lars Oxelheim and Trond Randøy, "The impact of foreign board membership on firm value," *Journal of Banking and Finance,* Volume 27, Number 12, 2003, p. 2,569.

In Chapter 15, we describe the experiences of firms that have successfully tapped global securities markets and the financial strategies and instruments they have used.

The Cost of Capital for MNEs Compared to Domestic Firms

Is the weighted average cost of capital for MNEs higher or lower than for their domestic counterparts? The answer is a function of the marginal cost of capital, the relative after-tax cost of debt, the optimal debt ratio, and the relative cost of equity.

Availability of Capital

Earlier in this chapter we discussed that international availability of capital to MNEs, or to other large firms that can attract international portfolio investors, may allow them to lower their cost of equity and debt compared with most domestic firms. In addition, international availability permits an MNE to maintain its desired debt ratio, even when significant amounts of new funds must be raised. In other words, an MNE's marginal cost of capital is constant for considerable ranges of its capital budget. This statement is not true for most domestic firms. They must either rely on internally generated funds or borrow in the short and medium term from commercial banks.

Financial Structure, Systematic Risk, and the Cost of Capital for MNEs

Theoretically, MNEs should be in a better position than their domestic counterparts to support higher debt ratios, because their cash flows are diversified internationally. The probability of a firm's covering fixed charges under varying conditions in product, financial, and foreign exchange markets should improve if the variability of its cash flows is minimized. By diversifying cash flows internationally, the MNE might be able to achieve the same kind of reduction in cash flow variability as portfolio investors receive from diversifying their security holdings internationally. The same argument applies—namely, that returns are not perfectly correlated between countries.

Despite the theoretical elegance of this hypothesis, empirical studies have come to the opposite conclusion.[4] Despite the favorable effect of international diversification of cash flows, bankruptcy risk was only about the same for MNEs as for domestic firms. However, MNEs faced higher agency costs, political risk, foreign exchange risk, and asymmetric information. These have been identified as the factors leading to lower debt ratios and even a higher cost of long-term debt for MNEs. Domestic firms rely much more heavily on short and intermediate debt, which lie at the low cost end of the yield curve.

Even more surprising, one study found that MNEs have a higher level of systematic risk than their domestic counterparts.[5] The same factors caused this phenomenon as caused the lower debt ratios for MNEs. The study concluded that the increased standard deviation of cash flows from internationalization more than offset the lower correlation from diversification.

As we stated earlier in this chapter, the systematic risk term, β_j, is defined as follows:

$$\beta_j = \frac{\rho_{jm} \sigma_j}{\sigma_m}$$

[4]Kwang Chul Lee and Chuck C.Y. Kwok, "Multinational Corporations vs. Domestic Corporations: International Environmental Factors and Determinants of Capital Structure," *Journal of International Business Studies,* Summer 1988, pp. 195–217.

[5]David M. Reeb, Chuck C.Y. Kwok, and H. Young Baek, "Systematic Risk of the Multinational Corporation," *Journal of International Business Studies,* Second Quarter 1998, pp. 263–279.

where ρ_{jm} is the correlation coefficient between security j and the market; σ_j is the standard deviation of the return on firm j; and σ_m is the standard deviation of the market return. The MNE's systematic risk could increase if the decrease in the correlation coefficient, ρ_{jm}, due to international diversification, is more than offset by an increase in σ_j, the MNE's standard deviation due to the aforementioned risk factors. This conclusion is consistent with the observation that many MNEs use a higher hurdle rate to discount expected foreign project cash flows. In essence, they are accepting projects that they consider to be riskier than domestic projects, thus potentially skewing upward their perceived systematic risk. At the least, MNEs need to earn a higher rate of return than their domestic equivalents in order to maintain their market value.

A more recent study found that internationalization actually allowed emerging-market MNEs to carry a higher level of debt and lowered their systematic risk.[6] This occurred because the emerging market MNEs are investing in more stable economies abroad, a strategy that lowers their operating, financial, foreign exchange, and political risks. The reduction in risk more than offsets their increased agency costs and allows the emerging market MNEs to enjoy higher leverage and lower systematic risk than their U.S.-based MNE counterparts.

Solving a Riddle: Is the Weighted Average Cost of Capital for MNEs Really Higher Than for Their Domestic Counterparts?

The riddle is that the MNE is supposed to have a lower marginal cost of capital (MCC) than a domestic firm, because of the MNE's access to a global cost and availability of capital. On the other hand, the empirical studies we mentioned show that the MNE's weighted average cost of capital (WACC) is actually higher than for a comparable domestic firm because of agency costs, foreign exchange risk, political risk, asymmetric information, and other complexities of foreign operations.

The answer to this riddle lies in the link between the cost of capital, its availability, and the opportunity set of projects. As the opportunity set of projects increases, eventually the firm needs to increase its capital budget to the point where its marginal cost of capital is increasing. The optimal capital budget would still be at the point where the rising marginal cost of capital equals the declining rate of return on the opportunity set of projects. However, this would be at a higher weighted average cost of capital than would have occurred for a lower level of the optimal capital budget.

To illustrate this linkage, Exhibit 14.8 shows the marginal cost of capital given different optimal capital budgets. Assume that there are two different demand schedules based on the opportunity set of projects for both the multinational enterprise (MNE) and domestic counterpart (DC).

The line MRR_{DC} depicts a modest set of potential projects. It intersects the line MCC_{MNE} at 15% and a $100 million budget level. It intersects the line MCC_{DC} at 10% and a $140 million budget level. At these low budget levels the MCC_{MNE} has a higher MCC and probably weighted average cost of capital than its domestic counterpart (MCC_{DC}), as discovered in the recent empirical studies.

[6]Chuck C.Y. Kwok and David M. Reeb, "Internationalization and Firm Risk: An Upstream-Downstream Hypothesis," *Journal of International Business Studies,* Volume 31, Issue 4, 2000, pp. 611–630.

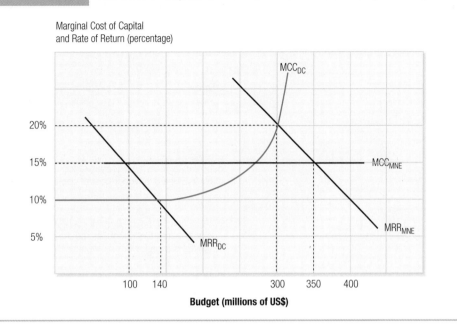

EXHIBIT 14.8   The Cost of Capital for MNE and Domestic Counterpart Compared

The line MRR_{MNE} depicts a more ambitious set of projects for both the MNE and its domestic counterpart. It intersects the line MCC_{MNE} still at 15% and a $350 million budget. However, it intersects the MCC_{DC} at 20% and a budget level of $300 million. At these higher budget levels, the MCC_{MNE} has a lower MCC and probably WACC than its domestic counterpart, as predicted earlier in this chapter.

In order to extend this conclusion to the general case, we would need to know under what conditions a domestic firm would be willing to undertake the optimal capital budget despite its increasing the firm's marginal cost of capital. At some point, the MNE might also have an optimal capital budget at the point where its MCC is rising.

Empirical studies show that neither mature domestic firms nor MNEs are typically willing to assume the higher agency costs or bankruptcy risk associated with higher MCCs and capital budgets. In fact, most mature firms demonstrate some degree of stakeholder wealth-maximizing behavior. They are somewhat risk-averse and tend to avoid returning to the market to raise fresh equity. They prefer to limit their capital budgets to what can be financed with free cash flows. Indeed, they have a so-called "pecking order" that determines the priority of which sources of funds they tap and in what order. This behavior motivates shareholders to monitor management more closely. They tie management's compensation to stock performance (options). They may also require other types of contractual arrangements that are collectively part of agency costs.

In conclusion, if both MNEs and domestic firms do actually limit their capital budgets to what can be financed without increasing their MCC, then the empirical findings that MNEs have higher WACC stands. If the domestic firm has such good growth opportunities that it chooses to undertake growth despite an increasing marginal cost of capital, then the MNE would have a lower WACC. Exhibit 14.9 summarizes these conclusions.

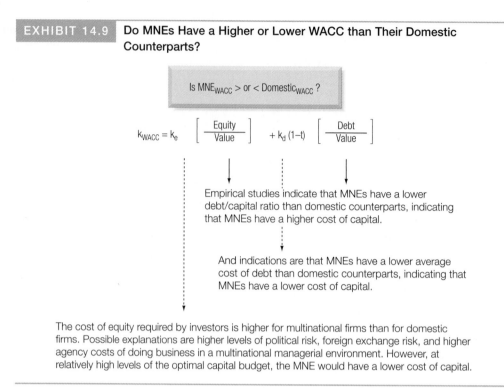

EXHIBIT 14.9   Do MNEs Have a Higher or Lower WACC than Their Domestic Counterparts?

Is $MNE_{WACC} >$ or $< Domestic_{WACC}$?

$$k_{WACC} = k_e \left[\frac{Equity}{Value} \right] + k_d (1-t) \left[\frac{Debt}{Value} \right]$$

Empirical studies indicate that MNEs have a lower debt/capital ratio than domestic counterparts, indicating that MNEs have a higher cost of capital.

And indications are that MNEs have a lower average cost of debt than domestic counterparts, indicating that MNEs have a lower cost of capital.

The cost of equity required by investors is higher for multinational firms than for domestic firms. Possible explanations are higher levels of political risk, foreign exchange risk, and higher agency costs of doing business in a multinational managerial environment. However, at relatively high levels of the optimal capital budget, the MNE would have a lower cost of capital.

SUMMARY POINTS

- Gaining access to global capital markets should allow a firm to lower its cost of capital.

- This can be achieved by increasing the market liquidity of its shares and by escaping from segmentation of its home capital market.

- The cost and availability of capital is directly linked to the degree of market liquidity and segmentation. Firms having access to markets with high liquidity and a low level of segmentation should have a lower cost of capital and greater ability to raise new capital.

- A firm is able to increase its market liquidity by raising debt in the Euromarket, by selling security issues in individual national capital markets and as Euroequities, and tapping local capital markets through foreign subsidiaries. Increased market liquidity causes the marginal cost of capital line to "flatten out to the right." This results in the firm being able to raise more capital at the same low marginal cost of capital, and thereby justify investing in more capital projects. The key is to attract international portfolio investors.

- A national capital market is segmented if the required rate of return on securities in that market differs from the required rate of return on securities of comparable expected return and risk that are traded on other national securities markets. Capital market segmentation is a financial market imperfection caused by government constraints and investor perceptions. The most important imperfections are: 1) asymmetric information; 2) transaction costs; 3) foreign exchange risk; 4) corporate governance differences; 5) political risk; and 6) regulatory barriers.

- Segmentation results in a higher cost of capital and less availability of capital.

- If a firm is resident in a segmented capital market, it can still escape from this market by sourcing its debt and equity abroad. The result should be a lower marginal cost of capital, improved liquidity for its shares, and a larger capital budget. The experience of Novo was suggested as a possible model for firms resident in small or emerging markets that are partially segmented and illiquid.

- Whether or not MNEs have a lower cost of capital than their domestic counterparts depends on their optimal financial structures, systematic risk, availability of capital, and the level of the optimal capital budget.

MINI-CASE   # Novo Industri A/S (Novo)

Novo is a Danish multinational firm that produces industrial enzymes and pharmaceuticals (mostly insulin). In 1977, Novo's management decided to "internationalize" its capital structure and sources of funds. This decision was based on the observation that the Danish securities market was both illiquid and segmented from other capital markets. In particular, the lack of availability and high cost of equity capital in Denmark resulted in Novo having a higher cost of capital than its main multinational competitors, such as Eli Lilly (U.S.), Miles Laboratories (U.S.—a subsidiary of Bayer, Germany), and Gist Brocades (the Netherlands).

Apart from the cost of capital, Novo's projected growth opportunities signaled the eventual need to raise new long-term capital beyond what could be raised in the illiquid Danish market. As Novo is a technology leader in its specialties, planned capital investments in plant, equipment, and research could not be postponed until internal financing from cash flow became available. Novo's competitors would preempt any markets not served by Novo.

Even if an equity issue of the size required could have been raised in Denmark, the required rate of return would have been unacceptably high. For example, Novo's price/earnings ratio was typically around 5; that of its foreign competitors was well over 10. Yet Novo's business and financial risk appeared to be about equal to that of its competitors. A price/earnings ratio of 5 appeared appropriate for Novo only within a domestic Danish context, when Novo was compared with other domestic firms of comparable business and financial risk.

If Denmark's securities markets were integrated with world markets, one would expect foreign investors to rush in and buy "undervalued" Danish securities. In that case, firms like Novo would enjoy an international cost of capital comparable to that of their foreign competitors. Strangely enough, no Danish governmental restrictions existed that would have prevented foreign investors from holding Danish securities. Therefore, one must look for investor perception as the main cause of market segmentation in Denmark at that time.

At least six characteristics of the Danish equity market were responsible for market segmentation: 1) asymmetric information base of Danish and foreign investors, 2) taxation, 3) alternative sets of feasible portfolios, 4) financial risk, 5) foreign exchange risk, and 6) political risk.

Asymmetric Information

Certain institutional characteristics of Denmark caused Danish and foreign investors to be uninformed about each other's equity securities. The most important information barrier was a Danish regulation that prohibited Danish investors from holding foreign private sector securities. Therefore, Danish investors had no incentive to follow developments in foreign securities markets or to factor such information into their evaluation of Danish securities. As a result, Danish securities might have been priced correctly in the efficient market sense relative to one another, considering the Danish information base, but priced incorrectly considering the combined foreign and Danish information base. Another detrimental effect of this regulation was that foreign securities firms did not locate offices or personnel in Denmark, as they had no product to sell. Lack of a physical presence in Denmark reduced the ability of foreign security analysts to follow Danish securities.

A second information barrier was lack of enough Danish security analysts following Danish securities. Only one professional Danish securities analysis service was published (Børsinformation), and that was in Danish. A few Danish institutional investors employed in-house analysts, but their findings were not available to the public. Almost no foreign security analysts followed Danish securities, because they had no product to sell and the Danish market was too small (small-country bias).

Other information barriers included language and accounting principles. Naturally, financial information was normally published in Danish, using Danish accounting principles. A few firms, such as Novo, published English versions, but almost none used U.S. or British accounting principles or attempted to show any reconciliation with such principles.

Taxation

Danish taxation policy had all but eliminated investment in common stock by individuals. Until a tax law change in July 1981, capital gains on shares held for over two years were taxed at a 50% rate. Shares held for less than two years, or for "speculative" purposes, were taxed at personal income tax rates, with the top marginal rate being 75%. In contrast, capital gains on bonds were tax-free. This situation resulted in bonds being issued at deep discounts because the redemption at par at maturity was considered a capital gain. Thus, most individual investors held bonds rather than stocks. This factor reduced the liquidity of the stock market and increased the required rate of return on stocks if they were to compete with bonds.

Feasible Set of Portfolios

Because of the prohibition on foreign security ownership, Danish investors had a very limited set of securities from which to choose a portfolio. In practice, Danish institutional portfolios were composed of Danish stocks, government bonds, and mortgage bonds. Because Danish stock price movements are closely correlated with each other, Danish portfolios possessed a rather high level of systematic risk. In addition, government policy had been to provide a relatively high real rate of return on government bonds after adjusting for inflation. The net result of taxation policies on individuals, and attractive real yields on government bonds was that required rates of return on stocks were relatively high by international standards.

From a portfolio perspective, Danish stocks provided an opportunity for foreign investors to diversify internationally. If Danish stock price movements were not closely correlated with world stock price movements, inclusion of Danish stocks in foreign portfolios should reduce the systematic risk of these portfolios. Furthermore, foreign investors were not subject to the high Danish income tax rates, because they are normally protected by tax treaties that typically limit their tax to 15% on dividends and capital gains. As a result of the international diversification potential, foreign investors might have required a lower rate of return on Danish stocks than Danish investors, other things being equal. However, other things were not equal, because foreign investors perceived Danish stocks to carry more financial, foreign exchange, and political risk than their own domestic securities.

Financial, Foreign Exchange, and Political Risks

Financial leverage utilized by Danish firms was relatively high by U.S. and U.K. standards, but not abnormal for Scandinavia, Germany, Italy, or Japan. In addition, most of the debt was short-term with variable interest rates. Just how foreign investors viewed financial risk in Danish firms depended on what norms they follow in their home countries. We know from Novo's experience in tapping the Eurobond market in 1978 that Morgan Grenfell, its British investment banker, advised Novo to maintain a

debt ratio (debt/total capitalization) closer to 50% rather than the traditional Danish 65% to 70%.

Foreign investors in Danish securities are subject to foreign exchange risk. Whether this is a plus or minus factor depends on the investor's home currency, perception about the future strength of the Danish krone, and its impact on a firm's operating exposure. Through personal contacts with foreign investors and bankers, Novo's management did not believe foreign exchange risk was a factor in Novo's stock price, because its operations were perceived as being well-diversified internationally. Over 90% of its sales were to customers located outside of Denmark.

With respect to political risk, Denmark was perceived as a stable Western democracy, but one with the potential to cause periodic problems for foreign investors. In particular, Denmark's national debt was regarded as too high for comfort, although this judgment had not yet shown up in the form of risk premiums on Denmark's Eurocurrency syndicated loans.

The Road to Globalization

Although Novo's management in 1977 wished to escape from the shackles of Denmark's segmented and illiquid capital market, many barriers had to be overcome. It is worthwhile to describe some of these obstacles, because they typify the barriers faced by other firms from segmented markets that wish to internationalize their capital sources.

Closing the Information Gap. Novo had been a family-owned firm from its founding in the 1920s by the two Pedersen brothers until 1974, when it went public and listed its "B" shares on the Copenhagen Stock Exchange. The "A" shares were held by the Novo Foundation; the "A" shares were sufficient to maintain voting control. However, Novo was essentially unknown in investment circles outside of Denmark. To overcome this disparity in the information base, Novo increased the level of its financial and technical disclosure in both Danish and English versions.

The information gap was further closed when Morgan Grenfell successfully organized a syndicate to underwrite and sell a $20 million convertible Eurobond issue for Novo in 1978. In connection with this offering, Novo listed its shares on the London Stock Exchange to facilitate conversion and to gain visibility. These twin actions were the key to dissolving the information barrier; of course, they also raised a large amount of long-term capital on favorable terms, which would have been unavailable in Denmark.

Despite the favorable impact of the Eurobond issue on availability of capital, Novo's cost of capital actually increased when Danish investors reacted negatively to the potential dilution effect of the conversion right. During 1979, Novo's share price in Danish kroner (Dkr) declined from around Dkr300 per share to around Dkr220 per share.

The Biotechnology Boom. During 1979, a fortuitous event occurred. Biotechnology began to attract the interest of the U.S. investment community, with several sensationally oversubscribed stock issues by such startup firms as Genentech and Cetus. Thanks to the aforementioned domestic information gap, Danish investors were unaware of these events and continued to value Novo at a low price/earnings ratio of 5, compared with over 10 for its established competitors and 30 or more for these new potential competitors.

In order to profile itself as a biotechnology firm with a proven track record, Novo organized a seminar in New York City on April 30, 1980. Soon after the seminar, a few sophisticated individual U.S. investors began buying Novo's shares and convertibles through the London Stock Exchange. Danish investors were only too happy to supply this foreign demand. Therefore, despite relatively strong demand from U.S. and British investors, Novo's share price increased only gradually, climbing back to the Dkr300 level by mid-summer. However, during the following months, foreign interest began to snowball, and by the end of 1980, Novo's stock price had reached the Dkr600 level. Moreover, foreign investors had increased their proportion of share ownership from virtually nothing to around 30%. Novo's price/earnings ratio had risen to around 16, which was now in line with that of its international competitors but not with the Danish market. At this point, one must conclude that Novo had succeeded in internationalizing its cost of capital. Other Danish securities remained locked in a segmented capital market. Exhibit 1 shows that the movement in the Danish stock market in general did not parallel the rise in Novo's share price, nor could it be explained by movement in the U.S. or U.K. stock markets as a whole.

Directed Share Issue in the United States. During the first half of 1981, under the guidance of Goldman Sachs and with the assistance of Morgan Grenfell and

EXHIBIT 1	Novo's B-Share Prices Compared with Stock Market Indices

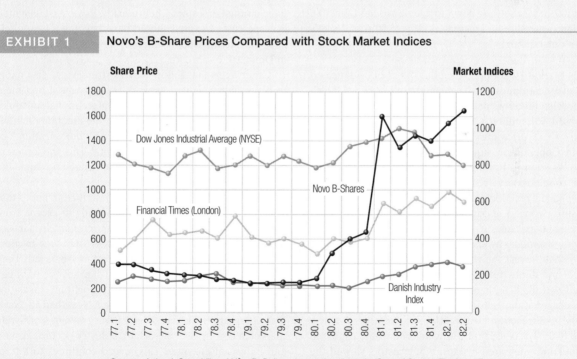

Source: Arthur I. Stonehill and Kåre B. Dullum, *Internationalizing the Cost of Capital: The Novo Experience and National Policy Implications*, London: John Wiley, 1982, p. 73. Reprinted with permission.

Copenhagen Handelsbank, Novo prepared a prospectus for SEC registration of a U.S. share offering and eventual listing on the New York Stock Exchange. The main barriers encountered in this effort, which would have general applicability, were connected with preparing financial statements that could be reconciled with U.S. accounting principles and the higher level of disclosure required by the SEC. In particular, industry segment reporting was a problem both from a disclosure perspective and an accounting perspective because the accounting data were not available internally in that format. As it turned out, the investment barriers in the U.S. were relatively tractable, although expensive and time-consuming to overcome.

The more serious barriers were caused by a variety of institutional and governmental regulations in Denmark. The latter were never designed so that firms could issue shares at market value, because Danish firms typically issued stock at par value with preemptive rights. By this time, however, Novo's share price, driven by continued foreign buying, was so high that virtually nobody in Denmark thought it was worth the price that foreigners were willing to pay. In fact, prior to the time of the share issue in July 1981, Novo's share price had risen to over Dkr1500, before settling down to a level around Dkr1400. Foreign ownership had increased to over 50% of Novo's shares outstanding!

Stock Market Reactions. One final piece of evidence on market segmentation can be gleaned from the way Danish and foreign investors reacted to the announcement of the proposed $61 million U.S. share issue on May 29, 1981. Novo's share price dropped 156 points the next trading day in Copenhagen, equal to about 10% of its market value. As soon as trading started in New York, the stock price immediately recovered all of its loss. The Copenhagen reaction was typical for an illiquid market. Investors worried about the dilution effect of the new share issue because it would increase the number of shares outstanding by about 8%. They did not believe that Novo could invest the new funds at a rate of return that would not dilute future earnings per share. They also feared that the U.S. shares would eventually flow back to Copenhagen if biotechnology lost its glitter.

The U.S. reaction to the announcement of the new share issue was consistent with what one would expect in a liquid and integrated market. U.S. investors viewed the new issue as creating additional demand for the shares, as Novo became more visible due to the selling efforts of a large aggressive syndicate. Furthermore, the marketing effort was directed at institutional investors who were previously underrepresented among Novo's U.S. investors. They had been underrepresented because U.S. institutional investors want to be assured of a liquid market in a stock in order to be able to get out, if desired, without depressing the share price. The wide distribution effected by the new issue, plus SEC registration and a New York Stock Exchange listing, all added up to more liquidity and a global cost of capital.

Effect on Novo's Weighted Average Cost of Capital. During most of 1981 and the years thereafter, Novo's share price was driven by international portfolio investors transacting on the New York, London, and Copenhagen stock exchanges. This situation reduced Novo's weighted average cost of capital and lowered its marginal cost of capital. Novo's systematic risk was reduced from its previous level, which was determined by nondiversified (internationally) Danish institutional investors and the Novo Foundation. However, its appropriate debt ratio level was also reduced to match the standards expected by international portfolio investors trading in the United States, United Kingdom, and other important markets. In essence, the U.S. dollar became Novo's functional currency when being evaluated by international investors. Theoretically, its revised weighted average cost of capital should have become a new reference hurdle rate when evaluating new capital investments in Denmark or abroad.

Other firms that follow Novo's strategy are also likely to have their weighted average cost of capital become a function of the requirements of international portfolio investors. Firms resident in some of the emerging market countries have already experienced "dollarization" of trade and financing for working capital. This phenomenon might be extended to long-term financing and the weighted average cost of capital.

The Novo experience has been described in hopes that it can be a model for other firms wishing to escape from segmented and illiquid home equity markets. In particular, MNEs based in emerging markets often face barriers and lack of visibility similar to what Novo faced. They could benefit by following Novo's proactive strategy employed to attract international portfolio investors. However, a word of caution is advised. Novo had an excellent operating track record and a very strong worldwide market niche in two important industry sectors: insulin and industrial enzymes. This record continues to attract investors in Denmark and abroad. Other companies would also need to have such a favorable track record to attract foreign investors.

QUESTIONS

1. **Dimensions of the Cost and Availability of Capital.** Global integration has given many firms access to new and cheaper sources of funds beyond those available in their home markets. What are the dimensions of a strategy to capture this lower cost and greater availability of capital?

2. **Benefits.** What are the benefits of achieving a lower cost and greater availability of capital?

3. **Definitions.** Define the following terms:
   a. Systematic risk
   b. Unsystematic risk
   c. Beta (in the Capital Asset Pricing Model)

4. **Equity Risk Premiums**
   a. What is an equity risk premium?
   b. What is the difference between calculating an equity risk premium using arithmetic returns and using geometric returns?
   c. In Exhibit 14.4, why are arithmetic mean risk premiums always higher than geometric mean risk premiums?

5. **Portfolio Investors.** Both domestic and international portfolio managers are *asset allocators*.
   a. What is their portfolio management objective?
   b. What is the main advantage that international portfolio managers have compared to portfolio managers limited to domestic-only asset allocation?

6. **Dimensions of Asset Allocation.** Portfolio asset allocation can be accomplished along many dimensions depending on the investment objective of the portfolio manager. Identify the various dimensions.

7. **Market Liquidity**
   a. Define what is meant by the term *market liquidity*.
   b. What are the main disadvantages for a firm located in an illiquid market?
   c. If a firm is limited to raising funds in its domestic capital market, what happens to its marginal cost of capital as it expands?
   d. If a firm can raise funds abroad, what happens to its marginal cost of capital as it expands?

8. **Market Segmentation**
   a. Define market segmentation.
   b. What are the six main causes of market segmentation?
   c. What are the main disadvantages for a firm to be located in a segmented market?

9. **Market Liquidity and Segmentation Effects.** What is the effect of market liquidity and segmentation on a firm's cost of capital?

10. **Novo Industri (A).** Why did Novo believe that its cost of capital was too high compared to its competitors? Why did Novo's relatively high cost of capital create a competitive disadvantage?

11. **Novo Industri (B).** Novo believed that the Danish capital market was segmented from world capital markets. Explain the six characteristics of the Danish equity market that were responsible for its segmentation.

12. **Novo Industri (C)**
    a. What was Novo's strategy to internationalize its cost of capital?
    b. What is the evidence that Novo's strategy succeeded?

13. **Emerging Markets.** It has been suggested that firms located in illiquid and segmented emerging markets could follow Novo's proactive strategy to internationalize their own cost of capital. What are the preconditions that would be necessary to succeed in such a proactive strategy?

14. **Cost of Capital for MNEs Compared to Domestic Firms.** Theoretically, MNEs should be in a better position than their domestic counterparts to support higher debt ratios, because their cash flows are diversified internationally. However, recent empirical studies have come to the opposite conclusion. These studies also concluded that MNEs have higher betas than their domestic counterparts.
    a. According to these empirical studies, why do MNEs have lower debt ratios than their domestic counterparts?
    b. According to these empirical studies, why do MNEs have higher betas than their domestic counterparts?

15. **The "Riddle."** The riddle is an attempt to explain under what conditions an MNE would have a higher or lower debt ratio and beta than its domestic counterpart. Explain and diagram these conditions.

16. **Emerging-Market MNEs.** Apart from improving liquidity and escaping from a segmented home market, why might emerging-market MNEs further lower their cost of capital by listing and selling equity abroad?

PROBLEMS

*1. Trident's Cost of Capital. Exhibit 14.2 showed the calculation of Trident's weighted average cost of capital. Assuming that financial conditions have worsened, and using the following current data, recalculate:

$k_{rf} = 4.000\%$	$k_m = 9.000\%$	$\beta = 1.3$
$k_d = 7.000\%$	$T = 30\%$	$E/V = 50\%$
$D/V = 50\%$	$V = 100\%$	

  a. Trident's cost of equity
  b. Trident's cost of debt
  c. Trident's weighted average cost of capital

2. Curacao Pharmaceuticals. Curacao Pharmaceuticals's cost of debt is 7%. The risk-free rate of interest is 3%. The expected return on the market portfolio is 8%. After effective taxes Curacao's effective tax rate is 25%. Its optimal capital structure is 60% debt and 40% equity.

  a. If Curacao's beta is estimated at 1.1, what is its weighted average cost of capital?
  b. If Curacao's beta is estimated at 0.8, significantly lower because of the continuing profit prospects in the global energy sector, what is its weighted average cost of capital?

3. Deming Pipelines, Inc. Deming Pipelines, Inc. is a large U.S. natural gas pipeline company that wants to raise $120 million to finance expansion. Deming wants a capital structure that is 50% debt and 50% equity. Its corporate combined federal and state income tax rate is 40%.

  Deming finds that it can finance in the domestic U.S. capital market at the following rates. Both debt and equity would have to be sold in multiples of $20 million, and these cost figures show the component costs, each, of debt and equity if raised half by equity and half by debt.

	Cost of Domestic Equity	Cost of Domestic Debt
Up to $40 million of new capital	12%	8%
$41 million to $80 million of new capital	18%	12%
Above $80 million	22%	16%

  A London bank advises Deming that U.S. dollars could be raised in Europe at the following costs, also in multiples of $20 million while maintaining the 50/50 capital structure.

	Cost of European Equity	Cost of European Debt
Up to $40 million of new capital	14%	6%
$41 million to $80 million of new capital	16%	10%
Above $80 million	24%	18%

  Each increment of cost would be influenced by the total amount of capital raised. That is, if Deming first borrowed $20 million in the European market at 6% and matched this with an additional $20 million of equity, additional debt beyond this amount would cost 12% in the United States and 10% in Europe. The same relationship holds for equity financing.

  a. Calculate the lowest average cost of capital for each increment of $40 million of new capital, where Deming raises $20 million in the equity market and an additional $20 million in the debt market at the same time.
  b. If Deming plans an expansion of only $60 million, how should that expansion be financed? What will be the weighted average cost of capital for the expansion?

*4. Tata's Cost of Capital. Tata is the largest and most successful specialty goods company based in India. It has not entered the North American marketplace yet, but is considering establishing both manufacturing and distribution facilities in the United States through a wholly owned subsidiary. It has approached two different investment banking advisers, Goldman Sachs and Bank of New York, for estimates of what its costs of capital would be several years into the future when it planned to list its American subsidiary on a U.S. stock exchange. Using the assumptions by the two different advisers (shown in the table at the top of the next page), calculate the prospective costs of debt, equity, and the WACC for Tata.

5. Country Equity Risk Premiums. Using the century of equity market data presented in Exhibit 14.3, answer the following questions:

  a. Which country had the largest differential between the arithmetic mean and geometric mean?
  b. If a Swiss firm were attempting to calculate its cost of equity using this data, assuming a risk-free rate of 2.0% and a security beta of 1.4, what would be its estimated cost of equity using both the arith-

Capital Cost Component	Symbol	Goldman Sachs	Bank of NY
Risk-free rate of interest	k_{rf}	3.0%	3.0%
Average equity market return	k_m	9.0%	12.0%
Estimated cost of debt, single-A	k_d	7.5%	7.8%
Estimated correlation of Tata with market	ρ_{jm}	0.90	0.85
Estimated standard deviation of Tata's returns	σ_j	24.0%	30.0%
Estimated standard deviation of market's returns	σ_m	18.0%	22.0%
Recommended debt to capital structure	D/V	35%	40%
Recommended equity to capital structure	E/V	65%	60%
Estimated effective U.S. tax rate	t	35%	35%

metic mean and geometric means for the equity risk premium?

6. **The Tombs.** You have joined your friends at the local watering hole, The Tombs, for your weekly debate on international finance. The topic this week is whether the cost of equity can ever be cheaper than the cost of debt. The group has chosen Brazil in the mid-1990s as the subject of the debate. One of the group members has pulled the following historical data describing Brazil from an Internet site.

Brazilian Economic Performance	1995	1996	1997	1998	1999
Inflation rate (IPC)	23.2%	10.0%	4.8%	−1.0%	10.5%
Bank lending rate (CDI)	53.1%	27.1%	24.7%	29.2%	30.7%
Exchange rate (reais/$)	0.972	1.039	1.117	1.207	1.700
Stock market index (Bovespa)	16.0%	28.0%	30.2%	−33.5%	151.9%

Larry argues that "it's all about *expected* versus *delivered*. You can talk about what equity investors expect, but they often find that what is delivered for years at a time is so small—even sometimes negative—that in effect the cost of equity is cheaper than the cost of debt."

Mohammed—he goes by Mo—interrupts: "But you're missing the point. The cost of capital is what the investor *requires* in compensation for the risk taken going *into* the investment. If he doesn't end up getting it, and that was happening here, then he pulls his capital out and walks."

Curly is the theoretician. "Ladies, this is not about empirical results; it is about the fundamental concept of risk-adjusted returns. An investor in equities knows he will reap returns only after all compensa-

tion has been made to debt-providers. He is therefore always subject to a higher level of risk to his return than debt instruments, and as the *capital asset pricing model* states, equity investors set their expected returns as a risk-adjusted factor over and above the returns to risk-free instruments."

At this point, both Larry and Mo simply stared at Curly, paused, and both ordered another beer. Using the Brazilian data presented, comment on this week's debate at The Tombs.

7. **Cargill's Cost of Capital.** Cargill is generally considered to be one of the three largest privately held companies in the world. Headquartered in Minneapolis, Minnesota, the company has been averaging sales of over $50 billion per year over the past five years. Although the company does not have publicly traded shares, it is still extremely important for it to calculate its weighted average cost of capital properly in order to make rational decisions on new investment proposals.

	Company A	Company B	Cargill
Company sales	$4.5 billion	$26 billion	$50 billion
Company's beta	0.86	0.78	??
Credit rating	AA	A	AA
Weighted average cost of debt	6.885%	7.125%	6.820%
Debt to total capital	34%	41%	28%
International sales/Sales	12%	26%	45%

Assuming a risk-free rate of 2.50%, an effective tax rate of 40%, and a market risk premium of 5.50%, estimate the weighted average cost of capital first for companies A and B, and then make a 'guesstimate' of what you believe a comparable WACC would be for Cargill.

Stevenson-Kwo and the Riddle.

Use the information in the table below to answer questions 8 through 10. Stevenson-Kwo is an American conglomerate that is actively debating the impacts of international diversification of its operations on its capital structure and cost of capital. The firm is planning on reducing consolidated debt after diversification.

	Symbol	Before Diversification	After Diversification
Debt to capital ratio	D/V	38%	32%
Equity to capital ratio	E/V	62%	68%
Corporate tax rate	t	35%	35%
Correlation of S-C's returns with market	ρ_{jm}	0.88	0.76
Standard deviation of S-C's returns	σ_j	28.0%	26.0%
Standard deviation of market's returns	σ_m	18.0%	18.0%
Market risk premium	$k_m - k_{rf}$	5.50%	5.50%
Corporate cost of debt	k_d	7.20%	7.00%
Risk-free rate of interest	k_{rf}	3.00%	3.00%

8. **Stevenson-Kwo's Cost of Equity.** Senior management at Stevenson-Kwo is actively debating the implications of diversification on its cost of equity. Although both parties agree that the company's returns will be less correlated with the reference market return in the future, the financial advisers believe that the market will assess an additional 3.0% risk premium for "going international" to the basic CAPM cost of equity. Calculate Stevenson-Kwo's cost of equity before and after international diversification of its operations, with and without the hypothetical additional risk premium, and comment on the discussion.

9. **Stevenson-Kwo's WACC.** Calculate the weighted average cost of capital for Stevenson-Kwo for before and after international diversification.
   a. Did the reduction in debt costs reduce the firm's weighted average cost of capital? How would you describe the impact of international diversification on its costs of capital?
   b. Adding the hypothetical risk premium to the cost of equity introduced in question 8 (an added 3.0% to the cost of equity because of international diversification), what is the firm's WACC?

10. **Stevenson-Kwo's WACC and Effective Tax Rate.** Many MNEs have greater ability to control and reduce their effective tax rates when expanding international operations. If Stevenson-Kwo was able to reduce its consolidated effective tax rate from 35% to 32%, what would be the impact on its WACC?

INTERNET EXERCISES

1. **Weighted Average Cost of Capital Calculator.** The *Financial Times* has a simple online way to use a weighted average cost of capital calculator. Use the link below to explore the impacts of changing capital structures on the firm's cost of capital. According to this, would an all-equity firm benefit from leverage?

   Financial Times   www.ft.com/personal-finance/tools
   Cost of Capital

2. **The Data Page.** Aswath Damodaran, a distinguished professor at the NYU Stern School of Business, maintains a detailed financial data page on a variety of topics—one of which is the cost of capital. Visit the following Web site to find estimates for the latest calculations on the cost of capital across industries:

   Aswath Damodaran   pages.stern.nyu.edu/
                           ~adamodar/

3. **Novo Industri.** Novo Industri A/S merged with Nordisk Gentofte in 1989. Nordisk Gentofte was Novo's main European competitor. The combined company, now called Novo Nordisk, has become the leading producer of insulin worldwide. Its main competitor is still Eli Lilly of the United States. Using standard investor information, and the Web site for Novo Nordisk and Eli Lilly, determine whether during the most recent five years Novo Nordisk has maintained a cost of capital competitive with Eli Lilly. In particular, examine the P/E ratios, share prices, debt ratios, and betas. Try to calculate each firm's actual cost of capital.

   Novo Nordisk   www.novonordisk.com
   Eli Lilly and Company   www.lilly.com
   BigCharts.com   bigcharts.com

CHAPTER 15

Sourcing Equity Globally

Do what you will, the capital is at hazard. . . All that can be required of a trustee to invest, is, that he shall conduct himself faithfully and exercise a sound discretion. He is to observe how men of prudence, discretion, and intelligence manage their own affairs, not in regard to speculation, but in regard to the permanent disposition of their funds, considering the probable income, as well as the probable safety of the capital to be invested.

—*Prudent Man Rule*, Justice Samuel Putnam, 1830.

Chapter 14 analyzed why gaining access to global capital markets should lower a firm's marginal cost of capital and increase its availability by improving the market liquidity of its shares and by overcoming market segmentation. In order to implement such a lofty goal it is necessary to start by designing a strategy that will ultimately attract international investors. This involves identifying and choosing among alternative paths to access global markets. It also usually requires some restructuring of the firm, improving the quality and level of its disclosure, and making its accounting and reporting standards more transparent to potential foreign investors. The Novo mini-case in Chapter 14 is a good example of the steps that need to be taken and barriers that might be faced.

A focus of this chapter is on firms resident in less liquid or segmented markets. They are the ones that need to tap liquid and unsegmented markets in order to attain the global cost and availability of capital. These firms are typically resident in emerging market countries and many of the smaller industrial country markets. Firms resident in the United States and United Kingdom already have full access to their own domestic liquid and unsegmented markets. Although they too source equity and debt abroad, it is unlikely to have as favorable an impact on their cost and availability of capital. In fact, sourcing funds abroad is often motivated only by the need to fund large foreign acquisitions rather than existing domestic or foreign operations.

This chapter starts with the design of a strategy to source both equity and debt capital globally. Then it describes depositary receipts. These are the most important instruments that facilitate cross-border trading in securities. The chapter continues with the specifics of cross-listing and selling equity issues abroad. (Selling of debt issues abroad is delayed until Chapter 16, It concludes with an analysis of alternative instruments to source equity abroad.

Designing a Strategy to Source Equity Globally

Designing a capital sourcing strategy requires management to agree upon a long-run financial objective and then choose among the various alternative paths to get there. Exhibit 15.1 is a visual presentation of alternative paths to the ultimate objective of attaining a global cost and availability of capital.

Normally, the choice of paths and implementation is aided by an early appointment of an investment bank as official adviser to the firm. Investment bankers are in touch with the potential foreign investors and what they are currently requiring. They can also help navigate the various institutional requirements and barriers that must be satisfied. Their services include advising if, when, and where a cross-listing should be initiated. They usually prepare the required stock prospectus if an equity issue is desired, help to price the issue, and maintain an aftermarket to prevent the share price from falling below its initial price.

Alternative Paths

Most firms raise their initial capital in their own domestic market (see Exhibit 15.1). Next, they are tempted to skip all the intermediate steps and drop to the bottom line, a Euroequity issue in global markets. This is the time when a good investment bank adviser will offer a "reality check." Most firms that have only raised capital in their domestic market are not well known enough to attract foreign investors. Remember from Chapter 14 that Novo was advised by its investment bankers to start with a convertible Eurobond issue and simultane-

EXHIBIT 15.1   Alternative Paths to Globalize the Cost and Availability of Capital

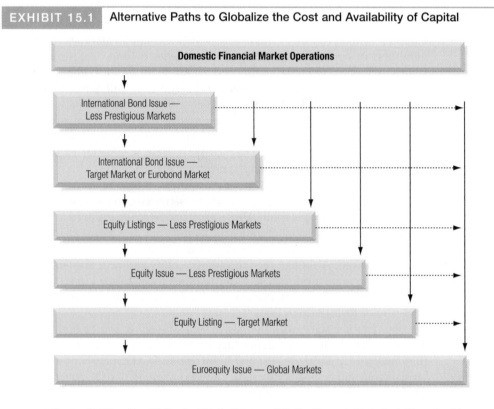

Source: Oxelhiem, Stonehill, Randøy, Vikkula, Dullum, and Modén, *Corporate Strategies in Internationalizing the Cost of Capital*, Copenhagen: Copenhagen Business School Press, 1998, p. 119.

ously cross-list their shares (and the bonds) in London. This was despite the fact that Novo had an outstanding track record with respect to growth, profitability, and dominance of two worldwide market niches (insulin and industrial enzymes).

Exhibit 15.1 shows that most firms should start sourcing abroad with an international bond issue. It could be placed on a less prestigious foreign market. This could be followed by an international bond issue in a target market or in the Eurobond market. The next step might be to cross-list and issue equity in one of the less prestigious markets so as to attract international investor attention. The next step could be to cross-list shares on a highly liquid prestigious foreign stock exchange such as London (LSE), NYSE (NYSE-Euronext), or NASDAQ. The ultimate step would be to place a directed equity issue in a prestigious target market or a Euroequity issue in global equity markets.

Depositary Receipts

Depositary receipts (depositary shares) are negotiable certificates issued by a bank to represent the underlying shares of stock, which are held in trust at a foreign custodian bank. Global depositary receipts (GDRs) refer to certificates traded outside of the United States. American depositary receipts (ADRs) refer to certificates traded in the United States and denominated in U.S. dollars. ADRs are sold, registered, and transferred in the United States in the same manner as any share of stock, with each ADR representing some multiple of the underlying foreign share. This multiple allows the ADRs to possess a price per share appropriate for the U.S. market (typically between $20 and $50 per share) even if the price of the foreign share is inappropriate when converted to U.S. dollars directly. Exhibit 15.2 illustrates the underlying issuance structure of an ADR.

ADRs can be exchanged for the underlying foreign shares, or vice versa, so arbitrage keeps foreign and U.S. prices of any given share the same after adjusting for transfer costs. For example, investor demand in one market will cause a price rise there, which will cause an arbitrage rise in the other market even when investors there are not as bullish on the stock.

ADRs convey certain technical advantages to U.S. shareholders. Dividends paid by a foreign firm are passed to its custodial bank and then to the bank that issued the ADR. The

EXHIBIT 15.2   Mechanics of American Depositary Receipts (ADRs)

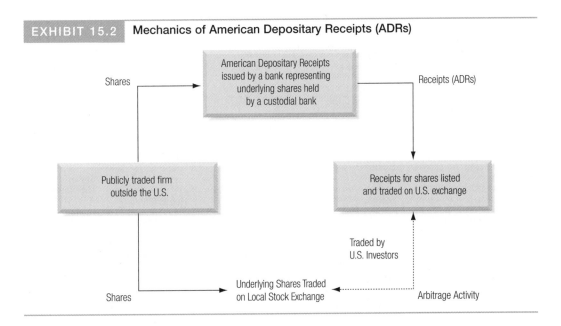

issuing bank exchanges the foreign currency dividends for U.S. dollars and sends the dollar dividend to the ADR holders. ADRs are in registered form, rather than in bearer form. Transfer of ownership is facilitated because it is done in the United States in accordance with U.S. laws and procedures. In the event of death of a shareholder, the estate does not need to go through probate in a foreign court system. Normally, trading costs are lower than when buying or selling the underlying shares in their home market. Settlement is usually faster in the United States. Withholding taxes are simpler because they're handled by the depositary bank.

ADRs are either *sponsored* or *unsponsored*. Sponsored ADRs are created at the request of a foreign firm wanting its shares traded in the United States. The firm applies to the Security and Exchange Commission (SEC) and a U.S. bank for registration and issuance of ADRs. The foreign firm pays all costs of creating such sponsored ADRs. If a foreign firm does not seek to have its shares traded in the United States but U.S. investors are interested, a U.S. securities firm may initiate creation of the ADRs. Such an ADR would be unsponsored, but the SEC still requires that all new ADR programs must have approval by the firm itself even if it is not a sponsored ADR.

Exhibit 15.3 summarizes the characteristics of ADRs in the United States. It shows three levels of commitment, distinguished by the necessary accounting standards, SEC registration requirement, time to completion, and costs. Level I ("over the counter" or pink sheets) is the easiest to satisfy. It facilitates trading in foreign securities that have been acquired by U.S. investors but the securities are not registered with the SEC. It is the least costly approach but might have a minimal impact on liquidity.

Level II applies to firms that want to list existing shares on the NYSE, ASE, or NASDAQ markets. They must meet the full registration requirements of the SEC. This means reconciling their financial accounts with those used under United States GAAP. This raises the cost considerably. Level III applies to the sale of a new equity issued in the United States. It too requires full registration with the SEC and an elaborate stock prospectus. This is the most expensive alternative but is the most likely to improve the stock's liquidity and escape from home market segmentation. So-called 144A programs will be described later in this chapter.

EXHIBIT 15.3   Characteristics of Depositary Receipt Programs

Type	Degree of Disclosure	Listing Alternatives	Ability to Raise Capital	Accounting Standards	Implementation Timetable
Over-the-Counter ADR Program (Level I)	None; home country standards apply	Over-the-Counter (OTC)/OTCQX	Must upgrade DR facility	U.S. GAAP/IFRS	6 weeks
Rule 144A/Regulations S GDR Program (Level I GDR)	None	Not listed	Yes, available to QIBs	U.S. GAAP/IFRS	3 weeks
U.S.-Listed ADR Program (Level II)	Detailed Sarbanes Oxley	NYSE, NASDAQ, NYSE Alternext U.S.	Must upgrade DR facility	U.S. GAAP/IFRS	13 weeks
U.S.-Listed ADR Program (Level III)	Rigorous Sarbanes Oxley	NYSE, NASDAQ, NYSE Alternext U.S.	Yes, Public Offering	U.S. GAAP/IFRS	14 weeks
Rule 144A/Regulation S GDR Program (Level II GDR)	None	DIFX	None	U.S. GAAP/IFRS	2 weeks
Rule 144A/Regulation S GDR Program (Level III GDR)	EU Prospectus Directive and/or U.S. Rule 144A	London, Luxembourg, DIFX, U.S. PORTAL	Yes, available to QIBs	U.S. GAAP/IFRS	8 weeks

Source: The Bank of New York Mellon, June 2, 2009.

Foreign Equity Listing and Issuance

According to the alternative paths presented earlier in Exhibit 15.1, a firm needs to choose one or more stock markets on which to cross-list its shares and sell new equity. Just where to go depends mainly on the firm's specific motives and the willingness of the host stock market to accept the firm. By cross-listing and selling its shares on a foreign exchange, a firm typically tries to accomplish one or more of the following objectives:

- Improve the liquidity of its existing shares and support a liquid secondary market for new equity issues in foreign markets

- Increase its share price by overcoming mispricing in a segmented and illiquid home capital market

- Increase the firm's visibility and political acceptance to its customers, suppliers, creditors, and host governments

- Establish a secondary market for shares used to acquire other firms in the host market

- Create a secondary market for shares that can be used to compensate local management and employees in foreign subsidiaries

Improving Liquidity

Quite often, foreign investors have acquired a firm's shares through normal brokerage channels, even though the shares are not listed in the investor's home market, or maybe not traded in the investor's preferred currency. Cross-listing is a way to encourage such investors to continue to hold and trade these shares, thus marginally improving secondary market liquidity. This is usually done through ADRs.

Firms domiciled in countries with small illiquid capital markets often outgrow those markets and are forced to raise new equity abroad. Listing on a stock exchange in the market in which these funds are to be raised is typically required by the underwriters to insure post-issue liquidity in the shares.

The introductory section of this chapter suggested that firms start by cross-listing in a less prestigious market followed by an equity issue in that market (see Exhibit 15.1). In order to maximize liquidity, however, the ideal is to cross-list and issue equity in a prestigious market and eventually to be able to offer a global equity issue.

Global Registered Shares (GRSs)

Similar to ordinary shares, GRSs have the added benefit of being able to be traded on equity exchanges around the globe in a variety of currencies. ADRs, however, are quoted only in U.S. dollars and are traded only in the United States. Theoretically, GRSs can be traded with the sun, following markets as they open and close around the globe around the clock. The shares are traded electronically, therefore eliminating the specialized forms and depositaries required by share forms like ADRs.

GRSs are not really a recent innovation. In fact, they are nearly identical to the structure used for cross-border trading of Canadian company securities in the U.S. for decades. More than 70 Canadian firms are listed on the NYSE, and all of these shares trade as ordinary shares in both their home market in Canada and the U.S. market.

According to the NYSE, dealing fees levied on ADRs cost investors between 3 cents and 5 cents per share per trade. By comparison, GRSs carry a flat cost of $5 per trade, regardless of the quantity of shares traded. For foreign corporations expecting or hoping to become widely traded securities for large institutional investors, the flat rate per trade for GRSs may increase their cost efficiency. A two-way electronic linkage between the Depositary Trust

Company in the United States and the Deutsche Börse Clearing Company in Germany facilitates the efficient quoting, trading, and settlement of shares in the respective currencies.

In October 2001, Deutsche Bank (DB) of Germany chose to list on the New York Stock Exchange via Global Registered Shares (GRSs). Many critics argued that by listing through GRSs Deutsche Bank would experience lower trading in their shares. This lower-trading expectation was based on DaimlerChrysler's GRS experiences in 1998.

Size and Liquidity of the Market

In order to maximize liquidity, it is desirable to cross-list and/or sell equity in the most liquid markets. Stock markets have, however, been subject to two major forces in recent years, which are changing their very behavior and liquidity—*demutualization* and *diversification*.

Demutualisation is the on-going process by which the small controlling seat owners on a number of exchanges have been giving up their exclusive powers. As a result, the actual ownership of the exchanges has become increasingly public. *Diversification* represents the growing diversity of both products (derivatives, currencies, etc.) and foreign companies/shares being listed. This has increased the activities and profitability of many exchanges while simultaneously offering a more global mix for reduced cost and increased service.

Stock Exchanges

With respect to stock exchanges, New York and London are clearly the most liquid. The recent merger of the New York Stock Exchange (NYSE) and Euronext, which itself was a merger of stock exchanges in Amsterdam, Brussels, and Paris, has extended the NYSE lead over NASDAQ (New York) and the London Stock Exchange (LSE). Tokyo has fallen on hard times in recent years in terms of trading value, as many foreign firms have chosen to delist from the Tokyo exchange in recent years. Few foreign firms remain cross-listed now in Tokyo. Deutsche Börse (Germany) has a fairly liquid market for domestic shares but a much lower level of liquidity for trading foreign shares. On the other hand, it is an appropriate target market for firms resident in the European Union, especially those that have adopted the euro. It is also used as a supplementary cross-listing location for firms that are already cross-listed on the LSE, NYSE, or NASDAQ.

Why are New York and London so dominant? According to the recent survey by *The Economist*, they offer what global financial firms are looking for:[1] plenty of skilled people, ready access to capital, good infrastructure, attractive regulatory and tax environments, and low levels of corruption. Location and the use of English, increasingly acknowledged as the language of global finance, are also important factors.

According to *The Economist* "London's supporters say that it surpasses New York in structured finance and new stock listings. It is especially strong on the wholesale side, accounting for 24% of the world's exports of financial services (against 39% for all of the Americas), according to the City of London Corporation. It also has a two-thirds share of the European Unions's total foreign exchange and derivatives trading, and 42% of the EU's share trading. The LSE also has the most listing by international companies. As of mid-July 2007 it had about 320 international companies listed on its main market and 480 on the Alternative Investment Market (AIM) which is geared to smaller firms.

Global Derivatives

With respect to the global derivatives, Chicago continues to be the dominant location for derivative creation and trading. This lead was reinforced recently with the merger of the Chicago Mercantile Exchange (CME) with the Chicago Board of Trade (CBOT). Other derivative exchanges are actively considering mergers to gain competitiveness and liquidity.

[1]"Magnets for Money," *The Economist*, September 15, 2007.

The Outlook

Most exchanges have moved heavily into electronic trading in recent years. For example, the role of the specialist at the NYSE has been greatly reduced with a correspondent reduction in employment by specialist firms. They are no longer responsible for ensuring an orderly movement for their stocks, but are still important in making more liquid markets for the less traded shares.

The LSE is also increasingly dominated by electronic trading rather than relying solely on market-making dealers. The Sarbanes-Oxley Act in the United States has encouraged firms that might have been listed on the NYSE to list in London instead.

At the present time, a number of mergers are done or being contemplated. For example, the LSE has purchased control of the Milan Stock Exchange. In process, is a potential change in ownership in the LSE, subject to various government approvals.

Börse Dubai and the rival Qatar Investment Authority may end up with a 48% stake in the LSE. Dubai is rapidly becoming a regional financial and trading center. Börse Dubai and NASDAQ have teamed up to buy a large stake in OMX, a Swedish-controlled firm that invests in Nordic stock exchanges, but also has a strong electronic trading capability. Börse Dubai also would own a 20% interest in NASDAQ.

Effect of Cross-Listing and Equity Issuance on Share Price

Although cross-listing and equity issuance can occur together, their impacts are separable and significant in and of themselves.

Cross-Listing

Does merely cross-listing on a foreign stock exchange have a favorable impact on share prices? It depends on the degree to which markets are segmented.

If a firm's home capital market is segmented, the firm could theoretically benefit by cross-listing in a foreign market if that market values the firm or its industry more than does the home market. This was certainly the situation experienced by Novo when it listed on the NYSE in 1981 (see Chapter 14). However, most capital markets are becoming more integrated with global markets. Even emerging markets are less segmented than they were just a few years ago.

As early as the period from 1969 to 1982, when markets were more segmented than today, a research study found a positive share price effect for foreign firms that listed on the NYSE, AMEX, or NASDAQ.[2] A later study found that share prices increased for foreign firms that cross-listed their shares in ADR form on the NYSE and AMEX during the period from 1982 to 1992.[3] The authors concluded that cross-listing in the United States enhanced share value by reducing the overall effect of segmentation among different national securities markets.

A more recent and comprehensive study consisted of 181 firms from 35 countries that instituted their first ADR program in the United States over the period from 1985 to 1995.[4] The author measured the stock price impact of the announcement of a cross-listing in the

[2]Gordon J. Alexander, Cheol S. Eun, and S. Janakiramanan, "International Listings and Stock Returns: Some Empirical Evidence," *Journal of Financial and Quantitative Analysis*, Volume 23, Number 2, June 1988, pp. 135–151.

[3]Sundaram, Anant K., and Dennis E. Logue, "Valuation Effects of Foreign Company Listings on U.S. Exchanges," *Journal of International Business Studies*, Volume 27, Number 1, First Quarter 1996, pp. 67–88.

[4]Darius P. Miller, "The Market Reaction to International Cross-Listings: Evidence from Depositary Receipts," *Journal of Financial Economics*, Volume 51, 1999, pp. 102–123.

United States and found significant positive abnormal returns around the announcement date. These were retained in the immediate following period. As expected, the study showed that the abnormal returns were greater for firms resident in emerging markets with a low level of legal barriers to capital flows, than for firms resident in developed markets. Firms resident in emerging markets with heavy restrictions on capital flows received some abnormal returns, but not as high as firms resident in the other markets. This was due to the perceived limited liquidity of firms resident in markets with too many restrictions on capital flows.

Finally, a still more recent study concluded as follows:[5]

> At the end of 1997, foreign companies with shares cross-listed in the U.S. had Tobin's q ratios that were 16.5% higher than the q ratios of non-cross-listed firms from the same country. The valuation difference is statistically significant and reaches 37% for those companies that list on major U.S. exchanges, even after controlling for a number of firm and country characteristics. We suggest that a U.S. listing reduces the extent to which controlling shareholders can engage in expropriation and thereby increases the firm's ability to take advantage of growth opportunities. We show that growth opportunities are more highly valued for firms that choose to cross-list in the U.S., particularly those from countries with poorer investor rights.

Tobin's q in this study is defined as follows: "For the numerator we take the book value of total assets, subtract the book value of equity, and add the market value of equity. For the denominator we use the book value of total assets."[6]

Equity Issuance

It is well known that the combined impact of a new equity issue undertaken simultaneously with a cross-listing has a more favorable impact on stock price than cross-listing alone. This occurs because the new issue creates an instantly enlarged shareholder base. Marketing efforts by the underwriters prior to the issue engender higher levels of visibility. Post-issue efforts by the underwriters to support at least the initial offering price also reduce investor risk.

The study of 181 firms cross-listing in the United States contained 30 firms that initiated new equity issues (Level III ADRs). The author found a statistically significant abnormal return for these firms, even higher than for the firms that just cross-listed (Levels I and II). Furthermore, the highest abnormal return was for Chilean firms (8.23 percent). The Chilean market has one of the highest levels of restrictions affecting foreign investors. Since it is well known that stock prices react negatively to new domestic issues in the United States, something truly significant must be happening when foreign ADRs are sold in the United States.

Even U.S. firms can benefit by issuing equity abroad. A recent study of U.S. firms that issued equity abroad concluded that increased name recognition and accessibility from global equity issues leads to increased investor recognition and participation in both the primary and secondary markets.[7] Moreover, the ability to issue global shares can validate firm quality by reducing the information asymmetry between insiders and investors. Another conclusion was that U.S. firms may seize a window of opportunity to switch to global offerings when domestic demand for their shares is weak. Finally, the study found that U.S. firms

[5]Craig Doidge, G. Andrew Karolyi, and René M. Stulz, "Why are foreign firms listed in the U.S. worth more?," *Journal of Financial Economics*, 71, 2004, p. 205.

[6]Ibid, p. 216.

[7]Congsheng Wu and Chuck C.Y. Kwok, "Why Do U.S. Firms Choose Global Equity Offerings?," *Financial Management*, Summer 2002, pp. 47–65.

announcing global equity offerings have significantly less negative market reactions by about one percentage point than what would have been expected had they limited their issues to the domestic market.

Increasing Visibility and Political Acceptance

MNEs list in markets where they have substantial physical operations. Commercial objectives are to enhance corporate image, advertise trademarks and products, get better local press coverage, and become more familiar with the local financial community in order to raise working capital locally.

Political objectives might include the need to meet local ownership requirements for a multinational firm's foreign joint venture. Local ownership of the parent firm's shares might provide a forum for publicizing the firm's activities and how they support the host country. This objective is the most important one for Japanese firms. The Japanese domestic market has both low-cost capital and high availability. Therefore, Japanese firms are not trying to increase the stock price, the liquidity of their shares, or the availability of capital.

Increasing Potential for Share Swaps with Acquisitions

Firms that follow a strategy of growth by acquisition are always looking for creative ways to fund these acquisitions rather than paying cash. Offering their shares as partial payment is considerably more attractive if those shares have a liquid secondary market. In that case, the target's shareholders have an easy way to convert their acquired shares to cash if they do not prefer a share swap. However, a share swap is often attractive as a tax-free exchange.

Compensating Management and Employees

If an MNE wishes to use stock options and share purchase compensation plans for local management and employees, local listing would enhance the perceived value of such plans. It should reduce transaction and foreign exchange costs for the local beneficiaries.

Barriers to Cross-Listing and Selling Equity Abroad

Although a firm may decide to cross-list and/or sell equity abroad, certain barriers exist. The most serious barriers are the future commitment to providing full and transparent disclosure of operating results and balance sheets as well as a continuous program of investor relations.

The Commitment to Disclosure and Investor Relations

A decision to cross-list must be balanced against the implied increased commitment to full disclosure and a continuing investor relations program. For firms resident in the Anglo-American markets, listing abroad might not appear to be much of a barrier. For example, the SEC's disclosure rules for listing in the United States are so stringent and costly that any other market's rules are mere child's play. Reversing the logic, however, non-U.S. firms must really think twice before cross-listing in the United States. Not only are the disclosure requirements breathtaking, but also continuous timely quarterly information is required by U.S. regulators and investors. As a result, the foreign firm must provide a costly continuous investor relations program for its U.S. shareholders, including frequent "road shows" and the time-consuming personal involvement of top management.

Disclosure Is a Double-Edged Sword

The U.S. school of thought is that the worldwide trend toward requiring fuller, more transparent, and more standardized financial disclosure of operating results and financial positions may have the desirable effect of lowering the cost of equity capital. As we observed in

2002, lack of full and accurate disclosure, and poor transparency worsened the U.S. stock market decline as investors fled to safer securities such as U.S. government bonds. This action increased the equity cost of capital for all firms. The other school of thought is that the U.S. level of required disclosure is an onerous, costly burden. It chases away many potential listers, thereby narrowing the choice of securities available to U.S. investors at reasonable transaction costs.

A study of 203 internationally traded shares concluded that there is a statistically significant relationship between the level of financial disclosure required and the markets on which the firms chose to list.[8] The higher the level of disclosure required, the less likely that a firm would list in that market. However, for those firms that do list despite the disclosure and cost barriers, the payoff could be needed access to additional equity funding of a large factory or an acquisition in the United States. Daimler Benz took the painful step of cross-listing on the NYSE prior to raising equity in the United States to fund a new auto plant and, as it turned out later, to merge with Chrysler Corporation.

Alternative Instruments to Source Equity in Global Markets

Alternative instruments to source equity in global markets include the following:

- Sale of a *directed public share* issue to investors in a target market
- Sale of a *Euroequity public issue* to investors in more than one market, including both foreign and domestic markets
- Private placements under SEC Rule 144A
- Sale of shares to *private equity* funds
- Sale of shares to a foreign firm as part of a *strategic alliance*

Directed Public Share Issues

A *directed public share issue* is defined as one that is targeted at investors in a single country and underwritten in whole or in part by investment institutions from that country. The issue might or might not be denominated in the currency of the target market. The shares might or might not be cross-listed on a stock exchange in the target market.

The $61 million U.S. share issue by Novo in 1981 (Chapter 14) was a good example of a successful directed share issue that both improved the liquidity of Novo's shares and lowered its cost of capital. Novo repeated this success in 1983 with a $100 million share issue at $53 per share (ADR), compared to $36 per share two years earlier.

A directed share issue might be motivated by a need to fund acquisitions or major capital investments in a target foreign market. This is an especially important source of equity for firms that reside in smaller capital markets and that have outgrown that market. A foreign share issue, plus cross-listing, can provide it with improved liquidity for its shares and the means to use those shares to pay for acquisitions.

Nycomed, a small but well respected Norwegian pharmaceutical firm, was an example of this type of motivation for a directed share issue combined with cross-listing. Its commercial strategy for growth was to leverage its sophisticated knowledge of certain market niches and technologies within the pharmaceutical field by acquiring other promising firms that possess relevant technologies, personnel, or market niches. Europe and the United States have pro-

[8]Saudagaran, Shahrokh M. and Gary C. Biddle, "Foreign Listing Location: A Study of MNEs and Stock Exchanges in Eight Countries," *Journal of International Business Studies*, Volume 26, Number 2, Second Quarter 1995, pp. 319–341.

vided fertile hunting grounds. The acquisitions were paid for partly with cash and partly with shares. Norway is too small a home capital market to fund these acquisitions for cash or to provide a liquid enough market to minimize Nycomed's marginal cost of capital.

Nycomed responded to the challenge by selling two successful directed share issues abroad. In June 1989, it cross-listed on the LSE (quoted on SEAQ International) and raised the equivalent of about $100 million in equity from foreign investors there. Then, in June 1992, it cross-listed on the NYSE and raised about $75 million with a share issue directed at U.S. investors. Nycomed eventually merged with Amersham, a British firm, and moved its headquarters to the United Kingdom.

Euroequity Public Issue

The gradual integration of the world's capital markets and increased international portfolio investment has spawned the emergence of a very viable Euroequity market. A firm can now issue equity underwritten and distributed in multiple foreign equity markets, sometimes simultaneously with distribution in the domestic market. The same financial institutions that had previously created an infrastructure for the Euronote and Eurobond markets (described in detail in Chapter 16) were responsible for the Euroequity market. The term "Euro" does not imply that the issuers or investors are located in Europe, nor does it mean the shares are sold in the currency "euro." It is a generic term for international securities issues originating and being sold anywhere in the world.

The largest and most spectacular issues have been made in conjunction with a wave of privatizations of government-owned enterprises. The Thatcher government in the United Kingdom created the model when it privatized British Telecom in December 1984. That issue was so large that it was necessary and desirable to sell *tranches* to foreign investors in addition to the sale to domestic investors. A *tranche* means an allocation of shares, typically to underwriters that are expected to sell to investors in their designated geographic markets. The objective is both to raise the funds and to ensure post-issue worldwide liquidity. Unfortunately, in the case of British Telecom, the issue was, in retrospect, underpriced. Most of the foreign shares, especially those placed in the United States, flowed back to London, leaving a nice profit behind for the U.S. underwriters and investors. Nevertheless, other large British privatization issues followed British Telecom, most notably British Steel in 1988.

Euroequity privatization issues have been particularly popular with international portfolio investors because most of the firms are very large, with excellent credit ratings and profitable quasi-government monopolies at the time of privatization. The British privatization model has been so successful that numerous others have followed. One of the largest Euroequity issues was made by Deutsche Telecom A.G. It was privatized by an initial public offering of $13.3 billion in November 1996.

Even government-owned firms in emerging capital markets have implemented privatization with the help of foreign tranches.

- Telefonos de Mexico, the giant Mexican telephone company, completed a $2 billion Euroequity issue in 1991. U.S.-based Southwestern Bell became a 10% shareholder, as did numerous other foreign institutional and individual investors. Telefonos de Mexico has a very liquid listing on the NYSE.

- One of the largest Euroequity offerings by a firm resident in an illiquid market was the 1993 sale of shares for $3.04 billion by YPF Sociedad Anonima, Argentina's state-owned oil company. About 75% of its shares were placed in tranches outside of Argentina, with 46% in the United States alone. Its underwriting syndicate represented a virtual who's who of the world's leading investment banks.

It appears that many of the privatized firms have performed well after being privatized. A study of privatization concluded that privatized firms showed strong performance improvements without reducing employment security. The firms in the study had been fully or partially privatized via public equity issues during the period from 1961 to 1990. After privatization, the firms increased real sales, raised capital investment levels, improved efficiency, and expanded their employment. With respect to financial performance, their profitability improved, debt levels were lowered, and dividend payments increased.[9]

Private Placement under SEC Rule 144A

One type of directed issue with a long history as a source of both equity and debt is the private placement market. A *private placement* is the sale of a security to a small set of qualified institutional buyers. The investors are traditionally insurance companies and investment companies. Since the securities are not registered for sale to the public, investors have typically followed a "buy and hold" policy. In the case of debt, terms are often custom designed on a negotiated basis. Private placement markets now exist in most countries.

As noted in Exhibit 15.3, in April 1990, the SEC approved Rule 144A. It permits qualified institutional buyers (QIBs) to trade privately placed securities without the previous holding period restrictions and without requiring SEC registration.

A *qualified institutional buyer* (QIB) is an entity (except a bank or a savings and loan) that owns and invests on a discretionary basis $100 million in securities of non-affiliates. Banks and savings and loans must meet this test but also must have a minimum net worth of $25 million. The SEC has estimated that about 4,000 QIBs exist, mainly investment advisers, investment companies, insurance companies, pension funds, and charitable institutions.

Simultaneously, the SEC modified its Regulation S to permit foreign issuers to tap the U.S. private placement market through an SEC Rule 144A issue, also without SEC registration. A screen-based automated trading system called PORTAL was established by the National Association of Securities Dealers (NASD) to support the distribution of primary issues and to create a liquid secondary market for these unregistered private placements.

Since SEC registration has been identified as the main barrier to foreign firms wishing to raise funds in the United States, SEC Rule 144A placements are proving attractive to foreign issuers of both equity and debt securities. Atlas Copco, the Swedish multinational engineering firm, was the first foreign firm to take advantage of SEC Rule 144A. It raised $49 million in the United States through an ADR equity placement as part of its larger $214 million Euroequity issue in 1990. Since then, several billion dollars a year have been raised by foreign issuers with private equity placements in the United States. However, it does not appear that such placements have a favorable effect on either liquidity or stock price.[10]

Private Equity Funds

Private equity funds are usually limited partnerships of institutional and wealthy investors, such as college endowment funds, that raise capital in the most liquid capital markets. They are best known for buying control of publicly owned firms, taking them private, improving management, and then reselling them after one to three years. They are resold in a variety of

[9]William L. Megginson, Robert C. Nash, and Mathias Ian Randenborgh, "The Financial and Operating Performance of Newly Privatized Firms: An International Empirical Analysis," *Journal of Finance*, June 1994, pp. 403–452.

[10]Boubakri, Narjess and Jean Claude Cosset, "The Financial and Operating Performance of Newly Privatized Firms: Evidence from Developing Countries," *The Journal of Finance*, Volume 53, Number 3, June 1998, pp. 1081–1110. This same conclusion was reached in the slightly more recent study by Miller 1999, op. cit.

ways including selling to other firms, selling to other private equity funds, or taking them back public. The private equity funds themselves are frequently very large, but may also utilize a large amount of debt to fund their takeovers. These "alternatives" as they are called, demand fees of 2% of assets plus 20% of profits. In addition, in the United States their gains are taxed at the capital gains rate of 15% on "carried interest" instead of the usual 35% rate on ordinary income. Equity funds have had some highly visible successes. *Global Finance in Practice 15.1* describes some leading equity funds and their assets.

Many mature family-owned firms resident in emerging markets are unlikely to qualify for a global cost and availability of capital even if they follow the strategy suggested in this chapter. Although they might be consistently profitable and growing, they are still too small, too invisible to foreign investors, lacking in managerial depth, and unable to fund the up-front costs of a globalization strategy. For these firms, *private equity funds* may be a solution.

Private equity funds differ from traditional venture capital funds. The latter usually operate mainly in highly developed countries. They typically invest in start-up firms with the goal of exiting the investment with an initial public offering (IPO) placed in those same highly liquid markets. Very little venture capital is available in emerging markets, partly because it would be difficult to exit with an IPO in an illiquid market. The same exiting problem faces the private equity funds, but they appear to have a longer time horizon. They invest in already mature and profitable companies. They are content with growing companies through better management and mergers with other firms.

The Exxel Group is an example of a successful private equity fund. Its founder and CEO, Juan Navarro, has been called the "buyout king of Argentina." From 1991 to 2002, the firm invested $4.8 billion in 74 companies in Argentina. In line with its mission, the company has continued to pursue full operational control over all acquisitions in order to implement its superior managerial, industrial, and market knowledge to create shareholder value.

GLOBAL FINANCE IN PRACTICE 15.1

Equity Firms and Their Assets (billions)

Assets	Some of Their Investments
$88	**Blackstone** (New York): Assets include a stake in Nielson Media, theme-park operation Universal Orlando and Allied Waste, a waste-management company
$59	**The Carlyle Group** (Washington, D.C.): Has investments in movie theater chain AMC Entertainment and Dunkin' Brands (Dunkin' Donuts and Baskin-Robbins)
$53	**Kohlberg Kravis Roberts** (New York): Owns retailer Dollar General, Toys 'R' Us stores and media company Primedia (publisher of *Surfer*, *Hot Rod*, and *AutoGuide*)
$50	**Bain Capital** (Boston): Invested in Internet companies ecredit.com and iwon.com; Ameritrade, a financial-services company, and luggage-maker Samsonite
$30	**Permira** (London): Recently acquired frozen food giant Iglo Birds Eye, and the Automobile Association (Britain's largest roadside emergency service)
$29	**CVC Capital Partners** (London): Has a stake in countertop manufacturer Formica, Formula 1 racing, and Tower Records Japan
$22	**Cerberus Capital Management** (New York): Partly owns the parent company for Air Canada. Owns GMAC Financial Services and Alamo Rent A Car. Took over a majority interest in Chrysler.

Data from *Newsweek*, July 23, 2007, p. 40.

Strategic Alliances

Strategic alliances are normally formed by firms that expect to gain synergies from one or more of the following joint efforts. They might share the cost of developing technology, or pursue complementary marketing activities. They might gain economies of scale or scope or a variety of other commercial advantages. However, one synergy that may sometimes be overlooked is the possibility for a financially strong firm to help a financially weak firm to lower its cost of capital by providing attractively priced equity or debt financing.

SUMMARY POINTS

- Designing a capital sourcing strategy requires management to agree upon a long-run financial objective.

- The firm must then choose among the various alternative paths to get there, including where to cross-list its shares, and where to issue new equity, and in what form.

- A firm cross-lists its shares on foreign stock exchanges for one or more of the following reasons:

  - Improve the liquidity of its existing shares by using depositary receipts

  - Increase its share price by overcoming mispricing by a segmented, illiquid home capital market

  - Support a new equity issue sold in a foreign market

  - Establish a secondary market for shares used in acquisitions

  - Increase the firm's visibility and political acceptance to its customers, suppliers, creditors, and host governments

  - Create a secondary market for shares that will be used to compensate local management and employees in foreign affiliates

  - If it is to support a new equity issue or to establish a market for share swaps, the target market should also be the listing market.

- If it is to increase the firm's commercial and political visibility or to compensate local management and employees, it should be the markets in which the firm has significant operations.

- The major liquid stock markets are the NASDAQ, NYSE, London, Euronext, Tokyo, and Deutsche Börse.

- The choice among these six markets depends on its size, and the sophistication of its market-making activities, including competitive transaction costs and competent crisis management.

- Increased commitment to full disclosure.

- A continuing investor relations program.

- A firm can lower its cost of capital and increase its liquidity by selling its shares to foreign investors in a variety of forms.

- Sale of a directed share issue to investors in one particular foreign equity market.

- Sale of a Euroequity share issue to foreign investors simultaneously in more than one market, including both foreign and domestic markets.

- Private placement under SEC Rule 144A.

- Sale of shares to private equity funds.

- Sale of shares to a foreign firm as part of a strategic alliance.

MINI-CASE   ## Petrobrás of Brazil and the Cost of Capital

Petrobrás stands out in terms of deepwater technology... but currently lags in the area of cost of capital. We believe that in the long term, if Petrobrás is to become a competitive player in what looks to be the future in underwater fuel exploration, it would be headed in the right direction by expanding internationally, securing its presence in the Golden Triangle, and lowering its cost of capital.

WACC reduction could be immediate. If Petrobrás were to acquire one of the North American independents—which we estimate on average have a WACC in the range of 6% to 8%—it could raise debt at the acquired company and subsequently lower its WACC in the short term. Petrobrás could even cancel some of its own debt and/or issue new debt through the newly acquired entity. We've seen other savvy Latin companies (i.e., Cemex via its Spanish subsidiary Valenciana) do this successfully in the past.

—"Foreign Expansion Makes Sense at the Right Price," Morgan Stanley Equity Research, January 18, 2002, p. 4

Petróleo Brasileiro S.A. (Petrobrás) was an integrated oil and gas company founded in 1954 by the Brazilian government as the national oil company of Brazil. In 1997, the Brazilian government initiated a number of major privatization efforts, including Petrobrás. The company was listed in São Paulo in 1997, and on the New York Stock Exchange (NYSE: PBR) in 2000. Despite the equity listings, the Brazilian government continued to be the controlling shareholder, with 33% of the total capital and 55% of the voting shares. As the national oil company of Brazil, the company's singular purpose was the reduction of Brazil's dependency on imported oil. A side effect of this focus, however, had been a lack of international diversification. Many of the company's critics argued that being both Brazilian and undiversified internationally resulted in an uncompetitive cost of capital.

Need for Diversification

In 2002, Petrobrás was the largest company in Brazil, and the largest publicly traded oil company in South America. It was not, however, international in its operations. This inherent lack of international diversification was clearly apparent to international investors, who assigned the company the same country risk factors and premiums they did all other Brazilian companies. As shown in Exhibit 1, the result was a cost of capital in 2002 that was 6% higher than all others. The equity strategists and markets considered this a distinct competitive disadvantage.

Petrobrás embarked on a globalization strategy, with several major transactions heading up the process. In December 2001, Repsol-YPF of Argentina and Petrobrás concluded an exchange of operating assets valued at $500 million. In the exchange, Petrobrás received 99% interest in the Eg3 S.A. service station chain, while Repsol-YPF gained a 30% stake in a refinery, a 10% stake in an offshore oil field, and a fuel resale right to 230 service stations in Brazil. The agreement included an eight-year guarantee against currency risks.

In October 2002, Petrobrás purchased Perez Companc (Pecom) of Argentina. Pecom had quickly come into play following the Argentine financial crisis in January 2002. Although Pecom had significant international reserves and production capability, the combined forces of a devalued Argentine peso, a largely dollar-denominated debt portfolio, and a multitude of Argentine government regulations that hindered its ability to hold and leverage hard currency resources, the company had moved quickly to find a buyer to refund its financial structure. Petrobrás took advantage of the opportunity. Pecom's ownership had been split between the owning family and foundation (58.6%), and public flotation (the remaining 41.4%).

| EXHIBIT 1 | Petrobrás Suffers an Uncompetitive Cost of Capital |

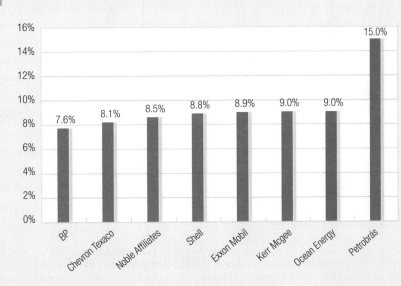

Source: MorganStanley Research, January 18, 2002, p. 5.

Petrobrás had purchased the controlling interest—the full 58.6% interest—outright from the family.

In the following three years, Petrobrás focused on restructuring much of its debt (and the debt it had acquired via the Pecom acquisition) and investing in its own growth. But progress in revitalizing its financial structure had come slowly, and by 2005 there was renewed discussion of a new equity issuance to increase its equity capital.[1] But at what cost? What was the company's cost of capital?

Cost of Capital and Country Risk

Exhibit 1 presents the cost of capital of a number of major oil and gas companies across the world, including Petrobrás in 2002. This comparison could occur only if all capital costs were calculated in a common currency; in this case, the U.S. dollar. The global oil and gas markets had long been considered "dollar-denominated," and any company operating in these markets, regardless of where it

actually operated in the world, was considered to have the dollar as its functional currency. Once that company listed its shares in a U.S. equity market like the NYSE, the dollarization of its capital costs became even more accepted.

But what was the cost of capital—in dollar terms—for a Brazilian business? Brazil has a long history of bouts with high inflation, economic instability, and currency devaluations and depreciations (depending on the regime de jure). One of the leading indicators of the global market's opinion of Brazilian country risk was the *sovereign spread,* the additional yield or cost of dollar funds that the Brazilian government had to pay on global markets over and above that which the U.S. Treasury paid to borrow dollar funds. As illustrated in Exhibit 2, the Brazilian sovereign spread had been both high and volatile over the past decade.[2] The spread was sometimes as low as 400 basis points (4.0%), as in recent years, or as high as 2,400 basis points (24%), during the 2002 financial crisis in which the reais was first devalued then floated. And that

---

EXHIBIT 2   The Brazilian Sovereign Spread (December 1997–August 2005)

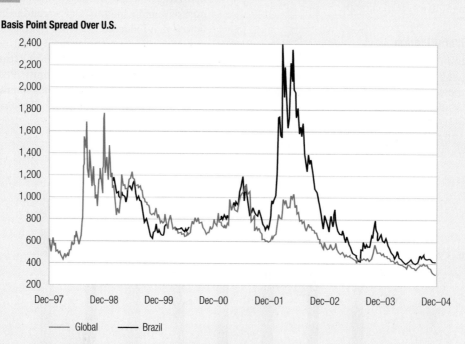

Source: JPMorgan s EMBI + Spread, as quoted by Latin Focus, http://www.latin-focus.com/latinfocus/countries/ brazilbisprd.htm, August 2005.

---

[1] By 2005, the company's financial strategy was showing significant diversification. Total corporate funding (not debt, in that project finance is nonrecourse to the company after operational startup) was well balanced: bonds, $4 billion; BNDES (bonds issued under the auspices of a Brazilian economic development agency), $3 billion; project finance, $5 billion; other, $4 billion.

[2] The measure of sovereign spread presented in Exhibit 2 is that calculated by JPMorgan in its Emerging Market Bond Index Plus (EMBI+) index. This is the most widely used measure of country risk by practitioners.

was merely the cost of debt for the government of Brazil. How was this sovereign spread reflected in the cost of debt and equity for a Brazilian company like Petrobrás?

One approach to the estimation of Petrobrás's cost of debt in U.S. dollar terms, $k_d^\$$, was to build it up—the government of Brazil's cost of dollar funds adjusted for a private corporate credit spread:

$$k_d^\$ = \text{U.S. Treasury risk-free rate} +$$
$$\text{Brazilian sovereign spread} +$$
$$\text{Petrobrás credit spread}$$
$$k_d^\$ = 4.000\% + 4.000\% + 1.000\% = 9.000\%$$

If the U.S. Treasury risk-free rate was estimated using the Treasury 10-year bond rate (yield), a base rate in August 2005 could be 4.0%. The Brazilian sovereign spread, as seen in Exhibit 2, appeared to be 400 basis points, or an additional 4.0%. Even if Petrobrás's credit spread was then only 1.0%, the company's current cost of dollar debt would be 9%. This cost was clearly higher than the cost of debt for most of the world's oil majors, who were probably paying only 5% on average for debt in late 2005.

Petrobrás's cost of equity would be similarly affected by the country risk–adjusted risk-free rate of interest. Using a simple expression of the Capital Asset Pricing Model (CAPM) to estimate the company's cost of equity capital in dollar terms ($k_e^\$$):

$$k_e^\$ = \text{risk-free rate} + \left(\beta_{\text{Petrobrás}} \times \text{market risk premium}\right)$$
$$= 8.000\% + \left(1.10 \times 5.500\%\right)$$
$$= 14.05\%$$

This calculation assumed the same risk-free rate as used in the cost of debt previously, with a beta (NYSE basis) of 1.10 and a market risk premium of 5.500%. Even with these relatively conservative assumptions (many would argue that the company's beta was actually higher or lower, and the market risk premium to be 6.0% or higher), the company's cost of equity was 14%.

Finally, the corporate cost of capital, WACC, could be calculated as follows:

$$\text{WACC} = \left(\text{Debt/capital}\right) \times k_d^\$ \times \left(1 - \text{Tax rate}\right) +$$
$$\left(\text{Equity/capital} \times k_e^\$\right)$$

Assuming a long-term target capital structure of one-third debt and two-thirds equity, and an effective corporate tax rate of 28% (after special tax concessions, surcharges, and incentives for the Brazilian oil and gas industry), Petrobrás' WACC was estimated at a little over 11.5%:

$$\text{WACC} = (0.333 \times 9.000\% \times 0.72) +$$
$$(0.667 \times 14.050\%) = 11.529\%$$

So, after all of the efforts to internationally diversify the firm and internationalize its cost of capital, why was Petrobrás' cost of capital still so much higher than its global counterparts? Not only was the company's WACC high compared to other major global players, but this was the same high cost of capital used as the basic discount rate in evaluating many potential investments and acquisitions.

A number of the investment banking firms that covered Petrobrás noted that the company's share price had shown a very high correlation with the EMBI + sovereign spread for Brazil (shown in Exhibit 2), hovering around 0.84 for a number of years. Similarly, Petrobrás' share price was also historically correlated—inversely—with the Brazilian reais/U.S. dollar exchange rate. This correlation had averaged –0.88 over the 2000–2004 period. Finally, the question of whether Petrobrás was considered an oil company or a Brazilian company was also somewhat in debate:

Petrobrás's stock performance appears more highly correlated to the Brazilian equity market and credit spreads based on historical trading patterns, suggesting that one's view on the direction of the broad Brazilian market is important in making an investment decision on the company. If the historical trend were to hold, an improvement in Brazilian risk perception should provide a fillip to Petrobrás's share price performance.

—"Petrobrás: A Diamond in the Rough,"
JPMorgan Latin American Equity Research,
June 18, 2004, p. 26–27.

Case Questions

1. Why do you think Petrobrás' cost of capital is so high? Are there better ways, or other ways, of calculating its weighted average cost of capital?

2. Does this method of using the sovereign spread also compensate for currency risk?

3. The final quote that "one's view on the direction of the broad Brazilian market" suggests that potential investors consider the relative attractiveness of Brazil in their investment decision. How does this perception show up in the calculation of the company's cost of capital?

4. Is the cost of capital really a relevant factor in the competitiveness and strategy of a company like Petrobrás? Does the corporate cost of capital really affect competitiveness?

QUESTIONS

1. **Designing a Strategy to Source Equity Globally.** Exhibit 15.1 illustrates alternative paths to globalizing the cost and availability of capital. Identify the specific steps in Exhibit 15.1 that were taken by Novo Industri (Chapter 14) in chronological order to gain an international cost and availability of capital.

2. **Depository Receipts—Definitions.** Define the following terms:
   a. ADRs
   b. GDRs
   c. Sponsored depositary receipts
   d. Unsponsored depositary receipts

3. **ADRs.** Distinguish between the three levels of commitment for ADRs traded in the United States.

4. **Foreign Equity Listing and Issuance.** Give five reasons why a firm might cross-list and sell its shares on a very liquid stock exchange.

5. **Cross-Listing Abroad.** What are the main reasons causing U.S. firms to cross-list abroad?

6. **Disclosure Debate.** The U.S. equity markets are generally considered to be the most demanding in the world in terms of financial disclosure. What are some pros and cons of this extremism?

7. **Barriers to Cross-Listing.** What are the main barriers to cross-listing abroad?

8. **Alternative Instruments.** What are five alternative instruments that can be used to source equity in global markets?

9. **Directed Public Share Issue.**
   a. Define what is meant by a "directed public share issue."
   b. Why did Novo choose to make a $61 million directed public share issue in the United States in 1981?

10. **Euroequity Public Share Issue.** Define what is meant by a "Euroequity public share issue."

11. **Private Placement under SEC Rule 144A.**
    a. What is SEC Rule 144A?
    b. Why might a foreign firm choose to sell its equity in the United States under SEC Rule 144A?

12. **Private Equity Funds.**
    a. What is a private equity fund?
    b. How do they differ from traditional venture capital firms?

   c. How do private equity funds raise their own capital, and how does this action give them a competitive advantage over local banks and investment funds?

13. **Strategic Alliances.**
    a. Why do firms form international strategic alliances?
    b. Why can an international strategic alliance lower a firm's cost of capital?

PROBLEMS

A Difference of Opinion: Petrobrás's WACC

Petrobrás of Brazil, the subject of the Mini-Case in this chapter, is a Brazilian oil company with shares listed in New York. A number of major investment banking firms cover Petrobrás, and as a result, there seems to be a great difference of opinion on how to calculate its weighted average cost of capital.

*1. **JPMorgan.** JPMorgan's Latin American Equity Research department produced the following WACC calculation for Petrobrás of Brazil versus Lukoil of Russia in their June 18, 2004, report. Evaluate the methodology and assumptions used in the calculation. Assume a 28% tax rate for both companies.

	Petrobrás	Lukoil
Risk-free rate	4.8%	4.8%
Sovereign risk	7.0%	3.0%
Equity risk premium	4.5%	5.7%
Market cost of equity	16.3%	13.5%
Beta (relevered)	0.87	1.04
Cost of debt	8.4%	6.8%
Debt/capital ratio	.333	.475
WACC	14.7%	12.3%

2. **UNIBANCO.** UNIBANCO estimated the weighted average cost of capital for Petrobrás to be 13.2% in Brazilian reais in its August 12, 2004, report. Evaluate the methodology and assumptions used in the calculation.

		Cost of debt	
Risk-free rate	4.5%	(after-taxes)	5.7%
Beta	0.99	Tax rate	34%
Market premium	6.0%	Debt/total capital	40%
Country risk premium	5.5%	WACC (R$)	13.2%
Cost of equity (US$)	15.9%		
Exchange rate	2.0%		
Cost of equity (R$)	18.3%		

3. **Citigroup SmithBarney (dollar).** Citigroup regularly performs a U.S. dollar-based discounted cash flow (DCF) valuation of Petrobrás in its coverage. That DCF analysis requires the use of a discount rate which they base on the company's weighted average cost of capital. Evaluate the methodology and assumptions of the 2003 Actual (2003A) and 2004 Estimates (2004E) of Petrobrás's WACC.

| | July 28, 2005 Report | | | March 8, 2005 Report | |
	2003A	2004E		2003A	2004E
Risk-free rate	9.4%	9.4%	Risk-free rate	9.0%	9.0%
Levered beta	1.07	1.09	Levered beta	1.08	1.10
Risk premium	5.5%	5.5%	Risk premium	5.5%	5.5%
Cost of equity	15.2%	15.3%	Cost of equity	14.9%	15.0%
Cost of debt	8.4%	8.4%	Cost of debt	9.0%	9.0%
Tax rate	28.5%	27.1%	Tax rate	28.5%	27.1%
Debt/capital ratio	32.7%	32.4%	Debt/capital ratio	33.4%	33.3%
WACC	12.2%	12.3%	WACC	12.1%	12.3%

4. **Citigroup SmithBarney (reais).** In a report dated June 17, 2003, Citigroup SmithBarney calculated a WACC for Petrobrás denominated in Brazilian reais (R$). Evaluate the methodology and assumptions of this cost of capital calculation.

Risk-free rate (Brazilian C-Bond)	9.9%
Petrobrás levered beta	1.40
Market risk premium	5.5%
Cost of equity	17.6%
Cost of debt	10.0%
Corporate tax rate	34.0%
Long-term debt ratio	50.6%
WACC (R$)	12.0%

5. **BBVA Investment Bank.** BBVA utilized a rather innovative approach to dealing with both country and currency risk in their December 20, 2004, report on Petrobrás. Use the table at the top of the next column to evaluate the methodology and assumptions used in this cost of capital calculation.

6. **Petrobrás's WACC Comparison.** Various estimates of the cost of capital for Petrobrás of Brazil appear to differ widely, but do they? Reorganize your answers to the previous five problems into those costs of capital which are in U.S. dollars versus Brazilian reais. Use the estimates for 2004 as the basis of comparison.

BBVA Investment Bank	2003	2004
U.S. 10-year risk-free rate (in US$)	4.1%	4.4%
Country risk premium (in US$)	6.0%	4.0%
Petrobrás premium (in US$)	−1.0%	−1.0%
Brazil risk-free rate (in US$)	9.1%	7.4%
Market risk premium (in US$)	6.0%	6.0%
Petrobrás beta	0.80	0.80
Cost of equity (in US$)	13.9%	12.2%
10-year (2004–2015) currency devaluation	2.50%	2.50%
Cost of equity (in R$)	16.75%	14.44%
Cost of debt after 35% tax (in R$)	5.5%	5.5%
Long-term equity ratio	69%	72%
Long-term debt ratio	31%	28%
WACC (in R$)	13.3%	12.0%

INTERNET EXERCISES

1. **Novo Industri.** Novo Industri merged with its main European competitor, Nordisk Gentofte, in 1989 to form Novo Nordisk. It is now the leading producer of insulin worldwide. Its main global competitor today is Eli Lilly (U.S.). Using standard investor information like P/E ratios, share prices, debt ratios, and betas pulled from various company Web sites, compare the cost of capital of these two major companies today.

Novo Nordisk	www.novonordisk.com
Eli Lilly and Company	www.lilly.com
BigCharts.com	bigcharts.com

2. **The Data Page.** Aswath Damodaran, a distinguished professor at the NYU Stern School of Business, maintains a detailed financial data page on a variety of topics—one of which is the cost of capital. Visit the following Web site to find estimates for the latest calculations on the cost of capital across industries:

Aswath Damodaran	pages.stern.nyu.edu/~adamodar/

3. **Weighted Average Cost of Capital Calculator.** The *Financial Times* has a simple online way to use a weighted average cost of capital calculator. Use the following link to explore the impacts of changing capital structures on the firm's cost of capital. Would an all-equity firm benefit from leverage?

Financial Times Cost of Capital	www.ft.com/lex/tools/costofcapital

CHAPTER 16

Sourcing Debt Globally

We are not ignorant of the theory of how increasing financial leverage results in maximizing returns. That having been said, over the years, we've seen repeated examples of others in this business who've fallen under the spell of erudite consultants and investment bankers, all using the right buzzwords espousing the benefits of some financial transaction, buttressed by financial theories that in reality only supported what we call "the clandestine rule of finance." (The Expeditors version of the Clandestine Rule of Finance is paraphrased "For every 'brilliant' transactional idea that is presented to management under the guise of maximizing shareholder returns, there exists a huge Fee that is inversely proportional to the actual return realized when the transaction occurs.")

—"Selected Inquiries Received Through November 9, 2006," Expeditors International.

We must modify the theory of optimal financial structure considerably to encompass the multinational firm. This chapter starts with a brief review of the domestic theory of optimal financial structure. We follow this with an analysis of the complexities involved in finding an optimal financial structure for an MNE. The next section highlights the unique complexities that influence the optimal financial structure for foreign subsidiaries of MNEs. The chapter continues with an analysis of the alternative debt instruments that an MNE can utilize to achieve an optimal financial structure.

Optimal Financial Structure

After many years of debate, most finance theorists now agree about whether an optimal financial structure exists for a firm, and if so, how it can be determined. The great debate between the so-called traditionalists and the Modigliani and Miller school of thought has apparently ended in a compromise. When taxes and bankruptcy costs are considered, a firm has an optimal financial structure determined by that particular mix of debt and equity that minimizes the firm's cost of capital for a given level of business risk. If the business risk of new projects differs from the risk of existing projects, the optimal mix of debt and equity would change to recognize trade-offs between business and financial risks.

Exhibit 16.1 illustrates how the cost of capital varies with the amount of debt employed. As the debt ratio (defined as total debt divided by total assets at market values) increases, the overall cost of capital (k_{WACC}) decreases because of the heavier weight of low-cost debt $[k_d(1 - t)]$ compared to high-cost equity (k_e). The low cost of debt is, of course, due to the tax deductibility of interest shown by the term $(1 - t)$.

Partly offsetting the favorable effect of more debt is an increase in the cost of equity (k_e), because investors perceive greater financial risk. Nevertheless, the overall weighted average after-tax cost of capital (k_{WACC}) continues to decline as the debt ratio increases, until financial risk becomes so serious that investors and management alike perceive a real danger of insolvency. This result causes a sharp increase in the cost of new debt and equity, thus increasing the weighted average cost of capital. The low point on the resulting U-shaped cost of capital curve, which is at 14% in Exhibit 16.1, defines the debt ratio range in which the cost of capital is minimized.

Most theorists believe that the low point is actually a rather broad, flat area encompassing a wide range of debt ratios, 30% to 60% in Exhibit 16.1, where little difference exists in the cost of capital. They also believe that, at least in the United States, the range of the flat area and the location of a particular firm's debt ratio within that range are determined by such variables as 1) the industry in which it competes, 2) volatility of its sales and operating income, and 3) the collateral value of its assets.

Optimal Financial Structure and the MNE

The domestic theory of optimal financial structures needs to be modified by four more variables in order to accommodate the case of the MNE. These variables, in order of appearance, are: 1) the availability of capital, 2) diversification of cash flows, 3) foreign exchange risk, and 4) the expectations of international portfolio investors.

EXHIBIT 16.1   **The Cost of Capital and Financial Structure**

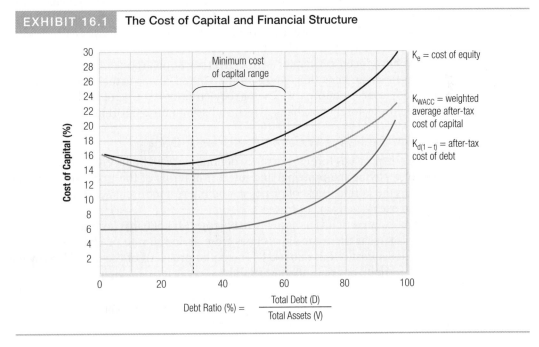

Availability of Capital

Chapter 14 demonstrated that access to capital in global markets allows an MNE to lower its cost of equity and debt compared with most domestic firms. It also permits an MNE to maintain its desired debt ratio, even when significant amounts of new funds must be raised. In other words, a multinational firm's marginal cost of capital is constant for considerable ranges of its capital budget. This statement is not true for most small domestic firms because they do not have access to the national equity or debt markets. They must either rely on internally generated funds or borrow for the short and medium term from commercial banks.

Multinational firms domiciled in countries that have illiquid capital markets are in almost the same situation as small domestic firms unless they have gained a global cost and availability of capital. They must rely on internally generated funds and bank borrowing. If they need to raise significant amounts of new funds to finance growth opportunities, they may need to borrow more than would be optimal from the viewpoint of minimizing their cost of capital. This is equivalent to saying that their *marginal cost of capital is increasing at higher budget levels.*

Risk Reduction through International Diversification of Cash Flows

As explained in Chapter 14, the theoretical possibility exists that multinational firms are in a better position than domestic firms to support higher debt ratios because their cash flows are diversified internationally. The probability of a firm's covering fixed charges under varying conditions in product, financial, and foreign exchange markets should increase if the variability of its cash flows is minimized.

By diversifying cash flows internationally, the MNE might be able to achieve the same kind of reduction in cash flow variability as portfolio investors receive from diversifying their security holdings internationally. Returns are not perfectly correlated between countries.

In contrast, a domestic German firm would not enjoy the benefit of cash flow international diversification but would have to rely entirely on its own net cash inflow from domestic operations. Perceived financial risk for the German firm would be greater than for a multinational firm because the variability of its German domestic cash flows could not be offset by positive cash flows elsewhere in the world.

As introduced in Chapter 14, the diversification argument has been challenged by empirical research findings that MNEs in the United States actually have lower debt ratios than their domestic counterparts. The agency costs of debt were higher for the MNEs, as were political risks, foreign exchange risks, and asymmetric information.

Foreign Exchange Risk and the Cost of Debt

When a firm issues foreign currency denominated debt, its effective cost equals the after-tax cost of repaying the principal and interest in terms of the firm's own currency. This amount includes the nominal cost of principal and interest in foreign currency terms, adjusted for any foreign exchange gains or losses.

For example, if a U.S.-based firm borrows Sfr1,500,000 for one year at 5.00% interest, and during the year the franc appreciates from an initial rate of Sfr1.5000/$ to Sfr1.4400/$, what is the dollar cost of this debt $(k_d^\$)$? The dollar proceeds of the initial borrowing are calculated at the current spot rate of Sfr1.5000/$:

$$\frac{\text{Sfr}1,500,000}{\text{Sfr}1.5000/\$} = \$1,000,000$$

At the end of one year, the U.S.-based firm is responsible for repaying the Sfr1,500,000 principal plus 5.00% interest, or a total of Sfr1,575,000. This repayment, however, must be made at an ending spot rate of Sfr1.4400/$:

$$\frac{\text{Sfr}1,500,000 \times 1.05}{\text{Sfr}1.4400/\$} = \$1,093,750$$

The actual dollar cost of the loan's repayment is not the nominal 5.00% paid in Swiss franc interest, but 9.375%:

$$\frac{\$1,093,750}{\$1,000,000} = 1.09375$$

The dollar cost is higher than expected due to appreciation of the Swiss franc against the U.S. dollar.

This total home-currency cost is actually the result of the combined percentage cost of debt and percentage change in the foreign currency's value. We can find the total cost of borrowing Swiss francs by a U.S. dollar-based firm, $k_d^\$$, by multiplying 1 plus the Swiss franc interest expense, k_d^{Sfr}, by 1 plus the percentage change in the Sfr/$ exchange rate, s:

$$k_d^\$ = \left[\left(1 + k_d^{\text{Sfr}}\right) \times \left(1 + s\right)\right] - 1$$

where $k_d^{\text{Sfr}} = 5.00\%$ and $S = 4.1667\%$. The percentage change in the value of the Swiss franc versus the U.S. dollar, when the home currency is the U.S. dollar, is

$$\frac{S_1 - S_2}{S_2} \times 100 = \frac{\text{Sfr}1.500/\$ - \text{Sfr}1.4400/\$}{\text{Sfr}1.4400/\$} \times 100 = +4.1667\%$$

The total expense, combining the nominal interest rate and the percentage change in the exchange rate, is

$$k_d^\$ = \left[\left(1 + .0500\right) \times \left(1 + .041667\right)\right] - 1 = .09375, \text{ or } 9.375\%$$

The total percentage cost of capital is 9.375%, not simply the foreign currency interest payment of 5%. The after-tax cost of this Swiss franc-denominated debt, when the U.S. income tax rate is 34%, is

$$k_d^\$ \left(1 - t\right) = 9.375\% \times 0.66 = 6.1875\%$$

The firm would report the added 4.1667% cost of this debt in terms of U.S. dollars as a foreign exchange transaction loss, and it would be deductible for tax purposes.

Expectations of International Portfolio Investors

The last two chapters highlighted the fact that the key to gaining a global cost and availability of capital is attracting and retaining international portfolio investors. Their expectations for a firm's debt ratio and overall financial structures are based on global norms that have developed over the past 30 years. Because a large proportion of international portfolio investors are based in the most liquid and unsegmented capital markets, such as the United States and the United Kingdom, their expectations tend to predominate and override individual national norms. Therefore, regardless of other factors, if a firm wants to raise capital in global markets, it must adopt global norms that are close to the U.S. and U.K. norms. Debt ratios up to 60% appear to be acceptable. Any higher debt ratio is more difficult to sell to international portfolio investors.

Financial Structure of Foreign Subsidiaries

If we accept the theory that minimizing the cost of capital for a given level of business risk and capital budget is an objective that should be implemented from the perspective of the consolidated MNE, then the financial structure of each subsidiary is relevant only to the extent that it affects this overall goal. In other words, an individual subsidiary does not really have an independent cost of capital. Therefore, its financial structure should not be based on an objective of minimizing it.

Financial structure norms for firms vary widely from one country to another but cluster for firms domiciled in the same country. This statement is the conclusion of a long line of empirical studies that have investigated the question, from 1969 to the present. Most of these international studies concluded that country-specific environmental variables are key determinants of debt ratios. Among these variables are historical development, taxation, corporate governance, bank influence, existence of a viable corporate bond market, attitude toward risk, government regulation, availability of capital, and agency costs.

Many other institutional differences also influence debt ratios in national capital markets, but firms trying to attract international portfolio investors must pay attention to debt ratio norms those investors expect. Since many international portfolio investors are influenced by the debt ratios that exist in the Anglo-American markets, there is a trend toward more global conformity. MNEs and other large firms dependent on attracting international portfolio investors are beginning to adopt similar debt ratio standards, even if domestic firms continue to use national standards.

Local Norms and the Financial Structure of Local Subsidiaries

Within the constraint of minimizing its consolidated worldwide cost of capital, should an MNE take differing country debt ratio norms into consideration when determining its desired debt ratio for foreign subsidiaries? For definition purposes, the debt considered here should be only that borrowed from sources outside the MNE. This debt would include local and foreign currency loans as well as Eurocurrency loans. The reason for this definition is that parent loans to foreign subsidiaries are often regarded as equivalent to equity investment both by host countries and by investing firms. A parent loan is usually subordinated to other debt and does not create the same threat of insolvency as an external loan. Furthermore, the choice of debt or equity investment is often arbitrary and subject to negotiation between host country and parent firm.

Main Advantages of Localization. The main advantages of a finance structure for foreign subsidiaries that conforms to local debt norms are as follows:

- A localized financial structure reduces criticism of foreign subsidiaries that have been operating with too high a proportion of debt (judged by local standards), often resulting in the accusation that they are not contributing a fair share of risk capital to the host country. At the other end of the spectrum, a localized financial structure would improve the image of foreign subsidiaries that have been operating with too little debt and thus appear to be insensitive to local monetary policy.

- A localized financial structure helps management evaluate return on equity investment relative to local competitors in the same industry. In economies where interest rates are relatively high as an offset to inflation, the penalty paid reminds management of the need to consider price level changes when evaluating investment performance.

- In economies where interest rates are relatively high because of a scarcity of capital, and real resources are fully utilized (full employment), the penalty paid for borrowing local funds reminds management that unless return on assets is greater than the local price of capital—that is, negative leverage—they are probably misallocating scarce domestic real resources such as land and labor. This factor may not appear relevant to management decisions, but it will certainly be considered by the host country in making decisions with respect to the firm.

Main Disadvantages of Localization. The main disadvantages of localized financial structures are as follows:

- An MNE is expected to have a comparative advantage over local firms in overcoming imperfections in national capital markets through better availability of capital and the ability to diversify risk. Why should it throw away these important competitive advantages to conform to local norms established in response to imperfect local capital markets, historical precedent, and institutional constraints that do not apply to the MNE?

- If each foreign subsidiary of an MNE localizes its financial structure, the resulting consolidated balance sheet might show a financial structure that does not conform to any particular country's norm. The debt ratio would be a simple weighted average of the corresponding ratio of each country in which the firm operates. This feature could increase perceived financial risk and thus the cost of capital for the parent, but only if two additional conditions are present:
    1. The consolidated debt ratio is pushed completely out of the discretionary range of acceptable debt ratios in the flat area of the cost of capital curve, as shown previously in Exhibit 16.1.
    2. The MNE is unable to offset high debt in one foreign subsidiary with low debt in other foreign or domestic subsidiaries at the same cost. If the international Fisher effect is working, replacement of debt should be possible at an equal after-tax cost after adjusting for foreign exchange risk. On the other hand, if market imperfections preclude this type of replacement, the possibility exists that the overall cost of debt, and thus the cost of capital, could increase if the MNE attempts to conform to local norms.

- The debt ratio of a foreign subsidiary is only cosmetic, because lenders ultimately look to the parent and its consolidated worldwide cash flow as the source of repayment. In many cases, debt of subsidiaries must be guaranteed by the parent firm. Even if no formal guarantee exists, an implied guarantee usually exists because almost no parent firm would dare to allow a subsidiary to default on a loan. If it did, repercussions would surely be felt with respect to the parent's own financial standing, with a resulting increase in its cost of capital.

Compromise Solution. In our opinion, a compromise position is possible. Both multinational and domestic firms should try to minimize their overall weighted average cost of capital for a given level of business risk and capital budget, as finance theory suggests. However, if debt is available to a foreign subsidiary at equal cost to that which could be raised elsewhere, after adjusting for foreign exchange risk, then localizing the foreign subsidiary's financial structure should incur no cost penalty and yet would also enjoy the advantages listed above.

Financing the Foreign Subsidiary

In addition to choosing an appropriate financial structure for foreign subsidiaries, financial managers of multinational firms need to choose among alternative sources of funds to finance foreign subsidiaries. Sources of funds available to foreign subsidiaries can be classified as *internal to the MNE* and *external to the MNE*.

Ideally, the choice among the sources of funds should minimize the cost of external funds after adjusting for foreign exchange risk. The firm should choose internal sources in order to minimize worldwide taxes and political risk. Simultaneously, the firm should ensure that managerial motivation in the foreign subsidiaries is geared toward minimizing the firm's consolidated worldwide cost of capital, rather than the foreign subsidiary's cost of capital. Needless to say, this task is difficult if not impossible, and the tendency is to place more emphasis on one variable at the expense of others.

Internal Sources of Funding. Exhibit 16.2 provides an overview of the *internal* sources of financing for foreign subsidiaries. In general, although the equity provided by the parent is required, it is frequently kept to legal and operational minimums to reduce risk of invested capital. Equity investment can take the form of either *cash* or *real goods* (machinery, equipment, inventory, and the like).

Debt is the preferable form of subsidiary financing, but access to local host country debt is limited in the early stages of a foreign subsidiary's life. Without a history of proven operational capability and debt service capability, the foreign subsidiary must acquire its debt from

EXHIBIT 16.2   Internal Financing of the Foreign Subsidiary

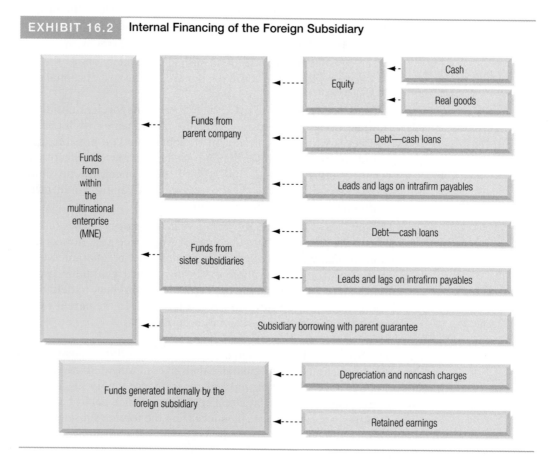

the parent company or sister subsidiaries (initially) and from unrelated parties with a parental guarantee (after operations have been initiated).

Once the operational and financial capabilities of the foreign subsidiary have been established, its ability to generate funds internally may become critical for the subsidiary's future growth. In special cases in which the subsidiary may be operating in a highly segmented market, such as an emerging market nation considered to be risky by the international investment and banking communities, the subsidiary's ability to generate its own funds from internal sources is important. These sources combine retained earnings, depreciation, and other noncash expenses. (A *noncash expense* is a deductible item such as depreciation, but the "expense" as a cash flow never leaves the firm.)

External Sources of Funding. Exhibit 16.3 provides an overview of the sources of foreign subsidiary financing *external* to the MNE. The sources are first decomposed into three categories: debt from the parent's country, debt from countries outside the parent's country, and local equity. Debt acquired from external parties in the parent's country reflects the lenders' familiarity with and confidence in the parent company itself, although the parent is in this case not providing explicit guarantees for the repayment of the debt.

Local currency debt, that is, debt acquired in the host country of the foreign subsidiary's residence, is particularly valuable to the foreign subsidiary that has substantial local currency cash inflows arising from its business activities. Local currency debt provides a foreign exchange financial hedge, matching currency of inflow with currency of outflow. Gaining access to local currency debt often takes time and patience by foreign subsidiary management in establishing operations and developing a local market credit profile. And in the case of many emerging markets, local currency debt is in short supply for all borrowers, local or foreign.

EXHIBIT 16.3   External Financing of the Foreign Subsidiary

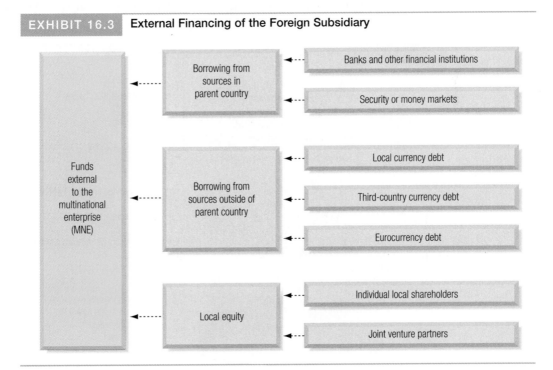

International Debt Markets

The international debt markets offer the borrower a variety of different maturities, repayment structures, and currencies of denomination. The markets and their many different instruments vary by source of funding, pricing structure, maturity, and subordination or linkage to other debt and equity instruments. Exhibit 16.4 provides an overview of the three basic categories described in the following sections, along with their primary components as issued or traded in the international debt markets today. The three major sources of debt funding on the international markets are *international bank loans and syndicated credits*, the *Euronote market*, and the *international bond market*.

An MNE will normally need debt in a variety of maturities, payment structures, and currencies, therefore often using all three markets in addition to its traditional domestic funding base. The following sections describe the basic attributes of these markets and instruments, as well as their relative advantages and disadvantages for meeting the funding needs of the individual MNE.

Bank Loans and Syndicated Credits

International Bank Loans. International bank loans have traditionally been sourced in the Eurocurrency markets. Eurodollar bank loans are also called *Eurodollar credits* or simply *Eurocredits*. The latter title is broader because it encompasses nondollar loans in the Eurocurrency market. The key factor attracting both depositors and borrowers to the Eurocurrency loan market is the narrow interest rate spread within that market. The difference between deposit and loan rates is often less than 1%.

Eurocredits. Eurocredits are bank loans to MNEs, sovereign governments, international institutions, and banks denominated in Eurocurrencies and extended by banks in countries other than the country in whose currency the loan is denominated. The basic borrowing interest rate for Eurodollar loans has long been tied to the London Interbank Offered Rate

---

EXHIBIT 16.4   International Debt Markets and Instruments

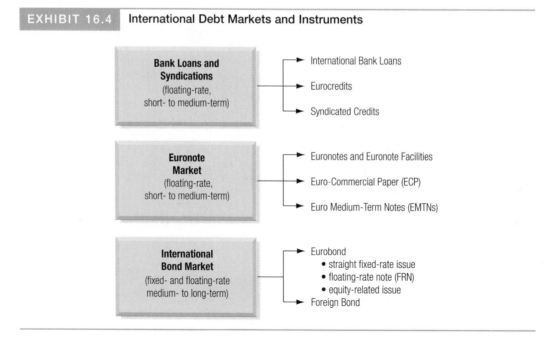

(LIBOR), which is the deposit rate applicable to interbank loans within London. Eurodollars are lent for both short- and medium-term maturities, with transactions for six months or less regarded as routine. Most Eurodollar loans are for a fixed term with no provision for early repayment.

Syndicated Credits. The syndication of loans has enabled banks to spread the risk of very large loans among a number of banks. Syndication is particularly important because many large MNEs need credit in excess of a single bank's loan limit. A *syndicated bank credit* is arranged by a lead bank on behalf of its client. Before finalizing the loan agreement, the lead bank seeks the participation of a group of banks, with each participant providing a portion of the total funds needed. The lead manager bank will work with the borrower to determine the amount of the total credit, the floating-rate base and spread over the base rate, maturity, and fee structure for managing the participating banks. The periodic expenses of the syndicated credit are composed of two elements:

1. The actual interest expense of the loan, normally stated as a spread in basis points over a variable-rate base such as LIBOR.

2. The commitment fees paid on any unused portions of the credit. The spread paid over LIBOR by the borrower is considered the *risk premium*, reflecting the general business and financial risk applicable to the borrower's repayment capability.

Global Finance in Practice 16.1 illustrates the pricing common to the syndicated loan markets, including interest expenses and the commitment and investment banking fees.

GLOBAL FINANCE IN PRACTICE 16.1

Pricing and Structure of a Syndicated Eurocredit

Borrower: Irish Aerospace, GPA Airbus, GPA Fokker, GPA Jetprop, GPA Rolls

Amount: US$1.25 billion; Revolving loans/guarantees/letters of credit

Terms: Eight years at 93.75 basis points over LIBOR, with a margin of 7/8% for GPA Airbus drawings

Arranger: Citicorp Investment Bank

Lead Managers and Underwriters: Citibank, Chase Investment Bank, Toronto-Dominion Bank, Citibank (Channel Islands) for a syndicate of Japanese leasing companies, Credit Suisse, Societe Generale (London), Amsterdam-Rotterdam Bank, Bank of Nova Scotia, Bank of Tokyo International, Daiwa Bank, IBJ, Irish Intercontinental

A typical syndicated loan of this type would have up-front fees totaling 1.5% of the principal. The fees would be divided between three groups: 1) the lead arranger bank(s), which organizes the loan and participants; 2) the lead managing and underwriting banks, which aid in the syndication of the loan; and 3) the participating banks, which actually provide the capital.

If the 1.5% total fee was subdivided equally among the three groups, the proceeds of the loan after expenses of issuance and arrangement are as follows:

$$\$1,250,000,000 - [(0.005 + 0.005 + 0.005) \times \$1,250,000,000] = \$1,231,250,000$$

The debt service payments over the eight-year period prior to principal repayment are LIBOR + 93.75 basis points; assuming an initial LIBOR rate of 9.00% (reset every six months for semiannual debt service payments):

$$\left[\frac{0.0900 + 0.009375}{2}\right] \times \$1,250,000,000 = \$62,109,375$$

The effective annual cost is thus:

$$\left[\frac{\$62,109,375}{\$1,231,250,000}\right] \times 2 \times 100 = 10.09\%$$

The syndicated credit will cost Irish Aerospace 10.09% at the current LIBOR rate of 9.000%.

Euronote Market

The Euronote market is the collective term used to describe short- to medium-term debt instruments sourced in the Eurocurrency markets. Although a multitude of differentiated financial products exists, they can be divided into two major groups—*underwritten facilities* and *nonunderwritten facilities*. Underwritten facilities are used for the sale of Euronotes in a number of different forms. Nonunderwritten facilities are used for the sale and distribution of *euro-commercial paper* (ECP) and *euro medium-term notes* (EMTNs).

Euronote Facilities. A major development in international money markets is the establishment of facilities for sales of short-term, negotiable, promissory notes—*Euronotes*. Among the facilities for their issuance are revolving underwriting facilities (rufs), note issuance facilities (nifs), and standby note issuance facilities (snifs). These facilities are provided by international investment and commercial banks. The Euronote is a substantially cheaper source of short-term funds than syndicated loans because the notes are placed directly with the investor public, and the securitized and underwritten form allows the ready establishment of liquid secondary markets. The banks receive substantial fees initially for their underwriting and placement services.

Euro-Commercial Paper (ECP). Euro-commercial paper (ECP), like commercial paper issued in domestic markets around the world, is a short-term debt obligation of a corporation or bank. Maturities are typically one, three, and six months. The paper is sold normally at a discount or occasionally with a stated coupon. Although the market is capable of supporting issues in any major currency, over 90% of issues outstanding are denominated in U.S. dollars.

Euro Medium-Term Notes (EMTNs). The Euro medium-term note is the latest major entrant to the world's debt markets. The EMTN effectively bridges the maturity gap between ECP and the longer-term and less flexible international bond. Although many of the notes were initially underwritten, most EMTNs are now nonunderwritten.

The rapid initial growth of the EMTN market followed directly on the heels of the same basic instrument that began in the U.S. domestic market when the U.S. Securities and Exchange Commission (SEC) instituted Rule #415, allowing companies to obtain *shelf registrations* for debt issues. This means that once the registration is obtained, the corporation can issue notes continuously without having to obtain new registrations for each additional issue. This in turn allows a firm to sell short- and medium-term notes through a much cheaper and more flexible issuance facility than ordinary bonds.

The EMTN's basic characteristics are similar to those of a bond, with principal, maturity, and coupon structures and rates being comparable. The EMTN's typical maturities range from as little as nine months to a maximum of 10 years. Coupons are typically paid semiannually, and coupon rates are comparable to similar bond issues. The EMTN does, however, have three unique characteristics. First, the EMTN is a facility, allowing continuous issuance over a period of time, unlike a bond issue which is essentially sold all at once. Second, because EMTNs are sold continuously, in order to make debt service (coupon redemption) manageable, coupons are paid on set calendar dates regardless of the date of issuance. Finally, EMTNs are issued in relatively small denominations, from $2 million to $5 million, making medium-term debt acquisition much more flexible than the large minimums customarily needed in the international bond markets.

International Bond Market

The international bond market sports a rich array of innovative instruments created by imaginative investment bankers, who are unfettered by the usual controls and regulations governing domestic capital markets. Indeed, the international bond market rivals the international banking market in terms of the quantity and cost of funds provided to international borrowers. All international bonds fall within two generic classifications, *Eurobonds* and *foreign bonds*. The distinction between categories is based on whether the borrower is a domestic or a foreign resident, and whether the issue is denominated in the local currency or a foreign currency.

Eurobonds. A *Eurobond* is underwritten by an international syndicate of banks and other securities firms, and is sold exclusively in countries other than the country in whose currency the issue is denominated. For example, a bond issued by a firm resident in the United States, denominated in U.S. dollars, but sold to investors in Europe and Japan (not to investors in the United States), would be a Eurobond.

Eurobonds are issued by multinational corporations, large domestic corporations, sovereign governments, governmental enterprises, and international institutions. They are offered simultaneously in a number of different national capital markets, but not in the capital market or to residents of the country in whose currency the bond is denominated. Almost all Eurobonds are in bearer form with call provisions and sinking funds.

The syndicate that offers a new issue of Eurobonds might be composed of underwriters from a number of countries, including European banks, foreign branches of U.S. banks, banks from offshore financial centers, investment and merchant banks, and nonbank securities firms.

- **The Straight Fixed-Rate Issue.** The straight fixed-rate issue is structured like most domestic bonds, with a fixed coupon, set maturity date, and full principal repayment upon final maturity. Coupons are normally paid annually, rather than semiannually, primarily because the bonds are bearer bonds and annual coupon redemption is more convenient for the holders.

- **The Floating-Rate Note (FRN).** The floating-rate note (FRN) was the new instrument of fashion on the international bond scene in the early 1980s. The FRN normally pays a semiannual coupon, which is determined using a variable-rate base. A typical coupon would be set at some fixed spread over LIBOR. This structure, like most variable-rate interest-bearing instruments, is designed to allow investors to shift more of the interest-rate risk of a financial investment to the borrower. It was a popular instrument in the early 1980s when world markets were characterized by relatively high and unpredictable interest rates. Although many FRNs have fixed maturities, a number of major issues since 1985 are perpetuities. The principal will never be repaid. Thus, they provide many of the same financial functions as equity.

- **The Equity-Related Issue.** The equity-related international bond resembles the straight fixed-rate issue in practically all price and payment characteristics, with the added feature that it is convertible to stock prior to maturity at a specified price per share (or alternatively, number of shares per bond). The borrower is able to issue debt with lower coupon payments due to the added value of the equity conversion feature.

Foreign Bonds. A *foreign bond* is underwritten by a syndicate composed of members from a single country, sold principally within that country, and denominated in the currency of that country. The issuer, however, is from another country. A bond issued by a firm resident in Sweden, denominated in dollars, and sold in the United States to U.S. investors by U.S. investment bankers, would be a foreign bond. Foreign bonds have nicknames: foreign bonds sold in the United States are "Yankee bonds"; foreign bonds sold in Japan are "Samurai bonds"; and foreign bonds sold in the United Kingdom are "Bulldogs."

Unique Characteristics of Eurobond Markets

Although the Eurobond market evolved at about the same time as the Eurodollar market, the two markets exist for different reasons, and each could exist independently of the other. The Eurobond market owes its existence to several unique factors, some of which have changed recently. Three of the original factors still of importance are absence of regulatory interference, less stringent disclosure practices, and favorable tax treatment.

Absence of Regulatory Interference. National governments often impose tight controls on foreign issuers of securities denominated in the local currency and sold within their national boundaries. However, governments in general have less stringent limitations for securities denominated in foreign currencies and sold within their markets to holders of those foreign currencies. In effect, Eurobond sales fall outside the regulatory domain of any single nation.

Less Stringent Disclosure. Disclosure requirements in the Eurobond market are much less stringent than those of the Securities and Exchange Commission (SEC) for sales within the United States. U.S. firms often find that the registration costs of a Eurobond offering are less than those of a domestic issue and that less time is needed to bring a new issue to market. Non-U.S. firms often prefer Eurodollar bonds over bonds sold within the United States because they do not wish to undergo the costs, and disclosure, needed to register with the SEC. However, the SEC has relaxed disclosure requirements for certain private placements (Rule #144A), which has improved the attractiveness of the U.S. domestic bond and equity markets.

Favorable Tax Status. Eurobonds offer tax anonymity and flexibility. Interest paid on Eurobonds is generally not subject to an income withholding tax. As one might expect, Eurobond interest is not always reported to tax authorities. Eurobonds are usually issued in bearer form, meaning that the name and country of residence of the owner is not on the certificate. To receive interest, the bearer cuts an interest coupon from the bond and turns it in at a banking institution listed on the issue as a paying agent. European investors are accustomed to the privacy provided by bearer bonds and are very reluctant to purchase registered bonds, which require holders to reveal their names before they receive interest. Bearer bond status, of course, is also tied to tax avoidance.

Rating of Eurobonds and Other International Issues

Purchasers of Eurobonds do not rely only on bond-rating services or on detailed analyses of financial statements. The general reputation of the issuing corporation and its underwriters has been a major factor in obtaining favorable terms. For this reason, larger and better-known MNEs, state enterprises, and sovereign governments are able to obtain the lowest interest rates. Firms whose names are better known to the general public, possibly because they manufacture consumer goods, are often believed to have an advantage over equally qualified firms whose products are less widely known.

Rating agencies, such as Moody's and Standard & Poor's (S&P), provide ratings for selected international bonds for a fee. Moody's ratings for international bonds imply the same creditworthiness as for domestic bonds of U.S. issuers. Moody's limits its evaluation to the issuer's ability to obtain the necessary currency to repay the issue according to the original terms of the bond. The agency excludes any assessment of risk to the investor caused by changing exchange rates.

Moody's rates international bonds upon request of the issuer. Based on supporting financial statements and other material obtained from the issuer, it makes a preliminary rating and then informs the issuer who has an opportunity to comment. After Moody's determines its final rating, the issuer may decide not to have the rating published. Consequently a disproportionately large number of published international ratings fall into the highest categories, since issuers about to receive a lower rating do not allow publication.

Moody's review of political risk includes study of the government system, the social environment, and the nation's external relations. Its review of economic risk looks at debt burden, international liquidity, balance of payments flexibility, economic structure, growth performance, economic management, and economic outlook. Moody's also evaluates the bonds of sovereign-supported entities by looking first at their creditworthiness on a standalone basis and then at the extent to which sovereign support either enhances or diminishes the borrower's financial strength. Credit ratings are critical to borrowers and investors alike. An MNE's credit rating determines its cost of funds.

Access to debt capital is, however, still a function of basic societal norms. Religion itself may play a part in the use and availability of debt capital. *Global Finance in Practice 16.2* illustrates one area rarely seen by Westerners: Islamic Finance.

GLOBAL FINANCE IN PRACTICE 16.2

Islamic Finance—Don't Call It Interest

How does a God-fearing Muslim finance a gas well? With sort of a sale-leaseback.

If you are a devout Muslim, you can't invest in a company that produces alcohol or pork. The Koran forbids interest, so a conventional home mortgage is verboten. So would be a debt-financed business asset. You can't use derivatives or buy into conventional hedge funds.

It's a tricky business to participate in a modern economy without running afoul of sharia, or Islamic law. But it can be done. For a fee you can get a consultant to arrange financial transactions that would pass muster with Allah. There may be extra steps or additional paperwork, but sometimes the outcome is the same as you'd get without sharia.

Big money is at stake. Moody's (nyse: MCO–news–people) says $800 billion is available for investing in sharia-compliant assets. UBS (nyse: UBS–news–people), HSBC (nyse: HBC–news–people), Barclays (nyse: BCS–news–people), Deutsche Bank (nyse: DB–news–people), Standard Chartered, AIG, Lloyds TSB (nyse: LYG–news–people), Morgan Stanley (nyse: MS–news–people) and Swiss Re are some of the Western financial institutions rushing sharia-compliant financial products to market.

How does one put that kind of money to work without breaking the rule on usury, given how ubiquitous interest is? A little creativity helps. Almost any hedge fund is off-limits, because of the genre's anything-goes investing style. So you don't buy a hedge fund, you buy a "structured note," whose return is tied to an index of hedge funds. Just such a product was introduced in June by Dubai Islamic Bank, Deutsche Bank and Goldman Sachs (nyse: GS–news–people) Asset Management (minimum investment $10,000). "The notes will reflect the performance of the index, so the customer's money will never go into the actual hedge fund," said Naveed

Ahmad, head of investments at Dubai Islamic Bank, at the product's unveiling.

Such blue-chip financial institutions rely largely on 20 or so rock-star sharia scholars to certify that their financial products are in accord with the Koran and the Prophet's teachings. These elite Islamic scholars may sit on 40 or 50 sharia boards each, typically at between $20,000 and $30,000 a seat annually.

In June Saudi Arabia's Prince Mishaal bin Abdullah bin Turki al-Saud joined forces with Bear Stearns (nyse: BSC–news–people) to create an asset management firm to guide wealthy Saudi families. As Eric Meyer, a Connecticut hedge fund executive and founder of his own Shariah Capital, explains, Western financial institutions are all eager to relieve the Gulf's "constipation of liquidity."

Mahmoud Amin El-Gamal, who holds the Islamic Finance Chair at Rice University in Houston, claims the sharia finance industry is selling overpriced products to the religiously naive. Indeed, some of the product specifications seem like hairsplitting. "Both the sophisticated investors and the ultrapuritans will see through this," says El-Gamal. "So you're left with the gullible who don't really understand the structure. You're feeling good for paying $500 to top law firms and 'religious' scholars? I think that's misplaced. Muslims around the world have among the worst rates of literacy and mortality. Take that same money and give it to charity."

Sheikh Yusuf disagrees. "Most of Islamic finance has been arranged for institutional and high-net-worth investors, all of whom represent the most knowledgeable investor."

Source: Abstracted from "Don't Call It Interest," *Forbes*, July 23, 2007. www.forbes.com/forbes/2007/0723/122.html.

SUMMARY POINTS

- The domestic theory of optimal financial structures needs to be modified by four variables in order to accommodate the case of the MNE. These variables are 1) the availability of capital, 2) diversification of cash flows, 3) foreign exchange risk, and 4) the expectations of international portfolio investors.

- A multinational firm's marginal cost of capital is constant for considerable ranges of its capital budget. This statement is not true for most small domestic firms because they do not have access to the national equity or debt markets.

- By diversifying cash flows internationally, the MNE may be able to achieve the kind of reduction in cash flow variability that portfolio investors receive from diversifying their security holdings internationally.

- When a firm issues foreign currency denominated debt, its effective cost equals the after-tax cost of repaying the principal and interest in terms of the firm's own currency. This amount includes the nominal cost of principal and interest in foreign currency terms, adjusted for any foreign exchange gains or losses.

- Regardless of other factors, if a firm wants to raise capital in global markets, it must adopt global norms that are close to the U.S. and U.K. norms. Debt ratios up to 60% appear to be acceptable. Any higher debt ratio is more difficult to sell to international portfolio investors.

- A compromise position between minimizing the global cost of capital and conforming to local capital norms (localization) is possible when determining the financial structure of a foreign subsidiary. Both multina-

tional and domestic firms should try to minimize their overall weighted average cost of capital for a given level of business risk and capital budget, as finance theory suggests.

- The debt ratio of a foreign subsidiary is in reality only cosmetic, because lenders ultimately look to the parent and its consolidated worldwide cash flow as the source of repayment. In many cases, debt of subsidiaries must be guaranteed by the parent firm.

- The international debt markets offer the borrower a variety of different maturities, repayment structures, and currencies of denomination. The markets and their many different instruments vary by source of funding, pricing structure, maturity, and subordination or linkage to other debt and equity instruments.

- The three major sources of debt funding on the international markets are *international bank loans and syndicated credits*, the *Euronote market*, and the *international bond market*.

- Eurocurrency markets serve two valuable purposes: 1) Eurocurrency deposits are an efficient and convenient money market device for holding excess corporate liquidity and 2) the Eurocurrency market is a major source of short-term bank loans to finance corporate working capital needs, including the financing of imports and exports.

- Three original factors in the evolution of the Eurobond markets are still of importance: absence of regulatory interference, less stringent disclosure practices, and favorable tax treatment.

MINI-CASE

Tirstrup BioMechanics (Denmark): Raising Dollar Debt

Although it was still August, Julie Harbjerg bent over against the first chill of autumn and hurried up Copenhagen's Strøget—the historic cobblestoned pedestrian street that begins at the City Hall and extends through the heart of the old city. She tried to keep her mind clear so that she could properly evaluate the various financing proposals that had been discussed in previous weeks with the many bankers who had visited Copenhagen. As assistant treasurer (international) for Tirstrup BioMechanics of Denmark, Julie was responsible

for the initial assessment of financing proposals for Tirstrup's international investments.

In 2003, the Tirstrup Group's products encompassed a full array of electromechanical medical devices. The product line included cardiac rhythm devices, pacing systems, and implantable defibrillators. A major corporate objective was to reduce Tirstrup's dependency on cardiac products. In 2003, 60% of its estimated US$2.1 billion sales (kr6.6044/$) were outside Denmark, although 85% of the Group's $2.4 billion in assets remained in the country.

Tirstrup was considering an acquisition of $410 million in the United States, and Julie Harbjerg was responsible for constructing a financing package. Tirstrup had roughly $30 million in cash on hand, and the seller had offered to carry a note for $75 million of the total. The note would be for five years at 7.50% per annum. Julie's boss, Knut Wicksell, director of finance, felt that funding should be such that repayment was deferred for at least seven years. Since Tirstrup had been burned during the last rise in short-term rates, it was generally understood that management's goal was to increase the proportion of fixed-rate debt. Julie had already been told by Wicksell that any equity issuance was out of the question.

Back in the office, Julie looked at the three U.S. dollar choices that she had previously considered and double-checked her all-in-cost (AIC) calculations again (see Exhibit 1).

■ **Eurodollar Bond.** Probably the most obvious choice to finance a U.S. acquisition was a Eurodollar bond. The bankers felt that Tirstrup's name was sufficiently well known in Europe that it could float a $100 million Eurobond at a fixed rate of 5.60% (12-year maturity). Fees would probably total 2%.

■ **Private Placement in the United States.** Several bankers had recommended a private placement of debt with an institutional investor in the United States. Nordeabank felt that their New York specialists could place as much as $200 million of Tirstrup's paper in this manner. The immediate cost would be about 5.3%, a little bit higher than a public issue in the United States (a *Yankee bond*), but the fees were significantly lower—about 7/8% of the principal.

■ **Yankee Bond.** As noted, Tirstrup could issue a bond in the United States. The problem was that the company currently had no real operations in the United States and had very little name recognition as a borrower. Bankers expected the company to pay about 5.75% for a seven-year issuance, with an additional 1.5% in up-front fees.

In addition to giving consideration to the dollar-denominated issuances, Julie was also considering two nondollar-denominated issuances, one euro and one Danish kroner.

■ €-Denominated Eurobond. Dresdner Bank (Germany) had recommended a euro-denominated

EXHIBIT 1

	Private Placement	US$ Eurobond	Yankee Bond	Euro-Eurobond	Danish Kroner
Principal (millions)	$200.000	$100,000	$100.000	€ 100.000	kr 650.000
Maturity (years)	10	12	7	7	7
Fixed Rate (per annum)	6.500%	5.600%	5.750%	4.800%	4.650%
Fees (of principal)	0.875%	2.000%	1.500%	2.000%	1.500%
Year	Cash Flows	Cash Flows	Cash Flows	Cash Flows	Cash Flows
0	$198.250	$98.000	$98.500	€ 98.000	kr 640.250
1	($11.000)	($5.600)	($5.750)	– € 4.800	(kr 30.225)
2	($11.000)	($5.600)	($5.750)	– € 4.800	(kr 30.225)
3	($11.000)	($5.600)	($5.750)	– € 4.800	(kr 30.225)
4	($11.000)	($5.600)	($5.750)	– € 4.800	(kr 30.225)
5	($11.000)	($5.600)	($5.750)	– € 4.800	(kr 30.225)
6	($11.000)	($5.600)	($5.750)	– € 4.800	(kr 30.225)
7	($11.000)	($5.600)	($105.750)	– € 104.800	(kr 680.225)
8	($11.000)	($5.600)			
9	($11.000)	($5.600)			
10	($211.000)	($5.600)			
11		($5.600)			
12		($105.600)			
All-in-cost (AIC)	5.617%	5.836%	6.019%	5.147%	4.908%

Note: All-in-cost is calculated as the internal rate of return of the complete series of cash flows associated with the issuance, including proceeds net of fees and complete repayment of principal and interest.

Eurobond for €100 million, $112 million at that day's exchange rate of $1.1160/€. The amount would be higher if the euro strengthened, as many economists expected would happen soon. Tirstrup would have to pay 4.80%, probably about 5.0% all-in for seven-year euro funds after the 2% fees were paid.

■ **Danish Kroner Bond.** Tirstrup's primary Copenhagen bank assured her that they could float an issue of kr650 million (approximately $98.4 million at the current spot rate of kr6.6044/$). The issue would be limited to about seven years, and her bankers assured her that the fees would be "as low as 1.5%."

Julie began to organize her thoughts—and her spreadsheets. She wanted to be able to recommend a package of financing that would meet the company's needs and minimize cost and risk. She then began to sketch out a funding matrix which would combine all elements in one form—one which would focus, after all fees and spreads, on the all-in-cost of capital (AIC). Exhibit 1 summarizes her calculations.

Case Questions

1. Which of the many debt characteristics—currency, maturity, cost, fixed versus floating rate—do you believe are of the highest priority for Julie and Tirstrup?

2. Does the currency of denomination depend on the currency of the parent or the currency of the business unit that will be responsible for servicing the debt?

3. Exhibit 1 is Julie's spreadsheet analysis of what she considers relevant choices. Using these, what would you recommend as a financing package?

QUESTIONS

1. **Objective.** What, in simple wording, is the objective sought by finding an optimal capital structure?

2. **Varying Debt Proportions.** As debt in a firm's capital structure is increased from no debt to a significant proportion of debt (say, 60%), what tends to happen to the cost of debt, to the cost of equity, and to the overall weighted average cost of capital?

3. **Availability of Capital.** How does the availability of capital influence the theory of optimal capital structure for a multinational enterprise?

4. **Diversified Cash Flows.** If a multinational firm is able to diversify its sources of cash inflow so as to receive those flows from several countries and in several currencies, do you think that tends to increase or decrease its weighted average cost of capital?

5. **Ex-Post Cost of Borrowing.** Many firms in many countries borrow at nominal costs that later prove to be very different. For example, Deutsche Bank recently borrowed at a nominal cost of 9.59% per annum, but later that debt was selling to yield 7.24%. At the same time, the Kingdom of Thailand borrowed at a nominal cost of 8.70%, but later found the debt was sold in the market at a yield of 11.87%. What caused these changes, and what might management do to benefit (as Deutsche Bank did) rather than suffer (as the Kingdom of Thailand did)?

6. **Local Norms.** Should foreign subsidiaries of multinational firms conform to the capital structure norms of the host country or to the norms of their parent's country? Discuss.

7. **Argentina.** In January 2002, the government of Argentina broke away from its currency board system that had tied the peso to the U.S. dollar and devalued the peso from APs1.0000/$ to APs1.40000$. This caused some Argentine firms with dollar-denominated debt to go bankrupt. Should a U.S. or European parent in good financial health "rescue" its Argentine subsidiary, which would otherwise go bankrupt because of Argentine political and economic management in the four or five years prior to January 2002? Assume the parent has not entered into a formal agreement to guarantee the debt of its Argentine subsidiary.

8. **Internal Financing.** What is the difference between "internal" financing and "external" financing for a subsidiary? List three types of internal financing and three types of external financing available to a foreign subsidiary.

9. **Eurodollars.** Which of the following are Eurodollars and which are not?
   a. A U.S. dollar deposit owned by a German corporation and held in Barclay's Bank in London
   b. A U.S. dollar deposit owned by a German corporation and held in Bank of America's office in London

c. A U.S. dollar deposit owned by a German corporation and held in Sumitomo Bank in Tokyo

d. A U.S. dollar deposit owned by a German corporation and held in Citibank in New York

e. A U.S. dollar deposit owned by a German corporation and held in the New York branch of Deutsche Bank

f. A U.S. dollar deposit owned by a U.S. resident and held in Overseas Banking Corporation in Singapore

g. A U.S. dollar deposit owned by a U.S. resident and held in the New York branch of Deutsche Bank

h. A deposit of euros in Paribas Bank in Paris

i. A deposit of euros in Citibank in New York

j. A deposit of Australian dollars in Paribas Bank in Paris

10. **Eurodollar Deposits.** Why would anyone, individual or corporation, want to deposit U.S. dollars in a bank outside of the United States when the natural location for such deposits would be a bank within the United States?

11. **Define the following terms:**
   a. LIBOR
   b. Euro LIBOR
   c. Eurocredits
   d. Syndicated bank credits

12. **International Debt Instruments.** Bank borrowing has long been the manner by which corporations and governments borrowed funds for short periods of time. What, then, is the advantage over bank borrowing for each of the following?
   a. Syndicated loans
   b. Euronotes
   c. Euro-commercial paper
   d. Euro medium-term notes
   e. International bonds

13. **Euro versus Foreign Bonds.** What is the difference between a Eurobond and a foreign bond, and why do two types of international bonds exist?

14. **Separation.** In project financing, the project is a legal entity separate from the corporations that are the equity owners. Why?

15. **Singular Project.** In the context of project financing, what is a "long-lived, capital-intensive, singular project"?

16. **Predictability.** Predictability of future cash flows is essential to induce creditors to participate in project financing. How does financial leverage increase the risk in highly leveraged projects, and how do the creators of investments financed by project financing manage to reduce the volatility of future cash flows?

17. **Infinite Lives.** Why do projects with infinite lives and grandiose growth projects not appeal to creditors who would engage in project financing, whereas those attributes are normally very desirable in a corporate investment?

18. **Maximizing Present Value.** Do the equity investors in investments based on project financing seek to maximize the present value of their investment, or are they compensated by some other manner?

PROBLEMS

*1. **Window Rock Manufacturing, Inc.** Window Rock Manufacturing, Inc., a U.S. multinational company, has the following debt components in its consolidated capital section:

U.S. dollar-denominated 25-year bonds at 6.00%	$10,000,000
U.S. dollar-denominated 5-year Euronotes at 4.00%	$4,000,000
Euro-denominated 10-year bonds at 5.00%	€ 6,000,000
Yen-denominated 20-year bonds at 2%	¥750,000,000
Common stock	$35,000,000
Retained earnings	$15,000,000

Window Rock's finance staff estimates their cost of equity to be 20%. Current exchange rates are:

European euros:	$1.24/€
British pounds sterling:	$1.86/£
Japanese yen:	¥109/$

Income taxes are 30% around the world after allowing for credits. Calculate Window Rock's weighted average cost of capital. Are any assumptions implicit in your calculation?

2. **The Flatiron Group (USA).** The Flatiron Group, a private equity firm headquartered in Boulder, Colorado, borrows £5,000,000 for one year at 7.375% interest.
   a. What is the dollar cost of this debt if the pound depreciates from $2.0625/£ to $1.9460/£ over the year?

b. What is the dollar cost of this debt if the pound appreciates from $2.0625/£ to $2.1640/£ over the year?

3. **Argosy Associates (USA).** Argosy Associates, a U.S.-based investment partnership, borrows €80,000,000 at a time when the exchange rate is $1.3460/€. The entire principal is to be repaid in three years, and interest is 6.250% per annum, paid annually in euros. The euro is expected to depreciate vis à vis the dollar at 3% per annum. What is the effective cost of this loan for Argosy?

4. **Quatrefoil Construction Company.** Quatrefoil Construction Company consists of a U.S. parent and wholly owned subsidiaries in Malaysia (Q-Malaysia) and Mexico (Q-Mexico). Selected portions of their nonconsolidated balance sheets, translated into U.S. dollars, are shown below.

Q-Malaysia (accounts in ringgits)		Q-Mexico (accounts in pesos)	
Long-term debt	RM 11,400,000	Long-term debt	Ps 20,000,000
Shareholders' equity	RM 15,200,000	Shareholders' equity	Ps 60,000,000

Quatrefoil Construction Company
(Nonconsolidated Balance Sheet—Selected Items Only)

Investment in Subsidiaries		Parent long-term debt	$ 12,000,000
In Q-Malaysia	$4,000,000	Common Stock	5,000,000
In Q-Mexico	6,000,000	Retained earnings	20,000,000
Current exchange rates are:		Malaysia:	RM3.80/$
		Mexico:	Ps 10/$

What are the debt and equity proportions in Quatrefoil's consolidated balance sheet?

*5. **Grupo Bimbo de Mexico.** Grupo Bimbo, although Mexican by incorporation, evaluates all business results, including financing costs, in U.S. dollars. The company needs to borrow $10,000,000 or the foreign currency equivalent for four years. For all issues, interest is payable once per year, at the end of the year. The following alternatives are available:

a. Sell Japanese yen bonds at par yielding 3% per annum. The current exchange rate is ¥106/$, and the yen is expected to strengthen against the dollar by 2% per annum.

b. Sell euro-denominated bonds at par yielding 7% per annum. The current exchange rate is $1.1960/€, and the euro is expected to weaken against the dollar by 2% per annum.

c. Sell U.S. dollar bonds at par yielding 5% per annum.

Which course of action do you recommend Grupo Bimbo take and why?

6. **Zermatte Air (Switzerland).** Zermatte Air of Switzerland retains $12,000,000 from tickets sold to U.S. dollar holders, after paying fuel and landing costs associated with its frequent flights between Dulles Airport in the United States and Geneva. These funds are currently deposited in Mid-Manhattan Bank in New York City where they are earning 5.00% per annum. Docklands Bank in London pays 5.50% interest on Eurodollar deposits, and Zermatte Air decides to move its funds from New York to London.

a. Show journal entries (debits and credits) on the books of Zermatte Air, Mid-Manhattan Bank, and Docklands Bank to reflect this transfer.

b. By how much have bank deposits of U.S. banks changed?

c. What happens if Docklands Bank invests the dollars in long-term U.S. government bonds?

7. **Gas du Ancy.** Gas du Ancy, a European gas company, is borrowing US$650,000,000 via a syndicated Eurocredit for six years at 82 basis points over LIBOR. LIBOR for the loan will be reset every six months. The funds will be provided by a syndicate of eight leading investment bankers, which will charge up-front fees totaling 1.2% of the principal amount. What is the effective interest cost for the first year if LIBOR is 4.00% for the first six months and 4.20% for the second six months?

8. **River Thames Insurance Company.** River Thames Insurance Company plans to sell US$2,000,000 of euro-commercial paper with a 60-day maturity and discounted to yield 4.60% per annum. What will be the immediate proceeds to River Thames Insurance?

9. **Sicilian Capital, S.A.** Sicilian Capital, S.A., is raising funds via a euro-medium-term note with the following characteristics:

Coupon rate: 8.00% payable semiannually on June 30 and December 31
Date of issuance: February 28, 2003
Maturity: August 31, 2005

How much in dollars will Sicilian Capital receive for each $1,000 note sold?

10. **AireAsia.** AireAsia, headquartered in Kunming, China, needs US$25,000,000 for one year to finance working capital. The airline has two alternatives for borrowing:

1. Borrow US$25,000,000 in Eurodollars in London at 7.250% per annum.
2. Borrow HK$39,000,000 in Hong Kong at 7.00% per annum, and exchange these Hong Kong dollars at the present exchange rate of HK$7.8/US$ for U.S. dollars.

At what ending exchange rate would AireAsia be indifferent between borrowing U.S. dollars and borrowing Hong Kong dollars?

INTERNET EXERCISES

1. **Country Credit Ratings History.** Fitch, the U.S.-based firm that provides detailed analysis and ratings of countries and companies maintains a historical time line of how the credit ratings of countries have changed over time. Use the Fitch sovereign ratings database to find the evolution of credit histories for the following emerging market countries: Argentina, Brazil, China, India, Indonesia, Malaysia, Romania, Russia, Slovakia, Slovenia, Thailand, Turkey, and Venezuela.

Fitch	www.fitchratings.com/web_content/ratings/sovereign_ratings_history.p

2. **Sovereign Credit Ratings Criteria.** The evaluation of credit risk and all other relevant risks associated with the multitude of borrowers on world debt markets requires a structured approach to international risk assessment. Check both Standard & Poor's and Moody's criteria described in depth on their Web pages to differentiate the various risks (local currency risk, default risk, currency risk, transfer risk, and so on) with major sovereign ratings worldwide.

Standard & Poor's	Go to www.standardandpoors.com, and click "Ratings" under "Products & Services."
Moody's	www.moodys.com/

3. **Dynamic Yield Curve.** This Internet site provides real-time data on the U.S. dollar fixed income securities markets. The dynamic yield curve that is presented allows the reader to see changing structures and rates along the 30-year maturity structure of the U.S. dollar government securities market.

Stockcharts.com	stockcharts.com/charts/YieldCurve.html

4. **Brady Bonds and Emerging Markets.** Emerging markets have repeatedly been beaten down with every major international financial crisis, whether it be the Mexican peso (1994), the Thai baht (1997), the Russian ruble (1998), or the Brazilian real (1999). Use the following Web sites to prepare an analysis of why these markets come under such severe pressure when a crisis occurs somewhere else around the globe.

Brady Network	www.bradynet.com/
Brady Bond Primer	www.emgmkts.com/research/bradydef.htm

PART V

Foreign Investment Decisions

CHAPTER 17

International Portfolio Theory and Diversification

It is not a case of choosing those which, to the best of one's judgement, are really the prettiest, nor even those which average opinion genuinely thinks the prettiest. We have reached the third degree where we devote our intelligences to anticipating what average opinion expects the average opinion to be.

—John Maynard Keynes, *The General Theory of Employment, Interest, and Money*, 1936.

This chapter explores how the application of portfolio theory can reduce risks of asset portfolios held by MNEs or individuals and risks incurred by MNEs in general from internationally diversified activities. In the first part of the chapter we extend portfolio theory from the domestic to the international business environment. Then we show how the risk of a portfolio, whether it is a securities portfolio or the general portfolio of activities of the MNE, is reduced through international diversification. The second part of the chapter details the theory and application of international portfolio theory and presents recent empirical results of the risk-return trade-offs of internationally diversified portfolios. The third and final section explores international diversification's impact on the cost of capital for the MNE.

International Diversification and Risk

The case for international diversification of portfolios can be decomposed into two components: the potential risk reduction benefits of holding international securities and the potential added foreign exchange risk.

Portfolio Risk Reduction

We first focus only on risk. The risk of a portfolio is measured by the ratio of the variance of the portfolio's return relative to the variance of the market return. This is the *beta* of the portfolio. As an investor increases the number of securities in a portfolio, the portfolio's risk declines rapidly at first, then asymptotically approaches the level of *systematic risk* of the market. A fully diversified domestic portfolio would have a beta of 1.0, as illustrated in Exhibit 17.1.

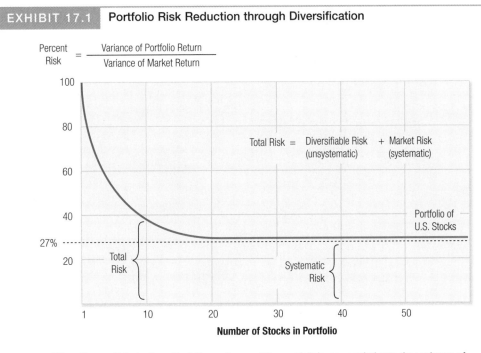

EXHIBIT 17.1   Portfolio Risk Reduction through Diversification

$$\text{Percent Risk} = \frac{\text{Variance of Portfolio Return}}{\text{Variance of Market Return}}$$

Total Risk = Diversifiable Risk + Market Risk
              (unsystematic)   (systematic)

Portfolio of U.S. Stocks

27%

Total Risk

Systematic Risk

Number of Stocks in Portfolio

When the portfolio is diversified, the variance of the portfolio's return relative to the variance of the market's return (beta) is reduced to the level of systematic risk—the risk of the market itself.

Exhibit 17.1 presents portfolio risk reduction for the U.S. economy. It shows that a fully diversified U.S. portfolio is only about 27% as risky as a typical individual stock. This relationship implies that about 73% of the risk associated with investing in a single stock is diversifiable in a fully diversified U.S. portfolio. Although we can reduce risk substantially through portfolio diversification, it is not possible to eliminate it totally because security returns are affected by a common set of factors—a set we characterize as the market.

The total risk of any portfolio is therefore composed of *systematic risk* (the market) and *unsystematic risk* (the individual securities). Increasing the number of securities in the portfolio reduces the unsystematic risk component leaving the systematic risk component unchanged.

Exhibit 17.2 illustrates the incremental gains of diversifying both domestically and internationally. The lowest line in Exhibit 17.2 (portfolio of international stocks) represents a portfolio in which foreign securities have been added. It has the same overall risk shape as the U.S. stock portfolio, but it has a lower portfolio beta. This means that the international portfolio's market risk is lower than that of a domestic portfolio. This situation arises because the returns on the foreign stocks are closely correlated not with returns on U.S. stocks, but rather with a global beta. We will return to the concept of a global beta later in this chapter.

Foreign Exchange Risk

The foreign exchange risks of a portfolio, whether it is a securities portfolio or the general portfolio of activities of the MNE, are reduced through international diversification. The construction of internationally diversified portfolios is both the same as and different from creating a traditional domestic securities portfolio. Internationally diversified portfolios are

| EXHIBIT 17.2 | Portfolio Risk Reduction through International Diversification |

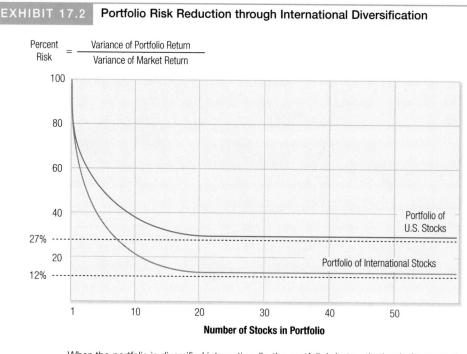

$$\text{Percent Risk} = \frac{\text{Variance of Portfolio Return}}{\text{Variance of Market Return}}$$

Number of Stocks in Portfolio

When the portfolio is diversified internationally, the portfolio's beta—the level of systematic risk that cannot be diversified away—is lowered.

the same in principle because the investor is attempting to combine assets that are less than perfectly correlated, reducing the total risk of the portfolio. In addition, by adding assets outside the home market—assets that previously were not available to be averaged into the portfolio's expected returns and risks—the investor is tapping into a larger pool of potential investments.

But international portfolio construction is also different in that when the investor acquires assets or securities outside the investor's home-country market, the investor may also be acquiring a foreign currency-denominated asset. This is not always the case. For example, many U.S.-based investors routinely purchase and hold Eurodollar bonds (on the secondary market only; it is illegal during primary issuance), which would not pose currency risk to the U.S.-based investor because they are denominated in the investor's home currency. Thus, the investor has actually acquired *two* additional assets—the currency of denomination and the asset subsequently purchased with the currency—one asset in principle, but two in expected returns and risks.

Japanese Equity Example. A numerical example can illustrate the difficulties associated with international portfolio diversification and currency risk. A U.S.-based investor takes US$1,000,000 on January 1, 2002, and invests in shares traded on the Tokyo Stock Exchange (TSE). On January 1, 2002, the spot exchange rate is ¥130.00/$. The US$1 million therefore yields ¥130,000,000. The investor uses ¥130,000,000 to acquire shares on the Tokyo Stock Exchange at ¥20,000 per share, acquiring 6,500 shares, and holds the shares for one year.

At the end of one year the investor sells the 6,500 shares at the market price, which is now ¥25,000 per share; the shares have risen ¥5,000 per share in price. The 6,500 shares at ¥25,000 per share yield proceeds of ¥162,500,000.

The Japanese yen are then changed back into the investor's home currency, the U.S. dollar, at the spot rate of ¥125.00/$ in effect on January 1, 2003. This results in total U.S. dollar proceeds of $1,300,000.00. The total return on the investment is then

$$\frac{\text{US\$1,300,000} - \text{US\$1,000,000}}{\text{US\$1,000,000}} = 30.00\%$$

The total U.S. dollar return is actually a combination of the return on the Japanese yen (which in this case was positive) and the return on the shares listed on the Tokyo Stock Exchange (which was also positive). This value is expressed by isolating the percentage change in the share price (r^{shares}) in combination with the percentage change in the currency value ($r^{¥/\$}$):

$$R^{\$} = \left[\left(1 + r^{¥/\$}\right)\left(1 + r^{shares, ¥}\right)\right] - 1$$

In this case, the value of the Japanese yen, in the eyes of a U.S.-based investor, rose 4.00% (from ¥130/$ to ¥125/$), while the shares traded on the Tokyo Stock Exchange rose 25.00%. The total investment return in U.S. dollars is therefore as follows:

$$R^{\$} = [(1 + .0400)(1 + .2500))] - 1 = .3000 \text{ or } 30.00\%$$

Obviously, the risk associated with international diversification, when it includes currency risk, is inherently more complex than that of domestic investments. You should also see, however, that the presence of currency risk may alter the correlations associated with securities in different countries and currencies, providing portfolio composition and diversification possibilities that domestic investment and portfolio construction may not. *Global Finance in Practice 17.1* details the debate regarding foreign exchange risk.

In conclusion:

- International diversification benefits induce investors to demand foreign securities (the so-called *buy-side*).
- If the addition of a foreign security to the portfolio of the investor aids in the reduction of risk for a given level of return, or if it increases the expected return for a given level of risk, then the security adds value to the portfolio.
- A security that adds value will be demanded by investors. Given the limits of the potential supply of securities, increased demand will bid up the price of that security, resulting in a lower cost of capital for the issuing firm. The firm issuing the security, the *sell-side*, is therefore able to raise capital at a lower cost.

Internationalizing the Domestic Portfolio

First, we review the basic principles of traditional domestic portfolio theory to aid in our identification of the incremental changes introduced through international diversification. Then, we illustrate how diversifying the portfolio internationally alters the potential set of portfolios available to the investor.

The Optimal Domestic Portfolio

Classic portfolio theory assumes a typical investor is risk-averse. This means that an investor is willing to accept some risk but is not willing to bear unnecessary risk. *The typical investor is therefore in search of a portfolio that maximizes expected portfolio return per unit of expected portfolio risk.*

GLOBAL FINANCE IN PRACTICE 17.1

Should Fund Managers Hedge Currency Risk?

In 2000, the impact of the decline of the euro on globally diversified portfolios reawakened the debate among portfolio managers as to whether currency components and their risks within the portfolios should be hedged. The decline of the euro over the year 2000, a drop of 19.6%, severely damaged the returns of many international portfolios.

The major international stock index used by most portfolio managers to benchmark performance is the Morgan Stanley Capital International European, Australian, and Far Eastern (EAFE) Index. The EAFE index fell 14.17% in 2000. If the currency component of the index was removed (effectively hedged), the index fell only 4.38%.

For example, by principle the Artisan Fund does not practice currency hedging. It believes that the currency risk component of an international portfolio is part and parcel to the principle of international diversification. The problem, however, is that the fund was exposed to the slide of the euro throughout 2000 and its investors suffered. Fund managers who argue against hedging are quick to point out that many of the world's major currencies experience large swings, fre-

quently moving back in the opposite direction, sometimes quickly, in subsequent periods.

Other funds, such as Janus Worldwide, used forward contracts and options to completely hedge their portfolios against currency fluctuations. They argue that removing the currency movements from the portfolio returns allows the fund to focus purely on stock-picking, the traditional competence of the fund manager. For example, Tweedy, Browne Company's Global Fund rose 12.4% in 2000, outperforming 95% of similar international funds sold to U.S.-based investors. According to the fund's manager, currency hedging added approximately 10 percentage points to the performance of the fund.

Still, other funds practice selective hedging, removing the risk associated with the currencies which the fund managers and its currency analysts feel are the most at risk in the current period. In the end it is a matter of taste. Similar to the question of whether financial managers should hedge or not hedge their transaction exposures, the debate over hedging currency components of international portfolios will continue.

The domestic investor may choose among a set of individual securities in the domestic market. The near infinite set of portfolio combinations of domestic securities form the *domestic portfolio opportunity set* shown in Exhibit 17.3. The set of portfolios formed along the extreme left edge of the domestic portfolio opportunity set is termed the *efficient frontier*. It represents the optimal portfolios of securities that possess the minimum expected risk for each level of expected portfolio return. The portfolio with the minimum risk among all those possible is the *minimum risk domestic portfolio* (MR_{DP}).

The individual investor will search out the optimal domestic portfolio (DP) that combines the risk-free asset and a portfolio of domestic securities found on the efficient frontier. He or she begins with the risk-free asset with return of R_f (and zero expected risk), and moves out along the security market line until reaching portfolio DP. This portfolio is defined as the optimal domestic portfolio because it moves out into risky space at the steepest slope—maximizing the slope of expected portfolio return over expected risk—while still touching the opportunity set of domestic portfolios. This line is called the *capital market line*, and portfolio theory assumes an investor who can borrow and invest at the risk-free rate can move to any point along this line.

Note that the optimal domestic portfolio is not the portfolio of minimum risk (MR_{DP}). A line stretching from the risk-free asset to the minimum risk domestic portfolio would have a lower slope than the capital market line, and the investor would not be receiving as great an expected return (vertical distance) per unit of expected risk (horizontal distance) as that found at DP.

International Diversification

Exhibit 17.4 illustrates the impact of allowing the investor to choose among an internationally diversified set of potential portfolios. The *internationally diversified portfolio opportunity*

EXHIBIT 17.3   Optimal Domestic Portfolio Construction

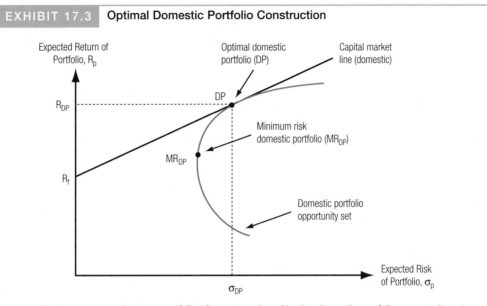

An investor may choose a portfolio of assets enclosed by the domestic portfolio opportunity set. The optimal domestic portfolio is found at DP, where the capital market line is tangent to the domestic portfolio opportunity set. The domestic portfolio with the minimum risk is designated MR_{DP}.

EXHIBIT 17.4   The Internationally Diversified Portfolio Opportunity Set

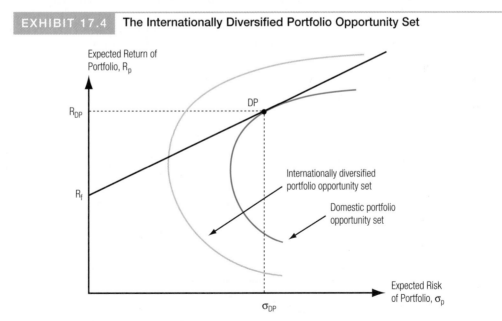

The addition of internationally diversified portfolios to the total opportunity set available to the investor shifts the total portfolio opportunity set left, providing lower expected risk portfolios for each level of expected portfolio return.

set shifts leftward of the purely domestic opportunity set. At any point on the efficient frontier of the internationally diversified portfolio opportunity set, the investor can find a portfolio of lower expected risk for each level of expected return.

It is critical to be clear as to exactly why the internationally diversified portfolio opportunity set is of lower expected risk than comparable domestic portfolios. The gains arise directly from the introduction of additional securities and/or portfolios which are of less than perfect correlation with the securities and portfolios within the domestic opportunity set.

For example, Sony Corporation is listed on the Tokyo Stock Exchange. Sony's share price derives its value from both the individual business results of the firm and the market in which it trades. If either or both are not perfectly positively correlated to the securities and markets available to a U.S.-based investor, then that investor would observe the opportunity set shift shown in Exhibit 17.4.

The Optimal International Portfolio

The investor can now choose an optimal portfolio that combines the same risk-free asset as before with a portfolio from the efficient frontier of the internationally diversified portfolio opportunity set. The *optimal international portfolio*, IP, is again found by locating that point on the capital market line (internationally diversified) that extends from the risk-free asset return of R_f to a point of tangency along the internationally diversified efficient frontier. We illustrate this in Exhibit 17.5.

The benefits of international diversification are now obvious. The investor's optimal portfolio IP possesses both higher expected portfolio return ($R_{IP} > R_{DP}$), and lower expected portfolio risk ($\sigma_{IP} < \sigma_{DP}$), than the purely domestic optimal portfolio. The optimal international portfolio is superior to the optimal domestic portfolio.

EXHIBIT 17.5   The Gains from International Portfolio Diversification

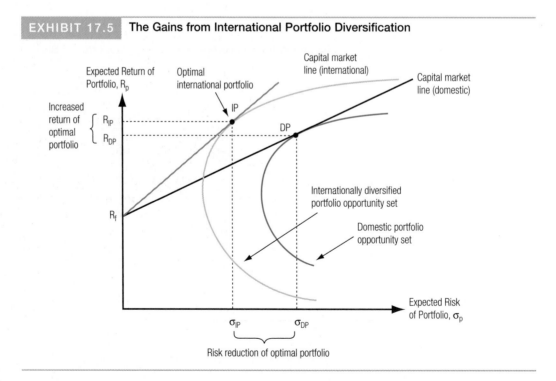

The Calculation of Portfolio Risk and Return

An investor may reduce investment risk by holding risky assets in a portfolio. As long as the asset returns are not perfectly positively correlated, the investor can reduce risk because some of the fluctuations of the asset returns will offset each other.

Two-Asset Model. Let us assume Trident's CFO Maria Gonzalez is considering investing Trident Corporation's marketable securities in two different risky assets, an index of the U.S. equity markets and an index of the German equity markets. The two equities are characterized by the following expected returns (the mean of recent returns) and expected risks (the standard deviation of recent returns):

	Expected Return	Expected Risk (σ)
United States equity index (US)	14%	15%
German equity index (GER)	18%	20%
Correlation coefficient ($\rho_{US\text{-}GER}$)	0.34	

If the weights of investment in the two assets are w_{US} and w_{GER} respectively, and $w_{US} + w_{GER} = 1$, the risk of the portfolio (σ_p), usually expressed in terms of the standard deviation of the portfolio's expected return, is given by the following equation:

$$\sigma_p = \sqrt{w_{US}^2\sigma_{US}^2 + w_{GER}^2\sigma_{GER}^2 + 2w_{US}w_{GER}\rho_{US\text{-}GER}\sigma_{US}\sigma_{GER}}$$

where σ_{US}^2 and σ_{GER}^2 are the squared standard deviations of the expected returns of risky assets in the United States and Germany (the variances), respectively. The Greek letter *rho*, $\rho_{US\text{-}GER}$, is the correlation coefficient between the two market returns over time.

We now plug in the values for the standard deviations of the United States (15%) and Germany (20%), and the correlation coefficient of 0.34. Assuming that Maria initially wishes to invest 40% of her funds in the United States (0.40), and 60% of her funds in German equities (0.60), the expected risk of the portfolio will be

$$\sigma_p = \sqrt{(0.40)^2(0.15)^2 + (0.60)^2(0.20)^2 + 2(0.40)(0.60)(0.34)(0.15)(0.20)}$$

which, when reduced is

$$\sqrt{0.0036 + 0.0144 + 0.0049} = 0.151 \approx 15.1\%$$

Note that the portfolio risk is *not* the weighted average of the risks of the individual assets. As long as the correlation coefficient (ρ) is smaller than 1.0, some of the fluctuations of the asset returns will offset each other, resulting in risk reduction. The lower the correlation coefficient, the greater the opportunity for risk diversification.

We obtain the expected return of the portfolio with

$$E(R_p) = w_{US}E(R_{US}) + w_{GER}E(R_{GER})$$

where $E(R_p)$, $E(R_{US})$, and $E(R_{GER})$ are the expected returns of the portfolio, the U.S. equity index, and the German equity index, respectively. Using the expected returns for the United States (14%) and German (18%) equity indexes above, we find the expected return of the portfolio to be

$$E(R_p) = (0.4)(0.14) + (0.6)(0.18) = 0.164 \approx 16.4\%.$$

Altering the Weights. Before Maria finalizes the desired portfolio, she wishes to evaluate the impact of changing the weights between the two equity indexes on the expected risk and expected returns of the portfolio. Using weight increments of 0.5, she graphs the alternative portfolios in the customary portfolio risk-return graphic. Exhibit 17.6 illustrates the result.

The different portfolios possible using different weights with the two equity assets provides Maria some interesting choices. The two extremes, the greatest expected return and the minimum expected risks, call for very different weight structures. The greatest expected return is, as we would expect from the original asset expectations, 100% German in composition. The minimum expected risk portfolio, with approximately 15.2% expected risk, is made up of approximately 70% U.S. and 30% German securities.

Multiple Asset Model. We can generalize the above equations to a portfolio consisting of multiple assets. The portfolio risk is

$$\sigma_P = \sqrt{\sum_{i=1}^{N} w_i^2 \sigma_j^2 + \sum_{i=1}^{N-1} \sum_{j=i+1}^{N} w_i w_j \rho_{ij} \sigma_i \sigma_j}$$

and the portfolio expected return is

$$E(R_P) = \sum_{i=1}^{N} w_i E(R_i)$$

where N stands for the total number of assets included in the portfolio.

By allowing investors to hold foreign assets, we substantially enlarge the feasible set of investments; higher return can be obtained at a given level of risk, or lower risk can be attained at the same level of return.

EXHIBIT 17.6   Alternative Portfolio Profiles under Varying Asset Weights

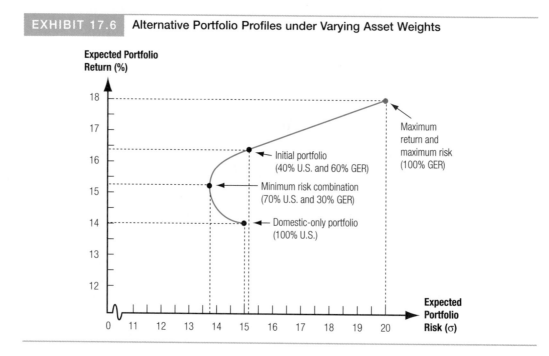

National Markets and Asset Performance

As demonstrated in the previous section, asset portfolios are traditionally constructed of both interest-bearing risk-free assets and risky assets. Exhibit 17.7 presents the performance of major individual national markets by asset category—bills, bonds, and equities—for the twentieth century (1900–2000). Risks and returns are presented on a real basis.

Exhibit 17.7 demonstrates that, at least for the 100-year period ending in 2000, the risk of investing in equity assets has been rewarded with substantial returns. U.S. equities delivered an inflation-adjusted mean return of 8.7%, versus mean returns of 2.1% on bonds and 1.0% on Treasury bills. But the U.S. market is also not exceptional, and in fact, equity markets in Australia, Germany, Japan, South Africa, and Sweden all exhibited higher mean returns for the century. It is also interesting to note that equity returns for all 16 countries listed demonstrated positive mean returns, the lowest being 4.8% in Belgium and the highest being 9.9% in Sweden.

As demonstrated by *Global Finance in Practice 17.2*, however, average performances over extended periods of time may be misleading, as they have a tendency to smooth returns which during the time of the crisis would indeed take an investor's breath away!

The true benefits of global diversification, however, arise from the fact that the returns of different stock markets around the world are not perfectly positively correlated. Because there are different industrial structures in different countries and because different

EXHIBIT 17.7	Real Returns and Risks on the Three Major Asset Classes, Globally, 1900–2000					
	Equities (%)		Bonds (%)		Bills (%)	
Country	Mean	S.D.	Mean	S.D.	Mean	S.D.
Australia	9.0	17.7	1.9	13.0	0.6	5.6
Belgium	4.8	22.8	0.3	12.1	0.0	8.2
Canada	7.7	16.8	2.4	10.6	1.8	5.1
Denmark	6.2	20.1	3.3	12.5	3.0	6.4
France	6.3	23.1	0.1	14.4	−2.6	11.4
Germany	8.8	32.3	0.3	15.9	0.1	10.6
Ireland	7.0	22.2	2.4	13.3	1.4	6.0
Italy	6.8	29.4	−0.8	14.4	−2.9	12.0
Japan	9.3	30.3	1.3	20.9	−0.3	14.5
The Netherlands	7.7	21.0	1.5	9.4	0.8	5.2
South Africa	9.1	22.8	1.9	10.6	1.0	6.4
Spain	5.8	22.0	1.9	12.0	0.6	6.1
Sweden	9.9	22.8	3.1	12.7	2.2	6.8
Switzerland	6.9	20.4	3.1	8.0	1.2	6.2
United Kingdom	7.6	20.0	2.3	14.5	1.2	6.6
United States	8.7	20.2	2.1	10.0	1.0	4.7

Source: Abstracted from Elroy Dimson, Paul Marsh, and Mike Staunton, *Triumph of the Optimists, 101 Years of Global Investment Returns*, Princeton University Press, 2002, p. 60. "Mean" is arithmetic mean; "S.D." is standard deviation of mean returns. Bond and bill statistics for Germany exclude the years 1922–1923; Swiss equities begin 1911.

GLOBAL FINANCE IN PRACTICE 17.2

Equity Market Crises in the Twentieth Century

The largest equity market losses in the past century were primarily related to war and terrorism, and their associated economic devastation.

Country	Event	Equity Market Losses (real returns, %)
U.S.	Terrorist attacks, September 11, 2001	−14%
U.S.	October 1987 stock market crash	−23%
U.S.	Bear market, 2000–2001	−37%
U.S.	Wall Street crash of 1929	−60%
U.K.	Bear market, 1973–1974	−71%
Germany	World War II, 1945–1948	−91%
Japan	World War II, 1944–1947	−97%

Source: Elroy Dimson, Paul Marsh, and Mike Staunton, *Triumph of the Optimists, 101 Years of Global Investment Returns*, Princeton University Press, 2002, p. 58.

economies do not exactly follow the same business cycle, we expect smaller return correlations between investments in different countries than between investments within a given country.

Exhibit 17.8 reports correlation coefficients between world equity markets for 1900–2000. The correlation coefficients in the lower bottom left of the exhibit are for the entire period, 1900–2000, while the upper top right of the exhibit are for the 1996–2000 period. The relatively low correlation coefficients among returns for the 16 countries for either period indicate great potential for international diversification. The returns, for the sake of comparison, have all been converted to the same currency basis (in this case the U.S. dollar) and are corrected for inflation.

As noted by the authors of the study, the correlations seem to be "plausible and linked to geography and distance" as national markets that are contiguous or near-contiguous seemingly demonstrate the higher correlation coefficients for the century. For example, among the lower bottom left correlation coefficients, the highest correlations are those between the United States and Canada (.80) and Ireland and the United Kingdom (.73).

The correlation coefficients among national equity markets in the upper top right of Exhibit 17.8, correlations for the 1996–2000 period, are noticeably higher than those for the entire century. The mean correlation coefficient for the entire century was 0.36, while that of the 1996–2000 period was 0.50. Although only for the most recent time segment, and one in which global equity market performance could have been atypical given the dot-com bubble in select industrial markets, the coefficients do indicate a higher degree of market performance integration.[1]

Additional multiple regression studies undertaken by the authors of the study found that when the twentieth century was divided in half "there was no discernible relationship between the two half centuries." They went on to determine that "it would not have been

[1]Elroy Dimson, Paul Marsh, and Mike Staunton, *Triumph of the Optimists, 101 Years of Global Investment Returns*, Princeton University Press, 2002, p. 115–116.

EXHIBIT 17.8	Correlation Coefficients between World Equity Markets, 1900–2000

Upper Top Right: Correlations based on 60 months of real dollar returns, 1996–2000, from FTSE World (Ireland and South Africa) and MSCI (all others).

Lower Bottom Left: Correlation based on 101 years of real dollar returns, 1900–2000.

	World	U.S.	U.K.	Swi	Swe	Spa	Saf	Neth	Jap	Ita	Ire	Ger	Fra	Den	Can	Bel	Aus
World		.93	.77	.59	.62	.67	.54	.73	.68	.52	.69	.69	.73	.57	.82	.54	.69
U.S.	.85		.67	.44	.46	.53	.46	.57	.49	.40	.66	.56	.56	.46	.78	.45	.57
U.K.	.70	.55		.58	.44	.63	.31	.71	.42	.39	.73	.58	.59	.57	.57	.59	.56
Swi	.68	.50	.62		.39	.60	.19	.72	.36	.45	.57	.53	.64	.58	.35	.63	.37
Swe	.62	.44	.42	.54		.63	.38	.63	.34	.49	.27	.76	.76	.44	.61	.29	.44
Spa	.41	.25	.25	.36	.37		.35	.63	.32	.64	.50	.64	.75	.56	.51	.55	.54
Saf	.55	.43	.49	.39	.34	.26		.30	.44	.24	.31	.42	.37	.25	.62	.10	.66
Neth	.57	.39	.42	.51	.43	.28	.29		.39	.59	.63	.74	.77	.64	.55	.70	.46
Jap	.45	.21	.33	.29	.39	.40	.31	.25		.18	.33	.25	.36	.24	.50	.17	.59
Ita	.54	.37	.43	.52	.39	.41	.41	.32	.34		.33	.55	.71	.50	.40	.51	.38
Ire	.58	.38	.73	.70	.42	.35	.42	.46	.29	.43		.42	.45	.49	.54	.57	.50
Ger	.30	.12	-.01	.22	.09	-.03	.05	.27	.06	.016	.03		.83	.61	.57	.59	.46
Fra	.62	.36	.45	.54	.44	.47	.38	.48	.25	.52	.53	.19		.63	.60	.66	.48
Den	.57	.38	.40	.51	.56	.34	.31	.50	.46	.38	.55	.22	.45		.55	.54	.30
Can	.80	.80	.55	.48	.53	.27	.54	.34	.30	.37	.41	.13	.35	.46		.30	.65
Bel	.58	.38	.40	.57	.43	.40	.29	.60	.25	.47	.49	.26	.68	.42	.35		.30
Aus	.66	.47	.66	.51	.50	.28	.56	.41	.28	.43	.62	.04	.47	.42	.62	.35	

Source: Elroy Dimson, Paul Marsh, and Mike Staunton, *Triumph of the Optimists, 101 Years of Global Investment Returns*, Princeton University Press, 2002, p. 115. Reprinted by permission of Princeton University Press.

possible to predict correlations for 1950–2000 from those estimated from annual data over the first half-century."[2]

Market Performance Adjusted for Risk: The Sharpe and Treynor Performance Measures

Although Exhibit 17.7 and Exhibit 17.8 provided some insights into the long-term historical performance of individual national markets and key assets, they do not provide a complete picture of how returns and risks must be considered in combination. Exhibit 17.9 presents summary statistics for the monthly returns across 18 major equity markets for the 1977–1996 period. In addition to the traditional measures of individual market performance of mean return and standard deviation (for risk), the individual national market's beta to the global portfolio is reported as well as two measures of risk-adjusted returns, the Sharpe and Treynor measures.

Investors should examine returns by the amount of return per unit of risk accepted, rather than in isolation (as in simply mean risks and returns). For example, in Exhibit 17.9, the Hong Kong market had the highest average monthly return at 1.50%, but also the highest risk, a standard deviation of 9.61%. (A major contributing factor to its high volatility was, perhaps, the political uncertainty about the future of the British colony after 1997.)

[2]Ibid., p. 116.

EXHIBIT 17.9	Summary Statistics of the Monthly Returns for 18 Major Stock Markets, 1977–1996 (all returns converted into U.S. dollars and include all dividends paid)

	Mean Return (%)	Standard Deviation (%)	Beta (β_i)	Sharpe M. (SHP$_i$)	Treynor M. (TRN$_i$)
Australia	1.00	7.44	1.02	0.078	0.0057
Austria	0.77	6.52	0.54	0.055	0.0066
Belgium	1.19	5.53	0.86	0.141	0.0091
Canada	0.82	5.34	0.93	0.076	0.0044
Denmark	0.99	6.25	0.68	0.092	0.0085
France	1.18	6.76	1.08	0.113	0.0071
Germany	0.97	6.17	0.84	0.089	0.0065
Hong Kong	1.50	9.61	1.09	0.113	0.0100
Italy	0.96	7.57	0.89	0.071	0.0061
Japan	1.08	6.66	1.21	0.099	0.0055
Netherlands	1.39	4.93	0.89	0.197	0.0109
Norway	1.00	7.94	1.02	0.073	0.0057
Singapore	1.09	7.50	1.01	0.090	0.0057
Spain	0.83	6.81	0.94	0.060	0.0044
Sweden	1.37	6.67	0.97	0.143	0.0099
Switzerland	1.10	5.39	0.86	0.127	0.0080
United Kingdom	1.35	5.79	1.06	0.162	0.0089
United States	1.01	4.16	0.82	0.143	0.0072
Average	1.09	6.51	0.93	0.107	0.0073

The results are computed with stock market data from Morgan Stanley's *Capital International Perspectives*, monthly.

To consider both risk and return in evaluating portfolio performance, we introduce two measures in Exhibit 17.9, the *Sharpe measure* (SHP) and the *Treynor measure* (TRN). The Sharpe measure calculates the average return over and above the risk-free rate of return per unit of portfolio risk:

$$\text{Sharpe measure} = \text{SHP}_i = \frac{\bar{R}_i - R_f}{\sigma_i}$$

where R_i is the average return for portfolio i during a specified time period, R_f is the average risk-free rate of return, and σ_i is the risk of portfolio i. The Treynor measure is very similar, but instead of using the standard deviation of the portfolio's total return as the measure of risk, it utilizes the portfolio's beta, β_i, the systematic risk of the portfolio, as measured against the world market portfolio:

$$\text{Treynor measure} = \text{TRN}_i = \frac{\bar{R}_i - R_f}{\beta_i}.$$

The Sharpe measure indicates on average how much excess return (above risk-free rate) an investor is rewarded per unit of portfolio risk the investor bears.

Though the equations of the Sharpe and Treynor measures look similar, the difference between them is important. If a portfolio is perfectly diversified (without any unsystematic risk), the two measures give similar rankings because the total portfolio risk is equivalent to the systematic risk. If a portfolio is poorly diversified, it is possible for it to show a high ranking on the basis of the Treynor measure, but a lower ranking on the basis of the Sharpe measure. The difference is attributable to the low level of portfolio diversification. The two measures, therefore, provide complementary but different information.

Hong Kong Example. The mean return for Hong Kong in Exhibit 17.9 was 1.5%. If we assume the average risk-free rate was 5% per year during this period (or 0.42% per month), the Sharpe measure would be calculated as

$$\text{SHP}_{\text{HKG}} = \frac{\bar{R}_i - R_f}{\sigma_i} = \frac{0.015 - 0.0042}{0.0961} = 0.113$$

For each unit (%) of portfolio total risk an investor bore, the Hong Kong market rewarded the investor with a monthly excess return of 0.113% in 1977–1996.

Alternatively, the Treynor measure was

$$\text{TRN}_{\text{HKG}} = \frac{\bar{R}_i - R_f}{\beta_i} = \frac{0.015 - 0.0042}{1.09} = 0.0100$$

Although the Hong Kong market had the second highest Treynor measure, its Sharpe measure was ranked eighth, indicating that the Hong Kong market portfolio was not very well diversified from the world market perspective. Instead, the highest ranking belonged to the Netherlands market, which had the highest Sharpe (0.197) and Treynor (0.0109) measures.

Does this mean that a U.S. investor would have been best rewarded by investing in the Netherlands market over this period? The answer is yes if the investor were allowed to invest in only one of these markets. It would definitely have been better than staying home in the U.S. market, which had a Sharpe measure of 0.143 for the period. However, if the investor were willing to combine these markets in a portfolio, the performance would have been even better. Since these market returns were not perfectly positively correlated, further risk reduction was possible through diversification across markets.

Are Markets Increasingly Integrated?

It is often said that as capital markets around the world become more and more integrated, the benefits of diversification will be reduced. To examine this question, we break the 20-year sample period of 1977–1996 into halves: 1977–1986 and 1987–1996. The official movement toward a single Europe coincides with 1986. At this time most EU countries deregulated their securities markets—or at least began the process of removing remaining restrictions on the free flow of capital across the borders.

Exhibit 17.10 reports selected stock markets' correlation coefficients with the United States for each subperiod. Only the Danish-U.S. market correlation actually fell from the first to the second period. The Canadian-U.S. correlation rose from an already high 0.66 to 0.77 in the latter period. Similarly, the correlations between the United States and both Singapore and the United Kingdom rose to 0.66 and 0.67, respectively.

The overall picture is that the correlations have increased over time. The answer to the question, "Are markets increasingly integrated?" is most likely yes. However, although capital market integration has decreased some benefits of international portfolio diversification, the correlation coefficients between markets are still far from 1.0. There are still plenty of risk-reducing opportunities for international portfolio diversification.

EXHIBIT 17.10	Comparison of Selected Correlation Coefficients between Stock Markets for Two Time Periods (dollar returns)		
Correlation to United States	**1977–1986**	**1987–1996**	**Change**
Canada	0.66	0.77	+0.11
Denmark	0.26	0.18	−0.08
France	0.37	0.55	+0.18
Germany	0.24	0.42	+0.18
Hong Kong	0.13	0.61	+0.48
Japan	0.16	0.26	+0.10
Singapore	0.31	0.66	+0.35
Switzerland	0.38	0.47	+0.09
United Kingdom	0.40	0.67	+0.27

Correlation coefficients computed from data from Morgan Stanley's *Capital International Perspectives*.

SUMMARY POINTS

- The total risk of any portfolio is composed of *systematic* (the market) and *unsystematic* (the individual securities) risk. Increasing the number of securities in the portfolio reduces the unsystematic risk component.

- An internationally diversified portfolio has a lower portfolio beta. This means that the portfolio's market risk is lower than that of a domestic portfolio. This situation arises because the returns on the foreign stocks are closely correlated not with returns on U.S. stocks, but rather with a global beta.

- Investors construct internationally diversified portfolios in an attempt to combine assets that are less than perfectly correlated, reducing the total risk of the portfolio. In addition, by adding assets outside the home market, the investor has now tapped into a larger pool of potential investments.

- International portfolio construction is also different in that when the investor acquires assets or securities outside the investor's home-country market, the investor may also be acquiring a foreign currency denominated asset.

- The investor has actually acquired two additional assets—the currency of denomination and the asset subsequently purchased with the currency—one asset in principle, but two in expected returns and risks.

- The foreign exchange risks of a portfolio, whether it is a securities portfolio or the general portfolio of activities of the MNE, are reduced through international diversification.

- The individual investor will search out the *optimal domestic portfolio* (DP), which combines the risk-free asset and a portfolio of domestic securities found on the efficient frontier. The investor begins with the risk-free asset with return of R_f (and zero expected risk) and moves out along the capital market line until reaching portfolio DP.

- This portfolio is called the *optimal domestic portfolio* because it moves out into risky space at the steepest slope—maximizing the slope of expected portfolio return over expected risk—while still touching the opportunity set of domestic portfolios.

- The *optimal international portfolio*, IP, is found by finding that point on the capital market line (internationally diversified) which extends from the risk-free asset return of R_f to a point of tangency along the internationally diversified efficient frontier.

- The investor's optimal portfolio IP possesses both higher expected portfolio return ($R_{IP} > R_{DP}$), and lower expected portfolio risk ($\sigma_{IP} < \sigma_{DP}$), than the purely domestic optimal portfolio. The optimal international portfolio is superior to the optimal domestic portfolio.

- Risk reduction is possible through international diversification because the returns of different stock markets around the world are not perfectly positively correlated.

- Because there are different industrial structures in different countries and because different economies do not exactly follow the same business cycle, we expect smaller return correlations between investments in different countries than between investments within a given country.

- The relatively low correlation coefficients among returns of 18 major stock markets around the world in the 20-year period from 1977 to 1996 indicate great potential for international diversification.

- The overall picture is that the correlations have increased over time.

- Nevertheless, 91 of the 153 correlations (59%) and the overall mean (0.46) were still below 0.5 in 1987–1996. The answer to the question, "Are markets increasingly integrated?" is yes.

- However, although capital market integration has decreased some benefits of international portfolio diversification, the correlation coefficients between markets are still far from 1.0. There are still plenty of risk-reducing opportunities for international portfolio diversification.

MINI-CASE   Is Modern Portfolio Theory Outdated?[1]

Who knew? The subprime borrowers had no idea the housing market was about to slump, preventing them from refinancing those teaser rates. The mortgage brokers didn't ask about jobs and such, because no one was demanding this information. The rating agencies didn't know that this confluence of easy credit, misplaced incentives, and overheated real estate would alter historical default rates, the more so because most housing downturns since the Great Depression have been regional in scope. And the people who packaged all those mortgages into securities have only just recovered from the shock of how easy it was to sell all that paper to greedy investors, only to be blindsided by the reality that nobody knows how much any of it is worth anymore.

In a quest for answers instead of excuses, I called up Niels Clemen Jensen, a former senior executive at Lehman Brothers who now runs Absolute Return Partners, a $400 million London fund of funds. Jensen is a pro well versed in the nuts and bolts of modern portfolio theory and risk management. I am here to testify that, in this case, knowledge is not bliss, more like a long leap into the unfathomable.

"Everything to do with modern portfolio theory, from the most simple tools like standard deviation to the more complicated tools such as value-at-risk, is based on the very simple assumption that the market is following the shape of the bell curve. And I guess you could make the case that if you go back probably not more than about 15, 20 years you could actually make the case that the vast majority of time markets—commodity markets, equity markets and fixed-income markets—were actually following the shape of the bell curve. In other words, returns were normally distributed. But a number of things have changed in the last 20 years. First of all, we have access to far more sophisticated instruments. Secondly, we use longs and shorts so with the emergence of the hedge-fund industry the different investors in the market have become a lot more sophisticated. So not only are we using instruments that didn't exist 20 years ago, we're also mixing those instruments in a way that makes things far more complicated. And for all these reasons returns are behaving differently today from the way they did 20 years ago."

I already knew about Jensen's claim that based on "normal" bell-curve distribution patterns, 10 market earthquakes that have occurred over the last 20 years—from the 1987 crash to the stock rout in August—could only have been expected to occur once every few billion years. Under the bell-curve model, which works best for relatively static systems, the '87 crash was so exceedingly unlikely that it shouldn't have occurred yet given the age of this universe. Sure does seem like we have a data problem on our hands.

[1] Abstracted from an article by Igor Greenwald entitled "Modern Portfolio Theory Looks Very Outdated" which appeared in *Smart Money* on November 20, 2007.

Jensen reels off the recent improbabilities: the October 1997 market rout, the Long-Term Capital Management fiasco the following year, right on through the dot-com bubble and the China selloff in February. "In isolation, none of these events should happen more than three, four, five, six, seven billion years," he says. "But if you have one-in-three-billion-year events every couple of years, then there's something wrong with the rules. As an industry, we need to come up with new tools because the old ones don't work anymore."

According to Jensen, part of the problem may lie with the limitations of the market data on which risk models are commonly built, since the stats only go back to 1970 or so. But that's hardly the only flaw. Not enough institutions, he says, take the common-sense approach of asking what might happen if the improbable comes to pass the way it has time and again in recent years. What happens if the market for your assets dries up? What happens if one can't meet the margin calls?

"I'm not saying everybody is in that boat," says Jensen. "I used to work at Goldman Sachs and I know Goldman has some pretty sophisticated models on their hands, so not everybody is guilty of this, but there are a surprising number of financial institutions out there who use relatively unsophisticated tools. You would be shocked to learn how many institutions in the world today have a very one-dimensional risk model. And in most cases it's based on value-at-risk." And value-at-risk is calculated based on a well-behaved bell curve, of course. I was starting to wish I'd scheduled this interview for a calmer day.

Jensen says the next generation of value-at-risk models—available in a year or two—will incorporate the Monte Carlo simulations already used by many individuals and personal financial planners. And it's high time too that Citigroup caught on to a methodology long available to every Jack and Jill. But that will still leave the problem that, essentially, Citigroup and everyone else are using the same approach to measure risk, virtually assuring a crisis eventually. "Part of the problem is that when everybody uses the same tools to manage their risk things are bound to go wrong sometime," says Jensen. "You're reacting the same way as everybody else. Not only is it based on an assumption that's not really reasonable, it's also the stan-dard model in the industry, which means everybody's using it and that will amplify the problem when the shit hits the fan."

Long-term investors with plenty of time left may be able to ride out the volatility. Those with shorter time horizons or less stomach for risk can devote a modest fraction of the portfolio to bear insurance, either as long-dated puts, bearish exchange-traded funds or even via a long-volatility hedge fund, Jensen says. "But buy them when everything is rosy and nobody really thinks of any need to buy put options," he adds. In other words, don't buy them now.

Not all the recent market shocks have been negative, of course. Jensen points to the Internet and Asian development as two hugely positive upsets of the recent years. But positive shocks are easier to absorb, since they tend to produce extended bull markets rather than crashes and financial panics. For our sake, we'd better hope that we are in fact living in extraordinary times, because Jensen thinks the above-average market returns of the past couple of decades may need to retest the long-term trend line of returns around 10% annually. And that could cause U.S. asset prices to decline as much as 25% from current levels.

Of course, that's a problem for the next three billion years or so—unless it happens in the next decade. In the shorter run, through the end of 2007, Jensen is quite hopeful that the oversold stock market can bounce back. Just as he's hopeful that better risk models are on the way. "I'm not a doomsayer," he says. "I'm actually a pretty optimistic person by nature. I don't think this is the end of the world but I think there's more bad news coming out in the spring." Of course there is. We optimists will need to stick together.

Case Questions

1. Why might the bell curve not be helpful when trying to construct and manage modern financial portfolios?

2. What risks are created if most of the major market agents are using the same models at the same times?

3. Since the time of the article, the world economy has suffered a significant crisis. What elements of the article may have proved correct?

QUESTIONS

1. **Diversification Benefits.** How does the diversification of a portfolio change its expected returns and expected risks? Is this in principle any different for internationally diversified portfolios?

2. **Risk Reduction.** What types of risk are present in a diversified portfolio? Which type of risk remains after the portfolio has been diversified?

3. **Measurement of Risk.** How, according to portfolio theory, is the risk of the portfolio measured exactly?

4. Market Risk. If all national markets have market risk, is all market risk the same?

5. Currency Risk. The currency risk associated with international diversification is a serious concern for portfolio managers. Is it possible for currency risk ever to benefit the portfolio's return?

6. Optimal Domestic Portfolio. Define in words (without graphics) how the optimal domestic portfolio is constructed.

7. Minimum Risk Portfolios. If the primary benefit of portfolio diversification is risk reduction, is the investor always better off choosing the portfolio with the lowest expected risk?

8. International Risk. When asked why they do not internationally diversify their portfolios, many portfolio managers answer that "the risks are not worth the expected returns." Using the theory of international diversification, how would you evaluate this statement?

9. Correlation Coefficients. The benefits of portfolio construction, domestically or internationally, arise from the lack of correlation among assets and markets. The increasing globalization of business is expected to change these correlations over time. How do you believe they will change and why?

10. Relative Risk and Return. Conceptually, how do the Sharpe and Treynor performance measures define risk differently? Which do you believe is a more useful measure in an internationally diversified portfolio?

11. International Equities and Currencies. As the newest member of the asset allocation team in your firm, you constantly find yourself being quizzed by your fellow group members. The topic is international diversification. One analyst asks you the following question:

Security prices are driven by a variety of factors, but corporate earnings are clearly one of the primary drivers. And corporate earnings—on average—follow business cycles. Exchange rates, as they taught you in college, reflect the market's assessment of the growth prospects for the economy behind the currency. So if securities go up with the business cycle, and currencies go up with the business cycle, why do we see currencies and securities prices across the globe not going up and down together?

What is the answer?

12. Are MNEs Global Investments? Firms with operations and assets across the globe, true MNEs, are in many ways as international in composition as the most internationally diversified portfolio of unrelated securities. Why do investors not simply invest in MNEs traded on their local exchanges and forego the complexity of purchasing securities traded on foreign exchanges?

13. ADRs versus Direct Holdings. When you are constructing your portfolio, you know you want to include Cementos de Mexico (Mexico), but you cannot decide whether you wish to hold it in the form of ADRs traded on the NYSE or directly through purchases on the Mexico City Bolsa.
   a. Does it make any difference in regard to currency risk?
   b. List the pros and cons of ADRs and direct purchases.
   c. What would you recommend if you were an asset investor for a corporation with no international operations or internationally diversified holdings?

PROBLEMS

1. Pacific Wietz. Giri Iyer is a European analyst and strategist for Tristar Funds, a New York-based mutual fund company. Giri is currently evaluating the recent performance of shares in Pacific Wietz, a publicly traded specialty chemical company in Germany listed on the Frankfurt DAX. The baseline investment amount used by Tristar is $200,000. He gathers the following quotes:

Element	Jan 1 Purchase	Dec 31 Sale	Distributions
Share price	€135.00	€157.60	€15.00
Exchange rate	$1.3460/€	$1.4250/€	

   a. What was the return on the security in local currency terms?
   b. What was the return on the security in U.S. dollar terms?
   c. Does this mean it was a good investment for a local investor, a U.S.-based investor, or both?

*2. Boeing and Unilever. An investor is evaluating a two-asset portfolio of the following securities:

Security	Expected Return (percent)	Std. Dev. (percent)
Boeing (U.S.)	18.6	22.8
Unilever (U.K.)	16.0	24.0

a. If the two securities have a correlation of +.6, what is the expected risk and return for a portfolio that is equally weighted?

b. If the two securities have a correlation of +.6, what is the expected risk and return for a portfolio that is 70% Boeing and 30% Unilever?

c. If the two securities have a correlation of +.6, what is the expected risk and return for a portfolio that is optimally weighted? Determine the weights that minimize the combined risk.

3. **Baltic Returns.** Assume the U.S. dollar returns (monthly averages) shown below for three Baltic republics. Calculate the Sharpe and Treynor measures of market performance.

Country	Mean Return	Standard Deviation	Risk-Free Rate	Beta
Estonia	1.12%	16.00%	0.42%	1.65
Latvia	0.75%	22.80%	0.42%	1.53
Lithuania	1.60%	13.50%	0.42%	1.20

4. **Anglo-American Equity Fund.** An investor is evaluating a two-asset portfolio of the following two securities:

Security	Expected Return (percent)	Std. Dev. (percent)
Anglo Equities	12.5	26.4
American Equities	10.8	22.5

a. If the two equity funds have a correlation of +.72, what is the expected risk and return for the following three portfolio weightings?

Portfolio A:	75% Anglo, 25% American
Portfolio B:	50% Anglo, 50% American
Portfolio C:	25% Anglo, 75% American

b. Which of the portfolios is preferable? On what basis?

Lancaster Technology (London Stock Exchange)

Lancaster Technology is an information technology services provider. Currently it operates primarily within the European marketplace, and therefore is not active or traded on any North American Stock Exchange. The company's share price and dividend distributions have been as follows in recent years:

	6/30/04	6/30/05	6/30/06	6/30/07
Share price (£)	37.40	42.88	40.15	44.60
Dividend (£)	1.50	1.60	1.70	1.80
Spot exchange rate ($/£)	1.8160	1.7855	1.8482	2.0164
Spot Exchange Rate (€/£)	1.4844	1.4812	1.4472	1.4845

*5. **Lancaster Technology: British Pound-Based Investors.** Using the data above, calculate the annual average capital appreciation rate on Lancaster shares, as well as the average total return (including dividends) to a British pound-based investor holding the shares for the entire period shown.

6. **Lancaster Technology: U.S. Dollar-Based Investors (A).** Using the data above, calculate the annual average total return (including dividends) to a U.S. dollar-based investor holding the shares for the entire period shown. Assume an investment of $100,000.

7. **Lancaster Technology: U.S.-Dollar-Based Investors (B).** Using the data above, now assume that the pound consistently appreciates versus the dollar 3.0% per year. Begin with the $1.8160/£ in June 2004. Calculate the annual average total return (including dividends) to a U.S. dollar-based investor holding the shares for the entire period shown.

8. **Lancaster Technology: Euro-Based Investors (A).** Using the data above, calculate the annual average total return (including dividends) to a Euro-based investor holding the shares for the entire period shown. Assume an investment of €100,000.

9. **Lancaster Technology: Euro-Based Investors (B).** Using the data above, now assume that the pound consistently appreciates versus the euro 1.5% per year. Begin with the €1.4844/£ in June 2004. Calculate the annual average total return (including dividends) to the euro-based investor holding the shares for the entire period shown.

10. **Brazilian Investors Diversify.** The Brazilian economy in 2001 and 2002 had gone up and down. The Brazilian reais (R$) had also been declining since 1999 (when it was floated). Investors wished to diversify internationally—into U.S. dollars for the most part—to protect themselves against the domestic economy and currency. A large private investor had, in April 2002, invested R$500,000 in Standard &

Poor's 500 Indexes, which are traded on the American Stock Exchange (AMSE: SPY). The beginning and ending index prices and exchange rates between the reais and the dollar were as follows:

	4/10/2002	4/10/2003
Share price of SPY (US$)	112.60	87.50
Exchange rate (R$/$)	2.27	3.22

a. What was the return on the index fund for the year to a U.S.-based investor?

b. What was the return to the Brazilian investor for the one year holding period? If the Brazilian investor could have invested locally in Brazil in an interest bearing account guaranteeing 12%, would that have been better than the American diversification strategy?

11. **Russian-U.S. Equity Portfolio (A).** An investor is evaluating a two-asset portfolio that combines a U.S. equity fund with a Russian equity fund. The expected returns, risks, and correlation coefficients for the coming one-year period are as follows:

Security	Expected Return (percent)	Expected Risk (percent)
U.S. equity fund	10.50	18.60
Russian equity fund	16.80	36.00

Assuming the expected correlation coefficient is 0.52 for the coming year, which weights (use increments of 5% such as 95/5, 90/10) result in the best trade-off between expected risk and expected return?

12. **Russian-U.S. Equity Portfolio (B).** Rework problem 11, but assume that you have reduced the expected correlation coefficient from 0.52 to 0.38. Which weights (use increments of 5% such as 95/5, 90/10) result in the best trade-off between expected risk and expected return?

INTERNET EXERCISES

1. **Modern Portfolio Theory.** Use the MoneyOnLine Internet site to review the fundamental theories, assumptions, and statistical tools that make up modern portfolio theory.

MoneyOnLine Limited   www.moneyonline.co.nz/calculator/theory.htm

2. **International Diversification via Mutual Funds.** All major mutual fund companies now offer a variety of internationally diversified mutual funds. The degree of international composition across funds, however, differs significantly. Use the Web sites of any of the major mutual fund providers (Fidelity, Scudder, Merrill Lynch, Kemper, and so on) and any others of interest, to do the following:

a. Distinguish between international funds, global funds, worldwide funds, and overseas funds.

b. Determine how international funds have been performing, in U.S. dollar terms, relative to mutual funds offering purely domestic portfolios.

c. Use the Security and Exchange Commission's Web site, www.sec.gov/pdf/ininvest.pdf, to review the risk-return issues related to international investing.

3. **Yahoo! Finance Investment Learning Center.** Yahoo! Finance provides detailed current basic and advanced research and reading materials related to all aspects of investing, including portfolio management. Use its Web site to refresh your memory on the benefits—and risks—of portfolio diversification.

Yahoo! Finance Learning   biz.yahoo.com/edu/ed_begin.html

CHAPTER 18

Foreign Direct Investment Theory and Political Risk

People don't want a quarter-inch drill. They want a quarter-inch hole.

—Theodore Levitt, Harvard Business School.

The strategic decision to undertake foreign direction investment (FDI), and thus become an MNE, starts with a self-evaluation. Does the firm have a sustainable competitive advantage? Next, should the firm enter foreign markets through foreign direct investment or some alternative mode such as licensing, joint ventures, strategic alliances, management contracts, or just plain exports? If foreign direct investment is the chosen method, where should the firm invest? Should the investment be via a greenfield investment or an acquisition? Is foreign direct investment exclusively the domain of large MNEs resident in the most advanced countries or can MNEs originate in less-developed countries?

Sustaining and Transferring Competitive Advantage

In deciding whether to invest abroad, management must first determine whether the firm has a sustainable competitive advantage that enables it to compete effectively in the home market. The competitive advantage must be firm-specific, transferable, and powerful enough to compensate the firm for the potential disadvantages of operating abroad (foreign exchange risks, political risks, and increased agency costs).

Based on observations of firms that have successfully invested abroad, we can conclude that some of the competitive advantages enjoyed by MNEs are 1) economies of scale and scope arising from their large size; 2) managerial and marketing expertise; 3) superior technology owing to their heavy emphasis on research; 4) financial strength; 5) differentiated products; and sometimes 6) competitiveness of their home markets.

Economies of Scale and Scope

Economies of scale and scope can be developed in production, marketing, finance, research and development, transportation, and purchasing. All of these areas have significant competitive advantages of being large, whether size is due to international or domestic operations. Production economies can come from the use of large-scale automated plant and equipment or from an ability to rationalize production through worldwide specialization.

For example, some automobile manufacturers, such as Ford, rationalize manufacturing by producing engines in one country, transmissions in another, and bodies in another and assembling still elsewhere, with the location often being dictated by comparative advantage.

Marketing economies occur when firms are large enough to use the most efficient advertising media to create worldwide brand identification, as well as to establish worldwide distribution, warehousing, and servicing systems. Financial economies derive from access to the full range of financial instruments and sources of funds, such as the Eurocurrency, Euroequity, and Eurobond markets. In-house research and development programs are typically restricted to large firms because of the minimum-size threshold for establishing a laboratory and scientific staff. Transportation economies accrue to firms that can ship in carload or shipload lots. Purchasing economies come from quantity discounts and market power.

Managerial and Marketing Expertise

Managerial expertise includes skill in managing large industrial organizations from both a human and a technical viewpoint. It also encompasses knowledge of modern analytical techniques and their application in functional areas of business. Managerial expertise can be developed through prior experience in foreign markets. In most empirical studies multinational firms have been observed to export to a market before establishing a production facility there. Likewise, they have prior experience sourcing raw materials and human capital in other foreign countries either through imports, licensing, or FDI. In this manner, the MNEs can partially overcome the supposed superior local knowledge of host country firms.

Advanced Technology

Advanced technology includes both scientific and engineering skills. It is not limited to MNEs, but firms in the most industrialized countries have had an advantage in terms of access to continuing new technology spin-offs from the military and space programs. Empirical studies have supported the importance of technology as a characteristic of MNEs.

Financial Strength

As discussed in Chapter 14, companies demonstrate financial strength by achieving and maintaining a global cost and availability of capital. This is a critical competitive cost variable that enables them to fund FDI and other foreign activities. MNEs that are resident in liquid and unsegmented capital markets are normally blessed with this attribute. However, MNEs that are resident in small industrial or emerging market countries can still follow a proactive strategy of seeking foreign portfolio and corporate investors.

Small- and medium-size firms often lack the characteristics that attract foreign (and maybe domestic) investors. They are too small or unattractive to achieve a global cost of capital. This limits their ability to fund FDI, and their higher marginal cost of capital reduces the number of foreign projects that can generate the higher required rate of return.

Differentiated Products

Firms create their own firm-specific advantages by producing and marketing differentiated products. Such products originate from research-based innovations or heavy marketing expenditures to gain brand identification. Furthermore, the research and marketing process continues to produce a steady stream of new differentiated products. It is difficult and costly for competitors to copy such products, and they always face a time lag if they try. Having developed differentiated products for the domestic home market, the firm may decide to market them worldwide, a decision consistent with the desire to maximize return on heavy research and marketing expenditures.

Competitiveness of the Home Market

A strongly competitive home market can sharpen a firm's competitive advantage relative to firms located in less competitive home markets. This phenomenon is known as the "diamond of national advantage." The diamond has four components, as illustrated in Exhibit 18.1.[1]

A firm's success in competing in a particular industry depends partly on the availability of factors of production (land, labor, capital, and technology) appropriate for that industry. Countries that are either naturally endowed with the appropriate factors or able to create them will probably spawn firms that are both competitive at home and potentially so abroad. For example, a well-educated work force in the home market creates a competitive advantage for firms in certain high-tech industries. Firms facing sophisticated and demanding customers in the home market are able to hone their marketing, production, and quality control skills. Japan is such a market.

Firms in industries that are surrounded by a critical mass of related industries and suppliers will be more competitive because of this supporting cast. For example, electronic firms located in centers of excellence, such as in the San Francisco Bay area, are surrounded by efficient, creative suppliers and enjoy access to educational institutions at the forefront of knowledge.

A competitive home market forces firms to fine-tune their operational and control strategies for their specific industry and country environment. Japanese firms learned how to organize to implement their famous just-in-time inventory control system. One key was to use numerous subcontractors and suppliers that were encouraged to locate near the final assembly plants.

EXHIBIT 18.1   **Determinants of National Competitive Advantage: Porter's Diamond**

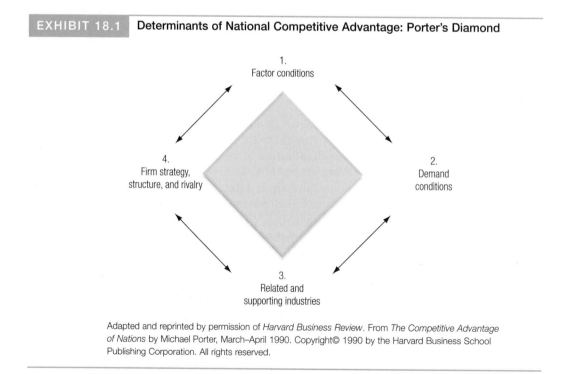

---

[1]Michael Porter, *The Competitive Advantage of Nations*, London: Macmillan Press, 1990.

In some cases, home country markets have not been large or competitive, but MNEs located there have nevertheless developed global niche markets served by foreign subsidiaries. Global competition in oligopolistic industries substitutes for domestic competition. For example, a number of MNEs resident in Scandinavia, Switzerland, and the Netherlands fall in this category. Some of these are Novo Nordisk (Denmark), Norske Hydro (Norway), Nokia (Finland), L.M. Ericsson (Sweden), Astra (Sweden), ABB (Sweden/Switzerland), Roche Holding (Switzerland), Royal Dutch Shell (the Netherlands), Unilever (the Netherlands), and Philips (the Netherlands).

Emerging market countries have also spawned aspiring global MNEs in niche markets even though they lack competitive home country markets. Some of these are traditional exporters in natural resource fields such as oil, agriculture, and minerals, but they are in transition to becoming MNEs. They typically start with foreign sales subsidiaries, joint ventures, and strategic alliances. Examples are Petrobrás (Brazil), YPF (Argentina), and Cemex (Mexico). Another category of firms is those that have been recently privatized in the telecommunications industry. Examples are Telefonos de Mexico and Telebras (Brazil). Still others started as electronic component manufacturers but are making the transition to manufacturing abroad. Examples are Samsung Electronics (Korea) and Acer Computer (Taiwan).

The OLI Paradigm and Internalization

The OLI Paradigm (Buckley and Casson, 1976; Dunning, 1977) is an attempt to create an overall framework to explain why MNEs choose FDI rather than serve foreign markets through alternative modes such as licensing, joint ventures, strategic alliances, management contracts, and exporting.[2]

The *OLI Paradigm* states that a firm must first have some competitive advantage in its home market—"O" or *owner-specific*—that can be transferred abroad if the firm is to be successful in foreign direct investment. Second, the firm must be attracted by specific characteristics of the foreign market—"L" or *location-specific*—that will allow it to exploit its competitive advantages in that market. Third, the firm will maintain its competitive position by attempting to control the entire value chain in its industry—"I" or *internalization*. This leads it to foreign direct investment rather than licensing or outsourcing.

Definitions

The "O" in OLI stands for owner-specific advantages. As described earlier, a firm must have competitive advantages in its home market. These must be firm-specific, not easily copied, and in a form that allows them to be transferred to foreign subsidiaries. For example, economies of scale and financial strength are not necessarily firm-specific because they can be achieved by many other firms. Certain kinds of technology can be purchased, licensed, or copied. Even differentiated products can lose their advantage to slightly altered versions, given enough marketing effort and the right price.

The "L" in OLI stands for location-specific advantages. These factors are typically market imperfections or genuine comparative advantages that attract FDI to particular locations. These factors might include a low-cost but productive labor force, unique sources of raw

[2]Peter J. Buckley and Mark Casson, *The Future of the Multinational Enterprise*, London: McMillan, 1976; and John H. Dunning, "Trade Location of Economic Activity and the MNE: A Search for an Eclectic Approach," in *The International Allocation of Economic Activity*, Bertil Ohlin, Per-Ove Hesselborn, and Per Magnus Wijkman, eds., New York: Holmes and Meier, 1977, pp. 395–418.

materials, a large domestic market, defensive investments to counter other competitors, or centers of technological excellence.

The "I" in OLI stands for internalization. According to the theory, the key ingredient for maintaining a firm-specific competitive advantage is possession of proprietary information and control of the human capital that can generate new information through expertise in research. Needless to say, once again large research-intensive firms are most likely to fit this description.

Minimizing transactions costs is the key factor in determining the success of an internalization strategy. Wholly owned FDI reduces the agency costs that arise from asymmetric information, lack of trust, and the need to monitor foreign partners, suppliers, and financial institutions. Self-financing eliminates the need to observe specific debt covenants on foreign subsidiaries that are financed locally or by joint venture partners. If a multinational firm has a low global cost and high availability of capital, why share it with joint venture partners, distributors, licensees, and local banks, all of which probably have a higher cost of capital?

The Financial Strategy

Financial strategies are directly related to the OLI Paradigm in explaining FDI, as shown in Exhibit 18.2. Proactive financial strategies can be controlled in advance by the MNE's financial managers. These include strategies necessary to gain an advantage from lower global cost and greater availability of capital and were explained in detail in Chapter 14. Other proactive financial strategies are negotiating financial subsidies and/or reduced taxation to increase free cash flows, reducing financial agency costs through FDI, and reducing operating and transaction exposure through FDI.

EXHIBIT 18.2   Finance-Specific Factors and the OLI Paradigm ("X" indicates a connection between FDI and finance-specific strategies)

	Ownership Advantages	Location Advantages	Internalization Advantages
Proactive Financial Strategies			
1. Gaining and maintaining a global cost and availability of capital			
▪ Competitive sourcing of capital globally	X	X	
▪ Strategic preparatory cross-listing	X		
▪ Providing accounting and disclosure transparency	X		
▪ Maintaining competitive commercial and financial banking relationships	X		
▪ Maintaining a competitive credit rating	X	X	X
2. Negotiating financial subsidies and/or reduced taxation to increase free cash flow	X	X	
3. Reducing financial agency cost through FDI			X
4. Reducing operating and transaction exposure through FDI	X		
Reactive Financial Strategies			
1. Exploiting undervalued or overvalued exchange rates		X	
2. Exploiting undervalued or overvalued stock prices		X	
3. Reacting to capital control that prevents the free movement of funds		X	
4. Minimizing taxation		X	X

Source: Reprinted from *International Business Review*, Volume 10, Lars Oxelheim, Arthur Stonehill, and Trond Randøy, "On the Treatment of Finance Specific Factors Within the OLI Paradigm," pp. 381–398, ©2001, with permission from Elsevier Science.

Reactive financial strategies, as illustrated in Exhibit 18.2, depend on discovering market imperfections. For example, the MNE can exploit misaligned exchange rates and stock prices. It also needs to react to capital controls that prevent the free movement of funds and react to opportunities to minimize worldwide taxation.

Deciding Where to Invest

The decision about where to invest abroad is influenced by behavioral factors. The decision about where to invest abroad for the first time is not the same as the decision about where to reinvest abroad. A firm learns from its first few investments abroad and what it learns influences subsequent investments.

In theory, a firm should identify its competitive advantages. Then it should search worldwide for market imperfections and comparative advantage until it finds a country where it expects to enjoy a competitive advantage large enough to generate a risk-adjusted return above the firm's hurdle rate.

In practice, firms have been observed to follow a sequential search pattern as described in the behavioral theory of the firm. Human rationality is bounded by one's ability to gather and process all the information that would be needed to make a perfectly rational decision based on all the facts. This observation lies behind two related behavioral theories of FDI. They are described next as the *behavioral approach* and *international network theory*.

Behavioral Approach to FDI

The behavioral approach to analyzing the FDI decision is typified by the so-called Swedish School of economists.[3] The Swedish School has rather successfully explained not just the initial decision to invest abroad but also later decisions to reinvest elsewhere and to change the structure of a firm's international involvement over time. Based on the internationalization process of a sample of Swedish MNEs, the economists observed that these firms tended to invest first in countries that were not too far distant in psychic terms. *Close psychic distance* defined countries with a cultural, legal, and institutional environment similar to Sweden's, such as Norway, Denmark, Finland, Germany, and the United Kingdom. The initial investments were modest in size to minimize the risk of an uncertain foreign environment. As the Swedish firms learned from their initial investments, they became willing to take greater risks with respect to both the psychic distance of the countries and the size of the investments.

MNEs in a Network Perspective

As the Swedish MNEs grew and matured, so did the nature of their international involvement. Today, each MNE is perceived as being a member of an international network, with nodes based in each of the foreign subsidiaries, as well as the parent firm itself. Centralized (hierarchical) control has given way to decentralized (heterarchical) control. Foreign subsidiaries compete with each other and with the parent for expanded resource commitments, thus influencing the strategy and reinvestment decisions. Many of these MNEs have become political coalitions with competing internal and external networks. Each subsidiary (and the parent) is embedded in its host country's network of suppliers and customers. It is also a member of a worldwide network based on its industry. Finally, it is a member of an organizational network under the nominal control of the parent firm. Complicating matters still fur-

[3]John Johansen and F. Wiedersheim-Paul, "The Internationalization of the Firm: Four Swedish Case Studies," *Journal of Management Studies*, Volume 12, Number 3, 1975; and John Johansen and Jan Erik Vahlne, "The Internationalization of the Firm: A Model of Knowledge Development and Increasing Foreign Market Commitments," *Journal of International Business Studies*, Volume 8, Number 1, 1977.

ther is the possibility that the parent itself may have evolved into a *transnational firm*, one that is owned by a coalition of investors located in different countries.[4]

Asea Brown Boveri (ABB) is an example of a Swedish-Swiss firm that has passed through the international evolutionary process all the way to being a transnational firm. ABB was formed through a merger of Sweden-based ASEA and Switzerland-based Brown Boveri in 1991. Both firms were already dominant players internationally in the electrotechnical and engineering industries. ABB has literally hundreds of foreign subsidiaries, which are managed on a much decentralized basis. ABB's "flat" organization structure and transnational ownership encourage local initiative, quick response, and decentralized FDI decisions. Although overall strategic direction is the legal responsibility of the parent firm, foreign subsidiaries play a major role in all decision making. Their input in turn is strongly influenced by their own membership in their local and worldwide industry networks.

How to Invest Abroad: Modes of Foreign Involvement

The globalization process includes a sequence of decisions regarding where production is to occur, who is to own or control intellectual property, and who is to own the actual production facilities. Exhibit 18.3 provides a roadmap to explain this FDI sequence.

EXHIBIT 18.3   The FDI Sequence: Foreign Presence and Foreign Investment

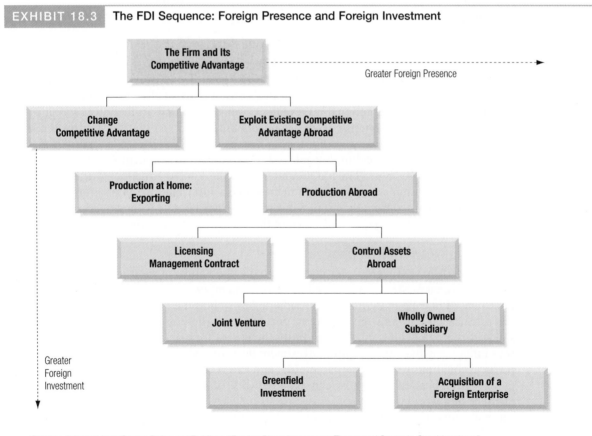

Source: Adapted from Gunter Dufey and R. Mirus, "Foreign Direct Investment: Theory and Strategic Considerations," unpublished, University of Michigan, 1985. Reprinted with permission from the authors. All rights reserved.

[4]Mats Forsgren, *Managing the Internationalization Process: The Swedish Case*, London: Routledge, 1989.

Exporting versus Production Abroad

There are several advantages to limiting a firm's activities to exports. *Exporting* has none of the unique risks facing FDI, joint ventures, strategic alliances, and licensing. Political risks are minimal. Agency costs, such as monitoring and evaluating foreign units, are avoided. The amount of front-end investment is typically lower than in other modes of foreign involvement. Foreign exchange risks remain, however. The fact that a significant share of exports (and imports) are executed between MNEs and their foreign subsidiaries and affiliates further reduces the risk of exports compared to other modes of involvement.

There are also disadvantages. A firm is not able to internalize and exploit the results of its research and development as effectively as if it invested directly. The firm also risks losing markets to imitators and global competitors that might be more cost efficient in production abroad and distribution. As these firms capture foreign markets, they might become so strong that they can export back into the domestic exporter's own market. Remember that defensive FDI is often motivated by the need to prevent this kind of predatory behavior as well as to preempt foreign markets before competitors can get started.

Licensing and Management Contracts versus Control of Assets Abroad

Licensing is a popular method for domestic firms to profit from foreign markets without the need to commit sizable funds. Since the foreign producer is typically wholly owned locally, political risk is minimized. In recent years, a number of host countries have demanded that MNEs sell their services in "unbundled form" rather than only through FDI. Such countries would like their local firms to purchase managerial expertise and knowledge of product and factor markets through management contracts, and purchase technology through licensing agreements.

The main disadvantage of licensing is that license fees are likely to be lower than FDI profits, although the return on the marginal investment might be higher. Other disadvantages include the following:

- Possible loss of quality control
- Establishment of a potential competitor in third-country markets
- Possible improvement of the technology by the local licensee, which then enters the original firm's home market
- Possible loss of opportunity to enter the licensee's market with FDI later
- Risk that technology will be stolen
- High agency costs

MNEs have not typically used licensing of independent firms. On the contrary, most licensing arrangements have been with their own foreign subsidiaries or joint ventures. License fees are a way to spread the corporate research and development cost among all operating units and a means of repatriating profits in a form more acceptable to some host countries than dividends.

Management contracts are similar to licensing insofar as they provide for some cash flow from a foreign source without significant foreign investment or exposure. Management contracts probably lessen political risk because repatriation of managers is easy. International consulting and engineering firms traditionally conduct their foreign business on the basis of a management contract.

Whether licensing and management contracts are cost effective compared to FDI depends on the price host countries will pay for the unbundled services. If the price were high enough, many firms would prefer to take advantage of market imperfections in an unbundled way, particularly in view of the lower political, foreign exchange, and business risks. Because we observe MNEs continuing to prefer FDI, we must assume that the price for selling unbundled services is still too low.

Why is the price of unbundled services too low? The answer may lie in the synergy created when services are bundled as FDI in the first place. Managerial expertise is often dependent on a delicate mix of organizational support factors that cannot be transferred abroad efficiently. Technology is a continuous process, but licensing usually captures only the technology at a particular point in time. Most important of all, however, economies of scale cannot be sold or transferred in small bundles. By definition they require large-scale operations. A relatively large operation in a small market can hardly achieve the same economies of scale as a large operation in a large market.

Despite the handicaps, some MNEs have successfully sold unbundled services. An example is sales of managerial expertise and technology to the OPEC countries. In this case, however, the OPEC countries are both willing and able to pay a price high enough to approach the returns on FDI (bundled services) while receiving only the lesser benefits of the unbundled services.

Joint Venture versus Wholly Owned Subsidiary

A *joint venture* is defined here as shared ownership in a foreign business. A foreign business unit that is partially owned by the parent company is typically termed a *foreign affiliate*. A foreign business unit that is 50% or more owned (and therefore controlled) by the parent company is typically designated a *foreign subsidiary*. A joint venture would therefore typically fall into the categorization of being a foreign affiliate but not a foreign subsidiary.

A joint venture between an MNE and a host country partner is a viable strategy if, and only if, the MNE finds the right local partner. Some of the obvious advantages of having a compatible local partner are as follows:

- The local partner understands the customs, mores, and institutions of the local environment. An MNE might need years to acquire such knowledge on its own with a wholly owned greenfield subsidiary.

- The local partner can provide competent management, not just at the top but also at the middle levels of management.

- If the host country requires that foreign firms share ownership with local firms or investors, 100% foreign ownership is not a realistic alternative to a joint venture.

- The local partner's contacts and reputation enhance access to the host country's capital markets.

- The local partner may possess technology that is appropriate for the local environment or perhaps can be used worldwide.

- The public image of a firm that is partially locally owned may improve its sales possibilities if the purpose of the investment is to serve the local market.

Despite this impressive list of advantages, joint ventures are not as common as wholly owned foreign subsidiaries because MNEs fear interference by the local partner in certain critical decision areas. Indeed, what is optimal from the viewpoint of the local venture may be suboptimal for the multinational operation as a whole. The following are the most important potential conflicts or difficulties:

- Political risk is increased rather than reduced if the wrong partner is chosen. Imagine the standing of joint ventures undertaken with the family or associates of

Suharto in Indonesia or Slobodan Milosevic in Serbia just before their overthrow. The local partner must be credible and ethical or the venture is worse off for being a joint venture.

- Local and foreign partners may have divergent views about the need for cash dividends, or about the desirability of growth financed from retained earnings versus new financing.

- Transfer pricing on products or components bought from or sold to related companies creates a potential for conflict of interest.

- Control of financing is another problem area. An MNE cannot justify its use of cheap or available funds raised in one country to finance joint venture operations in another country.

- Ability of a firm to rationalize production on a worldwide basis can be jeopardized if such rationalization would act to the disadvantage of local joint venture partners.

- Financial disclosure of local results might be necessary with locally traded shares, whereas if the firm is wholly owned from abroad such disclosure is not needed. Disclosure gives nondisclosing competitors an advantage in setting strategy.

Valuation of equity shares is difficult. How much should the local partner pay for its share? What is the value of contributed technology, or of contributed land in a country like China where all land is state owned? It is highly unlikely that foreign and host country partners have similar opportunity costs of capital, expectations about the required rate of return, or similar perceptions of appropriate premiums for business, foreign exchange, and political risks. Insofar as the venture is a component of the portfolio of each investor, its contribution to portfolio return and variance may be quite different for each.

Greenfield Investment versus Acquisition

A *greenfield investment* is defined as establishing a production or service facility starting from the ground up, that is, from a green field. A cross-border acquisition, in contrast, is defined as the purchase of an existing foreign-based firm or facility.

Strategic Alliances

The term *strategic alliance* conveys different meanings to different observers. In one form of cross-border strategic alliance, two firms exchange a share of ownership with one another. A strategic alliance can be a takeover defense if the prime purpose is for a firm to place some of its stock in stable and friendly hands. If that is all that occurs, it is just another form of portfolio investment.

In a more comprehensive strategic alliance, in addition to exchanging stock, the partners establish a separate joint venture to develop and manufacture a product or service. Numerous examples of such strategic alliances can be found in the automotive, electronics, telecommunications, and aircraft industries. Such alliances are particularly suited to high-tech industries where the cost of research and development is high and timely introduction of improvements is important.

A third level of cooperation might include joint marketing and servicing agreements in which each partner represents the other in certain markets. Some observers believe such arrangements begin to resemble the cartels prevalent in the 1920s and 1930s. Because they reduce competition, cartels have been banned by international agreements and many national laws.

Foreign Direct Investment Originating in Developing Countries

In recent years, developing countries with large home markets and some entrepreneurial talent have spawned a large number of rapidly growing and profitable MNEs. These MNEs have not only captured large shares of their home markets, but also have tapped global markets where they are increasingly competitive.

Exhibit 18.4 identifies 25 of the most successful MNEs, their countries of origin, their industry, and their strategy. Note that the countries of origin are dominated by those with the largest home markets. Of the 25 MNEs listed, eight originate in China, six in India, four in Brazil, and three in Russia. China and India also benefit from outsourcing that creates the infrastructure to support their home and export marketing capabilities.

EXHIBIT 18.4	Emerging Market Multinationals and Their Global Strategies			
Company	**Country**	**Industry**	**Revenues (bn$)**	**Corporate Strategy**
América Móvil	Mexico	Telecom services	$17.0	Export business model
Cemex	Mexico	Building materials	15.3	Export business model
China Mobile	China	Telecom services	30.1	Export business model
CNOOC	China	Oil and gas	8.7	Acquire offshore assets
CVRD	Brazil	Mining	15.1	Leverage natural resources
Embraer	Brazil	Aerospace	3.8	Engineering to innovation
Gazprom	Russia	Oil and gas	48.9	Leverage natural resources
Haier	China	Home appliances	12.8	Take brands global
Hisense	China	Electronics, appliances	4.2	Take brands global
Huawei Technologies	China	Telecom equipment	5.9	Engineering to innovation
Infosys Technologies	India	IT services	2.0	Engineering to innovation
Koc Holding	Turkey	Diversified industries	18.0	Take brands global
Lenovo Group	China	Computers, IT components	13.4	Take brands global
MMC Norilsk Nickel	Russia	Nonferrous metals	7.2	Leverage natural resources
Mahindra & Mahindra	India	Tractors, autos	2.9	Take brands global
Orascom Telecom	Egypt	Telecom services	3.3	Export business model
Petrobrás	Brazil	Oil and gas	56.3	Acquire offshore assets
Ranbaxy Laboratories	India	Pharmaceuticals	1.2	Engineering to innovation
Sadia	Brazil	Food and beverages	3.6	Leverage natural resources
Severstal	Russia	Steel	4.9	Leverage natural resources
Shanghai Baosteel	China	Steel	15.8	Acquire offshore assets
Tata Consultancy	India	IT services	2.8	Take brands global
Tata Motors	India	Autos	5.8	Engineering to innovation
Techtronic Industries	Hong Kong	Power tools	3.0	Target a niche
Wipro	India	IT services	2.3	Engineering to innovation

Source: "Emerging Giants," *Business Week*, July 31, 2006. This table is based on the work of the Boston Consulting Group, which has labeled this set "the new contenders."

In Exhibit 18.4, the Boston Consulting Group has identified six major corporate strategies employed by these emerging market MNEs:

1. *Taking brands global* means to establish primacy at home, expand in neighboring nations, and then move to the West.

2. *Engineering to innovation* means to tap low-cost talent at home, and then develop innovative products. *Global Finance in Practice 18.1* illustrates how Embraer (Brazil) has been able to innovate to compete with giants such as Airbus and Boeing.

3. *Leverage natural resources* means to take advantage of domestic oil, mineral, or timber resources to attain a cost edge, and then go global.

4. *Export business model* means to have a management system, and then replicate it globally through acquisitions.

GLOBAL FINANCE IN PRACTICE 18.1

Embraer of Brazil

A half-dozen freshly painted jets fill a mammoth hangar. One, emblazoned with the JetBlue (JBLU) logo, is being fitted with 100 leather seats and individual TV screens as well as 28 miles of electrical wiring. Lined up along the catwalk are planes for Delta Connection, Panama's Copa Airlines, United Express (UAL), and Republic Airways. This looks like a Boeing (BA) or Airbus assembly plant. But it's actually São José dos Campos, Brazil, home of Embraer, the world's third-largest aircraft maker.

Since 1969, Embraer has been the only company—and Brazil the only country—to make a successful entry into the commercial jet market. More than 1,000 of its planes are flying around the world, including a new generation of 118-seaters that are nibbling at the market served by Boeing Co.'s (BA) and Airbus' larger planes. Embraer delivered $446 million in profits on $3.83 billion in revenues last year, and 93% of those sales were outside Brazil.

How did Brazil succeed in such a capital-intensive, high-tech business? Surprisingly, wages, less than one-third of those at Boeing, are not the key factor. First, Embraer tapped into a long tradition of engineering spearheaded by the Brazilian air force's aerospace program created after World War II. For the past six years, Embraer has plowed 6% of revenues into research and development. It trains its newly hired engineers not only in aeronautics but also in market research and finance. Customers call the company's planes well designed, reliable, and cheaper to operate than rival aircraft.

Second, Brazilians who land jobs at Embraer know they're among the lucky few in a country with a limited number of high-tech positions. Customers sense the pride, says Dave Barger, JetBlue Airways Corp.'s chief operating officer. "If you work at Embraer in Brazil, you're something," he says. "It's a very cool culture. It plugs in nicely to JetBlue." Each time JetBlue takes delivery of a new Embraer aircraft, the airline donates $10,000 to an Embraer program that sends talented, poor students to college. JetBlue has ordered 101 planes, worth $3 billion.

Finally, Embraer has staying power. It has grown steadily since the former state-run company was privatized in 1994. Its high-performing, 50-seat regional jets put Embraer on the map, with more than 850 of them still flying. And its current wave of success stems from a decision in the late 1990s to invest $1 billion to design a new, larger plane that seats from 70 to 118 passengers for rapidly growing low-cost airlines.

Embraer engineers came up with a new fuselage design it called "double bubble" that allows plenty of head space, legroom, and luggage space, and eliminates the middle seat. More than 40 airlines provided input. That innovation has pushed Embraer ahead of archrival Bombardier of Canada and set the stage for an ambitious move into executive jets. "Years ago our competitors said: 'How dare those ugly ducklings from South America try to sell a jet in the Northern Hemisphere,'" says Satoshi Yokota, Embraer's executive vice-president for engineering and development. "Fortunately, they underestimated us."

Source: "An Ugly Duckling Finds Its Wings," *Business Week*, July 31, 2006, p. 44.

5. *Acquire offshore assets* means to become a global player by buying oil and mineral resources or partnering with other developing nation companies.

6. *Target a niche* means to focus on an industry, build scale and competence, and then expand globally by acquiring smaller players.

Foreign Direct Investment and Political Risk

In addition to business and foreign exchange risks, foreign direct investment faces political risks.

Defining Political Risk

For an MNE to identify, measure, and manage its political risks, it must define and classify these risks. Exhibit 18.5 classifies the political risks facing MNEs as being firm-specific, country-specific, or global-specific.

- *Firm-specific risks*, also known as *micro risks*, are those political risks that affect the MNE at the project or corporate level. *Governance risk,* due to goal conflict between an MNE and its host government, is the main political firm-specific risk. (An MNE also faces business risks and foreign exchange risks, which are covered extensively in other sections of this book.)

- *Country-specific risks*, also known as *macro risks*, are those political risks that also affect the MNE at the project or corporate level but originate at the country level. The two main political risk categories at the country level are *transfer risk* and *cultural and institutional risks.* Transfer risk concerns mainly the problem of blocked funds, but also peripherally sovereign credit risk. Cultural and institutional risks spring from ownership structure, human resource norms, religious heritage, nepotism and corruption, intellectual property rights, and protectionism.

- *Global-specific risks* are those political risks that affect the MNE at the project or corporate level but originate at the global level. Examples are terrorism, the antiglobalization movement, environmental concerns, poverty, and cyber attacks.

EXHIBIT 18.5   **Classification of Political Risks**

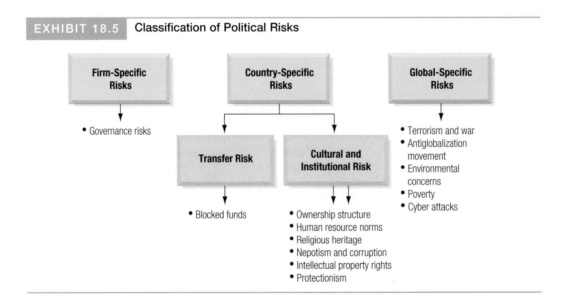

This method of classification differs sharply from the traditional method that classifies risks according to the disciplines of economics, finance, political science, sociology, and law. We prefer our classification system because it is easier to relate the identified political risks to existing and recommended strategies to manage these risks.

Assessing Political Risk

How can multinational firms anticipate government regulations that, from the firm's perspective, are discriminatory or wealth depriving? Normally a twofold approach is utilized.

At the macro level, prior to undertaking foreign direct investment, firms attempt to assess a host country's political stability and attitude toward foreign investors. At the micro level, firms analyze whether their firm-specific activities are likely to conflict with host-country goals as evidenced by existing regulations. The most difficult task, however, is to anticipate changes in host-country goal priorities, new regulations to implement reordered priorities, and the likely impact of such changes on the firm's operations.

Predicting Firm-Specific Risk (Micro Risk)

From the viewpoint of the MNE, assessing the political stability of a host country is only the first step, since the real objective is to anticipate the effect of political changes on activities of a specific firm. Indeed, different foreign firms operating within the same country may have very different degrees of vulnerability to changes in host-country policy or regulations. One does not expect a Kentucky Fried Chicken franchise to experience the same risk as a Ford manufacturing plant.

The need for firm-specific analyses of political risk has led to a demand for tailor-made studies undertaken in-house by professional political risk analysts. This demand is heightened by the observation that outside professional risk analysts rarely even agree on the degree of macro-political risk that exists in any set of countries.

In-house political risk analysts relate the macro risk attributes of specific countries to the particular characteristics and vulnerabilities of their client firms. Mineral extractive firms, manufacturing firms, multinational banks, private insurance carriers, and worldwide hotel chains are all exposed in fundamentally different ways to politically inspired restrictions. Even with the best possible firm-specific analysis, MNEs cannot be sure that the political or economic situation will not change. Thus, it is necessary to plan protective steps in advance to minimize the risk of damage from unanticipated changes.

Predicting Country-Specific Risk (Macro Risk)

Macro political risk analysis is still an emerging field of study. Political scientists in academia, industry, and government study country risk for the benefit of multinational firms, government foreign policy decision makers, and defense planners.

Political risk studies usually include an analysis of the historical stability of the country in question, evidence of present turmoil or dissatisfaction, indications of economic stability, and trends in cultural and religious activities. Data are usually assembled by reading local newspapers, monitoring radio and television broadcasts, reading publications from diplomatic sources, tapping the knowledge of outstanding expert consultants, contacting other business persons who have had recent experience in the host country, and finally conducting on-site visits.

Despite this impressive list of activities, the prediction track record of business firms, the diplomatic service, and the military has been spotty at best. When one analyzes trends, whether in politics or economics, the tendency is to predict an extension of the same trends into the future. It is a rare forecaster who is able to predict a cataclysmic change in direction. Who predicted the overthrow of Ferdinand Marcos in the Philippines? Indeed, who predicted the collapse of communism in the Soviet Union and the Eastern European satellites? Who predicted the fall of President Suharto in Indonesia in 1998 or Saddam Hussein in 2004?

Despite the difficulty of predicting country risk, the MNE must still attempt to do so in order to prepare itself for the unknown. A number of institutional services provide updated country risk ratings on a regular basis.

Predicting Global-Specific Risk

Predicting global-specific risk is even more difficult than predicting the other two types of political risk. Nobody predicted the surprise attacks on the World Trade Center and the Pentagon in the United States on September 11, 2001. On the other hand, the aftermath of this attack—the war on global terrorism, increased U.S. homeland security, and the destruction of part of the terrorist network in Afghanistan—was predictable. Nevertheless, we have come to expect future surprise terrorist attacks. U.S.-based MNEs are particularly exposed to not only Al Qaeda but also to other unpredictable groups willing to use terror or mob action to promote such diverse causes as antiglobalization, environmental protection, and even anarchy.

Since there is a great need to predict terrorism, we can expect to see a number of new indices, similar to country-specific indices, but devoted to ranking different types of terrorist threats, their locations, and potential targets.

Firm-Specific Risks

The firm-specific risks that confront MNEs include foreign exchange risks and governance risks. The various business and foreign exchange risks were detailed in Chapters 11–13. We focus our discussion here on governance risks.

Governance Risks

As introduced in Chapter 2, *governance risk* is the ability to exercise effective control over an MNE's operations within a country's legal and political environment. For an MNE, however, governance is a subject similar in structure to consolidated profitability—it must be addressed for the individual business unit and subsidiary, as well as for the MNE as a whole.

The most important type of governance risk for the MNE on the subsidiary level arises from a goal conflict between bona fide objectives of host governments and the private firms operating within their spheres of influence. Governments are normally responsive to a constituency of their citizens. Firms are responsive to a constituency of their owners and other stakeholders. The valid needs of these sets of constituents need not be the same, but governments set the rules. Consequently, governments impose constraints on the activities of private firms as part of their normal administrative and legislative functioning.

Historically, conflicts between objectives of MNEs and host governments have arisen over such issues as the firm's impact on economic development, perceived infringement on national sovereignty, foreign control of key industries, sharing or nonsharing of ownership and control with local interests, impact on a host country's balance of payments, influence on the foreign exchange value of its currency, control over export markets, use of domestic versus foreign executives and workers, and exploitation of national resources. Attitudes about conflicts are often colored by views about free enterprise versus state socialism, the degree of nationalism or internationalism present, or the place of religious views in determining appropriate economic and financial behavior.

The best approach to goal conflict management is to anticipate problems and negotiate understandings ahead of time. Different cultures apply different ethics to the question of honoring prior contracts, especially when they were negotiated with a previous administration. Nevertheless, prenegotiation of all conceivable areas of conflict provides a better basis for a successful future for both parties than does overlooking the possibility that divergent objectives will evolve over time. Preparation often includes negotiating investment agreements, buying investment insurance and guarantees, and designing risk-reducing operating strategies to be used after the foreign investment decision has been made.

Negotiating Investment Agreements

An *investment agreement* spells out specific rights and responsibilities of both the foreign firm and the host government. The presence of MNEs is as often sought by development-seeking host governments as a particular foreign location sought by an MNE. All parties have alternatives and so bargaining is appropriate.

An investment agreement should define policies on financial and managerial issues, including the following:

- The basis on which fund flows, such as dividends, management fees, royalties, patent fees, and loan repayments, may be remitted
- The basis for setting transfer prices
- The right to export to third-country markets
- Obligations to build, or fund, social and economic overhead projects, such as schools, hospitals, and retirement systems
- Methods of taxation, including the rate, the type, and the means by which the rate base is determined
- Access to host-country capital markets, particularly for long-term borrowing
- Permission for 100% foreign ownership versus required local ownership (joint venture) participation
- Price controls, if any, applicable to sales in the host-country markets
- Requirements for local sourcing versus import of raw materials and components
- Permission to use expatriate managerial and technical personnel, and to bring them and their personal possessions into the country free of exorbitant charges or import duties
- Provision for arbitration of disputes
- Provisions for planned divestment, should such be required, indicating how the going concern will be valued and to whom it will be sold

Investment Insurance and Guarantees: OPIC

MNEs can sometimes transfer political risk to a home-country public agency through an investment insurance and guarantee program. Many developed countries have such programs to protect investments by their nationals in developing countries.

The U.S. investment insurance and guarantee program is managed by the government-owned Overseas Private Investment Corporation (OPIC). OPIC's stated purpose is to mobilize and facilitate the participation of U.S. private capital and skills in the economic and social progress of less-developed friendly countries and areas, thereby complementing the developmental assistance of the United States. OPIC offers insurance coverage for four separate types of political risk, which have their own specific definitions for insurance purposes:

1. *Inconvertibility* is the risk that the investor will not be able to convert profits, royalties, fees, or other income, as well as the original capital invested, into dollars.

2. *Expropriation* is the risk that the host government takes a specific step that for one year prevents the investor or the foreign subsidiary from exercising effective control over use of the property.

3. *War, revolution, insurrection, and civil strife* coverage applies primarily to the damage of physical property of the insured, although in some cases inability of a foreign subsidiary to repay a loan because of a war may be covered.

4. *Business income* coverage provides compensation for loss of business income resulting from events of political violence that directly cause damage to the assets of a foreign enterprise.

Operating Strategies after the FDI Decision

Although an investment agreement creates obligations on the part of both foreign investor and host government, conditions change and agreements are often revised in the light of such changes. The changed conditions may be economic, or they may be the result of political changes within the host government. The firm that sticks rigidly to the legal interpretation of its original agreement may well find that the host government first applies pressure in areas not covered by the agreement and then possibly reinterprets the agreement to conform to the political reality of that country. Most MNEs, in their own self-interest, follow a policy of adapting to changing host-country priorities whenever possible.

The essence of such adaptation is anticipating host-country priorities and making the activities of the firm of continued value to the host country. Such an approach assumes the host government acts rationally in seeking its country's self-interest and is based on the idea that the firm should initiate reductions in goal conflict. Future bargaining position can be enhanced by careful consideration of policies in production, logistics, marketing, finance, organization, and personnel.

Local Sourcing. Host governments may require foreign firms to purchase raw material and components locally as a way to maximize value-added benefits and to increase local employment. From the viewpoint of the foreign firm trying to adapt to host-country goals, local sourcing reduces political risk, albeit at a trade-off with other factors. Local strikes or other turmoil may shut down the operation and such issues as quality control, high local prices because of lack of economies of scale, and unreliable delivery schedules become important. Often the MNE lowers political risk only by increasing its financial and commercial risk.

Facility Location. Production facilities may be located so as to minimize risk. The natural location of different stages of production may be resource-oriented, footloose, or market-oriented. Oil, for instance, is drilled in and around the Persian Gulf, Russia, Venezuela, and Indonesia. No choice exists for where this activity takes place. Refining, on the other hand, is footloose: A refining facility can be moved easily to another location or country. Whenever possible, oil companies have built refineries in politically safe countries, such as Western Europe, or small islands (such as Singapore or Curaçao), even though costs might be reduced by refining nearer the oil fields. They have traded reduced political risk and financial exposure for possibly higher transportation and refining costs.

Control of Transportation. Control of transportation has been an important means to reduce political risk. Oil pipelines that cross national frontiers, oil tankers, ore carriers, refrigerated ships, and railroads have all been controlled at times to influence the bargaining power of nations and companies.

Control of Technology. Control of key patents and processes is a viable way to reduce political risk. If a host country cannot operate a plant because it does not have technicians capable of running the process, or of keeping up with changed technology, abrogation of an investment agreement with a foreign firm is unlikely. Control of technology works best when the foreign firm is steadily improving its technology.

Control of Markets. Control of markets is a common strategy to enhance a firm's bargaining position. As effective as the OPEC cartel was in raising the price received for crude oil by its member countries in the 1970s, marketing was still controlled by the international oil companies. OPEC's need for the oil companies limited the degree to which its members could dictate terms. In more recent years OPEC members have established some marketing outlets of their own, such as Kuwait's extensive chain of Q8 gas stations in Europe.

Control of export markets for manufactured goods is also a source of leverage in dealings between MNEs and host governments. The MNE would prefer to serve world markets from sources of its own choosing, basing the decision on considerations of production cost, transportation, tariff barriers, political risk exposure, and competition. The selling pattern that maximizes long-run profits from the viewpoint of the worldwide firm rarely maximizes exports, or value added, from the perspective of the host countries. Some will argue that if the same plants were owned by local nationals and were not part of a worldwide integrated system, more goods would be exported by the host country. The contrary argument is that self-contained local firms might never obtain foreign market share because they lack economies of scale on the production side and are unable to market in foreign countries.

Brand Name and Trademark Control. Control of a brand name or trademark can have an effect almost identical to that of controlling technology. It gives the MNE a monopoly on something that may or may not have substantive value but quite likely represents value in the eyes of consumers. Ability to market under a world brand name is valuable for local firms and thus represents an important bargaining attribute for maintaining an investment position.

Thin Equity Base. Foreign subsidiaries can be financed with a thin equity base and a large proportion of local debt. If the debt is borrowed from locally owned banks, host-government actions that weaken the financial viability of the firm also endanger local creditors.

Multiple-Source Borrowing. If the firm must finance with foreign source debt, it may borrow from banks in a number of countries rather than just from home country banks. If, for example, debt is owed to banks in Tokyo, Frankfurt, London, and New York, nationals in a number of foreign countries have a vested interest in keeping the borrowing subsidiary financially strong. If the multinational is U.S.-owned, a fallout between the United States and the host government is less likely to cause the local government to move against the firm if it also owes funds to these other countries.

Country-Specific Risks: Transfer Risk

Country-specific risks affect all firms, domestic and foreign, that are resident in a host country. Exhibit 18.6 presents a taxonomy of most of the contemporary political risks and firm strategies that emanate from a specific country location. The main country-specific political risks are *transfer risk* and *cultural and institutional risks*.

Blocked Funds

Transfer risk is defined as limitations on the MNE's ability to transfer funds into and out of a host country without restrictions. When a government runs short of foreign exchange and cannot obtain additional funds through borrowing or attracting new foreign investment, it usually limits transfers of foreign exchange out of the country, a restriction known as *blocked funds*. In theory, this does not discriminate against foreign-owned firms because it applies to

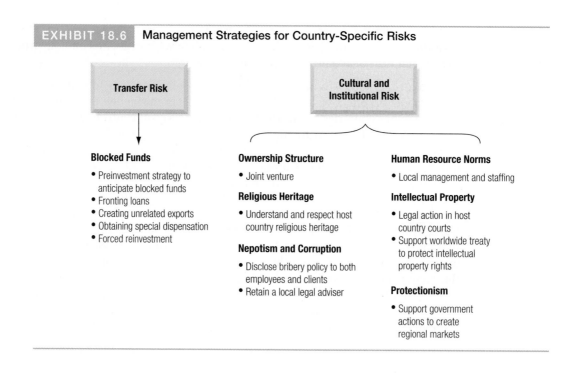

EXHIBIT 18.6   Management Strategies for Country-Specific Risks

Transfer Risk

Cultural and Institutional Risk

Blocked Funds
- Preinvestment strategy to anticipate blocked funds
- Fronting loans
- Creating unrelated exports
- Obtaining special dispensation
- Forced reinvestment

Ownership Structure
- Joint venture

Religious Heritage
- Understand and respect host country religious heritage

Nepotism and Corruption
- Disclose bribery policy to both employees and clients
- Retain a local legal adviser

Human Resource Norms
- Local management and staffing

Intellectual Property
- Legal action in host country courts
- Support worldwide treaty to protect intellectual property rights

Protectionism
- Support government actions to create regional markets

everyone; in practice, foreign firms have more at stake because of their foreign ownership. Depending on the size of a foreign exchange shortage, the host government might simply require approval of all transfers of funds abroad, thus reserving the right to set a priority on the use of scarce foreign exchange in favor of necessities rather than luxuries. In severe cases, the government might make its currency nonconvertible into other currencies, thereby fully blocking transfers of funds abroad. In between these positions are policies that restrict the size and timing of dividends, debt amortization, royalties, and service fees.

MNEs can react to the potential for blocked funds at three stages:

1. Prior to making an investment, a firm can analyze the effect of blocked funds on expected return on investment, the desired local financial structure, and optimal links with subsidiaries.

2. During operations a firm can attempt to move funds through a variety of repositioning techniques.

3. Funds that cannot be moved must be reinvested in the local country in a manner that avoids deterioration in their real value because of inflation or exchange depreciation.

Preinvestment Strategy to Anticipate Blocked Funds

Management can consider blocked funds in their capital budgeting analysis. Temporary blockage of funds normally reduces the expected net present value and internal rate of return on a proposed investment. Whether the investment should nevertheless be undertaken depends on whether the expected rate of return, even with blocked funds, exceeds the required rate of return on investments of the same risk class. Preinvestment analysis also includes the potential to minimize the effect of blocked funds by financing with local borrowing instead of parent equity, swap agreements, and other techniques to reduce local currency exposure and thus the need to repatriate funds. Sourcing and sales links with subsidiaries can be predetermined so as to maximize the potential for moving blocked funds.

Moving Blocked Funds

What can a multinational firm do to transfer funds out of countries having exchange or remittance restrictions? At least six popular strategies are used:

1. Providing alternative conduits for repatriating funds (analyzed in Chapter 21)
2. Transferring pricing goods and services between related units of the MNE (analyzed in Chapter 21)
3. Leading and lagging payments (described in Chapter 12)
4. Using fronting loans
5. Creating unrelated exports
6. Obtaining special dispensation

Fronting Loans. A *fronting loan* is a parent-to-subsidiary loan channeled through a financial intermediary, usually a large international bank. Fronting loans differ from parallel or back-to-back loans. The latter are offsetting loans between commercial businesses arranged outside the banking system. Fronting loans are sometimes referred to as *link financing*.

In a direct intracompany loan, a parent or sister subsidiary loans directly to the borrowing subsidiary, and at a later date the borrowing subsidiary repays the principal and interest. In a fronting loan, by contrast, the "lending" parent or subsidiary deposits funds in, say, a London bank, and that bank loans the same amount to the borrowing subsidiary in the host country. From the London bank's point of view the loan is risk-free, because the bank has 100% collateral in the form of the parent's deposit. In effect the bank fronts for the parent—hence the name *fronting loan*. Interest paid by the borrowing subsidiary to the bank is usually slightly higher than the rate paid by the bank to the parent, allowing the bank a margin for expenses and profit.

The bank chosen for the fronting loan is usually in a neutral country, away from both the lender's and the borrower's legal jurisdiction. Use of fronting loans increases chances for repayment should political turmoil occur between the home and host countries. Government authorities are more likely to allow a local subsidiary to repay a loan to a large international bank in a neutral country than to allow the same subsidiary to repay a loan directly to its parent. To stop payment to the international bank would hurt the international credit image of the country, whereas to stop payment to the parent corporation would have minimal impact on that image and might even provide some domestic political advantage.

Creating Unrelated Exports. Another approach to blocked funds that benefits both the subsidiary and host country is the creation of unrelated exports. Because the main reason for stringent exchange controls is usually a host country's persistent inability to earn hard currencies, anything an MNE can do to create new exports from the host country helps the situation and provides a potential means to transfer funds out.

Some new exports can often be created from present productive capacity with little or no additional investment, especially if they are in product lines related to existing operations. Other new exports may require reinvestment or new funds, although if the funds reinvested consist of those already blocked, little is lost in the way of opportunity costs.

Special Dispensation. If all else fails and the multinational firm is investing in an industry that is important to the economic development of the host country, the firm may bargain for special dispensation to repatriate some portion of the funds that otherwise would be blocked. Firms in "desirable" industries such as telecommunications, semiconductor manufacturing, instrumentation, pharmaceuticals, or other research and high-technology industries may receive preference over firms in mature industries. The amount of preference received depends on bargaining among the informed parties, the government and the business firm, either of which is free to back away from the proposed investment if unsatisfied with the terms.

Self-Fulfilling Prophecies. In seeking escape routes for blocked funds—or for that matter in trying to position funds through any of the techniques discussed in this chapter—the MNE may increase political risk and cause a change from partial blockage to full blockage. The possibility of such a self-fulfilling cycle exists any time a firm takes action that, no matter how legal, thwarts the underlying intent of politically motivated controls. In the statehouses of the world, as in the editorial offices of the local press and TV, MNEs and their subsidiaries are always a potential scapegoat.

Forced Reinvestment. If funds are indeed blocked from transfer into foreign exchange, they are by definition reinvested. Under such a situation the firm must find local opportunities that will maximize rate of return for a given acceptable level of risk.

If blockage is expected to be temporary, the most obvious alternative is to invest in local money market instruments. Unfortunately, in many countries such instruments are not available in sufficient quantity or with adequate liquidity. In some cases, government treasury bills, bank deposits, and other short-term instruments have yields that are kept artificially low relative to local rates of inflation or probable changes in exchange rates. Thus, the firm often loses real value during the period of blockage.

If short- or intermediate-term portfolio investments, such as bonds, bank time deposits, or direct loans to other companies, are not possible, investment in additional production facilities may be the only alternative. Often this investment is what the host country is seeking by its exchange controls, even if the existence of exchange controls is by itself counterproductive to the idea of additional foreign investment. Examples of forced direct reinvestment can be cited for Peru, where an airline invested in hotels and in maintenance facilities for other airlines; for Turkey, where a fish canning company constructed a plant to manufacture cans needed for packing the catch; and for Argentina, where an automobile company integrated vertically by acquiring a transmission manufacturing plant previously owned by a supplier.

If investment opportunities in additional production facilities are not available, funds may simply be used to acquire other assets expected to increase in value with local inflation. Typical purchases might be land, office buildings, or commodities that are exported to global markets. Even inventory stockpiling might be a reasonable investment, given the low opportunity cost of the blocked funds.

Country-Specific Risks: Cultural and Institutional Risks

When investing in some of the emerging markets, MNEs that are resident in the most industrialized countries face serious risks because of cultural and institutional differences. Among many such differences are the following:

- Differences in allowable ownership structures
- Differences in human resource norms
- Differences in religious heritage
- Nepotism and corruption in the host country
- Protection of intellectual property rights
- Protectionism

Ownership Structure

Historically, many countries have required that MNEs share ownership of their foreign subsidiaries with local firms or citizens. Thus, joint ventures were the only way an MNE could operate in some host countries. Prominent countries that used to require majority local ownership were Japan, Mexico, China, India, and Korea. This requirement has been eliminated or modified in more recent years by these countries and most others. However, firms in certain industries are still either excluded from ownership completely or must accept being a minority owner. These industries are typically related to national defense, agriculture, banking, or other sectors that are deemed critical for the host nation. Even the United States would not welcome foreign ownership of large key defense-related firms such as Boeing Aircraft.

Human Resource Norms

MNEs are often required by host countries to employ a certain proportion of host country citizens rather than staffing mainly with foreign expatriates. It is often very difficult to fire local employees due to host country labor laws and union contracts. This lack of flexibility to downsize in response to business cycles affects both MNEs and their local competitors. It also qualifies as a country-specific risk.

Cultural differences can also inhibit an MNE's staffing policies. For example, it is somewhat difficult for a woman manager to be accepted by local employees and managers in many Middle Eastern countries. The most extreme example of discrimination against women was highlighted in Afghanistan during the Taliban regime. Since the Taliban's downfall in late 2001, several women have been suggested for important government roles.

Religious Heritage

The current hostile environment for MNEs in some Middle Eastern countries such as Iran, Iraq, and Syria is being fed by some extremist Muslim clerics who are enraged about the continuing violence in Israel and the occupied Arab territories. However, the root cause of these conflicts is a mixture of religious fervor for some and politics for others. Although it is popular to blame the Muslim religion for its part in fomenting the conflict, a number of Middle Eastern countries, such as Egypt, Saudi Arabia, and Jordan, are relatively passive when it comes to *jihads*—calls for Muslims to attack the infidels (Jews and Christians). Osama bin Laden's call for jihad against the United States has not generated any great interest on the part of moderate Muslims. Indeed, Turkey, a Muslim country, has had a secular government for many decades and it strongly supported efforts to rid the world of bin Laden.

Despite religious differences, MNEs have operated successfully in emerging markets, especially in extractive and natural resource industries, such as oil, natural gas, minerals, and forest products. The main MNE strategy is to understand and respect the host country's religious traditions.

Nepotism and Corruption

MNEs must deal with endemic nepotism and corruption in a number of countries. Indonesia was famous for nepotism and corruption under the now deposed Suharto government. A number of African countries had a history of nepotism and corruption after they threw out their colonial governments following World War II. China and Russia have launched well-publicized crackdowns on these practices. Presently, one of the worst cases is that of Zimbabwe (formerly southern Rhodesia). *Global Finance in Practice 18.2* illustrates how that country's currency has deteriorated to reflect the destructive influence of nepotism and corruption.

GLOBAL FINANCE IN PRACTICE 18.2

Zimbabwe's Disposable Currency

Once one of the most prosperous countries in Africa, Zimbabwe seems to be nearing economic collapse.

What does it feel like to hold a few million dollars in your hands? If you're in Zimbabwe, and your wages are in Zimbabwean dollars, not very good. With hyperinflation running at 4,500 percent on an annual basis, all this cash is worth less than $100. Once one of the most prosperous countries in Africa, Zimbabwe seems to be nearing economic collapse. Unemployment is estimated at 80 percent. Electricity has been rationed to just four hours a day. A loaf of bread costs 44,000 Zimbabwean dollars, about 18 cents at black-market exchange rates—or $176 at the official rate.

To earn public support ahead of elections scheduled for March, President Robert Mugabe, who has been in power since 1980, imposed price controls in late June, which have been largely ignored. He also proposed legislation to transfer 51 percent of foreign-owned firms to local ownership and establish a government fund to help citizens buy stock in public companies.

The government would be able to reject any mergers, acquisitions or new investments in which indigenous Zimbabweans do not hold a majority stake. To many it is an echo of Mugabe's seizure of thousands of white-owned farms, mostly without compensation, in what he called a redistribution of land to poor blacks. Instead, choice farms were handed to government officials, and food production plummeted, leading to a humanitarian crisis. Along with their shrinking buying power, Zimbabweans now have the lowest life expectancy in the world: It has dropped under Mugabe from 60 to 37 for men and from 65 to 34 for women.

Source: "Zimbabwe's Disposable Currency," *Fortune*, August 6, 2007.

Bribery is not limited to emerging markets. It is also a problem in even the most industrialized countries, including the United States and Japan. In fact, the United States has an antibribery law that would imprison any U.S. business executive found guilty of bribing a foreign government official. This law was passed in reaction to an attempt by Lockheed Aircraft to bribe a Japanese Prime Minister.

Managing Bribery. MNEs are caught in a dilemma. Should they employ bribery if their local competitors use this strategy? The following are alternative strategies:

- Refuse bribery outright, or else demands will quickly multiply.
- Retain a local adviser to diffuse demands by local officials, customs agents, and other business partners.
- Do not count on the justice system in many emerging markets, because Western-oriented contract law may not agree with local norms.
- Educate both management and local employees about whatever bribery policy the firm intends to follow.

Intellectual Property Rights

Rogue businesses in some host countries have historically infringed on the *intellectual property rights* of both MNEs and individuals. *Intellectual property rights* grant the exclusive use of patented technology and copyrighted creative materials. Examples of patented technology are unique manufactured products, processing techniques, and prescription pharmaceutical drugs. Examples of copyrighted creative materials are software programs, educational materials (textbooks), and entertainment products (music, film, and art).

MNEs and individuals need to protect their intellectual property rights through the legal process. However, courts in some countries have historically not done a fair job of protecting intellectual property rights of anyone, much less of foreign MNEs. In those countries the legal process is costly and subject to bribery.

The agreement on Trade-Related Aspects of Intellectual Property Rights (TRIPS) to protect intellectual property rights has recently been ratified by most major countries. China signed the treaty as one of the conditions it needed to meet to join the World Trade Organization (WTO) in 2001. It remains to be seen whether host governments are strong enough to enforce their official efforts to stamp out intellectual piracy. Complicating this task is the thin line that exists between the real item being protected and look-alikes or generic versions of the same item.

Protectionism

Protectionism is defined as the attempt by a national government to protect certain of its designated industries from foreign competition. Industries that are protected are usually related to defense, agriculture, and "infant" industries.

Defense. Even though the United States is a vocal proponent of open markets, a foreign firm proposing to buy Lockheed Missile Division or other critical defense suppliers would not be welcome. The same attitude exists in many other countries, such as France, which has always wanted to maintain an independent defense capability.

Agriculture. Agriculture is another sensitive industry. No MNE would be foolish enough to attempt to buy agricultural properties, such as rice operations, in Japan. Japan has desperately tried to maintain an independent ability to feed its population. Agriculture is the "Mother Earth" industry that most countries want to protect for their own citizens.

Infant Industries. The traditional protectionist argument is that newly emerging industries need protection from foreign competition until they can get firmly established. The infant industry argument is usually directed at limiting imports but not necessarily MNEs. In fact, most host countries encourage MNEs to establish operations in industries that do not presently exist in the host country. Sometimes the host country offers foreign MNEs infant-industry status for a limited number of years. This status could lead to tax subsidies, construction of infrastructure, employee training, and other aids to help the MNE get started. Host countries are especially interested in attracting MNEs that promise to export, either to their own foreign subsidiaries elsewhere or to unrelated parties.

Tariff Barriers. The traditional methods for countries to implement protectionist barriers were through tariff and nontariff regulations. Negotiations under the General Agreements on Tariffs and Trade (GATT) have greatly reduced the general level of tariffs over the past decades. This process continues today under the auspices of the WTO. However, many nontariff barriers remain.

Nontariff Barriers. Nontariff barriers, which restrict imports by something other than a financial cost, are often difficult to identify because they are promulgated as health, safety, or sanitation requirements.

Strategies to Manage Protectionism. MNEs have only a very limited ability to overcome host country protectionism. However, MNEs do enthusiastically support efforts to reduce protectionism by joining together in regional markets. The best examples of regional markets are the European Union (EU), the North American Free Trade Association (NAFTA), and the Latin American Free Trade Association (MERCOSUR). Among the objectives of regional markets are elimination of internal trade barriers, such as tariffs and nontariff barriers, as well as the free movement of citizens for employment purposes. External trade barriers still exist.

The EU is trying to become a "United States of Europe," with a single internal market without barriers. It is not quite there, although the European Monetary Union and the euro have almost eliminated monetary policy differences. The EU still tolerates differences in fiscal policies, legal systems, and cultural identities. In any case, the movement toward regional markets is very favorable for MNEs serving those markets with foreign subsidiaries.

Global-Specific Risks

Global-specific risks faced by MNEs have come to the forefront in recent years. Exhibit 18.7 summarizes some of these risks and the strategies that can be used to manage them. The most visible recent risk was, of course, the attack by terrorists on the twin towers of the World Trade Center in New York on September 11, 2001. Many MNEs had major operations in the World Trade Center and suffered heavy casualties among their employees. In addition to terrorism, other global-specific risks include the antiglobalization movement, environmental concerns, poverty in emerging markets, and cyber attacks on computer information systems.

Terrorism and War

Although the World Trade Center attack and its aftermath, the war in Afghanistan, and the war in Iraq have affected nearly everyone in the world, many other acts of terrorism have been committed in recent years. More terrorist acts are expected to occur in the future. Particularly exposed are the foreign subsidiaries of MNEs and their employees. As mentioned earlier, foreign subsidiaries are especially exposed to war, ethnic strife, and terrorism because they are symbols of their respective parent countries.

No MNE has the tools to avert terrorism. Hedging, diversification, insurance, and the like are not suited to the task. Therefore, MNEs must depend on governments to fight terrorism and protect their foreign subsidiaries (and now even the parent firm). In return, governments expect financial, material, and verbal support from MNEs to support antiterrorist legislation and proactive initiatives to destroy terrorist cells wherever they exist.

Crisis Planning

MNEs can be subject to damage by being in harm's way. Nearly every year one or more host countries experience some form of ethnic strife, outright war with other countries, or terror-

---

EXHIBIT 18.7   Management Strategies for Global-Specific Risks

Terrorism and War
- Support government efforts to fight terrorism and war
- Crisis planning
- Cross-border supply chain integration

Antiglobalization
- Support government efforts to reduce trade barriers
- Recognize that MNEs are the targets

Environmental Concerns
- Show sensitivity to environmental concerns
- Support government efforts to maintain a level playing field for pollution controls

Poverty
- Provide stable, relatively well-paying jobs
- Establish the strictest of occupational safety standards

Cyber Attacks
- No effective strategy except Internet security efforts
- Support government anti-cyber attack efforts

Corporate Social Responsibility
- Corporate Sustainability

MNE movement toward multiple primary objectives:
Profitability, Sustainable Development, Corporate Social Responsibility

ism. It seems that foreign MNEs are often singled out as symbols of oppression because they represent their parent country, especially if it is the United States.

Resolving war and ethnic strife is beyond the ability of MNEs. Instead, they need to take defensive steps to limit the damage. *Crisis planning* has become a major activity for MNEs at both the foreign subsidiary and parent firm levels. Crisis planning means educating management and employees about how to react to various scenarios of violence. For example, MNE units must know how to stay in communication with each other; how to protect the MNE's property; how to escape the country; and how to protect themselves by maintaining a low profile.

Cross-Border Supply Chain Integration

The drive to increase efficiency in manufacturing has driven many MNEs to adopt just-in-time (JIT) near-zero inventory systems. Focusing on *inventory velocity*, the speed at which inventory moves through a manufacturing process, arriving only as needed and not before, has allowed these MNEs to generate increasing profits and cash flows with less capital being bottled up in the production cycle. This finely tuned supply chain system, however, is subject to significant political risk if the supply chain extends across borders.

Supply Chain Interruptions. Consider the cases of Dell Computer, Ford Motor Company, Dairy Queen, Apple Computer, Herman Miller, and The Limited in the days following the terrorist attacks of September 11, 2001. An immediate result of the event was the grounding of all aircraft into or out of the United States. Similarly, the land (Mexico and Canada) and sea borders of the United States were also shut down and not reopened for several days in some specific sites. Ford Motor Company shut down five of its manufacturing plants in the days following September 11 because of inadequate inventories of critical automotive inputs supplied from Canada. Dairy Queen experienced such significant delays in key confectionary ingredients that many of its stores were also temporarily closed.

Dell Computer, with one of the most highly acclaimed and admired virtually integrated supply chains, depends on computer parts and subassembly suppliers and manufacturers in Mexico and Canada to fulfill its everyday assembly and sales needs. In recent years, Dell has carried less than three full day's sales of total inventory—by cost-of-goods value. Suppliers are integrated electronically with Dell's order fulfillment system, and they deliver required components and subassemblies as sales demands require. But with the closure of borders and grounding of air freight, the company was brought to a near standstill because of its supply chain's reliance on the ability to treat business units and suppliers in different countries as if they were all part of a single seamless political unit.

As a result of these newly learned lessons, many MNEs are now evaluating the degree of exposure their supply chains possess in regard to cross-border stoppages or other cross-border political events. These companies are not, however, about to abandon JIT. It is estimated that U.S. companies alone have saved more than $1 billion a year in inventory carrying costs by using JIT methods over the past decade. This substantial benefit is now being weighed against the costs and risks associated with the post-September 11 supply chain interruptions.

To avoid suffering a similar fate in the future, manufacturers, retailers, and suppliers are now employing a range of tactics:

- **Inventory Management.** Manufacturers and assemblers are considering carrying more buffer inventory in order to hedge against supply and production-line disruptions. Retailers, meanwhile, should think about the timing and frequency of their replenishment. Rather than stocking up across the board, companies are focusing on the most critical parts to the product or service, and on those components that are uniquely available only from international sources.

- **Sourcing.** Manufacturers are now being more selective about where the critical inputs to their products come from. Although sourcing strategies will have to vary by location, firms are attempting to work more closely with existing suppliers to minimize cross-border exposures and reduce the potential costs with future stoppages.

- **Transportation.** Retailers and manufacturers alike are reassessing their cross-border shipping arrangements. For example, many inputs that currently are carried by passenger flights may be precluded from cohabitation on these flights in the future. Although the mode of transportation employed is a function of value, volume, and weight, many firms are now reassessing whether higher costs for faster shipment balance out the more tenuous their delivery under airline stoppages from labor, terrorist, or even bankruptcy disruptions in the future.

Antiglobalization Movement

During the past decade, there has been a growing negative reaction by some groups to reduced trade barriers and efforts to create regional markets, particularly to NAFTA and the European Union. NAFTA has been vigorously opposed by those sectors of the labor movement that could lose jobs to Mexico. Opposition within the European Union centers on loss of cultural identity, dilution of individual national control as new members are admitted, overcentralization of power in a large bureaucracy in Brussels, and most recently the disappearance of individual national currencies in mid-2002, when the euro became the only currency in 12 of the 15 member nations.

The antiglobalization movement has become more visible following riots in Seattle during the 2001 annual meeting of the World Trade Organization. Antiglobalization forces were not solely responsible for these riots, or for subsequent riots in Quebec and Prague in 2001. Other disaffected groups, such as environmentalists and even anarchists, joined in to make their causes more visible.

MNEs do not have the tools to combat antiglobalization movement. Indeed, they are blamed for fostering the problem in the first place. Once again, MNEs must rely on governments and crisis planning to manage these risks.

Environmental Concerns

MNEs have been accused of exporting their environmental problems to other countries. The accusation is that MNEs frustrated by pollution controls in their home country have relocated these activities to countries with weaker pollution controls. Another accusation is that MNEs contribute to the problem of global warming. However, that accusation applies to all firms in all countries. It is based on the manufacturing methods employed by specific industries and on consumers' desire for certain products such as large automobiles and sport vehicles that are not fuel efficient.

Once again, solving environmental problems is dependent on governments passing legislation and implementing pollution control standards. In 2001, the Kyoto Treaty, which attempted to reduce global warming, was ratified by most nations, with the notable exception of the United States. However, the United States has promised to combat global warming using its own strategies. The United States objected to provisions in the worldwide treaty that allowed emerging nations to follow less restrictive standards, while the economic burden would fall on the most industrialized countries, particularly the United States.

Poverty

MNEs have located foreign subsidiaries in countries plagued by extremely uneven income distribution. At one end of the spectrum is an elite class of well-educated, well-connected, and productive people. At the other end is a very large class of people living at or below the poverty level. They lack education, social and economic infrastructure, and political power.

MNEs might be contributing to this disparity by employing the elite class to manage their operations. On the other hand, MNEs are creating relatively stable and well-paying jobs for those who were otherwise unemployed and living below the poverty level. Despite being accused of supporting sweatshop conditions, MNEs usually compare favorably to their local competitors. For example, Nike, one of the targeted MNEs, usually pays better, provides more fringe benefits, maintains higher safety standards, and educates its workforce to allow personnel to advance up the career ladder. Of course, Nike cannot manage a country's poverty problems overall, but it can improve conditions for some people.

Cyber Attacks

The rapid growth of the Internet has fostered a whole new generation of scam artists and cranks who disrupt the usefulness of the World Wide Web. This is a domestic and an international problem. MNEs can face costly cyber attacks because of their visibility and the complexity of their internal information systems.

At this time, we know of no uniquely international strategies that MNEs can use to combat cyber attacks. MNEs are using the same strategies to manage foreign cyber attacks as they use for domestic attacks. Once again, they must rely on governments to control cyber attacks.

Corporate Social Responsibility

The first years of the twenty-first century have seen a rebirth in society's reflections on business. One of the most audible debates has been that regarding sustainable development, the principle that economic development today should not compromise the ability of future generations to achieve and enjoy similar standards of living. Although sustainable development initially focused on environmental concerns, it has evolved to include equal concerns that "incorporate the ambition for a just and caring society."[5] Although these debates have typically remained within areas of economic development, the debate in business circles has centered on corporate social responsibility.

SUMMARY POINTS

- In order to invest abroad, a firm must have a sustainable competitive advantage in the home market. This must be strong enough and transferable enough to overcome the disadvantages of operating abroad.

- Competitive advantages stem from economies of scale and scope arising from large size; managerial and marketing expertise; superior technology; financial strength; differentiated products; and competitiveness of the home market.

- The OLI Paradigm is an attempt to create an overall framework to explain why MNEs choose FDI rather than serve foreign markets through alternative modes, such as licensing, joint ventures, strategic alliances, management contracts, and exporting.

- Finance-specific strategies are directly related to the OLI Paradigm, including both proactive and reactive financial strategies.

- The decision about where to invest is influenced by economic and behavioral factors, as well as the stage of a firm's historical development.

- Psychic distance plays a role in determining the sequence of FDI and later reinvestment. As firms learn from their early investments they venture further afield and are willing to risk larger commitments.

- The most internationalized firms can be viewed from a network perspective. The parent firm and each of the foreign subsidiaries are members of networks. The networks are composed of relationships within a worldwide industry, within the host countries with suppliers and customers, and within the multinational firm itself.

- Exporting avoids political risk but not foreign exchange risk. It requires the least up-front investment but it might eventually lose markets to imitators and

[5]Dickson, Tim, "The Financial Case for Behaving Responsibly," *Financial Times*, August 19, 2002, p. 5.

global competitors that might be more cost efficient in production abroad and distribution.

- Alternative (to wholly owned foreign subsidiaries) modes of foreign involvement exist. They include joint venture, strategic alliances, licensing, management contracts, and traditional exporting.

- Licensing enables a firm to profit from foreign markets without a major front-end investment. However, disadvantages include limited returns, possible loss of quality control and potential of establishing a future competitor.

- The success of a joint venture depends primarily on the right choice of a partner. For this reason and a number of issues related to possible conflicts in decision making between a joint venture and a multinational parent, the 100%-owned foreign subsidiary approach is more common.

- The completion of the European Internal Market at end-of-year 1992 induced a surge in cross-border entry through strategic alliances. Although some forms of strategic alliances share the same characteristics as joint ventures, they often also include an exchange of stock.

- There are six major strategies employed by emerging market MNEs: taking brands global; engineering to innovation; leveraging natural resources; developing an export business model; acquiring offshore assets; and targeting a market niche.

- Political risks can be defined by classifying them on three levels: *firm-specific*, *country-specific*, and *global-specific*.

- *Firm-specific risks*, also known as *micro risks*, affect the MNE at the project or corporate level.

- *Country-specific risks*, also known as *macro risks*, affect the MNE at the project or corporate level but originate at the country level.

- *Global-specific risks* affect the MNE at the project or corporate level but originate at the global level.

- The main firm-specific risk is *governance risk*, which is the ability to exercise control over the MNE as a whole, globally, and within a specific country's legal and political environment on the individual subsidiary level.

- The most important type of governance risk arises from a goal conflict between bona fide objectives of governments and private firms.

- The main tools used to manage goal conflict are to negotiate an investment agreement; to purchase investment insurance and guarantees; and to modify operating strategies in production, logistics, marketing, finance, organization, and personnel.

- The main *country-specific risks* are *transfer risk*, known as *blocked funds*, and certain cultural and institutional risks.

- Blocked funds can be managed by any of five strategies: 1) including blocked funds in their original capital budgeting analysis; 2) fronting loans; 3) creating unrelated exports; 4) obtaining special dispensation; and 5) planning for forced reinvestment.

- Cultural and institutional risks emanate from host country policies with respect to ownership structure, human resource norms, religious heritage, nepotism and corruption, intellectual property rights, and protectionism.

- Managing cultural and institutional risks requires the MNE to understand the differences, take legal actions in host country courts, support worldwide treaties to protect intellectual property rights, and support government efforts to create regional markets.

- The main global-specific risks are currently caused by terrorism and war, the antiglobalization movement, environmental concerns, poverty, and cyber attacks.

- In order to manage global-specific risks, an MNE should adopt a crisis plan to protect its employees and property and to secure its supply chain integrity. However, the MNE largely relies on government to protect its citizens and firms from global-specific threats.

MINI-CASE   Mattel's Chinese Sourcing Crisis of 2007

Mattel was forced to deliver a humiliating public apology to 'the Chinese people' on Friday over the damaging succession of product recalls of China-made toys that

the US toy maker has announced in recent months. In a carefully stage-managed meeting in Beijing with a senior Chinese official, which, unusually, was open to the media, Thomas Debrowski, Mattel's executive vice-president for worldwide operations, read out a prepared text that played down the role of Chinese factories in the recalls.

"Mattel takes full responsibility for these recalls and apologises personally to you, the Chinese people, and all of our customers who received the toys," Mr Debrowski said. The apology was in stark contrast to recent comments from Robert Eckert, Mattel's chief executive. In testimony to the US Senate last week, he suggested that the fault for the group's recent product recalls lay with outside contractors. "We were let down, and so we let you down," he said.

—"Mattel in Apology to Chinese," Financial Times, September 22, 2007, p. 15.

Bob Eckert, CEO of Mattel (US), had a problem—a big problem. Mattel had discovered on July 30 that a number of its toys manufactured in China contained lead paint. The following month had seen a series of recalls, rising political tensions between the United States and Chinese governments, and a suicide. But no company had been in China longer than Mattel; the original Barbie had been created there in 1959. Mattel had a depth of experience and a longevity of relationships which should have prevented it. In the end it was those relationships and that longevity which may have contributed to the product safety failures.

Mattel's Sourcing

Mattel had long known the risks associated with a toy product's value stream. Toys were based on a global supply chain that was highly sensitive to petrochemical (plastics) and labor input costs, environmental and human rights sensitivities to socially responsible and sustainable business practices, transportation and logistics disruptions, border crossings, cost and time to market—all of which added to risk.

Growing concerns and controversies over labor practices had led Mattel to establish its *Global Manufacturing Principles* in 1997, in which it established principles and practices for all companies and sites that manufactured Mattel products, either company owned or licensed manufacturing. The *Global Manufacturing Principles* (GMP) were established to confirm the company's commitment to responsible manufacturing practices around the world. To support the GMP standards, the company created the Mattel Independent Monitoring Council (MIMCO). Mattel was highly regarded as the first global consumer products company to apply the system to both its own facilities and core contractors on a worldwide basis. But the problems had still happened.

The crisis had actually begun in June when U.S. toy maker RC2 recalled 1.5 million *Thomas the Tank Engine* products made in Guangdong, the Chinese province adjacent to Hong Kong and long the center for contract manufacturing by Western firms. Mattel had then followed with a disturbing series of three product recalls in less than one month.

- The first recall of 1.5 million toys of 83 different models was made on August 2, most of which were produced by Lee Der Industrial, a Mattel supplier for 15 years. The toys were found to contain high levels of lead paint, a chemical banned many years ago, but still secretly used by manufacturers around the globe in an effort to reduce costs (paint with lead often dried glossier and faster). Lee Der Industrial had knowingly used paint that was not approved by Mattel.

- The second recall, amounting to more than 18 million toys worldwide, was announced on August 14, only two weeks following the first recall. Products recalled were primarily products of Early Light Industrial in China, a Mattel partner for 20 years. The recall included just 436,000 Pixar toy cars over lead paint concerns, but nearly 18 million over the concern that small magnets on some products could be ingested. Early Light had subcontracted components of the Pixar cars to Hong Li Da, another Chinese company, that had actually used lead paint. This second announcement resulted in an immediate 6% drop in Mattel's share price on the New York Stock Exchange.

- The third recall, announced on September 4, was for 800,000 toys, most of which were accessories for Barbie dolls. Mattel explained that further product testing had indicated they possessed "impermissible levels" of lead paint. The products originated from seven different Chinese factories. This third announcement had prompted the EU to announce a two-month review of toy product safety for toys sold within the EU, regardless of the source of their manufacture.

Chinese manufacturers were the source of 65% of Mattel's toys. Of those, about one-half was owned by Mattel, and one-half was manufactured product for the company under a variety of licensed manufacturing agreements. Mattel still owns the 12 factories that make the majority of its core products like Barbie and Hot Wheels. But for the other roughly 50% of its product lines it relies on a set of vendors, which had included Lee Der Industrial and First Light. For long-standing relationships like those with Lee Der and First Light, Mattel allowed the companies to do most of their own product testing as a result of the long-term relationship and trust between the two parties. But regardless of who owned the actual manufacturing facility, many of the non-Mattel vendors had in-turn outsourced various components and parts to other businesses. All of the businesses in the complex supply chain were facing the same competitive cost pressures in China—rising wage rates, a shortage of skilled labor in coastal provinces, escalating material and commodity prices—some of which may have been the motivation for suppliers to cut corners and costs.

It was therefore not clear that outsourced manufacturing was really the culprit in this case, or simply the fact that much of the manufacturing and material industries operating throughout China were relatively fragmented, newly developed, under heavy cost pressures, and generally unregulated. Mattel had long held a very high reputation as being one of the very best at assuring healthy and safe product manufacturing, and had worked diligently with its suppliers to assure their conformity with manufacturing specifications and product safety. The resulting problem was that a number of suppliers in China had used lead paint instead of the paint that Mattel had specified and approved for use. They had done it to cut costs.

On September 5, Mattel had told an American Congressional committee that its recall of 17.4m toys containing a small magnet that could be swallowed by children was due to a flaw in the toys' design, rather than production flaws in China. As for some other toys recalled because of allegedly hazardous levels of lead in their paint, Mattel admitted that it had been overzealous and is likely to have recalled toys that did not contravene American regulations on lead content.

China Bears the Cost of Development

As Beijing cracks down on unsafe toy exports and demands more testing, many small toy producers in China are feeling a financial squeeze. The increased testing "has created real havoc for some . . . manufacturers" in China, says Ron Rycek, vice-president of toy sales at Hilco Corp., which sells toy such as Sonic Skillball to Toys 'R' Us and Amazon.com.

Even some companies that are able to keep operating feel the pinch. Manufacturers generally don't get paid until they ship their products, and they usually take out loans to buy materials, pay wages, and cover other expenses until customers transfer funds. With toys now waiting in warehouses while samples are sent to labs, producers can't repay those loans as quickly as they had expected. The testing "is holding up our capital and our warehouse space," says Leona Lam, CEO of

Leconcepts Holdings, a Hong Kong-based subcontractor that supplies parts to factories making plastic toys for the likes of Mattel Inc. and Fisher-Price.
—"Bottlenecks in Toyland," *Business Week*,
October 15, 2007, p. 52.

But regardless of how it had been presented in the press, a multitude of foreign firms selling everything from toothpaste to pet food to mobile phones had discovered a variety of product defects and health and safety risks in their Chinese-based manufacturing and supplier bases. The question remained, however, as to how much of this risk was inherently "Chinese" and how much was "low-cost country sourcing" in origin.

The rising anxieties over Chinese products and their associated risks and returns in 2007 reflected a multitude of different political, economic, and business difficulties. The rapid growth of the Chinese economy was already well known and well documented: approximately 5% of all manufactured goods in the world were now Chinese; 25% of all products sold in the United States had significant Chinese content; global commodity prices of oil, copper, molybdenum, steel, and others were seeing record levels as the rate of infrastructure and business development in China caused global shortages and market pressures. But the costs of such rapid economic development were only now starting to become painfully apparent.

The rate of manufacturing growth had far surpassed the ability of the Chinese government on all levels to manage the growth. Regulatory shortfalls—health, safety, and environmental—were now obvious. Although Mattel and other companies were now confessing their own guilt and accepting responsibility for managing their own product risks, the Chinese government was scurrying to close regulatory gaps and protect not only the export customers who were not protecting themselves, but trying to preserve the reputation of Chinese manufacturing and avoid increasing trade restrictions or barriers to their products in foreign markets.

The human costs were already high. Zheng Xiaoyu, a former boss of the Chinese State Food and Drug Administration (SFDA), had been executed earlier in the year for taking bribes to approve inferior drugs and certificates claiming that the paint used by Mattel's suppliers was lead-free. Mr. Zhang Shuhong, the CEO of Lee Der Industrial, the supplier for many of the products included within Mattel's first product recall, had committed suicide on August 14. Political pressure continued to build between the Chinese government and the United States as the list of products that had been banned by the Consumer Protection Council of the United States continued to grow (see Exhibit 1).

EXHIBIT 1	China-Manufactured Products Recalled by the U.S. Consumer Products Safety Commission between August 3 and September 6, 2007	
Company	**Product**	**Number of Units Affected**
Fisher-Price	Sesame Street, Geotrax, other toys	1 million
Mattel	Barbie accessories, Sarge toys	925,000
Springs Windows Fashions	Basic Blindz window blinds	140,000
Wal-Mart (Sam's Club)	Outdoor torches	138,000
Hayes	Outdoor candles	83,000
Jo-Ann Stores	Children's watering cans	6,000
Raleigh America	Bicycles	1,200
Life Is Good	Children's hooded sweatshirts	400

Source: "Supply Chain: Thomas and His Washington Friends," *CFO*, October 2007, p. 18; and the Consumer Products Safety Commission (CPSC).

The cost of increased regulation was already rising. A survey of consumers in the United Kingdom in September, for example, had found that 37% of the people surveyed noted that the crisis had affected their view of Chinese products overall. As a result, many stated they were much less likely to purchase products made in China. The fall-out from the crisis was indeed no single company, regulatory agency, or government's fault. But the damage was significant and lasting.

Case Questions

1. Mattel's global sourcing in China, like all other toy manufacturers, was based on low-cost manufacturing, low-cost labor, and a growing critical mass of facto-

ries competitively vying for contract manufacturing business. Do you think the product recalls and product quality problems are separate from or part of pursuing a low-cost country strategy?

2. Whether it is lead paint on toys or defective sliding sides on baby cribs, whose responsibility do you think it is to assure safety—the company, like Mattel, or the country, in this case China?

3. Many international trade and development experts argue that China is just now discovering the difference between being a major economic player in global business and its previous peripheral role as a low-cost manufacturing site on the periphery of the world economy. What do you think?

QUESTIONS

1. **Evolving into Multinationalism.** As a firm evolves from a pure domestic company into a true multinational enterprise, it must consider (a) its competitive advantages, (b) its production location, (c) the type of control it wants to have over any foreign operations, and (d) how much monetary capital to invest abroad. Explain how each of these considerations is important to the success of foreign operations.

2. **Theory of Comparative Advantage.** What is the essence of the theory of comparative advantage?

3. **Market Imperfections.** MNEs strive to take advantage of market imperfections in national markets for products, factors of production, and financial assets.

Large international firms are better able to exploit such imperfections. What are their main competitive advantages?

4. **Strategic Motives for Foreign Direct Investment (FDI).**

   a. Summarize the five main motives that drive the decision to initiate FDI.

   b. Match these motives with the following MNEs:

   General Motors (U.S.)
   Royal Dutch Shell (Netherlands/UK)
   Kentucky Fried Chicken (U.S.)
   Jardine Matheson (Hong Kong)
   Apple Computer (U.S.)
   NEC (Japan)

5. **Competitive Advantage.** In deciding whether to invest abroad, management must first determine whether the firm has a sustainable competitive advantage that enables it to compete effectively in the home market. What are the necessary characteristics of this competitive advantage?

6. **Economies of Scale and Scope.** Explain briefly how economies of scale and scope can be developed in production, marketing, finance, research and development, transportation, and purchasing.

7. **Competitiveness of the Home Market.** A strongly competitive home market can sharpen a firm's competitive advantage relative to firms located in less competitive markets. This phenomenon is known as Porter's "diamond of national advantage." Explain what is meant by the "diamond of national advantage."

8. **OLI Paradigm.** The OLI Paradigm is an attempt to create an overall framework to explain why MNEs choose FDI rather than serve foreign markets through alternative modes.
   a. Explain what is meant by the "O" in the OLI Paradigm.
   b. Explain what is meant by the "L" in the OLI Paradigm.
   c. Explain what is meant by the "I" in the OLI Paradigm.

9. **Financial Links to OLI.** Financial strategies are directly related to the OLI Paradigm.
   a. Explain how *proactive* financial strategies are related to OLI.
   b. Explain how *reactive* financial strategies are related to OLI.

10. **Where to Invest.** The decision about where to invest abroad is influenced by behavioral factors.
    a. Explain the *behavioral approach* to FDI.
    b. Explain the *international network theory* explanation of FDI.

11. **Exporting versus Producing Abroad.** What are the advantages and disadvantages of limiting a firm's activities to exporting compared to producing abroad?

12. **Licensing and Management Contracts versus Producing Abroad.** What are the advantages and disadvantages of licensing and management contracts compared to producing abroad?

13. **Joint Venture versus Wholly Owned Production Subsidiary.** What are the advantages and disadvantages of forming a joint venture to serve a foreign market compared to serving that market with a wholly owned production subsidiary?

14. **Greenfield Investment versus Acquisition.** What are the advantages and disadvantages of serving a foreign market through a greenfield foreign direct investment compared to an acquisition of a local firm in the target market?

15. **Cross-Border Strategic Alliance.** The term "cross-border strategic alliance" conveys different meanings to different observers. What are these meanings?

16. **Governance Risk.**
    a. What is meant by the term *governance risk*?
    b. What is the most important type of governance risk?

17. **Investment Agreement.** An investment agreement spells out the specific rights and responsibilities of a foreign firm and its host government. What are the main financial policies that should be included in an investment agreement?

18. **Investment Insurance and Guarantees (OPIC).**
    a. What is OPIC?
    b. What types of political risks can OPIC insure against?

19. **Operating Strategies after the FDI Decision.** The following operating strategies, among others, are expected to reduce damage from political risk. Explain each one and how it reduces damage.
    a. Local sourcing
    b. Facility location
    c. Control of technology
    d. Thin equity base
    e. Multiple-source borrowing

20. **Country-Specific Risk.** Define the following terms:
    a. Transfer risk
    b. Blocked funds
    c. Sovereign credit risk

21. **Blocked Funds.** Explain the strategies used by an MNE to counter blocked funds.

22. **Cultural and Institutional Risks.** Identify and explain the main types of cultural and institutional risks, except protectionism.

23. Strategies to Manage Cultural and Institutional Risks. Explain the strategies used by an MNE to manage each of the cultural and institutional risks that you identified in question 9, except protectionism.

24. Protectionism Defined.
a. Define protectionism and identify the industries that are typically protected.
b. Explain the "infant industry" argument for protectionism.

25. Managing Protectionism.
a. What are the traditional methods for countries to implement protectionism?
b. What are some typical nontariff barriers to trade?
c. How can MNEs overcome host-country protectionism?

26. Global-Specific Risks. What are the main types of political risks that are global in origin?

27. Managing Global-Specific Risks. What are the main strategies used by MNEs to manage the global-specific risks you identified in question 13?

28. U.S. Anti-Bribery Law. The United States has a law prohibiting U.S. firms from bribing foreign officials and business persons, even in countries where bribery is a normal practice. Some U.S. firms claim this places them at a disadvantage compared to host-country firms and other foreign firms that are not hampered by such a law. Discuss the ethics and practicality of the U.S. anti-bribery law.

29. Cool Cola Company. Cool Cola Company, one of the world's major manufacturers of cola soft drinks, is considering the establishment of a very large cola bottling plant in India. Cool Cola expects to sell half its product within India and to export the other half to Southeast Asian countries. If the Kashmir conflict could be resolved, Pakistan and even Afghanistan might become important markets.
a. Prepare an analysis of all the potential areas of goal conflict between Cool Cola and India.
b. Considering your answers to part (a), prepare a political risk forecast for Cool Cola's bottling plant in India. Consider the potential for political unrest in India or for war with Pakistan, as well as whether a foreign-owned soft drink plant would be affected by such unrest. Use current periodicals and newspapers to gather your data.
c. Assume Cool Cola decides to build a large bottling plant in India. Recommend operating strategies for Cool Cola Company that would reduce its political risk. Include strategies for marketing, production, finance, and organization.
d. Prepare a crisis plan for Cool Cola in India in case political conditions deteriorate.

30. Divestment: China. Assume that Cool Cola Company also has a network of soft drink bottling plants throughout China, but political stresses between the United States and China increase to the degree that Cool Cola would like to divest. What should Cool Cola consider in developing a plan that will enable it to divest its investment in bottling plants and distributions systems in China with minimum loss?

INTERNET EXERCISES

1. The World Bank. The World Bank provides a growing set of informational and analytical resources to aid in the assessment and management of cross-border risk. The Risk Management Support Group has a variety of political risk assessment tools, which are under constant development. Visit the following site and compose an executive briefing (one page or less) of what the political risk insurance provided by the World Bank will and will not cover.

World Bank Risk Management   www.worldbank.org/business/01risk_manage.html

2. Global Corruption Report. Transparency International (TI) is considered by many to be the leading nongovernmental anticorruption organization in the world today. It has recently introduced its own annual survey analyzing recent developments, identifying ongoing challenges, and offering potential solutions to individuals or organizations. One dimension of this analysis is the Bribe Payers Index. Visit TI's Web site to view the latest edition of the Bribe Payers Index.

Transparency International   www.transparency.org/surveys/index.html#bpi

3. Sovereign Credit Ratings Criteria. The evaluation of credit risk and all other relevant risks associated with the multitude of borrowers on world debt markets requires a structured approach to international risk assessment. Use Standard & Poor's criteria, described in depth on its Web site, to differentiate the various risks (local currency risk, default risk, currency risk, transfer risk, and so on) contained in major sovereign ratings worldwide.

Standard & Poor's   Go to www.standardandpoors.com and click "Ratings" under "Products & Services."

4. **Milken Capital Access Index.** The Milken Institute's Capital Access Index (CAI) is one of the newest informational indices that evaluates how accessible world capital markets are to MNEs and governments of many emerging market countries. According to the CAI, which countries have seen the largest deterioration in their access to capital in the last two years?

Milken Institute   www.milkeninstitute.org/

5. **Overseas Private Investment Corporation.** The Overseas Private Investment Corporation (OPIC) provides long-term political risk insurance and limited recourse project financing aid to U.S.-based firms investing abroad. Using the organization's Web site, answer the following questions:
   a. Exactly what types of risk will OPIC insure against?
   b. What financial limits and restrictions are there on this insurance protection?
   c. How should a project be structured to aid in its approval for OPIC coverage?

Overseas Private Investment Corp.   www.opic.gov/

CHAPTER 19

Multinational Capital Budgeting

Whales only get harpooned when they come to the surface, and turtles can only move forward when they stick their neck out, but investors face risk no matter what they do.

—Charles A. Jaffe.

This chapter describes in detail the issues and principles related to the investment in real productive assets in foreign countries, generally referred to as *multinational capital budgeting*.

Although the original decision to undertake an investment in a particular foreign country may be determined by a mix of strategic, behavioral, and economic decisions, the specific project, as well as all reinvestment decisions, should be justified by traditional financial analysis. For example, a production efficiency opportunity may exist for a U.S. firm to invest abroad, but the type of plant, mix of labor and capital, kinds of equipment, method of financing, and other project variables must be analyzed within the traditional financial framework of discounted cash flows. It must also consider the impact of the proposed foreign project on consolidated net earnings, cash flows from subsidiaries in other countries, and on the market value of the parent firm.

Multinational capital budgeting, like traditional domestic capital budgeting, focuses on the cash inflows and outflows associated with prospective long-term investment projects. Multinational capital budgeting techniques are used in traditional FDI analysis, such as the construction of a manufacturing plant in another country, as well as in the growing field of international mergers and acquisitions.

Capital budgeting for a foreign project uses the same theoretical framework as domestic capital budgeting—with a few very important differences. The basic steps are as follows:

1. Identify the initial capital invested or put at risk.
2. Estimate cash flows to be derived from the project over time, including an estimate of the terminal or salvage value of the investment.
3. Identify the appropriate discount rate for determining the present value of the expected cash flows.
4. Apply traditional capital budgeting decision criteria such as net present value (NPV) and internal rate of return (IRR) to determine the acceptability of or priority ranking of potential projects.

First, this chapter describes the complexities of budgeting for a foreign project. Second, we describe the insights gained by valuing a project from both the project's viewpoint and the parent's viewpoint. Next, we use a hypothetical investment by Cemex of Mexico in Indonesia to detail the process of multinational capital budgeting in practice. Then, we introduce the concept of real options analysis, an alternative method for evaluating the potential returns to a project or investment. We conclude with an analysis of project finance.

Complexities of Budgeting for a Foreign Project

Capital budgeting for a foreign project is considerably more complex than the domestic case. Several factors contribute to this greater complexity:

- Parent cash flows must be distinguished from project cash flows. Each of these two types of flows contributes to a different view of value.

- Parent cash flows often depend on the form of financing. Thus, we cannot clearly separate cash flows from financing decisions, as we can in domestic capital budgeting.

- Additional cash flows generated by a new investment in one foreign subsidiary may be in part or in whole taken away from another subsidiary, with the net result that the project is favorable from a single subsidiary's point of view but contributes nothing to worldwide cash flows.

- The parent must explicitly recognize remittance of funds because of differing tax systems, legal and political constraints on the movement of funds, local business norms, and differences in the way financial markets and institutions function.

- An array of nonfinancial payments can generate cash flows from subsidiaries to the parent, including payment of license fees and payments for imports from the parent.

- Managers must anticipate differing rates of national inflation because of their potential to cause changes in competitive position, and thus changes in cash flows over a period of time.

- Managers must keep the possibility of unanticipated foreign exchange rate changes in mind because of possible direct effects on the value of local cash flows, as well as indirect effects on the competitive position of the foreign subsidiary.

- Use of segmented national capital markets may create an opportunity for financial gains or may lead to additional financial costs.

- Use of host-government subsidized loans complicates both capital structure and the parent's ability to determine an appropriate weighted average cost of capital for discounting purposes.

- Managers must evaluate political risk because political events can drastically reduce the value or availability of expected cash flows.

- Terminal value is more difficult to estimate because potential purchasers from the host, parent, or third countries, or from the private or public sector, may have widely divergent perspectives on the value to them of acquiring the project.

Since the same theoretical capital budgeting framework is used to choose among competing foreign and domestic projects, it is critical that we have a common standard. Thus, all foreign complexities must be quantified as modifications to either expected cash flow or the rate of discount. Although in practice many firms make such modifications arbitrarily, readily available information, theoretical deduction, or just plain common sense can be used to make less arbitrary and more reasonable choices.

Project versus Parent Valuation

A strong theoretical argument exists in favor of analyzing any foreign project from the viewpoint of the parent. Cash flows to the parent are ultimately the basis for dividends to stockholders, reinvestment elsewhere in the world, repayment of corporate-wide debt, and other purposes that affect the firm's many interest groups. However, since most of a project's cash flows to its parent, or sister subsidiaries, are financial cash flows rather than operating cash flows, the parent viewpoint usually violates a cardinal concept of capital budgeting, namely, that financial cash flows should not be mixed with operating cash flows. Often the difference is not important because the two are almost identical, but in some instances a sharp divergence in these cash flows will exist. For example, funds that are permanently blocked from repatriation, or "forcibly reinvested," are not available for dividends to the stockholders or for repayment of parent corporate debt. Therefore, shareholders will not perceive the blocked earnings as contributing to the value of the firm, and creditors will not count on them in calculating interest coverage ratios and other evidence of ability to service debt.

Evaluation of a project from the local viewpoint serves some useful purposes, but it should be subordinated to evaluation from the parent's viewpoint. In evaluating a foreign project's performance relative to the potential of a competing project in the same host country, we must pay attention to the project's local return. Almost any project should at least be able to earn a cash return equal to the yield available on host government bonds with a maturity the same as the project's economic life, if a free market exists for such bonds. Host government bonds ordinarily reflect the local risk-free rate of return, including a premium equal to the expected rate of inflation. If a project cannot earn more than such a bond yield, the parent firm should buy host government bonds rather than invest in a riskier project—or, better yet, invest somewhere else!

Multinational firms should invest only if they can earn a risk-adjusted return greater than locally based competitors can earn on the same project. If they are unable to earn superior returns on foreign projects, their stockholders would be better off buying shares in local firms, where possible, and letting those companies carry out the local projects. Apart from these theoretical arguments, surveys over the past 35 years show that in practice multinational firms continue to evaluate foreign investments from both the parent and project viewpoint.

The attention paid to project returns in various surveys probably reflects emphasis on maximizing reported consolidated net earnings per share as a corporate financial goal. As long as foreign earnings are not blocked, they can be consolidated with the earnings of both the remaining subsidiaries and the parent. As mentioned previously, U.S. firms must consolidate foreign *subsidiaries* that are over 50% owned. If a firm is owned between 20% and 49% by a parent, it is called an *affiliate*. Affiliates are consolidated with the parent owner on a pro rata basis. Subsidiaries less than 20% owned are normally carried as unconsolidated investments. Even in the case of temporarily blocked funds, some of the most mature MNEs do not necessarily eliminate a project from financial consideration. They take a very long-run view of world business opportunities.

If reinvestment opportunities in the country where funds are blocked are at least equal to the parent firm's required rate of return (after adjusting for anticipated exchange rate changes), temporary blockage of transfer may have little practical effect on the capital budgeting outcome, because future project cash flows will be increased by the returns on forced reinvestment. Since large multinationals hold a portfolio of domestic and foreign projects, corporate liquidity is not impaired if a few projects have blocked funds; alternate sources of funds are available to meet all planned uses of funds. Furthermore, a long-run historical perspective on blocked funds does indeed lend support to the belief that funds are almost never permanently blocked. However, waiting for the release of such funds can be frustrating, and sometimes the blocked funds lose value while blocked because of inflation or unexpected exchange rate deterioration, even though they have been reinvested in the host country to protect at least part of their value in real terms.

In conclusion, most firms appear to evaluate foreign projects from both parent and project viewpoints. The parent's viewpoint gives results closer to the traditional meaning of net present value in capital budgeting. Project valuation provides a closer approximation of the effect on consolidated earnings per share, which all surveys indicate is of major concern to practicing managers. To illustrate the foreign complexities of multinational capital budgeting, we analyze a hypothetical market-seeking foreign direct investment by Cemex in Indonesia.

Illustrative Case: Cemex Enters Indonesia[1]

It is early in 1998. Cementos Mexicanos, Cemex, is considering the construction of a cement manufacturing facility on the Indonesian island of Sumatra. The project, Semen Indonesia (the Indonesian word for "cement" is *semen*), would be a wholly owned greenfield investment with a total installed capacity of 20 million metric tons per year (mmt/y). Although that is large by Asian production standards, Cemex believes that its latest cement manufacturing technology would be most efficiently utilized with a production facility of this scale.

Cemex has three driving reasons for the project: 1) the firm wishes to initiate a productive presence of its own in Southeast Asia, a relatively new market for Cemex; 2) the long-term prospects for Asian infrastructure development and growth appear very good over the longer term; and 3) there are positive prospects for Indonesia to act as a produce-for-export site as a result of the depreciation of the Indonesian rupiah (Rp) in 1997.

Cemex, the world's third-largest cement manufacturer, is an MNE headquartered in an emerging market but competing in a global arena. The firm competes in the global marketplace for both market share and capital. The international cement market, like markets in other commodities such as oil, is a dollar-based market. For this reason, and for comparisons against its major competitors in both Germany and Switzerland, Cemex considers the U.S. dollar its functional currency.

Cemex's shares are listed in both Mexico City and New York (OTC: CMXSY). The firm has successfully raised capital—both debt and equity—outside Mexico in U.S. dollars. Its investor base is increasingly global, with the U.S. share turnover rising rapidly as a percentage of total trading. As a result, its cost and availability of capital are internationalized and dominated by U.S. dollar investors. Ultimately, the Semen Indonesia project will be evaluated—in both cash flows and capital cost—in U.S. dollars.

Overview

A roadmap of the complete multinational capital budgeting analysis for Cemex in Indonesia is illustrated in Exhibit 19.1. The basic principle is that, starting at the top left, the parent company invests U.S. dollar-denominated capital, which flows clockwise through the creation and operation of an Indonesian subsidiary, which then generates cash flows that are eventually returned in a variety of forms to the parent company—in U.S. dollars. The first step is to construct a set of *pro forma* financial statements for Semen Indonesia, all in Indonesian rupiah (Rp). The next step is to create two capital budgets, the *project viewpoint* and the *parent viewpoint*.

Semen Indonesia will take only one year to build the plant, with actual operations commencing in year 1. The Indonesian government has only recently deregulated the heavier industries to allow foreign ownership. The following analysis is conducted assuming that pur-

---

[1]Cemex is a real company; the greenfield investment described here is hypothetical.

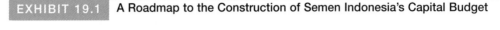

EXHIBIT 19.1   A Roadmap to the Construction of Semen Indonesia's Capital Budget

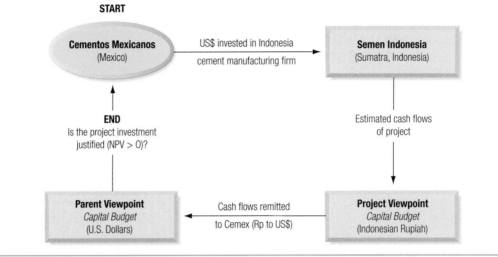

chasing power parity (PPP) holds for the Rp/US$ exchange rate for the life of the Indonesian project. This is a standard financial assumption made by Cemex for its foreign investments. The projected inflation rates for Indonesia and the United States are 30% per annum and 3% per annum, respectively.

If we assume an initial spot rate of Rp10,000/US$, and Indonesian and U.S. inflation rates of 30% and 3% per annum, respectively, for the life of the project, forecasted spot exchange rates follow the usual PPP calculation. For example, the forecasted exchange rate for year 1 of the project would be

$$\text{Spot rate (year 1)} = \text{Rp10,000/US\$} \times \frac{1+.30}{1+.03} = \text{Rp12,621/US\$}$$

Financial Assumptions

The following series of financial statements are based on these assumptions.

Capital Investment. Although the cost of building new cement manufacturing capacity anywhere in the industrial countries was estimated at roughly $150/ton of installed capacity, Cemex believed that it could build a state-of-the-art production and shipment facility in Sumatra at roughly $110/ton (see Exhibit 19.2). Assuming a 20 million metric tons per year capacity and a year 0 average exchange rate of Rp10,000/$, this cost will constitute an investment of Rp22 trillion ($2.2 billion). This figure includes an investment of Rp17.6 trillion in plant and equipment, giving rise to an annual depreciation charge of Rp1.76 trillion if we assume a 10-year straight-line depreciation schedule. The relatively short depreciation schedule is one of the policies of the Indonesian tax authorities meant to attract foreign investment.

Financing. This massive investment would be financed with 50% equity, all from Cemex, and 50% debt, 75% from Cemex and 25% from a bank consortium arranged by the Indonesian government. Cemex's own U.S. dollar-based weighted average cost of capital (WACC) was estimated at 11.98%. The WACC on a local Indonesian level in rupiah terms, for the project itself, was estimated at 33.257%. The details of this calculation are discussed later in this chapter.

| EXHIBIT 19.2 | Investment and Financing of the Semen Indonesia Project (all values in 000s unless otherwise noted) |

Investment		Financing	
Average exchange rate, Rp/$	10,000	Equity	Rp 11,000,000,000
Cost of installed capacity, $/tonne	$110	Debt	
Installed capacity	20,000	Rupiah debt	2,750,000,000
Investment in US$	$2,200,000	US$ debt, Rp	8,250,000,000
Investment in rupiah	22,000,000,000	Total	Rp 22,000,000,000
Plant and equipment, Rp	17,600,000,000		
Annual depreciation, Rp	1,760,000,000		
Costs of Capital: Cemex			
Risk-free rate	6.000%	Cemex beta	1.500
Credit premium	2.000%	Equity risk premium	7.000%
Cost of debt	8.000%	Cost of equity	16.500%
Cost of debt, after tax	5.200%	Percent equity	60%
Percent debt	40%	WACC	11.980%
Costs of Capital: Semen Indonesia			
Risk-free rate	33.000%	Semen Indonesia beta	1.000
Credit premium	2.000%	Equity risk premium	6.000%
Cost of rupiah debt	35.000%	Cost of equity	40.000%
Cost of US$ debt, after tax	5.200%	Percent equity	50%
Cost of US$ debt (rupiah equivalent)	38.835%		
Cost of US$ debt, after tax (rupiah equivalent)	27.184%		
Percent debt	50%	WACC	33.257%

Assumes corporate income tax rates of 35% and 30% in Mexico and Indonesia, respectively. The cost of the US$ loan is stated in rupiah terms assuming purchasing power parity and U.S. dollar and Indonesian rupiah inflation rates of 3% and 30%, respectively, throughout the subject period.

The explicit debt structures, including repayment schedules, are presented in Exhibit 19.3. The loan arranged by the Indonesian government, part of the government's economic development incentive program, is an eight-year loan, in rupiah, at 35% annual interest, fully amortizing. The interest payments are fully deductible against corporate tax liabilities.

The majority of the debt, however, is being provided by the parent company, Cemex. After raising the capital from its financing subsidiary, Cemex will relend the capital to Semen Indonesia. The loan is denominated in U.S. dollars, five years maturity, with an annual interest rate of 10%. Because the debt will have to be repaid from the rupiah earnings of the Indonesian enterprise, the *pro forma* financial statements are constructed so that the expected costs of servicing the dollar debt are included in the firm's *pro forma* income statement. The dollar loan, if the rupiah follows the purchasing power parity forecast, will have an effective interest expense in rupiah terms of 38.835%. We find this rate by determining the internal rate of return of repaying the dollar loan in full in rupiah (see Exhibit 19.3).

Revenues. Given that the existing cement manufacturing in Indonesia is depressed, all sales are based on export. The 20 mmt/y facility is expected to operate at only 40% capacity (producing 8 million metric tons). Cement produced will be sold in the export market at $58/ton

EXHIBIT 19.3	Semen Indonesia's Debt Service Schedules and Foreign Exchange Gains/Losses					
Spot rate (Rp/$)	10,000	12,621	15,930	20,106	25,376	32,028
Project year	**0**	**1**	**2**	**3**	**4**	**5**
Indonesian loan @ 35% for eight years (millions of rupiah):						
Loan principal	2,750,000					
Interest payment		(962,500)	(928,921)	(883,590)	(822,393)	(739,777)
Principal payment		(95,939)	(129,518)	(174,849)	(236,046)	(318,662)
Total payment		(1,058,439)	(1,058,439)	(1,058,439)	(1,058,439)	(1,058,439)
Cemex loan @ 10% for five years (millions of U.S. dollars):						
Principal	825					
Interest payment		(82.5)	(69.0)	(54.1)	(37.8)	(19.8)
Principal payment		(135.1)	(148.6)	(163.5)	(179.9)	(197.8)
Total payment		(217.6)	(217.6)	(217.6)	(217.6)	(217.6)
Cemex loan converted to Rp at scheduled and current spot rates (millions of rupiah):						
Scheduled at Rp10,000/$:						
Interest payment		(825,000)	(689,867)	(541,221)	(377,710)	(197,848)
Principal payment		(1,351,329)	(1,486,462)	(1,635,108)	(1,798,619)	(1,978,481)
Total payment		(2,176,329)	(2,176,329)	(2,176,329)	(2,176,329)	(2,176,329)
Actual (at current spot rate):						
Interest payment		(1,041,262)	(1,098,949)	(1,088,160)	(958,480)	(633,669)
Principal payment		(1,705,561)	(2,367,915)	(3,287,494)	(4,564,190)	(6,336,691)
Total payment		(2,746,823)	(3,466,864)	(4,375,654)	(5,522,670)	(6,970,360)
Cash flows in Rp on Cemex loan (millions of rupiah):						
Total actual cash flows	8,250,000	(2,746,823)	(3,466,864)	(4,375,654)	(5,522,670)	(6,970,360)
IRR of cash flows	38.835%					
Foreign exchange losses on Cemex loan (millions of rupiah):						
Foreign exchange losses on interest		(216,262)	(409,082)	(546,940)	(580,770)	(435,821)
Foreign exchange losses on principal		(354,232)	(881,453)	(1,652,385)	(2,765,571)	(4,358,210)
Total foreign exchange losses on debt		(570,494)	(1,290,535)	(2,199,325)	(3,346,341)	(4,794,031)

The loan by Cemex to the Indonesian subsidiary is denominated in U.S. dollars. Therefore , the loan will have to be repaid in U.S. dollars, not rupiah. At the time of the loan agreement, the spot exchange rate is Rp10,000/$. This is the assumption used in calculating the "scheduled" repaying of principal and interest in rupiah. The rupiah, however, is expected to depreciate in line with purchasing power parity. As it is repaid, the "actual" exchange rate will therefore give rise to a foreign exchange loss as it takes more and more rupiah to acquire U.S. dollars for debt service, both principal and interest. The foreign exchange losses on this debt service will be recognized on the Indonesian income statement.

(delivered). Note also that, at least for the conservative baseline analysis, we assume no increase in the price received over time.

Costs. The cash costs of cement manufacturing (labor, materials, power, and so on) are estimated at Rp115,000 per ton for project year 1, rising at about the rate of inflation, 30% per year. Additional production costs of Rp20,000 per ton for year 1 are also assumed to rise at the rate of inflation. As a result of all production being exported, loading costs of $2.00/ton and shipping of $10.00/ton must also be included. Note that these costs are originally stated in U.S. dollars, and for the purposes of Semen Indonesia's income statement, they must be converted to rupiah terms. This is the case because both loading and shipping costs are international services governed by contracts denominated in dollars. As a result, they are expected to rise over time only at the U.S. dollar rate of inflation (3%).

Semen Indonesia's *pro forma* income statement is illustrated in Exhibit 19.4. This is the typical financial statement measurement of the profitability of any business, whether domestic or international. The baseline analysis assumes a capacity utilization rate of only 40% (year 1), 50% (year 2), and 60% in the following years. Management believes this is necessary since existing in-country cement manufacturers are averaging only 40% of capacity at this time.

Additional expenses in the *pro forma* financial analysis include license fees paid by the subsidiary to the parent company of 2.0% of sales, and general and administrative expenses for Indonesian operations of 8.0% per year (and growing an additional 1% per year). Foreign exchange gains and losses are those related to the servicing of the U.S. dollar-denominated

EXHIBIT 19.4   Semen Indonesia's *Pro Forma* Income Statement (millions of rupiah)

Exchange Rate (Rp/$)	10,000	12,621	15,930	20,106	25,376	32,038
Project year	**0**	**1**	**2**	**3**	**4**	**5**
Sales volume		8,000	10,000	12,000	12,000	12,000
Sales price (US$)		58.00	58.00	58.00	58.00	58.00
Sales price (Rp)		732,039	923,933	1,166,128	1,471,808	1,857,627
Total revenue		5,856,311	9,239,325	13,993,541	17,661,751	22,291,530
Less cash costs		(920,000)	(1,495,000)	(2,332,200)	(3,031,860)	(3,941,418)
Less other production costs		(160,000)	(260,000)	(405,600)	(527,280)	(685,464)
Less loading costs		(201,942)	(328,155)	(511,922)	(665,499)	(865,149)
Less shipping costs		(1,009,709)	(1,640,777)	(2,559,612)	(3,327,495)	(4,325,744)
Total production costs		(2,291,650)	(3,723,932)	(5,809,334)	(7,552,134)	(9,817,774)
Gross profit		3,564,660	5,515,393	8,184,207	10,109,617	12,473,756
Gross margin		61%	60%	58%	57%	56%
Less license fees		(117,126)	(184,787)	(279,871)	(353,235)	(445,831)
Less general and administrative		(468,505)	(831,539)	(1,399,354)	(1,942,792)	(2,674,984)
EBITDA		2,979,029	4,499,067	6,504,982	7,813,589	9,352,941
Less depreciation and amortization		(1,760,000)	(1,760,000)	(1,760,000)	(1,760,000)	(1,760,000)
EBIT		1,219,029	2,739,067	4,744,982	6,053,589	7,592,941
Less interest on Cemex debt		(825,000)	(689,867)	(541,221)	(377,710)	(197,848)
Foreign exchange losses on debt		(570,494)	(1,290,535)	(2,199,325)	(3,346,341)	(4,794,031)
Less interest on local debt		(962,500)	(928,921)	(883,590)	(822,393)	(739,777)
EBT		(1,138,965)	(170,256)	1,120,846	1,507,145	1,861,285
Less income taxes (30%)		—	—	—	(395,631)	(558,386)
Net income		(1,138,965)	(170,256)	1,120,846	1,111,514	1,302,900
Net income (millions of US$)		(90)	(11)	56	44	41
Return on sales		−19%	−2%	8%	6%	6%

EBITDA = earnings before interest, taxes, depreciation, and amortization; EBIT = earnings before interest and taxes; EBT = earnings before taxes. Tax credits resulting from current period losses are carried forward toward next year's tax liabilities. Dividends are not distributed in the first year of operations as a result of losses, and are distributed at a 50% rate in years 2000–2003. All calculations are exact, but may appear not to add due to reported decimal places and rounding. The tax payment for year 3 is zero, and year 4 is less than 30%, as a result of tax loss carry-forwards from previous years.

debt provided by the parent and are drawn from the bottom of Exhibit 19.3. In summary, the subsidiary operation is expected to begin turning an accounting profit in its fourth year of operations (2000), with profits rising as capacity utilization increases over time.

Project Viewpoint Capital Budget

The capital budget for the Semen Indonesia manufacturing project from a project viewpoint is shown in Exhibit 19.5. We find the net cash flow, or *free cash flow* (FCF) as it is often called, by summing EBIT (earnings before interest and tax), recalculated taxes, depreciation, and changes in net working capital (the sum of the net additions to receivables, inventories, and payables necessary to support sales growth).

Note that EBIT, not EBT, is used in the capital budget. Depreciation and amortization are noncash expenses of the firm (there was no actual cash outflow, just an accounting entry) and therefore must be added back to capture all available cash flow. Because the capital budget creates cash flows that will be discounted to present value with a discount rate, and the discount rate includes the cost of debt—interest—we do not wish to subtract interest twice. Therefore, taxes are recalculated on the basis of EBIT. (This highlights the distinction between an income statement and a capital budget. The project's income statement shows losses the first two years of operations as a result of interest expenses and forecast foreign exchange losses, so it is not expected to pay taxes. But the capital budget, constructed on the basis of EBIT, before these financing and foreign exchange expenses, calculates a positive tax payment.) The firm's cost of capital used in discounting also includes the deductibility of debt interest in its calculation.

The initial investment of Rp22 trillion is the total capital invested to support these earnings. Although receivables average 50 to 55 days sales outstanding (DSO) and inventories 65 to 70 DSO, payables and trade credit are also relatively long at 114 DSO in the Indonesian cement industry. Semen Indonesia expects to add approximately 15 net DSO to its investment with sales growth. The remaining elements to complete the project viewpoint's capital budget are the terminal value (discussed below) and the discount rate of 33.257% (the firm's WACC).

Terminal Value. The terminal value (TV) of the project represents the continuing value of the cement manufacturing facility in the years after year 5, the last year of the detailed *pro*

| EXHIBIT 19.5 | Semen Indonesia's Capital Budget: Project Viewpoint (millions of rupiah) |

Exchange Rate (Rp/$)	10,000	12,621	15,930	20,106	25,376	32,038
Project year	**0**	**1**	**2**	**3**	**4**	**5**
EBIT		1,219,029	2,739,067	4,744,982	6,053,589	7,592,941
Less recalculated taxes at 30%		(365,709)	(821,720)	(1,423,495)	(1,816,077)	(2,277,882)
Add back depreciation		1,760,000	1,760,000	1,760,000	1,760,000	1,760,000
Net Operating Cash Flow		2,613,320	3,677,347	5,081,487	5,997,512	7,075,059
Less changes to NWC		(240,670)	(139,028)	(436,049)	(289,776)	(626,314)
Initial investment	(22,000,000)					
Terminal value						21,274,102
Free cash flow (FCF)	(22,000,000)	2,372,650	3,538,319	4,645,438	5,707,736	27,722,847
NPV @ 33.257%	(7,855,886)					
IRR	18.6 %					

NWC = net working capital. NPV = net present value. Discount rate is Semen Indonesia's WACC of 33.257%. IRR = internal rate of return, the rate of discount yielding an NPV of exactly zero. Values in exhibit are exact and are rounded to the nearest million.

forma financial analysis shown here. This value, like all asset values according to financial theory, is the present value of all future free cash flows that the asset is expected to yield. We calculate the TV as the present value of a perpetual net operating cash flow (NOCF) generated in the fifth year by Semen Indonesia, the growth rate assumed for that net operating cash flow (g), and the firm's weighted average cost of capital (k_{WACC}):

$$\text{Terminal value} = \frac{\text{NOCF}_5(1+g)}{k_{WACC} - g} = \frac{7,075,059(1+0)}{.33257 - 0} = RP21,274,102$$

or Rp21.274 trillion. The assumption that g = 0, that is, that NOCFs will not grow past year 5, is probably not true, but it is a prudent assumption for Cemex to make when estimating future cash flows so far into the future.

The results of the capital budget from the project viewpoint indicate a *negative* net present value (NPV) of Rp7,885,886 million (or about –Rp7.9 trillion) and an internal rate of return (IRR) of only 18.6% compared to the 33.257% cost of capital. These are the returns the project would yield to a local or Indonesian investor in Indonesian rupiah. The project, from this viewpoint, is not acceptable.

Repatriating Cash Flows to Cemex

Exhibit 19.6 now collects all incremental earnings to Cemex from the prospective investment project in Indonesia. As described in the section preceding the case, a foreign investor's assessment of a project's returns depends on the actual cash flows that are returned to it, in its own currency. For Cemex, this means that the investment must be analyzed in terms of U.S. dollar cash inflows and outflows associated with the investment over the life of the project, after tax, discounted at its appropriate cost of capital.

We build this *parent viewpoint capital budget* in two steps:

1. We isolate the individual cash flows, adjusted for any withholding taxes imposed by the Indonesian government and converted to U.S. dollars. (Statutory withholding taxes on international transfers are set by bilateral tax treaties, but individual firms may negotiate lower rates with governmental tax authorities. In the case of Semen Indonesia, dividends will be charged a 15% withholding tax, 10% interest payments, and 5% license fees.) Mexico does not tax repatriated earnings since they have already been taxed in Indonesia.

2. The actual parent viewpoint capital budget combines these U.S. dollar after-tax cash flows with the initial investment to determine the net present value of the proposed Semen Indonesia subsidiary in the eyes (and pocketbook) of Cemex. This is shown in Exhibit 19.6, which shows all incremental earnings to Cemex from the prospective investment project. A specific peculiarity of this parent viewpoint capital budget is that only the capital invested into the project by Cemex itself, $1,925 million, is included in the initial investment (the $1,100 million in equity and the $825 million loan). The Indonesian debt of Rp2.75 billion ($275 million) is not included in the Cemex parent viewpoint capital budget.

Parent Viewpoint Capital Budget

Finally, all cash flow estimates are now constructed to form the parent viewpoint's capital budget, detailed in Exhibit 19.6. The cash flows generated by Semen Indonesia from its Indonesian operations, dividends, license fees, debt service payments, and terminal value are now valued in U.S. dollar terms after tax.

In order to evaluate the project's cash flows that are returned to the parent company, Cemex must discount these at the corporate cost of capital. Remembering that Cemex consid-

EXHIBIT 19.6	Semen Indonesia's Remittance and Capital Budget: Parent Viewpoint (millions of rupiah and U.S. dollars)					

Exchange Rate (Rp/$)	10,000	12,621	15,930	20,106	25,376	32,038
Project year	**0**	**1**	**2**	**3**	**4**	**5**
Dividend Remittance						
Dividends paid (Rp)		—	—	560,423	555,757	651,450
Less withholding tax		—	—	(84,063)	(83,364)	(97,717)
Net dividend remitted (Rp)		—	—	476,360	472,393	553,732
Net dividend remitted (US$)				23.7	18.6	17.3
License Fees Remittance						
License fees remitted (Rp)		117,126	184,787	279,871	353,235	445,831
Less withholding tax		(5,856)	(9,239)	(13,994)	(17,662)	(22,292)
Net dividend remitted (Rp)		111,270	175,547	265,877	335,573	423,539
Net license fees remitted (US$)		8.8	11.0	13.2	13.2	13.2
Debt Service Remittance						
Promised interest paid (US$)		82.5	69.0	54.1	37.8	19.8
Less withholding tax @ 10%		(8.25)	(6.90)	(5.41)	(3.78)	(1.98)
Net interest remitted (US$)		74.25	62.09	48.71	33.99	17.81
Principal payments remitted (US$)		135.1	148.6	163.5	179.9	197.8
Capital Budget: Parent Viewpoint (millions of U.S. dollars)						
Dividends		—	—	23.7	18.6	17.3
License fees		8.8	11.0	13.2	13.2	13.2
Debt service		209.4	210.7	212.2	213.9	215.7
Total earnings		218.2	221.8	249.1	245.7	246.2
Initial investment	(1,925.0)					
Terminal value						614.7
Free cash flow (FCF)	(1,925.0)	218.2	221.8	249.1	245.7	860.8
NPV @ 17.98%	(925.6)					
IRR	−1.84 %					

NPV calculated using a company-determined discount rate of WACC + foreign investment premium, or 11.98% + 6.00% = 17.98%.

ers its functional currency to be the U.S. dollar, it calculates its cost of capital in U.S. dollars. As described in Chapter 14, the customary weighted average cost of capital formula is as follows:

$$k_{WACC} = k_e \frac{E}{V} + k_d(1-t)\frac{D}{V}$$

where

k_e = risk-adjusted cost of equity
k_d = before-tax cost of debt
t = marginal tax rate
E = market value of the firm's equity
D = market value of the firm's debt
V = total market value of the firm's securities (E + D)

Cemex's cost of equity is calculated using the capital asset pricing model (CAPM):

$$k_e = k_{rf} + (k_m - k_{rf}) \, \beta_{Cemex} = 6.00\% + (13.00\% - 6.00\%)1.5 = 16.50\%$$

where

k_e = risk-adjusted cost of equity

k_{rf} = risk-free rate of interest (U.S. Treasury intermediate bond yield)

k_m = expected rate of return in U.S. equity markets (large stock)

β_{Cemex} = measure of Cemex's individual risk relative to the market

The calculation assumes the current risk-free rate is 6.00%, the expected return on U.S. equities is 13.00%, and Cemex's beta is 1.5. The result is a cost of equity—required rate of return on equity investment in Cemex—of 16.50%.

The investment will be funded internally by the parent company, roughly in the same debt/equity proportions as the consolidated firm, 40% debt (D/V) and 60% equity (E/V). The current cost of debt for Cemex is 8.00%, and the effective tax rate is 35%. The cost of equity, when combined with the other components, results in a weighted average cost of capital for Cemex of

$$k_{WACC} = k_e \frac{E}{V} + k_d (1 - t) \frac{D}{V} = (16.50\%)(.60) + (8.00\%)(1 - .35)(.40) = 11.98\%$$

Cemex customarily uses this weighted average cost of capital of 11.98% to discount prospective investment cash flows for project ranking purposes. The Indonesian investment poses a variety of risks, however, which the typical domestic investment does not.

If Cemex were undertaking an investment of the same relative degree of risk as the firm itself, a simple discount rate of 11.980% might be adequate. Cemex, however, generally requires new investments to yield an additional 3% over the cost of capital for domestic investments, and 6% more for international projects. The discount rate for Semen Indonesia's cash flows repatriated to Cemex will therefore be discounted at 11.98% + 6.00%, or 17.98%. The project's baseline analysis indicates a negative NPV of US$925.6 million (IRR of −1.84%), which means that it is an unacceptable investment from the parent's viewpoint.

Most corporations require that new investments more than cover the cost of the capital employed in their undertaking. It is therefore not unusual for the firm to require a hurdle rate of 3% to 6% above its cost of capital in order to identify potential investments that will literally add value to stockholder wealth. An NPV of zero means the investment is "acceptable," but NPV values that exceed zero are literally the present value of wealth that is expected to be added to that of the firm and its shareholders. For foreign projects, as discussed previously, we must adjust for agency costs and foreign exchange risks and costs.

Sensitivity Analysis: Project Viewpoint Measurement

So far, the project investigation team has used a set of "most likely" assumptions to forecast rates of return. It is now time to subject the most likely outcome to sensitivity analyses. The same probabilistic techniques are available to test the sensitivity of results to political and foreign exchange risks as are used to test sensitivity to business and financial risks. Many decision makers feel more uncomfortable about the necessity to guess probabilities for unfamiliar political and foreign exchange events than they do about guessing their own more familiar business or financial risks. Therefore, it is more common to test sensitivity to political and foreign exchange risk by simulating what would happen to net present value and earnings under a variety of "what if" scenarios.

Political Risk. What if Indonesia should impose controls on the payment of dividends or license fees to Cemex? The impact of blocked funds on the rate of return from Cemex's perspective would depend on when the blockage occurs, what reinvestment opportunities exist for the blocked funds in Indonesia, and when the blocked funds would eventually be released to Cemex. We could simulate various scenarios for blocked funds and rerun the cash flow analysis in Exhibit 19.6 to estimate the effect on Cemex's rate of return.

What if Indonesia should expropriate Semen Indonesia? The effect of expropriation would depend on the following factors:

- When the expropriation occurs, in terms of number of years after the business began operation
- How much compensation the Indonesian government will pay, and how long after expropriation the payment will be made
- How much debt is still outstanding to Indonesian lenders, and whether the parent, Cemex, will have to pay this debt because of its parental guarantee
- The tax consequences of the expropriation
- Whether the future cash flows are foregone

Many expropriations eventually result in some form of compensation to the former owners. This compensation can come from a negotiated settlement with the host government or from payment of political risk insurance by the parent government. Negotiating a settlement takes time, and the eventual compensation is sometimes paid in installments over a further period of time. Thus, the present value of the compensation is often much lower than its nominal value. Furthermore, most settlements are based on book value of the firm at the time of expropriation rather than the firm's market value.

Repayment of parent guaranteed local debt would usually receive first claim on any compensation funds paid. If Cemex had guaranteed Semen Indonesia's debt to Indonesian lenders, they would be paid before Cemex could receive any settlement funds. In fact, the settlement agreement would probably provide for this. Alternatively, Cemex might have refused to guarantee Semen Indonesia's debt, protecting itself in the case of an expropriation but probably causing Semen Indonesia to pay a higher rate of interest and making the subsidiary less profitable to its parent.

If no compensation agreement is negotiated, Semen Indonesia, as an independently incorporated subsidiary of Cemex, might default on its debt. Cemex would not be obligated for Semen Indonesia's own debt, lacking a parent guarantee. As a practical matter, this is likely to occur only when the subsidiary's debt is borrowed locally, as in the case of Semen Indonesia. If Semen Indonesia had borrowed from, say, banks in Singapore, parent Cemex would feel an obligation to repay the debt even if it was not technically obligated.

The tax consequences of expropriation would depend on the timing and amount of capital loss recognized by Mexico. This loss would usually be based on the uncompensated book value of the Indonesian investment. The problem is that there is often some doubt as to when a write-off is appropriate for tax purposes, particularly if negotiations for a settlement drag on. In some ways a nice clear expropriation without hope of compensation, such as occurred in Cuba in the early 1960s, is preferred to a slow "bleeding death" in protracted negotiations. The former leads to an earlier use of the tax shield and a one-shot write-off against earnings, whereas the latter tends to depress earnings for years, as legal and other costs continue and no tax shelter is achieved.

Foreign Exchange Risk. The project team assumed that the Indonesian rupiah would depreciate versus the U.S. dollar at the purchasing power parity "rate" (approximately

20.767% per year in the baseline analysis). What if the rate of rupiah depreciation were greater? Although this event would make the assumed cash flows to Cemex worth less in dollars, operating exposure analysis would be necessary to determine whether the cheaper rupiah made Semen Indonesia more competitive. For example, since Semen Indonesia's exports to Taiwan are denominated in U.S. dollars, a weakening of the rupiah versus the dollar could result in greater rupiah earnings from those export sales. This serves to somewhat offset the imported components that Semen Indonesia purchases from the parent company that are also denominated in U.S. dollars. Semen Indonesia is representative of firms today which have both cash inflows and outflows denominated in foreign currencies, providing a partial natural hedge against currency movements.

What if the rupiah should *appreciate* against the dollar? The same kind of economic exposure analysis is needed. In this particular case we might guess that the effect would be positive on both local sales in Indonesia and the value in dollars of dividends and license fees paid to Cemex by Semen Indonesia. Note, however, that an appreciation of the rupiah might lead to more competition within Indonesia from firms in other countries with now-lower cost structures, lessening Semen Indonesia's sales.

Other Project Sensitivity Variables. The project rate of return to Cemex would also be sensitive to a change in the assumed terminal value, the capacity utilization rate, the size of the license fee paid by Semen Indonesia, the size of the initial project cost, the amount of working capital financed locally, and the tax rates in Indonesia and Mexico. Since some of these variables are within control of Cemex it is still possible that the Semen Indonesia project could be improved in its value to the firm and become acceptable.

Sensitivity Analysis: Parent Viewpoint Measurement

When a foreign project is analyzed from the parent's point of view, the additional risk that stems from its "foreign" location can be measured in at least two ways: *adjusting the discount rates* or *adjusting the cash flows*.

Adjusting Discount Rates. The first method is to treat all foreign risk as a single problem, by adjusting the discount rate applicable to foreign projects relative to the rate used for domestic projects to reflect the greater foreign exchange risk, political risk, agency costs, asymmetric information, and other uncertainties perceived in foreign operations. However, adjusting the discount rate applied to a foreign project's cash flow to reflect these uncertainties does not penalize net present value in proportion either to the actual amount at risk or to possible variations in the nature of that risk over time. Combining all risks into a single discount rate may thus cause us to discard much information about the uncertainties of the future.

In the case of foreign exchange risk, changes in exchange rates have a potential effect on future cash flows because of operating exposure. The direction of the effect, however, can either decrease or increase net cash inflows, depending on where the products are sold and where inputs are sourced. To increase the discount rate applicable to a foreign project, on the assumption that the foreign currency might depreciate more than expected, ignores the possible favorable effect of a foreign currency depreciation on the project's competitive position. Increased sales volume might more than offset a lower value of the local currency. Such an increase in the discount rate also ignores the possibility that the foreign currency may appreciate (two-sided risk).

Adjusting Cash Flows. In the second method, we incorporate foreign risks in adjustments to forecasted cash flows of the project. The discount rate for the foreign project is risk-adjusted only for overall business and financial risk, in the same manner as for domestic projects. Simulation-based assessment utilizes scenario development to estimate cash flows to the parent arising from the project over time under different alternative economic futures.

Certainty regarding the quantity and timing of cash flows in a prospective foreign investment is, to quote from *The Maltese Falcon*, "the stuff that dreams are made of." Due to the complexity of economic forces at work in major investment projects, it is paramount that the analyst realizes the subjectivity of the forecast cash flows. Humility in analysis is a valuable trait.

Shortcomings of Each. In many cases, however, neither adjusting the discount rate nor adjusting cash flows is optimal. For example, political uncertainties are a threat to the entire investment, not just the annual cash flows. Potential loss depends partly on the terminal value of the unrecovered parent investment, which will vary depending on how the project was financed, whether political risk insurance was obtained, and what investment horizon is contemplated. Furthermore, if the political climate were expected to be unfavorable in the near future, any investment would probably be unacceptable. Political uncertainty usually relates to possible adverse events that might occur in the more distant future, but that cannot be foreseen at the present. Adjusting the discount rate for political risk thus penalizes early cash flows too heavily while not penalizing distant cash flows enough.

Repercussions to the Investor. Apart from anticipated political and foreign exchange risks, MNEs sometimes worry that taking on foreign projects may increase the firm's overall cost of capital because of investors' perceptions of foreign risk. This worry seemed reasonable if a firm had significant investments in Iraq, Iran, Serbia, or Afghanistan in the 1990s. However, the argument loses persuasiveness when applied to diversified foreign investments with a heavy balance in the industrial countries of Canada, Western Europe, Australia, Latin America, and Asia where, in fact, the bulk of FDI is located. These countries have a reputation for treating foreign investments by consistent standards, and empirical evidence confirms that a foreign presence in these countries may not increase the cost of capital. In fact, some studies indicate that required returns on foreign projects may even be lower than those for domestic projects.

MNE Practices. Surveys of MNEs over the past 35 years have shown that about half of them adjust the discount rate and half adjust the cash flows. One recent survey indicated a rising use of adjusting discount rates over adjusting cash flows. However, the survey also indicated an increasing use of multifactor methods—discount rate adjustment, cash flow adjustment, real options analysis, and qualitative criteria—in evaluating foreign investments.[2]

Portfolio Risk Measurement

As we discussed in Chapter 17, the field of finance has distinguished two definitions of risk: 1) the risk of the individual security (standard deviation of expected return) and 2) the risk of the individual security as a component of a portfolio (*beta*). A foreign investment undertaken in order to enter a local or regional market—market seeking—will have returns that are more or less correlated with those of the local market. A portfolio-based assessment of the investment's prospects would then seem appropriate. A foreign investment undertaken for *resource-seeking* or *production-seeking* purposes may have returns related to those of the parent company or units located somewhere else in the world and have little to do with local markets. Cemex's proposed investment in Semen Indonesia is both *market seeking* and *production seeking* (for export). The decision about which approach is to be used by the

[2]Keck, Tom, Eric Levengood, and Al Longield, "Using Discounted Cash Flow Analysis in an International Setting: A Survey of Issues in Modeling the Cost of Capital," *Journal of Applied Corporate Finance,* Volume 11, Number 3, Fall 1998, pp. 82–99.

MNE in evaluating prospective foreign investments may be the single most important analytical decision it makes. An investment's acceptability may change dramatically from one criterion to the other.

For comparisons within the local host country, we should overlook a project's actual financing or parent-influenced debt capacity, since these would probably be different for local investors than they are for a multinational owner. In addition, the risks of the project to local investors might differ from those perceived by a foreign multinational owner because of the opportunities an MNE has to take advantage of market imperfections. Moreover, the local project may be only one out of an internationally diversified portfolio of projects for the multinational owner; if undertaken by local investors it might have to stand alone without international diversification. Since diversification reduces risk, the MNE can require a lower rate of return than is required by local investors.

Thus, the discount rate used locally must be a hypothetical rate based on a judgment as to what independent local investors would probably demand were they to own the business. Consequently, application of the local discount rate to local cash flows provides only a rough measure of the value of the project as a stand-alone local venture, rather than an absolute valuation.

Real Option Analysis

The discounted cash flow (DCF) approach used in the valuation of Semen Indonesia—and capital budgeting and valuation in general—has long had its critics. Investments that have long lives, cash flow returns in later years, or higher levels of risk than those typical of the firm's current business activities are often rejected by traditional DCF financial analysis. More importantly, when MNEs evaluate competitive projects, traditional discounted cash flow analysis is typically unable to capture the *strategic options* that an individual investment option may offer. This has led to the development of *real option analysis*. Real option analysis is the application of option theory to capital budgeting decisions.

Real options is a different way of thinking about investment values. At its core, it is a cross between decision-tree analysis and pure option-based valuation. It is particularly useful for analyzing investment projects that will follow very different value paths at decision points in time where management decisions are made regarding project pursuit. This wide range of potential outcomes is at the heart of real option theory. These wide ranges of value are *volatilities*, the basic element of option pricing theory described in Chapter 8.

Real option valuation also allows us to analyze a number of managerial decisions which in practice characterize many major capital investment projects:

- The option to defer
- The option to abandon
- The option to alter capacity
- The option to start up or shut down (switching)

Real option analysis treats cash flows in terms of future value in a positive sense, whereas DCF treats future cash flows negatively (on a discounted basis). Real option analysis is a particularly powerful device when addressing potential investment projects with extremely long life spans, or investments that do not commence until future dates. Real option analysis acknowledges the way information is gathered over time to support decision making. Management learns from both active (searching it out) and passive (observing market conditions) knowledge gathering and then uses this knowledge to make better decisions. This chapter's Mini-Case illustrates an application of real option analysis.

Project Financing

One of the hottest topics in international finance today is project finance. *Project finance* is the arrangement of financing for long-term capital projects, large in scale, long in life, and generally high in risk. This is a very general definition, however, because many forms and structures fall under this generic heading.

Project finance is not new. Examples go back centuries and include many famous early international businesses such as the Dutch East India Company and the British East India Company. These entrepreneurial importers financed their trade ventures to Asia on a voyage-by-voyage basis, with each voyage's financing being like venture capital; investors would be repaid when the shipper returned and the fruits of the Asian marketplace were sold at the docks to Mediterranean and European merchants. If all went well, the individual shareholders of the voyage were paid in full.

Project finance is used widely today by MNEs in the development of large-scale infrastructure projects in China, India, the Middle East, and many other emerging markets. Although each individual project has unique characteristics, most are highly leveraged transactions, with debt making up more than 60% of the total financing. Equity is a small component of project financing for two reasons: 1) the simple scale of the investment project often precludes a single investor or even a collection of private investors from being able to fund it and 2) many of these projects involve subjects traditionally funded by governments—such as electrical power generation, dam building, highway construction, energy exploration, production, and distribution.

This level of debt, however, places an enormous burden on cash flow for debt service. Therefore, project financing usually requires a number of additional levels of risk reduction. The lenders involved in these investments must feel secure that they will be repaid; bankers are not by nature entrepreneurs and do not enjoy entrepreneurial returns from project finance.

The following four basic properties are critical to the success of project financing:

1. **Separability of the Project from Its Investors.** The project is established as an individual legal entity, separate from the legal and financial responsibilities of its individual investors. This not only protects the assets of equity investors; but also it provides a controlled platform upon which creditors can evaluate the risks associated with the singular project. The ability of the project's cash flows to service all the debt itself assures that the debt service payments will be automatically allocated by and from the project itself (and not from a decision by management within an MNE).

2. **Long-Lived and Capital-Intensive Singular Projects.** Not only must the individual project be separable and large in proportion to the financial resources of its owners, its business line must be singular in its construction, operation, and size (capacity). The size is set at inception and is seldom, if ever, changed over the project's life.

3. **Cash Flow Predictability from Third-Party Commitments.** An oil field or electric power plant produces a homogeneous commodity product that can yield predictable cash flows if third-party commitments to take or pay can be established. Nonfinancial costs of production need to be controlled over time, usually through long-term supplier contracts with price adjustment clauses based on inflation. The predictability of net cash inflows to long-term contracts eliminates much of the individual project's business risk, allowing the financial structure to be heavily debt-financed and still safe from financial distress.

   The predictability of the project's revenue stream is essential in securing project financing. Typical contract provisions intended to ensure adequate cash flow normally include the following clauses: quantity and quality of the project's output; a pricing formula that enhances the predictability of adequate margin to cover operating costs and debt service payments, and a clear statement of the circumstances that permit significant changes in the contract, such as *force majeure* or adverse business conditions.

4. **Finite Projects with Finite Lives.** Even with a longer-term investment, it is critical that the project have a definite ending point at which all debt and equity have been repaid. Because the project is a stand-alone investment whose cash flows go directly to the servicing of its capital structure, and not to reinvestment for growth or other investment alternatives, investors of all kinds need assurances that the project's returns will be attained in a finite period. There is no capital appreciation, but only cash flow.

Examples of project finance include some of the largest individual investments undertaken in the past three decades, such as British Petroleum's financing of its interest in the North Sea and the Trans-Alaska Pipeline. The Trans-Alaska Pipeline was a joint venture

GLOBAL FINANCE IN PRACTICE 19.1

Project Finance Boom

Soaring oil revenues have brought boom times to the Middle East—and with them, unprecedented demand for project finance. Bankers say the Gulf has become the world's biggest market for project finance. According to HSBC, $33bn of the $98.5bn in project finance raised globally in the first half of this year was for the Middle East. This compares with $7bn five years ago.

Others agree. Simon Elliston, regional head of infrastructure and energy finance for Europe, Middle East and Africa at Citigroup, says: "New-build project finance transactions in the Middle East outstrips new-build anywhere else on the globe." The Gulf states are flush with cash from the rise in the price of oil. Regional energy companies are investing heavily to increase capacity, ranging from upstream oil and gas production to petrochemicals and electricity generation. But governments are also trying to diversify economies—most heavily dependent on hydrocarbons—by upgrading infrastructure, including vast property developments and airport and port expansions.

Florence Eid, senior economist for the Middle East and North Africa at JPMorgan, says the region's boom is driven by construction, property, infrastructure and petrochemicals. Declan Hegarty, managing director of the debt finance advisory for the Middle East at HSBC, says there is a huge amount of activity. But there is a difference between markets. "The busiest markets in the last few years have been Qatar, Abu Dhabi and Oman," he says. "But the balance of activity has been shifting in the last 12 months to Saudi Arabia, which has always been the market of tomorrow. For example, by

the time the Saudi Arabian private power programme is fully underway, it will have more private power capability than the rest of the Gulf region put together. Dubai has not been a project finance market although this may change given the extensive plans in infrastructure."

Banks, which provide the bulk of funding, are among those benefiting the most from the surge in activity. But while a breed of strong regional and local banks has emerged, international banks such as HSBC and Citigroup, have increased their presence. For instance, the Qatari government recently announced projects worth at least $130bn and said it wanted to finance at least half of these from foreign banks, some of which, including Barclays Capital, Credit Suisse and JPMorgan, are setting up in a financial centre in Doha, the capital.

There are advantages and disadvantages of looking to financing beyond banks. They are important, particularly at the early stages of a project, because they understand there might be delays in construction. "They can generally react because they usually have close relationships with the client," Mr Hegarty says. Nonetheless as a project matures, other sources of funding, including the bond market, securitisation markets and the Islamic finance market become increasingly relevant. Mr Hegarty says: "The more classic model of financing is breaking down because some of the projects are getting too big. We have to look harder at diversifying the financing sources."

Source: Abstracted from "Project Finance: Boom Brings Strong Demand," *Financial Times*, November 28, 2006.

between Standard Oil of Ohio, Atlantic Richfield, Exxon, British Petroleum, Mobil Oil, Philips Petroleum, Union Oil, and Amerada Hess. Each of these projects cost $1 billion or more and represented capital expenditures that no single firm would or could attempt to finance. Yet, through a joint venture arrangement, the higher-than-normal risk absorbed by the capital employed could be managed. *Global Finance in Practice 19.1* highlights the current hot bed of project financing, the Middle East.

SUMMARY POINTS

- The proposed greenfield investment in Indonesia by Cemex was analyzed within the traditional capital budgeting framework (base case).

- Foreign complications, including foreign exchange and political risks, were introduced to the analysis.

- Parent cash flows must be distinguished from project cash flows. Each of these two types of flows contributes to a different view of value.

- Parent cash flows often depend on the form of financing. Thus, cash flows cannot be clearly separated from financing decisions, as is done in domestic capital budgeting.

- Additional cash flows generated by a new investment in one foreign subsidiary may be in part or wholly taken away from another subsidiary, with the net result that the project is favorable from a single subsidiary point of view but contributes nothing to worldwide cash flows.

- Remittance of funds to the parent must be explicitly recognized because of differing tax systems, legal and political constraints on the movement of funds, local business norms, and differences in how financial markets and institutions function.

- Cash flows from subsidiaries to parent can be generated by an array of nonfinancial payments, including payment of license fees and payments for imports from the parent.

- Differing rates of national inflation must be anticipated because of their importance in causing changes in competitive position and thus cash flows over a period of time.

- A foreign project's capital budgeting analysis should be adjusted for potential foreign exchange and/or political risks associated with the investment.

- A number of alternative methods are used for adjusting for risk, including adding an additional risk premium to the discount factor used, decreasing expected cash flows, and conducting detailed sensitivity and scenario analysis on expected project outcomes.

- Real option is a different way of thinking about investment values. At its core, it is a cross between decision-tree analysis and pure option-based valuation.

- Real option valuation also allows us to evaluate the option to defer, the option to abandon, the option to alter capacity, and the option to start up or shut down a project.

MINI-CASE

Trident's Chinese Market Entry—An Application of Real Option Analysis

Trident is evaluating the possibility of entering the Chinese market. The senior management team, headed by CEO Charles Darwin, has concluded from a number of preliminary studies (code named *Beagle*) performed by a consultant that within three to five years this market could well determine who the major players are to be in Trident's telecommunications industry. The corporate finance team, headed by the CFO Maria Gonzalez, has concluded a preliminary financial analysis of its own on the basis of the numbers presented by the consultants.

The results of the corporate finance team's expected value analysis were not, however, encouraging. As illustrated in Exhibit 1, the expected gross profits of the venture were estimated to be only $10 million.

- Revenues were expected to follow one of two paths—either *high* (approximately $130 million at a 50% probability) or *low* ($50 million at a 50% probability). Therefore, using expected value analysis, revenues were estimated at $90 million.

EXHIBIT 1	Trident's Analysis of Chinese Market Entry		
Revenues	**Value (in millions)**	**Probability**	**Expected Value (in millions)**
High	$130	0.50	$65.00
Low	50	0.50	25.00
Expected value	$90.00		
Costs			
High	$120	0.33	$40.00
Medium	80	0.33	26.67
Low	40	0.33	13.33
Expected value			$80.00

Expected project gross profit = revenues − costs = $90 − $80 = $10.

- Costs were expected to be either high ($120 million), medium ($80 million), or low ($40 million), all with an equal 33.3% expected probability of occurrence. The expected value of costs was $80 million.

What made this $10 million gross profit all the more unattractive was that the market development group was requesting an additional $15 million for upfront research and development (R&D). This capital expense could not be justified. The expected total return on the project would then be a negative $5 million: ($15) + $10 = ($5). The corporate finance team concluded that the project was not an acceptable investment in its present form.

Charles was clearly frustrated with the corporate finance team during the presentation of their results. After some heated debate over individual values, Charles asked what specifically would be learned if the added $15 million in market research and development were actually spent. Would it improve the expected profitability of the project?

After some additional analysis, the corporate finance team concluded that nothing significant would be learned about the market which would change either the probabilities or expected values of revenues. However, after the additional R&D expenditure, the team felt certain that the cost of operations would be better known.

Charles then asked the corporate finance team about an alternative approach to viewing the project.

"What if the expenditure of $15 million were looked upon as the purchase of a call option on the project? What I mean is, if we spend the $15 million, we would then have the ability to identify the actual cost associated with undertaking the project. Even though we still would not really know the revenues—we still have business risk—we would be able to decide more intelligently whether to stop or proceed with the project at that point in time."

As shown in Exhibit 2, after the investment (or expenditure) of the $15 million in market research and development, the firm would know which of the three cost paths it would be on—high, medium, or low. Regardless of the expected revenue, still assumed to be $90 million, the firm could make an intelligent choice to either stop or proceed at that point. This was, in Charles' opinion, a much more logical way to pursue the analysis.

Maria Gonzalez and her finance team, however, were still not convinced. Maria said, "But we would still be spending the $15 million up front and still be looking at the same expected outcomes. I don't see how your approach changes anything."

Charles continued, "It changes a lot. After spending the $15 million we would know—with added certainty—what the likely outcome would be. If it is either the medium- or low-cost path, we would proceed and end up with a gross operating profit of either $10 or $50 million, depending on revenues. If it is the high-cost path, we would stop all work immediately, before incurring additional operating costs. The expected value, at least according to my calculations, is a positive $20 million":

$$\text{Expected Value} = (\$15) - [(0.333 \times \$0) + (0.333 \times \$10) + (0.333 \times \$50)] = \$20$$

It then dawned upon Maria what Charles was saying. The purchase of the call option, the expenditure of the $15 million, would allow Trident to avoid the loss-making option (the high-cost path with an expected outcome of negative $30 million), so the high-cost path would enter the calculation of expected value as zero. The purchase of the call option would indeed allow Trident to undertake the investment, if it wished, only after gaining additional time and knowledge.

EXHIBIT 2 Trident's Option Analysis of Chinese Market Entry

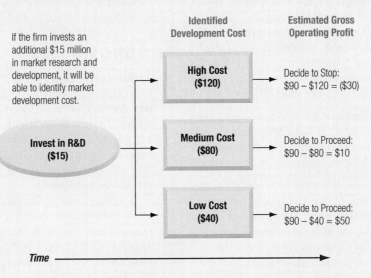

Investing in the market R&D is equivalent to buying a call option. Amounts are in millions.

Charles and the senior management team then concluded that they had won the argument (as senior management always does) and approved the project.

The Potential of Real Option Analysis

Real options analysis, like DCF and other investment analysis techniques, is nothing other than a tool. The two techniques are complementary. Management should employ both methods in the analysis of potential investments and gather information from both.

Unlike our example, real option analysis is not ordinarily a simple technique. There is an enormous amount of technical "comfort" required on the part of the analyst in order to implement the technique correctly. Like most techniques derived from financial theory, it is easily abused. Those who will utilize the information provided by real option analysis must be trained in the proper interpretation of its results.

But real option analysis is gaining in use and popularity. Consistent with the example of Trident, it is often favored first by senior management because it has two characteristics they like. Its structure acknowledges the time sequence of a project, describing cash inflows and outflows at different points in time. This is more consistent with the way management frequently sees a project unfold. Real option analysis also seems to value "management" by its very nature; it credits the ability of management to gain new information and make good business decisions at the points in time when those decisions must be made.

Case Questions

1. How does real option analysis differ from traditional expected value analysis?

2. How does real option analysis use information gathering differently from discounted cash flow analysis?

3. Recalculate both the expected return analysis and the real option analysis for the Chinese market entry assuming that the revenue probabilities were 25% high and 75% low. Is the project acceptable under either of the decision-making methodologies?

QUESTIONS

1. **Capital Budgeting Theoretical Framework.** Capital budgeting for a foreign project uses the same theoretical framework as domestic capital budgeting. What are the basic steps in domestic capital budgeting?

2. **Foreign Complexities.** Capital budgeting for a foreign project is considerably more complex than for a domestic project. What are the factors that add complexity?

3. **Project versus Parent Valuation.**
   a. Why should a foreign project be evaluated from both a project and a parent viewpoint?
   b. Which viewpoint, project or parent, gives results closer to the traditional meaning of net present value in capital budgeting?
   c. Which viewpoint gives results closer to the effect on consolidated earnings per share?

4. **Cash Flow.** Capital projects provide both operating cash flows and financial cash flows. Why are operating cash flows preferred for domestic capital budgeting but financial cash flows given major consideration in international projects?

5. **Risk-Adjusted Return.** Should the anticipated internal rate of return (IRR) for a proposed foreign project be compared to (a) alternative home country proposals, (b) returns earned by local companies in the same industry and/or risk class, or (c) both of the above? Justify your answer.

6. **Blocked Cash Flows.** In the context of evaluating foreign investment proposals, how should a multinational firm evaluate cash flows in the host foreign country that are blocked from being repatriated to the firm's home country?

7. **Host Country Inflation.** How should an MNE factor host country inflation into its evaluation of an investment proposal?

8. **Cost of Equity.** A foreign subsidiary does not have an independent cost of capital. However, in order to estimate the discount rate for a comparable host country firm, the analyst should try to calculate a hypothetical cost of capital. As part of this process, the analyst can estimate the subsidiary's proxy cost of equity by using the traditional equation: $k_e = k_{rf} + \beta(k_m - k_{rf})$. Define each variable in this equation and explain how the variable might be different for a proxy host country firm compared to the parent MNE.

9. **Viewpoints.** What are the differences in the cash flows used in a project point of view analysis and a parent point of view analysis?

10. **Foreign Exchange Risk.** How is foreign exchange risk sensitivity factored into the capital budgeting analysis of a foreign project?

11. **Expropriation Risk.** How is expropriation risk factored into the capital budgeting analysis of a foreign project?

12. **Real Option Analysis.** What is real option analysis? How is it a better method of making investment decisions than traditional capital budgeting analysis?

PROBLEMS

*1. **Trefica de Honduras.** Texas Pacific, a U.S.-based private equity firm, is trying to determine what it should pay for a tool manufacturing firm in Honduras named Trefica. Texas Pacific estimates that Trefica will generate a free cash flow of 13 million Honduran lempiras (Lp) next year (2003), and that this free cash flow will continue to grow at a constant rate of 8.0% per annum indefinitely.

A private equity firm like Texas Pacific, however, is not interested in owning a company for long, and plans to sell Trefica at the end of three years for approximately 10 times Trefica's free cash flow in that year. The current spot exchange rate is Lp14.80/$, but the Honduran inflation rate is expected to remain at a relatively high rate of 16.0% per annum compared to the U.S. dollar inflation rate of only 2.0% per annum. Texas Pacific expects to earn at least a 20% annual rate of return on international investments like Trefica.
   a. What is Trefica worth if the Honduran lempira were to remain fixed over the three-year investment period?
   b. What is Trefica worth if the Honduran lempira were to change in value over time according to purchasing power parity?

2. **Philadelphia Composite.** Philadelphia Composite Company (U.S.) is considering investing Rs50,000,000 in India to create a wholly owned tile manufacturing plant to export to the European market. After five years the subsidiary would be sold to Indian investors for Rs100,000,000. A *pro forma* income statement for the Indian operation predicts the generation of Rs7,000,000 of annual cash flow, as follows:

Annual sales revenue	Rs 30,000,000
Less cash operating expenses	−17,000,000
Less depreciation	−1,000,000
Income before interest and taxes	Rs 12,000,000
Less Indian taxes at 50%	−6,000,000
Net income	Rs 6,000,000
Add back depreciation	+1,000,000
Annual cash flow	Rs 7,000,000

The initial investment will be made on December 31, 2002, and cash flows will occur on December 31 of each succeeding year. Annual cash dividends to Philadelphia Composite from India will equal 75% of accounting income.

The U.S. corporate tax rate is 40% and the Indian corporate tax rate is 50%. Because the Indian tax rate is greater than the U.S. tax rate, annual dividends paid to Philadelphia Composite will not be subject to additional taxes in the United States. There are no capital gains taxes on the final sale. Philadelphia Composite uses a weighted average cost of capital of 14% on domestic investments, but will add six percentage points for the Indian investment because of perceived greater risk. Philadelphia Composite forecasts the rupee/dollar exchange rate for December 31 on the next six years to be as follows:

Year	Exchange Rate	Year	Exchange Rate
2002	Rs 50.00/$	2005	Rs 62.00/$
2003	Rs 54.00/$	2006	Rs 66.00/$
2004	Rs 58.00/$	2007	Rs 70.00/$

What is the net present value and internal rate of return on this investment?

3. **Atlantic Properties.** Atlantic Properties (U.S.) expects to receive cash dividends from a French joint venture over the coming three years. The first dividend, to be paid December 31, 2002, is expected to be €720,000. The dividend is then expected to grow 10.0% per year over the following two years. The current exchange rate (December 30, 2001) is $0.9180/€. Atlantic's weighted average cost of capital is 12%.
   a. What is the present value of the expected euro dividend stream if the euro is expected to appreciate 4.00% per annum against the dollar?
   b. What is the present value of the expected dividend stream if the euro were to depreciate 3.00% per annum against the dollar?

4. **Berkeley Devices.** Berkeley Devices, Inc. designs components for personal computers. Until the present, manufacturing has been subcontracted to other companies, but for reasons of quality control, Berkeley Devices has decided to manufacture components itself in Asia. Analysis has narrowed the choice to two possibilities: Penang, Malaysia and Manila, the Philippines. Currently, only the following summary of expected, after tax, cash flows is available. Although most operating outflows would be in Malaysian ringgit or Philippine pesos, some additional U.S. dollar cash outflows would be necessary, as shown in the table at the bottom of this page.

The Malaysia ringgit currently trades at RM3.80/$ and the Philippine peso trades at Ps50.00/$. Berkeley expects the Malaysian ringgit to appreciate 2.0% per year against the dollar, and the Philippine peso to depreciate 5.0% per year against the dollar. If the weighted average cost of capital for Berkeley Devices is 14.0%, which project looks most promising?

*5. **Koch Refining Company.** Privately owned Koch Refining Company is considering investing in the Czech Republic so as to have a refinery source closer to its European customers. The original investment in Czech korunas (K) would amount to K250 million, or $5,000,000 at the current spot rate of K32.50/$, all in fixed assets, which will be depreciated over 10 years by the straight-line method. An additional K100,000,000 will be needed for working capital.

For capital budgeting purposes, Koch assumes sale as a going concern at the end of the third year at a price, after all taxes, equal to the net book value of fixed assets alone (not including working capital). All free cash flow will be repatriated to the United States as soon as possible. The projected operational and financial results for the project are presented in U.S. dollars below.

Variable manufacturing costs are expected to be 50% of sales. No additional funds need be invested in the U.S. subsidiary during the period under consideration. The Czech Republic imposes no restrictions on repatriation of any funds of any sort. The Czech corporate tax rate is 25% and the United States rate is

Berkeley in Penang	2002	2003	2004	2005	2006	2007
Net ringgit cash flows	(26,000)	8,000	6,800	7,400	9,200	10,000
Net dollar cash flows	—	(100)	(120)	(150)	(150)	—
Berkeley in Manila						
Net peso cash flows	(560,000)	190,000	180,000	200,000	210,000	200,000
Dollar cash outflows	—	(100)	(200)	(300)	(400)	—

End of Year	Unit Demand	Unit Sales Price	Exchange Rate (Korunas/$)	Fixed Cash Operating Expenses	Depreciation
0			32.5		
1	700,000	$ 10.00	30.0	$ 1,000,000	$ 500,000
2	900,000	10.30	27.5	1,030,000	500,000
3	1,000,000	10.60	25.0	1,060,000	500,000

40%. Both countries allow a tax credit for taxes paid in other countries. Koch uses 18% as its weighted average cost of capital, and its objective is to maximize present value. Is the investment attractive to Koch Refining?

6. **Tostadas de Baja, S.A.** Tostadas de Baja, S.A., located in the state of Baja California, Mexico, manufactures frozen Mexican food, which enjoys a large following in California and Arizona. In order to be closer to its U.S. market, Tostadas de Baja is considering moving some of its manufacturing operations to southern California. Operations in California would begin in Year 1 and have the following attributes:

a. The Year 1 sales price in the United States would average $5 per package, and prices would increase 3% per annum.

b. The Year 1 production and sales total would be 1 million packets. Unit sales would grow at 10% per annum.

c. California production costs of an estimated $4 per packet in Year 1 would increase by 4% per annum. General and administration expenses would be $100,000 per year. Depreciation expenses would be $80,000 per year.

d. Tostadas de Baja uses a weighted average cost of capital of 16%.

e. Tostadas de Baja will assign an after-tax value to its California plant at the end of Year 3 equal to an infinite stream of Year 3 dividends, discounted at 20% per annum. The higher discount rate is because the company is concerned about the political risk of a Mexican firm manufacturing in California.

f. All production is for sale; hence, production volume equals sales volume. All sales are for cash.

g. Combined federal and state tax rate is 30% in the United States and 25% in Mexico.

h. Actual and expected exchange rates, by year, are as follows:

Year 0: Ps8.00/$.	Year 2: Ps10.00/$
Year 1: Ps9.00/$.	Year 3: Ps11.00/$

The California manufacturing plant will pay 80% of its accounting profit to Tostadas as an annual cash dividend. Mexican taxes are calculated on grossed up dividends from foreign countries, with a credit for host country taxes already paid. What is the maximum U.S. dollar price Tostadas de Baja should offer in Year 1 for the investment?

Santa Clara Electronics.

Use the following problem and assumptions to answer problems 7–10.

Santa Clara Electronics, Inc., of California exports 24,000 sets of low-density light bulbs per year to Argentina under an import license that expires in five years. In Argentina, the bulbs are sold for the Argentine peso equivalent of $60 per set. Direct manufacturing costs in the United States and shipping together amount to $40 per set. The market for this type of bulb in Argentina is stable, neither growing nor shrinking, and Santa Clara holds the major portion of the market.

The Argentine government has invited Santa Clara to open a manufacturing plant so imported bulbs can be replaced by local production. If Santa Clara makes the investment, it will operate the plant for five years and then sell the building and equipment to Argentine investors at net book value at the time of sale plus the value of any net working capital. (Net working capital is the amount of current assets less any portion financed by local debt.) Santa Clara will be allowed to repatriate all net income and depreciation funds to the United States each year. Santa Clara traditionally evaluates all foreign investments in U.S. dollar terms.

■ **Investment.** Santa Clara's anticipated cash outlay in U.S. dollars in 2010 would be as follows:

Building and equipment	$1,000,000
Net working capital	1,000,000
Total investment	$2,000,000

All investment outlays will be made in 2010, and all operating cash flows will occur at the end of years 2011 through 2015.

■ **Depreciation and Investment Recovery.** Building and equipment will be depreciated over five years on a straight-line basis. At the end of the fifth year, the $1,000,000 of net working capital may also be repatriated to the United States, as may the remaining net book value of the plant.

▪ **Sales Price of Bulbs.** Locally manufactured bulbs will be sold for the Argentine peso equivalent of $60 per set.

▪ **Operating Expenses per Set of Bulbs.** Material purchases are as follows:

Materials purchased in Argentina (U.S. dollar equivalent)	$20 per set
Materials imported from Santa Clara (U.S.)	$10 per set
Total variable costs	$30 per set

▪ **Transfer Prices.** The $10 transfer price per set for raw material sold by the parent consists of $5 of direct and indirect costs incurred in the United States on their manufacture, creating $5 of pre-tax profit to Santa Clara.

▪ **Taxes.** The corporate income tax rate is 40% in both Argentina and the United States (combined federal and state/province). There are no capital gains taxes on the future sale of the Argentine subsidiary, either in Argentina or the United States.

▪ **Discount Rate.** Santa Clara Electronics uses a 15% discount rate to evaluate all domestic and foreign projects.

7. **Santa Clara Electronics: Baseline Analysis.** Evaluate the proposed investment in Argentina by Santa Clara Electronics (U.S.). Santa Clara's management wishes the baseline analysis to be performed in U.S. dollars (and implicitly also assumes the exchange rate remains fixed throughout the life of the project). Create a project viewpoint capital budget and a parent viewpoint capital budget. What do you conclude from your analysis?

8. **Santa Clara Electronics: Revenue Growth Scenario.** As a result of their analysis in problem 7, Santa Clara wishes to explore the implications of being able to grow sales volume by 4% per year. Argentine inflation is expected to average 5% per year, so sales price and material cost increases of 7% and 6% per year, respectively, are thought to be reasonable. Although material costs in Argentina are expected to rise, U.S.-based costs are not expected to change over the five-year period. Evaluate this scenario for both the project and parent viewpoints. Is the project under this revenue growth scenario acceptable?

9. **Santa Clara Electronics: Revenue Growth and Sales Price Scenario.** In addition to the assumptions employed in problem 8, Santa Clara now wishes to evaluate the prospect of being able to sell the Argentine subsidiary at the end of year 5 at a multiple of the business's earnings in that year. Santa Clara believes that a multiple of six is a conservative estimate of the market value of the firm at that time. Evaluate the project and parent viewpoint capital budgets.

10. **Santa Clara Electronics: Revenue Growth, Sales Price and Currency Risk Scenario.** One of the new analysts at Santa Clara, a recent MBA graduate, believes that it is a fundamental error to evaluate the Argentine project's prospective earnings and cash flows in dollars, rather than first estimating their Argentine peso (Ps) value and then converting cash flow returns to the U.S. in dollars. She believes the correct method is to use the end-of-year spot rate in 2003 of Ps3.50/$ and assume it will change in relation to purchasing power. (She is assuming U.S. inflation to be 1% per annum and Argentine inflation to be 5% per annum.) She also believes that Santa Clara should use a risk-adjusted discount rate in Argentina that reflects Argentine capital costs (20% is her estimate) and a risk-adjusted discount rate for the parent viewpoint capital budget (18%) on the assumption that international projects in a risky currency environment should require a higher expected return than other lower risk projects. How do these assumptions and changes alter Santa Clara's perspective on the proposed investment?

INTERNET EXERCISES

1. **Capital Projects and the EBRD.** The European Bank for Reconstruction and Development (EBRD) was established to "foster the transition toward open market-oriented economies and to promote private and entrepreneurial initiative in the countries of central and eastern Europe and the Commonwealth of Independent States (CIS) committed to and applying the principles of multiparty democracy, pluralism and market economics." Use the EBRD Web site to determine which projects and companies EBRD is currently undertaking.

European Bank for
Reconstruction and
Development   www.ebrd.org

2. **Emerging Markets: China.** Long-term investment projects such as electrical power generation require a

thorough understanding of all attributes of doing business in that country, including import/export restrictions, labor relations, supplier financing, tax rules, depreciation schedules, currency properties and restrictions, sources of short-term and long-term debt, to name a few. China is currently the focus of investment and market penetration strategies of multinational firms worldwide. Using the Web (you might start with the following Web sites), build a database on doing business in China, and prepare an update of many of the factors such as average receivables outstanding and currency convertibility discussed in this chapter.

Ministry of Foreign Trade
and Economic
Cooperation, PRC   www.chinamarket.com.cn/

China Investment Trust
& Investment Corporation   www.citic.com/

PART VI

Managing Multinational Operations

CHAPTER 20

Multinational Tax Management

Over and over again courts have said that there is nothing sinister in so arranging one's affairs as to keep taxes as low as possible. Everybody does so, rich and poor, and all do right, for nobody owes any public duty to pay more than the law demands: taxes are enforced extractions, not voluntary contributions. To demand more in the name of morals is mere cant.

—Judge Learned Hand, Commissioner v. Newman, 159 F.2d 848 (CA-2, 1947).

Tax planning for multinational operations is an extremely complex, but vitally important aspect of international business. To plan effectively, MNEs must understand not only the intricacies of their own operations worldwide, but also the different structures and interpretations of tax liabilities across countries. *The primary objective of multinational tax planning is the minimization of the firm's worldwide tax burden.* This objective, however, must not be pursued without full recognition that decision making within the firm must always be based on the economic fundamentals of the firm's line of business, and not on convoluted policies undertaken purely for the reduction of tax liability. As evident from previous chapters, taxes have a major impact on corporate net income and cash flow through their influence on foreign investment decisions, financial structure, determination of the cost of capital, foreign exchange management, working capital management, and financial control.

The purpose of this chapter is to provide an overview of the way taxes are applied to MNEs globally. We do this in three parts. The first section acquaints you with the overall international tax environment. This includes a brief overview of the tax environments that an MNE is likely to encounter globally and the basics of most intercountry tax treaties. The second section examines transfer pricing. Although we use U.S. taxes as illustrations, our intention is not to make this chapter or this book U.S.-centric. Most of the U.S. practices that we describe have close parallels in other countries, albeit modified to fit their specific national overall tax system. The third and final section of the chapter examines the use of tax haven subsidiaries and international offshore financial centers.

Tax Principles

The following sections explain the most important aspects of the international tax environments and specific features that affect MNEs. Before we explain the specifics of multinational taxation in practice, however, it is necessary to introduce two areas of fundamental importance: *tax morality* and *tax neutrality*.

Tax Morality

The MNE faces not only a morass of foreign taxes but also an ethical question. In many countries, taxpayers—corporate or individual—do not voluntarily comply with the tax laws. Smaller domestic firms and individuals are the chief violators. The MNE must decide whether to follow a practice of full disclosure to tax authorities or adopt the philosophy of "when in Rome, do as the Romans do." Given the local prominence of most foreign subsidiaries and the political sensitivity of their position, most MNEs follow the full disclosure practice. Some firms, however, believe that their competitive position would be eroded if they did not avoid taxes to the same extent as their domestic competitors. There is obviously no prescriptive answer to the problem, since business ethics are partly a function of cultural heritage and historical development.

Some countries have imposed what seem to be arbitrary punitive tax penalties on MNEs for presumed violations of local tax laws. Property or wealth tax assessments are sometimes perceived by the foreign firm to be excessively large when compared with those levied on locally owned firms. The problem is then how to respond to tax penalties that are punitive or discriminatory.

Tax Neutrality

When a government decides to levy a tax, it must consider not only the potential revenue from the tax, or how efficiently it can be collected, but also the effect the proposed tax can have on private economic behavior. For example, the U.S. government's policy on taxation of foreign source income does not have as its sole objective the raising of revenue. Rather, it has multiple objectives, including the following:

- Neutralizing tax incentives that might favor (or disfavor) U.S. private investment in developed countries
- Providing an incentive for U.S. private investment in developing countries
- Improving the U.S. balance of payments by removing the advantages of artificial tax havens and encouraging repatriation of funds
- Raising revenue

The ideal tax should not only raise revenue efficiently but also have as few negative effects on economic behavior as possible. Some theorists argue that the ideal tax should be completely *neutral* in its effect on private decisions and completely *equitable* among taxpayers. However, other theorists claim that national policy objectives such as balance of payments or investment in developing countries should be encouraged through an active *tax incentive policy*. Most tax systems compromise between these two viewpoints.

One way to view neutrality is to require that the burden of taxation on each dollar, euro, pound, or yen of profit earned in home country operations by an MNE be equal to the burden of taxation on each currency-equivalent of profit earned by the same firm in its foreign operations. This is called *domestic neutrality*. A second way to view neutrality is to require that the tax burden on each foreign subsidiary of the firm is equal to the tax burden on its competitors in the same country. This is called *foreign neutrality*. The latter interpretation is often supported by MNEs because it focuses more on the competitiveness of the individual firm in individual country markets.

The issue of *tax equity* is also difficult to define and measure. In theory, an equitable tax is one that imposes the same total tax burden on all taxpayers who are similarly situated and located in the same tax jurisdiction. In the case of foreign investment income, the U.S. Treasury argues that since the United States uses the nationality principle to claim tax jurisdiction, U.S.-owned foreign subsidiaries are in the same tax jurisdiction as U.S. domestic subsidiaries. Therefore, a dollar earned in foreign operations should be taxed at the same rate and paid at the same time as a dollar earned in domestic operations.

National Tax Environments

Despite the fundamental objectives of national tax authorities, it is widely agreed that taxes affect economic decisions made by MNEs. Tax treaties between nations, and differential tax structures, rates, and practices all result in a less than level playing field for the MNEs competing on world markets.

Exhibit 20.1 provides an overview of corporate tax rates as applicable to Japan, Germany, and the United States. The categorizations of income (for example, distributed versus undistributed profits), the differences in tax rates, and the discrimination in tax rates applicable to income earned in specific countries serve to introduce the critical dimensions of tax planning for the MNE.

Nations typically structure their tax systems along one of two basic approaches: the *worldwide approach* or the *territorial approach*. Both approaches are attempts to determine which firms, foreign or domestic by incorporation, or which incomes, foreign or domestic in origin, are subject to the taxation of host country tax authorities.

Worldwide Approach. The *worldwide approach,* also referred to as the *residential* or *national approach,* levies taxes on the income earned by firms that are incorporated in the host country, regardless of where the income was earned (domestically or abroad). An MNE earning income both at home and abroad would therefore find its worldwide income taxed by its home country tax authorities. For example, a country like the United States taxes the

EXHIBIT 20.1	Comparison of Corporate Tax Rates: Japan, Germany, and the United States		
Taxable Income Category	**Japan**	**Germany**	**United States**
Corporate income tax rates:	41%	29.5%	40%
Withholding taxes on dividends (portfolio):			
with Japan	—	15%	5%
with Germany	15%	—	5%
with United States	10%	0/5/15%	—
Withholding taxes on dividends (substantial holdings):			
with Japan	—	15%	5%
with Germany	10%	—	5%
with United States	0/5%	0/5/15%	—
Withholding taxes on interest:			
with Japan	—	10%	10%
with Germany	10%	—	0%
with United States	10%	25%	—
Withholding taxes on royalties:			
with Japan	—	10%	0%
with Germany	10%	—	0%
with United States	0%	0%	—

Source: Corporate income tax rates drawn from "KPMG's Corporate and Indirect Tax Rate Survey, 2008,"KPMG.com. Tax rates as of April 1, 2008. Withholding tax rates extracted from Price Waterhouse Coopers, *Corporate Taxes: A Worldwide Summary, 2009.* "Substantial holdings" for the United States applies only to inter-corporate dividend payments. In Germany and Japan, "substantial holdings" applies to corporate shareholders of greater than 25%.

income earned by firms based in the United States regardless of whether the income earned by the firm is domestically or foreign sourced. In the case of the United States, ordinary foreign sourced income is taxed only as remitted to the parent firm. As with all questions of tax, however, numerous conditions and exceptions exist. The primary problem is that this does not address the income earned by foreign firms operating within the United States. Countries like the United States then apply the principle of *territorial taxation* to foreign firms within their legal jurisdiction, taxing all income earned by foreign firms within their borders as well.

Territorial Approach. The *territorial approach,* also termed the *source approach,* focuses on the income earned by firms within the legal jurisdiction of the host country, not on the country of firm incorporation. Countries like Germany that follow the territorial approach apply taxes equally to foreign and domestic firms on income earned within the country but in principle not on income earned outside the country. The territorial approach, like the worldwide approach, results in a major gap in coverage if resident firms earn income outside the country but are not taxed by the country in which the profits are earned. In this case, tax authorities extend tax coverage to income earned abroad if it is not covered by foreign tax jurisdictions. Once again, a mix of the two tax approaches is necessary for full coverage of income.

Tax Deferral. If the worldwide approach to international taxation is followed to the letter, it would end the *tax deferral* privilege for many MNEs. Foreign subsidiaries of MNEs pay host country corporate income taxes, but many parent countries defer claiming additional income taxes on that foreign source income *until it is remitted to the parent firm*. For example, U.S. corporate income taxes on some types of foreign source income of U.S.-owned subsidiaries incorporated abroad are deferred until the earnings are remitted to the U.S. parent. However, in October 2004, the U.S. tax laws were modified to encourage foreign source tax deferred income earned before 2003 to be repatriated to the United States at a low 5.25% tax rate. This money had to be repatriated before the end of 2005 and used to stimulate job creation in the United States to qualify for the low rate.

Tax Treaties

A network of bilateral tax treaties, many of which are modeled after one proposed by the Organisation for Economic Cooperation and Development (OECD), provides a means of reducing double taxation. Tax treaties normally define whether taxes are to be imposed on income earned in one country by the nationals of another, and if so, how. Tax treaties are bilateral, with the two signatories specifying what rates are applicable to which types of income between them alone. Exhibit 20.1's specification of withholding taxes on dividends, interest, and royalty payments between resident corporations of Japan, Germany, and the United States, is a classic example of the structure of tax treaties. Note that Germany, for example, imposes a 10% withholding tax on royalty payments to Japanese investors, while royalty payments to U.S. investors are withheld at a 0% rate.

The individual bilateral tax jurisdictions as specified through tax treaties are particularly important for firms that are primarily exporting to another country rather than doing business there through a "permanent establishment." The latter would be the case for manufacturing operations. A firm that only exports would not want any of its other worldwide income taxed by the importing country. Tax treaties define a "permanent establishment" and what constitutes a limited presence for tax purposes.

Tax treaties also typically result in reduced withholding tax rates between the two signatory countries, the negotiation of the treaty itself serving as a forum for opening and expanding business relationships between the two countries. This practice is important to both MNEs operating through foreign subsidiaries, earning *active income,* and individual portfolio investors simply receiving *passive income* in the form of dividends, interest, or royalties.

Tax Types

Taxes are classified on the basis of whether they are applied directly to income, called *direct taxes,* or on the basis of some other measurable performance characteristic of the firm, called *indirect taxes.* Exhibit 20.2 illustrates the wide range of corporate income taxes in the world today.

EXHIBIT 20.2	Corporate Income Tax Rates for Selected Countries, 2008				
Country	**2008**	**Country**	**2008**	**Country**	**2008**
Afghanistan	20%	Guatemala	31%	Papua New Guinea	30%
Albania	10%	Honduras	30%	Paraguay	10%
Angola	35%	Hong Kong	17%	Peru	30%
Argentina	35%	Hungary	16%	Philippines	35%
Aruba	28%	Iceland	15%	Poland	19%
Australia	30%	India	34%	Portugal	25%
Austria	25%	Indonesia	30%	Qatar	35%
Bahrain	0%	Iran	25%	Romania	16%
Bangladesh	30%	Ireland	13%	Russia	24%
Barbados	25%	Israel	27%	Saudi Arabia	20%
Belarus	24%	Italy	31%	Serbia	10%
Belgium	34%	Jamaica	33%	Singapore	18%
Bolivia	25%	Japan	41%	Slovak Republic	19%
Bosnia and Herzegovina	10%	Jordan	35%	Slovenia	22%
Botswana	25%	Kazakhstan	30%	South Africa	35%
Brazil	34%	Korea, Republic of	28%	Spain	30%
Bulgaria	10%	Kuwait	55%	Sri Lanka	35%
Canada	33.5%	Latvia	15%	Sudan	35%
Cayman Islands	0%	Libya	40%	Sweden	28%
Chile	17%	Lithuania	15%	Switzerland	19%
China	25%	Luxembourg	30%	Syria	28%
Colombia	33%	Macau	12%	Taiwan	25%
Costa Rica	30%	Malaysia	26%	Thailand	30%
Croatia	20%	Malta	35%	Tunisia	30%
Cyprus	10%	Mauritius	15%	Turkey	20%
Czech Republic	21%	Mexico	28%	Ukraine	25%
Denmark	25%	Montenegro	9%	United Arab Emirates	55%
Dominican Republic	25%	Mozambique	32%	United Kingdom	28%
Ecuador	25%	Netherlands	26%	United States	40%
Egypt	20%	Netherlands Antilles	35%	Uruguay	25%
Estonia	21%	New Zealand	30%	Venezuela	34%
Fiji	31%	Norway	28%	Vietnam	28%
Finland	26%	Oman	12%	Yemen	35%
France	33.33%	Pakistan	35%	Zambia	35%
Germany	29.51%	Palestine	16%		
Greece	25%	Panama	30%		

Source: "KPMG's Corporate and Indirect Tax Rate Survey, 2008," KPMG.com. Tax rates as of April 1, 2008.

The effective U.S. corporate income tax rate is 40% (Exhibit 20.2). This is relatively high compared to some important competitors such as China (25%), Japan (41%), Germany (29.51%), the Russian Federation (24%), Sweden (28%), and the United Kingdom (28%). *Global Finance in Practice 20.1* raises the growing question—Should the United States cut corporate income taxes?

Income Tax. Many governments rely on personal and corporate income taxes for their primary revenue source. Corporate income taxes are widely used today. Some countries impose different corporate tax rates on distributed income versus undistributed income. Corporate income tax rates vary over a relatively wide range, rising as high as 45% in Guyana and falling as low as 17% in Hong Kong, 15% in the British Virgin Islands, 10% in Cyprus, and effectively 0% in a number of offshore tax havens (discussed later in this chapter).

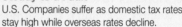

GLOBAL FINANCE IN PRACTICE 20.1

Taxed to the Max

As jobs vanish and Washington mulls a vast range of economic policy options, one that's conspicuously absent is corporate tax reform. That alarms many business advocates, who fear that current tax policy is outdated and will cripple U.S. companies if global growth resumes later this year or early next. "At this pivotal moment in history," warns David Lewis, chief tax executive for Eli Lilly and Co., "the U.S. must embrace an internationally competitive corporate tax system."

Exactly how badly higher tax rates harm U.S. companies is hard to measure and has long been a point of contention because the gap between nominal and effective rates can be substantial. But critics say that rapid globalization makes reform more urgent. More than two decades have passed since Congress overhauled corporate taxes. During that time global competition has surged and the United States has seen a fourfold increase in imports and an even larger jump in exports, two vital signs of a much more interconnected globe.

Canada, Germany, New Zealand, Spain, Italy, Switzerland, the United Kingdom, the Czech Republic, and Iceland all chopped their corporate tax rates last year. The U.S. business sector now grapples with the second-highest statutory income tax rates among the 30 industrialized nations in the Organization for Economic Co-operation and Development (OECD). Only Japanese companies face higher rates, by a slim margin.

Failure to align U.S. tax policy with reality imperils our industrial base, experts warn. "Ultimately, it means U.S. multinationals are probably going to lose market share to foreign multinationals," says Peter Merrill, director of the National Economics and Statistics Group at accounting firm PricewaterhouseCoopers. "And they may become takeover targets of foreign multinationals."

Steady to a Fault
U.S. Companies suffer as domestic tax rates stay high while overseas rates decline.

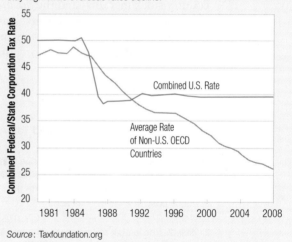

Source: Taxfoundation.org

Partisans of sweeping corporate tax reform insist the math should end any debate. Uncle Sam taxes U.S. corporate income at a top 35 percent rate, while states, on average, tack on 4.3 percentage points. The average among OECD countries is 26.6 percent. Thus, for every dollar earned in the global marketplace, U.S. companies appear to surrender nearly 13 cents more than a typical OECD member.

Source: "Taxed to the Max," Randy Myers, *CFO Magazine*, March 1, 2009.

Withholding Tax. Passive income (dividends, interest, royalties) earned by a resident of one country within the tax jurisdiction of a second country are normally subject to a withholding tax in the second country. The reason for the institution of withholding taxes is actually quite simple: governments recognize that most international investors will not file a tax return in each country in which they invest, and the government therefore wishes to assure that a minimum tax payment is received. As the term *withholding* implies, the taxes are withheld by the corporation from the payment made to the investor, and the withheld taxes are then turned over to government authorities. Withholding taxes are a major subject of bilateral tax treaties, and generally range between 0% and 25%.

Value-Added Tax. The *value-added tax* has achieved great prominence. It is a type of national sales tax collected at each stage of production or sale of consumption goods in proportion to the value added during that stage. In general, production goods such as plant and equipment have not been subject to the value-added tax. Certain basic necessities such as medicines and other health-related expenses, education and religious activities, and the postal service are usually exempt or taxed at lower rates. The value-added tax has been adopted as the main source of revenue from indirect taxation by all members of the European Union, most other countries in Western Europe, a number of Latin American countries, Canada, and scattered other countries. A numerical example of a value-added tax computation is shown in Exhibit 20.3.

Other National Taxes. There are a variety of other national taxes, which vary in importance from country to country. The *turnover tax* (tax on the purchase or sale of securities in some country stock markets) and the *tax on undistributed profits* were mentioned before. *Property and inheritance taxes,* also termed *transfer taxes,* are imposed in a variety of ways to achieve intended social redistribution of income and wealth as much as to raise revenue. There are a number of red tape charges for public services that are in reality user taxes. Sometimes

---

EXHIBIT 20.3   Value-Added Tax Applied to the Sale of a Wooden Fence Post

This is an example of how a wooden fence post would be assessed for value-added taxes in the course of its production and subsequent sale. A value-added tax of 10% is assumed.

1. **Step 1.** The original tree owner sells to the lumber mill, for $0.20, that part of a tree that ultimately becomes the fence post. The grower has added $0.20 in value up to this point by planting and raising the tree. While collecting $0.20 from the lumber mill, the grower must set aside $0.02 to pay the value-added tax to the government.

2. **Step 2.** The lumber mill processes the tree into fence posts and sells each post for $0.40 to the lumber wholesaler. The lumber mill has added $0.20 in value ($0.40 less $0.20) through its processing activities. Therefore, the lumber mill owner must set aside $0.02 to pay the mill's value-added tax to the government. In practice, the owner would probably calculate the mill's tax liability as 10% of $0.40, or $0.04, with a tax credit of $0.02 for the value-added tax already paid by the tree owner.

3. **Steps 3 and 4.** The lumber wholesaler and retailer also add value to the fence post through their selling and distribution activities. They are assessed $0.01 and $0.03 respectively, making the cumulative value-added tax collected by the government $0.08, or 10% of the final sales price.

Stage of Production	Sales Price	Value Added	Value-Added Tax at 10%	Cumulative Value-Added Tax
Tree owner	$0.20	$0.20	$0.02	$0.02
Lumber mill	$0.40	$0.20	$0.02	$0.04
Lumber wholesaler	$0.50	$0.10	$0.01	$0.05
Lumber retailer	$0.80	$0.30	$0.03	$0.08

foreign exchange purchases or sales are in effect hidden taxes, in as much as the government earns revenue rather than just regulates imports and exports for balance of payments reasons.

Foreign Tax Credits

To prevent double taxation of the same income, most countries grant a *foreign tax credit* for income taxes paid to the host country. Countries differ on how they calculate the foreign tax credit and what kinds of limitations they place on the total amount claimed. Normally, foreign tax credits are also available for withholding taxes paid to other countries on dividends, royalties, interest, and other income remitted to the parent. The value-added tax and other sales taxes are not eligible for a foreign tax credit but are typically deductible from pretax income as an expense.

A *tax credit* is a direct reduction of taxes that would otherwise be due and payable. It differs from a *deductible expense,* which is an expense used to reduce taxable income before the tax rate is applied. A $100 tax credit reduces taxes payable by the full $100, whereas a $100 deductible expense reduces taxable income by $100 and taxes payable by $100 × t, where t is the tax rate. Tax credits are more valuable on a dollar-for-dollar basis than are deductible expenses.

If there were no credits for foreign taxes paid, sequential taxation by the host government and then by the home government would result in a very high cumulative tax rate. To illustrate, assume the wholly owned foreign subsidiary of an MNE earns $10,000 before local income taxes and pays a dividend equal to all of its after-tax income. The host country income tax rate is 30%, and the home country of the parent tax rate is 35%. For simplicity, we will assume no withholding taxes. Total taxation with and without allowances for tax credits is shown in Exhibit 20.4.

If tax credits are not allowed, sequential levying of a 30% host country tax and then a 35% home country tax on the income that remains results in an effective 54.5% tax, a cumulative rate that would render many MNEs uncompetitive with single-country local firms. The effect of allowing tax credits is to limit total taxation on the *original* before-tax income to no more than the highest single rate among jurisdictions. In the case shown in Exhibit 20.4, the effective overall tax rate of 35% with foreign tax credits is equivalent to the higher tax rate of the home country (and is the tax rate payable if the income had been earned at home).

The $500 of additional home country tax under the tax credit system in Exhibit 20.4 is the amount needed to bring total taxation ($3,000 already paid plus the additional $500) up to but not beyond 35% of the original $10,000 of before-tax foreign income.

EXHIBIT 20.4   Foreign Tax Credits

Foreign Tax Credits	Without Foreign Tax Credits	With Foreign Tax Credits
Before-tax foreign income	$10,000	$10,000
Less foreign tax at 30%	–3,000	–3,000
Available to parent and paid as dividend	$ 7,000	$ 7,000
Less additional parent-country tax at 35%	–2,450	
Less incremental tax (after credits)	—	–500
Profit after all taxes	$ 4,550	$ 6,500
Total taxes, both jurisdictions	$ 5,450	$ 3,500
Effective overall tax rate (total taxes paid ÷ foreign income)	54.5%	35.0%

Transfer Pricing

Transfer pricing, the pricing of goods, services, and technology transferred to a foreign subsidiary from an affiliated company, is the first and foremost method of transferring funds out of a foreign subsidiary. These costs enter directly into the cost-of-goods-sold component of the subsidiary's income statement. This is a particularly sensitive problem for MNEs. Even purely domestic firms find it difficult to reach agreement on the best method for setting prices on transactions between related units. In the case of MNEs, managers must balance conflicting considerations such as fund positioning and income taxes.

Fund Positioning Effect

A parent company wishing to transfer funds out of a particular country can charge higher prices on goods sold to its subsidiary in that country, to the degree that government regulations allow. A foreign subsidiary can be financed by the reverse technique, a lowering of transfer prices. Payment by the subsidiary for imports from its parent or sister subsidiary transfers funds out of the subsidiary. A higher transfer price permits funds to be accumulated in the selling country. Transfer pricing may also be used to transfer funds between sister subsidiaries. Multiple sourcing of component parts on a worldwide basis allows switching between suppliers from within the corporate family to function as a device to transfer funds.

Income Tax Effect

A major consideration in setting a transfer price is the *income tax effect*. Worldwide corporate profits may be influenced by setting transfer prices to minimize taxable income in a country with a high income tax rate and maximize income in a country with a low income tax rate. A parent company wishing to reduce the taxable profits of a subsidiary in a high-tax environment may set transfer prices at a higher rate to increase the costs of the subsidiary thereby reducing taxable income.

The income tax effect is illustrated in Exhibit 20.5. Trident Europe is operating in a relatively high-tax environment (German corporate income taxes are 45%). Trident USA is in a significantly lower tax environment (U.S. corporate income tax rates are 35%), motivating Trident to charge Trident Europe a higher transfer price on goods produced in the United States and sold to Trident Europe.

If Trident Corporation adopts a high-markup policy by "selling" its merchandise at an intracompany sales price of $1,700,000, the same $800,000 of pretax consolidated income is allocated more heavily to low-tax Trident USA and less heavily to high-tax Trident Europe. (Note that Trident Corporation, the corporate parent, must adopt a transfer pricing policy that directly alters the profitability of each of the individual subsidiaries.) As a consequence, total taxes drop by $30,000 and consolidated net income increases by $30,000 to $500,000— all while total sales remain constant.

Trident would naturally prefer the high-markup policy for sales from the United States to Europe (Germany in this case). Needless to say, government tax authorities are aware of the potential income distortion from transfer price manipulation. There are a variety of regulations and court cases on the reasonableness of transfer prices, including fees and royalties as well as prices set for merchandise. If a government taxing authority does not accept a transfer price, taxable income will be deemed larger than was calculated by the firm and taxes will be increased.

Section 482 of the U.S. Internal Revenue Code is typical of laws circumscribing freedom to set transfer prices. Under this authority, the Internal Revenue Service (IRS) can reallocate gross income, deductions, credits, or allowances between related corporations in order to prevent tax evasion or to reflect more clearly a proper allocation of income. Under the IRS

EXHIBIT 20.5	Effect of Low versus High Transfer Price on Trident Europe's Net Income (thousands of U.S. dollars)		
Low-Markup Policy	**Trident USA (Subsidiary)**	**Trident Europe (Subsidiary)**	**Trident (Combined)**
Sales	$1,400	$2,000	$2,000
Less cost of goods sold*	(1,000)	(1,400)	(1,000)
Gross profit	$ 400	$ 600	$1,000
Less operating expenses	(100)	(100)	(200)
Taxable income	$ 300	$ 500	$ 800
Less income taxes	35% (105)	45% (225)	(330)
Net income	$ 195	$ 275	$ 470
High-Markup Policy			
Sales	$1,700	$2,000	$2,000
Less cost of goods sold˙	(1,000)	(1,700)	(1,000)
Gross profit	$ 700	$ 300	$ 1,000
Less operating expenses	(100)	(100)	(200)
Taxable income	$ 600	$ 200	$ 800
Less income taxes	35% (210)	45% (90)	(300)
Net income	$ 390	$ 110	$ 500

*Trident USA's sales price becomes cost of goods sold for Trident Europe.

guidelines and subsequent judicial interpretation, the burden of proof is on the taxpaying firm to show that the IRS has been arbitrary or unreasonable in reallocating income. This "guilty until proven innocent" approach means that MNEs must keep good documentation of the logic and costs behind their transfer prices. The "correct price" according to the guidelines is the one that reflects an *arm's length price*; that is, a sale of the same goods or service to a comparable unrelated customer.

IRS regulations provide three methods to establish arm's length prices: comparable uncontrolled prices, resale prices, and cost-plus calculations. All of these methods are recommended for use in member countries by the OECD Committee on Fiscal Affairs. In some cases, combinations of these three methods are used.

Managerial Incentives and Evaluation

When a firm is organized with decentralized profit centers, transfer pricing between centers can disrupt evaluation of managerial performance. This problem is not unique to MNEs, but it is a controversial issue in the "centralization versus decentralization" debate in domestic circles. In the domestic case, however, a modicum of coordination at the corporate level can alleviate some of the distortion that occurs when any profit center suboptimizes its profit for the corporate good. Also, in most domestic cases, the company can file a single (for that country) consolidated tax return, so the issue of cost allocation between related companies is not critical from a tax payment point of view.

In the multinational case, coordination is often hindered by longer and less efficient channels of communication, the need to consider the unique variables that influence international pricing, and separate taxation. Even with the best intentions, a manager in one country may find it difficult to know what is best for the firm as a whole when buying at a negotiated price from related companies in another country. Yet, if corporate headquarters establishes transfer prices and sourcing alternatives, one of the main advantages of a decentralized profit center system disappears: local management loses the incentive to act for its own benefit.

To illustrate, refer to Exhibit 20.5, where an increase in the transfer price led to a world-wide income gain: Trident Corporation's income rose by $195,000 (from $195,000 to $390,000) while Trident Europe's income fell by only $165,000 (from $275,000 to $110,000), for a net gain of $30,000. Should the managers of the European subsidiary lose their bonuses (or even their jobs) because of their "sub-par" performance? Bonuses are usually determined by a companywide formula based in part on the profitability of individual subsidiaries, but in this case Trident Europe "sacrificed" for the greater good of the whole. Arbitrarily changing transfer prices can create measurement problems.

Specifically, transferring profit from high-tax Trident Europe to low-tax Trident USA changes the following for one or both companies:

- Import tariffs paid (importer only) and hence profit levels
- Measurements of foreign exchange exposure, such as the amount of net exposed assets, because of changes in amounts of cash and receivables
- Liquidity tests, such as the current ratio, receivables turnover, and inventory turnover
- Operating efficiency, as measured by the ratio of gross profit to either sales or to total assets
- Income tax payments
- Profitability, as measured by the ratio of net income to either sales or capital invested
- Dividend payout ratio, in that a constant dividend will show a varied payout ratio as net income changes; alternatively, if the payout ratio is kept constant, the amount of dividend is changed by a change in transfer price
- Internal growth rate, as measured by the ratio of retained earnings to existing ownership equity

Effect on Joint-Venture Partners

Joint ventures pose a special problem in transfer pricing, because serving the interest of local stockholders by maximizing local profit may be suboptimal from the overall viewpoint of the MNE. Often the conflicting interests are irreconcilable. Indeed the local joint venture partner could be viewed as a potential Trojan horse if they complain to local authorities about the MNE's transfer pricing policy.

Tax Management at Trident

Exhibit 20.6 summarizes the key tax management issue for Trident when remitting dividend income back to the United States from Trident Europe and Trident Brazil as follows:

- Because corporate income tax rates in Germany (40%) are higher than those in the United States (35%), dividends remitted to the U.S. parent result in *excess* foreign tax credits. Any applicable withholding taxes on dividends between Germany and the United States only increase the amount of the excess foreign tax credit.
- Because corporate income tax rates in Brazil (25%) are lower than those in the United States (35%), dividends remitted to the U.S. parent result in *deficit* foreign tax credits. If there are withholding taxes applied to the dividends by Brazil on remittances to the United States, this will reduce the size of the deficit, but not eliminate it.

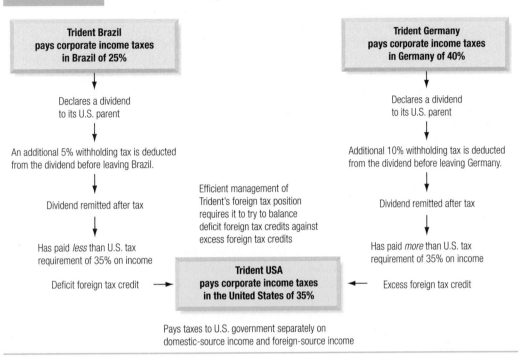

EXHIBIT 20.6   Trident's Tax Management of Foreign-Source Income

Trident's management would like to manage the two dividend remittances in order to match the deficits with the credits. The most straightforward method of doing this is to adjust the amount of dividend distributed from each foreign subsidiary so that, after all applicable income and withholding taxes have been applied, Trident's excess foreign tax credits from Trident Europe (Germany) exactly match the excess foreign tax deficits from Trident Brazil. There are a number of other methods of managing the global tax liabilities of Trident, so-called *repositioning of funds*, which are examined in detail in Chapter 21.

Tax Haven Subsidiaries and International Offshore Financial Centers

Many MNEs have foreign subsidiaries that act as tax havens for corporate funds awaiting reinvestment or repatriation. Tax haven subsidiaries, categorically referred to as *international offshore financial centers*, are partially a result of tax deferral features on earned foreign income allowed by some of the parent countries. Tax haven subsidiaries are typically established in a country that can meet the following requirements:

- A low tax on foreign investment or sales income earned by resident corporations and a low dividend withholding tax on dividends paid to the parent firm

- A stable currency to permit easy conversion of funds into and out of the local currency; this requirement can be met by permitting and facilitating the use of Eurocurrencies

- The facilities to support financial services such as good communications, professional qualified office workers, and reputable banking services

■   A stable government that encourages the establishment of foreign-owned financial and service facilities within its borders

Exhibit 20.7 provides a map of most of the world's major offshore financial centers. The typical tax haven subsidiary owns the common stock of its related operating foreign subsidiaries. There might be several tax haven subsidiaries scattered around the world. The tax haven subsidiary's equity is typically 100% owned by the parent firm. All transfers of funds might go through the tax haven subsidiaries, including dividends and equity financing. Thus, the parent country's tax on foreign source income, which might normally be paid when a dividend is declared by a foreign subsidiary, could continue to be deferred until the tax haven subsidiary itself pays a dividend to the parent firm. This event can be postponed indefinitely if foreign operations continue to grow and require new internal financing from the tax haven subsidiary. Thus, MNEs are able to operate a corporate pool of funds for foreign operations without having to repatriate foreign earnings through the parent country's tax machine.

For U.S. MNEs, the tax deferral privilege operating through a foreign subsidiary was not originally a tax loophole. On the contrary, it was granted by the U.S. government to allow U.S. firms to expand overseas and place them on a par with foreign competitors, which also enjoy similar types of tax deferral and export subsidies.

Unfortunately, some U.S. firms distorted the original intent of tax deferral into tax avoidance. Transfer prices on goods and services bought from or sold to related subsidiaries were artificially rigged to leave all the income from the transaction in the tax haven subsidiary. This manipulation could be done by routing the legal title to the goods or services through the tax haven subsidiary, even though the goods or services never physically entered the tax haven country. This maneuver left no residual tax base for either exporting or importing subsidiaries located outside the tax haven country. Needless to say, tax authorities of both exporting and importing countries were dismayed by the lack of taxable income in such transactions.

One purpose of the U.S. Internal Revenue Act of 1962 was to eliminate the tax advantages of these "paper" foreign corporations without destroying the tax deferral privilege for

EXHIBIT 20.7   International Offshore Financial Centers

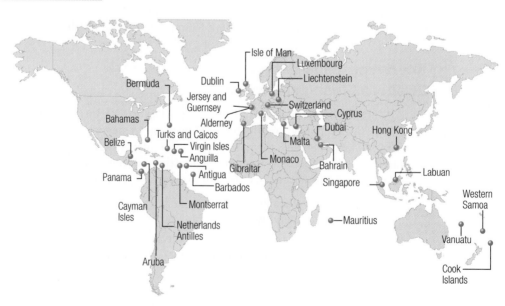

those foreign manufacturing and sales subsidiaries that were established for business and economic motives rather than tax motives. Although the tax motive has been removed, some firms have found these subsidiaries useful as finance control centers for foreign operations.

SUMMARY POINTS

- Nations typically structure their tax systems along one of two basic approaches: the *worldwide approach* or the *territorial approach*.

- Both approaches are attempts to determine which firms, foreign or domestic by incorporation, or which incomes, foreign or domestic in origin, are subject to the taxation of host country tax authorities.

- The *worldwide approach*, also referred to as the *residential* or *national approach*, levies taxes on the income earned by firms that are incorporated in the host country, regardless of where the income was earned (domestically or abroad).

- The *territorial approach*, also termed the *source approach*, focuses on the income earned by firms within the legal jurisdiction of the host country, not on the country of firm incorporation.

- A network of bilateral tax treaties, many of which are modeled after one proposed by the OECD, provides a means of reducing double taxation.

- Tax treaties normally define whether taxes are to be imposed on income earned in one country by the nationals of another, and if so, how. Tax treaties are bilateral, with the two signatories specifying what rates are applicable to which types of income between them alone.

- The *value-added tax* is a type of national sales tax collected at each stage of production or sale of consumption goods in proportion to the value added during that stage.

- Transfer pricing is the pricing of goods, services, and technology between related companies.

- High or low transfer prices have an effect on income taxes, fund positioning, managerial incentives and evaluation, and joint venture partners.

- To establish an arm's length price three methods are typically used: 1) comparable uncontrolled price, 2) resale prices, and 3) cost plus.

- MNEs have foreign subsidiaries that act as tax havens for corporate funds awaiting reinvestment or repatriation.

- Tax havens are typically located in countries that have a low corporate tax rate, a stable currency, facilities to support financial services, and a stable government.

MINI-CASE   ## Stanley Works and Corporate Inversion[1]

This strategic initiative will strengthen our company over the long-term. An important portion of our revenues and earnings are derived from outside the United States, where nearly 50% of our people reside. Moreover, an increasing proportion of our materials are being purchased from global sources. This change will create greater operational flexibility, better position us to manage international cash flows and help us to deal with our complex international tax structure. As a result, our competitiveness, one of the three legs of our vision to become a Great Brand, will be enhanced. The business, regulatory and tax environments in Bermuda are expected to create considerable value for share owners. In addition to operational flexibility, improved worldwide cash management and competitive advantages, the new corporate structure will enhance our ability to access international capital markets, which is favorable for organic growth, future strategic alliances and acquisitions, Finally, enhanced flexibility to manage worldwide tax liabilities should reduce our global effective tax rate from its current 32% to within the range of 23%–25%.

—Stanley Works, Form 14A, Securities and Exchange Commission, 8 February 2002.

[1]This mini-case was derived from *Stanley Works and Corporate Inversion*, Thunderbird Case Series, Copyright ©2003 Thunderbird, The American Graduate School of International Management, prepared by Professors Dale Davison and Michael H. Moffett. Reprinted with permission.

On February 8, 2002, Stanley Works (U.S.) announced that it would enter into a *corporate inversion*, whereby the company would reincorporate itself as a Bermuda-based corporation. This was termed an *outbound inversion*, as the reincorporation was to move the company's incorporation out of the United States to a foreign country. Currently, a U.S.-based corporation with head offices in New Britain, Connecticut, Stanley would make all U.S. operations a wholly owned subsidiary of a new parent company based in Bermuda—Stanley Tools, Ltd. Corporate headquarters, in fact all company offices and operational centers, would remain in Connecticut. The reasoning was simple: Stanley expected to save close to $30 million annually in corporate income taxes by changing its citizenship. On the date of the announcement the market value of Stanley increased by $199 million.

But the announcement was met with heated opposition from employees, stockholders, and local, state, and federal authorities. The change required a two-thirds approval by its stockholders. Stanley suffered through a controversial vote on the move in May 2002. Due to confusing corporate communiqués to shareholders, a second vote had to be scheduled. In August 2002 Stanley found itself a lightning rod for public debate on the responsibilities of a corporate citizen and the ethics of tax reduction and patriotism. Many regulators were now accusing the company of treaty shopping. The senior management team now wished to reevaluate their inversion decision.

Corporate Inversion

The purpose of a *corporate inversion* was—for all intents and purposes—to reduce tax liability. The United States taxed U.S.-based multinational companies on their worldwide income. As a U.S.-based company, Stanley paid corporate income taxes on all income generated in the United States (*domestic-source income*) and income earned abroad and repatriated or deemed repatriated to the parent company in the United States (*foreign source income*). It was this latter tax on foreign source income which was at the heart of the dilemma for companies like Stanley.

Other countries, for example Germany, taxed only income deemed earned *within* the country, termed *territorial taxation*. Multinational companies with their parent company located in countries like Germany had lower effective tax burdens imposed by their home country tax structures. Offshore tax havens—countries such as Bermuda, the Cayman Islands, and British Virgin Islands—imposed no taxes on foreign source income and few or negligible taxes on domestic income of multinational companies incorporated there. This provided a literal tax haven for a multinational company incorporated in that country although it had little or no operational or structural presence there.

History of Inversions

Corporate inversions were not a new tax strategy. The first outbound inversion of note was that undertaken by the McDermott Company in 1983. McDermott exchanged the shares held by its U.S. stockholders for shares in McDermott International, a Panamanian subsidiary of the company prior to the restructuring. The IRS had ruled the exchange of shares a taxable event, taxing all of the U.S. shareholders on the sale of their shares as capital gains. This unexpected consequence was thought to be a significant deterrent to future inversions, and the U.S. Congress soon followed with new tax legislation, Section 1248(i) of the IRS Code, which made it easier for the IRS to construe some inversions as taxable events for U.S. shareholders.

The next major corporate inversion of note was that undertaken by Helen of Troy, a beauty supply company located in Texas, in 1993. This was the first so-called *pure inversion* in that the company set up a completely new company offshore as its corporate headquarters (instead of selling the company's shares to an existing company or subsidiary). Management hoped that this strategy would be ruled a *reorganization*, rather than a taxable sale. The IRS once again, however, ruled the transaction a taxable event: "if US transferors owned, in the aggregate, 50% or more in the vote of value of the transferee foreign corporation immediately after the exchange." Although the McDermott and Helen of Troy tax rulings were thought to constitute significant deterrents to outbound corporate inversions, more and more companies have considered and, in some cases, completed the reorganization to offshore incorporation. The pace quickened in the late 1990s, with companies like Tyco and Ingersoll-Rand moving offshore to reduce tax liabilities.

An additional consideration was the equity market's response to inversions. On average, the market rewarded the announcement of an outbound inversion with a 1.7% appreciation in the company's share price.[2] This share price reaction was thought to represent the present value of cash flow savings resulting from the reduction in taxes due on foreign source income and the reduction of domestic (U.S.) tax savings on domestic income as a result of the restructuring of operations postinversion.

[2]Mihir A. Desai and James R. Hines, Jr., "Expectations and Expatriations: Tracing the Causes and Consequence of Corporate Inversions," *NBER Working Paper 9057*, July 2002, www.nber.org/papers/w9057.

Tax Strategy

Stanley, like many other U.S.-based multinational companies, felt increasingly burdened by the U.S. corporate income tax structure. Stanley's U.S. earnings were taxed at the U.S. corporate income tax rate of 35%. This U.S. corporate rate, which had only varied up or down by about 1% over 15 years, had become increasingly high relative to corporate tax rates globally, as many countries reduced corporate tax rates consistently and significantly throughout the 1990s.

The problem faced by Stanley and other multinationals was that more and more of their earnings were being generated outside of the United States, and U.S. tax authorities taxed those profits when remitted back to the parent company in the United States. As illustrated in Exhibit 1, if Stanley's European operations generated a profit, they would first pay local taxes to the host government in, say, France or Germany, and then additional taxes on those profits when the earnings were remitted back to the U.S. parent company.

However, under Subpart F of the U.S. Internal Revenue Service Tax Code, Sections 951–964, a U.S. parent company is subject to current U.S. tax on certain income earned by a foreign subsidiary, without regard to whether the income is remitted to the U.S. corporation or not.[3] This income, typically referred to as Subpart F income, was income generated by a controlled foreign corporation and earned

primarily through ownership of assets, not through the active production of goods or services. The U.S. tax authorities taxed this income as earned, rather than waiting to tax it when (or if) it was remitted to the U.S. parent company. This Subpart F provision had been specifically constructed to prevent foreign source income from being permanently parked in offshore tax havens, such as Bermuda, which assessed no corporate income taxes.

The U.S. tax code did have a number of features to eliminate the potential for double taxation (taxes paid in both Europe and the U.S., for example) or at least to lessen the burden. Many of the corporate taxes paid to host governments were credited against potential U.S. tax liabilities. This had proven quite effective when corporate tax rates abroad were higher than in the United States, but as many countries lowered their rates below those in the U.S., profits returned to the United States now resulted in additional taxes due.

As shown in Exhibit 2, the specific tax goals of the outbound corporate inversion were as follows:[4]

■ First, Bermuda, as is typical of most offshore financial centers, does not tax foreign source income. (In fact, Bermuda does not have a corporate income tax.) Stanley's profits generated throughout the world could be freely redistributed throughout the global business, including the parent, without creating additional tax liabilities in the country of the

---

EXHIBIT 1	Stanley Works U.S. Tax Liabilities before the Outbound Corporate Inversion

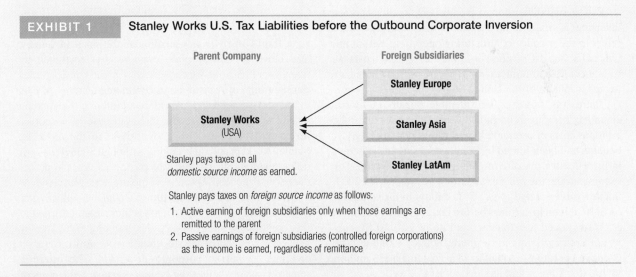

Stanley pays taxes on all *domestic source income* as earned.

Stanley pays taxes on *foreign source income* as follows:

1. Active earning of foreign subsidiaries only when those earnings are remitted to the parent
2. Passive earnings of foreign subsidiaries (controlled foreign corporations) as the income is earned, regardless of remittance

---

[3]This specifically applied to *controlled foreign corporations* or *CFCs*. A *CFC* was defined as any foreign corporation with more than 50% of its voting stock owned directly or indirectly by U.S. shareholders. Thus, most foreign subsidiaries of U.S-based multinationals were classified as CFCs.

[4]"Special Report: Outbound Inversion Transactions." *Tax Notes*, New York State Bar Association Tax Section, July 1, 2002, pp. 127–149.

EXHIBIT 2   Stanley Works U.S. Tax Liabilities after the Outbound Corporate Inversion

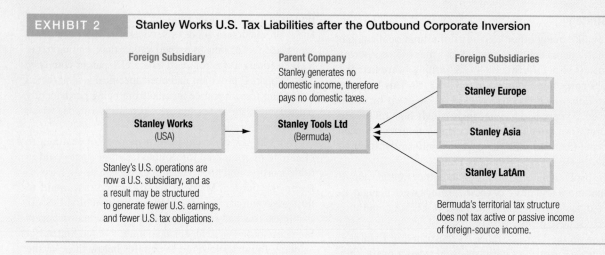

parent company (now Bermuda instead of the United States).

■ Second, the U.S. operations of Stanley would now be conducted as the U.S. subsidiary of a foreign corporation. This would most likely pose restructuring possibilities whereby the U.S. subsidiary would have increasing obligations to the Bermuda parent such as royalties, debt service, and licensing fees, which were legitimate deductible expenses in the U.S. but income to the parent company in Bermuda. The result would be a net reduction in U.S. tax liabilities from Stanley's business conducted in the United States.

This second dimension of the tax benefits of corporate inversion is often termed *earnings stripping*. The term refers to the practice of structuring operations within the United States to position as many corporate costs as legally possible to reduce taxable profits within the higher tax environment of the United States.

There was, however, considerable debate as to the actual tax benefits to be gained versus the growing public relations costs of inversion. The earnings per share (EPS) benefits had been touted by Stanley as a simple reduction in the effective tax rate for the overall organization. For example, using the *pro forma* earnings estimates for 2003, Stanley was expected to pay $134 million in taxes in 2003 on $420 million in earnings before tax, as shown in Exhibit 3. This assumed an effective tax rate of 32%. If Stanley were to reincorporate in Bermuda, Stanley estimated the effective tax rate would fall to 24%, yielding a $33 million savings for Stanley and its stockholders.[5]

Patriotism and Inversion

How would you like to keep living in your current home, but tell the Internal Revenue Service to go pound sand in Bermuda, because you're a legal resident of that lovely island? You can't, but toolmaker Stanley Works plans to save $30 million a year by moving. So what if our country is at war against terrorism and is spending billions extra for defense and homeland security? That's our problem, not the tax dodgers. Their problem is raising profits to get their stock price higher. What could possibly be more important, since a good stock market is good for America, right?

—Allan Sloan, "The Tax-Free Bermuda Getaway,"
Newsweek, April 15, 2002.

John Trani's other worries surrounded the image of Stanley. The move to reincorporate offshore was portrayed by many as unpatriotic—unsupportive of the United States during a time of recession and continuing terrorist threats in the post-September 11 world. In addition to the growing debate in Congress over the increasing use of corporate inversions, there was strong opposition to the move by Stanley workers and their unions. Although Stanley was not doing anything illegal, and was paying its taxes in accordance with current law, the company was portrayed as "working too hard" to avoid future income tax obligations.

John Trani and his senior management team returned to the conference room. Time was running out. Stanley needed to reschedule the stockholder vote now if it was to continue to pursue corporate inversion. The question remained as to whether the benefits exceeded the costs of *moving* offshore.

---

[5]Stanley had consistently followed a conservative estimate in its public discussions of a $30 million tax savings, as opposed to the $33 million calculation here.

EXHIBIT 3	Prospective Changes in Stanley Works' Earnings after Inversion		
	Pro Forma 2003 Earnings		
	Before	After	Savings
Earnings before tax	$420	$420	
Tax liability (32%/24%)	(134)	(101)	
Earnings after tax	$286	$319	+ $33
Shares outstanding (millions)	88.0	88.0	
Earnings per share (EPS)	$3.250	$3.625	+ $0.375 or 11.5%

Case Questions

1. If Stanley did indeed reincorporate offshore, how do you think the company would restructure its operations, both inside and outside the United States?

2. Do you believe that the U.S. government should allow a company like Stanley to reincorporate outside the country in order to pay lower taxes?

3. If you were John Trani, would you continue to pursue the outbound inversion or choose to stay put?

QUESTIONS

1. Tax Morality.
   a. What is meant by the term *tax morality*?
   b. Your company has a subsidiary in Russia, where tax evasion is a fine art. Discuss whether you should comply fully with Russian tax laws or should violate the laws, as do your local competitors.

2. Tax Neutrality.
   a. Define the term *tax neutrality*.
   b. What is the difference between *domestic neutrality* and *foreign neutrality*?
   c. What are a country's objectives when determining tax policy on foreign-source income?

3. Worldwide versus Territorial Approach. Nations typically structure their tax systems along one of two basic approaches: the *worldwide approach* or the *territorial approach*. Explain these two approaches and how they differ.

4. Tax Deferral.
   a. What is meant by the term *tax deferral*?
   b. Why do countries allow tax deferral on foreign-source income?

5. Tax Treaties.
   a. What is a bilateral tax treaty?
   b. What is the purpose of a bilateral tax treaty?
   c. What policies do most tax treaties cover?

6. Tax Types. Taxes are classified on the basis of whether they are applied directly to income, called *direct taxes*, or to some other measurable performance characteristic of the firm, called *indirect taxes*. Classify each of the following types of taxes as being direct or indirect or something else.
   a. Corporate income tax paid by a Japanese subsidiary on its operating income
   b. Royalties paid to Saudi Arabia for oil extracted and shipped to world markets
   c. Interest received by a U.S. parent on bank deposits held in London
   d. Interest received by a U.S. parent on a loan to a subsidiary in Mexico
   e. Principal repayment received by a U.S. parent from Belgium on a loan to a wholly owned subsidiary in Belgium
   f. Excise tax paid on cigarettes manufactured and sold within the United States
   g. Property taxes paid on the corporate headquarters building in Seattle
   h. A direct contribution to the International Committee of the Red Cross for refugee relief
   i. Deferred income tax, shown as a deduction on the U.S. parent's consolidated income tax
   j. Withholding taxes withheld by Germany on dividends paid to a U.K. parent corporation

7. **Foreign Tax Credit.** What is a foreign tax credit? Why do countries give credit for taxes paid on foreign-source income?

8. **Value-Added Tax.**
   a. What is a value-added tax?
   b. What are the advantages and disadvantages of a value-added tax?
   c. Although the value-added tax has been proposed numerous times, the Unites States has never adopted one. Why do you think the attitude toward value-added tax is negative in the United States when the value-added tax is widely used in the rest of the world?

9. **Transfer Pricing Motivation.** What is a transfer price and can a government regulate it? What difficulties and motives does a parent multinational firm face in setting transfer prices?

10. **Sister Subsidiaries.** Subsidiary Alpha in Country Able faces a 40% income tax rate. Subsidiary Beta in Country Baker faces only a 20% income tax rate. Presently, each subsidiary imports from the other an amount of goods and services exactly equal in monetary value to what each exports to the other. This method of balancing intracompany trade was imposed by a management keen to reduce all costs, including the costs (spread between bid and ask) of foreign exchange transactions. Both subsidiaries are profitable, and both could purchase all components domestically at approximately the same prices as they are paying to their foreign sister subsidiary. Does this seem like an optimal situation?

11. **Correct Pricing.** Section 482 of the U.S. Internal Revenue Code specifies use of a "correct" transfer price, and the burden of proof that the transfer price is "correct" lies with the company. What guidelines exist for determining the proper transfer price?

12. **Tax Haven Subsidiary.**
   a. What is meant by the term *tax haven*?
   b. What are the desired characteristics for a country if it expects to be used as a tax haven?
   c. Identify five tax havens.
   d. What are the advantages leading an MNE to use a tax haven subsidiary?
   e. What are the potential distortions of an MNE's taxable income that are opposed by tax authorities in nontax haven countries?

13. **Tax Treaties.** What do most bilateral tax treaties cover? How do they affect the operations and structure of MNEs?

PROBLEMS

*1. **Pfizer's Foreign-Source Income.** Pfizer is a U.S.-based global manufacturer and distributor of a wide array of pharmaceutical products. As part of the training in its corporate treasury offices, it has its interns build a spreadsheet analysis of the following hypothetical subsidiary earnings/distribution analysis. Use the spreadsheet presented in Exhibit 20.6 for your basic structure.

A foreign subsidiary has $3,400,000 in gross earnings, U.S. and foreign corporate income taxes are 35% and 28%, respectively, and foreign withholding taxes are 15%.
   a. What is the total tax payment, foreign and domestic combined, for this income?
   b. What is the effective tax rate paid on this income by the U.S.-based parent company?
   c. What would be the total tax payment and effective tax rate if the foreign corporate tax rate was 45% and there were no withholding taxes on dividends?
   d. What would be the total tax payment and effective tax rate if the income was earned by a branch of the U.S. corporation?

2. **Discovery Bay Airlines (Hong Kong).** Discovery Bay Airlines is a U.S.-based air freight firm with a wholly owned subsidiary in Hong Kong. The subsidiary, DBay-Hong Kong, has just completed a long-term planning report for the parent company in San Francisco, in which it has estimated the following expected earnings and payout rates for the years 2004–2007.

Discovery Bay-Hong Kong (Millions of U.S. dollars)	2004	2005	2006	2007
Earnings before interest and taxes (EBIT)	8,000	10,000	12,000	14,000
Less interest expenses	(800)	(1,000)	(1,200)	(1,400)
Earnings before taxes (EBT)	7,200	9,000	10,800	12,600

The current Hong Kong corporate tax rate on this category of income is 16.5%. Hong Kong imposes no withholding taxes on dividends remitted to U.S. investors (per the Hong Kong–United States bilateral tax treaty). The U.S. corporate income tax rate is 35%. The parent company wants to repatriate 75% of net income as dividends annually.
   a. Calculate the net income available for distribution by the Hong Kong subsidiary for the years 2004–2007.
   b. What is the amount of the dividend expected to be remitted to the U.S. parent each year?

c. After gross-up for U.S. tax liability purposes, what is the total dividend after tax (all Hong Kong and U.S. taxes) expected each year?

d. What is the effective tax rate on this foreign-sourced income per year?

3. **Jurgen-Strut of Germany.** Jurgen-Strut (JS) is a German-based company that manufactures electronic fuel-injection carburetor assemblies for several large automobile companies in Germany, including Mercedes, BMW, and Opel. The firm, like many firms in Germany today, is revising its financial policies in line with the increasing degree of disclosure required by firms if they wish to list their shares publicly in or out of Germany.

JS's primary problem is that the German corporate income tax code applies a different income tax rate to income depending on whether it is retained (45%) or distributed to stockholders (30%).

a. If Jurgen-Strut planned to distribute 50% of its net income, what would be its total net income and total corporate tax bills?

b. If Jurgen-Strut was attempting to choose between a 40% and 60% payout rate to stockholders, what arguments and values would management use in order to convince stockholders which of the two payouts is in everyone's best interest?

Wuzhou Blade Company.

Use the following company case to answer problems 4 through 6. Wuzhou Blade Company (Hong Kong) exports razor blades to its wholly owned parent company, Cranfield Eversharp (Great Britain). Hong Kong tax rates are 16% and British tax rates are 30%. Wuzhou calculates its profit per container as shown in the table (all values in British pounds):

Constructing Price	Wuzhou Blade	Cranfield Eversharp
Direct costs	£10,000	£16,100
Overhead	4,000	1,000
Total costs	£14,000	£17,100
Desired markup (15%)	2,100	2,565
Transfer price (sales price)	£16,100	£19,665

Income Statements (assumes a volume of 1,000 units)

	Wuzhou Blade		Cranfield Eversharp
Sales revenue	£16,100,000		£19,665,000
Less total costs	(14,000,000)		(17,100,000)
Taxable income	£2,100,000		£2,565,000
Less taxes	(16%) (336,000)	(30%)	(769,500)
Post-tax profit	£1,764,000		£1,795,500
Consolidated profit	£3,559,500		

4. **Wuzhou Blade (A).** Corporate management of Cranfield Eversharp is considering repositioning profits within the multinational company. What happens to the profits of Wuzhou Blade and Cranfield Eversharp, and the consolidated results of both if the markup at Wuzhou was increased to 20% and the markup at Cranfield was reduced to 10%? What is the impact of this repositioning on consolidated tax payments?

5. **Wuzhou Blade (B).** Encouraged by the results from problem 4's analysis, corporate management of Cranfield Eversharp wishes to continue to reposition profit in Hong Kong. It is, however, facing two constraints. First, the final sales price in Great Britain must be £20,000 or less to remain competitive. Second, the British tax authorities—in working with Cranfield Eversharp's cost accounting staff—has established a maximum transfer price allowed (from Hong Kong) of £17,800. What combination of markups do you recommend for Cranfield Eversharp to institute? What is the impact of this repositioning on consolidated profits after-tax and total tax payments?

6. **Wuzhou Blade (C).** Not to leave any potential tax repositioning opportunities unexplored, Cranfield Eversharp wants to combine the components of problem 4 with a redistribution of overhead costs. If overhead costs could be reallocated between the two units, but still total £5,000 per unit, and maintain a minimum of £1,750 per unit in Hong Kong, what is the impact of this repositioning on consolidated profits after-tax and total tax payments?

INTERNET EXERCISES

1. **International Taxation and Bulgaria.** The following Web site is a good resource for finding a multitude of global tax and accounting rules, regulations, and rates. Use it to find the specific tax issues facing a multinational organization that wishes to do business in Bulgaria today.

Taxsites.com   www.taxsites.com/international.html

2. **Global Taxes.** Sites like TaxWorld provide detailed insights into the conduct of business and the associated tax and accounting requirements of doing business in a variety of countries.

International Tax Resources   www.taxworld.org/OtherSites/International/international.htm

3. **International Taxpayer.** The United States Internal Revenue Service (IRS) provides detailed support and document requirements for international taxpayers. Use the IRS site to find out what the legal rules and regulations and definitions are for international residents tax liabilities when earning income and profits in the United States.

USIRS Taxpayer	www.irs.gov/businesses/small/international/index.html

4. **Official Government Tax Authorities.** Tax laws are constantly changing, and an MNE's tax planning and management processes must therefore include a continual updating of tax practices by country. Use the following government tax Web sites to address specific issues related to the respective countries:

Hong Kong's ownership change to China:	www.info.gov.hk/eindex.htm
Ireland's international financial services center:	www.revenue.ie/
Czech Republic's tax incentives for investment:	www.capitaltaxconsulting.com/international-tax/czech-republic/

5. **Tax Practices for International Business.** Many of the major accounting firms provide on-line information and advisory services for international business activities as related to tax and accounting practices. Use the following Web sites to gain up-to-date information on tax law changes or practices. According to the Web site, which five countries have the lowest corporate income tax rates today?

Ernst and Young	www.ey.com/tax/
Deloitte & Touche	www.dttus.com/
PriceWaterhouseCoopers	www.pwcglobal.com/

CHAPTER 21

Working Capital Management

Morality is all right, but what about dividends?

—Kaiser Wilhelm II.

Working capital management in an MNE requires repositioning cash flows, as well as managing current assets and liabilities, when faced with political, foreign exchange, tax, and liquidity constraints. The overall goal is to reduce funds tied up in working capital while simultaneously providing sufficient funding and liquidity for the conduct of global business. This should enhance return on assets and return on equity. It also should improve efficiency ratios and other evaluation of performance parameters.

The first section of this chapter describes Trident's operating cycle. The second section analyzes Trident's fund repositioning decisions. The third section examines the constraints that affect the repositioning of Trident's funds. The fourth section identifies alternative conduits for moving funds. The fifth section introduces the management of net working capital, including accounts receivable, inventory, and cash. The sixth and final section examines how working capital is financed, including the various types of banking services available.

Trident Brazil's Operating Cycle

The *operating* and *cash conversion cycles* for Trident Brazil are illustrated in Exhibit 21.1. The operating cycle can be decomposed into five periods, each with business, accounting, and potential cash flow implications.

Quotation Period

First noted in Chapter 11 when we introduced transaction exposure, the quotation period extends from the time of price quotation, t_0, to the point when the customer places an order, t_1. If the customer is requesting a price quote in foreign currency terms, say Chilean pesos, Trident Brazil would have a potential but uncertain foreign exchange transaction exposure. The quotation itself is not listed on any of the traditional financial statements of the firm, although a firm like Trident Brazil would keep a worksheet of quotations extended and their time periods.

Input Sourcing Period

Once a customer has accepted a quotation, the order is placed at time t_1. The buyer and seller sign a contract describing the product to be delivered, likely timing of delivery,

535

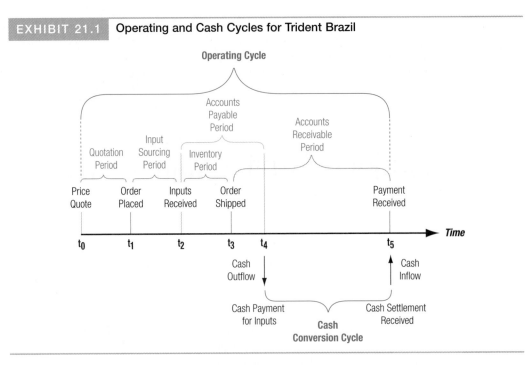

EXHIBIT 21.1   Operating and Cash Cycles for Trident Brazil

conditions of delivery, and price and financing terms. At this time Trident Brazil would order the material inputs that it requires to manufacture the product that it does not currently hold in inventory. Depending on the individual sale, the buyer may make a cash deposit or down payment. This would constitute the first actual cash flow associated with the order, a cash inflow to Trident Brazil, and that would initiate the cash conversion cycle for this transaction.

Inventory Period

As it receives inputs, Trident Brazil assembles and manufactures the goods. The length of this inventory-manufacturing period, from t_1 to t_2, depends on the type of product (off-the-shelf versus custom built-to-specification), the supply-chain integration of Trident Brazil with its various internal and external suppliers, and the technology employed by Trident.

Accounts Payable Period

As inputs arrive, Trident lists them as material and component inventories on the left-hand side of Trident Brazil's balance sheet, with corresponding accounts payable entries on the right-hand side of the balance sheet. If the inputs are invoiced in foreign currencies, whether from Trident USA, a sister subsidiary, or external suppliers, they constitute foreign currency transaction exposures to Trident Brazil.

Note that the accounts payable period shown in Exhibit 21.1 begins at the same time as the inventory period, t_2, but may extend in time to t_4, after the inventory period ends. If Trident Brazil's suppliers extend trade credit, Trident Brazil would be able to postpone paying for the inventory for an extended period. Of course, if Trident Brazil chooses not to accept trade credit, it may pay for the inputs as delivered. In this case, the accounts payable period would end before the inventory period—the manufacturing period—ends at time t_3. At whatever point in time Trident Brazil chooses to settle its outstanding accounts payable, it incurs a cash outflow.

Accounts Receivable Period

When the goods are finished and shipped, Trident Brazil records the transaction as a sale on its income statement and as an account receivable on its balance sheet. If it is a foreign currency-denominated invoice, the spot exchange rate on that date, t_4, is used to record the sale value in local currency. The exchange rate in effect on the date of cash settlement, t_5, would then be used in the calculation of any foreign exchange gains and losses associated with the transaction—the transaction exposure.

The length of the accounts receivable period depends on the credit terms offered by Trident Brazil, the choice made by the buyer to either accept trade credit or pay in cash, and country-specific and industry-specific payment practices. At cash settlement Trident Brazil receives a cash inflow (finally) in payment for goods delivered. At time t_5 the transaction is concluded and all accounting entries—inventory items, accounts payable, accounts receivable—are eliminated.

Trident's Repositioning Decisions

Next, we describe the variety of goals and constraints on the repositioning of funds within Trident Corporation. Exhibit 21.2 illustrates Trident, its wholly owned subsidiaries, the currency and tax rates applicable to each unit, and management's present conclusions regarding each subsidiary's growth prospects. Trident's three foreign subsidiaries each present a unique set of concerns.

- ■ *Trident Europe,* the oldest of the three, is operating in a relatively high-tax environment. It is operating in a relatively stable currency—the euro—and is free to move capital in and out of the country with few restrictions. The business itself is mature, with few significant growth prospects in the near future.

EXHIBIT 21.2 Trident's Foreign Subsidiaries

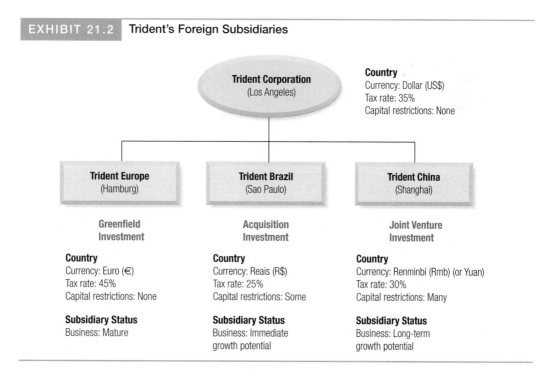

▧   *Trident Brazil,* the result of a recent acquisition, is operating in a low-tax environment, but historically a volatile currency environment. It is subject to only a few current capital restrictions. Trident believes the business has very good growth prospects in the short to medium term if it is able to inject additional capital and managerial expertise into the business.

▧   *Trident China,* a new joint venture with an in-country partner that is a former unit of the Chinese government, is operating in a relatively low-tax environment, with a fixed exchange rate (the renminbi is managed within a very narrow band relative to the U.S. dollar). It is subject to a number of restrictions on capital. The business is believed to have the greatest potential—in the long run.

In practice, Trident's senior management in the parent company (*corporate*) will first determine its strategic objectives regarding the business developments in each subsidiary, and then design a financial management plan for the repositioning of profits, cash flows, and capital for each subsidiary. As a result of this process, Trident will now attempt to pursue the following repositioning objectives by subsidiary:

▧   **Trident Europe:** Reposition profits from Germany to the United States while maintaining the value of the European market's maturity to Trident Corporation.

▧   **Trident Brazil:** Reposition or in some way manage the capital at risk in Brazil subject to foreign exchange rate risk while providing adequate capital for immediate growth prospects.

▧   **Trident China:** Reposition the quantity of funds in and out of China to protect against blocked funds (transfer risk), while balancing the needs of the joint venture partner. And in the end, not just Trident is affected. *Global Finance in Practice 21.1* illustrates a recent problem P&G had in India regarding payment terms.

GLOBAL FINANCE IN PRACTICE 21.1

P&G's Acquisition and Financial Management in India

The difficulties experienced by P&G and Gillette in India in 2006 highlighted the degree to which financial policies and management have on business operations. After P&G acquired Gillette in 2005, the complicated process of post-acquisition integration began globally. Both P&G and Gillette had operated successfully in India for decades. After the acquisition, P&G decided to keep the two businesses largely separate in Mumbai, India, but did believe significant benefits could be derived by combining purchasing and distribution.

In the first quarter of 2006 Gillette products were merged into the P&G distribution system. Problems arose almost immediately as both inventory and sales of Gillette products fell dramatically. Gillette's net sales for the first quarter of 2006 fell to Rs 37.95 *crore,* down from Rs 107.55 *crore* in the first quarter of 2005—roughly one-third of previous year sales. (Rs is the abbreviation for the Indian rupee; *crore* is 1 million rupee, while *lakh* stands for 100,000 rupees). At the current spot rate of Rs 33/$, this constituted a loss in sales of $2.3 million.

Whereas Gillette's distribution in India had always provided credit terms—payment terms—of 30 days, P&G's standing policy was either cash payment or payment in seven calendar days, depending on the size and nature of the retailer. Many of Gillette's smaller retailers, primarily chemists, stopped carrying Gillette products such as the Mach 3 shaving cartridges and razors after the shorter payment terms were instituted. The less friendly retail credit terms combined with significant price increases (razor blade cartridges now cost more than Rs 700 per pack of eight, while razors were priced over Rs 300) resulted in the massive loss in sales.

The world of post-acquisition integration includes understanding the impacts of financial management and credit term policies on product categories and distribution channels, everywhere in the world.

Source: Based on "Shift in Distribution Network Hits Gillette Stocks," *The Business Standard,* Hyderabad, India, Monday, May 15, 2006, p. 1.

Constraints on Repositioning Funds

Fund flows between units of a domestic business are generally unimpeded, but that is not the case in a multinational business. A firm operating globally faces a variety of political, tax, foreign exchange, and liquidity considerations that limit its ability to move funds easily and without cost from one country or currency to another. These constraints are why multinational financial managers must plan ahead for repositioning funds within an MNE. Advance planning is essential even when constraints do not exist, for at some future date political events may lead to unexpected restrictions.

Political Constraints

Political constraints can block the transfer of funds either overtly or covertly. Overt blockage occurs when a currency becomes inconvertible or is subject to government exchange controls that prevent its transfer at reasonable exchange rates. Covert blockage occurs when dividends or other forms of fund remittances are severely limited, heavily taxed, or excessively delayed by a bureaucratic approval process.

Tax Constraints

Tax constraints arise because of the complex and possibly contradictory tax structures of various national governments through whose jurisdictions funds might pass. A firm does not want funds in transit eroded by a sequence of nibbling tax collectors in every jurisdiction through which such funds might flow.

Transaction Costs

Foreign exchange transaction costs are incurred when one currency is exchanged for another. These costs, in the form of fees and/or the difference between bid and offer quotations, are revenue for the commercial banks and dealers that operate the foreign exchange market. Although usually a small percentage of the amount of money exchanged, such costs become significant for large or frequent transfers. Transaction costs are sufficiently large enough to warrant planning to avoid unnecessary back-and-forth transfers such as would occur if a subsidiary remitted a cash dividend to its parent at approximately the same time as the parent paid the subsidiary for goods purchased. Sending foreign exchange simultaneously in two directions is obviously a sheer waste of corporate resources, but it sometimes occurs when one part of a firm is not coordinated with another.

Liquidity Needs

Despite the overall advantage of worldwide cash handling, liquidity needs in each individual location must be satisfied and good local banking relationships maintained. The size of appropriate balances is in part a judgmental decision not easily measurable. Nevertheless, such needs constrain a pure optimization approach to worldwide cash positioning.

Conduits for Moving Funds by Unbundling Them

Multinational firms often *unbundle* their transfer of funds into separate flows for specific purposes. Host countries are then more likely to perceive that a portion of what might otherwise be called *remittance of profits* constitutes an essential purchase of specific benefits that command worldwide values and benefit the host country. Unbundling allows a multinational firm to recover funds from subsidiaries without piquing host country sensitivities over large dividend drains. For example, Trident might transfer funds from its foreign subsidiaries to the parent, Trident Corporation, by any of the conduits shown in Exhibit 21.3.

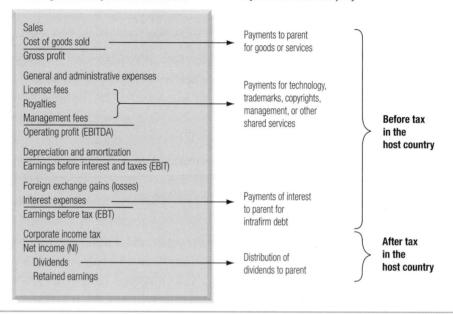

EXHIBIT 21.3   Potential Conduits for Moving Funds from Subsidiary to Parent

The conduits are separable into those that are *before-tax* and *after-tax* in the host country. Although not always the focus of intraunit fund movement, tax goals frequently make this a critical distinction for foreign subsidiary financial structures. An increase in the funds flow (charges) in any of the before-tax categories reduces the taxable profits of the foreign subsidiary *if* the host country tax authorities acknowledge the charge as a legitimate expense. The before-tax/after-tax distinction is also quite significant to a parent company attempting to repatriate funds in the most tax-efficient method if it is attempting to manage its own foreign tax credit/deficits between foreign units.

An item-by-item matching of remittance to input, such as royalties for intellectual property with fees for patents and advice, is equitable to host country and foreign investor alike. It allows each party to see the reason for each remittance and to judge its acceptance independently. If all investment inputs are *unbundled,* part of what might have been classified as residual profits may turn out to be tax-deductible expenses related to a specific purchased benefit. Unbundling also facilitates allocation of overhead from a parent's international division, so-called *shared services,* to each operating subsidiary in accordance with a predetermined formula. Predetermination of the allocation method means a host country is less likely to view a given remittance as capricious and thus inappropriate. Finally, unbundling facilitates the entry of local capital into joint-venture projects, because total remuneration to different owners can be in proportion to the value of the varied contributions of each, rather than only in proportion to the amount of monetary capital they have invested.

International Dividend Remittances

Payment of dividends is the classic method by which firms transfer profit back to owners, be those owners individual shareholders or parent corporations. International dividend policy now incorporates tax considerations, political risk, and foreign exchange risk, as well as a return for business guidance and technology.

Tax Implications

Host country tax laws influence the dividend decision. Countries such as Germany tax retained earnings at one rate and distributed earnings at a lower rate. Most countries levy withholding taxes on dividends paid to foreign parent firms and investors. Again, most (but not all) parent countries levy a tax on foreign dividends received, but allow a *tax credit* for foreign taxes already paid on that income stream. That said, dividends remain the most tax inefficient method for repatriating funds because they are distributed on an after-tax basis. This means that the parent company will frequently be faced with the generation of excess foreign tax credits on a dividend. Remittance of license or royalty fees is on a pretax basis in the foreign subsidiary; the only tax typically applied is that of withholding, a rate considerably below that of corporate income taxes.

Political Risk

Political risk may motivate parent firms to require foreign subsidiaries to remit all locally generated funds above that required to internally finance growth in sales (working capital requirements) and planned capital expansions (*capex* or capital expenditures). Such policies, however, are not universal.

One strategy employed by MNEs in response to potential government restrictions may be to maintain a constant dividend payout ratio so as to demonstrate that an established policy is being consistently carried out. This establishes a precedent for remittance of dividends and removes the perception of some host country governments that dividend distributions are by managerial election. (Note that even the terminology, *declare a dividend,* implies managerial discretion.)

Foreign Exchange Risk

If it anticipates a foreign exchange loss, an MNE may speed up the transfer of funds out of the country via dividends. This "lead" is usually part of a larger strategy of moving from weak currencies to strong currencies, and can include speeding up intrafirm payments on accounts receivable and payable. However, decisions to accelerate dividend payments ahead of what might be normal must take into account interest rate differences and the negative impact on host country relations.

Distributions and Cash Flows

Dividends are a cash payment to owners equal to all or a portion of earnings of a prior period. To pay dividends, a subsidiary needs both past earnings and available cash. Subsidiaries sometimes have earnings without cash because earnings are measured at the time of a sale but cash is received later, when the receivable is collected (a typical distinction between accounting profits and cash flow). Profits of rapidly growing subsidiaries are often tied up in ever-increasing receivables and inventory (working capital). Therefore, rapidly growing foreign subsidiaries may lack the cash to remit a dividend equal to even a portion of earnings.

The reverse may also be true; firms may be receiving cash from the collection of old receivables even when profits are down because current sales have fallen off or current expenses have risen relative to current sales prices. Such firms might want to declare a dividend in order to remove a bountiful supply of cash from a country, but lack the earnings against which to charge such payments. For either of these reasons a firm must look at both measured earnings and available cash before settling on a cash dividend policy.

Joint Venture Factors

Existence of joint venture partners or local stockholders also influences dividend policy. Optimal positioning of funds internationally cannot dominate the valid claims of independent partners or local stockholders for dividends. The latter do not benefit from the worldwide success of the MNE parent, but only from the success of the particular joint venture in which they own a share. Firms might hesitate to reduce dividends when earnings falter. They also might hesitate to increase dividends following a spurt in earnings because of possible adverse reaction to reducing dividends later should earnings decline. Many MNEs insist on 100% ownership of subsidiaries in order to avoid possible conflicts of interest with outside shareholders.

Net Working Capital

If Trident Brazil's business continues to expand, it will continually add to inventories and accounts payable (A/P) in order to fill increased sales in the form of accounts receivable (A/R). These three components make up *net working capital* (NWC). The combination is "net" as a result of the spontaneous funding capability of accounts payable; accounts payable provide part of the funding for increased levels of inventory and accounts receivable:

$$\text{Net Working Capital (NWC)} = (\text{A/R} + \text{Inventory}) - (\text{A/P}).$$

Because both A/R and inventory are components of current assets on the left-hand side of the balance sheet, as they grow they must be financed by additional liabilities of some form on the right-hand side of the balance sheet. A/P may provide a part of the funding. Exhibit 21.4 illustrates Trident Brazil's net working capital. Note that we do not include cash or short-term debt as part of net working capital. Although they are part of current assets and current liabilities, respectively, they are the result of management discretion, and do not spontaneously change with operations. Their determinate factors are discussed later in this chapter.

EXHIBIT 21.4   Trident Brazil's Net Working Capital Requirements

Net working capital (NWC) is the net inestment required of the firm to support ongoing sales. NWC components typically grow as the firm buys inputs, produces products, and sells finished goods.

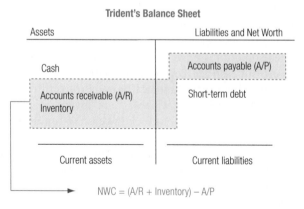

Trident's Balance Sheet

Note that NWC is *not* the same as current assets and current liabilities.

In principle, Trident attempts to minimize its net working capital balance. It reduces A/R if collections are accelerated. It reduces inventories by carrying lower levels of unfinished and finished goods, and by speeding the rate at which goods are manufactured—reducing so-called *cycle time*. All of these measures must be balanced with their customer costs. Sales could be reduced if inventories are not on hand, or if credit sales are reduced. On the other side of the balance sheet, NWC can be reduced by stretching A/P out. Again, if not done carefully, this could potentially damage the company's relationship with its key suppliers, thereby reducing reliability and supply-chain partnerships.

A/P versus Short-Term Debt

Exhibit 21.4 also illustrates one of the key managerial decisions for any subsidiary: Should A/P be paid off early, taking discounts if offered by suppliers? The alternative financing for NWC balances is short-term debt.

For example, in Brazil payment terms are quite long by global standards, often extending 60 to 90 days. Paraña Electronics is one of Trident Brazil's key suppliers. It delivers a shipment of electronic components and invoices Trident Brazil R$180,000. Paraña Electronics offers credit terms of 5/10 net 60. This means that the entire amount of the A/P, R$180,000, is due in 60 days. Alternatively, if Trident Brazil wishes to pay within the first 10 days, a 5% discount is given:

$$R\$180,000 \times (1 - 0.05) = R\$171,000$$

Trident Brazil's financial manager, Maria Gonzalez, must decide which is the lower-cost method of financing the NWC. Short-term debt in Brazilian reais, because of the relatively higher inflationary conditions common in Brazil, costs 24% per year.

What is the annual cost of the discount offered by Paraña Electronics? Trident Brazil is effectively paid 5% for giving up 50 days of financing (60 days less the 10-day period for discounts). Assuming a 365-day count for interest calculation,

$$\frac{365 \text{ days}}{50 \text{ days}} = 7.30$$

To calculate the effective annual interest cost of supplier financing, we must compound the 5% discount for 50 days 7.30 times, yielding a *cost of carry* provided by Paraña Electronics of

$$(1 + 0.05)^{7.3} = 1.428, \text{ or } 42.8\% \text{ per year.}$$

Paraña Electronics is therefore charging Trident Brazil 42.8% per year for financing. Alternatively, Trident Brazil could borrow reais from local banks in Sao Paulo for 24% per year, use the funds to pay Paraña Electronics early, and take the discounts offered. The latter is the obvious choice in this case.

The choice between taking supplier-provided financing and short-term debt is not always purely a matter of comparing interest costs. In many countries, the foreign subsidiaries of foreign MNEs have limited access to local currency debt. In other cases, the subsidiary may be offered funds from the parent company at competitive rates. We will return to this topic, *internal banking,* in the last section of this chapter.

Days Working Capital

A common method of benchmarking working capital management practice is to calculate the NWC of the firm on a "days sales" basis. If the value of A/R, inventories, and A/P on the balance sheet are divided by the annual daily sales (annual sales/365 days), we can summarize the firm's NWC in the number of days of sales NWC constitutes. Exhibit 21.5 provides the results of a survey by *CFO Magazine* in both the United States and Europe in 2001 for the technology hardware and equipment industry segment.

We must use care in viewing the survey results. First, the days sales values are for the consolidated companies, not for specific country-level subsidiaries. Therefore, the averages could reflect very different working capital structures for individual subsidiaries of the firms listed. Second, without knowing the specific business and country areas included, we have difficulty evaluating the short-term financing decisions discussed in the previous section as made by management of the listed firms.

Despite these reservations, there are some clear differences between the U.S. and European averages, as well as between individual firms. The days working capital average for the selected U.S. firms of 29 days is less than half the 75 days for the European sample. A closer look at the subcategories indicates a radically sparse attitude toward inventory among the U.S. firms, averaging 19 days sales. Days sales held in accounts receivable at 53 days on average is nearly 20 days less than the European average of 70. Payables are essentially identical between the two groups. Clearly, European-based technology hardware firms are carrying a significantly higher level of net working capital in their financial structures than comparable U.S.-based firms to support the same level of sales.

Among individual firms, Dell lives up to its billing as one of the most aggressive working capital managers across all industries. Dell's net working capital level of negative two days indicates exactly what it says—a level of A/P that surpasses the sum of receivables and inventory. Even with that accomplishment, its six days in inventory is still three times that of Apple Computer's two days in inventory.

EXHIBIT 21.5 Days Working Capital for Selected U.S. and European Technology Hardware and Equipment Firms

Company	Country	Days Working Capital	Days Receivables	Days Inventory	Days Payables
Intel Corporation	United States	48	47	21	20
Cisco Systems	United States	54	46	20	12
Dell Computer	United States	(2)	41	6	49
Texas Instruments	United States	34	65	32	63
Applied Materials	United States	41	82	52	93
Apple Computer	United States.	2	48	2	48
Sun Microsystems	United States	58	67	12	21
Gateway Inc.	United States	0	25	8	33
Average	United States	29	53	19	42
ST Microelectronics	France–Italy	58	65	52	59
Nokia	Finland	66	72	31	37
Philips Electronics	Netherlands	71	59	51	39
GN Store Nord	Denmark	100	92	40	32
Spirent	United Kingdom	107	66	63	22
Getronics	Netherlands	51	80	20	49
Infinecon Tech	Germany	75	57	69	51
Average	Europe	75	70	47	41

Source: CFO Magazine, "2001 Working Capital Survey," July 2, 2001, and CFO Europe Magazine, "2001 Working Capital Survey," July/August 2001. Days working capital = days receivables + days inventory – days payables.

Intrafirm Working Capital

The MNE itself poses some unique challenges in the management of working capital. Many multinationals manufacture goods in a few specific countries and then ship the intermediate products to other facilities globally for completion and distribution. The payables, receivables, and inventory levels of the various units are a combination of intrafirm and interfirm. The varying business practices observed globally regarding payment terms—both days and discounts—create severe mismatches in some cases.

For example, Exhibit 21.6 illustrates the challenges in working capital management faced by Trident Brazil. Because Trident Brazil purchases inputs from Trident USA and then uses additional local material input to finish the products for local distribution, it must manage two different sets of payables. Trident USA sells intrafirm on common U.S. payment terms, net 30 days. Local suppliers in Brazil, however, use payment terms closer to Brazilian norms of 60 days net (although in many cases this is still quite short for Brazilian practices, which have been known to extend to as long as 180 days). Similarly, since the customers of Trident Brazil are Brazilian, they expect the same common payment terms of 60 days. Trident Brazil is then "squeezed," having to pay Trident USA much faster than it pays other local suppliers and long before it receives a cash settlement from its customers.

In addition to Trident's need to determine intrafirm payment practices that do not put undue burdens on their foreign subsidiaries, the question of currency of invoice will also be extremely important. If Trident Brazil sells only domestically, it does not have natural inflows of U.S. dollars or other hard currencies—it earns only Brazilian reais. If Trident USA then invoices it for inputs in U.S. dollars, Trident Brazil will be constantly short dollars and will incur continuing currency management costs. Trident USA should invoice in Brazilian reais and manage the currency exposure centrally (possibly through a reinvoicing center, as discussed in Chapter 12).

EXHIBIT 21.6   **Trident's Multinational Working Capital Sequence**

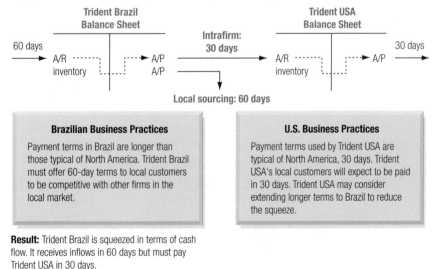

Cash inflows to Trident Brazil arise from local market sales. These cash flows are used to repay both intrafirm payables (to Trident USA) and local suppliers.

Brazilian Business Practices

Payment terms in Brazil are longer than those typical of North America. Trident Brazil must offer 60-day terms to local customers to be competitive with other firms in the local market.

U.S. Business Practices

Payment terms used by Trident USA are typical of North America, 30 days. Trident USA's local customers will expect to be paid in 30 days. Trident USA may consider extending longer terms to Brazil to reduce the squeeze.

Result: Trident Brazil is squeezed in terms of cash flow. It receives inflows in 60 days but must pay Trident USA in 30 days.

Managing Receivables

A firm's operating cash inflow is derived primarily from collecting its accounts receivable. Multinational accounts receivable are created by two separate types of transactions: sales to related subsidiaries and sales to independent or unrelated buyers.

Independent Customers. Management of accounts receivable from independent customers involves two types of decisions: In what currency should the transaction be denominated, and what should be the terms of payment? Domestic sales are almost always denominated in the local currency. At issue is whether export sales should be denominated in the currency of the exporter, the currency of the buyer, or a third-country currency. Competition or custom will often dictate the answer, but if negotiating room exists, the seller prefers to price and to invoice in the strongest currency, while an informed buyer prefers to pay in the weakest currency.

Payment Terms. Terms of payment is another bargaining factor. Considered by themselves, receivables from sales in weak currencies should be collected as soon as possible to minimize loss of exchange value between sales date and collection date. Accounts receivable resulting from sales in hard currencies may be allowed to remain outstanding longer. In fact, if the seller is expecting an imminent devaluation of its home currency, it might want to encourage slow payment of its hard currency receivables, especially if the home government requires immediate exchange of foreign currency receipts into the home currency. An alternative, if legal, would be for the seller to accept the proceeds abroad and keep them on deposit abroad rather than return them to the home country.

In inflationary economies, the demand for credit usually exceeds the supply. Often, however, a large business (be it multinational or a large local concern) has better access to the limited, cheaper credit that is available locally than do smaller domestic businesses, such as local distributors, retail merchants, or smaller manufacturers.

Self-Liquidating Bills. Some banking systems, often for reasons of tradition, have a predilection toward self-liquidating, discountable bills. In many European countries, it is easier to borrow from a bank on the security of bills (receivables in negotiable form) generated from sales than on the security of physical inventory. Napoleon is alleged to have had a philosophy that no good French merchant should be required to wait for funds if good merchandise has been sold to good people, provided a document exists showing the sale of the items. The document must have the signature of the buyer and the endorsement of the seller and the rediscounting bank. Thus, in France it is often possible to reduce net investment in receivables to zero by selling entirely on trade acceptances that can be discounted at the bank.

The European use of discountable bills has a very real rationale behind it. According to European commercial law, based on the Code Napoleon, the claim certified by the signature of the buyer on the bill is separated from the claim based on the underlying transaction. For example, a bill is easily negotiable because objections about the quality of the merchandise by the buyer do not affect the claim of the bill holder. In addition, defaulted bills can be collected through a particularly speedy judicial process that is much faster than the collection of normal receivables.

Other Terms. In many countries, government bodies facilitate inventory financing in the guise of receivable financing by extending export credit or by guaranteeing export credit from banks at advantageous interest rates. When the term of the special export financing can be extended to match the payment of the foreign purchaser, the foreign purchaser is in effect able to finance its inventory through the courtesy of the exporter's government.

In some environments, credit terms extended by manufacturers to retailers are of such long maturities as to constitute "purchase" of the retailer, such "purchase" being necessary to build an operational distribution system between manufacturer and ultimate customer. In Japan, for example, customer payment terms of 120 days are fairly common, and a manufacturer's sales effort is not competitive unless sufficient financial aid is provided to retailers to make it possible or beneficial for them to buy the manufacturer's product. Financial aid is reported to take the form of outright purchase of the retailer's capital stock, working capital loans, equipment purchase, subsidy or loan, and consideration of payment terms. Such manufacturer-supplied financing is a normal way of doing business in Japan—and contributes to the lack of domestic competition prevalent in that country.

Inventory Management

Operations in inflationary, devaluation-prone economies sometimes force management to modify its normal approach to inventory management. In some cases, management may choose to maintain inventory and reorder levels far in excess of what would be called for in an economic order-quantity model.

Under conditions where local currency devaluation is likely, management must decide whether to build up inventory of imported items in anticipation of the expected devaluation. After the devaluation, imported inventory will cost more in local currency terms. One trade-off is a higher holding cost because of the bloated level of inventory and high local interest rates that normally reflect the expected devaluation. A less obvious trade-off is the possibility that local government will enforce a price freeze following devaluation. This freeze would prevent the imported inventory from being sold for an appropriate markup above its now higher replacement value. Still worse, the devaluation may not occur as anticipated, leaving management holding an excessive level of inventory until it can be worked down. Disposing of excessive inventory will be particularly painful if competitors have followed the same strategy of speculating on imported inventory.

Free-Trade Zones and Free Industrial Zones

A *free-trade zone* combines the old idea of duty-free ports with legislation that reduces or eliminates customs duties to retailers or manufacturers who structure their operations to benefit from the technique. Income taxes may also be reduced for operations in a free-trade zone. The old duty-free ports, typically located in the dock area of major seaports, were where goods were held, duty free, until the owner was ready to deliver them within the country. Modern free-trade zones, by comparison, are often located away from a port area. For example, the Italian firm of Olivetti has such a zone in Harrisburg, Pennsylvania.

Free-trade zones function in several ways. As mentioned, they may be a place to off-load merchandise for subsequent sale within the country where the zone is located. An example of such a zone would be a storage area for imported Toyota automobiles in the Port of Los Angeles. A large quantity of differentiated models can be held until sold by a dealer, at which time the cars are "imported" into the United States from the free-trade zone. The advantage of such an arrangement is that a variety of models can be kept near the point of sale for quick delivery, but import duties need be paid only when the merchandise passes from the zone into California.

A second type of zone involves the assembly of components for subsequent sale within the country where the zone is located. An example is the Mercedes assembly line in Alabama. Components are imported into the free-trade zone where assembly work is finished. The import duty is paid only when the finished car is removed from the zone.

Furthermore, the duty is lower than it would be for a finished car because the charges on components are less than the charge on a finished vehicle.

A third type of zone is a full-fledged manufacturing center with a major portion of its output re-exported out of the country. Two examples are Penang, Malaysia, and Madagascar, where such zones are officially designated "free industrial zones." In Penang, companies as diverse as Dell, National Semiconductor, Sony, Bosch, and Trane Air Conditioning manufacture final products. A major portion of production is re-exported, avoiding Malaysian customs altogether but providing jobs for Malaysian workers and engineers. The portion of production sold in Malaysia is assessed duties only on the components originally imported. However, the variety of firms permits one to buy from another; Dell buys Pentium chips from Intel and disk drives from Seagate, both of which are located less than a mile from the Dell plant.

International Cash Management

International cash management is the set of activities that determine the levels of cash balances held throughout the MNE, and the facilitation of its movement cross-border. These activities are typically handled by the international treasury of the MNE.

Motives for Holding Cash

The level of cash maintained by an individual subsidiary is determined independently of the working capital management decisions discussed previously. Cash balances, including marketable securities, are held partly to enable normal day-to-day cash disbursements and partly to protect against unanticipated variations from budgeted cash flows. These motives are called the *transaction motive* and the *precautionary motive*.

Cash disbursed for operations is replenished from two sources: 1) internal working capital turnover and 2) external sourcing, traditionally short-term borrowing. Short-term borrowing can also be "negative," as when excess cash is used to repay outstanding short-term loans. In general, individual subsidiaries of MNEs typically maintain only minimal cash balances necessary to meet the transaction purposes. Efficient cash management aims to reduce cash tied up unnecessarily in the system, without diminishing profit or increasing risk, so as to increase the rate of return on invested assets.

International Cash Settlements and Processing

Multinational business increases the complexity of making payments and settling cash flows between related and unrelated firms. Over time a number of techniques and services have evolved that simplify and reduce the costs of making these cross-border payments. We focus here on four such techniques: wire transfers, cash pooling, payment netting, and electronic fund transfers.

Wire Transfers

Although there are a variety of computer-based networks used for effecting international transactions and settlements, two have come to dominate the international financial sector, CHIPS and SWIFT. The primary distinction among systems is whether they are for secure communications alone, or for actual transfer and settlement.

Chips. The Clearing House Interbank Payment System (CHIPS) is a computerized network that connects major banks globally. CHIPS is owned and operated by its member banks, making it the single largest privately operated and final-payments system in the world. Developed in 1970 when international currency transactions were dominated by the U.S. dollar, CHIPS has continued to dominate the transfer and settlement of U.S. dollar transactions for more than 34 years.

CHIPS is actually a subsidiary of the New York Clearing House, the oldest and largest payments processor of bank transactions. The New York Clearing House was first established in 1853 to provide a central place—a clearinghouse—where daily, all banks in New York City could settle transactions, such as the many personal checks written by private individuals and corporations, among themselves. CHIPS itself is simply a computer-based evolutionary result of this need. Because banks are still the primary financial service provider for MNEs, businesses transferring payments both interfirm and intrafirm globally use banks for effecting the payments and the banks in turn utilize CHIPS.

Swift. The Society for Worldwide Interbank Financial Telecommunications (SWIFT) also facilitates the wire transfer settlement process globally. Whereas CHIPS actually clears financial transactions, SWIFT is purely a communications system. By providing a secure and standardized transfer process, SWIFT has greatly reduced the errors and associated costs of effecting international cash transfers.

In recent years, SWIFT has expanded its messaging services beyond banks to broker-dealers and investment managers. In the mid-1990s, its services gained wider breadth as SWIFT expanded market infrastructure to payments in treasury, derivatives, and securities and trade services. It is now in the forefront of the evolution of Internet-based products and services for e-payments, expanding beyond banks to nonfinancial sector customers conducting business-to-business electronic commerce.

Cash Pooling and Centralized Depositories

Any business with widely dispersed operating subsidiaries can gain operational benefits by centralizing cash management. Internationally, the procedure calls for each subsidiary to hold minimum cash for its own transactions and no cash for precautionary purposes. However, the central pool has authority to override this general rule. All excess funds are remitted to a central cash depository, where a single authority invests the funds in such currencies and money market instruments as best serve the worldwide firm.

A central depository provides an MNE with at least four advantages:

1. Obtaining information
2. Holding precautionary cash balances
3. Reducing interest rate costs
4. Locating cost in desirable financial centers

Information Advantage. A central depository's size gives it an advantage in obtaining information. It should be located in one of the world's major financial centers so information needed for opinions about the relative strengths and weaknesses of various currencies can easily be obtained. Rate of return and risk information on alternative investments in each currency and facilities for executing orders must also be available. The information logic of centralization is that an office that specializes and operates with larger sums of money can get better information from banks, brokers, and other financial institutions, as well as better service in executing orders.

Precautionary Balance Advantage. A second reason for holding all precautionary balances in a central pool is that the total pool, if centralized, can be reduced in size without any loss in the level of protection. Trident USA, for example, has subsidiaries in Europe, Brazil, and China. Assume each of these subsidiaries maintains its own precautionary cash balance equal to its expected cash needs plus a safety margin of three standard deviations of historical variability of actual cash demands. Cash needs are assumed to be normally distributed in each country, and the needs are independent from one country to another. Three standard deviations means there exists a 99.87% chance that actual cash needs will be met; that is, only a 0.13% chance that any European subsidiary will run out of cash.

Cash needs of the individual subsidiaries, and the total precautionary cash balances held, are shown in Exhibit 21.7. Total precautionary cash balances held by Trident Europe, Brazil, and China, add up to $46,000,000, consisting of $28,000,000 in expected cash needs, and $18,000,000 in idle cash balances (the sum of three standard deviations of individual expected cash balances) held as a safety margin.

What would happen if the three Trident subsidiaries maintained all precautionary balances in a single account with Trident USA? Because variances are additive when probability distributions are independent (see footnote b to Exhibit 21.7), cash needed would drop from $46,000,000 to $39,224,972, calculated as follows:

$$
\begin{array}{lllll}
\text{Centralized} \\ \text{cash balance} & = & \text{Sum of expected cash needs} & + & \text{Three standard deviations} \\ & & & & \text{of expected sum} \\
& = & \$28,000,000 & + & (3 \times \$3,741,657) \\
& = & \$28,000,000 & + & \$11,224,972 \\
& = & \$39,224,972
\end{array}
$$

A budgeted cash balance three standard deviations above the aggregate expected cash need requires only $11,224,972 in potentially idle cash, as opposed to the previous cash balance of $18,000,000. Trident saves $6,755,028 in cash balances without reducing its safety.

EXHIBIT 21.7   Decentralized versus Centralized Cash Depositories

Decentralized Cash Depositories

Subsidiary	Expected Cash Need (A)	One Standard Deviation (B)	Cash Balance Budgeted for Adequate Protection[a] (A + 3B)
Trident Europe	$10,000,000	$1,000,000	$13,000,000
Trident Brazil	6,000,000	2,000,000	12,000,000
Trident China	12,000,000	3,000,000	21,000,000
Total	$28,000,000	$6,000,000	$46,000,000

Centralized Cash Depository

Subsidiary	Expected Cash Need (A)	One Standard Deviation (B)	Cash Balance Budgeted for Adequate Protection[a] (A + 3B)
Trident Europe	$10,000,000		
Trident Brazil	6,000,000		
Trident China	12,000,000		
Total	$28,000,000	$3,741,657[b]	$39,224,972

[a]Adequate protection is defined as the expected cash balance plus three standard deviations, assuming that the cash flows of all three individual units are normally distributed.

[b]The standard deviation of the expected cash balance of the centralized depository is calculated as follows:

$$\text{Standard deviation} = \sqrt{(1,000,000)^2 + (2,000,000)^2 + (3,000,000)^2} = \$3,741,657.$$

Interest Rate Advantage. A third advantage of centralized cash management is that one subsidiary will not borrow at high rates at the same that another holds surplus funds idle or invests them at low rates. Managers of the central pool can locate the least expensive locations to borrow and the most advantageous returns to be earned on excess funds. When additional cash is needed, the central pool manager determines the location of such borrowing. A local subsidiary manager can avoid borrowing at a rate above the minimum available to the pool manager. If the firm has a worldwide cash surplus, the central pool manager can evaluate comparative rates of return in various markets, transaction costs, exchange risks, and tax effects.

Location. Central money pools are usually maintained in major money centers such as London, New York, Zurich, Singapore, and Tokyo. Additional popular locations for money pools include Liechtenstein, Luxembourg, the Bahamas, and Bermuda. Although these countries do not have strong diversified economies, they offer most of the other prerequisites for a corporate financial center: freely convertible currency, political and economic stability, access to international communications, and clearly defined legal procedures. Their additional advantage as a so-called tax haven is desirable.

The need for a centralized depository system means that multinational banks have an advantage over single-country banks in designing and offering competitive services. However single-country banks can be incorporated into the system if the desired results can still be achieved, for the essence of the operation is centralized information and decisions. MNEs can place actual funds in as many banks as they desire.

Multilateral Netting

Multilateral netting is defined as the process that cancels, via offset, all or part of the debt owed by one entity to another related entity. Multilateral netting of payments is useful primarily when a large number of separate foreign exchange transactions occur between subsidiaries in the normal course of business. Netting reduces the settlement cost of what would otherwise be a large number of crossing spot transactions.

Multilateral netting is an extension of bilateral netting. Assume Trident Brazil owes Trident China $5,000,000, and Trident China simultaneously owes Trident Brazil $3,000,000. A bilateral settlement calls for a single payment of $2,000,000 from Brazil to China and the cancellation, via offset, of the remainder of the debt.

A multilateral system is an expanded version of this simple bilateral concept. Assume that payments are due between Trident's operations at the end of each month. Each obligation reflects the accumulated transactions of the prior month. These obligations for a particular month might be as shown in Exhibit 21.8.

Without netting, Trident Brazil makes three separate payments and receives three separate receipts at the end of the month. If Trident Brazil paid its intracompany obligations daily, or even weekly, rather than accumulating a balance to settle at the end of the month, it would generate a multitude of costly small bank transactions. The daily totals would add up to the monthly accumulated balances shown in the diagram.

In order to reduce bank transaction costs, such as the spread between foreign exchange bid and ask quotations and transfer fees, MNEs like Trident establish in-house multilateral netting centers. Other firms contract with banks to manage their netting system. Assume that Trident's net intracompany obligations for a given month can be summarized as shown in Exhibit 21.9.

Note that payment obligations and expected receipts add up to $43,000,000 because one subsidiary's debts are another's receivables. If the cost of foreign exchange transactions and transfer fees were 0.5%, the total cost of settlement would be $205,000. Using information

EXHIBIT 21.8   Multilateral Matrix before Netting (thousands of U.S. dollars)

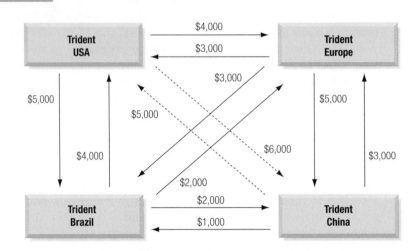

Prior to netting, the four sister Trident companies have numerous intrafirm payments between them. Each payment results in transfer charges.

EXHIBIT 21.9   Calculation of Trident Intrasubsidiary Net Obligations (thousands of U.S. dollars)

Receiving Subsidiary	Paying Subsidiary				Total Receipts	Net Receipts (Payments)
	United States	Brazil	Europe	China		
United States	—	$4,000	$3,000	$5,000	$12,000	($3,000)
Brazil	5,000	—	3,000	1,000	9,000	$1,000
Europe	4,000	2,000	—	3,000	9,000	($2,000)
China	6,000	2,000	5,000	—	13,000	$4,000
Total payments	$15,000	$8,000	$11,000	$9,000	$43,000	—

from the netting matrix in Exhibit 21.9, the netting center at Trident USA can order three payments to settle the entire set of obligations. Trident USA will itself remit $3,000,000 to China, and Europe will be instructed to send $1,000,000 each to Brazil and China. Total foreign exchange transfers are reduced to $5,000,000, and transaction costs at 0.5% are reduced to $25,000. This is shown in Exhibit 21.10.

Some countries limit or prohibit netting, while others permit netting on a "gross payment" basis only. For a single settlement period all payments may be combined into a single payment, and all receipts will be received as a single transfer. However, these two may not be netted and thus must pass through the local banking system.

Financing Working Capital

The MNE enjoys a much greater choice of banking sources to fund its working capital needs than do domestic firms. Banking sources available to MNEs include in-house banks funded by unrepatriated capital, international banks, and local banks where subsidiaries are located.

EXHIBIT 21.10 Multilateral Matrix after Netting (thousands of U.S. dollars)

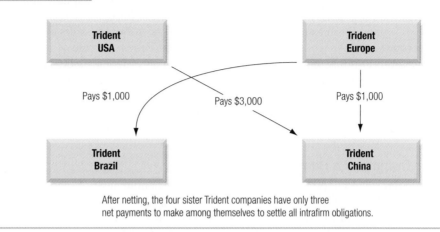

After netting, the four sister Trident companies have only three
net payments to make among themselves to settle all intrafirm obligations.

In-house banks and the various types of external commercial banking offices are described in the remainder of this chapter.

In-House Banks

Some MNEs have found that their financial resources and needs are either too large or too sophisticated for the financial services available in many locations where they operate. One solution to this has been the establishment of an *in-house* or *internal bank* within the firm. An in-house bank is not a separate corporation; rather, it is a set of functions performed by the existing treasury department. Acting as an independent entity, the central treasury of the firm transacts with the various business units of the firm on an arm's length basis. The purpose of the in-house bank is to provide bank-like services to the various units of the firm. The in-house bank may be able to provide services not available in many countries, and do so at lower cost when they are available. In addition to traditional banking activities, the in-house bank may be able to offer services to units of the firm, which aid in the management of ongoing transaction exposures. Lastly, because it is in-house, credit analysis is not a part of the bank's decision making.

For example, the in-house bank of Trident Corporation could work with Trident Europe and Trident Brazil. Trident Brazil sells all its receivables to the in-house bank as they arise, reducing some of its domestic working capital needs. Additional working capital needs are supplied by the in-house bank directly to Trident Brazil. Because the in-house bank is part of the same company, the interest rates it charges may be significantly lower than what Trident Brazil could obtain on its own. The source of funds for the in-house bank may arise from the deposits of excess cash balances from Trident Europe. If the in-house bank can pay Trident Europe a higher deposit rate than it could obtain on its own, and if the in-house bank can lend these funds to Trident Brazil at an interest rate lower than it could obtain on its own in Brazil, then both operating units benefit. Assuming the loan rate is greater than the deposit rate, the in-house bank profits by the margin between the two, but this margin or spread must be smaller than would be available from a commercial bank.

How can the in-house bank operate with a smaller spread than a regular commercial bank? First, its costs are lower because it does not have to conform to the stringent capital requirements imposed on commercial banks worldwide. Second, in-house banks do not have the overhead costs of supporting large dealing rooms, branch networks, retail "store fronts," and other services required for commercial bank competitiveness. Third, they do not need to assess the creditworthiness of the corporate units with which they deal, since the units are all in the same family—nor do they need to provide for credit losses.

In addition to providing financing benefits, in-house banks allow for more effective currency risk management. In the case of Trident Brazil, the sale of foreign currency receivables to the in-house bank shifts transaction exposure to the bank. The in-house bank is better equipped to deal with currency exposures and has a greater volume of international cash flows allowing Trident USA overall to gain from more effective use of netting and matching. This frees the units of the firm from struggling to manage transaction exposures and allows them to focus on their primary business activities.

Commercial Banking Offices

MNEs depend on their commercial banks to handle most of their trade financing needs, such as letters of credit, but also to provide advice on government support, country risk assessment, introductions to foreign firms and banks, and general financing availability. MNEs interface with their banks through a variety of types of banking offices, many of which perform specialized functions. Therefore, it is important for financial managers to understand which bank offices provide which kinds of activities. The main points of bank contact are with correspondent banks, representative offices, branch banks, and subsidiaries. In the United States, a more specialized banking facility is available: the Edge Act Corporation.

Correspondent Banks. Most major banks of the world maintain correspondent banking relationships with local banks in each of the major foreign cities of the world. The two-way link between banks is essentially one of correspondence via fax, cable, and mail, and a mutual deposit relationship. For example, a U.S. bank may have a correspondent bank in Kuala Lumpur, Malaysia, and the U.S. bank will in turn be the correspondent bank for the Malaysian bank. Each will maintain a deposit in the other in local currency.

Correspondent services include accepting drafts, honoring letters of credit, and furnishing credit information. Services are centered on collecting or paying foreign funds, often because of import or export transactions. However, a visiting business person can use the home bank's introduction to meet local bankers. Under a correspondent banking relationship, neither of the correspondent banks maintains its own personnel in the other country. Direct contact between the banks is usually limited to periodic visits between members of the banks' management.

For the business person, the main advantage of banking at home with a bank having a large number of foreign correspondent relationships is having the ability to handle financial matters in a large number of foreign countries through local bankers whose knowledge of local customs should be extensive. The disadvantages are the lack of ability to deposit in, borrow from, or disburse from a branch of one's own home bank. There is a possibility that correspondents will put a lower priority on serving the foreign banks' customer than on serving their own permanent customers.

Representative Offices. A bank establishes a representative office in a foreign country primarily to help parent bank clients when they are doing business in that country or in neighboring countries. It also functions as a geographically convenient location from which to visit correspondent banks in its region rather than sending bankers from the parent bank at greater financial and physical cost. A representative office is not a bank office. It cannot accept deposits, make loans, commit the parent bank to a loan, or deal in drafts, letters of credit, or the Eurocurrency market. Indeed, a tourist cannot even cash a traveler's check from the parent bank in the representative office.

If the parent bank eventually decides to open a local general banking office, the existence of a representative office for some prior period usually provides a valuable base of contacts and expertise to facilitate the change. However, representative offices are not necessarily a prelude to a general banking office, nor need an eventual general banking office be the major reason for opening a representative office.

Branch Banks. A foreign branch bank is a legal and operational part of the parent bank, with the full resources of that parent behind the local office. A branch bank does not have its own corporate charter, its own board of directors, or any shares of stock outstanding. Although for managerial and regulatory purposes it will maintain its own set of books, its assets and liabilities are in fact those of the parent bank. However, branch deposits are not subject to reserve requirements or FDIC insurance, in the case of U.S. banks, unless the deposits are reloaned to the U.S. parent bank.

Branch banks are subject to two sets of banking regulations. As part of the parent, they are subject to home-country regulations. However, they are also subject to regulations of the host country, which may provide any of a variety of restrictions on their operations.

The major advantage to a business of using a branch bank is that the branch will conduct a full range of banking services under the name and legal obligation of the parent. A deposit in a branch is a legal obligation of the parent. Services to customers are based on the worldwide value of the client relationship rather than just on the relationship to the local office. Legal loan limits are a function of the size of the parent, not of the branch.

From the point of view of a banker, the profits of a foreign branch are subject to immediate taxation at home, and losses of a foreign branch are deductible against taxable income at home. A new office expected to have losses in its early years creates a tax advantage if it is initially organized as a branch, even if eventually the intent is to change it to a separately incorporated subsidiary. From an organizational point of view, a foreign branch is usually simpler to create and staff than is a separately incorporated subsidiary.

The major disadvantage of a branch bank is one that accrues to the bank rather than to its customers. The parent bank (not just the branch) may be sued at the local level for debts or other activities of the branch.

Banking Subsidiaries. A subsidiary bank is a separately incorporated bank, owned entirely or in major part by a foreign parent, that conducts a general banking business. As a separate corporation, the banking subsidiary must comply with all the laws of the host country. Its lending limit is based on its own equity capital rather than that of the parent bank. This limits its ability to service large borrowers, but local incorporation also limits the liability of the parent bank to its equity investment in the subsidiary.

A foreign banking subsidiary often appears as a local bank in the eyes of potential customers in host countries and is thus often able to attract additional local deposits. This will especially be true if the bank was independent prior to being purchased by the foreign parent. Management may well be local, giving the bank greater access to the local business community. A foreign-owned bank subsidiary is more likely to be involved in both domestic and international business than is a foreign branch, which is more likely to appeal to the foreign business community but may well encounter difficulty in attracting banking business from local firms.

Edge Act Corporations. Edge Act corporations are subsidiaries of U.S. banks, incorporated in the United States under Section 25 of the Federal Reserve Act as amended, to engage in international banking and financing operations. Not only may such subsidiaries engage in general international banking, they may also finance commercial, industrial, or financial projects in foreign countries through long-term loans or equity participation. Such participation, however, is subject to the day-to-day practices and policies of the Federal Reserve System.

Edge Act corporations generally engage in two types of activities: direct international banking, including acting as a holding company for the stock of one or more foreign banking subsidiaries, and financing development activities not closely related to traditional banking operations.

SUMMARY POINTS

- The *operating cycle* of a business generates funding needs, cash inflows and outflows—the cash conversion cycle—and potential foreign exchange rate and credit risks.

- The funding needs generated by the *operating cycle* of the firm constitute *working capital.* The operating cycle of a business extends along a time line from the point at which a customer requests a price quote to the time at which payment is received from the customer for goods delivered.

- The *cash conversion cycle,* a subcomponent of the operating cycle, is that period of time extending between cash outflows for purchased inputs and materials and when cash inflow is received from a cash settlement.

- The MNE is constantly striving to create shareholder value by maximizing the after-tax profitability of the firm. One dimension of this task is to *reposition the profits* of the firm, as legally and practically possible, in low-tax environments.

- Repositioning profits allows the firm to increase its after-tax profits by lowering its tax liabilities with the same amount of sales.

- In addition to tax management, repositioning is useful when an MNE wishes to move cash flows or funds in general from where they are not needed to where they may be redeployed in more value-creating activities, or to minimize exposure to a potential currency collapse or potential political or economic crisis.

- *Royalty fees* are compensation for the use of intellectual property belonging to some other party. Royalty fees are usually a stated percentage of sales revenue (price × volume) so that the owner is compensated in proportion to the volume of sales.

- *License fees* are remuneration paid to the owners of technology, patents, trade names, and copyrighted material (including moving pictures, video tapes, compact disks, software, and books).

- License fees are usually based on a percentage of the value of the product or on the volume of production. As such, they are calculated independently of the amount of sales.

- International dividend policy now incorporates tax considerations, political risk, and foreign exchange risk, as well as a return for business guidance and technology.

- Dividends are the most tax-inefficient method for repatriating funds because they are distributed on an after-tax basis. This means that the parent company will frequently be faced with the generation of excess foreign tax credits on a dividend.

- Remittance of license or royalty fees is on a pretax basis in the foreign subsidiary, the only tax that is typically applied is withholding, at a rate considerably below that of corporate income taxes.

- In principle, firms attempt to minimize their net working capital balance. A/R is reduced if collections are accelerated. Inventories held by the firm are reduced by carrying lower levels of both unfinished and finished goods, and by speeding the rate at which goods are manufactured, reducing so-called *cycle time.*

- All firms must determine whether A/P should be paid off early, taking discounts if offered by suppliers, and whether to finance these payments with short-term debt. Note that short-term debt is not included within NWC because it does not spontaneously increase with operations, but must be acquired as part of management's financing choices.

- Over time, a number of techniques and services have evolved which simplify and reduce the costs of making cross-border payments. This includes wire transfers, cash pooling, payment netting, and electronic fund transfers.

- MNEs can finance working capital needs through in-house banks, international banks, and local banks where subsidiaries are located.

- International banks finance MNEs and service these accounts through representative offices, correspondent banking relationships, branch banks, banking subsidiaries, affiliates, and Edge Act corporations (United States only).

MINI-CASE   Honeywell and Pakistan International Airways

The Space and Avionics Control Group (SAC) of Honeywell, Incorporated (U.S.) was quite frustrated in June of 1997. The cockpit retrofit proposal with Pakistan International Airlines had been under negotiation for seven months, and over the past weekend a new request had been thrown in—to accept payment in Pakistan rupee. This was against corporate policy at Honeywell, but if an exception was not made, the deal—worth $23.7 million—was most likely dead.

Pakistan International Airlines (PIA)

Pakistan International Airlines Corporation (PIA) was the national carrier of the Islamic Republic of Pakistan. Founded in 1954, PIA operated scheduled passenger and cargo services. The firm was 57% state owned, with the remaining 43% held by private investors internal to Pakistan.

PIA's fleet was aging. Although the airline had planned a significant modernization program, recent restrictions placed on government spending by the International Monetary Fund (IMF) had killed the program. With the cancellation of the fleet modernization program, PIA now had to move fast to ensure compliance with U.S. Federal Aviation Administration (FAA) safety mandates. If it did not comply with the FAA mandates for quieter engines and upgraded avionics by June 30, 1998, PIA would be locked out of its very profitable U.S. gates. PIA would first retrofit the aircraft utilized on the long-haul flights to the United States, primarily the Boeing 747 classics. Due to SAC's extensive experience with a variety of control systems for Boeing and its recent work on cockpit retrofit for McDonnell Douglas aircraft, SAC felt it was the preferred supplier for PIA. However, SAC had not undertaken Boeing cockpit retrofits to date (no one had), and looked to the PIA deal as an opportunity to build a new competitive base. PIA's insistence on payment in local currency terms was now thought to be a tactic to extract better concessions from SAC and their agent, Makran.

Ibrahim Makran Pvt. Ltd.

In countries like Pakistan, the use of an agent is often considered a necessary evil. The agent can often help to bridge two business cultures and provide invaluable information, but at some cost. Honeywell's agent, Ibrahim Makran Pvt. Ltd., based in Hyderabad, was considered one of the most reliable and well connected in Pakistan. Makran traced its roots back to a long association with the Sperry Aerospace and Marine Group, the precursor to Honeywell's SAC unit (Sperry was acquired in 1986). Makran was also one of the largest import/export trading houses in Pakistan. It was 100% family owned and managed.

Standard practice in the avionics business was to provide the agent with a 10% commission, although this was negotiable. The 10% was based on the final sales and was paid after all payments were received. Typically, it was the agent who spotted the business opportunity and submitted a proposal to SAC Marketing.

When PIA contacted Makran regarding their latest demand, Makran knew that SAC would want to maintain the deal in U.S. dollars. Makran had therefore inquired as to the availability of dollar funds for a deal of this size from its own finance department. The finance department confirmed that they had the necessary U.S. dollar funds to pay SAC, but warned that policy was to charge 5% for services rendered and currency risks.

Makran advised SAC that it would be willing to purchase the receivable for an additional 5% (in addition to the 10% commission). Makran's U.S. subsidiary in Los Angeles would credit SAC within 30 days of SAC invoicing Makran. PIA advised Makran that if SAC accepted payment in Pakistan rupees, then local (Pakistan) payment terms would apply. This meant 180 days in principle, but often was much longer in practice. The agent also advised SAC that the Pakistan rupee was due for another devaluation. When pressed for more information, Makran simply replied that the company president, the elder Ibrahim Makran, had "good connections."

Pakistan Rupee

A central part of the IMF's austerity program was a devaluation of the Pakistan rupee by 7.86% against the U.S. dollar on October 22, 1996. Now, roughly six months later, there was renewed speculation that another devaluation was imminent in order to limit imports and help the export sector earn badly needed hard currency. Another recent economic setback had been the ruling by the European Union that Pakistan was guilty of dumping cotton, and had imposed anti-dumping fines on Pakistani cotton. This was a painful blow to the export sector. The current exchange rate of 40.4795 Pakistan rupee (Rp) per dollar was maintained by the Pakistani Central Bank. The parallel market rate—*the black market rate*—was approaching Rp50/US$. At present, there was no forward market for the Pakistan rupee.

Honeywell's Working Capital

Honeywell's finance department was attempting to reduce net working capital and had just concluded a thorough review of existing payment terms and worldwide days sales receivable (DSR) rates. The department's goal was to reduce worldwide DSR rates from 55 to 45 days in the current fiscal year. The *pay for performance* target for the current year (the annual performance bonus system at Honeywell) included net working capital goals. There was concern in the organization that the net working capital goal could prove the obstacle to achieving a bonus despite excellent sales growth. The latest DSR report follows:

SAC Control Systems' Average Days Sales Receivables by Region

Region	Actual	Target	Amount
North America	44	40	$31.0 million
South America	129	70	$2.1 million
Europe	55	45	$5.7 million
Middle East	93	60	$3.2 million
Asia	75	55	$11.0 million
PIA	264	180	$0.7 million
Boeing	39	30	$41.0 million
McDonnell Douglas	35	30	$18.0 million
Airbus Industries	70	45	$13.0 million

Notes:

A. U.S.-based airline trading companies distort the actual local payment terms.

B. The spread between individual customers within regions can be extremely large.

C. Some collection activity is assumed. Specific customers are periodically targeted.

D. Disputed invoices are included. Amount is for all products, services, and exchanges.

E. One of the criteria for granting "preferred" pricing is a 30-day DSR. The 10% reduction can be substantial but typically only motivates the larger customers.

Honeywell payment terms were net 30 from date of invoice. However, payment terms and practices varied dramatically across country and region. Payment terms were generally not published, with the exception of some private reports by credit rating agencies. Honeywell had not in the past enforced stringent credit terms on many customers. For example, neither contracts nor invoices stated any penalties for late payment. Many airlines did pay on time, but others availed themselves of Honeywell's cheap financing.

A review of PIA's account receivable history indicated that they consistently paid their invoices late. The current average DSR was 264 days. PIA had been repeatedly put on hold by the collections department, forcing marketing staff representatives to press the agent who in turn pressed PIA for payment. Honeywell was very concerned about this deal. It had in fact asked for guarantees that PIA would pay promptly. Honeywell's concern was also reflected in the 20% advance payment clause in the contract. Although marketing took the high DSR rate up with PIA and the agent, the current proposed deal was expected to be the same if not worse.

One positive attribute of the proposed contract was that delivery would not occur until one year after the contract was signed. The invoice for the full amount outstanding would be issued at that time. If the expected improvements to the DSR were made in the meantime, maybe the high DSR rate on the PIA deal could be averaged with the rest of Asia. The 20% advance payment would be used to fund the front-end engineering work.

Global treasury at Honeywell was headquartered along with corporate in Minneapolis, Minnesota. Corporate treasury was a profit center and charged 1% commission on all sales. Treasury, however, passed on the currency risk to the business unit. If a local subsidiary required local currency, treasury would try to match those requirements by accepting the A/R in the local currency. They had advised SAC that for many developing countries where Honeywell had little or no activities, such as Pakistan, this was done only on an exception basis. Global treasury also evaluated all deals in present value terms given the extended payment periods, and the corporate cost of capital was set at 12%.

Negotiations

Honeywell now speculated that the local currency request was a result of the 20% advance payment clause. The project was considered one of the riskiest SAC had undertaken, and the 20% advance payment would help reach the group's DSR goals. The DSR was being watched on a daily basis by division management. This project had already been forced to secure group-level approval because it fell below the minimum return-on-sales target. SAC's management had counted on the deal to make its annual sales targets, and that now seemed in jeopardy. It would need to act soon if it was to reach its targets.

Case Questions

1. Estimate what cash flows in which currencies the proposal would probably yield. What is the expected U.S. dollar value that would, in the end, be received?

2. Do you think the services that Makran is offering are worth the costs?

3. What would you do if you were heading the Honeywell SAC group negotiating the deal?

QUESTIONS

1. **Constraints on Positioning Funds.** Each of the following factors is sometimes a constraint on the free movement of funds internationally. Why would a government impose such a constraint? How might the management of a multinational argue that such a constraint is not in the best interests of the government that has imposed it?
   a. Government-mandated restrictions on moving funds out of the country
   b. Withholding taxes on dividend distributions to foreign owners
   c. Dual-currency regimes, with one rate for imports and another rate for exports
   d. Refusal to allow foreign firms in the country to net cash inflows and outflows into a single payment

2. **Unbundling.** What does this term mean? Why would unbundling be needed for international cash flows from foreign subsidiaries, but not for domestic cash flows between related domestic subsidiaries and their parent?

3. **Conduits.** In the context of unbundling cash flows from subsidiary to parent, explain how each of the following creates a conduit. What are the tax consequences of each?
   a. Imports of components from the parent
   b. Payment to cover overhead expenses of parent managers temporarily assigned to the subsidiary
   c. Payment of royalties for the use of proprietary technology
   d. Subsidiary borrowing of funds on an intermediate or long-term maturity from the parent
   e. Payment of dividends to the parent

4. **Sister Subsidiaries.** Subsidiary Alpha in Country Able faces a 40% income tax rate. Subsidiary Beta in Country Baker faces only a 20% income tax rate. Presently, each subsidiary imports from the other an amount of goods and services exactly equal in monetary value to what each exports to the other. This method of balancing intracompany trade was imposed by a management keen to reduce all costs, including the costs (spread between bid and ask) of foreign exchange transactions. Both subsidiaries are profitable, and both could purchase all components domestically at approximately the same prices as they are paying to their foreign sister subsidiary. Does this seem like an optimal situation?

5. **Allocated Fees—A.** What is the difference between a license fee and a royalty fee? Do you think license and royalty fees should be covered by the tax rules that regulate transfer pricing? Why?

6. **Allocated Fees—B.** What are the differences between a management fee, a technical assistance fee, and a license fee for patent usage? Should they be treated differently for income tax purposes?

7. **Distributed Overhead.** What methods might the U.S. Internal Revenue Service use to determine whether allocations of distributed overhead are being fairly allocated to foreign subsidiaries?

8. **Fee Treatment.** In the context of unbundling cash flows from subsidiary to parent, why might a host government be more lenient in its treatment of fees than in its treatment of dividends? What difference does it make to the subsidiary and to the parent?

9. **The Cycle.** The operating cycle of a firm, domestic or multinational, consists of the following time periods:
   a. Quotation period
   b. Input sourcing period
   c. Inventory period
   d. Accounts receivable period

   For each of these periods, explain whether a cash outflow or a cash inflow is associated with the beginning and the end of the period.

10. **Accounts Payable Period.** Exhibit 21.1 shows the accounts payable period to be longer than the inventory period. Could this be otherwise, and what would be the cash implications?

11. **Payables and Receivables.** As a financial manager, would you prefer that the accounts payable period

end before, at the same time, or after the beginning of the accounts receivable period? Explain.

12. **Transaction Exposure.** Assuming the flow illustrated in Exhibit 21.1, where does transaction exposure begin and end if inputs are purchased with one currency at t_1 and proceeds from the sale are received at t_5? Is there more than one interval of transaction exposure?

13. **Operating Exposure.** Is any operating exposure created during the course of a firm's operating cycle?

14. **Accounting Exposure.** Is any accounting exposure created during the course of a firm's operating cycle?

15. **Reducing NWC.** Assume a firm purchases inventory with one foreign currency and sells it for another foreign currency, neither currency being the home currency of the parent or subsidiary where the manufacturing process takes place. What can the firm do to reduce the amount of net working capital?

16. **Trade Terms.** Roberts and Sons, Inc., of Great Britain has just purchased inventory items costing kronor 1,000,000 from a Swedish supplier. The supplier has quoted terms 3/15, net 45. Under what conditions might Roberts and Sons reasonably take the discount, and when might it be a reasonable idea to wait the full 45 days to pay?

17. **Inventory Turnover.** Japanese industry is often praised for its just-in-time inventory practice between industrial buyers and industrial sellers. In the context of the "Days Receivables" turnover in Exhibit 21.5, what is the comparative impact of the just-in-time system in Japan? Are there any risks associated with this system? Do you think this applies equally to Japanese manufacturing firms sourcing raw material and components in Japan and those sourcing similar items from Thailand and Malaysia?

18. **Receivables Turnover.** Why might the time lag for multinational intrafirm accounts receivable and payable (that is, all received or paid to a parent or sister subsidiary) differ substantially from the time lags reported for transactions with nonaffiliated companies?

19. **Devaluation Risk.** Merlin Corporation of the United States imports raw material from Indonesia on terms of 2/10, net 30. Merlin expects a 36% devaluation of the Indonesian rupiah at any moment. Should Merlin take the discount? Discuss aspects of the problem.

20. **Free-Trade Zones.** What are the advantages of a free-trade zone?

21. **Motives.** Explain the difference between the transaction motive and the precautionary motive for holding cash.

22. **Cash Cycle.** The operating cash cycle of a multinational firm goes from cash collection from customers, cash holding for anticipated transaction needs (the transaction motive for holding cash), possible cash repositioning into another currency, and eventual cash disbursements to pay operating expenses. Assuming the initial cash collection is in one currency and the eventual cash disbursement is in another currency, what can a multinational firm do to shorten its cash cycle and what risks are involved?

23. **Electro-Beam Company.** Electro-Beam Company generates and disburses cash in the currencies of four countries: Singapore, Malaysia, Thailand, and Vietnam. What would be the characteristics you might consider if charged with designing a centralized cash depository system for Electro-Beam Company's Southeast Asian subsidiaries?

24. **France.** During the era of the French franc, France imposed a rule on its banks and subsidiaries of international companies operating in France that precluded those subsidiaries from netting cash flow obligations between France and non-French entities. Why do you suppose the French government imposed such a rule, and what if anything could subsidiaries in France have done about it?

25. **Foreign Bank Office.** What is the difference between a foreign branch and a foreign subsidiary of a home-country bank?

PROBLEMS

*1. **Asahi-Do, K.K.** Asahi-Do, K.K., the Japanese subsidiary of a U.S. company has ¥100,000,000 in accounts receivable for sales billed to customers on terms of 2/30 n/60. Customers usually pay in 30 days. Super-Do also has ¥60,000,000 of accounts payable billed to it on terms of 3/10 n/60. Super-Do delays payment until the last minute because it is normally short of cash. Super-Do, K.K. normally carries an average cash balance for transactions of ¥30,000,000. How much cash could Super-Do, K.K. save by taking the discount?

2. **Extreme Ski.** Extreme Ski of Grenoble, France, manufactures and sells in France, Switzerland, and Italy, and also maintains a corporate account in Frankfurt, Germany. Extreme has been setting separate operating cash balance in each country at a level equal to expected cash needs plus two standard deviations above those needs, based on a statistical analysis of cash flow volatility. Expected operating cash needs and one standard deviation of those needs are as follows:

	Expected Cash Need	One Standard Deviation
Switzerland	€5,000,000	€1,000,000
Italy	3,000,000	400,000
France	2,000,000	300,000
Germany	800,000	40,000
	€10,800,000	€1,740,000

Extreme's Frankfurt bank suggests that the same level of safety could be maintained if all precautionary balances were combined in a central account at the Frankfurt headquarters.

a. How much lower would Extreme Ski Company's total cash balances be if all precautionary balances were combined? Assume cash needs in each country are normally distributed and are independent of each other.

b. What other advantages might accrue to Extreme Ski Company from centralizing its cash holdings? Are these advantages realistic?

3. **Futebal do Brasil, S.A.** Futebal do Brazil, S.A. purchases newly sewn soccer balls from Pakistani manufacturers and distributes them in Argentina, Brazil, and Chile. All operations are through wholly owned subsidiaries. The three subsidiaries have submitted the following daily cash reports, with all amounts in thousands of U.S. dollars, which the Brazilian company uses for cash management purposes. Each of the two foreign subsidiaries is allowed to carry a $1,000,000 cash balance overnight, with the remainder remitted to a U.S. dollar account maintained in Sao Paulo unless instructed otherwise by the Brazilian financial staff. As a general matter, the cost of moving funds is such that funds should not be moved for one day and then returned the next, but a movement for two days which is then reversed is financially advantageous. The Brazilian headquarters invests surplus cash balance over US$5,000,000 in U.S. money market instruments purchased through the Miami correspondent bank of the firm's Brazilian

bank. Anticipated cash flows, in thousands of U.S. dollars are as follows:

	Companhia Futebal do Brasil	Compañía Fútbal de Argentina	Compañía Fútbal de Chile
Day-end cash balance	$6,000	$5,000	$5,000
Minimum operating balance required:	$5,000	$1,000	$1,000
Expected receipts (+) or disbursements (–):			
+1 day	+3,000	–2,000	+5,000
+2 days	0	+1,000	–3,000
+3 days	–5,000	–3,000	+2,000

Design an advantageous cash movement plan that complies with Futebal do Brasil general policies.

4. **GeoTech Agriculture.** GeoTech Agriculture, Inc. (U.S.) manufactures basic farm equipment in China, Spain, and Iowa in the United States. Each subsidiary has monthly unsettled balances due to or from other subsidiaries. At the end of December, unsettled intracompany debts in U.S. dollars were as follows:

GeoTech,China:	Owes $8 million to Spanish subsidiary
	Owes $9 million to Iowa parent
GeoTech,Spain:	Owes $5 million to Chinese subsidiary
	Owes $6 million to Iowa parent
GeoTech,Iowa:	Owes $4 million to Chinese subsidiary
	Owes $10 million to Spanish subsidiary

Foreign exchange transaction spreads average 0.4% of funds transferred.

a. How could GeoTech net these intracompany debts? How much would be saved in transaction expenses over the no-netting alternative?

b. Before settling the above accounts, GeoTech decides to invest $6,000,000 of parent funds in a new farm equipment manufacturing plant in the new Free Industrial Zone at Subic Bay, The Philippines. How can this decision be incorporated into the settlement process? What would be total bank charges? Explain.

5. **Crystal Publishing Company.** Crystal Publishing Company publishes books in Europe through separate subsidiaries in several countries. On a Europe-wide basis, Crystal publishing experiences uneven cash flows. Any given book creates a cash outflow during the period of writing and publishing, followed by a cash inflow in subsequent months and years as

the book is sold. To handle these imbalances, Crystal decided to create an in-house bank.

At the beginning of April, Crystal's in-house bank held deposits, on which it paid 4.8% interest, as follows:

From Crystal Germany	€20,000,000
From Crystal Spain	€5,000,000
From Crystal Britain	£12,000,000

At the beginning of April, Crystal's in-house bank advanced funds at an annual rate of 5.4% as follows:

To Crystal France	€12,000,000
To Crystal Italy	€8,000,000
To Crystal Greece	€6,000,000

The exchange rate between pounds sterling and the euro is €1.6000/£.

a. What would be the net interest earnings (interest earned less interest paid, before administrative expenses), of Crystal's in-house bank for the month of April?

b. If parent Crystal Publishing subsidized the in-house for all of its operating expenses, how much more could the in-house bank loan at the beginning of April?

6. **Balanced Tire Company (A).** Balanced Tire Company manufactures automobile tires for sale to retail outlets in the United States and, through a wholly owned distribution subsidiary, in neighboring Canada. Annual capacity of the U.S. factory is 700,000 tires per year, but present production is only 450,000, of which 300,000 are sold in the United States and 150,000 are exported to Canada. Federal and state income tax rates in both countries add up to 40%.

Within the United States, Balanced Tire sells to retail outlets for the U.S. dollar equivalent of C$80 per tire. After-tax profit is equivalent to C$10.80 per

tire calculated as shown in the following table, with all prices expressed in the Canadian dollar equivalent of U.S. dollars.

Balanced Tire's U.S. Profit Calculation, Expressed in Canadian Dollars:

Balanced Tire's U.S. sales price tire	C$80.00
less direct labor in U.S.	20.00
less direct material in U.S.	20.00
less U.S. manufacturing overhead	12.00
Total manufacturing costs	52.00
U.S. factory margin	28.00
less selling and administrative costs	10.00
Pre-tax profit per tire	18.00
less 40% U.S. income taxes	7.20
After-tax profit per tire in the United States	C$10.80

Direct labor consists of hourly payroll costs for factory workers, and direct material is for raw material purchased in the United States. Manufacturing overhead is a fixed cost that includes supervision and depreciation. Selling and administrative costs are fixed expenses for management salaries, office expenses and rent.

For its exports to Canada, Balanced Tire sells sets to its Canadian subsidiary at a U.S. dollar transfer price equal to C$56 per tire, this being U.S. manufacturing cost of C$52 plus a C$4.00 profit. Transportation and distribution costs add an additional C$2.00 per tire, and the tires are resold to Canadian retail outlets for C$80, the same equivalent price as in the United States. This price was arrived at independently, based on the analysis of elasticity of demand in Canada shown in the table below.

Maximum profit is at a sales price of C$80.00.

In making this calculation, Balanced Tire determined that unit demand in Canada was a function only of the sales price. Hence, it seemed self-evident to Balanced Tire's management that a transfer price

Sales in Canada (C$)					
Unit sales price in Canada	85.00	80.00	75.00	70.00	65.00
less import	56.00	56.00	56.00	56.00	56.00
less shipping	2.00	2.00	2.00	2.00	2.00
Unit profit before tax	27.00	22.00	17.00	12.00	7.00
less 40% Canadian tax	10.80	8.80	6.80	4.80	5.40
Unit profit after tax	16.20	13.20	10.20	7.20	4.20
expected unit volume	110,000	150,000	180,000	250,000	400,000
Total profit (000)	1,782	1,980	1,836	1,800	1,680

to Canada of C$80.00 per tire maximized Canada's contribution to profits at a total figure of C$1,980,000. Is Balanced Tire's present pricing strategy for Canada correct?

7. **Balanced Tire Company (B).** Assume Balanced Tire (previous problem) decided to set the Canadian price at C$65. Both countries, however, have decreased their corporate income tax rates: the United States to 35% and Canada to 38%.
   a. Given the change in tax rates, what final Canadian dollar price now would maximize the company's consolidated profits?
   b. Would reducing the transfer price from C$56 to C$54 increase or decrease consolidated profits?

*8. **Surgical Tools, Inc.** Surgical Tools, Inc. of Illinois wants to set up a regular procedure for transferring funds from its newly opened manufacturing subsidiary in Korea to the United States. The precedent set by the transfer method or methods is likely to prevail over any government objections that might otherwise arise in future years. The Korean subsidiary manufactures surgical tools for export to all Asian countries. The *pro forma* financial information shown in the table below portrays the results expected in the first full year of operations.

Sales	Won2,684,000,000
Cash manufacturing expenses	1,342,000,000
Depreciation	335,500,000
Pre-tax profit	1,006,500,000
Korean taxes at 28%	281,820,000
Profit after taxes	Won724,680,000
Exchange rate	Won1342/$
Korean income tax rate	28%
U.S. income tax rate	34%

Surgical Tool's CFO is pondering the following approaches:
   a. Declare a dividend of Won362,340,000, equal to 50% of profit after taxes. The dividend would be taxable in the United States after a gross-up for Korean taxes already paid.
   b. Add a license fee of Won362,340,000 to the above expenses, and remit that amount annually. The license fee would be fully taxable in the United States.

9. **Adams Corporation (A).** Adams Corporation (U.S.), a recently divested unit of Pfizer and the owner of a series of valuable consumer brands such as Listerine and Halls, owns 100% of Adams Brazil, S.A. This year Adams Brazil, S.A. earned R$52,000,000, equal to $20,000,000 at the current exchange rate of R$2.60/$. The exchange rate is not expected to change.

Adams Corporation wants to transfer half of Brazilian earnings to the United States and wonders if this sum should be remitted 1) by a cash dividend of $10,000,000 or 2) by a cash dividend of $5,000,000 and a royalty of $5,000,000. Brazilian income taxes are 15% and U.S. income taxes are 30%. Which do you recommend and why?

10. **Adams Corporation (B).** The Brazilian government under President Lula has instituted a new tax policy aimed at encouraging foreign MNEs to come to Brazil but reinvest their profits in the country, rather than pulling them out. Assume that all of the same conditions exist as in the previous problem, but now assume Brazil has instituted the following withholding taxes on dividends, royalties, and licensing fee remittances:

Type of Remittance	Withholding Tax Rate
Dividends	30%
Royalty payments	5%
License fees	5%

Now which of the alternatives do you recommend Adams use in remitting the $10 million to Adams (U.S.)?

11. **Quinlan Company (France).** The following events take place:

March 1: Quinlan Company seeks a sale at a price of €10,000,000 for items to be sold to a long-standing client in Poland. To achieve the order, Quinlan offered to denominate the order in zlotys (Z), Poland's currency, for Z20,000,000. This price was arrived at by multiplying the euro price by Z2.00/€, the exchange rate on the day of the quote. The zloty is expected to fall in value by 0.5% per month versus the euro.

April 1: Quinlan receives an order worth Z20,000,000 from that customer. On the same day, Quinlan places orders with its vendors for €4,000,000 of components needed to complete the sale.

May 1: Quinlan receives the components and is billed €4,000,000 by the vendor on terms of 2/20, net 60. During the next two months, Quinlan assigns direct labor to work on the project. The expense of direct labor was €5,000,000.

July 1: Quinlan ships the order to the customer and bills the customer Z20,000,000. On its corporate books, Quinlan debits accounts receivable and credits sales.

Sept 1: Quinlan's customer pays Z20,000,000 to Quinlan.

a. Draw a cash flow diagram for this transaction in the style of Exhibit 21.1 and explain the steps involved.

b. What working capital management techniques might Quinlan use to better its position vis-à-vis this particular customer?

INTERNET EXERCISES

1. **Going Global with CFO.** One of the most useful Internet sites with current analysis and thinking on a variety of corporate finance issues is the on-line version of CFO magazine. Use the three different regionally focused sites to explore the growing integration of cash management, currency management, operations control, and IT services.

CFO.com	www.cfo.com
CFOEurope.com	www.cfo.com/europe
CFOAsia.com	www.cfoasia.com

2. **Working Capital Management (A).** Many major multinational banks provide a variety of working capital and multinational cash management services described in this chapter. Using the Web sites of a variety of these cross-border banks, search out which banks offer multinational cash management services that would combine banking with foreign exchange management. Which banks provide specific services through regional or geographic service centers?

Bank of America	www.bankamerica.com/corporate/
Bank of Montreal	www.bmo.com/cebssite/

3. **Working Capital Management (B).** Use the New Zealand government's definition and analysis of working capital and compare that presented in this chapter. How does the New Zealand definition of working capital result in different management practices?

New Zealand Government Working Capital	www.treasury.govt.nz/publicsector/workingcapital/chap2.asp

4. **Clearinghouse Associations.** Associations like the New York Clearinghouse Association have played major roles in the international financial system for centuries. Use the following Web sites to prepare a two-page executive briefing on the role of clearing houses in history and in contemporary finance. Use the Web site for the Clearing House Interbank Payments System (CHIPS) to estimate the volume of international financial transactions.

New York Clearinghouse Association	www.theclearinghouse.org/
Clearing House Interbank Payments System	www.chips.org/

CHAPTER 22

International Trade Finance

Financial statements are like fine perfume: to be sniffed but not swallowed.

—Abraham Brilloff.

The purpose of this chapter is to explain how international trade—exports and imports—is financed. The contents are of direct practical relevance to domestic firms that just import and export and to multinational firms that trade with related and unrelated entities.

The chapter begins by explaining the types of trade relationships. Next, we explain the trade dilemma: exporters want to be paid before they export and importers do not want to pay until they receive the goods. The next section explains the benefits of the current international trade protocols. This is followed by a section that describes the elements of a trade transaction and the various documents that are used to facilitate the trade's completion and financing. The next section identifies international trade risks, namely, currency risk and noncompletion risk. The following sections describe the key trade documents, including letter of credit, draft, and bill of lading. The next section summarizes the documentation of a typical trade transaction. This is followed by a description of government programs to help finance exports, including export credit insurance and specialized banks such as the Export-Import Bank of the United States. Next, we compare the various types of short-term receivables financing and then the use of forfaiting for longer term receivables. The Mini-Case at the end of the chapter, *Crosswell International's Precious Ultra-Thin Diapers*, illustrates how an export requires the integration of management, marketing, and finance.

The Trade Relationship

As we discussed in Chapter 1, the first significant global activity by a domestic firm is the importing and exporting of goods and services. The purpose of this chapter is to analyze the *international trade phase* for a domestic firm that begins to import goods and services from foreign suppliers and to export to foreign buyers. In the case of Trident, this trade phase began with suppliers from Mexico and buyers from Canada.

Trade financing shares a number of common characteristics with the traditional value chain activities conducted by all firms. All companies must search out suppliers for the many goods and services required as inputs to their own goods production or service provision processes. Trident's Purchasing and Procurement Department must determine whether each potential supplier is capable of producing the product to required quality specifications, producing and delivering in a timely and reliable manner, and continuing to work with Trident in the ongoing process of product and process improvement for continued competitiveness. All must be at an acceptable price and payment terms. As presented in Exhibit 22.1, these issues apply to potential customers as well, because their continued business is equally as critical to Trident's operations and success.

Understanding the nature of the relationship between the exporter and the importer is critical to understanding the methods for import-export financing used in industry. Exhibit 22.2 provides an overview of the three categories of relationships: *unaffiliated unknown*, *unaffiliated known*, and *affiliated*.

- A foreign importer with which Trident has not previously conducted business would be considered *unaffiliated unknown*. In this case, the two parties would need to enter into a detailed sales contract, outlining the specific responsibilities and expectations of the business agreement. Trident would also need to seek out protection against the possibility that the importer would not make payment in full in a timely fashion.

- A foreign importer with which Trident has previously conducted business successfully would be considered *unaffiliated known*. In this case, the two parties may still enter into a detailed sales contract, but specific terms and shipments or provisions of services may be significantly looser in definition. Depending on the depth of the relationship, Trident may seek some third-party protection against noncompletion or conduct the business on an open-account basis.

- A foreign importer that is a subsidiary business unit of Trident, such as Trident Brazil, would be an *affiliated party* (sometimes referred to as *intrafirm trade*). Because both businesses are part of the same MNE, the most common practice would be to conduct the trade transaction without a contract or protection against nonpayment. This is not, however, always the case. In a variety of international business situations it may still be in Trident's best interest to detail the conditions for the business transaction, and possibly to protect against any political or country-based interruption to the completion of the trade transaction.

EXHIBIT 22.1   Financing Trade: The Flow of Goods and Funds

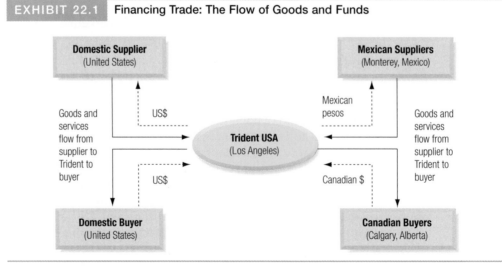

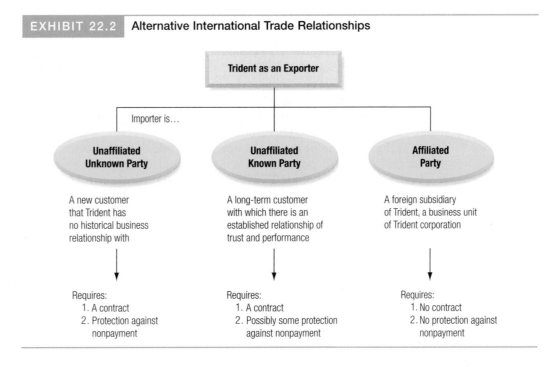

EXHIBIT 22.2   Alternative International Trade Relationships

The Trade Dilemma

International trade must work around a fundamental dilemma. Imagine an importer and an exporter who would like to do business with one another. Because of the distance between the two, it is not possible to hand over goods with one hand and accept payment with the other simultaneously. The importer would prefer the arrangement at the top of Exhibit 22.3, while the exporter would prefer the arrangement shown at the bottom.

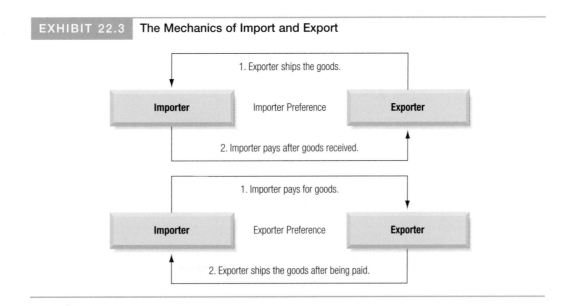

EXHIBIT 22.3   The Mechanics of Import and Export

The fundamental dilemma of being unwilling to trust a stranger in a foreign land is solved by using a highly respected bank as intermediary. A greatly simplified view is described in Exhibit 22.4. In this example, the importer obtains the bank's promise to pay on its behalf, knowing that the exporter will trust the bank. The bank's promise to pay is called a *letter of credit*.

The exporter ships the merchandise to the importer's country. Title to the merchandise is given to the bank on a document called an *order bill of lading*. The exporter asks the bank to pay for the goods, and the bank does so. The document to request payment is a *sight draft*. The bank, having paid for the goods, now passes title to the importer, whom the bank trusts. At that time or later, depending on their agreement, the importer reimburses the bank.

Financial managers of MNEs must understand these three basic documents. Their firms will often trade with unaffiliated parties, and the system of documentation provides a source of short-term capital that can be drawn upon even when shipments are to sister subsidiaries.

Benefits of the System

The three key documents and their interaction are described later in this chapter. They constitute a system developed and modified over centuries to protect both importer and exporter from the risk of noncompletion and foreign exchange risk, as well as to provide a means of financing.

Protection against Risk of Noncompletion

As stated, once importer and exporter agree on terms, the seller usually prefers to maintain legal title to the goods until paid, or at least until assured of payment. The buyer, however, will be reluctant to pay before receiving the goods, or at least before receiving title to them. Each wants assurance that the other party will complete its portion of the transaction. The letter of credit, sight draft, and bill of lading are part of a system carefully constructed to determine who suffers the financial loss if one of the parties defaults at any time.

EXHIBIT 22.4   The Bank as the Import-Export Intermediary

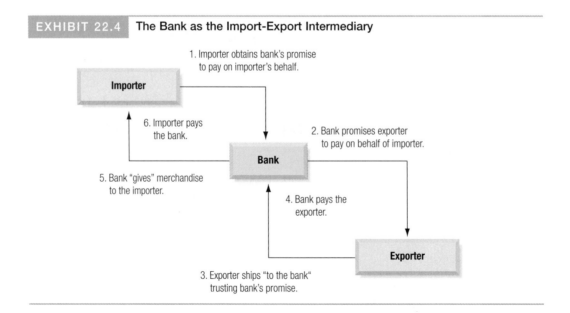

Protection against Foreign Exchange Risk

In international trade, foreign exchange risk arises from *transaction exposure*. If the transaction requires payment in the exporter's currency, the importer carries the foreign exchange risk. If the transaction calls for payment in the importer's currency, the exporter has the foreign exchange risk.

Transaction exposure can be hedged by the techniques described in Chapter 11, but in order to hedge, the exposed party must be certain that payment of a specified amount will be made on or near a particular date. The three key documents described in this chapter ensure both amount and time of payment and thus lay the groundwork for effective hedging.

The risk of noncompletion and foreign exchange risk are most important when the international trade is episodic, with no outstanding agreement for recurring shipments and no sustained relationship between buyer and seller. When the import-export relationship is of a recurring nature, as in the case of manufactured goods shipped weekly or monthly to a final assembly or retail outlet in another country, and when it is between countries whose currencies are considered strong, the exporter may well bill the importer on open account after a normal credit check. Banks provide credit information and collection services outside of the system of processing drafts drawn against letters of credit.

Financing the Trade

Most international trade involves a time lag during which funds are tied up while the merchandise is in transit. Once the risks of noncompletion and of exchange rate changes are disposed of, banks are willing to finance goods in transit. A bank can finance goods in transit, as well as goods held for sale, based on the key documents, without exposing itself to questions about the quality of the merchandise or other physical aspects of the shipment.

International Trade: Timeline and Structure

In order to understand the risks associated with international trade transactions, it is helpful to understand the sequence of events in any such transaction. Exhibit 22.5 illustrates, in principle, the series of events associated with a single export transaction.

EXHIBIT 22.5   The Trade Transaction Timeline and Structure

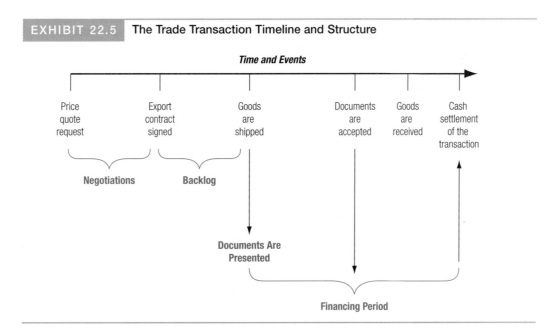

From a financial management perspective, the two primary risks associated with an international trade transaction are *currency risk* and *risk of noncompletion*. Exhibit 22.5 illustrates the traditional business problem of credit management: The exporter quotes a price, finalizes a contract, and ships the goods, losing physical control over the goods based on trust of the buyer or the promise of a bank to pay based on documents presented. The risk of default on the part of the importer is present as soon as the financing period begins, as illustrated in Exhibit 22.5.

In many cases, the initial task of analyzing the credit worth of foreign customers is similar to procedures for analyzing domestic customers. If Trident has had no experience with a foreign customer but that customer is a large, well-known firm in its home country, Trident may simply ask for a bank credit report on that firm. Trident may also talk to other firms that have had dealings with the foreign customer. If these investigations show the foreign customer (and country) to be completely trustworthy, Trident would likely ship to them on open account, with a credit limit, just as they would for a domestic customer. This is the least costly method of handling exports because there are no heavy documentation or bank charges. However, before a regular trading relationship has been established with a new or unknown firm, Trident must face the possibility of nonpayment for its exports or noncompletion of its imports. The risk of nonpayment can be eliminated through the use of a letter of credit issued by a creditworthy bank.

Letter of Credit (L/C)

A *letter of credit* (L/C) is a bank's promise to pay issued by a bank at the request of an importer (the applicant/buyer), in which the bank promises to pay an exporter (the beneficiary of the letter) upon presentation of documents specified in the L/C. An L/C reduces the risk of noncompletion because the bank agrees to pay against documents rather than actual merchandise. The relationship between the three parties is illustrated in Exhibit 22.6.

An importer (buyer) and exporter (seller) agree on a transaction, and the importer then applies to its local bank for the issuance of an L/C. The importer's bank issues an L/C and cuts a sales contract based on its assessment of the importer's creditworthiness, or the bank might require a cash deposit or other collateral from the importer in advance. The importer's bank will want to know the type of transaction, the amount of money involved, and what documents must accompany the draft that will be drawn against the L/C.

EXHIBIT 22.6   Parties to a Letter of Credit (L/C)

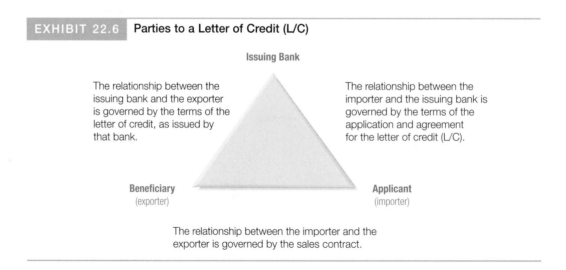

Issuing Bank

The relationship between the issuing bank and the exporter is governed by the terms of the letter of credit, as issued by that bank.

The relationship between the importer and the issuing bank is governed by the terms of the application and agreement for the letter of credit (L/C).

Beneficiary
(exporter)

Applicant
(importer)

The relationship between the importer and the exporter is governed by the sales contract.

If the importer's bank is satisfied with the credit standing of the applicant, it will issue an L/C guaranteeing to pay for the merchandise if shipped in accordance with the instructions and conditions contained in the L/C.

The essence of an L/C is the promise of the issuing bank to pay *against specified documents*, which must accompany any draft drawn against the credit. The L/C is not a guarantee of the underlying commercial transaction. Indeed, the L/C is a separate transaction from any sales or other contracts on which it might be based.

Irrevocable versus Revocable. An irrevocable L/C obligates the issuing bank to honor drafts drawn in compliance with the credit and can be neither canceled nor modified without the consent of all parties, including in particular the beneficiary (exporter). A revocable L/C can be canceled or amended at any time before payment; it is intended to serve as a means of arranging payment but not as a guarantee of payment.

Confirmed versus Unconfirmed. An L/C issued by one bank can be confirmed by another, in which case the confirming bank undertakes to honor drafts drawn in compliance with the credit. An unconfirmed L/C is the obligation only of the issuing bank. An exporter is likely to want a foreign bank's L/C confirmed by a domestic bank when the exporter has doubts about the foreign bank's ability to pay. Such doubts can arise when the exporter is unsure of the financial standing of the foreign bank, or if political or economic conditions in the foreign country are unstable. The essence of an L/C is shown in Exhibit 22.7.

Most commercial letters of credit are *documentary*, meaning that certain documents must be included with any drafts drawn under their terms. Required documents usually include an order bill of lading (discussed in more detail later in the chapter), a commercial invoice, and any of the following: consular invoice, insurance certificate or policy, and packing list.

EXHIBIT 22.7   Essence of a Letter of Credit (L/C)

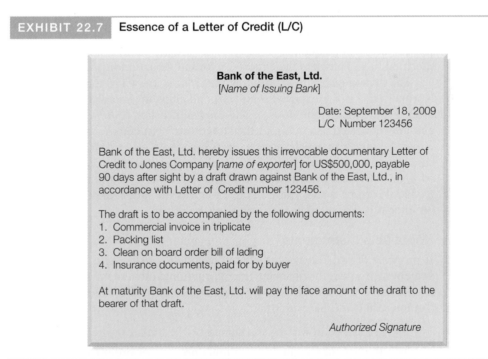

Bank of the East, Ltd.
[Name of Issuing Bank]

Date: September 18, 2009
L/C Number 123456

Bank of the East, Ltd. hereby issues this irrevocable documentary Letter of Credit to Jones Company [*name of exporter*] for US$500,000, payable 90 days after sight by a draft drawn against Bank of the East, Ltd., in accordance with Letter of Credit number 123456.

The draft is to be accompanied by the following documents:
1. Commercial invoice in triplicate
2. Packing list
3. Clean on board order bill of lading
4. Insurance documents, paid for by buyer

At maturity Bank of the East, Ltd. will pay the face amount of the draft to the bearer of that draft.

Authorized Signature

Advantages and Disadvantages of Letters of Credit

The primary advantage of an L/C is that it reduces risk—the exporter can sell against a bank's promise to pay rather than against the promise of a commercial firm. The exporter is also in a more secure position as to the availability of foreign exchange to pay for the sale, since banks are more likely to be aware of foreign exchange conditions and rules than is the importing firm itself. If the importing country should change its foreign exchange rules during the course of a transaction, the government is likely to allow already outstanding bank letters of credit to be honored for fear of throwing its own domestic banks into international disrepute. Of course, if the L/C is confirmed by a bank in the exporter's country, the exporter avoids any problem of blocked foreign exchange.

An exporter may find that an order backed by an irrevocable L/C will facilitate obtaining pre-export financing in the home country. If the exporter's reputation for delivery is good, a local bank may lend funds to process and prepare the merchandise for shipment. Once the merchandise is shipped in compliance with the terms and conditions of the credit, payment for the business transaction is made and funds will be generated to repay the pre-export loan.

The major advantage of an L/C to the importer is that the importer need not pay out funds until the documents have arrived at a local port or airfield and unless all conditions stated in the credit have been fulfilled. The main disadvantages are the fee charged by the importer's bank for issuing its L/C and the possibility that the L/C reduces the importer's borrowing line of credit with its bank. It may, in fact, be a competitive disadvantage for the exporter to demand automatically an L/C from an importer, especially if the importer has a good credit record and there is no concern regarding the economic or political conditions of the importer's country.

Draft

A *draft*, sometimes called a *bill of exchange* (B/E), is the instrument normally used in international commerce to effect payment. A draft is simply an order written by an exporter (seller) instructing an importer (buyer) or its agent to pay a specified amount of money at a specified time. Thus, it is the exporter's formal demand for payment from the importer.

The person or business initiating the draft is known as the *maker*, *drawer*, or *originator*. Normally this is the exporter who sells and ships the merchandise. The party to whom the draft is addressed is the *drawee*. The drawee is asked to *honor* the draft, that is, to pay the amount requested according to the stated terms. In commercial transactions, the drawee is either the buyer, in which case the draft is called a *trade draft*, or the buyer's bank, in which case the draft is called a *bank draft*. Bank drafts are usually drawn according to the terms of an L/C. A draft may be drawn as a bearer instrument, or it may designate a person to whom payment is to be made. This person, known as the *payee*, may be the drawer itself or it may be some other party such as the drawer's bank.

Negotiable Instruments

If properly drawn, drafts can become *negotiable instruments*. As such, they provide a convenient instrument for financing the international movement of the merchandise. To become a negotiable instrument, a draft must conform to the following requirements (Uniform Commercial Code, Section 3104(1)):

- It must be in writing and signed by the maker or drawer.
- It must contain an unconditional promise or order to pay a definite sum of money.

- It must be payable on demand or at a fixed or determinable future date.
- It must be payable to order or to bearer.

If a draft is drawn in conformity with the above requirements, a person receiving it with proper endorsements becomes a "holder in due course." This is a privileged legal status that enables the holder to receive payment despite any personal disagreements between drawee and maker because of controversy over the underlying transaction. If the drawee dishonors the draft, payment must be made to any holder in due course by any prior endorser or by the maker. This clear definition of the rights of parties who hold a negotiable instrument as a holder in due course has contributed significantly to the widespread acceptance of various forms of drafts, including personal checks.

Types of Drafts

Drafts are of two types: *sight drafts* and *time drafts*. A sight draft is payable on presentation to the drawee; the drawee must pay at once or dishonor the draft. A time draft, also called a *usance draft*, allows a delay in payment. It is presented to the drawee, who accepts it by writing or stamping a notice of acceptance on its face. Once accepted, the time draft becomes a promise to pay by the accepting party (the buyer). When a time draft is drawn on and accepted by a bank, it becomes a *banker's acceptance*; when drawn on and accepted by a business firm, it becomes a *trade acceptance*.

The time period of a draft is referred to as its *tenor*. To qualify as a negotiable instrument, and so be attractive to a holder in due course, a draft must be payable on a fixed or determinable future date. For example, "60 days after sight" is a fixed date, which is established precisely at the time the draft is accepted. However, payment "on arrival of goods" is not determinable since the date of arrival cannot be known in advance. Indeed, there is no assurance that the goods will arrive at all.

Bankers' Acceptances

When a draft is accepted by a bank, it becomes a bankers' acceptance. As such, it is the unconditional promise of that bank to make payment on the draft when it matures. In quality, the bankers' acceptance is practically identical to a marketable bank certificate of deposit (CD). The holder of a bankers' acceptance need not wait until maturity to liquidate the investment, but may sell the acceptance in the money market, where constant trading in such instruments occurs. The amount of the discount depends entirely on the credit rating of the bank that signed the acceptance, or another bank that reconfirmed the bankers' acceptance, for a fee. The all-in-cost of using a bankers' acceptance compared to other short-term financing instruments is analyzed later in this chapter.

Bill of Lading (B/L)

The third key document for financing international trade is the *bill of lading* (B/L). The bill of lading is issued to the exporter by a common carrier transporting the merchandise. It serves three purposes: as a receipt, as a contract, and as a document of title.

As a receipt, the bill of lading indicates that the carrier has received the merchandise described on the face of the document. The carrier is not responsible for ascertaining that the containers hold what is alleged to be their contents, so descriptions of merchandise on bills of lading are usually short and simple. If shipping charges are paid in advance, the bill of lading will usually be stamped "freight paid" or "freight prepaid." If merchandise is shipped collect—a less common procedure internationally than domestically—the carrier maintains a lien on the goods until freight is paid.

As a contract, the bill of lading indicates the obligation of the carrier to provide certain transportation in return for certain charges. Common carriers cannot disclaim responsibility for their negligence through inserting special clauses in a bill of lading. The bill of lading may specify alternative ports in the event that delivery cannot be made to the designated port, or it may specify that the goods will be returned to the exporter at the exporter's expense.

As a document of title, the bill of lading is used to obtain payment or a written promise of payment before the merchandise is released to the importer. The bill of lading can also function as collateral against which funds may be advanced to the exporter by its local bank prior to or during shipment and before final payment by the importer.

Characteristics of the Bill of Lading

The bill of lading is typically made payable to the order of the exporter, who thus retains title to the goods after they have been handed to the carrier. Title to the merchandise remains with the exporter until payment is received, at which time the exporter endorses the order bill of lading (which is negotiable) in blank or to the party making the payment, usually a bank. The most common procedure would be for payment to be advanced against a documentary draft accompanied by the endorsed order bill of lading. After paying the draft, the exporter's bank forwards the documents through bank clearing channels to the bank of the importer. The importer's bank, in turn, releases the documents to the importer after payment (sight drafts); after acceptance (time drafts addressed to the importer and marked D/A); or after payment terms have been agreed upon (drafts drawn on the importer's bank under provisions of an L/C).

Example: Documentation in a Typical Trade Transaction

Although a trade transaction could conceivably be handled in many ways, we will now turn to a hypothetical example, which illustrates the interaction of the various documents. Assume that Trident USA receives an order from a Canadian buyer. For Trident, this will be an export financed under an L/C requiring a bill of lading, with the exporter collecting via a time draft accepted by the Canadian buyer's bank. Such a transaction is illustrated in Exhibit 22.8.

1. The Canadian buyer places an order with Trident, asking if Trident is willing to ship under an L/C.

2. Trident agrees to ship under an L/C and specifies relevant information such as prices and terms.

3. The Canadian buyer applies to its bank, Northland Bank (Bank I), for an L/C to be issued in favor of Trident for the merchandise it wishes to buy.

4. Northland Bank issues the L/C in favor of Trident and sends it to the Southland Bank (Bank X—Trident's bank).

5. Southland Bank advises Trident of the opening of an L/C in Trident's favor. Southland Bank may or may not confirm the L/C to add its own guarantee to the document.

6. Trident ships the goods to the Canadian buyer.

7. Trident prepares a time draft and presents it to Southland Bank. The draft is drawn (addressed to) Northland Bank in accordance with Northland Bank's L/C and accompanied by other documents as required, including the bill of lading. Trident endorses the bill of lading in blank (making it a bearer instrument) so that title to the goods goes with the holder of the documents—Southland Bank at this point in the transaction.

EXHIBIT 22.8   Steps in a Typical Trade Transaction

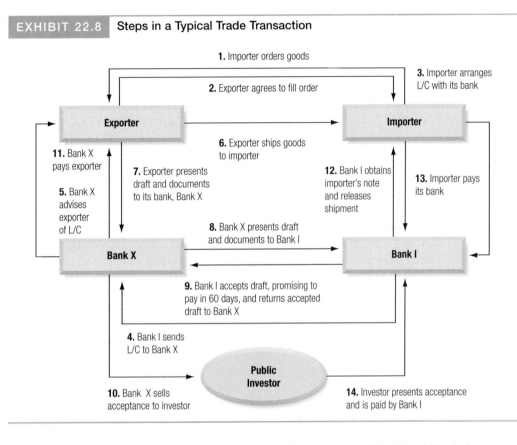

8. Southland Bank presents the draft and documents to Northland Bank for acceptance. Northland Bank accepts the draft by stamping and signing it making it a bankers' acceptance, takes possession of the documents, and promises to pay the now accepted draft at maturity—say, 60 days.

9. Northland Bank returns the accepted draft to Southland Bank. Alternatively, Southland Bank might ask Northland Bank to accept and discount the draft. Should this occur, Northland Bank would remit the cash less a discount fee rather than return the accepted draft to Southland Bank.

10. Southland Bank, having received the accepted draft, now a *bankers' acceptance*, may choose between several alternatives. Southland Bank may sell the acceptance in the open market at a discount to a portfolio investor. The investor will typically be a corporation or financial institution with excess cash it wants to invest for a short period of time. Southland Bank may also hold the acceptance in its own portfolio.

11. If Southland Bank discounted the acceptance with Northland Bank (mentioned in step 9) or discounted it in the local money market, Southland Bank will transfer the proceeds less any fees and discount to Trident. Another possibility would be for Trident itself to take possession of the acceptance, hold it for 60 days, and present it for collection. Normally, however, exporters prefer to receive the discounted cash value of the acceptance at once rather than wait for the acceptance to mature and receive a slightly greater amount of cash at a later date.

12. Northland Bank notifies the Canadian buyer of the arrival of the documents. The Canadian buyer signs a note or makes some other agreed upon plan to pay

Northland Bank for the merchandise in 60 days. Northland Bank releases the underlying documents so that the Canadian buyer can obtain physical possession of the shipment at once.

13. After 60 days, Northland Bank receives funds from the Canadian buyer to pay the maturing acceptance.

14. On the same day, the sixtieth day after acceptance, the holder of the matured acceptance presents it for payment and receives its face value. The holder may present it directly to Northland Bank, as shown in Exhibit 22.8, or return it to Southland Bank and have Southland Bank collect it through normal banking channels.

Although this is a typical transaction involving an L/C, few international trade transactions are ever truly typical. Business, and more specifically international business, requires flexibility and creativity by management at all times as illustrated by *Global Finance in Practice 22.1.* The Mini-Case at the end of this chapter presents an application of the mechanics of a real business situation. The result is a classic challenge to management: when and on what basis do you compromise typical procedure in order to accomplish strategic goals?

Government Programs to Help Finance Exports

Governments of most export-oriented industrialized countries have special financial institutions that provide some form of subsidized credit to their own national exporters. These export finance institutions offer terms that are better than those generally available from the competitive private sector. Thus, domestic taxpayers are subsidizing lower financial costs for foreign buyers in order to create employment and maintain a technological edge. The most important institutions usually offer export credit insurance and a government-supported bank for export financing.

GLOBAL FINANCE IN PRACTICE 22.1

The Resurgence of Transaction Banking and Letters of Credit

Why this sudden resurgence of interest in what is probably the oldest segment of the banking industry? Ashish Bajaj, Managing Director (Transaction Banking) at Citibank, says: "Transaction banking is an annuity business, and has stable and predictable revenues flows." In volatile times, that's a huge attraction. Then, the business is growing at over 40–50 per cent annually. No wonder every banker is keen on this segment.

A cash management client also brings trade business to a bank. Over the years, banks have been handling remittances and opening letters of credit (LCS) for their clients. Today, the trend is of clients shifting from the traditional LC system to electronic channels as this is more efficient. "There is an opportunity for banks to do more open account financing as they understand the risk better," says Ramesh Ganesan, head (Transaction Banking) at ABN AMRO Bank. This is a new trend; banks are taking exposures through open

accounts where there are no bank guarantees; the traditional LCS are backed by a guarantee. All this requires a high level of technology integrated from the front- to the back-end, both within India and across the globe.

Strong competition in the T-banking space is resulting in a fall in the (still high) margins. Result: the "float" income of banks is down and many are now making a strong case for a "fee" system. Today, about 70 per cent of a bank's earnings come from the former and only 30 per cent from fees. "Companies don't pay any fees for cash management services because of the float advantage enjoyed by banks," says a banker. "There is a need to price the transaction scientifically," says Natasha Patel, Head (Global Payments and Cash Management), HSBC India. This, however, does not always happen.

Source: "The Return of T-Banking," *Business Today—New Delhi*, October 7, 2007.

Export Credit Insurance

The exporter who insists on cash or an L/C payment for foreign shipments is likely to lose orders to competitors from other countries that provide more favorable credit terms. Better credit terms are often made possible by means of export credit insurance, which provides assurance to the exporter or the exporter's bank that, should the foreign customer default on payment, the insurance company will pay for a major portion of the loss. Because of the availability of export credit insurance, commercial banks are willing to provide medium- to long-term financing (five to seven years) for exports. Importers prefer that the exporter purchase export credit insurance to pay for nonperformance risk by the importer. In this way, the importer does not need to pay to have an L/C issued and does not reduce its credit line.

Competition between nations to increase exports by lengthening the period for which credit transactions can be insured may lead to a credit war and to unsound credit decisions. To prevent such an unhealthy development, a number of leading trading nations joined in 1934 to create the Berne Union (officially, the Union d' Assureurs des Credits Internationaux) for the purpose of establishing a voluntary international understanding on export credit terms. The Berne Union recommends maximum credit terms for many items, including heavy capital goods (five years), light capital goods (three years), and consumer durable goods (one year).

Export Credit Insurance in the United States

In the United States, export credit insurance is provided by the Foreign Credit Insurance Association (FCIA). This is an unincorporated association of private commercial insurance companies operating in cooperation with the Export-Import Bank.

The FCIA provides policies protecting U.S. exporters against the risk of nonpayment by foreign debtors as a result of commercial and political risks. Losses due to commercial risk are those that result from the insolvency or protracted payment default of the buyer. Political losses arise from actions of governments beyond the control of buyer or seller.

Export-Import Bank and Export Financing

The Export-Import Bank of the United States (Ex-Im Bank) is another independent agency of the U.S. government, established in 1934 to stimulate and facilitate the foreign trade of the United States. Interestingly, the Ex-Im Bank was originally created primarily to facilitate exports to the Soviet Union. In 1945, the Ex-Im Bank was rechartered "to aid in financing and to facilitate exports and imports and the exchange of commodities between the United States and any foreign country or the agencies or nationals thereof."

The Ex-Im Bank facilitates the financing of U.S. exports through various loan guarantee and insurance programs. The Ex-Im Bank guarantees repayment of medium-term (181 days to 5 years) and long-term (5 years to 10 years) export loans extended by U.S. banks to foreign borrowers. The Ex-Im Bank's medium- and long-term, direct-lending operation is based on participation with private sources of funds. Essentially, the Ex-Im Bank lends dollars to borrowers outside the United States for the purchase of U.S. goods and services. Proceeds of such loans are paid to U.S. suppliers. The loans themselves are repaid with interest in dollars to the Ex-Im Bank. The Ex-Im Bank requires private participation in these direct loans in order to 1) ensure that it complements rather than competes with private sources of export financing; 2) spread its resources more broadly; and 3) ensure that private financial institutions will continue to provide export credit.

The Ex-Im Bank also guarantees lease transactions; finances the costs involved in the preparation by U.S. firms of engineering, planning, and feasibility studies for non-U.S. clients on large capital projects; and supplies counseling for exporters, banks, or others needing help in finding financing for U.S. goods.

Trade Financing Alternatives

In order to finance international trade receivables, firms use the same financing instruments as they use for domestic trade receivables, plus a few specialized instruments that are only available for financing international trade. Exhibit 22.9 identifies the main short-term financing instruments and their typical approximate costs. The last section describes a longer term instrument called *forfaiting*.

Bankers' Acceptances

Bankers' acceptances, described earlier in this chapter, can be used to finance both domestic and international trade receivables. Exhibit 22.9 shows that bankers' acceptances typically earn a yield comparable to other money market instruments, especially marketable bank certificates of deposit. However, the all-in-cost to a firm of creating and discounting a bankers' acceptance also depends upon the commission charged by the bank that accepts the firm's draft.

The first owner of the bankers' acceptance created from an international trade transaction will be the exporter, who receives the accepted draft back after the bank has stamped it "accepted." The exporter may hold the acceptance until maturity and then collect. On an acceptance of, say, $100,000 for three months, the exporter would receive the face amount less the bank's acceptance commission of 1.5% per annum:

Face amount of the acceptance	$100,000	
Less 1.5% per annum commission for three months	−375	(.015 × 3/12 × $100,000)
Amount received by exporter in three months	$99,625	

Alternatively, the exporter may "discount"—that is, sell at a reduced price—the acceptance to its bank in order to receive funds at once. The exporter will then receive the face amount of the acceptance less both the acceptance fee and the going market rate of discount for bankers' acceptances. If the discount rate were 1.14% per annum as shown in Exhibit 22.9, the exporter would receive the following:

Face amount of the acceptance	$100,000	
Less 1.5% per annum commission for three months	−375	(.015 × 3/12 × $100,000)
Less 1.14% per annum discount rate for three months	−285	(.0114 × 3/12 × $100,000)
Amount received by exporter at once	$99,340	

EXHIBIT 22.9   Instruments for Financing Short-Term Domestic and International Trade Receivables

Instrument	Typical Cost or Yield for Three-Month Maturity
Bankers' acceptances*	1.14% yield annualized
Trade acceptances*	1.17% yield annualized
Factoring	Variable rate but much higher cost than bank credit lines
Securitization	Variable rate but competitive with bank credit lines
Bank credit lines (covered by export credit insurance)	4.25% plus points (fewer points if covered by export credit insurance)
Commercial paper*	1.15% yield annualized

*These instruments compete with three-month marketable bank time certificates of deposit.

Therefore, the annualized all-in-cost of financing this bankers' acceptance is as follows:

$$\frac{\text{Commission} + \text{discount}}{\text{Proceeds}} \times \frac{360}{90} = \frac{\$375 + \$285}{\$99,340} \times \frac{360}{90} = .0266 \text{ or } 2.66\%$$

The discounting bank may hold the acceptance in its own portfolio, earning for itself the 1.14% per annum discount rate, or the acceptance may be resold in the acceptance market to portfolio investors. Investors buying bankers' acceptances provide the funds that finance the transaction.

Trade Acceptances

Trade acceptances are similar to bankers' acceptances except that the accepting entity is a commercial firm, like General Motors Acceptance Corporation (GMAC), rather than a bank. The cost of a trade acceptance depends on the credit rating of the accepting firm plus the commission it charges. Like bankers' acceptances, trade acceptances are sold at a discount to banks and other investors at a rate that is competitive with other money market instruments (see Exhibit 22.9).

Factoring

Specialized firms, known as *factors*, purchase receivables at a discount on either a *nonrecourse* or *recourse* basis. Nonrecourse means that the factor assumes the credit, political, and foreign exchange risk of the receivables it purchases. Recourse means that the factor can give back receivables that are not collectible. Since the factor must bear the cost and risk of assessing the credit worth of each receivable, the cost of factoring is usually quite high. It is more than borrowing at the prime rate plus points.

The all-in-cost of factoring nonrecourse receivables is similar in structure to acceptances. The factor charges a commission to cover the nonrecourse risk, typically 1.5% to 2.5%, plus interest deducted as a discount from the initial proceeds. On the other hand, the firm selling the nonrecourse receivables avoids the cost of determining the credit worth of its customers. It also does not have to show debt borrowed to finance these receivables on its balance sheet. Furthermore, the firm avoids both foreign exchange and political risk on these nonrecourse receivables. *Global Finance in Practice 22.2* illustrates current factoring activities in Africa.

GLOBAL FINANCE IN PRACTICE 22.2

Tunisian Private Equity and Factoring

In an interview, Aziz Mebarek, founding partner, Tuninvest, talked about the private equity group's second fund and its investments. The AfricInvest Financial Sector Fund will invest in financial institutions in Africa and in general into financial services-related activities: banking, leasing, factoring, consumer credit, brokerage, credit bureau, rating, asset management and insurance. It will particularly focus on new or existing financing institutions in countries with nascent financial sectors, in post-war countries and in least-developed countries. The Nedherlands Development Finance Co, FMO, is for the time-being the only shareholder in the fund. Tuninvest brings companies to the stock market and will invest into listed companies as long as it has seats on the board to be able to influence the growth and strategy of the company. But it is not in the business of buying and selling stock, which is what asset managers do.

Source: "Tuninvest Sustainable Profits," *African Business*, October 2007, Issue 335, p. S42.

Securitization

The *securitization* of export receivables for financing trade is an attractive supplement to bankers' acceptance financing and factoring. A firm can *securitize* its export receivables by selling them to a legal entity established to create marketable securities based on a package of individual export receivables. An advantage of this technique is to remove the export receivables from the exporter's balance sheet because they have been sold without recourse.

The receivables are normally sold at a discount. The size of the discount depends on four factors:

1. The historic collection risk of the exporter
2. The cost of credit insurance
3. The cost of securing the desirable cash flow stream to the investors
4. The size of the financing and services fees

Securitization is more cost effective if there is a large volume of transactions with a known credit history and default probability. A large exporter could establish its own securitization entity. While the initial setup cost is high, the entity can be used on an ongoing basis. As an alternative, smaller exporters could use a common securitization entity provided by a financial institution, thereby saving the expensive setup costs.

Bank Credit Line Covered by Export Credit Insurance

A firm's bank credit line can typically be used to finance up to a fixed upper limit, say 80%, of accounts receivable. Export receivables can be eligible for inclusion in bank credit line financing. However, credit information on foreign customers may be more difficult to collect and assess. If a firm covers its export receivables with export credit insurance, it can greatly reduce the credit risk of those receivables. This insurance enables the bank credit line to cover more export receivables and lower the interest rate for that coverage. Of course, any foreign exchange risk must be handled by the transaction exposure techniques described in Chapter 11.

The cost of using a bank credit line is usually the prime rate of interest plus *points* to reflect a particular firm's credit risk. As usual, 100 points is equal to 1%. In the United States, borrowers are also expected to maintain a compensating deposit balance at the lending institution. In Europe and many other places, lending is done on an *overdraft* basis. An overdraft agreement allows a firm to overdraw its bank account up to the limit of its credit line. Interest at prime plus points is based only on the amount of overdraft borrowed. In either case, the all-in-cost of bank borrowing using a credit line is higher than acceptance financing as shown in Exhibit 22.9.

Commercial Paper

A firm can issue *commercial paper*—unsecured promissory notes—to fund its short-term financing needs, including both domestic and export receivables. However, only the large, well-known firms with favorable credit ratings have access to the domestic or euro commercial paper market. As shown in Exhibit 22.9, commercial paper interest rates lie at the low end of the yield curve and compete directly with marketable bank time certificates of deposit.

Forfaiting: Medium- and Long-Term Financing

Forfaiting is a specialized technique to eliminate the risk of nonpayment by importers in instances where the importing firm and/or its government is perceived by the exporter to be too risky for open account credit. The name of the technique comes from the French *à forfait*, a term that implies "to forfeit or surrender a right."

Role of the Forfaiter

The essence of forfaiting is the nonrecourse sale by an exporter of bank-guaranteed promissory notes, bills of exchange, or similar documents received from an importer in another country. The exporter receives cash at the time of the transaction by selling the notes or bills at a discount from their face value to a specialized finance firm called a *forfaiter*. The forfaiter arranges the entire operation prior to the actual transaction taking place. Although the exporting firm is responsible for the quality of delivered goods, it receives a clear and unconditional cash payment at the time of the transaction. All political and commercial risk of nonpayment by the importer is carried by the guaranteeing bank. Small exporters who trust their clients to pay find the forfaiting technique invaluable because it eases cash flow problems.

A Typical Forfaiting Transaction

A typical forfaiting transaction involves five parties, as shown in Exhibit 22.10. The steps in the process are as follows:

Step 1: Agreement. Importer and exporter agree on a series of imports to be paid for over a period of time, typically 3 to 5 years. However, periods up to 10 years or as short as 180 days have been financed by the technique. The importer agrees to make periodic payments, often against progress on delivery or completion of a project.

Step 2: Commitment. The forfaiter promises to finance the transaction at a fixed discount rate, with payment to be made when the exporter delivers to the forfaiter the appropriate promissory notes or other specified paper. The agreed upon discount rate is based on the cost of funds in the Euromarket, usually on LIBOR for the average life of the transaction, plus a margin over LIBOR to reflect the perceived risk in the deal. This risk premium is influenced by the size and tenor of the deal, country risk, and the quality of the guarantor institution. On a 5-year deal, for example, with 10 semiannual payments, the rate used would be based on the 2.25-year LIBOR rate. This discount rate is normally added to the invoice value of the transaction so that the cost of financing is ultimately borne by the importer. The forfaiter charges an additional commitment fee of from 0.5% per annum to as high as 6.0% per annum from

EXHIBIT 22.10   **Typical Forfaiting Transaction**

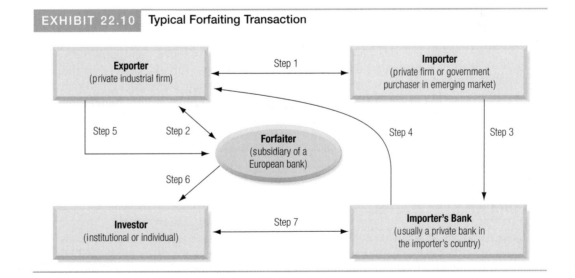

the date of its commitment to finance until receipt of the actual discount paper issued in accordance with the finance contract. This fee is also normally added to the invoice cost and passed on to the importer.

Step 3: *Aval* or Guarantee. The importer obligates itself to pay for its purchases by issuing a series of promissory notes, usually maturing every 6 or 12 months, against progress on delivery or completion of the project. These promissory notes are first delivered to the importer's bank where they are endorsed (that is, guaranteed) by that bank. In Europe, this unconditional guarantee is referred to as an *aval*, which translates into English as "backing." At this point, the importer's bank becomes the primary obligor in the eyes of all subsequent holders of the notes. The bank's aval or guarantee must be irrevocable, unconditional, divisible, and assignable. Because U.S. banks do not issue avals, U.S. transactions are guaranteed by a standby letter of credit (L/C), which is functionally similar to an aval but more cumbersome. For example, L/Cs can normally be transferred only once.

Step 4: Delivery of Notes. The now-endorsed promissory notes are delivered to the exporter.

Step 5: Discounting. The exporter endorses the notes "without recourse" and discounts them with the forfaiter, receiving the agreed upon proceeds. Proceeds are usually received two days after the documents are presented. By endorsing the notes "without recourse," the exporter frees itself from any liability for future payment on the notes and thus receives the discounted proceeds without having to worry about any further payment difficulties.

Step 6: Investment. The forfaiting bank either holds the notes until full maturity as an investment or endorses and rediscounts them in the international money market. Such subsequent sale by the forfaiter is usually without recourse. The major rediscount markets are in London and Switzerland, plus New York for notes issued in conjunction with Latin American business.

Step 7: Maturity. At maturity the investor holding the notes presents them for collection to the importer or to the importer's bank. The promise of the importer's bank is what gives the documents their value.

In effect, the forfaiter functions both as a money market firm and a specialist in packaging financial deals involving country risk. As a money market firm, the forfaiter divides the discounted notes into appropriately sized packages and resells them to various investors having different maturity preferences. As a country risk specialist, the forfaiter assesses the risk that the notes will eventually be paid by the importer or the importer's bank and puts together a deal that satisfies the needs of both exporter and importer.

Success of the forfaiting technique springs from the belief that the aval or guarantee of a commercial bank can be depended on. Although commercial banks are the normal and preferred guarantors, guarantees by government banks or government ministries of finance are accepted in some cases. On occasion, large commercial enterprises have been accepted as debtors without a bank guarantee. An additional aspect of the technique is that the endorsing bank's aval is perceived to be an "off balance sheet" obligation, the debt is presumably not considered by others in assessing the financial structure of the commercial banks.

SUMMARY POINTS

- International trade takes place between three categories of relationships: unaffiliated unknown parties, unaffiliated known parties, and affiliated parties.

- International trade transactions between affiliated parties typically do not require contractual arrangements or external financing. Trade transactions between unaffiliated parties typically require contracts and some type of external financing, such as that available through letters of credit.

- Over many years, established procedures have arisen to finance international trade. The basic procedure rests on the interrelationship between three key documents: the letter of credit, the draft, and the bill of lading.

- Variations in each of the three key documents—the letter of credit, the draft, and the bill of lading—provide a variety of ways to accommodate any type of transaction.

- In the simplest transaction, in which all three documents are used and in which financing is desirable, an importer applies for and receives an L/C from its bank.

- In the L/C, the bank substitutes its credit for that of the importer and promises to pay if certain documents are submitted to the bank. The exporter may now rely on the promise of the bank rather than on the promise of the importer.

- The exporter typically ships on an order bill of lading, attaches the order bill of lading to a draft ordering payment from the importer's bank, and presents these documents, plus any of a number of additional documents, through its own bank to the importer's bank.

- If the documents are in order, the importer's bank either pays the draft (a sight draft) or accepts the draft (a time draft). In the latter case, the bank promises to pay in the future. At this step the importer's bank acquires title to the merchandise through the bill of lading; it then releases the merchandise to the importer against payment or promise of future payment.

- If a sight draft is used, the exporter is paid at once. If a time draft is used, the exporter receives the accepted draft, now a bankers' acceptance, back from the bank.

The exporter may hold the bankers' acceptance until maturity or sell it at a discount in the money market.

- The total costs of an exporter entering a foreign market include the transaction costs of the trade financing, the import and export duties and tariffs applied by exporting and importing nations, and the costs of foreign market penetration, which include distribution expenses, inventory costs, and transportation expenses.

- Export credit insurance provides assurance to exporters (or exporters' banks) that should the foreign customer default on payment, the insurance company will pay for a major portion of the loss.

- In the United States, export credit insurance is provided by the Foreign Credit Insurance Association (FCIA), an unincorporated association of private commercial insurance companies operating in cooperation with the Export-Import Bank of the United States.

- The Export-Import Bank (Ex-Im Bank) is an independent agency established to stimulate and facilitate the foreign trade of the United States.

- Trade financing uses the same financing instruments as domestic receivables financing, plus some specialized instruments that are only available for financing international trade.

- A popular instrument for short-term financing is a bankers' acceptance. Its all-in-cost is comparable to other money market instruments, such as marketable bank certificates of deposit.

- Other short-term financing instruments with a domestic counterpart are trade acceptances, factoring, securitization, bank credit lines (usually covered by export credit insurance), and commercial paper.

- Forfaiting is an international trade technique that can provide medium- and long-term financing.

MINI-CASE Crosswell International's Precious Ultra-Thin Diapers

Crosswell International is a U.S.-based manufacturer and distributor of health care products, including children's diapers. Crosswell has been approached by Leonardo Sousa, the president of Material Hospitalar, a distributor of health care products throughout Brazil. Sousa is interested in distributing Crosswell's major diaper product, Precious, but only if an acceptable arrangement regarding pricing and payment terms can be reached.

Exporting to Brazil

Crosswell's manager for export operations, Geoff Mathieux, followed up the preliminary discussions by putting together an estimate of export costs and pricing for discussion purposes with Sousa. Crosswell needs to know all of the costs and pricing assumptions for the entire supply and value chain as it reaches the consumer. Mathieux believes it is critical that any arrangement that Crosswell enters into results in a price to consumers in the Brazilian marketplace that is both fair to all parties involved and competitive, given the market niche Crosswell hopes to penetrate. This first cut on pricing Precious diapers' entry into Brazil is presented in Exhibit 1.

Crosswell proposes to sell the basic diaper line to the Brazilian distributor for $34.00 per case, *FAS* (free alongside ship) Miami docks. This means that the seller,

Crosswell, agrees to cover all costs associated with getting the diapers to the Miami docks. The cost of loading the diapers aboard ship, the actual cost of shipping (freight), and associated documents is $4.32 per case. The running subtotal, $38.32 per case, is termed *CFR* (cost and freight). Finally, the insurance expenses related to the potential loss of the goods while in transit to final port of destination, export insurance, are $0.86 per case. The total *CIF* (cost,

---

EXHIBIT 1	Export Pricing for the Precious Diaper Line to Brazil

The Precious Ultra-Thin Diaper will be shipped via container. Each container will hold 968 cases of diapers. The costs and prices below are calculated on a per-case basis, although some costs and fees are assessed by container.

Exports Costs and Pricing to Brazil	Per Case	Rates and Calculation
FAS price per case, Miami	$34.00	
Freight, loading, and documentation	4.32	$4,180 per container/968 = $4.32
CFR price per case, Brazilian port (Santos)	$38.32	
Export insurance	0.86	2.25% of CIF
CIF to Brazilian port	$39.18	
CIF to Brazilian port, in Brazilian reais	R$97.95	2.50 Reais/US$ × $39.18
Brazilian Importation Costs		
Import duties	1.96	2.00% of CIF
Merchant marine renovation fee	2.70	25.00% of freight
Port storage fees	1.27	1.30% of CIF
Port handling fees	0.01	R$12 per container
Additional handling fees	0.26	20.00% of storage and handling
Customs brokerage fees	1.96	2.00% of CIF
Import license fee	0.05	R$50 per container
Local transportation charges	1.47	1.50% of CIF
Total cost to distributor in reais	R$107.63	
Distributor's Costs and Pricing		
Storage cost	1.47	1.50% of CIF × months
Cost of financing diaper inventory	6.86	7.00% of CIF × months
Distributor's margin	23.19	20.00% of price + storage + financing
Price to retailer in reais	R$139.15	
Brazilian Retailer Costs and Pricing		
Industrial product tax (IPT)	20.87	15.00% of price to retailer
Mercantile circulation services tax (MCS)	28.80	18.00% of price + IPT
Retailer costs and markup	56.65	30.00% of price + IPT + MCS
Price to consumer in reais	R$245.48	

Diaper Prices to Consumers	Diapers per Case	Price per Diaper
Small size	352	R$0.70
Medium size	256	R$0.96
Large size	192	R$1.28

insurance, and freight) is $39.18 per case, or 97.95 Brazilian reais per case, assuming an exchange rate of 2.50 Brazilian reais (R$) per U.S. dollar ($). In summary, the CIF cost of R$97.95 is the price charged by the exporter to the importer on arrival in Brazil, and is calculated as follows:

$$CIF = FAS + freight + export\ insurance$$
$$= (\$34.00 + \$4.32 + \$0.86) \times R\$2.50/\$$$
$$= R\$97.95.$$

The actual cost to the distributor of getting the diapers through the port and customs warehouses must also be calculated in terms of what Leonardo Sousa's costs are in reality. The various fees and taxes detailed in Exhibit 1 raise the fully landed cost of the Precious diapers to R$107.63 per case. The distributor would now bear storage and inventory costs totaling R$8.33 per case, which would bring the costs to R$115.96. The distributor then adds a margin for distribution services of 20% (R$23.19), raising the price as sold to the final retailer to R$139.15 per case.

Finally, the retailer (a supermarket or other retailer of consumer health care products) would include its expenses, taxes, and markup to reach the final shelf price of R$245.48 per case. This final retail price estimate now allows both Crosswell and Material Hospitalar to evaluate the price competitiveness of the Precious Ultra-Thin Diaper in the Brazilian marketplace, and provides a basis for further negotiations between the two parties.

Mathieux provides the above export price quotation, an outline of a potential representation agreement (for Sousa to represent Crosswell's product lines in the Brazilian marketplace), and payment and credit terms to Leonardo Sousa. Crosswell's payment and credit terms are that Sousa either pay in full in cash in advance, or with a confirmed irrevocable documentary L/C with a time draft specifying a tenor of 60 days.

Crosswell also requests from Sousa financial statements, banking references, foreign commercial references, descriptions of regional sales forces, and sales forecasts for the Precious diaper line. These last requests by Crosswell are very important for Crosswell to be able to assess Material Hospitalar's ability to be a dependable, creditworthy, and capable long-term partner and representative of the firm in the Brazilian marketplace. The discussions that follow focus on finding acceptable common ground between the two parties and working to increase the competitiveness of the Precious diaper in the Brazilian marketplace.

Crosswell's Proposal

The proposed sale by Crosswell to Material Hospitalar, at least in the initial shipment, is for 10 containers of 968 cases of diapers at $39.18 per case, CIF Brazil, payable in U.S. dollars. This is a total invoice amount of $379,262.40. Payment terms are that a confirmed L/C will be required of Material Hospitalar on a U.S. bank. The payment will be based on a time draft of 60 days, presentation to the bank for acceptance with other documents on the date of shipment. Both the exporter and the exporter's bank will expect payment from the importer or importer's bank 60 days from this date of shipment.

What should Crosswell expect? Assuming Material Hospitalar acquires the L/C and it is confirmed by Crosswell's bank in the United States, Crosswell will ship the goods after the initial agreement, say 15 days, as illustrated in Exhibit 2.

Simultaneous with the shipment, in which Crosswell has lost physical control over the goods, Crosswell will present the bill of lading acquired at the time of shipment with the other needed documents to its bank requesting payment. Because the export is under a confirmed L/C, assuming all documents are in order, Crosswell's bank will give Crosswell two choices:

1. Wait the full period of the time draft (60 days) and receive the entire payment in full ($379,262.40).

2. Receive the discounted value of this amount today.

The discounted amount, assuming U.S. dollar interest rate of 6.00% per annum (1.00% per 60 days), is as follows:

$$\frac{\$379,262.40}{(1+0.01)} = \frac{\$379,262.40}{1.01} = \$375,507.33$$

Because the invoice is denominated in U.S. dollars, Crosswell need not worry about currency value changes (currency risk). And, because its bank has confirmed the L/C, it is protected against changes or deteriorations in Material Hospitalar's ability to pay on the future date.

What should Material Hospitalar expect? Material Hospitalar will receive the goods on or before day 60. It will then move the goods through its distribution system to retailers. Depending on the payment terms between Material Hospitalar and its buyers (retailers), it could receive either cash or terms for payment for the goods. Because Material Hospitalar purchased the goods via the 60-day time draft and an L/C from its Brazilian bank, total payment of $379,262.40 is due on day 90 (shipment and presentation of documents was on day 30 + 60 day time draft) to the Brazilian bank. Material Hospitalar, because it is a Brazilian-based company and has agreed to make payment in U.S. dollars (foreign currency), carries the currency risk of the transaction.

Crosswell/Material Hospitalar's Concern

The concern the two companies have, however, is that the total price to the consumer in Brazil, R$245.48 per case, or

EXHIBIT 2   **Export Payment Terms on Crosswell's Export to Brazil**

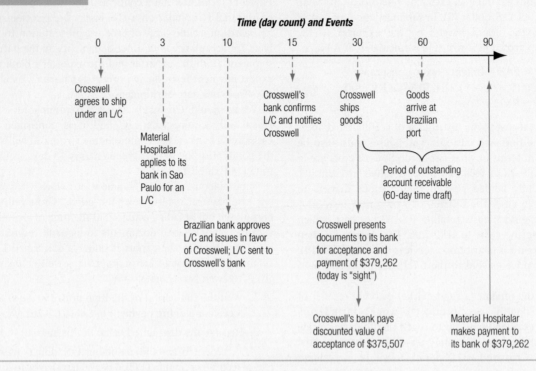

R$0.70/diaper (small size), is too high. The major competitors in the Brazilian market for premium quality diapers, Kenko do Brasil (Japan), Johnson & Johnson (U.S.), and Procter & Gamble (U.S.), are cheaper (see Exhibit 3). The competitors all manufacture in-country, thus avoiding the series of import duties and tariffs, which have added significantly to Crosswell's landed prices in the Brazilian marketplace.

Case Questions

1. How are pricing, currency of denomination, and financing interrelated in the value chain for Crosswell's penetration of the Brazilian market? Summarize them using Exhibit 2.

2. How important is Sousa to the value chain of Crosswell? What worries might Crosswell have regarding Sousa's ability to fulfill his obligations?

3. If Crosswell is to penetrate the market, some way of reducing its prices will be required. What do you suggest?

EXHIBIT 3   **Competitive Diaper Prices in the Brazilian Market (in Brazilian Reais)**

		Price per Diaper by Size		
Company (Country)	Brand	Small	Medium	Large
Kenko (Japan)	Monica Plus	0.68	0.85	1.18
Procter & Gamble (U.S.)	Pampers Uni	0.65	0.80	1.08
Johnson & Johnson (U.S.)	Sempre Seca Plus	0.65	0.80	1.08
Crosswell (U.S.)	Precious	0.70	0.96	1.40

QUESTIONS

1. **Unaffiliated Buyers.** Why might different documentation be used for an export to a nonaffiliated foreign buyer who is a new customer, as compared with an export to a nonaffiliated foreign buyer to whom the exporter has been selling for many years?

2. **Affiliated Buyers.** For what reason might an exporter use standard international trade documentation (letter of credit, draft, order bill of lading) on an intrafirm export to its parent or sister subsidiary?

3. **Related Party Trade.** What reasons can you give for the observation that intrafirm trade is now greater than trade between nonaffiliated exporters and importers?

4. **Documents.** Explain the difference between a letter of credit (L/C) and a draft. How are they linked?

5. **Risks.** What is the major difference between currency risk and risk of noncompletion? How are these risks handled in a typical international trade transaction?

6. **Letter of Credit.** Identify each party to a letter of credit (L/C) and indicate its responsibility.

7. **Confirming a Letter of Credit.** Why would an exporter insist on a confirmed letter of credit?

8. **Documenting an Export of Hard Drives.** List the steps involved in the export of computer hard disk drives from Penang, Malaysia to San Jose, California, using an unconfirmed letter of credit authorizing payment on sight.

9. **Documenting an Export of Lumber from Portland to Yokohama.** List the steps involved in the export of lumber from Portland, Oregon, to Yokohama, Japan, using a confirmed letter of credit, payment to be made in 120 days.

10. **Inca Breweries of Peru.** Inca Breweries of Lima, Peru, has received an order for 10,000 cartons of beer from Alicante Importers of Alicante, Spain. The beer will be exported to Spain under the terms of a letter of credit issued by a Madrid bank on behalf of Alicante Importers. The letter of credit specifies that the face value of the shipment, $720,000, will be paid 90 days after the Madrid bank accepts a draft drawn by Inca Breweries in accordance with the terms of the letter of credit.

    The current discount rate on three-month banker's acceptances is 8% per annum, and Inca Breweries estimates its weighted average cost of capital to be 20% per annum. The commission for selling a banker's acceptance in the discount market is 1.2% of the face amount.

    How much cash will Inca Breweries receive from the sale if it holds the acceptance until maturity? Do you recommend that Inca Breweries hold the acceptance until maturity or discount it at once in the U.S. banker's acceptance market?

11. **Swishing Shoe Company.** Swishing Shoe Company of Durham, North Carolina, has received an order for 50,000 cartons of athletic shoes from Southampton Footware, Ltd., of Great Britain, payment to be in British pounds sterling. The shoes will be shipped to Southampton Footware under the terms of a letter of credit issued by a London bank on behalf of Southampton Footware. The letter of credit specifies that the face value of the shipment, £400,000, will be paid 120 days after the London bank accepts a draft drawn by Southampton Footware in accordance with the terms of the letter of credit.

    The current discount rate in London on 120-day banker's acceptances is 12% per annum, and Southampton Footware estimates its weighted average cost of capital to be 18% per annum. The commission for selling a banker's acceptance in the discount market is 2.0% of the face amount.
    a. Would Swishing Shoe Company gain by holding the acceptance to maturity, as compared to discounting the banker's acceptance at once?
    b. Does Swishing Shoe Company incur any other risks in this transaction?

12. **Going Abroad.** Assume that Great Britain charges a duty of 10% on shoes imported into the United Kingdom. Swishing Shoe Company, in question 11, discovers that it can manufacture shoes in Ireland and import them into Great Britain free of any import duty.

    What factors should Swishing consider in deciding to continue to export shoes from North Carolina versus manufacture them in Ireland?

13. **Governmentally Supplied Credit.** Various governments have established agencies to insure against nonpayment for exports and/or to provide export credit. This shifts credit risk away from private banks and to the citizen taxpayers of the country whose government created and backs the agency. Why would such an arrangement be of benefit to the citizens of that country?

PROBLEMS

*1. **Indian Motorcycles (A).** Indian Motorcycles exports large-engine motorcycles (greater than 700cc) to Australia and invoices its customers in U.S. dollars. Sydney Wholesale Imports has purchased $3,000,000 of merchandise from Indian Motorcycles, with payment due in six months. The payment will be made with a bankers' acceptance issued by Charter Bank of Sydney at a fee of 1.75% per annum. Indian Motorcycles has a weighted average cost of capital of 10%. If Indian holds this acceptance to maturity, what is its annualized percentage all-in-cost?

2. **Indian Motorcycles (B).** Assuming the facts in problem 1, Bank of America is now willing to buy Indian Motorcycles's bankers' acceptance for a discount of 6% per annum. What would be Indian's annualized percentage all-in-cost of financing its $1,000,000 Australian receivable?

*3. **Takagi Toyota.** Takagi Toyota buys its cars from Toyota Motors-USA, and sells them to U.S. customers. One of its customers is Green Transport, a car rental firm that buys cars from Takagi Toyota at a wholesale price. Final payment is due to Takagi Toyota in six months. Green Transport has bought $200,000 worth of cars from Takagi, with a cash down payment of $40,000 and the balance due in six months without any interest charged as a sales incentive. Takagi Toyota will have the Green Transport receivable accepted by Alliance Acceptance for a 2% fee, and then sell it at a 3% per annum discount to Wells Fargo Bank.
   a. What is the annualized percentage all-in-cost to Takagi Toyota?
   b. What are Takagi Transport's net cash proceeds, including the cash down payment?

4. **Sun Microsystems (A).** Assume Sun Microsystems has sold Internet servers to Telecom Italia for €700,000. Payment is due in three months and will be made with a trade acceptance from Telecom Italia Acceptance. The acceptance fee is 1.0% per annum of the face amount of the note. This acceptance will be sold at a 4% per annum discount. What is the annualized percentage all-in-cost in euros of this method of trade financing?

5. **Sun Microsystems (B).** Assume that Sun Microsystems prefers to receive U.S. dollars rather than euros for the trade transaction described in problem 4. It is considering two alternatives: 1) It can sell the acceptance for euros at once and convert the euros immediately to U.S. dollars at the spot rate of exchange of $1.00/€ or 2) It can hold the euro acceptance until maturity but at the start sell the expected euro proceeds forward for dollars at the three-month forward rate of $1.02/€.
   a. What are the U.S. dollar net proceeds received at once from the discounted trade acceptance in alternative 1?
   b. What are the U.S. dollar net proceeds received in three months in alternative 2?
   c. What is the break-even investment rate that would equalize the net U.S. dollar proceeds from both alternatives?
   d. Which alternative should Sun Microsystems choose?

6. **Hollywood Entertainment (A).** Hollywood Entertainment has sold a combination of films and DVDs to Hong Kong Media Incorporated for US$100,000, with payment due in six months. Hollywood Entertainment has the following alternatives for financing this receivable: 1) Use its bank credit line. Interest would be at the prime rate of 5% plus 150 basis points per annum. Hollywood Enterprises would need to maintain a compensating balance of 20% of the loan's face amount. No interest will be paid on the compensating balance by the bank or 2) Use its bank credit line but purchase export credit insurance for a 1% fee. Because of the reduced risk, the bank interest rate would be reduced to 5% per annum without any points.
   a. What are the annualized percentage all-in-costs of each alternative?
   b. What are the advantages and disadvantages of each alternative?
   c. Which alternative would you recommend?

7. **Hollywood Entertainment (B).** Hollywood Entertainment has been approached by a factor that offers to purchase the Hong Kong Media Imports receivable at a 16% per annum discount plus a 2% charge for a nonrecourse clause.
   a. What is the annualized percentage all-in-cost of this factoring alternative?
   b. What are the advantages and disadvantages of the factoring alternative compared to the alternatives in Hollywood Entertainment (A)?

8. **Forfaiting at Kaduna Oil (Nigeria).** Kaduna Oil of Nigeria has purchased $1,000,000 of oil drilling equipment from Unicorn Drilling of Houston, Texas. Kaduna Oil must pay for this purchase over the next five years at a rate of $200,000 per year due on March 1 of each year.

Bank of Zurich, a Swiss forfaiter, has agreed to buy the five notes of $200,000 each at a discount. The discount rate would be approximately 8% per annum based on the expected three-year LIBOR rate plus 200 basis points, paid by Kaduna Oil. Bank of Zurich also would charge Kaduna Oil an additional commitment fee of 2% per annum from the date of its commitment to finance until receipt of the actual discounted notes issued in accordance with the financing contract. The $200,000 promissory notes will come due on March 1 in successive years.

The promissory notes issued by Kaduna Oil will be endorsed by their bank, Lagos City Bank, for a 1% fee and delivered to Unicorn Drilling. At this point Unicorn Drilling will endorse the notes *without recourse* and discount them with the forfaiter, Bank of Zurich, receiving the full $200,000 principal amount. Bank of Zurich will sell the notes by rediscounting them to investors in the international money market without recourse. At maturity, the investors holding the notes will present them for collection at Lagos City Bank. If Lagos City Bank defaults on payment, the investors will collect on the notes from Bank of Zurich.

a. What is the annualized percentage all-in-cost to Kaduna Oil of financing the first $200,000 note due March 1, 2004?

b. What might motivate Kaduna Oil to use this relatively expensive alternative for financing?

9. **Andersen Sports (A).** Andersen Sports (Andersen) is considering bidding to sell $100,000 of ski equipment to Kim Family Enterprises of Seoul, Korea. Payment would be due in six months. Since Andersen cannot find good credit information on Kim, Andersen wants to protect its credit risk. It is considering the following financing solution:

Kim's bank issues a letter of credit on behalf of Kim and agrees to accept Andersen's draft for $100,000 due in six months. The acceptance fee would cost Andersen $500, plus reduce Kim's available credit line by $100,000. The bankers' acceptance note of $100,000 would be sold at a 2% per annum discount in the money market. What is the annualized percentage all-in-cost to Andersen of this bankers' acceptance financing?

10. **Andersen Sports (B): Bank Credit Line with Export Credit Insurance.** Andersen could also buy export credit insurance from FCIA for a 1.5% premium. It finances the $100,000 receivable from Kim from its

credit line at 6% per annum interest. No compensating bank balance would be required.

a. What is Andersen's annualized percentage all-in-cost of financing?

b. What are Kim's costs?

c. What are the advantages and disadvantages of this alternative compared to the bankers' acceptance financing in Andersen (A)? Which alternative would you recommend?

INTERNET EXERCISES

1. **Going Global with CFO.** One of the most useful Internet sites with current analysis and thinking on a variety of corporate finance issues is the online version of CFO magazine. Use the three different regionally focused sites to explore the growing integration of cash management, currency management, operations control, and IT services.

CFO.com	www.cfo.com
CFO Europe.com	www.cfo.com/europe
CFO Asia.com	www.cfoasia.com

2. **Letter of Credit Services.** Commercial banks worldwide provide a variety of services to aid in the financing of foreign trade. Contact some of the many major multinational banks (a few are listed here) and determine what types of letter of credit services and other trade financing services they provide.

Bank of America	www.bankofamerica.com/index.jsp
Citibank	www.citibank.com/us/index.htm
Barclays	www.barclays.com
Deutsche Bank	www.db.com
Union Bank of Switzerland	www.ubs.com

3. **Export-Import Bank of the United States.** The EXIM Bank of the United States provides financing for U.S.-based exporters. Like most major industrial country trade-financing organizations, it is intended to aid in the export sale of products in which the buyer needs attractive financing terms. Use the EXIM Bank's Web site to determine the current country limits, fees, and other restrictions which currently apply. (*Note*: The Export-Import Bank's Web page provides some of the best Web site links in international business and statistics.)

| Export-Import Bank of the United States | www.exim.gov |

Answers to Selected Problems

Chapter 1: Globalization and the Multinational Enterprise

6. a. $14.77
   b. United States—30.5%, Brazil—27.1%, Germany—40.1%, China—2.4%
   c. 69.5%

9. Appreciation case: Consolidated EPS rises by 13.9%.
   Depreciation case: Consolidated EPS falls by 13.9%.

Chapter 2: Financial Goals and Corporate Governance

1. a. 12.500%
   b. 18.750%
   c. Dividend yield is 6.250%; capital gains are 12.500%.

3. a. 28.00%
   b. 16.57%
   c. 49.21%

Chapter 3: The International Monetary System

2. –41.82%

7. C$1.2601/$

13. $629,644.07

Chapter 4: The Balance of Payments

Australia	1998	1999	2000	2001	2002	2003	2004	2005	2006
1. Balance on goods	–5,331	–9,761	–4,813	1,786	–5,431	–15,369	–18,031	–13,403	–9,596
2. Balance on services	–1,091	–931	289	–259	–201	–433	–678	–918	869
3. Balance on goods and services	–6,422	–10,692	–4,524	1,527	–5,632	–15,802	–18,709	–14,321	–8,727
4. Current account balance	–18,014	–22,295	–15,103	–8,721	–17,385	–30,674	–40,066	–41,461	–41,504

Chapter 5: Current Multinational Financial Challenges: The Credit Crisis of 2007–2009

		3-month	6-month
1.	a. Discount on sale	$6.07	$23.26
	b. Simple yield	0.0607%	0.2331%
	c. Annualized yield	0.2432%	0.4668%

Chapter 6: The Foreign Exchange Market

1. a. 35.29
   b. 352,935

			Bid	Ask	Spread
2.	a.	1-month	1.2585	1.2600	.0015
		3-month	1.2589	1.2607	.0018
		6-month	1.2595	1.2615	.0020

   b. It widens, most likely a result of thinner and thinner trading volume.

Chapter 7: International Parity Conditions

6. a. 1.17
   b. −63.307%
   c. Inflation and balance of payments crisis
10. a. $28,211.81
   b. ¥112.72/$
   c. $28,832.47
   d. $28,677.30
15. Yes, Luis should take the arbitrage profit. He will make $5,238.13 on every $1 million invested.

Chapter 8: Foreign Currency Derivatives

1. a. He should buy a call on Singapore dollars.
   b. $0.65046
   c. Gross profit = $0.05000; net profit = $0.04954.
   d. Gross profit = $0.15000; net profit = $0.14954.

Chapter 9: Interest Rate and Currency Swaps

1. New York = $77,777.78
   Great Britain = $76,712.33
   Switzerland = $83,333.33
4. If LIBOR falls 50 basis points per year = 7.092%.
   If LIBOR rises 50 basis points per year = 7.458%.
   Not a good deal.

Chapter 10: Foreign Exchange Rate Determination and Forecasting

2. −15.38%
5. −40.00%

Chapter 11: Transaction Exposure

3. 1. $107,158.89
   2. $111,755.82
11. 1. Uncovered is uncertain; $209,580.84 at current rate; $216,049.38 if at the 3-month forward rate.
   2. Forward is $216, 049.38 and certain.
   3. Money market hedge is $212,973.80.
   Discussion: Forward contract is probably the most acceptable alternative, if the bank will allow it.

Chapter 12: Operating Exposure

2. Case #1: Same yuan price yields $33,913,043.
   Case #2: Same dollar price yields $54,000,000, which is better.

Chapter 13: Translation Exposure

5. A net exposure of $U420,000 or $21,000.

Chapter 14: The Global Cost and Availability of Capital

1. a. New cost of equity is 10.500%.
   b. New cost of debt, after-tax, is 4.900%.
   c. New weighted average cost of capital is 7.700%.

	Goldman Sachs	*Bank of New York*
4. Estimated beta	1.20	1.16
Estimated cost of equity	10.200%	13.432%
Estimated cost of debt	4.875%	5.070%
Estimated WACC	8.336%	10.087%

Chapter 15: Sourcing Equity Globally

	Petrobrás	*Lukoil*
1. Calculated WACC	14.674%	12.286%
I-Bank report WACC	14.700%	12.300%

Chapter 16: Sourcing Debt Globally

1. 13.9027%

5. IRR of Japanese bond is 5.060%.
   IRR of euro bond is 4.860%.
   IRR of dollar bond is 5.000%.

Chapter 17: International Portfolio Theory and Diversification

	Expected Return	*Expected Risk*
2. a. Equally weighted portfolio	17.30%	20.93%
b. 70% Boeing, 30% Unilever	17.82%	21.08%
c. Minimum risk is 55% Boeing, 45% Unilever	17.43%	20.89%

5. Share price appreciation = 6.456%.
   Annual return, including dividends = 10.698%.

Chapter 19: Multinational Capital Budgeting

1. a. $7,912,725
   b. $5,587,094

5. Project viewpoint = $265,073.
   Parent viewpoint = ($2,249,812).

Chapter 20: Multinational Tax Management

1. Case 1: 38.8%
   Case 2: 45.0%

Chapter 21: Working Capital Management

1. a. 19.41%
   b. 1,800,000

8. Dividend only: Total return, after-tax = $247,500.
   License fee only: Total return, after-tax = $178,200.

Chapter 22: International Trade Finance

1. 11.765%

3. a. 5.128%
   b. $196,000

Glossary

A/P. In international trade documentation, an abbreviation for authority to purchase or authority to pay. In accounting, an abbreviation for accounts payable.

Accounting exposure. Another name for translation exposure. *See* Translation exposure.

ADB. Asian Development Bank.

Ad valorem duty. A customs duty levied as a percentage of the assessed value of goods entering a country.

Adjusted present value. A type of present value analysis in capital budgeting in which operating cash flows are discounted separately from (1) the various tax shields provided by the deductibility of interest and other financial charges, and (2) the benefits of project-specific concessional financing. Each component cash flow is discounted at a rate appropriate for the risk involved.

ADR. *See* American Depositary Receipt.

AfDB. African Development Bank.

Affiliate. A foreign enterprise in which the parent company owns a minority interest.

Agency for International Development (AID). A unit of the U.S. government dealing with foreign aid.

All-equity discount rate. A discount rate in capital budgeting that would be appropriate for discounting operating cash flows if the project were financed entirely with owners' equity.

Alt-A Mortgage. A mortgage type which, although not prime, is considered a relatively low-risk loan to a creditworthy borrower, but lacks some technical qualifications to be categorized as "conforming."

American Depositary Receipt (ADR). A certificate of ownership, issued by a U.S. bank, representing a claim on underlying foreign securities. ADRs may be traded in lieu of trading in the actual underlying shares.

American option. An option that can be exercised at any time up to and including the expiration date.

American selling price (ASP). For customs purposes, the use of the domestic price of competing merchandise in the United States as a tax base for determining import duties. The ASP is generally higher than the actual foreign price, so its use is a protectionist technique.

American terms. Foreign exchange quotations for the U.S. dollar, expressed as the number of U.S. dollars per unit of non-U.S. currency.

Appreciation. In the context of exchange rate changes, a rise in the foreign exchange value of a currency that is pegged to other currencies or to gold. Also called revaluation.

Arbitrage. A trading strategy based on the purchase of a commodity, including foreign exchange, in one market at one price while simultaneously selling it in another market at a more advantageous price, in order to obtain a risk-free profit on the price differential.

Arbitrageur. An individual or company that practices arbitrage.

Arithmetic return. A calculation in which the mean equals the average of the annual percentage changes in capital appreciation plus dividend distributions.

Arm's-length price. The price at which a willing buyer and a willing unrelated seller freely agree to carry out a transaction. In effect, a free market price. Applied by tax authorities in judging the appropriateness of transfer prices between related companies.

Asset Backed Security (ABS). A derivative security which typically includes second mortgages and home-equity loans based on mortgages, in addition to credit card receivables and auto loans.

Asian currency unit. A trading department within a Singaporean bank that deals in foreign (non-Singaporean) currency deposits and loans.

Ask price. The price at which a dealer is willing to sell foreign exchange, securities or commodities. Also called offer price.

Asset market approach. A strategy that determines whether foreigners are willing to hold claims in monetary form, depending on an extensive set of investment considerations or drivers.

At-the-money. An option whose exercise price is the same as the spot price of the underlying currency.

Back-to-back loan. A loan in which two companies in separate countries borrow each other's currency for a specific period of time and repay the other's currency at an agreed maturity. Sometimes the two loans are channeled through an intermediate bank. Back-to-back financing is also called link financing.

Balance of payments. A financial statement summarizing the flow of goods, services, and investment funds between residents of a given country and residents of the rest of the world.

Balance of trade. An entry in the balance of payments measuring the difference between the monetary value of merchandise exports and merchandise imports.

Balance sheet hedge. An accounting strategy that requires an equal amount of exposed foreign currency assets and liabilities on a firm's consolidated balance sheet.

593

Bank for International Settlements (BIS). A bank in Basle, Switzerland, that functions as a bank for European central banks.

Bank rate. The interest rate at which central banks for various countries lend to their own monetary institutions.

Bankers' acceptance. An unconditional promise by a bank to make payment on a draft when it matures. This comes in the form of the bank's endorsement (acceptance) of a draft drawn against that bank in accordance with the terms of a letter of credit issued by the bank.

Barter. International trade conducted by the direct exchange of physical goods, rather than by separate purchases and sales at prices and exchange rates set by a free market.

Basic balance. In a country's balance of payments, the net of exports and imports of goods and services, unilateral transfers, and long-term capital flows.

Basis point. One one-hundredth of one percentage point, often used in quotations of spreads between interest rates or to describe changes in yields in securities.

Basis risk. A type of interest rate risk in which the interest rate base is mismatched.

Bearer bond. Corporate or governmental debt in bond form that is not registered to any owner. Possession of the bond implies ownership, and interest is obtained by clipping a coupon attached to the bond. The advantage of the bearer form is easy transfer at the time of a sale, easy use as collateral for a debt, and what some cynics call taxpayer anonymity, meaning that governments find it hard to trace interest payments in order to collect income taxes. Bearer bonds are common in Europe, but are seldom issued any more in the United States. The alternate form to a bearer bond is a registered bond.

Beta. Second letter of the Greek alphabet, used as a statistical measure of risk in the Capital Asset Pricing Model. Beta is the covariance between returns on a given asset and returns on the market portfolio, divided by the variance of returns on the market portfolio.

Bid. The price that a dealer is willing to pay to purchase foreign exchange or a security.

Bid-ask spread. The difference between a bid and an ask quotation.

Big Bang. The October 1986 liberalization of the London capital markets.

Bill of exchange (B/E). A written order requesting one party (such as an importer) to pay a specified amount of money at a specified time to the writer of the bill. Also called a draft. *See* Sight draft.

Bill of lading (B/L). A contract between a common carrier and a shipper to transport goods to a named destination. The bill of lading is also a receipt for the goods. Bills of lading are usually negotiable, meaning they are made to the order of a particular party and can be endorsed to transfer title to another party.

Black market. An illegal foreign exchange market.

Blocked funds. Funds in one country's currency that may not be exchanged freely for foreign currencies because of exchange controls.

Border tax adjustments. The fiscal practice, under the General Agreement on Tariffs and Trade, by which imported goods are subject to some or all of the tax charged in the importing country and re-exported goods are exempt from some or all of the tax charged in the exporting country.

Branch. A foreign operation not incorporated in the host country, in contrast to a subsidiary.

Bretton Woods Conference. An international conference in 1944 that established the international monetary system that was in effect from 1945 to 1971. The conference was held in Bretton Woods, New Hampshire, USA.

Bridge financing. Short-term financing from a bank, used while a borrower obtains medium- or long-term fixed-rate financing from capital markets.

Bulldogs. British pound-denominated bonds issued within the United Kingdom by a foreign borrower.

Cable. The U.S. dollar per British pound cross rate.

CAD. Cash against documents. International trade term.

Call option. The right, but not the obligation, to buy foreign exchange or another financial contract at a specified price within a specified time. *See* Option.

Capital account. A section of the balance of payments accounts. Under the revised format of the International Monetary Fund, the capital account measures capital transfers and the acquisition and disposal of nonproduced, nonfinancial assets. Under traditional definitions, still used by many countries, the capital account measures public and private international lending and investment. Most of the traditional definition of the capital account is now incorporated into IMF statements as the financial account.

Capital Asset Pricing Model (CAPM). A theoretical model that relates the return on an asset to its risk, where risk is the contribution of the asset to the volatility of a portfolio. Risk and return are presumed to be determined in competitive and efficient financial markets.

Capital budgeting. The analytical approach used to determine whether investment in long-lived assets or projects is viable.

Capital flight. Movement of funds out of a country because of political risk.

Capital markets. The financial markets of various countries in which various types of long-term debt and/or ownership securities, or claims on those securities, are purchased and sold.

Capital mobility. The degree to which private capital moves freely from country to country in search of the most promising investment opportunities.

Cash budgeting. Planning for future receipts and disbursements of cash.

Cash flow return on investment (CFROI). A measure of corporate performance in which the numerator equals profit from continuing operations less cash taxes and depreciation. This is divided by cash investment, which is taken to mean the replacement cost of capital employed.

Collateralized Debt Obligation (CDO). A portfolio of debt instruments of varying credit qualities created and packaged for resale as an asset-backed security. The collateral in the CDO is the real estate, aircraft, heavy equipment, or other property the loan was used to purchase.

Credit Default Swap (CDS). A derivative contract that derives its value from the credit quality and performance of any specified asset. The CDS was invented by a team at JPMorgan in 1997, and designed to shift the risk of default to a third party. It is a way to bet whether a specific mortgage or security will either fail to pay on time or fail to pay at all.

Certificate of Deposit (CD). A negotiable receipt issued by a bank for funds deposited for a certain period of time. CDs can be purchased or sold prior to their maturity in a secondary market, making them an interest-earning marketable security.

CIF. *See* Cost, insurance, and freight.

CKD. Completely knocked down. International trade term for components shipped into a country for assembly there. Often used in the automobile industry.

Clearing house. An institution through which financial obligations are cleared by the process of settling the obligations of various members.

Clearinghouse Interbank Payments System (CHIPS). A New York-based computerized clearing system used by banks to settle interbank foreign exchange obligations (mostly U.S. dollars) between members.

Collar option. The simultaneous purchase of a put option and sale of a call option, or vice versa, resulting in a form of hybrid option.

COMECON. Acronym for Council for Mutual Economic Assistance. An association of the former Soviet Union and Eastern European governments formed to facilitate international trade among European Communist countries. COMECON ceased to exist after the breakup of the Soviet Union.

Commercial risk. In banking, the likelihood that a foreign debtor will be unable to repay its debts because of business events, as distinct from political ones.

Common market. An association through treaty of two or more countries that agree to remove all trade barriers between themselves. The best known is the European Common Market, now called the European Union.

Comparative advantage. A theory that everyone gains if each nation specializes in the production of those goods that it produces relatively most efficiently and imports those goods that other countries produce relatively most efficiently. The theory supports free trade arguments.

Competitive exposure. *See* Operating exposure.

Concession agreement. An understanding or contract between a foreign corporation and a host government defining the rules under which the corporation may operate in that country.

Consolidated financial statement. A corporate financial statement in which accounts of a parent company and its subsidiaries are added together to produce a statement which reports the status of the worldwide enterprise as if it were a single corporation. Internal obligations are eliminated in consolidated statements.

Consolidation. In the context of accounting for multinational corporations, the process of preparing a single reporting currency financial statement, which combines financial statements of subsidiaries that are in fact measured in different currencies.

Contagion. The spread of a crisis in one country to its neighboring countries and other countries with similar characteristics—at least in the eyes of cross-border investors.

Controlled foreign corporation (CFC). A foreign corporation in which U.S. shareholders own more than 50% of the combined voting power or total value. Under U.S. tax law, U.S. shareholders may be liable for taxes on undistributed earnings of the controlled foreign corporation.

Convertible bond. A bond or other fixed-income security that may be exchanged for a number of shares of common stock.

Convertible currency. A currency that can be exchanged freely for any other currency without government restrictions.

Corporate governance. The relationship among stakeholders used to determine and control the strategic direction and performance of an organization.

Corporate wealth maximization. The corporate goal of maximizing the total wealth of the corporation rather than just the shareholders' wealth. Wealth is defined to include not just financial wealth but also the technical, marketing and human resources of the corporation.

Correspondent bank. A bank that holds deposits for and provides services to another bank, located in another geographic area, on a reciprocal basis.

Cost and freight (C&F). Price, quoted by an exporter, that includes the cost of transportation to the named port of destination.

Cost, insurance, and freight (CIF). Exporter's quoted price including the cost of packaging, freight or carriage, insurance premium, and other charges paid in respect of the goods from the time of loading in the country of export to their arrival at the named port of destination or place of transshipment.

Counterparty. The opposite party in a double transaction, which involves an exchange of financial instruments or obligations now and a reversal of that same transaction at an agreed-upon later date.

Counterparty risk. The potential exposure any individual firm bears that the second party to any financial contract may be unable to fulfill its obligations under the contract's specifications.

Countertrade. A type of international trade in which parties exchange goods directly rather than for money, a type of barter.

Countervailing duty. An import duty charged to offset an export subsidy by another country.

Country risk. In banking, the likelihood that unexpected events within a host country will influence a client's or a government's ability to repay a loan. Country risk is often divided into sovereign (political) risk and foreign exchange (currency) risk.

Country-specific risk. Political risks that affect the MNE at the country level, such as transfer risk (blocked funds) and cultural and institutional risks.

Covered interest arbitrage. The process whereby an investor earns a risk-free profit by (1) borrowing funds in one currency, (2) exchanging those funds in the spot market for a foreign currency, (3) investing the foreign currency at interest rates in a foreign country, (4) selling forward, at the time of original investment, the investment proceeds to be received at maturity, (5) using the proceeds of the forward sale to repay the original loan, and (6) sustaining a remaining profit balance.

Covering. A transaction in the forward foreign exchange market or money market that protects the value of future cash flows. Covering is another term for hedging. *See* Hedge.

Crawling peg. A foreign exchange rate system in which the exchange rate is adjusted very frequently to reflect prevailing rate of inflation.

Credit risk. The possibility that a borrower's credit worth, at the time of renewing a credit, is reclassified by the lender.

Crisis planning. The process of educating management and other employees about how to react to various scenarios of violence or other disruptive events.

Cross-border acquisition. A purchase in which one firm acquires another firm located in a different country.

Cross-currency swap. *See* Currency swap.

Cross-listing. The listing of shares of common stock on two or more stock exchanges.

Cross rate. An exchange rate between two currencies derived by dividing each currency's exchange rate with a third currency. For example, if ¥/$ is 108 and DKr/$ is 6.80, the cross rate between ¥ and DKr is ¥108 ÷ DKr6.80 = ¥15.88/DKr.

Cumulative translation adjustment (CTA) account. An entry in a translated balance sheet in which gains and/or losses from translation have been accumulated over a period of years.

Currency basket. The value of a portfolio of specific amounts of individual currencies, used as the basis for setting the market value of another currency. Also called currency cocktail.

Currency board. A currency board exists when a country's central bank commits to back its money supply entirely with foreign reserves at all times.

Currency swap. A transaction in which two counterparties exchange specific amounts of two different currencies at the outset, and then repay over time according to an agreed-upon contract that reflects interest payments and possibly amortization of principal. In a currency swap, the cash flows are similar to those in a spot and forward foreign exchange transaction. *See also* Swap.

Current account. In the balance of payments, the net flow of goods, services, and unilateral transfers (such as gifts) between a country and all foreign countries.

Current rate method. A method of translating the financial statements of foreign subsidiaries into the parent's reporting currency. All assets and liabilities are translated at the current exchange rate.

Current/noncurrent method. A method of translating the financial statements of foreign subsidiaries into the parent's reporting currency. All current assets and current liabilities are translated at the current rate, and all noncurrent accounts at their historical rates.

D/A. Documents against acceptance. International trade term.

D/P. Documents against payment. International trade term.

D/S. Days after sight. International trade term.

Deemed-paid tax. That portion of taxes paid to a foreign government that is allowed as a credit (reduction) in taxes due to a home government.

Delta. The change in an option's price divided by the change in the price of the underlying instrument. Hedging strategies are based on delta ratios.

Demand deposit. A bank deposit that can be withdrawn or transferred at any time without notice, in contrast to a time deposit where (theoretically) the bank may require a waiting period before the deposit can be withdrawn. Demand deposits may or may not earn interest. A time deposit is the opposite of a demand deposit.

Depositary receipt. *See* American Depositary Receipt.

Depreciate. In the context of foreign exchange rates, a drop in the spot foreign exchange value of a floating currency, i.e., a currency whose value is determined by open market transactions.

Devaluation. The action of a government or central bank authority to drop the spot foreign exchange value of a currency that is pegged to another currency or to gold.

Direct quote. The price of a unit of foreign exchange expressed in the home country's currency. The term has meaning only when the home country is specified.

Directed public share issue. An issue that is targeted at investors in a single country and underwritten in whole or in part by investment institutions from that country.

Dirty float. A system of floating (i.e., market-determined) exchange rates in which the government intervenes from time to time to influence the foreign exchange value of its currency.

Discount. In the foreign exchange market, the amount by which a currency is cheaper for future delivery than for spot (immediate) delivery. The opposite of discount is premium.

Dollarization. The use of the U.S. dollar as the official currency of a country.

Domestic International Sales Corporation (DISC). Under the U.S. tax code, a type of subsidiary formed to reduce taxes on exported U.S.-produced goods. It has been ruled illegal by the World Trade Organization.

Draft. An unconditional written order requesting one party (such as an importer) to pay a specified amount of money at a specified time to the order of the writer of the draft. Also called a bill of exchange. Personal checks are one type of draft.

Dragon bond. A U.S. dollar-denominated bond sold in the so-called Dragon economies of Asia, such as Hong Kong, Taiwan, and Singapore.

Dumping. The practice of offering goods for sale in a foreign market at a price that is lower than that of the same product in the home market or a third country. As used in GATT, a special case of differential pricing.

Economic exposure. Another name for operating exposure. *See* Operating exposure.

Economic Value Added (EVA). A widely used measure of corporate financial performance. It is calculated as the difference between net operating profits after tax for the business and the cost of capital invested (both debt and equity). EVA is a registered trademark of Stern Stewart & Company.

Edge Act and Agreement Corporation. Subsidiary of a U.S. bank incorporated under federal law to engage in various international banking and financing operations, including equity participations that are not allowed to regular domestic banks. The Edge Act subsidiary may be located in a state other than that of the parent bank.

Effective exchange rate. An index measuring the change in value of a foreign currency determined by calculating a weighted average of bilateral exchange rates. The weighting reflects the importance of each foreign country's trade with the home country.

Efficient market. A market in which all relevant information is already reflected in market prices. The term is most frequently applied to foreign exchange markets and securities markets.

EOM. End of month. International trade term.

Equity risk premium. The average annual return of the market expected by investors over and above riskless debt.

Euro. A new currency unit that replaced the individual currencies of 12 European countries that belong to the European Union.

Euro equity public issue. A new equity issue that is underwritten and distributed in multiple foreign equity markets, sometimes simultaneously with distribution in the domestic market.

Eurobank. A bank, or bank department, which bids for time deposits and makes loans in currencies other than that of the country where the bank is located.

Eurobond. A bond originally offered outside the country in whose currency it is denominated. For example, a dollar-denominated bond originally offered for sale to investors outside the United States.

Euro-Commercial Paper. Short-term notes (30, 60, 90, 120, 180, 270, and 360 days) sold in international money markets.

Eurocredit. Bank loans to MNEs, sovereign governments, international institutions, and banks denominated in Eurocurrencies and extended by banks in countries other than the country in whose currency the loan is denominated.

Eurocurrency. A currency deposited in a bank located in a country other than the country issuing the currency.

Eurodollar. A U.S. dollar deposited in a bank outside the United States. A Eurodollar is a type of Eurocurrency.

Euronote. Short- to medium-term debt instruments sold in the Eurocurrency market.

European Central Bank (ECB). Conducts monetary policy of the European Monetary Union. Its goal is to safeguard the stability of the euro and minimize inflation.

European Currency Unit (ECU). A composite currency created by the European Monetary System prior to the euro, which was designed to function as a reserve currency numeraire. The ECU was used as the numeraire for denominating a number of financial instruments and obligations.

European Economic Community (EEC). The European common market composed of Austria, Belgium, Denmark, Finland, France, Germany, Greece, Ireland,

Italy, Luxembourg, the Netherlands, Portugal, Spain, and the United Kingdom. Officially renamed the European Union (EU) January 1, 1994.

European Free Trade Association (EFTA). European countries not part of the European Union but having no internal tariffs.

European Monetary System (EMS). A monetary alliance of fifteen European countries (same members as the European Union).

European option. An option that can be exercised only on the day on which it expires.

European terms. Foreign exchange quotations for the U.S. dollar, expressed as the number of non-U.S. currency units per U.S. dollar.

European Union (EU). The official name of the former European Economic Community (EEC) as of January 1, 1994.

Ex dock. Followed by the name of a port of import. International trade term in which seller agrees to pay for the costs (shipping, insurance, customs duties, etc.) of placing the goods on the dock at the named port.

Exchange Rate Mechanism (ERM). The means by which members of the EMS formerly maintained their currency exchange rates within an agreed-upon range with respect to the other member currencies.

Exchange rate. The price of a unit of one country's currency expressed in terms of the currency of some other country.

Exchange rate pass-through. The degree to which the prices of imported and exported goods change as a result of exchange rate changes.

Export credit insurance. Provides assurance to the exporter or the exporter's bank that, should the foreign customer default on payment, the insurance company will pay for a major portion of the loss. *See also* Foreign Credit Insurance Association (FCIA).

Export-Import Bank (Eximbank). A U.S. government agency created to finance and otherwise facilitate imports and exports.

Expropriation. Official government seizure of private property, recognized by international law as the right of any sovereign state provided expropriated owners are given prompt compensation and fair market value in convertible currencies.

Factoring. Specialized firms, known as factors, purchase receivables at a discount on either a non-recourse or recourse basis.

FAF. Fly away free. International trade term.

FAQ. Free at quay. International trade term.

FAS. Free alongside. An international trade term in which the seller's quoted price for goods includes all costs of delivery of the goods alongside a vessel at the port of embarkation.

FASB 52. A regulation of the Financial Accounting Standards Board requiring U.S. companies to translate foreign subsidiary financial statements by the current rate (closing rate) method. FASB 52 became effective in 1981.

FASB 8. A regulation of the Financial Accounting Standards Board requiring U.S. companies to translate foreign affiliate financial statements by the temporal method. FASB 8 was in effect from 1976 to 1981. It is still used under specific circumstances.

FI. Free in. International trade term meaning that all expenses for loading into the hold of a vessel apply to the account of the consignee.

Financial account. A section of the balance of payments accounts. Under the revised format of the International Monetary Fund, the financial account measures long-term financial flows including direct foreign investment, portfolio investments, and other long-term movements. Under the traditional definition, which is still used by many countries, items in the financial account were included in the capital account.

Financial derivative. A financial instrument, such as a futures contract or option, whose value is derived from an underlying asset like a stock or currency.

Financial engineering. Those basic building blocks, such as spot positions, forwards, and options, used to construct positions that provide the user with desired risk and return characteristics.

Firm-specific risks. Political risks that affect the MNE at the project or corporate level. Governance risk due to goal conflict between an MNE and its host government is the main political firm-specific risk.

First in, first out (FIFO). An inventory valuation approach in which the cost of the earliest inventory purchases is charged against current sales. The opposite is LIFO, or last in, first out.

Fisher Effect. A theory that nominal interest rates in two or more countries should be equal to the required real rate of return to investors plus compensation for the expected amount of inflation in each country.

Fixed exchange rates. Foreign exchange rates tied to the currency of a major country (such as the United States), to gold, or to a basket of currencies such as Special Drawing Rights.

Flexible exchange rates. The opposite of fixed exchange rates. The foreign exchange rate is adjusted periodically by the country's monetary authorities in accordance with their judgment and/or an external set of economic indicators.

Floating exchange rates. Foreign exchange rates determined by demand and supply in an open market that is presumably free of government interference.

Floating rate note (FRN). Medium-term securities with interest rates pegged to LIBOR and adjusted quarterly or semiannually.

FOB. Free on board. International trade term in which exporter's quoted price includes the cost of loading goods into transport vessels at a named point.

Foreign affiliate. A foreign business unit that is less than 50% owned by the parent company.

Foreign bond. A bond issued by a foreign corporation or government for sale in the domestic capital market of another country, and denominated in the currency of that country.

Foreign Corrupt Practices Act of 1977. A U.S. law that punishes companies and their executives if they pay bribes or make other improper payments to foreigners.

Foreign Credit Insurance Association (FCIA). An unincorporated association of private commercial insurance companies, in cooperation with the Export-Import Bank of the United States, that provides export credit insurance to U.S. firms.

Foreign currency translation. The process of restating foreign currency accounts of subsidiaries into the reporting currency of the parent company in order to prepare a consolidated financial statement.

Foreign direct investment (FDI). Purchase of physical assets, such as plant and equipment, in a foreign country, to be managed by the parent corporation. FDI is distinguished from foreign portfolio investment.

Foreign exchange broker. An individual or firm that arranges foreign exchange transactions between two parties, but is not itself a principal in the trade. Foreign exchange brokers earn a commission for their efforts.

Foreign exchange dealer (or trader). An individual or firm that buys foreign exchange from one party (at a bid price), and then sells it (at an ask price) to another party. The dealer is a principal in two transactions and profits via the spread between the bid and ask prices.

Foreign exchange rate. The price of one country's currency in terms of another currency, or in terms of a commodity such as gold or silver. *See also* Exchange rate.

Foreign exchange risk. The likelihood that an unexpected change in exchange rates will alter the home currency value of foreign currency cash payments expected from a foreign source. Also, the likelihood that an unexpected change in exchange rates will alter the amount of home currency needed to repay a debt denominated in a foreign currency.

Foreign sales corporation (FSC). Under U.S. tax code, a type of foreign corporation that provides tax-exempt or tax-deferred income for U.S. persons or corporations having export-oriented activities.

Foreign tax credit. The amount by which a domestic firm may reduce (credit) domestic income taxes for income tax payments to a foreign government.

Forfaiting. A technique for arranging nonrecourse medium-term export financing, used most frequently to finance imports into Eastern Europe. A third party, usually a specialized financial institution, guarantees the financing.

Forward contract. An agreement to exchange currencies of different countries at a specified future date and at a specified forward rate.

Forward differential. The difference between spot and forward rates, expressed as an annual percentage.

Forward discount or premium. The same as forward differential.

Forward rate. An exchange rate quoted for settlement at some future date. The rate used in a forward transaction.

Forward rate agreement. An interbank-traded contract to buy or sell interest rate payments on a notional principal.

Forward transaction. An agreed-upon foreign exchange transaction to be settled at a specified future date, often one, two, or three months after the transaction date.

Free trade zone. An area within a country into which foreign goods may be brought duty free, often for purposes of additional manufacture, inventory storage, or packaging. Such goods are subject to duty only when they leave the duty-free zone to enter other parts of the country.

Freely floating exchange rates. Exchange rates determined in a free market without government interference, in contrast to dirty float.

Fronting loan. A parent-to-subsidiary loan that is channeled through a financial intermediary such as a large international bank in order to reduce political risk. Presumably government authorities are less likely to prevent a foreign subsidiary repaying an established bank than repaying the subsidiary's corporate parent.

Functional currency. In the context of translating financial statements, the currency of the primary economic environment in which a foreign subsidiary operates and in which it generates cash flows.

Futures, or futures contracts. Exchange-traded agreements calling for future delivery of a standard amount of any good, e.g., foreign exchange, at a fixed time, place, and price.

Gamma. A measure of the sensitivity of an option's delta ratio to small unit changes in the price of the underlying security.

Gap risk. A type of interest rate risk in which the timing of maturities is mismatched.

General Agreement on Tariffs and Trade (GATT). A framework of rules for nations to manage their trade policies, negotiate lower international tariff barriers, and settle trade disputes.

Generally Accepted Accounting Principles (GAAP). Approved accounting principles for U.S. firms, defined by the Financial Accounting Standards Board (FASB).

Geometric return. A calculation that uses the beginning and ending returns to calculate the annual average rate of compounded growth, similar to an internal rate of return.

Global registered shares. Similar to ordinary shares, global registered shares have the added benefit of being tradable on equity exchanges around the globe in a variety of currencies.

Global-specific risks. Political risks that originate at the global level, such as terrorism, the anti-globalization movement, environmental concerns, poverty, and cyber attacks.

Gold standard. A monetary system in which currencies are defined in terms of their gold content, and payment imbalances between countries are settled in gold.

Greenfield investment. An initial investment in a new foreign subsidiary with no predecessor operation in that location. This is in contrast to a new subsidiary created by the purchase of an already existing operation. Thus, a greenfield investment starts, conceptually if not literally, with an undeveloped "green field."

Gross up. *See* Deemed-paid tax.

Hard currency. A freely convertible currency that is not expected to depreciate in value in the foreseeable future.

Hedge. The purchase of a contract (including forward foreign exchange) or tangible good that will rise in value and offset a drop in value of another contract or tangible good. Hedges are undertaken to reduce risk by protecting an owner from loss.

Hedge accounting. An accounting procedure which specifies that gains and losses on hedging instruments be recognized in earnings at the same time that the effects of changes in the value of the items being hedged are recognized.

Historical exchange rate. In accounting, the exchange rate in effect when an asset or liability was acquired.

Hot money. Money which moves internationally from one currency and/or country to another in response to interest rate differences, and moves away immediately when the interest advantage disappears.

Hybrid foreign currency options. Purchase of a put option and the simultaneous sale of a call (or vice versa) so that the overall cost is less than the cost of a straight option.

Hyperinflation countries. Countries with a very high rate of inflation. Under United States FASB 52, these are defined as countries where the cumulative three-year inflation amounts to 100% or more.

IMM. International Monetary Market. A division of the Chicago Mercantile Exchange.

Impossible Trinity. An ideal currency would have exchange rate stability, full financial integration, and monetary independence.

Indirect quote. The price of a unit of a home country's currency expressed in terms of a foreign country's currency.

In-house bank. An internal bank established within an MNE if its needs are either too large or too sophisticated for local banks. The in-house bank is not a separate corporation but performs a set of functions by the existing treasury department. Acting as an independent entity, the in-house bank transacts with various internal business units of the firm on an arm's length basis.

Integrated foreign entity. An entity that operates as an extension of the parent company, with cash flows and general business lines that are highly interrelated with those of the parent.

Intellectual property rights. Legislation that grants the exclusive use of patented technology and copyrighted creative materials. A worldwide treaty to protect intellectual property rights has been ratified by most major countries, including most recently by China.

Interest rate futures. *See* Futures, or futures contracts.

Interest rate parity. A theory that the differences in national interest rates for securities of similar risk and maturity should be equal to but opposite in sign (positive or negative) to the forward exchange rate discount or premium for the foreign currency.

Interest rate swap. A transaction in which two counterparties exchange interest payment streams of different character (such as floating vs. fixed), based on an underlying notional principal amount.

Interest rate swaps. Contractual agreements to exchange or swap a series of interest cash flows.

Internal rate of return (IRR). A capital budgeting approach in which a discount rate is found that matches the present value of expected future cash inflows with the present value of outflows.

Internalization. A theory that the key ingredient for maintaining a firm-specific competitive advantage in international competition is the possession of proprietary information and control of human capital that can generate new information through expertise in research, management, marketing, or technology.

International Bank for Reconstruction and Development (IBRD, or World Bank). International development bank owned by member nations that makes development loans to member countries.

International Banking Facility (IBF). A department within a U.S. bank that may accept foreign deposits and make loans to foreign borrowers as if it were a foreign subsidiary. IBFs are free of U.S. reserve requirements, deposit insurance, and interest rate regulations.

International Capital Asset Pricing Model. A strategy in which the primary distinction in the estimation of the cost of equity for an individual firm using an internationalized version of the domestic capital asset pricing model is the definition of the "market" and a recalculation of the firm's beta for that market.

International Fisher Effect. A theory that the spot exchange rate should change by an amount equal to the difference in interest rates between two countries.

International Monetary Fund (IMF). An international organization created in 1944 to promote exchange rate stability and provide temporary financing for countries experiencing balance of payments difficulties.

International Monetary Market (IMM). A branch of the Chicago Mercantile Exchange which specializes in trading currency and financial futures contracts.

International monetary system. The structure within which foreign exchange rates are determined, international trade and capital flows are accommodated, and balance of payments adjustments made.

In-the-money. Circumstance in which an option is profitable, excluding the cost of the premium, if exercised immediately.

Intrinsic value. The financial gain if an option is exercised immediately.

Investment agreement. An agreement that spells out specific rights and responsibilities of both the investing foreign firm and the host government.

Joint venture. A business venture that is owned by two or more entities, often from different countries.

Jumbo loans. Loans of $1 billion or more.

Kangaroo bonds. Australian dollar-denominated bonds issued within Australia by a foreign borrower.

Lag. In the context of leads and lags, payment of a financial obligation later than is expected or required.

Lambda. A measure of the sensitivity of an option premium to a unit change in volatility.

Last in, first out (LIFO). An inventory valuation approach in which the cost of the latest inventory purchases is charged against current sales. The opposite is FIFO, or first in, first out.

Law of one price. The concept that if an identical product or service can be sold in two different markets, and no restrictions exist on the sale or transportation costs of moving the product between markets, the product's price should be the same in both markets.

Lead. In the context of leads and lags, the payment of a financial obligation earlier than is expected or required.

Letter of credit (L/C). An instrument issued by a bank, in which the bank promises to pay a beneficiary upon presentation of documents specified in the letter.

Link financing. *See* Back-to-back loan or Fronting loan.

Location-specific advantage. Market imperfections or genuine comparative advantages that attract foreign direct investment to particular locations.

London Interbank Offered Rate (LIBOR). The deposit rate applicable to interbank loans in London. LIBOR is used as the reference rate for many international interest rate transactions.

Long position. A position in which foreign currency assets exceed foreign currency liabilities. The opposite of a long position is a short position.

Maastricht Treaty. A treaty among the 12 European Union countries that specified a plan and timetable for the introduction of a single European currency, to be called the euro.

Macro risk. *See* Country-specific risk.

Macroeconomic uncertainty. Operating exposure's sensitivity to key macroeconomic variables, such as exchange rates, interest rates, and inflation rates.

Managed float. A country allows its currency to trade within a given band of exchange rates.

Margin. A deposit made as security for a financial transaction otherwise financed on credit.

Marked to market. The condition in which the value of a futures contract is assigned to market value daily, and all changes in value are paid in cash daily. The value of the contract is revalued using the closing price for the day. The amount to be paid is called the variation margin.

Market liquidity. The degree to which a firm can issue a new security without depressing the existing market price, as well as the degree to which a change in price of its securities elicits a substantial order flow.

Market segmentation. The divergence within a national market of required rates of return. If all capital markets are fully integrated, securities of comparable expected return and risk should have the same required rate of return in each national market after adjusting for foreign exchange risk and political risk.

Matching currency cash flows. The strategy of offsetting anticipated continuous long exposure to a particular currency by acquiring debt denominated in that currency.

Merchant bank. A bank that specializes in helping corporations and governments finance by any of a variety of market and/or traditional techniques. European merchant banks are sometimes differentiated from clearing banks, which tend to focus on bank deposits and clearing balances for the majority of the population.

Micro risk. *See* Firm-specific risk.

Monetary assets or liabilities. Assets in the form of cash or claims to cash (such as accounts receivable), or liabilities payable in cash. Monetary assets minus monetary liabilities are called net monetary assets.

Monetary/nonmonetary method. A method of translating the financial statements of foreign subsidiaries into the parent's reporting currency. All monetary accounts are translated at the current rate, and all nonmonetary accounts are translated at their historical rates. Sometimes called temporal method in the United States.

Money market hedge. The use of foreign currency borrowing to reduce transaction or accounting foreign exchange exposure.

Money markets. The financial markets in various countries in which various types of short-term debt instruments, including bank loans, are purchased and sold.

Mortgage Backed Security (MBO). A derivative security composed of residential or commercial real estate mortgages.

Most-favored-nation (MFN) treatment. The application by a country of import duties on the same, or most favored, basis to all countries accorded such treatment. Any tariff reduction granted in a bilateral negotiation will be extended to all other nations granted most-favored-nation status.

Multinational enterprise (MNE). A firm that has operating subsidiaries, branches, or affiliates located in foreign countries.

NSF. Not-sufficient funds. Term used by a bank when a draft or check is drawn on an account not having a sufficient credit balance.

Negotiable instrument. A written draft or promissory note, signed by the maker or drawer, that contains an unconditional promise or order to pay a definite sum of money on demand or at a determinable future date, and is payable to order or to bearer. A holder of a negotiable instrument is entitled to payment despite any personal disagreements between the drawee and maker.

Nepotism. The practice of showing favor to relatives over other qualified persons in conferring such benefits as the awarding of contracts, granting of special prices, promotions to various ranks, etc.

Net present value. A capital budgeting approach in which the present value of expected future cash inflows is subtracted from the present value of outflows.

Netting. The mutual offsetting of sums due between two or more business entities.

Nominal exchange rate. The actual foreign exchange quotation, in contrast to real exchange rate, which is adjusted for changes in purchasing power.

Nontariff barrier. Trade restrictive practices other than custom tariffs, such as import quotas, voluntary restrictions, variable levies, and special health regulations.

North American Free Trade Agreement (NAFTA). A treaty allowing free trade and investment between Canada, the United States, and Mexico.

Note issuance facility (NIF). An agreement by which a syndicate of banks indicates a willingness to accept short-term notes from borrowers and resell those notes in the Eurocurrency markets. The discount rate is often tied to LIBOR.

Notional principal. The size of a derivative contract, in total currency value, as used in futures contracts, forward contracts, option contracts, or swap agreements.

NPV. *See* Net present value.

O/A. Open account. Arrangement in which the importer (or other buyer) pays for the goods only after the goods are received and inspected. The importer is billed directly after shipment, and payment is not tied to any promissory notes or similar documents.

Offer. The price at which a trader is willing to sell foreign exchange, securities, or commodities. Also called ask.

Official reserves account. Total reserves held by official monetary authorities within the country, such as gold, SDRs, and major currencies.

Offshore finance subsidiary. A foreign financial subsidiary owned by a corporation in another country. Offshore finance subsidiaries are usually located in tax-free or low-tax jurisdictions to enable the parent multinational firm to finance international operations without being subject to home country taxes or regulations.

OLI paradigm. An attempt to create an overall framework to explain why MNEs choose foreign direct investment rather than serve foreign markets through alternative modes such as licensing, joint ventures, strategic alliances, management contracts, and exporting.

Operating exposure. The potential for a change in expected cash flows, and thus in value, of a foreign subsidiary as a result of an unexpected change in exchange rates. Also called economic exposure.

Option. In foreign exchange, a contract giving the purchaser the right, but not the obligation, to buy or sell a given amount of foreign exchange at a fixed price per unit for a specified time period. Options to buy are calls and options to sell are puts.

Order bill of lading. A shipping document through which possession and title to the shipment reside with the owner of the bill.

Organization of Petroleum Exporting Countries (OPEC). An alliance of most major crude oil producing countries, formed for the purpose of allocating and controlling production quotas so as to influence the price of crude oil in world markets.

Originate-to-Distribute (OTD). A common practice in the U.S. real estate market during the 2001–2007 real estate boom in which a real estate lender, or originator, makes loans expressly for the purpose of immediate resale.

Out-of-the-money. An option that would not be profitable, excluding the cost of the premium, if exercised immediately.

Outright quotation. The full price, in one currency, of a unit of another currency. *See* Points quotation.

Outsourcing. *See* Supply chain management.

Overseas Private Investment Corporation (OPIC). A U.S. government-owned insurance company that insures U.S. corporations against various political risks.

Over-the-counter market. A market for share of stock, options (including foreign currency options), or other financial contracts conducted via electronic connections between dealers. The over-the-counter market has no physical location or address, and is thus differentiated from organized exchanges which have a physical location where trading takes place.

Overvalued currency. A currency with a current foreign exchange value (i.e., current price in the foreign exchange market) greater than the worth of that currency. Because "worth" is a subjective concept, overvaluation is a matter of opinion. If the euro has a current market value of $1.20 (i.e., the current exchange rate is $1.20/€) at a time when its "true" value as derived from purchasing power parity or some other method is deemed to be $1.10, the euro is overvalued. The opposite of overvalued is undervalued.

Owner-specific advantage. A firm must have competitive advantages in its home market. These must be firm-specific, not easily copied, and in a form that allows them to be transferred to foreign subsidiaries.

Parallel loan. Another name for a back-to-back loan, in which two companies in separate countries borrow each other's currency for a specific period of time, and repay the other's currency at an agreed maturity.

Parallel market. An unofficial foreign exchange market tolerated by a government but not officially sanctioned. The exact boundary between a parallel market and a black market is not very clear, but official tolerance of what would otherwise be a black market leads to use of the term parallel market.

Parity conditions. In the context of international finance, a set of basic economic relationships that provide for equilibrium between spot and forward foreign exchange rates, interest rates, and inflation rates.

Participating forward. A complex option position which combines a bought put and a sold call option at the same strike price to create a net zero position. Also called zero-cost option and forward participation agreement.

Phi. The expected change in an option premium caused by a small change in the foreign interest rate (interest rate for the foreign currency).

Points. The smallest units of price change quoted, given a conventional number of digits in which a quotation is stated.

Points quotation. A forward quotation expressed only as the number of decimal points (usually four decimal points) by which it differs from the spot quotation.

Political risk. The possibility that political events in a particular country will influence the economic well-being of firms in that country. *See also* Sovereign risk.

Portfolio investment. Purchase of foreign stocks and bonds, in contrast to foreign direct investment.

Possessions corporation. A U.S. corporation, the subsidiary of another U.S. corporation located in a U.S. possession such as Puerto Rico, which for tax purposes is treated as if it were a foreign corporation.

Premium. In a foreign exchange market, the amount by which a currency is more expensive for future delivery than for spot (immediate) delivery. The opposite of premium is discount.

Prime mortgage. A mortgage categorized as conforming (also referred to as conventional loans), meaning it would meet the guarantee requirements for resale to Government-Sponsored Enterprises (GSEs) Fannie Mae and Freddie Mac.

Private placement. The sale of a security issue to a small set of qualified institutional buyers.

Project finance. Arrangement of financing for long-term capital projects, large in scale, long in life, and generally high in risk.

Protectionism. A political attitude or policy intended to inhibit or prohibit the import of foreign goods and services. The opposite of free trade policies.

Psychic distance. Firms tend to invest first in countries with a similar cultural, legal, and institutional environment.

Purchasing power parity. A theory that the price of internationally traded commodities should be the same in every country, and hence the exchange rate between the two currencies should be the ratio of prices in the two countries.

Put. An option to sell foreign exchange or financial contracts. *See* Option.

Qualified institutional buyer. An entity (except a bank or a savings and loan) that owns and invests on a discretionary basis a minimum of $100 million in securities of non-affiliates.

Quota. A limit, mandatory or voluntary, set on the import of a product.

Quotation. In foreign exchange trading, the pair of prices (bid and ask) at which a dealer is willing to buy or sell foreign exchange.

Range forward. A complex option position that combines the purchase of a put option and the sale of a call option with strike prices equidistant from the forward rate. Also called flexible forward, cylinder option, option fence, mini-max, and zero-cost tunnel.

Real exchange rate. An index of foreign exchange adjusted for relative price-level changes from a base point in time, typically a month or a year. Sometimes referred to as real effective exchange rate, it is used to measure purchasing-power-adjusted changes in exchange rates.

Real option analysis. The application of option theory to capital budgeting decisions.

Reference rate. The rate of interest used in a standardized quotation, loan agreement, or financial derivative valuation.

Registered bond. Corporate or governmental debt in a bond form in which the owner's name appears on the bond and in the issuer's records, and interest payments are made to the owner.

Reinvoicing center. A central financial subsidiary used by a multinational firm to reduce transaction exposure by having all home country exports billed in the home currency and then reinvoiced to each operating subsidiary in that subsidiary's local currency.

Relative purchasing power parity. A theory that if the spot exchange rate between two countries starts in equilibrium, any change in the differential rate of inflation between them tends to be offset over the long run by an equal but opposite change in the spot exchange rate.

Reporting currency. In the context of translating financial statements, the currency in which a parent firm prepares its own financial statements. Usually this is the parent's home currency.

Repositioning funds. The movement of funds from one currency or country to another. An MNE faces a variety of political, tax, foreign exchange, and liquidity constraints that limit its ability to move funds easily and without cost.

Representative office. A representative office established by a bank in a foreign country to help clients doing business in that country. It also functions as a geographically convenient location from which to visit correspondent banks in its region rather than sending bankers from the parent bank at greater financial and physical cost.

Repricing risk. The risk of changes in interest rates charged or earned at the time a financial contract's rate is reset.

Revaluation. A rise in the foreign exchange value of a currency that is pegged to other currencies or to gold. Also called appreciation.

Rho. The expected change in an option premium caused by a small change in the domestic interest rate (interest rate for the home currency).

Risk. The likelihood that an actual outcome will differ from an expected outcome. The actual outcome could be better or worse than expected (two-sided risk), although in common practice risk is more often used only in the context of an adverse outcome (one-sided risk). Risk can exist for any number of uncertain future situations, including future spot rates or the results of political events.

Risk-sharing agreement. A contractual arrangement in which the buyer and seller agree to share or split currency movement impacts on payments between them.

Rules of the Game. The basis of exchange rate determination under the international gold standard during most of the 19th and early 20th centuries. All countries agreed informally to follow the rule of buying and selling their currency at a fixed and predetermined price against gold.

Samurai bonds. Yen-denominated bonds issued within Japan by a foreign borrower.

Sarbanes-Oxley Act. An act passed in 2002 to regulate corporate governance in the United States.

SEC Rule 144A. Permits qualified institutional buyers to trade privately placed securities without requiring SEC registration.

Section 482. The set of U.S. Treasury regulations governing transfer prices.

Securitization. The replacement of nonmarketable loans (such as direct bank loans) with negotiable securities (such as publicly traded marketable notes and bonds), so that the risk can be spread widely among many investors, each of whom can add or subtract the amount of risk carried by buying or selling the marketable security.

Self-sustaining foreign entity. One that operates in the local economic environment independent of the parent company.

Shared services. A charge to compensate the parent for costs incurred in the general management of international operations and for other corporate services provided to foreign subsidiaries that must be recovered by the parent firm.

Shareholder wealth maximization. The corporate goal of maximizing the total value of the shareholders' investment in the company.

Sharpe measure. Calculates the average return over and above the risk-free rate of return per unit of portfolio risk. It uses the standard deviation of a portfolio's total return as the measure of risk.

Shogun bonds. Foreign currency-denominated bonds issued within Japan by Japanese corporations.

Short position. *See* Long position.

SIBOR. Singapore interbank offered rate.

Sight draft. A bill of exchange (B/E) that is due on demand; i.e., when presented to the bank. *See also* Bill of exchange.

SIMEX. Singapore International Monetary Exchange.

SIV. Structure Investment Vehicle. The SIV is an off-balance-sheet entity first created by Citigroup in 1988. It was designed to allow a bank to create an investment entity which would invest in long term and higher yielding assets such as speculative grade bonds, mortgage-backed securities (MBSs) and collateralized debt obligations (CDOs), while funding itself through commercial paper (CP) issuances.

Society for Worldwide Interbank Financial Telecommunications (SWIFT). A dedicated computer network providing funds transfer messages between member banks around the world.

Soft currency. A currency expected to drop in value relative to other currencies. Free trading in a currency deemed soft is often restricted by the monetary authorities of the issuing country.

Sovereign risk. The risk that a host government may unilaterally repudiate its foreign obligations or may prevent local firms from honoring their foreign obligations. Sovereign risk is often regarded as a subset of political risk.

Special Drawing Right (SDR). An international reserve asset, defined by the International Monetary Fund as the value of a weighted basket of five currencies.

Speculation. An attempt to make a profit by trading on expectations about future prices.

Spot rate. The price at which foreign exchange can be purchased (its bid) or sold (its ask) in a spot transaction. *See* Spot transaction.

Spot transaction. A foreign exchange transaction to be settled (paid for) on the second following business day.

Spread. The difference between the bid (buying) quote and the ask (selling) quote.

Stakeholder capitalism. Another name for corporate wealth maximization.

Strategic alliance. A formal relationship, short of a merger or acquisition, between two companies, formed for the purpose of gaining synergies because in some aspect the two companies complement each other.

Stripped bonds. Bonds issued by investment bankers against coupons or the maturity (corpus) portion of original bearer bonds, where the original bonds are held in trust by the investment banker. Whereas the original bonds will have coupons promising interest at each interest date (say June and December for each of the next twenty years), a given stripped bond will represent a claim against all interest payments from the entire original issue due on a particular interest date. A stripped bond is in effect a zero coupon bond manufactured by the investment banker.

Subpart F. A type of foreign income, as defined in the U.S. tax code, which under certain conditions is taxed immediately in the United States even though it has not been repatriated to the United States. It is income of a type that is otherwise easily shifted offshore to avoid current taxation.

Subprime mortgage. Subprime borrowers have a higher perceived risk of default, normally as a result of credit history elements which may include bankruptcy, loan delinquency, default, or simply a borrower with limited experience or history of debt. They are nearly exclusively floating-rate structures, and carry significantly higher interest rate spreads over the floating bases like LIBOR.

Subsidiary. A foreign operation incorporated in the host country and owned 50% or more by a parent corporation. Foreign operations that are not incorporated are called branches.

Supply chain management. A strategy that focuses on cost reduction through imports from less costly foreign locations with lower wages.

Sushi bonds. Eurodollar or other non-yen-denominated bonds issued by a Japanese corporation for sale to Japanese investors.

Swap. This term is used in many contexts. In general it is the simultaneous purchase and sale of foreign exchange or securities, with the purchase executed at once and the sale back to the same party carried out at an agreed-upon price to be completed at a specified future date. Swaps include interest rate swaps, currency swaps, and credit swaps. A swap rate is a forward foreign exchange quotation expressed in terms of the number of points by which the forward rate differs from the spot rate.

SWIFT. *See* Society for Worldwide Interbank Financial Telecommunications.

Syndicated loan. A large loan made by a group of banks to a large multinational firm or government. Syndicated loans allow the participating banks to maintain diversification by not lending too much to a single borrower.

Synthetic forward. A complex option position which combines the purchase of a put option and the sale of a call option, or vice versa, both at the forward rate.

Systematic risk. In portfolio theory, the risk of the market itself, i.e., risk that cannot be diversified away.

T/A. Trade acceptance. International trade term.

Tariff. A duty or tax on imports that can be levied as a percentage of cost or as a specific amount per unit of import.

Tax deferral. Foreign subsidiaries of MNEs pay host country corporate income taxes, but many parent countries, including the United States, defer claiming additional taxes on that foreign source income until it is remitted to the parent firm.

Tax exposure. The potential for tax liability on a given income stream or on the value of an asset. Usually used in the context of a multinational firm being able to minimize its tax liabilities by locating some portion of operations in a country where the tax liability is minimized.

Tax haven. A country with either no or very low tax rates that uses its tax structure to attract foreign investment or international financial dealings.

Tax morality. The consideration of conduct by an MNE to decide whether to follow a practice of full disclosure to local tax authorities or adopt the philosophy, "When in Rome, do as the Romans do."

Tax neutrality. In domestic tax, the requirement that the burden of taxation on earnings in home country operations by an MNE be equal to the burden of taxation on each currency equivalent of profit earned by the same firm in its foreign operations. Foreign tax neutrality requires that the tax burden on each foreign subsidiary of the firm be equal to the tax burden on its competitors in the same country.

Tax treaties. A network of bilateral treaties that provide a means of reducing double taxation.

Technical analysis. The focus on price and volume data to determine past trends that are expected to continue into the future. Analysts believe that future exchange rates are based on the current exchange rate.

TED Spread. Treasury Eurodollar Spread. The difference, in basis points, between the 3-month interest rate swap index or the 3-month LIBOR interest rate, and the 90-day U.S. Treasury bill rate. It is sometimes used as an indicator of credit crisis or fear over bank credit quality.

Temporal method. In the United States, term for a codification of a translation method essentially similar to the monetary/nonmonetary method.

Tequila effect. Term used to describe how the Mexican peso crisis of December 1994 quickly spread to other Latin American currency and equity markets through the contagion effect.

Terms of trade. The weighted average exchange ratio between a nation's export prices and its import prices, used to measure gains from trade. Gains from trade refers to increases in total consumption resulting from production specialization and international trade.

Territorial approach to taxes. Taxation of income earned by firms within the legal jurisdiction of the host country, not on the country of the firm's incorporation.

Theta. The expected change in an option premium caused by a small change in the time to expiration.

Time draft. A draft that allows a delay in payment. It is presented to the drawee, who accepts it by writing a notice of acceptance on its face. Once accepted, the time draft becomes a promise to pay by the accepting party. *See also* Bankers' acceptance.

Total Shareholder Return (TSR). A measure of corporate performance based on the sum of share price appreciation and current dividends.

Tranche. An allocation of shares, typically to underwriters that are expected to sell to investors in their designated geographic markets.

Transaction exposure. The potential for a change in the value of outstanding financial obligations entered into prior to a change in exchange rates but not due to be settled until after the exchange rates change.

Transfer pricing. The setting of prices to be charged by one unit (such as a foreign subsidiary) of a multiunit corporation to another unit (such as the parent corporation) for goods or services sold between such related units.

Translation exposure. The potential for an accounting-derived change in owners' equity resulting from exchange rate changes and the need to restate financial statements of foreign subsidiaries in the single currency of the parent corporation. *See also* Accounting exposure.

Transnational firm. A company owned by a coalition of investors located in different countries.

Transparency. The degree to which an investor can discern the true activities and value drivers of a company from the disclosures and financial results reported.

Treynor measure. A calculation of the average return over and above the risk-free rate of return per unit of portfolio risk. It uses the portfolio's beta as the measure of risk.

Unbiased predictor. A theory that spot prices at some future date will be equal to today's forward rates.

Unbundling. Dividing cash flows from a subsidiary to a parent into their many separate components, such as royalties, lease payments, dividends, etc., so as to increase the likelihood that some fund flows will be allowed during economically difficult times.

Uncovered interest arbitrage. The process by which investors borrow in countries and currencies exhibiting relatively low interest rates and convert the proceeds into currencies that offer much higher interest rates. The transaction is "uncovered" because the investor does not sell the higher yielding currency proceeds forward.

Undervalued. The status of currency with a current foreign exchange value (i.e., current price in the foreign exchange market) below the worth of that currency. Because "worth" is a subjective concept, undervaluation is a matter of opinion. If the euro has a current market value of $1.20 (i.e., the current exchange rate is $1.20/€) at a time when its "true" value as derived from purchasing power parity or some other method is deemed to be $1.30, the euro is undervalued. The opposite of undervalued is overvalued.

Unsystematic risk. In a portfolio, the amount of risk that can be eliminated by diversification.

Value-added tax. A type of national sales tax collected at each stage of production or sale of consumption goods, and levied in proportion to the value added during that stage.

Value date. The date when value is given (i.e., funds are deposited) for foreign exchange transactions between banks.

Value today. A spot foreign exchange transaction in which delivery and payment are made on the same day as the contract. Normal delivery is two business days after the contract.

Value tomorrow. A spot foreign exchange transaction in which delivery and payment are made on the next business day after the contract. Normal delivery is two business days after the contract.

Volatility. In connection with options, the standard deviation of daily spot price movement.

Weighted average cost of capital (WACC). The sum of the proportionally weighted costs of different sources of capital, used as the minimum acceptable target return on new investments.

World Bank. *See* International Bank for Reconstruction and Development.

Worldwide approach to taxes. The principle that taxes are levied on the income earned by firms that are incorporated in a host country, regardless of where the income was earned.

Yankee bonds. Dollar-denominated bonds issued within the United States by a foreign borrower.

Yield to maturity. The rate of interest (discount) which equates future cash flows of a bond, both interest and principal, with the present market price. Yield to maturity is thus the time-adjusted rate of return earned by a bond investor.

Zero coupon bond. A bond which pays no periodic interest, but returns a given amount of principal at a stated maturity date. Zero coupon bonds are sold at a discount from the maturity amount to provide the holder a compound rate of return for the holding period.

Index

Credits

Chapter 1

Global Finance in Practice 1.1	From "US Companies Choose: National Multinational or 'A-National'?," Francesco Guerrera, *Financial Times*, August 16, 2007, p. 7. ©2007 *Financial Times*. Reproduced by permission.
Chapter 1 Mini-Case	©2007 Thunderbird School of Global Management. Reprinted by permission of the author.

Chapter 2

Global Finance in Practice 2.1	©June 2007, *Le Figaro*, Reproduced by permission.
Exhibit 2.4	Country Governance Rankings as of September 23, 2008, from www.gmiratings.com. Reproduced by permission of Governance Metrics International.
Exhibits 2.5 and 2.6	Harbula, Peter. "The Ownership Structure, Governance, and Performance of French Companies" from *Journal of Applied Corporate Finance*, Volume 19, Number 1, Winter 2007. Reproduced by permission of Wiley-Blackwell Publishing.
Global Finance in Practice 2.2	From "Shortcomings in China's Corporate Governance Regime," Johnny K. W. Cheung, China Law & Practice, February 2007. ©2007 China Law & Practice. Reproduced by permission.

Chapter 3

Exhibit 3.2	From International Financial Statistics, www.imfstatistics.org. Reproduced by permission of International Monetary Fund.
Exhibit 3.4	Adapted from Lars Oxelheim, *International Financial Integration*, Springer-Verlag, 1990, p. 10. Reproduced with kind permission of Springer Science+Business Media.
Exhibits 3.5 and 3.7	©2001 Pacific Exchange Rate Service (fx.sauder.ubc.ca). Reprinted by permission of Werner Antweiler.
Chapter 3 Mini-Case	©2005 Thunderbird School of Global Management. Reprinted by permission of the author.
Chapter 3 Mini-Case Exhibit 1	©2005 Pacific Exchange Rate Service (fx.sauder.ubc.ca). Reprinted by permission of Werner Antweiler.

Chapter 4

Exhibits 4.2–4.7	From *Balance of Payments Statistics Yearbook*, 2008. Reprinted by permission of International Monetary Fund.
Global Finance in Practice 4.2	©2003 The Economist Newspaper Limited, London. Reproduced by permission.
Exhibit 4.9	Obstfeld, M. and A. M. Taylor, "A Stylized View of Capital Mobility in Modern History," from M. D. Bordo, A. M. Taylor, and J. G. Williamson, eds., *Globalization in Historical Perspective*, Chicago: University of Chicago Press, 2001. Reprinted by permission of University of Chicago Press.
Chapter 4 Mini-Case, Exhibits 2 and 3	From *Balance of Payments Statistics Yearbook*, 2001. Reprinted by permission of International Monetary Fund.

Chapter 5

Exhibit 5.10	British Bankers Association (BBA), Overnight Lending Rates. Reproduced by permission.
Global Finance in Practice 5.2	*Berkshire Hathaway Annual Report*, 2008, Letter to Shareholders, pp. 14–15. Reproduced by permission.

Chapter 6

Exhibit 6.1	©2001. Reprinted by permission of Federal Reserve Bank of New York.
Global Finance in Practice 6.1	Foreign Exchange and Money Market Transactions, UBS Investment Bank, Spring 2004. ©2004 UBS. All rights reserved. Reproduced with permission.
Global Finance in Practice 6.2	"A Hedge Against Forex Exposure," *Financial Times*, August 2, 2005. ©2005 *Financial Times*. Reproduced by permission.
Chapter 6 Mini-Case	©2004 Thunderbird School of Global Management. Reprinted by permission of the author.

Chapter 7

Exhibit 7.1	©2008 The Economist Newspaper Limited, London. Reproduced by permission.
Exhibit 7.3	From *International Financial Statistics*, December 2008, annual, series REU. Reprinted by permission of International Monetary Fund.
Global Finance in Practice 7.1	Dimson, Elroy. *Triumph of the Optimists.* ©2002 Elroy Dimson, Paul Marsh, and Mike Staunton. Published by Princeton University Press. Reproduced by permission of Princeton University Press.
Global Finance in Practice 7.2	"Shopping, Cooking, Cleaning . . . Playing the Yen Carry Trade; Stories—Inquiry; Why Japanese housewives added international finance to their list of daily chores." *Financial Times*, Feb 21, 2009. ©2009 *Financial Times*. Reproduced by permission.
Table, p. 190	Copyright ©1999 The Economist Newspaper Limited, London. Reproduced by permission.

Chapter 8

Extract, p. 221	From "The New Religion of Risk Management" by Peter L. Bernstein, March–April 1996. ©1996 Harvard Business School Publishing Corporation; all rights reserved. Reprinted by permission of *Harvard Business Review*.
Chapter 8 Mini-Case	*Berkshire Hathaway Annual Report*, 2008, Letter to Shareholders, pp. 14–15. Reproduced by permission.
Exhibit 8A.1	From Stoll, Hans R. and Robert E. Whaley, *Futures and Options*, 1E. ©1993 South-Western, a part of Cengage Learning, Inc. www.cengage.com/permissions. Reproduced by permission.

Chapter 9

Exhibit 9.1	*Hedging Instruments for Foreign Exchange, Monday Market, and Precious Metals.* ©UBS. All rights reserved. Reproduced with permission.

Chapter 10

Extract, p. 261	Solnik, International Investments, ©2000 Pearson Education, Inc. Reproduced by permission of Pearson Education, Inc.
Exhibit 10.2	From *International Financial Statistics*, October–November 1997. Reprinted by permission of International Monetary Fund.
Exhibit 10.3	©1999 Pacific Exchange Rate Service (fx.sauder.ubc.ca). Reprinted by permission of Werner Antweiler.
Exhibits 10.4 and 10.5	From *Political Risk Services*, Argentina Economic Development Agency. Reprinted by permission of International Monetary Fund.
Exhibit 10.6	©2002 Pacific Exchange Rate Service (fx.sauder.ubc.ca). Reprinted by permission of Werner Antweiler.
Problems 1, 4, and 9, graphs, pp. 277 and 278	©2007 Pacific Exchange Rate Service (fx.sauder.ubc.ca). Reprinted by permission of Werner Antweiler.

Chapter 12

Global Finance in Practice 12.2	"Detroit Winners," *Financial Times*, Wednesday, September 5, 2007, p. 12. ©2007 *Financial Times*. Reproduced by permission.

Chapter 13

Exhibit 13.1	From FASB Statement No. 52, Foreign Currency Translation. Reprinted with permission of the FASB.
Global Finance in Practice 13.1	"Gyrus Hurt by Dollar Weakness," *Financial Times*, September 18, 2007. ©2007 *Financial Times*. Reproduced by permission.
Global Finance in Practice 13.2, table	©2000 The McGraw-Hill Companies, Inc. Reprinted from December 4, 2000 issue of *BusinessWeek* by special permission.
Ch 13 Mini-Case, diagrams	©2004 Pacific Exchange Rate Service (fx.sauder.ubc.ca). Reprinted by permission of Werner Antweiler.

Chapter 14

Exhibit 14.4	Elroy Dimson, Paul Marsh, and Mike Staunton, "Global Evidence on the Equity Risk Premium," *Journal of Applied Corporate Finance*, 2003, Volume 15, Number 4, p. 31. Reproduced by permission of Wiley-Blackwell Publishing.

| Chapter 14 Mini-Case | Stonehill, Arthur I. and Kare B. Dullum, *Internationalizing the Cost of Capital in Theory and Practice: The Novo Experience and National Policy Implications*. ©1982 John Wiley & Sons, Ltd. Reproduced by permission of John Wiley & Sons Ltd. |

Chapter 15

| Exhibit 15.1 | Oxelheim, Stonehill, Randoy, Vikkula, Dullum, and Moden, *Corporate Strategies in Internationalizing the Cost of Capital*. ©1998 Copenhagen Business School Press. Reproduced by permission. |
| Exhibit 15.3 | ©The Bank of New York Mellon. Reproduced by permission. |

Chapter 16

| Global Finance in Practice 16.2 | Abstracted from Morais, Richard C., "Islamic Finance—'Don't Call It Interest'", *Forbes*, July 23, 2007. Reprinted by permission of *Forbes Magazine*. ©2009 Forbes LLC. |

Chapter 17

Exhibits 17.7 and 17.8	Dimson, Elroy. *Triumph of the Optimists*. ©2002 Elroy Dimson, Paul Marsh, and Mike Staunton. Published by Princeton University Press. Reproduced by permission of Princeton University Press.
Global Finance in Practice 17.2	Dimson, Elroy. *Triumph of the Optimists*. ©2002 Elroy Dimson, Paul Marsh, and Mike Staunton. Published by Princeton University Press. Reproduced by permission of Princeton University Press.
Chapter 17 Mini-Case	©2007 SmartMoney. All rights reserved. SmartMoney is a registered trademark of SmartMoney a Joint Venture of Dow Jones & Co., Inc & Hearst SM Partnership. Reproduced by permission of SmartMoney.

Chapter 18

Exhibit 18.1	From "The Competitive Advantage of Nations" by Michael Porter, March-April 1990. ©1990 Harvard Business School Publishing Corporation. All rights reserved. Reprinted by permission of *Harvard Business Review*.
Exhibit 18.2	From *International Business Review*, Volume 10, Lars Oxelheim, Arthur Stonehill, and Trond Randoy, "On the Treatment of Finance Specific Factors Within the OLI Paradigm," pp. 381–398, ©2001. Reprinted with permission from Elsevier Science.
Exhibit 18.3	Adapted from Dufey, Gunter and R. Mirus, "Foreign Direct Investment: Theory and Strategic Considerations," unpublished, University of Michigan, 1985. All rights reserved. Reprinted with permission from the authors.
Exhibit 18.4	©2006 The McGraw-Hill Companies, Inc. Reprinted from July 31, 2006 *BusinessWeek* by special permission.
Global Finance in Practice 18.2	Prasso, Sheridan. "Zimbabwe's Disposable Currency" from *Fortune*, August 6, 2007. ©2007 Time Inc. All rights reserved. Reproduced by permission.

Chapter 19

| Global Finance in Practice 19.1 | Abstracted from "Project Finance: Boom Brings Strong Demand," *Financial Times*, November 28, 2006. ©2006 *Financial Times*. Reproduced by permission. |

Chapter 20

Exhibit 20.1	©2009 PricewaterhouseCoopers. All rights reserved. Reproduced by permission.
Exhibit 20.2	©2008 KPMG. Reproduced by permission.
Global Finance in Practice 20.1	Myers, Randy, "Taxed to the Max," *CFO Magazine*, March 1, 2009. ©2009 CFO Publishing Corporation. All rights reserved. Reproduced by permission.
Global Finance in Practice 20.1, graph	From Taxfoundation.org. Reproduced by permission.

Chapter 21

| Global Finance in Practice 21.1 | Based on "Shift in Distribution Network Hits Gillette Stocks," *The Business Standard*, Hyderabad, India, Monday, May 15, 2006. ©2006 Business Standard Limited. Reproduced by permission. |

Chapter 22

| Global Finance in Practice 22.1 | ©2009 The India Today Group. |
| Global Finance in Practice 22.2 | From Yedder, Omar Ben, "Tuninvest Sustainable Profits," *African Business*, October 2007. Reproduced by permission of IC Publications Ltd. |

Currencies of the World

Country	Currency	ISO-4217 Code	Symbol
Afghanistan	Afghan afghani	AFN	
Albania	Albanian lek	ALL	
Algeria	Algerian dinar	DZD	
American Samoa	see United States		
Andorra	see Spain and France		
Angola	Angolan kwanza	AOA	
Anguilla	East Caribbean dollar	XCD	EC$
Antigua and Barbuda	East Caribbean dollar	XCD	EC$
Argentina	Argentine peso	ARS	
Armenia	Armenian dram	AMD	
Aruba	Aruban florin	AWG	f
Australia	Australian dollar	AUD	$
Austria	European euro	EUR	€
Azerbaijan	Azerbaijani manat	AZN	
Bahamas	Bahamian dollar	BSD	B$
Bahrain	Bahraini dinar	BHD	
Bangladesh	Bangladeshi taka	BDT	
Barbados	Barbadian dollar	BBD	Bds$
Belarus	Belarusian ruble	BYR	Br
Belgium	European euro	EUR	€
Belize	Belize dollar	BZD	BZ$
Benin	West African CFA franc	XOF	CFA
Bermuda	Bermudian dollar	BMD	BD$
Bhutan	Bhutanese ngultrum	BTN	Nu.
Bolivia	Bolivian boliviano	BOB	Bs.
Bosnia-Herzegovina	Bosnia and Herzegovina konvertibilna marka	BAM	KM
Botswana	Botswana pula	BWP	P
Brazil	Brazilian real	BRL	R$
British Indian Ocean Territory	see United Kingdom		
Brunei	Brunei dollar	BND	B$
Bulgaria	Bulgarian lev	BGN	
Burkina Faso	West African CFA franc	XOF	CFA
Burma	see Myanmar		
Burundi	Burundi franc	BIF	FBu
Cambodia	Cambodian riel	KHR	
Cameroon	Central African CFA franc	XAF	CFA
Canada	Canadian dollar	CAD	$
Canton and Enderbury Islands	see Kiribati		
Cape Verde	Cape Verdean escudo	CVE	Esc
Cayman Islands	Cayman Islands dollar	KYD	KY$
Central African Republic	Central African CFA franc	XAF	CFA
Chad	Central African CFA franc	XAF	CFA
Chile	Chilean peso	CLP	$
China	Chinese renminbi	CNY	¥
Christmas Island	see Australia		
Cocos (Keeling) Islands	see Australia		
Colombia	Colombian peso	COP	Col$
Comoros	Comorian franc	KMF	
Congo	Central African CFA franc	XAF	CFA
Congo, Democratic Republic	Congolese franc	CDF	F
Cook Islands	see New Zealand		
Costa Rica	Costa Rican colon	CRC	₡
Côte d'Ivoire	West African CFA franc	XOF	CFA
Croatia	Croatian kuna	HRK	kn
Cuba	Cuban peso	CUC	$
Cyprus	Cypriot pound	CYP	£
Czech Republic	Czech koruna	CZK	Kč
Denmark	Danish krone	DKK	Kr
Djibouti	Djiboutian franc	DJF	Fdj
Dominica	East Caribbean dollar	XCD	EC$
Dominican Republic	Dominican peso	DOP	RD$
Dronning Maud Land	see Norway		
East Timor	East Timor-Leste		
Ecuador	uses the U.S. Dollar		
Egypt	Egyptian pound	EGP	£
El Salvador	uses the U.S. Dollar		
Equatorial Guinea	Central African CFA franc	GQE	CFA
Eritrea	Eritrea nakfa	ERN	Nfa
Estonia	Estonian kroon	EEK	KR
Ethiopia	Ethiopian birr	ETB	Br
Faeroe Islands (Føroyar)	see Denmark		
Falkland Islands	Falkland Islands pound	FKP	£
Fiji	Fijian dollar	FJD	FJ$
Finland	European euro	EUR	€
France	European euro	EUR	€
French Guiana	see France		
French Polynesia	CFP franc	XPF	F
Gabon	Central African CFA franc	XAF	CFA
Gambia	Gambian dalasi	GMD	D
Georgia	Georgian lari	GEL	
Germany	European euro	EUR	€
Ghana	Ghanaian cedi	GHS	
Gibraltar	Gibraltar pound	GIP	£
Great Britain	see United Kingdom		
Greece	European euro	EUR	€
Greenland	see Denmark		

Currencies of the World (continued)

Country	Currency	ISO-4217 Code	Symbol	Country	Currency	ISO-4217 Code	Symbol
Grenada	East Caribbean dollar	XCD	EC$	Liechtenstein	uses the Swiss Franc		
Guadeloupe	see France			Lithuania	Lithuanian litas	LTL	Lt
Guam	see United States			Luxembourg	European euro	EUR	€
Guatemala	Guatemalan quetzal	GTQ	Q	Macau	Macanese pataca	MOP	P
Guernsey	see United Kingdom			Macedonia (Former Yug. Rep.)	Macedonian denar	MKD	
Guinea-Bissau	West African CFA franc	XOF	CFA	Madagascar	Malagasy ariary	MGA	FMG
Guinea	Guinean franc	GNF	FG	Malawi	Malawian kwacha	MWK	MK
Guyana	Guyanese dollar	GYD	GY$	Malaysia	Malaysian ringgit	MYR	RM
Haiti	Haitian gourde	HTG	G	Maldives	Maldivian rufiyaa	MVR	Rf
Heard and McDonald Islands	see Australia			Mali	West African CFA franc	XOF	CFA
Honduras	Honduran lempira	HNL	L	Malta	Maltese lira	MTL	Lm
Hong Kong	Hong Kong dollar	HKD	HK$	Martinique	see France		
Hungary	Hungarian forint	HUF	Ft	Mauritania	Mauritanian ouguiya	MRO	UM
Iceland	Icelandic króna	ISK	kr	Mauritius	Mauritian rupee	MUR	Rs
India	Indian rupee	INR	Rs	Mayotte	see France		
Indonesia	Indonesian rupiah	IDR	Rp	Micronesia	see United States		
International Monetary Fund	Special Drawing Rights	XDR	SDR	Midway Islands	see United States		
Iran	Iranian rial	IRR		Mexico	Mexican peso	MXN	$
Iraq	Iraqi dinar	IQD		Moldova	Moldovan leu	MDL	
Ireland	European euro	EUR	€	Monaco	see France		
Isle of Man	see United Kingdom			Mongolia	Mongolian tugrik	MNT	₮
Israel	Israeli new sheqel	ILS		Montenegro	see Italy		
Italy	European euro	EUR	€	Montserrat	East Caribbean dollar	XCD	EC$
Ivory Coast	see Côte d'Ivoire			Morocco	Moroccan dirham	MAD	
Jamaica	Jamaican dollar	JMD	J$	Mozambique	Mozambican metical	MZM	MTn
Japan	Japanese yen	JPY	¥	Myanmar	Myanma kyat	MMK	K
Jersey	see United Kingdom			Nauru	see Australia		
Johnston Island	see United States			Namibia	Namibian dollar	NAD	N$
Jordan	Jordanian dinar	JOD		Nepal	Nepalese rupee	NPR	NRs
Kampuchea	see Cambodia			Netherlands Antilles	Netherlands Antillean gulden	ANG	NAƒ
Kazakhstan	Kazakhstani tenge	KZT	T	Netherlands	European euro	EUR	€
Kenya	Kenyan shilling	KES	KSh	New Caledonia	CFP franc	XPF	F
Kiribati	see Australia			New Zealand	New Zealand dollar	NZD	NZ$
Korea, North	North Korean won	KPW	W	Nicaragua	Nicaraguan cordoba	NIO	C$
Korea, South	South Korean won	KRW	W	Niger	West African CFA franc	XOF	CFA
Kuwait	Kuwaiti dinar	KWD		Nigeria	Nigerian naira	NGN	₦
Kyrgyzstan	Kyrgyzstani som	KGS		Niue	see New Zealand		
Laos	Lao kip	LAK	KN	Norfolk Island	see Australia		
Latvia	Latvian lats	LVL	Ls	Northern Mariana Islands	see United States		
Lebanon	Lebanese lira	LBP		Norway	Norwegian krone	NOK	kr
Lesotho	Lesotho loti	LSL	M	Oman	Omani rial	OMR	
Liberia	Liberian dollar	LRD	L$	Pakistan	Pakistani rupee	PKR	Rs.
Libya	Libyan dinar	LYD	LD	Palau	see United States		